CALIFORNIA LEGISL

CALIFORNIA

CODE OF CIVIL PROCEDURE

2024 EDITION

Division - TITLE OF ACT ... 22
Division - PRELIMINARY PROVISIONS ... 22
Part 1 - OF COURTS OF JUSTICE ... 24
- Title 1 - ORGANIZATION AND JURISDICTION ... 24
  - Chapter 1 - COURTS OF JUSTICE IN GENERAL ... 24
  - Chapter 3 - SUPREME COURT ... 25
  - Chapter 4 - SUPERIOR COURTS ... 26
  - Chapter 5 - MUNICIPAL COURTS ... 27
  - Chapter 5.1 - LIMITED CIVIL CASES ... 27
  - Article 1 - JURISDICTION IN LIMITED CIVIL CASES ... 27
  - Article 2 - ECONOMIC LITIGATION FOR LIMITED CIVIL CASES ... 28
  - Chapter 5.5 - SMALL CLAIMS COURT ... 30
  - Article 1 - GENERAL PROVISIONS ... 30
  - Article 2 - SMALL CLAIMS COURT ... 30
  - Article 3 - ACTIONS ... 33
  - Article 4 - PARTIES ... 34
  - Article 5 - HEARING ... 34
  - Article 6 - JUDGMENT ... 36
  - Article 7 - MOTION TO VACATE, APPEAL, AND RELATED MATTERS ... 37
  - Article 8 - SATISFACTION AND ENFORCEMENT OF JUDGMENT ... 38
  - Article 9 - ADMINISTRATION ... 40
  - Chapter 6 - GENERAL PROVISIONS RESPECTING COURTS OF JUSTICE ... 41
  - Article 1 - OPEN COURT ACCESS ... 41
  - Article 2 - INCIDENTAL POWERS AND DUTIES OF COURTS ... 42
  - Article 3 - JUDICIAL HOLIDAYS ... 45
  - Article 4 - PROCEEDINGS IN CASE OF ABSENCE OF JUDGE ... 45
  - Article 6 - SEALS OF COURTS ... 46
  - Chapter 7 - SPECIAL IMMIGRANT JUVENILE FINDINGS ... 46
- Title 2 - JUDICIAL OFFICERS ... 46
  - Chapter 2 - POWERS OF JUDGES AT CHAMBERS ... 46
  - Chapter 3 - DISQUALIFICATIONS OF JUDGES ... 47
  - Chapter 4 - INCIDENTAL POWERS AND DUTIES OF JUDICIAL OFFICERS ... 51
  - Chapter 5 - MISCELLANEOUS PROVISIONS RESPECTING COURTS OF JUSTICE ... 52
- Title 3 - PERSONS SPECIALLY INVESTED WITH POWERS OF A JUDICIAL NATURE ... 52
  - Chapter 1 - TRIAL JURY SELECTION AND MANAGEMENT ACT ... 52
  - Chapter 2 - COURT COMMISSIONERS ... 64
- Title 4 - MINISTERIAL OFFICERS OF COURTS OF JUSTICE ... 64

- Chapter 1 - OF MINISTERIAL OFFICERS GENERALLY 64
- Chapter 2 - LEVYING OFFICER ELECTRONIC TRANSACTIONS ACT 65
- Chapter 3 - PHONOGRAPHIC REPORTERS 66
- Title 5 - PERSONS SPECIALLY INVESTED WITH MINISTERIAL POWERS RELATING TO COURTS OF JUSTICE 67
  - Chapter 1 - ATTORNEYS AND COUNSELORS AT LAW 67

Part 2 - OF CIVIL ACTIONS 68

- Title 1 - OF THE FORM OF CIVIL ACTIONS 68
- Title 2 - OF THE TIME OF COMMENCING CIVIL ACTIONS 68
  - Chapter 1 - THE TIME OF COMMENCING ACTIONS IN GENERAL 68
  - Chapter 2 - THE TIME OF COMMENCING ACTIONS FOR THE RECOVERY OF REAL PROPERTY 69
  - Chapter 3 - THE TIME OF COMMENCING ACTIONS OTHER THAN FOR THE RECOVERY OF REAL PROPERTY 70
  - Chapter 4 - GENERAL PROVISIONS AS TO THE TIME OF COMMENCING ACTIONS 80
  - Chapter 5 - THE COMMENCEMENT OF ACTIONS BASED UPON PROFESSIONAL NEGLIGENCE 84
  - Chapter 6 - TIME OF COMMENCEMENT OF ACTION AFTER PERSON'S DEATH 84
- Title 3 - OF THE PARTIES TO CIVIL ACTIONS 85
  - Chapter 1 - GENERAL PROVISIONS 85
  - Chapter 2 - MARRIED PERSON 89
  - Chapter 3 - DISABILITY OF PARTY 89
  - Chapter 4 - EFFECT OF DEATH 91
    - Article 1 - DEFINITIONS 91
    - Article 2 - SURVIVAL AND CONTINUATION 92
    - Article 3 - DECEDENT'S CAUSE OF ACTION 92
    - Article 4 - CAUSE OF ACTION AGAINST DECEDENT 93
    - Article 5 - INSURED CLAIMS 93
    - Article 6 - WRONGFUL DEATH 93
  - Chapter 5 - PERMISSIVE JOINDER 94
  - Chapter 6 - INTERPLEADER 94
  - Chapter 7 - INTERVENTION 95
  - Chapter 8 - COMPULSORY JOINDER 96
- Title 3A - VEXATIOUS LITIGANTS 96
- Title 4 - OF THE PLACE OF TRIAL, RECLASSIFICATION, AND COORDINATION OF CIVIL ACTIONS 98
  - Chapter 1 - PLACE OF TRIAL 98
  - Chapter 2 - RECLASSIFICATION OF CIVIL ACTIONS AND PROCEEDINGS 101
  - Chapter 3 - COORDINATION 103
- Title 4.5 - RECORDING NOTICE OF CERTAIN ACTIONS 104
  - Chapter 1 - DEFINITIONS AND GENERAL PROVISIONS 104
    - Article 3 - EXPUNGEMENT AND OTHER RELIEF 105

- Article 4 - WITHDRAWAL 106
- Article 5 - EFFECT OF WITHDRAWAL OR EXPUNGEMENT OF NOTICE 106

Title 5 - JURISDICTION AND SERVICE OF PROCESS 106
- Chapter 1 - JURISDICTION AND FORUM 106
- Article 1 - JURISDICTION 106
- Article 2 - FORUM 106
- Article 3 - JURISDICTION IN ACTION 106
- Chapter 2 - COMMENCING CIVIL ACTIONS 107
- Chapter 3 - SUMMONS 109
- Chapter 4 - SERVICE OF SUMMONS 109
- Article 1 - GENERAL 109
- Article 2 - PERSONS WHO MAY SERVE SUMMONS 110
- Article 3 - MANNER OF SERVICE OF SUMMONS 110
- Article 4 - PERSONS UPON WHOM SUMMONS MAY BE SERVED 112
- Article 5 - PROOF OF SERVICE 113
- Chapter 5 - OBJECTION TO JURISDICTION 113

Title 6 - OF THE PLEADINGS IN CIVIL ACTIONS 114
- Chapter 1 - THE PLEADINGS IN GENERAL 114
- Chapter 2 - PLEADINGS DEMANDING RELIEF 114
- Article 1 - GENERAL PROVISIONS 114
- Article 2 - COMPULSORY CROSS-COMPLAINTS 119
- Article 3 - PERMISSIVE JOINDER OF CAUSES OF ACTION 119
- Article 4 - CROSS-COMPLAINTS 119
- Article 5 - CONTENTS OF DOCUMENTS IN PARTICULAR ACTIONS OR PROCEEDINGS 120
- Chapter 3 - OBJECTIONS TO PLEADINGS; DENIALS AND DEFENSES 120
- Article 1 - OBJECTIONS TO PLEADINGS 120
- Article 2 - DENIALS AND DEFENSES 122
- Article 3 - TIME TO RESPOND TO CROSS-COMPLAINT 123
- Chapter 4 - MOTION TO STRIKE 123
- Chapter 5 - SUMMARY JUDGMENTS AND MOTIONS FOR JUDGMENT ON THE PLEADINGS 124
- Chapter 6 - VERIFICATION OF PLEADINGS 128
- Chapter 7 - GENERAL RULES OF PLEADING 128
- Chapter 8 - VARIANCE-MISTAKES IN PLEADINGS AND AMENDMENTS 129

Title 6.5 - ATTACHMENT 131
- Chapter 1 - WORDS AND PHRASES DEFINED 131
- Chapter 2 - GENERAL PROVISIONS 133
- Chapter 3 - ACTIONS IN WHICH ATTACHMENT AUTHORIZED 134
- Chapter 4 - NOTICED HEARING PROCEDURE FOR OBTAINING WRIT OF ATTACHMENT 135

- Article 1 - RIGHT TO ATTACH ORDER; ISSUANCE OF WRIT OF ATTACHMENT 135
- Article 2 - NOTICED HEARING PROCEDURE FOR OBTAINING ADDITIONAL WRITS 137
- Article 3 - EX PARTE PROCEDURE FOR OBTAINING ADDITIONAL WRITS 138
- Chapter 5 - EX PARTE HEARING PROCEDURE FOR OBTAINING WRIT OF ATTACHMENT 138
  - Article 1 - GREAT OR IRREPARABLE INJURY REQUIREMENT 138
  - Article 2 - ORDER DETERMINING RIGHT TO ATTACH; ISSUANCE OF WRIT OF ATTACHMENT .. 139
  - Article 3 - PROCEDURE FOR OBTAINING ADDITIONAL WRITS 139
  - Article 4 - CLAIM OF EXEMPTION 140
- Chapter 6 - TEMPORARY PROTECTIVE ORDER 140
- Chapter 7 - PROPERTY SUBJECT TO ATTACHMENT 141
- Chapter 8 - LEVY PROCEDURES; LIEN OF ATTACHMENT; MANAGEMENT AND DISPOSITION OF ATTACHED PROPERTY 142
  - Article 1 - GENERAL PROVISIONS 142
  - Article 2 - METHODS OF LEVY 144
  - Article 3 - LIEN OF ATTACHMENT 148
  - Article 4 - DUTIES AND LIABILITIES OF THIRD PERSONS AFTER LEVY 149
  - Article 5 - MANAGEMENT AND DISPOSITION OF ATTACHED PROPERTY 149
- Chapter 9 - UNDERTAKINGS 151
  - Article 1 - GENERAL PROVISIONS 151
  - Article 2 - UNDERTAKINGS TO OBTAIN WRIT OF ATTACHMENT OR PROTECTIVE ORDER 151
  - Article 3 - UNDERTAKING TO OBTAIN RELEASE OF ATTACHMENT OR PROTECTIVE ORDER 151
  - Article 4 - UNDERTAKING ON APPEAL 151
- Chapter 10 - LIABILITY FOR WRONGFUL ATTACHMENT 152
- Chapter 11 - ATTACHING PLAINTIFF'S MISCELLANEOUS REMEDIES 152
  - Article 1 - EXAMINATION OF THIRD PERSON 152
  - Article 2 - CREDITOR'S SUIT 154
  - Article 3 - LIEN IN PENDING ACTION OR PROCEEDING 154
- Chapter 12 - NONRESIDENT ATTACHMENT 156
- Chapter 13 - EFFECT OF BANKRUPTCY PROCEEDINGS AND GENERAL ASSIGNMENTS FOR THE BENEFIT OF CREDITORS 157

Title 7 - OTHER PROVISIONAL REMEDIES IN CIVIL ACTIONS 158
- Chapter 1 - GENERAL PROVISIONS 158
- Chapter 2 - CLAIM AND DELIVERY OF PERSONAL PROPERTY 158
  - Article 1 - WORDS AND PHRASES DEFINED 158
  - Article 2 - WRIT OF POSSESSION 158
  - Article 3 - TEMPORARY RESTRAINING ORDER 160
  - Article 4 - LEVY AND CUSTODY 160
  - Article 5 - UNDERTAKINGS 161
  - Article 6 - MISCELLANEOUS PROVISIONS 161

- Chapter 3 - INJUNCTION ... 161
- Chapter 5 - RECEIVERS ... 174
- Chapter 5A - UNDERTAKING OF PERSONS HANDLING PRIVATE PROPERTY OR FUNDS ... 176
- Chapter 6 - DEPOSIT IN COURT ... 176

Title 7a - PRETRIAL CONFERENCES ... 176

Title 8 - OF THE TRIAL AND JUDGMENT IN CIVIL ACTIONS ... 177
- Chapter 1 - JUDGMENT IN GENERAL ... 177
- Chapter 1.5 - DISMISSAL FOR DELAY IN PROSECUTION ... 180
- Article 1 - DEFINITIONS AND GENERAL PROVISIONS ... 180
- Article 2 - MANDATORY TIME FOR SERVICE OF SUMMONS ... 181
- Article 3 - MANDATORY TIME FOR BRINGING ACTION TO TRIAL OR NEW TRIAL ... 181
- Article 4 - DISCRETIONARY DISMISSAL FOR DELAY ... 182
- Chapter 2 - JUDGMENT UPON FAILURE TO ANSWER ... 182
- Chapter 3 - ISSUES-THE MODE OF TRIAL AND POSTPONEMENTS ... 184
- Chapter 4 - TRIAL BY JURY ... 186
- Article 2 - CONDUCT OF THE TRIAL ... 186
- Article 3 - THE VERDICT ... 187
- Article 4.5 - VOLUNTARY EXPEDITED JURY TRIALS ... 188
- Chapter 4.6 - MANDATORY EXPEDITED JURY TRIALS IN LIMITED CIVIL CASES ... 190
- Chapter 5 - TRIAL BY THE COURT ... 191
- Chapter 6 - OF REFERENCES AND TRIALS BY REFEREES ... 193
- Chapter 7 - PROVISIONS RELATING TO TRIALS IN GENERAL ... 194
- Article 1 - EXCEPTIONS ... 194
- Article 1.5 - VIEW BY TRIER OF FACT ... 195
- Article 2 - NEW TRIALS ... 195
- Chapter 8 - THE MANNER OF GIVING AND ENTERING JUDGMENT ... 197

Title 8.5 - UNIFORM FOREIGN-MONEY CLAIMS ACT ... 200

Title 9 - ENFORCEMENT OF JUDGMENTS ... 202
- Division 1 - DEFINITIONS AND GENERAL PROVISIONS ... 202
- Chapter 1 - DEFINITIONS AND GENERAL PROVISIONS ... 202
- Chapter 2 - GENERAL PROVISIONS ... 203
- Chapter 3 - PERIOD FOR ENFORCEMENT AND RENEWAL OF JUDGMENTS ... 204
- Article 1 - PERIOD FOR ENFORCEMENT OF JUDGMENTS ... 204
- Article 2 - RENEWAL OF JUDGMENTS ... 204
- Article 3 - APPLICATION OF CHAPTER ... 206
- Chapter 4 - MANNER OF SERVICE OF WRITS, NOTICES, AND OTHER PAPERS ... 206
- Article 1 - SERVICE ON ATTORNEY OF CREDITOR OR DEBTOR ... 206
- Article 2 - MANNER OF SERVICE GENERALLY ... 207

Article 3 - PROOF OF SERVICE	209
Article 4 - APPLICATION OF CHAPTER	209
Chapter 5 - INTEREST AND COSTS	209
Chapter 6 - ENFORCEMENT AFTER DEATH OF JUDGMENT CREDITOR OR JUDGMENT DEBTOR	211
Chapter 7 - LEVYING OFFICERS	211
Chapter 8 - ENFORCEMENT OF STATE TAX LIABILITY	212
Article 1 - ENFORCEMENT PURSUANT TO WARRANT OR NOTICE OF LEVY	212
Article 2 - ENFORCEMENT OF JUDGMENT FOR TAXES	213
Chapter 9 - ENFORCEMENT OF SUPPORT JUDGMENTS	213
Chapter 10 - ENFORCEMENT OF JUDGMENTS BY LABOR COMMISSIONER	214
Chapter 20 - TRANSITIONAL PROVISIONS	214
Division 2 - ENFORCEMENT OF MONEY JUDGMENTS	215
Chapter 1 - GENERAL PROVISIONS	215
Article 1 - PROPERTY SUBJECT TO ENFORCEMENT OF MONEY JUDGMENT	215
Article 2 - AMOUNT TO SATISFY MONEY JUDGMENT	216
Chapter 2 - LIENS	217
Article 1 - GENERAL PROVISIONS	217
Article 2 - JUDGMENT LIEN ON REAL PROPERTY	217
Article 3 - JUDGMENT LIEN ON PERSONAL PROPERTY	219
Article 4 - EXECUTION LIEN	223
Article 5 - OTHER LIENS CREATED BY ENFORCEMENT PROCESS	224
Chapter 3 - EXECUTION	224
Article 1 - GENERAL PROVISIONS	224
Article 2 - WRIT OF EXECUTION AND NOTICE OF LEVY	225
Article 3 - PROPERTY SUBJECT TO EXECUTION	227
Article 4 - METHODS OF LEVY	228
Article 5 - DUTIES AND LIABILITIES OF THIRD PERSONS AFTER LEVY	232
Article 6 - SALE AND COLLECTION	233
Article 7 - DISTRIBUTION OF PROCEEDS OF SALE OR COLLECTION	236
Chapter 4 - EXEMPTIONS	237
Article 1 - GENERAL PROVISIONS	237
Article 2 - PROCEDURE FOR CLAIMING EXEMPTIONS AFTER LEVY	240
Article 3 - EXEMPT PROPERTY	242
Article 4 - HOMESTEAD EXEMPTION	248
Article 5 - DECLARED HOMESTEADS	250
Chapter 5 - WAGE GARNISHMENT	252
Article 1 - SHORT TITLE; DEFINITIONS	252
Article 2 - GENERAL PROVISIONS	252

Article 3 - RESTRICTIONS ON EARNINGS WITHHOLDING 255

Article 4 - EARNINGS WITHHOLDING ORDER FOR TAXES 256

Article 5 - PROCEDURE FOR EARNINGS WITHHOLDING ORDERS AND EXEMPTION CLAIMS 257

Article 6 - FORMS; EMPLOYER'S INSTRUCTIONS 260

Article 7 - ADMINISTRATION AND ENFORCEMENT 261

Chapter 6 - MISCELLANEOUS CREDITORS' REMEDIES 261

Article 1 - WRITTEN INTERROGATORIES TO JUDGMENT DEBTOR 261

Article 2 - EXAMINATION PROCEEDINGS 262

Article 3 - CREDITOR'S SUIT 264

Article 4 - CHARGING ORDERS 265

Article 5 - LIEN IN PENDING ACTION OR PROCEEDING 265

Article 6 - ASSIGNMENT ORDER 267

Article 7 - RECEIVER TO ENFORCE JUDGMENT 268

Article 8 - COLLECTION OF JUDGMENT WHERE JUDGMENT DEBTOR IS CREDITOR OF PUBLIC ENTITY 268

Article 9 - ENFORCEMENT AGAINST FRANCHISE 271

Article 10 - OTHER ENFORCEMENT PROCEDURES 272

Division 3 - ENFORCEMENT OF NONMONEY JUDGMENTS 272

Chapter 1 - GENERAL PROVISIONS 272

Chapter 2 - JUDGMENT FOR POSSESSION OF PERSONAL PROPERTY 273

Chapter 3 - JUDGMENT FOR POSSESSION OF REAL PROPERTY 273

Chapter 4 - JUDGMENT FOR SALE OF PROPERTY 274

Chapter 5 - OTHER JUDGMENTS 274

Division 4 - THIRD-PARTY CLAIMS AND RELATED PROCEDURES 275

Chapter 1 - DEFINITIONS 275

Chapter 2 - THIRD-PARTY CLAIMS OF OWNERSHIP AND POSSESSION 275

Chapter 3 - THIRD-PARTY CLAIM OF SECURITY INTEREST OR LIEN 276

Chapter 4 - HEARING ON THIRD-PARTY CLAIM 277

Chapter 5 - CREDITOR'S DEMAND FOR THIRD-PARTY CLAIM BY SECURED PARTY OR LIENHOLDER 278

Chapter 6 - THIRD-PARTY UNDERTAKING TO RELEASE PROPERTY 279

Chapter 7 - UNDERTAKINGS 280

Division 5 - SATISFACTION OF JUDGMENT 280

Chapter 1 - SATISFACTION OF JUDGMENT 280

Chapter 2 - ACKNOWLEDGMENT OF PARTIAL SATISFACTION OF JUDGMENT 281

Chapter 3 - ACKNOWLEDGMENT OF SATISFACTION OF MATURED INSTALLMENTS UNDER INSTALLMENT JUDGMENT 282

Title 10 - ACTIONS IN PARTICULAR CASES 282

Chapter 1 - ACTIONS FOR THE FORECLOSURE OF MORTGAGES 282

Chapter 2 - ACTIONS FOR NUISANCE, WASTE, AND WILLFUL TRESPASS, IN CERTAIN CASES, ON REAL PROPERTY 287

Chapter 3 - ACTIONS FOR THE RECOVERY OF REAL PROPERTY, AND OTHER PROVISIONS RELATING TO ACTIONS CONCERNING REAL PROPERTY 289

Chapter 3.5 - ACTIONS TO RE-ESTABLISH DESTROYED LAND RECORDS.............................290

Chapter 3.6 - CULLEN EARTHQUAKE ACT 293

Chapter 4 - QUIET TITLE 294

Article 1 - GENERAL PROVISIONS...294

Article 2 - COMMENCEMENT OF ACTION 295

Article 3 - DEFENDANTS 295

Article 4 - SERVICE OF PROCESS 296

Article 5 - JUDGMENT..296

Article 6 - LIENS AND ENCUMBRANCES 297

Chapter 4.5 - SPECIAL ACTIONS AND PROCEEDINGS TO CLEAR TITLE 298

Article 1 - IDENTITY OF PERSON IN CHAIN OF TITLE 298

Article 2 - LAND DEDICATED FOR PUBLIC IMPROVEMENT 298

Article 3 - RIGHT OF ENTRY OR OCCUPATION OF SURFACE LANDS UNDER OIL OR GAS LEASE 299

Chapter 4.6 - ACTIONS CONCERNING REAL PROPERTY TITLES AFFECTED BY PUBLIC IMPROVEMENT ASSESSMENTS 300

Chapter 5 - ACTIONS FOR THE USURPATION OF AN OFFICE OR FRANCHISE 301

Chapter 7 - ACTIONS RELATING TO GROUNDWATER RIGHTS 301

Article 1 - GENERAL PROVISIONS...301

Article 2 - SCOPE OF ACTION 302

Article 3 - NOTICE AND SERVICE OF COMPLAINT...302

Article 4 - INTERVENTION...304

Article 5 - JUDGE 304

Article 6 - ELECTRONIC SERVICE..305

Article 7 - CASE MANAGEMENT 305

Article 8 - BASIN BOUNDARIES 305

Article 9 - INITIAL DISCLOSURES..305

Article 10 - EXPERT WITNESSES 306

Article 11 - WRITTEN TESTIMONY 306

Article 12 - SPECIAL MASTER 307

Article 13 - PRELIMINARY INJUNCTION 307

Article 14 - STAY...307

Article 15 - PHYSICAL SOLUTION..307

Article 16 - JUDGMENT 307

Article 17 - JUDGMENT BINDING ON SUCCESSORS 308

Article 18 - CONTINUING JURISDICTION ... 308
Chapter 8 - ACTIONS AGAINST COOWNERS OF MINES ... 308
Chapter 9 - VALIDATING PROCEEDINGS ... 308
Chapter 10 - GOOD FAITH IMPROVER OF PROPERTY OWNED BY ANOTHER ... 310
Chapter 11 - ACTIONS TO RECOVER COVID-19 RENTAL DEBT ... 310

Title 10.5 - PARTITION OF REAL AND PERSONAL PROPERTY ... 311
Chapter 1 - GENERAL PROVISIONS ... 311
Article 1 - PRELIMINARY PROVISIONS ... 311
Article 2 - POWERS OF COURT ... 311
Chapter 2 - COMMENCEMENT OF ACTION ... 312
Article 1 - COMPLAINT AND LIS PENDENS ... 312
Article 2 - SUMMONS ... 312
Article 3 - ANSWER ... 312
Article 4 - PARTIES ... 313
Chapter 3 - TRIAL ... 313
Article 1 - DETERMINATION OF INTERESTS OF PARTIES ... 313
Article 2 - DETERMINATION OF RIGHT TO PARTITION ... 313
Article 3 - DETERMINATION OF MANNER OF PARTITION ... 314
Chapter 4 - REFEREES ... 314
Article 1 - GENERAL PROVISIONS ... 314
Article 2 - CONTRACTS OF REFEREE ... 315
Chapter 5 - DIVISION OF THE PROPERTY ... 315
Chapter 6 - SALE OF THE PROPERTY ... 316
Article 1 - MANNER OF SALE ... 316
Article 2 - SALES PROCEDURES ... 316
Article 3 - CONSUMMATION OF SALE ... 317
Article 4 - DISPOSITION OF PROCEEDS OF SALE ... 318
Chapter 7 - PARTITION BY APPRAISAL ... 318
Chapter 8 - COSTS OF PARTITION ... 319
Article 1 - ALLOWANCE AND APPORTIONMENT OF COSTS OF PARTITION ... 319
Article 2 - PAYMENT OF COSTS OF PARTITION ... 319
Chapter 9 - JUDGMENT ... 320
Chapter 10 - PARTITION OF REAL PROPERTY ACT ... 320

Title 11 - CONTRIBUTION AMONG JOINT JUDGMENT DEBTORS ... 323
Chapter 1 - RELEASES FROM AND CONTRIBUTION AMONG JOINT TORTFEASORS ... 323
Chapter 2 - CONTRIBUTION AMONG OTHER JUDGMENT DEBTORS ... 324

Title 13 - APPEALS IN CIVIL ACTIONS ... 324
Chapter 1 - APPEALS IN GENERAL ... 324

- Chapter 2 - STAY OF ENFORCEMENT AND OTHER PROCEEDINGS 326
- Title 14 - OF MISCELLANEOUS PROVISIONS 329
  - Chapter 1 - PROCEEDINGS AGAINST JOINT DEBTORS 329
  - Chapter 2 - BONDS AND UNDERTAKINGS 329
    - Article 1 - PRELIMINARY PROVISIONS AND DEFINITIONS 329
    - Article 2 - GENERAL PROVISIONS 330
    - Article 3 - EXECUTION AND FILING 331
    - Article 4 - APPROVAL AND EFFECT 332
    - Article 5 - PERSONAL SURETIES 332
    - Article 6 - ADMITTED SURETY INSURERS 332
    - Article 7 - DEPOSIT IN LIEU OF BOND 333
    - Article 8 - BONDS TO THE STATE OF CALIFORNIA 334
    - Article 9 - OBJECTIONS TO BONDS 335
    - Article 10 - INSUFFICIENT AND EXCESSIVE BONDS 335
    - Article 11 - RELEASE OR SUBSTITUTION OF SURETIES ON BOND GIVEN IN ACTION OR PROCEEDING 336
    - Article 12 - NEW, ADDITIONAL, AND SUPPLEMENTAL BONDS 336
    - Article 13 - CANCELLATION OF BOND OR WITHDRAWAL OF SURETIES 337
    - Article 14 - LIABILITY OF PRINCIPAL AND SURETIES 337
    - Article 15 - ENFORCEMENT LIEN 338
  - Chapter 3 - OFFERS BY A PARTY TO COMPROMISE 339
  - Chapter 3.2 - TIME-LIMITED DEMANDS 340
  - Chapter 3.5 - CONFIDENTIAL SETTLEMENT AGREEMENTS 340
  - Chapter 3.6 - AGREEMENTS SETTLING EMPLOYMENT DISPUTES 341
  - Chapter 3.7 - ENROLLMENT AGREEMENTS 342
  - Chapter 4 - MOTIONS AND ORDERS 342
  - Chapter 5 - NOTICES, AND FILING AND SERVICE OF PAPERS 343
  - Chapter 6 - OF COSTS 348
  - Chapter 7 - GENERAL PROVISIONS 354
  - Chapter 8 - DECLARATORY RELIEF 355
  - Chapter 9 - ACTIONS TO ENFORCE REAL PROPERTY AND MOBILEHOME SALES AGREEMENTS 356
  - Chapter 10 - COMPUTER ASSISTANCE 356
- Part 3 - OF SPECIAL PROCEEDINGS OF A CIVIL NATURE 356
  - Title - PRELIMINARY PROVISIONS 356
  - Title 1 - OF WRITS OF REVIEW, MANDATE, AND PROHIBITION 356
    - Chapter 1 - WRIT OF REVIEW 356
    - Chapter 2 - WRIT OF MANDATE 357
    - Chapter 3 - WRIT OF PROHIBITION 360

- Chapter 4 - WRITS OF REVIEW, MANDATE, AND PROHIBITION MAY ISSUE AND BE HEARD AT CHAMBERS 361
- Chapter 5 - RULES OF PRACTICE AND APPEALS 361

Title 3 - OF SUMMARY PROCEEDINGS 361
- Chapter 1 - CONFESSION OF JUDGMENT WITHOUT ACTION 361
- Chapter 2 - SUBMITTING A CONTROVERSY WITHOUT ACTION 361
- Chapter 2.5 - JUDICIAL ARBITRATION 362
- Chapter 4 - SUMMARY PROCEEDINGS FOR OBTAINING POSSESSION OF REAL PROPERTY IN CERTAIN CASES 364
- Chapter 5 - COVID-19 TENANT RELIEF ACT 376
- Chapter 6 - COVID-19 RENTAL HOUSING RECOVERY ACT 383

Title 4 - OF THE ENFORCEMENT OF LIENS 386
- Chapter 1 - LIENS IN GENERAL 386
- Chapter 2.5 - OIL AND GAS LIENS 386
- Chapter 3 - CERTAIN LIENS AND PRIORITIES FOR SALARIES, WAGES AND CONSUMER DEBTS 388
- Chapter 4 - CERTAIN LIENS UPON ANIMALS 390
- Chapter 5 - LIENS ON AIRCRAFT 390

Title 5 - OF CONTEMPTS 391

Title 7 - EMINENT DOMAIN LAW 394
- Chapter 1 - GENERAL PROVISIONS 394
- Chapter 2 - PRINCIPLES OF CONSTRUCTION; DEFINITIONS 394
  - Article 1 - CONSTRUCTION 394
  - Article 2 - WORDS AND PHRASES DEFINED 395
- Chapter 3 - THE RIGHT TO TAKE 396
  - Article 1 - GENERAL LIMITATIONS ON EXERCISE OF POWER OF EMINENT DOMAIN 396
  - Article 2 - RIGHTS INCLUDED IN GRANT OF EMINENT DOMAIN AUTHORITY 397
  - Article 3 - FUTURE USE 398
  - Article 4 - SUBSTITUTE CONDEMNATION 398
  - Article 5 - EXCESS CONDEMNATION 399
  - Article 6 - CONDEMNATION FOR COMPATIBLE USE 399
  - Article 7 - CONDEMNATION FOR MORE NECESSARY PUBLIC USE 399
- Chapter 4 - PRECONDEMNATION ACTIVITIES 401
  - Article 1 - PRELIMINARY LOCATION, SURVEY, AND TESTS 401
  - Article 2 - RESOLUTION OF NECESSITY 401
  - Article 3 - RESOLUTION CONSENTING TO EMINENT DOMAIN PROCEEDING BY QUASI-PUBLIC ENTITY 405
- Chapter 5 - COMMENCEMENT OF PROCEEDING 406
  - Article 1 - JURISDICTION AND VENUE 406
  - Article 2 - COMMENCEMENT OF PROCEEDING GENERALLY 406

Article 3 - PARTIES; JOINDER OF PROPERTY ... 406
Article 4 - PLEADINGS ... 407
Article 5 - OBJECTIONS TO RIGHT TO TAKE ... 408
Article 6 - SETTLEMENT OFFERS AND ALTERNATIVE DISPUTE RESOLUTION ... 408
Chapter 6 - DEPOSIT AND WITHDRAWAL OF PROBABLE COMPENSATION; POSSESSION PRIOR TO JUDGMENT ... 409
Article 1 - DEPOSIT OF PROBABLE COMPENSATION ... 409
Article 2 - WITHDRAWAL OF DEPOSIT ... 410
Article 3 - POSSESSION PRIOR TO JUDGMENT ... 411
Chapter 7 - DISCOVERY; EXCHANGE OF VALUATION DATA ... 412
Article 1 - DISCOVERY ... 412
Article 2 - EXCHANGE OF VALUATION DATA ... 413
Chapter 8 - PROCEDURES FOR DETERMINING RIGHT TO TAKE AND COMPENSATION ... 414
Article 1 - GENERAL PROVISIONS ... 414
Article 2 - CONTESTING RIGHT TO TAKE ... 415
Article 3 - PROCEDURES RELATING TO DETERMINATION OF COMPENSATION ... 415
Chapter 9 - COMPENSATION ... 416
Article 1 - GENERAL PROVISIONS ... 416
Article 2 - DATE OF VALUATION ... 416
Article 3 - COMPENSATION FOR IMPROVEMENTS ... 417
Article 4 - MEASURE OF COMPENSATION FOR PROPERTY TAKEN ... 418
Article 5 - COMPENSATION FOR INJURY TO REMAINDER ... 418
Article 6 - COMPENSATION FOR LOSS OF GOODWILL ... 418
Article 7 - MISCELLANEOUS PROVISIONS ... 419
Article 8 - REMEDIATION OF HAZARDOUS MATERIALS ON PROPERTY TO BE ACQUIRED BY SCHOOL DISTRICTS ... 419
Chapter 10 - DIVIDED INTERESTS ... 421
Article 1 - GENERAL PROVISIONS ... 421
Article 2 - LEASES ... 421
Article 3 - ENCUMBRANCES ... 421
Article 4 - FUTURE INTERESTS ... 422
Chapter 11 - POSTJUDGMENT PROCEDURE ... 422
Article 1 - PAYMENT OF JUDGMENT; FINAL ORDER OF CONDEMNATION ... 422
Article 2 - DEPOSIT AND WITHDRAWAL OF AWARD ... 423
Article 3 - POSSESSION AFTER JUDGMENT ... 424
Article 4 - INTEREST ... 424
Article 5 - PRORATION OF PROPERTY TAXES ... 424
Article 6 - ABANDONMENT ... 425

Article 7 - LITIGATION EXPENSES AND DAMAGES UPON DISMISSAL OR DEFEAT OF RIGHT TO TAKE 425

Article 8 - COSTS 426

Chapter 12 - ARBITRATION OF COMPENSATION IN ACQUISITIONS OF PROPERTY FOR PUBLIC USE 426

Title 8 - CHANGE OF NAMES 426

Title 9 - ARBITRATION 429

Chapter 1 - GENERAL PROVISIONS 429

Chapter 2 - ENFORCEMENT OF ARBITRATION AGREEMENTS 430

Chapter 3 - CONDUCT OF ARBITRATION PROCEEDINGS 434

Chapter 4 - ENFORCEMENT OF THE AWARD 438

Article 1 - CONFIRMATION, CORRECTION OR VACATION OF THE AWARD 438

Article 2 - LIMITATIONS OF TIME 439

Chapter 5 - GENERAL PROVISIONS RELATING TO JUDICIAL PROCEEDINGS 439

Article 1 - PETITIONS AND RESPONSES 439

Article 2 - VENUE, JURISDICTION AND COSTS 440

Article 3 - APPEALS 440

Title 9.1 - ARBITRATION OF MEDICAL MALPRACTICE 441

Title 9.2 - PUBLIC CONSTRUCTION CONTRACT ARBITRATION 441

Title 9.3 - ARBITRATION AND CONCILIATION OF INTERNATIONAL COMMERCIAL DISPUTES 442

Chapter 1 - APPLICATION AND INTERPRETATION 442

Article 1 - SCOPE OF APPLICATION 442

Article 2 - INTERPRETATION 442

Article 3 - RECEIPT OF WRITTEN COMMUNICATIONS 443

Article 4 - WAIVER OF RIGHT TO OBJECT 443

Article 5 - EXTENT OF JUDICIAL INTERVENTION 443

Article 6 - FUNCTIONS 443

Chapter 2 - ARBITRATION AGREEMENTS AND JUDICIAL MEASURES IN AID OF ARBITRATION 443

Article 1 - DEFINITION AND FORM OF ARBITRATION AGREEMENTS 443

Article 2 - STAY OF PROCEEDINGS 443

Article 3 - INTERIM MEASURES 443

Chapter 3 - COMPOSITION OF ARBITRAL TRIBUNALS 444

Article 1 - NUMBER OF ARBITRATORS 444

Article 2 - APPOINTMENT OF ARBITRATORS 444

Article 3 - GROUNDS FOR CHALLENGE 444

Article 4 - CHALLENGE PROCEDURE 445

Article 5 - FAILURE OR IMPOSSIBILITY TO ACT 445

Article 6 - TERMINATION OF MANDATE AND SUBSTITUTION OF ARBITRATORS 446

Chapter 4 - JURISDICTION OF ARBITRAL TRIBUNALS 446

Article 1 - COMPETENCE OF AN ARBITRAL TRIBUNAL TO RULE ON ITS JURISDICTION............446

Article 2 - INTERIM MEASURES ORDERED BY ARBITRAL TRIBUNALS 446

Chapter 5 - MANNER AND CONDUCT OF ARBITRATION 446

Article 1 - EQUAL TREATMENT OF PARTIES 446

Article 1.5 - REPRESENTATION BY FOREIGN AND OUT-OF-STATE ATTORNEYS 447

Article 2 - DETERMINATION OF RULES OF PROCEDURE 447

Article 3 - PLACE OF ARBITRATION 447

Article 4 - COMMENCEMENT OF ARBITRAL PROCEEDINGS 448

Article 5 - LANGUAGE 448

Article 6 - STATEMENTS OF CLAIM AND DEFENSE 448

Article 7 - HEARINGS AND WRITTEN PROCEEDINGS 448

Article 8 - DEFAULT OF A PARTY 448

Article 9 - EXPERT APPOINTED BY ARBITRAL TRIBUNAL 448

Article 10 - COURT ASSISTANCE IN TAKING EVIDENCE AND CONSOLIDATING ARBITRATIONS 449

Chapter 6 - MAKING OF ARBITRAL AWARD AND TERMINATION OF PROCEEDINGS....................449

Article 1 - RULES APPLICABLE TO SUBSTANCE OF DISPUTE 449

Article 2 - DECISIONMAKING BY PANEL OF ARBITRATORS 449

Article 3 - SETTLEMENT 449

Article 4 - FORM AND CONTENT OF ARBITRAL AWARD 450

Article 5 - TERMINATION OF PROCEEDINGS 450

Article 6 - CORRECTION AND INTERPRETATION OF AWARDS AND ADDITIONAL AWARDS........450

Chapter 7 - CONCILIATION 451

Article 1 - APPOINTMENT OF CONCILIATORS 451

Article 2 - REPRESENTATION AND ASSISTANCE 451

Article 3 - REPORT OF CONCILIATORS 451

Article 4 - CONFIDENTIALITY 451

Article 5 - STAY OF ARBITRATION AND RESORT TO OTHER PROCEEDINGS 451

Article 6 - TERMINATION 452

Article 7 - ENFORCEABILITY OF DECREE 452

Article 8 - COSTS 452

Article 9 - EFFECT ON JURISDICTION 452

Article 10 - IMMUNITY OF CONCILIATORS AND PARTIES 452

Title 9.4 - REAL ESTATE CONTRACT ARBITRATION...452

Title 9.5 - ARBITRATION OF FIREFIGHTER AND LAW ENFORCEMENT OFFICER LABOR DISPUTES 453

Title 10 - UNCLAIMED PROPERTY 455

Chapter 1 - GENERAL PROVISIONS 455

Article 1 - DEFINITIONS 455

Article 2 - PURPOSE AND SCOPE 455
Chapter 2 - RECEIPT AND EXPENDITURE OF FUNDS 455
Article 1 - DEPOSIT OF UNCLAIMED PROPERTY 455
Article 2 - APPROPRIATION 457
Chapter 3 - PAYMENT OF CLAIMS 457
Article 1 - GENERAL 457
Article 2 - REFUND OF ERRONEOUS RECEIPTS 457
Article 3 - CLAIMS 457
Chapter 4 - MANAGEMENT OF UNCLAIMED PROPERTY 459
Article 1 - GENERAL PROVISIONS 459
Article 2 - POWERS OF THE CONTROLLER 459
Article 3 - SALE OR DISPOSAL OF PROPERTY 459
Article 4 - DISPOSAL OF PROCEEDS OF SALE OR LEASE 460
Chapter 5 - ESCHEAT PROCEEDINGS 460
Article 1 - ESCHEAT PROCEEDINGS ON UNCLAIMED PROPERTY 460
Article 2 - ESCHEAT BY NOTICE AND PUBLICATION 461
Article 3 - ESCHEAT PROCEEDINGS IN DECEDENTS' ESTATES 461
Article 4 - PERMANENT ESCHEAT 462
Chapter 6 - DISPOSITION OF UNCLAIMED PROPERTY 463
Article 1 - ESTATES OF DECEASED PERSONS 463
Article 2 - ABANDONED PROPERTY 464
Chapter 7 - UNCLAIMED PROPERTY LAW 464
Article 1 - SHORT TITLE; DEFINITIONS; APPLICATION 464
Article 2 - ESCHEAT OF UNCLAIMED PERSONAL PROPERTY 465
Article 3 - IDENTIFICATION OF ESCHEATED PROPERTY 472
Article 4 - PAYMENT OF CLAIMS 474
Article 5 - ADMINISTRATION OF UNCLAIMED PROPERTY 475
Article 6 - COMPLIANCE AND ENFORCEMENT 477
Article 7 - MISCELLANEOUS 478
Chapter 8 - PROPERTY IN CUSTODY OF FEDERAL OFFICERS, AGENCIES, AND DEPARTMENTS.479
Title 11 - MONEY JUDGMENTS OF OTHER JURISDICTIONS 481
Chapter 1 - SISTER STATE MONEY JUDGMENTS 481
Chapter 2 - FOREIGN-COUNTRY MONEY JUDGMENTS 482
Chapter 3 - TRIBAL COURT CIVIL MONEY JUDGMENT ACT 484
Title 11.6 - CIVIL ACTION MEDIATION 487
Title 11.7 - RECOVERY OF PREFERENCES AND EXEMPT PROPERTY IN AN ASSIGNMENT FOR THE BENEFIT OF CREDITORS 489
Title 12 - TRIBAL INJUNCTIONS 492
Title 13 - INSPECTION WARRANTS 492

Part 4 - MISCELLANEOUS PROVISIONS 493
    Title 1 - OF THE GENERAL PRINCIPLES OF EVIDENCE...493
    Title 2 - OF THE KINDS AND DEGREES OF EVIDENCE...494
        Chapter 2 - WITNESSES..494
        Chapter 3 - WRITINGS...494
        Article 2 - PUBLIC WRITINGS 494
        Article 3 - PRIVATE WRITINGS...495
        Article 4 - RECORDS DESTROYED IN FIRE OR CALAMITY 496
        Article 4.5 - PRIVATE RECORDS DESTROYED IN DISASTER OR CALAMITY 497
        Chapter 6 - INDISPENSABLE EVIDENCE..497
    Title 3 - OF THE PRODUCTION OF EVIDENCE...497
        Chapter 2 - MEANS OF PRODUCTION...497
        Chapter 3 - MANNER OF PRODUCTION 504
        Article 1 - MODE OF TAKING THE TESTIMONY OF WITNESSES...504
        Article 2 - AFFIDAVITS...505
    Title 4 - CIVIL DISCOVERY ACT 505
        Chapter 1 - GENERAL PROVISIONS 505
        Chapter 2 - SCOPE OF DISCOVERY 507
        Article 1 - GENERAL PROVISIONS 507
        Article 2 - SCOPE OF DISCOVERY IN SPECIFIC CONTEXTS 507
        Article 3 - VIOLATION OF THE ELDER ABUSE AND DEPENDENT ADULT CIVIL PROTECTION ACT 507
        Chapter 3 - USE OF TECHNOLOGY IN CONDUCTING DISCOVERY IN A COMPLEX CASE...............508
        Chapter 4 - ATTORNEY WORK PRODUCT 508
        Chapter 5 - METHODS AND SEQUENCE OF DISCOVERY 509
        Article 1 - GENERAL PROVISIONS 509
        Article 2 - METHODS AND SEQUENCE OF DISCOVERY IN SPECIFIC CONTEXTS 509
        Chapter 6 - NONPARTY DISCOVERY 509
        Article 1 - GENERAL PROVISIONS 509
        Article 2 - PROCEDURES APPLICABLE TO ALL TYPES OF DEPOSITION SUBPOENAS 509
        Article 3 - SUBPOENA COMMANDING ONLY ATTENDANCE AND TESTIMONY OF THE DEPONENT 510
        Article 4 - SUBPOENA COMMANDING ONLY PRODUCTION OF BUSINESS RECORDS FOR COPYING 2020.410...511
        Article 5 - SUBPOENA COMMANDING BOTH PRODUCTION OF BUSINESS RECORDS AND ATTENDANCE AND TESTIMONY OF THE DEPONENT 2020.510 511
        Chapter 7 - SANCTIONS 512
        Chapter 8 - TIME FOR COMPLETION OF DISCOVERY 513
        Chapter 9 - ORAL DEPOSITION INSIDE CALIFORNIA..513

Article 1 - GENERAL PROVISIONS 513

Article 2 - DEPOSITION NOTICE 514

Article 3 - CONDUCT OF DEPOSITION 516

Article 4 - OBJECTIONS, SANCTIONS, PROTECTIVE ORDERS, MOTIONS TO COMPEL, AND SUSPENSION OF DEPOSITIONS 517

Article 5 - TRANSCRIPT OR RECORDING 520

Article 6 - POST-DEPOSITION PROCEDURES 2025.610 522

Chapter 10 - ORAL DEPOSITION OUTSIDE CALIFORNIA 523

Chapter 11 - DEPOSITION BY WRITTEN QUESTIONS 523

Chapter 12 - DISCOVERY IN ACTION PENDING OUTSIDE CALIFORNIA 524

Article 1 - INTERSTATE AND INTERNATIONAL DEPOSITIONS AND DISCOVERY ACT 524

Chapter 13 - WRITTEN INTERROGATORIES 526

Article 1 - PROPOUNDING INTERROGATORIES 526

Article 2 - RESPONSE TO INTERROGATORIES 528

Article 3 - USE OF INTERROGATORY ANSWER 530

Chapter 14 - INSPECTION, COPYING, TESTING, SAMPLING, AND PRODUCTION OF DOCUMENTS, ELECTRONICALLY STORED INFORMATION, TANGIBLE THINGS, LAND, AND OTHER PROPERTY 530

Article 1 - INSPECTION DEMAND 530

Article 2 - RESPONSE TO INSPECTION DEMAND 532

Article 3 - INSPECTION AND PRODUCTION OF DOCUMENTS AND OTHER PROPERTY IN SPECIFIC CONTEXTS 535

Chapter 15 - PHYSICAL OR MENTAL EXAMINATION 535

Article 1 - GENERAL PROVISIONS 535

Article 2 - PHYSICAL EXAMINATION OF PERSONAL INJURY PLAINTIFF 535

Article 3 - MOTION FOR PHYSICAL OR MENTAL EXAMINATION 536

Article 4 - FAILURE TO SUBMIT TO OR PRODUCE ANOTHER FOR PHYSICAL OR MENTAL EXAMINATION 536

Article 5 - CONDUCT OF EXAMINATION 536

Article 6 - REPORTS OF EXAMINATION 537

Chapter 16 - REQUESTS FOR ADMISSION 537

Article 1 - REQUESTS FOR ADMISSION 537

Article 2 - RESPONSE TO REQUESTS FOR ADMISSION 539

Article 3 - EFFECT OF ADMISSION 540

Chapter 17 - FORM INTERROGATORIES AND REQUESTS FOR ADMISSION 541

Chapter 18 - SIMULTANEOUS EXCHANGE OF EXPERT WITNESS INFORMATION 541

Article 1 - GENERAL PROVISIONS 541

Article 2 - DEMAND FOR EXCHANGE OF EXPERT WITNESS INFORMATION 541

Article 3 - DEPOSITION OF EXPERT WITNESS 543

Article 4 - MOTION TO AUGMENT OR AMEND EXPERT WITNESS LIST OR DECLARATION 544

Article 5 - MOTION TO SUBMIT TARDY EXPERT WITNESS INFORMATION 544

Chapter 19 - PERPETUATION OF TESTIMONY OR PRESERVATION OF EVIDENCE BEFORE FILING ACTION 545

Chapter 20 - PERPETUATION OF TESTIMONY OR PRESERVATION OF INFORMATION PENDING APPEAL 546

Title 5 - OF THE RIGHTS AND DUTIES OF WITNESSES 546

Title 6 - OF EVIDENCE IN PARTICULAR CASES, AND MISCELLANEOUS AND GENERAL PROVISIONS 546

Chapter 1 - EVIDENCE IN PARTICULAR CASES 546

Chapter 3 - ADMINISTRATION OF OATHS AND AFFIRMATIONS 547

Title 7 - UNIFORM FEDERAL LIEN REGISTRATION ACT 548

Division - TITLE OF ACT

Section 1 - Title of act, parts

This act shall be known as the Code of Civil Procedure, and is divided into four parts, as follows:

Part I.	Of Courts of Justice.
II.	Of Civil Actions.
III.	Of Special Proceedings of a Civil Nature.
IV.	Miscellaneous Provisions.

Amended by Stats. 1965, Ch. 299.

Division - PRELIMINARY PROVISIONS

Section 2 - Effective date

This Code takes effect at twelve o'clock noon, on the first day of January, eighteen hundred and seventy-three.
Enacted 1872.

Section 3 - Retroactive effect

No part of it is retroactive, unless expressly so declared.
Enacted 1872.

Section 4 - Code establishes law of state

The rule of the common law, that statutes in derogation thereof are to be strictly construed, has no application to this Code. The Code establishes the law of this State respecting the subjects to which it relates, and its provisions and all proceedings under it are to be liberally construed, with a view to effect its objects and to promote justice.
Enacted 1872.

Section 5 - Provisions substantially same as existing statutes construed as continuations

The provisions of this Code, so far as they are substantially the same as existing statutes, must be construed as continuations thereof, and not as new enactments.
Enacted 1872.

Section 6 - Continuation in office of persons holding office under repealed acts

All persons who at the time this Code takes effect hold office under any of the Acts repealed, continue to hold the same according to the tenure thereof, except those offices which are not continued by one of the Codes adopted at this session of the Legislature.
Enacted 1872.

Section 7 - Cessation of office abolished by repeal of act

When any office is abolished by the repeal of any Act, and such Act is not in substance reënacted or continued in either of the Codes, such office ceases at the time the Codes take effect.
Enacted 1872.

Section 8 - Proceedings commenced and rights accrued before effective date

No action or proceeding commenced before this Code takes effect, and no right accrued, is affected by its provisions, but the proceedings therein must conform to the requirements of this Code as far as applicable.
Enacted 1872.

Section 9 - Limitation or period of time in existing statute has begun to run before effective date

When a limitation or period of time prescribed in any existing statute for acquiring a right or barring a remedy, or for any other purpose, has begun to run before this code goes into effect, and the same or any limitation is prescribed in this code, the time that has already run shall be deemed part of the time prescribed as such limitation by this code.
Amended by Stats 2017 ch 561 (AB 1516),s 20, eff. 1/1/2018.

Section 10 - Holidays within meaning of code

Holidays within the meaning of this code are every Sunday and any other days that are specified or provided for as judicial holidays in Section 135.
Amended by Stats 2001 ch 542 (SB 1112), s 1, eff. 1/1/2002.

Section 11 - Notice or communication required to be mailed by registered mail

Wherever any notice or other communication is required by this code to be mailed by registered mail by or to any person or corporation, the mailing of such notice or communication by certified mail shall be deemed to be a sufficient compliance with the requirements of law.
Added by Stats. 1959, Ch. 426.

Section 12 - Computation of time in which act provided bylaw to be done

The time in which any act provided by law is to be done is computed by excluding the first day, and including the last, unless the last day is a holiday, and then it is also excluded.
Enacted 1872.

Section 12a - Last day for performing act holiday

(a) If the last day for the performance of any act provided or required by law to be performed within a specified period of time is a holiday, then that period is hereby extended to and including the next day that is not a holiday. For purposes of this section, "holiday" means all day on Saturdays, all holidays specified in Section 135 and, to the extent provided in Section 12b, all days that by terms of Section 12b are required to be considered as holidays.
(b) This section applies to Sections 659, 659a, and 921, and to all other provisions of law providing or requiring an act to be performed on a particular day or within a specified period of time, whether expressed in this or any other code or statute, ordinance, rule, or regulation.
Amended by Stats 2007 ch 263 (AB 310),s 3, eff. 1/1/2008.
Amended by Stats 2001 ch 542 (SB 1112), s 2, eff. 1/1/2002.

Section 12b - Day office closed considered holiday

If any city, county, state, or public office, other than a branch office, is closed for the whole of any day, insofar as the business of that office is concerned, that day shall be considered as a holiday for the purposes of computing time under Sections 12 and 12a.
Added by Stats. 1951, Ch. 655.

Section 12c - Act to be performed no later than specified of days before hearing date

(a) Where any law requires an act to be performed no later than a specified number of days before a hearing date, the last day to perform that act shall be determined by counting backward from the hearing date, excluding the day of the hearing as provided by Section 12.

(b) Any additional days added to the specified number of days because of a particular method of service shall be computed by counting backward from the day determined in accordance with subdivision (a).

Added by Stats 2010 ch 41 (AB 2119),s 1, eff. 1/1/2011.

Section 13 - Act of secular nature falls upon holiday

Whenever any act of a secular nature, other than a work of necessity or mercy, is appointed by law or contract to be performed upon a particular day, which day falls upon a holiday, such act may be performed upon the next business day with the same effect as if it had been performed upon the day appointed.

Enacted 1872.

Section 13a - Act performed on special holiday

Any act required by law to be performed on a particular day or within a specified period of time may be performed (but is not hereby required to be performed) on a special holiday as that term is used in Section 6705 of the Government Code, with like effect as if performed on a day which is not a holiday.

Amended by Stats. 1959, Ch. 594.

Section 13b - Act performed on Saturday

Any act required by law to be performed on a particular day or within a specified period may be performed (but is not hereby required to be performed) on a Saturday, with like effect as if performed on a day which is not a holiday.

Added by Stats. 1961, Ch. 1370.

Section 14 - Seal required to be affixed to paper

When the seal of a Court, public officer, or person is required by law to be affixed to any paper, the word "seal" includes an impression of such seal upon the paper alone as well as upon wax or a wafer affixed thereto.

Enacted 1872.

Section 15 - Joint authority given to three or more public officers or persons

Words giving a joint authority to three or more public officers or other persons are construed as giving such authority to a majority of them, unless it is otherwise expressed in the Act giving the authority.

Enacted 1872.

Section 16 - Construction of words and phrases, technical words and phrases

Words and phrases are construed according to the context and the approved usage of the language; but technical words and phrases, and such others as have acquired a peculiar and appropriate meaning in law, or are defined in the succeeding section, are to be construed according to such peculiar and appropriate meaning or definition.

Enacted 1872.

Section 17 - Rules of construction

(a) Words used in this code in the present tense include the future as well as the present. Words used in the masculine gender include the feminine and neuter. The singular number includes the plural and the plural number includes the singular.

(b) As used in this code, the following words have the following meanings, unless otherwise apparent from the context:

(1) "Affinity" signifies the connection existing in consequence of marriage, between each of the married persons and the blood relatives of the other when applied to the marriage relation.

(2) "County" includes "city and county."

(3) "Electronic signature" means an electronic sound, symbol, or process attached to or logically associated with an electronic record and executed or adopted by a person with the intent to sign the electronic record.

(4) "Month" means a calendar month, unless otherwise expressed.

(5) "Oath" includes an affirmation or declaration.

(A) "Depose" includes any written statement made under oath or affirmation.

(B) "Testify" includes any mode of oral statement made under oath or affirmation.

(6) "Person" includes a corporation as well as a natural person.

(7) "Process" signifies a writ or summons issued in the course of a judicial proceeding.

(8) "Property" includes both personal and real property.

(A) "Personal property" includes money, goods, chattels, things in action, and evidences of debt.

(B) "Real property" is coextensive with lands, tenements, and hereditaments.

(9) "Section" refers to a section of this code, unless some other code or statute is expressly mentioned.

(10) "Sheriff" includes marshal.

(11) "Signature" or "subscription" includes a mark of a person's name, if the person cannot write, with his or her name being written near it by a person who writes his or her own name as a witness. In order that a mark may be acknowledged or serve as the signature to any sworn statement, it shall be witnessed by two persons who shall subscribe their own names as witnesses thereto.

(12) "Spouse" includes "registered domestic partner," as required by Section 297.5 of the Family Code.

(13) "State" includes the District of Columbia and the territories when applied to the different parts of the United States, and the words "United States" may include the district and territories.

(14) "Will" includes codicil.

(15) "Writ" means an order or precept in writing, issued in the name of the people, or of a court or judicial officer.

(16) "Writing" includes printing and typewriting.

Amended by Stats 2016 ch 50 (SB 1005),s 13, eff. 1/1/2017.
Amended by Stats 2015 ch 32 (AB 432),s 1, eff. 1/1/2016.
Amended by Stats 2003 ch 62 (SB 600),s 21, eff. 1/1/2004.
Amended by Stats 2002 ch 784 (SB 1316),s 21, eff. 1/1/2003.

Section 18 - Statutes, laws and rules repealed and abrogated

No statute, law, or rule is continued in force because it is consistent with the provisions of this Code on the same subject; but in all cases provided for by this Code, all statutes, laws, and rules heretofore in force in this State, whether consistent or not with the provisions of this Code, unless expressly continued in force by it, are repealed and abrogated. This repeal or abrogation does not revive any former law heretofore repealed, nor does it affect any right already existing or accrued, or any action or proceeding already taken, except as in this Code provided; nor does it affect any private statute not expressly repealed.

Enacted 1872.

Section 19 - Designation of act

This Act, whenever cited, enumerated, referred to, or amended, may be designated simply as "The Code of Civil Procedure," adding, when necessary, the number of the section.

Enacted 1872.

Section 20 - Judicial remedies

Judicial remedies are such as are administered by the Courts of justice, or by judicial officers empowered for that purpose by the Constitution and statutes of this State.

Enacted 1872.

Section 21 - Classes of remedies

These remedies are divided into two classes:

1. Actions; and,

2. Special proceedings.

Enacted 1872.

Section 22 - Action

An action is an ordinary proceeding in a court of justice by which one party prosecutes another for the declaration, enforcement, or protection of a right, the redress or prevention of a wrong, or the punishment of a public offense.

Amended by Stats. 1933, Ch. 742.

Section 23 - Special proceeding

Every other remedy is a special proceeding.

Enacted 1872.

Section 24 - Kinds of actions

Actions are of two kinds:

1. Civil; and,

2. Criminal.

Enacted 1872.

Section 25 - Civil action

A civil action arises out of:

1. An obligation;

2. An injury.

Enacted 1872.

Section 26 - Obligation

An obligation is a legal duty, by which one person is bound to do or not to do a certain thing, and arises from either of the following:

(a) Contract.

(b) Operation of law.

Amended by Stats 2017 ch 561 (AB 1516),s 21, eff. 1/1/2018.

Section 27 - Kinds of injury

An injury is of two kinds:

1. To the person; and,

2. To property.

Enacted 1872.

Section 28 - Injury to property

An injury to property consists in depriving its owner of the benefit of it, which is done by taking, withholding, deteriorating, or destroying it.

Enacted 1872.

Section 29 - Injury to person

Every other injury is an injury to the person.

Enacted 1872.

Section 30 - Remedies in civil action

A civil action is prosecuted by one party against another for the declaration, enforcement or protection of a right, or the redress or prevention of a wrong.

Amended by Stats. 1933, Ch. 742.

Section 31 - Prosecution of criminal action

The Penal Code defines and provides for the prosecution of a criminal action.

Enacted 1872.

Section 32 - Merger of right to prosecute

When the violation of a right admits of both a civil and criminal remedy, the right to prosecute the one is not merged in the other.

Enacted 1872.

Section 32.5 - Jurisdictional classification

The "jurisdictional classification" of a case means its classification as a limited civil case or an unlimited civil case.

Amended by Stats 2002 ch 784 (SB 1316),s 22, eff. 1/1/2003.

Section 33 - Assistance by prosecuting attorney in civil resolution of Title 13, Part 1, Penal Code violation

A prosecuting attorney, in his or her discretion, may assist in the civil resolution of a violation of an offense described in Title 13 (commencing with Section 450) of Part 1 of the Penal Code in lieu of filing a criminal complaint.

Added by Stats. 1982, Ch. 1518, Sec. 1.

Section 34 - Electronic signature

An electronic signature, as defined in Section 17, by a court or judicial officer shall be as effective as an original signature.

Added by Stats 2015 ch 32 (AB 432),s 2, eff. 1/1/2016.

Part 1 - OF COURTS OF JUSTICE

Title 1 - ORGANIZATION AND JURISDICTION

Chapter 1 - COURTS OF JUSTICE IN GENERAL

Section 35 - [Effective until 1/1/2027] Precedence given proceedings regarding elections

(a) Proceedings in cases involving the registration or denial of registration of voters, the certification or denial of certification of candidates, the certification or denial of certification of ballot measures, election contests, and actions under Section 20010 of the Elections Code shall be placed on the calendar in the order of their date of filing and shall be given precedence.

(b) This section shall remain in effect only until January 1, 2027, and as of that date is repealed, unless a later enacted statute, that is enacted before January 1, 2027, deletes or extends that date.

Amended by Stats 2022 ch 745 (AB 972),s 1, eff. 1/1/2023.

Amended by Stats 2019 ch 493 (AB 730),s 1, eff. 1/1/2020.

Section 35 - [Operative 1/1/2027] Precedence given proceedings regarding elections

(a) Proceedings in cases involving the registration or denial of registration of voters, the certification or denial of certification of candidates, the certification or denial of certification of ballot measures, and election contests shall be placed on the calendar in the order of their date of filing and shall be given precedence.

(b) This section shall become operative January 1, 2027.

Amended by Stats 2022 ch 745 (AB 972),s 2, eff. 1/1/2023.
Added by Stats 2019 ch 493 (AB 730),s 2, eff. 1/1/2020.

Section 36 - Motion for preference

(a) A party to a civil action who is over 70 years of age may petition the court for a preference, which the court shall grant if the court makes both of the following findings:

(1) The party has a substantial interest in the action as a whole.

(2) The health of the party is such that a preference is necessary to prevent prejudicing the party's interest in the litigation.

(b) A civil action to recover damages for wrongful death or personal injury shall be entitled to preference upon the motion of any party to the action who is under 14 years of age unless the court finds that the party does not have a substantial interest in the case as a whole. A civil action subject to subdivision (a) shall be given preference over a case subject to this subdivision.

(c) Unless the court otherwise orders:

(1) A party may file and serve a motion for preference supported by a declaration of the moving party that all essential parties have been served with process or have appeared.

(2) At any time during the pendency of the action, a party who reaches 70 years of age may file and serve a motion for preference.

(d) In its discretion, the court may also grant a motion for preference that is accompanied by clear and convincing medical documentation that concludes that one of the parties suffers from an illness or condition raising substantial medical doubt of survival of that party beyond six months, and that satisfies the court that the interests of justice will be served by granting the preference.

(e) Notwithstanding any other provision of law, the court may in its discretion grant a motion for preference that is supported by a showing that satisfies the court that the interests of justice will be served by granting this preference.

(f) Upon the granting of such a motion for preference, the court shall set the matter for trial not more than 120 days from that date and there shall be no continuance beyond 120 days from the granting of the motion for preference except for physical disability of a party or a party's attorney, or upon a showing of good cause stated in the record. Any continuance shall be for no more than 15 days and no more than one continuance for physical disability may be granted to any party.

(g) Upon the granting of a motion for preference pursuant to subdivision (b), a party in an action based upon a health provider's alleged professional negligence, as defined in Section 364, shall receive a trial date not sooner than six months and not later than nine months from the date that the motion is granted.

Amended by Stats 2008 ch 218 (AB 1949),s 1, eff. 1/1/2009.

Section 36.5 - Affidavit in support of motion for preference

An affidavit submitted in support of a motion for preference under subdivision (a) of Section 36 may be signed by the attorney for the party seeking preference based upon information and belief as to the medical diagnosis and prognosis of any party. The affidavit is not admissible for any purpose other than a motion for preference under subdivision (a) of Section 36.

Added by Stats. 1990, Ch. 1232, Sec. 1.

Section 37 - Preference in action for damages caused by defendant in commission of felony

(a) A civil action shall be entitled to preference, if the action is one in which the plaintiff is seeking damages which were alleged to have been caused by the defendant during the commission of a felony offense for which the defendant has been criminally convicted.

(b) The court shall endeavor to try the action within 120 days of the grant of preference.

Amended by Stats. 1983, Ch. 938, Sec. 1. Effective September 20, 1983.

Section 38 - Reference in statutes to judicial district

Unless the provision or context otherwise requires, a reference in a statute to a judicial district means:

(a) As it relates to a court of appeal, the court of appeal district.

(b) As it relates to a superior court, the county.

Amended by Stats 2018 ch 92 (SB 1289),s 39, eff. 1/1/2019.

Chapter 3 - SUPREME COURT

Section 41 - Business transacted at any time

The Supreme Court and the courts of appeal may transact business at any time.

Added by renumbering Section 61.4 by Stats. 1967, Ch. 17.

Section 42 - Adjournments construed as recesses

Adjournments from day to day, or from time to time, are to be construed as recesses in the sessions, and shall not prevent the Supreme Court or the courts of appeal from sitting at any time.

Added by renumbering Section 48 by Stats. 1967, Ch. 17.

Section 43 - Authority of court in proceedings before courts; questions determined if new trial granted

The Supreme Court, and the courts of appeal, may affirm, reverse, or modify any judgment or order appealed from, and may direct the proper judgment or order to be entered, or direct a new trial or further proceedings to be had. In giving its decision, if a new trial be granted, the court shall pass upon and determine all the questions of law involved in the case, presented upon such appeal, and necessary to the final determination of the case. Its judgment in appealed cases shall be remitted to the court from which the appeal was taken.

Added by renumbering Section 53 by Stats. 1967, Ch. 17.

Section 44 - Preference of appeals in probate proceedings and certain election cases

Appeals in probate proceedings, in contested election cases, and in actions for libel or slander by a person who holds any elective public office or a candidate for any such office alleged to have occurred during the course of an election campaign shall be given preference in hearing in the courts of appeal, and in the Supreme Court when transferred thereto. All these cases shall be placed on the calendar in the order of their date of issue, next after cases in which the people of the state are parties.

Amended by Stats. 1982, Ch. 1642, Sec. 1. Operative June 6, 1984, pursuant to Sec. 3 of Ch. 1642.

Section 45 - Precedence of cases regarding freeing minor from parental control

An appeal from a judgment freeing a minor who is a dependent child of the juvenile court from parental custody and control, or denying a recommendation to free a minor from parental custody or control, shall have precedence over all cases in the court to which an appeal in the matter is taken. In order to enable the child to be available for adoption as soon as possible and to minimize the anxiety to all parties, the appellate court shall grant an extension of time to a court reporter or to counsel only upon an exceptional showing of good cause.

Amended by Stats. 1997, Ch. 510, Sec. 1. Effective January 1, 1998.

Chapter 4 - SUPERIOR COURTS

Section 71 - Process extends throughout state

The process of superior courts shall extend throughout the state.

Added by Stats. 1967, Ch. 17.

Section 73c - Hearings relating to sale, exchange or disposition of property of savings and loan association

Notwithstanding anything to the contrary contained in any other law of this state, the judges of the superior court of the county in which is located the principal office in this state of any savings and loan association of whose business, property and assets possession shall have been taken by the Commissioner of Financial Institutions, may, in their discretion, whenever those judges deem it necessary or advisable, hold hearings relating to the sale, exchange or other disposition of any parcel of real property or any item of personal property of the association, regardless of the location of the property, at the county seat of any county in this state or at the places in the county in which the principal office in this state of the association is located at which sessions of the superior court are held.

Amended by Stats 2003 ch 149 (SB 79),s 1, eff. 1/1/2004.

Section 73d - Travel expenses for judge, clerk, deputy clerk, court report or bailiff to attend hearings pursuant to section 73c

Whenever, under Section 73c, it becomes necessary for a judge, clerk, deputy clerk, court reporter or bailiff of or sitting in the superior court of the county in this state in which is located the principal office of any savings and loan association whose business, property and assets are in the possession of the Commissioner of Financial Institutions, to travel to another county, there temporarily to attend hearings relating to the sale, exchange or other disposition of real or personal property of the association, each judge, clerk, deputy clerk, court reporter or bailiff shall be allowed the necessary expenses in going to, returning from and attending upon the business of the court. The expenses shall, upon order of the court, be a charge against the funds of the association and paid out of those funds by the Commissioner of Financial Institutions.

Amended by Stats 2003 ch 149 (SB 79),s 2, eff. 1/1/2004.

Section 73e - Sessions of court in county in which juvenile hall located

Notwithstanding any other provisions of law, in each county wherein the juvenile hall is not located at the county seat of the county, a majority of the judges of the superior court in and for such county may by an order filed with the clerk of the court direct that a session or sessions of the superior court, while sitting for the purpose of hearing and determining cases and proceedings arising under Chapter 2 of Part 1 of Division 2 or Chapter 2 of Part 1 of Division 6 or Chapter 4 of Part 4 of Division 6 of the Welfare and Institutions Code, may be held or continued in any place in the county in which the juvenile hall is located and thereafter such session or sessions of the court may be held or continued in the location designated in such order. In a county having two superior court judges the presiding judge may make the order.

Amended by Stats 2002 ch 784 (SB 1316),s 24, eff. 1/1/2003.

Section 74 - Adjournments construed as recesses

Adjournments from day to day, or from time to time, are to be construed as recesses in the sessions, and shall not prevent the Court from sitting at any time.

Repealed and added by Code Amendments 1880, Ch. 35.

Section 75 - When noncontested matter deemed submitted when all judges absent from county

The superior court in any county may by rule provide that, whenever all judges are absent from the county, any noncontested matter in which no evidence is required, or which may be submitted upon affidavits, shall be deemed submitted upon the filing with the clerk of a statement of submission by the party or the party's attorney or upon the date set for the hearing.

Amended by Stats 2002 ch 784 (SB 1316),s 25, eff. 1/1/2003.

Section 77 - Appellate division of superior court

(a) In every county there is an appellate division of the superior court consisting of three judges or, when the Chief Justice finds it necessary, four judges. The Chief Justice shall assign judges to the appellate division for specified terms pursuant to rules, not inconsistent with statute, adopted by the Judicial Council to promote the independence and quality of each appellate division. Each judge assigned to the appellate division of a superior court shall be a judge of that court, a judge of the superior court of another county, or a judge retired from the superior court or a court of higher jurisdiction in this state.

The Chief Justice shall designate one of the judges of each appellate division as the presiding judge of the division.

(b) In each appellate division, no more than three judges shall participate in a hearing or decision. The presiding judge of the division shall designate the three judges who shall participate.

(c) In addition to their other duties, the judges designated as members of the appellate division of the superior court shall serve for the period specified in the order of designation. Whenever a judge is designated to serve in the appellate division of the superior court of a county other than the county in which that judge was elected or appointed as a superior court judge, or if the judge is retired, in a county other than the county in which the judge resides, the judge shall receive expenses for travel, board, and lodging. If the judge is out of the judge's county overnight or longer, by reason of the designation, that judge shall be paid a per diem allowance in lieu of expenses for board and lodging in the same amounts as are payable for those purposes to justices of the Supreme Court under the rules of the Department of General Services. In addition, a retired judge shall receive for the time so served, amounts equal to that which the judge would have received if the judge had been assigned to the superior court of the county.

(d) The concurrence of two judges of the appellate division of the superior court shall be necessary to render the decision in every case in, and to transact any other business except business that may be done at chambers by the presiding judge of, the division. A judgment of the appellate division in an appeal shall contain a brief statement of the reasons for the judgment. A judgment stating only "affirmed" or "reversed" is insufficient. The presiding judge shall convene the appellate division when necessary. The presiding judge shall also supervise its business and transact any business that may be done at chambers.

(e) The appellate division of the superior court has jurisdiction on appeal in all cases in which an appeal may be taken to the superior court or the appellate division of the superior court as provided by law, except where the appeal is a retrial in the superior court.

(f) The powers of each appellate division shall be the same as are now or may hereafter be provided by law or rule of the Judicial Council relating to appeals to the appellate division of the superior courts.

(g) The Judicial Council shall promulgate rules, not inconsistent with law, to promote the independence of, and govern the practice and procedure and the disposition of the business of, the appellate division.

(h) Notwithstanding subdivisions (b) and (d), appeals from convictions of traffic infractions may be heard and decided by one judge of the appellate division of the superior court.

Amended by Stats 2018 ch 92 (SB 1289),s 40, eff. 1/1/2019.

Amended by Stats 2016 ch 31 (SB 836),s 10, eff. 6/27/2016.

Amended by Stats 2014 ch 58 (AB 1932),s 1, eff. 1/1/2015.

Amended by Stats 2006 ch 538 (SB 1852),s 60, eff. 1/1/2007.

Amended by Stats 2002 ch 784 (SB 1316),s 26, eff. 1/1/2003.

Previously Amended October 10, 1999 (Bill Number: SB 832) (Chapter 853).

Amended September 7, 1999 (Bill Number: SB 210) (Chapter 344).

Chapter 5 - MUNICIPAL COURTS
Section 81 through 84 - [Repealed]
Repealed by Stats 2002 ch 784 (SB 1316),s 27, eff. 1/1/2003.

Chapter 5.1 - LIMITED CIVIL CASES
Article 1 - JURISDICTION IN LIMITED CIVIL CASES

Section 85 - Action or special proceeding treated as limited civil case
An action or special proceeding shall be treated as a limited civil case if all of the following conditions are satisfied, and, notwithstanding any statute that classifies an action or special proceeding as a limited civil case, an action or special proceeding shall not be treated as a limited civil case unless all of the following conditions are satisfied:

(a) The amount in controversy does not exceed twenty-five thousand dollars ($25,000). As used in this section, "amount in controversy" means the amount of the demand, or the recovery sought, or the value of the property, or the amount of the lien, that is in controversy in the action, exclusive of attorneys' fees, interest, and costs.

(b) The relief sought is a type that may be granted in a limited civil case.

(c) The relief sought, whether in the complaint, a cross-complaint, or otherwise, is exclusively of a type described in one or more statutes that classify an action or special proceeding as a limited civil case or that provide that an action or special proceeding is within the original jurisdiction of the municipal court, including, but not limited to, the following provisions:

(1) Section 798.61 or 798.88 of the Civil Code.
(2) Section 1719 of the Civil Code.
(3) Section 3342.5 of the Civil Code.
(4) Section 86.
(5) Section 86.1.
(6) Section 1710.20.
(7) Section 7581 of the Food and Agricultural Code.
(8) Section 12647 of the Food and Agricultural Code.
(9) Section 27601 of the Food and Agricultural Code.
(10) Section 31503 of the Food and Agricultural Code.
(11) Section 31621 of the Food and Agricultural Code.
(12) Section 52514 of the Food and Agricultural Code.
(13) Section 53564 of the Food and Agricultural Code.
(14) Section 53069.4 of the Government Code.
(15) Section 53075.6 of the Government Code.
(16) Section 53075.61 of the Government Code.
(17) Section 5411.5 of the Public Utilities Code.
(18) Section 9872.1 of the Vehicle Code.
(19) Section 10751 of the Vehicle Code.
(20) Section 14607.6 of the Vehicle Code.
(21) Section 40230 of the Vehicle Code.
(22) Section 40256 of the Vehicle Code.

Amended by Stats 2015 ch 176 (SB 244),s 3, eff. 1/1/2016.
Amended by Stats 2012 ch 99 (AB 2272),s 3, eff. 1/1/2013.

Section 85.1 - [Repealed]
Repealed by Stats 2002 ch 784 (SB 1316),s 28, eff. 1/1/2003.

Section 86 - Cases or proceedings deemed limited civil cases
(a) The following civil cases and proceedings are limited civil cases:

(1) A case at law in which the demand, exclusive of interest, or the value of the property in controversy amounts to twenty-five thousand dollars ($25,000) or less. This paragraph does not apply to a case that involves the legality of any tax, impost, assessment, toll, or municipal fine, except an action to enforce payment of delinquent unsecured personal property taxes if the legality of the tax is not contested by the defendant.

(2) An action for dissolution of partnership where the total assets of the partnership do not exceed twenty-five thousand dollars ($25,000); an action of interpleader where the amount of money or the value of the property involved does not exceed twenty-five thousand dollars ($25,000).

(3) An action to cancel or rescind a contract when the relief is sought in connection with an action to recover money not exceeding twenty-five thousand dollars ($25,000) or property of a value not exceeding twenty-five thousand dollars ($25,000), paid or delivered under, or in consideration of, the contract; an action to revise a contract where the relief is sought in an action upon the contract if the action otherwise is a limited civil case.

(4) A proceeding in forcible entry or forcible or unlawful detainer where the whole amount of damages claimed is twenty-five thousand dollars ($25,000) or less.

(5) An action to enforce and foreclose a lien on personal property where the amount of the lien is twenty-five thousand dollars ($25,000) or less.

(6) An action to enforce and foreclose, or a petition to release, a lien arising under Chapter 4 (commencing with Section 8400) of Title 2 of Part 6 of Division 4 of the Civil Code, or to enforce and foreclose an assessment lien on a common interest development as defined in Section 4100 or 6534 of the Civil Code, where the amount of the liens is twenty-five thousand dollars ($25,000) or less. However, if an action to enforce the lien affects property that is also affected by a similar pending action that is not a limited civil case, or if the total amount of liens sought to be foreclosed against the same property aggregates an amount in excess of twenty-five thousand dollars ($25,000), the action is not a limited civil case.

(7) An action for declaratory relief when brought pursuant to either of the following:

(A) By way of cross-complaint as to a right of indemnity with respect to the relief demanded in the complaint or a cross-complaint in an action or proceeding that is otherwise a limited civil case.

(B) To conduct a trial after a nonbinding fee arbitration between an attorney and client, pursuant to Article 13 (commencing with Section 6200) of Chapter 4 of Division 3 of the Business and Professions Code, where the amount in controversy is twenty-five thousand dollars ($25,000) or less.

(8) An action to issue a temporary restraining order or preliminary injunction; to take an account, where necessary to preserve the property or rights of any party to a limited civil case; to make any order or perform any act, pursuant to Title 9 (commencing with Section 680.010) of Part 2 (enforcement of judgments) in a limited civil case; to appoint a receiver pursuant to Section 564 in a limited civil case; to determine title to personal property seized in a limited civil case.

(9) An action under Article 3 (commencing with Section 708.210) of Chapter 6 of Division 2 of Title 9 of Part 2 for the recovery of an interest in personal property or to enforce the liability of the debtor of a judgment debtor where the interest claimed adversely is of a value not exceeding twenty-five thousand dollars ($25,000) or the debt denied does not exceed twenty-five thousand dollars ($25,000).

(10) An arbitration-related petition filed pursuant to either of the following:

(A) Article 2 (commencing with Section 1292) of Chapter 5 of Title 9 of Part 3, except for uninsured motorist arbitration proceedings in accordance with Section 11580.2 of the Insurance Code, if the petition is filed before the arbitration award becomes final and the matter to be resolved by arbitration is a limited civil case under paragraphs (1) to (9), inclusive, of subdivision (a) or if the petition is filed after the arbitration award becomes final and the amount of the award and all other rulings, pronouncements, and decisions made in the award are within paragraphs (1) to (9), inclusive, of subdivision (a).

(B) To confirm, correct, or vacate a fee arbitration award between an attorney and client that is binding or has become binding, pursuant to Article 13 (commencing with Section 6200) of Chapter 4 of Division 3 of the Business and Professions Code, where the arbitration award is twenty-five thousand dollars ($25,000) or less.

(b) The following cases in equity are limited civil cases:

(1) A case to try title to personal property when the amount involved is not more than twenty-five thousand dollars ($25,000).

(2) A case when equity is pleaded as a defensive matter in any case that is otherwise a limited civil case.

(3) A case to vacate a judgment or order of the court obtained in a limited civil case through extrinsic fraud, mistake, inadvertence, or excusable neglect.

Amended by Stats 2013 ch 605 (SB 752),s 22, eff. 1/1/2014.
Amended by Stats 2012 ch 181 (AB 806),s 42, eff. 1/1/2013, op. 1/1/2014.
Amended by Stats 2010 ch 697 (SB 189),s 21, eff. 1/1/2011, op. 7/1/2012.
Amended by Stats 2001 ch 44 (SB 562), s 1, eff. 1/1/2002.

Section 86.1 - Action pursuant to Long-Term Care, Health, Safety and Security Act of 1973 deemed limited civil case

An action brought pursuant to the Long-Term Care, Health, Safety, and Security Act of 1973 (Chapter 2.4 (commencing with Section 1417) of Division 2 of the Health and Safety Code) is a limited civil case if civil penalties are not sought or amount to twenty-five thousand dollars ($25,000) or less.

Amended by Stats 2002 ch 784 (SB 1316),s 29, eff. 1/1/2003.

Section 87 - Limited civil case brought in small claims division

(a) A limited civil case may be brought in the small claims division if the case is within the jurisdiction of the small claims division as otherwise provided by statute. Where a statute or rule applicable to a small claims case conflicts with a statute or rule applicable to a limited civil case, the statute or rule applicable to a small claims case governs the small claims case and the statute or rule applicable to a limited civil case does not.

(b) Nothing in this section affects the jurisdiction of the small claims division as otherwise provided by statute.

Added 9/7/1999 (Bill Number: SB 210) (Chapter 344).

Section 88 - Action or proceeding referred to unlimited civil case

A civil action or proceeding other than a limited civil case may be referred to as an unlimited civil case.

Added 9/7/1999 (Bill Number: SB 210) (Chapter 344).

Section 89 - Authority of court in limited or unlimited civil cases

(a) The existence of a statute relating to the authority of the court in a limited civil case does not, by itself, imply that the same authority does or does not exist in an unlimited civil case.

(b) The existence of a statute relating to the authority of the court in an unlimited civil case does not, by itself, imply that the same authority does or does not exist in a limited civil case.

Added by Stats 2001 ch 44 (SB 562), s 2, eff. 1/1/2002.

Article 2 - ECONOMIC LITIGATION FOR LIMITED CIVIL CASES

Section 90 - Generally

Except where changed by the provisions of this article, all provisions of law applicable to civil actions generally apply to actions subject to this article.

Amended by Stats 2003 ch 149 (SB 79),s 3, eff. 1/1/2004.

Section 91 - Applicability of article; withdrawal of action from provisions of article

(a) Except as otherwise provided in this section, the provisions of this article apply to every limited civil case.

(b) The provisions of this article do not apply to any action under Chapter 5.5 (commencing with Section 116.110) or any proceeding under Chapter 4 (commencing with Section 1159) of Title 3 of Part 3.

(c) Any action may, upon noticed motion, be withdrawn from the provisions of this article, upon a showing that it is impractical to prosecute or defend the action within the limitations of these provisions.

Amended by Stats. 1998, Ch. 931, Sec. 36. Effective September 28, 1998.

Section 92 - Pleadings allowed

(a) The pleadings allowed are complaints, answers, cross-complaints, answers to cross-complaints and general demurrers.

(b) The answer need not be verified, even if the complaint or cross-complaint is verified.

(c) Special demurrers are not allowed.

(d) Motions to strike are allowed only on the ground that the damages or relief sought are not supported by the allegations of the complaint.

(e) Except as limited by this section, all other motions are permitted.

Amended by Stats. 1983, Ch. 102, Sec. 2. Effective June 16, 1983.

Section 93 - Case questionnaires

(a) The plaintiff has the option to serve case questionnaires with the complaint, using forms approved by the Judicial Council. The questionnaires served shall include a completed copy of the plaintiff's completed case questionnaire, and a blank copy of the defendant's case questionnaire.

(b) Any defendant upon whom a case questionnaire is served shall serve a completed defendant's case questionnaire upon the requesting plaintiff with the answer.

(c) The case questionnaire shall be designed to elicit fundamental information about each party's case, including names and addresses of all witnesses with knowledge of any relevant facts, a list of all documents relevant to the case, a statement of the nature and amount of damages, and information covering insurance coverages, injuries and treating physicians. The Judicial Council shall design and develop forms for case questionnaires.

(d) Approved forms shall be made available by the clerk of the court.

(e) If a party on whom a case questionnaire has been served under subdivision (a) or (b) fails to serve a timely or a complete response to that questionnaire, the party serving the questionnaire may move for an order compelling a response or a further response and for a monetary sanction under Chapter 7 (commencing with Section 2023.010) of Title 4 of Part 4. If a party then fails to obey an order compelling a response or a further response, the court may make those orders that are just, including the imposition of an issue sanction, an evidence sanction, or a terminating

sanction under Chapter 7 (commencing with Section 2023.010) of Title 4 of Part 4. In lieu of or in addition to that sanction, the court may impose a monetary sanction under Chapter 7 (commencing with Section 2023.010) of Title 4 of Part 4.
Amended by Stats 2004 ch 182 (AB 3081),s 5, eff. 7/1/2005
Amended by Stats. 1987, Ch. 86, Sec. 1. Effective July 2, 1987. Operative July 1, 1987, by Sec. 21 of Ch. 86.

Section 94 - Discovery
Discovery is permitted only to the extent provided by this section and Section 95. This discovery shall comply with the notice and format requirements of the particular method of discovery, as provided in Title 4 (commencing with Section 2016.010) of Part 4. As to each adverse party, a party may use the following forms of discovery:

(a) Any combination of 35 of the following:

(1) Interrogatories (with no subparts) under Chapter 13 (commencing with Section 2030.010) of Title 4 of Part 4.

(2) Demands to produce documents or things under Chapter 14 (commencing with Section 2031.010) of Title 4 of Part 4.

(3) Requests for admission (with no subparts) under Chapter 16 (commencing with Section 2033.010) of Title 4 of Part 4.

(b) One oral or written deposition under Chapter 9 (commencing with Section 2025.010), Chapter 10 (commencing with Section 2026.010), or Chapter 11 (commencing with Section 2028.010) of Title 4 of Part 4. For purposes of this subdivision, a deposition of an organization shall be treated as a single deposition even though more than one person may be designated or required to testify pursuant to Section 2025.230.

(c) Any party may serve on any person a deposition subpoena duces tecum requiring the person served to mail copies of documents, books, or records to the party's counsel at a specified address, along with an affidavit complying with Section 1561 of the Evidence Code. The party who issued the deposition subpoena shall mail a copy of the response to any other party who tenders the reasonable cost of copying it.

(d) Physical and mental examinations under Chapter 15 (commencing with Section 2032.010) of Title 4 of Part 4.

(e) The identity of expert witnesses under Chapter 18 (commencing with Section 2034.010) of Title 4 of Part 4.

Amended by Stats 2006 ch 538 (SB 1852),s 61, eff. 1/1/2007.
Amended by Stats 2005 ch 294 (AB 333),s 2, eff. 1/1/2006
Amended by Stats 2004 ch 182 (AB 3081),s 6, eff. 7/1/2005

Section 95 - Additional discovery
(a) The court may, on noticed motion and subject to such terms and conditions as are just, authorize a party to conduct additional discovery, but only upon a showing that the moving party will be unable to prosecute or defend the action effectively without the additional discovery. In making a determination under this section, the court shall take into account whether the moving party has used all applicable discovery in good faith, and whether the party has attempted to secure the additional discovery by stipulation or by means other than formal discovery.

(b) The parties may stipulate to additional discovery.

Added by Stats. 1982, Ch. 1581, Sec. 1.

Section 96 - Statement of names and addresses of witnesses party intends to call at trial
(a) Any party may serve on any other party a request in substantially the following form:

TO: ,
attorney for :

You are requested to serve on the undersigned, within 20 days, a statement of: the names and addresses of witnesses (OTHER THAN A PARTY WHO IS AN INDIVIDUAL) you intend to call at trial; a description of physical evidence you intend to offer; and a description and copies of documentary evidence you intend to offer or, if the documents are not available to you, a description of them. Witnesses and evidence that will be used only for impeachment need not be included. YOU WILL NOT BE PERMITTED TO CALL ANY WITNESS, OR INTRODUCE ANY EVIDENCE, NOT INCLUDED IN THE STATEMENT SERVED IN RESPONSE TO THIS REQUEST, EXCEPT AS OTHERWISE PROVIDED BY LAW.

(b) The request shall be served no more than 45 days or less than 30 days prior to the date first set for trial, unless otherwise ordered.

(c) A statement responding to the request shall be served within 20 days from the service of the request.

(d) No additional, amended or late statement is permitted except by written stipulation or unless ordered for good cause on noticed motion.

(e) No request or statement served under this section shall be filed, unless otherwise ordered.

(f) The clerk shall furnish forms for requests under this rule.

(g) The time for performing acts required under this section shall be computed as provided by law, including Section 1013.

Added by Stats. 1982, Ch. 1581, Sec. 1.

Section 97 - Calling witness or introducing evidence against objecting party
(a) Except as provided in this section, upon objection of a party who served a request in compliance with Section 96, no party required to serve a responding statement may call a witness or introduce evidence, except for purposes of impeachment, against the objecting party unless the witness or evidence was included in the statement served.

(b) The exceptions to subdivision (a) are:

(1) A person who, in his or her individual capacity, is a party to the litigation and who calls himself or herself as a witness.

(2) An adverse party.

(3) Witnesses and evidence used solely for purposes of impeachment.

(4) Documents obtained by discovery authorized by this chapter.

(5) The court may, upon such terms as may be just (including, but not limited to, continuing the trial for a reasonable period of time and awarding costs and litigation expenses), permit a party to call a witness or introduce evidence which is required to be, but is not included in such party's statement so long as the court finds that such party has made a good faith effort to comply with subdivision (c) of Section 96 or that the failure to comply was the result of his or her mistake, inadvertence, surprise or excusable neglect as provided in Section 473.

(c) Nothing in this article limits the introduction of evidence in any hearing pursuant to Section 585.

Amended by Stats. 1983, Ch. 102, Sec. 3. Effective June 16, 1983.

Section 98 - Prepared testimony offered by affidavit or declaration under penalty of perjury
A party may, in lieu of presenting direct testimony, offer the prepared testimony of revelant witnesses in the form of affidavits or declarations under penalty of perjury. The prepared testimony may include, but need not be limited to, the opinions of expert witnesses, and testimony which authenticates documentary evidence. To the extent the contents of the prepared testimony would have been admissible were the witness to testify orally thereto, the prepared testimony shall be received as evidence in the case, provided that either of the following applies:

(a) A copy has been served on the party against whom it is offered at least 30 days prior to the trial, together with a current address of the affiant that is within 150 miles of the place of trial, and the affiant is available for service of process at that place for a reasonable period of time, during the 20 days immediately prior to trial.

(b) The statement is in the form of all or part of a deposition in the case, and the party against whom it is offered had an opportunity to participate in the deposition. The court shall determine whether the affidavit or declaration shall be read into the record in lieu of oral testimony or admitted as a documentary exhibit.

Amended by Stats. 1983, Ch. 102, Sec. 4. Effective June 16, 1983.

Section 99 - When judgment or final order does not operate as collateral estoppel
A judgment or final order, in respect to the matter directly adjudged, is conclusive between the parties and their successors in interest but does not operate as collateral estoppel of a party or a successor in interest to a party in other litigation with a person who was not a party or a successor in interest to a party to the action in which the judgment or order is rendered.
Added by Stats. 1982, Ch. 1581, Sec. 1.

Section 100 - Right to appeal judgment or final order
Any party shall have the right to appeal any judgment or final order consistent with the law governing appeals.
Added by Stats. 1982, Ch. 1581, Sec. 1.

Chapter 5.5 - SMALL CLAIMS COURT
Article 1 - GENERAL PROVISIONS

Section 116.110 - Title of act
This chapter shall be known and may be cited as "The Small Claims Act."
Added by Stats. 1990, Ch. 1305, Sec. 3. Note: Prior to 1991, this subject matter was in Chapter 5A, comprising Sections 116 to 117.24.

Section 116.120 - Legislative findings and declaration
The Legislature hereby finds and declares as follows:
(a) Individual minor civil disputes are of special importance to the parties and of significant social and economic consequence collectively.
(b) In order to resolve minor civil disputes expeditiously, inexpensively, and fairly, it is essential to provide a judicial forum accessible to all parties directly involved in resolving these disputes.
(c) The small claims divisions have been established to provide a forum to resolve minor civil disputes, and for that reason constitute a fundamental element in the administration of justice and the protection of the rights and property of individuals.
(d) The small claims divisions, the provisions of this chapter, and the rules of the Judicial Council regarding small claims actions shall operate to ensure that the convenience of parties and witnesses who are individuals shall prevail, to the extent possible, over the convenience of any other parties or witnesses.
Amended by Stats. 1998, Ch. 931, Sec. 37. Effective September 28, 1998.

Section 116.130 - Definitions
In this chapter, unless the context indicates otherwise:
(a) "Plaintiff" means the party who has filed a small claims action. The term includes a defendant who has filed a claim against a plaintiff.
(b) "Defendant" means the party against whom the plaintiff has filed a small claims action. The term includes a plaintiff against whom a defendant has filed a claim.
(c) "Judgment creditor" means the party, whether plaintiff or defendant, in whose favor a money judgment has been rendered.
(d) "Judgment debtor" means the party, whether plaintiff or defendant, against whom a money judgment has been rendered.
(e) "Person" means an individual, corporation, partnership, limited liability partnership, limited liability company, firm, association, or other entity.
(f) "Individual" means a natural person.
(g) "Party" means a plaintiff or defendant.
(h) "Motion" means a party's written request to the court for an order or other action. The term includes an informal written request to the court, such as a letter.
(i) "Declaration" means a written statement signed by an individual which includes the date and place of signing, and a statement under penalty of perjury under the laws of this state that its contents are true and correct.
(j) "Good cause" means circumstances sufficient to justify the requested order or other action, as determined by the judge.
(k) "Mail" means first-class mail with postage fully prepaid, unless stated otherwise.
Amended by Stats 2003 ch 449 (AB 1712),s 4, eff. 1/1/2004.

Section 116.140 - Provisions inapplicable
The following do not apply in small claims actions:
(a) Subdivision (a) of Section 1013 and subdivision (b) of Section 1005, on the extension of the time for taking action when notice is given by mail.
(b) Title 6.5 (commencing with Section 481.010) of Part 2, on the issuance of prejudgment attachments.
Added by Stats. 1991, Ch. 915, Sec. 2.

Article 2 - SMALL CLAIMS COURT

Section 116.210 - Generally
In each superior court there shall be a small claims division. The small claims division may be known as the small claims court.
Amended by Stats 2002 ch 784 (SB 1316),s 30, eff. 1/1/2003.

Section 116.220 - Jurisdiction
(a) The small claims court has jurisdiction in the following actions:
  (1) Except as provided in subdivisions (c), (e), and (f), for recovery of money, if the amount of the demand does not exceed five thousand dollars ($5,000).
  (2) Except as provided in subdivisions (c), (e), and (f), to enforce payment of delinquent unsecured personal property taxes in an amount not to exceed five thousand dollars ($5,000), if the legality of the tax is not contested by the defendant.
  (3) To issue the writ of possession authorized by Sections 1861.5 and 1861.10 of the Civil Code if the amount of the demand does not exceed five thousand dollars ($5,000).
  (4) To confirm, correct, or vacate a fee arbitration award not exceeding five thousand dollars ($5,000) between an attorney and client that is binding or has become binding, or to conduct a hearing de novo between an attorney and client after nonbinding arbitration of a fee dispute involving no more than five thousand dollars ($5,000) in controversy, pursuant to Article 13 (commencing with Section 6200) of Chapter 4 of Division 3 of the Business and Professions Code.
  (5) For an injunction or other equitable relief only when a statute expressly authorizes a small claims court to award that relief.
(b) In any action seeking relief authorized by paragraphs (1) to (4), inclusive, of subdivision (a), the court may grant equitable relief in the form of rescission, restitution, reformation, and specific performance, in lieu of, or in addition to, money damages. The court may issue a conditional judgment. The court shall retain jurisdiction until full payment and performance of any judgment or order.
(c) Notwithstanding subdivision (a), the small claims court has jurisdiction over a defendant guarantor as follows:
  (1) For any action brought by a natural person against the Registrar of the Contractors' State License Board as the defendant guarantor, the small claims jurisdictional limit stated in Section 116.221 shall apply.
  (2) For any action against a defendant guarantor that does not charge a fee for its guarantor or surety services, if the amount of the demand does not exceed two thousand five hundred dollars ($2,500).

(3) For any action brought by a natural person against a defendant guarantor that charges a fee for its guarantor or surety services, if the amount of the demand does not exceed six thousand five hundred dollars ($6,500).

(4) For any action brought by an entity other than a natural person against a defendant guarantor that charges a fee for its guarantor or surety services or against the Registrar of the Contractors' State License Board as the defendant guarantor, if the amount of the demand does not exceed four thousand dollars ($4,000).

(d) In any case in which the lack of jurisdiction is due solely to an excess in the amount of the demand, the excess may be waived, but any waiver is not operative until judgment.

(e) Notwithstanding subdivision (a), in any action filed by a plaintiff incarcerated in a Department of Corrections and Rehabilitation facility, the small claims court has jurisdiction over a defendant only if the plaintiff has alleged in the complaint that he or she has exhausted his or her administrative remedies against that department, including compliance with Sections 905.2 and 905.4 of the Government Code. The final administrative adjudication or determination of the plaintiff's administrative claim by the department may be attached to the complaint at the time of filing in lieu of that allegation.

(f) In any action governed by subdivision (e), if the plaintiff fails to provide proof of compliance with the requirements of subdivision (e) at the time of trial, the judicial officer shall, at his or her discretion, either dismiss the action or continue the action to give the plaintiff an opportunity to provide that proof.

(g) For purposes of this section, "department" includes an employee of a department against whom a claim has been filed under this chapter arising out of his or her duties as an employee of that department.

Amended by Stats 2009 ch 468 (AB 712),s 1, eff. 1/1/2010.
Amended by Stats 2008 ch 157 (SB 1432),s 4, eff. 1/1/2009.
Amended by Stats 2006 ch 150 (AB 2455),s 1, eff. 1/1/2007.
Amended October 10, 1999 (Bill Number: AB 1678) (Chapter 982).

Section 116.221 - Jurisdictional amount

In addition to the jurisdiction conferred by Section 116.220, the small claims court has jurisdiction in an action brought by a natural person, if the amount of the demand does not exceed ten thousand dollars ($10,000), except as otherwise prohibited by subdivision (c) of Section 116.220 or subdivision (a) of Section 116.231.

Amended by Stats 2018 ch 92 (SB 1289),s 41, eff. 1/1/2019.
Amended by Stats 2011 ch 64 (SB 221),s 1, eff. 1/1/2012.
Added by Stats 2005 ch 600 (SB 422),s 2, eff. 1/1/2006.

Section 116.222 - Statement of calculation of liability in action to enforce payment of debt

If the action is to enforce the payment of a debt, the statement of calculation of liability shall separately state the original debt, each payment credited to the debt, each fee and charge added to the debt, each payment credited against those fees and charges, all other debits or charges to the account, and an explanation of the nature of those fees, charges, debits, and all other credits to the debt, by source and amount.

Amended by Stats 2015 ch 303 (AB 731),s 36, eff. 1/1/2016.
Added by Stats 2005 ch 618 (AB 1459),s 3, eff. 1/1/2006.
Added by Stats 2005 ch 600 (SB 422),s 3, eff. 1/1/2006.

Section 116.223 - [Effective until 10/1/2025] Jurisdiction for actions for recovery of COVID-19 rental debt; declaration of legislature

(a) The Legislature hereby finds and declares as follows:

(1) There is anticipated to be an unprecedented number of claims arising out of nonpayment of residential rent that occurred between March 1, 2020, and September 30, 2021, related to the COVID-19 pandemic.

(2) These disputes are of special importance to the parties and of significant social and economic consequence collectively as the people of the State of California grapple with the health, economic, and social impacts of the COVID-19 pandemic.

(3) It is essential that the parties have access to a judicial forum to resolve these disputes expeditiously, inexpensively, and fairly.

(4) It is the intent of the Legislature that landlords of residential real property and their tenants have the option to litigate disputes regarding rent which is unpaid for the time period between March 1, 2020, and September 30, 2021, in the small claims court. It is the intent of the Legislature that the jurisdictional limits of the small claims court not apply to these disputes over COVID-19 rental debt.

(b)

(1) Notwithstanding paragraph (1) of subdivision (a) Section 116.220, Section 116.221, or any other law, the small claims court has jurisdiction in any action for recovery of COVID-19 rental debt, as defined in Section 1179.02, and any defenses thereto, regardless of the amount demanded.

(2) In an action described in paragraph (1), the court shall reduce the damages awarded for any amount of COVID-19 rental debt sought by payments made to the landlord to satisfy the COVID-19 rental debt, including payments by the tenant, rental assistance programs, or another third party pursuant to paragraph (3) of subdivision (a) of Section 1947.3 of the Civil Code.

(3) An action to recover COVID-19 rental debt, as defined in Section 1179.02, brought pursuant to this subdivision shall not be commenced before November 1, 2021.

(c) Any claim for recovery of COVID-19 rental debt, as defined in Section 1179.02, shall not be subject to Section 116.231, notwithstanding the fact that a landlord of residential rental property may have brought two or more small claims actions in which the amount demanded exceeded two thousand five hundred dollars ($2,500) in any calendar year.

(d) This section shall remain in effect until October 1, 2025, and as of that date is repealed.

Amended by Stats 2021 ch 27 (AB 832),s 7, eff. 6/28/2021.
Amended by Stats 2021 ch 2 (SB 91),s 9, eff. 1/29/2021.
Added by Stats 2020 ch 37 (AB 3088),s 14, eff. 8/31/2020.

Section 116.225 - Agreement establishing forum outside of state for action within small claims court jurisdiction

An agreement entered into or renewed on or after January 1, 2003, establishing a forum outside of California for an action arising from an offer or provision of goods, services, property, or extensions of credit primarily for personal, family, or household purposes that is otherwise within the jurisdiction of a small claims court of this state is contrary to public policy and is void and unenforceable.

Added by Stats 2002 ch 247 (AB 2949),s 1, eff. 1/1/2003.

Section 116.230 - Fees

(a) In a small claims case, the clerk of the court shall charge and collect only those fees authorized under this chapter.

(b) If the party filing a claim has filed 12 or fewer small claims in the state within the previous 12 months, the filing fee is the following:

(1) Thirty dollars ($30) if the amount of the demand is one thousand five hundred dollars ($1,500) or less.

(2) Fifty dollars ($50) if the amount of the demand is more than one thousand five hundred dollars ($1,500) but less than or equal to five thousand dollars ($5,000).

(3) Seventy-five dollars ($75) if the amount of the demand is more than five thousand dollars ($5,000).

(c) If the party has filed more than 12 other small claims in the state within the previous 12 months, the filing fee is one hundred dollars ($100).

(d)

(1) If, after having filed a claim and paid the required fee under paragraph (1) of subdivision (b), a party files an amended claim or amendment to a claim that raises the amount of the demand so that the filing fee under paragraph (2) of subdivision (b) would be charged, the filing fee for the amended claim or amendment is twenty dollars ($20).

(2) If, after having filed a claim and paid the required fee under paragraph (2) of subdivision (b), a party files an amended claim or amendment to a claim that raises the amount of the demand so that the filing fee under paragraph (3) of subdivision (b) would be charged, the filing fee for the amended claim or amendment is twenty-five dollars ($25).

(3) If, after having filed a claim and paid the required fee under paragraph (1) of subdivision (b), a party files an amended claim or amendment to a claim that raises the amount of the demand so that the filing fee under paragraph (3) of subdivision (b) would be charged, the filing fee for the amended claim or amendment is forty-five dollars ($45).

(4) The additional fees paid under this subdivision are due upon filing. The court shall not reimburse a party if the party's claim is amended to demand a lower amount that falls within the range for a filing fee lower than that originally paid.

(e) Each party filing a claim shall file a declaration with the claim stating whether that party has filed more than 12 other small claims in the state within the last 12 months.

(f) The clerk of the court shall deposit fees collected under this section into a bank account established for this purpose by the Administrative Office of the Courts and maintained under rules adopted by or trial court financial policies and procedures authorized by the Judicial Council under subdivision (a) of Section 77206 of the Government Code. The deposits shall be made as required under Section 68085.1 of the Government Code and trial court financial policies and procedures authorized by the Judicial Council.

(g)

(1) The Administrative Office of the Courts shall distribute six dollars ($6) of each thirty-dollar ($30) fee, eight dollars ($8) of each fifty-dollar ($50) fee, ten dollars ($10) of each seventy-five-dollar ($75) fee, and fourteen dollars ($14) of each one hundred-dollar ($100) fee collected under subdivision (b) or (c) to a special account in the county in which the court is located to be used for the small claims advisory services described in Section 116.940, or, if the small claims advisory services are administered by the court, to the court. The Administrative Office of the Courts shall also distribute two dollars ($2) of each seventy-five-dollar ($75) fee collected under subdivision (b) to the law library fund in the county in which the court is located.

(2) From the fees collected under subdivision (d), the Administrative Office of the Courts shall distribute two dollars ($2) to the law library fund in the county in which the court is located, and three dollars ($3) to the small claims advisory services described in Section 116.940, or, if the small claims advisory services are administered by the court, to the court.

(3) Records of these moneys shall be available from the Administrative Office of the Courts for inspection by the public on request.

(4) Nothing in this section precludes the court or county from contracting with a third party to provide small claims advisory services as described in Section 116.940.

(h) The remainder of the fees collected under subdivisions (b), (c), and (d) shall be transmitted monthly to the Controller for deposit in the Trial Court Trust Fund.

(i) All money distributed under this section to be used for small claims advisory services shall be used only for providing those services as described in Section 116.940. Nothing in this section shall preclude the county or the court from procuring other funding to comply with the requirements of Section 116.940.

Amended by Stats 2007 ch 738 (AB 1248),s 3, eff. 1/1/2008.
Amended by Stats 2005 ch 706 (AB 1742),s 3, eff. 1/1/2006
Added by Stats 2005 ch 75 (AB 145),s 19, eff. 7/19/2005, op. 1/1/2006.
See Stats 2005 ch 75 (AB 145), s 154.

Section 116.231 - Filing more than two small claims actions in which amount demanded exceeds $2,500

(a) Except as provided in subdivision (d), no person may file more than two small claims actions in which the amount demanded exceeds two thousand five hundred dollars ($2,500), anywhere in the state in any calendar year.

(b) Except as provided in subdivision (d), if the amount demanded in any small claims action exceeds two thousand five hundred dollars ($2,500), the party making the demand shall file a declaration under penalty of perjury attesting to the fact that not more than two small claims actions in which the amount of the demand exceeded two thousand five hundred dollars ($2,500) have been filed by that party in this state within the calendar year.

(c) The Legislature finds and declares that the pilot project conducted under the authority of Chapter 1196 of the Statutes of 1991 demonstrated the efficacy of the removal of the limitation on the number of actions public entities may file in the small claims courts on claims exceeding two thousand five hundred dollars ($2,500).

(d) The limitation on the number of filings exceeding two thousand five hundred dollars ($2,500) does not apply to filings where the claim does not exceed five thousand dollars ($5,000) that are filed by a city, county, city and county, school district, county office of education, community college district, local district, or any other local public entity. If any small claims action is filed by a city, county, city and county, school district, county office of education, community college district, local district, or any other local public entity pursuant to this section, and the defendant informs the court either in advance of the hearing by written notice or at the time of the hearing, that he or she is represented in the action by legal counsel, the action shall be transferred out of the small claims division. A city, county, city and county, school district, county office of education, community college district, local district, or any other local public entity may not file a claim within the small claims division if the amount of the demand exceeds five thousand dollars ($5,000).

Amended by Stats. 1998, Ch. 931, Sec. 39. Effective September 28, 1998.

Section 116.232 - Fee charged plaintiff for each defendant to whom copy of claim mailed

A fee of fifteen dollars ($15) shall be charged and collected from the plaintiff for each defendant to whom the court clerk mails a copy of the claim under Section 116.340. This fee shall be distributed to the court in which it was collected.

Amended by Stats 2013 ch 31 (SB 75),s 1, eff. 6/27/2013.
Added by Stats 2005 ch 75 (AB 145),s 20, eff. 7/19/2005, op. 1/1/2006.

Section 116.240 - Case heard by temporary judge

(a) With the consent of the parties who appear at the hearing, the court may order a case to be heard by a temporary judge who is a member of the State Bar, and who has been sworn and empowered to act until final determination of the case.

(b) Prior to serving as a temporary judge in small claims court, on and after July 1, 2006, and at least every three years thereafter, each temporary judge shall take the course of study offered by the courts on ethics and substantive law under rules adopted by the Judicial Council. The course shall include, but not be limited to, state and federal consumer laws, landlord-tenant law along with any applicable county specific rent deposit law, the state and federal Fair Debt Collection Practices Acts, the federal Truth in Lending Act, the federal Fair Credit Billing Act, the federal Electronic Fund Transfer Act, tort law, and contract law, including defenses to contracts and defenses to debts. On substantive law, the courts may receive assistance from the Department of Consumer Affairs, to the extent that the department is fiscally able to provide that assistance.

Amended by Stats 2005 ch 618 (AB 1459),s 4, eff. 1/1/2006
Amended by Stats 2005 ch 600 (SB 422),s 4, eff. 1/1/2006

Section 116.250 - Sessions; night sessions

(a) Sessions of the small claims court may be scheduled at any time and on any day, including Saturdays, but excluding other judicial holidays.
(b) Each small claims division of a superior court with seven or more judicial officers shall conduct at least one night session or Saturday session each month for the purpose of hearing small claims cases other than small claims appeals. The term "session" includes, but is not limited to, a proceeding conducted by a member of the State Bar acting as a mediator or referee.
Amended by Stats 2003 ch 149 (SB 79),s 4, eff. 1/1/2004.
Amended by Stats 2002 ch 784 (SB 1316),s 31, eff. 1/1/2003.

Section 116.260 - Assistance to advise litigants
In each county, individual assistance shall be made available to advise small claims litigants and potential litigants without charge as provided in Section 116.940 and by rules adopted by the Judicial Council.
Added by Stats. 1990, Ch. 1305, Sec. 3. Note: Prior to 1991, this subject matter was in Chapter 5A, comprising Sections 116 to 117.24.

Section 116.270 - Law clerks
Any small claims division may use law clerks to assist the judge with legal research of small claims cases.
Added by Stats. 1990, Ch. 1305, Sec. 3. Note: Prior to 1991, this subject matter was in Chapter 5A, comprising Sections 116 to 117.24.

Article 3 - ACTIONS

Section 116.310 - No formal pleading except claim; pretrial discovery not permitted
(a) No formal pleading, other than the claim described in Section 116.320 or 116.360, is necessary to initiate a small claims action.
(b) The pretrial discovery procedures described in Section 2019.010 are not permitted in small claims actions.
Amended by Stats 2004 ch 182 (AB 3081),s 7, eff. 7/1/2005
Amended by Stats 2003 ch 149 (SB 79),s 5, eff. 1/1/2004.

Section 116.320 - Commencement of action by filing claim
(a) A plaintiff may commence an action in the small claims court by filing a claim under oath with the clerk of the small claims court in person, by mail, by facsimile transmission if authorized pursuant to Section 1010.5, or by electronic means as authorized by Section 1010.6.
(b) The claim form shall be a simple nontechnical form approved or adopted by the Judicial Council. The claim form shall set forth a place for (1) the name and address of the defendant, if known; (2) the amount and the basis of the claim; (3) that the plaintiff, where possible, has demanded payment and, in applicable cases, possession of the property; (4) that the defendant has failed or refused to pay, and, where applicable, has refused to surrender the property; and (5) that the plaintiff understands that the judgment on his or her claim will be conclusive and without a right of appeal.
(c) The form or accompanying instructions shall include information that the plaintiff (1) may not be represented by an attorney, (2) has no right of appeal, and (3) may ask the court to waive fees for filing and serving the claim on the ground that the plaintiff is unable to pay them, using the forms approved by the Judicial Council for that purpose.
Amended by Stats 2007 ch 738 (AB 1248),s 4, eff. 1/1/2008.

Section 116.330 - Scheduling case for hearing and issuing order to appear
(a) When a claim is filed, the clerk shall schedule the case for hearing and shall issue an order directing the parties to appear at the time set for the hearing with witnesses and documents to prove their claim or defense. The case shall be scheduled for hearing no earlier than 20 days but not more than 70 days from the date of the order.
(b) In lieu of the method of setting the case for hearing described in subdivision (a), at the time a claim is filed the clerk may do all of the following:
(1) Cause a copy of the claim to be mailed to the defendant by any form of mail providing for a return receipt.
(2) On receipt of proof that the claim was served as provided in paragraph (1), issue an order scheduling the case for hearing in accordance with subdivision (a) and directing the parties to appear at the time set for the hearing with witnesses and documents to prove their claim or defense.
(3) Cause a copy of the order setting the case for hearing and directing the parties to appear, to be served upon the parties by any form of mail providing for a return receipt.
Amended by Stats 2005 ch 706 (AB 1742),s 4, eff. 1/1/2006

Section 116.340 - Service of claim and order
(a) Service of the claim and order on the defendant may be made by any one of the following methods:
(1) The clerk may cause a copy of the claim and order to be mailed to the defendant by any form of mail providing for a return receipt.
(2) The plaintiff may cause a copy of the claim and order to be delivered to the defendant in person.
(3) The plaintiff may cause service of a copy of the claim and order to be made by substituted service as provided in subdivision (a) or (b) of Section 415.20 without the need to attempt personal service on the defendant. For these purposes, substituted service as provided in subdivision (b) of Section 415.20 may be made at the office of the sheriff or marshal who shall deliver a copy of the claim and order to any person authorized by the defendant to receive service, as provided in Section 416.90, who is at least 18 years of age, and thereafter mailing a copy of the claim and order to the defendant's usual mailing address.
(4) The clerk may cause a copy of the claim to be mailed, the order to be issued, and a copy of the order to be mailed as provided in subdivision (b) of Section 116.330.
(b) Service of the claim and order on the defendant shall be completed at least 15 days before the hearing date if the defendant resides within the county in which the action is filed, or at least 20 days before the hearing date if the defendant resides outside the county in which the action is filed.
(c) Proof of service of the claim and order shall be filed with the small claims court at least five days before the hearing.
(d) Service by the methods described in subdivision (a) shall be deemed complete on the date that the defendant signs the mail return receipt, on the date of the personal service, as provided in Section 415.20, or as established by other competent evidence, whichever applies to the method of service used.
(e) Service shall be made within this state, except as provided in subdivisions (f) and (g).
(f) The owner of record of real property in California who resides in another state and who has no lawfully designated agent in California for service of process may be served by any of the methods described in this section if the claim relates to that property.
(g) A nonresident owner or operator of a motor vehicle involved in an accident within this state may be served pursuant to the provisions on constructive service in Sections 17450 to 17461, inclusive, of the Vehicle Code without regard to whether the defendant was a nonresident at the time of the accident or when the claim was filed. Service shall be made by serving both the Director of the California Department of Motor Vehicles and the defendant, and may be made by any of the methods authorized by this chapter or by registered mail as authorized by Section 17454 or 17455 of the Vehicle Code.
(h) If an action is filed against a principal and his or her guaranty or surety pursuant to a guarantor or suretyship agreement, a reasonable attempt shall be made to complete service on the principal. If service is not completed on the principal, the action shall be transferred to the court of appropriate jurisdiction.
Amended by Stats 2005 ch 706 (AB 1742),s 5, eff. 1/1/2006
Amended by Stats 2002 ch 806 (AB 3027),s 3, eff. 1/1/2003.

Section 116.360 - Claim filed by defendant against plaintiff in same action

(a) The defendant may file a claim against the plaintiff in the same action in an amount not to exceed the jurisdictional limits stated in Sections 116.220, 116.221, and 116.231. The claim need not relate to the same subject or event as the plaintiff's claim.

(b) The defendant's claim shall be filed and served in the manner provided for filing and serving a claim of the plaintiff under Sections 116.330 and 116.340.

(c) The defendant shall cause a copy of the claim and order to be served on the plaintiff at least five days before the hearing date, unless the defendant was served 10 days or less before the hearing date, in which event the defendant shall cause a copy of the defendant's claim and order to be served on the plaintiff at least one day before the hearing date.

Amended by Stats 2006 ch 167 (AB 2618),s 4, eff. 1/1/2007.

Section 116.370 - Venue and court location requirements

(a) Venue and court location requirements in small claims actions shall be the same as in other civil actions. The court may prescribe by local rule the proper court locations for small claims actions.

(b) A defendant may challenge venue or court location by writing to the court and mailing a copy of the challenge to each of the other parties to the action, without personally appearing at the hearing.

(c) In all cases, including those in which the defendant does not either challenge venue or court location or appear at the hearing, the court shall inquire into the facts sufficiently to determine whether venue and court location are proper, and shall make its determination accordingly.

(1) If the court determines that the action was not commenced in the proper venue, the court, on its own motion, shall dismiss the action without prejudice, unless all defendants are present and agree that the action may be heard. If the court determines that the action was not commenced in the proper court location, the court may transfer the action to a proper location pursuant to local rule.

(2) If the court determines that the action was commenced in the proper venue and court location, the court may hear the case if all parties are present. If the defendant challenged venue or court location and all parties are not present, the court shall postpone the hearing for at least 15 days and shall notify all parties by mail of the court's decision and the new hearing date, time, and place.

Amended by Stats 2002 ch 806 (AB 3027),s 4, eff. 1/1/2003.

Section 116.390 - Request to transfer small claims action if defendant's claim exceeds jurisdictional amount

(a) If a defendant has a claim against a plaintiff that exceeds the jurisdictional limits stated in Sections 116.220, 116.221, and 116.231, and the claim relates to the contract, transaction, matter, or event which is the subject of the plaintiff's claim, the defendant may commence an action against the plaintiff in a court of competent jurisdiction and request the small claims court to transfer the small claims action to that court.

(b) The defendant may make the request by filing with the small claims court in which the plaintiff commenced the action, at or before the time set for the hearing of that action, a declaration stating the facts concerning the defendant's action against the plaintiff with a true copy of the complaint so filed by the defendant against the plaintiff. The defendant shall cause a copy of the declaration and complaint to be personally delivered to the plaintiff at or before the time set for the hearing of the small claims action.

(c) In ruling on a motion to transfer, the small claims court may do any of the following:

(1) render judgment on the small claims case prior to the transfer;

(2) not render judgment and transfer the small claims case;

(3) refuse to transfer the small claims case on the grounds that the ends of justice would not be served. If the small claims action is transferred prior to judgment, both actions shall be tried together in the transferee court.

(d) When the small claims court orders the action transferred, it shall transmit all files and papers to the transferee court.

(e) The plaintiff in the small claims action shall not be required to pay to the clerk of the transferee court any transmittal, appearance, or filing fee unless the plaintiff appears in the transferee court, in which event the plaintiff shall be required to pay the filing fee and any other fee required of a defendant in the transferee court. However, if the transferee court rules against the plaintiff in the action filed in that court, the court may award to the defendant in that action the costs incurred as a consequence of the transfer, including attorney's fees and filing fees.

Amended by Stats 2006 ch 167 (AB 2618),s 5, eff. 1/1/2007.

Amended by Stats 2005 ch 75 (AB 145),s 21, eff. 7/19/2005, op. 1/1/2006

Article 4 - PARTIES

Section 116.410 - Generally; appearance by guardian ad litem

(a) Any person who is at least 18 years of age, or legally emancipated, and mentally competent may be a party to a small claims action.

(b) A minor or incompetent person may appear by a guardian ad litem appointed by a judge of the court in which the action is filed.

Amended by Stats 2004 ch 171 (AB 3078),s 1, eff. 1/1/2005.

Section 116.420 - Assignee of claim filing or maintaining claim

(a) No claim shall be filed or maintained in small claims court by the assignee of the claim.

(b) This section does not prevent the filing or defense of an action in the small claims court by (1) a trustee in bankruptcy in the exercise of the trustee's duties as trustee, or (2) by the holder of a security agreement, retail installment contract, or lien contract subject to the Unruh Act (Chapter 1 (commencing with Section 1801) of Title 2 of Part 4 of Division 3 of the Civil Code) or the Automobile Sales Finance Act (Chapter 2b (commencing with Section 2981) of Title 14 of Part 4 of Division 3 of the Civil Code), purchased by the holder for the holder's portfolio of investments, provided that the holder is not an assignee for the purpose of collection.

(c) This section does not prevent the filing in small claims court by a local government which is self-insured for purposes of workers' compensation and is seeking subrogation pursuant to Section 3852 of the Labor Code.

Amended by Stats. 1994, Ch. 231, Sec. 1. Effective January 1, 1995.

Section 116.430 - Declaration if plaintiff's business operates under fictitious business name

(a) If the plaintiff operates or does business under a fictitious business name and the claim relates to that business, the claim shall be accompanied by the filing of a declaration stating that the plaintiff has complied with the fictitious business name laws by executing, filing, and publishing a fictitious business name statement as required.

(b) A small claims action filed by a person who has not complied with the applicable fictitious business name laws by executing, filing, and publishing a fictitious business name statement as required shall be dismissed without prejudice.

(c) For purposes of this section, "fictitious business name" means the term as defined in Section 17900 of the Business and Professions Code, and "fictitious business name statement" means the statement described in Section 17913 of the Business and Professions Code.

Amended by Stats. 1991, Ch. 915, Sec. 12.

Article 5 - HEARING

Section 116.510 - Generally

The hearing and disposition of the small claims action shall be informal, the object being to dispense justice promptly, fairly, and inexpensively.

Amended by Stats. 1991, Ch. 915, Sec. 13.

Section 116.520 - Evidence offered

(a) The parties have the right to offer evidence by witnesses at the hearing or, with the permission of the court, at another time.

(b) If the defendant fails to appear, the court shall still require the plaintiff to present evidence to prove his or her claim.

(c) The court may consult witnesses informally and otherwise investigate the controversy with or without notice to the parties.
Added by Stats. 1990, Ch. 1305, Sec. 3.

Section 116.530 - Appearance by attorney
(a) Except as permitted by this section, no attorney may take part in the conduct or defense of a small claims action.
(b) Subdivision (a) does not apply if the attorney is appearing to maintain or defend an action in any of the following capacities:
   (1) By or against himself or herself.
   (2) By or against a partnership in which he or she is a general partner and in which all the partners are attorneys.
   (3) By or against a professional corporation of which he or she is an officer or director and of which all other officers and directors are attorneys.
(c) Nothing in this section shall prevent an attorney from doing any of the following:
   (1) Providing advice to a party to a small claims action, either before or after the commencement of the action.
   (2) Testifying to facts of which he or she has personal knowledge and about which he or she is competent to testify.
   (3) Representing a party in an appeal to the superior court.
   (4) Representing a party in connection with the enforcement of a judgment.
Amended by Stats 2003 ch 449 (AB 1712),s 5, eff. 1/1/2004.

Section 116.531 - Assistance rendered party by representative of insurer or expert in matter
Nothing in this article shall prevent a representative of an insurer or other expert in the matter before the small claims court from rendering assistance to a party in the litigation except during the conduct of the hearing, either before or after the commencement of the action, unless otherwise prohibited by law; nor shall anything in this article prevent those individuals from testifying to facts of which they have personal knowledge and about which they are competent to testify.
Added by Stats. 1990, Ch. 1683, Sec. 5.

Section 116.540 - Party other than plaintiff and defendant taking part in action
(a) Except as permitted by this section, no individual other than the plaintiff and the defendant may take part in the conduct or defense of a small claims action.
(b) Except as additionally provided in subdivision (i), a corporation may appear and participate in a small claims action only through a regular employee, or a duly appointed or elected officer or director, who is employed, appointed, or elected for purposes other than solely representing the corporation in small claims court.
(c) A party who is not a corporation or a natural person may appear and participate in a small claims action only through a regular employee, or a duly appointed or elected officer or director, or in the case of a partnership, a partner, engaged for purposes other than solely representing the party in small claims court.
(d) If a party is an individual doing business as a sole proprietorship, the party may appear and participate in a small claims action by a representative and without personally appearing if both of the following conditions are met:
   (1) The claim can be proved or disputed by evidence of an account that constitutes a business record as defined in Section 1271 of the Evidence Code, and there is no other issue of fact in the case.
   (2) The representative is a regular employee of the party for purposes other than solely representing the party in small claims actions and is qualified to testify to the identity and mode of preparation of the business record.
(e) A plaintiff who is a service member is not required to personally appear, and may submit declarations to serve as evidence supporting their claim, appear via video appearance, or allow another individual to appear and participate on their behalf, if the service member is assigned to a location more than 100 miles from the court where the action is proceeding, or is otherwise unable to personally appear due to the performance of military duty, the representative is serving without compensation, other than compensation from the United States or the State of California, and, except as to representatives who are employed by the United States or the State of California, the representative has appeared in small claims actions on behalf of others no more than four times during the calendar year. The defendant may file a claim in the same action in an amount not to exceed the jurisdictional limits stated in Sections 116.220, 116.221, and 116.231.
(f) A party incarcerated in a county jail, a Department of Corrections and Rehabilitation facility, or a Division of Juvenile Facilities facility is not required to personally appear, and may submit declarations to serve as evidence supporting their claim, or may authorize another individual to appear and participate on their behalf if that individual is serving without compensation and has appeared in small claims actions on behalf of others no more than four times during the calendar year.
(g) A defendant who is a nonresident owner of real property may defend against a claim relating to that property without personally appearing by (1) submitting written declarations to serve as evidence supporting their defense, (2) allowing another individual to appear and participate on their behalf if that individual is serving without compensation and has appeared in small claims actions on behalf of others no more than four times during the calendar year, or (3) taking the action described in both (1) and (2).
(h) A party who is an owner of rental real property may appear and participate in a small claims action through a property agent under contract with the owner to manage the rental of that property, if (1) the owner has retained the property agent principally to manage the rental of that property and not principally to represent the owner in small claims court, and (2) the claim relates to the rental property.
(i) A party that is an association created to manage a common interest development, as defined in Section 4100 or in Sections 6528 and 6534 of the Civil Code, may appear and participate in a small claims action through an agent, a management company representative, or bookkeeper who appears on behalf of that association.
(j) At the hearing of a small claims action, the court shall require any individual who is appearing as a representative of a party under subdivisions (b) to (i), inclusive, to file a declaration stating (1) that the individual is authorized to appear for the party, and (2) the basis for that authorization. If the representative is appearing under subdivision (b), (c), (d), (h), or (i), the declaration also shall state that the individual is not employed solely to represent the party in small claims court. If the representative is appearing under subdivision (e), (f), or (g), the declaration also shall state that the representative is serving without compensation, and has appeared in small claims actions on behalf of others no more than four times during the calendar year.
(k) A spouse who sues or who is sued with their spouse may appear and participate on behalf of their spouse if (1) the claim is a joint claim, (2) the represented spouse has given their consent, and (3) the court determines that the interests of justice would be served.
(l) If the court determines that a party cannot properly present their claim or defense and needs assistance, the court may in its discretion allow another individual to assist that party.
(m) Nothing in this section shall operate or be construed to authorize an attorney to participate in a small claims action except as expressly provided in Section 116.530.
Amended by Stats 2022 ch 620 (SB 1311),s 3, eff. 1/1/2023.
Amended by Stats 2016 ch 50 (SB 1005),s 14, eff. 1/1/2017.
Amended by Stats 2013 ch 605 (SB 752),s 23, eff. 1/1/2014.
Amended by Stats 2012 ch 181 (AB 806),s 43, eff. 1/1/2013, op. 1/1/2014.
Amended by Stats 2006 ch 167 (AB 2618),s 6, eff. 1/1/2007.
Amended by Stats 2005 ch 452 (SB 137),s 7, eff. 1/1/2006

Section 116.541 - Appearance by Department of Corrections or Department of Youth Authority

(a) Notwithstanding Section 116.540 or any other provision of law, the Department of Corrections or the Department of the Youth Authority may appear and participate in a small claims action through a regular employee, who is employed or appointed for purposes other than solely representing that department in small claims court.

(b) Where the Department of Corrections or the Department of the Youth Authority is named as a defendant in small claims court, the representative of the department is not required to personally appear to challenge the plaintiff's compliance with the pleading requirements and may submit pleadings or declarations to assert that challenge.

(c) At the hearing of a small claims action, the court shall require any individual who is appearing as a representative of the Department of Corrections or the Department of the Youth Authority under subdivision (a) to file a declaration stating (1) that the individual is authorized to appear for the party, (2) the basis for that authorization, and (3) that the individual is not employed solely to represent the party in small claims court.

(d) Nothing in this section shall operate or be construed to authorize an attorney to participate in a small claims action except as expressly provided in Section 116.530.

(e) For purposes of this section, all references to the Department of Corrections or the Department of the Youth Authority include an employee thereof, against whom a claim has been filed under this chapter arising out of his or her duties as an employee of that department.

Added by Stats. 1995, Ch. 366, Sec. 2. Effective January 1, 1996.

Section 116.550 - [Repealed]

Repealed by Stats 2018 ch 852 (SB 1155),s 1, eff. 1/1/2019.

Section 116.560 - Claim filed against person operating business under fictitious names relates to defendant's business

(a) Whenever a claim that is filed against a person operating or doing business under a fictitious business name relates to the defendant's business, the court shall inquire at the time of the hearing into the defendant's correct legal name and the name or names under which the defendant does business. If the correct legal name of the defendant, or the name actually used by the defendant, is other than the name stated on the claim, the court shall amend the claim to state the correct legal name of the defendant, and the name or names actually used by the defendant.

(b) The plaintiff may request the court at any time, whether before or after judgment, to amend the plaintiff's claim or judgment to include both the correct legal name and the name or names actually used by the defendant. Upon a showing of good cause, the court shall amend the claim or judgment to state the correct legal name of the defendant, and the name or names actually used by the defendant.

(c) For purposes of this section, "fictitious business name" means the term as defined in Section 17900 of the Business and Professions Code.

Added by Stats. 1991, Ch. 915, Sec. 17.

Section 116.570 - Request to postpone hearing date

(a) Any party may submit a written request to postpone a hearing date for good cause.

(1) The written request may be made either by letter or on a form adopted or approved by the Judicial Council.

(2) The request shall be filed at least 10 days before the hearing date, unless the court determines that the requesting party has good cause to file the request at a later date.

(3) On the date of making the written request, the requesting party shall mail or personally deliver a copy to each of the other parties to the action.

(4)

(A) If the court finds that the interests of justice would be served by postponing the hearing, the court shall postpone the hearing, and shall notify all parties by mail of the new hearing date, time, and place.

(B) On one occasion, upon the written request of a defendant guarantor, the court shall postpone the hearing for at least 30 days, and the court shall take this action without a hearing. This subparagraph does not limit the discretion of the court to grant additional postponements under subparagraph (A).

(5) The court shall provide a prompt response by mail to any person making a written request for postponement of a hearing date under this subdivision.

(b) If service of the claim and order upon the defendant is not completed within the number of days before the hearing date required by subdivision (b) of Section 116.340, and the defendant has not personally appeared and has not requested a postponement, the court shall postpone the hearing for at least 15 days. If a postponement is ordered under this subdivision, the clerk shall promptly notify all parties by mail of the new hearing date, time, and place.

(c) This section does not limit the inherent power of the court to order postponements of hearings in appropriate circumstances.

(d) A fee of ten dollars ($10) shall be charged and collected for the filing of a request for postponement and rescheduling of a hearing date after timely service pursuant to subdivision (b) of Section 116.340 has been made upon the defendant.

Amended by Stats 2002 ch 806 (AB 3027),s 5, eff. 1/1/2003.

Article 6 - JUDGMENT

Section 116.610 - Generally

(a) The small claims court shall give judgment for damages, or equitable relief, or both damages and equitable relief, within the jurisdictional limits stated in Sections 116.220, 116.221, and 116.231, and may make any orders as to time of payment or otherwise as the court deems just and equitable for the resolution of the dispute.

(b) The court may, at its discretion or on request of any party, continue the matter to a later date in order to permit and encourage the parties to attempt resolution by informal or alternative means.

(c) The judgment shall include a determination whether the judgment resulted from a motor vehicle accident on a California highway caused by the defendant's operation of a motor vehicle, or by the operation by some other individual, of a motor vehicle registered in the defendant's name.

(d) If the defendant has filed a claim against the plaintiff, or if the judgment is against two or more defendants, the judgment, and the statement of decision if one is rendered, shall specify the basis for and the character and amount of the liability of each of the parties, including, in the case of multiple judgment debtors, whether the liability of each is joint or several.

(e) If specific property is referred to in the judgment, whether it be personal or real, tangible or intangible, the property shall be identified with sufficient detail to permit efficient implementation or enforcement of the judgment.

(f) In an action against several defendants, the court may, in its discretion, render judgment against one or more of them, leaving the action to proceed against the others, whenever a several judgment is proper.

(g)

(1) The prevailing party is entitled to the costs of the action, including the costs of serving the order for the appearance of the defendant.

(2) Notwithstanding paragraph (1) of this subdivision and subdivision (b) of Section 1032, the amount of the small claims court fee paid by a party pursuant to subdivision (c) of Section 116.230 that exceeds the amount that would have been paid if the party had paid the fee pursuant to subdivision (b) of Section 116.230 shall not be recoverable as costs.

(h) When the court renders judgment, the clerk shall promptly deliver or mail notice of entry of the judgment to the parties, and shall execute a certificate of personal delivery or mailing and place it in the file.

(i) The notice of entry of judgment shall be on a form approved or adopted by the Judicial Council.

Amended by Stats 2006 ch 167 (AB 2618),s 7, eff. 1/1/2007.
Amended by Stats 2005 ch 618 (AB 1459),s 5, eff. 1/1/2006
Amended by Stats 2005 ch 600 (SB 422),s 5, eff. 1/1/2006

Section 116.620 - Payment of judgment
(a) The judgment debtor shall pay the amount of the judgment either immediately or at the time and upon the terms and conditions, including payment by installments, which the court may order.
(b) The court may at any time, for good cause, upon motion by a party and notice by the clerk to all affected parties at their last known address, amend the terms and conditions for payment of the judgment to provide for payment by installment. The determination shall be made without regard to the nature of the underlying debt and without regard to whether the moving party appeared before entry of the judgment.
(c) In determining the terms and conditions of payment, the court may consider any factors which would be relevant to a claim of exemption under Chapter 4 (commencing with Section 703.010) of Division 2 of Title 9 of Part 2.
Added by Stats. 1990, Ch. 1305, Sec. 3. Note: Prior to 1991, this subject matter was in Chapter 5A, comprising Sections 116 to 117.24.

Section 116.630 - Amendment of name of party to include correct legal name
The court may, at any time after judgment, for good cause, upon motion by a party and notice by the clerk to all affected parties at their last known address, amend the name of any party to include both the correct legal name and the actually used name or names of that party.
Added by Stats. 1990, Ch. 1305, Sec. 3. Note: Prior to 1991, this subject matter was in Chapter 5A, comprising Sections 116 to 117.24.

Article 7 - MOTION TO VACATE, APPEAL, AND RELATED MATTERS

Section 116.710 - Right to appeal
(a) The plaintiff in a small claims action shall have no right to appeal the judgment on the plaintiff's claim, but a plaintiff who did not appear at the hearing may file a motion to vacate the judgment in accordance with Section 116.720.
(b) The defendant with respect to the plaintiff's claim, and a plaintiff with respect to a claim of the defendant, may appeal the judgment to the superior court in the county in which the action was heard.
(c) With respect to the plaintiff's claim, the insurer of the defendant may appeal the judgment to the superior court in the county in which the matter was heard if the judgment exceeds two thousand five hundred dollars ($2,500) and the insurer stipulates that its policy with the defendant covers the matter to which the judgment applies.
(d) A defendant who did not appear at the hearing has no right to appeal the judgment, but may file a motion to vacate the judgment in accordance with Section 116.730 or 116.740 and also may appeal the denial of that motion.
Amended (as added by Stats. 1990, Ch. 1305) by Stats. 1990, Ch. 1683, Sec. 6.

Section 116.720 - Motion to vacate by plaintiff who did not appear at hearing
(a) A plaintiff who did not appear at the hearing in the small claims court may file a motion to vacate the judgment with the clerk of the small claims court. The motion shall be filed within 30 days after the clerk has mailed notice of entry of the judgment to the parties.
(b) The clerk shall schedule the hearing on the motion to vacate for a date no earlier than 10 days after the clerk has mailed written notice of the date, time, and place of the hearing to the parties.
(c) Upon a showing of good cause, the small claims court may grant the motion. If the defendant is not present, the court shall hear the motion in the defendant's absence.
(d) If the motion is granted, and if all parties are present and agree, the court may hear the case without rescheduling it. If the defendant is not present, the judge or clerk shall reschedule the case and give notice in accordance with Section 116.330.
Amended by Stats. 1991, Ch. 915, Sec. 20.

Section 116.725 - Motion to correct clerical error or set aside and vacate incorrect or erroneous judgment
(a) A motion to correct a clerical error in a judgment or to set aside and vacate a judgment on the ground of an incorrect or erroneous legal basis for the decision may be made as follows:
  (1) By the court on its own motion at any time.
  (2) By a party within 30 days after the clerk mails notice of entry of judgment to the parties.
(b) Each party may file only one motion to correct a clerical error or to set aside and vacate the judgment on the ground of an incorrect or erroneous legal basis for the decision.
Added by Stats 2005 ch 706 (AB 1742),s 7, eff. 1/1/2006.
Repealed by Stats 2005 ch 706 (AB 1742),s 6, eff. 1/1/2006.

Section 116.730 - Motion to vacate filed by defendant who did not appear at hearing
(a) A defendant who did not appear at the hearing in the small claims court may file a motion to vacate the judgment with the clerk of the small claims court. The motion shall be filed within 30 days after the clerk has mailed notice of entry of the judgment to the parties.
(b) The defendant shall appear at any hearing on the motion, or submit written justification for not appearing together with a declaration in support of the motion.
(c) Upon a showing of good cause, the court may grant the motion to vacate the judgment. If the plaintiff is not present, the court shall hear the motion in the plaintiff's absence.
(d) If the motion is granted, and if all parties are present and agree, the court may hear the case without rescheduling it. If the plaintiff is not present, the judge or clerk shall reschedule the case and give notice in accordance with Section 116.330.
(e) If the motion is denied, the defendant may appeal to the superior court only on the denial of the motion to vacate the judgment. The defendant shall file the notice of appeal with the clerk of the small claims court within 10 days after the small claims court has mailed or delivered notice of the court's denial of the motion to vacate the judgment.
(f) If the superior court determines that the defendant's motion to vacate the judgment should have been granted, the superior court may hear the claims of all parties without rescheduling the matter, provided that all parties are present and the defendant has previously complied with this article, or may order the case transferred to the small claims court for a hearing.
Amended by Stats. 1991, Ch. 915, Sec. 21.

Section 116.740 - Defendant not properly served and did not appear
(a) If the defendant was not properly served as required by Section 116.330 or 116.340 and did not appear at the hearing in the small claims court, the defendant may file a motion to vacate the judgment with the clerk of the small claims court. The motion shall be accompanied by a supporting declaration, and shall be filed within 180 days after the defendant discovers or should have discovered that judgment was entered against the defendant.
(b) The court may order that the enforcement of the judgment shall be suspended pending a hearing and determination of the motion to vacate the judgment.
(c) Upon a showing of good cause, the court may grant the motion to vacate the judgment. If the plaintiff is not present, the court shall hear the motion in the plaintiff's absence.
(d) Subdivisions (d), (e), and (f) of Section 116.730 apply to any motion to vacate a judgment.
Amended by Stats. 1991, Ch. 915, Sec. 22.

Section 116.745 - Fee for filing motion to vacate

The clerk shall collect a fee of twenty dollars ($20) for the filing of a motion to vacate.

Amended by Stats 2005 ch 75 (AB 145),s 22, eff. 7/19/2005, op. 1/1/2006

Section 116.750 - Notice of appeal

(a) An appeal from a judgment in a small claims action is taken by filing a notice of appeal with the clerk of the small claims court.

(b) A notice of appeal shall be filed not later than 30 days after the clerk has delivered or mailed notice of entry of the judgment to the parties. A notice of appeal filed after the 30-day period is ineffective for any purpose.

(c) The time for filing a notice of appeal is not extended by the filing of a request to correct a mistake or by virtue of any subsequent proceedings on that request, except that a new period for filing notice of appeal shall begin on the delivery or mailing of notice of entry of any modified judgment.

Amended by Stats. 1991, Ch. 915, Sec. 23.

Section 116.760 - Fee for filing notice of appeal

(a) The appealing party shall pay a fee of seventy-five dollars ($75) for filing a notice of appeal.

(b) A party who does not appeal shall not be charged any fee for filing any document relating to the appeal.

(c) The fee shall be distributed as follows:

(1) To the county law library fund, as provided in Section 6320 of the Business and Professions Code, the amount specified in Section 6321 and 6322.1 of the Business and Professions Code.

(2) To the Trial Court Trust Fund, the remainder of the fee.

Amended by Stats 2005 ch 75 (AB 145),s 23, eff. 7/19/2005, op. 1/1/2006

Amended by Stats 2000 ch 447 (SB 1533), s 1, eff. 1/1/2001.

Section 116.770 - Appeal to superior court

(a) The appeal to the superior court shall consist of a new hearing before a judicial officer other than the judicial officer who heard the action in the small claims division.

(b) The hearing on an appeal to the superior court shall be conducted informally. The pretrial discovery procedures described in Section 2019.010 are not permitted, no party has a right to a trial by jury, and no tentative decision or statement of decision is required.

(c) Article 5 (commencing with Section 116.510) on hearings in the small claims court applies in hearings on appeal in the superior court, except that attorneys may participate.

(d) The scope of the hearing shall include the claims of all parties who were parties to the small claims action at the time the notice of appeal was filed. The hearing shall include the claim of a defendant that was heard in the small claims court.

(e) The clerk of the superior court shall schedule the hearing for the earliest available time and shall mail written notice of the hearing to the parties at least 14 days prior to the time set for the hearing.

(f) The Judicial Council may prescribe by rule the practice and procedure on appeal and the time and manner in which the record on appeal shall be prepared and filed.

Amended by Stats 2004 ch 182 (AB 3081),s 8, eff. 7/1/2005

Section 116.780 - Judgment of superior court after hearing appeal

(a) The judgment of the superior court after a hearing on appeal is final and not appealable.

(b) Article 6 (commencing with Section 116.610) on judgments of the small claims court applies to judgments of the superior court after a hearing on appeal, except as provided in subdivision (c).

(c) For good cause and where necessary to achieve substantial justice between the parties, the superior court may award a party to an appeal reimbursement of (1) attorney's fees actually and reasonably incurred in connection with the appeal, not exceeding one hundred fifty dollars ($150), and (2) actual loss of earnings and expenses of transportation and lodging actually and reasonably incurred in connection with the appeal, not exceeding one hundred fifty dollars ($150).

Amended by Stats 2011 ch 308 (SB 647),s 1, eff. 1/1/2012.

Amended by Stats 2005 ch 706 (AB 1742),s 8, eff. 1/1/2006

Section 116.790 - Attorney's fees and award for loss of earnings and transportation and lodging expenses

If the superior court finds that the appeal was without substantial merit and not based on good faith, but was intended to harass or delay the other party, or to encourage the other party to abandon the claim, the court may award the other party (a) attorney's fees actually and reasonably incurred in connection with the appeal, not exceeding one thousand dollars ($1,000), and (b) any actual loss of earnings and any expenses of transportation and lodging actually and reasonably incurred in connection with the appeal, not exceeding one thousand dollars ($1,000), following a hearing on the matter.

Amended by Stats. 1991, Ch. 915, Sec. 27.

Section 116.795 - Dismissal of appeal for failure to appear or appeal not timely heard

(a) The superior court may dismiss the appeal if the appealing party does not appear at the hearing or if the appeal is not heard within one year from the date of filing the notice of appeal with the clerk of the small claims court.

(b) Upon dismissal of an appeal by the superior court, the small claims court shall thereafter have the same jurisdiction as if no appeal had been filed.

Added by Stats. 1990, Ch. 1305, Sec. 3. Note: Prior to 1991, this subject matter was in Chapter 5A, comprising Sections 116 to 117.24.

Section 116.798 - Petition seeking writ of review, mandate or prohibition

(a)

(1) A petition that seeks a writ of review, a writ of mandate, or a writ of prohibition relating to an act of the small claims division, other than a postjudgment enforcement order, may be heard by a judge who is assigned to the appellate division of the superior court.

(2) A petition described by paragraph (1) may also be heard by the court of appeal or by the Supreme Court.

(3) Where a judge described in paragraph (1) grants a writ directed to the small claims division, the small claims division is an inferior tribunal for purposes of Title 1 (commencing with Section 1067) of Part 3.

(4) The fee for filing a writ petition in the superior court under paragraph (1) is the same as the fee for filing a notice of appeal under Section 116.760.

(5) The Judicial Council shall promulgate procedural rules for a writ proceeding under paragraph (1).

(6) An appeal shall not be taken from a judgment granting or denying a petition under paragraph (1) for issuance of a writ. An appellate court may, in its discretion, upon petition for extraordinary writ, review the judgment.

(b) A petition that seeks a writ of review, a writ of mandate, or a writ of prohibition relating to an act of a superior court in a small claims appeal may be heard by the court of appeal or by the Supreme Court.

(c) A petition that seeks a writ of review, a writ of mandate, or a writ of prohibition relating to a postjudgment enforcement order of the small claims division may be heard by the appellate division of the superior court, by the court of appeal, or by the Supreme Court.

Added by Stats 2012 ch 470 (AB 1529),s 3, eff. 1/1/2013.

Article 8 - SATISFACTION AND ENFORCEMENT OF JUDGMENT

Section 116.810 - Suspension of enforcement of judgment

(a) Enforcement of the judgment of a small claims court, including the issuance or recording of any abstract of the judgment, is automatically suspended, without the filing of a bond by the defendant, until the expiration of the time for appeal.
(b) If an appeal is filed as provided in Article 7 (commencing with Section 116.710), enforcement of the judgment of the small claims court is suspended unless (1) the appeal is dismissed by the superior court pursuant to Section 116.795, or (2) the superior court determines that the small claims court properly denied the defendant's motion to vacate filed under Section 116.730 or 116.740. In either of those events, the judgment of the small claims court may be enforced.
(c) The scope of the suspension of enforcement under this section and, unless otherwise ordered, of any suspension of enforcement ordered by the court, shall include any enforcement procedure described in Title 9 (commencing with Section 680.010) of Part 2 and in Sections 674 and 1174.
Amended by Stats. 1991, Ch. 915, Sec. 28.

Section 116.820 - Enforcement of judgment
(a) The judgment of a small claims court, or the judgment of the superior court after a hearing on appeal, may be enforced by the small claims court as provided in Title 9 (commencing with Section 680.010) of Part 2 and in Sections 674 and 1174 on the enforcement of judgments of other courts.
(b) The clerk of the court shall charge and collect all fees associated with the enforcement of judgments under Title 9 (commencing with Section 680.010) of Part 2. The clerk shall immediately deposit all the fees collected under this section into a bank account established for this purpose by the Administrative Office of the Courts. The money shall be remitted to the State Treasury under rules adopted by, or trial court financial policies and procedures authorized by, the Judicial Council under subdivision (a) of Section 77206 of the Government Code. The Controller shall distribute the fees to the Trial Court Trust Fund as provided in Section 68085.1 of the Government Code.
(c) The prevailing party in any action subject to this chapter is entitled to the costs of enforcing the judgment and accrued interest.
Amended by Stats 2011 ch 308 (SB 647),s 2, eff. 1/1/2012.
Amended by Stats 2009 ch 596 (SB 556),s 1, eff. 1/1/2010.
Amended by Stats 2005 ch 75 (AB 145),s 24, eff. 7/19/2005, op. 1/1/2006
Amended by Stats 2003 ch 159 (AB 1759), eff. 8/2/2003.

Section 116.830 - Form mailed to judgment debtor regarding nature and location of assets
(a) At the time judgment is rendered, or notice of entry of the judgment is mailed to the parties, the clerk shall deliver or mail to the judgment debtor a form containing questions regarding the nature and location of any assets of the judgment debtor.
(b) Within 30 days after the clerk has mailed notice of entry of the judgment, unless the judgment has been satisfied, the judgment debtor shall complete the form and cause it to be delivered to the judgment creditor.
(c) In the event a motion is made to vacate the judgment or a notice of appeal is filed, a judgment debtor shall complete and deliver the form within 30 days after the clerk has delivered or mailed notice of denial of the motion to vacate, or notice of dismissal of or entry of judgment on the appeal, whichever is applicable.
(d) In case of the judgment debtor's willful failure to comply with subdivision (b) or (c), the judgment creditor may request the court to apply the sanctions, including arrest and attorney's fees, as provided in Section 708.170, on contempt of court.
(e) The Judicial Council shall approve or adopt the form to be used for the purpose of this section.
Amended by Stats. 1991, Ch. 915, Sec. 30.

Section 116.840 - Payment of judgment; entry of satisfaction of judgment
(a) At the option of the judgment debtor, payment of the judgment may be made either (1) to the judgment creditor in accordance with Section 116.850, or (2) to the court in which the judgment was entered in accordance with Section 116.860.
(b) The small claims court may order entry of satisfaction of judgment in accordance with subdivisions (c) and (d) of Section 116.850, or subdivision (b) of Section 116.860.
Added by Stats. 1990, Ch. 1305, Sec. 3. Note: Prior to 1991, this subject matter was in Chapter 5A, comprising Sections 116 to 117.24.

Section 116.850 - Execution and filing acknowledgment of satisfaction of judgment
(a) If full payment of the judgment is made to the judgment creditor or to the judgment creditor's assignee of record, then immediately upon receipt of payment, the judgment creditor or assignee shall file with the clerk of the court an acknowledgment of satisfaction of the judgment.
(b) Any judgment creditor or assignee of record who, after receiving full payment of the judgment and written demand by the judgment debtor, fails without good cause to execute and file an acknowledgment of satisfaction of the judgment with the clerk of the court in which the judgment is entered within 14 days after receiving the request, is liable to the judgment debtor or the judgment debtor's grantees or heirs for all damages sustained by reason of the failure and, in addition, the sum of fifty dollars ($50).
(c) The clerk of the court shall enter a satisfaction of judgment at the request of the judgment debtor if the judgment debtor either (1) establishes a rebuttable presumption of full payment under subdivision (d), or (2) establishes a rebuttable presumption of partial payment under subdivision (d) and complies with subdivision (c) of Section 116.860.
(d) A rebuttable presumption of full or partial payment of the judgment, whichever is applicable, is created if the judgment debtor files both of the following with the clerk of the court in which the judgment was entered:
    (1) Either a canceled check or money order for the full or partial amount of the judgment written by the judgment debtor after judgment and made payable to and endorsed by the judgment creditor, or a cash receipt for the full or partial amount of the judgment written by the judgment debtor after judgment and signed by the judgment creditor.
    (2) A declaration stating that (A) the judgment debtor has made full or partial payment of the judgment including accrued interest and costs; (B) the judgment creditor has been requested to file an acknowledgment of satisfaction of the judgment and refuses to do so, or refuses to accept subsequent payments, or the present address of the judgment creditor is unknown; and (C) the documents identified in and accompanying the declaration constitute evidence of the judgment creditor's receipt of full or partial payment.
Amended by Stats. 1991, Ch. 915, Sec. 31.

Section 116.860 - Request to make payment to court
(a) A judgment debtor who desires to make payment to the court in which the judgment was entered may file a request to make payment, which shall be made on a form approved or adopted by the Judicial Council.
(b) Upon the filing of the request to make payment and the payment to the clerk of the amount of the judgment and any accrued interest and costs after judgment, plus any required fee authorized by this section, the clerk shall enter satisfaction of the judgment and shall remit payment to the judgment creditor as provided in this section.
(c) If partial payment of the judgment has been made to the judgment creditor, and the judgment debtor files the declaration and evidence of partial payment described in subdivision (d) of Section 116.850, the clerk shall enter satisfaction of the judgment upon receipt by the clerk of the balance owing on the judgment, including any accrued interest and costs after judgment, and the fee required by this section.
(d) If payment is made by means other than money order, certified or cashier's check, or cash, entry of satisfaction of the judgment shall be delayed for 30 days.
(e) The clerk shall notify the judgment creditor, at his or her last known address, that the judgment debtor has satisfied the judgment by making payment to the court. The notification shall explain the procedures which the judgment creditor has to follow to receive payment.

(f) For purposes of this section, "costs after judgment" consist of only those costs itemized in a memorandum of costs filed by the judgment creditor or otherwise authorized by the court.
(g) Payments that remain unclaimed for three years shall go to the superior court pursuant to Section 68084.1 of the Government Code.
(h) A fee of twenty dollars ($20) shall be paid by the judgment debtor for the costs of administering this section.
Amended by Stats 2005 ch 75 (AB 145),s 25, eff. 7/19/2005, op. 1/1/2006

Section 116.870 - Suspension of judgment debtor's privilege to operate motor vehicle for failure to satisfy judgment
(a) Sections 16250 to 16381, inclusive, of the Vehicle Code, regarding the suspension of the judgment debtor's privilege to operate a motor vehicle for failing to satisfy a judgment, apply if the judgment (1) was for damage to property in excess of one thousand dollars ($1,000) or for bodily injury to, or death of, a person in any amount, and (2) resulted from the operation of a motor vehicle upon a California highway by the defendant, or by any other person for whose conduct the defendant was liable, unless the liability resulted from the defendant's signing the application of a minor for a driver's license.
(b) This section shall become operative on January 1, 2017.
Added by Stats 2015 ch 451 (SB 491),s 2, eff. 1/1/2016.

Section 116.880 - Notice requesting suspension of judgment debtor's privilege to operate motor vehicle
(a) If the judgment (1) was for one thousand dollars ($1,000) or less, (2) resulted from a motor vehicle accident occurring on a California highway caused by the defendant's operation of a motor vehicle, and (3) has remained unsatisfied for more than 90 days after the judgment became final, the judgment creditor may file with the Department of Motor Vehicles a notice requesting a suspension of the judgment debtor's privilege to operate a motor vehicle.
(b) The notice shall state that the judgment has not been satisfied, and shall be accompanied by (1) a fee set by the department, (2) the judgment of the court determining that the judgment resulted from a motor vehicle accident occurring on a California highway caused by the judgment debtor's operation of a motor vehicle, and (3) a declaration that the judgment has not been satisfied. The fee shall be used by the department to finance the costs of administering this section and shall not exceed the department's actual costs.
(c) Upon receipt of a notice, the department shall attempt to notify the judgment debtor by telephone, if possible, otherwise by certified mail, that the judgment debtor's privilege to operate a motor vehicle will be suspended for a period of 90 days, beginning 20 days after receipt of notice by the department from the judgment creditor, unless satisfactory proof, as provided in subdivision (e), is provided to the department before that date.
(d) At the time the notice is filed, the department shall give the judgment creditor a copy of the notice that indicates the filing fee paid by the judgment creditor, and includes a space to be signed by the judgment creditor acknowledging payment of the judgment by the judgment debtor. The judgment creditor shall mail or deliver a signed copy of the acknowledgment to the judgment debtor once the judgment is satisfied.
(e) The department shall terminate the suspension, or the suspension proceedings, upon the occurrence of one or more of the following:
    (1) Receipt of proof that the judgment has been satisfied, either (A) by a copy of the notice required by this section signed by the judgment creditor acknowledging satisfaction of the judgment, or (B) by a declaration of the judgment debtor stating that the judgment has been satisfied.
    (2) Receipt of proof that the judgment debtor is complying with a court-ordered payment schedule.
    (3) Proof that the judgment debtor had insurance covering the accident sufficient to satisfy the judgment.
    (4) A deposit with the department of the amount of the unsatisfied judgment, if the judgment debtor presents proof, satisfactory to the department, of inability to locate the judgment creditor.
    (5) At the end of 90 days.
(f) If the suspension has been terminated under subdivision (e), the action is final and shall not be reinstituted. If the suspension is terminated, Section 14904 of the Vehicle Code shall apply. Money deposited with the department under this section shall be handled in the same manner as money deposited under paragraph (4) of subdivision (a) of Section 16377 of the Vehicle Code.
(g) A public agency is not liable for an injury caused by the suspension, termination of suspension, or the failure to suspend a person's privilege to operate a motor vehicle as authorized by this section.
(h) This section shall become operative on January 1, 2017.
Added by Stats 2015 ch 451 (SB 491),s 4, eff. 1/1/2016.

Article 9 - ADMINISTRATION

Section 116.920 - Rules of practice and procedure and forms
(a) The Judicial Council shall provide by rule for the practice and procedure and for the forms and their use in small claims actions. The rules and forms so adopted shall be consistent with this chapter.
(b) The Judicial Council, in consultation with the Department of Consumer Affairs, shall adopt rules to ensure that litigants receive adequate notice of the availability of assistance from small claims advisors, to prescribe other qualifications and the conduct of advisors, to prescribe training standards for advisors and for temporary judges hearing small claims matters, to prescribe, where appropriate, uniform rules and procedures regarding small claims actions and judgments, and to address other matters that are deemed necessary and appropriate.
Amended by Stats. 1991, Ch. 915, Sec. 35.

Section 116.930 - Division to provide copy of publication describing small claims law and procedures; manual on small claims rules and procedures
(a) Each small claims division shall provide in each courtroom in which small claims actions are heard a current copy of a publication describing small claims court law and the procedures that are applicable in the small claims courts, including the law and procedures that apply to the enforcement of judgments. The Small Claims Court and Consumer Law California Judge's Bench Book developed by the California Center for Judicial Education and Research is illustrative of a publication that satisfies the requirement of this subdivision.
(b) Each small claims division may formulate and distribute to litigants and the public a manual on small claims court rules and procedures. The manual shall explain how to complete the necessary forms, how to determine the proper court in which small claims actions may be filed, how to present and defend against claims, how to appeal, how to enforce a judgment, how to protect property that is exempt from execution, and such other matters that the court deems necessary or desirable.
(c) If the Department of Consumer Affairs determines there are sufficient private or public funds available in addition to the funds available within the department's current budget, the department, in cooperation with the Judicial Council, shall prepare a manual or information booklet on small claims court rules and procedures. The department shall distribute copies to the general public and to each small claims division.
(d) If funding is available, the Judicial Council, in cooperation with the Department of Consumer Affairs, shall prepare and distribute to each judge who sits in a small claims court a bench book describing all state and federal consumer protection laws reasonably likely to apply in small claims actions.
Added by Stats. 1990, Ch. 1305, Sec. 3. Note: Prior to 1991, this subject matter was in Chapter 5A, comprising Sections 116 to 117.24.

Section 116.940 - Small claims advisory service
(a) Except as otherwise provided in this section or in rules adopted by the Judicial Council, which are consistent with the requirements of this section, the characteristics of the small claims advisory service required by Section 116.260 shall be determined by each county, or by the superior court in a county where the small claims advisory service is administered by the court, in accordance with local needs and conditions.
(b) Each advisory service shall provide the following services:

(1) Individual personal advisory services, in person or by telephone, and by any other means reasonably calculated to provide timely and appropriate assistance. The topics covered by individual personal advisory services shall include, but not be limited to, preparation of small claims court filings, procedures, including procedures related to the conduct of the hearing, and information on the collection of small claims court judgments.

(2) Recorded telephone messages may be used to supplement the individual personal advisory services, but shall not be the sole means of providing advice available in the county.

(3) Adjacent counties, superior courts in adjacent counties, or any combination thereof, may provide advisory services jointly.

(c) In a county in which the number of small claims actions filed annually is 1,000 or less as averaged over the immediately preceding two fiscal years, the county or the superior court may elect to exempt itself from the requirements set forth in subdivision (b). If the small claims advisory service is administered by the county, this exemption shall be formally noticed through the adoption of a resolution by the board of supervisors. If the small claims advisory service is administered by the superior court, this exemption shall be formally noticed through adoption of a local rule. If a county or court so exempts itself, the county or court shall nevertheless provide the following minimum advisory services in accordance with rules adopted by the Judicial Council:

(1) Recorded telephone messages providing general information relating to small claims actions filed in the county shall be provided during regular business hours.

(2) Small claims information booklets shall be provided in the court clerk's office of each superior court, appropriate county offices, and in any other location that is convenient to prospective small claims litigants in the county.

(d) The advisory service shall operate in conjunction and cooperation with the small claims division, and shall be administered so as to avoid the existence or appearance of a conflict of interest between the individuals providing the advisory services and any party to a particular small claims action or any judicial officer deciding small claims actions.

(e) Advisers may be volunteers, and shall be members of the State Bar, law students, paralegals, or persons experienced in resolving minor disputes, and shall be familiar with small claims court rules and procedures. Advisers may not appear in court as an advocate for any party.

(f) Advisers, including independent contractors, other employees, and volunteers, have the immunity conferred by Section 818.9 of the Government Code with respect to advice provided as a public service on behalf of a court or county to small claims litigants and potential litigants under this chapter.

(g) This section does not preclude a court or county from contracting with a third party to provide small claims advisory services as described in this section.

Amended by Stats 2013 ch 76 (AB 383),s 21, eff. 1/1/2014.
Amended by Stats 2012 ch 470 (AB 1529),s 4, eff. 1/1/2013.
Amended by Stats 2005 ch 618 (AB 1459),s 6, eff. 1/1/2006
Amended by Stats 2005 ch 600 (SB 422),s 6, eff. 1/1/2006
Amended by Stats 2002 ch 806 (AB 3027),s 6, eff. 1/1/2003.

Section 116.950 - Advisory committee to study small claims practice and procedure

(a) This section shall become operative only if the Department of Consumer Affairs determines that sufficient private or public funds are available in addition to the funds available in the department's current budget to cover the costs of implementing this section.

(b) There shall be established an advisory committee, constituted as set forth in this section, to study small claims practice and procedure, with particular attention given to the improvement of procedures for the enforcement of judgments.

(c) The members of the advisory committee shall serve without compensation, but shall be reimbursed for expenses actually and necessarily incurred by them in the performance of their duties.

(d) The advisory committee shall be composed as follows:

(1) The Attorney General or a representative.

(2) Two consumer representatives from consumer groups or agencies, appointed by the Secretary of the State and Consumer Services Agency.

(3) One representative appointed by the Speaker of the Assembly and one representative appointed by the President pro Tempore of the Senate.

(4) Two representatives appointed by the Board of Governors of the State Bar.

(5) Two representatives of the business community, appointed by the Secretary of Technology, Trade, and Commerce.

(6) Six judicial officers who have extensive experience presiding in small claims court, appointed by the Judicial Council. Judicial officers appointed under this subdivision may include judicial officers of the superior court, judges of the appellate courts, retired judicial officers, and temporary judges.

(7) One representative appointed by the Governor.

(8) Two clerks of the court appointed by the Judicial Council.

(e) Staff assistance to the advisory committee shall be provided by the Department of Consumer Affairs, with the assistance of the Judicial Council, as needed.

Amended by Stats 2002 ch 664 (AB 3034),s 46, eff. 1/1/2003.
Amended by Stats 2002 ch 784 (SB 1316),s 32, eff. 1/1/2003.
Amended by Stats 2001 ch 745 (SB 1191), s 8, eff. 10/11/2001.
Previously Amended September 7, 1999 (Bill Number: SB 210) (Chapter 344).

Chapter 6 - GENERAL PROVISIONS RESPECTING COURTS OF JUSTICE

Article 1 - OPEN COURT ACCESS

Section 124 - Court to be public; remote access; public audio stream

(a) Except as provided in Section 214 of the Family Code or any other law, the sittings of every court shall be public.

(b)

(1) The court shall not exclude the public from physical access because remote access is available, unless it is necessary to restrict or limit physical access to protect the health or safety of the public or court personnel.

(2) When a courthouse is physically closed, to the extent permitted by law, the court shall provide, at a minimum, a public audio stream or telephonic means by which to listen to the proceedings. This paragraph does not apply to proceedings pursuant to Section 214 of the Family Code or other law that authorizes or requires a proceeding to be closed.

(3) For purposes of this subdivision, "remote access" shall include, but is not limited to, an audio stream that is available on an internet website or telephonic means to listen to a court proceeding.

Amended by Stats 2021 ch 526 (AB 716),s 3, eff. 1/1/2022.
Amended by Stats 2021 ch 526 (AB 716),s 2, eff. 1/1/2022.
Amended by Stats 2021 ch 526 (AB 716),s 1, eff. 1/1/2022.
Amended by Stats. 1992, Ch. 163, Sec. 12. Effective January 1, 1993. Operative January 1, 1994, by Sec. 161 of Ch. 163.

Article 2 - INCIDENTAL POWERS AND DUTIES OF COURTS

Section 128 - Generally

(a) Every court shall have the power to do all of the following:

(1) To preserve and enforce order in its immediate presence.

(2) To enforce order in the proceedings before it, or before a person or persons empowered to conduct a judicial investigation under its authority.

(3) To provide for the orderly conduct of proceedings before it, or its officers.

(4) To compel obedience to its judgments, orders, and process, and to the orders of a judge out of court, in an action or proceeding pending therein.

(5) To control in furtherance of justice, the conduct of its ministerial officers, and of all other persons in any manner connected with a judicial proceeding before it, in every matter pertaining thereto.

(6) To compel the attendance of persons to testify in an action or proceeding pending therein, in the cases and manner provided in this code.

(7) To administer oaths in an action or proceeding pending therein, and in all other cases where it may be necessary in the exercise of its powers and duties.

(8) To amend and control its process and orders so as to make them conform to law and justice. An appellate court shall not reverse or vacate a duly entered judgment upon an agreement or stipulation of the parties unless the court finds both of the following:

(A) There is no reasonable possibility that the interests of nonparties or the public will be adversely affected by the reversal.

(B) The reasons of the parties for requesting reversal outweigh the erosion of public trust that may result from the nullification of a judgment and the risk that the availability of stipulated reversal will reduce the incentive for pretrial settlement.

(b) Notwithstanding Section 1211 or any other law, if an order of contempt is made affecting an attorney, his or her agent, investigator, or any person acting under the attorney's direction, in the preparation and conduct of any action or proceeding, the execution of any sentence shall be stayed pending the filing within three judicial days of a petition for extraordinary relief testing the lawfulness of the court's order, the violation of which is the basis of the contempt except for the conduct as may be proscribed by subdivision (b) of Section 6068 of the Business and Professions Code, relating to an attorney's duty to maintain respect due to the courts and judicial officers.

(c) Notwithstanding Section 1211 or any other law, if an order of contempt is made affecting a public safety employee acting within the scope of employment for reason of the employee's failure to comply with a duly issued subpoena or subpoena duces tecum, the execution of any sentence shall be stayed pending the filing within three judicial days of a petition for extraordinary relief testing the lawfulness of the court's order, a violation of which is the basis for the contempt. As used in this subdivision, "public safety employee" includes any peace officer, firefighter, paramedic, or any other employee of a public law enforcement agency whose duty is either to maintain official records or to analyze or present evidence for investigative or prosecutorial purposes.

(d) Notwithstanding Section 1211 or any other law, if an order of contempt is made affecting the victim of a sexual assault, where the contempt consists of refusing to testify concerning that sexual assault, the execution of any sentence shall be stayed pending the filing within three judicial days of a petition for extraordinary relief testing the lawfulness of the court's order, a violation of which is the basis for the contempt. As used in this subdivision, "sexual assault" means any act made punishable by Section 261, 262, 264.1, 285, 286, 287, 288, or 289 of, or former Section 288a of, the Penal Code.

(e) Notwithstanding Section 1211 or any other law, if an order of contempt is made affecting the victim of domestic violence, where the contempt consists of refusing to testify concerning that domestic violence, the execution of any sentence shall be stayed pending the filing within three judicial days of a petition for extraordinary relief testing the lawfulness of the court's order, a violation of which is the basis for the contempt. As used in this subdivision, the term "domestic violence" means "domestic violence" as defined in Section 6211 of the Family Code.

(f) Notwithstanding Section 1211 or any other provision of law, no order of contempt shall be made affecting a county government or any member of its governing body acting pursuant to its constitutional or statutory authority unless the court finds, based on a review of evidence presented at a hearing conducted for this purpose, that either of the following conditions exist:

(1) That the county has the resources necessary to comply with the order of the court.

(2) That the county has the authority, without recourse to voter approval or without incurring additional indebtedness, to generate the additional resources necessary to comply with the order of the court, that compliance with the order of the court will not expose the county, any member of its governing body, or any other county officer to liability for failure to perform other constitutional or statutory duties, and that compliance with the order of the court will not deprive the county of resources necessary for its reasonable support and maintenance.

Amended by Stats 2018 ch 423 (SB 1494),s 7, eff. 1/1/2019.

Amended 9/27/1999 (Bill Number: AB 1676) (Chapter 508).

Section 128.5 - Expenses awarded against party or attorney for bad faith actions or tactics

(a) A trial court may order a party, the party's attorney, or both, to pay the reasonable expenses, including attorney's fees, incurred by another party as a result of actions or tactics, made in bad faith, that are frivolous or solely intended to cause unnecessary delay. This section also applies to judicial arbitration proceedings under Chapter 2.5 (commencing with Section 1141.10) of Title 3 of Part 3.

(b) For purposes of this section:

(1) "Actions or tactics" include, but are not limited to, the making or opposing of motions or the filing and service of a complaint, cross-complaint, answer, or other responsive pleading. The mere filing of a complaint without service thereof on an opposing party does not constitute "actions or tactics" for purposes of this section.

(2) "Frivolous" means totally and completely without merit or for the sole purpose of harassing an opposing party.

(c) Expenses pursuant to this section shall not be imposed except on notice contained in a party's moving or responding papers or, on the court's own motion, after notice and opportunity to be heard. An order imposing expenses shall be in writing and shall recite in detail the action or tactic or circumstances justifying the order.

(d) In addition to any award pursuant to this section for an action or tactic described in subdivision (a), the court may assess punitive damages against the plaintiff on a determination by the court that the plaintiff's action was an action maintained by a person convicted of a felony against the person's victim, or the victim's heirs, relatives, estate, or personal representative, for injuries arising from the acts for which the person was convicted of a felony, and that the plaintiff is guilty of fraud, oppression, or malice in maintaining the action.

(e) This section shall not apply to disclosures and discovery requests, responses, objections, and motions.

(f) Sanctions ordered pursuant to this section shall be ordered pursuant to the following conditions and procedures:

(1) If, after notice and a reasonable opportunity to respond, the court issues an order pursuant to subdivision (a), the court may, subject to the conditions stated below, impose an appropriate sanction upon the party, the party's attorneys, or both, for an action or tactic described in subdivision (a). In determining what sanctions, if any, should be ordered, the court shall consider whether a party seeking sanctions has exercised due diligence.

(A) A motion for sanctions under this section shall be made separately from other motions or requests and shall describe the specific alleged action or tactic, made in bad faith, that is frivolous or solely intended to cause unnecessary delay.

(B) If the alleged action or tactic is the making or opposing of a written motion or the filing and service of a complaint, cross-complaint, answer, or other responsive pleading that can be withdrawn or appropriately corrected, a notice of motion shall be served as provided in Section

1010, but shall not be filed with or presented to the court, unless 21 days after service of the motion or any other period as the court may prescribe, the challenged action or tactic is not withdrawn or appropriately corrected.

(C) If warranted, the court may award to the party prevailing on the motion the reasonable expenses and attorney's fees incurred in presenting or opposing the motion. Absent exceptional circumstances, a law firm shall be held jointly responsible for violations committed by its partners, associates, and employees.

(D) If the alleged action or tactic is the making or opposing of a written motion or the filing and service of a complaint, cross-complaint, answer, or other responsive pleading that can be withdrawn or appropriately corrected, the court on its own motion may enter an order describing the specific action or tactic, made in bad faith, that is frivolous or solely intended to cause unnecessary delay, and direct an attorney, law firm, or party to show cause why it has made an action or tactic as defined in subdivision (b), unless, within 21 days of service of the order to show cause, the challenged action or tactic is withdrawn or appropriately corrected.

(2) An order for sanctions pursuant to this section shall be limited to what is sufficient to deter repetition of the action or tactic or comparable action or tactic by others similarly situated. Subject to the limitations in subparagraphs (A) and (B), the sanction may consist of, or include, directives of a nonmonetary nature, an order to pay a penalty into court, or, if imposed on motion and warranted for effective deterrence, an order directing payment to the movant of some or all of the reasonable attorney's fees and other expenses incurred as a direct result of the action or tactic described in subdivision (a).

(A) Monetary sanctions may not be awarded against a represented party for a violation of presenting a claim, defense, and other legal contentions that are warranted by existing law or by a nonfrivolous argument for the extension, modification, or reversal of existing law or the establishment of new law.

(B) Monetary sanctions may not be awarded on the court's motion unless the court issues its order to show cause before a voluntary dismissal or settlement of the claims made by or against the party that is, or whose attorneys are, to be sanctioned.

(g) A motion for sanctions brought by a party or a party's attorney primarily for an improper purpose, such as to harass or to cause unnecessary delay or needless increase in the cost of litigation, shall itself be subject to a motion for sanctions. It is the intent of the Legislature that courts shall vigorously use its sanction authority to deter the improper actions or tactics or comparable actions or tactics of others similarly situated.

(h) The liability imposed by this section is in addition to any other liability imposed by law for acts or omissions within the purview of this section.

(i) This section applies to actions or tactics that were part of a civil case filed on or after January 1, 2015.

Amended by Stats 2017 ch 169 (AB 984),s 1, eff. 8/7/2017.

Amended by Stats 2014 ch 425 (AB 2494),s 1, eff. 1/1/2015.

Section 128.6 - [Repealed]

Repealed by Stats 2010 ch 328 (SB 1330),s 31, eff. 1/1/2011.

Section 128.7 - Attorney or unrepresented party to sign pleadings, petitions, notice, etc.; certification; sanctions for violations

(a) Every pleading, petition, written notice of motion, or other similar paper shall be signed by at least one attorney of record in the attorney's individual name, or, if the party is not represented by an attorney, shall be signed by the party. Each paper shall state the signer's address and telephone number, if any. Except when otherwise provided by law, pleadings need not be verified or accompanied by affidavit. An unsigned paper shall be stricken unless omission of the signature is corrected promptly after being called to the attention of the attorney or party.

(b) By presenting to the court, whether by signing, filing, submitting, or later advocating, a pleading, petition, written notice of motion, or other similar paper, an attorney or unrepresented party is certifying that to the best of the person's knowledge, information, and belief, formed after an inquiry reasonable under the circumstances, all of the following conditions are met:

(1) It is not being presented primarily for an improper purpose, such as to harass or to cause unnecessary delay or needless increase in the cost of litigation.

(2) The claims, defenses, and other legal contentions therein are warranted by existing law or by a nonfrivolous argument for the extension, modification, or reversal of existing law or the establishment of new law.

(3) The allegations and other factual contentions have evidentiary support or, if specifically so identified, are likely to have evidentiary support after a reasonable opportunity for further investigation or discovery.

(4) The denials of factual contentions are warranted on the evidence or, if specifically so identified, are reasonably based on a lack of information or belief.

(c) If, after notice and a reasonable opportunity to respond, the court determines that subdivision (b) has been violated, the court may, subject to the conditions stated below, impose an appropriate sanction upon the attorneys, law firms, or parties that have violated subdivision (b) or are responsible for the violation. In determining what sanctions, if any, should be ordered, the court shall consider whether a party seeking sanctions has exercised due diligence.

(1) A motion for sanctions under this section shall be made separately from other motions or requests and shall describe the specific conduct alleged to violate subdivision (b). Notice of motion shall be served as provided in Section 1010, but shall not be filed with or presented to the court unless, within 21 days after service of the motion, or any other period as the court may prescribe, the challenged paper, claim, defense, contention, allegation, or denial is not withdrawn or appropriately corrected. If warranted, the court may award to the party prevailing on the motion the reasonable expenses and attorney's fees incurred in presenting or opposing the motion. Absent exceptional circumstances, a law firm shall be held jointly responsible for violations committed by its partners, associates, and employees.

(2) On its own motion, the court may enter an order describing the specific conduct that appears to violate subdivision (b) and directing an attorney, law firm, or party to show cause why it has not violated subdivision (b), unless, within 21 days of service of the order to show cause, the challenged paper, claim, defense, contention, allegation, or denial is withdrawn or appropriately corrected.

(d) A sanction imposed for violation of subdivision (b) shall be limited to what is sufficient to deter repetition of this conduct or comparable conduct by others similarly situated. Subject to the limitations in paragraphs (1) and (2), the sanction may consist of, or include, directives of a nonmonetary nature, an order to pay a penalty into court, or, if imposed on motion and warranted for effective deterrence, an order directing payment to the movant of some or all of the reasonable attorney's fees and other expenses incurred as a direct result of the violation.

(1) Monetary sanctions may not be awarded against a represented party for a violation of paragraph (2) of subdivision (b).

(2) Monetary sanctions may not be awarded on the court's motion unless the court issues its order to show cause before a voluntary dismissal or settlement of the claims made by or against the party that is, or whose attorneys are, to be sanctioned.

(e) When imposing sanctions, the court shall describe the conduct determined to constitute a violation of this section and explain the basis for the sanction imposed.

(f) In addition to any award pursuant to this section for conduct described in subdivision (b), the court may assess punitive damages against the plaintiff upon a determination by the court that the plaintiff's action was an action maintained by a person convicted of a felony against the person's victim, or the victim's heirs, relatives, estate, or personal representative, for injuries arising from the acts for which the person was convicted of a felony, and that the plaintiff is guilty of fraud, oppression, or malice in maintaining the action.

(g) This section shall not apply to disclosures and discovery requests, responses, objections, and motions.

(h) A motion for sanctions brought by a party or a party's attorney primarily for an improper purpose, such as to harass or to cause unnecessary delay or needless increase in the cost of litigation, shall itself be subject to a motion for sanctions. It is the intent of the Legislature that courts shall vigorously use its sanctions authority to deter that improper conduct or comparable conduct by others similarly situated.

(i) This section shall apply to a complaint or petition filed on or after January 1, 1995, and any other pleading, written notice of motion, or other similar paper filed in that matter.

Amended by Stats 2005 ch 706 (AB 1742),s 9, eff. 1/1/2006

Amended by Stats 2002 ch 491 (SB 2009),s 1, eff. 1/1/2003.

Section 129 - Dissemination of copies of photographs of deceased taken by coroner as part of post mortem examination or autopsy

(a) Notwithstanding any other law, a copy, reproduction, or facsimile of any kind of a photograph, negative, or print, including instant photographs and video recordings, of the body, or any portion of the body, of a deceased person, taken by or for the coroner at the scene of death or in the course of a post mortem examination or autopsy, shall not be made or disseminated except as follows:

(1) For use in a criminal action or proceeding in this state that relates to the death of that person.

(2) As a court of this state permits, by order after good cause has been shown and after written notification of the request for the court order has been served, at least five days before the order is made, upon the district attorney of the county in which the post mortem examination or autopsy has been made or caused to be made.

(3) For use or potential use in a civil action or proceeding in this state that relates to the death of that person, if either of the following applies:

(A) The coroner receives written authorization from a legal heir or representative of that person before the action is filed or while the action is pending. To verify the identity of the legal heir or representative, all of the following shall be provided to the coroner:

(i) A declaration under penalty of perjury that the individual is a legal heir or representative of the deceased person.

(ii) A valid form of identification.

(iii) A certified death certificate.

(B) A subpoena is issued by a party who is a legal heir or representative of the deceased person in a pending civil action.

(b) This section shall not apply to the making or dissemination of a copy, reproduction, or facsimile for use in the field of forensic pathology, in medical or scientific education or research, or by a coroner or any law enforcement agency in the United States for investigative purposes, including identification and identification confirmation.

(c) This section shall apply to a copy, reproduction, or facsimile, and to a photograph, negative, or print, regardless of when it was made.

(d) A coroner is not personally liable for monetary damages in a civil action for any act or omission in compliance with this section.

Amended by Stats 2016 ch 467 (AB 2427),s 1, eff. 1/1/2017.

Amended by Stats 2013 ch 53 (AB 957),s 1, eff. 1/1/2014.

Amended by Stats 2009 ch 88 (AB 176),s 16, eff. 1/1/2010.

Section 130 - Request by family member that autopsy report and evidence regarding child under 18 killed as result of criminal act be sealed and not disclosed, disclosure exceptions

(a) Subject to the provisions of this section, when a child who is under 18 years of age is killed as a result of a criminal act and a person has been convicted and sentenced for the commission of that criminal act, or a person has been found to have committed that offense by the juvenile court and adjudged a ward of the juvenile court, upon the request of a qualifying family member of the deceased child, the autopsy report and evidence associated with the examination of the victim in the possession of a public agency, as defined in Section 7920.525 of the Government Code, shall be sealed and not disclosed, except that an autopsy report and evidence associated with the examination of the victim that has been sealed pursuant to this section may be disclosed, as follows:

(1) To law enforcement, prosecutorial agencies and experts hired by those agencies, public social service agencies, child death review teams, or the hospital that treated the child immediately prior to death, to be used solely for investigative, prosecutorial, or review purposes, and may not be disseminated further.

(2) To the defendant and the defense team in the course of criminal proceedings or related habeas proceedings, to be used solely for investigative, criminal defense, and review purposes, including review for the purpose of initiating any criminal proceeding or related habeas proceeding, and may not be disseminated further. The "defense team" includes, but is not limited to, all of the following: attorneys, investigators, experts, paralegals, support staff, interns, students, and state and privately funded legal assistance projects hired or consulted for the purposes of investigation, defense, appeal, or writ of habeas corpus on behalf of the person accused of killing the deceased child victim.

(3) To civil litigants in a cause of action related to the victim's death with a court order upon a showing of good cause and proper notice under Section 129, to be used solely to pursue the cause of action, and may not be disseminated further.

(b) Nothing in this section shall prohibit the use of autopsy reports and evidence in relation to court proceedings.

(c) Nothing in this section shall abrogate the rights of victims, their authorized representatives, or insurance carriers to request the release of information pursuant to Article 1 (commencing with Section 7923.600) of Chapter 1 of Part 5 of Division 10 of Title 1 of the Government Code. However, if a seal has been requested, an insurance carrier receiving items pursuant to a request under that article is prohibited from disclosing the requested items except as necessary in the normal course of business. An insurance carrier shall not, under any circumstances, disclose to the general public items received pursuant to Article 1 (commencing with Section 7923.600) of Chapter 1 of Part 5 of Division 10 of Title 1 of the Government Code.

(d) This section may not be invoked by a qualifying family member who has been charged with or convicted of any act in furtherance of the victim's death. Upon the filing of those charges against a qualifying family member, any seal maintained at the request of that qualifying family member under this section shall be removed.

(e) A coroner or medical examiner shall not be liable for damages in a civil action for any reasonable act or omission taken in good faith in compliance with this section.

(f) If sealing of the autopsy report has been requested by a qualifying family member and another qualifying family member opposes sealing, the opposing party may request a hearing in the superior court in the county with jurisdiction over the crime leading to the child's death for a determination of whether the sealing should be maintained. The opposing party shall notify all other qualifying family members, the medical examiner's office that conducted the autopsy, and the district attorney's office with jurisdiction over the crime at least 10 court days in advance of the hearing. At the hearing, the court shall consider the interests of all qualifying family members, the protection of the memory of the deceased child, any evidence that the qualifying family member requesting the seal was involved in the crime that resulted in the death of the child, the public interest in scrutiny of the autopsy report or the performance of the medical examiner, any impact that unsealing would have on pending investigations or pending litigation, and any other relevant factors. Official information in the possession of a public agency necessary to the determination of the hearing shall be received in camera upon a proper showing. In its discretion, the court may, to the extent allowable by law and with good cause shown, restrict the dissemination of an autopsy report or evidence associated with the examination of a victim. This section shall not apply if a public agency has independently determined that the autopsy report may not be disclosed pursuant to Article 1 (commencing with Section 7923.600) of Chapter 1 of Part 5 of Division 10 of Title 1 of the Government Code because it is an investigative file. In that instance, nothing in this section shall preclude the application of Part 5 (commencing with Section 7923.000) of Division 10 of Title 1 of the Government Code.

(g) If a seal has been maintained pursuant to this section, a qualifying family member, or a biological or adoptive aunt, uncle, sibling, first cousin, child, or grandparent of the deceased child may request that the seal be removed. The request to remove the seal shall be adjudicated pursuant to subdivision (f), with the party requesting the removal of the seal being the opposing party.

(h) Nothing in this section shall limit the public access to information contained in the death certificate including: name, age, gender, race, date, time and location of death, the name of a physician reporting a death in a hospital, the name of the certifying pathologist, date of certification, burial information, and cause of death.

(i) When a medical examiner declines a request to provide a copy of an autopsy report that has been sealed pursuant to this section, the examiner shall cite this section as the reason for declining to provide a copy of the report.

(j) For purposes of this section:

    (1) A "child who is under 18 years of age" does not include any child who comes within either of the following descriptions:

        (A) The child was a dependent child of the juvenile court pursuant to Section 300 of the Welfare and Institutions Code at the time of the child's death, or, pursuant to subdivision (b) of Section 10850.4 of the Welfare and Institutions Code, abuse or neglect is determined to have led to the child's death.

        (B) The child was residing in a state or county juvenile facility, or a private facility under contract with the state or county for the placement of juveniles, as a ward of the juvenile court pursuant to Section 602 of the Welfare and Institutions Code at the time of the child's death.

    (2) "Evidence associated with the examination of a victim" means any object, writing, diagram, recording, computer file, photograph, video, DVD, CD, film, digital device, or other item that was collected during, or serves to document, the autopsy of a deceased child.

    (3) "Qualifying family member" means the biological or adoptive parent, spouse, or legal guardian.

(k) Nothing in this section shall limit the discovery provisions set forth in Chapter 10 (commencing with Section 1054) of Title 6 of the Penal Code.

(l) Nothing in this section shall be construed to limit the authority of the court to seal records or restrict the dissemination of an autopsy report or evidence associated with the examination of a victim under case law, other statutory law, or the rules of court.

(m) The provisions of this section are severable. If any provision of this section or its application is held invalid, that invalidity shall not affect other provisions or applications that can be given effect without the invalid provision or application.

Amended by Stats 2021 ch 615 (AB 474),s 55, eff. 1/1/2022, op. 1/1/2023.
Added by Stats 2010 ch 302 (SB 5),s 3, eff. 9/25/2010.

Section 131.3 through 131.7 - [Repealed]
Repealed by Stats 2001 ch 473 (SB 485), ss 1-5, eff. 1/1/2002.

Article 3 - JUDICIAL HOLIDAYS

Section 133 - Generally
Courts of justice may be held and judicial business transacted on any day, except as provided in this article.
Repealed and added by Stats. 1985, Ch. 1450, Sec. 2. Operative January 1, 1989, by Sec. 6 of Ch. 1450.

Section 134 - Courts closed for transaction of business on judicial holidays, exceptions

(a) Except as provided in subdivision (c), the courts shall be closed for the transaction of judicial business on judicial holidays for all but the following purposes:

    (1) To give, upon their request, instructions to a jury when deliberating on their verdict.

    (2) To receive a verdict or discharge a jury.

    (3) For the conduct of arraignments and the exercise of the powers of a magistrate in a criminal action, or in a proceeding of a criminal nature.

    (4) For the conduct of Saturday small claims court sessions pursuant to the Small Claims Act set forth in Chapter 5.5 (commencing with Section 116.110).

(b) Injunctions and writs of prohibition may be issued and served on any day.

(c) In any superior court, one or more departments of the court may remain open and in session for the transaction of any business that may come before the department in the exercise of the civil or criminal jurisdiction of the court, or both, on a judicial holiday or at any hours of the day or night, or both, as the judges of the court prescribe.

(d) The fact that a court is open on a judicial holiday shall not make that day a nonholiday for purposes of computing the time required for the conduct of any proceeding nor for the performance of any act. Any paper lodged with the court at a time when the court is open pursuant to subdivision (c), shall be filed by the court on the next day that is not a judicial holiday, if the document meets appropriate criteria for filing.

Amended by Stats 2002 ch 784 (SB 1316),s 33, eff. 1/1/2003.

Section 135 - Judicial holidays
Every full day designated as a holiday by Section 6700 of the Government Code, including that Thursday of November declared by the President to be Thanksgiving Day, is a judicial holiday, except the date corresponding with the second new moon following the winter solstice, or the third new moon following the winter solstice should an intercalary month intervene, known as "Lunar New Year," April 24, known as "Genocide Remembrance Day," September 9, known as "Admission Day," the second Monday in October, known as "Columbus Day," and any other day appointed by the President, but not by the Governor, for a public fast, thanksgiving, or holiday. If a judicial holiday falls on a Saturday or a Sunday, the Judicial Council may designate an alternative day for observance of the holiday. Every Saturday and the day after Thanksgiving Day are judicial holidays. Officers and employees of the courts shall observe only the judicial holidays established pursuant to this section.

Amended by Stats 2022 ch 792 (AB 2596),s 1.5, eff. 1/1/2023.
Amended by Stats 2022 ch 761 (AB 1801),s 2, eff. 1/1/2023.
Amended by Stats 2021 ch 283 (AB 855),s 1, eff. 1/1/2022.
Amended by Stats 2015 ch 26 (SB 85),s 2, eff. 6/24/2015.
Amended by Stats 2001 ch 542 (SB 1112), s 3, eff. 1/1/2002.

Section 136 - Day appointed for holding court falls on judicial holiday
If a day appointed for the holding or sitting of a court, or to which it is adjourned, falls on a judicial holiday, it shall be deemed appointed for or adjourned to the next day.
Added by Stats. 1985, Ch. 1450, Sec. 2. Operative January 1, 1989, by Sec. 6 of Ch. 1450.

Article 4 - PROCEEDINGS IN CASE OF ABSENCE OF JUDGE

Section 139 - Adjournment if no judge attends
If no judge attends on the day appointed for the holding or sitting of a court, or on the day to which it may have been adjourned, within one hour after the time appointed, the sheriff, marshal, or clerk shall adjourn the same until the next day, at 10 o'clock a.m., and if no judge attend on that day, before noon, the sheriff, marshal, or clerk shall adjourn the same until the following day at the same hour; and so on, from day to day unless the judge, by written order, directs it to be adjourned to some day certain, fixed in said order, in which case it shall be so adjourned.
Amended by Stats. 1996, Ch. 872, Sec. 6. Effective January 1, 1997.

Article 6 - SEALS OF COURTS

Section 153 - Affixing to proceedings

Except as otherwise expressly provided by law, the seal of a court need not be affixed to any proceeding therein, or to any document, except to the following:

(a) A writ.

(b) A summons.

(c) A warrant of arrest.

Prior heading repealed by Stats 2015 ch 303 (AB 731),s 37, eff. 1/1/2016.

Amended by Stats. 1988, Ch. 1199, Sec. 2. Operative July 1, 1989, by Sec. 119 of Ch. 1199.

Chapter 7 - SPECIAL IMMIGRANT JUVENILE FINDINGS

Section 155 - Jurisdiction of superior court

(a)

(1) A superior court has jurisdiction under California law to make judicial determinations regarding the custody and care of children within the meaning of the federal Immigration and Nationality Act (8 U.S.C. Sec. 1101 et seq. and 8 C.F.R. Sec. 204.11), which includes, but is not limited to, the juvenile, probate, and family court divisions of the superior court. These courts have jurisdiction to make the factual findings necessary to enable a child to petition the United States Citizenship and Immigration Services for classification as a special immigrant juvenile pursuant to Section 1101(a)(27)(J)(a)(27)(J) of Title 8 of the United States Code.

(2) The factual findings set forth in paragraph (1) of subdivision (b) may be made at any point in a proceeding regardless of the division of the superior court or type of proceeding if the prerequisites of that subdivision are met.

(b)

(1) If an order is requested from the superior court making the necessary findings regarding special immigrant juvenile status pursuant to Section 1101(a)(27)(J)(a)(27)(J) of Title 8 of the United States Code, and there is evidence to support those findings, which may consist solely of, but is not limited to, a declaration by the child who is the subject of the petition, the court shall issue the order, which shall include all of the following findings:

(A) The child was either of the following:

(i) Declared a dependent of the court.

(ii) Legally committed to, or placed under the custody of, a state agency or department, or an individual or entity appointed by the court. The court shall indicate the date on which the dependency, commitment, or custody was ordered.

(B) That reunification of the child with one or both of the child's parents was determined not to be viable because of abuse, neglect, abandonment, or a similar basis pursuant to California law. The court shall indicate the date on which reunification was determined not to be viable.

(C) That it is not in the best interest of the child to be returned to the child's, or his or her parent's, previous country of nationality or country of last habitual residence.

(2) The superior the court may make additional findings under this section that are supported by evidence only if requested by a party. The asserted, purported, or perceived motivation of the child seeking classification as a special immigrant juvenile shall not be admissible in making the findings under this section. The court shall not include nor reference the asserted, purported, or perceived motivation of the child seeking classification as a special immigrant juvenile in the court's findings under this section.

(c) In any judicial proceedings in response to a request that the superior court make the findings necessary to support a petition for classification as a special immigrant juvenile, information regarding the child's immigration status that is not otherwise protected by state confidentiality laws shall remain confidential and shall be available for inspection only by the court, the child who is the subject of the proceeding, the parties, the attorneys for the parties, the child's counsel, and the child's guardian.

(d) In any judicial proceedings in response to a request that the superior court make the findings necessary to support a petition for classification as a special immigrant juvenile, records of the proceedings that are not otherwise protected by state confidentiality laws may be sealed using the procedure set forth in California Rules of Court 2.550 and 2.551.

(e) The Judicial Council shall adopt any rules and forms needed to implement this section.

Amended by Stats 2016 ch 25 (AB 1603),s 1, eff. 6/27/2016.

Added by Stats 2014 ch 685 (SB 873),s 1, eff. 9/27/2014.

Title 2 - JUDICIAL OFFICERS

Chapter 2 - POWERS OF JUDGES AT CHAMBERS

Section 165 - Justices of Supreme Court and courts of appeal

The justices of the Supreme Court and of the courts of appeal, or any of them, may, at chambers, grant all orders and writs which are usually granted in the first instance upon an ex parte application, except writs of mandamus, certiorari, and prohibition; and may, in their discretion, hear applications to discharge such orders and writs.

Prior heading repealed by Stats 2015 ch 303 (AB 731),s 38, eff. 1/1/2016.

Amended by Stats. 1967, Ch. 17.

Section 166 - Judges of superior courts

(a) The judges of the superior courts may, in chambers:

(1) Grant all orders and writs that are usually granted in the first instance upon an ex parte application, and hear and dispose of those orders and writs, appoint referees, require and receive inventories and accounts to be filed, order notice of settlement of supplemental accounts, suspend the powers of personal representatives, guardians, or conservators in the cases allowed by law, appoint special administrators, grant letters of temporary guardianship or conservatorship, approve or reject claims, and direct the issuance from the court of all writs and process necessary in the exercise of their powers in matters of probate.

(2) Hear and determine all motions made pursuant to Section 657 or 663.

(3) Hear and determine all uncontested actions, proceedings, demurrers, motions, petitions, applications, and other matters pending before the court other than actions for dissolution of marriage, for legal separation, or for a judgment of nullity of the marriage, and except also applications for confirmation of sale of real property in probate proceedings.

(4) Hear and determine motions to tax costs of enforcing a judgment.

(5) Approve bonds and undertakings.

(b) A judge may, out of court, anywhere in the state, exercise all the powers and perform all the functions and duties conferred upon a judge as contradistinguished from the court, or that a judge may exercise or perform in chambers.

Amended by Stats 2002 ch 784 (SB 1316),s 34, eff. 1/1/2003.

Section 166.1 - Commentary by judge in interlocutory order

Upon the written request of any party or his or her counsel, or at the judge's discretion, a judge may indicate in any interlocutory order a belief that there is a controlling question of law as to which there are substantial grounds for difference of opinion, appellate resolution of which may materially advance the conclusion of the litigation. Neither the denial of a request for, nor the objection of another party or counsel to, such a commentary in the interlocutory order, may be grounds for a writ or appeal.
Added by Stats 2002 ch 708 (AB 2865),s 1, eff. 1/1/2003.

Section 167 - Judge may perform acts required or permitted to be performed by clerk
Any act required or permitted to be performed by the clerk of a court may be performed by a judge thereof.
Amended by Stats. 1989, Ch. 1417, Sec. 1.

Chapter 3 - DISQUALIFICATIONS OF JUDGES

Section 170 - Duty of judge to decide any proceeding
A judge has a duty to decide any proceeding in which he or she is not disqualified.
Repealed and added by Stats. 1984, Ch. 1555, Sec. 2.

Section 170.1 - Grounds for disqualification
(a) A judge shall be disqualified if any one or more of the following are true:
(1)
(A) The judge has personal knowledge of disputed evidentiary facts concerning the proceeding.
(B) A judge shall be deemed to have personal knowledge within the meaning of this paragraph if the judge, or the spouse of the judge, or a person within the third degree of relationship to either of them, or the spouse of such a person is to the judge's knowledge likely to be a material witness in the proceeding.
(2)
(A) The judge served as a lawyer in the proceeding, or in any other proceeding involving the same issues he or she served as a lawyer for a party in the present proceeding or gave advice to a party in the present proceeding upon a matter involved in the action or proceeding.
(B) A judge shall be deemed to have served as a lawyer in the proceeding if within the past two years:
(i) A party to the proceeding, or an officer, director, or trustee of a party, was a client of the judge when the judge was in the private practice of law or a client of a lawyer with whom the judge was associated in the private practice of law.
(ii) A lawyer in the proceeding was associated in the private practice of law with the judge.
(C) A judge who served as a lawyer for, or officer of, a public agency that is a party to the proceeding shall be deemed to have served as a lawyer in the proceeding if he or she personally advised or in any way represented the public agency concerning the factual or legal issues in the proceeding.
(3)
(A) The judge has a financial interest in the subject matter in a proceeding or in a party to the proceeding.
(B) A judge shall be deemed to have a financial interest within the meaning of this paragraph if:
(i) A spouse or minor child living in the household has a financial interest.
(ii) The judge or the spouse of the judge is a fiduciary who has a financial interest.
(C) A judge has a duty to make reasonable efforts to inform himself or herself about his or her personal and fiduciary interests and those of his or her spouse and the personal financial interests of children living in the household.
(4) The judge, or the spouse of the judge, or a person within the third degree of relationship to either of them, or the spouse of such a person is a party to the proceeding or an officer, director, or trustee of a party.
(5) A lawyer or a spouse of a lawyer in the proceeding is the spouse, former spouse, child, sibling, or parent of the judge or the judge's spouse or if such a person is associated in the private practice of law with a lawyer in the proceeding.
(6)
(A) For any reason:
(i) The judge believes his or her recusal would further the interests of justice.
(ii) The judge believes there is a substantial doubt as to his or her capacity to be impartial.
(iii) A person aware of the facts might reasonably entertain a doubt that the judge would be able to be impartial.
(B) Bias or prejudice toward a lawyer in the proceeding may be grounds for disqualification.
(7) By reason of permanent or temporary physical impairment, the judge is unable to properly perceive the evidence or is unable to properly conduct the proceeding.
(8)
(A) The judge has a current arrangement concerning prospective employment or other compensated service as a dispute resolution neutral or is participating in, or, within the last two years has participated in, discussions regarding prospective employment or service as a dispute resolution neutral, or has been engaged in that employment or service, and any of the following applies:
(i) The arrangement is, or the prior employment or discussion was, with a party to the proceeding.
(ii) The matter before the judge includes issues relating to the enforcement of either an agreement to submit a dispute to an alternative dispute resolution process or an award or other final decision by a dispute resolution neutral.
(iii) The judge directs the parties to participate in an alternative dispute resolution process in which the dispute resolution neutral will be an individual or entity with whom the judge has the arrangement, has previously been employed or served, or is discussing or has discussed the employment or service.
(iv) The judge will select a dispute resolution neutral or entity to conduct an alternative dispute resolution process in the matter before the judge, and among those available for selection is an individual or entity with whom the judge has the arrangement, with whom the judge has previously been employed or served, or with whom the judge is discussing or has discussed the employment or service.
(B) For the purposes of this paragraph, all of the following apply:
(i) "Participating in discussions" or "has participated in discussion" means that the judge solicited or otherwise indicated an interest in accepting or negotiating possible employment or service as an alternative dispute resolution neutral, or responded to an unsolicited statement regarding, or an offer of, that employment or service by expressing an interest in that employment or service, making an inquiry regarding the employment or service, or encouraging the person making the statement or offer to provide additional information about that possible employment or service. If a judge's response to an unsolicited statement regarding, a question about, or offer of, prospective employment or other compensated service as a dispute resolution neutral is limited to responding negatively, declining the offer, or declining to discuss that employment or service, that response does not constitute participating in discussions.
(ii) "Party" includes the parent, subsidiary, or other legal affiliate of any entity that is a party and is involved in the transaction, contract, or facts that gave rise to the issues subject to the proceeding.
(iii) "Dispute resolution neutral" means an arbitrator, mediator, temporary judge appointed under Section 21 of Article VI of the California Constitution, referee appointed under Section 638 or 639, special master, neutral evaluator, settlement officer, or settlement facilitator.
(9)

(A) The judge has received a contribution in excess of one thousand five hundred dollars ($1500) from a party or lawyer in the proceeding, and either of the following applies:

(i) The contribution was received in support of the judge's last election, if the last election was within the last six years.

(ii) The contribution was received in anticipation of an upcoming election.

(B) Notwithstanding subparagraph (A), the judge shall be disqualified based on a contribution of a lesser amount if subparagraph (A) of paragraph (6) applies.

(C) The judge shall disclose any contribution from a party or lawyer in a matter that is before the court that is required to be reported under subdivision (f) of Section 84211 of the Government Code, even if the amount would not require disqualification under this paragraph. The manner of disclosure shall be the same as that provided in Canon 3E of the Code of Judicial Ethics.

(D) Notwithstanding paragraph (1) of subdivision (b) of Section 170.3, the disqualification required under this paragraph may be waived by the party that did not make the contribution unless there are other circumstances that would prohibit a waiver pursuant to paragraph (2) of subdivision (b) of Section 170.3.

(b) A judge before whom a proceeding was tried or heard shall be disqualified from participating in any appellate review of that proceeding.

(c) At the request of a party or on its own motion an appellate court shall consider whether in the interests of justice it should direct that further proceedings be heard before a trial judge other than the judge whose judgment or order was reviewed by the appellate court.

Amended by Stats 2010 ch 686 (AB 2487),s 1, eff. 1/1/2011.
Amended by Stats 2005 ch 332 (AB 1322),s 1, eff. 9/22/2005.
Amended by Stats 2002 ch 1094 (AB 2504),s 1, eff. 1/1/2003.

Section 170.2 - Not grounds for disqualification

It shall not be grounds for disqualification that the judge:

(a) Is or is not a member of a racial, ethnic, religious, sexual or similar group and the proceeding involves the rights of such a group.

(b) Has in any capacity expressed a view on a legal or factual issue presented in the proceeding, except as provided in paragraph (2) of subdivision (a) of, or subdivision (b) or (c) of, Section 170.1.

(c) Has as a lawyer or public official participated in the drafting of laws or in the effort to pass or defeat laws, the meaning, effect or application of which is in issue in the proceeding unless the judge believes that his or her prior involvement was so well known as to raise a reasonable doubt in the public mind as to his or her capacity to be impartial.

Added by Stats. 1984, Ch. 1555, Sec. 6.

Section 170.3 - Judge determining himself or herself to be disqualified

(a)

(1) If a judge determines himself or herself to be disqualified, the judge shall notify the presiding judge of the court of his or her recusal and shall not further participate in the proceeding, except as provided in Section 170.4, unless his or her disqualification is waived by the parties as provided in subdivision (b).

(2) If the judge disqualifying himself or herself is the only judge or the presiding judge of the court, the notification shall be sent to the person having authority to assign another judge to replace the disqualified judge.

(b)

(1) A judge who determines himself or herself to be disqualified after disclosing the basis for his or her disqualification on the record may ask the parties and their attorneys whether they wish to waive the disqualification, except where the basis for disqualification is as provided in paragraph (2). A waiver of disqualification shall recite the basis for the disqualification, and is effective only when signed by all parties and their attorneys and filed in the record.

(2) There shall be no waiver of disqualification if the basis therefor is either of the following:

(A) The judge has a personal bias or prejudice concerning a party.

(B) The judge served as an attorney in the matter in controversy, or the judge has been a material witness concerning that matter.

(3) The judge shall not seek to induce a waiver and shall avoid any effort to discover which lawyers or parties favored or opposed a waiver of disqualification.

(4) If grounds for disqualification are first learned of or arise after the judge has made one or more rulings in a proceeding, but before the judge has completed judicial action in a proceeding, the judge shall, unless the disqualification be waived, disqualify himself or herself, but in the absence of good cause the rulings he or she has made up to that time shall not be set aside by the judge who replaces the disqualified judge.

(c)

(1) If a judge who should disqualify himself or herself refuses or fails to do so, any party may file with the clerk a written verified statement objecting to the hearing or trial before the judge and setting forth the facts constituting the grounds for disqualification of the judge. The statement shall be presented at the earliest practicable opportunity after discovery of the facts constituting the ground for disqualification. Copies of the statement shall be served on each party or his or her attorney who has appeared and shall be personally served on the judge alleged to be disqualified, or on his or her clerk, provided that the judge is present in the courthouse or in chambers.

(2) Without conceding his or her disqualification, a judge whose impartiality has been challenged by the filing of a written statement may request any other judge agreed upon by the parties to sit and act in his or her place.

(3) Within 10 days after the filing or service, whichever is later, the judge may file a consent to disqualification in which case the judge shall notify the presiding judge or the person authorized to appoint a replacement of his or her recusal as provided in subdivision (a), or the judge may file a written verified answer admitting or denying any or all of the allegations contained in the party's statement and setting forth any additional facts material or relevant to the question of disqualification. The clerk shall forthwith transmit a copy of the judge's answer to each party or his or her attorney who has appeared in the action.

(4) A judge who fails to file a consent or answer within the time allowed shall be deemed to have consented to his or her disqualification and the clerk shall notify the presiding judge or person authorized to appoint a replacement of the recusal as provided in subdivision (a).

(5) A judge who refuses to recuse himself or herself shall not pass upon his or her own disqualification or upon the sufficiency in law, fact, or otherwise, of the statement of disqualification filed by a party. In that case, the question of disqualification shall be heard and determined by another judge agreed upon by all the parties who have appeared or, in the event they are unable to agree within five days of notification of the judge's answer, by a judge selected by the chairperson of the Judicial Council, or if the chairperson is unable to act, the vice chairperson. The clerk shall notify the executive officer of the Judicial Council of the need for a selection. The selection shall be made as expeditiously as possible. No challenge pursuant to this subdivision or Section 170.6 may be made against the judge selected to decide the question of disqualification.

(6) The judge deciding the question of disqualification may decide the question on the basis of the statement of disqualification and answer and any written arguments as the judge requests, or the judge may set the matter for hearing as promptly as practicable. If a hearing is ordered, the judge shall permit the parties and the judge alleged to be disqualified to argue the question of disqualification and shall for good cause shown hear evidence on any disputed issue of fact. If the judge deciding the question of disqualification determines that the judge is disqualified, the judge hearing the question shall notify the presiding judge or the person having authority to appoint a replacement of the disqualified judge as provided in subdivision (a).

(d) The determination of the question of the disqualification of a judge is not an appealable order and may be reviewed only by a writ of mandate from the appropriate court of appeal sought only by the parties to the proceeding. The petition for the writ shall be filed and served within 10 days after service of written notice of entry of the court's order determining the question of disqualification. If the notice of entry is served by mail, that time shall be extended as provided in subdivision (a) of Section 1013.

Amended by Stats 2006 ch 567 (AB 2303),s 4, eff. 1/1/2007.

Section 170.4 - Acts allowed by disqualified judge

(a) A disqualified judge, notwithstanding his or her disqualification may do any of the following:

(1) Take any action or issue any order necessary to maintain the jurisdiction of the court pending the assignment of a judge not disqualified.

(2) Request any other judge agreed upon by the parties to sit and act in his or her place.

(3) Hear and determine purely default matters.

(4) Issue an order for possession prior to judgment in eminent domain proceedings.

(5) Set proceedings for trial or hearing.

(6) Conduct settlement conferences.

(b) Notwithstanding paragraph (5) of subdivision (c) of Section 170.3, if a statement of disqualification is untimely filed or if on its face it discloses no legal grounds for disqualification, the trial judge against whom it was filed may order it stricken.

(c)

(1) If a statement of disqualification is filed after a trial or hearing has commenced by the start of voir dire, by the swearing of the first witness or by the submission of a motion for decision, the judge whose impartiality has been questioned may order the trial or hearing to continue, notwithstanding the filing of the statement of disqualification. The issue of disqualification shall be referred to another judge for decision as provided in subdivision (a) of Section 170.3, and if it is determined that the judge is disqualified, all orders and rulings of the judge found to be disqualified made after the filing of the statement shall be vacated.

(2) For the purposes of this subdivision, if (A) a proceeding is filed in a single judge court or has been assigned to a single judge for comprehensive disposition, and (B) the proceeding has been set for trial or hearing 30 or more days in advance before a judge whose name was known at the time, the trial or hearing shall be deemed to have commenced 10 days prior to the date scheduled for trial or hearing as to any grounds for disqualification known before that time.

(3) A party may file no more than one statement of disqualification against a judge unless facts suggesting new grounds for disqualification are first learned of or arise after the first statement of disqualification was filed. Repetitive statements of disqualification not alleging facts suggesting new grounds for disqualification shall be stricken by the judge against whom they are filed.

(d) Except as provided in this section, a disqualified judge shall have no power to act in any proceeding after his or her disqualification or after the filing of a statement of disqualification until the question of his or her disqualification has been determined.

Added by Stats. 1984, Ch. 1555, Sec. 8.

Section 170.5 - Definitions

For the purposes of Sections 170 to 170.5, inclusive, the following definitions apply:

(a) "Judge" means judges of the superior courts, and court commissioners and referees.

(b) "Financial interest" means ownership of more than a 1 percent legal or equitable interest in a party, or a legal or equitable interest in a party of a fair market value in excess of one thousand five hundred dollars ($1,500), or a relationship as director, advisor or other active participant in the affairs of a party, except as follows:

(1) Ownership in a mutual or common investment fund that holds securities is not a "financial interest" in those securities unless the judge participates in the management of the fund.

(2) An office in an educational, religious, charitable, fraternal, or civic organization is not a "financial interest" in securities held by the organization.

(3) The proprietary interest of a policyholder in a mutual insurance company, or a depositor in a mutual savings association, or a similar proprietary interest, is a "financial interest" in the organization only if the outcome of the proceeding could substantially affect the value of the interest.

(c) "Officer of a public agency" does not include a Member of the Legislature or a state or local agency official acting in a legislative capacity.

(d) The third degree of relationship shall be calculated according to the civil law system.

(e) "Private practice of law" includes a fee for service, retainer, or salaried representation of private clients or public agencies, but excludes lawyers as full-time employees of public agencies or lawyers working exclusively for legal aid offices, public defender offices, or similar nonprofit entities whose clientele is by law restricted to the indigent.

(f) "Proceeding" means the action, case, cause, motion, or special proceeding to be tried or heard by the judge.

(g) "Fiduciary" includes any executor, trustee, guardian, or administrator.

Amended by Stats 2002 ch 784 (SB 1316),s 35, eff. 1/1/2003.

Section 170.6 - Judge or court commissioner prejudiced against party or attorney or interest of party or attorney

(a)

(1) A judge, court commissioner, or referee of a superior court of the State of California shall not try a civil or criminal action or special proceeding of any kind or character nor hear any matter therein that involves a contested issue of law or fact when it is established as provided in this section that the judge or court commissioner is prejudiced against a party or attorney or the interest of a party or attorney appearing in the action or proceeding.

(2) A party to, or an attorney appearing in, an action or proceeding may establish this prejudice by an oral or written motion without prior notice supported by affidavit or declaration under penalty of perjury, or an oral statement under oath, that the judge, court commissioner, or referee before whom the action or proceeding is pending, or to whom it is assigned, is prejudiced against a party or attorney, or the interest of the party or attorney, so that the party or attorney cannot, or believes that he or she cannot, have a fair and impartial trial or hearing before the judge, court commissioner, or referee. If the judge, other than a judge assigned to the case for all purposes, court commissioner, or referee assigned to, or who is scheduled to try, the cause or hear the matter is known at least 10 days before the date set for trial or hearing, the motion shall be made at least 5 days before that date. If directed to the trial of a cause with a master calendar, the motion shall be made to the judge supervising the master calendar not later than the time the cause is assigned for trial. If directed to the trial of a criminal cause that has been assigned to a judge for all purposes, the motion shall be made to the assigned judge or to the presiding judge by a party within 10 days after notice of the all purpose assignment, or if the party has not yet appeared in the action, then within 10 days after the appearance. If directed to the trial of a civil cause that has been assigned to a judge for all purposes, the motion shall be made to the assigned judge or to the presiding judge by a party within 15 days after notice of the all purpose assignment, or if the party has not yet appeared in the action, then within 15 days after the appearance. If the court in which the action is pending is authorized to have no more than one judge, and the motion claims that the duly elected or appointed judge of that court is prejudiced, the motion shall be made before the expiration of 30 days from the date of the first appearance in the action of the party who is making the motion or whose attorney is making the motion. In no event shall a judge, court commissioner, or referee entertain the motion if it is made after the drawing of the name of the first juror, or if there is no jury, after the making of an opening statement by counsel for plaintiff, or if there is no opening statement by counsel for plaintiff, then after swearing in the first witness or the giving of any evidence or after trial of the

cause has otherwise commenced. If the motion is directed to a hearing, other than the trial of a cause, the motion shall be made not later than the commencement of the hearing. In the case of trials or hearings not specifically provided for in this paragraph, the procedure specified herein shall be followed as nearly as possible. The fact that a judge, court commissioner, or referee has presided at, or acted in connection with, a pretrial conference or other hearing, proceeding, or motion prior to trial, and not involving a determination of contested fact issues relating to the merits, shall not preclude the later making of the motion provided for in this paragraph at the time and in the manner herein provided. A motion under this paragraph may be made following reversal on appeal of a trial court's decision, or following reversal on appeal of a trial court's final judgment, if the trial judge in the prior proceeding is assigned to conduct a new trial on the matter. Notwithstanding paragraph (4), the party who filed the appeal that resulted in the reversal of a final judgment of a trial court may make a motion under this section regardless of whether that party or side has previously done so. The motion shall be made within 60 days after the party or the party's attorney has been notified of the assignment.

(3) A party to a civil action making that motion under this section shall serve notice on all parties no later than five days after making the motion.

(4) If the motion is duly presented, and the affidavit or declaration under penalty of perjury is duly filed or an oral statement under oath is duly made, thereupon and without any further act or proof, the judge supervising the master calendar, if any, shall assign some other judge, court commissioner, or referee to try the cause or hear the matter. In other cases, the trial of the cause or the hearing of the matter shall be assigned or transferred to another judge, court commissioner, or referee of the court in which the trial or matter is pending or, if there is no other judge, court commissioner, or referee of the court in which the trial or matter is pending, the Chair of the Judicial Council shall assign some other judge, court commissioner, or referee to try the cause or hear the matter as promptly as possible. Except as provided in this section, no party or attorney shall be permitted to make more than one such motion in any one action or special proceeding pursuant to this section. In actions or special proceedings where there may be more than one plaintiff or similar party or more than one defendant or similar party appearing in the action or special proceeding, only one motion for each side may be made in any one action or special proceeding.

(5) Unless required for the convenience of the court or unless good cause is shown, a continuance of the trial or hearing shall not be granted by reason of the making of a motion under this section. If a continuance is granted, the cause or matter shall be continued from day to day or for other limited periods upon the trial or other calendar and shall be reassigned or transferred for trial or hearing as promptly as possible.

(6) Any affidavit filed pursuant to this section shall be in substantially the following form:

(Here set forth court and cause)
State of California,   ss.   PEREMPTORY CHALLENGE
County of

____, being duly sworn, deposes and says: That he or she is a party (or attorney for a party) to the within action (or special proceeding). That ____ the judge, court commissioner, or referee before whom the trial of the (or a hearing in the) action (or special proceeding) is pending (or to whom it is assigned) is prejudiced against the party (or his or her attorney) or the interest of the party (or his or her attorney) so that affiant cannot or believes that he or she cannot have a fair and impartial trial or hearing before the judge, court commissioner, or referee.
Subscribed and sworn to before me this
____ day of ____, 20__.
(Clerk or notary public or other officer administering oath)

(7) Any oral statement under oath or declaration under penalty of perjury made pursuant to this section shall include substantially the same contents as the affidavit above.

(b) Nothing in this section shall affect or limit Section 170 or Title 4 (commencing with Section 392) of Part 2, and this section shall be construed as cumulative thereto.

(c) If any provision of this section or the application to any person or circumstance is held invalid, that invalidity shall not affect other provisions or applications of the section that can be given effect without the invalid provision or application and, to this end, the provisions of this section are declared to be severable.

Amended by Stats 2010 ch 131 (AB 1894),s 1, eff. 1/1/2011.
Amended by Stats 2003 ch 62 (SB 600),s 22, eff. 1/1/2004.
Amended by Stats 2002 ch 784 (SB 1316),s 36, eff. 1/1/2003.

Section 170.65 - [Repealed]
This section was repealed effective 1/1/ 2001, pursuant to its own terms. .

Section 170.7 - Inapplicability of section 170.6 to judge assigned to serve on appellate division of superior court
Section 170.6 does not apply to a judge designated or assigned to serve on the appellate division of a superior court in the judge's capacity as a judge of that division.
Amended by Stats. 1998, Ch. 931, Sec. 48. Effective September 28, 1998.

Section 170.8 - No judge or court qualified to hear action or proceeding
When there is no judge of a court qualified to hear an action or proceeding, the clerk shall forthwith notify the Chairman of the Judicial Council of that fact. The judge assigned by the Chairman of the Judicial Council shall hear the action or proceeding at the time fixed therefor or, if no time has been fixed or good cause appears for changing the time theretofore fixed, the judge shall fix a time for hearing in accordance with law and rules and hear the action or proceeding at the time so fixed.
Amended by Stats. 1989, Ch. 1417, Sec. 2.

Section 170.9 - Acceptance of gifts by judge from single source in calendar year of more than $250
(a) A judge shall not accept gifts from a single source in a calendar year with a total value of more than two hundred fifty dollars ($250). This section shall not be construed to authorize the receipt of gifts that would otherwise be prohibited by the Code of Judicial Ethics adopted by the California Supreme Court or any other law.

(b) This section shall not prohibit or limit the following:
(1) Payments, advances, or reimbursements for travel and related lodging and subsistence permitted by subdivision (e).
(2) Wedding gifts and gifts exchanged between individuals on birthdays, holidays, and other similar occasions, if the gifts exchanged are not substantially disproportionate in value.
(3) A gift, bequest, favor, or loan from a person whose preexisting relationship with a judge would prevent the judge from hearing a case involving that person, under the Code of Judicial Ethics adopted by the California Supreme Court.

(c) For purposes of this section, "judge" includes all of the following:
(1) Judges of the superior courts.

(2) Justices of the courts of appeal and the Supreme Court.

(3) Subordinate judicial officers, as defined in Section 71601 of the Government Code.

(d) The gift limitation amounts in this section shall be adjusted biennially by the Commission on Judicial Performance to reflect changes in the Consumer Price Index, rounded to the nearest ten dollars ($10).

(e) Payments, advances, or reimbursements for travel, including actual transportation and related lodging and subsistence that is reasonably related to a judicial or governmental purpose, or to an issue of state, national, or international public policy, are not prohibited or limited by this section if any of the following apply:

(1) The travel is in connection with a speech, practice demonstration, or group or panel discussion given or participated in by the judge, the lodging and subsistence expenses are limited to the day immediately preceding, the day of, and the day immediately following the speech, demonstration, or discussion, and the travel is within the United States.

(2) The travel is provided by a government, a governmental agency or authority, a foreign government, a foreign bar association, an international service organization, a bona fide public or private educational institution, as defined in Section 203 of the Revenue and Taxation Code, or a nonprofit charitable or religious organization that is exempt from taxation under Section 501(c)(3)(c)(3) of the Internal Revenue Code, or by a person domiciled outside the United States who substantially satisfies the requirements for tax-exempt status under Section 501(c)(3)(c)(3) of the Internal Revenue Code. For purposes of this section, "foreign bar association" means an association of attorneys located outside the United States (A) that performs functions substantially equivalent to those performed by state or local bar associations in this state and (B) that permits membership by attorneys in that country representing various legal specialties and does not limit membership to attorneys generally representing one side or another in litigation. "International service organization" means a bona fide international service organization of which the judge is a member. A judge who accepts travel payments from an international service organization pursuant to this subdivision shall not preside over or participate in decisions affecting that organization, its state or local chapters, or its local members.

(3) The travel is provided by a state or local bar association or judges professional association in connection with testimony before a governmental body or attendance at any professional function hosted by the bar association or judges professional association, the lodging and subsistence expenses are limited to the day immediately preceding, the day of, and the day immediately following the professional function.

(f) Payments, advances, and reimbursements for travel not described in subdivision (e) are subject to the limit in subdivision (a).

(g) No judge shall accept any honorarium.

(h) "Honorarium" means a payment made in consideration for any speech given, article published, or attendance at a public or private conference, convention, meeting, social event, meal, or like gathering.

(i) "Honorarium" does not include earned income for personal services that are customarily provided in connection with the practice of a bona fide business, trade, or profession, such as teaching or writing for a publisher, and does not include fees or other things of value received pursuant to Section 94.5 of the Penal Code for performance of a marriage. For purposes of this section, "teaching" shall include presentations to impart educational information to lawyers in events qualifying for credit under mandatory continuing legal education, to students in bona fide educational institutions, and to associations or groups of judges.

(j) Subdivisions (a) and (e) shall apply to all payments, advances, and reimbursements for travel and related lodging and subsistence.

(k) This section does not apply to any honorarium that is not used and, within 30 days after receipt, is either returned to the donor or delivered to the Controller for deposit in the General Fund without being claimed as a deduction from income for tax purposes.

(l) "Gift" means a payment to the extent that consideration of equal or greater value is not received and includes a rebate or discount in the price of anything of value unless the rebate or discount is made in the regular course of business to members of the public without regard to official status. A person, other than a defendant in a criminal action, who claims that a payment is not a gift by reason of receipt of consideration has the burden of proving that the consideration received is of equal or greater value. However, the term "gift" does not include any of the following:

(1) Informational material such as books, reports, pamphlets, calendars, periodicals, cassettes and discs, or free or reduced-price admission, tuition, or registration, for informational conferences or seminars. No payment for travel or reimbursement for any expenses shall be deemed "informational material."

(2) Gifts that are not used and, within 30 days after receipt, are returned to the donor or delivered to a charitable organization without being claimed as a charitable contribution for tax purposes.

(3) Gifts from a judge's spouse, child, parent, grandparent, grandchild, brother, sister, parent-in-law, brother-in-law, sister-in-law, nephew, niece, aunt, uncle, or first cousin or the spouse of any such person. However, a gift from any of those persons shall be considered a gift if the donor is acting as an agent or intermediary for a person not covered by this paragraph.

(4) Campaign contributions required to be reported under Chapter 4 (commencing with Section 84100) of Title 9 of the Government Code.

(5) Any devise or inheritance.

(6) Personalized plaques and trophies with an individual value of less than two hundred fifty dollars ($250).

(7) Admission to events hosted by state or local bar associations or judges professional associations, and provision of related food and beverages at those events, when attendance does not require "travel," as described in paragraph (3) of subdivision (e).

(m) The Commission on Judicial Performance shall enforce the prohibitions of this section with regard to judges of the superior courts and justices of the courts of appeal and the Supreme Court. With regard to subordinate judicial officers, consistent with Section 18.1 of Article VI of the California Constitution, the court employing the subordinate judicial officer shall exercise initial jurisdiction to enforce the prohibitions of this section, and the Commission on Judicial Performance shall exercise discretionary jurisdiction with respect to the enforcement of the prohibitions of this section.

Amended by Stats 2011 ch 296 (AB 1023),s 36, eff. 1/1/2012.
Amended by Stats 2010 ch 206 (AB 2116),s 1, eff. 1/1/2011.
Amended by Stats 2002 ch 784 (SB 1316),s 37, eff. 1/1/2003.

Chapter 4 - INCIDENTAL POWERS AND DUTIES OF JUDICIAL OFFICERS

Section 177 - Generally

A judicial officer shall have power:

(a) To preserve and enforce order in the officer's immediate presence, and in proceedings before the officer, when the officer is engaged in the performance of official duty.

(b) To compel obedience to the officer's lawful orders as provided in this code.

(c) To compel the attendance of persons to testify in a proceeding before the officer, in the cases and manner provided in this code.

(d) To administer oaths to persons in a proceeding pending before the officer, and in all other cases where it may be necessary in the exercise of the officer's powers and duties.

(e) To prohibit activities that threaten access to state courthouses and court proceedings, and to prohibit interruption of judicial administration, including protecting the privilege from civil arrest at courthouses and court proceedings.

Amended by Stats 2019 ch 787 (AB 668),s 3, eff. 1/1/2020.

Section 177.5 - Imposition of money sanctions

A judicial officer shall have the power to impose reasonable money sanctions, not to exceed fifteen hundred dollars ($1,500), notwithstanding any other provision of law, payable to the court, for any violation of a lawful court order by a person, done without good cause or substantial justification. This power shall not apply to advocacy of counsel before the court. For the purposes of this section, the term "person" includes a witness, a party, a party's attorney, or both.

Sanctions pursuant to this section shall not be imposed except on notice contained in a party's moving or responding papers; or on the court's own motion, after notice and opportunity to be heard. An order imposing sanctions shall be in writing and shall recite in detail the conduct or circumstances justifying the order.

Amended by Stats 2005 ch 75 (AB 145),s 27, eff. 7/19/2005, op. 1/1/2006

Section 178 - Power to punish for contempt

For the effectual exercise of the powers conferred by the last section, a judicial officer may punish for contempt in the cases provided in this Code.

Repealed and added by Code Amendments 1880, Ch. 35.

Section 179 - Power to take and certify proof and acknowledgment of conveyance, acknowledgment of satisfaction of judgment, affidavit or deposition

Each of the justices of the Supreme Court and of any court of appeal and the judges of the superior courts, shall have power in any part of the state to take and certify:

(a) The proof and acknowledgment of a conveyance of real property, or of any other written instrument.

(b) The acknowledgment of satisfaction of a judgment of any court.

(c) An affidavit or deposition to be used in this state.

Amended by Stats 2003 ch 62 (SB 600),s 23, eff. 1/1/2004.

Amended by Stats 2002 ch 784 (SB 1316),s 38, eff. 1/1/2003.

Chapter 5 - MISCELLANEOUS PROVISIONS RESPECTING COURTS OF JUSTICE

Section 182 - Chapter heading not to govern or limit scope and meaning of chapter

The heading to this chapter shall not be deemed to govern or limit the scope or meaning of this chapter.

Added by Stats. 1955, Ch. 59.

Section 184 - Vacancy in office not to affect proceeding

No proceeding in any court of justice, in an action or special proceeding pending therein, shall be affected by a vacancy in the office of all or any of the judges or justices thereof.

Amended by Stats. 1933, Ch. 743.

Section 185 - Proceedings written and conducted in English language; translations of domestic violence protective orders

(a) Every written proceeding in a court of justice in this state shall be in the English language, and judicial proceedings shall be conducted, preserved, and published in no other. Nothing in this section shall prohibit a court from providing an unofficial translation of a court order issued pursuant to Section 527.6 or 527.8 of the Code of Civil Procedure, or Part 1 (commencing with Section 6200) of Division 10 of the Family Code, or Section 136.2 of the Penal Code, in a language other than English.

(b) The Judicial Council shall, by July 1, 2001, make available to all courts, translations of domestic violence protective order forms in languages other than English, as the Judicial Council deems appropriate, for protective orders issued pursuant to Section 527.6 or 527.8 of the Code of Civil Procedure, or Part 1 (commencing with Section 6200) of Division 10 of the Family Code, or Section 136.2 of the Penal Code.

Amended 10/10/1999 (Bill Number: SB 218) (Chapter 662).

Section 186 - Use of abbreviations; numbers expressed in figures or numerals

Such abbreviations as are in common use may be used, and numbers may be expressed by figures or numerals in the customary manner.

Repealed and added by Code Amendments 1880, Ch. 35.

Section 187 - All means necessary to carry into effect jurisdiction given court or judicial officer

When jurisdiction is, by the Constitution or this Code, or by any other statute, conferred on a Court or judicial officer, all the means necessary to carry it into effect are also given; and in the exercise of this jurisdiction, if the course of proceeding be not specifically pointed out by this Code or the statute, any suitable process or mode of proceeding may be adopted which may appear most conformable to the spirit of this Code.

Repealed and added by Code Amendments 1880, Ch. 35.

Title 3 - PERSONS SPECIALLY INVESTED WITH POWERS OF A JUDICIAL NATURE

Chapter 1 - TRIAL JURY SELECTION AND MANAGEMENT ACT

Section 190 - Title of act

This chapter shall be known and may be cited as the Trial Jury Selection and Management Act.

Repealed and added by Stats. 1988, Ch. 1245, Sec. 2.

Section 191 - Policy of state

The Legislature recognizes that trial by jury is a cherished constitutional right, and that jury service is an obligation of citizenship.

It is the policy of the State of California that all persons selected for jury service shall be selected at random from the population of the area served by the court; that all qualified persons have an equal opportunity, in accordance with this chapter, to be considered for jury service in the state and an obligation to serve as jurors when summoned for that purpose; and that it is the responsibility of jury commissioners to manage all jury systems in an efficient, equitable, and cost-effective manner, in accordance with this chapter.

Repealed and added by Stats. 1988, Ch. 1245, Sec. 2.

Section 192 - Applicability for both civil and criminal cases

This chapter applies to the selection of jurors, and the formation of trial juries, for both civil and criminal cases, in all trial courts of the state.

Repealed and added by Stats. 1988, Ch. 1245, Sec. 2.

Section 193 - Three kinds of jurors

Juries are of three kinds:

(a) Grand juries established pursuant to Title 4 (commencing with Section 888) of Part 2 of the Penal Code.

(b) Trial juries.

(c) Juries of inquest.

Repealed and added by Stats. 1988, Ch. 1245, Sec. 2.

Section 194 - Definitions

The following definitions govern the construction of this chapter:

(a) "County" means any county or any coterminous city and county.

(b) "Court" means a superior court of this state, and includes, when the context requires, any judge of the court.

(c) "Deferred jurors" are those prospective jurors whose request to reschedule their service to a more convenient time is granted by the jury commissioner.

(d) "Excused jurors" are those prospective jurors who are excused from service by the jury commissioner for valid reasons based on statute, state or local court rules, and policies.
(e) "Juror pool" means the group of prospective qualified jurors appearing for assignment to trial jury panels.
(f) "Jury of inquest" is a body of persons summoned from the citizens before the sheriff, coroner, or other ministerial officers, to inquire of particular facts.
(g) "Master list" means a list of names randomly selected from the source lists.
(h) "Potential juror" means any person whose name appears on a source list.
(i) "Prospective juror" means a juror whose name appears on the master list.
(j) "Qualified juror" means a person who meets the statutory qualifications for jury service.
(k) "Qualified juror list" means a list of qualified jurors.
(l) "Random" means that which occurs by mere chance indicating an unplanned sequence of selection where each juror's name has substantially equal probability of being selected.
(m) "Source list" means a list used as a source of potential jurors.
(n) "Summons list" means a list of prospective or qualified jurors who are summoned to appear or to be available for jury service.
(o) "Trial jurors" are those jurors sworn to try and determine by verdict a question of fact.
(p) "Trial jury" means a body of persons selected from the citizens of the area served by the court and sworn to try and determine by verdict a question of fact.
(q) "Trial jury panel" means a group of prospective jurors assigned to a courtroom for the purpose of voir dire.
Amended by Stats 2002 ch 784 (SB 1316),s 39, eff. 1/1/2003.

Section 195 - Jury commissioners
(a) In each county, there shall be one jury commissioner who shall be appointed by, and serve at the pleasure of, a majority of the judges of the superior court. In any county where there is a superior court administrator or executive officer, that person shall serve as ex officio jury commissioner. In any court jurisdiction where any person other than a court administrator or clerk/administrator is serving as jury commissioner on the effective date of this section, that person shall continue to so serve at the pleasure of a majority of the judges of the appointing court.
(b) Any jury commissioner may, whenever the business of court requires, appoint deputy jury commissioners. Salaries and benefits of those deputies shall be fixed in the same manner as salaries and benefits of other court employees.
(c) The jury commissioner shall be primarily responsible for managing the jury system under the general supervision of the court in conformance with the purpose and scope of this act. He or she shall have authority to establish policies and procedures necessary to fulfill this responsibility.
Amended by Stats 2002 ch 784 (SB 1316),s 40, eff. 1/1/2003.

Section 196 - Inquiry by commissioners as to qualifications; response when prospective juror unable to respond; failure to respond
(a) The jury commissioner or the court shall inquire as to the qualifications of persons on the master list or source list who are or may be summoned for jury service. The commissioner or the court may require any person to answer, under oath, orally or in written form, all questions as may be addressed to that person, regarding the person's qualifications and ability to serve as a prospective trial juror. The commissioner and his or her assistants shall have power to administer oaths and shall be allowed actual traveling expenses incurred in the performance of their duties.
(b) Response to the jury commissioner or the court concerning an inquiry or summons may be made by any person having knowledge that the prospective juror is unable to respond to such inquiry or summons.
(c) Any person who fails to respond to jury commissioner or court inquiry as instructed, may be summoned to appear before the jury commissioner or the court to answer the inquiry, or may be deemed to be qualified for jury service in the absence of a response to the inquiry. Any information thus acquired by the court or jury commissioner shall be noted in jury commissioner or court records.
Amended by Stats 2003 ch 149 (SB 79),s 6, eff. 1/1/2004.

Section 197 - Random selection; source lists
(a) All persons selected for jury service shall be selected at random, from a source or sources inclusive of a representative cross section of the population of the area served by the court. Sources may include, in addition to other lists, customer mailing lists, telephone directories, or utility company lists.
(b)
(1) The list of registered voters and the Department of Motor Vehicles' list of licensed drivers and identification cardholders resident within the area served by the court, are appropriate source lists for selection of jurors. Until January 1, 2022, only these two source lists, when substantially purged of duplicate names, shall be considered inclusive of a representative cross section of the population, within the meaning of subdivision (a).
(2) The list of resident state tax filers is an appropriate source list for selection of jurors. Beginning on January 1, 2022, the list of resident state tax filers, the list of registered voters, and the Department of Motor Vehicles' list of licensed drivers and identification cardholders resident within the area served by the court, when substantially purged of duplicate names, shall be considered inclusive of a representative cross section of the population, within the meaning of subdivision (a).
(c) The Department of Motor Vehicles shall furnish the jury commissioner of each county with the current list of the names, addresses, and other identifying information of persons residing in the county who are age 18 years or older and who are holders of a current driver's license or identification card issued pursuant to Article 3 (commencing with Section 12800) of, or Article 5 (commencing with Section 13000) of, Chapter 1 of Division 6 of the Vehicle Code. The conditions under which these lists shall be compiled semiannually shall be determined by the director, consistent with any rules which may be adopted by the Judicial Council. This service shall be provided by the Department of Motor Vehicles pursuant to Section 1812 of the Vehicle Code. The jury commissioner shall not disclose the information furnished by the Department of Motor Vehicles pursuant to this section to any person, organization, or agency.
(d)
(1) The Franchise Tax Board shall annually furnish the jury commissioner of each county with a list of resident state tax filers for their county in consultation with the Judicial Council.
(2) The list of resident state tax filers shall be submitted to the jury commissioner of each county by November 1, 2021, and each November 1 thereafter.
(3)
(A) For purposes of this section, "list of resident state tax filers" means a list that includes the name, date of birth, principal residence address, and county of principal residence, of persons who are 18 years of age or older and have filed a California resident income tax return for the preceding taxable year.
(B) For purposes of this paragraph, "county of principal residence" means the county in which the taxpayer has their principal residence on the date that the taxpayer filed their California resident income tax return.
(C) For the purposes of this paragraph, "principal residence" is used in the same manner it is used in Section 121 of the Internal Revenue Code.
Amended by Stats 2020 ch 230 (SB 592),s 1, eff. 1/1/2021.

Section 198 - Master and qualified juror lists

(a) Random selection shall be utilized in creating master and qualified juror lists, commencing with selection from source lists, and continuing through selection of prospective jurors for voir dire.

(b) The jury commissioner shall, at least once in each 12-month period, randomly select names of prospective trial jurors from the source list or lists, to create a master list.

(c) The master jury list shall be used by the jury commissioner, as provided by statute and state and local court rules, for the purpose of (1) mailing juror questionnaires and subsequent creation of a qualified juror list, and (2) summoning prospective jurors to respond or appear for qualification and service.

Repealed and added by Stats. 1988, Ch. 1245, Sec. 2.

Section 198.5 - Selection if court sessions held in location other than county seat

If sessions of the superior court are held in a location other than the county seat, the names for master jury lists and qualified jury lists to serve in a session may be selected from the area in which the session is held, pursuant to a local superior court rule that divides the county in a manner that provides all qualified persons in the county an equal opportunity to be considered for jury service. Nothing in this section precludes the court, in its discretion, from ordering a countywide venire in the interest of justice.

Amended by Stats 2003 ch 449 (AB 1712),s 6, eff. 1/1/2004.
Amended by Stats 2002 ch 784 (SB 1316),s 41, eff. 1/1/2004

Section 199 through 200 - [Repealed]

Repealed by Stats 2002 ch 784 (SB 1316),s 42 through 46, eff. 1/1/2004.

Section 201 - Separate trial jury list

In any superior court, a separate trial jury panel may be drawn, summoned, and impaneled for each judge, or any one panel may be drawn, summoned, and impaneled by any one of the judges, for use in the trial of cases before any of the judges, as occasion may require. In those courts, when a panel of jurors is in attendance for service before one or more of the judges, whether impaneled for common use or not, the whole or any number of the jurors from such panel may be required to attend and serve in the trial of cases, or to complete a panel, or jury, before any other of the judges.

Amended by Stats 2002 ch 784 (SB 1316),s 47, eff. 1/1/2003.

Section 202 - Use of mechanical, electric or electronic equipment for selection

Mechanical, electric, or electronic equipment, which in the opinion of the jury commissioner is satisfactory therefor, may be used in the performance of any function specified by this chapter for the selection and drawing of jurors.

Added by Stats. 1988, Ch. 1245, Sec. 2.

Section 203 - Persons not eligible and qualified to be prospective jurors

(a) All persons are eligible and qualified to be prospective trial jurors, except the following:

(1) Persons who are not citizens of the United States.

(2) Persons who are less than 18 years of age.

(3) Persons who are not domiciliaries of the State of California, as determined pursuant to Article 2 (commencing with Section 2020) of Chapter 1 of Division 2 of the Elections Code.

(4) Persons who are not residents of the jurisdiction wherein they are summoned to serve.

(5) Persons who have been convicted of malfeasance in office and whose civil rights have not been restored.

(6) Persons who are not possessed of sufficient knowledge of the English language, provided that no person shall be deemed incompetent solely because of the loss of sight or hearing in any degree or other disability which impedes the person's ability to communicate or which impairs or interferes with the person's mobility.

(7) Persons who are serving as grand or trial jurors in any court of this state.

(8) Persons who are the subject of conservatorship.

(9) Persons while they are incarcerated in any prison or jail.

(10) Persons who have been convicted of a felony and are currently on parole, postrelease community supervision, felony probation, or mandated supervision for the conviction of a felony.

(11) Persons who are currently required to register as a sex offender pursuant to Section 290 of the Penal Code based on a felony conviction.

(b) No person shall be excluded from eligibility for jury service in the State of California, for any reason other than those reasons provided by this section.

(c) The provisions of this section are severable. If any provision of this section or its application is held invalid, that invalidity shall not affect other provisions or applications that can be given effect without the invalid provision or application.

Amended by Stats 2019 ch 591 (SB 310),s 1, eff. 1/1/2020.

Section 204 - Eligible person not exempt by reason of occupation, economic status or characteristics; excused from service for undue hardship

(a) No eligible person shall be exempt from service as a trial juror by reason of occupation, economic status, or any characteristic listed or defined in Section 11135 of the Government Code, or for any other reason. No person shall be excused from service as a trial juror except as specified in subdivision (b).

(b) An eligible person may be excused from jury service only for undue hardship, upon themselves or upon the public, as defined by the Judicial Council.

Amended by Stats 2007 ch 568 (AB 14),s 15, eff. 1/1/2008.
Amended by Stats 2000 ch 43 (AB 2418), s 2, eff. 1/1/2001.

Section 205 - Questionnaires

(a) If a jury commissioner requires a person to complete a questionnaire, the questionnaire shall ask only questions related to juror identification, qualification, and ability to serve as a prospective juror.

(b) Except as ordered by the court, the questionnaire referred to in subdivision (a) shall be used solely for qualifying prospective jurors, and for management of the jury system, and not for assisting in the courtroom voir dire process of selecting trial jurors for specific cases.

(c) The court may require a prospective juror to complete such additional questionnaires as may be deemed relevant and necessary for assisting in the voir dire process or to ascertain whether a fair cross section of the population is represented as required by law, if such procedures are established by local court rule.

(d) The trial judge may direct a prospective juror to complete additional questionnaires as proposed by counsel in a particular case to assist the voir dire process.

Repealed and added by Stats. 1988, Ch. 1245, Sec. 2.

Section 206 - Discussion of jury deliberation and verdict in criminal case

(a) Prior to discharging the jury from the case, the judge in a criminal action shall inform the jurors that they have an absolute right to discuss or not to discuss the deliberation or verdict with anyone. The judge shall also inform the jurors of the provisions set forth in subdivisions (b), (d), and (e).

(b) Following the discharge of the jury in a criminal case, the defendant, or his or her attorney or representative, or the prosecutor, or his or her representative, may discuss the jury deliberation or verdict with a member of the jury, provided that the juror consents to the discussion and that the discussion takes place at a reasonable time and place.

(c) If a discussion of the jury deliberation or verdict with a member of the jury pursuant to subdivision (b) occurs at any time more than 24 hours after the verdict, prior to discussing the jury deliberation or verdict with a member of a jury pursuant to subdivision (b), the defendant or his or her attorney or representative, or the prosecutor or his or her representative, shall inform the juror of the identity of the case, the party in that case which the person represents, the subject of the interview , the absolute right of the juror to discuss or not discuss the deliberations or verdict in the case with the person, and the juror's right to review and have a copy of any declaration filed with the court.

(d) Any unreasonable contact with a juror by the defendant, or his or her attorney or representative, or by the prosecutor, or his or her representative, without the juror's consent shall be immediately reported to the trial judge.

(e) Any violation of this section shall be considered a violation of a lawful court order and shall be subject to reasonable monetary sanctions in accordance with Section 177.5 of the Code of Civil Procedure.

(f) Nothing in the section shall prohibit a peace officer from investigating an allegation of criminal conduct.

(g) Pursuant to Section 237, a defendant or defendant's counsel may, following the recording of a jury's verdict in a criminal proceeding, petition the court for access to personal juror identifying information within the court's records necessary for the defendant to communicate with jurors for the purpose of developing a motion for new trial or any other lawful purpose. This information consists of jurors' names, addresses, and telephone numbers. The court shall consider all requests for personal juror identifying information pursuant to Section 237.

Amended by Stats 2000 ch 242 (AB 2567), s 1, eff. 1/1/2001.

Section 207 - Records maintained by commissioners

(a) The jury commissioner shall maintain records regarding selection, qualification, and assignment of prospective jurors.

(b) The jury commissioner shall maintain records providing a clear audit trail regarding a juror's attendance, jury fees, and mileage.

(c) All records and papers maintained or compiled by the jury commissioner in connection with the selection or service of a juror may be kept on an electronic or microfilm medium and such records shall be preserved for at least three years after the list used in their selection is prepared, or for any longer period ordered by the court or the jury commissioner.

Added by Stats. 1988, Ch. 1245, Sec. 2.

Section 208 - Estimation of number of prospective jurors required; summoning

The jury commissioner shall estimate the number of prospective jurors that may be required to serve the needs of the court, and shall summon prospective jurors for service. Prospective jurors shall be summoned by mailing a summons by first-class mail or by personal service or, in urgency situations, as elsewhere provided by law. The summons, when served by mail, shall be mailed at least 10 days prior to the date of required appearance. Once a prospective juror has been summoned, the date, time, or place of appearance may be modified or further specified by the jury commissioner, by means of written, telegraphic, telephonic, or direct oral communication with the prospective juror.

Amended by Stats 2003 ch 149 (SB 79),s 7, eff. 1/1/2004.

Section 209 - Failure to attend; contempt of court

(a) Any prospective trial juror who has been summoned for service, and who fails to attend as directed or to respond to the court or jury commissioner and to be excused from attendance, may be attached and compelled to attend. Following an order to show cause hearing, the court may find the prospective juror in contempt of court, punishable by fine, incarceration, or both, as otherwise provided by law.

(b) In lieu of imposing sanctions for contempt as set forth in subdivision (a), the court may impose reasonable monetary sanctions, as provided in this subdivision, on a prospective juror who has not been excused pursuant to Section 204 after first providing the prospective juror with notice and an opportunity to be heard. If a juror fails to respond to the initial summons the court may issue a second summons indicating that the person failed to appear in response to a previous summons and ordering the person to appear for jury duty. The second summons may be issued no earlier than 90 days after the initial failure to appear. Upon the failure of the juror to appear in response to the second summons, the court may issue a failure to appear notice informing the person that failure to respond may result in the imposition of money sanctions. If the prospective juror does not attend the court within the time period as directed by the failure to appear notice, the court shall issue an order to show cause. Payment of monetary sanctions imposed pursuant to this subdivision does not relieve the person of his or her obligation to perform jury duty.

(c)

(1) The court may give notice of its intent to impose sanctions by either of the following means:

(A) Verbally to a prospective juror appearing in person in open court.

(B) The issuance on its own motion of an order to show cause requiring the prospective juror to demonstrate reasons for not imposing sanctions. The court may serve the order to show cause by certified or first-class mail.

(2) The monetary sanctions imposed pursuant to subdivision (b) may not exceed two hundred fifty dollars ($250) for the first violation, seven hundred fifty dollars ($750) for the second violation, and one thousand five hundred dollars ($1,500) for the third and any subsequent violation. Monetary sanctions may not be imposed on a prospective juror more than once during a single juror pool cycle. The prospective juror may be excused from paying sanctions pursuant to subdivision (b) of Section 204 or in the interests of justice. The full amount of any sanction paid shall be deposited in a bank account established for this purpose by the Administrative Office of the Courts and transmitted from that account monthly to the Controller for deposit in the Trial Court Trust Fund, as provided in Section 68085.1 of the Government Code. It is the intent of the Legislature that the funds derived from the monetary sanctions authorized in this section be allocated, to the extent feasible, to the family courts and the civil courts. The Judicial Council shall, by rule, provide for a procedure by which a prospective juror against whom a sanction has been imposed by default may move to set aside the default.

Amended by Stats 2009 ch 44 (SB 319),s 1, eff. 1/1/2010.

Amended by Stats 2006 ch 567 (AB 2303),s 5, eff. 1/1/2007.

Added by Stats 2003 ch 359 (AB 1180),s 2, eff. 1/1/2007.

Amended by Stats 2005 ch 75 (AB 145),s 28, eff. 7/19/2005, op. 1/1/2006

Amended by Stats 2003 ch 359 (AB 1180),s 1, eff. 1/1/2004.

Repealed by Stats 2003 ch 359 (AB 1180),s 1, eff. 1/1/2007.

Section 210 - Contents of summons

The summons shall contain the date, time, and place of appearance required of the prospective juror or, alternatively, instructions as to the procedure for calling the jury commissioner for telephonic instructions for appearance as well as such additional juror information as deemed appropriate by the jury commissioner.

Added by Stats. 1988, Ch. 1245, Sec. 2.

Section 210.5 - Standardized jury summons

The Judicial Council shall adopt a standardized jury summons for use, with appropriate modifications, around the state, that is understandable and has consumer appeal. The standardized jury summons shall include a specific reference to the rules for breast-feeding mothers. The use of the standardized jury summons shall be voluntary, unless otherwise prescribed by the rules of court.

Added by Stats 2000 ch 266 (AB 1814), s 2, eff. 1/1/2001.

Section 211 - No prospective jurors remaining available for voir dire

When a court has no prospective jurors remaining available for voir dire from panels furnished by, or available from, the jury commissioner, and finds that not proceeding with voir dire will place a party's right to a trial by jury in jeopardy, the court may direct the sheriff or marshal to summon, serve, and immediately attach the person of a sufficient number of citizens having the qualifications of jurors, to complete the panel.
Amended by Stats. 1996, Ch. 872, Sec. 7. Effective January 1, 1997.

Section 213 - One-hour telephone notice to appear for service
Unless excused by reason of undue hardship, all or any portion of the summoned prospective jurors shall be available on one-hour notice by telephone to appear for service, when the jury commissioner determines that it will efficiently serve the operational requirements of the court. Jurors available on one-hour telephone notice shall receive credit for each day of such availability towards their jury service obligation, but they shall not be paid unless they are actually required to make an appearance.
Added by Stats. 1988, Ch. 1245, Sec. 2.

Section 214 - Orientation for new jurors
The jury commissioner shall provide orientation for new jurors, which shall include necessary basic information concerning jury service. The jury commissioner shall notify each juror of the provisions of Section 230 of the Labor Code.
Amended by Stats. 1989, Ch. 1416, Sec. 8.

Section 215 - Fee for jurors in superior court; mileage; access to existing public transit services at no cost
(a) Except as provided in subdivision (b), on and after July 1, 2000, the fee for jurors in the superior court, in civil and criminal cases, is fifteen dollars ($15) a day for each day's attendance as a juror after the first day.
(b) A juror who is employed by a federal, state, or local government entity, or by any other public entity as defined in Section 481.200, and who receives regular compensation and benefits while performing jury service, shall not be paid the fee described in subdivision (a).
(c) All jurors in the superior court, in civil and criminal cases, shall be reimbursed for mileage at the rate of thirty-four cents ($0.34) per mile for each mile actually traveled in attending and returning from court as a juror after the first day.
(d) All jurors and prospective jurors who have been summoned shall be provided with access to existing public transit services at no cost utilizing one of the following options:
(1) Courts may partner with public transit operators in their county to create new programs or continue existing public transit programs that provide no-cost service for jurors and prospective jurors who have been summoned.
(2) A method of reimbursement determined by the court up to a daily maximum of twelve dollars ($12).
(e) Subdivision (d) does not apply to a court in an area where a public transit operator does not provide existing service that is reasonably available to the court facility.
(f) In determining whether transit service is reasonably available to the court facility, the court shall consider factors that include, but are not limited to, all of the following:
(1) Proximity of transit service to the court location.
(2) Hours of operation of transit service in the vicinity of the court location.
(3) Frequency of operation of transit service in the vicinity of the court location.
(4) Availability of transit access to all areas of the court's jurisdiction from which a potential juror may reside.
(g) Prior to determining that transit service is not reasonably available to the court facility, the court shall contact the public transit operator to inquire whether new transit options may be implemented near the court.
Amended by Stats 2022 ch 326 (AB 1981),s 2, eff. 1/1/2023.
Amended by Stats 2004 ch 227 (SB 1102),s 9, eff. 8/16/2004.
Amended by Stats 2002 ch 144 (AB 2925),s 1, eff. 1/1/2003.
Amended by Stats 2002 ch 784 (SB 1316),s 48, eff. 1/1/2003.
Amended by Stats 2000 ch 123 (AB 2866), s 1, eff. 7/8/2000.

Section 216 - Deliberation room or rooms provided by board of supervisors
(a) At each court facility where jury cases are heard, the court shall provide a deliberation room or rooms for use of jurors when they have retired for deliberation. The deliberation rooms shall be designed to minimize unwarranted intrusions by other persons in the court facility, shall have suitable furnishings, equipment, and supplies, and shall also have restroom accommodations for male and female jurors.
(b) Unless authorized by the jury commissioner, jury assembly facilities shall be restricted to use by jurors and jury commissioner staff.
Amended by Stats 2020 ch 210 (AB 1984),s 1, eff. 1/1/2021.

Section 217 - Food and lodging and necessities provided jury ordered to be kept together in criminal case
In criminal cases only, while the jury is kept together, either during the progress of the trial or after their retirement for deliberation, the court may direct the sheriff or marshal to provide the jury with suitable and sufficient food and lodging, or other reasonable necessities. The expenses incurred under this section shall be charged against the Trial Court Operations Fund of the county in which the court is held. All those expenses shall be paid on the order of the court.
Amended by Stats 2002 ch 784 (SB 1316),s 49, eff. 1/1/2003.

Section 218 - Commissioner to hear excuses of jurors
The jury commissioner shall hear the excuses of jurors summoned, in accordance with the standards prescribed by the Judicial Council. It shall be left to the discretion of the jury commissioner to accept an excuse under subdivision (b) of Section 204 without a personal appearance. All excuses shall be in writing setting forth the basis of the request and shall be signed by the juror.
Added by Stats. 1988, Ch. 1245, Sec. 2.

Section 219 - Random selection of jurors for jury panels for voir dire; peace officers not selected
(a) Except as provided in subdivision (b), the jury commissioner shall randomly select jurors for jury panels to be sent to courtrooms for voir dire.
(b)
(1) Notwithstanding subdivision (a), no peace officer, as defined in Section 830.1, subdivision (a) of Section 830.2, and subdivision (a) of Section 830.33, of the Penal Code, shall be selected for voir dire in civil or criminal matters.
(2) Notwithstanding subdivision (a), no peace officer, as defined in subdivisions (b) and (c) of Section 830.2 of the Penal Code, shall be selected for voir dire in criminal matters.
Amended by Stats 2001 ch 55 (SB 303), s 1, eff. 1/1/2002.

Section 219.5 - Scheduling accommodations for peace officers
The Judicial Council shall adopt a rule of court, on or before January 1, 2005, requiring the trial courts to establish procedures for jury service that gives peace officers, as defined by Section 830.5 of the Penal Code, scheduling accommodations when necessary.
Added by Stats 2003 ch 353 (AB 513),s 1, eff. 1/1/2004.

Section 220 - Number of persons making up trial jury
A trial jury shall consist of 12 persons, except that in civil actions and cases of misdemeanor, it may consist of 12 or any number less than 12, upon which the parties may agree.
Added by Stats. 1988, Ch. 1245, Sec. 2.

Section 221 - [Repealed]

Repealed by Stats 2001 ch 115 (SB 153), s 1, eff. 1/1/2002.

Section 222 - Selection when action is called for trial by jury

(a) Except as provided in subdivision (b), when an action is called for trial by jury, the clerk shall randomly select the names of the jurors for voir dire, until the jury is selected or the panel is exhausted.

(b) When the jury commissioner has provided the court with a listing of the trial jury panel in random order, the court shall seat prospective jurors for voir dire in the order provided by the panel list.

Amended by Stats 2007 ch 263 (AB 310),s 4, eff. 1/1/2008.

Section 222.5 - Examination of prospective jurors in civil cases

(a) To select a fair and impartial jury in a civil jury trial, the trial judge shall conduct an initial examination of prospective jurors. At the final status conference or at the first practical opportunity prior to voir dire, whichever comes first, the trial judge shall consider and discuss with counsel the form and subject matter of voir dire questions. Before voir dire by the trial judge, the parties may submit questions to the trial judge. The trial judge may include additional questions requested by the parties as the trial judge deems proper.

(b)

(1) Upon completion of the trial judge's initial examination, counsel for each party shall have the right to examine, by oral and direct questioning, any of the prospective jurors in order to enable counsel to intelligently exercise both peremptory challenges and challenges for cause. The scope of the examination conducted by counsel shall be within reasonable limits prescribed by the trial judge in the judge's sound discretion subject to the provisions of this chapter. During any examination conducted by counsel for the parties, the trial judge shall permit liberal and probing examination calculated to discover bias or prejudice with regard to the circumstances of the particular case before the court. The fact that a topic has been included in the trial judge's examination shall not preclude appropriate followup questioning in the same area by counsel. The trial judge shall permit counsel to conduct voir dire examination without requiring prior submission of the questions unless a particular counsel engages in improper questioning.

(2) The trial judge shall not impose specific unreasonable or arbitrary time limits or establish an inflexible time limit policy for voir dire.

(3) For purposes of this section, an "improper question" is any question that, as its dominant purpose, attempts to precondition the prospective jurors to a particular result, indoctrinate the jury, or question the prospective jurors concerning the pleadings or the applicable law.

(c)

(1) In exercising the judge's sound discretion, the trial judge shall give due consideration to all of the following:

(A) The amount of time requested by trial counsel.

(B) Any unique or complex elements, legal or factual, in the case.

(C) Length of the trial.

(D) Number of parties.

(E) Number of witnesses.

(F) Whether the case is designated as a complex or long cause.

(2) As voir dire proceeds, the judge shall permit supplemental time for questioning based on any of the following:

(A) Individual responses or conduct of jurors that may evince attitudes inconsistent with suitability to serve as a fair and impartial juror in the particular case.

(B) Composition of the jury panel.

(C) An unusual number of for cause challenges.

(d) Upon the request of a party, the trial judge shall allow a brief opening statement by counsel for each party prior to the commencement of the oral questioning phase of the voir dire process.

(e) In civil cases, the trial judge may, upon stipulation by counsel for all the parties appearing in the action, permit counsel to examine the prospective jurors outside a judge's presence.

(f) A trial judge shall not arbitrarily or unreasonably refuse to submit reasonable written questionnaires, the contents of which are determined by the court in its sound discretion, when requested by counsel. If a questionnaire is utilized, the parties shall be given reasonable time to evaluate the responses to the questionnaires before oral questioning commences.

(g) To help facilitate the jury selection process, at the earliest practical time, the judge in a civil trial shall provide the parties with both the alphabetical list and the list of prospective jurors in the order in which they will be called.

Amended by Stats 2017 ch 337 (SB 658),s 1, eff. 1/1/2018.

Amended by Stats 2011 ch 409 (AB 1403),s 1, eff. 1/1/2012.

Section 223 - Examination of prospective jurors in criminal cases

(a) To select a fair and impartial jury in a criminal jury trial, the trial judge shall conduct an initial examination of prospective jurors. At the first practical opportunity prior to voir dire, the trial judge shall consider the form and subject matter of voir dire questions. Before voir dire by the trial judge, the parties may submit questions to the trial judge. The trial judge may include additional questions requested by the parties as the trial judge deems proper.

(b)

(1) Upon completion of the trial judge's initial examination, counsel for each party shall have the right to examine, by oral and direct questioning, any of the prospective jurors. The scope of the examination conducted by counsel shall be within reasonable limits prescribed by the trial judge in the judge's sound discretion subject to the provisions of this chapter. During any examination conducted by counsel for the parties, the trial judge shall permit liberal and probing examination calculated to discover bias or prejudice with regard to the circumstances of the particular case or the parties before the court. The fact that a topic has been included in the trial judge's examination shall not preclude appropriate followup questioning in the same area by counsel. The trial judge should permit counsel to conduct voir dire examination without requiring prior submission of the questions unless a particular counsel engages in improper questioning.

(2) The trial judge shall not impose specific unreasonable or arbitrary time limits or establish an inflexible time limit policy for voir dire. As voir dire proceeds, the trial judge shall permit supplemental time for questioning based on individual responses or conduct of jurors that may evince attitudes inconsistent with suitability to serve as a fair and impartial juror in the particular case.

(3) For purposes of this section, an "improper question" is any question that, as its dominant purpose, attempts to precondition the prospective jurors to a particular result or indoctrinate the jury.

(c) In exercising the judge's sound discretion, the trial judge shall consider all of the following:

(1) The amount of time requested by trial counsel.

(2) Any unique or complex legal or factual elements in the case.

(3) The length of the trial.

(4) The number of parties.

(5) The number of witnesses.

(d) Voir dire of any prospective jurors shall, where practicable, take place in the presence of the other jurors in all criminal cases, including death penalty cases. Examination of prospective jurors shall be conducted only in aid of the exercise of challenges for cause.

(e) The trial judge shall, in his or her sound discretion, consider reasonable written questionnaires when requested by counsel. If a questionnaire is utilized, the parties shall be given reasonable time to evaluate the responses to the questionnaires before oral questioning commences.

(f) To help facilitate the jury selection process, at the earliest practical time, the trial judge in a criminal trial shall provide the parties with the list of prospective jurors in the order in which they will be called.

(g) The trial judge's exercise of discretion in the manner in which voir dire is conducted, including any limitation on the time that will be allowed for direct questioning of prospective jurors by counsel and any determination that a question is not in aid of the exercise of challenges for cause, is not cause for a conviction to be reversed, unless the exercise of that discretion results in a miscarriage of justice, as specified in Section 13 of Article VI of the California Constitution.

Added by Stats 2017 ch 302 (AB 1541),s 2, eff. 1/1/2018.

Note: This section was added on June 5, 1990, by initiative Prop. 115 (the Crime Victims Justice Reform Act).

Section 224 - Service providers for jurors with disabilities

(a) If a party does not cause the removal by challenge of an individual juror who is deaf, hard of hearing, blind, visually impaired, or speech impaired and who requires auxiliary services to facilitate communication, the party shall stipulate to the presence of a service provider in the jury room during jury deliberations, and prepare and deliver to the court proposed jury instructions to the service provider.

(b) As used in this section, "service provider" includes, but is not limited to, a person who is a sign language interpreter, oral interpreter, deaf-blind interpreter, reader, or speech interpreter. If auxiliary services are required during the course of jury deliberations, the court shall instruct the jury and the service provider that the service provider for the juror with a disability is not to participate in the jury's deliberations in any manner except to facilitate communication between the juror with a disability and other jurors.

(c) The court shall appoint a service provider whose services are needed by a juror with a disability to facilitate communication or participation. A sign language interpreter, oral interpreter, or deaf-blind interpreter appointed pursuant to this section shall be a qualified interpreter, as defined in subdivision (f) of Section 754 of the Evidence Code. Service providers appointed by the court under this subdivision shall be compensated in the same manner as provided in subdivision (i) of Section 754 of the Evidence Code.

Amended by Stats 2016 ch 94 (AB 1709),s 3, eff. 1/1/2017.

Section 225 - Challenge defined; challenge to panel; challenge to prospective juror

A challenge is an objection made to the trial jurors that may be taken by any party to the action, and is of the following classes and types:

(a) A challenge to the trial jury panel for cause.

    (1) A challenge to the panel may only be taken before a trial jury is sworn. The challenge shall be reduced to writing, and shall plainly and distinctly state the facts constituting the ground of challenge.

    (2) Reasonable notice of the challenge to the jury panel shall be given to all parties and to the jury commissioner, by service of a copy thereof.

    (3) The jury commissioner shall be permitted the services of legal counsel in connection with challenges to the jury panel.

(b) A challenge to a prospective juror by either:

    (1) A challenge for cause, for one of the following reasons:

        (A) General disqualification-that the juror is disqualified from serving in the action on trial.

        (B) Implied bias-as, when the existence of the facts as ascertained, in judgment of law disqualifies the juror.

        (C) Actual bias-the existence of a state of mind on the part of the juror in reference to the case, or to any of the parties, which will prevent the juror from acting with entire impartiality, and without prejudice to the substantial rights of any party.

    (2) A peremptory challenge to a prospective juror.

Repealed and added by Stats. 1988, Ch. 1245, Sec. 2.

Section 226 - Challenge to individual juror

(a) A challenge to an individual juror may only be made before the jury is sworn.

(b) A challenge to an individual juror may be taken orally or may be made in writing, but no reason need be given for a peremptory challenge, and the court shall exclude any juror challenged peremptorily.

(c) All challenges for cause shall be exercised before any peremptory challenges may be exercised.

(d) All challenges to an individual juror, except a peremptory challenge, shall be taken, first by the defendants, and then by the people or plaintiffs.

Repealed and added by Stats. 1988, Ch. 1245, Sec. 2.

Section 227 - Challenges for cause

The challenges of either party for cause need not all be taken at once, but they may be taken separately, in the following order, including in each challenge all the causes of challenge belonging to the same class and type:

(a) To the panel.

(b) To an individual juror, for a general disqualification.

(c) To an individual juror, for an implied bias.

(d) To an individual juror, for an actual bias.

Repealed and added by Stats. 1988, Ch. 1245, Sec. 2.

Section 228 - Challenges for general disqualification

Challenges for general disqualification may be taken on one or both of the following grounds, and for no other:

(a) A want of any of the qualifications prescribed by this code to render a person competent as a juror.

(b) The existence of any incapacity which satisfies the court that the challenged person is incapable of performing the duties of a juror in the particular action without prejudice to the substantial rights of the challenging party.

Amended by Stats 2002 ch 1008 (AB 3028),s 1, eff. 1/1/2003.

Section 229 - Challenge for implied bias

A challenge for implied bias may be taken for one or more of the following causes, and for no other:

(a) Consanguinity or affinity within the fourth degree to any party, to an officer of a corporation which is a party, or to any alleged witness or victim in the case at bar.

(b) Standing in the relation of, or being the parent, spouse, or child of one who stands in the relation of, guardian and ward, conservator and conservatee, master and servant, employer and clerk, landlord and tenant, principal and agent, or debtor and creditor, to either party or to an officer of a corporation which is a party, or being a member of the family of either party; or a partner in business with either party; or surety on any bond or obligation for either party, or being the holder of bonds or shares of capital stock of a corporation which is a party; or having stood within one year previous to the filing of the complaint in the action in the relation of attorney and client with either party or with the attorney for either party. A depositor of a bank or a holder of a savings account in a savings and loan association shall not be deemed a creditor of that bank or savings and loan association for the purpose of this paragraph solely by reason of his or her being a depositor or account holder.

(c) Having served as a trial or grand juror or on a jury of inquest in a civil or criminal action or been a witness on a previous or pending trial between the same parties, or involving the same specific offense or cause of action; or having served as a trial or grand juror or on a jury within one year previously in any criminal or civil action or proceeding in which either party was the plaintiff or defendant or in a criminal action where either party was the defendant.

(d) Interest on the part of the juror in the event of the action, or in the main question involved in the action, except his or her interest as a member or citizen or taxpayer of a county, city and county, incorporated city or town, or other political subdivision of a county, or municipal water district.

(e) Having an unqualified opinion or belief as to the merits of the action founded upon knowledge of its material facts or of some of them.

(f) The existence of a state of mind in the juror evincing enmity against, or bias towards, either party.

(g) That the juror is party to an action pending in the court for which he or she is drawn and which action is set for trial before the panel of which the juror is a member.

(h) If the offense charged is punishable with death, the entertaining of such conscientious opinions as would preclude the juror finding the defendant guilty; in which case the juror may neither be permitted nor compelled to serve.

Added by Stats. 1988, Ch. 1245, Sec. 2.

Section 230 - Challenges for cause tried by court

Challenges for cause shall be tried by the court. The juror challenged and any other person may be examined as a witness in the trial of the challenge, and shall truthfully answer all questions propounded to them.

Added by Stats. 1988, Ch. 1245, Sec. 2.

Section 231 - Peremptory challenges in criminal cases

(a) In criminal cases, if the offense charged is punishable with death, or with imprisonment in the state prison for life, the defendant is entitled to 20 and the people to 20 peremptory challenges. Except as provided in subdivision (b), in a trial for any other offense, the defendant is entitled to 10 and the state to 10 peremptory challenges. When two or more defendants are jointly tried, their challenges shall be exercised jointly, but each defendant shall also be entitled to five additional challenges which may be exercised separately, and the people shall also be entitled to additional challenges equal to the number of all the additional separate challenges allowed the defendants.

(b) If the offense charged is punishable with a maximum term of imprisonment of 90 days or less, the defendant is entitled to six and the state to six peremptory challenges. When two or more defendants are jointly tried, their challenges shall be exercised jointly, but each defendant shall also be entitled to four additional challenges which may be exercised separately, and the state shall also be entitled to additional challenges equal to the number of all the additional separate challenges allowed the defendants.

(c) In civil cases, each party shall be entitled to six peremptory challenges. If there are more than two parties, the court shall, for the purpose of allotting peremptory challenges, divide the parties into two or more sides according to their respective interests in the issues. Each side shall be entitled to eight peremptory challenges. If there are several parties on a side, the court shall divide the challenges among them as nearly equally as possible. If there are more than two sides, the court shall grant such additional peremptory challenges to a side as the interests of justice may require, provided that the peremptory challenges of one side shall not exceed the aggregate number of peremptory challenges of all other sides. If any party on a side does not use his or her full share of peremptory challenges, the unused challenges may be used by the other party or parties on the same side.

(d) Peremptory challenges shall be taken or passed by the sides alternately, commencing with the plaintiff or people, and each party shall be entitled to have the panel full before exercising any peremptory challenge. When each side passes consecutively, the jury shall then be sworn, unless the court, for good cause, shall otherwise order. The number of peremptory challenges remaining with a side shall not be diminished by any passing of a peremptory challenge.

(e) If all the parties on both sides pass consecutively, the jury shall then be sworn, unless the court, for good cause, shall otherwise order. The number of peremptory challenges remaining with a side shall not be diminished by any passing of a peremptory challenge.

(f) This section shall become operative on January 1, 2021.

Added by Stats 2016 ch 33 (SB 843),s 3, eff. 6/27/2016.

Section 231.5 - Peremptory challenge used to remove juror on basis of bias because of race, color, religion, etc.

A party shall not use a peremptory challenge to remove a prospective juror on the basis of an assumption that the prospective juror is biased merely because of a characteristic listed or defined in Section 11135 of the Government Code, or similar grounds.

Amended by Stats 2015 ch 115 (AB 87),s 1, eff. 1/1/2016.

Added by Stats 2000 ch 43 (AB 2418), s 3, eff. 1/1/2001.

Section 231.7 - [Effective until 1/1/2026] Peremptory challenge to remove prospective juror based on membership - perceived or actual - in protected group

(a) A party shall not use a peremptory challenge to remove a prospective juror on the basis of the prospective juror's race, ethnicity, gender, gender identity, sexual orientation, national origin, or religious affiliation, or the perceived membership of the prospective juror in any of those groups.

(b) A party, or the trial court on its own motion, may object to the improper use of a peremptory challenge under subdivision (a). After the objection is made, any further discussion shall be conducted outside the presence of the panel. The objection shall be made before the jury is impaneled, unless information becomes known that could not have reasonably been known before the jury was impaneled.

(c) Notwithstanding Section 226, upon objection to the exercise of a peremptory challenge pursuant to this section, the party exercising the peremptory challenge shall state the reasons the peremptory challenge has been exercised.

(d)

(1) The court shall evaluate the reasons given to justify the peremptory challenge in light of the totality of the circumstances. The court shall consider only the reasons actually given and shall not speculate on, or assume the existence of, other possible justifications for the use of the peremptory challenge. If the court determines there is a substantial likelihood that an objectively reasonable person would view race, ethnicity, gender, gender identity, sexual orientation, national origin, or religious affiliation, or perceived membership in any of those groups, as a factor in the use of the peremptory challenge, then the objection shall be sustained. The court need not find purposeful discrimination to sustain the objection. The court shall explain the reasons for its ruling on the record. A motion brought under this section shall also be deemed a sufficient presentation of claims asserting the discriminatory exclusion of jurors in violation of the United States and California Constitutions.

(2)

(A) For purposes of this section, an objectively reasonable person is aware that unconscious bias, in addition to purposeful discrimination, have resulted in the unfair exclusion of potential jurors in the State of California.

(B) For purposes of this section, a "substantial likelihood" means more than a mere possibility but less than a standard of more likely than not.

(C) For purposes of this section, "unconscious bias" includes implicit and institutional biases.

(3) In making its determination, the circumstances the court may consider include, but are not limited to, any of the following:

(A) Whether any of the following circumstances exist:

(i) The objecting party is a member of the same perceived cognizable group as the challenged juror.

(ii) The alleged victim is not a member of that perceived cognizable group.

(iii) Witnesses or the parties are not members of that perceived cognizable group.

(B) Whether race, ethnicity, gender, gender identity, sexual orientation, national origin, or religious affiliation, or perceived membership in any of those groups, bear on the facts of the case to be tried.

(C) The number and types of questions posed to the prospective juror, including, but not limited to, any the following:

(i) Consideration of whether the party exercising the peremptory challenge failed to question the prospective juror about the concerns later stated by the party as the reason for the peremptory challenge pursuant to subdivision (c).

(ii) Whether the party exercising the peremptory challenge engaged in cursory questioning of the challenged potential juror.

(iii) Whether the party exercising the peremptory challenge asked different questions of the potential juror against whom the peremptory challenge was used in contrast to questions asked of other jurors from different perceived cognizable groups about the same topic or whether the party phrased those questions differently.

(D) Whether other prospective jurors, who are not members of the same cognizable group as the challenged prospective juror, provided similar, but not necessarily identical, answers but were not the subject of a peremptory challenge by that party.

(E) Whether a reason might be disproportionately associated with a race, ethnicity, gender, gender identity, sexual orientation, national origin, or religious affiliation, or perceived membership in any of those groups.

(F) Whether the reason given by the party exercising the peremptory challenge was contrary to or unsupported by the record.

(G) Whether the counsel or counsel's office exercising the challenge has used peremptory challenges disproportionately against a given race, ethnicity, gender, gender identity, sexual orientation, national origin, or religious affiliation, or perceived membership in any of those groups, in the present case or in past cases, including whether the counsel or counsel's office who made the challenge has a history of prior violations under Batson v. Kentucky (1986) 476 U.S. 79, People v. Wheeler (1978) 22 Cal.3d 258, Section 231.5, or this section.

(e) A peremptory challenge for any of the following reasons is presumed to be invalid unless the party exercising the peremptory challenge can show by clear and convincing evidence that an objectively reasonable person would view the rationale as unrelated to a prospective juror's race, ethnicity, gender, gender identity, sexual orientation, national origin, or religious affiliation, or perceived membership in any of those groups, and that the reasons articulated bear on the prospective juror's ability to be fair and impartial in the case:

(1) Expressing a distrust of or having a negative experience with law enforcement or the criminal legal system.

(2) Expressing a belief that law enforcement officers engage in racial profiling or that criminal laws have been enforced in a discriminatory manner.

(3) Having a close relationship with people who have been stopped, arrested, or convicted of a crime.

(4) A prospective juror's neighborhood.

(5) Having a child outside of marriage.

(6) Receiving state benefits.

(7) Not being a native English speaker.

(8) The ability to speak another language.

(9) Dress, attire, or personal appearance.

(10) Employment in a field that is disproportionately occupied by members listed in subdivision (a) or that serves a population disproportionately comprised of members of a group or groups listed in subdivision (a).

(11) Lack of employment or underemployment of the prospective juror or prospective juror's family member.

(12) A prospective juror's apparent friendliness with another prospective juror of the same group as listed in subdivision (a).

(13) Any justification that is similarly applicable to a questioned prospective juror or jurors, who are not members of the same cognizable group as the challenged prospective juror, but were not the subject of a peremptory challenge by that party. The unchallenged prospective juror or jurors need not share any other characteristics with the challenged prospective juror for peremptory challenge relying on this justification to be considered presumptively invalid.

(f) For purposes of subdivision (e), the term "clear and convincing" refers to the degree of certainty the factfinder must have in determining whether the reasons given for the exercise of a peremptory challenge are unrelated to the prospective juror's cognizable group membership, bearing in mind conscious and unconscious bias. To determine that a presumption of invalidity has been overcome, the factfinder shall determine that it is highly probable that the reasons given for the exercise of a peremptory challenge are unrelated to conscious or unconscious bias and are instead specific to the juror and bear on that juror's ability to be fair and impartial in the case.

(g)

(1) The following reasons for peremptory challenges have historically been associated with improper discrimination in jury selection:

(A) The prospective juror was inattentive, or staring or failing to make eye contact.

(B) The prospective juror exhibited either a lack of rapport or problematic attitude, body language, or demeanor.

(C) The prospective juror provided unintelligent or confused answers.

(2) The reasons set forth in paragraph (1) are presumptively invalid unless the trial court is able to confirm that the asserted behavior occurred, based on the court's own observations or the observations of counsel for the objecting party. Even with that confirmation, the counsel offering the reason shall explain why the asserted demeanor, behavior, or manner in which the prospective juror answered questions matters to the case to be tried.

(h) Upon a court granting an objection to the improper exercise of a peremptory challenge, the court shall do one or more of the following:

(1) Quash the jury venire and start jury selection anew. This remedy shall be provided if requested by the objecting party.

(2) If the motion is granted after the jury has been impaneled, declare a mistrial and select a new jury if requested by the defendant.

(3) Seat the challenged juror.

(4) Provide the objecting party additional challenges.

(5) Provide another remedy as the court deems appropriate.

(i) This section applies in all jury trials in which jury selection begins on or after January 1, 2022.

(j) The denial of an objection made under this section shall be reviewed by the appellate court de novo, with the trial court's express factual findings reviewed for substantial evidence. The appellate court shall not impute to the trial court any findings, including findings of a prospective juror's demeanor, that the trial court did not expressly state on the record. The reviewing court shall consider only reasons actually given under subdivision (c) and shall not speculate as to or consider reasons that were not given to explain either the party's use of the peremptory challenge or the party's failure to challenge similarly situated jurors who are not members of the same cognizable group as the challenged juror, regardless of whether the moving party made a comparative analysis argument in the trial court. Should the appellate court determine that the objection was erroneously denied, that error shall be deemed prejudicial, the judgment shall be reversed, and the case remanded for a new trial.

(k) This section shall not apply to civil cases.

(l) It is the intent of the Legislature that enactment of this section shall not, in purpose or effect, lower the standard for judging challenges for cause or expand use of challenges for cause.

(m) The provisions of this section are severable. If any provision of this section or its application is held invalid, that invalidity shall not affect other provisions or applications that can be given effect without the invalid provision or application.

(n) This section shall remain in effect only until January 1, 2026, and as of that date is repealed.

Added by Stats 2020 ch 318 (AB 3070),s 2, eff. 1/1/2021.

Section 231.7 - [Operative 1/1/2026] Peremptory challenge to remove prospective juror based on membership - perceived or actual - in protected group

(a) A party shall not use a peremptory challenge to remove a prospective juror on the basis of the prospective juror's race, ethnicity, gender, gender identity, sexual orientation, national origin, or religious affiliation, or the perceived membership of the prospective juror in any of those groups.

(b) A party, or the trial court on its own motion, may object to the improper use of a peremptory challenge under subdivision (a). After the objection is made, any further discussion shall be conducted outside the presence of the panel. The objection shall be made before the jury is impaneled, unless information becomes known that could not have reasonably been known before the jury was impaneled.

(c) Notwithstanding Section 226, upon objection to the exercise of a peremptory challenge pursuant to this section, the party exercising the peremptory challenge shall state the reasons the peremptory challenge has been exercised.

(d)

(1) The court shall evaluate the reasons given to justify the peremptory challenge in light of the totality of the circumstances. The court shall consider only the reasons actually given and shall not speculate on, or assume the existence of, other possible justifications for the use of the peremptory challenge. If the court determines there is a substantial likelihood that an objectively reasonable person would view race, ethnicity, gender, gender identity, sexual orientation, national origin, or religious affiliation, or perceived membership in any of those groups, as a factor in the use of the peremptory challenge, then the objection shall be sustained. The court need not find purposeful discrimination to sustain the objection. The court shall explain the reasons for its ruling on the record. A motion brought under this section shall also be deemed a sufficient presentation of claims asserting the discriminatory exclusion of jurors in violation of the United States and California Constitutions.

(2)

(A) For purposes of this section, an objectively reasonable person is aware that unconscious bias, in addition to purposeful discrimination, have resulted in the unfair exclusion of potential jurors in the State of California.

(B) For purposes of this section, a "substantial likelihood" means more than a mere possibility but less than a standard of more likely than not.

(C) For purposes of this section, "unconscious bias" includes implicit and institutional biases.

(3) In making its determination, the circumstances the court may consider include, but are not limited to, any of the following:

(A) Whether any of the following circumstances exist:

(i) The objecting party is a member of the same perceived cognizable group as the challenged juror.

(ii) The alleged victim is not a member of that perceived cognizable group.

(iii) Witnesses or the parties are not members of that perceived cognizable group.

(B) Whether race, ethnicity, gender, gender identity, sexual orientation, national origin, or religious affiliation, or perceived membership in any of those groups, bear on the facts of the case to be tried.

(C) The number and types of questions posed to the prospective juror, including, but not limited to, any the following:

(i) Consideration of whether the party exercising the peremptory challenge failed to question the prospective juror about the concerns later stated by the party as the reason for the peremptory challenge pursuant to subdivision (c).

(ii) Whether the party exercising the peremptory challenge engaged in cursory questioning of the challenged potential juror.

(iii) Whether the party exercising the peremptory challenge asked different questions of the potential juror against whom the peremptory challenge was used in contrast to questions asked of other jurors from different perceived cognizable groups about the same topic or whether the party phrased those questions differently.

(D) Whether other prospective jurors, who are not members of the same cognizable group as the challenged prospective juror, provided similar, but not necessarily identical, answers but were not the subject of a peremptory challenge by that party.

(E) Whether a reason might be disproportionately associated with a race, ethnicity, gender, gender identity, sexual orientation, national origin, or religious affiliation, or perceived membership in any of those groups.

(F) Whether the reason given by the party exercising the peremptory challenge was contrary to or unsupported by the record.

(G) Whether the counsel or counsel's office exercising the challenge has used peremptory challenges disproportionately against a given race, ethnicity, gender, gender identity, sexual orientation, national origin, or religious affiliation, or perceived membership in any of those groups, in the present case or in past cases, including whether the counsel or counsel's office who made the challenge has a history of prior violations under Batson v. Kentucky (1986) 476 U.S. 79, People v. Wheeler (1978) 22 Cal.3d 258, Section 231.5, or this section.

(e) A peremptory challenge for any of the following reasons is presumed to be invalid unless the party exercising the peremptory challenge can show by clear and convincing evidence that an objectively reasonable person would view the rationale as unrelated to a prospective juror's race, ethnicity, gender, gender identity, sexual orientation, national origin, or religious affiliation, or perceived membership in any of those groups, and that the reasons articulated bear on the prospective juror's ability to be fair and impartial in the case:

(1) Expressing a distrust of or having a negative experience with law enforcement or the criminal legal system.

(2) Expressing a belief that law enforcement officers engage in racial profiling or that criminal laws have been enforced in a discriminatory manner.

(3) Having a close relationship with people who have been stopped, arrested, or convicted of a crime.

(4) A prospective juror's neighborhood.

(5) Having a child outside of marriage.

(6) Receiving state benefits.

(7) Not being a native English speaker.

(8) The ability to speak another language.

(9) Dress, attire, or personal appearance.

(10) Employment in a field that is disproportionately occupied by members listed in subdivision (a) or that serves a population disproportionately comprised of members of a group or groups listed in subdivision (a).

(11) Lack of employment or underemployment of the prospective juror or prospective juror's family member.

(12) A prospective juror's apparent friendliness with another prospective juror of the same group as listed in subdivision (a).

(13) Any justification that is similarly applicable to a questioned prospective juror or jurors, who are not members of the same cognizable group as the challenged prospective juror, but were not the subject of a peremptory challenge by that party. The unchallenged prospective juror or jurors need not share any other characteristics with the challenged prospective juror for peremptory challenge relying on this justification to be considered presumptively invalid.

(f) For purposes of subdivision (e), the term "clear and convincing" refers to the degree of certainty the factfinder must have in determining whether the reasons given for the exercise of a peremptory challenge are unrelated to the prospective juror's cognizable group membership, bearing in mind conscious and unconscious bias. To determine that a presumption of invalidity has been overcome, the factfinder shall determine that it is highly probable that the reasons given for the exercise of a peremptory challenge are unrelated to conscious or unconscious bias and are instead specific to the juror and bear on that juror's ability to be fair and impartial in the case.

(g)

(1) The following reasons for peremptory challenges have historically been associated with improper discrimination in jury selection:

(A) The prospective juror was inattentive, or staring or failing to make eye contact.

(B) The prospective juror exhibited either a lack of rapport or problematic attitude, body language, or demeanor.

(C) The prospective juror provided unintelligent or confused answers.

(2) The reasons set forth in paragraph (1) are presumptively invalid unless the trial court is able to confirm that the asserted behavior occurred, based on the court's own observations or the observations of counsel for the objecting party. Even with that confirmation, the counsel offering the reason shall explain why the asserted demeanor, behavior, or manner in which the prospective juror answered questions matters to the case to be tried.

(h) Upon a court granting an objection to the improper exercise of a peremptory challenge, the court shall do one or more of the following:

(1) Quash the jury venire and start jury selection anew. This remedy shall be provided if requested by the objecting party.

(2) If the motion is granted after the jury has been impaneled, declare a mistrial and select a new jury if requested by the defendant.

(3) Seat the challenged juror.

(4) Provide the objecting party additional challenges.

(5) Provide another remedy as the court deems appropriate.

(i) This section applies in all jury trials in which jury selection begins on or after January 1, 2022.

(j) The denial of an objection made under this section shall be reviewed by the appellate court de novo, with the trial court's express factual findings reviewed for substantial evidence. The appellate court shall not impute to the trial court any findings, including findings of a prospective juror's demeanor, that the trial court did not expressly state on the record. The reviewing court shall consider only reasons actually given under subdivision (c) and shall not speculate as to or consider reasons that were not given to explain either the party's use of the peremptory challenge or the party's failure to challenge similarly situated jurors who are not members of the same cognizable group as the challenged juror, regardless of whether the moving party made a comparative analysis argument in the trial court. Should the appellate court determine that the objection was erroneously denied, that error shall be deemed prejudicial, the judgment shall be reversed, and the case remanded for a new trial.

(k) It is the intent of the Legislature that enactment of this section shall not, in purpose or effect, lower the standard for judging challenges for cause or expand use of challenges for cause.

(l) The provisions of this section are severable. If any provision of this section or its application is held invalid, that invalidity shall not affect other provisions or applications that can be given effect without the invalid provision or application.

(m) This section shall become operative January 1, 2026.

Added by Stats 2020 ch 318 (AB 3070),s 3, eff. 1/1/2021.

Section 232 - Perjury acknowledgment and agreement prior to examination

(a) Prior to the examination of prospective trial jurors in the panel assigned for voir dire, the following perjury acknowledgement and agreement shall be obtained from the panel, which shall be acknowledged by the prospective jurors with the statement "I do": "Do you, and each of you, understand and agree that you will accurately and truthfully answer, under penalty of perjury, all questions propounded to you concerning your qualifications and competency to serve as a trial juror in the matter pending before this court; and that failure to do so may subject you to criminal prosecution."

(b) As soon as the selection of the trial jury is completed, the following acknowledgment and agreement shall be obtained from the trial jurors, which shall be acknowledged by the statement "I do": "Do you and each of you understand and agree that you will well and truly try the cause now pending before this court, and a true verdict render according only to the evidence presented to you and to the instructions of the court."

Amended by Stats. 1989, Ch. 1416, Sec. 10.

Section 233 - Discharge of juror found unable to perform duty; alternate juror designated to take juror's place

If, before the jury has returned its verdict to the court, a juror becomes sick or, upon other good cause shown to the court, is found to be unable to perform his or her duty, the court may order the juror to be discharged. If any alternate jurors have been selected as provided by law, one of them shall then be designated by the court to take the place of the juror so discharged. If after all alternate jurors have been made regular jurors or if there is no alternate juror, a juror becomes sick or otherwise unable to perform the juror's duty and has been discharged by the court as provided in this section, the jury shall be discharged and a new jury then or afterwards impaneled, and the cause may again be tried. Alternatively, with the consent of all parties, the trial may proceed with only the remaining jurors, or another juror may be sworn and the trial begin anew.

Added by Stats. 1988, Ch. 1245, Sec. 2.

Section 234 - Drawing of alternate jurors for trial likely to be protracted trial

Whenever, in the opinion of a judge of a superior court about to try a civil or criminal action or proceeding, the trial is likely to be a protracted one, or upon stipulation of the parties, the court may cause an entry to that effect to be made in the minutes of the court and thereupon, immediately after the jury is impaneled and sworn, the court may direct the calling of one or more additional jurors, in its discretion, to be known as "alternate jurors."

These alternate jurors shall be drawn from the same source, and in the same manner, and have the same qualifications, as the jurors already sworn, and shall be subject to the same examination and challenges. However, each side, or each defendant, as provided in Section 231, shall be entitled to as many peremptory challenges to the alternate jurors as there are alternate jurors called.

The alternate jurors shall be seated so as to have equal power and facilities for seeing and hearing the proceedings in the case, and shall take the same oath as the jurors already selected, and shall, unless excused by the court, attend at all times upon the trial of the cause in company with the other jurors, but shall not participate in deliberation unless ordered by the court, and for a failure to do so are liable to be punished for contempt. They shall obey the orders of and be bound by the admonition of the court, upon each adjournment of the court; but if the regular jurors are ordered to be kept in the custody of the sheriff or marshal during the trial of the cause, the alternate jurors shall also be kept in confinement with the other jurors; and upon final submission of the case to the jury, the alternate jurors shall be kept in the custody of the sheriff or marshal who shall not suffer any communication to be made to them except by order of the court, and shall not be discharged until the original jurors are discharged, except as provided in this section.

If at any time, whether before or after the final submission of the case to the jury, a juror dies or becomes ill, or upon other good cause shown to the court is found to be unable to perform his or her duty, or if a juror requests a discharge and good cause appears therefor, the court may order the juror to be discharged and draw the name of an alternate, who shall then take his or her place in the jury box, and be subject to the same rules and regulations as though he or she had been selected as one of the original jurors.

All laws relative to fees, expenses, and mileage or transportation of jurors shall be applicable to alternate jurors, except that in civil cases the sums for fees and mileage or transportation need not be deposited until the judge directs alternate jurors to be impaneled.

Amended by Stats 2010 ch 328 (SB 1330),s 33, eff. 1/1/2011.

Amended by Stats 2002 ch 784 (SB 1316),s 50, eff. 1/1/2003.

Section 235 - Prospective jurors provided at request of sheriff, coroner or other ministerial officer

At the request of the sheriff, coroner, or other ministerial officer, the jury commissioner shall provide such prospective jurors as may be required to form a jury of inquest. Prospective jurors so provided shall be selected, obligated, and compensated in the same manner as other jurors selected under the provisions of this chapter.

Added by Stats. 1988, Ch. 1245, Sec. 2.

Section 236 - Duty of jurors sworn in at coroner's inquest

When six or more prospective jurors of inquest attend, they shall be sworn by the coroner to inquire who the person was, and when, where, and by what means the person came to his or her death, to inquire into the circumstances attending the death, and to render a true verdict thereon, according to the evidence offered them or arising from the inspection of the body.

Added by Stats. 1988, Ch. 1245, Sec. 2.

Section 237 - Release of names of qualified jurors drawn from qualified juror list to public

(a)

(1) The names of qualified jurors drawn from the qualified juror list for the superior court shall be made available to the public upon request unless the court determines that a compelling interest, as defined in subdivision (b), requires that this information should be kept confidential or its use limited in whole or in part.

(2) Upon the recording of a jury's verdict in a criminal jury proceeding, the court's record of personal juror identifying information of trial jurors, as defined in Section 194, consisting of names, addresses, and telephone numbers, shall be sealed until further order of the court as provided by this section.

(3) For purposes of this section, "sealed" or "sealing" means extracting or otherwise removing the personal juror identifying information from the court record.

(4) This subdivision applies only to cases in which a jury verdict was returned on or after January 1, 1996.

(b) Any person may petition the court for access to these records. The petition shall be supported by a declaration that includes facts sufficient to establish good cause for the release of the juror's personal identifying information. The court shall set the matter for hearing if the petition and supporting declaration establish a prima facie showing of good cause for the release of the personal juror identifying information, but shall not set the matter for hearing if there is a showing on the record of facts that establish a compelling interest against disclosure. A compelling interest includes, but is not limited to, protecting jurors from threats or danger of physical harm. If the court does not set the matter for hearing, the court shall by minute order set forth the reasons and make express findings either of a lack of a prima facie showing of good cause or the presence of a compelling interest against disclosure.

(c) If a hearing is set pursuant to subdivision (b), the petitioner shall provide notice of the petition and the time and place of the hearing at least 20 days prior to the date of the hearing to the parties in the criminal action. The court shall provide notice to each affected former juror by personal service or by first-class mail, addressed to the last known address of the former juror as shown in the records of the court. In a capital case, the petitioner shall also serve notice on the Attorney General. Any affected former juror may appear in person, in writing, by telephone, or by counsel to protest the granting of the petition. A former juror who wishes to appear at the hearing to oppose the unsealing of the personal juror identifying information may request the court to close the hearing in order to protect the former juror's anonymity.

(d) After the hearing, the records shall be made available as requested in the petition, unless a former juror's protest to the granting of the petition is sustained. The court shall sustain the protest of the former juror if, in the discretion of the court, the petitioner fails to show good cause, the record establishes the presence of a compelling interest against disclosure as defined in subdivision (b), or the juror is unwilling to be contacted by the petitioner. The court shall set forth reasons and make express findings to support the granting or denying of the petition to disclose. The court may require the person to whom disclosure is made, or his or her agent or employee, to agree not to divulge jurors' identities or identifying information to others; the court may otherwise limit disclosure in any manner it deems appropriate.

(e) Any court employee who has legal access to personal juror identifying information sealed under subdivision (a), who discloses the information, knowing it to be a violation of this section or a court order issued under this section, is guilty of a misdemeanor.

(f) Any person who intentionally solicits another to unlawfully access or disclose personal juror identifying information contained in records sealed under subdivision (a), knowing that the records have been sealed, or who, knowing that the information was unlawfully secured, intentionally discloses it to another person is guilty of a misdemeanor.

Amended by Stats. 1996, Ch. 636, Sec. 2. Effective September 19, 1996.

Section 239 - [Repealed]

Section 240 - [Effective until 1/1/2025] Pilot program to determine if paying low-income trial jurors increased fee promotes a more diverse trial jury panel

(a) Notwithstanding any other law, including Section 215, the Superior Court of San Francisco, in conjunction with the City and County of San Francisco and their justice partners, is authorized to conduct a pilot program pursuant to the requirements of this section to analyze and determine whether paying certain low-income trial jurors an increased fee for service as a trial juror in a criminal case promotes a more economically and racially diverse trial jury panel that more accurately reflects the demographics of the community. This pilot program shall be developed and implemented at no cost to the Superior Court of San Francisco.

(b) The fee for service as a trial juror in a criminal case paid pursuant to the pilot program shall be as follows:

(1) Except as provided in paragraph (2), a trial juror in a criminal case shall be paid the fee required by Section 215.

(2) A trial juror in a criminal case shall be paid a fee of one hundred dollars ($100) per day for each day they are required to report for service as a trial juror if the trial juror's household income for the past 12 months is less than 80 percent of the San Francisco Bay area median income and the trial juror meets one of the additional following criteria:

(A) The trial juror's employer does not compensate for any trial jury service.

(B) The trial juror's employer does not compensate for trial jury service for the estimated duration of the criminal jury trial.

(C) The trial juror is self-employed.

(D) The trial juror is unemployed.

(c) The pilot program court shall determine whether a trial juror is eligible for the one-hundred-dollar ($100) fee for service in a criminal jury trial pursuant to paragraph (2) of subdivision (b).

(d) The pilot program court shall only fund the one-hundred-dollar ($100) fee to eligible trial jurors using funding provided by The Financial Justice Project of the City and County of San Francisco.

(e) The pilot program court shall provide information about the pilot program with every mailed jury summons and all information that is provided regarding excuse from jury service based on a hardship. The pilot program court and court staff shall also provide information about the pilot program whenever applicable under the circumstances. The justice partners shall develop the materials and language to describe the pilot program to prospective jurors. There shall be no additional cost to the pilot program court to provide information about the pilot program, including all printing and mailing costs, which shall be covered through funds provided by The Financial Justice Project of the City and County of San Francisco.

(f) The pilot program court shall implement a juror self-reporting data collection effort to collect data during the pilot program that allows a thorough analysis of whether paying certain low-income trial jurors an increased fee for service as a trial juror in a criminal case promotes a more economically and racially diverse trial jury panel that more accurately reflects the demographics of the community. The data collected shall include, to the maximum extent possible, the race, ethnicity, and income level of all trial jurors that receive the one-hundred-dollar ($100) fee for service as a trial juror. The justice partners shall design the self-reporting data collection survey and the pilot program court shall use existing resources and leverage technology to disseminate and collect surveys from jurors, and shall not require additional funding to support this data collection effort.

(g) The pilot program court and the justice partners shall select a third-party entity to prepare an analysis and report of the data collected pursuant to subdivision (f) without any cost to the pilot program court. Any funding required to support the third-party entity shall be made available through funds provided by The Financial Justice Project of the City and County of San Francisco. The third-party entity shall prepare a report of its analysis of the data and conclusion whether paying certain low-income trial jurors an increased fee for service as a trial juror in a criminal case promotes a more economically and racially diverse trial jury panel that more accurately reflects the demographics of the community. The third-party entity shall transmit its report to the pilot program court and the Legislature, in compliance with Section 9795 of the Government Code, within six months of the conclusion of the pilot program.
(h) The pilot program court shall terminate the pilot program on or before December 31, 2023. The pilot program court shall terminate the pilot program if at any time it determines the increased financial reimbursement is causing prejudice to the rights of litigants or the interests of justice.
(i) For the purposes of this section only, "pilot program court" means the Superior Court of San Francisco.
(j) For the purposes of this section only, "justice partners" means the San Francisco Financial Justice Project within the Treasurer's Office, the San Francisco Public Defender's Office, the San Francisco District Attorney's Office, and the San Francisco Bar Association.
(k) This section shall remain in effect only until January 1, 2025, and as of that date is repealed.
Added by Stats 2021 ch 717 (AB 1452),s 2, eff. 1/1/2022.

Section 241 - [Effective until 1/1/2027] Pilot program to study whether increases in juror compensation and mileage reimbursement rates increase juror diversity and participation
(a) The Judicial Council shall sponsor a pilot program for two fiscal years to study whether increases in juror compensation and mileage reimbursement rates increase juror diversity and participation. The Judicial Council shall select at least six trial courts, in counties with regional and geographic diversity, including the County of Alameda, to participate in the pilot program.
(b) As part of the pilot program, the participating pilot courts shall collect demographic information, as reported by jurors.
(c) No later than September 1, 2026, the Judicial Council shall provide a report to the Legislature pursuant to Section 9795 of the Government Code describing the findings of the pilot program and providing information for promoting juror diversity.
(d) The Judicial Council may enlist the services of a consultant to conduct the study.
(e) This section shall remain in effect only until January 1, 2027, and as of that date is repealed.
Added by Stats 2022 ch 326 (AB 1981),s 3, eff. 1/1/2023.

Chapter 2 - COURT COMMISSIONERS

Section 259 - Powers
Subject to the supervision of the court, every court commissioner shall have power to do all of the following:
(a) Hear and determine ex parte motions for orders and alternative writs and writs of habeas corpus in the superior court for which the court commissioner is appointed.
(b) Take proof and make and report findings thereon as to any matter of fact upon which information is required by the court. Any party to any contested proceeding may except to the report and the subsequent order of the court made thereon within five days after written notice of the court's action. A copy of the exceptions shall be filed and served upon opposing party or counsel within the five days. The party may argue any exceptions before the court on giving notice of motion for that purpose within 10 days from entry thereof. After a hearing before the court on the exceptions, the court may sustain, or set aside, or modify its order.
(c) Take and approve any bonds and undertakings in actions or proceedings, and determine objections to the bonds and undertakings.
(d) Act as temporary judge when otherwise qualified so to act and when appointed for that purpose, on stipulation of the parties litigant. While acting as temporary judge the commissioner shall receive no compensation therefor other than compensation as commissioner.
(e) Hear and report findings and conclusions to the court for approval, rejection, or change, all preliminary matters including motions or petitions for the custody and support of children, the allowance of temporary spousal support, costs and attorneys' fees, and issues of fact in contempt proceedings in proceedings for support, dissolution of marriage, nullity of marriage, or legal separation.
(f) Hear actions to establish paternity and to establish or enforce child and spousal support pursuant to subdivision (a) of Section 4251 of the Family Code.
(g) Hear, report on, and determine all uncontested actions and proceedings subject to the requirements of subdivision (d).
Amended by Stats 2004 ch 49 (SB 1225),s 1, eff. 1/1/2005

Title 4 - MINISTERIAL OFFICERS OF COURTS OF JUSTICE
Chapter 1 - OF MINISTERIAL OFFICERS GENERALLY

Section 262 - Liability of sheriff for execution of process or return at direction of party or attorney
The direction or authority of a party or his or her attorney to a sheriff, in respect to the execution of process or return thereof, or to any related act or omission, is not available to discharge or excuse the sheriff from a liability for neglect or misconduct, unless it is contained in written instructions by the attorney of the party, including the signature and name of the attorney of the party, or by the party, if he or she has no attorney. Subject to subdivision (c) of Section 263, the instructions may be transmitted electronically pursuant to Chapter 2 (commencing with Section 263).
Amended by Stats 2010 ch 680 (AB 2394),s 1, eff. 1/1/2011.

Section 262.1 - Execution of process and orders regular on face and issued by competent authority justified
A sheriff or other ministerial officer is justified in the execution of, and shall execute, all process and orders regular on their face and issued by competent authority, whatever may be the defect in the proceedings upon which they were issued.
Added by Stats. 1951, Ch. 655.

Section 262.2 - Authority to show process to any interested party
Except as otherwise provided, the officer executing process shall, so long as he or she retains the original process, show it to any interested person, upon request. The officer shall show the process, with all papers, or electronic copies of all papers, attached, at his or her office whenever the office is open for business.
Amended by Stats 2010 ch 680 (AB 2394),s 2, eff. 1/1/2011.

Section 262.3 - Execution of process by successor in office
When any process remains with the sheriff unexecuted, in whole or in part, at the time of his death, resignation of office, or at the expiration of his term of office, such process shall be executed by his successor or successors in office.
Added by Stats. 1951, Ch. 655.

Section 262.4 - Execution and delivery of deeds and conveyances by sheriff to purchaser of real property at sheriff's sale
If the sheriff sells real estate, under and by virtue of an execution or order of court, the sheriff, or his or her successors in office, shall execute and deliver to the purchaser or purchasers all deeds and conveyances required by law and necessary for the purpose, and those deeds and conveyances shall be valid in law as if they had been executed by the sheriff who made the sale. The deeds and conveyances may be recorded electronically pursuant to Chapter 2 (commencing with Section 263) if they comply with the Electronic Recording Delivery Act of 2004 (Article 6 (commencing with Section 27390) of Chapter 6 of Part 3 of Division 2 of Title 3 of the Government Code).
Amended by Stats 2010 ch 680 (AB 2394),s 3, eff. 1/1/2011.

Section 262.5 - Service of paper other than process upon sheriff

Service of a paper, other than process, upon the sheriff may be made by delivering it to him or to one of his deputies, or to a person in charge of the office during office hours, or, if no such person is there, by leaving it in a conspicuous place in the office.

Added by Stats. 1951, Ch. 655.

Section 262.6 - Execution of process and orders when sheriff party to proceeding

When the sheriff is a party to an action or proceeding, the process and orders therein, which it would otherwise be the duty of the sheriff to execute, shall be executed by the coroner of the county.

Added by Stats. 1951, Ch. 655.

Section 262.7 - Persons serving process and orders when action begun against sheriff

If an action is begun against a sheriff, all process and orders may be served by any person in the manner provided in this code.

Amended by Stats 2014 ch 470 (AB 2256),s 1, eff. 1/1/2015.

Section 262.8 - Persons serving process and orders denominated elisor

Process or orders in an action or proceeding may be executed by a person residing in the county, designated by the court, or the judge thereof, and denominated an elisor, in the following cases:

(a) When the sheriff and coroner are both parties.

(b) When either of these officers is a party, and the process is against the other.

(c) When either of these officers is a party, and there is a vacancy in the office of the other, or where it appears, by affidavit, to the satisfaction of the court in which the proceeding is pending, or the judge thereof, that both of these officers are disqualified, or by reason of any bias, prejudice, or other cause would not act promptly or impartially.

Added by Stats. 1951, Ch. 655.

Section 262.9 - Execution and return of process delivered to elisor

When process is delivered to an elisor, he shall execute and return it in the same manner as the sheriff is required to execute similar process.

Added by Stats. 1951, Ch. 655.

Section 262.10 - Compensation for execution of process or act performed by coroner or elisor

Whenever process is executed, or any act performed by a coroner or elisor, he shall receive a reasonable compensation, to be fixed by the court, to be paid by the plaintiff in case of the summoning of jurors to complete the panel, and by the person or party requiring the service in all other cases in private action. If rendered at the instance of the people, it shall be audited and paid as a county charge.

Added by Stats. 1951, Ch. 655.

Section 262.11 - Execution of process by sheriff of new county in which real estate situated

In all cases where new counties have been or may hereafter be created, and executions, orders of sale upon foreclosures of mortgages, or other process affecting specific real estate have been or may hereafter be adjudged by the final judgment or decree of a court of competent jurisdiction, to be executed by the sheriff of the county in which such real estate was originally situated, such process may be executed by the sheriff of the new county in which such real estate is found to be situated, with the like effect as if he were the sheriff of the county designated in the judgment, decree, or order of sale to execute the same.

Added by Stats. 1955, Ch. 59.

Chapter 2 - LEVYING OFFICER ELECTRONIC TRANSACTIONS ACT

Section 263 - Title of act; legislative findings and declaration; compliance with act

(a) This chapter may be cited as the Levying Officer Electronic Transactions Act.

(b) The Legislature finds and declares that modern technologies offer alternatives to paper-based systems and provide the means to create, store, retrieve, and transmit records and documents in electronic form resulting in increased efficiency, taxpayer savings, and improved public access to levying officers. It is the intent of the Legislature in enacting this act to accommodate current and future technologies based on industry standards.

(c) Nothing in this chapter shall be construed to require a court or levying officer to comply with any of its provisions unless the court and the levying officer have (1) jointly determined that both the court and the sheriff's department have the resources and the technological capacity to do so, and (2) have mutually agreed to electronically act upon documents as provided in this chapter.

Added by Stats 2010 ch 680 (AB 2394),s 4, eff. 1/1/2011.

Section 263.1 - Definitions

As used in this chapter, the following terms have the following definitions:

(a) "Electronic mail" or "e-mail" means an electronic message that is sent to an e-mail address and transmitted between two or more telecommunications devices, computers, or electronic devices capable of receiving electronic messages through a local, regional, or global computer network, whether or not the message is converted to hard copy format after receipt, viewed upon transmission, or stored for later retrieval.

(b) "Electronic record" means a document or record created, generated, sent, communicated, received, or stored by electronic means.

(c) "Electronic signature" means an electronic sound, symbol, or process attached to, or logically associated with, an electronic record and executed or adopted by a person with the intent to sign the electronic record.

(d) "Fax" is an abbreviation for "facsimile" and refers, as indicated by the context, to a facsimile transmission or to a document so transmitted.

(e) "Fax machine" means a machine that can send and receive a facsimile transmission using industry standards and includes a fax modem connected to a computer.

(f) "Fax transmission" means the electronic transmission and reconstruction of a document that prints a duplicate of the original document at the receiving end. "Fax transmission" includes, but is not limited to, the use of a facsimile machine or the process of integrating an electronic fax software application to automate the sending and receiving of a faxed document as an electronic record, in portable data format, by e-mail or similar electronic means.

(g) "Information processing system" means an electronic system for creating, generating, sending, receiving, storing, displaying, retrieving, or processing information, but does not include a fax machine.

(h) "Instructions" and "levying officer instructions" mean a written request to a levying officer to serve process, perform a levy, execute an arrest warrant, or perform some other act.

(i) "Legal entity" means the legal form of an artificial person and includes a corporation, defunct corporation, unincorporated association, partnership, public agency, limited liability company, joint stock company or association, and limited liability partnership.

(j) "Levying officer" means the sheriff or marshal acting as a ministerial officer pursuant to Section 26608 of the Government Code.

(k) "Record" means information that is inscribed on a tangible medium, or that is stored in an electronic or other medium and is retrievable in perceivable form.

(l) "Transmission record" means the electronic record or document printed by the sending fax machine, stating the telephone number of the receiving fax machine, the number of pages sent, the transmission time and date, and an indication of any errors in transmission.

Added by Stats 2010 ch 680 (AB 2394),s 4, eff. 1/1/2011.

Section 263.2 - Authority to utilize information processing system; system problem preventing officer from receiving electronic transmissions

(a) A levying officer may utilize an information processing system to create, generate, send, receive, store, display, retrieve, or process information, electronic records, and documents when based on industry standards and only to the extent that the levying officer has the resources and technological capacity to do so.

(b) If a technical problem with the levying officer's system prevents the levying officer from receiving an electronic transmission during regular business hours on a particular court day, and the electronic sender demonstrates an attempt to electronically transmit the document on that day, the levying officer shall deem the document or record as filed on that day.

Added by Stats 2010 ch 680 (AB 2394),s 4, eff. 1/1/2011.

Section 263.3 - Rules applicable when fax transmission authorized

Whenever the fax transmission of a document or record to a levying officer is authorized pursuant to this chapter, all of the following shall apply:

(a) A levying officer may act upon an electronic record or document transmitted by a facsimile machine in the same manner as the paper record or document upon which the electronic record or document is based.

(b) A facsimile cover sheet shall accompany the faxed record or document and include all of the following information:

   (1) The name of the sender.

   (2) The fax number of the sender.

   (3) The name of the levying officer.

   (4) The fax number of the levying officer.

   (5) A description of the record or document, including its name, if any, and the number of pages.

   (6) A statement directing the recipient of the faxed document or record to fax to the sender a confirmation, if true, that the fax was properly received.

(c) A person authorized to fax a record or document to the levying officer pursuant to this chapter shall do all of the following:

   (1) Retain the paper version of the record or document.

   (2) Print or otherwise retain a transmission record of the fax transmission.

   (3) Deliver the paper version of the record, document, or transmission record to the levying officer within five days after a request to do so has been mailed to the sender by the levying officer.

(d) The levying officer shall retain the facsimile cover sheet together with the faxed record or document.

(e) The levying officer may electronically copy and store the printed cover sheet, record, or document as an electronic record.

Added by Stats 2010 ch 680 (AB 2394),s 4, eff. 1/1/2011.

Section 263.4 - Electronic records

(a) A levying officer may create, store, print, or transmit an electronic record in the place of, and in the same manner as, the paper record or document upon which the electronic record is based.

(b) An electronic record transmitted to a levying officer shall be accompanied by all of the following information:

   (1) The name of the sender.

   (2) The electronic address of the sender.

   (3) The name of the levying officer.

   (4) The electronic address or fax number of the levying officer.

(c) The person transmitting the electronic record shall do both of the following:

   (1) Retain the paper version of the record or document.

   (2) Deliver the paper version of the record or document to the levying officer within five days after a request to do so has been mailed to the sender by the levying officer.

(d) For the purpose of this section, "transmission" of an electronic record includes sending the electronic record included in, or in conjunction with, an electronic mail message, as defined in Section 263.1.

Added by Stats 2010 ch 680 (AB 2394),s 4, eff. 1/1/2011.

Section 263.6 - Return of officer's actions filed in lieu of returning original paper version of writ of execution

(a) In lieu of returning to court the paper version of an original writ of execution, the levying officer may retain the original writ or an electronic copy of the original writ and file only a return of the levying officer's actions.

(b) If the original writ is not returned to court as provided in subdivision (a), the levying officer shall retain, for not less than two years after the levying officer's return is filed with court, each of the following, as applicable:

   (1) The original paper writ or digital image of the writ.

   (2) The memorandum of garnishee.

   (3) The employer's return.

   (4) An inventory of the levied property.

(c) A creditor seeking the issuance of a writ directed to another county may direct the levying officer to file an accounting of the levying officer's actions with the court.

   (1) The filing of the accounting described in this subdivision does not constitute a return of the writ.

   (2) The accounting shall indicate that the levying officer is in possession of an active writ.

Added by Stats 2010 ch 680 (AB 2394),s 4, eff. 1/1/2011.

Section 263.7 - Identifiers excluded or redacted from record available to public

(a) A levying officer shall exclude or redact the following identifiers from any record or document made available to the public:

   (1) Social security number.

   (2) Financial account number.

(b) If an identifier is redacted, only the last four digits of the number may be used.

(c) A levying officer also shall exclude or redact the identifiers listed in subdivision (a) from any writ return filed with the court.

(d) The term "public" does not include the creditor, debtor, garnishee, or third-party claimant.

Added by Stats 2010 ch 680 (AB 2394),s 4, eff. 1/1/2011.

Chapter 3 - PHONOGRAPHIC REPORTERS

Section 269 - Duty of reporters; transcripts requested; record on appeal

(a) An official reporter or official reporter pro tempore of the superior court shall take down in shorthand all testimony, objections made, rulings of the court, exceptions taken, arraignments, pleas, sentences, arguments of the attorneys to the jury, and statements and remarks made and oral instructions given by the judge or other judicial officer, in the following cases:

   (1) In a civil case, on the order of the court or at the request of a party.

   (2) In a felony case, on the order of the court or at the request of the prosecution, the defendant, or the attorney for the defendant.

   (3) In a misdemeanor or infraction case, on the order of the court.

(b) If a transcript is ordered by the court or requested by a party, or if a nonparty requests a transcript that the nonparty is entitled to receive, regardless of whether the nonparty was permitted to attend the proceeding to be transcribed, the official reporter or official reporter pro tempore shall, within a reasonable time after the trial of the case that the court designates, write the transcripts out, or the specific portions thereof as may be requested, in plain and legible longhand, or by typewriter, or other printing machine, and certify that the transcripts were correctly reported and transcribed, and when directed by the court, file the transcripts with the clerk of the court.

(c) If a defendant is convicted of a felony, after a trial on the merits, the record on appeal shall be prepared immediately after the verdict or finding of guilt is announced unless the court determines that it is likely that no appeal from the decision will be made. The court's determination of a likelihood of appeal shall be based upon standards and rules adopted by the Judicial Council.

Amended by Stats 2002 ch 71 (SB 1371),s 1, eff. 1/1/2003.

Section 270 - [Repealed]
Repealed by Stats 2001 ch 115 (SB 153), s 2, eff. 1/1/2002.

Section 271 - Delivery of transcript in electronic form
(a) An official reporter or official reporter pro tempore shall deliver a transcript in electronic form, in compliance with the California Rules of Court, to any court, party, or person entitled to the transcript, unless any of the following apply:

   (1) The party or person entitled to the transcript requests the reporter's transcript in paper form.

   (2) Prior to January 1, 2023, the court lacks the technical ability to use or store a transcript in electronic form pursuant to this section and provides advance notice of this fact to the official reporter or official reporter pro tempore.

   (3) Prior to January 1, 2023, the official reporter or official reporter pro tempore lacks the technical ability to deliver a transcript in electronic form pursuant to this section and provides advance notice of this fact to the court, party, or person entitled to the transcript.

(b) If a paper transcript is delivered in lieu of an electronic transcript described in subdivision (a), within 120 days of the official reporter or official reporter pro tempore filing or delivering the paper transcript, the official reporter or official reporter pro tempore shall provide, upon request, a copy of the original transcript in full text-searchable portable document format (PDF) if the proceedings were produced with computer-aided transcription equipment. The copy of the original transcript in full text-searchable PDF format shall not be deemed to be an original transcript.

(c) Nothing in this section changes any requirement set forth in Section 69950 or 69954 of the Government Code, regardless of whether a transcript is delivered in electronic or paper form.

(d) Except as provided in subdivision (b), an electronic transcript delivered in accordance with this section shall be deemed to be an original transcript for all purposes, including any obligation of an attorney to maintain or deliver a file to a client.

(e) An electronic transcript shall comply with any format requirement imposed pursuant to subdivision (a). However, an official reporter or official reporter pro tempore shall not be required to use a specific vendor, technology, or software to comply with this section, unless the official reporter or official reporter pro tempore agrees with the court, party, or person entitled to the transcript to use a specific vendor, technology, or software. Absent that agreement, an official reporter or official reporter pro tempore may select the vendor, technology, and software to comply with this section and the California Rules of Court. In adopting transcript format requirements for the California Rules of Court, consideration shall be given on a technology-neutral basis to the availability of relevant vendors of transcript products, technologies, and software.

(f) After January 1, 2023, if new or updated rule of court format requirements for electronic transcripts necessitate a significant change in equipment or software owned by official reporters or official reporters pro tempore, the official reporters and official reporters pro tempore shall be given no less than one year to comply with the format requirements. If the change is necessary to address a security issue, then a reasonable time shall be given to comply with the new format requirements.

Added by Stats 2017 ch 532 (AB 1450),s 2, eff. 1/1/2018.

Section 273 - Report of reporter certified as correct transcript; rough draft transcript
(a) The report of the official reporter, or official reporter pro tempore, of any court, duly appointed and sworn, when transcribed and certified as being a correct transcript of the testimony and proceedings in the case, is prima facie evidence of that testimony and proceedings.

(b) The report of the official reporter, or official reporter pro tempore, of any court, duly appointed and sworn, when prepared as a rough draft transcript, shall not be certified and cannot be used, cited, distributed, or transcribed as the official certified transcript of the proceedings. A rough draft transcript shall not be cited or used in any way or at any time to rebut or contradict the official certified transcript of the proceedings as provided by the official reporter or official reporter pro tempore. The production of a rough draft transcript shall not be required.

(c) This section shall become operative on January 1, 2022.

Amended by Stats 2016 ch 703 (AB 2881),s 7, eff. 1/1/2017.
Added by Stats 2009 ch 87 (AB 170),s 2, eff. 1/1/2010.

Section 274a - Opinion rendered by superior court judge transcribed by reporter
Any judge of the superior court may have any opinion given or rendered by the judge in the trial of a felony case or an unlimited civil case, pending in that court, or any necessary order, petition, citation, commitment or judgment in any probate proceeding, proceeding concerning new or additional bonds of county officials or juvenile court proceeding, or the testimony or judgment relating to the custody or support of minor children in any proceeding in which the custody or support of minor children is involved, taken down in shorthand and transcribed together with such copies as the court may deem necessary by the official reporter or an official reporter pro tempore of the court.

Amended by Stats 2002 ch 784 (SB 1316),s 51, eff. 1/1/2003.

Section 274c - [Repealed]
Repealed by Stats 2002 ch 71 (SB 1371),s 3, eff. 1/1/2003.

Title 5 - PERSONS SPECIALLY INVESTED WITH MINISTERIAL POWERS RELATING TO COURTS OF JUSTICE
Chapter 1 - ATTORNEYS AND COUNSELORS AT LAW

Section 283 - Authority bind client and receive money claimed by client
An attorney and counselor shall have authority:

1. To bind his client in any of the steps of an action or proceeding by his agreement filed with the Clerk, or entered upon the minutes of the Court, and not otherwise;

2. To receive money claimed by his client in an action or proceeding during the pendency thereof, or after judgment, unless a revocation of his authority is filed, and upon the payment thereof, and not otherwise, to discharge the claim or acknowledge satisfaction of the judgment.

Repealed and added by Code Amendments 1880, Ch. 35.

Section 284 - Change of attorney in action or special proceeding
The attorney in an action or special proceeding may be changed at any time before or after judgment or final determination, as follows:

1. Upon the consent of both client and attorney, filed with the clerk, or entered upon the minutes;

2. Upon the order of the court, upon the application of either client or attorney, after notice from one to the other.

Amended by Stats. 1967, Ch. 161.

Section 285 - Notice of change and substitution of new attorney

When an attorney is changed, as provided in the last section, written notice of the change and of the substitution of a new attorney, or of the appearance of the party in person, must be given to the adverse party. Until then he must recognize the former attorney.
Repealed and added by Code Amendments 1880, Ch. 35.

Section 285.1 - Withdrawal of attorney of record in proceeding for dissolution of marriage, legal separation, declaration of void marriage, support, etc.

An attorney of record for any party in any civil action or proceeding for dissolution of marriage, legal separation, or for a declaration of void or voidable marriage, or for the support, maintenance or custody of minor children may withdraw at any time subsequent to the time when any judgment in such action or proceeding, other than an interlocutory judgment, becomes final, and prior to service upon him of pleadings or motion papers in any proceeding then pending in said cause, by filing a notice of withdrawal. Such notice shall state (a) date of entry of final decree or judgment, (b) the last known address of such party, (c) that such attorney withdraws as attorney for such party. A copy of such notice shall be mailed to such party at his last known address and shall be served upon the adverse party.
Amended by Stats. 1969, Ch. 1608.

Section 285.2 - Withdrawal of legal service agency attorney if reduction of public funding impairs ability to represent indigent client

If a reduction in public funding for legal service materially impairs a legal service agency attorney's ability to represent an indigent client, the court, on its own motion or on the motion of either the client or attorney, shall permit the withdrawal of such attorney upon a showing that all of the following apply:

(a) There are not adequate public funds to continue the effective representation of the indigent client.
(b) A good faith effort was made to find alternate representation for such client.
(c) All reasonable steps to reduce the legal prejudice to the client have been taken. A showing of indigency of the client, in and of itself, will not be deemed sufficient cause to deny the application for withdrawal.
Added by Stats. 1983, Ch. 279, Sec. 1.

Section 285.3 - Tolling certain time period upon granting withdrawal pursuant to section 285.2

The court, upon the granting of a motion for withdrawal pursuant to Section 285.2, may toll the running of any statute of limitations, filing requirement, statute providing for mandatory dismissal, notice of appeal, or discovery requirement, for a period not to exceed 90 days, on the court's own motion or on motion of any party or attorney, when the court finds that tolling is required to avoid legal prejudice caused by the withdrawal of the legal service agency attorney.
Added by Stats. 1983, Ch. 279, Sec. 2.

Section 285.4 - Appointment of attorney by court upon granting withdrawal motion pursuant to section 285.2

The court, upon the granting of a motion for withdrawal pursuant to Section 285.2, may appoint any member of the bar or any law firm or professional law corporation to represent the indigent client without compensation, upon a showing of good cause. Nothing herein shall preclude the appointed attorney from recovering any attorneys' fees and costs to which the client may be entitled by law. In determining the existence of good cause, the court may consider, but is not limited to, the following factors:

(a) The probable merit of the client's claim.
(b) The client's financial ability to pay for legal services.
(c) The availability of alternative legal representation.
(d) The need for legal representation to avoid irreparable legal prejudice to the indigent client.
(e) The ability of appointed counsel to effectively represent the indigent client.
(f) Present and recent pro bono work of the appointed attorney, law firm or private law corporation.
(g) The ability of the indigent client to represent himself.
(h) The workload of the appointed attorney.
Added by Stats. 1983, Ch. 279, Sec. 3.

Section 286 - Death, removal or suspension or cessation to act as attorney

When an attorney dies, or is removed or suspended, or ceases to act as such, a party to an action, for whom he was acting as attorney, must, before any further proceedings are had against him, be required by the adverse party, by written notice, to appoint another attorney, or to appear in person.
Repealed and added by Code Amendments 1880, Ch. 35.

Part 2 - OF CIVIL ACTIONS

Title 1 - OF THE FORM OF CIVIL ACTIONS

Section 307 - One form of civil action

There is in this State but one form of civil actions for the enforcement or protection of private rights and the redress or prevention of private wrongs.
Enacted 1872.

Section 308 - Parties

In such action the party complaining is known as the plaintiff, and the adverse party as the defendant.
Enacted 1872.

Section 309 - Question of fact not put in issue by pleadings tried by jury

A question of fact not put in issue by the pleadings may be tried by a jury, upon an order for the trial, stating distinctly and plainly the question of fact to be tried; and such order is the only authority necessary for a trial.
Enacted 1872.

Title 2 - OF THE TIME OF COMMENCING CIVIL ACTIONS

Chapter 1 - THE TIME OF COMMENCING ACTIONS IN GENERAL

Section 312 - Generally

Civil actions, without exception, can only be commenced within the periods prescribed in this title, after the cause of action shall have accrued, unless where, in special cases, a different limitation is prescribed by statute.
Amended by Stats. 1897, Ch. 21.

Section 313 - Presentation of claims against governmental entity as prerequisite to commencement of action

The general procedure for the presentation of claims as a prerequisite to commencement of actions for money or damages against the State of California, counties, cities, cities and counties, districts, local authorities, and other political subdivisions of the State, and against the officers, employees, and servants thereof, is prescribed by Division 3.6 (commencing with Section 810) of Title 1 of the Government Code.
Amended by Stats. 1963, Ch. 1715.

Chapter 2 - THE TIME OF COMMENCING ACTIONS FOR THE RECOVERY OF REAL PROPERTY

Section 315 - State suing person
The people of this State will not sue any person for or in respect to any real property, or the issues or profits thereof, by reason of the right or title of the people to the same, unless:
1. Such right or title shall have accrued within ten years before any action or other proceeding for the same is commenced; or,
2. The people, or those from whom they claim, shall have received the rents and profits of such real property, or of some part thereof, within the space of ten years.
Enacted 1872.

Section 316 - Person claiming under letters patent or grants from state
No action can be brought for or in respect to real property by any person claiming under letters patent or grants from this State, unless the same might have been commenced by the people as herein specified, in case such patent had not been issued or grant made.
Enacted 1872.

Section 317 - Recovery of property conveyed when letters patent or grants declare void
Section Three Hundred and Seventeen. When letters patent or grants of real property issued or made by the people of this State, are declared void by the determination of a competent Court, an action for the recovery of the property so conveyed may be brought, either by the people of the State, or by any subsequent patentee or grantee of the property, his heirs or assigns, within five years after such determination, but not after that period.
Amended by Code Amendments 1873-74, Ch. 383.

Section 318 - Action for recovery of real property or possession of real property
No action for the recovery of real property, or for the recovery of the possession thereof, can be maintained, unless it appear that the plaintiff, his ancestor, predecessor, or grantor, was seized or possessed of the property in question, within five years before the commencement of the action.
Enacted 1872.

Section 319 - Action or defense to action arising out of title to real property or rents or profits
No cause of action, or defense to an action, arising out of the title to real property, or to rents or profits out of the same, can be effectual, unless it appear that the person prosecuting the action, or making the defense, or under whose title the action is prosecuted, or the defense is made, or the ancestor, predecessor, or grantor of such person was seized or possessed of the premises in question within five years before the commencement of the Act in respect to which such action is prosecuted or defense made.
Enacted 1872.

Section 320 - Entry upon real estate deemed sufficient or valid as claim
No entry upon real estate is deemed sufficient or valid as a claim, unless an action be commenced thereupon within one year after making such entry, and within five years from the time when the right to make it descended or accrued.
Enacted 1872.

Section 321 - Presumption in action for recovery of property when legal title to property established
In every action for the recovery of real property, or the possession thereof, the person establishing a legal title to the property is presumed to have been possessed thereof within the time required by law, and the occupation of the property by any other person is deemed to have been under and in subordination to the legal title, unless it appear that the property has been held and possessed adversely to such legal title, for five years before the commencement of the action.
Enacted 1872.

Section 322 - Property deemed been held adversely by occupant under claim of title founded upon written instrument or decree or judgment
When it appears that the occupant, or those under whom he claims, entered into the possession of the property under claim of title, exclusive of other right, founding such claim upon a written instrument, as being a conveyance of the property in question, or upon the decree or judgment of a competent Court, and that there has been a continued occupation and possession of the property included in such instrument, decree, or judgment, or of some part of the property, under such claim, for five years, the property so included is deemed to have been held adversely, except that when it consists of a tract divided into lots, the possession of one lot is not deemed a possession of any other lot of the same tract.
Enacted 1872.

Section 323 - Land deemed possessed and occupied by person claiming title founded upon instrument or decree or judgment
For the purpose of constituting an adverse possession by any person claiming a title founded upon a written instrument, or a judgment or decree, land is deemed to have been possessed and occupied in the following cases:
1. Where it has been usually cultivated or improved;
2. Where it has been protected by a substantial inclosure;
3. Where, although not inclosed, it has been used for the supply of fuel, or of fencing timber for the purposes of husbandry, or for pasturage, or for the ordinary use of the occupant;
4. Where a known farm or single lot has been partly improved, the portion of such farm or lot that may have been left not cleared, or not inclosed according to the usual course and custom of the adjoining country, shall be deemed to have been occupied for the same length of time as the part improved and cultivated.
Enacted 1872.

Section 324 - Property deemed held adversely by occupant under claim of title not founded upon written instrument or decree or judgment
Where it appears that there has been an actual continued occupation of land, under a claim of title, exclusive of any other right, but not founded upon a written instrument, judgment, or decree, the land so actually occupied, and no other, is deemed to have been held adversely.
Enacted 1872.

Section 325 - Land deemed possessed and occupied by person claiming title not founded on instrument or decree or judgment
(a) For the purpose of constituting an adverse possession by a person claiming title, not founded upon a written instrument, judgment, or decree, land is deemed to have been possessed and occupied in the following cases only:
  (1) Where it has been protected by a substantial enclosure.
  (2) Where it has been usually cultivated or improved.
(b) In no case shall adverse possession be considered established under the provision of any section of this code, unless it shall be shown that the land has been occupied and claimed for the period of five years continuously, and the party or persons, their predecessors and grantors, have timely paid all state, county, or municipal taxes that have been levied and assessed upon the land for the period of five years during which the land has been occupied and claimed. Payment of those taxes by the party or persons, their predecessors and grantors shall be established by certified records of the county tax collector.
Amended by Stats 2010 ch 55 (AB 1684),s 1, eff. 1/1/2011.

Section 326 - Possession of tenant deemed possession of landlord
When the relation of landlord and tenant has existed between any persons, the possession of the tenant is deemed the possession of the landlord until the expiration of five years from the termination of the tenancy, or, where there has been no written lease, until the expiration of five years from the time of the last payment of rent, notwithstanding that such tenant may have acquired another title, or may have claimed to hold adversely to his landlord. But such presumptions cannot be made after the periods herein limited.
Enacted 1872.

Section 327 - Right to possession not impaired or affected by descent cast in consequence of death
The right of a person to the possession of real property is not impaired or affected by a descent cast in consequence of the death of a person in possession of such property.
Enacted 1872.

Section 328 - Person entitled to commence action under age of majority or lacking legal capacity
If a person entitled to commence an action for the recovery of real property, or for the recovery of the possession thereof, or to make an entry or defense founded on the title to real property, or to rents or services out of the property, is, at the time title first descends or accrues, either under the age of majority or lacking legal capacity to make decisions, the time, not exceeding 20 years, during which the disability continues is not deemed a portion of the time in this chapter limited for the commencement of the action, or the making of the entry or defense, but the action may be commenced, or entry or defense made, within the period of five years after the disability shall cease, or after the death of the person entitled, who shall die under the disability. The action shall not be commenced, or entry or defense made, after that period.
Amended by Stats 2014 ch 144 (AB 1847),s 3, eff. 1/1/2015.

Section 328.5 - Person entitled to commence action imprisoned
If a person entitled to commence an action for the recovery of real property, or for the recovery of the possession thereof, or to make any entry or defense founded on the title to real property, or to rents or services out of the property, is, at the time the title first descends or accrues, imprisoned on a criminal charge, or in execution upon conviction of a criminal offense, for a term less than life, the time, not exceeding two years, during which imprisonment continues is not deemed any portion of the time in this chapter limited for the commencement of the action, or the making of the entry or defense, but the action may be commenced, or entry or defense made, within the period of five years after the imprisonment ceases, or after the death of the person entitled, who dies while imprisoned; but the action shall not be commenced, or entry or defense made, after that period.
Added by Stats. 1994, Ch. 1083, Sec. 3. Effective January 1, 1995.

Section 329 - Action for foreclosure of lien securing assessment for street improvement
The time within which an action for the foreclosure of a lien securing an assessment against real property for street improvements, the proceedings for which are prescribed by legislation of any political unit other than the state, may be commenced, shall be two years from and after the date on which the assessment, or any bond secured thereby, or the last installment of the assessment or bond, shall be due, or, as to existing rights of action not heretofore barred, one year after the effective date hereof, whichever time is later. After that time, if the lien has not been otherwise removed, the lien ceases to exist and the assessment is conclusively presumed to be paid. The official having charge of the records of the assessment shall mark it "Conclusively presumed paid," if, at the expiration of the time within which such action might be brought he has received no written notice of the pendency of the action.
Amended by Stats. 1981, Ch. 714, Sec. 68.

Section 329.5 - Contesting validity of assessment or supplemental assessment for public improvements
The validity of an assessment or supplemental assessment against real property for public improvements, the proceedings for which are prescribed by the legislative body of any chartered city, shall not be contested in any action or proceeding unless the action or proceeding is commenced within 30 days after the assessment is levied, or such longer period as the legislative body may provide. Any appeal from a final judgment in such an action or proceeding shall be perfected within 30 days after the entry of judgment.
Added by Stats. 1959, Ch. 1007.

Section 330 - Sale of land upon which lien to secure payment of public improvement assessment represented by public improvement bond
In all cases in which there is now vested or there shall hereafter be vested in a treasurer, street superintendent, or other public official the power to sell at public auction, after demand upon him by the holder of any public improvement bond, any lot or parcel of land upon which exists or which shall hereafter exist a lien to secure the payment of a public improvement assessment represented by said bond, and the act or law establishing such power fails to prescribe the time within which such official may act, said official may sell at any time prior to the expiration of four years after the due date of said bond or of the last installment thereof or of the last principal coupon attached thereto, or prior to January 1, 1947, whichever is later, but not thereafter. This section is not intended to extend, enlarge or revive any power of sale which has heretofore been lost by reason of lapse of time or otherwise.
Added by Stats. 1945, Ch. 360.

Chapter 3 - THE TIME OF COMMENCING ACTIONS OTHER THAN FOR THE RECOVERY OF REAL PROPERTY

Section 335 - Generally
The periods prescribed for the commencement of actions other than for the recovery of real property, are as follows:
Enacted 1872.

Section 335.1 - Assault, battery or injury or death caused by wrongful act or negligence
Within two years: An action for assault, battery, or injury to, or for the death of, an individual caused by the wrongful act or neglect of another.
Added by Stats 2002 ch 448 (SB 688),s 2, eff. 1/1/2003.

Section 336 - Mesne profits; violation of restriction as defined in section 784, Civil Code
Within five years:
(a) An action for mesne profits of real property.
(b) An action for violation of a restriction, as defined in Section 784 of the Civil Code. The period prescribed in this subdivision runs from the time the person seeking to enforce the restriction discovered or, through the exercise of reasonable diligence, should have discovered the violation. A failure to commence an action for violation of a restriction within the period prescribed in this subdivision does not waive the right to commence an action for any other violation of the restriction and does not, in itself, create an implication that the restriction is abandoned, obsolete, or otherwise unenforceable. This subdivision shall not bar commencement of an action for violation of a restriction before January 1, 2001, and until January 1, 2001, any other applicable statutory or common law limitation shall continue to apply to that action.
Amended by Stats. 1998, Ch. 14, Sec. 3. Effective January 1, 1999.

Section 336a - Bonds, notes or debentures; mortgage, trust deed or other agreement on bonds, notes or debentures
Within six years:

(a) An action upon any bonds, notes, or debentures issued by any corporation or pursuant to permit of the Commissioner of Financial Protection and Innovation, or upon any coupons issued with the bonds, notes, or debentures, if those bonds, notes, or debentures shall have been issued to or held by the public.

(b) An action upon any mortgage, trust deed, or other agreement pursuant to which the bonds, notes, or debentures were issued. This section does not apply to bonds or other evidences of indebtedness of a public district or corporation.

Amended by Stats 2022 ch 452 (SB 1498),s 37, eff. 1/1/2023.
Amended by Stats 2020 ch 370 (SB 1371),s 33, eff. 1/1/2021.
Amended by Stats 2019 ch 143 (SB 251),s 18, eff. 1/1/2020.

Section 337 - Contract, obligation or liability founded upon written instrument; book account; rescission of contract

Within four years:

(a) An action upon any contract, obligation or liability founded upon an instrument in writing, except as provided in Section 336a; provided, that the time within which any action for a money judgment for the balance due upon an obligation for the payment of which a deed of trust or mortgage with power of sale upon real property or any interest therein was given as security, following the exercise of the power of sale in such deed of trust or mortgage, may be brought shall not extend beyond three months after the time of sale under such deed of trust or mortgage.

(b) An action to recover (1) upon a book account whether consisting of one or more entries; (2) upon an account stated based upon an account in writing, but the acknowledgment of the account stated need not be in writing; (3) a balance due upon a mutual, open and current account, the items of which are in writing; provided, however, that if an account stated is based upon an account of one item, the time shall begin to run from the date of the item, and if an account stated is based upon an account of more than one item, the time shall begin to run from the date of the last item.

(c) An action based upon the rescission of a contract in writing. The time begins to run from the date upon which the facts that entitle the aggrieved party to rescind occurred. Where the ground for rescission is fraud or mistake, the time shall not begin to run until the discovery by the aggrieved party of the facts constituting the fraud or mistake. Where the ground for rescission is misrepresentation under Section 359 of the Insurance Code, the time shall not begin to run until the representation becomes false.

(d) When the period in which an action must be commenced under this section has run, a person shall not bring suit or initiate an arbitration or other legal proceeding to collect the debt. The period in which an action may be commenced under this section shall only be extended pursuant to Section 360.

Amended by Stats 2018 ch 247 (AB 1526),s 2, eff. 1/1/2019.

Section 337a - Book account defined

The term "book account" means a detailed statement which constitutes the principal record of one or more transactions between a debtor and a creditor arising out of a contract or some fiduciary relation, and shows the debits and credits in connection therewith, and against whom and in favor of whom entries are made, is entered in the regular course of business as conducted by such creditor or fiduciary, and is kept in a reasonably permanent form and manner and is (1) in a bound book, or (2) on a sheet or sheets fastened in a book or to backing but detachable therefrom, or (3) on a card or cards of a permanent character, or is kept in any other reasonably permanent form and manner.

Added by Stats. 1959, Ch. 1010.

Section 337.1 - Recovery of damages against person performing design, specifications, surveying, planning, observation of construction

(a) Except as otherwise provided in this section, no action shall be brought to recover damages from any person performing or furnishing the design, specifications, surveying, planning, supervision or observation of construction or construction of an improvement to real property more than four years after the substantial completion of such improvement for any of the following:

(1) Any patent deficiency in the design, specifications, surveying, planning, supervision or observation of construction or construction of an improvement to, or survey of, real property;

(2) Injury to property, real or personal, arising out of any such patent deficiency; or

(3) Injury to the person or for wrongful death arising out of any such patent deficiency.

(b) If, by reason of such patent deficiency, an injury to property or the person or an injury causing wrongful death occurs during the fourth year after such substantial completion, an action in tort to recover damages for such an injury or wrongful death may be brought within one year after the date on which such injury occurred, irrespective of the date of death, but in no event may such an action be brought more than five years after the substantial completion of construction of such improvement.

(c) Nothing in this section shall be construed as extending the period prescribed by the laws of this state for the bringing of any action.

(d) The limitation prescribed by this section shall not be asserted by way of defense by any person in actual possession or the control, as owner, tenant or otherwise, of such an improvement at the time any deficiency in such an improvement constitutes the proximate cause of the injury or death for which it is proposed to bring an action.

(e) As used in this section, "patent deficiency" means a deficiency which is apparent by reasonable inspection.

(f) Subdivisions (a) and (b) shall not apply to any owner-occupied single-unit residence.

Added by Stats. 1967, Ch. 1326.

Section 337.15 - Recovery of damages from person developing real property or performing or furnishing design, specifications, surveying, supervision testing, observation of construction

(a) No action may be brought to recover damages from any person, or the surety of a person, who develops real property or performs or furnishes the design, specifications, surveying, planning, supervision, testing, or observation of construction or construction of an improvement to real property more than 10 years after the substantial completion of the development or improvement for any of the following:

(1) Any latent deficiency in the design, specification, surveying, planning, supervision, or observation of construction or construction of an improvement to, or survey of, real property.

(2) Injury to property, real or personal, arising out of any such latent deficiency.

(b) As used in this section, "latent deficiency" means a deficiency which is not apparent by reasonable inspection.

(c) As used in this section, "action" includes an action for indemnity brought against a person arising out of that person's performance or furnishing of services or materials referred to in this section, except that a cross-complaint for indemnity may be filed pursuant to subdivision (b) of Section 428.10 in an action which has been brought within the time period set forth in subdivision (a) of this section.

(d) Nothing in this section shall be construed as extending the period prescribed by the laws of this state for bringing any action.

(e) The limitation prescribed by this section shall not be asserted by way of defense by any person in actual possession or the control, as owner, tenant or otherwise, of such an improvement, at the time any deficiency in the improvement constitutes the proximate cause for which it is proposed to bring an action.

(f) This section shall not apply to actions based on willful misconduct or fraudulent concealment.

(g) The 10-year period specified in subdivision (a) shall commence upon substantial completion of the improvement, but not later than the date of one of the following, whichever first occurs:

(1) The date of final inspection by the applicable public agency.

(2) The date of recordation of a valid notice of completion.

(3) The date of use or occupation of the improvement.

(4) One year after termination or cessation of work on the improvement. The date of substantial completion shall relate specifically to the performance or furnishing design, specifications, surveying, planning, supervision, testing, observation of construction or construction services by each profession or trade rendering services to the improvement.
Amended by Stats. 1981, Ch. 88, Sec. 1.

Section 337.2 - Breach of lease and abandonment of real property or termination of lessee's right to possession
Where a lease of real property is in writing, no action shall be brought under Section 1951.2 of the Civil Code more than four years after the breach of the lease and abandonment of the property, or more than four years after the termination of the right of the lessee to possession of the property, whichever is the earlier time.
Added by Stats. 1970, Ch. 89.

Section 337.5 - General obligation bonds; judgment or decree
Within 10 years:

(a) An action upon any general obligation bonds or coupons, not secured in whole or in part by a lien on real property, issued by any county, city and county, municipal corporation, district (including school districts), or other political subdivision of the State of California.

(b) An action upon a judgment or decree of any court of the United States or of any state within the United States.
Amended by Stats 2010 ch 719 (SB 856),s 7, eff. 10/19/2010.

Section 337.6 - Bonds or coupons against which statute of limitations ran on or after August 27, 1937
Notwithstanding the provisions of Section 337.5 of this code actions may be brought on bonds or coupons as set forth in subsection 2 of said section, against which the statute of limitations ran on or after August 27, 1937; provided, such actions are brought on or before June 30, 1959. Upon presentation for payment they shall be registered and payment shall not be made thereon until the next fiscal year following presentation unless available funds are sufficient to first pay obligations which are due or will become due from the same fund during the fiscal year of presentation and during the next succeeding six months. Interest shall not be paid on bonds or coupons registered for the purpose of this section.
Amended by Stats. 1957, Ch. 719.

Section 338 - Liability created by statute; trespass or injury to real property; taking, detaining or injuring goods or chattels; fraud or mistake; bond of public official; notary's bond; slander of title; section 17536, Business and Professions Code; Water Quality Control Act; Section 19, Article 1, California Constitution; division 26, Health and Safety Code; sections 1603.1, 1615, 5650.1, Fish and Game Code; validity of special tax levy; violation of FPA or Forestry and Fire Protection rules and regulations
Within three years:

(a) An action upon a liability created by statute, other than a penalty or forfeiture.

(b) An action for trespass upon or injury to real property.

(c)

(1) An action for taking, detaining, or injuring goods or chattels, including an action for the specific recovery of personal property.

(2) The cause of action in the case of theft, as described in Section 484 of the Penal Code, of an article of historical, interpretive, scientific, or artistic significance is not deemed to have accrued until the discovery of the whereabouts of the article by the aggrieved party, the aggrieved party's agent, or the law enforcement agency that originally investigated the theft.

(3)

(A) Notwithstanding paragraphs (1) and (2), an action for the specific recovery of a work of fine art brought against a museum, gallery, auctioneer, or dealer, in the case of an unlawful taking or theft, as described in Section 484 of the Penal Code, of a work of fine art, including a taking or theft by means of fraud or duress, shall be commenced within six years of the actual discovery by the claimant or the claimant's agent, of both of the following:

(i) The identity and the whereabouts of the work of fine art. In the case where there is a possibility of misidentification of the object of fine art in question, the identity can be satisfied by the identification of facts sufficient to determine that the work of fine art is likely to be the work of fine art that was unlawfully taken or stolen.

(ii) Information or facts that are sufficient to indicate that the claimant has a claim for a possessory interest in the work of fine art that was unlawfully taken or stolen.

(B) This paragraph shall apply to all pending and future actions commenced on or before December 31, 2017, including an action dismissed based on the expiration of statutes of limitations in effect prior to the date of enactment of this statute if the judgment in that action is not yet final or if the time for filing an appeal from a decision on that action has not expired, provided that the action concerns a work of fine art that was taken within 100 years prior to the date of enactment of this statute.

(C) For purposes of this paragraph:

(i) "Actual discovery," notwithstanding Section 19 of the Civil Code, does not include constructive knowledge imputed by law.

(ii) "Auctioneer" means an individual who is engaged in, or who by advertising or otherwise holds the individual out as being available to engage in, the calling for, the recognition of, and the acceptance of, offers for the purchase of goods at an auction as defined in subdivision (b) of Section 1812.601 of the Civil Code.

(iii) "Dealer" means a person who holds a valid seller's permit and who is actively and principally engaged in, or conducting the business of, selling works of fine art.

(iv) "Duress" means a threat of force, violence, danger, or retribution against an owner of the work of fine art in question, or the owner's family member, sufficient to coerce a reasonable person of ordinary susceptibilities to perform an act that otherwise would not have been performed or to acquiesce to an act to which the person would otherwise not have acquiesced.

(v) "Fine art" has the same meaning as defined in paragraph (1) of subdivision (d) of Section 982 of the Civil Code.

(vi) "Museum or gallery" shall include any public or private organization or foundation operating as a museum or gallery.

(4) Section 361 shall not apply to an action brought pursuant to paragraph (3).

(5) A party in an action to which paragraph (3) applies may raise all equitable and legal affirmative defenses and doctrines, including, without limitation, laches and unclean hands.

(d) An action for relief on the ground of fraud or mistake. The cause of action in that case is not deemed to have accrued until the discovery, by the aggrieved party, of the facts constituting the fraud or mistake.

(e) An action upon a bond of a public official except any cause of action based on fraud or embezzlement is not deemed to have accrued until the discovery, by the aggrieved party or the aggrieved party's agent, of the facts constituting the cause of action upon the bond.

(f)

(1) An action against a notary public on the notary public's bond or in the notary public's official capacity except that a cause of action based on malfeasance or misfeasance is not deemed to have accrued until discovery, by the aggrieved party or the aggrieved party's agent, of the facts constituting the cause of action.

(2) Notwithstanding paragraph (1), an action based on malfeasance or misfeasance shall be commenced within one year from discovery, by the aggrieved party or the aggrieved party's agent, of the facts constituting the cause of action or within three years from the performance of the notarial act giving rise to the action, whichever is later.

(3) Notwithstanding paragraph (1), an action against a notary public on the notary public's bond or in the notary public's official capacity shall be commenced within six years.

(g) An action for slander of title to real property.

(h) An action commenced under Section 17536 of the Business and Professions Code. The cause of action in that case shall not be deemed to have accrued until the discovery by the aggrieved party, the Attorney General, the district attorney, the county counsel, the city prosecutor, or the city attorney of the facts constituting grounds for commencing the action.

(i) An action commenced under the Porter-Cologne Water Quality Control Act (Division 7 (commencing with Section 13000) of the Water Code). The cause of action in that case shall not be deemed to have accrued until the discovery by the State Water Resources Control Board or a regional water quality control board of the facts constituting grounds for commencing actions under their jurisdiction.

(j) An action to recover for physical damage to private property under Section 19 of Article I of the California Constitution.

(k) An action commenced under Division 26 (commencing with Section 39000) of the Health and Safety Code. These causes of action shall not be deemed to have accrued until the discovery by the State Air Resources Board or by a district, as defined in Section 39025 of the Health and Safety Code, of the facts constituting grounds for commencing the action under its jurisdiction.

(l) An action commenced under Section 1602, 1615, or 5650.1 of the Fish and Game Code. These causes of action shall not be deemed to have accrued until discovery by the agency bringing the action of the facts constituting the grounds for commencing the action.

(m) An action challenging the validity of the levy upon a parcel of a special tax levied by a local agency on a per parcel basis.

(n) An action commencing under Section 51.7 of the Civil Code.

(o) An action commenced under Section 4601.1 of the Public Resources Code, if the underlying violation is of Section 4571, 4581, or 4621 of the Public Resources Code, or of Section 1103.1 of Title 14 of the California Code of Regulations, and the underlying violation is related to the conversion of timberland to nonforestry-related agricultural uses. These causes of action shall not be deemed to have accrued until discovery by the Department of Forestry and Fire Protection.

(p) An action for civil penalties commenced under Section 26038 of the Business and Professions Code.

Amended by Stats 2021 ch 264 (AB 287),s 1, eff. 1/1/2022.
Amended by Stats 2018 ch 796 (SB 1453),s 1, eff. 1/1/2019.
Amended by Stats 2015 ch 683 (SB 798),s 1, eff. 1/1/2016.
Amended by Stats 2010 ch 691 (AB 2765),s 2, eff. 1/1/2011.
Amended by Stats 2006 ch 538 (SB 1852),s 62, eff. 1/1/2007.
Amended by Stats 2005 ch 383 (SB 1110),s 1.5, eff. 1/1/2006
Amended by Stats 2005 ch 123 (AB 378),s 2, eff. 7/19/2005, op. 1/1/2006

Section 338.1 - [Operative Until 1/1/2024] Civil penalties or punitive damages authorized under Division 20, Health and Safety Code
An action for civil penalties or punitive damages authorized under Chapter 6.5 (commencing with Section 25100), Chapter 6.67 (commencing with Section 25270), Chapter 6.7 (commencing with Section 25280), Chapter 6.8 (commencing with Section 25300), or Chapter 6.95 (commencing with Section 25500) of Division 20 of the Health and Safety Code shall be commenced within five years after the discovery by the agency bringing the action of the facts constituting the grounds for commencing the action.

Amended by Stats 2018 ch 141 (AB 1980),s 1, eff. 1/1/2019.
Amended by Stats 2009 ch 429 (AB 305),s 1, eff. 1/1/2010.
This section is set out more than once due to postponed, multiple, or conflicting amendments.

Section 338.1 - [Operative 1/1/2024] Civil penalties or punitive damages authorized under Division 20, Health and Safety Code
An action for civil penalties or punitive damages authorized under Chapter 6.5 (commencing with Section 25100), Chapter 6.67 (commencing with Section 25270), Chapter 6.7 (commencing with Section 25280), or Chapter 6.95 (commencing with Section 25500) of Division 20 of, or Part 2 (commencing with Section 78000) of Division 45 of, the Health and Safety Code shall be commenced within five years after the discovery by the agency bringing the action of the facts constituting the grounds for commencing the action.

Amended by Stats 2022 ch 258 (AB 2327),s 7, eff. 1/1/2023, op. 1/1/2024.
Amended by Stats 2018 ch 141 (AB 1980),s 1, eff. 1/1/2019.
Amended by Stats 2009 ch 429 (AB 305),s 1, eff. 1/1/2010.
This section is set out more than once due to postponed, multiple, or conflicting amendments.

Section 339 - Contract, obligation not founded on written instrument; against sheriff or coroner for doing official act; rescission of contract not in writing

Within two years:

1. An action upon a contract, obligation or liability not founded upon an instrument of writing, except as provided in Section 2725 of the Commercial Code or subdivision 2 of Section 337 of this code; or an action founded upon a contract, obligation or liability, evidenced by a certificate, or abstract or guaranty of title of real property, or by a policy of title insurance; provided, that the cause of action upon a contract, obligation or liability evidenced by a certificate, or abstract or guaranty of title of real property or policy of title insurance shall not be deemed to have accrued until the discovery of the loss or damage suffered by the aggrieved party thereunder.

2. An action against a sheriff or coroner upon a liability incurred by the doing of an act in an official capacity and in virtue of office, or by the omission of an official duty including the nonpayment of money collected in the enforcement of a judgment.

3. An action based upon the rescission of a contract not in writing. The time begins to run from the date upon which the facts that entitle the aggrieved party to rescind occurred. Where the ground for rescission is fraud or mistake, the time does not begin to run until the discovery by the aggrieved party of the facts constituting the fraud or mistake.

Amended by Stats. 1996, Ch. 872, Sec. 11. Effective January 1, 1997.

Section 339.5 - Breach of lease of real property not in writing and abandonment of property or termination of lessee's right to possession
Where a lease of real property is not in writing, no action shall be brought under Section 1951.2 of the Civil Code more than two years after the breach of the lease and abandonment of the property, or more than two years after the termination of the right of the lessee to possession of the property, whichever is the earlier time.

Added by Stats. 1970, Ch. 89.

Section 340 - Penalty or forfeiture; libel, slander, false imprisonment, seduction, payment on forged check, neglect of animal; officer seizing property; good faith improver

Within one year:

(a) An action upon a statute for a penalty or forfeiture, if the action is given to an individual, or to an individual and the state, except if the statute imposing it prescribes a different limitation.

(b) An action upon a statute for a forfeiture or penalty to the people of this state.

(c) An action for libel, slander, false imprisonment, seduction of a person below the age of legal consent, or by a depositor against a bank for the payment of a forged or raised check, or a check that bears a forged or unauthorized endorsement, or against any person who boards or feeds an animal or fowl or who engages in the practice of veterinary medicine as defined in Section 4826 of the Business and Professions Code, for that person's neglect resulting in injury or death to an animal or fowl in the course of boarding or feeding the animal or fowl or in the course of the practice of veterinary medicine on that animal or fowl.

(d) An action against an officer to recover damages for the seizure of any property for a statutory forfeiture to the state, or for the detention of, or injury to property so seized, or for damages done to any person in making that seizure.

(e) An action by a good faith improver for relief under Chapter 10 (commencing with Section 871.1) of Title 10 of Part 2. The time begins to run from the date upon which the good faith improver discovers that the good faith improver is not the owner of the land upon which the improvements have been made.

Amended by Stats 2002 ch 448 (SB 688),s 3, eff. 1/1/2003.

Section 340.1 - Childhood sexual abuse

(a)In an action for recovery of damages suffered as a result of childhood sexual assault, the time for commencement of the action shall be within 22 years of the date the plaintiff attains the age of majority or within five years of the date the plaintiff discovers or reasonably should have discovered that psychological injury or illness occurring after the age of majority was caused by the sexual assault, whichever period expires later, for any of the following actions:

(1)An action against any person for committing an act of childhood sexual assault.

(2)An action for liability against any person or entity who owed a duty of care to the plaintiff, if a wrongful or negligent act by that person or entity was a legal cause of the childhood sexual assault that resulted in the injury to the plaintiff.

(3)An action for liability against any person or entity if an intentional act by that person or entity was a legal cause of the childhood sexual assault that resulted in the injury to the plaintiff.

(b)

(1)In an action described in subdivision (a), a person who is sexually assaulted and proves it was as the result of a cover up may recover up to treble damages against a defendant who is found to have covered up the sexual assault of a minor, unless prohibited by another law.

(2)For purposes of this subdivision, a "cover up" is a concerted effort to hide evidence relating to childhood sexual assault.

(c)An action described in paragraph (2) or (3) of subdivision (a) shall not be commenced on or after the plaintiff's 40th birthday unless the person or entity knew or had reason to know, or was otherwise on notice, of any misconduct that creates a risk of childhood sexual assault by an employee, volunteer, representative, or agent, or the person or entity failed to take reasonable steps or to implement reasonable safeguards to avoid acts of childhood sexual assault. For purposes of this subdivision, providing or requiring counseling is not sufficient, in and of itself, to constitute a reasonable step or reasonable safeguard. Nothing in this subdivision shall be construed to constitute a substantive change in negligence law.

(d)"Childhood sexual assault" as used in this section includes any act committed against the plaintiff that occurred when the plaintiff was under the age of 18 years and that would have been proscribed by Section 266j of the Penal Code; Section 285 of the Penal Code; paragraph (1) or (2) of subdivision (b), or of subdivision (c), of Section 286 of the Penal Code; subdivision (a) or (b) of Section 288 of the Penal Code; paragraph (1) or (2) of subdivision (b), or of subdivision (c), of Section 287 or of former Section 288a of the Penal Code; subdivision (h), (i), or (j) of Section 289 of the Penal Code; any sexual conduct as defined in paragraph (1) of subdivision (d) of Section 311.4 of the Penal Code; Section 647.6 of the Penal Code; or any prior laws of this state of similar effect at the time the act was committed. This subdivision does not limit the availability of causes of action permitted under subdivision (a), including causes of action against persons or entities other than the alleged perpetrator of the abuse.

(e)This section shall not be construed to alter the otherwise applicable burden of proof, as defined in Section 115 of the Evidence Code, that a plaintiff has in a civil action subject to this section.

(f)Every plaintiff 40 years of age or older at the time the action is filed shall file certificates of merit as specified in subdivision (g).

(g)Certificates of merit shall be executed by the attorney for the plaintiff and by a licensed mental health practitioner selected by the plaintiff declaring, respectively, as follows, setting forth the facts which support the declaration:

(1)That the attorney has reviewed the facts of the case, consulted with at least one mental health practitioner who the attorney reasonably believes is knowledgeable of the relevant facts and issues involved in the particular action, and concluded on the basis of that review and consultation that there is reasonable and meritorious cause for the filing of the action.

(2)That the mental health practitioner consulted is licensed to practice and practices in this state and is not a party to the action, that the practitioner is not treating and has not treated the plaintiff, and that the practitioner has interviewed the plaintiff and is knowledgeable of the relevant facts and issues involved in the particular action, and has concluded, on the basis of the practitioner's knowledge of the facts and issues, that in the practitioner's professional opinion there is a reasonable basis to believe that the plaintiff had been subject to childhood sexual abuse.

(3)That the attorney was unable to obtain the consultation required by paragraph (1) because a statute of limitations would impair the action and that the certificates required by paragraphs (1) and (2) could not be obtained before the impairment of the action. If a certificate is executed pursuant to this paragraph, the certificates required by paragraphs (1) and (2) shall be filed within 60 days after filing the complaint.

(h)If certificates are required pursuant to subdivision (f), the attorney for the plaintiff shall execute a separate certificate of merit for each defendant named in the complaint.

(i)In any action subject to subdivision (f), a defendant shall not be served, and the duty to serve a defendant with process does not attach, until the court has reviewed the certificates of merit filed pursuant to subdivision (g) with respect to that defendant, and has found, in camera, based solely on those certificates of merit, that there is reasonable and meritorious cause for the filing of the action against that defendant. At that time, the duty to serve that defendant with process shall attach.

(j)A violation of this section may constitute unprofessional conduct and may be the grounds for discipline against the attorney.

(k)The failure to file certificates in accordance with this section shall be grounds for a demurrer pursuant to Section 430.10 or a motion to strike pursuant to Section 435.

(l)In any action subject to subdivision (f), a defendant shall be named by "Doe" designation in any pleadings or papers filed in the action until there has been a showing of corroborative fact as to the charging allegations against that defendant.

(m)At any time after the action is filed, the plaintiff may apply to the court for permission to amend the complaint to substitute the name of the defendant or defendants for the fictitious designation, as follows:

(1)The application shall be accompanied by a certificate of corroborative fact executed by the attorney for the plaintiff. The certificate shall declare that the attorney has discovered one or more facts corroborative of one or more of the charging allegations against a defendant or defendants, and shall set forth in clear and concise terms the nature and substance of the corroborative fact. If the corroborative fact is evidenced by the statement of a witness or the contents of a document, the certificate shall declare that the attorney has personal knowledge of the statement of the witness or of the contents of the document, and the identity and location of the witness or document shall be included in the certificate. For purposes of this section, a fact is corroborative of an allegation if it confirms or supports the allegation. The opinion of any mental health practitioner concerning the plaintiff shall not constitute a corroborative fact for purposes of this section.

(2)If the application to name a defendant is made before that defendant's appearance in the action, neither the application nor the certificate of corroborative fact by the attorney shall be served on the defendant or defendants, nor on any other party or their counsel of record.

(3)If the application to name a defendant is made after that defendant's appearance in the action, the application shall be served on all parties and proof of service provided to the court, but the certificate of corroborative fact by the attorney shall not be served on any party or their counsel of record.

(n)The court shall review the application and the certificate of corroborative fact in camera and, based solely on the certificate and any reasonable inferences to be drawn from the certificate, shall, if one or more facts corroborative of one or more of the charging allegations against a defendant has been shown, order that the complaint may be amended to substitute the name of the defendant or defendants.

(o)The court shall keep under seal and confidential from the public and all parties to the litigation, other than the plaintiff, any and all certificates of corroborative fact filed pursuant to subdivision (m).

(p)Upon the favorable conclusion of the litigation with respect to any defendant for whom a certificate of merit was filed or for whom a certificate of merit should have been filed pursuant to this section, the court may, upon the motion of a party or upon the court's own motion, verify compliance with this section by requiring the attorney for the plaintiff who was required by subdivision (g) to execute the certificate to reveal the name, address, and telephone number of the person or persons consulted with pursuant to subdivision (g) that were relied upon by the attorney in preparation of the certificate of merit. The name, address, and telephone number shall be disclosed to the trial judge in camera and in the absence of the moving party. If the court finds there has been a failure to comply with this section, the court may order a party, a party's attorney, or both, to pay any reasonable expenses, including attorney's fees, incurred by the defendant for whom a certificate of merit should have been filed.

(q)Notwithstanding any other law, a claim for damages described in paragraphs (1) through (3), inclusive, of subdivision (a) that has not been litigated to finality and that would otherwise be barred as of January 1, 2020, because the applicable statute of limitations, claim presentation deadline, or any other time limit had expired, is revived, and these claims may be commenced within three years of January 1, 2020. A plaintiff shall have the later of the three-year time period under this subdivision or the time period under subdivision (a) as amended by the act that added this subdivision.

(r)The changes made to the time period under subdivision (a) as amended by the act that amended this subdivision in 2019 apply to and revive any action commenced on or after the date of enactment of that act, and to any action filed before the date of enactment, and still pending on that date, including any action or causes of action that would have been barred by the laws in effect before the date of enactment.

(s)Notwithstanding any other law, including Chapter 1 of Part 3 of Division 3.6 of Title 1 of the Government Code (commencing with Section 900) and Chapter 2 of Part 3 of Division 3.6 of Title 1 of the Government Code (commencing with Section 910), a claim for damages described in paragraphs (1) through (3), inclusive, of subdivision (a), is not required to be presented to any government entity prior to the commencement of an action.

Amended by Stats 2022 ch 444 (AB 2959),s 1, eff. 1/1/2023.
Amended by Stats 2019 ch 861 (AB 218),s 1, eff. 1/1/2020.
Amended by Stats 2018 ch 423 (SB 1494),s 8, eff. 1/1/2019.
Amended by Stats 2002 ch 149 (SB 1779),s 1, eff. 1/1/2003.
Previously Amended July 14, 1999 (Bill Number: SB 674) (Chapter 120).

Section 340.15 - Domestic violence

(a) In any civil action for recovery of damages suffered as a result of domestic violence, the time for commencement of the action shall be the later of the following:

(1) Within three years from the date of the last act of domestic violence by the defendant against the plaintiff.

(2) Within three years from the date the plaintiff discovers or reasonably should have discovered that an injury or illness resulted from an act of domestic violence by the defendant against the plaintiff.

(b) As used in this section, "domestic violence" has the same meaning as defined in Section 6211 of the Family Code.

Amended by Stats. 1998, Ch. 123, Sec. 1. Effective January 1, 1999.

Section 340.16 - Sexual assault after plaintiff's 18th birthday

(a)In any civil action for recovery of damages suffered as a result of sexual assault, where the assault occurred on or after the plaintiff's 18th birthday, the time for commencement of the action shall be the later of the following:

(1)Within 10 years from the date of the last act, attempted act, or assault with the intent to commit an act, of sexual assault against the plaintiff.

(2)Within three years from the date the plaintiff discovers or reasonably should have discovered that an injury or illness resulted from an act, attempted act, or assault with the intent to commit an act, of sexual assault against the plaintiff.

(b)

(1)As used in this section, "sexual assault" means any of the crimes described in Section 243.4, 261, 264.1, 286, 287, or 289, or former Sections 262 and 288a, of the Penal Code, assault with the intent to commit any of those crimes, or an attempt to commit any of those crimes.

(2)For the purpose of this section, it is not necessary that a criminal prosecution or other proceeding have been brought as a result of the sexual assault or, if a criminal prosecution or other proceeding was brought, that the prosecution or proceeding resulted in a conviction or adjudication. This subdivision does not limit the availability of causes of action permitted under subdivision (a), including causes of action against persons or entities other than the alleged person who committed the crime.

(3)This section applies to any action described in subdivision (a) that is based upon conduct that occurred on or after January 1, 2009, and is commenced on or after January 1, 2019, that would have been barred solely because the applicable statute of limitations has or had expired. Such claims are hereby revived and may be commenced until December 31, 2026. This subdivision does not revive any of the following claims:

(A)A claim that has been litigated to finality in a court of competent jurisdiction before January 1, 2023.

(B)A claim that has been compromised by a written settlement agreement between the parties entered into before January 1, 2023.

(c)

(1)Notwithstanding any other law, any claim seeking to recover more than two hundred fifty thousand dollars ($250,000) in damages arising out of a sexual assault or other inappropriate contact, communication, or activity of a sexual nature by a physician occurring at a student health center between January 1, 1988, and January 1, 2017, that would otherwise be barred before January 1, 2020, solely because the applicable statute of limitations has or had expired, is hereby revived and, a cause of action may proceed if already pending in court on October 2, 2019, or, if not filed by that date, may be commenced between January 1, 2020, and December 31, 2020.

(2)This subdivision does not revive any of the following claims:

(A)A claim that has been litigated to finality in a court of competent jurisdiction before January 1, 2020.

(B)A claim that has been compromised by a written settlement agreement between the parties entered into before January 1, 2020.

(C)A claim brought against a public entity.

(3)An attorney representing a claimant seeking to recover under this subdivision shall file a declaration with the court under penalty of perjury stating that the attorney has reviewed the facts of the case and consulted with a mental health practitioner, and that the attorney has concluded on the basis of this review and consultation that it is the attorney's good faith belief that the claim value is more than two hundred fifty thousand dollars ($250,000). The declaration shall be filed upon filing the complaint, or for those claims already pending, by December 1, 2019.

(d)

(1) Notwithstanding any other law, any claim seeking to recover damages arising out of a sexual assault or other inappropriate contact, communication, or activity of a sexual nature by a physician while employed by a medical clinic owned and operated by the University of California, Los Angeles, or a physician who held active privileges at a hospital owned and operated by the University of California, Los Angeles, at the time that the sexual assault or other inappropriate contact, communication, or activity of a sexual nature occurred, between January 1, 1983, and January 1, 2019, that would otherwise be barred before January 1, 2021, solely because the applicable statute of limitations has or had expired, is hereby revived, and a cause of action may proceed if already pending in court on January 1, 2021, or, if not filed by that date, may be commenced between January 1, 2021, and December 31, 2021.

(2) This subdivision does not revive either of the following claims:

(A) A claim that has been litigated to finality in a court of competent jurisdiction before January 1, 2021.

(B) A claim that has been compromised by a written settlement agreement between the parties entered into before January 1, 2021.

(e)

(1) Notwithstanding any other law, any claim seeking to recover damages suffered as a result of a sexual assault that occurred on or after the plaintiff's 18th birthday that would otherwise be barred before January 1, 2023, solely because the applicable statute of limitations has or had expired, is hereby revived, and a cause of action may proceed if already pending in court on January 1, 2023, or, if not filed by that date, may be commenced between January 1, 2023, and December 31, 2023.

(2) This subdivision revives claims brought by a plaintiff who alleges all of the following:

(A) The plaintiff was sexually assaulted.

(B) One or more entities are legally responsible for damages arising out of the sexual assault.

(C) The entity or entities, including, but not limited to, their officers, directors, representatives, employees, or agents, engaged in a cover up or attempted a cover up of a previous instance or allegations of sexual assault by an alleged perpetrator of such abuse.

(3) Failure to allege a cover up as required by subparagraph (C) of paragraph (2) as to one entity does not affect revival of the plaintiff's claim or claims against any other entity.

(4) For purposes of this subdivision:

(A) "Cover up" means a concerted effort to hide evidence relating to a sexual assault that incentivizes individuals to remain silent or prevents information relating to a sexual assault from becoming public or being disclosed to the plaintiff, including, but not limited to, the use of nondisclosure agreements or confidentiality agreements.

(B) "Entity" means a sole proprietorship, partnership, limited liability company, corporation, association, or other legal entity.

(C) "Legally responsible" means that the entity or entities are liable under any theory of liability established by statute or common law, including, but not limited to, negligence, intentional torts, and vicarious liability.

(5) This subdivision revives any related claims, including, but not limited to, wrongful termination and sexual harassment, arising out of the sexual assault that is the basis for a claim pursuant to this subdivision.

(6) This subdivision does not revive either of the following claims:

(A) A claim that has been litigated to finality in a court of competent jurisdiction before January 1, 2023.

(B) A claim that has been compromised by a written settlement agreement between the parties entered into before January 1, 2023.

(7) This subdivision shall not be construed to alter the otherwise applicable burden of proof, as defined in Section 115 of the Evidence Code, that a plaintiff has in a civil action subject to this section.

(8) Nothing in this subdivision precludes a plaintiff from bringing an action for sexual assault pursuant to subdivisions (a) and (b).

Amended by Stats 2022 ch 442 (AB 2777), s 3, eff. 1/1/2023.
Amended by Stats 2020 ch 246 (AB 3092), s 1, eff. 1/1/2021.
Amended by Stats 2019 ch 462 (AB 1510), s 1, eff. 10/2/2019.
Added by Stats 2018 ch 939 (AB 1619), s 1, eff. 1/1/2019.

Stats 2022 ch 442 (AB 2777) shall be known and may be cited as the Sexual Abuse and Cover Up Accountability Act.

Section 340.2 - Exposure to asbestos

(a) In any civil action for injury or illness based upon exposure to asbestos, the time for the commencement of the action shall be the later of the following:

(1) Within one year after the date the plaintiff first suffered disability.

(2) Within one year after the date the plaintiff either knew, or through the exercise of reasonable diligence should have known, that such disability was caused or contributed to by such exposure.

(b) "Disability" as used in subdivision (a) means the loss of time from work as a result of such exposure which precludes the performance of the employee's regular occupation.

(c) In an action for the wrongful death of any plaintiff's decedent, based upon exposure to asbestos, the time for commencement of an action shall be the later of the following:

(1) Within one year from the date of the death of the plaintiff's decedent.

(2) Within one year from the date the plaintiff first knew, or through the exercise of reasonable diligence should have known, that the death was caused or contributed to by such exposure.

Added by Stats. 1979, Ch. 513.

Section 340.3 - Damages based on defendant's commission of felony offense

(a) Unless a longer period is prescribed for a specific action, in any action for damages against a defendant based upon the defendant's commission of a felony offense for which the defendant has been convicted, the time for commencement of the action shall be within one year after judgment is pronounced.

(b)

(1) Notwithstanding subdivision (a), an action for damages against a defendant based upon the defendant's commission of a felony offense for which the defendant has been convicted may be commenced within 10 years of the date on which the defendant is discharged from parole if the conviction was for any offense specified in paragraph (1), except voluntary manslaughter, (2), (3), (4), (5), (6), (7), (9), (16), (17), (20), (22), (25), (34), or (35) of subdivision (c) of Section 1192.7 of the Penal Code.

(2) No civil action may be commenced pursuant to paragraph (1) if any of the following applies:

(A) The defendant has received either a certificate of rehabilitation as provided in Chapter 3.5 (commencing with Section 4852.01) of Title 6 of Part 3 of the Penal Code or a pardon as provided in Chapter 1 (commencing with Section 4800) or Chapter 3 (commencing with Section 4850) of Title 6 of Part 3 of the Penal Code.

(B) Following a conviction for murder or attempted murder, the defendant has been paroled based in whole or in part upon evidence presented to the Board of Prison Terms that the defendant committed the crime because he or she was the victim of intimate partner battering.

(C) The defendant was convicted of murder or attempted murder in the second degree in a trial at which substantial evidence was presented that the person committed the crime because he or she was a victim of intimate partner battering.

(D) The defendant was unlawfully imprisoned or restrained but has been released from prison after successfully prosecuting a writ of habeas corpus pursuant to Chapter 1 (commencing with Section 1473) of Title 12 of Part 2 of the Penal Code.

(c) If the sentence or judgment is stayed, the time for the commencement of the action shall be tolled until the stay is lifted. For purposes of this section, a judgment is not stayed if the judgment is appealed or the defendant is placed on probation.

(d)

(1) Subdivision (b) shall apply to any action commenced before, on, or after the effective date of this section, including any action otherwise barred by a limitation of time in effect prior to the effective date of this section, thereby reviving those causes of action that had lapsed or expired under the law in effect prior to the effective date of this section.

(2) Paragraph (1) does not apply to either of the following:

(A) Any claim that has been litigated to finality on the merits in any court of competent jurisdiction prior to January 1, 2003. For purposes of this section, termination of a prior action on the basis of the statute of limitations does not constitute a claim that has been litigated to finality on the merits.

(B) Any written, compromised settlement agreement that has been entered into between a plaintiff and a defendant if the plaintiff was represented by an attorney who was admitted to practice law in this state at the time of the settlement, and the plaintiff signed the agreement.

(e) Any restitution paid by the defendant to the victim shall be credited against any judgment, award, or settlement obtained pursuant to this section. Any judgment, award, or settlement obtained pursuant to an action under this section shall be subject to the provisions of Section 13963 of the Government Code.

Amended by Stats 2015 ch 465 (AB 538),s 1, eff. 1/1/2016.
Amended by Stats 2005 ch 215 (AB 220),s 1, eff. 1/1/2006
Amended by Stats 2002 ch 633 (SB 1887),s 1, eff. 9/17/2002.

Section 340.35 - Childhood sexual abuse and action commenced before January 1, 2006

(a) This section shall apply if both of the following conditions are met:

(1) A complaint, information, or indictment was filed in a criminal case initiated pursuant to subdivision (f), (g), or (h) of Section 803 of the Penal Code.

(2) The case was dismissed or overturned pursuant to the United States Supreme Court's decision in Stogner v. California (2003) 156 L.Ed.2d 544.

(b) Unless a longer period is prescribed for a specific action, any action for damages against an individual for committing an act of childhood sexual abuse shall be commenced before January 1, 2006.

(c) This section shall apply to any action commenced before, on, or after the effective date of this section, including any action otherwise barred by a limitation of time in effect prior to the effective date of this section, thereby reviving those causes of action that had lapsed or expired under the law in effect prior to the effective date of this section.

(d) This section shall not apply to any of the following:

(1) Any claim against a person or entity other than the individual against whom a complaint, information, or indictment was filed as described in paragraph (1) of subdivision (a).

(2) Any claim that has been litigated to finality on the merits in any court of competent jurisdiction prior to the effective date of this section. For purposes of this section, termination of a prior action on the basis of the statute of limitations does not constitute a claim that has been "litigated to finality on the merits."

(3) Any written, compromised settlement agreement that has been entered into between a plaintiff and a defendant, if the plaintiff was represented by an attorney who was admitted to practice law in this state at the time of the settlement, and the plaintiff signed the agreement.

(e) Any restitution paid by the defendant to the victim shall be credited against any judgment, award, or settlement obtained pursuant to this section. Any judgment, award, or settlement obtained pursuant to an action under this section shall be subject to Section 13966.01 of the Government Code.

Added by Stats 2004 ch 741 (SB 1678),s 1, eff. 1/1/2005.

Section 340.4 - Injuries suffered by minor before or in course of birth

An action by or on behalf of a minor for personal injuries sustained before or in the course of his or her birth must be commenced within six years after the date of birth, and the time the minor is under any disability mentioned in Section 352 shall not be excluded in computing the time limited for the commencement of the action.

Added by Stats. 1992, Ch. 163, Sec. 16. Effective January 1, 1993. Operative January 1, 1994, by Sec. 161 of Ch. 163.

Section 340.5 - Health care provider's professional negligence

In an action for injury or death against a health care provider based upon such person's alleged professional negligence, the time for the commencement of action shall be three years after the date of injury or one year after the plaintiff discovers, or through the use of reasonable diligence should have discovered, the injury, whichever occurs first. In no event shall the time for commencement of legal action exceed three years unless tolled for any of the following:

(1) upon proof of fraud,

(2) intentional concealment, or

(3) the presence of a foreign body, which has no therapeutic or diagnostic purpose or effect, in the person of the injured person. Actions by a minor shall be commenced within three years from the date of the alleged wrongful act except that actions by a minor under the full age of six years shall be commenced within three years or prior to his eighth birthday whichever provides a longer period. Such time limitation shall be tolled for minors for any period during which parent or guardian and defendant's insurer or health care provider have committed fraud or collusion in the failure to bring an action on behalf of the injured minor for professional negligence.

For the purposes of this section:

(1) "Health care provider" means any person licensed or certified pursuant to Division 2 (commencing with Section 500) of the Business and Professions Code, or licensed pursuant to the Osteopathic Initiative Act, or the Chiropractic Initiative Act, or licensed pursuant to Chapter 2.5 (commencing with Section 1440) of Division 2 of the Health and Safety Code; and any clinic, health dispensary, or health facility, licensed pursuant to Division 2 (commencing with Section 1200) of the Health and Safety Code. "Health care provider" includes the legal representatives of a health care provider;

(2) "Professional negligence" means a negligent act or omission to act by a health care provider in the rendering of professional services, which act or omission is the proximate cause of a personal injury or wrongful death, provided that such services are within the scope of services for which the provider is licensed and which are not within any restriction imposed by the licensing agency or licensed hospital.

Amended by Stats. 1975, 2nd Ex. Sess., Ch. 2.

Section 340.6 - Attorney's wrongful act or omission in performance of professional services

(a) An action against an attorney for a wrongful act or omission, other than for actual fraud, arising in the performance of professional services shall be commenced within one year after the plaintiff discovers, or through the use of reasonable diligence should have discovered, the facts constituting the wrongful act or omission, or four years from the date of the wrongful act or omission, whichever occurs first. If the plaintiff is required to establish the plaintiff's factual innocence for an underlying criminal charge as an element of the plaintiff's claim, the action shall be commenced within two years after the plaintiff achieves postconviction exoneration in the form of a final judicial disposition of the criminal case.

Except for a claim for which the plaintiff is required to establish the plaintiff's factual innocence, the time for commencement of legal action shall not exceed four years except that the period shall be tolled during the time that any of the following exist:

(1) The plaintiff has not sustained actual injury.

(2) The attorney continues to represent the plaintiff regarding the specific subject matter in which the alleged wrongful act or omission occurred.

(3) The attorney willfully conceals the facts constituting the wrongful act or omission when those facts are known to the attorney, except that this subdivision shall toll only the four-year limitation.

(4) The plaintiff is under a legal or physical disability that restricts the plaintiff's ability to commence legal action.

(5) A dispute between the lawyer and client concerning fees, costs, or both is pending resolution under Article 13 (commencing with Section 6200) of Chapter 4 of Division 3 of the Business and Professions Code. As used in this paragraph, "pending" means from the date a request for arbitration is filed until 30 days after receipt of notice of the award of the arbitrators, or receipt of notice that the arbitration is otherwise terminated, whichever occurs first.

(b) In an action based upon an instrument in writing, the effective date of which depends upon some act or event of the future, the period of limitations provided for by this section shall commence to run upon the occurrence of that act or event.

Amended by Stats 2019 ch 13 (AB 692),s 2, eff. 1/1/2020.

Amended by Stats 2009 ch 432 (AB 316),s 2, eff. 1/1/2010.

Section 340.7 - Dalkon Shield victims

(a) Notwithstanding Section 335.1, a civil action brought by, or on behalf of, a Dalkon Shield victim against the Dalkon Shield Claimants' Trust, shall be brought in accordance with the procedures established by A.H. Robins Company, Inc. Plan of Reorganization, and shall be brought within 15 years of the date on which the victim's injury occurred, except that the statute shall be tolled from August 21, 1985, the date on which the A.H. Robins Company filed for Chapter 11 Reorganization in Richmond, Virginia.

(b) This section applies regardless of when the action or claim shall have accrued or been filed and regardless of whether it might have lapsed or otherwise be barred by time under California law. However, this section shall only apply to victims who, prior to January 1, 1990, filed a civil action, a timely claim, or a claim that is declared to be timely under the sixth Amended and Restated Disclosure Statement filed pursuant to Section 1125 of the Federal Bankruptcy Code in re: A.H. Robins Company, Inc., dated March 28, 1988, U.S. Bankruptcy Court, Eastern District of Virginia (case number 85-01307-R).

Amended by Stats 2008 ch 179 (SB 1498),s 34, eff. 1/1/2009.

Amended by Stats 2007 ch 130 (AB 299),s 35, eff. 1/1/2008.

Section 340.8 - Exposure to hazardous material or toxic substance

(a) In any civil action for injury or illness based upon exposure to a hazardous material or toxic substance, the time for commencement of the action shall be no later than either two years from the date of injury, or two years after the plaintiff becomes aware of, or reasonably should have become aware of, (1) an injury, (2) the physical cause of the injury, and (3) sufficient facts to put a reasonable person on inquiry notice that the injury was caused or contributed to by the wrongful act of another, whichever occurs later.

(b) In an action for the wrongful death of any plaintiff's decedent, based upon exposure to a hazardous material or toxic substance, the time for commencement of an action shall be no later than either (1) two years from the date of the death of the plaintiff's decedent, or (2) two years from the first date on which the plaintiff is aware of, or reasonably should have become aware of, the physical cause of the death and sufficient facts to put a reasonable person on inquiry notice that the death was caused or contributed to by the wrongful act of another, whichever occurs later.

(c) For purposes of this section:

(1) A "civil action for injury or illness based upon exposure to a hazardous material or toxic substance" does not include an action subject to Section 340.2 or 340.5.

(2) Media reports regarding the hazardous material or toxic substance contamination do not, in and of themselves, constitute sufficient facts to put a reasonable person on inquiry notice that the injury or death was caused or contributed to by the wrongful act of another.

(d) Nothing in this section shall be construed to limit, abrogate, or change the law in effect on the effective date of this section with respect to actions not based upon exposure to a hazardous material or toxic substance.

Added by Stats 2003 ch 873 (SB 331),s 1, eff. 1/1/2004.

See Stats 2003 ch 873 (SB 331), s 2.

Section 340.9 - Insurance claim for damages arising out of Northridge earthquake of 1994

(a) Notwithstanding any other provision of law or contract, any insurance claim for damages arising out of the Northridge earthquake of 1994 which is barred as of the effective date of this section solely because the applicable statute of limitations has or had expired is hereby revived and a cause of action thereon may be commenced provided that the action is commenced within one year of the effective date of this section. This subdivision shall only apply to cases in which an insured contacted an insurer or an insurer's representative prior to January 1, 2000, regarding potential Northridge earthquake damage.

(b) Any action pursuant to this section commenced prior to, or within one year from, the effective date of this section shall not be barred based upon this limitations period.

(c) Nothing in this section shall be construed to alter the applicable limitations period of an action that is not time barred as of the effective date of this section.

(d) This section shall not apply to either of the following:

(1) Any claim that has been litigated to finality in any court of competent jurisdiction prior to the effective date of this section.

(2) Any written compromised settlement agreement which has been made between an insurer and its insured where the insured was represented by counsel admitted to the practice of law in California at the time of the settlement, and who signed the agreement.

Added by Stats 2000 ch 1090 (SB 1899), s 1, eff. 1/1/2001.

Section 340.10 - Injury or death of terrorist victim of September 11, 2001 attacks

(a) For purposes of this section, "terrorist victim" means any individual who died or was injured as a consequence of the terrorist-related aircraft crashes of September 11, 2001, including persons who were present at the World Trade Center in New York City, New York, the Pentagon in Arlington, Virginia, or at the site of the crash at Shanksville, Pennsylvania, or in the immediate aftermath of the terrorist-related aircraft crashes of September 11, 2001, including members of the flight crew and passengers on American Airlines Flight 11, American Airlines Flight 77, United Airlines Flight 175, and United Airlines Flight 93, and who suffered physical harm or death as a result of any of the crashes, as defined in Section 40101 of Title 49 of the United States Code and the related, applicable regulations, other than an individual identified by the Attorney General of the United States as a participant or conspirator in the terrorist-related aircraft crashes, or a representative or heir of such an individual.

(b) The statute of limitations for injury or death set forth in Section 335.1 shall apply to any action brought for injury to, or for the death of, any terrorist victim described in subdivision (a) and caused by the wrongful act or neglect of another, regardless of whether that action lapsed or was otherwise barred by time under California law predating the passage of this section and Section 335.1.

Added by Stats 2002 ch 448 (SB 688),s 4, eff. 1/1/2003.

Section 341 - Against officer for seizure as tax collector; recovery of stock sold for delinquent assessment; invalidate action of trustees of dissolved corporation

Within six months:
An action against an officer, or officer de facto:

1. To recover any goods, wares, merchandise, or other property, seized by any such officer in his official capacity as tax collector, or to recover the price or value of any goods, wares, merchandise, or other personal property so seized, or for damages for the seizure, detention, sale of, or injury to any goods, wares, merchandise, or other personal property seized, or for damages done to any person or property in making any such seizure.
2. To recover stock sold for a delinquent assessment, as provided in section three hundred forty-seven of the Civil Code.
3. To set aside or invalidate any action taken or performed by a majority of the trustees of any corporation heretofore or hereafter dissolved by operation of law, including the revivor of any such corporation.

Amended by Stats. 1917, Ch. 217.

Section 341.5 - Action against state by local agency challenging constitutionality of statute relating to state funding

Notwithstanding any other provision of law, any action or proceeding in which a county, city, city and county, school district, special district, or any other local agency is a plaintiff or petitioner, that is brought against the State of California challenging the constitutionality of any statute relating to state funding for counties, cities, cities and counties, school districts, special districts, or other local agencies, shall be commenced within 90 days of the effective date of the statute at issue in the action. For purposes of this section, "State of California" means the State of California itself, or any of its agencies, departments, commissions, boards, or public officials.

Amended by Stats. 1994, Ch. 156, Sec. 1. Effective July 11, 1994.

Section 341a - Recovery for conversion of personal property left at hotel, hospital, rest home, sanitarium, boarding house, etc.

All civil actions for the recovery or conversion of personal property, wearing apparel, trunks, valises or baggage alleged to have been left at a hotel, hospital, rest home, sanitarium, boarding house, lodging house, furnished apartment house, or furnished bungalow court, shall be begun within 90 days from and after the date of the departure of the owner of said personal property, wearing apparel, trunks, valises or baggage from said hotel, hospital, rest home, sanitarium, boarding house, lodging house, furnished apartment house, or furnished bungalow court.

Amended by Stats. 1943, Ch. 405.

Section 342 - Action against public entity for which claim required to be presented

An action against a public entity upon a cause of action for which a claim is required to be presented in accordance with Chapter 1 (commencing with Section 900) and Chapter 2 (commencing with Section 910) of Part 3 of Division 3.6 of Title 1 of the Government Code must be commenced within the time provided in Section 945.6 of the Government Code.

Added by Stats. 1963, Ch. 1715.

Section 343 - Action for relief not provided

An action for relief not hereinbefore provided for must be commenced within four years after the cause of action shall have accrued.

Enacted 1872.

Section 344 - Recovery of balance due upon account where reciprocal demands between parties

In an action brought to recover a balance due upon a mutual, open, and current account, where there have been reciprocal demands between the parties, the cause of action is deemed to have accrued from the time of the last item proved in the account on either side.

Enacted 1872.

Section 345 - Applicability to actions brought in name state or county; accounts for support of state or county hospital patients deemed book accounts

The limitations prescribed in this chapter apply to actions brought in the name of the state or county or for the benefit of the state or county, in the same manner as to actions by private parties. Accounts for the support of patients at state or county hospitals are book accounts as defined in Section 337a, and actions on them may be commenced at any time within four years after the last date of service or the last date of payment.

Amended by Stats. 1984, Ch. 797, Sec. 1.

Section 346 - Redemption of mortgage with or without account of rents and profits

An action to redeem a mortgage of real property, with or without an account of rents and profits, may be brought by the mortgagor or those claiming under him, against the mortgagee in possession, or those claiming under him, unless he or they have continuously maintained an adverse possession of the mortgaged premises for five years after breach of some condition of the mortgage.

Enacted 1872.

Section 347 - Redemption of mortgaged premises by mortgagor not entitled to maintain action

If there is more than one such mortgagor, or more than one person claiming under a mortgagor, some of whom are not entitled to maintain such an action under the provisions of this Chapter, any one of them who is entitled to maintain such an action may redeem therein a divided or undivided part of the mortgaged premises, according as his interest may appear and have an accounting, for a part of the rents and profits proportionate to his interest in the mortgaged premises, on payment of a part of the mortgage money, bearing the same proportion to the whole of such money as the value of his divided or undivided interest in the premises bears to the whole of such premises.

Enacted 1872.

Section 348 - Recovery of money or other property deposited with bank, banker, trust company, etc.

To actions brought to recover money or other property deposited with any bank, banker, trust company, building and loan association, or savings and loan society or evidenced by a certificate issued by an industrial loan company or credit union there is no limitation.

This section shall not apply to banks, bankers, trust companies, building and loan associations, industrial loan companies, credit unions, and savings and loan societies which have become insolvent and are in process of liquidation and in such cases the statute of limitations shall be deemed to have commenced to run from the beginning of the process of liquidation; provided, however, nothing herein contained shall be construed so as to relieve any stockholder of any banking corporation or trust company from stockholders' liability as shall at any time, be provided by law.

Amended by Stats. 1955, Ch. 208.

Section 348.5 - Bonds or coupons issued by state

An action upon any bonds or coupons issued by the State of California shall have no limitation.

Added by Stats 2010 ch 719 (SB 856),s 8, eff. 10/19/2010.

Section 349 - [Repealed]

Repealed by Stats 2010 ch 328 (SB 1330),s 33.5, eff. 1/1/2011.

Section 349.05 - Removal of oil, gas or other liquid

Within one hundred eighty days:

(a) An action to enjoin, abate, or for damages on account of, an underground trespass, use or occupancy, by means of a well drilled for oil or gas or both from a surface location on land other than real property in which the aggrieved party has some right, title or interest or in respect to which the aggrieved party has some right, title or interest.

(b) An action for conversion or for the taking or removing of oil, gas or other liquid, or fluids by means of any such well. When any of said acts is by means of a new well the actual drilling of which is commenced after this section becomes effective, and such act was knowingly committed with actual intent to commit such act, the cause of action in such case shall not be deemed to have accrued until the discovery, by the aggrieved party, of the act or acts complained of; but in all other cases, and as to wells heretofore or hereafter drilled, the cause of action shall be deemed to have accrued ten days after the time when the well which is the subject of the cause of action was first placed on production.

Notwithstanding the continuing character of any such act, there shall be but one cause of action for any such act, and the cause of action shall accrue as aforesaid.

In all cases where oil or gas has been heretofore or is hereafter extracted from any existing or subsequently drilled well in this State, by a person without right but asserting a claim of right in good faith or acting under an honest mistake of law or fact, the measure of damages, if there be any right of recovery under existing law, shall be the value of the oil or gas at the time of extraction, without interest, after deducting all costs of development, operation and production, which costs shall include taxes and interest on all expenditures from the date thereof.

This section shall apply to causes of action existing when this section becomes effective. The time for commencement of existing causes of action which would be barred by this section within the first one hundred eighty days after this section becomes effective, shall be the said first one hundred eighty days.

Whenever the term "oil" is used in this section it shall be taken to include "petroleum," and the term "gas" shall mean natural gas coming from the earth.

The limitations prescribed by this section shall not apply to rights of action or actions to be brought in the name of or for the benefit of the people of this State, or of any county, city and county, city or other political subdivision of this State.

Renumbered from Ca. Civ. Proc. Code § 349 3/4 by Stats 2020 ch 370 (SB 1371),s 34, eff. 1/1/2021.

Section 349.1 - Acts or proceedings taken under color of law for formation, organization, incorporation, etc. of city, county, city or county, etc.

The validity of any acts or proceedings taken under color of law for the formation, organization, incorporation, dissolution, consolidation, change of organization or reorganization of, or for any change in the territorial boundaries of, any city, county, city and county, special district, public corporation or other public entity, or improvement district within any of the foregoing, shall not be contested in any action unless such action shall have been brought within six months from the date of completion of said acts or proceedings. Unless an action is commenced within said period all said acts or proceedings shall be held valid and in every respect legal and incontestable.

This section shall not amend or repeal any existing statute prescribing a shorter period of limitation than that specified herein.

Amended by Stats. 1965, Ch. 2044.

Section 349.2 - Acts or proceedings taken by city, county, city or county, etc. for authorization, sale or issuance of bonds

Where any acts or proceedings are taken under color of law by or on behalf of any city, county, city and county, special district, public corporation or other public entity for the authorization, sale or issuance of bonds:

(1) The validity of any such acts or proceedings for the authorization of bonds shall not be contested in any action unless such action shall have been brought within six months from the date of election authorizing said bonds, in cases where said bonds are required by law to be authorized at an election, or within six months from the date of adoption of a resolution or ordinance authorizing such bonds, in cases where bonds are not required by law to be authorized at an election;

(2) The validity of any such acts or proceedings for the sale of bonds (including all acts or proceedings taken prior thereto and providing for the issuance of such bonds) shall not be contested in any action unless such action shall have been brought within six months from the date of sale of said bonds;

(3) The validity of any such acts or proceedings for the issuance and delivery of, or payment for, bonds shall not be contested in any action unless such action shall have been brought within six months from the date of issuance and delivery of, or payment for, said bonds. Unless an action is commenced within the applicable time hereinabove specified, said acts or proceedings for the authorization, sale or issuance of bonds shall be held valid and in every respect legal and incontestable.

This section shall not amend or repeal any existing statute prescribing a shorter period of limitation than that specified herein.

As used in this section, the term "bonds" means all instruments evidencing indebtedness incurred or to be incurred for any public purpose, all instruments evidencing the borrowing of money in anticipation of taxes, revenues or other income of a public body, all instruments payable from revenues or special funds, and all instruments funding or refunding any thereof or any indebtedness, but shall not include any special assessment bonds, special assessment refunding bonds, or bonds or other instruments issued to represent special assessments which are, directly or indirectly, secured by or payable from specific assessments levied against lands benefited, including bonds or other instruments issued under or pursuant to any statute, charter or ordinance providing for the improvement of streets, the opening and widening of streets, the provision for off-street parking, or the refunding of any of the same.

Added by Stats. 1957, Ch. 1345.

Section 349.4 - Confirmation or validation of acts or proceedings

All acts and proceedings heretofore or hereafter taken under color of law for the formation, organization or incorporation of, or for any change in the territorial boundaries of, any city, county, city and county, special district, public corporation or other public entity, or improvement district, annexed area or zone within any of the foregoing, and for the authorization, issuance, sale, or exchange of bonds of the entity or the territory thereof may be confirmed, validated, and declared legally effective in the manner provided in this section.

The legislative body of the entity may instruct its clerk or secretary to mail a notice to all owners of property within the entity, within the improvement district or zone, or within the annexed area, as the case may be, as their names and addresses appear on the last equalized county assessment roll, or as known to the clerk or secretary. Such notice shall include the name of the entity, the date the entity or the zone or improvement district therein was ordered formed or its territory changed by annexation or otherwise, as the case may be, the amount of bonds authorized, if any, and a statement that commencing with the date of mailing of said notice there shall be a 60-calendar-day period during which period any property owner may file an action contesting the validity of the formation of the entity, or of such improvement district or zone, or of such change of boundaries by annexation or otherwise, as the case may be, or the validity of the bond authorization, if any. The clerk or secretary shall make and file with the legislative body of the entity a certificate of mailing of the notices. The legislative body of the entity may order the clerk or secretary to include in such notice such other additional information that it deems pertinent.

If no action is filed during such 60-day period, the formation of the entity or of such improvement district or zone, or the change of boundaries by annexation or otherwise, as the case may be, and the bond authorization, if any, are valid and uncontestable.

Added by Stats. 1977, Ch. 7.

Chapter 4 - GENERAL PROVISIONS AS TO THE TIME OF COMMENCING ACTIONS

Section 350 - Action commenced when complaint filed

An action is commenced, within the meaning of this Title, when the complaint is filed.

Enacted 1872.

Section 351 - Accrual of action against person out of state

If, when the cause of action accrues against a person, he is out of the State, the action may be commenced within the term herein limited, after his return to the State, and if, after the cause of action accrues, he departs from the State, the time of his absence is not part of the time limited for the commencement of the action.

Enacted 1872.

Section 352 - Person entitled to bring action under age of majority or lacking legal capacity at time action accrued

(a) If a person entitled to bring an action, mentioned in Chapter 3 (commencing with Section 335) is, at the time the cause of action accrued either under the age of majority or lacking the legal capacity to make decisions, the time of the disability is not part of the time limited for the commencement of the action.

(b) This section shall not apply to an action against a public entity or public employee upon a cause of action for which a claim is required to be presented in accordance with Chapter 1 (commencing with Section 900) or Chapter 2 (commencing with Section 910) of Part 3, or Chapter 3 (commencing with Section 950) of Part 4, of Division 3.6 of Title 1 of the Government Code. This subdivision shall not apply to any claim presented to a public entity prior to January 1, 1971.

Amended by Stats 2014 ch 144 (AB 1847),s 4, eff. 1/1/2015.

Section 352.1 - Person entitled to bring action imprisoned at time action accrued

(a) If a person entitled to bring an action, mentioned in Chapter 3 (commencing with Section 335), is, at the time the cause of action accrued, imprisoned on a criminal charge, or in execution under the sentence of a criminal court for a term less than for life, the time of that disability is not a part of the time limited for the commencement of the action, not to exceed two years.

(b) This section does not apply to an action against a public entity or public employee upon a cause of action for which a claim is required to be presented in accordance with Chapter 1 (commencing with Section 900) or Chapter 2 (commencing with Section 910) of Part 3, or Chapter 3 (commencing with Section 950) of Part 4, of Division 3.6 of Title 1 of the Government Code. This subdivision shall not apply to any claim presented to a public entity prior to January 1, 1971.

(c) This section does not apply to an action, other than an action to recover damages or that portion of an action that is for the recovery of damages, relating to the conditions of confinement, including an action brought by that person pursuant to Section 1983 of Title 42 of the United States Code.

Added by Stats. 1994, Ch. 1083, Sec. 5. Effective January 1, 1995.

Section 352.5 - Person under order of restitution as condition of probation with respect to act or omission giving rise to liability

If, after a cause of action accrues against a person, that person comes under an order for restitution as a condition of probation with respect to the specific act or omission giving rise to such person's liability, the time during which the order is in effect is not a part of the time limited for the commencement of such an action based upon that act or omission.

Added by Stats. 1976, Ch. 282.

Section 353.1 - Person entitled to bring action represented by attorney whose practice court has assumed jurisdiction

If a person entitled to bring an action or other proceeding, which action or other proceeding has not been filed or otherwise instituted, is represented by an attorney over whose practice a court of this state has assumed jurisdiction pursuant to Section 6180 or Section 6190 of the Business and Professions Code, and the application for the court to assume jurisdiction is filed prior to the expiration of the applicable statute of limitation or claim statute, the person shall have six months from the date of entry of the order assuming jurisdiction within which to file or otherwise institute the matter, if the applicable statute of limitation otherwise would have expired.

Added by Stats. 1983, Ch. 254, Sec. 3.

Section 354 - Person under disability to commence action by reason of existence of state of war

When a person is, by reason of the existence of a state of war, under a disability to commence an action, the time of the continuance of such disability is not part of the period limited for the commencement of the action whether such cause of action shall have accrued prior to or during the period of such disability.

Amended by Stats. 1943, Ch. 151.

Section 354.3 - Owner or heir or beneficiary of owner of Holocaust-era artwork

(a) The following definitions govern the construction of this section:

(1) "Entity" means any museum or gallery that displays, exhibits, or sells any article of historical, interpretive, scientific, or artistic significance.

(2) "Holocaust-era artwork" means any article of artistic significance taken as a result of Nazi persecution during the period of 1929 to 1945, inclusive.

(b) Notwithstanding any other provision of law, any owner, or heir or beneficiary of an owner, of Holocaust-era artwork, may bring an action to recover Holocaust-era artwork from any entity described in paragraph (1) of subdivision (a). Subject to Section 410.10, that action may be brought in a superior court of this state, which court shall have jurisdiction over that action until its completion or resolution. Section 361 does not apply to this section.

(c) Any action brought under this section shall not be dismissed for failure to comply with the applicable statute of limitation, if the action is commenced on or before December 31, 2010.

Added by Stats 2002 ch 332 (AB 1758),s 2, eff. 1/1/2003.

Section 354.4 - Armenian Genocide victim with claim arising out of insurance purchased in Europe or Asia between 1875 and 1923

(a) The following definitions govern the construction of this section:

(1) "Armenian Genocide victim" means any person of Armenian or other ancestry living in the Ottoman Empire during the period of 1915 to 1923, inclusive, who died, was deported, or escaped to avoid persecution during that period.

(2) "Insurer" means an insurance provider doing business in the state, or whose contacts in the state satisfy the constitutional requirements for jurisdiction, that sold life, property, liability, health, annuities, dowry, educational, casualty, or any other insurance covering persons or property to persons in Europe or Asia at any time between 1875 and 1923.

(b) Notwithstanding any other provision of law, any Armenian Genocide victim, or heir or beneficiary of an Armenian Genocide victim, who resides in this state and has a claim arising out of an insurance policy or policies purchased or in effect in Europe or Asia between 1875 and 1923 from an insurer described in paragraph (2) of subdivision (a), may bring a legal action or may continue a pending legal action to recover on that claim in any court of competent jurisdiction in this state, which court shall be deemed the proper forum for that action until its completion or resolution.

(c) Any action, including any pending action brought by an Armenian Genocide victim or the heir or beneficiary of an Armenian Genocide victim, whether a resident or nonresident of this state, seeking benefits under the insurance policies issued or in effect between 1875 and 1923 shall not be dismissed for failure to comply with the applicable statute of limitation, provided the action is filed on or before December 31, 2016.

(d) The provisions of this section are severable. If any provision of this section or its application is held invalid, that invalidity shall not affect other provisions or applications that can be given effect without the invalid provision or application.

Amended by Stats 2011 ch 70 (AB 173),s 1, eff. 7/7/2011.

Added by Stats 2000 ch 543 (SB 1915), s 2, eff. 9/18/2000.

Section 354.45 - Armenian Genocide victim with claim arising out of bank's failure to pay over deposited or looted assets

(a) For purposes of this section, the following terms have the following meanings:

(1) "Armenian Genocide victim" means any person of Armenian or other ancestry living in the Ottoman Empire during the period of 1890 to 1923, inclusive, who died, was injured in person or property, was deported, or escaped to avoid persecution during that period.

(2) "Bank" means any banking or financial institution, including any institution that issued bonds, that conducted business in Ottoman Turkey at any time during the period of 1890 to 1923, inclusive.

(3) "Deposited assets" means any and all cash, securities, bonds, gold, jewels or jewelry, or any other tangible or intangible items of personal property, or any documents indicating ownership or possessory interests in real, personal, or intangible property, that were deposited with and held by a bank.

(4) "Looted assets" means any and all personal, commercial, real, and intangible property, including cash, securities, gold, jewelry, businesses, artwork, equipment, and intellectual property, that was taken from the ownership or control of an individual, organization, or entity, by theft, forced transfer, or exploitation, during the period of 1890 to 1923, inclusive, by any person, organization, or entity acting on behalf of, or in furtherance of the acts of, the Turkish Government, that were received by and deposited with a bank.

(b) Notwithstanding any other law, any Armenian Genocide victim, or heir or beneficiary of an Armenian Genocide victim, who resides in this state and has a claim arising out of a failure of a bank to pay or turn over deposited assets, or to turn over looted assets, may bring an action or may continue a pending action, to recover on that claim in any court of competent jurisdiction in this state, which court shall be deemed the proper forum for that action until its completion or resolution.

(c) Any action, including any pending action brought by an Armenian Genocide victim, or the heir or beneficiary of an Armenian Genocide victim, who resides in this state, seeking payment for, or the return of, deposited assets, or the return of looted assets, shall not be dismissed for failure to comply with the applicable statute of limitation, if the action is filed on or before December 31, 2016.

(d) The provisions of this section are severable. If any provision of this section or its application is held invalid, that invalidity shall not affect other provisions or applications that can be given effect without the invalid provision or application.

Added by Stats 2006 ch 443 (SB 1524),s 2, eff. 1/1/2007.

Section 354.5 - Holocaust victim or victim's heir or beneficiary having claim arising out insurance purchased in Europe before 1945

(a) The following definitions govern the construction of this section:

(1) "Holocaust victim" means any person who was persecuted during the period of 1929 to 1945, inclusive, by Nazi Germany, its allies, or sympathizers.

(2) "Related company" means any parent, subsidiary, reinsurer, successor in interest, managing general agent, or affiliate company of the insurer.

(3) "Insurer" means an insurance provider doing business in the state, or whose contacts in the state satisfy the constitutional requirements for jurisdiction, that sold life, property, liability, health, annuities, dowry, educational, casualty, or any other insurance covering persons or property to persons in Europe at any time before 1945, directly or through a related company, whether the sale of the insurance occurred before or after the insurer and the related company became related.

(b) Notwithstanding any other provision of law, any Holocaust victim, or heir or beneficiary of a Holocaust victim, who resides in this state and has a claim arising out of an insurance policy or policies purchased or in effect in Europe before 1945 from an insurer described in paragraph (3) of subdivision (a), may bring a legal action to recover on that claim in any superior court of the state for the county in which the plaintiff or one of the plaintiffs resides, which court shall be vested with jurisdiction over that action until its completion or resolution.

(c) Any action brought by a Holocaust victim or the heir or beneficiary of a Holocaust victim, whether a resident or nonresident of this state, seeking proceeds of the insurance policies issued or in effect before 1945 shall not be dismissed for failure to comply with the applicable statute of limitation, provided the action is commenced on or before December 31, 2010.

Effective 10/10/1999 (Bill Number: AB 600) (Chapter 827).

Section 354.6 - Second World War slave labor or forced labor victims

(a) As used in this section:

(1) "Second World War slave labor victim" means any person taken from a concentration camp or ghetto or diverted from transportation to a concentration camp or from a ghetto to perform labor without pay for any period of time between 1929 and 1945, by the Nazi regime, its allies and sympathizers, or enterprises transacting business in any of the areas occupied by or under control of the Nazi regime or its allies and sympathizers.

(2) "Second World War forced labor victim" means any person who was a member of the civilian population conquered by the Nazi regime, its allies or sympathizers, or prisoner-of-war of the Nazi regime, its allies or sympathizers, forced to perform labor without pay for any period of time between 1929 and 1945, by the Nazi regime, its allies and sympathizers, or enterprises transacting business in any of the areas occupied by or under control of the Nazi regime or its allies and sympathizers.

(3) "Compensation" means the present value of wages and benefits that individuals should have been paid and damages for injuries sustained in connection with the labor performed. Present value shall be calculated on the basis of the market value of the services at the time they were performed, plus interest from the time the services were performed, compounded annually to date of full payment without diminution for wartime or postwar currency devaluation.

(b) Any Second World War slave labor victim, or heir of a Second World War slave labor victim, Second World War forced labor victim, or heir of a Second World War forced labor victim, may bring an action to recover compensation for labor performed as a Second World War slave labor victim or Second World War forced labor victim from any entity or successor in interest thereof, for whom that labor was performed, either directly or through a subsidiary or affiliate. That action may be brought in a superior court of this state, which court shall have jurisdiction over that action until its completion or resolution.

(c) Any action brought under this section shall not be dismissed for failure to comply with the applicable statute of limitation, if the action is commenced on or before December 31, 2010.

EFFECTIVE 7/28/99. Added 7/28/1999 (Bill Number: SB 1245) (Chapter 216).

Section 354.7 - Bracero for claim arising out of failure to pay over savings amounts

(a) The following definitions govern the construction of this section:

(1) "Bracero" means any person who participated in the labor importation program known as the Bracero program between January 1, 1942, and January 1, 1950, pursuant to agreements between the United States and Mexico.

(2) "Savings fund" means funds withheld from the wages of braceros as savings to be paid to braceros upon their return to Mexico.

(b) Notwithstanding any other provision of law, any bracero, or heir or beneficiary of a bracero, who has a claim arising out of a failure to pay or turn over savings fund amounts may bring a legal action or may continue a pending legal action to recover on that claim in any court of competent jurisdiction in this state, which court shall be deemed a proper forum for that action until its completion or resolution.

(c) Notwithstanding any other provision of law, any action brought by a bracero, or heir or beneficiary of a bracero, arising out of a failure to pay or turn over savings fund amounts shall not be dismissed for failure to comply with the otherwise applicable statute of limitations, provided the action is filed on or before December 31, 2005.

(d) The provisions of this section are severable. If any provision of this section or its application is held invalid, that invalidity shall not affect other provisions or applications that can be given effect without the invalid provision or application.

Added by Stats 2002 ch 1070 (AB 2913),s 2, eff. 9/29/2002.

Section 354.8 - Actions to be commenced within 10 years

(a) Notwithstanding any other law, including, but not limited to Section 335.1, the following actions shall be commenced within 10 years:

(1) An action for assault, battery, or both, where the conduct constituting the assault or battery would also constitute any of the following:

(A) An act of torture, as described in Section 206 of the Penal Code.

(B) An act of genocide, as described in Section 1091(a)(a) of Title 18 of the United States Code.
(C) A war crime, as defined in Section 2441 of Title 18 of the United States Code.
(D) An attempted extrajudicial killing, as defined in Section 3(a) of Public Law 102-256.
(E)
(i) Crimes against humanity.
(ii) For purposes of this paragraph, "crimes against humanity" means any of the following acts as part of a widespread or systematic attack directed against a civil population, with knowledge of the attack:
(I) Murder.
(II) Extermination.
(III) Enslavement.
(IV) Forcible transfer of population.
(V) Arbitrary detention.
(VI) Rape, sexual slavery, enforced prostitution, forced pregnancy, enforced sterilization, or any other form of sexual violence of comparable gravity.
(VII) Persecution on political, race, national, ethnic, cultural, religious, or gender grounds.
(VIII) Enforced disappearance of persons.
(IX) Other inhuman acts of similar character intentionally causing great suffering, serious bodily injury, or serious mental injury.
(2) An action for wrongful death, where the death arises out of conduct constituting any of the acts described in paragraph (1), or where the death would constitute an extrajudicial killing, as defined in Section 3(a) of Public Law 102-256.
(3) An action for the taking of property in violation of international law, in which either of the following apply:
(A) That property, or any property exchanged for such property, is present in the United States in connection with a commercial activity carried on in the United States by a foreign state.
(B) That property, or any property exchanged for such property, is owned or operated by an agency or instrumentality of a foreign state and that agency or instrumentality is engaged in a commercial activity in the United States.
(4) An action seeking benefits under an insurance policy where the insurance claim arises out of any of the conduct described in paragraphs (1) to (3), inclusive.
(b) An action brought under this section shall not be dismissed for failure to comply with any previously applicable statute of limitations.
(c) Section 361 shall not apply to an action brought pursuant to this section if all or part of the unlawful act or acts out of which the action arises occurred in this state.
(d) A prevailing plaintiff may be awarded reasonable attorney's fees and litigation costs including, but not limited to, expert witness fees and expenses as part of the costs.
(e) This section shall apply to all actions commenced concerning an act described in paragraphs (1) to (4), inclusive, of subdivision (a), that occurs on or after January 1, 2016.
(f) The provisions of this section are severable. If any provision of this section or its application is held invalid, that invalidity shall not affect other provisions or applications that can be given effect without the invalid provision or application.
Added by Stats 2015 ch 474 (AB 15),s 2, eff. 1/1/2016.

Section 355 - Commencement of new action after plaintiff's judgment reversed on appeal
If an action is commenced within the time prescribed therefor, and a judgment therein for the plaintiff be reversed on appeal other than on the merits, a new action may be commenced within one year after the reversal.
Amended by Stats. 1992, Ch. 178, Sec. 7. Effective January 1, 1993.

Section 356 - Commencement stayed by injunction or statutory prohibition
When the commencement of an action is stayed by injunction or statutory prohibition, the time of the continuance of the injunction or prohibition is not part of the time limited for the commencement of the action.
Enacted 1872.

Section 357 - Disability
No person can avail himself of a disability, unless it existed when his right of action accrued.
Enacted 1872.

Section 358 - Two or more disabilities coexisting
When two or more disabilities coexist at the time the right of action accrues, the limitation does not attach until they are removed.
Enacted 1872.

Section 359 - Actions against directors, shareholders or members of corporations to recover penalty or forfeiture
This title does not affect actions against directors, shareholders, or members of a corporation, to recover a penalty or forfeiture imposed, or to enforce a liability created by law; but such actions must be brought within three years after the discovery by the aggrieved party of the facts upon which the penalty or forfeiture attached, or the liability was created.
Amended by Stats. 1978, Ch. 1305.

Section 359.5 - Obligations under surety bond continued upon performance of principal
If the obligations under a surety bond are conditioned upon performance of the principal, the expiration of the statute of limitations with respect to the obligations of the principal, other than the obligations of the principal under the bond, shall also bar an action against the principal or surety under the bond, unless the terms of the bond provide otherwise.
Added by Stats. 1982, Ch. 106, Sec. 1.

Section 360 - Acknowledgment or promise of new or continuing contract
No acknowledgment or promise is sufficient evidence of a new or continuing contract, by which to take the case out of the operation of this title, unless the same is contained in some writing, signed by the party to be charged thereby, provided that any payment on account of principal or interest due on a promissory note made by the party to be charged shall be deemed a sufficient acknowledgment or promise of a continuing contract to stop, from time to time as any such payment is made, the running of the time within which an action may be commenced upon the principal sum or upon any installment of principal or interest due on such note, and to start the running of a new period of time, but no such payment of itself shall revive a cause of action once barred.
Amended by Stats. 1955, Ch. 417.

Section 360.5 - Waiver to defense that action not commenced within time
No waiver shall bar a defense to any action that the action was not commenced within the time limited by this title unless the waiver is in writing and signed by the person obligated. No waiver executed prior to the expiration of the time limited for the commencement of the action by this title shall be effective for a period exceeding four years from the date of expiration of the time limited for commencement of the action by this title and no waiver executed after the expiration of such time shall be effective for a period exceeding four years from the date thereof, but any such waiver may be renewed for a further period of not exceeding four years from the expiration of the immediately preceding waiver. Such waivers may be made successively. The provisions of this section shall not be applicable to any acknowledgment, promise or any form of waiver

which is in writing and signed by the person obligated and given to any county to secure repayment of indigent aid or the repayment of moneys fraudulently or illegally obtained from the county.
Amended by Stats. 1953, Ch. 655.

Section 361 - Lapse of time barring action arising in another state or foreign country
When a cause of action has arisen in another State, or in a foreign country, and by the laws thereof an action thereon cannot there be maintained against a person by reason of the lapse of time, an action thereon shall not be maintained against him in this State, except in favor of one who has been a citizen of this State, and who has held the cause of action from the time it accrued.
Enacted 1872.

Section 362 - Inapplicability of title to actions already commenced or time prescribed in statute has run
This Title does not extend to actions already commenced, nor to cases where the time prescribed in any existing statute for acquiring a right or barring a remedy has fully run, but the laws now in force are applicable to such actions and cases, and are repealed subject to the provisions of this section.
Enacted 1872.

Section 363 - Action construed to include special proceeding
The word "action" as used in this Title is to be construed, whenever it is necessary so to do, as including a special proceeding of a civil nature.
Enacted 1872.

Chapter 5 - THE COMMENCEMENT OF ACTIONS BASED UPON PROFESSIONAL NEGLIGENCE

Section 364 - Notice to health care provider of intention to commence action
(a) No action based upon the health care provider's professional negligence may be commenced unless the defendant has been given at least 90 days' prior notice of the intention to commence the action.
(b) No particular form of notice is required, but it shall notify the defendant of the legal basis of the claim and the type of loss sustained, including with specificity the nature of the injuries suffered.
(c) The notice may be served in the manner prescribed in Chapter 5 (commencing with Section 1010) of Title 14 of Part 2.
(d) If the notice is served within 90 days of the expiration of the applicable statute of limitations, the time for the commencement of the action shall be extended 90 days from the service of the notice.
(e) The provisions of this section shall not be applicable with respect to any defendant whose name is unknown to the plaintiff at the time of filing the complaint and who is identified therein by a fictitious name, as provided in Section 474.
(f) For the purposes of this section:
  (1) "Health care provider" means any person licensed or certified pursuant to Division 2 (commencing with Section 500) of the Business and Professions Code, or licensed pursuant to the Osteopathic Initiative Act, or the Chiropractic Initiative Act, or licensed pursuant to Chapter 2.5 (commencing with Section 1440) of Division 2 of the Health and Safety Code; and any clinic, health dispensary, or health facility, licensed pursuant to Division 2 (commencing with Section 1200) of the Health and Safety Code. "Health care provider" includes the legal representatives of a health care provider;
  (2) "Professional negligence" means negligent act or omission to act by a health care provider in the rendering of professional services, which act or omission is the proximate cause of a personal injury or wrongful death, provided that such services are within the scope of services for which the provider is licensed and which are not within any restriction imposed by the licensing agency or licensed hospital.
Amended by Stats. 1975, 2nd Ex. Sess., Ch. 2.

Section 365 - Failure to comply with chapter
Failure to comply with this chapter shall not invalidate any proceedings of any court of this state, nor shall it affect the jurisdiction of the court to render a judgment therein. However, failure to comply with such provisions by any attorney at law shall be grounds for professional discipline and the State Bar of California shall investigate and take appropriate action in any such cases brought to its attention.
Added by Stats. 1975, 2nd Ex. Sess., Ch. 1.

Chapter 6 - TIME OF COMMENCEMENT OF ACTION AFTER PERSON'S DEATH

Section 366.1 - Death of person entitled to bring action before expiration of limitations period
If a person entitled to bring an action dies before the expiration of the applicable limitations period, and the cause of action survives, an action may be commenced before the expiration of the later of the following times:
(a) Six months after the person's death.
(b) The limitations period that would have been applicable if the person had not died.
Added by Stats. 1992, Ch. 178, Sec. 8. Effective January 1, 1993.

Section 366.2 - Death of person against whom action brought before expiration of limitations period
(a) If a person against whom an action may be brought on a liability of the person, whether arising in contract, tort, or otherwise, and whether accrued or not accrued, dies before the expiration of the applicable limitations period, and the cause of action survives, an action may be commenced within one year after the date of death, and the limitations period that would have been applicable does not apply.
(b) The limitations period provided in this section for commencement of an action shall not be tolled or extended for any reason except as provided in any of the following, where applicable:
  (1) Sections 12, 12a, and 12b of this code.
  (2) Part 4 (commencing with Section 9000) of Division 7 of the Probate Code (creditor claims in administration of estates of decedents).
  (3) Part 8 (commencing with Section 19000) of Division 9 of the Probate Code (payment of claims, debts, and expenses from revocable trust of deceased settlor).
  (4) Former Part 3 (commencing with Section 21300) of Division 11 of the Probate Code (no contest clauses), as that part read prior to its repeal by Chapter 174 of the Statutes of 2008.
(c) This section applies to actions brought on liabilities of persons dying on or after January 1, 1993.
Amended by Stats 2009 ch 348 (SB 308),s 2, eff. 1/1/2010.
Amended by Stats 2006 ch 221 (AB 2864),s 1, eff. 1/1/2007.

Section 366.3 - Action to enforce claim of distribution from decedent's estate or trust
(a) If a person has a claim that arises from a promise or agreement with a decedent to distribution from an estate or trust or under another instrument, whether the promise or agreement was made orally or in writing, an action to enforce the claim to distribution may be commenced within one year after the date of death, and the limitations period that would have been applicable does not apply.
(b) The limitations period provided in this section for commencement of an action shall not be tolled or extended for any reason except as provided in Sections 12, 12a, and 12b of this code, and former Part 3 (commencing with Section 21300) of Division 11 of the Probate Code, as that part read prior to its repeal by Chapter 174 of the Statutes of 2008.
(c) This section applies to actions brought on claims concerning persons dying on or after the effective date of this section.
Amended by Stats 2009 ch 348 (SB 308),s 3, eff. 1/1/2010.

Amended by Stats 2006 ch 221 (AB 2864),s 2, eff. 1/1/2007.
Added by Stats 2000 ch 17 (AB 1491), s 1, eff. 1/1/2001.

Title 3 - OF THE PARTIES TO CIVIL ACTIONS
Chapter 1 - GENERAL PROVISIONS

Section 367 - Real party in interest
Every action must be prosecuted in the name of the real party in interest, except as otherwise provided by statute.
Amended by Stats. 1992, Ch. 178, Sec. 10. Effective January 1, 1993.

Section 367.3 - Right of protected person to proceed under pseudonym
(a) For purposes of this section, the following definitions apply:

(1) "Identifying characteristics" means the name or any part thereof, address or any part thereof, city or unincorporated area of residence, age, marital status, relationship to other parties, and race or ethnic background, telephone number, email address, social media profiles, online identifiers, contact information, or any other information, including images of the protected person, from which the protected person's identity can be discerned.

(2) "Online identifiers" means any personally identifying information or signifiers that would tie an individual to a particular electronic service, device, or internet application, website, or platform account, including, access names, access codes, account names, aliases, avatars, credentials, gamer tags, display names, handles, login names, member names, online identities, pseudonyms, screen names, user accounts, user identifications, usernames, Uniform Resource Locators (URLs), domain names, Internet Protocol (IP) addresses, and media access control (MAC) addresses.

(3) "Protected person" means a person who is an active participant in the address confidentiality program created pursuant to Chapter 3.1 (commencing with Section 6205) of Division 7 of Title 1 of the Government Code.

(b)

(1) A protected person who is a party in a civil proceeding may proceed using a pseudonym, either John Doe, Jane Doe, or Doe, for the true name of the protected person and may exclude or redact from all pleadings and documents filed in the action other identifying characteristics of the protected person. A protected person who proceeds using a pseudonym as provided in this section shall file with the court and serve upon all other parties to the proceeding a confidential information form for this purpose that includes the protected person's name and other identifying characteristics being excluded or redacted. The court shall keep the confidential information form confidential.

(2) In cases where a protected person proceeds using a pseudonym under this section, the following provisions shall apply, subject to sanction for an intentional violation:

(A) Except as provided in subparagraph (B), all parties and their agents and attorneys shall use the pseudonym in all pleadings, discovery requests or discovery motion documents, and other documents filed or served in the action, and at hearings, trial, and other court proceedings that are open to the public.

(B) A party seeking discovery in which the true name of the protected person and identifying information must be divulged for the purposes of fair and reasonable discovery, may use the true name of the protected person and identifying information for purposes of that discovery. The discovery request and all information collected through the discovery process shall not be made public and, if filed in court, shall be subject to subparagraph (C).

(C)

(i) A party filing a pleading, discovery document, or other document in the action shall exclude or redact any identifying characteristics of the protected person from the pleading, discovery document, or other document, except for a confidential information form filed pursuant to this subdivision.

(ii) A party excluding or redacting identifying characteristics shall file with the court and serve upon all other parties a confidential information form that includes the protected person's name and other identifying characteristics being excluded or redacted. The court shall keep the confidential information form confidential.

(D) Following final disposition of the proceedings a party in possession of any pleading, discovery document, or other document containing confidential information of the protected person obtained in the course of the action shall treat the documents as a nonpublic consumer record in accordance with Section 1798.81 of the Civil Code, subject to penalty for violations of that section.

(E) If the protected person is a minor dependent or minor ward of the state, the minor's parent, guardian, or attorney shall inform the minor's social worker or probation officer of the minor's participation in the action. The social worker or probation officer shall keep this information confidential.

(3) The responsibility to exclude or redact identifying characteristics of the protected person from documents filed with the court rests solely with the parties and their attorneys. This section does not require the court to review pleadings or other papers for compliance.

(4) The court, on motion of the protected person, may order a record or part of a record to be filed under seal in accordance with Rules 2.550 and 2.551 of the California Rules of Court, as those rules may be amended.

(c) In an action filed under this section, the plaintiff shall state in the caption of the complaint "ACTION BASED ON CODE OF CIVIL PROCEDURE SECTION 367.3."

(d) This section does not alter or negate any rights, obligations, or immunities of an interactive service provider under Section 230 of Title 47 of the United States Code. This section does not limit or preclude a plaintiff from securing or recovering any other available remedy.

(e) The Judicial Council shall coordinate with the Secretary of State to adopt or revise as appropriate rules and forms to implement this section, on or before January 1, 2021.

(f) The provisions of this section are severable. If any provision of this section or its application is held invalid, that invalidity shall not affect other provisions or applications that can be given effect without the invalid provision or application.
Added by Stats 2019 ch 439 (AB 800),s 1, eff. 1/1/2020.

Section 367.5 - [Repealed]
Repealed by Stats 2022 ch 979 (SB 233),s 1, eff. 1/1/2023.
Added by Stats 2007 ch 268 (AB 500),s 1, eff. 1/1/2008.

Section 367.6 - [Repealed]
Repealed by Stats 2022 ch 979 (SB 233),s 2, eff. 1/1/2023.
Amended by Stats 2012 ch 41 (SB 1021),s 1, eff. 6/27/2012.
Added by Stats 2010 ch 720 (SB 857),s 3, eff. 10/19/2010.

Section 367.75 - [Effective until 1/1/2026] Parties appearing remotely; conducting conferences, hearings, and proceedings
(a)

(1) Except as provided in subdivisions (b) and (d), in civil cases, when a party has provided notice to the court and all other parties that it intends to appear remotely, a party may appear remotely and the court may conduct conferences, hearings, and proceedings, in whole or in part, through the use of remote technology.

(2) This section does not apply to any of the following type of proceedings:

(A) Any proceeding in matters identified in paragraph (1) of subdivision (a) of section 367.76.
(B) A juvenile justice proceeding covered by Section 679.5 of the Welfare and Institutions Code.
(b) Except as otherwise provided by law, the court may require a party or witness to appear in person at a conference, hearing, or proceeding described in subdivision (a), or under subdivisions (e) and (h), if any of the following conditions are present:
(1) The court with jurisdiction over the case does not have the technology necessary to conduct the conference, hearing, or proceeding remotely.
(2) Although the court has the requisite technology, the quality of the technology or audibility at a conference, hearing, or proceeding prevents the effective management or resolution of the conference, hearing, or proceeding.
(3) The court determines on a hearing-by-hearing basis that an in-person appearance would materially assist in the determination of the conference, hearing, or proceeding or in the effective management or resolution of the particular case.
(4) The quality of the technology or audibility at a conference, hearing, or proceeding inhibits the court reporter's ability to accurately prepare a transcript of the conference, hearing, or proceeding.
(5) The quality of the technology or audibility at a conference, hearing, or proceeding prevents an attorney from being able to provide effective representation to the attorney's client.
(6) The quality of the technology or audibility at a conference, hearing, or proceeding inhibits a court interpreter's ability to provide language access to a court user or authorized individual.
(c) Notwithstanding paragraph (3) of subdivision (b), an expert witness may appear remotely absent good cause to compel in-person testimony.
(d)
(1) Except as otherwise provided by law and subject to the limitations of subdivision (b), upon its own motion or the motion of any party, the court may conduct a trial or evidentiary hearing, in whole or in part, through the use of remote technology, absent a showing by the opposing party as to why a remote appearance or testimony should not be allowed.
(2)
(A) Except as provided in Section 269 of the Code of Civil Procedure and Section 69957 of the Government Code, if the court conducts a trial, in whole or in part, through the use of remote technology, the official reporter or official reporter pro tempore shall be physically present in the courtroom.
(B) If the court conducts a trial, in whole or in part, through the use of remote technology, upon request, the court interpreter shall be physically present in the courtroom.
(e)
(1) Before the court with jurisdiction over the case may proceed with a remote conference, hearing, proceeding, or trial, the court shall have a process for a party, witness, official reporter, official reporter pro tempore, court interpreter, or other court personnel to alert the judicial officer of technology or audibility issues that arise during the conference, hearing, proceeding, or trial.
(2) The court shall require that a remote appearance by a party or witness have the necessary privacy and security appropriate for the conference, hearing, proceeding, or trial.
(3) The court shall inform all parties, particularly parties without legal representation, about the potential technological or audibility issues that could arise when using remote technology, which may require a delay of or halt the conference, hearing, proceeding, or trial. The court shall make information available to self-represented parties regarding the options for appearing in person and through the use of remote technology.
(f) The court shall not require a party to appear through the use of remote technology. If the court permits an appearance through remote technology, the court must ensure that technology in the courtroom enables all parties, whether appearing remotely or in person, to fully participate in the conference, hearing, or proceeding.
(g) A self-represented party may appear remotely in a conference, hearing, or proceeding conducted through the use of remote technology only if they agree to do so.
(h) Any juvenile dependency proceeding may be conducted in whole or in part through the use of remote technology subject to the following:
(1) Any person authorized to be present may request to appear remotely.
(2) Any party to the proceeding may request that the court compel the physical presence of a witness or party. A witness, including a party providing testimony, may appear through remote technology only with the consent of all parties and if the witness has access to the appropriate technology.
(3) A court shall not require a party to appear through the use of remote technology.
(4) The confidentiality requirements that apply to an in-person juvenile dependency proceeding shall apply to a juvenile dependency proceeding conducted through the use of remote technology.
(i)
(1) Notwithstanding Section 8613.5 of the Family Code, in an adoption proceeding under Division 13 (commencing with Section 8500) of the Family Code, the court may conduct an adoption finalization hearing, in whole or in part, through the use of remote technology, without the court finding that it is impossible or impracticable for either prospective adoptive parent to make the appearance in person.
(2) A court shall not require a party to appear through the use of remote technology.
(3) The confidentiality and privacy requirements that apply to an in-person adoption finalization hearing, including, but not limited to, the requirements in Section 8611 of the Family Code, apply to an adoption finalization hearing conducted through the use of remote technology.
(j) For purposes of this section, a party includes a nonparty subject to Chapter 6 of Title 4 of Part 4 (commencing with Section 2020.010).
(k) Subject to the limitations in subdivision (b), this section is not intended to prohibit the use of appearances through the use of remote technology when stipulated by attorneys for represented parties.
(l) Consistent with its constitutional rulemaking authority, the Judicial Council shall adopt rules to implement the policies and provisions in this section to promote statewide consistency, including, but not limited to, the following procedures:
(1) A deadline by which a party must notify the court and the other parties of their request to appear remotely.
(2) Procedures and standards for a judicial officer to determine when a conference, hearing, or proceeding may be conducted through the use of remote technology. The procedures and standards shall require that a judicial officer give consideration to the limited access to technology or transportation that a party or witness might have.
(m) This section shall remain in effect only until January 1, 2026, and as of that date is repealed.
Amended by Stats 2023 ch 34 (SB 133),s 3, eff. 6/30/2023.
Added by Stats 2021 ch 214 (SB 241),s 5, eff. 1/1/2022.

Section 367.76 - Applicability to proceedings
(a)
(1) This section applies to proceedings in the following matters:
(A) Judicial commitments under Part 2 (commencing with Section 6250) of Division 6 of the Welfare and Institutions Code, except for delinquency proceedings.

(B) Involuntary treatment and conservatorships of gravely disabled persons under Chapter 1 (commencing with Section 5000), Chapter 2 (commencing with Section 5150), and Chapter 3 (commencing with Section 5350) of Part 1 of Division 5 of the Welfare and Institutions Code, including Murphy conservatorships.

(C) Contempt proceedings under Title 5 (commencing with Section 1209) of Part 3 of this code.

(D) Mentally disordered offender proceedings under Article 4 (commencing with Section 2960) of Chapter 7 of Title 1 of Part 3 of the Penal Code.

(E) Commitment proceedings under Section 1026, et seq. of the Penal Code.

(F) Competency proceedings under Chapter 6 (commencing with Section 1367) of Title 10 of Part 2 of the Penal Code.

(G) Placement and revocation proceedings pursuant to Section 1600 et seq. of the Penal Code.

(H) Involuntary medication and treatment hearings for individuals committed or awaiting admission to a State Department of State Hospitals facility as described in Section 4100 of the Welfare and Institutions Code.

(2) This section does not apply to proceedings in matters brought pursuant to Sections 601 and 602 of the Welfare and Institutions Code.

(b) For the purposes of this section, the following definitions apply:

(1) "Person" means the person subject to any proceeding in matters described in paragraph (1) of subdivision (a).

(2) "Proceeding" or "proceedings" includes, but is not limited to, all hearings, conferences, and trials in matters described in paragraph (1) of subdivision (a).

(3) "Remote technology" means technology that provides for the two-way transmission of video and audio signals except that audio signals alone may be permitted where specifically authorized by law. Remote technology shall include, but not be limited to, a computer, tablet, telephone, cellular telephone, or other electronic or communications device. Notwithstanding the foregoing and subject to subdivision (h), the person subject to the proceeding, in consultation with counsel if represented, may, at their request, participate through audio-only technology.

(c) Proceedings in matters arising under subdivision (a) may be conducted through the use of remote technology subject to the following:

(1) A person has the right to be physically present for all proceedings and shall not be required to appear through the use of remote technology.

(2) A person may waive their right to be physically present and may elect to appear remotely.

(3) Except as provided in subdivisions (d), (e), and (h), a party, counsel for a party, or witness may appear through the use of remote technology.

(4) The confidentiality requirements that apply to inperson proceedings shall apply with equal force and effect when conducted through the use of remote technology.

(d) If the person is physically present in court the following shall apply:

(1) Absent exceptional circumstances and except as provided in paragraphs (3) and (4), counsel for the person, counsel for the other party or parties, the other party or parties, and the judicial officer shall be physically present in the courtroom.

(2) Except as provided in paragraphs (3) and (4) and paragraph (3) of subdivision (b) of Section 1370 of the Penal Code, absent a waiver by the person or a finding of good cause by the court, any witness the other party or parties calls shall be physically present in the courtroom. In determining whether good cause exists to excuse the physical presence of a witness, the court shall consider the distance the witness must travel, the nature of the testimony, and the nature of the proceeding.

(3) Notwithstanding paragraphs (1) and (2), counsel and witnesses for the State Department of Developmental Services shall not be required to be physically present in the courtroom absent a finding of good cause by the court.

(4) Notwithstanding paragraphs (1) and (2), counsel and witnesses for the State Department of State Hospitals shall not be required to be physically present in the courtroom in any nonjury trial matters or proceedings described in paragraph (1) of subdivision (a) absent a finding of good cause by the court.

(e) Notwithstanding any other law, unless good cause exists, a court shall not compel the physical presence of the person who is a patient in a State Department of State Hospitals or State Department of Developmental Services facility or other inpatient or outpatient treatment facility absent consent of the person in consultation with counsel. In determining whether good cause exists to compel the physical presence of a patient, the court shall consider the nature of the hearing and whether requiring the physical presence of the patient would interfere with the person's program of treatment or be detrimental to their mental or physical health.

(f)

(1) Until July 1, 2024, when the court conducts proceedings that will be reported by an official reporter or official reporter pro tempore, the reporter shall be physically present in the same room as the judicial officer except where the court finds that, as the result of unusual circumstances, this requirement would place extreme or undue hardship on the court or the litigants. For purposes of this paragraph, "unusual circumstances" means a work stoppage, a circumstance described in subdivision (a) of Section 68115 of the Government Code, an unforeseen emergency, court proceedings conducted in a remote court location to which a judicial officer is not regularly assigned to sit, or when a judicial officer has to travel to a location outside of a courthouse to conduct the proceeding.

(2) Beginning July 1, 2024, when the court conducts proceedings that will be reported by an official reporter or official reporter pro tempore, the reporter shall be physically present in the same room as the judicial officer if the court cannot provide the technology standards described in subdivision (o).

(g) If the court conducts a trial, in whole or in part, through the use of remote technology, upon request, the court interpreter shall be physically present in the courtroom.

(h)

(1) If any of the following conditions are present and cannot be resolved, the court shall not permit any party, counsel, or witness to appear or participate in proceedings through the use of remote technology, and shall continue any proceeding being conducted with the use of remote technology:

(A) The court does not have the technology necessary to conduct the proceeding remotely.

(B) Although the court has the requisite technology, the quality of the technology or audibility at a proceeding prevents the effective management or resolution of the proceeding.

(C) The quality of the technology or audibility at a proceeding inhibits the court reporter's ability to accurately prepare and certify a transcript of the proceeding.

(D) The court reporter is unable to capture the verbatim record and certify a transcript of any proceeding that is conducted remotely, in whole or in part, to the same extent and in the same manner as if it were not conducted remotely.

(E) The quality of the technology or audibility at a proceeding inhibits the ability of the person to understand or participate in the proceeding.

(F) The quality of the technology or audibility at a proceeding inhibits counsel from being able to provide effective representation to the person.

(G) The court does not have the technology necessary for secure, confidential communication between counsel and the person.

(H) The quality of the technology or audibility at a proceeding inhibits a court interpreter's ability to provide language access, including to communicate and interpret directly with the person and the court during the proceedings.

(2) Except as provided in subdivision (e) or otherwise provided by law, the court may require a party or witness to appear in person at a proceeding if the court determines on a hearing-by-hearing basis that an inperson appearance would materially assist in the determination of the proceeding or resolution of the case. The court's determination shall be based on the individual case before the court and shall be entered into the minutes or otherwise made on the record. In making its determination, the court shall consider the request of the person, the nature of the proceedings, and whether requiring the physical presence of the person would disrupt the person's program of treatment or be detrimental to their mental or physical health.

(3) The court shall not continue proceedings beyond statutory time limits pursuant to this section absent a waiver by the person in consultation with counsel.

(i) Subject to the limitations in subdivision (h), this section is not intended to prohibit the use of appearances through the use of remote technology when stipulated by attorneys for represented parties.

(j) Before the court may conduct proceedings through the use of remote technology, the court shall have a process for a party, witness, official reporter, official reporter pro tempore, court interpreter, or other court personnel to alert the judicial officer of technology or audibility issues that arise during the proceedings.

(k) The court shall inform all parties, particularly parties without legal representation, about the potential technological or audibility issues that could arise when using remote technology, which may require a delay of or halt the proceedings. The court shall make information available to self-represented parties regarding the options for appearing in person and through the use of remote technology.

(l) A self-represented party may appear remotely in a proceeding conducted through the use of remote technology only if they agree to do so.

(m) For purposes of this section, a party includes a nonparty subject to Chapter 6 (commencing with Section 2020.010) of Title 4 of Part 4.

(n) Consistent with its constitutional rulemaking authority, the Judicial Council shall adopt such other rules and standards as are necessary to implement the policies and provisions of this section and the intent of the Legislature.

(o) By April 1, 2024, the Judicial Council shall adopt, and trial courts shall implement by July 1, 2024, minimum standards for the courtroom technology necessary to permit remote participation in proceedings subject to this section. Those standards shall include, but not be limited to, hard-wired or other reliable high-speed internet connections in the courtroom for the judicial officer and court reporter, and monitors, dedicated cameras, speakers, and microphones so the judicial officer, court reporter, and court interpreter can appropriately see and hear remote participants, as well as to ensure that remote participants can appropriately see and hear the judicial officer and other courtroom participants.

(p) Consistent with federal and California labor law, a trial court shall not retaliate or threaten to retaliate against an official reporter or an official reporter pro tempore who notifies the judicial officer that technology or audibility issues are impeding the creation of the verbatim record of a proceeding that includes participation through remote technology. This subdivision shall only apply to an official reporter and an official reporter pro tempore when they meet the definition of "trial court employee" under subdivision (l) of Section 71601 of the Government Code.

(q) This section shall remain in effect only until January 1, 2026, and as of that date is repealed.

Added by Stats 2023 ch 34 (SB 133),s 4, eff. 6/30/2023.

Section 367.8 - [Effective until 7/1/2023] Report on the use of remote technology in civil actions by the trial courts

(a) The Judicial Council shall, by January 1, 2023, submit a report to the Legislature and the Governor on the use of remote technology in civil actions by the trial courts. The report shall report county-specific data that includes, but is not limited to, the following:

(1) The number of proceedings conducted with use of remote technology.
(2) Technology issues affecting remote proceedings.
(3) Any relevant expenditure information related to remote proceedings.
(4) The impact of remote proceedings on court users' ability to access the courts.
(5) The impact of the use of remote proceedings on case backlogs as a result of the COVID-19 pandemic.
(6) Information regarding court workers' and court users' experience using remote technology.
(7) Any other information necessary to evaluate the use of remote proceedings by the courts.

(b) A report to be submitted pursuant to this section shall be submitted in compliance with Section 9795 of the Government Code.

(c) This section shall remain in effect only until July 1, 2023, and as of that date is repealed.

Added by Stats 2021 ch 257 (AB 177),s 4, eff. 9/23/2021.

Section 367.8 - Report regarding technology issues or problems affecting remote proceedings

(a) Each superior court shall report to the Judicial Council on or before October 1, 2023, and annually thereafter, and the Judicial Council shall report to the Legislature on or before December 31, 2023, and annually thereafter, to assess the impact of technology issues or problems affecting remote proceedings, as included under Sections 367.75 and 367.76 of this code, and Section 679.5 of the Welfare and Institutions Code, and all purchases and leases of technology or equipment to facilitate remote conferences, hearings, or proceedings. The report by each superior court and the Judicial Council shall specify all of the following for each annual reporting period:

(1) The number of proceedings conducted with the use of remote technology.
(2) Any superior court in which technology issues or problems occurred.
(3) The superior courts in which remote technology was used.
(4) The types of trial court conferences, hearings, or proceedings in which remote technology was used.
(5) The cost of purchasing, leasing, or upgrading remote technology.
(6) The type of technology and equipment purchased or leased.
(7) Any other information necessary to evaluate the use of remote proceedings by the courts.

(b) A report to be submitted to the Legislature pursuant to this section shall be submitted in compliance with Section 9795 of the Government Code.

Added by Stats 2023 ch 34 (SB 133),s 5, eff. 6/30/2023.

Section 367.9 - [Repealed]

Added by Stats 2021 ch 257 (AB 177),s 5, eff. 9/23/2021.

Section 367.10 - Rules regarding remote court proceedings from locations other than courtroom

Consistent with its constitutional rulemaking authority, the Judicial Council shall adopt rules that include standards for when a judicial officer, in limited situations and in the interest of justice, may preside over a remote court proceeding from a location other than a courtroom.

Added by Stats 2023 ch 34 (SB 133),s 6, eff. 6/30/2023.

Section 368 - Action by assignee without prejudice to set-off or other defenses

In the case of an assignment of a thing in action, the action by the assignee is without prejudice to any set-off, or other defense existing at the time of, or before, notice of the assignment; but this section does not apply to a negotiable promissory note or bill of exchange, transferred in good faith, and upon good consideration, before maturity.

Enacted 1872.

Section 368.5 - Transfer of interest in action

An action or proceeding does not abate by the transfer of an interest in the action or proceeding or by any other transfer of an interest. The action or proceeding may be continued in the name of the original party, or the court may allow the person to whom the transfer is made to be substituted in the action or proceeding.

Added by Stats. 1992, Ch. 178, Sec. 11. Effective January 1, 1993.

Section 369 - Persons allowed to sue without joining persons for whose benefit action prosecuted

(a) The following persons may sue without joining as parties the persons for whose benefit the action is prosecuted:

(1) A personal representative, as defined in subdivision (a) of Section 58 of the Probate Code.

(2) A trustee of an express trust.

(3) Except for a person upon whom a power of sale has been conferred pursuant to a deed of trust or mortgage, a person with whom, or in whose name, a contract is made for the benefit of another.

(4) Any other person expressly authorized by statute.

(b) Notwithstanding subdivision (a), a trustee upon whom a power of sale has been conferred pursuant to a deed of trust or mortgage may sue to exercise the trustee's powers and duties pursuant to Chapter 2 (commencing with Section 2920) of Title 14 of Part 4 of Division 3 of the Civil Code.

Amended by Stats. 1992, Ch. 178, Sec. 12. Effective January 1, 1993.

Section 369.5 - Partnerships or other unincorporated association sued in name assumed; member joined as party; judgment against member based on personal liability

(a) A partnership or other unincorporated association, whether organized for profit or not, may sue and be sued in the name it has assumed or by which it is known.

(b) A member of the partnership or other unincorporated association may be joined as a party in an action against the unincorporated association. If service of process is made on the member as an individual, whether or not the member is also served as a person upon whom service is made on behalf of the unincorporated association, a judgment against the member based on the member's personal liability may be obtained in the action, whether the liability is joint, joint and several, or several.

Added by Stats. 1992, Ch. 178, Sec. 13. Effective January 1, 1993.

Chapter 2 - MARRIED PERSON

Section 370 - Generally

A married person may be sued without his or her spouse being joined as a party, and may sue without his or her spouse being joined as a party in all actions.

Amended by Stats. 1975, Ch. 1241.

Section 371 - Spouses sued together

If spouses are sued together, each may defend for his or her own right, but if one spouse neglects to defend, the other spouse may defend for that spouse's right also.

Amended by Stats 2016 ch 50 (SB 1005),s 15, eff. 1/1/2017.

Chapter 3 - DISABILITY OF PARTY

Section 372 - Appearance by guardian, conservator of estate or guardian ad litem

(a)

(1) When a minor, a person who lacks legal capacity to make decisions, or a person for whom a conservator has been appointed is a party, that person shall appear either by a guardian or conservator of the estate or by a guardian ad litem appointed by the court in which the action or proceeding is pending, or by a judge thereof, in each case.

(2)

(A) A guardian ad litem may be appointed in any case when it is deemed by the court in which the action or proceeding is prosecuted, or by a judge thereof, expedient to appoint a guardian ad litem to represent the minor, person who lacks legal capacity to make decisions, or person for whom a conservator has been appointed, notwithstanding that the person may have a guardian or conservator of the estate and may have appeared by the guardian or conservator of the estate.

(B) If application is made for appointment of a guardian ad litem for a person described in paragraph (1), and that person has a guardian or conservator of the estate, the application may be granted only if all of the following occur:

(i) The applicant gives notice and a copy of the application to the guardian or conservator of the estate upon filing the application.

(ii) The application discloses the existence of a guardian or conservator of the estate.

(iii) The application sets forth the reasons why the guardian or conservator of the estate is inadequate to represent the interests of the proposed ward in the action.

(C) The guardian or conservator of the estate shall have five court days from receiving notice of the application to file any opposition to the application.

(3) The guardian or conservator of the estate or guardian ad litem so appearing for any minor, person who lacks legal capacity to make decisions, or person for whom a conservator has been appointed shall have power, with the approval of the court in which the action or proceeding is pending, to compromise the same, to agree to the order or judgment to be entered therein for or against the ward or conservatee, and to satisfy any judgment or order in favor of the ward or conservatee or release or discharge any claim of the ward or conservatee pursuant to that compromise. Money or other property to be paid or delivered pursuant to the order or judgment for the benefit of a minor, person lacking legal capacity to make decisions, or person for whom a conservator has been appointed shall be paid and delivered as provided in Chapter 4 (commencing with Section 3600) of Part 8 of Division 4 of the Probate Code.

(4) Where reference is made in this chapter to "a person who lacks legal capacity to make decisions," the reference shall be deemed to include all of the following:

(A) A person who lacks capacity to understand the nature or consequences of the action or proceeding.

(B) A person who lacks capacity to assist the person's attorney in the preparation of the case.

(C) A person for whom a conservator may be appointed pursuant to Section 1801 of the Probate Code.

(5) Nothing in this section, or in any other provision of this code, the Civil Code, the Family Code, or the Probate Code is intended by the Legislature to prohibit a minor from exercising an intelligent and knowing waiver of the minor's constitutional rights in a proceeding under the Juvenile Court Law (Chapter 2 (commencing with Section 200) of Part 1 of Division 2 of the Welfare and Institutions Code).

(b)

(1) Notwithstanding subdivision (a), a minor 12 years of age or older may appear in court without a guardian, counsel, or guardian ad litem, for the purpose of requesting or opposing a request for any of the following:

(A) An injunction or temporary restraining order or both to prohibit harassment pursuant to Section 527.6.

(B) An injunction or temporary restraining order or both against violence or a credible threat of violence in the workplace pursuant to Section 527.8.

(C) A protective order pursuant to Division 10 (commencing with Section 6200) of the Family Code.

(D) A protective order pursuant to Sections 7710 and 7720 of the Family Code. The court may, either upon motion or in its own discretion, and after considering reasonable objections by the minor to the appointment of specific individuals, appoint a guardian ad litem to assist the minor in obtaining or opposing the order, provided that the appointment of the guardian ad litem does not delay the issuance or denial of the order being sought. In making the determination concerning the appointment of a particular guardian ad litem, the court shall consider whether the minor and the guardian have divergent interests.

(2) For purposes of this subdivision only, upon the issuance of an order pursuant to paragraph (1), if the minor initially appeared in court seeking an order without a guardian or guardian ad litem, and if the minor is residing with a parent or guardian, the court shall send a copy of the order to at least one parent or guardian designated by the minor, unless, in the discretion of the court, notification of a parent or guardian would be contrary to the best interest of the minor. The court is not required to send the order to more than one parent or guardian.

(c)

(1) Notwithstanding subdivision (a), a minor may appear in court without a guardian ad litem in the following proceedings if the minor is a parent of the child who is the subject of the proceedings:

(A) Family court proceedings pursuant to Part 3 (commencing with Section 7600) of Division 12 of the Family Code.

(B) Dependency proceedings pursuant to Chapter 2 (commencing with Section 200) of Part 1 of Division 2 of the Welfare and Institutions Code.

(C) Guardianship proceedings for a minor child pursuant to Part 2 (commencing with Section 1500) of Division 4 of the Probate Code.

(D) Any other proceedings concerning child custody, visitation, or support.

(2) If the court finds that the minor parent is unable to understand the nature of the proceedings or to assist counsel in preparing the case, the court shall, upon its own motion or upon a motion by the minor parent or the minor parent's counsel, appoint a guardian ad litem.

(d) Before a court appoints a guardian ad litem pursuant to this chapter, a proposed guardian ad litem shall disclose both of the following to the court and all parties to the action or proceeding:

(1) Any known actual or potential conflicts of interest that would or might arise from the appointment.

(2) Any familial or affiliate relationship the proposed guardian ad litem has with any of the parties.

(e) If a guardian ad litem becomes aware that a potential conflict of interest has become an actual conflict of interest or that a new potential or actual conflict of interest exists, the guardian ad litem shall promptly disclose the conflict of interest to the court.

Amended by Stats 2022 ch 843 (SB 1279),s 1, eff. 1/1/2023.
Amended by Stats 2014 ch 144 (AB 1847),s 5, eff. 1/1/2015.
Amended by Stats 2008 ch 181 (SB 1612),s 1, eff. 1/1/2009.

Section 372.5 - Appointment of guardian under pseudonym

(a) The court may appoint a guardian ad litem under a pseudonym pursuant to the requirements of this section.

(b) A person who applies for appointment as a guardian ad litem under a pseudonym shall, at the same time that the application is filed, file an ex parte request for leave to appear under a pseudonym. The ex parte request shall allege facts and circumstances establishing the guardian ad litem's overriding interest in preserving his or her anonymity.

(c) To permit an applicant for appointment as a guardian ad litem to appear under pseudonym, the court shall make each of the following findings:

(1) That the applicant has an overriding interest in preserving anonymity that supports permitting the applicant to appear under a pseudonym.

(2) That there is a substantial probability that the applicant's interest in preserving anonymity will be prejudiced if the applicant is not permitted to appear under a pseudonym.

(3) That permitting the applicant to appear under a pseudonym is narrowly tailored to serve the applicant's interest in preserving anonymity without unduly prejudicing the public's right of access or the ability of the other parties to prosecute, defend, or resolve the action.

(4) That there are no less restrictive means of protecting the applicant's interest in preserving his or her anonymity.

(d)

(1) The court may make any further orders necessary to preserve the applicant's anonymity or to allow the other parties or financial institutions to know the applicant's identity to the extent necessary to prosecute, defend, or resolve the action.

(2) In addition to any other orders, the court may require a guardian ad litem who is permitted to appear under a pseudonym and is not represented by counsel to designate a mailing or electronic address for service of process and to consent to accept service of process under the pseudonym at that address for purposes of the action.

(e)

(1) If a guardian ad litem is permitted to appear under a pseudonym, all court decisions, orders, petitions, and any documents filed with the court shall be written in a manner that protects the name and personal identifying information of the guardian ad litem from public disclosure, except to the extent the information is necessary for the parties to prosecute, defend, or resolve the action.

(2) For purposes of this subdivision, "personal identifying information" includes the guardian ad litem's name or any part thereof, his or her address or any part thereof, and the city or unincorporated area of the guardian ad litem's residence.

(f) The responsibility for excluding the name and personal identifying information of the guardian ad litem from documents filed with the court rests solely with the parties and their attorneys. This section does not require the court to review pleadings or other papers for compliance with this subdivision.

(g) After granting permission for a guardian ad litem to appear under a pseudonym pursuant to this section, the court shall retain discretion to reconsider its decision.

(h) This section does not affect the right of a plaintiff or petitioner to pursue litigation under a pseudonym in appropriate circumstances.

Added by Stats 2018 ch 817 (AB 2185),s 1, eff. 1/1/2019.

Section 373 - Appointment of guardian ad litem

When a guardian ad litem is appointed, he or she shall be appointed as follows:

(a) If the minor is the plaintiff the appointment must be made before the summons is issued, upon the application of the minor, if the minor is 14 years of age or older, or, if under that age, upon the application of a relative or friend of the minor.

(b) If the minor is the defendant, upon the application of the minor, if the minor is 14 years of age or older, and the minor applies within 10 days after the service of the summons, or, if under that age or if the minor neglects to apply, then upon the application of a relative or friend of the minor, or of any other party to the action, or by the court on its own motion.

(c) If the person lacking legal competence to make decisions is a party to an action or proceeding, upon the application of a relative or friend of the person lacking legal competence to make decisions, or of any other party to the action or proceeding, or by the court on its own motion.

Amended by Stats 2014 ch 144 (AB 1847),s 6, eff. 1/1/2015.

Section 373.5 - Guardian ad litem for person not ascertained, not in being or unknown

If under the terms of a written instrument, or otherwise, a person or persons of a designated class who are not ascertained or who are not in being, or a person or persons who are unknown, may be or may become legally or equitably interested in any property, real or personal, the court in which any action, petition or proceeding of any kind relative to or affecting the property is pending, may, upon the representation of any party thereto, or of any person interested, appoint a suitable person to appear and act therein as guardian ad litem of the person or persons not ascertained, not in being, or who are unknown; and the judgment, order or decree in the proceedings, made after the appointment, shall be conclusive upon all persons for whom the guardian ad litem was appointed.

The guardian ad litem shall have power, with the approval of the court in which the action, petition or proceeding is pending, to compromise the same, to agree to the order or judgment to be entered therein for or against the persons for whom the guardian ad litem was appointed, and to satisfy any judgment or order in favor of the persons, or release, or discharge any claim of the persons pursuant to the compromise. The court shall have the same power with respect to the money or other property to be paid or delivered under such order or judgment as is provided in Section 372 of this code.

The reasonable expenses of the guardian ad litem, including compensation and counsel fees, shall be determined by the court and paid as it may order, either out of the property or by plaintiff or petitioner. If the expenses are to be paid by the plaintiff or petitioner, execution therefor may issue in the name of the guardian ad litem.

Amended by Stats. 1961, Ch. 435.

Section 374 - Appearance by minor under age 12 without counsel to request or oppose injunction or temporary restraining order or protective order

(a) A minor under 12 years of age, accompanied by a duly appointed and acting guardian ad litem, shall be permitted to appear in court without counsel for the limited purpose of requesting or opposing a request for (1) an injunction or temporary restraining order or both to prohibit harassment pursuant to Section 527.6, (2) an injunction or temporary restraining order or both against violence or a credible threat of violence in the workplace pursuant to Section 527.8, (3) a protective order pursuant to Division 10 (commencing with Section 6200) of the Family Code, or (4) a protective order pursuant to Sections 7710 and 7720 of the Family Code.

(b) In making the determination concerning appointment of a particular guardian ad litem for purposes of this section, the court shall consider whether the minor and the guardian have divergent interests.

(c) The Judicial Council shall adopt forms by July 1, 1999, to implement this section. The forms shall be designed to facilitate the appointment of the guardian ad litem for purposes of this section.

Added by Stats. 1998, Ch. 706, Sec. 2. Effective September 22, 1998.

Section 374.5 - Court hearing proceedings pursuant to section 372 or 374

A proceeding initiated by or brought against a minor for any of the injunctions or orders described in paragraph (1) of subdivision (b) of Section 372 or subdivision (a) of Section 374 shall be heard in the court assigned to hear those matters; except that, if the minor bringing the action or against whom the action is brought has previously been adjudged a dependent child or a ward of the juvenile court, the matter shall be heard in the juvenile court having jurisdiction over the minor.

Added by Stats. 1998, Ch. 706, Sec. 3. Effective September 22, 1998.

Section 375 - Action not abated by disability; continued by or against representative

An action or proceeding does not abate by the disability of a party. The court, on motion, shall allow the action or proceeding to be continued by or against the party's representative.

Added by Stats. 1992, Ch. 178, Sec. 17. Effective January 1, 1993.

Section 376 - Action by parents of legitimate unmarried minor child for injury to child

(a) The parents of a legitimate unmarried minor child, acting jointly, may maintain an action for injury to the child caused by the wrongful act or neglect of another. If either parent fails on demand to join as plaintiff in the action or is dead or cannot be found, then the other parent may maintain the action. The parent, if living, who does not join as plaintiff shall be joined as a defendant and, before trial or hearing of any question of fact, shall be served with summons either in the manner provided by law for the service of a summons in a civil action or by sending a copy of the summons and complaint by registered mail with proper postage prepaid addressed to that parent's last known address with request for a return receipt. If service is made by registered mail, the production of a return receipt purporting to be signed by the addressee creates a rebuttable presumption that the summons and complaint have been duly served. The presumption established by this section is a presumption affecting the burden of producing evidence. The respective rights of the parents to any award shall be determined by the court.

(b) A parent may maintain an action for such an injury to his or her illegitimate unmarried minor child if a guardian has not been appointed. Where a parent who does not have care, custody, or control of the child brings the action, the parent who has care, custody, or control of the child shall be served with the summons either in the manner provided by law for the serving of a summons in a civil action or by sending a copy of the summons and complaint by registered mail, with proper postage prepaid, addressed to the last known address of that parent, with request for a return receipt. If service is made by registered mail, the production of a return receipt purporting to be signed by the addressee creates a rebuttable presumption that the summons and complaint have been duly served. The presumption established by this section is a presumption affecting the burden of producing evidence. The respective rights of the parents to any award shall be determined by the court.

(c) The father of an illegitimate child who maintains an action under this section shall have acknowledged in writing prior to the child's injury, in the presence of a competent witness, that he is the father of the child, or, prior to the child's injury, have been judicially determined to be the father of the child.

(d) A parent of an illegitimate child who does not maintain an action under this section may be joined as a party thereto.

(e) A guardian may maintain an action for such an injury to his or her ward.

(f) An action under this section may be maintained against the person causing the injury. If any other person is responsible for the wrongful act or neglect, the action may also be maintained against the other person. The death of the child or ward does not abate the parents' or guardian's cause of action for the child's injury as to damages accruing before the child's death.

(g) In an action under this section, damages may be awarded that, under all of the circumstances of the case, may be just, except that:

(1) In an action maintained after the death of the child, the damages recoverable are as provided in Section 377.34.

(2) Where the person causing the injury is deceased, the damages recoverable in an action against the decedent's personal representative are as provided in Section 377.42.

(h) If an action arising out of the same wrongful act or neglect may be maintained pursuant to Section 377.60 for wrongful death of a child described in this section, the action authorized by this section may be consolidated therewith for trial as provided in Section 1048.

Amended by Stats. 1992, Ch. 178, Sec. 18. Effective January 1, 1993.

Chapter 4 - EFFECT OF DEATH
Article 1 - DEFINITIONS

Section 377.10 - Beneficiary of the decedent's estate

For the purposes of this chapter, "beneficiary of the decedent's estate" means:

(a) If the decedent died leaving a will, the sole beneficiary or all of the beneficiaries who succeed to a cause of action, or to a particular item of property that is the subject of a cause of action, under the decedent's will.

(b) If the decedent died without leaving a will, the sole person or all of the persons who succeed to a cause of action, or to a particular item of property that is the subject of a cause of action, under Sections 6401 and 6402 of the Probate Code or, if the law of a sister state or foreign nation governs succession to the cause of action or particular item of property, under the law of the sister state or foreign nation.

Added by Stats. 1992, Ch. 178, Sec. 20. Effective January 1, 1993.

Section 377.11 - Decedent's successor in interest

For the purposes of this chapter, "decedent's successor in interest" means the beneficiary of the decedent's estate or other successor in interest who succeeds to a cause of action or to a particular item of the property that is the subject of a cause of action.
Added by Stats. 1992, Ch. 178, Sec. 20. Effective January 1, 1993.

Article 2 - SURVIVAL AND CONTINUATION

Section 377.20 - Generally
(a) Except as otherwise provided by statute, a cause of action for or against a person is not lost by reason of the person's death, but survives subject to the applicable limitations period.
(b) This section applies even though a loss or damage occurs simultaneously with or after the death of a person who would have been liable if the person's death had not preceded or occurred simultaneously with the loss or damage.
Added by Stats. 1992, Ch. 178, Sec. 20. Effective January 1, 1993.

Section 377.21 - Pending action or proceeding
A pending action or proceeding does not abate by the death of a party if the cause of action survives.
Added by Stats. 1992, Ch. 178, Sec. 20. Effective January 1, 1993.

Section 377.22 - Assignability of action not affected
Nothing in this chapter shall be construed as affecting the assignability of causes of action.
Added by Stats. 1992, Ch. 178, Sec. 20. Effective January 1, 1993.

Article 3 - DECEDENT'S CAUSE OF ACTION

Section 377.30 - Commencement by personal representation or successor in interest
A cause of action that survives the death of the person entitled to commence an action or proceeding passes to the decedent's successor in interest, subject to Chapter 1 (commencing with Section 7000) of Part 1 of Division 7 of the Probate Code, and an action may be commenced by the decedent's personal representative or, if none, by the decedent's successor in interest.
Added by Stats. 1992, Ch. 178, Sec. 20. Effective January 1, 1993.

Section 377.31 - Continuance of action by personal representative or successor in interest
On motion after the death of a person who commenced an action or proceeding, the court shall allow a pending action or proceeding that does not abate to be continued by the decedent's personal representative or, if none, by the decedent's successor in interest.
Added by Stats. 1992, Ch. 178, Sec. 20. Effective January 1, 1993.

Section 377.32 - Affidavit or declaration by successor in interest
(a) The person who seeks to commence an action or proceeding or to continue a pending action or proceeding as the decedent's successor in interest under this article, shall execute and file an affidavit or a declaration under penalty of perjury under the laws of this state stating all of the following:

(1) The decedent's name.

(2) The date and place of the decedent's death.

(3) "No proceeding is now pending in California for administration of the decedent's estate."

(4) If the decedent's estate was administered, a copy of the final order showing the distribution of the decedent's cause of action to the successor in interest.

(5) Either of the following, as appropriate, with facts in support thereof:

(A) "The affiant or declarant is the decedent's successor in interest (as defined in Section 377.11 of the California Code of Civil Procedure) and succeeds to the decedent's interest in the action or proceeding."

(B) "The affiant or declarant is authorized to act on behalf of the decedent's successor in interest (as defined in Section 377.11 of the California Code of Civil Procedure) with respect to the decedent's interest in the action or proceeding."

(6) "No other person has a superior right to commence the action or proceeding or to be substituted for the decedent in the pending action or proceeding."

(7) "The affiant or declarant affirms or declares under penalty of perjury under the laws of the State of California that the foregoing is true and correct."

(b) Where more than one person executes the affidavit or declaration under this section, the statements required by subdivision (a) shall be modified as appropriate to reflect that fact.
(c) A certified copy of the decedent's death certificate shall be attached to the affidavit or declaration.
Added by Stats. 1992, Ch. 178, Sec. 20. Effective January 1, 1993.

Section 377.33 - Orders ensuring proper administration
The court in which an action is commenced or continued under this article may make any order concerning parties that is appropriate to ensure proper administration of justice in the case, including appointment of the decedent's successor in interest as a special administrator or guardian ad litem.
Added by Stats. 1992, Ch. 178, Sec. 20. Effective January 1, 1993.

Section 377.34 - Damages recoverable
(a) In an action or proceeding by a decedent's personal representative or successor in interest on the decedent's cause of action, the damages recoverable are limited to the loss or damage that the decedent sustained or incurred before death, including any penalties or punitive or exemplary damages that the decedent would have been entitled to recover had the decedent lived, and do not include damages for pain, suffering, or disfigurement.
(b) Notwithstanding subdivision (a), in an action or proceeding by a decedent's personal representative or successor in interest on the decedent's cause of action, the damages recoverable may include damages for pain, suffering, or disfigurement if the action or proceeding was granted a preference pursuant to Section 36 before January 1, 2022, or was filed on or after January 1, 2022, and before January 1, 2026.
(c) A plaintiff who recovers damages pursuant to subdivision (b) between January 1, 2022, and January 1, 2025, inclusive, shall, within 60 days after obtaining a judgment, consent judgment, or court-approved settlement agreement entitling the plaintiff to the damages, submit to the Judicial Council a copy of the judgment, consent judgment, or court-approved settlement agreement, along with a cover sheet detailing all of the following information:

(1) The date the action was filed.

(2) The date of the final disposition of the action.

(3) The amount and type of damages awarded, including economic damages and damages for pain, suffering, or disfigurement.

(d)

(1) On or before January 1, 2025, the Judicial Council shall transmit to the Legislature a report detailing the information received pursuant to subdivision (c) for all judgements, consent judgements, or court-approved settlement agreements rendered from January 1, 2022, to July 31, 2024, inclusive, in which damages were recovered pursuant to subdivision (b). The report shall comply with Section 9795 of the Government Code.

(2) This subdivision shall become inoperative on January 1, 2029, pursuant to Section 10231.5 of the Government Code.

(e) Nothing in this section alters Section 3333.2 of the Civil Code.
(f) Nothing in this section affects claims brought pursuant to Chapter 11 (commencing with Section 15600) of Part 3 of Division 9 of the Welfare and Institutions Code.
Amended by Stats 2021 ch 448 (SB 447),s 1, eff. 1/1/2022.
Added by Stats. 1992, Ch. 178, Sec. 20. Effective January 1, 1993.

Section 377.35 - Effective date of article
On or after January 1, 1993, this article applies to the commencement of an action or proceeding the decedent was entitled to commence, and to the continuation of an action or proceeding commenced by the decedent, regardless of whether the decedent died before, on, or after January 1, 1993.
Added by Stats. 1992, Ch. 178, Sec. 20. Effective January 1, 1993.

Article 4 - CAUSE OF ACTION AGAINST DECEDENT

Section 377.40 - Assertion of action against personal representative or successor in interest
Subject to Part 4 (commencing with Section 9000) of Division 7 of the Probate Code governing creditor claims, a cause of action against a decedent that survives may be asserted against the decedent's personal representative or, to the extent provided by statute, against the decedent's successor in interest.
Added by Stats. 1992, Ch. 178, Sec. 20. Effective January 1, 1993.

Section 377.41 - Continuance of action against personal representative or successor in interest
On motion, the court shall allow a pending action or proceeding against the decedent that does not abate to be continued against the decedent's personal representative or, to the extent provided by statute, against the decedent's successor in interest, except that the court may not permit an action or proceeding to be continued against the personal representative unless proof of compliance with Part 4 (commencing with Section 9000) of Division 7 of the Probate Code governing creditor claims is first made.
Added by Stats. 1992, Ch. 178, Sec. 20. Effective January 1, 1993.

Section 377.42 - Damages recoverable
In an action or proceeding against a decedent's personal representative or, to the extent provided by statute, against the decedent's successor in interest, on a cause of action against the decedent, all damages are recoverable that might have been recovered against the decedent had the decedent lived except damages recoverable under Section 3294 of the Civil Code or other punitive or exemplary damages.
Added by Stats. 1992, Ch. 178, Sec. 20. Effective January 1, 1993.

Section 377.43 - Effective date of article
This article applies to the commencement on or after January 1, 1993, of an action or proceeding against the decedent's personal representative or successor in interest, or to the making of a motion on or after January 1, 1993, to continue a pending action or proceeding against the decedent's personal representative or successor in interest, regardless of whether the decedent died before, on, or after January 1, 1993.
Added by Stats. 1992, Ch. 178, Sec. 20. Effective January 1, 1993.

Article 5 - INSURED CLAIMS

Section 377.50 - Action to establish decedent's liability for which decedent protected by insurance
An action to establish the decedent's liability for which the decedent was protected by insurance may be commenced or continued against the decedent's estate as provided in Chapter 1 (commencing with Section 550) of Part 13 of Division 2 of the Probate Code.
Added by Stats. 1992, Ch. 178, Sec. 20. Effective January 1, 1993.

Article 6 - WRONGFUL DEATH

Section 377.60 - Persons who may assert action
A cause of action for the death of a person caused by the wrongful act or neglect of another may be asserted by any of the following persons or by the decedent's personal representative on their behalf:
(a) The decedent's surviving spouse, domestic partner, children, and issue of deceased children, or, if there is no surviving issue of the decedent, the persons, including the surviving spouse or domestic partner, who would be entitled to the property of the decedent by intestate succession. If the parents of the decedent would be entitled to bring an action under this subdivision, and the parents are deceased, then the legal guardians of the decedent, if any, may bring an action under this subdivision as if they were the decedent's parents.
(b)
    (1) Whether or not qualified under subdivision (a), if they were dependent on the decedent, the putative spouse, children of the putative spouse, stepchildren, parents, or the legal guardians of the decedent if the parents are deceased.
    (2) As used in this subdivision, "putative spouse" means the surviving spouse of a void or voidable marriage who is found by the court to have believed in good faith that the marriage to the decedent was valid.
(c) A minor, whether or not qualified under subdivision (a) or (b), if, at the time of the decedent's death, the minor resided for the previous 180 days in the decedent's household and was dependent on the decedent for one-half or more of the minor's support.
(d) This section applies to any cause of action arising on or after January 1, 1993.
(e) The addition of this section by Chapter 178 of the Statutes of 1992 was not intended to adversely affect the standing of any party having standing under prior law, and the standing of parties governed by that version of this section as added by Chapter 178 of the Statutes of 1992 shall be the same as specified herein as amended by Chapter 563 of the Statutes of 1996.
(f)
    (1) For the purpose of this section, "domestic partner" means a person who, at the time of the decedent's death, was the domestic partner of the decedent in a registered domestic partnership established in accordance with subdivision (b) of Section 297 of the Family Code.
    (2) Notwithstanding paragraph (1), for a death occurring prior to January 1, 2002, a person may maintain a cause of action pursuant to this section as a domestic partner of the decedent by establishing the factors listed in paragraphs (1) to (6), inclusive, of subdivision (b) of Section 297 of the Family Code, as it read pursuant to Section 3 of Chapter 893 of the Statutes of 2001, prior to its becoming inoperative on January 1, 2005.
    (3) The amendments made to this subdivision during the 2003-04 Regular Session of the Legislature are not intended to revive any cause of action that has been fully and finally adjudicated by the courts, or that has been settled, or as to which the applicable limitations period has run.
Amended by Stats 2020 ch 51 (AB 2445),s 1, eff. 9/9/2020.
Amended by Stats 2004 ch 947 (AB 2580),s 1, eff. 1/1/2005
Amended by Stats 2001 ch 893 (AB 25), s 2, eff. 1/1/2002.

Section 377.61 - Damages
In an action under this article, damages may be awarded that, under all the circumstances of the case, may be just, but may not include damages recoverable under Section 377.34. The court shall determine the respective rights in an award of the persons entitled to assert the cause of action.
Added by Stats. 1992, Ch. 178, Sec. 20. Effective January 1, 1993.

Section 377.62 - Joinder or consolidation of actions
(a) An action under Section 377.30 may be joined with an action under Section 377.60 arising out of the same wrongful act or neglect.

(b) An action under Section 377.60 and an action under Section 377.31 arising out of the same wrongful act or neglect may be consolidated for trial as provided in Section 1048.

Added by Stats. 1992, Ch. 178, Sec. 20. Effective January 1, 1993.

Chapter 5 - PERMISSIVE JOINDER

Section 378 - Joinder as plaintiffs

(a) All persons may join in one action as plaintiffs if:

(1) They assert any right to relief jointly, severally, or in the alternative, in respect of or arising out of the same transaction, occurrence, or series of transactions or occurrences and if any question of law or fact common to all these persons will arise in the action; or

(2) They have a claim, right, or interest adverse to the defendant in the property or controversy which is the subject of the action.

(b) It is not necessary that each plaintiff be interested as to every cause of action or as to all relief prayed for. Judgment may be given for one or more of the plaintiffs according to their respective right to relief.

Amended by Stats. 1971, Ch. 244.

Section 379 - Joinder as defendants

(a) All persons may be joined in one action as defendants if there is asserted against them:

(1) Any right to relief jointly, severally, or in the alternative, in respect of or arising out of the same transaction, occurrence, or series of transactions or occurrences and if any question of law or fact common to all these persons will arise in the action; or

(2) A claim, right, or interest adverse to them in the property or controversy which is the subject of the action.

(b) It is not necessary that each defendant be interested as to every cause of action or as to all relief prayed for. Judgment may be given against one or more defendants according to their respective liabilities.

(c) Where the plaintiff is in doubt as to the person from whom he or she is entitled to redress, he or she may join two or more defendants, with the intent that the question as to which, if any, of the defendants is liable, and to what extent, may be determined between the parties.

Amended by Stats. 1975, Ch. 1241.

Section 379.5 - Orders to prevent embarrassment, delay or undue expenses, for separate trials

When parties have been joined under Section 378 or 379, the court may make such orders as may appear just to prevent any party from being embarrassed, delayed, or put to undue expense, and may order separate trials or make such other order as the interests of justice may require.

Added by Stats. 1971, Ch. 244.

Section 382 - Party not consenting to joinder as plaintiff made defendant

If the consent of any one who should have been joined as plaintiff cannot be obtained, he may be made a defendant, the reason thereof being stated in the complaint; and when the question is one of a common or general interest, of many persons, or when the parties are numerous, and it is impracticable to bring them all before the court, one or more may sue or defend for the benefit of all.

Amended by Stats. 1971, Ch. 244.

Section 382.4 - Notification of connection of relationship with nonparty recipient of distribution

If a proposed settlement in a class action established pursuant to Section 382, including a consent judgment, decree, or settlement agreement, provides for the distribution of money or any other thing of value to a person or entity that is not a party to the action, an attorney for a party to the action shall, in connection with the hearing for preliminary approval pursuant to subdivision (c) of Rule 3.769 of the California Rules of Court, notify the court if the attorney has a connection to or a relationship with a nonparty recipient of the distribution that could reasonably create the appearance of impropriety as between the selection of the recipient of the money or thing of value and the interests of the class.

Added by Stats 2018 ch 45 (SB 847),s 1, eff. 6/27/2018.

Section 384 - Payment and distribution of unpaid residue of class action judgment

(a) It is the policy of the State of California to ensure that the unpaid cash residue and unclaimed or abandoned funds in class action litigation are distributed, to the fullest extent possible, in a manner designed either to further the purposes of the underlying class action or causes of action, or to promote justice for all Californians. The Legislature finds that the use of funds for these purposes is in the public interest, is a proper use of the funds, and is consistent with essential public and governmental purposes.

(b) Except as provided in subdivision (c), before the entry of a judgment in a class action established pursuant to Section 382 that provides for the payment of money to members of the class, the court shall determine the total amount that will be payable to all class members if all class members are paid the amount to which they are entitled pursuant to the judgment. The court shall also set a date when the parties shall report to the court the total amount that was actually paid to the class members. After the report is received, the court shall amend the judgment to direct the defendant to pay the sum of the unpaid residue or unclaimed or abandoned class member funds, plus any interest that has accrued thereon, to nonprofit organizations or foundations to support projects that will benefit the class or similarly situated persons, or that promote the law consistent with the objectives and purposes of the underlying cause of action, to child advocacy programs, or to nonprofit organizations providing civil legal services to the indigent. The court shall ensure that the distribution of any unpaid residue or unclaimed or abandoned class member funds derived from multistate or national cases brought under California law shall provide substantial or commensurate benefit to California consumers. For purposes of this subdivision, "judgment" includes a consent judgment, decree, or settlement agreement that has been approved by the court.

(c) This section shall not apply to any class action brought against any public entity, as defined in Section 811.2 of the Government Code, or against any public employee, as defined in Section 811.4 of the Government Code. However, this section shall not be construed to abrogate any equitable cy pres remedy that may be available in any class action with regard to all or part of the cash residue or unclaimed or abandoned class member funds.

Amended by Stats 2018 ch 776 (AB 3250),s 6, eff. 1/1/2019.

Amended by Stats 2018 ch 45 (SB 847),s 2, eff. 6/27/2018.

Amended by Stats 2017 ch 17 (AB 103),s 4, eff. 6/27/2017.

Amended by Stats 2001 ch 96 (SB 1218), s 2, eff. 1/1/2002.

Section 384.5 - Judgments providing for distribution to non-party recipients

If a judgment in a class action established pursuant to Section 382, including a consent judgment, decree, or settlement agreement that has been approved by a court, provides for a distribution of money or any other thing of value to a person or entity that is not a party to the action, the court shall transmit a copy of the order, judgment, or decree to the Judicial Council. The order, judgment, or decree shall contain, at a minimum, the information necessary for the California Research Bureau to complete the report required by Section 68520 of the Government Code.

Added by Stats 2018 ch 45 (SB 847),s 3, eff. 6/27/2018.

Chapter 6 - INTERPLEADER

Section 386 - Cross-complaint in interpleader

(a) A defendant, against whom an action is pending upon a contract, or for specific personal property, may, at any time before answer, upon affidavit that a person not a party to the action makes against him, and without any collusion with him, a demand upon such contract, or for such property, upon notice to such person and the adverse party, apply to the court for an order to substitute such person in his place, and discharge him from liability to either party, on his depositing in court the amount claimed on the contract, or delivering the property or its value to such person as the court may direct; and the court may, in its discretion, make the order; or such defendant may file a verified cross-complaint in interpleader, admitting that he has no interest in such amount or such property claimed, or in a portion of such amount or such property and alleging that all or such portion of the amount or property is demanded by parties to such action or cross-action and apply to the court upon notice to such parties for an order to deliver such property or portion thereof or its value to such person as the court shall direct. And whenever conflicting claims are or may be made upon a person for or relating to personal property, or the performance of an obligation, or any portion thereof, such person may bring an action against the conflicting claimants to compel them to interplead and litigate their several claims. The order of substitution may be made and the action of interpleader may be maintained, and the applicant or interpleading party be discharged from liability to all or any of the conflicting claimants, although their titles or claims have not a common origin, or are not identical but are adverse to and independent of one another.

(b) Any person, firm, corporation, association or other entity against whom double or multiple claims are made, or may be made, by two or more persons which are such that they may give rise to double or multiple liability, may bring an action against the claimants to compel them to interplead and litigate their several claims. When the person, firm, corporation, association or other entity against whom such claims are made, or may be made, is a defendant in an action brought upon one or more of such claims, it may either file a verified cross-complaint in interpleader, admitting that it has no interest in the money or property claimed, or in only a portion thereof, and alleging that all or such portion is demanded by parties to such action, and apply to the court upon notice to such parties for an order to deliver such money or property or such portion thereof to such person as the court shall direct; or may bring a separate action against the claimants to compel them to interplead and litigate their several claims. The action of interpleader may be maintained although the claims have not a common origin, are not identical but are adverse to and independent of one another, or the claims are unliquidated and no liability on the part of the party bringing the action or filing the cross-complaint has arisen. The applicant or interpleading party may deny liability in whole or in part to any or all of the claimants. The applicant or interpleading party may join as a defendant in such action any other party against whom claims are made by one or more of the claimants or such other party may interplead by cross-complaint; provided, however, that such claims arise out of the same transaction or occurrence.

(c) Any amount which a plaintiff or cross-complainant admits to be payable may be deposited by him with the clerk of the court at the time of the filing of the complaint or cross-complaint in interpleader without first obtaining an order of the court therefor. Any interest on amounts deposited and any right to damages for detention of property so delivered, or its value, shall cease to accrue after the date of such deposit or delivery.

(d) A defendant named in a complaint to compel conflicting claimants to interplead and litigate their claims, or a defendant named in a cross-complaint in interpleader, may, in lieu of or in addition to any other pleading, file an answer to the complaint or cross-complaint which shall be served upon all other parties to the action and which shall contain allegations of fact as to his ownership of or other interest in the amount or property and any affirmative defenses and relief requested. The allegations in such answer shall be deemed denied by all other parties to the action, unless otherwise admitted in the pleadings.

(e) Except in cases where by the law a right to a jury trial is now given, conflicting claims to funds or property or the value thereof so deposited or delivered shall be deemed issues triable by the court, and such issues may be first tried. In the event the amount deposited shall be less than the amount claimed to be due by one or more of the conflicting claimants thereto, or in the event the property or the value thereof delivered is less than all of the property or the value thereof claimed by one or more of such conflicting claimants, any issues of fact involved in determining whether there is a deficiency in such deposit or delivery shall be tried by the court or a jury as provided in Title 8 (commencing with Section 577) of Part 2 of this code.

(f) After any such complaint or cross-complaint in interpleader has been filed, the court in which it is filed may enter its order restraining all parties to the action from instituting or further prosecuting any other proceeding in any court in this state affecting the rights and obligations as between the parties to the interpleader until further order of the court.

Amended by Stats. 1975, Ch. 670.

Section 386.1 - Investment of deposit

Where a deposit has been made pursuant to Section 386, the court shall, upon the application of any party to the action, order such deposit to be invested in an insured interest-bearing account. Interest on such amount shall be allocated to the parties in the same proportion as the original funds are allocated.

Amended by Stats. 1979, Ch. 173.

Section 386.5 - Discharge from liability and dismissal from action upon deposit of amount in dispute with clerk

Where the only relief sought against one of the defendants is the payment of a stated amount of money alleged to be wrongfully withheld, such defendant may, upon affidavit that he is a mere stakeholder with no interest in the amount or any portion thereof and that conflicting demands have been made upon him for the amount by parties to the action, upon notice to such parties, apply to the court for an order discharging him from liability and dismissing him from the action on his depositing with the clerk of the court the amount in dispute and the court may, in its discretion, make such order.

Added by Stats. 1953, Ch. 328.

Section 386.6 - Costs and attorney's fees

(a) A party to an action who follows the procedure set forth in Section 386 or 386.5 may insert in his motion, petition, complaint, or cross complaint a request for allowance of his costs and reasonable attorney fees incurred in such action. In ordering the discharge of such party, the court may, in its discretion, award such party his costs and reasonable attorney fees from the amount in dispute which has been deposited with the court. At the time of final judgment in the action the court may make such further provision for assumption of such costs and attorney fees by one or more of the adverse claimants as may appear proper.

(b) A party shall not be denied the attorney fees authorized by subdivision (a) for the reason that he is himself an attorney, appeared in pro se, and performed his own legal services.

Amended by Stats. 1974, Ch. 273.

Chapter 7 - INTERVENTION

Section 387 - Generally

(a) For purposes of this section:
  (1) "Defendant" includes a cross-defendant.
  (2) "Plaintiff" includes a cross-complainant.

(b) An intervention takes place when a nonparty, deemed an intervenor, becomes a party to an action or proceeding between other persons by doing any of the following:
  (1) Joining a plaintiff in claiming what is sought by the complaint.
  (2) Uniting with a defendant in resisting the claims of a plaintiff.
  (3) Demanding anything adverse to both a plaintiff and a defendant.

(c) A nonparty shall petition the court for leave to intervene by noticed motion or ex parte application. The petition shall include a copy of the proposed complaint in intervention or answer in intervention and set forth the grounds upon which intervention rests.

(d)
  (1) The court shall, upon timely application, permit a nonparty to intervene in the action or proceeding if either of the following conditions is satisfied:

(A) A provision of law confers an unconditional right to intervene.

(B) The person seeking intervention claims an interest relating to the property or transaction that is the subject of the action and that person is so situated that the disposition of the action may impair or impede that person's ability to protect that interest, unless that person's interest is adequately represented by one or more of the existing parties.

(2) The court may, upon timely application, permit a nonparty to intervene in the action or proceeding if the person has an interest in the matter in litigation, or in the success of either of the parties, or an interest against both.

(e) If leave to intervene is granted by the court, the intervenor shall do both of the following:

(1) Separately file the complaint in intervention, answer in intervention, or both.

(2) Serve a copy of the order, or notice of the court's decision or order, granting leave to intervene and the pleadings in intervention as follows:

(A) A party to the action or proceeding who has not yet appeared shall be served in the same manner for service of summons pursuant to Article 3 (commencing with Section 415.10) of Chapter 4 of Title 5 of Part 2.

(B) A party who has appeared in the action or proceeding, whether represented by an attorney or not represented by an attorney, shall be served in the same manner for service of summons pursuant to Article 3 (commencing with Section 415.10) of Chapter 4 of Title 5 of Part 2, or in the manner provided by Chapter 5 (commencing with Section 1010) of Title 14 of Part 2.

(f) Within 30 days after service of a complaint in intervention or answer in intervention, a party may move, demur, or otherwise plead to the complaint in intervention or answer in intervention in the same manner as to an original complaint or answer.

Amended by Stats 2017 ch 131 (AB 1693),s 1, eff. 1/1/2018.

Section 388 - Copy of pleading in action alleging pollution or adverse environmental effects furnished Attorney General

In an action brought by a party for relief of any nature other than solely for money damages where a pleading alleges facts or issues concerning alleged pollution or adverse environmental effects which could affect the public generally, the party filing the pleading shall furnish a copy to the Attorney General of the State of California. The copy shall be furnished by the party filing the pleading within 10 days after filing.

Repealed and added by Stats. 1992, Ch. 178, Sec. 26. Effective January 1, 1993.

Chapter 8 - COMPULSORY JOINDER

Section 389 - Generally

(a) A person who is subject to service of process and whose joinder will not deprive the court of jurisdiction over the subject matter of the action shall be joined as a party in the action if (1) in his absence complete relief cannot be accorded among those already parties or (2) he claims an interest relating to the subject of the action and is so situated that the disposition of the action in his absence may (i) as a practical matter impair or impede his ability to protect that interest or (ii) leave any of the persons already parties subject to a substantial risk of incurring double, multiple, or otherwise inconsistent obligations by reason of his claimed interest. If he has not been so joined, the court shall order that he be made a party.

(b) If a person as described in paragraph (1) or (2) of subdivision (a) cannot be made a party, the court shall determine whether in equity and good conscience the action should proceed among the parties before it, or should be dismissed without prejudice, the absent person being thus regarded as indispensable. The factors to be considered by the court include:

(1) to what extent a judgment rendered in the person's absence might be prejudicial to him or those already parties;

(2) the extent to which, by protective provisions in the judgment, by the shaping of relief, or other measures, the prejudice can be lessened or avoided;

(3) whether a judgment rendered in the person's absence will be adequate;

(4) whether the plaintiff or cross-complainant will have an adequate remedy if the action is dismissed for nonjoinder.

(c) A complaint or cross-complaint shall state the names, if known to the pleader, of any persons as described in paragraph (1) or (2) of subdivision (a) who are not joined, and the reasons why they are not joined.

(d) Nothing in this section affects the law applicable to class actions.

Amended by Stats. 1971, Ch. 244.

Section 389.5 - Person making application to be made party brought in by proper amendment

When, in an action for the recovery of real or personal property, or to determine conflicting claims thereto, a person not a party to the action but having an interest in the subject thereof makes application to the court to be made a party, it may order him to be brought in by the proper amendment.

Added by Stats. 1957, Ch. 1498.

Title 3A - VEXATIOUS LITIGANTS

Section 391 - Definitions

As used in this title, the following terms have the following meanings:

(a) "Litigation" means any civil action or proceeding, commenced, maintained or pending in any state or federal court.

(b) "Vexatious litigant" means a person who does any of the following:

(1) In the immediately preceding seven-year period has commenced, prosecuted, or maintained in propria persona at least five litigations other than in a small claims court that have been (i) finally determined adversely to the person or (ii) unjustifiably permitted to remain pending at least two years without having been brought to trial or hearing.

(2) After a litigation has been finally determined against the person, repeatedly relitigates or attempts to relitigate, in propria persona, either (i) the validity of the determination against the same defendant or defendants as to whom the litigation was finally determined or (ii) the cause of action, claim, controversy, or any of the issues of fact or law, determined or concluded by the final determination against the same defendant or defendants as to whom the litigation was finally determined.

(3) In any litigation while acting in propria persona, repeatedly files unmeritorious motions, pleadings, or other papers, conducts unnecessary discovery, or engages in other tactics that are frivolous or solely intended to cause unnecessary delay.

(4) Has previously been declared to be a vexatious litigant by any state or federal court of record in any action or proceeding based upon the same or substantially similar facts, transaction, or occurrence.

(5) After being restrained pursuant to a restraining order issued after a hearing pursuant to Chapter 1 (commencing with Section 6300) of Part 4 of Division 10 of the Family Code, and while the restraining order is still in place, they commenced, prosecuted, or maintained one or more litigations against a person protected by the restraining order in this or any other court or jurisdiction that are determined to be meritless and caused the person protected by the order to be harassed or intimidated.

(c) "Security" means an undertaking to assure payment, to the party for whose benefit the undertaking is required to be furnished, of the party's reasonable expenses, including attorney's fees and not limited to taxable costs, incurred in or in connection with a litigation instituted, caused to be instituted, or maintained or caused to be maintained by a vexatious litigant.

(d) "Plaintiff" means the person who commences, institutes or maintains a litigation or causes it to be commenced, instituted or maintained, including an attorney at law acting in propria persona.

(e) "Defendant" means a person (including corporation, association, partnership and firm or governmental entity) against whom a litigation is brought or maintained or sought to be brought or maintained.
Amended by Stats 2022 ch 84 (AB 2391),s 1, eff. 1/1/2023.
Amended by Stats. 1994, Ch. 587, Sec. 3.5. Effective January 1, 1995.

Section 391.1 - Motion for order requiring plaintiff furnish security or dismissal of litigation
(a) In any litigation pending in any court of this state, at any time until final judgment is entered, a defendant may move the court, upon notice and hearing, for an order requiring the plaintiff to furnish security or for an order dismissing the litigation pursuant to subdivision (b) of Section 391.3. The motion for an order requiring the plaintiff to furnish security shall be based upon the ground, and supported by a showing, that the plaintiff is a vexatious litigant and that there is not a reasonable probability that they will prevail in the litigation against the moving defendant.
(b) A motion pursuant to subdivision (a) on the grounds that plaintiff is a vexatious litigant pursuant to paragraph (5) of subdivision (b) of Section 391 may be brought only by a person protected by the restraining order. A person filing a motion as described in this subdivision shall not be required to pay a filing fee.
Amended by Stats 2022 ch 84 (AB 2391),s 2, eff. 1/1/2023.
Amended by Stats 2012 ch 417 (AB 2274),s 1, eff. 1/1/2013, op. 1/1/2014.

Section 391.2 - Determination upon motion
At the hearing upon the motion the court shall consider any evidence, written or oral, by witnesses or affidavit, as may be material to the ground of the motion. Except for an order dismissing the litigation pursuant to subdivision (b) of Section 391.3, no determination made by the court in determining or ruling upon the motion shall be or be deemed to be a determination of any issue in the litigation or of the merits thereof.
Amended by Stats 2012 ch 417 (AB 2274),s 2, eff. 1/1/2013, op. 1/1/2014.

Section 391.3 - Order requiring plaintiff to furnish security; order dismissing litigation
(a) Except as provided in subdivision (b), if, after hearing the evidence upon the motion, the court determines that the plaintiff is a vexatious litigant and that there is no reasonable probability that the plaintiff will prevail in the litigation against the moving defendant, the court shall order the plaintiff to furnish, for the benefit of the moving defendant, security in such amount and within such time as the court shall fix.
(b) If, after hearing evidence on the motion, the court determines that the litigation has no merit and has been filed for the purposes of harassment or delay, the court shall order the litigation dismissed. This subdivision shall only apply to litigation filed in a court of this state by a vexatious litigant subject to a prefiling order pursuant to Section 391.7 who was represented by counsel at the time the litigation was filed and who became in propria persona after the withdrawal of his or her attorney.
(c) A defendant may make a motion for relief in the alternative under either subdivision (a) or (b) and shall combine all grounds for relief in one motion.
Amended by Stats 2012 ch 417 (AB 2274),s 3, eff. 1/1/2013, op. 1/1/2014.

Section 391.4 - Security not furnished as ordered
When security that has been ordered furnished is not furnished as ordered, the litigation shall be dismissed as to the defendant for whose benefit it was ordered furnished.
Added by Stats. 1963, Ch. 1471.

Section 391.6 - Stay of litigation when motion filed
Except as provided in subdivision (b) of Section 391.3, when a motion pursuant to Section 391.1 is filed prior to trial the litigation is stayed, and the moving defendant need not plead, until 10 days after the motion shall have been denied, or if granted, until 10 days after the required security has been furnished and the moving defendant given written notice thereof. When a motion pursuant to Section 391.1 is made at any time thereafter, the litigation shall be stayed for such period after the denial of the motion or the furnishing of the required security as the court shall determine.
Amended by Stats 2012 ch 417 (AB 2274),s 4, eff. 1/1/2013, op. 1/1/2014.

Section 391.7 - Prefiling order preventing vexatious litigation
(a) In addition to any other relief provided in this title, the court may, on its own motion or the motion of any party, enter a prefiling order which prohibits a vexatious litigant from filing any new litigation in the courts of this state in propria persona without first obtaining leave of the presiding justice or presiding judge of the court where the litigation is proposed to be filed. Disobedience of the order by a vexatious litigant may be punished as a contempt of court.
(b) The presiding justice or presiding judge shall permit the filing of that litigation only if it appears that the litigation has merit and has not been filed for the purposes of harassment or delay. The presiding justice or presiding judge may condition the filing of the litigation upon the furnishing of security for the benefit of the defendants as provided in Section 391.3.
(c) The clerk may not file any litigation presented by a vexatious litigant subject to a prefiling order unless the vexatious litigant first obtains an order from the presiding justice or presiding judge permitting the filing. If the clerk mistakenly files the litigation without the order, any party may file with the clerk and serve, or the presiding justice or presiding judge may direct the clerk to file and serve, on the plaintiff and other parties a notice stating that the plaintiff is a vexatious litigant subject to a prefiling order as set forth in subdivision (a). The filing of the notice shall automatically stay the litigation. The litigation shall be automatically dismissed unless the plaintiff within 10 days of the filing of that notice obtains an order from the presiding justice or presiding judge permitting the filing of the litigation as set forth in subdivision (b). If the presiding justice or presiding judge issues an order permitting the filing, the stay of the litigation shall remain in effect, and the defendants need not plead, until 10 days after the defendants are served with a copy of the order.
(d) For purposes of this section, "litigation" includes any petition, application, or motion other than a discovery motion, in a proceeding under the Family Code or Probate Code, for any order.
(e) The presiding justice or presiding judge of a court may designate a justice or judge of the same court to act on his or her behalf in exercising the authority and responsibilities provided under subdivisions (a) to (c), inclusive.
(f) The clerk of the court shall provide the Judicial Council a copy of any prefiling orders issued pursuant to subdivision (a). The Judicial Council shall maintain a record of vexatious litigants subject to those prefiling orders and shall annually disseminate a list of those persons to the clerks of the courts of this state.
Amended by Stats 2011 ch 49 (SB 731),s 1, eff. 1/1/2012.
Amended by Stats 2002 ch 1118 (AB 1938),s 1, eff. 1/1/2003.

Section 391.8 - Application to vacate prefiling order
(a) A vexatious litigant subject to a prefiling order under Section 391.7 may file an application to vacate the prefiling order and remove his or her name from the Judicial Council's list of vexatious litigants subject to prefiling orders. The application shall be filed in the court that entered the prefiling order, either in the action in which the prefiling order was entered or in conjunction with a request to the presiding justice or presiding judge to file new litigation under Section 391.7. The application shall be made before the justice or judge who entered the order, if that justice or judge is available. If that justice or judge who entered the order is not available, the application shall be made before the presiding justice or presiding judge, or his or her designee.
(b) A vexatious litigant whose application under subdivision (a) was denied shall not be permitted to file another application on or before 12 months has elapsed after the date of the denial of the previous application.

(c) A court may vacate a prefiling order and order removal of a vexatious litigant's name from the Judicial Council's list of vexatious litigants subject to prefiling orders upon a showing of a material change in the facts upon which the order was granted and that the ends of justice would be served by vacating the order.

Added by Stats 2011 ch 49 (SB 731),s 2, eff. 1/1/2012.

Title 4 - OF THE PLACE OF TRIAL, RECLASSIFICATION, AND COORDINATION OF CIVIL ACTIONS

Chapter 1 - PLACE OF TRIAL

Section 392 - Real property subject of action or proceeding; unlawful detainer

(a) Subject to the power of the court to transfer actions and proceedings as provided in this title, the superior court in the county where the real property that is the subject of the action, or some part thereof, is situated, is the proper court for the trial of the following actions:

(1) For the recovery of real property, or of an estate or interest therein, or for the determination in any form, of that right or interest, and for injuries to real property.

(2) For the foreclosure of all liens and mortgages on real property.

(b) In the court designated as the proper court in subdivision (a), the proper court location for trial of a proceeding for an unlawful detainer, as defined in Section 1161, is the location where the court tries that type of proceeding that is nearest or most accessible to where the real property that is the subject of the action, or some part thereof, is situated. Otherwise any location of the superior court designated as the proper court in subdivision (a) is a proper court location for the trial. The court may specify by local rule the nearest or most accessible court location where the court tries that type of case.

Amended by Stats 2002 ch 806 (AB 3027),s 7, eff. 1/1/2003.

Section 393 - Recovery of penalty or forfeiture; act done by public officer or person in virtue of office

Subject to the power of the court to transfer actions and proceedings as provided in this title, the county in which the cause, or some part of the cause, arose, is the proper county for the trial of the following actions:

(a) For the recovery of a penalty or forfeiture imposed by statute, except, that when it is imposed for an offense committed on a lake, river, or other stream of water, situated in two or more counties, the action may be tried in any county bordering on the lake, river, or stream, and opposite to the place where the offense was committed.

(b) Against a public officer or person especially appointed to execute the duties of a public officer, for an act done by the officer or person in virtue of the office, or against a person who, by the officer's command or in the officer's aid, does anything touching the duties of the officer.

Amended by Stats 2003 ch 449 (AB 1712),s 7, eff. 1/1/2004.

Section 394 - Action against county or city and county, city or local agency

(a) An action or proceeding against a county, or city and county, a city, or local agency, may be tried in the county, or city and county, or the county in which the city or local agency is situated, unless the action or proceeding is brought by a county, or city and county, a city, or local agency, in which case it may be tried in any county, or city and county, not a party thereto and in which the city or local agency is not situated. Except for actions initiated by the local child support agency pursuant to Section 17400, 17402, 17404, or 17416 of the Family Code, any action or proceeding brought by a county, city and county, city, or local agency within a certain county, or city and county, against a resident of another county, city and county, or city, or a corporation doing business in the latter, shall be, on motion of either party, transferred for trial to a county, or city and county, other than the plaintiff, if the plaintiff is a county, or city and county, and other than that in which the plaintiff is situated, if the plaintiff is a city, or a local agency, and other than that in which the defendant resides, or is doing business, or is situated. Whenever an action or proceeding is brought against a county, city and county, city, or local agency, in any county, or city and county, other than the defendant, if the defendant is a county, or city and county, or, if the defendant is a city, or local agency, other than that in which the defendant is situated, or the action or proceeding must be, on motion of that defendant, transferred for trial to a county, or city and county, other than that in which the plaintiff, or any of the plaintiffs, resides, or is doing business, or is situated, and other than the plaintiff county, or city and county, or county in which that plaintiff city or local agency is situated, and other than the defendant county, or city and county, or county in which the defendant city or local agency is situated; provided, however, that any action or proceeding against the city, county, city and county, or local agency for injury occurring within the city, county, or city and county, or within the county in which the local agency is situated, to person or property or person and property caused by the negligence or alleged negligence of the city, county, city and county, local agency, or its agents or employees, shall be tried in that county, or city and county, or if a city is a defendant, in the city or in the county in which the city is situated, or if a local agency is a defendant, in the county in which the local agency is situated. In that action or proceeding, the parties thereto may, by stipulation in writing, or made in open court, and entered in the minutes, agree upon any county, or city and county, for the place of trial thereof. When the action or proceeding is one in which a jury is not of right, or in case a jury is waived, then in lieu of transferring the cause, the court in the original county may request the chairperson of the Judicial Council to assign a disinterested judge from a neutral county to hear that cause and all proceedings in connection therewith. When the action or proceeding is transferred to another county for trial, a witness required to respond to a subpoena for a hearing within the original county shall be compelled to attend hearings in the county to which the cause is transferred. If the demand for transfer is made by one party and the opposing party does not consent thereto, the additional costs of the nonconsenting party occasioned by the transfer of the cause, including living and traveling expenses of the nonconsenting party and material witnesses, found by the court to be material, and called by the nonconsenting party, not to exceed five dollars ($5) per day each in excess of witness fees and mileage otherwise allowed by law, shall be assessed by the court hearing the cause against the party requesting the transfer. To the extent of that excess, those costs shall be awarded to the nonconsenting party regardless of the outcome of the trial. This section shall apply to actions or proceedings now pending or hereafter brought.

(b) For the purposes of this section, "local agency" shall mean any governmental district, board, or agency, or any other local governmental body or corporation, but shall not include the State of California or any of its agencies, departments, commissions, or boards.

Amended by Stats 2002 ch 784 (SB 1316),s 52, eff. 1/1/2003.

Amended by Stats 2002 ch 927 (AB 3032),s 1, eff. 1/1/2003.

Section 395 - Action for injury to person or personal property or death from wrongful act or negligence; offer or provision of goods, services, loans or extension of credit for family or household use

(a) Except as otherwise provided by law and subject to the power of the court to transfer actions or proceedings as provided in this title, the superior court in the county where the defendants or some of them reside at the commencement of the action is the proper court for the trial of the action. If the action is for injury to person or personal property or for death from wrongful act or negligence, the superior court in either the county where the injury occurs or the injury causing death occurs or the county where the defendants, or some of them reside at the commencement of the action, is a proper court for the trial of the action. In a proceeding for dissolution of marriage, the superior court in the county where either the petitioner or respondent has been a resident for three months next preceding the commencement of the proceeding is the proper court for the trial of the proceeding. In a proceeding for nullity of marriage or legal separation of the parties, the superior court in the county where either the petitioner or the respondent resides at the commencement of the proceeding is the proper court for the trial of the proceeding. In a proceeding to enforce an obligation of support under Section 3900 of the Family Code, the superior court in the county where the child resides is the proper court for the trial of the action. In a proceeding to establish and enforce a foreign judgment or court order for the support of a minor child, the superior court in the county where the child resides is the proper court for the trial of the action. Subject to subdivision (b), if a defendant has contracted to perform an obligation in a particular county, the superior court in the county where the obligation is to be performed, where the contract in fact was entered into, or where the defendant or any defendant resides at the commencement of the action is a proper court for the trial of an action founded on that obligation, and the county where the obligation is incurred is the county where it is to be performed, unless there is a special contract in writing to the contrary. If none of the defendants reside in the state or if they reside in the state and the county where they reside is unknown to the plaintiff, the action may be tried in the superior court in any county that the plaintiff may designate in his or her complaint, and, if the defendant is about to depart from the state, the action may be tried in the superior court in any county where either of the parties reside or service is made. If any person is improperly joined as a defendant or has been made a defendant solely for the purpose of having the action tried in the superior court in the county where he or she resides, his or her residence shall not be considered in determining the proper place for the trial of the action.

(b) Subject to the power of the court to transfer actions or proceedings as provided in this title, in an action arising from an offer or provision of goods, services, loans or extensions of credit intended primarily for personal, family or household use, other than an obligation described in Section 1812.10 or Section 2984.4 of the Civil Code, or an action arising from a transaction consummated as a proximate result of either an unsolicited telephone call made by a seller engaged in the business of consummating transactions of that kind or a telephone call or electronic transmission made by the buyer or lessee in response to a solicitation by the seller, the superior court in the county where the buyer or lessee in fact signed the contract, where the buyer or lessee resided at the time the contract was entered into, or where the buyer or lessee resides at the commencement of the action is the proper court for the trial of the action. In the superior court designated in this subdivision as the proper court, the proper court location for trial of a case is the location where the court tries that type of case that is nearest or most accessible to where the buyer or lessee resides, where the buyer or lessee in fact signed the contract, where the buyer or lessee resided at the time the contract was entered into, or where the buyer or lessee resides at the commencement of the action. Otherwise, any location of the superior court designated as the proper court in this subdivision is a proper court location for the trial. The court may specify by local rule the nearest or most accessible court location where the court tries that type of case.

(c) Any provision of an obligation described in subdivision (b) waiving that subdivision is void and unenforceable.

Amended by Stats 2002 ch 806 (AB 3027),s 8, eff. 1/1/2003.

Section 395.1 - Defendant sued in official or representative capacity on claim for payment of money or recovery of personal property

Except as otherwise provided in Section 17005 of the Probate Code pertaining to trustees, when a defendant is sued in an official or representative capacity as executor, administrator, guardian, conservator, or trustee on a claim for the payment of money or for the recovery of personal property, the county which has jurisdiction of the estate which the defendant represents shall be the proper county for the trial of the action.

Amended by Stats. 1986, Ch. 820, Sec. 16. Operative July 1, 1987, by Sec. 43 of Ch. 820.

Section 395.2 - Action against unincorporated association

If an unincorporated association has filed a statement with the Secretary of State pursuant to statute, designating its principal office in this state, the proper county for the trial of an action against the unincorporated association is the same as it would be if the unincorporated association were a corporation and, for the purpose of determining the proper county, the principal place of business of the unincorporated association shall be deemed to be the principal office in this state listed in the statement.

Amended by Stats 2004 ch 178 (SB 1746),s 2, eff. 1/1/2005

Section 395.5 - Action against corporation or association on contract

A corporation or association may be sued in the county where the contract is made or is to be performed, or where the obligation or liability arises, or the breach occurs; or in the county where the principal place of business of such corporation is situated, subject to the power of the court to change the place of trial as in other cases.

Added by Stats. 1972, Ch. 118.

Section 395.9 - [Repealed]

Repealed 9/7/1999 (Bill Number: SB 210) (Chapter 344).

Section 396 - Appeal or petition not filed in proper state court; appeal or petition transferred to court having jurisdiction

(a) No appeal or petition filed in the superior court shall be dismissed solely because the appeal or petition was not filed in the proper state court.

(b) If the superior court lacks jurisdiction of an appeal or petition, and a court of appeal or the Supreme Court would have jurisdiction, the appeal or petition shall be transferred to the court having jurisdiction upon terms as to costs or otherwise as may be just, and proceeded with as if regularly filed in the court having jurisdiction.

Added by Stats 2008 ch 56 (SB 1182),s 2, eff. 1/1/2009.

Section 396a - Affidavit filed in unlawful detainer proceeding showing proceeding commenced in proper court and location

In a case that is subject to Sections 1812.10 and 2984.4 of the Civil Code, or subdivision (b) of Section 395 of the Code of Civil Procedure, or in an action or proceeding for an unlawful detainer as defined in Section 1161 of the Code of Civil Procedure:

(a) The plaintiff shall state facts in the complaint, verified by the plaintiff's oath, or the oath of the plaintiff's attorney, or in an affidavit of the plaintiff or of the plaintiff's attorney filed with the complaint, showing that the action has been commenced in the proper superior court and the proper court location for the trial of the action or proceeding, and showing that the action is subject to the provisions of Sections 1812.10 and 2984.4 of the Civil Code or subdivision (b) of Section 395 of the Code of Civil Procedure, or is an action for an unlawful detainer. When the affidavit is filed with the complaint, a copy thereof shall be served with the summons. Except as provided in this section, if the complaint or affidavit is not filed pursuant to this subdivision, no further proceedings may occur in the action or proceeding, except to dismiss the action or proceeding without prejudice. However, the court may, on terms that are just, permit the affidavit to be filed after the filing of the complaint, and a copy of the affidavit shall be served on the defendant and the time to answer or otherwise plead shall date from that service.

(b) If it appears from the complaint or affidavit, or otherwise, that the superior court or court location where the action or proceeding is commenced is not the proper court or court location for the trial, the court where the action or proceeding is commenced, or a judge thereof, shall, whenever that fact appears, transfer it to the proper court or court location, on its own motion, or on motion of the defendant, unless the defendant consents in writing, or in open court (consent in open court being entered in the minutes of the court), to the keeping of the action or proceeding in the court or court location where commenced. If that consent is given, the action or proceeding may continue in the court or court location where commenced. Notwithstanding Section 1801.1 and subdivision (f) of Section 2983.7 of the Civil Code, that consent may be given by a defendant who is represented by counsel at the time the consent is given, and if an action or proceeding is subject to subdivision (b) of Section 395 or is for an unlawful detainer, that consent may only be given by a defendant who is represented by counsel at the time the consent is given.

(c) In any case where the transfer of the action or proceeding is ordered under subdivision (a) or (b), if summons is served prior to the filing of the action or proceeding in the superior court or court location to which it is transferred, as to any defendant, so served, who has not appeared in the action or proceeding, the time to answer or otherwise plead shall date from service upon that defendant of written notice of the filing.

(d) If it appears from the complaint or affidavit of the plaintiff that the superior court and court location where the action or proceeding is commenced are a proper court and court location for the trial thereof, all proper proceedings may be had, and the action or proceeding may be tried in that court at that location.

(e) A motion for a transfer of the action or proceeding to a different superior court may be made as in other cases, within the time, upon the grounds, and in the manner provided in this title, and if upon that motion it appears that the action or proceeding is not pending in the proper court, or should for other cause be transferred, the action or proceeding shall be ordered transferred as provided in this title. If any action or proceeding is ordered transferred to another court as provided in this section, proceedings shall be had, and the costs and fees shall be paid, as provided in Sections 398 and 399.

(f) If a motion is made for transfer of an action or proceeding to a different court location within the same superior court as provided in this section, proceedings shall be had as provided by local rules of the superior court.

Amended by Stats 2007 ch 263 (AB 310),s 5, eff. 1/1/2008.

Amended by Stats 2002 ch 806 (AB 3027),s 10, eff. 1/1/2003.

Section 396b - Notice or motion for order transferring action or proceeding; expenses and attorney's fees to prevailing party

(a) Except as otherwise provided in Section 396a, if an action or proceeding is commenced in a court having jurisdiction of the subject matter thereof, other than the court designated as the proper court for the trial thereof, under this title, the action may, notwithstanding, be tried in the court where commenced, unless the defendant, at the time he or she answers, demurs, or moves to strike, or, at his or her option, without answering, demurring, or moving to strike and within the time otherwise allowed to respond to the complaint, files with the clerk, a notice of motion for an order transferring the action or proceeding to the proper court, together with proof of service, upon the adverse party, of a copy of those papers. Upon the hearing of the motion the court shall, if it appears that the action or proceeding was not commenced in the proper court, order the action or proceeding transferred to the proper court.

(b) In its discretion, the court may order the payment to the prevailing party of reasonable expenses and attorney's fees incurred in making or resisting the motion to transfer whether or not that party is otherwise entitled to recover his or her costs of action. In determining whether that order for expenses and fees shall be made, the court shall take into consideration (1) whether an offer to stipulate to change of venue was reasonably made and rejected, and (2) whether the motion or selection of venue was made in good faith given the facts and law the party making the motion or selecting the venue knew or should have known. As between the party and his or her attorney, those expenses and fees shall be the personal liability of the attorney not chargeable to the party. Sanctions shall not be imposed pursuant to this subdivision except on notice contained in a party's papers, or on the court's own noticed motion, and after opportunity to be heard.

(c) The court in a proceeding for dissolution of marriage or legal separation or under the Uniform Parentage Act (Part 3 (commencing with Section 7600) of Division 12 of the Family Code) may, prior to the determination of the motion to transfer, consider and determine motions for allowance of temporary spousal support, support of children, and counsel fees and costs, and motions to determine custody of and visitation with children, and may make all necessary and proper orders in connection therewith.

(d) In any case, if an answer is filed, the court may consider opposition to the motion to transfer, if any, and may retain the action in the county where commenced if it appears that the convenience of the witnesses or the ends of justice will thereby be promoted.

(e) If the motion to transfer is denied, the court shall allow the defendant time to move to strike, demur, or otherwise plead if the defendant has not previously filed a response.

Amended by Stats 2005 ch 706 (AB 1742),s 10, eff. 1/1/2006

Section 397 - Grounds for changing place of trial on motion

The court may, on motion, change the place of trial in the following cases:

(a) When the court designated in the complaint is not the proper court.

(b) When there is reason to believe that an impartial trial cannot be had therein.

(c) When the convenience of witnesses and the ends of justice would be promoted by the change.

(d) When from any cause there is no judge of the court qualified to act.

(e) When a proceeding for dissolution of marriage has been filed in the county in which the petitioner has been a resident for three months next preceding the commencement of the proceeding, and the respondent at the time of the commencement of the proceeding is a resident of another county in this state, to the county of the respondent's residence when the ends of justice would be promoted by the change. If a motion to change the place of trial is made pursuant to this paragraph, the court may, prior to the determination of such motion, consider and determine motions for allowance of temporary spousal support, support of children, temporary restraining orders, attorneys' fees, and costs, and make all necessary and proper orders in connection therewith.

Amended by Stats. 1992, Ch. 163, Sec. 19. Effective January 1, 1993. Operative January 1, 1994, by Sec. 161 of Ch. 163.

Section 397.5 - Transfer of dissolution of marriage or legal separation proceedings to county of residence of either party

In any proceeding for dissolution or nullity of marriage or legal separation of the parties under the Family Code, where it appears that both petitioner and respondent have moved from the county rendering the order, the court may, when the ends of justice and the convenience of the parties would be promoted by the change, order that the proceedings be transferred to the county of residence of either party.

Amended by Stats. 1994, Ch. 1269, Sec. 2.6. Effective January 1, 1995.

Section 398 - Court to which action or proceeding transferred

(a) If a court orders the transfer of an action or proceeding for a cause specified in subdivisions (b), (c), and (d) of Section 397, the action or proceeding shall be transferred to a court having jurisdiction of the subject matter of the action upon agreement of the parties by stipulation in writing, or in open court and entered in the minutes or docket. If the parties do not so agree, the action or proceeding shall be transferred to the nearest or most accessible court where the like objection or cause for making the order does not exist.

(b) If an action or proceeding is commenced in a court other than one designated as a proper court for the trial thereof by the provisions of this title, and the same is ordered transferred for that reason, the action or proceeding shall be transferred to a proper court upon agreement of the parties by stipulation in writing, or in open court and entered in the minutes or docket. If the parties do not so agree, the action or proceeding shall be transferred to a proper court in the county in which the action or proceeding was commenced which the defendant may designate or, if there is no proper court in that county, to a proper court, in a proper county, designated by the defendant. If the defendant does not designate the court as herein provided, or if the court orders the transfer of an action on its own motion as provided in this title, the action or proceeding shall be transferred to the proper court as determined by the court in which the action or proceeding is pending.

(c) The designation of the court by the defendant as provided for in subdivision (b), may be made in the notice of motion for change of venue or in open court and entered in the minutes or docket at the time the order for transfer is made.

Amended by Stats 2015 ch 303 (AB 731),s 39, eff. 1/1/2016.

Section 399 - Transmission of pleading and papers to clerk of court to which proceeding transferred; payment of costs and fees

(a) If an order is made transferring an action or proceeding under any provision of this title, the clerk shall, after expiration of the time within which a petition for writ of mandate could have been filed pursuant to Section 400, or if a writ petition is filed after judgment denying the writ becomes final, and upon payment of the costs and fees, transmit the pleadings and papers of the action or proceeding, or, if the pleadings are oral, a transcript of the pleadings, to the clerk of the court to which the action or proceeding is transferred. If the transfer is sought on any ground specified in subdivision (b), (c), (d), or (e) of Section 397, the costs and fees of the transfer, and of filing the papers in the court to which the transfer is ordered, shall be paid at the time the notice of motion is filed by the party making the motion for the transfer. If the transfer is sought solely, or is ordered, because the action or proceeding was commenced in a court other than that designated as proper by this title, those costs and fees, including any expenses and attorney's fees awarded to the defendant pursuant to Section 396b, shall be paid by the plaintiff before the transfer is made. If the defendant has paid those costs and fees at the time of filing a notice of motion, those costs and fees shall be repaid to the defendant, upon the making of the transfer order. If those costs and fees have not been paid by the plaintiff within five days after service of notice of the transfer order, any other party interested in the action or proceeding, whether named in the complaint as a party or not, may pay those costs and fees, and the clerk shall transmit the papers and pleadings of the action or proceeding as if those costs and fees had been originally paid by the plaintiff, and those costs and fees shall be a proper item of costs of the party paying them, recoverable by that party if that party prevails in the action. Otherwise, those costs and fees shall be offset against and deducted from the amount, if any, awarded the plaintiff if the plaintiff prevails against that party in the action. The cause of action shall not be further prosecuted in any court until those costs and fees are paid. If those costs and fees are not paid within 30 days after service of notice of the transfer order, if a copy of a petition for writ of mandate pursuant to Section 400 is filed in the trial court, or if an appeal is taken pursuant to Section 904.2, then, within 30 days after notice of finality of the order of transfer, the court on a duly noticed motion by any party may dismiss the action without prejudice to the cause on the condition that no other action on the cause may be commenced in another court before satisfaction of the court's order for costs and fees. If a petition for writ of mandate or appeal does not result in a stay of proceedings, the time for payment of those costs and fees shall be 60 days after service of the notice of the order.

(b) At the time of transmittal of the papers and pleadings, the clerk shall mail notice to all parties who have appeared in the action or special proceeding, stating the date on which the transmittal occurred. Promptly upon receipt of the papers and pleadings, the clerk of the court to which the action or proceeding is transferred shall mail notice to all parties who have appeared in the action or special proceeding, stating the date of the filing of the case and number assigned to the case in the court.

(c) The court to which an action or proceeding is transferred under this title shall have and exercise over the action or proceeding the like jurisdiction as if it had been originally commenced in that court, all prior proceedings being saved, and the court may require amendment of the pleadings, the filing and service of amended, additional, or supplemental pleadings, and the giving of notice, as may be necessary for the proper presentation and determination of the action or proceeding in the court.

(d) Notwithstanding subdivision (c), the court transferring jurisdiction of a family law action or proceeding pursuant to Section 398 shall, if another court has not assumed jurisdiction over the action or proceeding, retain jurisdiction to make orders designed to prevent:

    (1) Immediate danger or irreparable harm to a party or to the children involved in the matter.

    (2) Immediate loss or damage to property subject to disposition in the matter.

(e) By January 1, 2019, the Judicial Council shall, by rule of court, establish:

    (1) The timeframe for a court to transfer jurisdiction over a family law action or proceeding.

    (2) The timeframe for a court to assume jurisdiction over a family law action or proceeding.

Amended by Stats 2017 ch 316 (AB 712),s 1, eff. 1/1/2018.
Amended by Stats 2007 ch 43 (SB 649),s 4, eff. 1/1/2008.

Section 399.5 - [Repealed]
Repealed 9/7/1999 (Bill Number: SB 210) (Chapter 344).

Section 400 - Petition for writ of mandate requiring trial in proper court
When an order is made by the superior court granting or denying a motion to change the place of trial, the party aggrieved by the order may, within 20 days after service of a written notice of the order, petition the court of appeal for the district in which the court granting or denying the motion is situated for a writ of mandate requiring trial of the case in the proper court. The superior court may, for good cause, and prior to the expiration of the initial 20-day period, extend the time for one additional period not to exceed 10 days. The petitioner shall file a copy of the petition in the trial court immediately after the petition is filed in the court of appeal. The court of appeal may stay all proceedings in the case, pending judgment on the petition becoming final. The clerk of the court of appeal shall file with the clerk of the trial court, a copy of any final order or final judgment immediately after the order or judgment becomes final.

Amended 9/7/1999 (Bill Number: SB 210) (Chapter 344).

Section 401 - Removal of action by or against state or state agency which may be commenced in Sacramento County
(1) Whenever it is provided by any law of this State that an action or proceeding against the State or a department, institution, board, commission, bureau, officer or other agency thereof shall or may be commenced in, tried in, or removed to the County of Sacramento, the same may be commenced and tried in any city or city and county of this State in which the Attorney General has an office.

(2) Whenever it is provided by any law of this State that the State or a department, institution, board, commission, bureau, officer or other agency thereof shall or may commence an action or proceeding in the County of Sacramento, the same, on motion of the defendants or some of them, shall be removed for trial to the county or city and county in which the Attorney General has an office nearest to the county in which the defendants or some of them reside or have their principal office in this State.

Added by Stats. 1947, Ch. 306.

Section 402 - Location specified by local rule of superior court
(a) Except as otherwise provided by law:

    (1) A superior court may specify by local rule the locations where certain types of actions or proceedings are to be filed.

    (2) A superior court may specify by local rule the locations where certain types of actions or proceedings are to be heard or tried.

    (3) A superior court may not dismiss a case, and the clerk may not reject a case for filing, because it is filed, or a person seeks to file it, in a court location other than the location specified by local rule. However, the court may transfer the case on its own motion to the proper court location.

(b) A superior court may transfer an action or proceeding filed in one location to another location of the superior court. This section does not affect the authority of the presiding judge to apportion the business of the court as provided by the California Rules of Court.

Added by Stats 2002 ch 806 (AB 3027),s 12, eff. 1/1/2003.

Section 402.5 - [Repealed]
Repealed by Stats 2002 ch 806 (AB 3027),s 13, eff. 1/1/2003.

Section 403 - Transfer for coordination with action involving common question of fact or law
A judge may, on motion, transfer an action or actions from another court to that judge's court for coordination with an action involving a common question of fact or law within the meaning of Section 404. The motion shall be supported by a declaration stating facts showing that the actions meet the standards specified in Section 404.1, are not complex as defined by the Judicial Council and that the moving party has made a good faith effort to obtain agreement to the transfer from all parties to each action. Notice of the motion shall be served on all parties to each action and on each court in which an action is pending. Any party to that action may file papers opposing the motion within the time permitted by rule of the Judicial Council. The court to which a case is transferred may order the cases consolidated for trial pursuant to Section 1048 without any further motion or hearing.

The Judicial Council may adopt rules to implement this section, including rules prescribing procedures for preventing duplicative or conflicting transfer orders issued by different courts.

Amended by Stats 2002 ch 784 (SB 1316),s 55, eff. 1/1/2003.
Amended by Stats 2000 ch 688 (AB 1669), s 2, eff. 1/1/2001.

Chapter 2 - RECLASSIFICATION OF CIVIL ACTIONS AND PROCEEDINGS

Section 403.010 - Chapter not to affect amendment of pleadings

Nothing in this chapter expands or limits the law on whether a plaintiff, cross-complainant, or petitioner may file an amended complaint or other amended initial pleading. Nothing in this chapter expands or limits the law on whether, and to what extent, an amendment relates back to the date of filing the original complaint or other initial pleading.
Amended by Stats 2002 ch 784 (SB 1316),s 56, eff. 1/1/2003.
Added September 7, 1999 (Bill Number: SB 210) (Chapter 344).

Section 403.020 - Pleading changes jurisdictional classification from limited to unlimited
(a) If a plaintiff, cross-complainant, or petitioner files an amended complaint or other amended initial pleading that changes the jurisdictional classification from limited to unlimited, the party at the time of filing the pleading shall pay the reclassification fee provided in Section 403.060, and the clerk shall promptly reclassify the case. If the amendment changes the jurisdictional classification from unlimited to limited, no reclassification fee is required, and the clerk shall promptly reclassify the case.
(b) For purposes of this chapter, an amendment to an initial pleading shall be treated in the same manner as an amended initial pleading.
Amended by Stats 2001 ch 824 (AB 1700), s 2, eff. 1/1/2002.
Added September 7, 1999 (Bill Number: SB 210) (Chapter 344).
This section was also amended by Stats 2001 ch 159 (SB 662), s 38, but was superseded. See Ca. Gov't Code § 9510.

Section 403.030 - Limited civil case reclassified by cross-complaint
If a party in a limited civil case files a cross-complaint that causes the action or proceeding to exceed the maximum amount in controversy for a limited civil case or otherwise fail to satisfy the requirements for a limited civil case as prescribed by Section 85, the caption of the cross-complaint shall state that the action or proceeding is a limited civil case to be reclassified by cross-complaint, or words to that effect. The party at the time of filing the cross-complaint shall pay the reclassification fees provided in Section 403.060, and the clerk shall promptly reclassify the case.
Amended by Stats 2001 ch 824 (AB 1700), s 3, eff. 1/1/2002.
Added September 7, 1999 (Bill Number: SB 210) (Chapter 344).

Section 403.040 - Motion for reclassification
(a) The plaintiff, cross-complainant, or petitioner may file a motion for reclassification within the time allowed for that party to amend the initial pleading. The defendant or cross-defendant may file a motion for reclassification within the time allowed for that party to respond to the initial pleading. The court, on its own motion, may reclassify a case at any time. A motion for reclassification does not extend the moving party's time to amend or answer or otherwise respond. The court shall grant the motion and enter an order for reclassification, regardless of any fault or lack of fault, if the case has been classified in an incorrect jurisdictional classification.
(b) If a party files a motion for reclassification after the time for that party to amend that party's initial pleading or to respond to a complaint, cross-complaint, or other initial pleading, the court shall grant the motion and enter an order for reclassification only if both of the following conditions are satisfied:
(1) The case is incorrectly classified.
(2) The moving party shows good cause for not seeking reclassification earlier.
(c) If the court grants a motion for reclassification, the payment of the reclassification fee shall be determined, unless the court orders otherwise, as follows:
(1) If a case is reclassified as an unlimited civil case, the party whose pleading causes the action or proceeding to exceed the maximum amount in controversy for a limited civil case or otherwise fails to satisfy the requirements of a limited civil case under Section 85 shall pay the reclassification fee provided in Section 403.060.
(2) If a case is reclassified as a limited civil case, no reclassification fee is required.
(d) If the court grants an order for reclassification of an action or proceeding pursuant to this section, the reclassification shall proceed as follows:
(1) If the required reclassification fee is paid pursuant to Section 403.060 or no reclassification fee is required, the clerk shall promptly reclassify the case.
(2) An action that has been reclassified pursuant to this section shall not be further prosecuted in any court until the required reclassification fee is paid. If the required reclassification fee has not been paid within five days after service of notice of the order for reclassification, any party interested in the case, regardless of whether that party is named in the complaint, may pay the fee, and the clerk shall promptly reclassify the case as if the fee had been paid as provided in Section 403.060. The fee shall then be a proper item of costs of the party paying it, recoverable if that party prevails in the action or proceeding. Otherwise, the fee shall be offset against and deducted from the amount, if any, awarded to the party responsible for the fee, if that party prevails in the action or proceeding.
(3) If the fee is not paid within 30 days after service of notice of an order of reclassification, the court on its own motion or the motion of any party may order the case to proceed as a limited civil case, dismiss the action or cross-action without prejudice on the condition that no other action or proceeding on the same matters may be commenced in any other court until the reclassification fee is paid, or take such other action as the court may deem appropriate.
(e) Nothing in this section shall be construed to require the superior court to reclassify an action or proceeding because the judgment to be rendered, as determined at the trial or hearing, is one that might have been rendered in a limited civil case.
(f) In any case where the misclassification is due solely to an excess in the amount of the demand, the excess may be remitted and the action may continue as a limited civil case.
Amended by Stats 2001 ch 824 (AB 1700), s 4, eff. 1/1/2002.
Added September 7, 1999 (Bill Number: SB 210) (Chapter 344).

Section 403.050 - Stipulation to reclassification
(a) The parties to the action or proceeding may stipulate to reclassification of the case within the time allowed to respond to the initial pleading.
(b) If the stipulation for reclassification changes the jurisdictional classification of the case from limited to unlimited, the reclassification fee provided in Section 403.060 shall be paid at the time the stipulation is filed.
(c) Upon filing of the stipulation and, if required under subdivision (b), the payment of the reclassification fee provided in Section 403.060, the clerk shall promptly reclassify the case.
Added by Stats 2001 ch 824 (AB 1700), s 6, eff. 1/1/2002.
Former § 403.050 was repealed by Stats 2001 ch 824 (AB 1700), s 5. .

Section 403.060 - Reclassification fee
(a) For reclassification of a case from a limited civil case to an unlimited civil case, a fee shall be charged as provided in Section 70619 of the Government Code. This reclassification fee shall be in addition to any other fee due for that appearance or filing in a limited civil case. No additional amounts shall be charged for appearance or filing fees paid prior to reclassification. After reclassification, the fees ordinarily charged in an unlimited case shall be charged.
(b) If a reclassification fee is required and is not paid at the time an amended complaint or other initial pleading, a cross-complaint, or a stipulation for reclassification is filed under Section 403.020, 403.030, or 403.050, the clerk shall not reclassify the case and the case shall remain and proceed as a limited civil case.

(c) No fee shall be charged for reclassification of a case from an unlimited civil case to a limited civil case. The fees ordinarily required for filing or appearing in a limited civil case shall be charged at the time of filing a pleading that reclassifies the case. Parties are not entitled to a refund of the difference between any fees previously paid for appearance or filing in an unlimited civil case and the fees due in a limited civil case. After reclassification, the fees ordinarily charged in a limited civil case shall be charged.
Amended by Stats 2005 ch 75 (AB 145),s 29, eff. 7/19/2005, op. 1/1/2006
Added by Stats 2001 ch 824 (AB 1700), s 8, eff. 1/1/2002.
Former § 403.060 was repealed by Stats 2001 ch 824 (AB 1700), s 7. .

Section 403.070 - When reclassified action deemed commenced; authority of court
(a) An action or proceeding that is reclassified shall be deemed to have been commenced at the time the complaint or petition was initially filed, not at the time of reclassification.
(b) The court shall have and exercise over the reclassified action or proceeding the same authority as if the action or proceeding had been originally commenced as reclassified, all prior proceedings being saved. The court may allow or require whatever amendment of the pleadings, filing and service of amended, additional, or supplemental pleadings, or giving of notice, or other appropriate action, as may be necessary for the proper presentation and determination of the action or proceeding as reclassified.
Added 9/7/1999 (Bill Number: SB 210) (Chapter 344).

Section 403.080 - Petition for writ of mandate requiring proper classification
When an order is made by the superior court granting or denying a motion to reclassify an action or proceeding pursuant to Section 403.040, the party aggrieved by the order may, within 20 days after service of a written notice of the order, petition the court of appeal for the district in which the court granting or denying the motion is situated for a writ of mandate requiring proper classification of the action or proceeding pursuant to Section 403.040. The superior court may, for good cause, and prior to the expiration of the initial 20-day period, extend the time for one additional period not to exceed 10 days. The petitioner shall file a copy of the petition in the superior court immediately after the petition is filed in the court of appeal. The court of appeal may stay all proceedings in the case, pending judgment on the petition becoming final. The clerk of the court of appeal shall file with the clerk of the superior court, a copy of any final order or final judgment immediately after the order or judgment becomes final.
Added 9/7/1999 (Bill Number: SB 210) (Chapter 344).

Section 403.090 - Rules governing procedure for reclassification
The Judicial Council may prescribe rules, not inconsistent with statute, governing the procedure for reclassification of civil actions and proceedings.
Added 9/7/1999 (Bill Number: SB 210) (Chapter 344).

Chapter 3 - COORDINATION

Section 404 - Petition for coordination when actions sharing common question pending in different courts
When civil actions sharing a common question of fact or law are pending in different courts, a petition for coordination may be submitted to the Chairperson of the Judicial Council, by the presiding judge of any such court, or by any party to one of the actions after obtaining permission from the presiding judge, or by all of the parties plaintiff or defendant in any such action. A petition for coordination, or a motion for permission to submit a petition, shall be supported by a declaration stating facts showing that the actions are complex, as defined by the Judicial Council and that the actions meet the standards specified in Section 404.1. On receipt of a petition for coordination, the Chairperson of the Judicial Council may assign a judge to determine whether the actions are complex, and if so, whether coordination of the actions is appropriate, or the Chairperson of the Judicial Council may authorize the presiding judge of a court to assign the matter to judicial officers of the court to make the determination in the same manner as assignments are made in other civil cases.
Amended by Stats 2002 ch 784 (SB 1316),s 57, eff. 1/1/2003.
Amended by Stats 2000 ch 688 (AB 1669), s 3, eff. 1/1/2001.

Section 404.1 - When coordination appropriate
Coordination of civil actions sharing a common question of fact or law is appropriate if one judge hearing all of the actions for all purposes in a selected site or sites will promote the ends of justice taking into account whether the common question of fact or law is predominating and significant to the litigation; the convenience of parties, witnesses, and counsel; the relative development of the actions and the work product of counsel; the efficient utilization of judicial facilities and manpower; the calendar of the courts; the disadvantages of duplicative and inconsistent rulings, orders, or judgments; and, the likelihood of settlement of the actions without further litigation should coordination be denied.
Added by Stats. 1972, Ch. 1162.

Section 404.2 - Selection of reviewing court having appellate jurisdiction
A judge assigned pursuant to Section 404 who determines that coordination is appropriate shall select the reviewing court having appellate jurisdiction if the actions to be coordinated are within the jurisdiction of more than one reviewing court. The assigned judge shall select the reviewing court which will promote the ends of justice as determined under the standards specified in Section 404.1.
Amended by Stats. 1996, Ch. 713, Sec. 4. Effective September 23, 1996.

Section 404.3 - Assignment of judge to hear and determine actions
A judge assigned pursuant to Section 404 who determines that coordination is appropriate shall order the actions coordinated, report that fact to the Chairperson of the Judicial Council, and the Chairperson of the Judicial Council shall either assign a judge to hear and determine the actions in the site or sites the assigned judge finds appropriate or authorize the presiding judge of a court to assign the matter to judicial officers of the court in the same manner as assignments are made in other civil cases.
Amended by Stats 2002 ch 784 (SB 1316),s 58, eff. 1/1/2003.

Section 404.4 - Requesting judge assigned to hear coordinated actions to order coordinating pending action
The presiding judge of any court in which there is pending an action sharing a common question of fact or law with actions coordinated pursuant to Section 404, on the court's own motion or the motion of any party supported by an affidavit stating facts showing that the action meets the standards specified in Section 404.1, or all the parties plaintiff or defendant in any such action, supported by an affidavit stating facts showing that the action meets the standards specified in Section 404.1, may request the judge assigned to hear the coordinated actions for an order coordinating the action. Coordination of the action shall be determined under the standards specified in Section 404.1.
Amended by Stats. 1996, Ch. 713, Sec. 6. Effective September 23, 1996.

Section 404.5 - Stay
Pending any determination of whether coordination is appropriate, the judge making that determination may stay any action being considered for, or affecting an action being considered for, coordination.
Added by Stats. 1972, Ch. 1162.

Section 404.6 - Petition for writ of mandate requiring reviewing court to make appropriate order
Within 20 days after service upon him or her of a written notice of entry of an order of the court under this chapter, any party may petition the appropriate reviewing court for a writ of mandate to require the court to make such order as the reviewing court finds appropriate. The superior court may, for good cause, and prior to the expiration of the initial 20-day period, extend the time for one additional period not to exceed 10 days.
Amended by Stats. 1989, Ch. 1416, Sec. 13.

Section 404.7 - Rules for practice and procedure for coordination
Notwithstanding any other provision of law, the Judicial Council shall provide by rule the practice and procedure for coordination of civil actions in convenient courts, including provision for giving notice and presenting evidence.
Added by Stats. 1972, Ch. 1162.

Section 404.8 - Payment or reimbursement of expenses
Expenses of the assigned judge, other necessary judicial officers and employees, and facilities for cases coordinated under Section 404 shall be paid or reimbursed by the state from funds appropriated to the Judicial Council.
Amended by Stats. 1996, Ch. 713, Sec. 7. Effective September 23, 1996.

Section 404.9 - Delegation by presiding judge of duties to another judge
Any duties of the presiding judge specified in this chapter may be delegated by the presiding judge to another judge of the court.
Amended by Stats 2002 ch 784 (SB 1316),s 59, eff. 1/1/2003.

Title 4.5 - RECORDING NOTICE OF CERTAIN ACTIONS
Chapter 1 - DEFINITIONS AND GENERAL PROVISIONS

Section 405 - Generally
The definitions in this chapter govern the construction of this title.
Added by Stats. 1992, Ch. 883, Sec. 2. Effective January 1, 1993.

Section 405.1 - Claimant
"Claimant" means a party to an action who asserts a real property claim and records a notice of the pendency of the action.
Added by Stats. 1992, Ch. 883, Sec. 2. Effective January 1, 1993.

Section 405.2 - Notice of pendency of action or notice
"Notice of pendency of action" or "notice" means a notice of the pendency of an action in which a real property claim is alleged.
Added by Stats. 1992, Ch. 883, Sec. 2. Effective January 1, 1993.

Section 405.3 - Probable validity
"Probable validity," with respect to a real property claim, means that it is more likely than not that the claimant will obtain a judgment against the defendant on the claim.
Added by Stats. 1992, Ch. 883, Sec. 2. Effective January 1, 1993.

Section 405.4 - Real property claim
"Real property claim" means the cause or causes of action in a pleading which would, if meritorious, affect (a) title to, or the right to possession of, specific real property or (b) the use of an easement identified in the pleading, other than an easement obtained pursuant to statute by any regulated public utility.
Added by Stats. 1992, Ch. 883, Sec. 2. Effective January 1, 1993.

Section 405.5 - Applicability of title to actions pending in United States District Court
This title applies to an action pending in any United States District Court in the same manner that it applies to an action pending in the courts of this state.
Added by Stats. 1992, Ch. 883, Sec. 2. Effective January 1, 1993.

Section 405.6 - Law governing action in eminent domain by public agency
In an action by a public agency in eminent domain pursuant to Title 7 (commencing with Section 1230.010) of Part 3, the issuance, service, and recordation of a notice of pendency of action shall be governed by Section 1250.150 and shall not be subject to Chapter 2 (commencing with Section 405.20).
Added by Stats. 1992, Ch. 883, Sec. 2. Effective January 1, 1993.

Section 405.7 - Action commenced to declare building uninhabitable
Whenever an action is commenced to declare a building uninhabitable, the plaintiff public agency, at the time of filing the complaint, shall record in the office of the recorder of the county in which the building is situated, a notice of the pendency of the action, containing the names of the parties and a description of the real property upon which the building affected by the action is situated.
Added by Stats. 1992, Ch. 883, Sec. 2. Effective January 1, 1993.

Section 405.8 - Party may seek attachment, injunction, other relief in connection with real property or expungement of notice
Nothing in this title precludes any party from seeking an attachment, injunction, or other relief in connection with a real property claim or the expungement of a notice of pending action.
Added by Stats. 1992, Ch. 883, Sec. 2. Effective January 1, 1993.

Section 405.20 - Recording notice in action asserting real property claim
A party to an action who asserts a real property claim may record a notice of pendency of action in which that real property claim is alleged. The notice may be recorded in the office of the recorder of each county in which all or part of the real property is situated. The notice shall contain the names of all parties to the action and a description of the property affected by the action.
Amended by Stats 2004 ch 227 (SB 1102),s 10, eff. 8/16/2004.

Section 405.21 - Signing notice; approval of notice by judge
An attorney of record in an action may sign a notice of pendency of action. Alternatively, a judge of the court in which an action that includes a real property claim is pending may, upon request of a party thereto, approve a notice of pendency of action. A notice of pendency of action shall not be recorded unless (a) it has been signed by the attorney of record, (b) it is signed by a party acting in propria persona and approved by a judge as provided in this section, or (c) the action is subject to Section 405.6.
Amended by Stats. 1994, Ch. 146, Sec. 20. Effective January 1, 1995.

Section 405.22 - Mailing copy of notice in action asserting real property claim
Except in actions subject to Section 405.6, the claimant shall, prior to recordation of the notice, cause a copy of the notice to be mailed, by registered or certified mail, return receipt requested, to all known addresses of the parties to whom the real property claim is adverse and to all owners of record of the real property affected by the real property claim as shown by the latest county assessment roll. If there is no known address for service on an adverse party or owner, then as to that party or owner a declaration under penalty of perjury to that effect may be recorded instead of the proof of service required above, and the service on that party or owner shall not be required. Immediately following recordation, a copy of the notice shall also be filed with the court in which the action is pending. Service shall also be made immediately and in the same manner upon each adverse party later joined in the action.
Amended by Stats 2004 ch 227 (SB 1102),s 11, eff. 8/16/2004.

Section 405.23 - Void or invalid notice
Any notice of pendency of action shall be void and invalid as to any adverse party or owner of record unless the requirements of Section 405.22 are met for that party or owner and a proof of service in the form and content specified in Section 1013a has been recorded with the notice of pendency of action.
Added by Stats. 1992, Ch. 883, Sec. 2. Effective January 1, 1993.

Section 405.24 - Constructive notice
From the time of recording the notice of pendency of action, a purchaser, encumbrancer, or other transferee of the real property described in the notice shall be deemed to have constructive notice of the pendency of the noticed action as it relates to the real property and only of its pendency against parties not fictitiously named. The rights and interest of the claimant in the property, as ultimately determined in the pending noticed action, shall relate back to the date of the recording of the notice.
Added by Stats. 1992, Ch. 883, Sec. 2. Effective January 1, 1993.

Article 3 - EXPUNGEMENT AND OTHER RELIEF

Section 405.30 - Application to expunge notice; intervention by person not party to action; evidence; burden of proof
At any time after notice of pendency of action has been recorded, any party, or any nonparty with an interest in the real property affected thereby, may apply to the court in which the action is pending to expunge the notice. However, a person who is not a party to the action shall obtain leave to intervene from the court at or before the time the party brings the motion to expunge the notice. Evidence or declarations may be filed with the motion to expunge the notice. The court may permit evidence to be received in the form of oral testimony, and may make any orders it deems just to provide for discovery by any party affected by a motion to expunge the notice. The claimant shall have the burden of proof under Sections 405.31 and 405.32.
Added by Stats. 1992, Ch. 883, Sec. 2. Effective January 1, 1993.

Section 405.31 - Pleading does not contain real property claim
In proceedings under this chapter, the court shall order the notice expunged if the court finds that the pleading on which the notice is based does not contain a real property claim. The court shall not order an undertaking to be given as a condition of expunging the notice where the court finds the pleading does not contain a real property claim.
Added by Stats. 1992, Ch. 883, Sec. 2. Effective January 1, 1993.

Section 405.32 - Claimant has not established probable validity of real property claim
In proceedings under this chapter, the court shall order that the notice be expunged if the court finds that the claimant has not established by a preponderance of the evidence the probable validity of the real property claim. The court shall not order an undertaking to be given as a condition of expunging the notice if the court finds the claimant has not established the probable validity of the real property claim.
Added by Stats. 1992, Ch. 883, Sec. 2. Effective January 1, 1993.

Section 405.33 - Expungement order conditioned on giving undertaking
In proceedings under this chapter, the court shall order that the notice be expunged if the court finds that the real property claim has probable validity, but adequate relief can be secured to the claimant by the giving of an undertaking. The expungement order shall be conditioned upon the giving of the undertaking of such nature and in such amount as will indemnify the claimant for all damages proximately resulting from the expungement which the claimant may incur if the claimant prevails upon the real property claim. In its order conditionally expunging the notice, the court shall set a return date for the moving party to show fulfillment of the condition, and if the moving party fails to show fulfillment of the condition on the return day, the court shall deny the motion to expunge without further notice or hearing. Recovery may be had on the undertaking pursuant to Section 996.440.
For purposes only of determining under this section whether the giving of an undertaking will secure adequate relief to the claimant, the presumption of Section 3387 of the Civil Code that real property is unique shall not apply, except in the case of real property improved with a single-family dwelling which the claimant intends to occupy.
Added by Stats. 1992, Ch. 883, Sec. 2. Effective January 1, 1993.

Section 405.34 - Undertaking as condition of maintaining notice in record title
Subject to the provisions of Sections 405.31 and 405.32, at any time after a notice of pendency of action has been recorded, and regardless of whether a motion to expunge has been filed, the court may, upon motion by any person with an interest in the property, require the claimant to give the moving party an undertaking as a condition of maintaining the notice in the record title. However, a person who is not a party to the action shall obtain leave to intervene from the court at or before the time the person moves to require an undertaking. The court may permit evidence to be received in the form of oral testimony and may make any orders it deems just to provide for discovery by any affected party. An undertaking required pursuant to this section shall be of such nature and in such amount as the court may determine to be just. In its order requiring an undertaking, the court shall set a return date for the claimant to show compliance and if the claimant fails to show compliance on the return date, the court shall order the notice of pendency of action expunged without further notice or hearing.
Recovery on an undertaking required pursuant to this section may be had in an amount not to exceed the undertaking, pursuant to Section 996.440, upon a showing (a) that the claimant did not prevail on the real property claim and (b) that the person seeking recovery suffered damages as a result of the maintenance of the notice. In assessing these damages, the court shall not consider the claimant's intent or the presence or absence of probable cause.
Added by Stats. 1992, Ch. 883, Sec. 2. Effective January 1, 1993.

Section 405.35 - When order effective and recorded
No order expunging a notice of pendency of action shall be effective, nor shall it be recorded in the office of any county recorder, until the time within which a petition for writ of mandate may be filed pursuant to Section 405.39 has expired. No order expunging a notice of pendency of action shall be effective, nor shall it be recorded in the office of any county recorder, after a petition for writ of mandate has been timely filed pursuant to Section 405.39, until the proceeding commenced by the petition is finally adjudicated. This section imposes no duty on the county recorder to determine whether the requirements of this section or of any order expunging a notice of pendency of action have been met.
Added by Stats. 1992, Ch. 883, Sec. 2. Effective January 1, 1993.

Section 405.36 - Recording another notice after notice expunged
Once a notice of pending action has been expunged, the claimant may not record another notice of pending action as to the affected property without leave of the court in which the action is pending.
Added by Stats. 1992, Ch. 883, Sec. 2. Effective January 1, 1993.

Section 405.37 - Authority of court to exonerate or modify undertaking
After notice and hearing, for good cause and upon such terms as are just, the court may exonerate or modify any undertaking required by an order issued pursuant to Section 405.33 or 405.34 or pursuant to a stipulation made in lieu of such an order. An order of the court under this section may be made conditional upon the giving of a new undertaking under Section 405.33 or 405.34.
Added by Stats. 1992, Ch. 883, Sec. 2. Effective January 1, 1993.

Section 405.38 - Attorney's fees and costs
The court shall direct that the party prevailing on any motion under this chapter be awarded the reasonable attorney's fees and costs of making or opposing the motion unless the court finds that the other party acted with substantial justification or that other circumstances make the imposition of attorney's fees and costs unjust.
Added by Stats. 1992, Ch. 883, Sec. 2. Effective January 1, 1993.

Section 405.39 - Petition for writ of mandate
No order or other action of the court under this chapter shall be appealable. Any party aggrieved by an order made on a motion under this chapter may petition the proper reviewing court to review the order by writ of mandate. The petition for writ of mandate shall be filed and served within

20 days of service of written notice of the order by the court or any party. The court which issued the order may, within the initial 20-day period, extend the initial 20-day period for one additional period not to exceed 10 days. A copy of the petition for writ of mandate shall be delivered to the clerk of the court which issued the order with a request that it be placed in the court file.
Added by Stats. 1992, Ch. 883, Sec. 2. Effective January 1, 1993.

Article 4 - WITHDRAWAL

Section 405.50 - Generally

At any time after notice of pendency of an action has been recorded pursuant to this title or other law, the notice may be withdrawn by recording in the office of the recorder in which the notice of pendency was recorded a notice of withdrawal executed by the party who recorded the notice of pendency of action or by the party's successor in interest. The notice of withdrawal shall be acknowledged.
Added by Stats. 1992, Ch. 883, Sec. 2. Effective January 1, 1993.

Article 5 - EFFECT OF WITHDRAWAL OR EXPUNGEMENT OF NOTICE

Section 405.60 - Notice and information recorded deemed not to constitute actual or constructive notice

Upon the withdrawal of a notice of pendency of action pursuant to Section 405.50 or upon recordation of a certified copy of an order expunging a notice of pendency of action pursuant to this title, neither the notice nor any information derived from it, prior to the recording of a certified copy of the judgment or decree issued in the action, shall constitute actual or constructive notice of any of the matters contained, claimed, alleged, or contended therein, or of any of the matters related to the action, or create a duty of inquiry in any person thereafter dealing with the affected property.
Added by Stats. 1992, Ch. 883, Sec. 2. Effective January 1, 1993.

Section 405.61 - No purchaser, transferee, mortgagee or other encumbrancer deemed to have actual knowledge

Upon the withdrawal of a notice of pendency of action pursuant to Section 405.50 or upon recordation of a certified copy of an order expunging a notice of pendency of action pursuant to this title, no person except a nonfictitious party to the action at the time of recording of the notice of withdrawal or order, who thereafter becomes, by conveyance recorded prior to the recording of a certified copy of the judgment or decree issued in the action, a purchaser, transferee, mortgagee, or other encumbrancer for a valuable consideration of any interest in the real property subject to the action, shall be deemed to have actual knowledge of the action or any of the matters contained, claimed, or alleged therein, or of any of the matters related to the action, irrespective of whether that person possessed actual knowledge of the action or matter and irrespective of when or how the knowledge was obtained.
It is the intent of the Legislature that this section shall provide for the absolute and complete free transferability of real property after the expungement or withdrawal of a notice of pendency of action.
Added by Stats. 1992, Ch. 883, Sec. 2. Effective January 1, 1993.

Title 5 - JURISDICTION AND SERVICE OF PROCESS

Chapter 1 - JURISDICTION AND FORUM

Article 1 - JURISDICTION

Section 410.10 - Generally

A court of this state may exercise jurisdiction on any basis not inconsistent with the Constitution of this state or of the United States.
Added by Stats. 1969, Ch. 1610.

Article 2 - FORUM

Section 410.30 - Action should be heard in forum outside state

(a) When a court upon motion of a party or its own motion finds that in the interest of substantial justice an action should be heard in a forum outside this state, the court shall stay or dismiss the action in whole or in part on any conditions that may be just.
(b) The provisions of Section 418.10 do not apply to a motion to stay or dismiss the action by a defendant who has made a general appearance.
Amended by Stats. 1972, Ch. 601. Note: This version was suspended from Sept. 22, 1986, until Jan. 1, 1992, during operation of the temporary amendment by Stats. 1986, Ch. 968.

Section 410.40 - Action against foreign corporation or nonresident person in California court

Any person may maintain an action or proceeding in a court of this state against a foreign corporation or nonresident person where the action or proceeding arises out of or relates to any contract, agreement, or undertaking for which a choice of California law has been made in whole or in part by the parties thereto and which (a) is a contract, agreement, or undertaking, contingent or otherwise, relating to a transaction involving in the aggregate not less than one million dollars ($1,000,000), and (b) contains a provision or provisions under which the foreign corporation or nonresident agrees to submit to the jurisdiction of the courts of this state.
This section applies to contracts, agreements, and undertakings entered into before, on, or after its effective date; it shall be fully retroactive. Contracts, agreements, and undertakings selecting California law entered into before the effective date of this section shall be valid, enforceable, and effective as if this section had been in effect on the date they were entered into; and actions and proceedings commencing in a court of this state before the effective date of this section may be maintained as if this section were in effect on the date they were commenced.
Added by Stats. 1992, Ch. 615, Sec. 5. Effective January 1, 1993.

Section 410.42 - Provisions of contract for construction of work of improvement prohibiting resolution of disputes in state

(a) The following provisions of a contract between the contractor and a subcontractor with principal offices in this state, for the construction of a public or private work of improvement in this state, shall be void and unenforceable:
   (1) A provision which purports to require any dispute between the parties to be litigated, arbitrated, or otherwise determined outside this state.
   (2) A provision which purports to preclude a party from commencing such a proceeding or obtaining a judgment or other resolution in this state or the courts of this state.
(b) For purposes of this section, "construction" means any work or services performed on, or materials provided for, a work of improvement, as defined in Section 8050 of the Civil Code, and for which a lien may be claimed pursuant to Section 8400 of the Civil Code (whether or not a lien is in fact claimed) or for which such a lien could be claimed but for Section 8160 of the Civil Code.
Amended by Stats 2010 ch 697 (SB 189),s 22, eff. 1/1/2011, op. 7/1/2012.

Article 3 - JURISDICTION IN ACTION

Section 410.50 - Jurisdiction from time summons served; general appearance equivalent to personal service; continued jurisdiction

(a) Except as otherwise provided by statute, the court in which an action is pending has jurisdiction over a party from the time summons is served on him as provided by Chapter 4 (commencing with Section 413.10). A general appearance by a party is equivalent to personal service of summons on such party.
(b) Jurisdiction of the court over the parties and the subject matter of an action continues throughout subsequent proceedings in the action.
Added by Stats. 1969, Ch. 1610.

Section 410.60 - Action against corporation which has forfeited charter or right to do business or dissolved

In an action against a corporation which has forfeited its charter or right to do business, or has dissolved, the court in which the action is pending has jurisdiction over all the trustees of such corporation and of its stockholders or members from the time summons is served on one of the trustees as provided by Chapter 4 (commencing with Section 413.10).
Added by Stats. 1969, Ch. 1610.

Section 410.70 - Action against persons jointly, jointly and severally or severally liable on contract
In an action against two or more persons who are jointly, jointly and severally, or severally liable on a contract, the court in which the action is pending has jurisdiction to proceed against such of the defendants as are served as if they were the only defendants.
Added by Stats. 1969, Ch. 1610.

Chapter 2 - COMMENCING CIVIL ACTIONS

Section 411.10 - Filing complaint
A civil action is commenced by filing a complaint with the court.
Added by Stats. 1969, Ch. 1610.

Section 411.20 - Payment made by check later returned without payment
(a) If the clerk accepts for filing a complaint or other first paper, or any subsequent filing, and payment is made by check which is later returned without payment, the clerk shall, by mail, notify the party who tendered the check that (1) the check has been returned without payment, (2) the administrative charge specified in subdivision (g) has been imposed to reimburse the court for the costs of processing the returned check and providing the notice specified in this subdivision, and (3) the party has 20 days from the date of mailing of the notice within which to pay the filing fee and the administrative charge, except as provided in subdivision (e). The notice also shall state that the administrative charge and the filing fee shall be paid in cash, by certified check, or by other means specified by the court, but not by traveler's check or personal check. If the person who tendered the check is not a party to the action or proposed action, but only is acting on behalf of a party, the clerk shall notify not only the person who tendered the check, but also the party or that party's attorney if the party is represented. The clerk's certificate as to the mailing of notice pursuant to this section establishes a rebuttable presumption that the fees were not paid. This presumption is a presumption affecting the burden of producing evidence.
(b) The clerk shall void the filing if the party who tendered a returned check or on whose behalf a returned check was tendered has not paid the full amount of the fee and the administrative charge by a means specified in subdivision (a) within 20 days of the date on which the notice required by subdivision (a) was mailed. Any filing voided by this section can be disposed of immediately after the 20 days have elapsed without preserving a copy in the court records, notwithstanding Section 68152 of the Government Code.
(c) If an adverse party files a response to a complaint, paper or filing referred to in subdivision (a), together with a filing fee, and the original filing is voided pursuant to subdivision (b), the responsive filing is not required and shall be voided. The court shall, by mail, provide notice to the parties or their attorneys that the initial paper and the response have been voided. The responding party's filing fee shall be refunded upon request, provided that the request for a refund is made within 20 days from the date on which the notice was mailed. Upon receipt of the request, the court shall refund the responding party's filing fee without imposing any administrative charge. A refund under this subdivision is available if the adverse party has filed only a responsive pleading, but not if the party has also filed a cross-complaint or other first paper seeking affirmative relief for which there is a filing fee.
(d) If an adverse party, or a person acting on behalf of the adverse party, tenders a check for a required filing fee that is later returned without payment, the procedures in subdivisions (a) and (b) shall apply.
(e) If any trial or other hearing is scheduled to be heard prior to the expiration of the 20-day period provided for in subdivision (a), the fee shall be paid prior to the trial or hearing. Failure of the party to pay the fee prior to the trial or hearing date shall cause the court to void the filing and proceed as if it had not been filed.
(f) If the clerk performs a service or issues any document for which a fee is required and payment is made by check which is later returned without payment, the court may order further proceedings suspended as to the party for whom the check was tendered. If the court so orders, the clerk shall, by mail, notify the party who tendered the check that proceedings have been suspended until the receipt of payment of the required fee and the administrative charge specified in subdivision (g), by cash cashier's check, or other means specified by the court, but not by personal check or traveler's check. If the person who tendered the check is not a party to the action or proposed action, but only is acting on behalf of a party, the clerk shall notify not only the person who tendered the check, but also the party or that party's attorney if the party is represented. The clerk's certificate as to the mailing of notice pursuant to this section establishes a rebuttable presumption that the fees were not paid. This presumption is a presumption affecting the burden of producing evidence.
(g) The clerk shall impose an administrative charge for providing notice that a check submitted for a filing fee has been returned without payment and for all related administrative, clerical, and other costs incurred under this section. The administrative charge shall, in each instance, be either twenty-five dollars ($25) or a reasonable amount that does not exceed the actual cost incurred by the court, as determined by the court. The notices provided by the court under subdivisions (a) and (f) shall state the specific amount of the administrative charge that shall be paid to the court. Each administrative charge collected shall be distributed to the court that incurred the charge as described in Section 68085.1 of the Government Code.
Amended by Stats 2005 ch 75 (AB 145),s 30, eff. 7/19/2005, op. 1/1/2006
Amended by Stats 2004 ch 171 (AB 3078),s 2, eff. 1/1/2005.

Section 411.20.5 - Unpaid fees; sanctions
If an electronic filing is made to the clerk by an electronic filing service provider acting as the agent of the court for purposes of collecting and remitting filing fees, and fees owed to the electronic filing service provider remain unpaid for a period of five days after notice to the attorney of record, and the filing was made by the attorney of record and not a self-represented party, the electronic filing service provider may notify the clerk that fees remain unpaid despite notice to the attorney of record. The clerk may then notify the attorney of record that the attorney of record may be sanctioned by the court for nonpayment of fees. The court may sanction the attorney of record if the fees to the electronic filing service provider remain unsatisfied 20 days after notice by the clerk.
Added by Stats 2018 ch 248 (AB 1531),s 1, eff. 1/1/2019.

Section 411.21 - Payment by check in amount less than required fee
(a) If a complaint or other first paper is accompanied by payment by check in an amount less than the required fee, the clerk shall accept the paper for filing, but shall not issue a summons until the court receives full payment of the required fee. The clerk shall, by mail, notify the party tendering the check that (1) the check was made out for an amount less than the required filing fee, (2) the administrative charge specified in subdivision (g) has been imposed to reimburse the court for the costs of processing the partial payment and providing the notice specified in this subdivision, and (3) the party has 20 days from the date of mailing of the notice within which to pay the remainder of the required fee and the administrative charge, except as provided in subdivision (f). If the person who tendered the check is not a party to the action or proposed action, but only is acting on behalf of a party, the clerk shall notify not only the person who tendered the check, and also the party or that party's attorney, if the party is represented. The clerk's certificate as to the mailing of notice pursuant to this section establishes a rebuttable presumption that the fees were not paid. This presumption is a presumption affecting the burden of producing evidence. This subdivision does not apply to an unlawful detainer action.

(b) The clerk shall void the filing if the party who tendered a check in an amount less than the required filing fee or on whose behalf a check in an amount less than the required filing fee was tendered has not paid the full amount of the fee and the administrative charge by a means specified in subdivision (a) within 20 days of the date on which the notice required by subdivision (a) was mailed. Any filing voided by this section may be disposed of immediately after the 20 days have elapsed without preserving a copy in the court records notwithstanding Section 68152 of the Government Code.

(c) If a check for less than the required fee was tendered, the remainder of the required fee and the administrative charge were not paid within the period specified in subdivision (a), and a refund of the partial payment has not been requested in a writing mailed or presented by the party or person who tendered the check within 20 days from the date on which the remainder of the required fee was due, the partial payment shall be remitted to the State Treasurer to be deposited in the Trial Court Trust Fund, except for the amount of the administrative charge described in subdivision (g), that shall be deducted from the partial payment and shall be distributed as described in subdivision (g) to the court which incurred the charge. If the party or person who tendered the check for partial payment requests a refund of the partial payment, in writing, within the time specified in this subdivision, the clerk shall refund the amount of the partial payment less the amount of the administrative charge imposed by that court. All partial payments that the court received before January 1, 2006, and that remain on deposit for filings that the clerk voided pursuant to this section, once three years have passed from the date that the filing was voided, shall be remitted to the State Treasurer for deposit into the Trial Court Trust Fund.

(d) If an adverse party files a response to a complaint or other first paper referred to in subdivision (a), together with a filing fee, and the original filing is voided pursuant to subdivision (b), the responsive filing is not required and shall be voided. The court shall, by mail, provide notice to the parties that the initial paper and the response have been voided. The responding party's filing fee shall be refunded upon request, provided that the request for a refund is made in writing within 20 days from the date on which the notice was mailed. Upon receipt of the request, the court shall reimburse the responding party's filing fee without imposing any administrative charge. A refund under this subdivision is available if the adverse party has filed only a responsive pleading, but not if the party has also filed a cross-complaint or other first paper seeking affirmative relief for which there is a filing fee.

(e) If an adverse party, or a person acting on behalf of the adverse party, tenders a check for a required filing fee in an amount less than the required fee, the procedures in subdivisions (a), (b), and (c) shall apply.

(f) If any trial or other hearing is scheduled to be heard prior to the expiration of the 20-day period provided for in subdivision (a), the fee shall be paid prior to the trial or hearing. Failure of the party to pay the fee prior to the trial or hearing date shall cause the court to void the filing and proceed as if it had not been filed.

(g) The clerk shall impose an administrative charge for providing notice that a check submitted for a filing fee is in an amount less than the required fee and for all related administrative, clerical, and other costs incurred under this section. The administrative charge shall, in each instance, be either twenty-five dollars ($25) or a reasonable amount that does not exceed the actual cost incurred by the court, as determined by the court. The notices provided by the court under subdivision (a) shall state the specific amount of the administrative charge that shall be paid to the court. Each administrative charge collected shall be distributed to the court that incurred the charge as described in Section 68085.1 of the Government Code. When a partial payment is to be remitted to the State Treasurer under subdivision (c), the court shall notify the Administrative Office of the Courts of the amount of (1) the partial payment collected, and (2) the administrative charge to be deducted from the payment and to be distributed to the court.

Amended by Stats 2007 ch 738 (AB 1248),s 5, eff. 1/1/2008.
Added by Stats 2005 ch 75 (AB 145),s 31, eff. 7/19/2005, op. 1/1/2006.

Section 411.35 - Certificate filed and served by attorney for plaintiff or cross-complainant in professional negligence action against architect, professional engineer or land surveyor

(a) In every action, including a cross-complaint for damages or indemnity, arising out of the professional negligence of a person holding a valid architect's certificate issued pursuant to Chapter 3 (commencing with Section 5500) of Division 3 of the Business and Professions Code, or of a person holding a valid registration as a professional engineer issued pursuant to Chapter 7 (commencing with Section 6700) of Division 3 of the Business and Professions Code, or a person holding a valid land surveyor's license issued pursuant to Chapter 15 (commencing with Section 8700) of Division 3 of the Business and Professions Code on or before the date of service of the complaint or cross-complaint on any defendant or cross-defendant, the attorney for the plaintiff or cross-complainant shall file and serve the certificate specified by subdivision (b).

(b) A certificate shall be executed by the attorney for the plaintiff or cross-complainant declaring one of the following:

(1) That the attorney has reviewed the facts of the case, that the attorney has consulted with and received an opinion from at least one architect, professional engineer, or land surveyor who is licensed to practice and practices in this state or any other state, or who teaches at an accredited college or university and is licensed to practice in this state or any other state, in the same discipline as the defendant or cross-defendant and who the attorney reasonably believes is knowledgeable in the relevant issues involved in the particular action, and that the attorney has concluded on the basis of this review and consultation that there is reasonable and meritorious cause for the filing of this action. The person consulted may not be a party to the litigation. The person consulted shall render his or her opinion that the named defendant or cross-defendant was negligent or was not negligent in the performance of the applicable professional services.

(2) That the attorney was unable to obtain the consultation required by paragraph (1) because a statute of limitations would impair the action and that the certificate required by paragraph (1) could not be obtained before the impairment of the action. If a certificate is executed pursuant to this paragraph, the certificate required by paragraph (1) shall be filed within 60 days after filing the complaint.

(3) That the attorney was unable to obtain the consultation required by paragraph (1) because the attorney had made three separate good faith attempts with three separate architects, professional engineers, or land surveyors to obtain this consultation and none of those contacted would agree to the consultation.

(c) Where a certificate is required pursuant to this section, only one certificate shall be filed, notwithstanding that multiple defendants have been named in the complaint or may be named at a later time.

(d) Where the attorney intends to rely solely on the doctrine of "res ipsa loquitur," as defined in Section 646 of the Evidence Code, or exclusively on a failure to inform of the consequences of a procedure, or both, this section shall be inapplicable. The attorney shall certify upon filing of the complaint that the attorney is solely relying on the doctrines of "res ipsa loquitur" or failure to inform of the consequences of a procedure or both, and for that reason is not filing a certificate required by this section.

(e) For purposes of this section, and subject to Section 912 of the Evidence Code, an attorney who submits a certificate as required by paragraph (1) or (2) of subdivision (b) has a privilege to refuse to disclose the identity of the architect, professional engineer, or land surveyor consulted and the contents of the consultation. The privilege shall also be held by the architect, professional engineer, or land surveyor so consulted. If, however, the attorney makes a claim under paragraph (3) of subdivision (b) that he or she was unable to obtain the required consultation with the architect, professional engineer, or land surveyor, the court may require the attorney to divulge the names of architects, professional engineers, or land surveyors refusing the consultation.

(f) A violation of this section may constitute unprofessional conduct and be grounds for discipline against the attorney, except that the failure to file the certificate required by paragraph (1) of subdivision (b), within 60 days after filing the complaint and certificate provided for by paragraph (2) of subdivision (b), shall not be grounds for discipline against the attorney.

(g) The failure to file a certificate in accordance with this section shall be grounds for a demurrer pursuant to Section 430.10 or a motion to strike pursuant to Section 435.

(h) Upon the favorable conclusion of the litigation with respect to any party for whom a certificate of merit was filed or for whom a certificate of merit should have been filed pursuant to this section, the trial court may, upon the motion of a party or upon the court's own motion, verify compliance with this section, by requiring the attorney for the plaintiff or cross-complainant who was required by subdivision (b) to execute the certificate to reveal the name, address, and telephone number of the person or persons consulted with pursuant to subdivision (b) that were relied upon by the attorney in preparation of the certificate of merit. The name, address, and telephone number shall be disclosed to the trial judge in an in-camera proceeding at which the moving party shall not be present. If the trial judge finds there has been a failure to comply with this section, the court may order a party, a party's attorney, or both, to pay any reasonable expenses, including attorney's fees, incurred by another party as a result of the failure to comply with this section.

(i) For purposes of this section, "action" includes a complaint or cross-complaint for equitable indemnity arising out of the rendition of professional services whether or not the complaint or cross-complaint specifically asserts or utilizes the terms "professional negligence" or "negligence."

EFFECTIVE 1/1/2000. Amended July 26, 1999 (Bill Number: AB 540) (Chapter 176).

Chapter 3 - SUMMONS

Section 412.10 - Issuance generally

After payment of all applicable fees, the plaintiff may have the clerk issue one or more summons for any defendant. The clerk shall keep each original summons in the court records and provide a copy of each summons issued to the plaintiff who requested issuance of the summons.

Amended by Stats 2005 ch 300 (AB 496),s 2, eff. 1/1/2006

Section 412.20 - Requirements

(a) Except as otherwise required by statute, a summons shall be directed to the defendant, signed by the clerk and issued under the seal of the court in which the action is pending, and it shall contain:

   (1) The title of the court in which the action is pending.

   (2) The names of the parties to the action.

   (3) A direction that the defendant file with the court a written pleading in response to the complaint within 30 days after summons is served on him or her.

   (4) A notice that, unless the defendant so responds, his or her default will be entered upon application by the plaintiff, and the plaintiff may apply to the court for the relief demanded in the complaint, which could result in garnishment of wages, taking of money or property, or other relief.

   (5) The following statement in boldface type: "You may seek the advice of an attorney in any matter connected with the complaint or this summons. Such attorney should be consulted promptly so that your pleading may be filed or entered within the time required by this summons."

   (6) The following introductory legend at the top of the summons above all other matter, in boldface type, in English and Spanish: "Notice! You have been sued. The court may decide against you without your being heard unless you respond within 30 days. Read information below."

(b) Each county may, by ordinance, require that the legend contained in paragraph (6) of subdivision (a) be set forth in every summons issued out of the courts of that county in any additional foreign language, if the legend in the additional foreign language is set forth in the summons in the same manner as required in that paragraph.

(c) A summons in a form approved by the Judicial Council is deemed to comply with this section.

Amended by Stats. 1989, Ch. 1105, Sec. 6.

Section 412.30 - Notice in summons served in action against corporation or unincorporated association

In an action against a corporation or an unincorporated association (including a partnership), the copy of the summons that is served shall contain a notice stating in substance: "To the person served: You are hereby served in the within action (or special proceeding) on behalf of (here state the name of the corporation or the unincorporated association) as a person upon whom a copy of the summons and of the complaint may be delivered to effect service on said party under the provisions of (here state appropriate provisions of Chapter 4 (commencing with Section 413.10) of the Code of Civil Procedure)." If service is also made on such person as an individual, the notice shall also indicate that service is being made on such person as an individual as well as on behalf of the corporation or the unincorporated association.

If such notice does not appear on the copy of the summons served, no default may be taken against such corporation or unincorporated association or against such person individually, as the case may be.

Added by Stats. 1969, Ch. 1610.

Chapter 4 - SERVICE OF SUMMONS

Article 1 - GENERAL

Section 413.10 - Generally

Except as otherwise provided by statute, a summons shall be served on a person:

(a) Within this state, as provided in this chapter.

(b) Outside this state but within the United States, as provided in this chapter or as prescribed by the law of the place where the person is served.

(c) Outside the United States, as provided in this chapter or as directed by the court in which the action is pending, or, if the court before or after service finds that the service is reasonably calculated to give actual notice, as prescribed by the law of the place where the person is served or as directed by the foreign authority in response to a letter rogatory. These rules are subject to the provisions of the Convention on the "Service Abroad of Judicial and Extrajudicial Documents" in Civil or Commercial Matters (Hague Service Convention).

Amended by Stats. 1984, Ch. 191, Sec. 1.

Section 413.20 - Extension of time if summons served by mail

If a summons is served by mail pursuant to this chapter, the provisions of Section 1013 that extend the time for exercising a right or doing an act shall not extend any time specified in this title.

Added by Stats. 1969, Ch. 1610.

Section 413.30 - No provision made in chapter or other law for service of summons

Where no provision is made in this chapter or other law for the service of summons, the court in which the action is pending may direct that summons be served in a manner which is reasonably calculated to give actual notice to the party to be served and that proof of such service be made as prescribed by the court.

Added by Stats. 1969, Ch. 1610.

Section 413.40 - Service in compliance with chapter made by person in violation of Chapter 16, Division 8, Business and Professions Code

Any service of summons which complies with the provisions of this chapter shall not be rendered invalid or ineffective because it was made by a person in violation of Chapter 16 (commencing with Section 22350) of Division 8 of the Business and Professions Code.

Added by Stats. 1971, Ch. 1661.

Article 2 - PERSONS WHO MAY SERVE SUMMONS

Section 414.10 - Generally

A summons may be served by any person who is at least 18 years of age and not a party to the action.
Added by Stats. 1969, Ch. 1610.

Article 3 - MANNER OF SERVICE OF SUMMONS

Section 415.10 - Personal delivery

A summons may be served by personal delivery of a copy of the summons and of the complaint to the person to be served. Service of a summons in this manner is deemed complete at the time of such delivery.

The date upon which personal delivery is made shall be entered on or affixed to the face of the copy of the summons at the time of its delivery. However, service of a summons without such date shall be valid and effective.
Amended by Stats. 1976, Ch. 789.

Section 415.20 - Leaving copy of summons and complaint at office or at usual mailing address and mailing copy of summons and compliant to person to be served

(a) In lieu of personal delivery of a copy of the summons and complaint to the person to be served as specified in Section 416.10, 416.20, 416.30, 416.40, or 416.50, a summons may be served by leaving a copy of the summons and complaint during usual office hours in his or her office or, if no physical address is known, at his or her usual mailing address, other than a United States Postal Service post office box, with the person who is apparently in charge thereof, and by thereafter mailing a copy of the summons and complaint by first-class mail, postage prepaid to the person to be served at the place where a copy of the summons and complaint were left. When service is effected by leaving a copy of the summons and complaint at a mailing address, it shall be left with a person at least 18 years of age, who shall be informed of the contents thereof. Service of a summons in this manner is deemed complete on the 10th day after the mailing.

(b) If a copy of the summons and complaint cannot with reasonable diligence be personally delivered to the person to be served, as specified in Section 416.60, 416.70, 416.80, or 416.90, a summons may be served by leaving a copy of the summons and complaint at the person's dwelling house, usual place of abode, usual place of business, or usual mailing address other than a United States Postal Service post office box, in the presence of a competent member of the household or a person apparently in charge of his or her office, place of business, or usual mailing address other than a United States Postal Service post office box, at least 18 years of age, who shall be informed of the contents thereof, and by thereafter mailing a copy of the summons and of the complaint by first-class mail, postage prepaid to the person to be served at the place where a copy of the summons and complaint were left. Service of a summons in this manner is deemed complete on the 10th day after the mailing.

(c) Notwithstanding subdivision (b), if the only address reasonably known for the person to be served is a private mailbox obtained through a commercial mail receiving agency, service of process may be effected on the first delivery attempt by leaving a copy of the summons and complaint with the commercial mail receiving agency in the manner described in subdivision (d) of Section 17538.5 of the Business and Professions Code.

Amended by Stats 2017 ch 129 (AB 1093),s 1, eff. 1/1/2018.
Amended by Stats 2003 ch 128 (AB 418),s 1, eff. 1/1/2004.

Section 415.21 - Access to gated community or covered multifamily dwelling for purpose of service

(a) Notwithstanding any other law, any person shall be granted access to a gated community or a covered multifamily dwelling for a reasonable period of time for the sole purpose of performing lawful service of process or service of a subpoena upon displaying a current driver's license or other identification, and one of the following:

(1) A badge or other confirmation that the individual is acting in the individual's capacity as a representative of a county sheriff or marshal, or as an investigator employed by an office of the Attorney General, a county counsel, a city attorney, a district attorney, or a public defender.

(2) Evidence of current registration as a process server pursuant to Chapter 16 (commencing with Section 22350) of Division 8 of the Business and Professions Code or of licensure as a private investigator pursuant to Chapter 11.3 (commencing with Section 7512) of Division 3 of the Business and Professions Code.

(b) This section shall only apply to a gated community or a covered multifamily dwelling that is staffed at the time service of process is attempted by a guard or other security personnel assigned to control access to the community or dwelling.

(c) For purposes of this section, "covered multifamily dwelling" means either of the following:

(1) An apartment building, including a timeshare apartment building not considered a place of public accommodation or transient lodging, with three or more dwelling units.

(2) A condominium, including a timeshare condominium not considered a place of public accommodation or transient lodging, with four or more dwelling units.

Amended by Stats 2019 ch 12 (AB 622),s 1, eff. 1/1/2020.
Amended by Stats 2016 ch 88 (SB 1431),s 1, eff. 1/1/2017.
Amended by Stats 2014 ch 470 (AB 2256),s 2, eff. 1/1/2015.
Amended by Stats 2012 ch 113 (AB 1720),s 1, eff. 1/1/2013.
Amended by Stats 2005 ch 706 (AB 1742),s 11, eff. 1/1/2006
See Stats 2012 ch 113 (AB 1720), s 2.

Section 415.30 - Mail service

(a) A summons may be served by mail as provided in this section. A copy of the summons and of the complaint shall be mailed (by first-class mail or airmail, postage prepaid) to the person to be served, together with two copies of the notice and acknowledgment provided for in subdivision (b) and a return envelope, postage prepaid, addressed to the sender.

(b) The notice specified in subdivision (a) shall be in substantially the following form: (Title of court and cause, with action number, to be inserted by the sender prior to mailing)

NOTICE

To:(Here state the name of the person to be served.)

This summons is served pursuant to Section 415.30 of the California Code of Civil Procedure. Failure to complete this form and return it to the sender within 20 days may subject you (or the party on whose behalf you are being served) to liability for the payment of any expenses incurred in serving a summons upon you in any other manner permitted by law. If you are served on behalf of a corporation, unincorporated association (including a partnership), or other entity, this form must be signed in the name of such entity by you or by a person authorized to receive service of process on behalf of such entity. In all other cases, this form must be signed by you personally or by a person authorized by you to acknowledge receipt of summons. Section 415.30 provides that this summons is deemed served on the date of execution of an acknowledgment of receipt of summons.

Signature of sender

ACKNOWLEDGMENT OF RECEIPT OF SUMMONS

This acknowledges receipt on (insert date) of a copy of the summons and of the complaint at (insert address).

Date:(Date this acknowledgement is executed)

Signature of person acknowledging receipt, with title if acknowledgment is made on behalf of another person

(c) Service of a summons pursuant to this section is deemed complete on the date a written acknowledgement of receipt of summons is executed, if such acknowledgement thereafter is returned to the sender.
(d) If the person to whom a copy of the summons and of the complaint are mailed pursuant to this section fails to complete and return the acknowledgment form set forth in subdivision (b) within 20 days from the date of such mailing, the party to whom the summons was mailed shall be liable for reasonable expenses thereafter incurred in serving or attempting to serve the party by another method permitted by this chapter, and, except for good cause shown, the court in which the action is pending, upon motion, with or without notice, shall award the party such expenses whether or not he is otherwise entitled to recover his costs in the action.
(e) A notice or acknowledgment of receipt in form approved by the Judicial Council is deemed to comply with this section.
Added by Stats. 1969, Ch. 1610.

Section 415.40 - Service on person outside state
A summons may be served on a person outside this state in any manner provided by this article or by sending a copy of the summons and of the complaint to the person to be served by first-class mail, postage prepaid, requiring a return receipt. Service of a summons by this form of mail is deemed complete on the 10th day after such mailing.
Amended by Stats. 1982, Ch. 249, Sec. 1.

Section 415.45 - Service in action for unlawful detainer of real property
(a) A summons in an action for unlawful detainer of real property may be served by posting if upon affidavit it appears to the satisfaction of the court in which the action is pending that the party to be served cannot with reasonable diligence be served in any manner specified in this article other than publication and that:
(1) A cause of action exists against the party upon whom service is to be made or he is a necessary or proper party to the action; or
(2) The party to be served has or claims an interest in real property in this state that is subject to the jurisdiction of the court or the relief demanded in the action consists wholly or in part in excluding such party from any interest in such property.
(b) The court shall order the summons to be posted on the premises in a manner most likely to give actual notice to the party to be served and direct that a copy of the summons and of the complaint be forthwith mailed by certified mail to such party at his last known address.
(c) Service of summons in this manner is deemed complete on the 10th day after posting and mailing.
(d) Notwithstanding an order for posting of the summons, a summons may be served in any other manner authorized by this article, except publication, in which event such service shall supersede any posted summons.
Amended by Stats. 1978, Ch. 625.

Section 415.46 - Prejudgment claim of right to possession
(a) In addition to the service of a summons and complaint in an action for unlawful detainer upon a tenant and subtenant, if any, as prescribed by this article, a prejudgment claim of right to possession may also be served on any person who appears to be or who may claim to have occupied the premises at the time of the filing of the action. Service upon occupants shall be made pursuant to subdivision (c) by serving a copy of a prejudgment claim of right to possession, as specified in subdivision (f), attached to a copy of the summons and complaint at the same time service is made upon the tenant and subtenant, if any.
(b) Service of the prejudgment claim of right to possession in this manner shall be effected by a marshal, sheriff, or registered process server.
(c)
(1) When serving the summons and complaint upon a tenant and subtenant, if any, the marshal, sheriff, or registered process server shall make a reasonably diligent effort to ascertain whether there are other adult occupants of the premises who are not named in the summons and complaint by inquiring of the person or persons who are being personally served, or any person of suitable age and discretion who appears to reside upon the premises, whether there are other occupants of the premises.
(2) If the identity of such an occupant is disclosed to the officer or process server and the occupant is present at the premises, the officer or process server shall serve that occupant with a copy of the prejudgment claim of right to possession attached to a copy of the summons and complaint. If personal service cannot be made upon that occupant at that time, service may be effected by leaving a copy of a prejudgment claim of right to possession attached to a copy of the summons and complaint addressed to that occupant with a person of suitable age and discretion at the premises, affixing the same so that it is not readily removable in a conspicuous place on the premises in a manner most likely to give actual notice to that occupant, and sending the same addressed to that occupant by first-class mail.
(3) In addition to the service on an identified occupant, or if no occupant is disclosed to the officer or process server, or if substituted service is made upon the tenant and subtenant, if any, the officer or process server shall serve a prejudgment claim of right to possession for all other persons who may claim to occupy the premises at the time of the filing of the action by leaving a copy of a prejudgment claim of right to possession attached to a copy of the summons and complaint at the premises at the same time service is made upon the tenant and subtenant, if any, affixing the same so that it is not readily removable in a conspicuous place on the premises so that it is likely to give actual notice to an occupant, and sending the same addressed to "all occupants in care of the named tenant" to the premises by first-class mail.
(4) The person serving process shall state the date of service on the prejudgment claim of right to possession form. However, the absence of the date of service on the prejudgment claim of right to possession does not invalidate the claim.
(d) Proof of service under this section shall be filed with the court and shall include a statement that service was made pursuant to this section. Service on occupants in accordance with this section shall not alter or affect service upon the tenant or subtenant, if any.
(e)
(1) If an owner or his or her agent has directed and obtained service of a prejudgment claim of right to possession in accordance with this section, no occupant of the premises, whether or not that occupant is named in the judgment for possession, may object to the enforcement of that judgment as prescribed in Section 1174.3.
(2) In any action for unlawful detainer resulting from a foreclosure sale of a rental housing unit pursuant to Section 1161a, paragraph (1) shall not limit the right of any tenant or subtenant of the property to file a prejudgment claim of right of possession pursuant to subdivision (a) of Section 1174.25 at any time before judgment, or to object to enforcement of a judgment for possession as prescribed in Section 1174.3, regardless of whether the tenant or subtenant was served with a prejudgment claim of right to possession.
(f) The prejudgment claim of right to possession shall be made on the following form: [SEE PRINTED VERSION OF THE BILL]
Amended by Stats 2014 ch 913 (AB 2747),s 7, eff. 1/1/2015.
Amended by Stats 2012 ch 562 (AB 2610),s 2, eff. 1/1/2013.

Section 415.47 - Service upon lessee in action for unlawful detainer of real property
(a) Where the lessee has given the lessor written notice of the lessee's intent not to abandon leased real property as provided in Section 1951.3 of the Civil Code, the summons in an action for unlawful detainer of the real property may be served on the lessee by certified mail, postage prepaid,

addressed to the lessee at the address stated in the lessee's notice of intent not to abandon if such summons is deposited in the mail within 60 days from the date the lessee's notice of intent not to abandon is received by the lessor. Service in this manner is deemed completed on the 10th day after such mailing.

(b) Where the lessee has given the lessor written notice of the lessee's intent not to abandon leased real property as provided in Section 1951.3 of the Civil Code, but failed to include in such notice an address at which the lessee may be served by certified mail in any action for unlawful detainer of the real property, the summons in an action for unlawful detainer of the real property may be served on the lessee by certified mail, postage prepaid, addressed to the lessee at (1) the same address or addresses to which the lessor's notice of belief of abandonment was addressed if that notice was given by mail or (2) the address of the real property if the lessor's notice of belief of abandonment was personally served on the lessee. Service may not be made pursuant to this subdivision unless the summons is deposited in the mail within 60 days from the date the lessee's notice of intent not to abandon is received by the lessor. Service in the manner authorized by this subdivision is deemed completed on the 10th day after such mailing.

(c) This section provides an alternative method of service on the lessee and does not preclude service in any other manner authorized by this chapter.

Added by Stats. 1974, Ch. 332.

Section 415.50 - Publication

(a) A summons may be served by publication if upon affidavit it appears to the satisfaction of the court in which the action is pending that the party to be served cannot with reasonable diligence be served in another manner specified in this article and that either:

(1) A cause of action exists against the party upon whom service is to be made or he or she is a necessary or proper party to the action.

(2) The party to be served has or claims an interest in real or personal property in this state that is subject to the jurisdiction of the court or the relief demanded in the action consists wholly or in part in excluding the party from any interest in the property.

(b) The court shall order the summons to be published in a named newspaper, published in this state, that is most likely to give actual notice to the party to be served. If the party to be served resides or is located out of this state, the court may also order the summons to be published in a named newspaper outside this state that is most likely to give actual notice to that party. The order shall direct that a copy of the summons, the complaint, and the order for publication be forthwith mailed to the party if his or her address is ascertained before expiration of the time prescribed for publication of the summons. Except as otherwise provided by statute, the publication shall be made as provided by Section 6064 of the Government Code unless the court, in its discretion, orders publication for a longer period.

(c) Service of a summons in this manner is deemed complete as provided in Section 6064 of the Government Code.

(d) Notwithstanding an order for publication of the summons, a summons may be served in another manner authorized by this chapter, in which event the service shall supersede any published summons.

(e) As a condition of establishing that the party to be served cannot with reasonable diligence be served in another manner specified in this article, the court may not require that a search be conducted of public databases where access by a registered process server to residential addresses is prohibited by law or by published policy of the agency providing the database, including, but not limited to, voter registration rolls and records of the Department of Motor Vehicles.

Amended by Stats 2003 ch 449 (AB 1712),s 8, eff. 1/1/2004.
Amended by Stats 2002 ch 197 (AB 2493),s 2, eff. 1/1/2003.

Section 415.95 - Service on business organization form unknown

(a) A summons may be served on a business organization, form unknown, by leaving a copy of the summons and complaint during usual office hours with the person who is apparently in charge of the office of that business organization, and by thereafter mailing a copy of the summons and complaint by first-class mail, postage prepaid, to the person to be served at the place where a copy of the summons and complaint was left. Service of a summons in this manner is deemed complete on the 10th day after the mailing.

(b) Service of a summons pursuant to this section is not valid for a corporation with a registered agent for service of process listed with the Secretary of State.

Added by Stats 2003 ch 128 (AB 418),s 2, eff. 1/1/2004.

Article 4 - PERSONS UPON WHOM SUMMONS MAY BE SERVED

Section 416.10 - Service on corporation

A summons may be served on a corporation by delivering a copy of the summons and the complaint by any of the following methods:

(a) To the person designated as agent for service of process as provided by any provision in Section 202, 1502, 2105, or 2107 of the Corporations Code (or Sections 3301 to 3303, inclusive, or Sections 6500 to 6504, inclusive, of the Corporations Code, as in effect on December 31, 1976, with respect to corporations to which they remain applicable).

(b) To the president, chief executive officer, or other head of the corporation, a vice president, a secretary or assistant secretary, a treasurer or assistant treasurer, a controller or chief financial officer, a general manager, or a person authorized by the corporation to receive service of process.

(c) If the corporation is a bank, to a cashier or assistant cashier or to a person specified in subdivision (a) or (b).

(d) If authorized by any provision in Section 1701, 1702, 2110, or 2111 of the Corporations Code (or Sections 3301 to 3303, inclusive, or Sections 6500 to 6504, inclusive, of the Corporations Code, as in effect on December 31, 1976, with respect to corporations to which they remain applicable), as provided by that provision.

Amended by Stats 2006 ch 567 (AB 2303),s 7, eff. 1/1/2007.

Section 416.20 - Service on corporation that has forfeited charter or right to do business

A summons may be served on a corporation that has forfeited its charter or right to do business, or has dissolved, by delivering a copy of the summons and of the complaint:

(a) To a person who is a trustee of the corporation and of its stockholders or members; or

(b) When authorized by any provision in Sections 2011 or 2114 of the Corporations Code (or Sections 3301 to 3303, inclusive, or Sections 6500 to 6504, inclusive, of the Corporations Code as in effect on December 31, 1976, with respect to corporations to which they remain applicable), as provided by such provision.

Amended by Stats. 1977, Ch. 235.

Section 416.30 - Service on joint stock company or association

A summons may be served on a joint stock company or association by delivering a copy of the summons and of the complaint as provided by Section 416.10 or 416.20.

Added by Stats. 1969, Ch. 1610.

Section 416.40 - Service on unincorporated association including partnership

A summons may be served on an unincorporated association (including a partnership) by delivering a copy of the summons and of the complaint:

(a) If the association is a general or limited partnership, to the person designated as agent for service of process in a statement filed with the Secretary of State or to a general partner or the general manager of the partnership;

(b) If the association is not a general or limited partnership, to the person designated as agent for service of process in a statement filed with the Secretary of State or to the president or other head of the association, a vice president, a secretary or assistant secretary, a treasurer or assistant treasurer, a general manager, or a person authorized by the association to receive service of process;
(c) When authorized by Section 18220 of the Corporations Code, as provided by that section.
Amended by Stats 2004 ch 178 (SB 1746),s 3, eff. 1/1/2005

Section 416.50 - Service on public entity
(a) A summons may be served on a public entity by delivering a copy of the summons and of the complaint to the clerk, secretary, president, presiding officer, or other head of its governing body.
(b) As used in this section, "public entity" includes the state and any office, department, division, bureau, board, commission, or agency of the state, the Regents of the University of California, a county, city, district, public authority, public agency, and any other political subdivision or public corporation in this state.
Added by Stats. 1969, Ch. 1610.

Section 416.60 - Service on minor
A summons may be served on a minor by delivering a copy of the summons and of the complaint to his parent, guardian, conservator, or similar fiduciary, or, if no such person can be found with reasonable diligence, to any person having the care or control of such minor or with whom he resides or by whom he is employed, and to the minor if he is at least 12 years of age.
Amended by Stats. 1972, Ch. 579.

Section 416.70 - Service on person for whom guardian, conservator or similar fiduciary appointed
A summons may be served on a person (other than a minor) for whom a guardian, conservator, or similar fiduciary has been appointed by delivering a copy of the summons and of the complaint to his guardian, conservator, or similar fiduciary and to such person, but, for good cause shown, the court in which the action is pending may dispense with delivery to such person.
Amended by Stats. 1972, Ch. 579.

Section 416.80 - Service as provided in section 12, Elections Code
When authorized by Section 12 of the Elections Code, a summons may be served as provided by that section.
Amended by Stats 2009 ch 140 (AB 1164),s 38, eff. 1/1/2010.

Section 416.90 - Service on person not otherwise specified in article
A summons may be served on a person not otherwise specified in this article by delivering a copy of the summons and of the complaint to such person or to a person authorized by him to receive service of process.
Added by Stats. 1969, Ch. 1610.

Article 5 - PROOF OF SERVICE

Section 417.10 - Proof summons served on person within state
Proof that a summons was served on a person within this state shall be made:
(a) If served under Section 415.10, 415.20, or 415.30, by the affidavit of the person making the service showing the time, place, and manner of service and facts showing that the service was made in accordance with this chapter. The affidavit shall recite or in other manner show the name of the person to whom a copy of the summons and of the complaint were delivered, and, if appropriate, his or her title or the capacity in which he or she is served, and that the notice required by Section 412.30 appeared on the copy of the summons served, if in fact it did appear. If service is made by mail pursuant to Section 415.30, proof of service shall include the acknowledgment of receipt of summons in the form provided by that section or other written acknowledgment of receipt of summons satisfactory to the court.
(b) If served by publication pursuant to Section 415.50, by the affidavit of the publisher or printer, or his or her foreperson or principal clerk, showing the time and place of publication, and an affidavit showing the time and place a copy of the summons and of the complaint were mailed to the party to be served, if in fact mailed.
(c) If served pursuant to another law of this state, in the manner prescribed by that law or, if no manner is prescribed, in the manner prescribed by this section for proof of a similar manner of service.
(d) By the written admission of the party.
(e) If served by posting pursuant to Section 415.45, by the affidavit of the person who posted the premises, showing the time and place of posting, and an affidavit showing the time and place copies of the summons and of the complaint were mailed to the party to be served, if in fact mailed.
(f) All proof of personal service shall be made on a form adopted by the Judicial Council.
Amended by Stats 2006 ch 538 (SB 1852),s 63, eff. 1/1/2007.

Section 417.20 - Proof summons served on person outside state
Proof that a summons was served on a person outside this state shall be made:
(a) If served in a manner specified in a statute of this state, as prescribed by Section 417.10, and if service is made by mail pursuant to Section 415.40, proof of service shall include evidence satisfactory to the court establishing actual delivery to the person to be served, by a signed return receipt or other evidence;
(b) In the manner prescribed by the court order pursuant to which the service is made;
(c) Subject to any additional requirements that may be imposed by the court in which the action is pending, in the manner prescribed by the law of the place where the person is served for proof of service in an action in its courts of general jurisdiction; or
(d) By the written admission of the party.
(e) If served by posting pursuant to Section 415.45, by the affidavit of the person who posted the premises, showing the time and place of posting, and an affidavit showing the time and place copies of the summons and of the complaint were mailed to the party to be served, if in fact mailed.
Amended by Stats. 1972, Ch. 719.

Section 417.30 - Filing proof
After a summons has been served on a person, proof of service of the summons as provided in Section 417.10 or 417.20 shall be filed, unless the defendant has previously made a general appearance.
Amended by Stats 2005 ch 300 (AB 496),s 3, eff. 1/1/2006

Section 417.40 - Proof signed by person registered under Chapter 16, Division 8, Business and Professions Code
Any proof of service which is signed by a person registered under Chapter 16 (commencing with Section 22350) of Division 8 of the Business and Professions Code or his employee or independent contractor shall indicate the county in which he is registered and the number assigned to him pursuant to Section 22355 of the Business and Professions Code.
Added by Stats. 1971, Ch. 1661.

Chapter 5 - OBJECTION TO JURISDICTION

Section 418.10 - Serving and filing notice of motion
(a) A defendant, on or before the last day of his or her time to plead or within any further time that the court may for good cause allow, may serve and file a notice of motion for one or more of the following purposes:
   (1) To quash service of summons on the ground of lack of jurisdiction of the court over him or her.

(2) To stay or dismiss the action on the ground of inconvenient forum.

(3) To dismiss the action pursuant to the applicable provisions of Chapter 1.5 (commencing with Section 583.110) of Title 8.

(b) The notice shall designate, as the time for making the motion, a date not more than 30 days after filing of the notice. The notice shall be served in the same manner, and at the same times, prescribed by subdivision (b) of Section 1005. The service and filing of the notice shall extend the defendant's time to plead until 15 days after service upon him or her of a written notice of entry of an order denying his or her motion, except that for good cause shown the court may extend the defendant's time to plead for an additional period not exceeding 20 days.

(c) If the motion is denied by the trial court, the defendant, within 10 days after service upon him or her of a written notice of entry of an order of the court denying his or her motion, or within any further time not exceeding 20 days that the trial court may for good cause allow, and before pleading, may petition an appropriate reviewing court for a writ of mandate to require the trial court to enter its order quashing the service of summons or staying or dismissing the action. The defendant shall file or enter his or her responsive pleading in the trial court within the time prescribed by subdivision (b) unless, on or before the last day of the defendant's time to plead, he or she serves upon the adverse party and files with the trial court a notice that he or she has petitioned for a writ of mandate. The service and filing of the notice shall extend the defendant's time to plead until 10 days after service upon him or her of a written notice of the final judgment in the mandate proceeding. The time to plead may for good cause shown be extended by the trial court for an additional period not exceeding 20 days.

(d) No default may be entered against the defendant before expiration of his or her time to plead, and no motion under this section, or under Section 473 or 473.5 when joined with a motion under this section, or application to the court or stipulation of the parties for an extension of the time to plead, shall be deemed a general appearance by the defendant.

(e) A defendant or cross-defendant may make a motion under this section and simultaneously answer, demur, or move to strike the complaint or cross-complaint.

(1) Notwithstanding Section 1014, no act by a party who makes a motion under this section, including filing an answer, demurrer, or motion to strike constitutes an appearance, unless the court denies the motion made under this section. If the court denies the motion made under this section, the defendant or cross-defendant is not deemed to have generally appeared until entry of the order denying the motion.

(2) If the motion made under this section is denied and the defendant or cross-defendant petitions for a writ of mandate pursuant to subdivision (c), the defendant or cross-defendant is not deemed to have generally appeared until the proceedings on the writ petition have finally concluded.

(3) Failure to make a motion under this section at the time of filing a demurrer or motion to strike constitutes a waiver of the issues of lack of personal jurisdiction, inadequacy of process, inadequacy of service of process, inconvenient forum, and delay in prosecution.

Amended by Stats 2002 ch 69 (SB 1325),s 1, eff. 1/1/2003.

Section 418.11 - Appearance at hearing for ex parte relief

An appearance at a hearing at which ex parte relief is sought, or an appearance at a hearing for which an ex parte application for a provisional remedy is made, is not a general appearance and does not constitute a waiver of the right to make a motion under Section 418.10.

Added by Stats. 1987, Ch. 62, Sec. 1.

Title 6 - OF THE PLEADINGS IN CIVIL ACTIONS
Chapter 1 - THE PLEADINGS IN GENERAL

Section 420 - Definition

The pleadings are the formal allegations by the parties of their respective claims and defenses, for the judgment of the Court.

Enacted 1872.

Section 421 - Generally

The forms of pleading in civil actions, and the rules by which the sufficiency of the pleadings is to be determined, are those prescribed in this Code.

Enacted 1872.

Section 422.10 - Pleadings allowed

The pleadings allowed in civil actions are complaints, demurrers, answers, and cross-complaints.

Added by Stats. 1971, Ch. 244.

Section 422.30 - Caption

(a) Every pleading shall contain a caption setting forth:

(1) The name of the court and county in which the action is brought.

(2) The title of the action.

(b) In a limited civil case, the caption shall state that the case is a limited civil case, and the clerk shall classify the case accordingly.

Amended by Stats 2002 ch 784 (SB 1316),s 60, eff. 1/1/2003.

Previously Amended September 7, 1999 (Bill Number: SB 210) (Chapter 344).

Section 422.40 - Title of action in complaint

In the complaint, the title of the action shall include the names of all the parties; but, except as otherwise provided by statute or rule of the Judicial Council, in other pleadings it is sufficient to state the name of the first party on each side with an appropriate indication of other parties.

Added by Stats. 1971, Ch. 244.

Chapter 2 - PLEADINGS DEMANDING RELIEF
Article 1 - GENERAL PROVISIONS

Section 425.10 - Requirements of complaint or cross-complaint; amount demanded in damages not stated

(a) A complaint or cross-complaint shall contain both of the following:

(1) A statement of the facts constituting the cause of action, in ordinary and concise language.

(2) A demand for judgment for the relief to which the pleader claims to be entitled. If the recovery of money or damages is demanded, the amount demanded shall be stated.

(b) Notwithstanding subdivision (a), where an action is brought to recover actual or punitive damages for personal injury or wrongful death, the amount demanded shall not be stated, but the complaint shall comply with Section 422.30 and, in a limited civil case, with subdivision (b) of Section 70613 of the Government Code.

Amended by Stats 2005 ch 75 (AB 145),s 32, eff. 7/19/2005, op. 1/1/2006

Amended by Stats 2001 ch 812 (AB 223), s 1, eff. 1/1/2002.

Section 425.11 - Request by defendant for statement setting forth nature and amount of damages sought

(a) As used in this section:

(1) "Complaint" includes a cross-complaint.

(2) "Plaintiff" includes a cross-complainant.

(3) "Defendant" includes a cross-defendant.

(b) When a complaint is filed in an action to recover damages for personal injury or wrongful death, the defendant may at any time request a statement setting forth the nature and amount of damages being sought. The request shall be served upon the plaintiff, who shall serve a responsive statement as to the damages within 15 days. In the event that a response is not served, the defendant, on notice to the plaintiff, may petition the court in which the action is pending to order the plaintiff to serve a responsive statement.
(c) If no request is made for the statement referred to in subdivision (b), the plaintiff shall serve the statement on the defendant before a default may be taken.
(d) The statement referred to in subdivision (b) shall be served in the following manner:
(1) If a party has not appeared in the action, the statement shall be served in the same manner as a summons.
(2) If a party has appeared in the action, the statement shall be served upon the party's attorney, or upon the party if the party has appeared without an attorney, in the manner provided for service of a summons or in the manner provided by Chapter 5 (commencing with Section 1010) of Title 14 of Part 2.
(e) The statement referred to in subdivision (b) may be combined with the statement described in Section 425.115.
Amended by Stats 2006 ch 538 (SB 1852),s 63.5, eff. 1/1/2007.
Amended by Stats 2001 ch 812 (AB 223), s 2, eff. 1/1/2002.

Section 425.115 - Preservation by plaintiff of right to seek punitive damages on default judgment
(a) As used in this section:
(1) "Complaint" includes a cross-complaint.
(2) "Plaintiff" includes a cross-complainant.
(3) "Defendant" includes a cross-defendant.
(b) The plaintiff preserves the right to seek punitive damages pursuant to Section 3294 of the Civil Code on a default judgment by serving upon the defendant the following statement, or its substantial equivalent:

NOTICE TO :
(Insert name of defendant or cross-defendant)
reserves the right to seek
(Insert name of plaintiff or cross-complainant)
$ in punitive damages
(Insert dollar amount)
when seeks a judgment in the
(Insert name of plaintiff orcross-complainant)
suit filed against you.

(Insert name of attorney orparty appearing in propria persona)   (Date)

(c) If the plaintiff seeks punitive damages pursuant to Section 3294 of the Civil Code, and if the defendant appears in the action, the plaintiff shall not be limited to the amount set forth in the statement served on the defendant pursuant to this section.
(d) A plaintiff who serves a statement on the defendant pursuant to this section shall be deemed to have complied with Sections 425.10 and 580 of this code and Section 3295 of the Civil Code.
(e) The plaintiff may serve a statement upon the defendant pursuant to this section, and may serve the statement as part of the statement required by Section 425.11.
(f) The plaintiff shall serve the statement upon the defendant pursuant to this section before a default may be taken, if the motion for default judgment includes a request for punitive damages.
(g) The statement referred to in subdivision (b) shall be served by one of the following methods:
(1) If the party has not appeared in the action, the statement shall be served in the same manner as a summons pursuant to Article 3 (commencing with Section 415.10) of Chapter 4 of Title 5 of Part 2 of the Code of Civil Procedure.
(2) If the party has appeared in the action, the statement shall be served upon his or her attorney, or upon the party if he or she has appeared without an attorney, either in the same manner as a summons pursuant to Article 3 (commencing with Section 415.10) of Chapter 4 or in the manner provided by Chapter 5 (commencing with Section 1010) of Title 14.
Amended by Stats 2005 ch 706 (AB 1742),s 12, eff. 1/1/2006

Section 425.12 - Development and approval of forms
(a) The Judicial Council shall develop and approve official forms for use in trial courts of this state for any complaint, cross-complaint or answer in any action based upon personal injury, property damage, wrongful death, unlawful detainer, breach of contract or fraud.
(b) The Judicial Council shall develop and approve an official form for use as a statement of damages pursuant to Sections 425.11 and 425.115.
(c) In developing the forms required by this section, the Judicial Council shall consult with a representative advisory committee which shall include, but not be limited to, representatives of the plaintiff's bar, the defense bar, the public interest bar, court administrators and the public. The forms shall be drafted in nontechnical language and shall be made available through the office of the clerk of the appropriate trial court.
Amended by Stats. 1995, Ch. 796, Sec. 4. Effective January 1, 1996.

Section 425.13 - Claim for punitive damages in action for professional negligence of health care provider
(a) In any action for damages arising out of the professional negligence of a health care provider, no claim for punitive damages shall be included in a complaint or other pleading unless the court enters an order allowing an amended pleading that includes a claim for punitive damages to be filed. The court may allow the filing of an amended pleading claiming punitive damages on a motion by the party seeking the amended pleading and on the basis of the supporting and opposing affidavits presented that the plaintiff has established that there is a substantial probability that the plaintiff will prevail on the claim pursuant to Section 3294 of the Civil Code. The court shall not grant a motion allowing the filing of an amended pleading that includes a claim for punitive damages if the motion for such an order is not filed within two years after the complaint or initial pleading is filed or not less than nine months before the date the matter is first set for trial, whichever is earlier.
(b) For the purposes of this section, "health care provider" means any person licensed or certified pursuant to Division 2 (commencing with Section 500) of the Business and Professions Code, or licensed pursuant to the Osteopathic Initiative Act, or the Chiropractic Initiative Act, or licensed pursuant to Chapter 2.5 (commencing with Section 1440) of Division 2 of the Health and Safety Code; and any clinic, health dispensary, or health facility, licensed pursuant to Division 2 (commencing with Section 1200) of the Health and Safety Code. "Health care provider" includes the legal representatives of a health care provider.
Amended by Stats. 1988, Ch. 1205, Sec. 1.

Section 425.14 - Claim for punitive damages in action against religious corporation or religious corporation sole
No claim for punitive or exemplary damages against a religious corporation or religious corporation sole shall be included in a complaint or other pleading unless the court enters an order allowing an amended pleading that includes a claim for punitive or exemplary damages to be filed. The court may allow the filing of an amended pleading claiming punitive or exemplary damages on a motion by the party seeking the amended

pleading and upon a finding, on the basis of the supporting and opposing affidavits presented, that the plaintiff has established evidence which substantiates that plaintiff will meet the clear and convincing standard of proof under Section 3294 of the Civil Code.
Nothing in this section is intended to affect the plaintiff's right to discover evidence on the issue of punitive or exemplary damages.
Added by Stats. 1988, Ch. 1410, Sec. 1.

Section 425.15 - Action against person serving without compensation as director or officer of nonprofit corporation

(a) No cause of action against a person serving without compensation as a director or officer of a nonprofit corporation described in this section, on account of any negligent act or omission by that person within the scope of that person's duties as a director acting in the capacity of a board member, or as an officer acting in the capacity of, and within the scope of the duties of, an officer, shall be included in a complaint or other pleading unless the court enters an order allowing the pleading that includes that claim to be filed after the court determines that the party seeking to file the pleading has established evidence that substantiates the claim. The court may allow the filing of a pleading that includes that claim following the filing of a verified petition therefor accompanied by the proposed pleading and supporting affidavits stating the facts upon which the liability is based. The court shall order service of the petition upon the party against whom the action is proposed to be filed and permit that party to submit opposing affidavits prior to making its determination. The filing of the petition, proposed pleading, and accompanying affidavits shall toll the running of any applicable statute of limitations until the final determination of the matter, which ruling, if favorable to the petitioning party, shall permit the proposed pleading to be filed.

(b) Nothing in this section shall affect the right of the plaintiff to discover evidence on the issue of damages.

(c) Nothing in this section shall be construed to affect any action against a nonprofit corporation for any negligent action or omission of a volunteer director or officer occurring within the scope of the person's duties.

(d) For the purposes of this section, "compensation" means remuneration whether by way of salary, fee, or other consideration for services rendered. However, the payment of per diem, mileage, or other reimbursement expenses to a director or officer shall not constitute compensation.

(e)

(1) This section applies only to officers and directors of nonprofit corporations that are subject to Part 2 (commencing with Section 5110), Part 3 (commencing with Section 7110), or Part 4 (commencing with Section 9110) of Division 2 of Title 1 of the Corporations Code that are organized to provide charitable, educational, scientific, social, or other forms of public service and that are exempt from federal income taxation under Section 501(c)(1)(c)(1), except any credit union, or Section 501(c)(4)(c)(4), 501(c)(5)(c)(5), 501(c)(7)(c)(7), or 501(c)(19)(c)(19) of the Internal Revenue Code.

(2) This section does not apply to any corporation that unlawfully restricts membership, services, or benefits conferred on the basis of political affiliation, age, or any characteristic listed or defined in subdivision (b) or (e) of Section 51 of the Civil Code.
Amended by Stats 2007 ch 568 (AB 14),s 16, eff. 1/1/2008.

Section 425.16 - California anti-SLAPP law

(a) The Legislature finds and declares that there has been a disturbing increase in lawsuits brought primarily to chill the valid exercise of the constitutional rights of freedom of speech and petition for the redress of grievances. The Legislature finds and declares that it is in the public interest to encourage continued participation in matters of public significance, and that this participation should not be chilled through abuse of the judicial process. To this end, this section shall be construed broadly.

(b)

(1) A cause of action against a person arising from any act of that person in furtherance of the person's right of petition or free speech under the United States Constitution or the California Constitution in connection with a public issue shall be subject to a special motion to strike, unless the court determines that the plaintiff has established that there is a probability that the plaintiff will prevail on the claim.

(2) In making its determination, the court shall consider the pleadings, and supporting and opposing affidavits stating the facts upon which the liability or defense is based.

(3) If the court determines that the plaintiff has established a probability that the plaintiff will prevail on the claim, neither that determination nor the fact of that determination shall be admissible in evidence at any later stage of the case, or in any subsequent action, and no burden of proof or degree of proof otherwise applicable shall be affected by that determination in any later stage of the case or in any subsequent proceeding.

(c)

(1) Except as provided in paragraph (2), in any action subject to subdivision (b), a prevailing defendant on a special motion to strike shall be entitled to recover that defendant's attorney's fees and costs. If the court finds that a special motion to strike is frivolous or is solely intended to cause unnecessary delay, the court shall award costs and reasonable attorney's fees to a plaintiff prevailing on the motion, pursuant to Section 128.5.

(2) A defendant who prevails on a special motion to strike in an action subject to paragraph (1) shall not be entitled to attorney's fees and costs if that cause of action is brought pursuant to Section 11130, 11130.3, 54960, or 54960.1 of the Government Code, or pursuant to Chapter 2 (commencing with Section 7923.100) of Part 4 of Division 10 of Title 1 of the Government Code. Nothing in this paragraph shall be construed to prevent a prevailing defendant from recovering attorney's fees and costs pursuant to Section 7923.115, 11130.5, or 54960.5 of the Government Code.

(d) This section shall not apply to any enforcement action brought in the name of the people of the State of California by the Attorney General, district attorney, or city attorney, acting as a public prosecutor.

(e) As used in this section, "act in furtherance of a person's right of petition or free speech under the United States or California Constitution in connection with a public issue" includes:

(1) any written or oral statement or writing made before a legislative, executive, or judicial proceeding, or any other official proceeding authorized by law,

(2) any written or oral statement or writing made in connection with an issue under consideration or review by a legislative, executive, or judicial body, or any other official proceeding authorized by law,

(3) any written or oral statement or writing made in a place open to the public or a public forum in connection with an issue of public interest, or

(4) any other conduct in furtherance of the exercise of the constitutional right of petition or the constitutional right of free speech in connection with a public issue or an issue of public interest.

(f) The special motion may be filed within 60 days of the service of the complaint or, in the court's discretion, at any later time upon terms it deems proper. The motion shall be scheduled by the clerk of the court for a hearing not more than 30 days after the service of the motion unless the docket conditions of the court require a later hearing.

(g) All discovery proceedings in the action shall be stayed upon the filing of a notice of motion made pursuant to this section. The stay of discovery shall remain in effect until notice of entry of the order ruling on the motion. The court, on noticed motion and for good cause shown, may order that specified discovery be conducted notwithstanding this subdivision.

(h) For purposes of this section, "complaint" includes "cross-complaint" and "petition," "plaintiff" includes "cross-complainant" and "petitioner," and "defendant" includes "cross-defendant" and "respondent."

(i) An order granting or denying a special motion to strike shall be appealable under Section 904.1.

(j)

(1) Any party who files a special motion to strike pursuant to this section, and any party who files an opposition to a special motion to strike, shall, promptly upon so filing, transmit to the Judicial Council, by email or facsimile, a copy of the endorsed, filed caption page of the motion or opposition, a copy of any related notice of appeal or petition for a writ, and a conformed copy of any order issued pursuant to this section, including any order granting or denying a special motion to strike, discovery, or fees.

(2) The Judicial Council shall maintain a public record of information transmitted pursuant to this subdivision for at least three years, and may store the information on microfilm or other appropriate electronic media.

Amended by Stats 2021 ch 615 (AB 474),s 56, eff. 1/1/2022, op. 1/1/2023.
Amended by Stats 2014 ch 71 (SB 1304),s 17, eff. 1/1/2015.
Amended by Stats 2010 ch 328 (SB 1330),s 34, eff. 1/1/2011.
Amended by Stats 2009 ch 65 (SB 786),s 1, eff. 1/1/2010.
Amended by Stats 2005 ch 535 (AB 1158),s 1, eff. 10/5/2005.
Effective October 10, 1999 (Bill Number: AB 1675) (Chapter 960).

Section 425.17 - Inapplicability of anti-SLAPP law

(a) The Legislature finds and declares that there has been a disturbing abuse of Section 425.16, the California Anti-SLAPP Law, which has undermined the exercise of the constitutional rights of freedom of speech and petition for the redress of grievances, contrary to the purpose and intent of Section 425.16. The Legislature finds and declares that it is in the public interest to encourage continued participation in matters of public significance, and that this participation should not be chilled through abuse of the judicial process or Section 425.16.

(b) Section 425.16 does not apply to any action brought solely in the public interest or on behalf of the general public if all of the following conditions exist:

(1) The plaintiff does not seek any relief greater than or different from the relief sought for the general public or a class of which the plaintiff is a member. A claim for attorney's fees, costs, or penalties does not constitute greater or different relief for purposes of this subdivision.

(2) The action, if successful, would enforce an important right affecting the public interest, and would confer a significant benefit, whether pecuniary or nonpecuniary, on the general public or a large class of persons.

(3) Private enforcement is necessary and places a disproportionate financial burden on the plaintiff in relation to the plaintiff's stake in the matter.

(c) Section 425.16 does not apply to any cause of action brought against a person primarily engaged in the business of selling or leasing goods or services, including, but not limited to, insurance, securities, or financial instruments, arising from any statement or conduct by that person if both of the following conditions exist:

(1) The statement or conduct consists of representations of fact about that person's or a business competitor's business operations, goods, or services, that is made for the purpose of obtaining approval for, promoting, or securing sales or leases of, or commercial transactions in, the person's goods or services, or the statement or conduct was made in the course of delivering the person's goods or services.

(2) The intended audience is an actual or potential buyer or customer, or a person likely to repeat the statement to, or otherwise influence, an actual or potential buyer or customer, or the statement or conduct arose out of or within the context of a regulatory approval process, proceeding, or investigation, except where the statement or conduct was made by a telephone corporation in the course of a proceeding before the California Public Utilities Commission and is the subject of a lawsuit brought by a competitor, notwithstanding that the conduct or statement concerns an important public issue.

(d) Subdivisions (b) and (c) do not apply to any of the following:

(1) Any person enumerated in subdivision (b) of Section 2 of Article I of the California Constitution or Section 1070 of the Evidence Code, or any person engaged in the dissemination of ideas or expression in any book or academic journal, while engaged in the gathering, receiving, or processing of information for communication to the public.

(2) Any action against any person or entity based upon the creation, dissemination, exhibition, advertisement, or other similar promotion of any dramatic, literary, musical, political, or artistic work, including, but not limited to, a motion picture or television program, or an article published in a newspaper or magazine of general circulation.

(3) Any nonprofit organization that receives more than 50 percent of its annual revenues from federal, state, or local government grants, awards, programs, or reimbursements for services rendered.

(e) If any trial court denies a special motion to strike on the grounds that the action or cause of action is exempt pursuant to this section, the appeal provisions in subdivision (i) of Section 425.16 and paragraph (13) of subdivision (a) of Section 904.1 do not apply to that action or cause of action.

Amended by Stats 2011 ch 296 (AB 1023),s 36.5, eff. 1/1/2012.
Added by Stats 2003 ch 338 (SB 515),s 1, eff. 1/1/2004.

Section 425.18 - Special motion to strike SLAPPback

(a) The Legislature finds and declares that a SLAPPback is distinguishable in character and origin from the ordinary malicious prosecution action. The Legislature further finds and declares that a SLAPPback cause of action should be treated differently, as provided in this section, from an ordinary malicious prosecution action because a SLAPPback is consistent with the Legislature's intent to protect the valid exercise of the constitutional rights of free speech and petition by its deterrent effect on SLAPP (strategic lawsuit against public participation) litigation and by its restoration of public confidence in participatory democracy.

(b) For purposes of this section, the following terms have the following meanings:

(1) "SLAPPback" means any cause of action for malicious prosecution or abuse of process arising from the filing or maintenance of a prior cause of action that has been dismissed pursuant to a special motion to strike under Section 425.16.

(2) "Special motion to strike" means a motion made pursuant to Section 425.16.

(c) The provisions of subdivisions (c), (f), (g), and (i) of Section 425.16, and paragraph (13) of subdivision (a) of Section 904.1, shall not apply to a special motion to strike a SLAPPback.

(d)

(1) A special motion to strike a SLAPPback shall be filed within any one of the following periods of time, as follows:

(A) Within 120 days of the service of the complaint.

(B) At the court's discretion, within six months of the service of the complaint.

(C) At the court's discretion, at any later time in extraordinary cases due to no fault of the defendant and upon written findings of the court stating the extraordinary case and circumstance.

(2) The motion shall be scheduled by the clerk of the court for a hearing not more than 30 days after the service of the motion unless the docket conditions of the court require a later hearing.

(e) A party opposing a special motion to strike a SLAPPback may file an ex parte application for a continuance to obtain necessary discovery. If it appears that facts essential to justify opposition to that motion may exist, but cannot then be presented, the court shall grant a reasonable continuance to permit the party to obtain affidavits or conduct discovery or may make any other order as may be just.

(f) If the court finds that a special motion to strike a SLAPPback is frivolous or solely intended to cause unnecessary delay, the court shall award costs and reasonable attorney's fees to a plaintiff prevailing on the motion, pursuant to Section 128.5.

(g) Upon entry of an order denying a special motion to strike a SLAPPback claim, or granting the special motion to strike as to some but less than all causes of action alleged in a complaint containing a SLAPPback claim, an aggrieved party may, within 20 days after service of a written notice of the entry of the order, petition an appropriate reviewing court for a peremptory writ.

(h) A special motion to strike may not be filed against a SLAPPback by a party whose filing or maintenance of the prior cause of action from which the SLAPPback arises was illegal as a matter of law.

(i) This section does not apply to a SLAPPback filed by a public entity.

Added by Stats 2005 ch 535 (AB 1158),s 2, eff. 10/5/2005.

Section 425.50 - Allegation of construction-related accessibility claim in complaint

(a) An allegation of a construction-related accessibility claim in a complaint, as defined in subdivision (a) of Section 55.52 of the Civil Code, shall state facts sufficient to allow a reasonable person to identify the basis of the violation or violations supporting the claim, including all of the following:

(1) A plain language explanation of the specific access barrier or barriers the individual encountered, or by which the individual alleges he or she was deterred, with sufficient information about the location of the alleged barrier to enable a reasonable person to identify the access barrier.

(2) The way in which the barrier denied the individual full and equal use or access, or in which it deterred the individual, on each particular occasion.

(3) The date or dates of each particular occasion on which the claimant encountered the specific access barrier, or on which he or she was deterred.

(4)

(A) Except in complaints that allege physical injury or damage to property, a complaint filed by or on behalf of a high-frequency litigant shall also state all of the following:

(i) Whether the complaint is filed by, or on behalf of, a high-frequency litigant.

(ii) In the case of a high-frequency litigant who is a plaintiff, the number of complaints alleging a construction-related accessibility claim that the high-frequency litigant has filed during the 12 months prior to filing the complaint.

(iii) In the case of a high-frequency litigant who is a plaintiff, the reason the individual was in the geographic area of the defendant's business.

(iv) In the case of a high-frequency litigant who is a plaintiff, the reason why the individual desired to access the defendant's business, including the specific commercial, business, personal, social, leisure, recreational, or other purpose.

(B) As used in this section "high-frequency litigant" has the same meaning as set forth in subdivision (b) of Section 425.55.

(b)

(1) A complaint alleging a construction-related accessibility claim, as those terms are defined in subdivision (a) of Section 55.3 of the Civil Code, shall be verified by the plaintiff. A complaint filed without verification shall be subject to a motion to strike.

(2) A complaint alleging a construction-related accessibility claim filed by, or on behalf of, a high-frequency litigant shall state in the caption "ACTION SUBJECT TO THE SUPPLEMENTAL FEE IN GOVERNMENT CODE SECTION 70616.5."

(c) A complaint alleging a construction-related accessibility claim shall be signed by at least one attorney of record in the attorney's individual name, or, if the party is not represented by an attorney, shall be signed by the party. By signing the complaint, the attorney or unrepresented party is certifying that, to the best of the person's knowledge, information, and belief, formed after an inquiry reasonable under the circumstances, all of the following conditions are met:

(1) It is not being presented primarily for an improper purpose, such as to harass or to cause unnecessary delay or needless increase in the cost of litigation.

(2) The claims, defenses, and other legal contentions therein are warranted by existing law or by a nonfrivolous argument for the extension, modification, or reversal of existing law or the establishment of new law.

(3) The allegations and other factual contentions have evidentiary support or, if specifically so identified, are likely to have evidentiary support after a reasonable opportunity for further investigation or discovery.

(4) The denials of factual contentions are warranted on the evidence or, if specifically so identified, are reasonably based on a lack of information or belief.

(d) A court may, after notice and a reasonable opportunity to respond, determine whether subdivision (c) has been violated and, if so, impose sanctions as provided in Section 128.7 for violations of subdivision (b) of Section 128.7.

(e) Nothing in this section shall limit the right of a plaintiff to amend a complaint under Section 472, or with leave of the court under Section 473. However, an amended pleading alleging a construction-related accessibility claim shall be pled as required by subdivision (a).

(f) The determination whether an attorney is a high-frequency litigant shall be made solely on the basis of the verified complaint and any other publicly available documents. Notwithstanding any other law, no party to the proceeding may conduct discovery with respect to whether an attorney is a high-frequency litigant.

(g) This section shall become operative on January 1, 2013.

Amended by Stats 2015 ch 755 (AB 1521),s 5, eff. 10/10/2015.
Amended by Stats 2013 ch 76 (AB 383),s 22, eff. 1/1/2014.
Added by Stats 2012 ch 383 (SB 1186),s 13, eff. 9/19/2012.

Section 425.55 - Construction-related accessibility claims; high-frequency litigant defined

(a) The Legislature finds and declares all of the following:

(1) Protection of the civil rights of persons with disabilities is of the utmost importance to this state, and private enforcement is the essential means of achieving that goal, as the law has been designed.

(2) According to information from the California Commission on Disability Access, more than one-half, or 54 percent, of all construction-related accessibility complaints filed between 2012 and 2014 were filed by two law firms. Forty-six percent of all complaints were filed by a total of 14 parties. Therefore, a very small number of plaintiffs have filed a disproportionately large number of the construction-related accessibility claims in the state, from 70 to 300 lawsuits each year. Moreover, these lawsuits are frequently filed against small businesses on the basis of boilerplate complaints, apparently seeking quick cash settlements rather than correction of the accessibility violation. This practice unfairly taints the reputation of other innocent disabled consumers who are merely trying to go about their daily lives accessing public accommodations as they are entitled to have full and equal access under the state's Unruh Civil Rights Act (Section 51 of the Civil Code) and the federal Americans with Disabilities Act of 1990 (Public Law 101-336).

(3) Therefore, given these special and unique circumstances, the provisions of this section are warranted for this limited group of plaintiffs.

(b) For the purposes of this article, "high-frequency litigant" means a person, except as specified in paragraph (3), who utilizes court resources in actions arising from alleged construction-related access violations at such a high level that it is appropriate that additional safeguards apply so as to ensure that the claims are warranted. A "high-frequency litigant" means one or more of the following:

(1) A plaintiff who has filed 10 or more complaints alleging a construction-related accessibility violation within the 12-month period immediately preceding the filing of the current complaint alleging a construction-related accessibility violation.

(2) An attorney who has represented as attorney of record 10 or more high-frequency litigant plaintiffs in actions that were resolved within the 12-month period immediately preceding the filing of the current complaint alleging a construction-related accessibility violation, excluding all of the following actions:

(A) An action in which an early evaluation conference was held pursuant to Section 55.54 of the Civil Code.

(B) An action in which judgment was entered in favor of the plaintiff.

(C) An action in which the construction-related accessibility violations alleged in the complaint were remedied in whole or in part, or a favorable result was achieved, after the plaintiff filed a complaint or provided a demand letter, as defined in Section 55.3 of the Civil Code.

(3) This section does not apply to an attorney employed or retained by a qualified legal services project or a qualified support center, as defined in Section 6213 of the Business and Professions Code, when acting within the scope of employment to represent a client in asserting a construction-related accessibility claim, or the client in such a case.

Added by Stats 2015 ch 755 (AB 1521),s 6, eff. 10/10/2015.

Article 2 - COMPULSORY CROSS-COMPLAINTS

Section 426.10 - Definitions

As used in this article:

(a) "Complaint" means a complaint or cross-complaint.

(b) "Plaintiff" means a person who files a complaint or cross-complaint.

(c) "Related cause of action" means a cause of action which arises out of the same transaction, occurrence, or series of transactions or occurrences as the cause of action which the plaintiff alleges in his complaint.

Added by Stats. 1971, Ch. 244.

Section 426.30 - Failure to allege related cause of action against plaintiff in cross-complaint

(a) Except as otherwise provided by statute, if a party against whom a complaint has been filed and served fails to allege in a cross-complaint any related cause of action which (at the time of serving his answer to the complaint) he has against the plaintiff, such party may not thereafter in any other action assert against the plaintiff the related cause of action not pleaded.

(b) This section does not apply if either of the following are established:

(1) The court in which the action is pending does not have jurisdiction to render a personal judgment against the person who failed to plead the related cause of action.

(2) The person who failed to plead the related cause of action did not file an answer to the complaint against him.

Added by Stats. 1971, Ch. 244.

Section 426.40 - Inapplicability of article

This article does not apply if any of the following are established:

(a) The cause of action not pleaded requires for its adjudication the presence of additional parties over whom the court cannot acquire jurisdiction.

(b) Both the court in which the action is pending and any other court to which the action is transferrable pursuant to Section 396 are prohibited by the federal or state constitution or by a statute from entertaining the cause of action not pleaded.

(c) At the time the action was commenced, the cause of action not pleaded was the subject of another pending action.

Added by Stats. 1971, Ch. 244.

Section 426.50 - Amendment of pleading or filing cross-complaint to assert cause of action subject to requirements of article

A party who fails to plead a cause of action subject to the requirements of this article, whether through oversight, inadvertence, mistake, neglect, or other cause, may apply to the court for leave to amend his pleading, or to file a cross-complaint, to assert such cause at any time during the course of the action. The court, after notice to the adverse party, shall grant, upon such terms as may be just to the parties, leave to amend the pleading, or to file the cross-complaint, to assert such cause if the party who failed to plead the cause acted in good faith. This subdivision shall be liberally construed to avoid forfeiture of causes of action.

Added by Stats. 1971, Ch. 244.

Section 426.60 - Inapplicability of article to small claims court actions or declaration of rights and duties of parties

(a) This article applies only to civil actions and does not apply to special proceedings.

(b) This article does not apply to actions in the small claims court.

(c) This article does not apply where the only relief sought is a declaration of the rights and duties of the respective parties in an action for declaratory relief under Chapter 8 (commencing with Section 1060) of Title 14 of this part.

Added by Stats. 1971, Ch. 244.

Section 426.70 - Applicability to eminent domain proceedings

(a) Notwithstanding subdivision (a) of Section 426.60, this article applies to eminent domain proceedings.

(b) The related cause of action may be asserted by cross-complaint in an eminent domain proceeding whether or not the party asserting such cause of action has presented a claim in compliance with Part 3 (commencing with Section 900) of Division 3.6 of Title 1 of the Government Code to the plaintiff in the original eminent domain proceeding.

Added by Stats. 1975, Ch. 1240.

Article 3 - PERMISSIVE JOINDER OF CAUSES OF ACTION

Section 427.10 - Generally

(a) A plaintiff who in a complaint, alone or with coplaintiffs, alleges a cause of action against one or more defendants may unite with such cause any other causes which he has either alone or with any coplaintiffs against any of such defendants.

(b) Causes of action may be joined in a cross-complaint in accordance with Sections 428.10 and 428.30.

Added by Stats. 1971, Ch. 244.

Article 4 - CROSS-COMPLAINTS

Section 428.10 - Generally

A party against whom a cause of action has been asserted in a complaint or cross-complaint may file a cross-complaint setting forth either or both of the following:

(a) Any cause of action he has against any of the parties who filed the complaint or cross-complaint against him. Nothing in this subdivision authorizes the filing of a cross-complaint against the plaintiff in an action commenced under Title 7 (commencing with Section 1230.010) of Part 3.

(b) Any cause of action he has against a person alleged to be liable thereon, whether or not such person is already a party to the action, if the cause of action asserted in his cross-complaint (1) arises out of the same transaction, occurrence, or series of transactions or occurrences as the cause brought against him or (2) asserts a claim, right, or interest in the property or controversy which is the subject of the cause brought against him.

Amended by Stats. 1975, Ch. 1240.

Section 428.20 - Joinder of person as cross-complainant or cross-defendant

When a person files a cross-complaint as authorized by Section 428.10, he may join any person as a cross-complainant or cross-defendant, whether or not such person is already a party to the action, if, had the cross-complaint been filed as an independent action, the joinder of that party would have been permitted by the statutes governing joinder of parties.

Added by Stats. 1971, Ch. 244.

Section 428.30 - Action united with action asserted in cross-complaint

Where a person files a cross-complaint as authorized by Section 428.10, he may unite with the cause of action asserted in the cross-complaint any other causes of action he has against any of the cross-defendants, other than the plaintiff in an eminent domain proceeding, whether or not such cross-defendant is already a party to the action.

Added by Stats. 1971, Ch. 244.

Section 428.40 - Separate document

The cross-complaint shall be a separate document.

Added by Stats. 1971, Ch. 244.

Section 428.50 - Time for filing

(a) A party shall file a cross-complaint against any of the parties who filed the complaint or cross-complaint against him or her before or at the same time as the answer to the complaint or cross-complaint.

(b) Any other cross-complaint may be filed at any time before the court has set a date for trial.

(c) A party shall obtain leave of court to file any cross-complaint except one filed within the time specified in subdivision (a) or (b). Leave may be granted in the interest of justice at any time during the course of the action.

Amended by Stats. 1983, Ch. 176, Sec. 1.

Section 428.60 - Service

A cross-complaint shall be served on each of the parties in an action in the following manner:

(1) If a party has not appeared in the action, a summons upon the cross-complaint shall be issued and served upon him in the same manner as upon commencement of an original action.

(2) If a party has appeared in the action, the cross-complaint shall be served upon his attorney, or upon the party if he has appeared without an attorney, in the manner provided for service of summons or in the manner provided by Chapter 5 (commencing with Section 1010) of Title 14 of Part 2 of this code.

Amended by Stats. 1974, Ch. 429.

Section 428.70 - Special answer filed by third-party defendant

(a) As used in this section:

(1) "Third-party plaintiff" means a person against whom a cause of action has been asserted in a complaint or cross-complaint, who claims the right to recover all or part of any amounts for which he may be held liable on such cause of action from a third person, and who files a cross-complaint stating such claim as a cause of action against the third person.

(2) "Third-party defendant" means the person who is alleged in a cross-complaint filed by a third-party plaintiff to be liable to the third-party plaintiff if the third-party plaintiff is held liable on the claim against him.

(b) In addition to the other rights and duties a third-party defendant has under this article, he may, at the time he files his answer to the cross-complaint, file as a separate document a special answer alleging against the person who asserted the cause of action against the third-party plaintiff any defenses which the third-party plaintiff has to such cause of action. The special answer shall be served on the third-party plaintiff and on the person who asserted the cause of action against the third-party plaintiff.

Added by Stats. 1971, Ch. 244.

Section 428.80 - Counterclaim abolished

The counterclaim is abolished. Any cause of action that formerly was asserted by a counterclaim shall be asserted by a cross-complaint. Where any statute refers to asserting a cause of action as a counterclaim, such cause shall be asserted as a cross-complaint. The erroneous designation of a pleading as a counterclaim shall not affect its validity, but such pleading shall be deemed to be a cross-complaint.

Added by Stats. 1971, Ch. 244.

Article 5 - CONTENTS OF DOCUMENTS IN PARTICULAR ACTIONS OR PROCEEDINGS

Section 429.30 - Demand for relief on account of alleged infringement of plaintiff's rights in and to literary, artistic or intellectual production

(a) As used in this section:

(1) "Complaint" includes a cross-complaint.

(2) "Plaintiff" includes the person filing a cross-complaint.

(b) If the complaint contains a demand for relief on account of the alleged infringement of the plaintiff's rights in and to a literary, artistic, or intellectual production, there shall be attached to the complaint a copy of the production as to which the infringement is claimed and a copy of the alleged infringing production. If, by reason of bulk or the nature of the production, it is not practicable to attach a copy to the complaint, that fact and the reasons why it is impracticable to attach a copy of the production to the complaint shall be alleged; and the court, in connection with any demurrer, motion, or other proceedings in the cause in which a knowledge of the contents of such production may be necessary or desirable, shall make such order for a view of the production not attached as will suit the convenience of the court to the end that the contents of such production may be deemed to be a part of the complaint to the same extent and with the same force as though such production had been capable of being and had been attached to the complaint. The attachment of any such production in accordance with the provisions of this section shall not be deemed a making public of the production within the meaning of Section 983 of the Civil Code.

Added by Stats. 1971, Ch. 244.

Chapter 3 - OBJECTIONS TO PLEADINGS; DENIALS AND DEFENSES

Article 1 - OBJECTIONS TO PLEADINGS

Section 430.10 - Grounds for objection by party against whom complaint or cross-complaint filed

The party against whom a complaint or cross-complaint has been filed may object, by demurrer or answer as provided in Section 430.30, to the pleading on any one or more of the following grounds:

(a) The court has no jurisdiction of the subject of the cause of action alleged in the pleading.

(b) The person who filed the pleading does not have the legal capacity to sue.

(c) There is another action pending between the same parties on the same cause of action.

(d) There is a defect or misjoinder of parties.

(e) The pleading does not state facts sufficient to constitute a cause of action.

(f) The pleading is uncertain. As used in this subdivision, "uncertain" includes ambiguous and unintelligible.

(g) In an action founded upon a contract, it cannot be ascertained from the pleading whether the contract is written, is oral, or is implied by conduct.
(h) No certificate was filed as required by Section 411.35.
Amended by Stats 2020 ch 370 (SB 1371),s 35, eff. 1/1/2021.

Section 430.20 - Grounds for objection by party against whom answer filed
A party against whom an answer has been filed may object, by demurrer as provided in Section 430.30, to the answer upon any one or more of the following grounds:
(a) The answer does not state facts sufficient to constitute a defense.
(b) The answer is uncertain. As used in this subdivision, "uncertain" includes ambiguous and unintelligible.
(c) Where the answer pleads a contract, it cannot be ascertained from the answer whether the contract is written or oral.
Added by Stats. 1971, Ch. 244.

Section 430.30 - Objection taken by demurrer; by answer
(a) When any ground for objection to a complaint, cross-complaint, or answer appears on the face thereof, or from any matter of which the court is required to or may take judicial notice, the objection on that ground may be taken by a demurrer to the pleading.
(b) When any ground for objection to a complaint or cross-complaint does not appear on the face of the pleading, the objection may be taken by answer.
(c) A party objecting to a complaint or cross-complaint may demur and answer at the same time.
Added by Stats. 1971, Ch. 244.

Section 430.40 - Time for demur to complaint or cross-complaint; demur to answer
(a) A person against whom a complaint or cross-complaint has been filed may, within 30 days after service of the complaint or cross-complaint, demur to the complaint or cross-complaint.
(b) A party who has filed a complaint or cross-complaint may, within 10 days after service of the answer to his pleading, demur to the answer.
Added by Stats. 1971, Ch. 244.

Section 430.41 - Meeting required before filing demurrer
(a) Before filing a demurrer pursuant to this chapter, the demurring party shall meet and confer in person or by telephone with the party who filed the pleading that is subject to demurrer for the purpose of determining whether an agreement can be reached that would resolve the objections to be raised in the demurrer. If an amended complaint, cross-complaint, or answer is filed, the responding party shall meet and confer again with the party who filed the amended pleading before filing a demurrer to the amended pleading.
　(1) As part of the meet and confer process, the demurring party shall identify all of the specific causes of action that it believes are subject to demurrer and identify with legal support the basis of the deficiencies. The party who filed the complaint, cross-complaint, or answer shall provide legal support for its position that the pleading is legally sufficient or, in the alternative, how the complaint, cross-complaint, or answer could be amended to cure any legal insufficiency.
　(2) The parties shall meet and confer at least five days before the date the responsive pleading is due. If the parties are not able to meet and confer at least five days prior to the date the responsive pleading is due, the demurring party shall be granted an automatic 30-day extension of time within which to file a responsive pleading, by filing and serving, on or before the date on which a demurrer would be due, a declaration stating under penalty of perjury that a good faith attempt to meet and confer was made and explaining the reasons why the parties could not meet and confer. The 30-day extension shall commence from the date the responsive pleading was previously due, and the demurring party shall not be subject to default during the period of the extension. Any further extensions shall be obtained by court order upon a showing of good cause.
　(3) The demurring party shall file and serve with the demurrer a declaration stating either of the following:
　　(A) The means by which the demurring party met and conferred with the party who filed the pleading subject to demurrer, and that the parties did not reach an agreement resolving the objections raised in the demurrer.
　　(B) That the party who filed the pleading subject to demurrer failed to respond to the meet and confer request of the demurring party or otherwise failed to meet and confer in good faith.
　(4) A determination by the court that the meet and confer process was insufficient shall not be grounds to overrule or sustain a demurrer.
(b) A party demurring to a pleading that has been amended after a demurrer to an earlier version of the pleading was sustained shall not demur to any portion of the amended complaint, cross-complaint, or answer on grounds that could have been raised by demurrer to the earlier version of the complaint, cross-complaint, or answer.
(c) If a court sustains a demurrer to one or more causes of action and grants leave to amend, the court may order a conference of the parties before an amended complaint or cross-complaint or a demurrer to an amended complaint or cross-complaint, may be filed. If a conference is held, the court shall not preclude a party from filing a demurrer and the time to file a demurrer shall not begin until after the conference has concluded. This section does not prohibit the court from ordering a conference on its own motion at any time or prevent a party from requesting that the court order a conference to be held.
(d) This section does not apply to the following civil actions:
　(1) An action in which a party not represented by counsel is incarcerated in a local, state, or federal correctional institution.
　(2) A proceeding in forcible entry, forcible detainer, or unlawful detainer.
(e)
　(1) In response to a demurrer and prior to the case being at issue, a complaint or cross-complaint shall not be amended more than three times, absent an offer to the trial court as to such additional facts to be pleaded that there is a reasonable possibility the defect can be cured to state a cause of action. The three-amendment limit shall not include an amendment made without leave of the court pursuant to Section 472, provided the amendment is made before a demurrer to the original complaint or cross-complaint is filed.
　(2) Nothing in this section affects the rights of a party to amend its pleading or respond to an amended pleading after the case is at issue.
(f) Nothing in this section affects appellate review or the rights of a party pursuant to Section 430.80.
(g) If a demurrer is overruled as to a cause of action and that cause of action is not further amended, the demurring party preserves its right to appeal after final judgment without filing a further demurrer.
Amended by Stats 2020 ch 36 (AB 3364),s 15, eff. 1/1/2021.
Added by Stats 2015 ch 418 (SB 383),s 1, eff. 1/1/2016.

Section 430.50 - Demurrer to whole complaint or any cause of action stated; demurrer to whole answer or to any defenses set up
(a) A demurrer to a complaint or cross-complaint may be taken to the whole complaint or cross-complaint or to any of the causes of action stated therein.
(b) A demurrer to an answer may be taken to the whole answer or to any one or more of the several defenses set up in the answer.
Added by Stats. 1971, Ch. 244.

Section 430.60 - Demurrer to distinctly specify grounds of objections
A demurrer shall distinctly specify the grounds upon which any of the objections to the complaint, cross-complaint, or answer are taken. Unless it does so, it may be disregarded.
Added by Stats. 1971, Ch. 244.

Section 430.70 - Demurrer based on matter which court may take judicial notice

When the ground of demurrer is based on a matter of which the court may take judicial notice pursuant to Section 452 or 453 of the Evidence Code, such matter shall be specified in the demurrer, or in the supporting points and authorities for the purpose of invoking such notice, except as the court may otherwise permit.

Added by Stats. 1971, Ch. 244.

Section 430.80 - Failure to object deemed waiver of objection

(a) If the party against whom a complaint or cross-complaint has been filed fails to object to the pleading, either by demurrer or answer, that party is deemed to have waived the objection unless it is an objection that the court has no jurisdiction of the subject of the cause of action alleged in the pleading or an objection that the pleading does not state facts sufficient to constitute a cause of action.

(b) If the party against whom an answer has been filed fails to demur thereto, that party is deemed to have waived the objection unless it is an objection that the answer does not state facts sufficient to constitute a defense.

Amended by Stats. 1983, Ch. 1167, Sec. 2.

Section 430.90 - Time to respond when case remanded for improper removal to federal court

(a) Where the defendant has removed a civil action to federal court without filing a response in the original court and the case is later remanded for improper removal, the time to respond shall be as follows:

  (1) If the defendant has not generally appeared in either the original or federal court, then 30 days from the day the original court receives the case on remand to move to dismiss the action pursuant to Section 583.250 or to move to quash service of summons or to stay or dismiss the action pursuant to Section 418.10, if the court has not ruled on a similar motion filed by the defendant prior to the removal of the action to federal court.

  (2) If the defendant has not filed an answer in the original court, then 30 days from the day the original court receives the case on remand to do any of the following:

    (A) Answer the complaint.

    (B) Demur or move to strike all or a portion of the complaint if:

      (i) an answer was not filed in the federal court, and

      (ii) a demurrer or motion to strike raising the same or similar issues was not filed and ruled upon by the original court prior to the removal of the action to federal court or was not filed and ruled upon in federal court prior to the remand. If the demurrer or motion to strike is denied by the court, the defendant shall have 30 days to answer the complaint unless an answer was filed with the demurrer or motion to strike.

(b) For the purposes of this section, time shall be calculated from the date of the original court's receipt of the order of remand.

Added by Stats. 1995, Ch. 796, Sec. 5. Effective January 1, 1996.

Article 2 - DENIALS AND DEFENSES

Section 431.10 - Material allegation defined; immaterial allegation defined

(a) A material allegation in a pleading is one essential to the claim or defense and which could not be stricken from the pleading without leaving it insufficient as to that claim or defense.

(b) An immaterial allegation in a pleading is any of the following:

  (1) An allegation that is not essential to the statement of a claim or defense.

  (2) An allegation that is neither pertinent to nor supported by an otherwise sufficient claim or defense.

  (3) A demand for judgment requesting relief not supported by the allegations of the complaint or cross-complaint.

(c) An "immaterial allegation" means "irrelevant matter" as that term is used in Section 436.

Amended by Stats. 1986, Ch. 540, Sec. 2.

Section 431.20 - Material allegation not controverted taken as true; statement of new matter in answer deemed controverted

(a) Every material allegation of the complaint or cross-complaint, not controverted by the answer, shall, for the purposes of the action, be taken as true.

(b) The statement of any new matter in the answer, in avoidance or constituting a defense, shall, on the trial, be deemed controverted by the opposite party.

Added by Stats. 1971, Ch. 244.

Section 431.30 - General denial; denial made positively or according to information and belief of defendant

(a) As used in this section:

  (1) "Complaint" includes a cross-complaint.

  (2) "Defendant" includes a person filing an answer to a cross-complaint.

(b) The answer to a complaint shall contain:

  (1) The general or specific denial of the material allegations of the complaint controverted by the defendant.

  (2) A statement of any new matter constituting a defense.

(c) Affirmative relief may not be claimed in the answer.

(d) If the complaint is subject to Article 2 (commencing with Section 90) of Chapter 5.1 of Title 1 of Part 1 or is not verified, a general denial is sufficient but only puts in issue the material allegations of the complaint. If the complaint is verified, unless the complaint is subject to Article 2 (commencing with Section 90) of Chapter 5.1 of Title 1 of Part 1, the denial of the allegations shall be made positively or according to the information and belief of the defendant. However, if the cause of action is a claim assigned to a third party for collection and the complaint is verified, the denial of the allegations shall be made positively or according to the information and belief of the defendant, even if the complaint is subject to Article 2 (commencing with Section 90) of Chapter 5.1 of Title 1 of Part 1.

(e) If the defendant has no information or belief upon the subject sufficient to enable him or her to answer an allegation of the complaint, he or she may so state in his or her answer and place his or her denial on that ground.

(f) The denials of the allegations controverted may be stated by reference to specific paragraphs or parts of the complaint; or by express admission of certain allegations of the complaint with a general denial of all of the allegations not so admitted; or by denial of certain allegations upon information and belief, or for lack of sufficient information or belief, with a general denial of all allegations not so denied or expressly admitted.

(g) The defenses shall be separately stated, and the several defenses shall refer to the causes of action which they are intended to answer, in a manner by which they may be intelligibly distinguished.

Amended by Stats 2003 ch 149 (SB 79),s 8, eff. 1/1/2004.

Section 431.40 - General written denial and statement of new matter constituting defense if amount in controversy not in excess of $1,000

(a) Any provision of law to the contrary notwithstanding, in any action in which the demand, exclusive of interest, or the value of the property in controversy does not exceed one thousand dollars ($1000), the defendant at his option, in lieu of demurrer or other answer, may file a general written denial and a brief statement of any new matter constituting a defense.

(b) Nothing in this section excuses the defendant from complying with the provisions of law applicable to a cross-complaint, and any cross-complaint of the defendant shall be subject to the requirements applicable in any other action.

(c) The general written denial described in subdivision (a) shall be on a blank available at the place of filing and shall be in a form prescribed by the Judicial Council. This form need not be verified.
Amended by Stats. 1977, Ch. 93.

Section 431.50 - Exemption from liability because loss insured against was remotely caused or would not have occurred but for peril excepted

In an action to recover upon a contract of insurance wherein the defendant claims exemption from liability upon the ground that, although the proximate cause of the loss was a peril insured against, the loss was remotely caused by or would not have occurred but for a peril excepted in the contract of insurance, the defendant shall in his answer set forth and specify the peril which was the proximate cause of the loss, in what manner the peril excepted contributed to the loss or itself caused the peril insured against, and if he claims that the peril excepted caused the peril insured against, he shall in his answer set forth and specify upon what premises or at what place the peril excepted caused the peril insured against.
Added by Stats. 1971, Ch. 244.

Section 431.70 - Defense of payment in that two demands compensated so far as they equal each other

Where cross-demands for money have existed between persons at any point in time when neither demand was barred by the statute of limitations, and an action is thereafter commenced by one such person, the other person may assert in the answer the defense of payment in that the two demands are compensated so far as they equal each other, notwithstanding that an independent action asserting the person's claim would at the time of filing the answer be barred by the statute of limitations. If the cross-demand would otherwise be barred by the statute of limitations, the relief accorded under this section shall not exceed the value of the relief granted to the other party. The defense provided by this section is not available if the cross-demand is barred for failure to assert it in a prior action under Section 426.30. Neither person can be deprived of the benefits of this section by the assignment or death of the other. For the purposes of this section, a money judgment is a "demand for money" and, as applied to a money judgment, the demand is barred by the statute of limitations when enforcement of the judgment is barred under Chapter 3 (commencing with Section 683.010) of Division 1 of Title 9.
Amended by Stats. 1982, Ch. 497, Sec. 32. Operative July 1, 1983, by Sec. 185 of Ch. 497.

Article 3 - TIME TO RESPOND TO CROSS-COMPLAINT

Section 432.10 - Generally

A party served with a cross-complaint may within 30 days after service move, demur, or otherwise plead to the cross-complaint in the same manner as to an original complaint.
Added by Stats. 1971, Ch. 244.

Chapter 4 - MOTION TO STRIKE

Section 435 - Service and filing of notice of motion to strike

(a) As used in this section:
    (1) The term "complaint" includes a cross-complaint.
    (2) The term "pleading" means a demurrer, answer, complaint, or cross-complaint.
(b)
    (1) Any party, within the time allowed to respond to a pleading may serve and file a notice of motion to strike the whole or any part thereof, but this time limitation shall not apply to motions specified in subdivision (e).
    (2) A notice of motion to strike the answer or the complaint, or a portion thereof, shall specify a hearing date set in accordance with Section 1005.
    (3) A notice of motion to strike a demurrer, or a portion thereof, shall set the hearing thereon concurrently with the hearing on the demurrer.
(c) If a party serves and files a notice of motion to strike without demurring to the complaint, the time to answer is extended and no default may be entered against that defendant, except as provided in Sections 585 and 586.
(d) The filing of a notice of motion to strike an answer or complaint, or portion thereof, shall not extend the time within which to demur.
(e) A motion to strike, as specified in this section, may be made as part of a motion pursuant to subparagraph (A) of paragraph (1) of subdivision (i) of Section 438.
Amended by Stats. 1993, Ch. 456, Sec. 3.5. Effective January 1, 1994.

Section 435.5 - Meeting before filing motion to strike

(a) Before filing a motion to strike pursuant to this chapter, the moving party shall meet and confer in person or by telephone with the party who filed the pleading that is subject to the motion to strike for the purpose of determining if an agreement can be reached that resolves the objections to be raised in the motion to strike. If an amended pleading is filed, the responding party shall meet and confer again with the party who filed the amended pleading before filing a motion to strike the amended pleading.
    (1) As part of the meet and confer process, the moving party shall identify all of the specific allegations that it believes are subject to being stricken and identify with legal support the basis of the deficiencies. The party who filed the pleading shall provide legal support for its position that the pleading is legally sufficient, or, in the alternative, how the pleading could be amended to cure any legal insufficiency.
    (2) The parties shall meet and confer at least five days before the date a motion to strike must be filed. If the parties are unable to meet and confer at least five days before the date the motion to strike must be filed, the moving party shall be granted an automatic 30-day extension of time within which to file a motion to strike, by filing and serving, on or before the date a motion to strike must be filed, a declaration stating under penalty of perjury that a good faith attempt to meet and confer was made and explaining the reasons why the parties could not meet and confer. The 30-day extension shall commence from the date the motion to strike was previously due, and the moving party shall not be subject to default during the period of the extension. Any further extensions shall be obtained by court order upon a showing of good cause.
    (3) The moving party shall file and serve with the motion to strike a declaration stating either of the following:
        (A) The means by which the moving party met and conferred with the party who filed the pleading subject to the motion to strike, and that the parties did not reach an agreement resolving the objections raised by the motion to strike.
        (B) That the party who filed the pleading subject to the motion to strike failed to respond to the meet and confer request of the moving party or otherwise failed to meet and confer in good faith.
    (4) A determination by the court that the meet and confer process was insufficient shall not be grounds to grant or deny the motion to strike.
(b) A party moving to strike a pleading that has been amended after a motion to strike an earlier version of the pleading was granted shall not move to strike any portion of the pleadings on grounds that could have been raised by a motion to strike as to the earlier version of the pleading.
(c)
    (1) If a court grants a motion to strike and grants leave to amend, the court may order a conference of the parties before an amended pleading, or a motion to strike an amended pleading, may be filed. If the conference is held, the court shall not preclude a party from filing a motion to strike and the time to file a motion to strike shall not begin until after the conference has concluded.
    (2) This section does not prohibit the court from ordering a conference on its own motion at any time or prevent a party from requesting that the court order that a conference be held.
(d) This section does not apply to any of the following:
    (1) An action in which a party not represented by counsel is incarcerated in a local, state, or federal correctional institution.

(2) A proceeding in forcible entry, forcible detainer, or unlawful detainer.
(3) A special motion brought pursuant to Section 425.16.
(4) A motion brought less than 30 days before trial.

(e)

(1) In response to a motion to strike and before the case is at issue, a pleading shall not be amended more than three times, absent an offer to the trial court of additional facts to be pleaded that, if pleaded, would result in a reasonable possibility that the defect can be cured. The three-amendment limit does not include an amendment made without leave of the court pursuant to Section 472, if the amendment is made before a motion to strike as to the original pleading is filed.

(2) This section does not affect the rights of a party to amend its pleading or respond to an amended pleading after the case is at issue.

(f) This section does not affect appellate review or the rights of a party pursuant to Section 430.80.

(g) If a motion to strike is denied and the pleading is not further amended, the moving party preserves its right to appeal after final judgment without filing a further motion to strike.

Amended by Stats 2020 ch 36 (AB 3364),s 16, eff. 1/1/2021.
Added by Stats 2017 ch 273 (AB 644),s 1, eff. 1/1/2018.

Section 436 - Authority of court upon motion

The court may, upon a motion made pursuant to Section 435, or at any time in its discretion, and upon terms it deems proper:
(a) Strike out any irrelevant, false, or improper matter inserted in any pleading.
(b) Strike out all or any part of any pleading not drawn or filed in conformity with the laws of this state, a court rule, or an order of the court.
Amended by Stats. 1983, Ch. 1167, Sec. 4.

Section 437 - Grounds for motion to appear on face of challenged pleading; motion based on matter subject to judicial notice

(a) The grounds for a motion to strike shall appear on the face of the challenged pleading or from any matter of which the court is required to take judicial notice.
(b) Where the motion to strike is based on matter of which the court may take judicial notice pursuant to Section 452 or 453 of the Evidence Code, such matter shall be specified in the notice of motion, or in the supporting points and authorities, except as the court may otherwise permit.
Added by Stats. 1982, Ch. 704, Sec. 4.

Chapter 5 - SUMMARY JUDGMENTS AND MOTIONS FOR JUDGMENT ON THE PLEADINGS

Section 437c - Motion for summary judgment

(a)

(1) A party may move for summary judgment in an action or proceeding if it is contended that the action has no merit or that there is no defense to the action or proceeding. The motion may be made at any time after 60 days have elapsed since the general appearance in the action or proceeding of each party against whom the motion is directed or at any earlier time after the general appearance that the court, with or without notice and upon good cause shown, may direct.

(2) Notice of the motion and supporting papers shall be served on all other parties to the action at least 75 days before the time appointed for hearing. If the notice is served by mail, the required 75-day period of notice shall be increased by 5 days if the place of address is within the State of California, 10 days if the place of address is outside the State of California but within the United States, and 20 days if the place of address is outside the United States. If the notice is served by facsimile transmission, express mail, or another method of delivery providing for overnight delivery, the required 75-day period of notice shall be increased by two court days.

(3) The motion shall be heard no later than 30 days before the date of trial, unless the court for good cause orders otherwise. The filing of the motion shall not extend the time within which a party must otherwise file a responsive pleading.

(b)

(1) The motion shall be supported by affidavits, declarations, admissions, answers to interrogatories, depositions, and matters of which judicial notice shall or may be taken. The supporting papers shall include a separate statement setting forth plainly and concisely all material facts that the moving party contends are undisputed. Each of the material facts stated shall be followed by a reference to the supporting evidence. The failure to comply with this requirement of a separate statement may in the court's discretion constitute a sufficient ground for denying the motion.

(2) An opposition to the motion shall be served and filed not less than 14 days preceding the noticed or continued date of hearing, unless the court for good cause orders otherwise. The opposition, where appropriate, shall consist of affidavits, declarations, admissions, answers to interrogatories, depositions, and matters of which judicial notice shall or may be taken.

(3) The opposition papers shall include a separate statement that responds to each of the material facts contended by the moving party to be undisputed, indicating if the opposing party agrees or disagrees that those facts are undisputed. The statement also shall set forth plainly and concisely any other material facts the opposing party contends are disputed. Each material fact contended by the opposing party to be disputed shall be followed by a reference to the supporting evidence. Failure to comply with this requirement of a separate statement may constitute a sufficient ground, in the court's discretion, for granting the motion.

(4) A reply to the opposition shall be served and filed by the moving party not less than five days preceding the noticed or continued date of hearing, unless the court for good cause orders otherwise.

(5) Evidentiary objections not made at the hearing shall be deemed waived.

(6) Except for subdivision (c) of Section 1005 relating to the method of service of opposition and reply papers, Sections 1005 and 1013, extending the time within which a right may be exercised or an act may be done, do not apply to this section.

(7) An incorporation by reference of a matter in the court's file shall set forth with specificity the exact matter to which reference is being made and shall not incorporate the entire file.

(c) The motion for summary judgment shall be granted if all the papers submitted show that there is no triable issue as to any material fact and that the moving party is entitled to a judgment as a matter of law. In determining if the papers show that there is no triable issue as to any material fact, the court shall consider all of the evidence set forth in the papers, except the evidence to which objections have been made and sustained by the court, and all inferences reasonably deducible from the evidence, except summary judgment shall not be granted by the court based on inferences reasonably deducible from the evidence if contradicted by other inferences or evidence that raise a triable issue as to any material fact.

(d) Supporting and opposing affidavits or declarations shall be made by a person on personal knowledge, shall set forth admissible evidence, and shall show affirmatively that the affiant is competent to testify to the matters stated in the affidavits or declarations. An objection based on the failure to comply with the requirements of this subdivision, if not made at the hearing, shall be deemed waived.

(e) If a party is otherwise entitled to summary judgment pursuant to this section, summary judgment shall not be denied on grounds of credibility or for want of cross-examination of witnesses furnishing affidavits or declarations in support of the summary judgment, except that summary judgment may be denied in the discretion of the court if the only proof of a material fact offered in support of the summary judgment is an affidavit or declaration made by an individual who was the sole witness to that fact; or if a material fact is an individual's state of mind, or lack thereof, and that fact is sought to be established solely by the individual's affirmation thereof.

(f)

(1) A party may move for summary adjudication as to one or more causes of action within an action, one or more affirmative defenses, one or more claims for damages, or one or more issues of duty, if the party contends that the cause of action has no merit, that there is no affirmative defense to the cause of action, that there is no merit to an affirmative defense as to any cause of action, that there is no merit to a claim for damages, as specified in Section 3294 of the Civil Code, or that one or more defendants either owed or did not owe a duty to the plaintiff or plaintiffs. A motion for summary adjudication shall be granted only if it completely disposes of a cause of action, an affirmative defense, a claim for damages, or an issue of duty.

(2) A motion for summary adjudication may be made by itself or as an alternative to a motion for summary judgment and shall proceed in all procedural respects as a motion for summary judgment. A party shall not move for summary judgment based on issues asserted in a prior motion for summary adjudication and denied by the court unless that party establishes, to the satisfaction of the court, newly discovered facts or circumstances or a change of law supporting the issues reasserted in the summary judgment motion.

(g) Upon the denial of a motion for summary judgment on the ground that there is a triable issue as to one or more material facts, the court shall, by written or oral order, specify one or more material facts raised by the motion that the court has determined there exists a triable controversy. This determination shall specifically refer to the evidence proffered in support of and in opposition to the motion that indicates that a triable controversy exists. Upon the grant of a motion for summary judgment on the ground that there is no triable issue of material fact, the court shall, by written or oral order, specify the reasons for its determination. The order shall specifically refer to the evidence proffered in support of and, if applicable, in opposition to the motion that indicates no triable issue exists. The court shall also state its reasons for any other determination. The court shall record its determination by court reporter or written order.

(h) If it appears from the affidavits submitted in opposition to a motion for summary judgment or summary adjudication, or both, that facts essential to justify opposition may exist but cannot, for reasons stated, be presented, the court shall deny the motion, order a continuance to permit affidavits to be obtained or discovery to be had, or make any other order as may be just. The application to continue the motion to obtain necessary discovery may also be made by ex parte motion at any time on or before the date the opposition response to the motion is due.

(i) If, after granting a continuance to allow specified additional discovery, the court determines that the party seeking summary judgment has unreasonably failed to allow the discovery to be conducted, the court shall grant a continuance to permit the discovery to go forward or deny the motion for summary judgment or summary adjudication. This section does not affect or limit the ability of a party to compel discovery under the Civil Discovery Act (Title 4 (commencing with Section 2016.010) of Part 4).

(j) If the court determines at any time that an affidavit was presented in bad faith or solely for the purpose of delay, the court shall order the party who presented the affidavit to pay the other party the amount of the reasonable expenses the filing of the affidavit caused the other party to incur. Sanctions shall not be imposed pursuant to this subdivision except on notice contained in a party's papers or on the court's own noticed motion, and after an opportunity to be heard.

(k) Unless a separate judgment may properly be awarded in the action, a final judgment shall not be entered on a motion for summary judgment before the termination of the action, but the final judgment shall, in addition to any matters determined in the action, award judgment as established by the summary proceeding provided for in this section.

(l) In an action arising out of an injury to the person or to property, if a motion for summary judgment is granted on the basis that the defendant was without fault, no other defendant during trial, over plaintiff's objection, may attempt to attribute fault to, or comment on, the absence or involvement of the defendant who was granted the motion.

(m)

(1) A summary judgment entered under this section is an appealable judgment as in other cases. Upon entry of an order pursuant to this section, except the entry of summary judgment, a party may, within 20 days after service upon him or her of a written notice of entry of the order, petition an appropriate reviewing court for a peremptory writ. If the notice is served by mail, the initial period within which to file the petition shall be increased by five days if the place of address is within the State of California, 10 days if the place of address is outside the State of California but within the United States, and 20 days if the place of address is outside the United States. If the notice is served by facsimile transmission, express mail, or another method of delivery providing for overnight delivery, the initial period within which to file the petition shall be increased by two court days. The superior court may, for good cause, and before the expiration of the initial period, extend the time for one additional period not to exceed 10 days.

(2) Before a reviewing court affirms an order granting summary judgment or summary adjudication on a ground not relied upon by the trial court, the reviewing court shall afford the parties an opportunity to present their views on the issue by submitting supplemental briefs. The supplemental briefs may include an argument that additional evidence relating to that ground exists, but the party has not had an adequate opportunity to present the evidence or to conduct discovery on the issue. The court may reverse or remand based upon the supplemental briefs to allow the parties to present additional evidence or to conduct discovery on the issue. If the court fails to allow supplemental briefs, a rehearing shall be ordered upon timely petition of a party.

(n)

(1) If a motion for summary adjudication is granted, at the trial of the action, the cause or causes of action within the action, affirmative defense or defenses, claim for damages, or issue or issues of duty as to the motion that has been granted shall be deemed to be established and the action shall proceed as to the cause or causes of action, affirmative defense or defenses, claim for damages, or issue or issues of duty remaining.

(2) In the trial of the action, the fact that a motion for summary adjudication is granted as to one or more causes of action, affirmative defenses, claims for damages, or issues of duty within the action shall not bar any cause of action, affirmative defense, claim for damages, or issue of duty as to which summary adjudication was either not sought or denied.

(3) In the trial of an action, neither a party, a witness, nor the court shall comment to a jury upon the grant or denial of a motion for summary adjudication.

(o) A cause of action has no merit if either of the following exists:

(1) One or more of the elements of the cause of action cannot be separately established, even if that element is separately pleaded.

(2) A defendant establishes an affirmative defense to that cause of action.

(p) For purposes of motions for summary judgment and summary adjudication:

(1) A plaintiff or cross-complainant has met his or her burden of showing that there is no defense to a cause of action if that party has proved each element of the cause of action entitling the party to judgment on the cause of action. Once the plaintiff or cross-complainant has met that burden, the burden shifts to the defendant or cross-defendant to show that a triable issue of one or more material facts exists as to the cause of action or a defense thereto. The defendant or cross-defendant shall not rely upon the allegations or denials of its pleadings to show that a triable issue of material fact exists but, instead, shall set forth the specific facts showing that a triable issue of material fact exists as to the cause of action or a defense thereto.

(2) A defendant or cross-defendant has met his or her burden of showing that a cause of action has no merit if the party has shown that one or more elements of the cause of action, even if not separately pleaded, cannot be established, or that there is a complete defense to the cause of action. Once the defendant or cross-defendant has met that burden, the burden shifts to the plaintiff or cross-complainant to show that a triable issue of one or more material facts exists as to the cause of action or a defense thereto. The plaintiff or cross-complainant shall not rely upon the allegations or denials of its pleadings to show that a triable issue of material fact exists but, instead, shall set forth the specific facts showing that a triable issue of material fact exists as to the cause of action or a defense thereto.

(q) In granting or denying a motion for summary judgment or summary adjudication, the court need rule only on those objections to evidence that it deems material to its disposition of the motion. Objections to evidence that are not ruled on for purposes of the motion shall be preserved for appellate review.
(r) This section does not extend the period for trial provided by Section 1170.5.
(s) Subdivisions (a) and (b) do not apply to actions brought pursuant to Chapter 4 (commencing with Section 1159) of Title 3 of Part 3.
(t) Notwithstanding subdivision (f), a party may move for summary adjudication of a legal issue or a claim for damages other than punitive damages that does not completely dispose of a cause of action, affirmative defense, or issue of duty pursuant to this subdivision.

(1)
(A) Before filing a motion pursuant to this subdivision, the parties whose claims or defenses are put at issue by the motion shall submit to the court both of the following:
(i) A joint stipulation stating the issue or issues to be adjudicated.
(ii) A declaration from each stipulating party that the motion will further the interest of judicial economy by decreasing trial time or significantly increasing the likelihood of settlement.
(B) The joint stipulation shall be served on any party to the civil action who is not also a party to the motion.
(2) Within 15 days of receipt of the stipulation and declarations, unless the court has good cause for extending the time, the court shall notify the stipulating parties if the motion may be filed. In making this determination, the court may consider objections by a nonstipulating party made within 10 days of the submission of the stipulation and declarations.
(3) If the court elects not to allow the filing of the motion, the stipulating parties may request, and upon request the court shall conduct, an informal conference with the stipulating parties to permit further evaluation of the proposed stipulation. The stipulating parties shall not file additional papers in support of the motion.
(4)
(A) A motion for summary adjudication made pursuant to this subdivision shall contain a statement in the notice of motion that reads substantially similar to the following: "This motion is made pursuant to subdivision (t) of Section 437c of the Code of Civil Procedure. The parties to this motion stipulate that the court shall hear this motion and that the resolution of this motion will further the interest of judicial economy by decreasing trial time or significantly increasing the likelihood of settlement."
(B) The notice of motion shall be signed by counsel for all parties, and by those parties in propria persona, to the motion.
(5) A motion filed pursuant to this subdivision may be made by itself or as an alternative to a motion for summary judgment and shall proceed in all procedural respects as a motion for summary judgment.
(u) For purposes of this section, a change in law does not include a later enacted statute without retroactive application.
Amended by Stats 2016 ch 86 (SB 1171),s 22, eff. 1/1/2017.
Amended by Stats 2015 ch 345 (AB 1141),s 1.5, eff. 1/1/2016.
Amended by Stats 2015 ch 161 (SB 470),s 1, eff. 1/1/2016.
Added by Stats 2011 ch 419 (SB 384),s 4, eff. 1/1/2012.

Section 438 - Motion for judgment on pleadings
(a) As used in this section:
(1) "Complaint" includes a cross-complaint.
(2) "Plaintiff" includes a cross-complainant.
(3) "Defendant" includes a cross-defendant.
(b)
(1) A party may move for judgment on the pleadings.
(2) The court may upon its own motion grant a motion for judgment on the pleadings.
(c)
(1) The motion provided for in this section may only be made on one of the following grounds:
(A) If the moving party is a plaintiff, that the complaint states facts sufficient to constitute a cause or causes of action against the defendant and the answer does not state facts sufficient to constitute a defense to the complaint.
(B) If the moving party is a defendant, that either of the following conditions exist:
(i) The court has no jurisdiction of the subject of the cause of action alleged in the complaint.
(ii) The complaint does not state facts sufficient to constitute a cause of action against that defendant.
(2) The motion provided for in this section may be made as to either of the following:
(A) The entire complaint or cross-complaint or as to any of the causes of action stated therein.
(B) The entire answer or one or more of the affirmative defenses set forth in the answer.
(3) If the court on its own motion grants the motion for judgment on the pleadings, it shall be on one of the following bases:
(A) If the motion is granted in favor of the plaintiff, it shall be based on the grounds that the complaint states facts sufficient to constitute a cause or causes of action against the defendant and the answer does not state facts sufficient to constitute a defense to the complaint.
(B) If the motion is granted in favor of the defendant, that either of the following conditions exist:
(i) The court has no jurisdiction of the subject of the cause of action alleged in the complaint.
(ii) The complaint does not state facts sufficient to constitute a cause of action against that defendant.
(d) The grounds for motion provided for in this section shall appear on the face of the challenged pleading or from any matter of which the court is required to take judicial notice. Where the motion is based on a matter of which the court may take judicial notice pursuant to Section 452 or 453 of the Evidence Code, the matter shall be specified in the notice of motion, or in the supporting points and authorities, except as the court may otherwise permit.
(e) No motion may be made pursuant to this section if a pretrial conference order has been entered pursuant to Section 575, or within 30 days of the date the action is initially set for trial, whichever is later, unless the court otherwise permits.
(f) The motion provided for in this section may be made only after one of the following conditions has occurred:
(1) If the moving party is a plaintiff, and the defendant has already filed his or her answer to the complaint and the time for the plaintiff to demur to the answer has expired.
(2) If the moving party is a defendant, and the defendant has already filed his or her answer to the complaint and the time for the defendant to demur to the complaint has expired.
(g) The motion provided for in this section may be made even though either of the following conditions exist:
(1) The moving party has already demurred to the complaint or answer, as the case may be, on the same grounds as is the basis for the motion provided for in this section and the demurrer has been overruled, provided that there has been a material change in applicable case law or statute since the ruling on the demurrer.
(2) The moving party did not demur to the complaint or answer, as the case may be, on the same grounds as is the basis for the motion provided for in this section.
(h)

(1) The motion provided for in this section may be granted with or without leave to file an amended complaint or answer, as the case may be.

(2) Where a motion is granted pursuant to this section with leave to file an amended complaint or answer, as the case may be, then the court shall grant 30 days to the party against whom the motion was granted to file an amended complaint or answer, as the case may be.

(3) If the motion is granted with respect to the entire complaint or answer without leave to file an amended complaint or answer, as the case may be, then judgment shall be entered forthwith in accordance with the motion granting judgment to the moving party.

(4) If the motion is granted with leave to file an amended complaint or answer, as the case may be, then the following procedures shall be followed:

(A) If an amended complaint is filed after the time to file an amended complaint has expired, then the court may strike the complaint pursuant to Section 436 and enter judgment in favor of that defendant against that plaintiff or a plaintiff.

(B) If an amended answer is filed after the time to file an amended answer has expired, then the court may strike the answer pursuant to Section 436 and proceed to enter judgment in favor of that plaintiff and against that defendant or a defendant.

(C) Except where subparagraphs (A) and (B) apply, if the motion is granted with respect to the entire complaint or answer with leave to file an amended complaint or answer, as the case may be, but an amended complaint or answer is not filed, then after the time to file an amended complaint or answer, as the case may be, has expired, judgment shall be entered forthwith in favor of the moving party.

(i)

(1) Where a motion for judgment on the pleadings is granted with leave to amend, the court shall not enter a judgment in favor of a party until the following proceedings are had:

(A) If an amended pleading is filed and the moving party contends that pleading is filed after the time to file an amended pleading has expired or that the pleading is in violation of the court's prior ruling on the motion, then that party shall move to strike the pleading and enter judgment in its favor.

(B) If no amended pleading is filed, then the party shall move for entry of judgment in its favor.

(2) All motions made pursuant to this subdivision shall be made pursuant to Section 1010.

(3) At the hearing on the motion provided for in this subdivision, the court shall determine whether to enter judgment in favor of a particular party.

Amended by Stats. 1994, Ch. 493, Sec. 2. Effective September 12, 1994.

Section 439 - Meeting before filing motion for judgment

(a) Before filing a motion for judgment on the pleadings pursuant to this chapter, the moving party shall meet and confer in person or by telephone with the party who filed the pleading that is subject to the motion for judgment on the pleadings for the purpose of determining if an agreement can be reached that resolves the claims to be raised in the motion for judgment on the pleadings. If an amended pleading is filed, the responding party shall meet and confer again with the party who filed the amended pleading before filing a motion for judgment on the pleadings against the amended pleading.

(1) As part of the meet and confer process, the moving party shall identify all of the specific allegations that it believes are subject to judgment and identify with legal support the basis of the claims. The party who filed the pleading shall provide legal support for its position that the pleading is not subject to judgment, or, in the alternative, how the pleading could be amended to cure any claims it is subject to judgment.

(2) The parties shall meet and confer at least five days before the date a motion for judgment on the pleadings is filed. If the parties are unable to meet and confer by that time, the moving party shall be granted an automatic 30-day extension of time within which to file a motion for judgment on the pleadings, by filing and serving, on or before the date a motion for judgment on the pleadings must be filed, a declaration stating under penalty of perjury that a good faith attempt to meet and confer was made and explaining the reasons why the parties could not meet and confer. The 30-day extension shall commence from the date the motion for judgment on the pleadings was previously filed, and the moving party shall not be subject to default during the period of the extension. Any further extensions shall be obtained by court order upon a showing of good cause.

(3) The moving party shall file and serve with the motion for judgment on the pleadings a declaration stating either of the following:

(A) The means by which the moving party met and conferred with the party who filed the pleading subject to the motion for judgment on the pleadings, and that the parties did not reach an agreement resolving the claims raised by the motion for judgment on the pleadings.

(B) That the party who filed the pleading subject to the motion for judgment on the pleadings failed to respond to the meet and confer request of the moving party or otherwise failed to meet and confer in good faith.

(4) A determination by the court that the meet and confer process was insufficient shall not be grounds to grant or deny the motion for judgment on the pleadings.

(b) A party moving for judgment on a pleading that has been amended after a motion for judgment on the pleadings on an earlier version of the pleading was granted shall not move for judgment on any portion of the pleadings on grounds that could have been raised by a motion for judgment on the pleadings as to the earlier version of the pleading.

(c)

(1) If a court grants a motion for judgment on the pleadings and grants leave to amend, the court may order a conference of the parties before an amended pleading, or a motion for judgment on an amended pleading, may be filed. If the conference is held, the court shall not preclude a party from filing a motion for judgment on the pleadings and the time to file a motion for judgment on the pleadings shall not begin until after the conference has concluded.

(2) This section does not prohibit the court from ordering a conference on its own motion at any time or prevent a party from requesting that the court order that a conference be held.

(d) This section does not apply to any of the following:

(1) An action in which a party not represented by counsel is incarcerated in a local, state, or federal correctional institution.

(2) A proceeding in forcible entry, forcible detainer, or unlawful detainer.

(3) A special motion brought pursuant to Section 425.16.

(4) A motion brought less than 30 days before trial.

(e)

(1) In response to a motion for judgment on the pleadings and before the case is at issue, a pleading shall not be amended more than three times, absent an offer to the trial court of additional facts to be pleaded that, if pleaded, would result in a reasonable possibility that the defect can be cured. The three-amendment limit does not include an amendment made without leave of the court pursuant to Section 472, if the amendment is made before a motion for judgments on the pleadings as to the original pleading is filed.

(2) This section does not affect the rights of a party to amend its pleading or respond to an amended pleading after the case is at issue.

(f) This section does not affect appellate review or the rights of a party pursuant to Section 430.80.

(g) If a motion for judgment on the pleadings is denied and the pleading is not further amended, the moving party preserves its right to appeal after final judgment without filing a further motion for judgment on the pleadings.

Amended by Stats 2020 ch 36 (AB 3364),s 17, eff. 1/1/2021.
Added by Stats 2017 ch 273 (AB 644),s 2, eff. 1/1/2018.

Chapter 6 - VERIFICATION OF PLEADINGS

Section 446 - Generally

(a) Every pleading shall be subscribed by the party or his or her attorney. When the state, any county thereof, city, school district, district, public agency, or public corporation, or any officer of the state, or of any county thereof, city, school district, district, public agency, or public corporation, in his or her official capacity, is plaintiff, the answer shall be verified, unless an admission of the truth of the complaint might subject the party to a criminal prosecution, or, unless a county thereof, city, school district, district, public agency, or public corporation, or an officer of the state, or of any county, city, school district, district, public agency, or public corporation, in his or her official capacity, is defendant. When the complaint is verified, the answer shall be verified. In all cases of a verification of a pleading, the affidavit of the party shall state that the same is true of his own knowledge, except as to the matters which are therein stated on his or her information or belief, and as to those matters that he or she believes it to be true; and where a pleading is verified, it shall be by the affidavit of a party, unless the parties are absent from the county where the attorney has his or her office, or from some cause unable to verify it, or the facts are within the knowledge of his or her attorney or other person verifying the same. When the pleading is verified by the attorney, or any other person except one of the parties, he or she shall set forth in the affidavit the reasons why it is not made by one of the parties. When a corporation is a party, the verification may be made by any officer thereof. When the state, any county thereof, city, school district, district, public agency, or public corporation, or an officer of the state, or of any county thereof, city, school district, district, public agency, or public corporation, in his or her official capacity is plaintiff, the complaint need not be verified; and if the state, any county thereof, city, school district, district, public agency, or public corporation, or an officer of such state, county, city, school district, district, public agency, or public corporation, in his or her official capacity is defendant, its or his or her answer need not be verified.

When the verification is made by the attorney for the reason that the parties are absent from the county where he or she has his or her office, or from some other cause are unable to verify it, or when the verification is made on behalf of a corporation or public agency by any officer thereof, the attorney's or officer's affidavit shall state that he or she has read the pleading and that he or she is informed and believes the matters therein to be true and on that ground alleges that the matters stated therein are true. However, in those cases the pleadings shall not otherwise be considered as an affidavit or declaration establishing the facts therein alleged.

A person verifying a pleading need not swear to the truth or his or her belief in the truth of the matters stated therein but may, instead, assert the truth or his or her belief in the truth of those matters "under penalty of perjury."

(b) This section shall become operative on January 1, 1999, unless a statute that becomes effective on or before this date extends or deletes the repeal date of Section 446, as amended by Assembly Bill 3594 of the 1993-94 Regular Session.

Repealed (in Sec. 4) and added by Stats. 1994, Ch. 1062, Sec. 5. Effective January 1, 1995. Section operative January 1, 1999, by its own provisions.

Chapter 7 - GENERAL RULES OF PLEADING

Section 452 - Allegations liberally construed

In the construction of a pleading, for the purpose of determining its effect, its allegations must be liberally construed, with a view to substantial justice between the parties.

Enacted 1872.

Section 454 - Items of account

It is not necessary for a party to set forth in a pleading the items of an account therein alleged, but he must deliver to the adverse party, within ten days after a demand thereof in writing, a copy of the account, or be precluded from giving evidence thereof. The court or judge thereof may order a further account when the one delivered is too general, or is defective in any particular.

If the pleading is verified the account must be verified by the affidavit of the party to the effect that he believes it to be true; or if the facts are within the personal knowledge of the agent or attorney for the party, or the party is not within the county where the attorney has his office or from some cause unable to make the affidavit, by the affidavit of the agent or attorney.

Amended by Stats. 1939, Ch. 63.

Section 455 - Description of real property

In an action for the recovery of real property, it must be described in the complaint with such certainty as to enable an officer, upon execution, to identify it.

Enacted 1872.

Section 456 - Judgment or determination stated as duly given or made and to be final

In pleading a judgment or other determination of a court, officer, or board, it is not necessary to state the facts conferring jurisdiction, but such judgment or determination may be stated to have been duly given or made and to have become final. If such allegation be controverted, the party pleading must establish on the trial the facts conferring jurisdiction and creating finality.

Amended by Stats. 1957, Ch. 1365.

Section 457 - Performance of conditions precedent in contract

In pleading the performance of conditions precedent in a contract, it is not necessary to state the facts showing such performance, but it may be stated generally that the party duly performed all the conditions on his part, and if such allegation be controverted, the party pleading must establish, on the trial, the facts showing such performance.

Enacted 1872.

Section 458 - Statute of limitations

In pleading the Statute of Limitations it is not necessary to state the facts showing the defense, but it may be stated generally that the cause of action is barred by the provisions of Section ____ (giving the number of the section and subdivision thereof, if it is so divided, relied upon) of The Code of Civil Procedure; and if such allegation be controverted, the party pleading must establish, on the trial, the facts showing that the cause of action is so barred.

Enacted 1872.

Section 459 - Private statute or ordinance or right derived from

In pleading a private statute, or an ordinance of a county or municipal corporation, or a right derived therefrom, it is sufficient to refer to such statute or ordinance by its title and the day of its passage. In pleading the performance of conditions precedent under a statute or an ordinance of a county or municipal corporation, or of a right derived therefrom, it is not necessary to state the facts showing such performance, but it may be stated generally that the party duly performed all the conditions on his part required thereby; if such allegations be controverted the party pleading must establish on the trial the facts showing such performance.

Amended by Stats. 1907, Ch. 372.

Section 460 - Action for libel and slander

In an action for libel or slander it is not necessary to state in the complaint any extrinsic facts for the purpose of showing the application to the plaintiff of the defamatory matter out of which the cause of action arose; but it is sufficient to state, generally, that the same was published or spoken concerning the plaintiff; and if such allegation be controverted, the plaintiff must establish on the trial that it was so published or spoken.

Enacted 1872.

Section 460.5 - Order to respond to complaint for libel and slander shortened to 20 days after service
(a) In any action for libel or slander, for good cause shown upon ex parte written application, the court may order that the time to respond to the complaint is 20 days after the service of summons on the defendant. The application shall be supported by an affidavit stating facts showing, among other things, that the alleged defamatory matter has been continuously published and that there is a reasonable likelihood that the publication will continue. The order shall direct the clerk to endorse the summons to show that the time to respond has been shortened pursuant to this section. A copy of the application, affidavit, and order shall be served with the summons.
(b) In any such action, unless otherwise ordered by the court for good cause shown, the time allowed the defendant to respond to the complaint or amend the answer under Section 586 shall not exceed 10 days.
(c) The court shall give any such action precedence over all other civil actions, except actions to which special precedence is given by law, in the matter of the setting the case for hearing or trial, and in hearing the case, to the end that all such actions shall be quickly heard and determined. Except for good cause shown, the court shall not grant a continuance in excess of 10 days without the consent of the adverse party.
(d) For purposes of this section, "continuously published" means three or more publications within 15 days.
Added by Stats. 1972, Ch. 594.

Section 460.7 - Order to respond shortened in action by candidate for libel and slander
(a) In any action by a candidate or former candidate for elective public office against a holder of elective public office or an opposing candidate for libel or slander that is alleged to have occurred during the course of an election campaign, the court shall order that the time to respond to the complaint is 20 days after the service of summons on the defendant. The order shall direct the clerk to endorse the summons to show that the time to respond has been shortened pursuant to this section. A copy of the affidavit and order shall be served with the summons.
(b) In any action described in subdivision (a), unless otherwise ordered by the court for good cause shown, the time allowed the defendant to respond to the complaint or amend the answer under Section 586 shall not exceed 10 days.
(c) The court shall give any action described in subdivision (a) precedence over all other civil actions, except actions to which special precedence is given by law, in the matter of the setting of the case of hearing or trial, and in hearing the case, to the end that all actions described in subdivision (a) shall be quickly heard and determined. Except for good cause shown, the court shall not grant a continuance in excess of 10 days without the consent of the adverse party.
Amended by Stats 2006 ch 538 (SB 1852),s 64, eff. 1/1/2007.

Section 461 - Alleging truth of matter charged as defamatory and mitigating circumstances
In any action within Section 460 or 460.5, the defendant may, in his answer, allege both the truth of the matter charged as defamatory, and any mitigating circumstances, to reduce the amount of damages. Whether he proves the justification or not, he may give in evidence the mitigating circumstances.
Amended by Stats. 1972, Ch. 594.

Section 464 - Supplemental complaint or answer; action seeking child support
(a) The plaintiff and defendant, respectively, may be allowed, on motion, to make a supplemental complaint or answer, alleging facts material to the case occurring after the former complaint or answer.
(b) The plaintiff and defendant, or petitioner and respondent, may, in any action in which the support of children is an issue, file a supplemental complaint seeking a judgment or order of paternity or support for a child of the mother and father of the child whose paternity and support are already in issue before the court. A supplemental complaint for paternity or child support may be filed without leave of court either before or after final judgment in the underlying action.
(c) Upon the filing of a supplemental complaint, the court clerk shall issue an amended or supplemental summons pursuant to Section 412.10. Service of the supplemental summons and complaint shall be made in the manner provided for the initial service of a summons by this code.
Amended by Stats. 1994, Ch. 1269, Sec. 2.8. Effective January 1, 1995.

Section 465 - Filing and service of pleading subsequent to complaint
Except with leave of the court, all pleadings subsequent to the complaint, together with proof of service unless a summons need be issued, shall be filed with the clerk or judge, and copies thereof served upon the adverse party or his or her attorney.
Amended by Stats. 1986, Ch. 953, Sec. 3.

Chapter 8 - VARIANCE-MISTAKES IN PLEADINGS AND AMENDMENTS

Section 469 - Variance misleading adverse party deemed material
Variance between the allegation in a pleading and the proof shall not be deemed material, unless it has actually misled the adverse party to his or her prejudice in maintaining his or her action or defense upon the merits. If it appears that a party has been so misled, the court may order the pleading to be amended, upon such terms as may be just.
Amended by Stats 2017 ch 561 (AB 1516),s 22, eff. 1/1/2018.

Section 470 - Where variance not material
Where the variance is not material, as provided in Section 469 the court may direct the fact to be found according to the evidence, or may order an immediate amendment, without costs.
Amended by Stats. 1986, Ch. 540, Sec. 4.

Section 471 - Unproven allegation not deemed variance but failure of proof
Where, however, the allegation of the claim or defense to which the proof is directed, is unproved, not in some particular or particulars only, but in its general scope and meaning, it is not to be deemed a case of variance, within the meaning of Sections 469 and 470, but a failure of proof.
Amended by Stats. 1986, Ch. 540, Sec. 5.

Section 471.5 - Filing and service of amendments; time for answering amendments after service
(a) If the complaint is amended, a copy of the amendments shall be filed, or the court may, in its discretion, require the complaint as amended to be filed, and a copy of the amendments or amended complaint must be served upon the defendants affected thereby. The defendant shall answer the amendments, or the complaint as amended, within 30 days after service thereof, or such other time as the court may direct, and judgment by default may be entered upon failure to answer, as in other cases. For the purposes of this subdivision, "complaint" includes a cross-complaint, and "defendant" includes a person against whom a cross-complaint is filed.
(b) If the answer is amended, the adverse party has 10 days after service thereof, or such other time as the court may direct, in which to demur to the amended answer.
Repealed and added by Stats. 1972, Ch. 73.

Section 472 - Time for amending pleading by party of course
(a) A party may amend its pleading once without leave of the court at any time before the answer, demurrer, or motion to strike is filed, or after a demurrer or motion to strike is filed but before the demurrer or motion to strike is heard if the amended pleading is filed and served no later than the date for filing an opposition to the demurrer or motion to strike. A party may amend the pleading after the date for filing an opposition to the demurrer or motion to strike, upon stipulation by the parties. The time for responding to an amended pleading shall be computed from the date of service of the amended pleading.
(b) This section shall not apply to a special motion brought pursuant to Section 425.16.
Amended by Stats 2020 ch 36 (AB 3364),s 19, eff. 1/1/2021.

Amended by Stats 2017 ch 273 (AB 644),s 3, eff. 1/1/2018.
Amended by Stats 2015 ch 418 (SB 383),s 2, eff. 1/1/2016.
Section 472a - Demurrer; motion to strike granted; motion to dismiss denied
(a) A demurrer is not waived by an answer filed at the same time.
(b) Except as otherwise provided by rule adopted by the Judicial Council, if a demurrer to a complaint or to a cross-complaint is overruled and there is no answer filed, the court shall allow an answer to be filed upon such terms as may be just. If a demurrer to the answer is overruled, the action shall proceed as if no demurrer had been interposed, and the facts alleged in the answer shall be considered as denied to the extent mentioned in Section 431.20.
(c) Subject to the limitations imposed by subdivision (e) of Section 430.41, if a demurrer is sustained, the court may grant leave to amend the pleading upon any terms as may be just and shall fix the time within which the amendment or amended pleading shall be filed. If a demurrer is stricken pursuant to Section 436 and there is no answer filed, the court shall allow an answer to be filed on terms that are just.
(d) If a motion to strike is granted pursuant to Section 436, the court may order that an amendment or amended pleading be filed upon terms it deems proper. If a motion to strike a complaint or cross-complaint, or portion thereof, is denied, the court shall allow the party filing the motion to strike to file an answer.
(e) If a motion to dismiss an action pursuant to Article 2 (commencing with Section 583.210) of Chapter 1.5 of Title 8 is denied, the court shall allow a pleading to be filed.
Amended by Stats 2020 ch 36 (AB 3364),s 20, eff. 1/1/2021.
Amended by Stats 2015 ch 418 (SB 383),s 4, eff. 1/1/2016.
Section 472b - Running of time to amend or answer when demurrer sustained or overruled
When a demurrer to any pleading is sustained or overruled, and time to amend or answer is given, the time so given runs from the service of notice of the decision or order, unless the notice is waived in open court, and the waiver entered in the minutes. When an order sustaining a demurrer without leave to amend is reversed or otherwise remanded by any order issued by a reviewing court, any amended complaint shall be filed within 30 days after the clerk of the reviewing court mails notice of the issuance of the remittitur.
Amended by Stats 2001 ch 44 (SB 562), s 3, eff. 1/1/2002.
Section 472c - Orders open to appeal
(a) When any court makes an order sustaining a demurrer without leave to amend the question as to whether or not such court abused its discretion in making such an order is open on appeal even though no request to amend such pleading was made.
(b) The following orders shall be deemed open on appeal where an amended pleading is filed after the court's order:
(1) An order sustaining a demurrer to a cause of action within a complaint or cross-complaint where the order did not sustain the demurrer as to the entire complaint or cross-complaint.
(2) An order sustaining a demurrer to an affirmative defense within an answer where the order sustaining the demurrer did not sustain the demurrer as to the entire answer.
(3) An order granting a motion to strike a portion of a pleading where the order granting the motion to strike did not strike the entire pleading.
(c) As used in this section, "open on appeal" means that a party aggrieved by an order listed in subdivision (b) may claim the order as error in an appeal from the final judgment in the action.
Amended by Stats. 1993, Ch. 456, Sec. 7. Effective January 1, 1994.
Section 472d - Statement of specific grounds in decision sustaining demurrer
Whenever a demurrer in any action or proceeding is sustained, the court shall include in its decision or order a statement of the specific ground or grounds upon which the decision or order is based which may be by reference to appropriate pages and paragraphs of the demurrer.
The party against whom a demurrer has been sustained may waive these requirements.
Added by Stats. 1961, Ch. 727.
Section 473 - Mistake, inadvertence, surprise or excusable neglect
(a)
(1) The court may, in furtherance of justice, and on any terms as may be proper, allow a party to amend any pleading or proceeding by adding or striking out the name of any party, or by correcting a mistake in the name of a party, or a mistake in any other respect; and may, upon like terms, enlarge the time for answer or demurrer. The court may likewise, in its discretion, after notice to the adverse party, allow, upon any terms as may be just, an amendment to any pleading or proceeding in other particulars; and may upon like terms allow an answer to be made after the time limited by this code.
(2) When it appears to the satisfaction of the court that the amendment renders it necessary, the court may postpone the trial, and may, when the postponement will by the amendment be rendered necessary, require, as a condition to the amendment, the payment to the adverse party of any costs as may be just.
(b) The court may, upon any terms as may be just, relieve a party or his or her legal representative from a judgment, dismissal, order, or other proceeding taken against him or her through his or her mistake, inadvertence, surprise, or excusable neglect. Application for this relief shall be accompanied by a copy of the answer or other pleading proposed to be filed therein, otherwise the application shall not be granted, and shall be made within a reasonable time, in no case exceeding six months, after the judgment, dismissal, order, or proceeding was taken. However, in the case of a judgment, dismissal, order, or other proceeding determining the ownership or right to possession of real or personal property, without extending the six-month period, when a notice in writing is personally served within the State of California both upon the party against whom the judgment, dismissal, order, or other proceeding has been taken, and upon his or her attorney of record, if any, notifying that party and his or her attorney of record, if any, that the order, judgment, dismissal, or other proceeding was taken against him or her and that any rights the party has to apply for relief under the provisions of Section 473 of the Code of Civil Procedure shall expire 90 days after service of the notice, then the application shall be made within 90 days after service of the notice upon the defaulting party or his or her attorney of record, if any, whichever service shall be later. No affidavit or declaration of merits shall be required of the moving party. Notwithstanding any other requirements of this section, the court shall, whenever an application for relief is made no more than six months after entry of judgment, is in proper form, and is accompanied by an attorney's sworn affidavit attesting to his or her mistake, inadvertence, surprise, or neglect, vacate any (1) resulting default entered by the clerk against his or her client, and which will result in entry of a default judgment, or (2) resulting default judgment or dismissal entered against his or her client, unless the court finds that the default or dismissal was not in fact caused by the attorney's mistake, inadvertence, surprise, or neglect. The court shall, whenever relief is granted based on an attorney's affidavit of fault, direct the attorney to pay reasonable compensatory legal fees and costs to opposing counsel or parties. However, this section shall not lengthen the time within which an action shall be brought to trial pursuant to Section 583.310.
(c)
(1) Whenever the court grants relief from a default, default judgment, or dismissal based on any of the provisions of this section, the court may do any of the following:
(A) Impose a penalty of no greater than one thousand dollars ($1,000) upon an offending attorney or party.
(B) Direct that an offending attorney pay an amount no greater than one thousand dollars ($1,000) to the State Bar Client Security Fund.
(C) Grant other relief as is appropriate.

(2) However, where the court grants relief from a default or default judgment pursuant to this section based upon the affidavit of the defaulting party's attorney attesting to the attorney's mistake, inadvertence, surprise, or neglect, the relief shall not be made conditional upon the attorney's payment of compensatory legal fees or costs or monetary penalties imposed by the court or upon compliance with other sanctions ordered by the court.
(d) The court may, upon motion of the injured party, or its own motion, correct clerical mistakes in its judgment or orders as entered, so as to conform to the judgment or order directed, and may, on motion of either party after notice to the other party, set aside any void judgment or order.
Amended by Stats. 1996, Ch. 60, Sec. 1. Effective January 1, 1997.

Section 473.1 - Relief from judgment when court assumes jurisdiction over law practice of attorney for party
The court may, upon such terms as may be just, relieve a party from a judgment, order, or other proceeding taken against him or her, including dismissal of an action pursuant to Section 581 or Chapter 1.5 (commencing with Section 583.110) of Title 8, where a court of this state has assumed jurisdiction, pursuant to Section 6180 or 6190 of the Business and Professions Code, over the law practice of the attorney for the party and the judgment, order or other proceeding was taken against the party after the application for the court to assume jurisdiction over the practice was filed. Application for this relief shall be made within a reasonable period of time, in no case exceeding six months, after the court takes jurisdiction over the practice. However, in the case of a judgment, order, or other proceeding determining the ownership or right to possession of real or personal property, without extending the six-month period, when a notice in writing is personally served within the state both upon the party against whom the judgment, order, or other proceeding has been taken, and upon the attorney appointed pursuant to Section 6180.5 of the Business and Professions Code to act under the court's direction, notifying the party and the appointed attorney that the order, judgment, or other proceeding was taken against him or her and that any rights the party has to apply for relief under the provisions of the section shall expire 90 days after service of notice, then application for relief must be made within 90 days after service of the notice upon the defaulting party or the attorney appointed to act under the court's direction pursuant to Section 6180.5 of the Business and Professions Code, whichever service is later. No affidavit or declaration of merits shall be required of the moving party.
Amended by Stats. 1993, Ch. 589, Sec. 25. Effective January 1, 1994.

Section 473.5 - Notice or motion to set aside default or default judgment and leave to defend
(a) When service of a summons has not resulted in actual notice to a party in time to defend the action and a default or default judgment has been entered against him or her in the action, he or she may serve and file a notice of motion to set aside the default or default judgment and for leave to defend the action. The notice of motion shall be served and filed within a reasonable time, but in no event exceeding the earlier of:
    (i) two years after entry of a default judgment against him or her; or
    (ii) 180 days after service on him or her of a written notice that the default or default judgment has been entered.
(b) A notice of motion to set aside a default or default judgment and for leave to defend the action shall designate as the time for making the motion a date prescribed by subdivision (b) of Section 1005, and it shall be accompanied by an affidavit showing under oath that the party's lack of actual notice in time to defend the action was not caused by his or her avoidance of service or inexcusable neglect. The party shall serve and file with the notice a copy of the answer, motion, or other pleading proposed to be filed in the action.
(c) Upon a finding by the court that the motion was made within the period permitted by subdivision (a) and that his or her lack of actual notice in time to defend the action was not caused by his or her avoidance of service or inexcusable neglect, it may set aside the default or default judgment on whatever terms as may be just and allow the party to defend the action.
Amended by Stats. 1990, Ch. 1491, Sec. 5.

Section 474 - Plaintiff ignorant of name of defendant
When the plaintiff is ignorant of the name of a defendant, he must state that fact in the complaint, or the affidavit if the action is commenced by affidavit, and such defendant may be designated in any pleading or proceeding by any name, and when his true name is discovered, the pleading or proceeding must be amended accordingly; provided, that no default or default judgment shall be entered against a defendant so designated, unless it appears that the copy of the summons or other process, or, if there be no summons or process, the copy of the first pleading or notice served upon such defendant bore on the face thereof a notice stating in substance: "To the person served: You are hereby served in the within action (or proceedings) as (or on behalf of) the person sued under the fictitious name of (designating it)." The certificate or affidavit of service must state the fictitious name under which such defendant was served and the fact that notice of identity was given by endorsement upon the document served as required by this section. The foregoing requirements for entry of a default or default judgment shall be applicable only as to fictitious names designated pursuant to this section and not in the event the plaintiff has sued the defendant by an erroneous name and shall not be applicable to entry of a default or default judgment based upon service, in the manner otherwise provided by law, of an amended pleading, process or notice designating defendant by his true name.
Amended by Stats. 1955, Ch. 886.

Section 475 - Error, improper ruling, instruction or defect not affecting substantial rights of parties
The court must, in every stage of an action, disregard any error, improper ruling, instruction, or defect, in the pleadings or proceedings which, in the opinion of said court, does not affect the substantial rights of the parties. No judgment, decision, or decree shall be reversed or affected by reason of any error, ruling, instruction, or defect, unless it shall appear from the record that such error, ruling, instruction, or defect was prejudicial, and also that by reason of such error, ruling, instruction, or defect, the said party complaining or appealing sustained and suffered substantial injury, and that a different result would have been probable if such error, ruling, instruction, or defect had not occurred or existed. There shall be no presumption that error is prejudicial, or that injury was done if error is shown.
Amended by Stats. 1897, Ch. 47.

Title 6.5 - ATTACHMENT
Chapter 1 - WORDS AND PHRASES DEFINED

Section 481.010 - Generally
Unless the provision or context otherwise requires, the definitions in this chapter govern the construction of this title.
Added by Stats. 1974, Ch. 1516.

Section 481.020 - Account debtor
"Account debtor" means "account debtor" as defined in paragraph (3) of subdivision (a) of Section 9102 of the Commercial Code.
EFFECTIVE 7/1/2001. Amended October 10, 1999 (Bill Number: SB 45) (Chapter 991).

Section 481.030 - Account receivable
"Account receivable" means "account" as defined in paragraph (2) of subdivision (a) of Section 9102 of the Commercial Code.
EFFECTIVE 7/1/2001. Amended October 10, 1999 (Bill Number: SB 45) (Chapter 991).

Section 481.040 - Chattel paper
"Chattel paper" means "chattel paper" as defined in paragraph (11) of subdivision (a) of Section 9102 of the Commercial Code.
EFFECTIVE 7/1/2001. Amended October 10, 1999 (Bill Number: SB 45) (Chapter 991).

Section 481.055 - Costs
"Costs" means costs and disbursements, including, but not limited to, statutory fees, charges, commissions, and expenses.
Added by Stats. 1982, Ch. 1198, Sec. 5. Operative July 1, 1983, by Sec. 70 of Ch. 1198.

Section 481.060 - Complaint
"Complaint" includes a cross-complaint.
Added by Stats. 1974, Ch. 1516.

Section 481.070 - Defendant
"Defendant" includes a cross-defendant.
Added by Stats. 1974, Ch. 1516.

Section 481.080 - Deposit account
"Deposit account" means "deposit account" as defined in paragraph (29) of subdivision (a) of Section 9102 of the Commercial Code.
EFFECTIVE 7/1/2001. Amended October 10, 1999 (Bill Number: SB 45) (Chapter 991).

Section 481.090 - Document of title
"Document of title" means "document" as defined in paragraph (30) of subdivision (a) of Section 9102 of the Commercial Code. A document of title is negotiable if it is negotiable within the meaning of Section 7104 of the Commercial Code.
EFFECTIVE 7/1/2001. Amended October 10, 1999 (Bill Number: SB 45) (Chapter 991).

Section 481.100 - Equipment
"Equipment" means tangible personal property in the possession of the defendant and used or bought for use primarily in the defendant's trade, business, or profession if it is not included in the definitions of inventory or farm products.
Added by Stats. 1974, Ch. 1516.

Section 481.110 - Farm products
"Farm products" means crops or livestock or supplies used or produced in farming operations or products of crops or livestock in their unmanufactured states (such as ginned cotton, wool clip, maple syrup, milk, and eggs), while in the possession of a defendant engaged in raising, fattening, grazing, or other farming operations. If tangible personal property is a farm product, it is neither equipment nor inventory.
Amended by Stats. 1982, Ch. 1198, Sec. 8. Operative July 1, 1983, by Sec. 70 of Ch. 1198.

Section 481.113 - Financial institution
"Financial institution" means a state or national bank, state or federal savings and loan association or credit union, or like organization, and includes a corporation engaged in a safe deposit business.
Added by Stats. 1982, Ch. 1198, Sec. 9. Operative July 1, 1983, by Sec. 70 of Ch. 1198.

Section 481.115 - General intangibles
"General intangibles" means "general intangibles," as defined in paragraph (42) of subdivision (a) of Section 9102 of the Commercial Code, consisting of rights to payment.
EFFECTIVE 7/1/2001. Amended October 10, 1999 (Bill Number: SB 45) (Chapter 991).

Section 481.117 - Instrument
"Instrument" means "instrument" as defined in paragraph (47) of subdivision (a) of Section 9102 of the Commercial Code.
EFFECTIVE 7/1/2001. Amended October 10, 1999 (Bill Number: SB 45) (Chapter 991).

Section 481.120 - Inventory
"Inventory" means tangible personal property in the possession of a defendant that (a) is held by the defendant for sale or lease or to be furnished under contracts of service or (b) is raw materials, work in process, or materials used or consumed in his trade, business, or profession. Inventory of a person is not to be classified as his equipment.
Added by Stats. 1974, Ch. 1516.

Section 481.140 - Levying officer
"Levying officer" means the sheriff or marshal who is directed to execute a writ or order issued under this title.
Amended by Stats. 1996, Ch. 872, Sec. 12. Effective January 1, 1997.

Section 481.170 - Person
"Person" includes a natural person, a corporation, a partnership or other unincorporated association, a limited liability company, and a public entity.
Amended by Stats. 1994, Ch. 1010, Sec. 58. Effective January 1, 1995.

Section 481.175 - Personal property
"Personal property" includes both tangible and intangible personal property.
Added by Stats. 1982, Ch. 1198, Sec. 15. Operative July 1, 1983, by Sec. 70 of Ch. 1198.

Section 481.180 - Plaintiff
"Plaintiff" means a person who files a complaint or cross-complaint.
Added by Stats. 1974, Ch. 1516.

Section 481.190 - Probable validity
A claim has "probable validity" where it is more likely than not that the plaintiff will obtain a judgment against the defendant on that claim.
Added by Stats. 1974, Ch. 1516.

Section 481.195 - Property
"Property" includes real and personal property and any interest therein.
Added by Stats. 1982, Ch. 1198, Sec. 16. Operative July 1, 1983, by Sec. 70 of Ch. 1198.

Section 481.200 - Public entity
"Public entity" includes the state, the Regents of the University of California, a county, a city, district, public authority, public agency, and any other political subdivision or public corporation in the state.
Added by Stats. 1974, Ch. 1516.

Section 481.203 - Real property
"Real property" includes any right in real property, including, but not limited to, a leasehold interest in real property.
Added by Stats. 1982, Ch. 1198, Sec. 17. Operative July 1, 1983, by Sec. 70 of Ch. 1198.

Section 481.205 - Registered process server
"Registered process server" means a person registered as a process server pursuant to Chapter 16 (commencing with Section 22350) of Division 8 of the Business and Professions Code.
Added by Stats. 1982, Ch. 1198, Sec. 18. Operative July 1, 1983, by Sec. 70 of Ch. 1198.

Section 481.207 - Secured party
"Secured party" means "secured party" as defined in paragraph (73) of subdivision (a) of Section 9102 of the Commercial Code.
Amended by Stats 2013 ch 531 (AB 502),s 2, eff. 1/1/2014, op. 7/1/2014.
EFFECTIVE 7/01/2001. Amended October 10, 1999 (Bill Number: SB 45) (Chapter 991).

Section 481.210 - Security
"Security" means a "security" as defined by Section 8102 of the Commercial Code.
Added by Stats. 1974, Ch. 1516.

Section 481.220 - Security agreement
"Security agreement" means a "security agreement" as defined by paragraph (74) of subdivision (a) of Section 9102 of the Commercial Code.
Amended by Stats 2013 ch 531 (AB 502),s 3, eff. 1/1/2014, op. 7/1/2014.
EFFECTIVE 7/01/2001. Amended October 10, 1999 (Bill Number: SB 45) (Chapter 991).
Section 481.223 - Security interest
"Security interest" means "security interest" as defined in Section 1201 of the Commercial Code.
Added by Stats. 1982, Ch. 1198, Sec. 20. Operative July 1, 1983, by Sec. 70 of Ch. 1198.
Section 481.225 - Tangible personal property
"Tangible personal property" includes chattel paper, documents of title, instruments, securities, and money.
Added by Stats. 1982, Ch. 1198, Sec. 21. Operative July 1, 1983, by Sec. 70 of Ch. 1198.

Chapter 2 - GENERAL PROVISIONS

Section 482.010 - Title of law
This title shall be known and may be cited as "The Attachment Law."
Added by Stats. 1974, Ch. 1516.
Section 482.020 - Relief pursuant to Chapter 3, Title 7
Nothing in this title precludes the granting of relief pursuant to Chapter 3 (commencing with Section 525) of Title 7.
Added by Stats. 1974, Ch. 1516.
Section 482.030 - Rules; forms
(a) The Judicial Council may provide by rule for the practice and procedure in proceedings under this title.
(b) The Judicial Council shall prescribe the form of the applications, notices, orders, and other documents required by this title.
Added by Stats. 1974, Ch. 1516.
Section 482.040 - Affidavit requirements
The facts stated in each affidavit filed pursuant to this title shall be set forth with particularity. Except where matters are specifically permitted by this title to be shown by information and belief, each affidavit shall show affirmatively that the affiant, if sworn as a witness, can testify competently to the facts stated therein. As to matters shown by information and belief, the affidavit shall state the facts on which the affiant's belief is based, showing the nature of his information and the reliability of his informant. The affiant may be any person, whether or not a party to the action, who has knowledge of the facts. A verified complaint that satisfies the requirements of this section may be used in lieu of or in addition to an affidavit.
Added by Stats. 1974, Ch. 1516.
Section 482.050 - Request that fact of filing complaint not be made public; inspection of file by party
(a) If the plaintiff so requests in writing at the time he files his complaint, the clerk of the court with whom the complaint is filed shall not make available to the public the records and documents in such action before either (1) 30 days after the filing of the complaint or (2) the filing pursuant to this title of the return of service of the notice of hearing and any temporary protective order, or of the writ of attachment if issued without notice, whichever event occurs first.
(b) Notwithstanding subdivision (a), the clerk of the court shall make the entire file in the action available for inspection at any time to any party named in the complaint or to his attorney.
(c) The request by plaintiff that the fact of filing of a complaint or application for relief not be made public may take the form of a notation to that effect, made by rubber stamp or other suitable means, at the top of the first page of the complaint filed with the clerk.
Added by Stats. 1974, Ch. 1516.
Section 482.060 - Subordinate judicial duties; duties not subordinate judicial duties
(a) Except as otherwise provided in subdivision (b), the judicial duties to be performed under this title are subordinate judicial duties within the meaning of Section 22 of Article VI of the California Constitution and may be performed by appointed officers such as court commissioners.
(b) The judicial duties to be performed in the determination of the following matters are not subordinate judicial duties:
    (1) A contested claim of exemption.
    (2) A contested motion for determination of the liability and damages for wrongful attachment.
    (3) A contested third-party claim.
    (4) A contested proceeding to enforce a third person's liability.
(c) Nothing in subdivision (b) limits the power of a court to appoint a temporary judge pursuant to Section 21 of Article VI of the California Constitution.
Amended by Stats. 1982, Ch. 1198, Sec. 23. Operative July 1, 1983, by Sec. 70 of Ch. 1198.
Section 482.070 - Service of legal process
(a)
    (1) Except as otherwise provided in this title, legal process required or permitted to be served under this title may be served personally or by mail.
    (2) For purposes of this title, the term "legal process" shall refer to each and all of the writs, notices, orders, or other papers required or permitted to be served pursuant to this title.
(b) Except as otherwise provided in this section, service of legal process under this title is governed by Article 1 (commencing with Section 684.010) and Article 2 (commencing with Section 684.110) of Chapter 4 of Division 1 of Title 9, including the provisions of Section 684.120 extending time when service is made by mail.
(c) For the purpose of subdivision (b), in Article 1 (commencing with Section 684.010) and Article 2 (commencing with Section 684.110) of Chapter 4 of Division 1 of Title 9:
    (1) References to the "judgment debtor" shall be deemed references to the defendant.
    (2) References to the "judgment creditor" shall be deemed references to the plaintiff.
    (3) References to a "writ" shall be deemed references to a writ of attachment.
    (4) References to a "notice of levy" shall be deemed references to a notice of attachment.
(d) If the defendant has not appeared in the action and legal process is required to be personally served on the defendant under this title, service shall be made in the same manner as a summons is served under Chapter 4 (commencing with Section 413.10) of Title 5.
(e) Except for service of a subpoena or other process to require the attendance of the defendant or service of a paper to bring the defendant into contempt, if the defendant has an attorney of record in the action, service shall be made on the attorney rather than on the defendant.
(f) Proof of service under this title is governed by Article 3 (commencing with Section 684.210) of Chapter 4 of Division 1 of Title 9.
Amended by Stats 2012 ch 484 (AB 2364),s 1, eff. 1/1/2013.
Section 482.080 - Order directing defendant transfer possession of property or documentary evidence to levying officer
(a) If a writ of attachment is issued, the court may also issue an order directing the defendant to transfer to the levying officer either or both of the following:
    (1) Possession of the property to be attached if the property is sought to be attached by taking it into custody.

(2) Possession of documentary evidence of title to property of or a debt owed to the defendant that is sought to be attached. An order pursuant to this paragraph may be served when the property or debt is levied upon or thereafter.

(b) The order shall be personally served on the defendant and shall contain a notice to the defendant that failure to comply with the order may subject the defendant to arrest and punishment for contempt of court.

Amended by Stats. 1982, Ch. 1198, Sec. 25. Operative July 1, 1983, by Sec. 70 of Ch. 1198.

Section 482.090 - Issuance of several writs; alias writ; date of issuance

(a) Several writs in the same form may be issued simultaneously or from time to time upon the same undertaking, whether or not any writ previously issued has been returned.

(b) After the return of the writ of attachment, or upon the filing by the plaintiff of an affidavit setting forth the loss of the writ of attachment, the clerk, upon demand of the plaintiff at any time before judgment, may issue an alias writ which shall be in the same form as the original without requirement of a new undertaking.

(c) The date of issuance of a writ of attachment shall be deemed to be the date the writ is first issued.

Added by Stats. 1974, Ch. 1516.

Section 482.100 - Claim of exemption by defendant

(a) The defendant may claim an exemption provided in Section 487.020 for property levied upon pursuant to a writ issued under this title if the right to the exemption is the result of a change in circumstances occurring after (1) the denial of a claim of exemption for the property earlier in the action or (2) the expiration of the time for claiming the exemption earlier in the action.

(b) A claim of exemption under this section shall follow the procedure provided in Article 2 (commencing with Section 703.510) of Chapter 4 of Division 2 of Title 9 except that, subject to subdivision (a), the defendant may claim the exemption at any time. For this purpose, references in Article 2 (commencing with Section 703.510) of Chapter 4 of Division 2 of Title 9 to the "judgment debtor" shall be deemed references to the defendant, and references to the "judgment creditor" shall be deemed references to the plaintiff.

(c) The exemption provided by subdivision (b) of Section 487.020 may be claimed at the defendant's option either pursuant to subdivision (b) of this section or by following the procedure provided in this subdivision. The claim shall be made by filing with the court and serving on the plaintiff a notice of motion. Service on the plaintiff shall be made not less than three days prior to the date set for the hearing. The hearing shall be held not more than five days after the filing of the notice of motion unless, for good cause shown, the court orders otherwise. The notice of motion shall state the relief requested and shall be accompanied by an affidavit supporting any factual issues raised and points and authorities supporting any legal issues raised. At the hearing on the motion, the defendant has the burden of showing that the property is exempt pursuant to subdivision (b) of Section 487.020. Upon this showing and the showing required by subdivision (a), the court shall order the release of the property.

Amended by Stats. 1982, Ch. 1198, Sec. 26. Operative July 1, 1983, by Sec. 70 of Ch. 1198.

Section 482.110 - Estimate of costs and allowable attorney's fees

(a) The plaintiff's application for a right to attach order and a writ of attachment pursuant to this title may include an estimate of the costs and allowable attorney's fees.

(b) In the discretion of the court, the amount to be secured by the attachment may include an estimated amount for costs and allowable attorney's fees.

Added by Stats. 1976, Ch. 437.

Section 482.120 - Order restricting amount of property to be levied on

If the court determines at the hearing on issuance of a writ of attachment under this title that the value of the defendant's interest in the property described in the plaintiff's application clearly exceeds the amount necessary to satisfy the amount to be secured by the attachment, the court may direct the order of levy on the property described in the writ or restrict the amount of the property to be levied upon.

Added by Stats. 1976, Ch. 437.

Chapter 3 - ACTIONS IN WHICH ATTACHMENT AUTHORIZED

Section 483.010 - Generally

(a) Except as otherwise provided by statute, an attachment may be issued only in an action on a claim or claims for money, each of which is based upon a contract, express or implied, where the total amount of the claim or claims is a fixed or readily ascertainable amount not less than five hundred dollars ($500) exclusive of costs, interest, and attorney's fees.

(b) An attachment may not be issued on a claim which is secured by any interest in real property arising from agreement, statute, or other rule of law (including any mortgage or deed of trust of realty and any statutory, common law, or equitable lien on real property, but excluding any security interest in fixtures subject to Division 9 (commencing with Section 9101) of the Commercial Code). However, an attachment may be issued where the claim was originally so secured but, without any act of the plaintiff or the person to whom the security was given, the security has become valueless or has decreased in value to less than the amount then owing on the claim, in which event the amount to be secured by the attachment shall not exceed the lesser of the amount of the decrease or the difference between the value of the security and the amount then owing on the claim.

(c) If the action is against a defendant who is a natural person, an attachment may be issued only on a claim which arises out of the conduct by the defendant of a trade, business, or profession. An attachment may not be issued on a claim against a defendant who is a natural person if the claim is based on the sale or lease of property, a license to use property, the furnishing of services, or the loan of money where the property sold or leased, or licensed for use, the services furnished, or the money loaned was used by the defendant primarily for personal, family, or household purposes.

(d) An attachment may be issued pursuant to this section whether or not other forms of relief are demanded.

Amended (as amended by Stats. 1995, Ch. 591, Sec. 1) by Stats. 1997, Ch. 222, Sec. 1. Effective January 1, 1998.

Section 483.012 - Remedy not action to for recovery of debt

Subject to the restrictions of Sections 580b and 580d, in an action to foreclose a mortgage or deed of trust on real property or an estate for years therein, pursuit of any remedy provided by this title shall not constitute an action for the recovery of a debt for purposes of subdivision (a) of Section 726 or a failure to comply with any other statutory or judicial requirement to proceed first against security.

Added by Stats. 1997, Ch. 222, Sec. 3. Effective January 1, 1998.

Section 483.013 - Exemption of federal disability benefits awarded to veterans for service-connected disabilities

Notwithstanding Section 483.010, federal disability benefits awarded to veterans for service-connected disabilities pursuant to Chapter 11 of Title 38 of the United States Code shall be exempt from the claim of creditors, and shall not be liable to attachment, levy, or seizure by or under any legal or equitable process whatsoever, as provided by federal law. This section does not apply to that portion of service-connected disability benefits that are subject to child and spousal support enforcement under Section 659(h)(1)(A)(ii)(V)(h)(1)(A)(ii)(V) of Title 42 of the United States Code.

Added by Stats 2009 ch 162 (SB 285),s 2, eff. 1/1/2010.

Section 483.015 - Amount to be secured by attachment

(a) Subject to subdivision (b) and to Section 483.020, the amount to be secured by an attachment is the sum of the following:

(1) The amount of the defendant's indebtedness claimed by the plaintiff.

(2) Any additional amount included by the court under Section 482.110.

(b) The amount described in subdivision (a) shall be reduced by the sum of the following:

(1) The amount of any money judgment in favor of the defendant and against the plaintiff that remains unsatisfied and is enforceable.

(2) The amount of any indebtedness of the plaintiff that the defendant has claimed in a cross-complaint filed in the action if the defendant's claim is one upon which an attachment could be issued.

(3) The amount of any claim of the defendant asserted as a defense in the answer pursuant to Section 431.70 if the defendant's claim is one upon which an attachment could be issued had an action been brought on the claim when it was not barred by the statute of limitations.

(4) The value of any security interest in the property of the defendant held by the plaintiff to secure the defendant's indebtedness claimed by the plaintiff, together with the amount by which the value of the security interest has decreased due to the act of the plaintiff or a prior holder of the security interest.

Amended (as amended by Stats. 1995, Ch. 591, Sec. 3) by Stats. 1997, Ch. 222, Sec. 4. Effective January 1, 1998.

Section 483.020 - Amount to be secured by attachment in unlawful detainer proceeding

(a) Subject to subdivisions (d) and (e), the amount to be secured by the attachment in an unlawful detainer proceeding is the sum of the following:

(1) The amount of the rent due and unpaid as of the date of filing the complaint in the unlawful detainer proceeding.

(2) Any additional amount included by the court under subdivision (c).

(3) Any additional amount included by the court under Section 482.110.

(b) In an unlawful detainer proceeding, the plaintiff's application for a right to attach order and a writ of attachment pursuant to this title may include (in addition to the rent due and unpaid as of the date of the filing of the complaint and any additional estimated amount authorized by Section 482.110) an amount equal to the rent for the period from the date the complaint is filed until the estimated date of judgment or such earlier estimated date as possession has been or is likely to be delivered to the plaintiff, such amount to be computed at the rate provided in the lease.

(c) The amount to be secured by the attachment in the unlawful detainer proceeding may, in the discretion of the court, include an additional amount equal to the amount of rent for the period from the date the complaint is filed until the estimated date of judgment or such earlier estimated date as possession has been or is likely to be delivered to the plaintiff, such amount to be computed at the rate provided in the lease.

(d) Except as provided in subdivision (e), the amount to be secured by the attachment as otherwise determined under this section shall be reduced by the amounts described in subdivision (b) of Section 483.015.

(e) Where the plaintiff has received a payment or holds a deposit to secure (1) the payment of rent and the performance of other obligations under the lease or (2) only the performance of other obligations under the lease, the amount of the payment or deposit shall not be subtracted in determining the amount to be secured by the attachment.

Amended by Stats. 1997, Ch. 222, Sec. 6. Effective January 1, 1998.

Chapter 4 - NOTICED HEARING PROCEDURE FOR OBTAINING WRIT OF ATTACHMENT
Article 1 - RIGHT TO ATTACH ORDER; ISSUANCE OF WRIT OF ATTACHMENT

Section 484.010 - Generally

Upon the filing of the complaint or at any time thereafter, the plaintiff may apply pursuant to this article for a right to attach order and a writ of attachment by filing an application for the order and writ with the court in which the action is brought.

Added by Stats. 1974, Ch. 1516.

Section 484.020 - Application requirements

The application shall be executed under oath and shall include all of the following:

(a) A statement showing that the attachment is sought to secure the recovery on a claim upon which an attachment may be issued.

(b) A statement of the amount to be secured by the attachment.

(c) A statement that the attachment is not sought for a purpose other than the recovery on the claim upon which the attachment is based.

(d) A statement that the applicant has no information or belief that the claim is discharged in a proceeding under Title 11 of the United States Code (Bankruptcy) or that the prosecution of the action is stayed in a proceeding under Title 11 of the United States Code (Bankruptcy).

(e) A description of the property to be attached under the writ of attachment and a statement that the plaintiff is informed and believes that such property is subject to attachment. Where the defendant is a corporation, a reference to "all corporate property which is subject to attachment pursuant to subdivision (a) of Code of Civil Procedure Section 487.010" satisfies the requirements of this subdivision. Where the defendant is a partnership or other unincorporated association, a reference to "all property of the partnership or other unincorporated association which is subject to attachment pursuant to subdivision (b) of Code of Civil Procedure Section 487.010" satisfies the requirements of this subdivision. Where the defendant is a natural person, the description of the property shall be reasonably adequate to permit the defendant to identify the specific property sought to be attached.

Amended by Stats. 1982, Ch. 1198, Sec. 30. Operative July 1, 1983, by Sec. 70 of Ch. 1198.

Section 484.030 - Affidavit supporting application

The application shall be supported by an affidavit showing that the plaintiff on the facts presented would be entitled to a judgment on the claim upon which the attachment is based.

Added by Stats. 1974, Ch. 1516.

Section 484.040 - Hearing required for issuance of order or writ; documents served upon defendant

No order or writ shall be issued under this article except after a hearing. At the times prescribed by subdivision (b) of Section 1005, the defendant shall be served with all of the following:

(a) A copy of the summons and complaint.

(b) A notice of application and hearing.

(c) A copy of the application and of any affidavit in support of the application.

Amended by Stats. 1989, Ch. 693, Sec. 2.

Section 484.050 - Notice of application and hearing

The notice of application and hearing shall inform the defendant of all of the following:

(a) A hearing will be held at a place and at a time, to be specified in the notice, on plaintiff's application for a right to attach order and a writ of attachment.

(b) The order will be issued if the court finds that the plaintiff's claim is probably valid and the other requirements for issuing the order are established. The hearing is not for the purpose of determining whether the claim is actually valid. The determination of the actual validity of the claim will be made in subsequent proceedings in the action and will not be affected by the decisions at the hearing on the application for the order.

(c) The amount to be secured by the attachment is determined pursuant to Sections 482.110, 483.010, 483.015, and 483.020, which statutes shall be summarized in the notice.

(d) If the right to attach order is issued, a writ of attachment will be issued to attach the property described in the plaintiff's application unless the court determines that such property is exempt from attachment or that its value clearly exceeds the amount necessary to satisfy the amount to be

secured by the attachment. However, additional writs of attachment may be issued to attach other nonexempt property of the defendant on the basis of the right to attach order.
(e) If the defendant desires to oppose the issuance of the order, the defendant shall file with the court and serve on the plaintiff a notice of opposition and supporting affidavit as required by Section 484.060 not later than five court days prior to the date set for hearing.
(f) If the defendant claims that the personal property described in the application, or a portion thereof, is exempt from attachment, the defendant shall include that claim in the notice of opposition filed and served pursuant to Section 484.060 or file and serve a separate claim of exemption with respect to the property as provided in Section 484.070. If the defendant does not do so, the claim of exemption will be barred in the absence of a showing of a change in circumstances occurring after the expiration of the time for claiming exemptions.
(g) The defendant may obtain a determination at the hearing whether real or personal property not described in the application or real property described in the application is exempt from attachment by including the claim in the notice of opposition filed and served pursuant to Section 484.060 or by filing and serving a separate claim of exemption with respect to the property as provided in Section 484.070, but the failure to so claim that the property is exempt from attachment will not preclude the defendant from making a claim of exemption with respect to the property at a later time.
(h) Either the defendant or the defendant's attorney or both of them may be present at the hearing.
(i) The notice shall contain the following statement: "You may seek the advice of an attorney as to any matter connected with the plaintiff's application. The attorney should be consulted promptly so that the attorney may assist you before the time set for hearing."
Amended by Stats. 1997, Ch. 222, Sec. 7. Effective January 1, 1998.

Section 484.060 - Notice of opposition
(a) If the defendant desires to oppose the issuance of the right to attach order sought by plaintiff or objects to the amount sought to be secured by the attachment, the defendant shall file and serve upon the plaintiff no later than five court days prior to the date set for the hearing a notice of opposition. The notice shall state the grounds on which the defendant opposes the issuance of the order or objects to the amount sought to be secured by the attachment and shall be accompanied by an affidavit supporting any factual issues raised and points and authorities supporting any legal issues raised. If the defendant fails to file a notice of opposition within the time prescribed, the defendant shall not be permitted to oppose the issuance of the order.
(b) If a defendant filing a notice of opposition desires to make any claim of exemption as provided in Section 484.070, the defendant may include that claim in the notice of opposition filed pursuant to this section.
(c) The plaintiff may file and serve upon the opposing party a reply two court days prior to the date set for the hearing.
Amended by Stats. 1990, Ch. 1491, Sec. 6.

Section 484.070 - Claim of exemption
(a) If the defendant claims that the personal property described in the plaintiff's application, or a portion of such property, is exempt from attachment, the defendant shall claim the exemption as provided in this section. If the defendant fails to make the claim or makes the claim but fails to prove that the personal property is exempt, the defendant may not later claim the exemption except as provided in Section 482.100.
(b) If the defendant desires to claim at the hearing that real or personal property not described in the plaintiff's application or real property described in the plaintiff's application is exempt from attachment, in whole or in part, the defendant shall claim the exemption as provided in this section. Failure to make the claim does not preclude the defendant from later claiming the exemption. If the claim is made as provided in this section but the defendant fails to prove that the property is exempt from attachment, the defendant may not later claim that the property, or a portion thereof, is exempt except as provided in Section 482.100.
(c) The claim of exemption shall:
  (1) Describe the property claimed to be exempt.
  (2) Specify the statute section supporting the claim.
(d) The claim of exemption shall be accompanied by an affidavit supporting any factual issues raised by the claim and points and authorities supporting any legal issues raised.
(e) The claim of exemption, together with any supporting affidavit and points and authorities, shall be filed and served on the plaintiff not less than five court days before the date set for the hearing.
(f) If the plaintiff desires to oppose the claim of exemption, the plaintiff shall file and serve on the defendant, not less than two days before the date set for the hearing, a notice of opposition to the claim of exemption, accompanied by an affidavit supporting any factual issues raised and points and authorities supporting any legal issues raised. If the plaintiff does not file and serve a notice of opposition as provided in this subdivision, no writ of attachment shall be issued as to the property claimed to be exempt. If all of the property described in the plaintiff's application is claimed to be exempt and the plaintiff does not file and serve a notice of opposition as provided in this subdivision, no hearing shall be held and no right to attach order or writ of attachment shall be issued and any temporary protective order issued pursuant to Chapter 6 (commencing with Section 486.010) immediately expires.
(g) If the plaintiff files and serves a notice of opposition to the claim as provided in this section, the defendant has the burden of proving that the property is exempt from attachment.
Amended by Stats. 1998, Ch. 932, Sec. 14. Effective January 1, 1999.

Section 484.080 - Continuance
(a) At the time set for the hearing, the plaintiff shall be ready to proceed. If the plaintiff is not ready, or if he has failed to comply with Section 484.040, the court may either deny the application for the order or, for good cause shown, grant the plaintiff a continuance for a reasonable period. If such a continuance is granted, the effective period of any protective order issued pursuant to Chapter 6 (commencing with Section 486.010) may be extended by the court for a period ending not more than 10 days after the new hearing date if the plaintiff shows a continuing need for such protective order.
(b) The court may, in its discretion and for good cause shown, grant the defendant a continuance for a reasonable period to enable him to oppose the issuance of the right to attach order. If such a continuance is granted, the court shall extend the effective period of any protective order issued pursuant to Chapter 6 (commencing with Section 486.010) for a period ending not more than 10 days after the new hearing date unless the defendant shows pursuant to Section 486.100 that the protective order should be modified or vacated.
Added by Stats. 1974, Ch. 1516.

Section 484.090 - Findings required for issuance of right to attach order
(a) At the hearing, the court shall consider the showing made by the parties appearing and shall issue a right to attach order, which shall state the amount to be secured by the attachment determined by the court in accordance with Section 483.015 or 483.020, if it finds all of the following:
  (1) The claim upon which the attachment is based is one upon which an attachment may be issued.
  (2) The plaintiff has established the probable validity of the claim upon which the attachment is based.
  (3) The attachment is not sought for a purpose other than the recovery on the claim upon which the attachment is based.
  (4) The amount to be secured by the attachment is greater than zero.
(b) If, in addition to the findings required by subdivision (a), the court finds that the defendant has failed to prove that all the property sought to be attached is exempt from attachment, it shall order a writ of attachment to be issued upon the filing of an undertaking as provided by Sections 489.210 and 489.220.

(c) If the court determines that property of the defendant is exempt from attachment, in whole or in part, the right to attach order shall describe the exempt property and prohibit attachment of the property.

(d) The court's determinations shall be made upon the basis of the pleadings and other papers in the record; but, upon good cause shown, the court may receive and consider at the hearing additional evidence, oral or documentary, and additional points and authorities, or it may continue the hearing for the production of the additional evidence or points and authorities.

Amended by Stats. 1997, Ch. 222, Sec. 8. Effective January 1, 1998.

Section 484.100 - Effect of court determinations

The court's determinations under this chapter shall have no effect on the determination of any issues in the action other than issues relevant to proceedings under this chapter nor shall they affect the rights of the plaintiff or defendant in any other action arising out of the same claim of the plaintiff or defendant. The court's determinations under this chapter shall not be given in evidence nor referred to at the trial of any such action.

Amended by Stats. 1982, Ch. 1198, Sec. 34. Operative July 1, 1983, by Sec. 70 of Ch. 1198.

Section 484.110 - Waiver of defense

(a) Neither the failure of the defendant to oppose the issuance of a right to attach order under this chapter nor the defendant's failure to rebut any evidence produced by the plaintiff in connection with proceedings under this chapter shall constitute a waiver of any defense to the plaintiff's claim in the action or any other action or have any effect on the right of the defendant to produce or exclude evidence at the trial of any such action.

(b) Neither the failure of the plaintiff to oppose the issuance of an order reducing the amount to be secured by the attachment under this chapter nor the plaintiff's failure to rebut any evidence produced by the defendant in connection with proceedings under this chapter shall constitute a waiver of any defense to the defendant's claim in the action or any other action or have any effect on the right of the plaintiff to produce or exclude evidence at the trial of any such action.

Amended by Stats. 1982, Ch. 1198, Sec. 35. Operative July 1, 1983, by Sec. 70 of Ch. 1198.

Article 2 - NOTICED HEARING PROCEDURE FOR OBTAINING ADDITIONAL WRITS

Section 484.310 - Time plaintiff may apply for writ by filing application

At any time after a right to attach order has been issued under Article 1 (commencing with Section 484.010) or after the court has found pursuant to Section 485.240 that the plaintiff is entitled to a right to attach order, the plaintiff may apply for a writ of attachment under this article by filing an application with the court in which the action is brought.

Added by Stats. 1974, Ch. 1516.

Section 484.320 - Application requirements

The application shall be executed under oath and shall include all of the following:

(a) A statement that the plaintiff has been issued a right to attach order under Article 1 (commencing with Section 484.010) or that the court has found pursuant to Section 485.240 that the plaintiff is entitled to a right to attach order.

(b) A statement of the amount to be secured by the attachment.

(c) A description of the property to be attached under the writ of attachment and a statement that the plaintiff is informed and believes that the property is subject to attachment. The description shall satisfy the requirements of Section 484.020.

(d) A statement that the applicant has no information or belief that the claim is discharged in a proceeding under Title 11 of the United States Code (Bankruptcy) or that the prosecution of the action is stayed in a proceeding under Title 11 of the United States Code (Bankruptcy).

Amended by Stats. 1982, Ch. 1198, Sec. 36. Operative July 1, 1983, by Sec. 70 of Ch. 1198.

Section 484.330 - Hearing required; service upon defendant

No writ of attachment shall be issued under this article except after a hearing. At least 15 days prior to the hearing, the defendant shall be served with both of the following:

(a) A notice of application and hearing.

(b) A copy of the application.

Amended by Stats. 1991, Ch. 1090, Sec. 2.

Section 484.340 - Notice of application and hearing

The notice of application and hearing shall inform the defendant of all of the following:

(a) The plaintiff has applied for a writ of attachment to attach the property described in the application.

(b) A hearing will be held at a place and at a time, to be specified in the notice, to determine whether the plaintiff is entitled to the writ.

(c) A writ of attachment will be issued to attach the property described in the plaintiff's application unless the court determines that the property is exempt from attachment or that its value clearly exceeds the amount necessary to satisfy the amount to be secured by the attachment.

(d) If the defendant claims that the property described in the application, or a portion thereof, is exempt from attachment, the defendant may file with the court and serve on the plaintiff a claim of exemption with respect to the property as provided in Section 484.350 not later than five days prior to the date set for hearing. If the defendant fails to make such a claim with respect to personal property, the defendant may not later claim the exemption in the absence of a showing of a change in circumstances occurring after the expiration of the time for claiming exemptions.

(e) Either the defendant or the defendant's attorney or both of them may be present at the hearing.

(f) The notice shall contain the following statement: "You may seek the advice of an attorney as to any matter connected with the plaintiff's application. The attorney should be consulted promptly so that the attorney may assist you before the time set for hearing."

Amended by Stats. 1982, Ch. 1198, Sec. 37. Operative July 1, 1983, by Sec. 70 of Ch. 1198.

Section 484.350 - Claim of exemption

(a) If the defendant claims that the property described in the plaintiff's application, or a portion of such property, is exempt from attachment, the defendant may claim the exemption as provided in this section. If the defendant fails to make a claim with respect to personal property, or makes a claim with respect to real or personal property but fails to prove that the property is exempt, the defendant may not later claim the exemption except as provided in Section 482.100.

(b) The claim of exemption shall:

(1) Describe the property claimed to be exempt.

(2) Specify the statute section supporting the claim.

(c) The claim of exemption shall be accompanied by an affidavit supporting any factual issues raised by the claim and points and authorities supporting any legal issues raised.

(d) The claim of exemption, together with any supporting affidavit and points and authorities, shall be filed and served on the plaintiff not less than five court days before the date set for the hearing.

Amended by Stats. 1998, Ch. 932, Sec. 15. Effective January 1, 1999.

Section 484.360 - Notice of opposition to claim of exemption

(a) If the defendant files and serves a claim of exemption and the plaintiff desires to oppose the claim, he shall file and serve on the defendant, not less than two days before the date set for the hearing, a notice of opposition to the claim of exemption, accompanied by an affidavit supporting any factual issues raised and points and authorities supporting any legal issues raised.

(b) If the defendant files and serves a claim of exemption and supporting affidavit as provided in Section 484.350 and the plaintiff does not file and serve a notice of opposition as provided in this section, no writ of attachment shall be issued as to the property claimed to be exempt. If all of the property described in the plaintiff's application is claimed to be exempt and the plaintiff does not file and serve a notice of opposition as provided in this section, no hearing shall be held and no writ of attachment shall be issued.
(c) If the plaintiff files and serves a notice of opposition to the claim as provided in this section, the defendant has the burden of proving that the property is exempt from attachment.
Added by Stats. 1974, Ch. 1516.

Section 484.370 - Conduct of hearing; findings required for ordering issuance of writ
The hearing shall be conducted in the manner prescribed in Section 484.090 and the court shall order a writ of attachment to be issued upon the filing of an undertaking as provided by Sections 489.210 and 489.220, if it finds both of the following:
(a) A right to attach order has been issued in the action pursuant to Article 1 (commencing with Section 484.010) or the court has found pursuant to Section 485.240 that the plaintiff is entitled to a right to attach order.
(b) The defendant has failed to prove that the property sought to be attached, or the portion thereof to be described in the writ, is exempt from attachment.
Amended by Stats. 1976, Ch. 437.

Article 3 - EX PARTE PROCEDURE FOR OBTAINING ADDITIONAL WRITS

Section 484.510 - Time plaintiff may apply for writ by filing application
(a) At any time after a right to attach order has been issued under Article 1 (commencing with Section 484.010) or after the court has found pursuant to Section 485.240 that the plaintiff is entitled to a right to attach order, the plaintiff may apply for a writ of attachment under this article by filing an application which meets the requirements of Section 484.320 with the court in which the action is brought.
(b) The application shall be accompanied by an affidavit showing that the property sought to be attached is not exempt from attachment. Such affidavit may be based on the affiant's information and belief.
Added by Stats. 1974, Ch. 1516.

Section 484.520 - Findings required for ordering issuance of writ
The court shall examine the application and supporting affidavit and shall order a writ of attachment to be issued upon the filing of an undertaking as provided by Sections 489.210 and 489.220, if it finds both of the following:
(a) A right to attach order has been issued in the action pursuant to Article 1 (commencing with Section 484.010) or the court has found pursuant to Section 485.240 that the plaintiff is entitled to a right to attach order.
(b) The affidavit accompanying the application shows that the property sought to be attached, or the portion thereof to be described in the writ, is not exempt from attachment.
Amended by Stats. 1976, Ch. 437.

Section 484.530 - Claim of exemption
(a) The defendant may claim an exemption as to real or personal property levied upon pursuant to a writ issued under this article by following the procedure set forth in Article 2 (commencing with Section 703.510) of Chapter 4 of Division 2 of Title 9, except that the defendant shall claim the exemption as to personal property not later than 30 days after the levying officer serves the defendant with the notice of attachment describing such property. For this purpose, references in Article 2 (commencing with Section 703.510) of Chapter 4 of Division 2 of Title 9 to the "judgment debtor" shall be deemed references to the defendant, and references to the "judgment creditor" shall be deemed references to the plaintiff.
(b) The defendant may claim the exemption provided by subdivision (b) of Section 487.020 within the time provided by subdivision (a) of this section either (1) by following the procedure set forth in Article 2 (commencing with Section 703. 510) of Chapter 4 of Division 2 of Title 9 or (2) by following the procedure set forth in subdivision (c) of Section 482.100 except that the requirement of showing changed circumstances under subdivision (a) of Section 482.100 does not apply.
(c) Notwithstanding subdivisions (a) and (b), a claim of exemption shall be denied if the claim has been denied earlier in the action and there is no change in circumstances affecting the claim.
Amended by Stats. 1982, Ch. 1198, Sec. 39. Operative July 1, 1983, by Sec. 70 of Ch. 1198.

Chapter 5 - EX PARTE HEARING PROCEDURE FOR OBTAINING WRIT OF ATTACHMENT
Article 1 - GREAT OR IRREPARABLE INJURY REQUIREMENT

Section 485.010 - Generally
(a) Except as otherwise provided by statute, no right to attach order or writ of attachment may be issued pursuant to this chapter unless it appears from facts shown by affidavit that great or irreparable injury would result to the plaintiff if issuance of the order were delayed until the matter could be heard on notice.
(b) The requirement of subdivision (a) is satisfied if any of the following are shown:
   (1) Under the circumstances of the case, it may be inferred that there is a danger that the property sought to be attached would be concealed, substantially impaired in value, or otherwise made unavailable to levy if issuance of the order were delayed until the matter could be heard on notice.
   (2) Under the circumstances of the case, it may be inferred that the defendant has failed to pay the debt underlying the requested attachment and the defendant is insolvent in the sense that the defendant is generally not paying his or her debts as those debts become due, unless the debts are subject to a bona fide dispute. Plaintiff's affidavit filed in support of the ex parte attachment shall state, in addition to the requirements of Section 485.530, the known undisputed debts of the defendant, that the debts are not subject to bona fide dispute, and the basis for plaintiff's determination that the defendant's debts are undisputed.
   (3) A bulk sales notice has been recorded and published pursuant to Division 6 (commencing with Section 6101) of the Commercial Code with respect to a bulk transfer by the defendant.
   (4) An escrow has been opened pursuant to the provisions of Section 24074 of the Business and Professions Code with respect to the sale by the defendant of a liquor license.
   (5) Any other circumstance showing that great or irreparable injury would result to the plaintiff if issuance of the order were delayed until the matter could be heard on notice.
(c) Upon a writ being issued solely on a showing under paragraph (2) of subdivision (b), if the defendant requests the court to review the issuance of the writ, the court shall conduct a hearing within five court days after the plaintiff is served with notice of the defendant's request. A writ issued solely on a showing under paragraph (3) of subdivision (b) shall be limited to the property covered by the bulk sales notice or the proceeds of the sale of such property. In addition to any other service required by this title, such writ shall be served by the levying officer on the transferee or auctioneer identified by the bulk sales notice not more than five days after the levy of such writ. A writ issued solely on a showing under paragraph (4) of subdivision (b) shall be limited to the plaintiff's pro rata share of the proceeds of the sale in escrow.
Amended by Stats. 1988, Ch. 727, Sec. 1.

Article 2 - ORDER DETERMINING RIGHT TO ATTACH; ISSUANCE OF WRIT OF ATTACHMENT

Section 485.210 - Application for order and writ
(a) Upon the filing of the complaint or at any time thereafter, the plaintiff may apply pursuant to this article for a right to attach order and a writ of attachment by filing an application for the order and writ with the court in which the action is brought.
(b) The application shall satisfy the requirements of Section 484.020 and, in addition, shall include a statement showing that the requirement of Section 485.010 is satisfied.
(c) The application shall be supported by an affidavit showing all of the following:
　(1) The plaintiff on the facts presented would be entitled to a judgment on the claim upon which the attachment is based.
　(2) The plaintiff would suffer great or irreparable injury (within the meaning of Section 485.010) if issuance of the order were delayed until the matter could be heard on notice.
　(3) The property sought to be attached is not exempt from attachment.
(d) An affidavit in support of the showing required by paragraph (3) of subdivision (c) may be based on the affiant's information and belief.
Added by Stats. 1974, Ch. 1516.

Section 485.220 - Findings required for ordering writ to issue
(a) The court shall examine the application and supporting affidavit and, except as provided in Section 486.030, shall issue a right to attach order, which shall state the amount to be secured by the attachment, and order a writ of attachment to be issued upon the filing of an undertaking as provided by Sections 489.210 and 489.220, if it finds all of the following:
　(1) The claim upon which the attachment is based is one upon which an attachment may be issued.
　(2) The plaintiff has established the probable validity of the claim upon which the attachment is based.
　(3) The attachment is not sought for a purpose other than the recovery upon the claim upon which the attachment is based.
　(4) The affidavit accompanying the application shows that the property sought to be attached, or the portion thereof to be specified in the writ, is not exempt from attachment.
　(5) The plaintiff will suffer great or irreparable injury (within the meaning of Section 485.010) if issuance of the order is delayed until the matter can be heard on notice.
　(6) The amount to be secured by the attachment is greater than zero.
(b) If the court finds that the application and the supporting affidavit do not satisfy the requirements of Section 485.010, it shall so state and deny the order. If denial is solely on the ground that Section 485.010 is not satisfied, the court shall so state and such denial does not preclude the plaintiff from applying for a right to attach order and writ of attachment under Chapter 4 (commencing with Section 484.010) with the same affidavits and supporting papers.
Amended by Stats. 1997, Ch. 222, Sec. 9. Effective January 1, 1998.

Section 485.230 - Discovery of identity, location and value of property
Where a right to attach order has been issued by the court, a plaintiff may discover, through any means provided for by, and subject to the protections included in, Title 4 (commencing with Section 2016.010) of Part 4, the identity, location, and value of property in which the defendant has an interest.
Amended by Stats 2004 ch 182 (AB 3081),s 10, eff. 7/1/2005

Section 485.240 - Application for order to set aside right to attach or quash writ
(a) Any defendant whose property has been attached pursuant to a writ issued under this chapter may apply for an order (1) that the right to attach order be set aside, the writ of attachment quashed, and any property levied upon pursuant to the writ be released, or (2) that the amount to be secured by the attachment be reduced as provided in Section 483.015. Such application shall be made by filing with the court and serving on the plaintiff a notice of motion.
(b) The notice of motion shall state the grounds on which the motion is based and shall be accompanied by an affidavit supporting any factual issues raised and points and authorities supporting any legal issues raised. It shall not be grounds to set aside an order that the plaintiff would not have suffered great or irreparable injury (within the meaning of Section 485.010) if issuance of the order had been delayed until the matter could have been heard on notice.
(c) At the hearing on the motion, the court shall determine whether the plaintiff is entitled to the right to attach order or whether the amount to be secured by the attachment should be reduced. If the court finds that the plaintiff is not entitled to the right to attach order, it shall order the right to attach order set aside, the writ of attachment quashed, and any property levied on pursuant to the writ released. If the court finds that the plaintiff is entitled to the right to attach order, thereafter the plaintiff may apply for additional writs pursuant to Article 2 (commencing with Section 484.310) or Article 3 (commencing with Section 484.510) of Chapter 4.
(d) The court's determinations shall be made upon the basis of the pleadings and other papers in the record; but, upon good cause shown, the court may receive and consider at the hearing additional evidence, oral or documentary, and additional points and authorities, or it may continue the hearing for the production of such additional evidence or points and authorities.
(e) The hearing provided for in this section shall take precedence over all other civil matters on the calendar of that day except older matters of the same character.
Amended by Stats. 1983, Ch. 155, Sec. 4. Effective June 30, 1983. Operative July 1, 1983, by Sec. 32 of Ch. 155.

Article 3 - PROCEDURE FOR OBTAINING ADDITIONAL WRITS

Section 485.510 - Application for additional writs
At any time after a right to attach order and writ of attachment have been issued under Article 2 (commencing with Section 485.210), the plaintiff may apply for an additional writ of attachment under this article by filing an application with the court in which the action is brought.
Added by Stats. 1974, Ch. 1516.

Section 485.520 - Application requirements
The application shall be executed under oath and shall include all of the following:
(a) A statement that the plaintiff has been issued a right to attach order and writ of attachment pursuant to Article 2 (commencing with Section 485.210) in the action.
(b) A statement of the amount to be secured by the attachment under the right to attach order.
(c) A description of the property to be attached under the writ of attachment and a statement that the plaintiff is informed and believes that the property is not exempt from attachment. The description shall satisfy the requirements of Section 484.020.
(d) A statement showing that the requirement of Section 485.010 has been satisfied.
Amended by Stats. 1982, Ch. 1198, Sec. 41. Operative July 1, 1983, by Sec. 70 of Ch. 1198.

Section 485.530 - Affidavit supporting application
(a) The application shall be supported by an affidavit showing both of the following:
　(1) The plaintiff would suffer great or irreparable injury (within the meaning of Section 485.010) if the issuance of the writ of attachment were delayed until the matter could be heard on notice.

(2) The property sought to be attached is not exempt from attachment.

(b) The affidavit in support of the showing required by paragraph (2) of subdivision (a) may be based on the affiant's information and belief.

Amended by Stats. 1976, Ch. 437.

Section 485.540 - Findings required for ordering issuance of writ

The court shall examine the application and supporting affidavit and shall order a writ of attachment to be issued upon the filing of an undertaking as provided by Sections 489.210 and 489.220, if it finds all of the following:

(a) A right to attach order has been issued in the action pursuant to Article 2 (commencing with Section 485.210).

(b) The affidavit accompanying the application shows that the property sought to be attached, or the portion thereof to be specified in the writ, is not exempt from attachment.

(c) The plaintiff will suffer great or irreparable injury (within the meaning of Section 485.010) if issuance of the writ of attachment is delayed until the matter can be heard on notice.

Amended by Stats. 1976, Ch. 437.

Article 4 - CLAIM OF EXEMPTION

Section 485.610 - Generally

(a) The defendant may claim an exemption as to real or personal property levied upon pursuant to a writ of attachment issued under this chapter by following the procedure set forth in Article 2 (commencing with Section 703.510) of Chapter 4 of Division 2 of Title 9, except that the defendant shall claim the exemption as to personal property not later than 30 days after the levying officer serves the defendant with the notice of attachment describing such property and may claim an exemption for real property within the time provided in Section 487.030. For this purpose, references in Article 2 (commencing with Section 703.510) of Chapter 4 of Division 2 of Title 9 to the "judgment debtor" shall be deemed references to the defendant, and references to the "judgment creditor" shall be deemed references to the plaintiff.

(b) The defendant may claim the exemption provided by subdivision (b) of Section 487.020 within the time provided by subdivision (a) of this section either (1) by following the procedure set forth in Article 2 (commencing with Section 703. 510) of Chapter 4 of Division 2 of Title 9 or (2) by following the procedure set forth in subdivision (c) of Section 482.100 except that the requirement of showing changed circumstances under subdivision (a) of Section 482.100 does not apply.

Amended by Stats. 1984, Ch. 538, Sec. 2.

Chapter 6 - TEMPORARY PROTECTIVE ORDER

Section 486.010 - Application for order

(a) At the time of applying for a right to attach order under Chapter 4 (commencing with Section 484.010), the plaintiff may apply pursuant to this chapter for a temporary protective order by filing an application for the order with the court in which the action is brought.

(b) The application shall state what relief is requested and shall be supported by an affidavit, which may be based on information and belief, showing that the plaintiff would suffer great or irreparable injury (within the meaning of Section 485.010) if the temporary protective order were not issued.

Added by Stats. 1974, Ch. 1516.

Section 486.020 - Findings required for issuance

The court shall examine the application, supporting affidavit, and other papers on record and shall issue a temporary protective order, which shall state the amount sought to be secured by the attachment under the application for the right to attach order, upon the filing of an undertaking as provided by Sections 489.210 and 489.220, if it finds all of the following:

(a) The claim upon which the application for attachment is based is one upon which an attachment may be issued.

(b) The plaintiff has established the probable validity of the claim upon which the application for the attachment is based.

(c) The order is not sought for a purpose other than the recovery upon the claim upon which the application for the attachment is based.

(d) The plaintiff will suffer great or irreparable injury (within the meaning of Section 485.010) if the temporary protective order is not issued.

Amended by Stats. 1982, Ch. 1198, Sec. 42.5. Operative July 1, 1983, by Sec. 70 of Ch. 1198.

Section 486.030 - Issuance of temporary order instead of right to attach order

(a) In any case where the plaintiff has applied for a right to attach order and writ of attachment under Chapter 5 (commencing with Section 485.010), the court may in its discretion deny the application for the order and writ and issue instead a temporary protective order under this chapter if it determines that the requirements of Section 485.220 are satisfied but that the issuance of the temporary protective order instead of the right to attach order and writ would be in the interest of justice and equity to the parties, taking into account the effect on the defendant of issuing a writ of attachment ex parte, the effect on the plaintiff of issuing the temporary protective order instead of the writ, and other factors that bear on equity and justice under the circumstances of the particular case.

(b) If the court issues a temporary protective order under this section, the plaintiff's application for a right to attach order and writ shall be treated as an application for a right to attach order and writ under Article 1 (commencing with Section 484.010) of Chapter 4 and the plaintiff shall comply with the requirements of service provided in Section 484.040.

Added by Stats. 1974, Ch. 1516.

Section 486.040 - Provisions contained in temporary order

The temporary protective order issued under this chapter shall contain such provisions as the court determines would be in the interest of justice and equity to the parties, taking into account the effects on both the defendant and the plaintiff under the circumstances of the particular case.

Added by Stats. 1974, Ch. 1516.

Section 486.050 - Order may prohibit transfer by defendant of any of defendant's property located in state

(a) Except as otherwise provided in Section 486.040, the temporary protective order may prohibit a transfer by the defendant of any of the defendant's property in this state subject to the levy of the writ of attachment. The temporary protective order shall describe the property in a manner adequate to permit the defendant to identify the property subject to the temporary protective order.

(b) Notwithstanding subdivision (a), if the property is farm products held for sale or is inventory, the temporary protective order shall not prohibit the defendant from transferring the property in the ordinary course of business, but the temporary protective order may impose appropriate restrictions on the disposition of the proceeds from that type of transfer.

Amended by Stats 2008 ch 179 (SB 1498),s 35, eff. 1/1/2009.

Section 486.060 - Checks issued by defendant against defendant's accounts

(a) Notwithstanding any terms of the temporary protective order, the defendant may issue any number of checks against any of the defendant's accounts in a financial institution in this state to the extent permitted by this section.

(b) The defendant may issue any number of checks in any amount for the following purposes:

(1) Payment of any payroll expense (including fringe benefits and taxes and premiums for workers' compensation and unemployment insurance) falling due in the ordinary course of business prior to the levy of a writ of attachment.

(2) Payment for goods thereafter delivered to the defendant C.O.D. for use in the defendant's trade, business, or profession.

(3) Payment of taxes if payment is necessary to avoid penalties which will accrue if there is any further delay in payment.

(4) Payment of reasonable legal fees and reasonable costs and expenses required for the representation of the defendant in the action.

(c) In addition to the checks permitted to be issued by subdivision (b), the defendant may issue any number of checks for any purpose so long as the total amount of the checks does not exceed the greater of the following:

(1) The amount by which the total amount on deposit exceeds the sum of the amount sought to be secured by the attachment and the amounts permitted to be paid pursuant to subdivision (b).

(2) One thousand dollars ($1,000).

Amended by Stats. 1982, Ch. 1198, Sec. 43. Operative July 1, 1983, by Sec. 70 of Ch. 1198.

Section 486.070 - Order binds only defendant

Except as otherwise provided by Section 486.110, a temporary protective order issued under this chapter binds only the defendant, whether or not any other person knows of or is served with a copy of the temporary protective order.

Amended by Stats. 1976, Ch. 437.

Section 486.080 - Order personally served on defendant

The temporary protective order shall be personally served on the defendant together with the documents referred to in Section 484.040.

Amended by Stats. 1982, Ch. 1198, Sec. 44. Operative July 1, 1983, by Sec. 70 of Ch. 1198.

Section 486.090 - Expiration

Except as otherwise provided in this title, the temporary protective order shall expire at the earliest of the following times:

(a) Forty days after the issuance of the order or, if an earlier date is prescribed by the court in the order, on such earlier date.

(b) As to specific property described in the order, when a levy of attachment upon that property is made by the plaintiff.

Amended by Stats. 1976, Ch. 437.

Section 486.100 - Modification or vacation

Upon ex parte application of the defendant or, if the court so orders, after a noticed hearing, the court may modify or vacate the temporary protective order if it determines that such action would be in the interest of justice and equity to the parties, taking into account the effect on the defendant of the continuance of the original order, the effect on the plaintiff of modifying or vacating the order, and any other factors.

Added by Stats. 1974, Ch. 1516.

Section 486.110 - Lien created by service of order upon defendant

(a) The service upon the defendant of a temporary protective order pursuant to Section 486.080 creates a lien upon any property, or the proceeds thereof, which is described in the order, is owned by the defendant at the time of such service, and is subject to attachment pursuant to this title. The lien continues on property subject to the lien, notwithstanding the transfer or encumbrance of the property subject to the lien, unless the person receiving the property, whether real or personal, is a person listed in Section 697.740.

(b) The lien terminates upon the date of expiration of the temporary protective order except with respect to property levied upon while the temporary protective order is in effect under a writ of attachment issued upon application of the plaintiff.

Amended by Stats. 1984, Ch. 538, Sec. 2.5.

Chapter 7 - PROPERTY SUBJECT TO ATTACHMENT

Section 487.010 - Generally

The following property of the defendant is subject to attachment:

(a) Where the defendant is a corporation, all corporate property for which a method of levy is provided by Article 2 (commencing with Section 488.300) of Chapter 8.

(b) Where the defendant is a partnership or other unincorporated association, all partnership or association property for which a method of levy is provided by Article 2 (commencing with Section 488.300) of Chapter 8.

(c) Where the defendant is a natural person, all of the following property:

(1) Interests in real property except leasehold estates with unexpired terms of less than one year.

(2) Accounts receivable, chattel paper, and general intangibles arising out of the conduct by the defendant of a trade, business, or profession, except any such individual claim with a principal balance of less than one hundred fifty dollars ($150).

(3) Equipment.

(4) Farm products.

(5) Inventory.

(6) Final money judgments arising out of the conduct by the defendant of a trade, business, or profession.

(7) Money on the premises where a trade, business, or profession is conducted by the defendant and, except for the first one thousand dollars ($1,000), money located elsewhere than on such premises and deposit accounts, but, if the defendant has more than one deposit account or has at least one deposit account and money located elsewhere than on the premises where a trade, business, or profession is conducted by the defendant, the court, upon application of the plaintiff, may order that the writ of attachment be levied so that an aggregate amount of one thousand dollars ($1,000) in the form of such money and in such accounts remains free of levy.

(8) Negotiable documents of title.

(9) Instruments.

(10) Securities.

(11) Minerals or the like (including oil and gas) to be extracted.

(d) In the case of a defendant described in subdivision (c), community property of a type described in subdivision (c) is subject to attachment if the community property would be subject to enforcement of the judgment obtained in the action in which the attachment is sought. Unless the provision or context otherwise requires, if community property that is subject to attachment is sought to be attached:

(1) Any provision of this title that applies to the property of the defendant or to obligations owed to the defendant also applies to the community property interest of the spouse of the defendant and to obligations owed to either spouse that are community property.

(2) Any provision of this title that applies to property in the possession or under the control of the defendant also applies to community property in the possession or under the control of the spouse of the defendant.

Amended by Stats. 1982, Ch. 1198, Sec. 46. Operative July 1, 1983, by Sec. 70 of Ch. 1198.

Section 487.020 - Exempt property

Except as provided in paragraph (2) of subdivision (a) of Section 3439.07 of the Civil Code, the following property is exempt from attachment:

(a) All property exempt from enforcement of a money judgment.

(b) Property which is necessary for the support of a defendant who is a natural person or the family of such defendant supported in whole or in part by the defendant.

(c) "Earnings" as defined by Section 706.011.

(d) All property not subject to attachment pursuant to Section 487.010.

Amended by Stats. 1986, Ch. 383, Sec. 7.

Section 487.025 - Homestead

(a) The recording of a homestead declaration (as defined in Section 704.910) does not limit or affect the right of a plaintiff to attach the declared homestead described in the homestead declaration, whether the homestead declaration is recorded before or after the declared homestead is attached.

(b) An attachment lien attaches to a homestead (as defined in Section 704.710) in the amount of any surplus over the total of the following:
  (1) All liens and encumbrances on the homestead at the time the attachment lien is created.
  (2) The homestead exemption set forth in Section 704.730.
(c) Nothing in subdivision (a) or (b) limits the right of the defendant to an exemption under subdivision (b) of Section 487.020.
(d) Notwithstanding subdivision (b), a homestead (as defined in Section 704.710) is exempt from sale to the extent provided in Section 704.800 when it is sought to be sold to enforce the judgment obtained in the action in which the attachment was obtained.
Added by Stats. 1982, Ch. 1198, Sec. 47.5. Operative July 1, 1983, by Sec. 70 of Ch. 1198.

Section 487.030 - Claim of exemption

(a) At any time prior to the entry of judgment in the action, the defendant may claim any exemption provided by subdivision (a) of Section 487.020 with respect to real property by following the procedure set forth in Article 2 (commencing with Section 703.510) of Chapter 4 of Division 2 of Title 9. A claim of exemption under this subdivision shall be denied if the claim has been denied earlier in the action.
(b) At any time prior to the entry of judgment in the action, the defendant may claim the exemption provided by subdivision (b) of Section 487.020 with respect to real property either (1) by following the procedure set forth in Article 2 (commencing with Section 703.510) of Chapter 4 of Division 2 of Title 9 or (2) by following the procedure set forth in subdivision (c) of Section 482.100 except that the requirement of showing changed circumstances under subdivision (a) of Section 482.100 does not apply. A claim of exemption under this subdivision shall be denied if the claim has been denied earlier in the action and there is no change in circumstances affecting the claim.
(c) For the purposes of this section, references in Article 2 (commencing with Section 703.510) of Chapter 4 of Division 2 of Title 9 to the "judgment debtor" shall be deemed references to the defendant, and references to the "judgment creditor" shall be deemed references to the plaintiff.
(d) Nothing in this section limits the right to claim after the entry of judgment a homestead exemption for real property under Article 4 (commencing with Section 704.710) of Chapter 4 of Division 2 of Title 9 unless prior to entry of judgment the defendant has claimed the exemption provided by subdivision (a) of Section 487.020 with respect to such property and the claim has been denied.
Added by Stats. 1982, Ch. 1198, Sec. 48. Operative July 1, 1983, by Sec. 70 of Ch. 1198.

Chapter 8 - LEVY PROCEDURES; LIEN OF ATTACHMENT; MANAGEMENT AND DISPOSITION OF ATTACHED PROPERTY

Article 1 - GENERAL PROVISIONS

Section 488.010 - Writ requirements

The writ of attachment shall include the following information:
(a) The date of issuance of the writ.
(b) The title of the court that issued the writ and the cause and number of the action.
(c) The name and address of the plaintiff and the name and last known address of the defendant.
(d) The amount to be secured by the attachment.
(e) A description of the property to be levied upon to satisfy the attachment.
Repealed and added by Stats. 1982, Ch. 1198, Sec. 50. Operative July 1, 1983, by Sec. 70 of Ch. 1198.

Section 488.020 - Writ directed to levying officer and process server; duty of levying officer to levy in accordance with instructions

(a) A writ of attachment shall be directed to a levying officer in the county in which property of the defendant described in the writ may be located and to any registered process server.
(b) Upon the receipt of written instructions from the plaintiff's attorney of record or, if the plaintiff has no attorney of record, from the plaintiff, the levying officer to whom the writ is directed and delivered shall levy the writ without delay in the manner provided in this chapter on the property described in the writ or so much thereof as is clearly sufficient to satisfy the amount to be secured by the attachment. The levying officer is not liable for a determination made in good faith under this subdivision.
(c) If a copy of the summons and complaint has not previously been served on the defendant, the instructions to the levying officer shall instruct the levying officer to make the service at the same time the levying officer serves the defendant with a copy of the writ of attachment.
Repealed and added by Stats. 1982, Ch. 1198, Sec. 50. Operative July 1, 1983, by Sec. 70 of Ch. 1198.

Section 488.030 - Instructions given levying officer by plaintiff

(a) The plaintiff shall give the levying officer instructions in writing. The instructions shall be signed by the plaintiff's attorney of record or, if the plaintiff does not have an attorney of record, by the plaintiff. The instructions shall contain the information needed or requested by the levying officer to comply with the provisions of this title, including but not limited to:
  (1) An adequate description of any property to be levied upon.
  (2) A statement whether the property is a dwelling.
  (3) If the property is a dwelling, whether it is real or personal property.
(b) Subject to subdivision (c), the levying officer shall act in accordance with the written instructions to the extent the actions are taken in conformance with the provisions of this title.
(c) Except to the extent the levying officer has actual knowledge that the information is incorrect, the levying officer may rely on any information contained in the written instructions.
Repealed and added by Stats. 1982, Ch. 1198, Sec. 50. Operative July 1, 1983, by Sec. 70 of Ch. 1198.

Section 488.040 - Correct name and address of person required to be served included in instructions

(a) If the levying officer is required by any provision of this title to serve any writ, order, notice, or other paper on any person, the plaintiff shall include in the instructions to the levying officer the correct name and address of the person. The plaintiff shall use reasonable diligence to ascertain the correct name and address of the person.
(b) Unless the levying officer has actual knowledge that the name or address included in the instructions is incorrect, the levying officer shall rely on the instructions in serving the writ, order, notice, or other paper on the person.
Repealed and added by Stats. 1982, Ch. 1198, Sec. 50. Operative July 1, 1983, by Sec. 70 of Ch. 1198.

Section 488.050 - Deposits by plaintiff as prerequisite to performance by officer and to taking property into custody

(a) Except as otherwise provided by law:
  (1) As a prerequisite to the performance by the levying officer of a duty under this title, the plaintiff shall deposit a sum of money with the levying officer sufficient to pay the costs of performing the duty.
  (2) As a prerequisite to the taking of property into custody by the levying officer under this chapter, whether by keeper or otherwise, the plaintiff shall deposit with the levying officer a sum of money sufficient to pay the costs of taking the property and keeping it safely for a period not to exceed 15 days. If continuation of the custody of the property is required, the levying officer shall, from time to time, demand orally or in writing that the plaintiff deposit additional amounts to cover estimated costs for periods not to exceed 30 days each. A written demand may be mailed or delivered to the plaintiff. The plaintiff has not less than three business days after receipt of the demand within which to comply with the demand. If the amount demanded is not paid within the time specified in the oral or written demand, the levying officer shall release the property.
(b) The levying officer is not liable for failure to take or hold property unless the plaintiff has complied with the provisions of this section.

Repealed and added by Stats. 1982, Ch. 1198, Sec. 50. Operative July 1, 1983, by Sec. 70 of Ch. 1198.

Section 488.060 - Notice of attachment

The notice of attachment shall inform the person notified of all of the following:

(a) The capacity in which the person is notified.

(b) The specific property which is sought to be attached.

(c) The person's rights under the attachment, including the right to make a third-party claim pursuant to Division 4 (commencing with Section 720.010) of Title 9.

(d) The person's duties under the attachment.

Repealed and added by Stats. 1982, Ch. 1198, Sec. 50. Operative July 1, 1983, by Sec. 70 of Ch. 1198.

Section 488.065 - Copy of original notice sufficient as notice of attachment

A copy of the original notice of attachment which has been served upon a third party holding the property sought to be attached, if served upon the defendant or any other party, shall suffice as the notice of attachment to that person.

Added by Stats. 1984, Ch. 759, Sec. 1.

Section 488.070 - Personal property sought to be attached located in private place of defendant

If a writ of attachment has been issued and personal property sought to be attached under the writ is located in a private place of the defendant:

(a) The levying officer shall comply with the provisions of Section 699.030.

(b) The plaintiff may obtain the relief provided under Section 699.030 in the manner and subject to the requirements of that section.

Repealed and added by Stats. 1982, Ch. 1198, Sec. 50. Operative July 1, 1983, by Sec. 70 of Ch. 1198.

Section 488.080 - Levy by registered process server

(a) A registered process server may levy under a writ of attachment on the following types of property:

(1) Real property, pursuant to Section 488.315.

(2) Growing crops, timber to be cut, or minerals or the like, including oil and gas, to be extracted or accounts receivable resulting from the sale thereof at the wellhead or minehead, pursuant to Section 488.325.

(3) Personal property in the custody of a levying officer, pursuant to Section 488.355.

(4) Equipment of a going business, pursuant to Section 488.375.

(5) Motor vehicles, vessels, mobilehomes, or commercial coaches used as equipment of a going business, pursuant to Section 488.385.

(6) Farm products or inventory of a going business, pursuant to Section 488.405.

(7) Personal property used as a dwelling, pursuant to subdivision (a) of Section 700.080.

(8) Deposit accounts, pursuant to Section 488.455.

(9) Property in a safe-deposit box, pursuant to Section 488.460.

(10) Accounts receivable or general intangibles, pursuant to Section 488.470.

(11) Final money judgments, pursuant to Section 488.480.

(12) Interest of a defendant in personal property in the estate of a decedent, pursuant to Section 488.485.

(b) Before levying under the writ of attachment, the registered process server shall cause to be deposited with the levying officer a copy of the writ and the fee, as provided by Section 26721 of the Government Code.

(c) If a registered process server levies on property pursuant to subdivision (a), the registered process server shall do both of the following:

(1) Comply with the applicable levy, posting, and service provisions of Article 2 (commencing with Section 488.300).

(2) Request any third person served to give a garnishee's memorandum to the levying officer in compliance with Section 488.610 on a form provided by the registered process server.

(d) Within five court days after levy under this section, all of the following shall be filed with the levying officer:

(1) The writ of attachment.

(2) A proof of service by the registered process server stating the manner of levy performed.

(3) Proof of service of the copy of the writ and notice of attachment on other persons, as required by Article 2 (commencing with Section 488.300).

(4) Instructions in writing, as required by the provisions of Section 488.030.

(e) If the fee provided by Section 26721 of the Government Code has been paid, the levying officer shall perform all other duties under the writ as if the levying officer had levied under the writ and shall return the writ to the court. If the registered process server does not comply with subdivisions (b) and (d), the levy is ineffective and the levying officer shall not be required to perform any duties under the writ, and may issue a release for any property sought to be attached. The levying officer is not liable for actions taken in conformance with the provisions of this title in reliance on information provided to the levying officer under subdivision (d), except to the extent that the levying officer has actual knowledge that the information is incorrect. Nothing in this subdivision limits any liability the plaintiff or registered process server may have if the levying officer acts on the basis of incorrect information provided under subdivision (d).

(f) The fee for services of a registered process server under this section is a recoverable cost pursuant to Section 1033.5.

Amended by Stats 2016 ch 102 (AB 2211),s 1, eff. 1/1/2017.

Amended by Stats 2007 ch 15 (AB 859),s 1, eff. 1/1/2008.

Section 488.090 - Methods for taking property into custody

Except as otherwise provided by statute, where the method of levy upon property requires that property be taken into custody or where the levying officer is otherwise directed to take property into custody, the levying officer may do so by any of the following methods:

(a) Removing the property to a place of safekeeping.

(b) Installing a keeper.

(c) Otherwise obtaining possession or control of the property.

Repealed and added by Stats. 1982, Ch. 1198, Sec. 50. Operative July 1, 1983, by Sec. 70 of Ch. 1198.

Section 488.100 - Special lien of levying officer

The levying officer has a special lien, dependent upon possession, on personal property levied upon in the amount of the levying officer's costs for which an advance has not been made.

Added by Stats. 1982, Ch. 1198, Sec. 50. Operative July 1, 1983, by Sec. 70 of Ch. 1198.

Section 488.110 - Third-party claims

A third person shall claim an interest in property attached in the manner provided for third-party claims under Division 4 (commencing with Section 720.010) of Title 9.

Added by Stats. 1982, Ch. 1198, Sec. 50. Operative July 1, 1983, by Sec. 70 of Ch. 1198.

Section 488.120 - Attachment lien not affected by failure to post, serve or mail copy of writ and notice

In any case where property has been levied upon and, pursuant to a levy, a copy of the writ of attachment and a notice of attachment are required by statute to be posted or to be served on or mailed to the defendant or other person, failure to post, serve, or mail the copy of the writ and the notice does not affect the attachment lien created by the levy.

Added by Stats. 1982, Ch. 1198, Sec. 50. Operative July 1, 1983, by Sec. 70 of Ch. 1198.

Section 488.130 - Return of writ by levying officer
(a) The levying officer to whom the writ of attachment is delivered shall return the writ to the court from which the writ issued, together with a report of the levying officer's actions. The return shall be made promptly in accordance with the plaintiff's instructions given to the levying officer but in no event later than 60 days after the levying officer receives the writ.
(b) The levying officer shall make a full inventory of property attached and return the inventory with the writ.
Added by Stats. 1982, Ch. 1198, Sec. 50. Operative July 1, 1983, by Sec. 70 of Ch. 1198.

Section 488.140 - No liability for actions taken in conformance with provisions of title
(a) The levying officer or registered process server is not liable for actions taken in conformance with the provisions of this title, including actions taken in conformance with the provisions of this title in reliance on information contained in the written instructions of the plaintiff except to the extent the levying officer or registered process server has actual knowledge that the information is incorrect. Nothing in this subdivision limits any liability the plaintiff may have if the levying officer or registered process server acts on the basis of incorrect information given in the written instructions.
(b) Unless the levying officer is negligent in the care or handling of the property, the levying officer is not liable to either the plaintiff or the defendant for loss by fire, theft, injury, or damage of any kind to personal property while (1) in the possession of the levying officer either in a warehouse or other storage place or in the custody of a keeper or (2) in transit to or from a warehouse or other storage place.
Amended by Stats. 1983, Ch. 155, Sec. 5.5. Effective June 30, 1983. Operative July 1, 1983, by Sec. 32 of Ch. 155.

Article 2 - METHODS OF LEVY

Section 488.300 - Construction of terms
If the method of levy under a writ of execution is incorporated by this article, for the purposes of this article references in Article 4 (commencing with Section 700.010) of Chapter 3 of Division 2 of Title 9 to:
(a) "Judgment creditor" shall be deemed references to the plaintiff.
(b) "Judgment debtor" shall be deemed references to the defendant.
(c) "Notice of levy" shall be deemed references to a notice of attachment.
(d) "Writ" shall be deemed references to a writ of attachment.
Added by Stats. 1982, Ch. 1198, Sec. 50. Operative July 1, 1983, by Sec. 70 of Ch. 1198.

Section 488.305 - Service of writ and notice on defendant
At the time of levy pursuant to this article or promptly thereafter, the levying officer shall serve a copy of the writ of attachment and a notice of attachment on the defendant.
Added by Stats. 1982, Ch. 1198, Sec. 50. Operative July 1, 1983, by Sec. 70 of Ch. 1198.

Section 488.315 - To attach real property
To attach real property, the levying officer shall comply with Section 700.015 and the recorder shall index the copy of the writ of attachment and a notice of attachment as provided in that section.
Added by Stats. 1982, Ch. 1198, Sec. 50. Operative July 1, 1983, by Sec. 70 of Ch. 1198.

Section 488.325 - To attach growing crops, timber to be cut or minerals
To attach (1) growing crops, (2) timber to be cut, or (3) minerals or the like (including oil and gas) to be extracted or accounts receivable resulting from the sale thereof at the wellhead or minehead, the levying officer shall comply with Section 700.020 and the recorder shall index the copy of the writ of attachment and a notice of attachment as provided in that section.
Added by Stats. 1982, Ch. 1198, Sec. 50. Operative July 1, 1983, by Sec. 70 of Ch. 1198.

Section 488.335 - To attach personal property in possession of defendant
Unless another method of attachment is provided by this article, to attach tangible personal property in the possession or under the control of the defendant, the levying officer shall take the property into custody.
Added by Stats. 1982, Ch. 1198, Sec. 50. Operative July 1, 1983, by Sec. 70 of Ch. 1198.

Section 488.345 - To attach tangible personal property in possession of defendant
Unless another method of attachment is provided by this article, to attach tangible personal property in the possession or under the control of a third person, the levying officer shall comply with Section 700.040.
Added by Stats. 1982, Ch. 1198, Sec. 50. Operative July 1, 1983, by Sec. 70 of Ch. 1198.

Section 488.355 - To attach personal property in custody of levying officer
(a) To attach personal property in the custody of a levying officer, the plaintiff or levying officer shall comply with subdivision (a) of Section 700.050.
(b) The levying officer having custody of the property shall comply with the writs in the order they are received and is not subject to the provisions of Article 4 (commencing with Section 488.600).
Added by Stats. 1982, Ch. 1198, Sec. 50. Operative July 1, 1983, by Sec. 70 of Ch. 1198.

Section 488.365 - To attach goods in possession of bailee
To attach goods in the possession of a bailee (as defined in Section 7102 of the Commercial Code) other than one who has issued a negotiable document of title therefor, the levying officer shall comply with Section 700.060.
Added by Stats. 1982, Ch. 1198, Sec. 50. Operative July 1, 1983, by Sec. 70 of Ch. 1198.

Section 488.375 - To attach equipment of going business in possession or under control of defendant
(a) Except as provided by Section 488.385, to attach equipment of a going business in the possession or under the control of the defendant, the levying officer shall file with the office of the Secretary of State a notice of attachment, in the form prescribed by the Secretary of State, which shall contain all of the following:
    (1) The name and mailing address of the plaintiff.
    (2) The name and last known mailing address of the defendant.
    (3) The title of the court where the action is pending and the cause and number of the action.
    (4) A description of the specific property attached.
    (5) A statement that the plaintiff has acquired an attachment lien on the specified property of the defendant.
(b) Upon presentation of a notice of attachment under this section for filing, and tender of the filing fee to the office of the Secretary of State, the notice of attachment shall be filed, marked, and indexed in the same manner as a financing statement. The fee for filing in the office of the Secretary of State is the same as the fee for filing a financing statement in the standard form.
(c) Upon the request of any person, the Secretary of State shall issue a certificate showing whether there is on file in that office on the date and hour stated therein any notice of attachment filed against the equipment of a particular person named in the request. If a notice of attachment is on file, the certificate shall state the date and hour of filing of each such notice and any notice affecting any such notice of attachment and the name and address of the plaintiff. Upon request, the Secretary of State shall furnish a copy of any notice of attachment or notice affecting a notice of attachment. The certificate shall be issued as part of a combined certificate pursuant to Section 9528 of the Commercial Code, and the fee for the certificate and copies shall be in accordance with that section.

(d) The fee for filing, indexing, and furnishing filing data for a notice of extension of attachment is the same as the fee for a continuation statement under Section 9525 of the Commercial Code. The fee for filing, indexing, and furnishing filing data for a notice of release of attachment is the same as the fee for a statement of release under Section 9525 of the Commercial Code.
(e) If property subject to an attachment lien under this section becomes a fixture (as defined in paragraph (41) of subdivision (a) of Section 9102 of the Commercial Code), the attachment lien under this section is extinguished.
Amended by Stats 2021 ch 124 (AB 938),s 7, eff. 1/1/2022.
EFFECTIVE 7/1/2001. Amended October 10, 1999 (Bill Number: SB 45) (Chapter 991).

Section 488.385 - To attach vehicle or vessel, mobilehome or commercial coach which is equipment of going business

(a) To attach a vehicle or vessel for which a certificate of ownership has been issued by the Department of Motor Vehicles, or a mobilehome or commercial coach for which a certificate of title has been issued by the Department of Housing and Community Development, which is equipment of a going business in the possession or under the control of the defendant, the levying officer shall file with the appropriate department a notice of attachment, in the form prescribed by the appropriate department, which shall contain all of the following:
 (1) The name and mailing address of the plaintiff.
 (2) The name and last known mailing address of the defendant.
 (3) The title of the court where the action is pending and the cause and number of the action.
 (4) A description of the specific property attached.
 (5) A statement that the plaintiff has acquired an attachment lien on the specific property of the defendant.
(b) Upon presentation of a notice of attachment, notice of extension, or notice of release under this section for filing and tender of the filing fee to the appropriate department, the notice shall be filed and indexed. The fee for filing and indexing the notice is fifteen dollars ($15).
(c) Upon the request of any person, the department shall issue its certificate showing whether there is on file in that department on the date and hour stated therein any notice of attachment filed against the property of a particular person named in the request. If a notice of attachment is on file, the certificate shall state the date and hour of filing of each such notice of attachment and any notice affecting any such notice of attachment and the name and address of the plaintiff. The fee for the certificate issued pursuant to this subdivision is fifteen dollars ($15). Upon request, the department shall furnish a copy of any notice of attachment or notice affecting a notice of attachment for a fee of one dollar ($1) per page.
(d) If property subject to an attachment lien under this section becomes a fixture (as defined in paragraph (41) of subdivision (a) of Section 9102 of the Commercial Code), the attachment lien under this section is extinguished.
Amended by Stats 2003 ch 719 (SB 1055),s 1, eff. 1/1/2004.
EFFECTIVE 7/01/2001. Amended October 10, 1999 (Bill Number: SB 45) (Chapter 991).

Section 488.395 - To attach farm products or inventory of going business

Except as specified in subdivision (e) and as provided by Sections 488.325 and 488.405:
(a) To attach farm products or inventory of a going business in the possession or under the control of the defendant, the levying officer shall place a keeper in charge of the property for the period prescribed by subdivisions (b) and (c). During the keeper period, the business may continue to operate in the ordinary course of business provided that all sales are final and are for cash or its equivalent. For the purpose of this subdivision, a check is the equivalent of cash. The levying officer is not liable for accepting payment in the form of a cash equivalent. The keeper shall take custody of the proceeds from all sales unless otherwise directed by the plaintiff.
(b) Subject to subdivision (c), the period during which the business may continue to operate under the keeper is:
 (1) Ten days, if the defendant is a natural person and the writ of attachment has been issued ex parte pursuant to Article 3 (commencing with Section 484.510) of Chapter 4 or pursuant to Chapter 5 (commencing with Section 485.010).
 (2) Two days, in cases not described in paragraph (1).
(c) Unless some other disposition is agreed upon by the plaintiff and the defendant, the levying officer shall take the farm products or inventory into exclusive custody at the earlier of the following times:
 (1) At any time the defendant objects to placement of a keeper in charge of the business.
 (2) At the conclusion of the applicable period prescribed by subdivision (b).
(d) A defendant described in paragraph (1) of subdivision (b) may claim an exemption pursuant to subdivision (b) of Section 487.020 by following the procedure set forth in subdivision (c) of Section 482.100 except that the requirement of showing changed circumstances under subdivision (a) of Section 482.100 does not apply. Upon a showing that the property is exempt pursuant to subdivision (b) of Section 487.020, the court shall order the release of the exempt property and may make such further order as the court deems appropriate to protect against frustration of the collection of the plaintiff's claim. The order may permit the plaintiff to attach farm products or inventory of the going business and proceeds or after-acquired property, or both, by filing pursuant to Section 488.405 and may provide reasonable restrictions on the disposition of the property previously attached.
(e) This section does not apply to the placement of a keeper in a business for the purpose of attaching tangible personal property consisting solely of money or equivalent proceeds of sales, which shall be conducted in the same manner as provided in Section 700.070.
Amended by Stats. 1996, Ch. 1159, Sec. 10. Effective January 1, 1997.

Section 488.405 - Alternative method to attach farm products or inventory

(a) This section provides an alternative method of attaching farm products or inventory of a going business in the possession or under the control of the defendant, but this section does not apply to property described in Section 488.325. This section applies if the plaintiff instructs the levying officer to attach the farm products or inventory under this section.
(b) To attach under this section farm products or inventory of a going business in the possession or under the control of the defendant, the levying officer shall file a notice of attachment with the Secretary of State.
(c) Except as provided in subdivisions (d) and (e), the filing of the notice of attachment gives the plaintiff an attachment lien on all of the following:
 (1) The farm products or inventory described in the notice.
 (2) Identifiable cash proceeds (as that term is used in Section 9315 of the Commercial Code).
 (3) If permitted by the writ of attachment or court order, after-acquired property.
(d) The attachment lien created by the filing of the notice of attachment under this section does not extend to either of the following:
 (1) A vehicle or vessel required to be registered with the Department of Motor Vehicles or a mobilehome or commercial coach required to be registered pursuant to the Health and Safety Code.
 (2) The inventory of a retail merchant held for sale except to the extent that the inventory of the retail merchant consists of durable goods having a unit retail value of at least five hundred dollars ($500). For the purposes of this paragraph, "retail merchant" does not include (A) a person whose sales for resale exceeded 75 percent in dollar volume of the person's total sales of all goods during the 12 months preceding the filing of the notice of attachment or (B) a cooperative association organized pursuant to Chapter 1 (commencing with Section 54001) of Division 20 of the Food and Agricultural Code (agricultural cooperative associations) or Part 3 (commencing with Section 13200) of Division 3 of Title 1 of the Corporations Code (Fish Marketing Act).
(e) If property subject to an attachment lien under this section becomes a fixture (as defined in paragraph (41) of subdivision (a) of Section 9102 of the Commercial Code), the attachment lien under this section is extinguished.

(f) The notice of attachment shall be in the form prescribed by the Secretary of State and shall contain all of the following:
  (1) The name and mailing address of the plaintiff.
  (2) The name and last known mailing address of the defendant.
  (3) The title of the court where the action is pending and the cause and number of the action.
  (4) A description of the farm products and inventory attached.
  (5) A statement that the plaintiff has acquired an attachment lien on the described property and on identifiable cash proceeds (as that term is used in Section 9315 of the Commercial Code) and, if permitted by the writ of attachment or court order, on after-acquired property.
(g) Upon presentation of a notice of attachment under this section for filing and tender of the filing fee to the office of the Secretary of State, the notice of attachment shall be filed, marked, and indexed in the same manner as a financing statement. The fee for filing in the office of the Secretary of State is the same as the fee for filing a financing statement in the standard form.
(h) Upon the request of any person, the Secretary of State shall issue a certificate showing whether there is on file in that office on the date and hour stated therein any notice of attachment filed against the farm products or inventory of a particular person named in the request. If a notice of attachment is on file, the certificate shall state the date and hour of filing of each such notice of attachment and any notice affecting any such notice of attachment and the name and address of the plaintiff. Upon request, the Secretary of State shall furnish a copy of any notice of attachment or notice affecting a notice of attachment. The certificate shall be issued as part of a combined certificate pursuant to Section 9528 of the Commercial Code, and the fee for the certificate and copies shall be in accordance with that section.
(i) The fee for filing, indexing, and furnishing filing data for a notice of extension of attachment is the same as the fee for a continuation statement under Section 9525 of the Commercial Code. The fee for filing, indexing, and furnishing filing data for a notice of release of attachment is the same as the fee for a statement of release under Section 9525 of the Commercial Code.
Amended by Stats 2021 ch 124 (AB 938),s 8, eff. 1/1/2022.
EFFECTIVE 7/1/2001. Amended October 10, 1999 (Bill Number: SB 45) (Chapter 991).

Section 488.415 - To attach personal property used in dwelling
To attach personal property used as a dwelling, the levying officer shall comply with Section 700.080.
Added by Stats. 1982, Ch. 1198, Sec. 50. Operative July 1, 1983, by Sec. 70 of Ch. 1198.

Section 488.425 - Certificate of ownership or certificate of title still in effect
If a vehicle or vessel is attached and a certificate of ownership has been issued by the Department of Motor Vehicles for the vehicle or vessel and the certificate of ownership is still in effect, or if a mobilehome or commercial coach is attached and a certificate of title has been issued by the Department of Housing and Community Development for the mobilehome or commercial coach and the certificate of title is still in effect, the levying officer shall comply with Section 700.090.
Added by Stats. 1982, Ch. 1198, Sec. 50. Operative July 1, 1983, by Sec. 70 of Ch. 1198.

Section 488.435 - To attach chattel paper
(a) To attach chattel paper, the levying officer shall comply with Section 700.100.
(b) In addition to any other rights created by a levy on chattel paper, the levy creates a lien on the defendant's rights in specific goods subject to the chattel paper.
Added by Stats. 1982, Ch. 1198, Sec. 50. Operative July 1, 1983, by Sec. 70 of Ch. 1198.

Section 488.440 - To attach instrument
To attach an instrument, the levying officer shall comply with Section 700.110.
Added by Stats. 1982, Ch. 1198, Sec. 50. Operative July 1, 1983, by Sec. 70 of Ch. 1198.

Section 488.445 - To attach negotiable document of title
To attach a negotiable document of title, the levying officer shall comply with Section 700.120.
Added by Stats. 1982, Ch. 1198, Sec. 50. Operative July 1, 1983, by Sec. 70 of Ch. 1198.

Section 488.450 - To attach security
To attach a security, the levying officer shall comply with Section 8112 of the Commercial Code. The legal process referred to in Section 8112 of the Commercial Code means the legal process required by the state in which the chief executive office of the issuer of the security is located and, where that state is California, means personal service by the levying officer of a copy of the writ of attachment and notice of attachment on the person who is to be served.
Amended by Stats. 1996, Ch. 497, Sec. 1.5. Effective January 1, 1997.

Section 488.455 - To attach deposit account
(a) Subject to Sections 488.465 and 684.115, to attach a deposit account, the levying officer shall personally serve a copy of the writ of attachment and a notice of attachment on the financial institution with which the deposit account is maintained.
(b) The attachment lien that arises upon service of a writ of attachment and notice of attachment reaches only amounts in a deposit account at the time of service on the financial institution, including the amount of any deposit not yet finally collected, unless the deposit is returned unpaid to the financial institution.
(c) The levying officer shall serve a copy of the writ of attachment and a notice of attachment on any third person in whose name any deposit account described therein stands. That service shall be made personally or by mail as follows:
  (1) At the time of levy or promptly thereafter, if the party seeking the levy informs the levying officer of that person and his, her, or its residence or business address.
  (2) Promptly following the levying officer's receipt of a garnishee's memorandum if service was not accomplished pursuant to paragraph (1), if the garnishee's memorandum identifies that person and his, her, or its residence or business address.
(d) The financial institution shall not honor a withdrawal request or a check or other order for the payment of money from the deposit account if presentation of that withdrawal request or item to the financial institution occurs during the time the attachment lien is in effect unless, following that withdrawal or payment, sufficient funds are available to cover the levy. For these purposes, a withdrawal from the deposit account to cover the financial institution's standard fee or charge for processing the levy shall not be considered a payment of money from the account in violation of this subdivision.
(e) During the time the attachment lien is in effect, the financial institution is not liable to any person for any of the following:
  (1) Performance of the duties of a garnishee under the levy.
  (2) Nonpayment of a check or other order for the payment or transfer of money drawn or presented against the deposit account if the nonpayment is pursuant to the requirements of subdivision (d).
  (3) Refusal to pay a withdrawal from the deposit account if the refusal is pursuant to the requirements of subdivision (d).
(f) For the purposes of this section, none of the following is a third person in whose name the deposit account stands:
  (1) A person who is only a person named as the beneficiary of a Totten trust account.
  (2) A person who is only a payee designated in a pay-on-death provision in an account pursuant to Section 18318.5 of the Financial Code or Section 5140 of the Probate Code, or other similar provision.

(3) A person who is only acting in a representative or custodial capacity with respect to benefits paid or payable by the United States government. Rather, accounts maintained by the representative or custodian shall be deemed to stand in that beneficiary's name, and the amounts therein shall be covered by a levy against that beneficiary.

(g) For purposes of this section, final payment of a deposit shall be deemed to have occurred in accordance with Section 4215 or 11210 of the Commercial Code or with automated clearinghouse or Federal Reserve System rule, regulation, operating circular, or similar governing document, as applicable to the deposit. If, for any reason, a deposit is returned by the financial institution upon which it is drawn, that deposit shall not be deemed finally collected for purposes of this subdivision regardless of any later payment by the financial institution upon which the deposit is drawn.

(h) When a deposit account has been attached, as an alternative to paying the amount of the deposit account that is attached to the levying officer as required by Section 488.600, the financial institution may continue to hold the deposit account until the deposit account is levied upon after judgment in the action or is earlier released, the deposit account to be held in one of the following manners:

(1) If the entire deposit account is attached, the financial institution may hold the deposit account on the terms applicable before the attachment, subject to the requirements of subdivision (d).

(2) If less than the entire deposit account is attached:

(A) With the consent of the defendant, and any third person in whose name the deposit account stands, the financial institution may hold in the deposit account on the same terms an amount larger than the attached amount as necessary to avoid a penalty or a reduction of the rate of interest.

(B) If the defendant, and any third person in whose name the deposit account stands, do not consent as provided in subparagraph (A), the financial institution may hold the attached amount on the same terms affecting the deposit account before the attachment, subject to the requirements of subdivision (d).

(3) The financial institution may hold the attached deposit account in any other manner agreed upon by the plaintiff, the defendant, and any third person in whose name the deposit account stands.

(i) Subdivision (h) does not prevent a financial institution that is holding an attached deposit account as provided in subdivision (h) from paying the attached amount to the levying officer before the time the financial institution otherwise is required to pay the amount under subdivision (h).

Amended by Stats 2012 ch 484 (AB 2364),s 2, eff. 1/1/2013.
Amended by Stats 2003 ch 110 (AB 690),s 1, eff. 1/1/2004.
Amended by Stats 2002 ch 664 (AB 3034),s 47, eff. 1/1/2003.

Section 488.460 - To attach property in safe-deposit box

(a) Subject to Sections 488.465 and 684.115, to attach property in a safe-deposit box, the levying officer shall personally serve a copy of the writ of attachment and a notice of attachment on the financial institution with which the safe-deposit box is maintained.

(b) At the time of levy or promptly thereafter, the levying officer shall serve a copy of the writ of attachment and a notice of attachment on any third person in whose name the safe-deposit box stands.

(c) During the time the attachment lien is in effect, the financial institution may not permit the removal of any of the contents of the safe-deposit box except as directed by the levying officer.

(d) Upon receipt of a garnishee's memorandum from the financial institution, as required by Section 488.610, indicating a safe-deposit box is under levy, the levying officer shall promptly mail a written notice to the judgment creditor demanding an additional fee as required by Section 26723 of the Government Code, plus the costs to open the safe-deposit box and seize and store the contents. The levying officer shall release the levy on the safe-deposit box if the plaintiff does not pay the required fee, plus costs, within three business days plus the extended time period specified in subdivision (a) of Section 1013 for service by mail by the levying officer.

(e) The levying officer may first give the person in whose name the safe-deposit box stands an opportunity to open the safe-deposit box to permit the removal pursuant to the attachment of the attached property. The financial institution may refuse to permit the forcible opening of the safe-deposit box to permit the removal of the attached property unless the plaintiff or levying officer pays in advance the cost of forcibly opening the safe-deposit box and of repairing any damage caused thereby.

(f) During the time the attachment lien is in effect, the financial institution is not liable to any person for any of the following:

(1) Performance of the duties of a garnishee under the attachment.

(2) Refusal to permit access to the safe-deposit box by the person in whose name it stands.

(3) Removal of any of the contents of the safe-deposit box pursuant to the attachment.

(g) If the levying officer removes any property from the safe-deposit box to satisfy the levy, but allows other property to remain in the safe-deposit box, the attachment lien is released automatically with respect to any property that remains in the safe-deposit box.

Amended by Stats 2012 ch 484 (AB 2364),s 3, eff. 1/1/2013.
Amended by Stats 2003 ch 888 (AB 394),s 1, eff. 1/1/2004.

Section 488.465 - Deposit account or safe-deposit box standing in name of person other than defendant

(a) Except as provided in subdivision (b), a deposit account or safe-deposit box standing in the name of a person other than the defendant, either alone or together with other third persons, is not subject to levy under Section 488.455 or 488.460 unless the levy is authorized by court order. The levying officer shall serve a copy of the court order on the third person at the time the copy of the writ of attachment and the notice of attachment are served on the third person.

(b) A court order is not required as a prerequisite to levy on a deposit account or safe-deposit box standing in the name of any of the following:

(1) The defendant, whether alone or together with third persons.

(2) The defendant's spouse, whether alone or together with other third persons. An affidavit showing that the person in whose name the account stands is the defendant's spouse shall be delivered to the financial institution at the time of levy.

(3) A fictitious business name if an unexpired fictitious business name statement filed pursuant to Chapter 5 (commencing with Section 17900) of Part 3 of Division 7 of the Business and Professions Code lists as the persons doing business under the fictitious business name either (A) the defendant or (B) the defendant's spouse or (C) the defendant and the defendant's spouse, but does not list any other person. A copy of a fictitious business name statement, certified as provided in Section 17926 of the Business and Professions Code, that satisfies these requirements shall be delivered to the financial institution at the time of levy and, if a person other than the defendant is listed in the statement, an affidavit showing that the other person is the defendant's spouse shall also be delivered to the financial institution at the time of levy.

(c) In any case where a deposit account in the name of a person other than the defendant, whether alone or together with the defendant, is levied upon, the financial institution shall not pay to the levying officer the amount levied upon until being notified to do so by the levying officer. The levying officer may not require the financial institution to pay the amount levied upon until the expiration of 15 days after service of notice of attachment on the third person.

Repealed and added by Stats. 1984, Ch. 538, Sec. 6.3.

Section 488.470 - To attach account receivable or general intangible

(a) Unless another method of attachment is provided by this article, to attach an account receivable or general intangible, the levying officer shall personally serve a copy of the writ of attachment and a notice of attachment on the account debtor.

(b) If an attachment is made under subdivision (a) and payments on the account receivable or general intangible are made to a person other than the defendant (whether pursuant to a security agreement, assignment for collection, or otherwise), the levying officer shall, if so instructed by the plaintiff, personally serve a copy of the writ of attachment and a notice of attachment on such third person. Service of the copy of the writ and notice of attachment on the third person is an attachment of any amounts owed to the defendant by the third person.

Added by Stats. 1982, Ch. 1198, Sec. 50. Operative July 1, 1983, by Sec. 70 of Ch. 1198.

Section 488.475 - Attachment of property subject of pending action or special proceeding

(a) The following property may be attached pursuant to this article notwithstanding that the property levied upon is the subject of a pending action or special proceeding:

(1) Real property.

(2) Growing crops, timber to be cut, or minerals or the like (including oil and gas) to be extracted or accounts receivable resulting from the sale thereof at the wellhead or minehead.

(3) Tangible personal property in the possession or under the control of the defendant or in the custody of a levying officer.

(4) The interest of a defendant in personal property in the estate of a decedent, whether the interest arises by testate or intestate succession.

(b) Except as provided in subdivision (a), attachment of property that is the subject of an action or special proceeding pending at the time of the attachment is not effective.

(c) If attachment is attempted but is ineffective under subdivision (b) and the levying officer has requested a garnishee's memorandum under Section 488.610 in connection with the ineffective attachment, the garnishee's memorandum shall include the following information in addition to that required by Section 488.610:

(1) A statement that the attachment of the property is not effective because the property is the subject of a pending action or special proceeding.

(2) The title of the court and the cause and number of the pending action or proceeding.

(d) For the purpose of this section, an action or proceeding is pending from the time the action or proceeding is commenced until judgment has been entered and the time for appeal has expired or, if an appeal is filed, until the appeal has been finally determined.

(e) Nothing in this section affects or limits the right of the plaintiff to obtain a lien pursuant to Article 3 (commencing with Section 491.410) of Chapter 11.

Added by Stats. 1982, Ch. 1198, Sec. 50. Operative July 1, 1983, by Sec. 70 of Ch. 1198.

Section 488.480 - To attach final money judgment

(a) As used in this section, "final money judgment" means a money judgment after the time for appeal from the judgment has expired or, if an appeal is filed, after the appeal has been finally determined.

(b) To attach a final money judgment, the levying officer shall file a copy of the writ of attachment and a notice of attachment with the clerk of the court that entered the final money judgment. The court clerk shall endorse upon the judgment a statement of the existence of the attachment lien and the time it was created. If an abstract of the judgment is issued, it shall include a statement of the attachment lien in favor of the plaintiff.

(c) At the time of levy or promptly thereafter, the levying officer shall serve a copy of the writ of attachment and a notice of attachment on the judgment debtor obligated to pay the final money judgment attached.

Amended by Stats. 1984, Ch. 538, Sec. 6.5.

Section 488.485 - To attach defendant's interest in property of estate of decedent

(a) To attach the interest of the defendant in personal property in the estate of a decedent, whether the interest arises by testate or intestate succession, the levying officer shall personally serve a copy of the writ of attachment and a notice of attachment on the personal representative of the decedent. The attachment does not impair the powers of the representative over the property for the purposes of administration.

(b) The personal representative shall report the attachment to the court in which the estate is being administered when any petition for distribution is filed. If a decree orders distribution to the defendant, the court making the decree shall order the attached property to be deliverd to the levying officer. The property may not be delivered to the levying officer until the decree distributing the propety has become final. To the extent the property delivered to the levying officer is not necessary to satisfy the attachment, it shall be released to the defendant.

(c) Promptly after the property is delivered to the levying officer pursuant to subdivision (b), the levying officer shall serve a notice describing the property on the defendant. Notwithstanding Sections 484.070, 484.350, 484.530, and 485.610, a claim of exemption for the property described in the notice may be made within 10 days after the notice was served on the defendant.

Added by Stats. 1982, Ch. 1198, Sec. 50. Operative July 1, 1983, by Sec. 70 of Ch. 1198.

Article 3 - LIEN OF ATTACHMENT

Section 488.500 - Generally

(a) A levy on property under a writ of attachment creates an attachment lien on the property from the time of levy until the expiration of the time provided by Section 488.510.

(b) Except as provided in subdivisions (c) and (d), if property subject to an attachment lien is transferred or encumbered, the property transferred or encumbered remains subject to the lien after the transfer or encumbrance to the same extent that the property would remain subject to an execution lien pursuant to Sections 697.720 to 697.750, inclusive.

(c) Except as otherwise provided in this title, if equipment is attached pursuant to Section 488.375 or farm products or inventory is attached pursuant to Section 488.405, the attachment lien on the property covered by the attachment lien has the same force and effect as a judgment lien on personal property created at the same time would have pursuant to Sections 697.590 to 697.620, inclusive.

(d) If equipment consisting of a vehicle, vessel, mobilehome, or commercial coach is attached pursuant to Section 488.385, the attachment lien on the specified property does not affect the rights of a person who is a bona fide purchaser or encumbrancer and obtains possession of both the property and its certificate of ownership issued by the Department of Motor Vehicles or its certificate of title or registration card issued by the Department of Housing and Community Development. If the levying officer obtains possession of the certificate of ownership or certificate of title or registration card, the attachment lien has the priority of the lien of a lien creditor under Sections 9317 and 9323 of the Commercial Code as of the time possession is obtained by the levying officer. If the levying officer does not obtain possession of the certificate of ownership or certificate of title or registration card, the attachment lien has the same force and effect as an unperfected security interest that attached at the same time as the notice of attachment was filed.

(e) If an attachment lien is created on property that is subject to the lien of a temporary protective order or a lien under Article 1 (commencing with Section 491.110) of Chapter 11, the priority of the attachment lien relates back to the date the earlier lien was created. Nothing in this subdivision affects priorities or rights of third persons established while the lien of the temporary protective order or the lien under Article 1 (commencing with Section 491.110) of Chapter 11 was in effect as determined under the law governing the effect of such lien.

EFFECTIVE 7/1/2001. Amended October 10, 1999 (Bill Number: SB 45) (Chapter 991).

Section 488.510 - Release from operation of attachment at expiration of 3 years from date of writ's issuance; extension

(a) Unless sooner released or discharged, any attachment shall cease to be of any force or effect, and the property levied upon shall be released from the operation of the attachment, at the expiration of three years from the date of issuance of the writ of attachment under which the levy was made.

(b) Notwithstanding subdivision (a), upon motion of the plaintiff, made not less than 10 or more than 60 days before the expiration of the three-year period and upon notice of not less than five days to the defendant whose property is attached, the court in which the action is pending may, by order filed prior to the expiration of the period and for good cause, extend the time of the attachment for a period not exceeding one year from the date on which the attachment would otherwise expire.

(c) The levying officer shall serve notice of the order upon any person holding property pursuant to an attachment and shall record or file the notice in any office where the writ and notice of attachment are recorded or filed prior to the expiration of the period described in subdivision (a) or any extension thereof. Where the attached property is real property, the plaintiff or the plaintiff's attorney, instead of the levying officer, may record the required notice.

(d) Any attachment may be extended from time to time in the manner prescribed in this section, but the maximum period of the attachment, including the extensions, shall not exceed eight years from the date of issuance of the writ of attachment under which the levy of attachment was made.

(e) The death of the defendant whose property is attached does not terminate the attachment.

Repealed and added by Stats. 1982, Ch. 1198, Sec. 50. Operative July 1, 1983, by Sec. 70 of Ch. 1198.

Article 4 - DUTIES AND LIABILITIES OF THIRD PERSONS AFTER LEVY

Section 488.600 - Generally

(a) Sections 701.010, 701.020, 701.040, 701.050, 701.060, and 701.070 prescribe duties and liabilities of a third person under a levy made under this title.

(b) For the purposes of this section, references in Sections 701.010, 701.020, 701.040, 701.050, and 701.060 to:

(1) "Amount required to satisfy the judgment" shall be deemed references to the amount required to satisfy the amount to be secured by the attachment.

(2) "Execution lien" or "lien" shall be deemed references to the attachment lien.

(3) "Judgment creditor" shall be deemed references to the plaintiff.

(4) "Judgment debtor" shall be deemed references to the defendant.

(5) "Levy" shall be deemed references to levy of attachment.

(6) "Notice of levy" shall be deemed references to notice of attachment.

(7) "Release" of property shall be deemed references to release of property pursuant to this title.

(8) "Satisfaction or discharge of the judgment" shall be deemed references to the satisfaction or termination of the attachment.

(9) "Writ" or "writ of execution" shall be deemed references to a writ of attachment.

(c) For the purposes of this section, references in Section 701.070 to:

(1) "Levy" shall be deemed references to levy of attachment.

(2) "Notice of the levy" shall be deemed references to notice of attachment.

Amended by Stats 2012 ch 484 (AB 2364),s 4, eff. 1/1/2013.

Section 488.610 - Garnishee's memorandum by third person

(a) At the time of service of a copy of the writ of attachment and a notice of attachment on a third person, the levying officer shall request the third person to give the levying officer a garnishee's memorandum containing the information required by this section. Within 10 days after the request is made, the third person shall mail or deliver the garnishee's memorandum to the levying officer whether or not the levy is effective.

(b) The garnishee's memorandum shall be executed under oath and shall contain the following information:

(1) A description of any property of the defendant sought to be attached that is not delivered to the levying officer and the reason for not delivering the property.

(2) A statement of the amount and terms of any obligation to the defendant sought to be attached that is due and payable and is not paid to the levying officer and the reason for not paying the obligation.

(3) A statement of the amount and terms of any obligation to the defendant sought to be attached that is not due and payable at the time of levy.

(4) A description of claims and rights of other persons to the attached property or obligation that are known to the third person and the names and addresses of those other persons.

(5) A statement that the garnishee holds neither any property nor any obligations in favor of the judgment debtor.

(c) If a garnishee's memorandum is received from the third person, the levying officer shall promptly mail or deliver a copy of the memorandum to the plaintiff and attach the original to the writ when it is returned to the court. If a garnishee's memorandum is not received from the third person, the levying officer shall so state in the return.

(d) Except as provided in subdivisions (e) and (f), if a third person does not give the levying officer a garnishee's memorandum within the time provided in subdivision (a) or does not provide complete information, the third person may, in the court's discretion, be required to pay the costs and reasonable attorney's fees incurred in any proceedings to obtain the information required in the garnishee's memorandum.

(e) Notwithstanding subdivision (a), where a deposit account or property in a safe-deposit box is attached, the financial institution need not give a garnishee's memorandum to the levying officer if the financial institution fully complies with the levy and, if a garnishee's memorandum is required, the garnishee's memorandum need provide information with respect only to property which is carried on the records available at the office or branch where the levy is made, unless the levy has been served at a central location designated by a financial institution in accordance with Section 684.115, in which case the garnishee's memorandum shall apply to all offices and branches of the financial institution except to the extent acceptance of the levy at that central location is limited pursuant to paragraph (3) of subdivision (a) of Section 684.115.

(f) Notwithstanding subdivision (a), the third person need not give a garnishee's memorandum to the levying officer if both of the following conditions are satisfied:

(1) The third person has delivered to the levying officer all of the property sought to be attached.

(2) The third person has paid to the levying officer the amount due at the time of levy on any obligation to the defendant that was attached and there is no additional amount that thereafter will become payable on the obligation levied upon.

Amended by Stats 2012 ch 484 (AB 2364),s 5, eff. 1/1/2013.

Section 488.620 - No liability for disclosure of information in memorandum

A third person who gives a garnishee's memorandum pursuant to this title is not liable to any person for the disclosure in the garnishee's memorandum of any information contained in the garnishee's memorandum.

Added by Stats. 1983, Ch. 155, Sec. 8.3. Effective June 30, 1983. Operative July 1, 1983, by Sec. 32 of Ch. 155.

Article 5 - MANAGEMENT AND DISPOSITION OF ATTACHED PROPERTY

Section 488.700 - Order to preserve value of property; sale of perishable property; daily fee if receiver appointed

(a) If property has been or is sought to be attached, the court may appoint a receiver or order the levying officer to take any action the court orders that is necessary to preserve the value of the property, including but not limited to selling the property, if the court determines that the property is perishable or will greatly deteriorate or greatly depreciate in value or that for some other reason the interests of the parties will be best served by the order. An order may be made under this subdivision upon application of the plaintiff, the defendant, or a person who has filed a third-party claim pursuant to Division 4 (commencing with Section 720.010) of Title 9. The application shall be made on noticed motion if the court so directs or a court rule so requires. Otherwise, the application may be made ex parte.

(b) If the levying officer determines that property is extremely perishable or will greatly deteriorate or greatly depreciate in value before a court order pursuant to subdivision (a) could be obtained, the levying officer may take any action necessary to preserve the value of the property or may sell the property. The levying officer is not liable for a determination made in good faith under this subdivision.

(c) Except as otherwise provided by order of the court, a sale of the property pursuant to this section shall be made in the manner provided by Article 6 (commencing with Section 701.510) of Chapter 3 of Division 2 of Title 9 and the proceeds shall be deposited in the court to abide the judgment in the action. Notwithstanding subdivisions (b) and (d) of Section 701.530, notice of sale shall be posted and served at a reasonable time before sale, considering the character and condition of the property.

(d) If a receiver is appointed, the court shall fix the daily fee of the receiver and may order the plaintiff to pay the fees and expenses of the receiver in advance or may direct that the whole or any part of the fees and expenses be paid from the proceeds of any sale of the property. Except as otherwise provided in this section, the provisions of Chapter 5 (commencing with Section 564) and Chapter 5a (commencing with Section 571) of Title 7 govern the appointment, qualifications, powers, rights, and duties of a receiver appointed under this section.

Added by Stats. 1982, Ch. 1198, Sec. 50. Operative July 1, 1983, by Sec. 70 of Ch. 1198.

Section 488.710 - Duty to endorse and present instrument for payment

(a) As used in this section, "instrument" means a check, draft, money order, or other order for the withdrawal of money from a financial institution, the United States, any state, or any public entity within any state.

(b) If an instrument is payable to the defendant on demand and comes into the possession of a levying officer pursuant to this title, the levying officer shall promptly endorse and present the instrument for payment.

(c) The levying officer shall endorse the instrument by writing on the instrument (1) the name of the defendant, (2) the name and official title of the levying officer, and (3) the title of the court and the cause in which the writ was issued. The endorsement is as valid as if the instrument were endorsed by the defendant. No financial institution or public entity on which the instrument is drawn is liable to any person for payment of the instrument to the levying officer rather than to the defendant by reason of the endorsement. No levying officer is liable by reason of endorsing, presenting, and obtaining payment of the instrument. The funds or credit resulting from the payment of the instrument shall be held by the levying officer subject to the lien of attachment.

(d) If it appears from the face of the instrument that it has been tendered to the defendant in satisfaction of a claim or demand and that endorsement of the instrument is considered a release and satisfaction by the defendant of the claim or demand, the levying officer shall not endorse the instrument unless the defendant has first endorsed it to the levying officer. If the defendant does not endorse the instrument to the levying officer, the levying officer shall hold the instrument for 30 days and is not liable to the defendant or to any other person for delay in presenting it for payment. At the end of the 30-day holding period, the levying officer shall return the instrument to the maker.

Added by Stats. 1982, Ch. 1198, Sec. 50. Operative July 1, 1983, by Sec. 70 of Ch. 1198.

Section 488.720 - Motion to release attachment to extent value of defendant's interest exceeds amount necessary to satisfy amount secured

(a) The defendant may apply by noticed motion to the court in which the action is pending or in which the judgment in the action was entered for an order releasing the attachment of property to the extent that the value of the defendant's interest in the property clearly exceeds the amount necessary to satisfy the amount to be secured by the attachment.

(b) The notice of motion shall state the grounds on which the motion is based and shall be accompanied by an affidavit supporting any factual issues raised and points and authorities supporting any legal issues raised.

(c) At the hearing on the motion, the court shall determine the value of the defendant's interest in the property and order the release of the attachment of the property to the extent that the value of the defendant's interest in the property attached clearly exceeds the amount necessary to satisfy the amount to be secured by the attachment. After entry of judgment in the action in which the property was attached, the court shall also take into consideration in determining whether the attachment is clearly excessive the value of any property not attached in the action that (1) has been levied upon pursuant to a writ of execution issued to satisfy the judgment in the action or (2) otherwise has been sought to be applied to the satisfaction of the judgment in the action.

(d) The court's determinations shall be made upon the basis of the pleadings and other papers in the record; but, upon good cause shown, the court may receive and consider at the hearing additional evidence, oral or documentary, and additional points and authorities, or it may continue the hearing for the production of the additional evidence or points and authorities.

Added by Stats. 1982, Ch. 1198, Sec. 50. Operative July 1, 1983, by Sec. 70 of Ch. 1198.

Section 488.730 - Release of attach property

(a) The levying officer shall release attached property when the levying officer receives a written direction to release the property from the plaintiff's attorney of record or, if the plaintiff does not have an attorney of record, from the plaintiff or when the levying officer receives a certified copy of a court order for release or when otherwise required to release the property. The release extinguishes any attachment lien in favor of the plaintiff on the property released.

(b) If the property to be released has been taken into custody under the levy, it shall be released to the person from whom it was taken unless otherwise ordered by the court. If the person does not claim the property to be released, the levying officer shall retain custody of the property and shall serve on the person a notice of where possession of the property may be obtained. If the person does not claim the property within 30 days after the notice is served, the levying officer shall sell the property (other than cash which does not have a value exceeding its face value) in the manner provided by Article 6 (commencing with Section 701.510) of Chapter 3 of Division 2 of Title 9. The levying officer shall deposit the proceeds of sale and cash, after first deducting the levying officer's costs, with the county treasurer of the county where the property is located payable to the order of the person. If the amount deposited is not claimed by the person or the legal representative of the person within five years after the deposit is made, by making application to the treasurer or other official designated by the county, it shall be paid into the general fund of the county.

(c) If the property to be released has not been taken into custody under the levy, the levying officer shall release the attachment by issuing a written notice of release and serving it on the person who was served with a copy of the writ and a notice of attachment to create the lien.

(d) If the property to be released was levied upon by recording or filing a copy of the writ and a notice of attachment, the levying officer shall record or file a written notice of release in the same office. If the notice of attachment had been filed with the Secretary of State, any release shall have the effect prescribed in Section 697.650.

(e) The levying officer is not liable for releasing an attachment in accordance with this section and no other person is liable for acting in conformity with the release.

Amended by Stats. 1989, Ch. 445, Sec. 1.

Section 488.740 - Delivery of money and property to person from whom collected or taken

If the defendant recovers judgment against the plaintiff and no timely motion for vacation of judgment or for judgment notwithstanding the verdict or for a new trial is filed and served and is pending and no appeal is perfected and undertaking executed and filed as provided in Section 921, any undertaking received from the defendant in the action, all the proceeds of sales and money collected by the levying officer, and all the

property attached remaining in the levying officer's hands shall be delivered to the person from whom it was collected or taken, unless otherwise ordered by the court; and the court shall order the discharge of any attachment made in the action and the release of any property held thereunder.
Added by Stats. 1982, Ch. 1198, Sec. 50. Operative July 1, 1983, by Sec. 70 of Ch. 1198.

Chapter 9 - UNDERTAKINGS
Article 1 - GENERAL PROVISIONS

Section 489.010 - Applicability of Bond and Undertaking Law
The Bond and Undertaking Law (Chapter 2 (commencing with Section 995. 010) of Title 14) applies to a bond given pursuant to this title, except to the extent this title prescribes a different rule or is inconsistent.
Added by Stats. 1985, Ch. 41, Sec. 2.

Section 489.060 - Presentment and filing
(a) Except as provided in subdivision (b), all undertakings given pursuant to this title shall be presented to a proper court for approval and upon approval shall be filed with the court in which the action is pending.
(b) If the surety on the undertaking is an admitted surety insurer, the undertaking is not required to be approved by the court.
Amended by Stats. 1982, Ch. 517, Sec. 107.

Section 489.130 - Plaintiff's failure to increase amount pursuant to court order not wrongful attachment
Where the court orders the amount of the undertaking increased pursuant to Section 489.220 or 489.410, the plaintiff's failure to increase the amount of the undertaking is not a wrongful attachment within the meaning of Section 490.010.
Added by Stats. 1976, Ch. 437.

Article 2 - UNDERTAKINGS TO OBTAIN WRIT OF ATTACHMENT OR PROTECTIVE ORDER

Section 489.210 - Undertaking filed before issuance of writ or order
Before issuance of a writ of attachment, a temporary protective order, or an order under subdivision (b) of Section 491.415, the plaintiff shall file an undertaking to pay the defendant any amount the defendant may recover for any wrongful attachment by the plaintiff in the action.
Amended by Stats. 1984, Ch. 538, Sec. 7.

Section 489.220 - Amount
(a) Except as provided in subdivision (b), the amount of an undertaking filed pursuant to this article shall be ten thousand dollars ($10,000).
(b) If, upon objection to the undertaking, the court determines that the probable recovery for wrongful attachment exceeds the amount of the undertaking, it shall order the amount of the undertaking increased to the amount it determines to be the probable recovery for wrongful attachment if it is ultimately determined that the attachment was wrongful.
Amended by Stats 2001 ch 812 (AB 223), s 3, eff. 1/1/2002.

Section 489.230 - Statement in notice that undertaking filed
(a) The notice of attachment shall include a statement, in a form adopted by the Judicial Council, advising the defendant that the undertaking has been filed and informing the defendant of the right to object to the undertaking.
(b) The form for the temporary protective order shall include a statement comparable to the one required by subdivision (a).
Amended by Stats. 1982, Ch. 517, Sec. 114.

Article 3 - UNDERTAKING TO OBTAIN RELEASE OF ATTACHMENT OR PROTECTIVE ORDER

Section 489.310 - Generally
(a) Whenever a writ is issued, a defendant who has appeared in the action may apply by noticed motion to the court in which the action is pending for an order permitting the defendant to substitute an undertaking for any of his property in the state which has been or is subject to being attached.
(b) In a case (1) where the defendant applies for an order to release a portion of property which has been attached or (2) where the defendant applies for an order preventing the attachment of property and the amount of the undertaking to be given is less than the amount to be secured by the attachment, the application shall include a statement, executed under oath, describing the property to be so released or so protected from attachment.
(c) The defendant shall file an undertaking to pay the plaintiff the value of the property released not exceeding the amount of any judgment which may be recovered by the plaintiff in the action against the defendant. The amount of the undertaking filed pursuant to this section shall be equal to the lesser of (1) the value of the property attached or prevented from being attached or (2) the amount specified by the writ to be secured by the attachment. The court shall issue such order upon the condition that a sufficient undertaking be filed.
(d) Where an action is against more than one defendant, any defendant may make such application. The filing of an undertaking by such defendant shall not subject him to any demand against any other defendant; however, the levying officer shall not be prevented thereby from attaching, or be obliged to release from attachment, any property of any other defendant. Where all the defendants do not join in the application, the application shall include a statement, executed under oath, describing the character of the defendant's title to the property and the manner in which the defendant acquired such title and stating whether any other defendant who has not joined in the application has an interest in the property. Where two or more defendants have an interest in the same property, a joint application and undertaking shall be filed to secure the release of such property.
Amended by Stats. 1976, Ch. 437.

Section 489.320 - Order terminating temporary protective order
(a) A defendant who has been served with a temporary protective order and who has appeared in the action may apply by noticed motion to the court in which the action is pending for an order terminating the temporary protective order with respect to that defendant.
(b) The defendant shall file an undertaking to pay the plaintiff the amount of any judgment recovered by the plaintiff in the action against the defendant. The amount of the undertaking filed pursuant to this section shall be equal to the amount sought to be secured by the attachment. The court shall issue the order terminating the temporary protective order with respect to the defendant upon the condition that a sufficient undertaking be filed.
Amended by Stats. 1982, Ch. 1198, Sec. 52. Operative July 1, 1983, by Sec. 70 of Ch. 1198.

Article 4 - UNDERTAKING ON APPEAL

Section 489.410 - Generally
(a) At any time after entry of judgment in favor of the defendant and before perfection of an appeal under Section 921, upon motion of the defendant, the trial court may order an increase in the amount of the original undertaking on attachment in such amount, if any, as is justified by the detriment reasonably to be anticipated by continuing the attachment. Unless such undertaking is filed within 10 days after such order, the attachment shall be set aside and the property released therefrom.

(b) If an order increasing the undertaking is made, the amount of the undertaking on appeal required by Section 921 shall be the same as the amount fixed by the trial court in such order.

(c) Neither the pendency nor granting of a motion timely filed and served by the plaintiff for vacation of judgment or for judgment notwithstanding the verdict or for new trial shall continue an attachment in force unless an undertaking is given by the plaintiff to pay all costs and damages sustained by continuing the attachment. The undertaking may be included in the undertaking specified in Section 921. If not so included, the same procedure shall apply as in case of an undertaking pursuant to Section 921.

Added by Stats. 1974, Ch. 1516.

Section 489.420 - Release of property upon failure of respondent to timely object to undertaking

If a defendant appeals and the enforcement of the judgment against the defendant is stayed by the filing of a sufficient undertaking on appeal as provided by this code, all property of the defendant which has been attached in the action shall be released from the attachment upon the failure of the respondent to object to the undertaking within the time prescribed by statute or, if an objection is made, upon a determination that the undertaking is sufficient.

Amended by Stats. 1982, Ch. 517, Sec. 115.

Chapter 10 - LIABILITY FOR WRONGFUL ATTACHMENT

Section 490.010 - Wrongful attachment

A wrongful attachment consists of any of the following:

(a) The levy under a writ of attachment or the service of a temporary protective order in an action in which attachment is not authorized, except that it is not a wrongful attachment if both of the following are established:

(1) The levy was not authorized solely because of the prohibition of subdivision (c) of Section 483.010.

(2) The person who sold or leased, or licensed for use, the property, furnished the services, or loaned the money reasonably believed that it would not be used primarily for personal, family, or household purposes.

(b) The levy under a writ of attachment or the service of a temporary protective order in an action in which the plaintiff does not recover judgment.

(c) The levy under writ of attachment obtained pursuant to Article 3 (commencing with Section 484.510) of Chapter 4 or Chapter 5 (commencing with Section 485.010) on property exempt from attachment except where the plaintiff shows that the plaintiff reasonably believed that the property attached was not exempt from attachment.

Amended by Stats. 1982, Ch. 1198, Sec. 53. Operative July 1, 1983, by Sec. 70 of Ch. 1198.

Section 490.020 - Liability of plaintiff

(a) The liability of a plaintiff for causing a wrongful attachment under Section 490.010 includes both of the following:

(1) All damages proximately caused to the defendant by the wrongful attachment.

(2) All costs and expenses, including attorney's fees, reasonably expended in defeating the attachment.

(b) The liability of a plaintiff for wrongful attachment pursuant to Section 490.010 is limited by the amount of the undertaking.

Amended by Stats. 1982, Ch. 1198, Sec. 54. Operative July 1, 1983, by Sec. 70 of Ch. 1198.

Section 490.040 - Amount recovered offset against unsatisfied amounts

The amount of any recovery for wrongful attachment shall be offset insofar as possible against any unsatisfied amounts owed to the plaintiff by the defendant on the judgment in the action for which wrongful attachment damages are awarded.

Added by Stats. 1974, Ch. 1516.

Section 490.060 - Right to recover damages on common law theory not limited

Nothing in this chapter limits the right to recover for damages caused by an attachment or protective order on any common law theory of recovery.

Added by Stats. 1974, Ch. 1516.

Chapter 11 - ATTACHING PLAINTIFF'S MISCELLANEOUS REMEDIES

Article 1 - EXAMINATION OF THIRD PERSON

Section 491.110 - Order directing third person to appear; Service of order; lien created; failure to appear; mileage fees

(a) Upon ex parte application by the plaintiff and proof by the plaintiff by affidavit or otherwise to the satisfaction of the proper court that the plaintiff has a right to attach order and that a third person has possession or control of property in which the defendant has an interest or is indebted to the defendant in an amount exceeding two hundred fifty dollars ($250), the court shall make an order directing the third person to appear before the court, or before a referee appointed by the court, at a time and place specified in the order, to answer concerning the property or debt. The affidavit in support of the plaintiff's application may be based on the affiant's information and belief.

(b) Not less than 10 days prior to the date set for the examination, a copy of the order shall be:

(1) Served personally on the third person.

(2) Served personally or by mail on the defendant.

(c) If the property or the debt is described in the affidavit or application for an order under subdivision (a) in a manner reasonably adequate to permit it to be identified, service of the order on the third person creates a lien on the defendant's interest in the property in the third person's possession or control or on the debt owed by the third person to the defendant. The lien continues for a period of one year from the date of the order unless extended or sooner terminated by the court.

(d) The order shall contain the following statement in 14-point boldface type if printed or in capital letters if typed: "NOTICE TO PERSON SERVED. If you fail to appear at the time and place specified in this order, you may be subject to arrest and punishment for contempt of court and the court may make an order requiring you to pay the reasonable attorney's fees incurred by the plaintiff in this proceeding."

(e) The order is not effective unless, at the time it is served on the third person, the person serving the order tenders to the third person fees for the mileage necessary to be traveled from the third person's residence to the place of examination. The fees shall be in the same amount generally provided for witnesses when legally required to attend civil proceedings in the court where the examination proceeding is to be conducted.

Added by Stats. 1982, Ch. 1198, Sec. 57. Operative July 1, 1983, by Sec. 70 of Ch. 1198.

Section 491.120 - Requiring witnesses to appear and testify

In any proceeding for the examination of a third person under this article, witnesses, including the defendant, may be required to appear and testify before the court or referee in the same manner as upon the trial of an issue.

Added by Stats. 1982, Ch. 1198, Sec. 57. Operative July 1, 1983, by Sec. 70 of Ch. 1198.

Section 491.130 - Powers of referee conducting proceedings

(a) The examination proceedings authorized by this article may be conducted by a referee appointed by the court. The referee may issue, modify, or vacate an order authorized by Section 491.190, may make a protective order authorized by Section 491.180, and may issue a warrant authorized by Section 491.160, and has the same power as the court to grant adjournments, to preserve order, and to subpoena witnesses to attend the examination, but only the court that ordered the reference has power to do any of the following:

(1) Punish for contempt for disobeying an order of the referee.

(2) Make an award of attorney's fees pursuant to Section 491.160.

(3) Determine a third-party claim under Section 491.170.
(b) Only a member of the State Bar of California is eligible for appointment as a referee pursuant to this article.
(c) Nothing in subdivision (a) limits the power of a court to appoint a temporary judge pursuant to Section 21 of Article VI of the California Constitution.
Added by Stats. 1982, Ch. 1198, Sec. 57. Operative July 1, 1983, by Sec. 70 of Ch. 1198.

Section 491.140 - Appearance by corporation, partnership, association, trust, other organization served with order
(a) If a corporation, partnership, association, trust, or other organization is served with an order to appear for an examination, it shall designate to appear and be examined one or more officers, directors, managing agents, or other persons who are familiar with its property and debts.
(b) If the order to appear for an examination requires the appearance of a specified individual, the specified individual shall appear for the examination and may be accompanied by one or more officers, directors, managing agents, or other persons familiar with the property and debts of the corporation, partnership, association, trust, or other organization.
(c) If the order to appear for the examination does not require the appearance of a specified individual, the order shall advise the corporation, partnership, association, trust, or other organization of its duty to make a designation under subdivision (a).
(d) A corporation, partnership, association, trust, or other organization, whether or not a party, may appear at an examination through any authorized officer, director, or employee, whether or not the person is an attorney.
Amended by Stats. 1984, Ch. 538, Sec. 7.5.

Section 491.150 - Proper court for examination
(a) Except as otherwise provided in this section, the proper court for examination of a person under this article is the court that issued the writ of attachment.
(b) A person sought to be examined may not be required to attend an examination before a court located outside the county in which the person resides or has a place of business unless the distance from the person's place of residence or place of business to the place of examination is less than 150 miles.
(c) If a person sought to be examined does not reside or have a place of business in the county where the court that issued the writ is located, the superior court in the county where the person resides or has a place of business is a proper court for examination of the person.
(d) If the plaintiff seeks an examination of a person before a court other than the court that issued the writ, the plaintiff shall file an application that shall include all of the following:
(1) A certified copy of the complaint in the pending action.
(2) An affidavit in support of the application stating the place of residence or place of business of the person sought to be examined.
(3) Any necessary affidavit or showing for the examination as required by Section 491.110.
(4) The filing fee for a motion as provided in subdivision (a) of Section 70617 of the Government Code.
Amended by Stats 2005 ch 75 (AB 145),s 33, eff. 7/19/2005, op. 1/1/2006

Section 491.160 - Failure to appear by person served by sheriff, marshal or court appointed person; improper service
(a) If an order requiring a person to appear for an examination was served by a sheriff, marshal, a person specially appointed by the court in the order, or a registered process server, and the person fails to appear:
(1) The court may do either of the following:
(A) Pursuant to a warrant, have the person brought before the court to answer for the failure to appear and may punish the person for contempt.
(B) Issue a warrant for the arrest of the person who failed to appear as required by the court order, pursuant to Section 1993.
(2) If the person's failure to appear is without good cause, the plaintiff shall be awarded reasonable attorney's fees incurred in the examination proceeding.
(b) A person who willfully makes an improper service of an order for an examination which subsequently results in the arrest pursuant to subdivision (a) of the person who fails to appear is guilty of a misdemeanor.
Amended by Stats 2006 ch 277 (AB 2369),s 1, eff. 1/1/2007.

Section 491.170 - Third person claims interest in property adverse to defendant or denies debt
(a) Subject to subdivision (b), if a third person examined pursuant to this article claims an interest in the property adverse to the defendant or denies the debt, the court may, if the plaintiff so requests, determine the interests in the property or the existence of the debt. Such a determination is conclusive as to the plaintiff, the defendant, and the third person, but an appeal may be taken from the determination in the manner provided for appeals from the court in which the proceeding takes place. The court may grant a continuance for a reasonable time for discovery proceedings, the production of evidence, or other preparation for the hearing.
(b) The court may not make the determination provided in subdivision (a) if the third person's claim is made in good faith and any of the following conditions is satisfied:
(1) The court would not be a proper court for the trial of an independent civil action (including a creditor's suit) for the determination of the interests in the property or the existence of the debt, and the third person objects to the determination of the matter under subdivision (a).
(2) At the time an order for examination pursuant to this article is served on the third person a civil action (including a creditor's suit) is pending with respect to the interests in the property or the existence of the debt.
(3) The court determines that the interests in the property or the existence of the debt should be determined in a creditor's suit.
(c) Upon application of the plaintiff made ex parte, the court may make an order forbidding transfer of the property to the defendant or payment of the debt to the defendant until the interests in the property or the existence of the debt is determined pursuant to subdivision (a) or until a creditor's suit may be commenced and an order obtained pursuant to Section 491.340. An undertaking may be required in the discretion of the court. The court may modify or vacate the order at any time with or without a hearing on such terms as are just.
(d) Upon application of the plaintiff upon noticed motion, the court, if it determines that the defendant probably owns an interest in the property or that the debt probably is owed to the defendant, may make an order forbidding the transfer or other disposition of the property to any person or forbidding payment of the debt until the interests in the property or the existence of the debt is determined pursuant to subdivision (a) or until a creditor's suit may be commenced and an order obtained pursuant to Section 491.340. The court shall require the plaintiff to furnish an undertaking as provided in Section 529. The court may modify or vacate the order at any time after notice and hearing on such terms as are just.
Added by Stats. 1982, Ch. 1198, Sec. 57. Operative July 1, 1983, by Sec. 70 of Ch. 1198.

Section 491.180 - Protective orders
In any proceeding under this article, the court may, on motion of the person to be examined or on its own motion, make such protective orders as justice may require.
Added by Stats. 1982, Ch. 1198, Sec. 57. Operative July 1, 1983, by Sec. 70 of Ch. 1198.

Section 491.190 - Court orders at conclusion of proceeding
(a) Except as provided in subdivision (b), at the conclusion of a proceeding pursuant to this article:
(1) The court may order the defendant's interest in the property in the possession or under the control of the third person or a debt owed by the third person to the defendant to be attached in the manner and under the conditions provided by this title or to be delivered or paid to the levying officer if the levying officer has a writ of attachment permitting the attachment of the property or debt. After the property or debt has been

attached, the order may be enforced as provided in Section 491.360. The order creates a lien on the property or debt. The lien continues for a period of one year from the date of the order unless the court extends or reduces the period of the existence of the lien.

(2) If the property or debt has previously been attached, the court may make an order determining the third person's liability, and the order may be enforced as provided in Section 491.360.

(b) If a third person examined pursuant to this article claims an interest in the property adverse to the defendant or denies the debt and the court does not determine the matter as provided in subdivision (a) of Section 491.170, the court may not make an order under subdivision (a) of this section, but may make an order pursuant to subdivision (c) or (d) of Section 491.170 forbidding transfer or payment to the extent authorized by that section.

Added by Stats. 1982, Ch. 1198, Sec. 57. Operative July 1, 1983, by Sec. 70 of Ch. 1198.

Section 491.200 - Continuance of lien

A lien created under this article continues on property subject to the lien notwithstanding the transfer or encumbrance of the property subject to the lien unless the transfer or encumbrance is made to a person listed in Section 697.740.

Added by Stats. 1982, Ch. 1198, Sec. 57. Operative July 1, 1983, by Sec. 70 of Ch. 1198.

Article 2 - CREDITOR'S SUIT

Section 491.310 - Action to enforce third person liability

If a third person has possession or control of property in which the defendant has an interest or is indebted to the defendant and the property or debt has been subjected to an attachment lien, the plaintiff may bring an action against the third person to enforce the third person's liability under this title.

Added by Stats. 1982, Ch. 1198, Sec. 57. Operative July 1, 1983, by Sec. 70 of Ch. 1198.

Section 491.320 - Joinder of defendant

The defendant shall be joined in an action brought pursuant to this article but is not an indispensable party. The residence of the defendant may not be considered in the determination of proper venue unless otherwise provided by contract between the defendant and the third person.

Added by Stats. 1982, Ch. 1198, Sec. 57. Operative July 1, 1983, by Sec. 70 of Ch. 1198.

Section 491.330 - Time limits on commencement of action

(a) Except as provided in subdivision (b), an action shall be commenced pursuant to this article before the expiration of the later of the following times:

(1) The time when the defendant may bring an action against the third person concerning the property or debt.

(2) One year after creation of an attachment lien on the property or debt pursuant to this title if the lien is created at the time when the defendant may bring an action against the third person concerning the property or debt.

(b) An action may not be commenced pursuant to this article if the attachment lien is not in effect.

(c) If an action is commenced pursuant to this article within the time permitted in this section, the action may be prosecuted to judgment so long as the attachment lien or a lien of the plaintiff on the same property pursuant to Title 9 (commencing with Section 680.010) is in effect.

Added by Stats. 1982, Ch. 1198, Sec. 57. Operative July 1, 1983, by Sec. 70 of Ch. 1198.

Section 491.340 - Orders restraining third person from transferring or disposing of property

The plaintiff may apply to the court in which an action under this article is pending for either or both of the following:

(a) An order restraining the third person from transferring the attached property to the defendant or from paying the attached debt to the defendant. The order shall be made on noticed motion if the court so directs or a court rule so requires. Otherwise, the order may be made on ex parte application. The order shall remain in effect until judgment is entered in the action or until such earlier time as the court may provide in the order. An undertaking may be required in the discretion of the court. The court may modify or vacate the order at any time with or without a hearing on such terms as are just.

(b) A temporary restraining order or a preliminary injunction or both, restraining the third person from transferring to any person or otherwise disposing of the attached property, pursuant to Chapter 3 (commencing with Section 525) of Title 7, and the court may make, dissolve, and modify such orders as provided therein.

Added by Stats. 1982, Ch. 1198, Sec. 57. Operative July 1, 1983, by Sec. 70 of Ch. 1198.

Section 491.350 - No right to jury trial

There is no right to a jury trial in an action under this article.

Added by Stats. 1982, Ch. 1198, Sec. 57. Operative July 1, 1983, by Sec. 70 of Ch. 1198.

Section 491.360 - Enforcement of judgment

If the plaintiff establishes the liability of the third person, the court shall render judgment accordingly. The judgment may be enforced in the same manner as it could be enforced if it had been obtained by the defendant against the third party; but, prior to entry of judgment in favor of the plaintiff against the defendant, any money or property obtained in enforcing the judgment against the third party shall be paid or delivered into court to abide the judgment in the action of the plaintiff against the defendant or shall be held by a levying officer, or otherwise held, as ordered by the court.

Added by Stats. 1982, Ch. 1198, Sec. 57. Operative July 1, 1983, by Sec. 70 of Ch. 1198.

Section 491.370 - Costs not recovered from defendant

Costs incurred by or taxed against the plaintiff in an action under this article may not be recovered from the defendant.

Added by Stats. 1982, Ch. 1198, Sec. 57. Operative July 1, 1983, by Sec. 70 of Ch. 1198.

Article 3 - LIEN IN PENDING ACTION OR PROCEEDING

Section 491.410 - Generally

(a) If the defendant is a party to a pending action or special proceeding, the plaintiff may obtain a lien under this article, to the extent required to secure the amount to be secured by the attachment, on both of the following:

(1) Any cause of action of the defendant for money or property that is the subject of the other action or proceeding, if the money or property would be subject to attachment if the defendant prevails in the action or proceedings.

(2) The rights of the defendant to money or property under any judgment subsequently procured in the other action or proceeding, if the money or property would be subject to attachment.

(b) To obtain a lien under this article, the plaintiff shall file all of the following in the other pending action or special proceeding:

(1) A notice of lien.

(2) A copy of the right to attach order.

(3) A copy of an order permitting creation of a lien under this article made by the court that issued the right to attach order.

(c) At the time of the filing under subdivision (b) or promptly thereafter, the plaintiff shall serve on all parties who, prior thereto, have made an appearance in the other action or special proceeding a copy of the notice of lien and a statement of the date when the notice of lien was filed in the other action or special proceeding. Failure to serve all parties as required by this subdivision does not affect the lien created by the filing under subdivision (b), but the rights of a party are not affected by the lien until the party has notice of the lien.

(d) For the purpose of this article, an action or special proceeding is pending until the time for appeal from the judgment has expired or, if an appeal is filed, until the appeal has been finally determined.
Amended by Stats. 1984, Ch. 538, Sec. 8.

Section 491.415 - Application for order permitting creation of lien
(a) For the purpose of applying for a right to attach order, the defendant's cause of action that is the subject of the pending action or proceeding and the defendant's rights to money or property under a judgment procured in the action or proceeding shall be treated as property subject to attachment.
(b) At the time the plaintiff applies for a right to attach order, the plaintiff may apply for an order permitting creation of a lien under this article. If the plaintiff has already obtained a right to attach order, an application for an order permitting creation of a lien under this article may be applied for in the same manner as a writ of attachment. As a prerequisite to obtaining an order under this subdivision, the plaintiff shall file an undertaking as provided by Sections 489.210 and 489.220.
(c) The defendant may, but is not required to, claim an exemption in a proceeding initiated by the plaintiff for an order permitting creation of a lien under this article. An exemption may be claimed if the money or property sought by the defendant would be exempt from attachment should the defendant prevail in the other action or proceeding. The exemption shall be claimed and determined pursuant to this subdivision in the same manner as an exemption is claimed and determined upon application for a writ of attachment.
Added by Stats. 1984, Ch. 538, Sec. 9.

Section 491.420 - Notice of lien
The notice of lien under Section 491.410 shall contain all of the following:
(a) A statement that a lien has been created under this article and the title of the court and the cause and number of the pending action or proceeding in which the notice of lien is filed.
(b) The name and last known address of the defendant.
(c) The name and address of the plaintiff.
(d) The title of the court where the plaintiff's action against the defendant is pending and the cause and number of the action.
(e) The amount required to secure the amount to be secured by the attachment at the time the notice of lien is filed in the action or proceeding.
(f) A statement that the lien attaches to any cause of action of the defendant that is the subject of such action or proceeding and to the defendant's rights to money or property under any judgment subsequently procured in the action or proceeding.
(g) A statement that no compromise, dismissal, settlement, or satisfaction of the pending action or proceeding or any of the defendant's rights to money or property under any judgment procured therein may be entered into by or on behalf of the defendant, and that the defendant may not enforce the defendant's rights to money or property under any judgment procured in the pending action or proceeding by a writ or otherwise, unless one of the following requirements is satisfied:
   (1) The prior approval by order of the court in which the action or proceeding is pending has been obtained.
   (2) The written consent of the plaintiff has been obtained or the plaintiff has released the lien.
Added by Stats. 1982, Ch. 1198, Sec. 57. Operative July 1, 1983, by Sec. 70 of Ch. 1198.

Section 491.430 - Intervention by plaintiff in action or special proceeding
(a) The court in which the action or special proceeding subject to the lien under this article is pending may permit the plaintiff who has obtained the lien to intervene in the action or proceeding pursuant to Section 387.
(b) For the purposes of subdivision (a) of Section 491.460 and Section 491.470, a plaintiff shall be deemed to be a party to the action or special proceeding even though the plaintiff has not become a party to the action or proceeding under subdivision (a).
Amended by Stats. 1984, Ch. 538, Sec. 10.

Section 491.440 - Consent of plaintiff or court authorization required to enforce judgment obtained by defendant
(a) Except as provided in subdivision (c) of Section 491.410, unless the lien is released, the judgment recovered in the action or special proceeding in favor of the defendant may not be enforced by a writ or otherwise, and no compromise, dismissal, settlement, or satisfaction of the pending action or special proceeding or the judgment procured therein may be entered into by or on behalf of the defendant, without the written consent of the plaintiff or authorization by order of the court obtained under subdivision (b).
(b) Upon application by the defendant, the court in which the action or special proceeding subject to the lien under this article is pending or the judgment procured therein is entered may, in its discretion, after a hearing, make an order described in subdivision (a) that may include such terms and conditions as the court deems necessary. The application for an order under this subdivision shall be made on noticed motion. The notice of motion shall be served on the plaintiff.
Added by Stats. 1982, Ch. 1198, Sec. 57. Operative July 1, 1983, by Sec. 70 of Ch. 1198.

Section 491.450 - Endorsement of lien's existence upon judgment
(a) If a lien is created pursuant to this article, the court clerk shall endorse upon the judgment recovered in the action or special proceeding a statement of the existence of the lien and the time it was created.
(b) Any abstract issued upon the judgment shall include a statement of the lien in favor of the plaintiff.
Added by Stats. 1982, Ch. 1198, Sec. 57. Operative July 1, 1983, by Sec. 70 of Ch. 1198.

Section 491.460 - Satisfaction of lien
(a) If the defendant is entitled to money or property under the judgment in the action or special proceeding and a lien created under this article exists, upon application of any party to the action or special proceeding, the court may order that the defendant's rights to money or property under the judgment be attached or otherwise applied to the satisfaction of the lien created under this article as ordered by the court. Application for an order under this section shall be on noticed motion. The notice of motion shall be served on all other parties.
(b) If the judgment determines that the defendant has an interest in property, the court may order the party having custody or control of the property not to transfer the property until it can be attached or otherwise applied to the satisfaction of the lien created under this article.
(c) If the court determines that a party (other than the defendant) having notice of the lien created under this article has transferred property that was subject to the lien, or has paid an amount to the defendant that was subject to the lien, the court shall render judgment against the party in an amount equal to the lesser of the following:
   (1) The value of the defendant's interest in the property or the amount paid to the defendant.
   (2) The amount of the plaintiff's lien created under this article.
(d) A judgment or order under this section may be enforced in the same manner as it could be enforced if it had been obtained by the defendant against the third party; but, prior to entry of judgment in favor of the plaintiff against the defendant, any money or property obtained in enforcing the judgment or order against the third party shall be paid or delivered into court to abide the judgment in the action of the plaintiff against the defendant or shall be held by a levying officer, or otherwise held, as ordered by the court.
Added by Stats. 1982, Ch. 1198, Sec. 57. Operative July 1, 1983, by Sec. 70 of Ch. 1198.

Section 491.470 - Claim of exemption by defendant
(a) If a lien is created under this article, the defendant may claim that all or any portion of the money or property that the defendant may recover in the action or special proceeding is exempt from attachment. The claim shall be made by application on noticed motion to the court in which the action or special proceeding is pending, filed, and served on the plaintiff not later than 30 days after the defendant has notice of the creation of

lien. The defendant shall execute an affidavit in support of the application that includes the matters set forth in subdivision (c) of Section 484.070. No notice of opposition to the claim of exemption is required. The failure of the defendant to make a claim of exemption under this section constitutes a waiver of the exemption.

(b) The court may determine the exemption claim at any time prior to the entry of judgment in the action or special proceeding or may consolidate the exemption hearing with the hearing on a motion pursuant to Section 491.460.

(c) If the defendant establishes to the satisfaction of the court that the money or property that the defendant may recover in the action or special proceeding is all or partially exempt from attachment, the court shall order the termination of the lien created under this article on the exempt portion of the money or property.

Added by Stats. 1984, Ch. 538, Sec. 11.

Chapter 12 - NONRESIDENT ATTACHMENT

Section 492.010 - Generally

Notwithstanding subdivision (a) of Section 483.010, an attachment may be issued in any action for the recovery of money brought against any of the following:

(a) A natural person who does not reside in this state.

(b) A foreign corporation not qualified to do business in this state under the provisions of Chapter 21 (commencing with Section 2100) of Division 1 of Title 1 of the Corporations Code.

(c) A foreign partnership which has not filed a designation pursuant to Section 15800 of the Corporations Code.

Amended by Stats 2021 ch 124 (AB 938),s 9, eff. 1/1/2022.
Amended by Stats. 1982, Ch. 1198, Sec. 58. Operative July 1, 1983, by Sec. 70 of Ch. 1198.

Section 492.020 - Application for right to attach order and writ of attachment

(a) Upon the filing of the complaint or at any time thereafter, the plaintiff may apply pursuant to this chapter for a right to attach order and a writ of attachment by filing an application for the order and writ with the court in which the action is brought.

(b) The application shall satisfy the requirements of Section 484.020 and shall be supported by an affidavit showing all of the following:

    (1) The action is one described in Section 492.010 and is brought against a defendant described in Section 492.010.

    (2) The plaintiff on the facts presented would be entitled to a judgment on the claim upon which the attachment is based.

    (3) The property sought to be attached is subject to attachment pursuant to Section 492.040.

(c) The affidavit in support of the showing required by paragraph (3) of subdivision (b) may be based on the affiant's information and belief.

Added by Stats. 1974, Ch. 1516.

Section 492.030 - Issuance or denial of order

(a) The court shall examine the application and supporting affidavit and shall issue a right to attach order, which shall state the amount to be secured by the attachment, and order a writ of attachment to be issued upon the filing of an undertaking as provided by Sections 489.210 and 489.220, if it finds all of the following:

    (1) The claim upon which the attachment is based is one upon which an attachment may be issued.

    (2) The plaintiff has established the probable validity of the claim upon which the attachment is based.

    (3) The defendant is one described in Section 492.010.

    (4) The attachment is not sought for a purpose other than the recovery on the claim upon which the attachment is based.

    (5) The affidavit accompanying the application shows that the property sought to be attached, or the portion thereof to be specified in the writ, is subject to attachment pursuant to Section 492.040.

    (6) The amount to be secured by the attachment is greater than zero.

(b) If the court finds that the application and supporting affidavit do not satisfy the requirements of this chapter, it shall so state and deny the order. If denial is solely on the ground that the defendant is not one described in Section 492.010, the judicial officer shall so state and such denial does not preclude the plaintiff from applying for a right to attach order and writ of attachment under Chapter 4 (commencing with Section 484.010) with the same affidavits and supporting papers.

Amended by Stats. 1997, Ch. 222, Sec. 10. Effective January 1, 1998.

Section 492.040 - Levy upon property

Notwithstanding Sections 487.010 and 487.020, a writ of attachment issued under this chapter may be levied upon any property of a defendant for which a method of levy is provided by Article 2 (commencing with Section 488.300) of Chapter 8. However, after the defendant has filed a general appearance in the action, only nonexempt property of the defendant may be levied upon and property previously levied upon which is exempt under Section 487.020 shall be released upon order of the court.

Amended by Stats. 1982, Ch. 1198, Sec. 59. Operative July 1, 1983, by Sec. 70 of Ch. 1198.

Section 492.050 - Application to set aside order, quash wit and release property

(a) Any defendant whose property has been attached pursuant to a writ issued under this chapter may apply for an order that the right to attach order be set aside, the writ of attachment quashed, and any property levied upon pursuant to the writ released. Such application shall be made by filing with the court and serving on the plaintiff a notice of motion.

(b) The notice of motion shall state the grounds on which the motion is based and shall be accompanied by an affidavit supporting any factual issues raised and points and authorities supporting any legal issues raised.

(c) If the defendant has filed a general appearance in the action, the right to attach order shall be set aside unless the plaintiff shows that his right to attach is authorized by a provision other than Section 492.010.

(d) At the hearing on the motion, the court shall determine whether the plaintiff is entitled to a right to attach order. If the court finds that the plaintiff is not entitled to a right to attach order, it shall order the right to attach order set aside, the writ of attachment quashed, and any property levied upon pursuant to the writ released. If the court finds that the plaintiff is entitled to a right to attach order, the attachment shall continue in effect except as provided in Section 492.040 and, thereafter, the plaintiff may apply for additional writs pursuant to Article 2 (commencing with Section 484.310) or Article 3 (commencing with Section 484.510) of Chapter 4.

(e) The court's determination shall be made upon the basis of the pleadings and other papers in the record; but, upon good cause shown, the court may receive and consider at the hearing additional evidence, oral or documentary, and additional points and authorities, or it may continue the hearing for the production of such additional evidence or points or authorities.

(f) The hearing provided for in this section shall take precedence over all other civil matters on the calendar of that day except older matters of the same character.

Added by Stats. 1974, Ch. 1516.

Section 492.060 - Application for additional writ

At any time after a right to attach order and writ of attachment have been issued under this chapter and before the hearing provided by Section 492.050, the plaintiff may apply for an additional writ of attachment under this chapter as provided in Sections 492.060 to 492.090, inclusive. The application shall be filed with the court in which the action is brought.

Added by Stats. 1974, Ch. 1516.

Section 492.070 - Application requirements

The application shall be executed under oath and shall include all of the following:
(a) A statement that the plaintiff has been issued a right to attach order and writ of attachment pursuant to Section 492.030.
(b) A statement of the amount to be secured by the attachment.
(c) A description of the property to be attached under the writ of attachment and a statement that the plaintiff is informed and believes that such property is subject to attachment pursuant to Section 492.040. The description shall satisfy the requirements of Section 484.020.
Amended by Stats. 1982, Ch. 1198, Sec. 60. Operative July 1, 1983, by Sec. 70 of Ch. 1198.

Section 492.090 - Findings required issuance of writ
The court shall examine the application and supporting affidavit and shall order a writ of attachment to be issued upon the filing of an undertaking as provided by Sections 489.210 and 489.220, if it finds both of the following:
(a) A right to attach order has been issued in the action pursuant to Section 492.030.
(b) The affidavit accompanying the application shows that the property sought to be attached, or the portion thereof to be specified in the writ, is subject to attachment pursuant to Section 492.040.
Amended by Stats. 1976, Ch. 437.

Chapter 13 - EFFECT OF BANKRUPTCY PROCEEDINGS AND GENERAL ASSIGNMENTS FOR THE BENEFIT OF CREDITORS

Section 493.010 - General assignment for the benefit of creditors defined
As used in this chapter, "general assignment for the benefit of creditors" means an assignment which satisfies all of the following requirements:
(a) The assignment is an assignment of all the defendant's assets that are transferable and not exempt from enforcement of a money judgment.
(b) The assignment is for the benefit of all the defendant's creditors.
(c) The assignment does not itself create a preference of one creditor or class of creditors over any other creditor or class of creditors, but the assignment may recognize the existence of preferences to which creditors are otherwise entitled.
Amended by Stats. 1982, Ch. 1198, Sec. 61. Operative July 1, 1983, by Sec. 70 of Ch. 1198.

Section 493.020 - Defendant authorized to make general assignment
Notwithstanding any other provision of this title, the defendant may make a general assignment for the benefit of creditors.
Added by Stats. 1977, Ch. 499.

Section 493.030 - Termination of lien of temporary protective order
(a) The making of a general assignment for the benefit of creditors terminates a lien of a temporary protective order or of attachment if the lien was created within 90 days prior to the making of the general assignment.
(b) The filing of a petition commencing a voluntary or involuntary case under Title 11 of the United States Code (Bankruptcy) terminates a lien of a temporary protective order or of attachment if the lien was created within 90 days prior to the filing of the petition.
(c) Subdivisions (a) and (b) do not apply unless all liens of attachment on the defendant's property in other states that were created within 90 days prior to the making of a general assignment for the benefit of creditors or the filing of a petition commencing a case under Title 11 of the United States Code (Bankruptcy) have terminated.
Amended by Stats. 1979, Ch. 177.

Section 493.040 - Request for release of attachment
(a) Where a lien of attachment terminates pursuant to Section 493.030, the assignee under a general assignment for the benefit of creditors or, in the case of a bankruptcy, the trustee, interim trustee, or the debtor in possession if there is no trustee or interim trustee, may secure the release of the attached property by filing with the levying officer a request for release of attachment stating the grounds for release and describing the property to be released, executed under oath, together with a copy thereof.
(b) In the case of an assignee, the request shall include two copies of the general assignment for the benefit of creditors.
(c) In the case of a trustee, interim trustee, or debtor in possession, the request shall include a certified copy of the petition in bankruptcy, together with a copy thereof.
(d) If immediate release of the attachment is sought, the request shall be accompanied by an undertaking to pay the plaintiff any damages resulting from an improper release of the attachment, in the amount to be secured by the attachment, executed by an admitted surety insurer.
(e) Within five days after the filing of the request for release of attachment, the levying officer shall mail to the plaintiff:
  (1) A copy of the request for release of the attachment, including the copy of the document filed pursuant to subdivision (b) or (c).
  (2) If an undertaking has not been given, a notice that the attachment will be released pursuant to the request for release of attachment unless otherwise ordered by a court within 10 days after the date of mailing the notice.
  (3) If an undertaking has been given, a notice that the attachment has been released.
(f) Unless otherwise ordered by a court, if an undertaking has not been given, the levying officer shall release the attachment pursuant to the request for release of attachment after the expiration of 10 days from the date of mailing the papers referred to in subdivision (e) to the plaintiff. If an undertaking has been given, the levying officer shall immediately release the attachment pursuant to the request for release of attachment.
(g) Where the attached property has been taken into custody, it shall be released to the person making the request for release of attachment or some other person designated in the request. Where the attached property has not been taken into custody, it shall be released as provided in subdivision (c) or (d) of Section 488.730.
(h) The levying officer is not liable for releasing an attachment in accordance with this section nor is any other person liable for acting in conformity with the release.
Amended by Stats. 1982, Ch. 1198, Sec. 62.5. Operative July 1, 1983, by Sec. 70 of Ch. 1198.

Section 493.050 - Reinstatement of lien or attachment
(a) The lien of a temporary protective order or of attachment, which has terminated pursuant to Section 493.030, is reinstated with the same effect as if it had not been terminated in the following cases:
  (1) Where the termination is the result of the making of a general assignment for the benefit of creditors and the general assignment for the benefit of creditors is set aside otherwise than by the filing of a petition commencing a case under Title 11 of the United States Code (Bankruptcy).
  (2) Where the termination is the result of the filing of a petition commencing a case under Title 11 of the United States Code (Bankruptcy) and the petition is dismissed.
  (3) Where the termination is the result of the filing of a petition commencing a case under Title 11 of the United States Code (Bankruptcy) and the trustee abandons property which had been subject to the lien of the temporary protective order or of attachment.
(b) The period from the making of a general assignment for the benefit of creditors until reinstatement of the lien of the temporary protective order or of attachment is not counted in determining the duration of the temporary protective order or the lien of attachment.
Amended by Stats. 1979, Ch. 177.

Section 493.060 - Subrogation to rights of plaintiff; preservation of lien for benefit of estate
(a) Upon the making of a general assignment for the benefit of creditors that terminates a lien under this chapter, the assignee is subrogated to the rights of the plaintiff under the temporary protective order or attachment.

(b) Upon the filing of a petition commencing a case under Title 11 of the United States Code (Bankruptcy), a lien terminated pursuant to this chapter is preserved for the benefit of the estate.

Amended by Stats. 1979, Ch. 177.

Title 7 - OTHER PROVISIONAL REMEDIES IN CIVIL ACTIONS
Chapter 1 - GENERAL PROVISIONS
Section 501 - Imprisonment prohibited
A person may not be imprisoned in a civil action for debt or tort, whether before or after judgment. Nothing in this section affects any power a court may have to imprison a person who violates a court order.

Added by Stats. 1974, Ch. 1516.

Chapter 2 - CLAIM AND DELIVERY OF PERSONAL PROPERTY
Article 1 - WORDS AND PHRASES DEFINED
Section 511.010 - Generally
Unless the provision or context otherwise requires, the definitions in this article govern the construction of this chapter.

Added by Stats. 1973, Ch. 526.

Section 511.020 - Complaint
"Complaint" includes a cross-complaint.

Added by Stats. 1973, Ch. 526.

Section 511.030 - Defendant
"Defendant" includes a cross-defendant.

Added by Stats. 1973, Ch. 526.

Section 511.040 - Farm products
"Farm products" means crops or livestock or supplies used or produced in farming operations or products of crops or livestock in their unmanufactured states (such as ginned cotton, wool clip, maple syrup, honey, milk, and eggs) while in the possession of a defendant engaged in raising, fattening, grazing, or other farming operations. If tangible personal property is a farm product, it is not inventory.

Added by Stats. 1973, Ch. 526.

Section 511.050 - Inventory
"Inventory" means tangible personal property in the possession of a defendant who holds it for sale or lease or to be furnished under contracts of service.

Added by Stats. 1973, Ch. 526.

Section 511.060 - Levying officer
"Levying officer" means the sheriff or marshal who is directed to execute a writ of possession issued under this chapter.

Amended by Stats. 1996, Ch. 872, Sec. 14. Effective January 1, 1997.

Section 511.070 - Person
"Person" includes an individual, a corporation, a partnership or other unincorporated association, a limited liability company, and a public entity.

Amended by Stats. 1994, Ch. 1010, Sec. 59. Effective January 1, 1995.

Section 511.080 - Plaintiff
"Plaintiff" means a person who files a complaint or cross-complaint.

Added by Stats. 1973, Ch. 526.

Section 511.090 - Probable validity
A claim has "probable validity" where it is more likely than not that the plaintiff will obtain a judgment against the defendant on that claim.

Added by Stats. 1973, Ch. 526.

Section 511.100 - Public entity
"Public entity" includes the state, the Regents of the University of California, a county, city, district, public authority, public agency, and any other political subdivision or public corporation in the state.

Added by Stats. 1973, Ch. 526.

Article 2 - WRIT OF POSSESSION
Section 512.010 - Application for writ
(a) Upon the filing of the complaint or at any time thereafter, the plaintiff may apply pursuant to this chapter for a writ of possession by filing a written application for the writ with the court in which the action is brought.

(b) The application shall be executed under oath and shall include all of the following:

(1) A showing of the basis of the plaintiff's claim and that the plaintiff is entitled to possession of the property claimed. If the basis of the plaintiff's claim is a written instrument, a copy of the instrument shall be attached.

(2) A showing that the property is wrongfully detained by the defendant, of the manner in which the defendant came into possession of the property, and, according to the best knowledge, information, and belief of the plaintiff, of the reason for the detention.

(3) A particular description of the property and a statement of its value.

(4) A statement, according to the best knowledge, information, and belief of the plaintiff, of the location of the property and, if the property, or some part of it, is within a private place which may have to be entered to take possession, a showing that there is probable cause to believe that such property is located there.

(5) A statement that the property has not been taken for a tax, assessment, or fine, pursuant to a statute; or seized under an execution against the property of the plaintiff; or, if so seized, that it is by statute exempt from such seizure.

(c) The requirements of subdivision (b) may be satisfied by one or more affidavits filed with the application.

Added by Stats. 1973, Ch. 526.

Section 512.020 - Issuance after hearing; ex parte issuance
(a) Except as otherwise provided in this section, no writ shall be issued under this chapter except after a hearing on a noticed motion.

(b) A writ of possession may be issued ex parte pursuant to this subdivision if probable cause appears that any of the following conditions exists:

(1) The defendant gained possession of the property by feloniously taking the property from the plaintiff. This subdivision shall not apply where the defendant has fraudulently appropriated property entrusted to him or obtained possession by false or fraudulent representation or pretense or by embezzlement.

(2) The property is a credit card.

(3) The defendant acquired possession of the property in the ordinary course of his trade or business for commercial purposes and:

(i) The property is not necessary for the support of the defendant or his family; and

(ii) There is an immediate danger that the property will become unavailable to levy by reason of being transferred, concealed, or removed from the state or will become substantially impaired in value by acts of destruction or by failure to take care of the property in a reasonable manner; and

(iii) The ex parte issuance of a writ of possession is necessary to protect the property. The plaintiff's application for the writ shall satisfy the requirements of Section 512.010 and, in addition, shall include a showing that the conditions required by this subdivision exist. A writ of possession may issue if the court finds that the conditions required by this subdivision exist and the requirements of Section 512.060 are met. Where a writ of possession has been issued pursuant to this subdivision, a copy of the summons and complaint, a copy of the application and any affidavit in support thereof, and a notice which satisfies the requirements of subdivisions (c) and (d) of Section 512.040 and informs the defendant of his rights under this subdivision shall be served upon the defendant and any other person required by Section 514.020 to be served with a writ of possession. Any defendant whose property has been taken pursuant to a writ of possession issued under this subdivision may apply for an order that the writ be quashed and any property levied on pursuant to the writ be released. Such application shall be made by noticed motion, and the provisions of Section 512.050 shall apply. Pending the hearing on the defendant's application, the court may order that delivery pursuant to Section 514.030 of any property previously levied upon be stayed. If the court determines that the plaintiff is not entitled to a writ of possession, the court shall quash the writ of possession and order the release and redelivery of any property previously levied upon, and shall award the defendant any damages sustained by him which were proximately caused by the levy of the writ of possession and the loss of possession of the property pursuant to such levy.

Added by Stats. 1973, Ch. 526.

Section 512.030 - Service on defendant prior to hearing

(a) Prior to the hearing required by subdivision (a) of Section 512.020, the defendant shall be served with all of the following:

(1) A copy of the summons and complaint.

(2) A Notice of Application and Hearing.

(3) A copy of the application and any affidavit in support thereof.

(b) If the defendant has not appeared in the action, and a writ, notice, order, or other paper is required to be personally served on the defendant under this title, service shall be made in the same manner as a summons is served under Chapter 4 (commencing with Section 413.10) of Title 5.

Amended by Stats 2007 ch 15 (AB 859),s 2, eff. 1/1/2008.

Section 512.040 - Notice of application and hearing

The "Notice of Application and Hearing" shall inform the defendant of all of the following:

(a) A hearing will be held at a place and at a time, to be specified in the notice, on plaintiff's application for a writ of possession.

(b) The writ will be issued if the court finds that the plaintiff's claim is probably valid and the other requirements for issuing the writ are established. The hearing is not for the purpose of determining whether the claim is actually valid. The determination of the actual validity of the claim will be made in subsequent proceedings in the action and will not be affected by the decision at the hearing on the application for the writ.

(c) If the defendant desires to oppose the issuance of the writ, he shall file with the court either an affidavit providing evidence sufficient to defeat the plaintiff's right to issuance of the writ or an undertaking to stay the delivery of the property in accordance with Section 515.020.

(d) The notice shall contain the following statement: "If you believe the plaintiff may not be entitled to possession of the property claimed, you may wish to seek the advice of an attorney. Such attorney should be consulted promptly so that he may assist you before the time set for the hearing."

Added by Stats. 1973, Ch. 526.

Section 512.050 - Affidavits and points and authorities; evidence at hearing

Each party shall file with the court and serve upon the other party within the time prescribed by rule any affidavits and points and authorities intended to be relied upon at the hearing. At the hearing, the court shall make its determinations upon the basis of the pleadings and other papers in the record; but, upon good cause shown, the court may receive and consider additional evidence and authority produced at the hearing or may continue the hearing for the production of such additional evidence, oral or documentary, or the filing of other affidavits or points and authorities.

Added by Stats. 1973, Ch. 526.

Section 512.060 - Finding for issuance of writ; entry of private place to take possession

(a) At the hearing, a writ of possession shall issue if both of the following are found:

(1) The plaintiff has established the probable validity of the plaintiff's claim to possession of the property.

(2) The undertaking requirements of Section 515.010 are satisfied.

(b) No writ directing the levying officer to enter a private place to take possession of any property shall be issued unless the plaintiff has established that there is probable cause to believe that the property is located there.

Amended by Stats 2002 ch 68 (SB 1322),s 1, eff. 1/1/2003.

Section 512.070 - Order directing transfer of possession to plaintiff

If a writ of possession is issued, the court may also issue an order directing the defendant to transfer possession of the property to the plaintiff. Such order shall contain a notice to the defendant that failure to turn over possession of such property to plaintiff may subject the defendant to being held in contempt of court.

Amended by Stats. 1976, Ch. 145.

Section 512.080 - Writ requirements

The writ of possession shall meet all of the following requirements:

(a) Be directed to the levying officer within whose jurisdiction the property is located.

(b) Describe the specific property to be seized.

(c) Specify any private place that may be entered to take possession of the property or some part of it.

(d) Direct the levying officer to levy on the property pursuant to Section 514.010 if found and to retain it in custody until released or sold pursuant to Section 514.030.

(e) Inform the defendant of the right to object to the plaintiff's undertaking, a copy of which shall be attached to the writ, or to obtain redelivery of the property by filing an undertaking as prescribed by Section 515.020.

Amended by Stats. 1982, Ch. 517, Sec. 118.

Section 512.090 - Endorsement directing seizure at private place not specified in writ

(a) The plaintiff may apply ex parte in writing to the court in which the action was brought for an endorsement on the writ directing the levying officer to seize the property at a private place not specified in the writ.

(b) The court shall make the endorsement if the plaintiff establishes by affidavit that there is probable cause to believe that the property or some part of it may be found at that place.

Added by Stats. 1973, Ch. 526.

Section 512.100 - Failure to oppose issuance or rebut evidence not waiver of defense or right to produce evidence

Neither the failure of the defendant to oppose the issuance of a writ of possession under this chapter nor his failure to rebut any evidence produced by the plaintiff in connection with proceedings under this chapter shall constitute a waiver of any defense to plaintiff's claim in the action or any other action or have any effect on the right of the defendant to produce or exclude evidence at the trial of any such action.

Added by Stats. 1973, Ch. 526.

Section 512.110 - Effect of determination of court on determination of issues

The determinations of the court under this chapter shall have no effect on the determination of any issues in the action other than the issues relevant to proceedings under this chapter, nor shall they affect the rights of any party in any other action arising out of the same claim. The determinations of the court under this chapter shall not be given in evidence nor referred to in the trial of any such action.

Added by Stats. 1973, Ch. 526.

Section 512.120 - Failure of plaintiff to recover judgment in action

If the plaintiff fails to recover judgment in the action, he shall redeliver the property to the defendant and be liable for all damages sustained by the defendant which are proximately caused by operation of the temporary restraining order and preliminary injunction, if any, the levy of the writ of possession, and the loss of possession of the property pursuant to levy of the writ of possession or in compliance with an order issued under Section 512.070.

Added by Stats. 1973, Ch. 526.

Article 3 - TEMPORARY RESTRAINING ORDER

Section 513.010 - Application; issued ex parte; dissolution

(a) Except as otherwise provided by this chapter, the provisions of Chapter 3 (commencing with Section 525) of this title relating to the issuance of a temporary restraining order apply. At or after the time he files his application for writ of possession, the plaintiff may apply for a temporary restraining order by setting forth in the application a statement of grounds justifying the issuance of such order.

(b) A temporary restraining order may issue ex parte if all of the following are found:

(1) The plaintiff has established the probable validity of his claim to possession of the property.

(2) The plaintiff has provided an undertaking as required by Section 515.010.

(3) The plaintiff has established the probability that there is an immediate danger that the property claimed may become unavailable to levy by reason of being transferred, concealed, or removed or may become substantially impaired in value.

(c) If at the hearing on issuance of the writ of possession the court determines that the plaintiff is not entitled to a writ of possession, the court shall dissolve any temporary restraining order; otherwise, the court may issue a preliminary injunction to remain in effect until the property claimed is seized pursuant to the writ of possession.

Added by Stats. 1973, Ch. 526.

Section 513.020 - Order prohibiting transferring interest, concealing or removing property, impairing value

In the discretion of the court, the temporary restraining order may prohibit the defendant from doing any or all of the following:

(a) Transferring any interest in the property by sale, pledge, or grant of security interest, or otherwise disposing of, or encumbering, the property. If the property is farm products held for sale or lease or is inventory, the order may not prohibit the defendant from transferring the property in the ordinary course of business, but the order may impose appropriate restrictions on the disposition of the proceeds from such transfer.

(b) Concealing or otherwise removing the property in such a manner as to make it less available to seizure by the levying officer.

(c) Impairing the value of the property either by acts of destruction or by failure to care for the property in a reasonable manner.

Added by Stats. 1973, Ch. 526.

Article 4 - LEVY AND CUSTODY

Section 514.010 - Duty of levying officer; keeper in charge of mobilehome or boat; demanding possession of private place

(a) Except as otherwise provided in this section, upon receipt of the writ of possession the levying officer shall search for and take custody of the specified property, if it be in the possession of the defendant or his agent, either by removing the property to a place of safekeeping or by installing a keeper.

(b) If the specified property is used as a dwelling, such as a mobilehome or boat, levy shall be made by placing a keeper in charge of the property for two days, at the plaintiff's expense, after which period the levying officer shall remove the occupants and any contents not specified in the writ and shall take exclusive possession of the property.

(c) If the specified property or any part of it is in a private place, the levying officer shall at the time he demands possession of the property announce his identity, purpose, and authority. If the property is not voluntarily delivered, the levying officer may cause any building or enclosure where the property may be located to be broken open in such a manner as he reasonably believes will cause the least damage and may call upon the power of the county to aid and protect him, but, if he reasonably believes that entry and seizure of the property will involve a substantial risk of death or serious bodily harm to any person, he shall refrain from seizing the property and shall promptly make a return to the court from which the writ issued setting forth the reasons for his belief that the risk exists. In such case, the court shall make such orders as may be appropriate.

(d) Nothing in this section authorizes the levying officer to enter or search any private place not specified in the writ of possession or other order of the court.

Added by Stats. 1973, Ch. 526.

Section 514.020 - Copy of writ and undertaking delivered to person in possession; service if no one in possession

(a) At the time of levy, the levying officer shall deliver to the person in possession of the property a copy of the writ of possession, a copy of the plaintiff's undertaking, if any, and a copy of the order for issuance of the writ.

(b) If no one is in possession of the property at the time of levy, the levying officer shall subsequently serve the writ and attached undertaking on the defendant. If the defendant has appeared in the action, service shall be accomplished in the manner provided by Chapter 5 (commencing with Section 1010) of Title 14. If the defendant has not appeared in the action, service shall be accomplished in the manner provided for the service of summons and complaint by Article 3 (commencing with Section 415.10) of Chapter 4 of Title 5.

Amended by Stats 2002 ch 68 (SB 1322),s 2, eff. 1/1/2003.

Section 514.030 - Duty of levying officer after taking possession

(a) After the levying officer takes possession pursuant to a writ of possession, the levying officer shall keep the property in a secure place. Except as otherwise provided by Sections 512.020 and 514.050:

(1) If notice of the filing of an undertaking for redelivery or notice of objection to the plaintiff's undertaking is not received by the levying officer within 10 days after levy of the writ of possession, the levying officer shall deliver the property to plaintiff, upon receiving the fees for taking and necessary expenses for keeping the property.

(2) If notice of the filing of an undertaking for redelivery is received by the levying officer within 10 days after levy of the writ of possession and defendant's undertaking is not objected to, the levying officer shall redeliver the property to defendant upon expiration of the time to so object, upon receiving the fees for taking and necessary expenses for keeping the property not already paid or advanced by the plaintiff.

(3) If notice of objection to the plaintiff's undertaking or notice of the filing of an undertaking for redelivery is received within 10 days after levy of the writ of possession and defendant's undertaking is objected to, the levying officer shall not deliver or redeliver the property until the time provided in Section 515.030.

(b) Notwithstanding subdivision (a), where not otherwise provided by contract and where an undertaking for redelivery has not been filed, upon a showing that the property is perishable or will greatly deteriorate or depreciate in value or for some other reason that the interests of the parties will be best served thereby, the court may order that the property be sold and the proceeds deposited in the court to abide the judgment in the action.

Amended by Stats. 1982, Ch. 517, Sec. 119.

Section 514.040 - Return of writ by levying officer

The levying officer shall return the writ of possession, with his proceedings thereon, to the court in which the action is pending within 30 days after levy but in no event more than 60 days after the writ is issued.

Added by Stats. 1973, Ch. 526.

Section 514.050 - Third person claiming property taken

Where the property taken is claimed by a third person, the rules and proceedings applicable in cases of third-party claims under Division 4 (commencing with Section 720.010) of Title 9 apply.

Amended by Stats. 1982, Ch. 497, Sec. 33. Operative July 1, 1983, by Sec. 185 of Ch. 497.

Article 5 - UNDERTAKINGS

Section 515.010 - Undertaking filed by plaintiff

(a) Except as provided in subdivision (b), the court shall not issue a temporary restraining order or a writ of possession until the plaintiff has filed an undertaking with the court. The undertaking shall provide that the sureties are bound to the defendant for the return of the property to the defendant, if return of the property is ordered, and for the payment to the defendant of any sum recovered against the plaintiff. The undertaking shall be in an amount not less than twice the value of the defendant's interest in the property or in a greater amount. The value of the defendant's interest in the property is determined by the market value of the property less the amount due and owing on any conditional sales contract or security agreement and all liens and encumbrances on the property, and any other factors necessary to determine the defendant's interest in the property.

(b) If the court finds that the defendant has no interest in the property, the court shall waive the requirement of the plaintiff's undertaking and shall include in the order for issuance of the writ the amount of the defendant's undertaking sufficient to satisfy the requirements of subdivision (b) of Section 515.020.

Amended by Stats 2002 ch 68 (SB 1322),s 3, eff. 1/1/2003.

Section 515.020 - Undertaking filed by defendant

(a) The defendant may prevent the plaintiff from taking possession of property pursuant to a writ of possession or regain possession of property so taken by filing with the court in which the action was brought an undertaking in an amount equal to the amount of the plaintiff's undertaking pursuant to subdivision (a) of Section 515.010 or in the amount determined by the court pursuant to subdivision (b) of Section 515.010.

(b) The undertaking shall state that, if the plaintiff recovers judgment on the action, the defendant shall pay all costs awarded to the plaintiff and all damages that the plaintiff may sustain by reason of the loss of possession of the property. The damages recoverable by the plaintiff pursuant to this section shall include all damages proximately caused by the plaintiff's failure to gain or retain possession.

(c) The defendant's undertaking may be filed at any time before or after levy of the writ of possession. A copy of the undertaking shall be mailed to the levying officer.

(d) If an undertaking for redelivery is filed and the defendant's undertaking is not objected to, the levying officer shall deliver the property to the defendant, or, if the plaintiff has previously been given possession of the property, the plaintiff shall deliver the property to the defendant. If an undertaking for redelivery is filed and the defendant's undertaking is objected to, the provisions of Section 515.030 apply.

Amended by Stats 2002 ch 68 (SB 1322),s 4, eff. 1/1/2003.

Section 515.030 - Objection to plaintiff's undertaking

(a) The defendant may object to the plaintiff's undertaking not later than 10 days after levy of the writ of possession. The defendant shall mail notice of objection to the levying officer.

(b) The plaintiff may object to the defendant's undertaking not later than 10 days after the defendant's undertaking is filed. The plaintiff shall mail notice of objection to the levying officer.

(c) If the court determines that the plaintiff's undertaking is insufficient and a sufficient undertaking is not filed within the time required by statute, the court shall vacate the temporary restraining order or preliminary injunction, if any, and the writ of possession and, if levy has occurred, order the levying officer or the plaintiff to return the property to the defendant. If the court determines that the plaintiff's undertaking is sufficient, the court shall order the levying officer to deliver the property to the plaintiff.

(d) If the court determines that the defendant's undertaking is insufficient and a sufficient undertaking is not filed within the time required by statute, the court shall order the levying officer to deliver the property to the plaintiff, or, if the plaintiff has previously been given possession of the property, the plaintiff shall retain possession. If the court determines that the defendant's undertaking is sufficient, the court shall order the levying officer or the plaintiff to deliver the property to the defendant.

Amended by Stats. 1984, Ch. 538, Sec. 14.

Article 6 - MISCELLANEOUS PROVISIONS

Section 516.010 - Rule providing for practice and procedure

The Judicial Council may provide by rule for the practice and procedure in proceedings under this chapter.

Added by Stats. 1973, Ch. 526.

Section 516.020 - Forms

The Judicial Council shall prescribe the form of the applications, notices, orders, and other documents required by this chapter.

Added by Stats. 1973, Ch. 526.

Section 516.030 - Requirements of affidavits

The facts stated in each affidavit filed pursuant to this chapter shall be set forth with particularity. Except where matters are specifically permitted by this chapter to be shown by information and belief, each affidavit shall show affirmatively that the affiant, if sworn as a witness, can testify competently to the facts stated therein. The affiant may be any person, whether or not a party to the action, who has knowledge of the facts. A verified complaint that satisfies the requirements of this section may be used in lieu of or in addition to an ordinary affidavit.

Added by Stats. 1973, Ch. 526.

Section 516.040 - Judicial duties performed by appointed officers

The judicial duties to be performed under this chapter are "subordinate judicial duties" within the meaning of Section 22 of Article VI of the California Constitution and may be performed by appointed officers such as court commissioners.

Added by Stats. 1973, Ch. 526.

Section 516.050 - Granting relief pursuant to chapter 3

Nothing in this chapter shall preclude the granting of relief pursuant to Chapter 3 (commencing with Section 525) of this title.

Added by Stats. 1973, Ch. 526.

Chapter 3 - INJUNCTION

Section 525 - Definition; granted by court or judge

An injunction is a writ or order requiring a person to refrain from a particular act. It may be granted by the court in which the action is brought, or by a judge thereof; and when granted by a judge, it may be enforced as an order of the court.

Amended by Stats. 1907, Ch. 272.

Section 526 - Cases in which injunction granted; cases in which injunction not granted

(a) An injunction may be granted in the following cases:

(1) When it appears by the complaint that the plaintiff is entitled to the relief demanded, and the relief, or any part thereof, consists in restraining the commission or continuance of the act complained of, either for a limited period or perpetually.

(2) When it appears by the complaint or affidavits that the commission or continuance of some act during the litigation would produce waste, or great or irreparable injury, to a party to the action.

(3) When it appears, during the litigation, that a party to the action is doing, or threatens, or is about to do, or is procuring or suffering to be done, some act in violation of the rights of another party to the action respecting the subject of the action, and tending to render the judgment ineffectual.

(4) When pecuniary compensation would not afford adequate relief.

(5) Where it would be extremely difficult to ascertain the amount of compensation which would afford adequate relief.

(6) Where the restraint is necessary to prevent a multiplicity of judicial proceedings.

(7) Where the obligation arises from a trust.

(b) An injunction cannot be granted in the following cases:

(1) To stay a judicial proceeding pending at the commencement of the action in which the injunction is demanded, unless the restraint is necessary to prevent a multiplicity of proceedings.

(2) To stay proceedings in a court of the United States.

(3) To stay proceedings in another state upon a judgment of a court of that state.

(4) To prevent the execution of a public statute by officers of the law for the public benefit.

(5) To prevent the breach of a contract the performance of which would not be specifically enforced, other than a contract in writing for the rendition of personal services from one to another where the promised service is of a special, unique, unusual, extraordinary, or intellectual character, which gives it peculiar value, the loss of which cannot be reasonably or adequately compensated in damages in an action at law, and where the compensation for the personal services is as follows:

(A) As to contracts entered into on or before December 31, 1993, the minimum compensation provided in the contract for the personal services shall be at the rate of six thousand dollars ($6,000) per annum.

(B) As to contracts entered into on or after January 1, 1994, the criteria of clause (i) or (ii), as follows, are satisfied:

(i) The compensation is as follows:

(I) The minimum compensation provided in the contract shall be at the rate of nine thousand dollars ($9,000) per annum for the first year of the contract, twelve thousand dollars ($12,000) per annum for the second year of the contract, and fifteen thousand dollars ($15,000) per annum for the third to seventh years, inclusive, of the contract.

(II) In addition, after the third year of the contract, there shall actually have been paid for the services through and including the contract year during which the injunctive relief is sought, over and above the minimum contractual compensation specified in subclause (I), the amount of fifteen thousand dollars ($15,000) per annum during the fourth and fifth years of the contract, and thirty thousand dollars ($30,000) per annum during the sixth and seventh years of the contract. As a condition to petitioning for an injunction, amounts payable under this clause may be paid at any time prior to seeking injunctive relief.

(ii) The aggregate compensation actually received for the services provided under a contract that does not meet the criteria of subparagraph (A), is at least 10 times the applicable aggregate minimum amount specified in subclauses (I) and (II) of clause (i) through and including the contract year during which the injunctive relief is sought. As a condition to petitioning for an injunction, amounts payable under this subparagraph may be paid at any time prior to seeking injunctive relief.

(C) Compensation paid in any contract year in excess of the minimums specified in clauses (i) and (ii) of subparagraph (B) shall apply to reduce the compensation otherwise required to be paid under those provisions in any subsequent contract years. However, an injunction may be granted to prevent the breach of a contract entered into between any nonprofit cooperative corporation or association and a member or stockholder thereof, in respect to any provision regarding the sale or delivery to the corporation or association of the products produced or acquired by the member or stockholder.

(6) To prevent the exercise of a public or private office, in a lawful manner, by the person in possession.

(7) To prevent a legislative act by a municipal corporation.

Amended by Stats. 1993, Ch. 836, Sec. 2. Effective January 1, 1994.

Section 526a - Action to restrain or prevent waste of or injury to estate, funds or property of local agency

(a) An action to obtain a judgment, restraining and preventing any illegal expenditure of, waste of, or injury to, the estate, funds, or other property of a local agency, may be maintained against any officer thereof, or any agent, or other person, acting in its behalf, either by a resident therein, or by a corporation, who is assessed for and is liable to pay, or, within one year before the commencement of the action, has paid, a tax that funds the defendant local agency, including, but not limited to, the following:

(1) An income tax.

(2) A sales and use tax or transaction and use tax initially paid by a consumer to a retailer.

(3) A property tax, including a property tax paid by a tenant or lessee to a landlord or lessor pursuant to the terms of a written lease.

(4) A business license tax.

(b) This section does not affect any right of action in favor of a local agency, or any public officer; provided, that no injunction shall be granted restraining the offering for sale, sale, or issuance of any municipal bonds for public improvements or public utilities.

(c) An action brought pursuant to this section to enjoin a public improvement project shall take special precedence over all civil matters on the calendar of the court except those matters to which equal precedence on the calendar is granted by law.

(d) For purposes of this section, the following definitions apply:

(1) "Local agency" means a city, town, county, or city and county, or a district, public authority, or any other political subdivision in the state.

(2) "Resident" means a person who lives, works, owns property, or attends school in the jurisdiction of the defendant local agency.

Amended by Stats 2018 ch 319 (AB 2376),s 1, eff. 1/1/2019.

Section 526b - Suit to restrain issuance, sale or delivery of bonds of city, town, county or other district

Every person or corporation bringing, instigating, exciting or abetting, any suit to obtain an injunction, restraining or enjoining the issuance, sale, offering for sale, or delivery, of bonds, or other securities, or the expenditure of the proceeds of the sale of such bonds or other securities, of any city, city and county, town, county, or other district organized under the laws of this state, or any other political subdivision of this state, proposed to be issued, sold, offered for sale or delivered by such city, city and county, town, county, district or other political subdivision, for the purpose of acquiring, constructing, completing, improving or extending water works, electric works, gas works or other public utility works or property, shall, if the injunction sought is finally denied, and if such person or corporation owns, controls, or is operating or interested in, a public utility

business of the same nature as that for which such bonds or other securities are proposed to be issued, sold, offered for sale, or delivered, be liable to the defendant for all costs, damages and necessary expenses resulting to such defendant by reason of the filing of such suit.
Added by Stats. 1921, Ch. 384.

Section 527 - Preliminary injunctions and temporary restraining orders

(a) A preliminary injunction may be granted at any time before judgment upon a verified complaint, or upon affidavits if the complaint in the one case, or the affidavits in the other, show satisfactorily that sufficient grounds exist therefor. No preliminary injunction shall be granted without notice to the opposing party.

(b) A temporary restraining order or a preliminary injunction, or both, may be granted in a class action, in which one or more of the parties sues or defends for the benefit of numerous parties upon the same grounds as in other actions, whether or not the class has been certified.

(c) No temporary restraining order shall be granted without notice to the opposing party, unless both of the following requirements are satisfied:

(1) It appears from facts shown by affidavit or by the verified complaint that great or irreparable injury will result to the applicant before the matter can be heard on notice.

(2) The applicant or the applicant's attorney certifies one of the following to the court under oath:

(A) That within a reasonable time prior to the application the applicant informed the opposing party or the opposing party's attorney at what time and where the application would be made.

(B) That the applicant in good faith attempted but was unable to inform the opposing party and the opposing party's attorney, specifying the efforts made to contact them.

(C) That for reasons specified the applicant should not be required to so inform the opposing party or the opposing party's attorney.

(d) In case a temporary restraining order is granted without notice in the contingency specified in subdivision (c):

(1) The matter shall be made returnable on an order requiring cause to be shown why a preliminary injunction should not be granted, on the earliest day that the business of the court will admit of, but not later than 15 days or, if good cause appears to the court, 22 days from the date the temporary restraining order is issued.

(2) The party who obtained the temporary restraining order shall, within five days from the date the temporary restraining order is issued or two days prior to the hearing, whichever is earlier, serve on the opposing party a copy of the complaint if not previously served, the order to show cause stating the date, time, and place of the hearing, any affidavits to be used in the application, and a copy of the points and authorities in support of the application. The court may for good cause, on motion of the applicant or on its own motion, shorten the time required by this paragraph for service on the opposing party.

(3) When the matter first comes up for hearing, if the party who obtained the temporary restraining order is not ready to proceed, or if the party has failed to effect service as required by paragraph (2), the court shall dissolve the temporary restraining order.

(4) The opposing party is entitled to one continuance for a reasonable period of not less than 15 days or any shorter period requested by the opposing party, to enable the opposing party to meet the application for a preliminary injunction. If the opposing party obtains a continuance under this paragraph, the temporary restraining order shall remain in effect until the date of the continued hearing.

(5) Upon the filing of an affidavit by the applicant that the opposing party could not be served within the time required by paragraph (2), the court may reissue any temporary restraining order previously issued. The reissued order shall be made returnable as provided by paragraph (1), with the time for hearing measured from the date of reissuance. No fee shall be charged for reissuing the order.

(e) The opposing party may, in response to an order to show cause, present affidavits relating to the granting of the preliminary injunction, and if the affidavits are served on the applicant at least two days prior to the hearing, the applicant shall not be entitled to any continuance on account thereof. On the day the order is made returnable, the hearing shall take precedence over all other matters on the calendar of the day, except older matters of the same character, and matters to which special precedence may be given by law. When the cause is at issue it shall be set for trial at the earliest possible date and shall take precedence over all other cases, except older matters of the same character, and matters to which special precedence may be given by law.

(f) Notwithstanding failure to satisfy the time requirements of this section, the court may nonetheless hear the order to show cause why a preliminary injunction should not be granted if the moving and supporting papers are served within the time required by Section 1005 and one of the following conditions is satisfied:

(1) The order to show cause is issued without a temporary restraining order.

(2) The order to show cause is issued with a temporary restraining order, but is either not set for hearing within the time required by paragraph (1) of subdivision (d), or the party who obtained the temporary restraining order fails to effect service within the time required by paragraph (2) of subdivision (d).

(g) This section does not apply to an order issued under the Family Code.

(h) As used in this section:

(1) "Complaint" means a complaint or a cross-complaint.

(2) "Court" means the court in which the action is pending.

Amended by Stats 2000 ch 688 (AB 1669), s 4, eff. 1/1/2001.

Section 527.3 - When restraining orders or injunctions prevented in labor disputes

(a) In order to promote the rights of workers to engage in concerted activities for the purpose of collective bargaining, picketing or other mutual aid or protection, and to prevent the evils which frequently occur when courts interfere with the normal processes of dispute resolution between employers and recognized employee organizations, the equity jurisdiction of the courts in cases involving or growing out of a labor dispute shall be no broader than as set forth in subdivision (b) of this section, and the provisions of subdivision (b) of this section shall be strictly construed in accordance with existing law governing labor disputes with the purpose of avoiding any unnecessary judicial interference in labor disputes.

(b) The acts enumerated in this subdivision, whether performed singly or in concert, shall be legal, and no court nor any judge nor judges thereof, shall have jurisdiction to issue any restraining order or preliminary or permanent injunction which, in specific or general terms, prohibits any person or persons, whether singly or in concert, from doing any of the following:

(1) Giving publicity to, and obtaining or communicating information regarding the existence of, or the facts involved in, any labor dispute, whether by advertising, speaking, patrolling any public street or any place where any person or persons may lawfully be, or by any other method not involving fraud, violence or breach of the peace.

(2) Peaceful picketing or patrolling involving any labor dispute, whether engaged in singly or in numbers.

(3) Assembling peaceably to do any of the acts specified in paragraphs (1) and (2) or to promote lawful interests.

(4) Except as provided in subparagraph (iv), for purposes of this section, "labor dispute" is defined as follows:

(i) A case shall be held to involve or to grow out of a labor dispute when the case involves persons who are engaged in the same industry, trade, craft, or occupation; or have direct or indirect interests therein; or who are employees of the same employer; or who are members of the same or an affiliated organization of employers or employees; whether such dispute is (a) between one or more employers or associations of employers and one or more employees or associations of employees; (b) between one or more employers or associations of employers and one or more employers or associations of employers; or (c) between one or more employees or associations of employees and one or more employees or associations of employees; or when the case involves any conflicting or competing interests in a "labor dispute" of "persons participating or interested" therein (as defined in subparagraph (ii)).

(ii) A person or association shall be held to be a person participating or interested in a labor dispute if relief is sought against him or it, and if he or it is engaged in the same industry, trade, craft, or occupation in which such dispute occurs, or has a direct or indirect interest therein, or is a member, officer, or agent of any association composed in whole or in part of employers or employees engaged in such industry, trade, craft, or occupation.

(iii) The term "labor dispute" includes any controversy concerning terms or conditions of employment, or concerning the association or representation of persons in negotiating, fixing, maintaining, changing, or seeking to arrange terms or conditions of employment regardless of whether or not the disputants stand in the proximate relation of employer and employee.

(iv) The term "labor dispute" does not include a jurisdictional strike as defined in Section 1118 of the Labor Code.

(c) Nothing contained in this section shall be construed to alter or supersede the provisions of Chapter 1 of the 1975-76 Third Extraordinary Session, and to the extent of any conflict between the provisions of this act and that chapter, the provisions of the latter shall prevail.

(d) Nothing contained in this section shall be construed to alter the legal rights of public employees or their employers, nor shall this section alter the rights of parties to collective-bargaining agreements under the provisions of Section 1126 of the Labor Code.

(e) It is not the intent of this section to permit conduct that is unlawful including breach of the peace, disorderly conduct, the unlawful blocking of access or egress to premises where a labor dispute exists, or other similar unlawful activity.

Added by Stats. 1975, Ch. 1156.

Section 527.6 - Prohibiting harassment

(a)

(1) A person who has suffered harassment as defined in subdivision (b) may seek a temporary restraining order and an order after hearing prohibiting harassment as provided in this section.

(2) A minor, under 12 years of age, accompanied by a duly appointed and acting guardian ad litem, shall be permitted to appear in court without counsel for the limited purpose of requesting or opposing a request for a temporary restraining order or order after hearing, or both, under this section as provided in Section 374.

(b) For purposes of this section, the following terms have the following meanings:

(1) "Course of conduct" is a pattern of conduct composed of a series of acts over a period of time, however short, evidencing a continuity of purpose, including following or stalking an individual, making harassing telephone calls to an individual, or sending harassing correspondence to an individual by any means, including, but not limited to, the use of public or private mails, interoffice mail, facsimile, or email. Constitutionally protected activity is not included within the meaning of "course of conduct."

(2) "Credible threat of violence" is a knowing and willful statement or course of conduct that would place a reasonable person in fear for the person's safety or the safety of the person's immediate family, and that serves no legitimate purpose.

(3) "Harassment" is unlawful violence, a credible threat of violence, or a knowing and willful course of conduct directed at a specific person that seriously alarms, annoys, or harasses the person, and that serves no legitimate purpose. The course of conduct must be that which would cause a reasonable person to suffer substantial emotional distress, and must actually cause substantial emotional distress to the petitioner.

(4) "Petitioner" means the person to be protected by the temporary restraining order and order after hearing and, if the court grants the petition, the protected person.

(5) "Respondent" means the person against whom the temporary restraining order and order after hearing are sought and, if the petition is granted, the restrained person.

(6) "Temporary restraining order" and "order after hearing" mean orders that include any of the following restraining orders, whether issued ex parte or after notice and hearing:

(A) An order enjoining a party from harassing, intimidating, molesting, attacking, striking, stalking, threatening, sexually assaulting, battering, abusing, telephoning, including, but not limited to, making annoying telephone calls, as described in Section 653m of the Penal Code, destroying personal property, contacting, either directly or indirectly, by mail or otherwise, or coming within a specified distance of, or disturbing the peace of, the petitioner. On a showing of good cause, in an order issued pursuant to this subparagraph in connection with an animal owned, possessed, leased, kept, or held by the petitioner, or residing in the residence or household of the petitioner, the court may do either or both of the following:

(i) Grant the petitioner exclusive care, possession, or control of the animal.

(ii) Order the respondent to stay away from the animal and refrain from taking, transferring, encumbering, concealing, molesting, attacking, striking, threatening, harming, or otherwise disposing of the animal.

(B) An order enjoining a party from specified behavior that the court determines is necessary to effectuate orders described in subparagraph (A).

(7) "Unlawful violence" is any assault or battery, or stalking as prohibited in Section 646.9 of the Penal Code, but does not include lawful acts of self-defense or defense of others.

(c) In the discretion of the court, on a showing of good cause, a temporary restraining order or order after hearing issued under this section may include other named family or household members.

(d) Upon filing a petition for orders under this section, the petitioner may obtain a temporary restraining order in accordance with Section 527, except to the extent this section provides an inconsistent rule. The temporary restraining order may include any of the restraining orders described in paragraph (6) of subdivision (b). A temporary restraining order may be issued with or without notice, based on a declaration that, to the satisfaction of the court, shows reasonable proof of harassment of the petitioner by the respondent, and that great or irreparable harm would result to the petitioner.

(e) A request for the issuance of a temporary restraining order without notice under this section shall be granted or denied on the same day that the petition is submitted to the court. If the petition is filed too late in the day to permit effective review, the order shall be granted or denied on the next day of judicial business in sufficient time for the order to be filed that day with the clerk of the court.

(f) A temporary restraining order issued under this section shall remain in effect, at the court's discretion, for a period not to exceed 21 days, or, if the court extends the time for hearing under subdivision (g), not to exceed 25 days, unless otherwise modified or terminated by the court.

(g) Within 21 days, or, if good cause appears to the court, 25 days from the date that a petition for a temporary order is granted or denied, a hearing shall be held on the petition. If a request for a temporary order is not made, the hearing shall be held within 21 days, or, if good cause appears to the court, 25 days, from the date that the petition is filed.

(h) The respondent may file a response that explains, excuses, justifies, or denies the alleged harassment, or may file a cross-petition under this section.

(i) At the hearing, the judge shall receive any testimony that is relevant, and may make an independent inquiry. If the judge finds by clear and convincing evidence that unlawful harassment exists, an order shall issue prohibiting the harassment.

(j)

(1) In the discretion of the court, an order issued after notice and hearing under this section may have a duration of no more than five years, subject to termination or modification by further order of the court either on written stipulation filed with the court or on the motion of a party. The order may be renewed, upon the request of a party, for a duration of no more than five additional years, without a showing of any further harassment since the issuance of the original order, subject to termination or modification by further order of the court either on written

stipulation filed with the court or on the motion of a party. A request for renewal may be brought any time within the three months before the order expires.

(2) The failure to state the expiration date on the face of the form creates an order with a duration of three years from the date of issuance.

(3) If an action is filed for the purpose of terminating or modifying a protective order before the expiration date specified in the order by a party other than the protected party, the party who is protected by the order shall be given notice, pursuant to subdivision (b) of Section 1005, of the proceeding by personal service or, if the protected party has satisfied the requirements of Chapter 3.1 (commencing with Section 6205) of Division 7 of Title 1 of the Government Code, by service on the Secretary of State. If the party who is protected by the order cannot be notified before the hearing for modification or termination of the protective order, the court shall deny the motion to modify or terminate the order without prejudice or continue the hearing until the party who is protected can be properly noticed and may, upon a showing of good cause, specify another method for service of process that is reasonably designed to afford actual notice to the protected party. The protected party may waive the protected party's right to notice if the protected party is physically present in court and does not challenge the sufficiency of the notice.

(k) This section does not preclude either party from representation by private counsel or from appearing on the party's own behalf.

(l) In a proceeding under this section, if there are allegations of unlawful violence or credible threats of violence, a support person may accompany a party in court and, if the party is not represented by an attorney, may sit with the party at the table that is generally reserved for the party and the party's attorney. The support person is present to provide moral and emotional support for a person who alleges they are a victim of violence. The support person is not present as a legal adviser and may not provide legal advice. The support person may assist the person who alleges they are a victim of violence in feeling more confident that they will not be injured or threatened by the other party during the proceedings if the person who alleges the person is a victim of violence and the other party are required to be present in close proximity. This subdivision does not preclude the court from exercising its discretion to remove the support person from the courtroom if the court believes the support person is prompting, swaying, or influencing the party assisted by the support person.

(m)

(1) Except as provided in paragraph (2), upon the filing of a petition under this section, the respondent shall be personally served with a copy of the petition, temporary restraining order, if any, and notice of hearing of the petition. Service shall be made at least five days before the hearing. The court may for good cause, on motion of the petitioner or on its own motion, shorten the time for service on the respondent.

(2) If the court determines at the hearing that, after a diligent effort, the petitioner has been unable to accomplish personal service, and that there is reason to believe that the respondent is evading service or cannot be located, then the court may specify another method of service that is reasonably calculated to give actual notice to the respondent and may prescribe the manner in which proof of service shall be made.

(n) A notice of hearing under this section shall notify the respondent that if the respondent does not attend the hearing, the court may make orders against the respondent that could last up to five years.

(o) The respondent shall be entitled, as a matter of course, to one continuance, for a reasonable period, to respond to the petition.

(p)

(1) Either party may request a continuance of the hearing, which the court shall grant on a showing of good cause. The request may be made in writing before or at the hearing, or orally at the hearing. The court may also grant a continuance on its own motion.

(2) If the court grants a continuance, any temporary restraining order that has been granted shall remain in effect until the end of the continued hearing, unless otherwise ordered by the court. In granting a continuance, the court may modify or terminate a temporary restraining order.

(q)

(1) If a respondent named in a restraining order issued after a hearing has not been served personally with the order but has received actual notice of the existence and substance of the order through personal appearance in court to hear the terms of the order from the court, additional proof of service is not required for enforcement of the order.

(2) If the respondent named in a temporary restraining order is personally served with the order and notice of hearing with respect to a restraining order or protective order based on the temporary restraining order, but the respondent does not appear at the hearing, either personally or by an attorney, and the terms and conditions of the restraining order or protective order issued at the hearing are identical to the temporary restraining order, except for the duration of the order, the restraining order or protective order issued at the hearing may be served on the respondent by first-class mail sent to the respondent at the most current address for the respondent available to the court.

(3) The Judicial Council form for temporary orders issued pursuant to this subdivision shall contain a statement in substantially the following form: "If you have been personally served with this temporary restraining order and notice of hearing, but you do not appear at the hearing either in person or by a lawyer, and a restraining order that is the same as this temporary restraining order except for the expiration date is issued at the hearing, a copy of the restraining order will be served on you by mail at the following address: ____.
If that address is not correct or you wish to verify that the temporary restraining order was converted to a restraining order at the hearing without substantive change and to find out the duration of that order, contact the clerk of the court."

(4) If information about a minor has been made confidential pursuant to subdivision (v), the notice shall identify the information, specifically, that has been made confidential and shall include a statement that disclosure or misuse of that information is punishable as a contempt of court.

(r)

(1) Information on a temporary restraining order or order after hearing relating to civil harassment issued by a court pursuant to this section shall be transmitted to the Department of Justice in accordance with either paragraph (2) or (3).

(2) The court shall order the petitioner or the attorney for the petitioner to deliver a copy of an order issued under this section, or reissuance, extension, modification, or termination of the order, and any subsequent proof of service, by the close of the business day on which the order, reissuance, extension, modification, or termination was made, to a law enforcement agency having jurisdiction over the residence of the petitioner and to any additional law enforcement agencies within the court's discretion as are requested by the petitioner.

(3) Alternatively, the court or its designee shall transmit, within one business day, to law enforcement personnel all information required under subdivision (b) of Section 6380 of the Family Code regarding any order issued under this section, or a reissuance, extension, modification, or termination of the order, and any subsequent proof of service, by either one of the following methods:

(A) Transmitting a physical copy of the order or proof of service to a local law enforcement agency authorized by the Department of Justice to enter orders into the California Law Enforcement Telecommunications System (CLETS).

(B) With the approval of the Department of Justice, entering the order or proof of service into CLETS directly.

(4) Each appropriate law enforcement agency shall make available information as to the existence and current status of orders issued under this section to law enforcement officers responding to the scene of reported harassment.

(5) An order issued under this section shall, on request of the petitioner, be served on the respondent, whether or not the respondent has been taken into custody, by any law enforcement officer who is present at the scene of reported harassment involving the parties to the proceeding. The petitioner shall provide the officer with an endorsed copy of the order and a proof of service that the officer shall complete and send to the issuing court.

(6) Upon receiving information at the scene of an incident of harassment that a protective order has been issued under this section, or that a person who has been taken into custody is the subject of an order, if the protected person cannot produce a certified copy of the order, a law enforcement officer shall immediately attempt to verify the existence of the order.

(7) If the law enforcement officer determines that a protective order has been issued but not served, the officer shall immediately notify the respondent of the terms of the order and shall at that time also enforce the order. Verbal notice of the terms of the order shall constitute service of the order and is sufficient notice for purposes of this section and for purposes of Section 29825 of the Penal Code. Verbal notice shall include the information required pursuant to paragraph (4) of subdivision (q).

(s) The prevailing party in an action brought pursuant to this section may be awarded court costs and attorney's fees, if any.

(t) Willful disobedience of a temporary restraining order or order after hearing granted pursuant to this section is punishable pursuant to Section 273.6 of the Penal Code.

(u)

(1) A person subject to a protective order issued pursuant to this section shall not own, possess, purchase, receive, or attempt to purchase or receive a firearm or ammunition while the protective order is in effect.

(2) The court shall order a person subject to a protective order issued pursuant to this section to relinquish any firearms the person owns or possesses pursuant to Section 527.9.

(3) A person who owns, possesses, purchases, or receives, or attempts to purchase or receive, a firearm or ammunition while the protective order is in effect is punishable pursuant to Section 29825 of the Penal Code.

(v)

(1) A minor or the minor's legal guardian may petition the court to have information regarding the minor that was obtained in connection with a request for a protective order pursuant to this section, including, but not limited to, the minor's name, address, and the circumstances surrounding the request for a protective order with respect to that minor, be kept confidential.

(2) The court may order the information specified in paragraph (1) be kept confidential if the court expressly finds all of the following:

    (A) The minor's right to privacy overcomes the right of public access to the information.

    (B) There is a substantial probability that the minor's interest will be prejudiced if the information is not kept confidential.

    (C) The order to keep the information confidential is narrowly tailored.

    (D) No less restrictive means exist to protect the minor's privacy.

(3)

    (A) If the request is granted, except as provided in paragraph (4), information regarding the minor shall be maintained in a confidential case file and shall not become part of the public file in the proceeding or any other civil proceeding involving the parties. Except as provided in subparagraph (B), if the court determines that disclosure of confidential information has been made without a court order, the court may impose a sanction of up to one thousand dollars ($1,000). A minor who has alleged harassment, as defined in subdivision (b), shall not be sanctioned for disclosure of the confidential information. If the court imposes a sanction, the court shall first determine whether the person has or is reasonably likely to have the ability to pay.

    (B) Confidential information may be disclosed without a court order only in the following circumstances:

        (i) By the minor's legal guardian who petitioned to keep the information confidential pursuant to this subdivision or the protected party in an order pursuant to this division, provided that the disclosure is necessary to prevent harassment or is in the minor's best interest. A legal guardian or a protected party who makes a disclosure under this clause is subject to the sanction in subparagraph (A) only if the disclosure was malicious.

        (ii) By a person to whom confidential information is disclosed, provided that the disclosure is necessary to prevent harassment or is in the best interest of the minor, no more information than necessary is disclosed, and a delay would be caused by first obtaining a court order to authorize the disclosure of the information. A person who makes a disclosure pursuant to this clause is subject to the sanction in subparagraph (A) if the person discloses the information in a manner that recklessly or maliciously disregards these requirements.

(4)

    (A) Confidential information shall be made available to both of the following:

        (i) Law enforcement pursuant to subdivision (r), to the extent necessary and only for the purpose of enforcing the order.

        (ii) The respondent to allow the respondent to comply with the order for confidentiality and to allow the respondent to comply with and respond to the protective order. A notice shall be provided to the respondent that identifies the specific information that has been made confidential and shall include a statement that disclosure is punishable by a monetary fine.

    (B) At any time, the court on its own may authorize a disclosure of any portion of the confidential information to certain individuals or entities as necessary to prevent harassment, as defined under subdivision (b), including implementation of the protective order, or if it is in the best interest of the minor.

    (C) The court may authorize a disclosure of any portion of the confidential information to any person that files a petition if necessary to prevent harassment, as defined under subdivision (b), or if it is in the best interest of the minor. The party who petitioned the court to keep the information confidential pursuant to this subdivision shall be served personally or by first-class mail with a copy of the petition and afforded an opportunity to object to the disclosure.

(w) This section does not apply to any action or proceeding covered by Title 1.6C (commencing with Section 1788) of Part 4 of Division 3 of the Civil Code or by Division 10 (commencing with Section 6200) of the Family Code. This section does not preclude a petitioner from using other existing civil remedies.

(x)

(1) The Judicial Council shall develop forms, instructions, and rules relating to matters governed by this section. The petition and response forms shall be simple and concise, and their use by parties in actions brought pursuant to this section is mandatory.

(2) A temporary restraining order or order after hearing relating to civil harassment issued by a court pursuant to this section shall be issued on forms adopted by the Judicial Council and that have been approved by the Department of Justice pursuant to subdivision (i) of Section 6380 of the Family Code. However, the fact that an order issued by a court pursuant to this section was not issued on forms adopted by the Judicial Council and approved by the Department of Justice shall not, in and of itself, make the order unenforceable.

(y) There is no filing fee for a petition that alleges that a person has inflicted or threatened violence against the petitioner, stalked the petitioner, or acted or spoken in any other manner that has placed the petitioner in reasonable fear of violence, and that seeks a protective or restraining order restraining stalking, future violence, or threats of violence, in an action brought pursuant to this section. A fee shall not be paid for a subpoena filed in connection with a petition alleging these acts. A fee shall not be paid for filing a response to a petition alleging these acts.

(z)

(1) Subject to paragraph (4) of subdivision (b) of Section 6103.2 of the Government Code, there shall not be a fee for the service of process by a sheriff or marshal of a protective or restraining order to be issued, if either of the following conditions apply:

    (A) The protective or restraining order issued pursuant to this section is based upon stalking, as prohibited by Section 646.9 of the Penal Code.

    (B) The protective or restraining order issued pursuant to this section is based upon unlawful violence or a credible threat of violence.

(2) The Judicial Council shall prepare and develop forms for persons who wish to avail themselves of the services described in this subdivision.

Amended by Stats 2021 ch 156 (AB 1143),s 1, eff. 1/1/2022.

Amended by Stats 2019 ch 294 (AB 925),s 1, eff. 1/1/2020.
Amended by Stats 2017 ch 384 (AB 953),s 1, eff. 1/1/2018.
Amended by Stats 2016 ch 86 (SB 1171),s 24, eff. 1/1/2017.
Amended by Stats 2015 ch 411 (AB 1081),s 1.5, eff. 1/1/2016.
Amended by Stats 2015 ch 401 (AB 494),s 1, eff. 1/1/2016.
Added by Stats 2013 ch 158 (AB 499),s 2, eff. 1/1/2014.

Section 527.7 - Enjoining actions in furtherance of unlawful acts of violence or force

(a) It shall be unlawful for any group, association, organization, society, or other assemblage of two or more persons to meet and to advocate, and to take substantial action in furtherance of, the commission of an unlawful act of violence or force directed to and likely to produce the imminent and unlawful infliction of serious bodily injury or death of another person within this state.

(b) Whenever it reasonably appears that any group, association, society, or other assemblage of two or more persons has met and taken substantial action in furtherance of the commission of an act of violence made unlawful by subdivision (a) and will engage in those acts in the future, any aggrieved individual may bring a civil action in the superior court to enjoin the advocacy of the commission of any act of violence made unlawful by subdivision (a) at any future meeting or meetings. Upon a proper showing by clear and convincing evidence, a permanent or preliminary injunction, restraining order, or writ of mandate shall be granted.

(c) Whenever it appears that an action brought under this section was groundless and brought in bad faith for the purpose of harassment, the trial court or any appellate court may award to the defendant attorney's fees and court costs incurred for the purpose of defending the action.

Added by Stats. 1982, Ch. 1624, Sec. 1.

Section 527.8 - Employer seeking to restrain on behalf of employees threat of violence that may be carried out at workplace

(a) Any employer, whose employee has suffered unlawful violence or a credible threat of violence from any individual, that can reasonably be construed to be carried out or to have been carried out at the workplace, may seek a temporary restraining order and an order after hearing on behalf of the employee and, at the discretion of the court, any number of other employees at the workplace, and, if appropriate, other employees at other workplaces of the employer.

(b) For purposes of this section:

(1) "Course of conduct" is a pattern of conduct composed of a series of acts over a period of time, however short, evidencing a continuity of purpose, including following or stalking an employee to or from the place of work; entering the workplace; following an employee during hours of employment; making telephone calls to an employee; or sending correspondence to an employee by any means, including, but not limited to, the use of the public or private mails, interoffice mail, facsimile, or computer email.

(2) "Credible threat of violence" is a knowing and willful statement or course of conduct that would place a reasonable person in fear for his or her safety, or the safety of his or her immediate family, and that serves no legitimate purpose.

(3) "Employer" and "employee" mean persons defined in Section 350 of the Labor Code. "Employer" also includes a federal agency, the state, a state agency, a city, county, or district, and a private, public, or quasi-public corporation, or any public agency thereof or therein. "Employee" also includes the members of boards of directors of private, public, and quasi-public corporations and elected and appointed public officers. For purposes of this section only, "employee" also includes a volunteer or independent contractor who performs services for the employer at the employer's worksite.

(4) "Petitioner" means the employer that petitions under subdivision (a) for a temporary restraining order and order after hearing.

(5) "Respondent" means the person against whom the temporary restraining order and order after hearing are sought and, if the petition is granted, the restrained person.

(6) "Temporary restraining order" and "order after hearing" mean orders that include any of the following restraining orders, whether issued ex parte or after notice and hearing:

(A) An order enjoining a party from harassing, intimidating, molesting, attacking, striking, stalking, threatening, sexually assaulting, battering, abusing, telephoning, including, but not limited to, making annoying telephone calls as described in Section 653m of the Penal Code, destroying personal property, contacting, either directly or indirectly, by mail or otherwise, or coming within a specified distance of, or disturbing the peace of, the employee.

(B) An order enjoining a party from specified behavior that the court determines is necessary to effectuate orders described in subparagraph (A).

(7) "Unlawful violence" is any assault or battery, or stalking as prohibited in Section 646.9 of the Penal Code, but shall not include lawful acts of self-defense or defense of others.

(c) This section does not permit a court to issue a temporary restraining order or order after hearing prohibiting speech or other activities that are constitutionally protected, or otherwise protected by Section 527.3 or any other provision of law.

(d) In the discretion of the court, on a showing of good cause, a temporary restraining order or order after hearing issued under this section may include other named family or household members, or other persons employed at the employee's workplace or workplaces.

(e) Upon filing a petition under this section, the petitioner may obtain a temporary restraining order in accordance with subdivision (a) of Section 527, if the petitioner also files a declaration that, to the satisfaction of the court, shows reasonable proof that an employee has suffered unlawful violence or a credible threat of violence by the respondent, and that great or irreparable harm would result to an employee. The temporary restraining order may include any of the protective orders described in paragraph (6) of subdivision (b).

(f) A request for the issuance of a temporary restraining order without notice under this section shall be granted or denied on the same day that the petition is submitted to the court, unless the petition is filed too late in the day to permit effective review, in which case the order shall be granted or denied on the next day of judicial business in sufficient time for the order to be filed that day with the clerk of the court.

(g) A temporary restraining order granted under this section shall remain in effect, at the court's discretion, for a period not to exceed 21 days, or if the court extends the time for hearing under subdivision (h), not to exceed 25 days, unless otherwise modified or terminated by the court.

(h) Within 21 days, or if good cause appears to the court, 25 days from the date that a petition for a temporary order is granted or denied, a hearing shall be held on the petition. If no request for temporary orders is made, the hearing shall be held within 21 days, or, if good cause appears to the court, 25 days, from the date that the petition is filed.

(i) The respondent may file a response that explains, excuses, justifies, or denies the alleged unlawful violence or credible threats of violence.

(j) At the hearing, the judge shall receive any testimony that is relevant and may make an independent inquiry. Moreover, if the respondent is a current employee of the entity requesting the order, the judge shall receive evidence concerning the employer's decision to retain, terminate, or otherwise discipline the respondent. If the judge finds by clear and convincing evidence that the respondent engaged in unlawful violence or made a credible threat of violence, an order shall issue prohibiting further unlawful violence or threats of violence.

(k)

(1) In the discretion of the court, an order issued after notice and hearing under this section may have a duration of not more than three years, subject to termination or modification by further order of the court either on written stipulation filed with the court or on the motion of a party. These orders may be renewed, upon the request of a party, for a duration of not more than three years, without a showing of any further violence or threats of violence since the issuance of the original order, subject to termination or modification by further order of the court either on written

stipulation filed with the court or on the motion of a party. The request for renewal may be brought at any time within the three months before the expiration of the order.

(2) The failure to state the expiration date on the face of the form creates an order with a duration of three years from the date of issuance.

(3) If an action is filed for the purpose of terminating or modifying a protective order prior to the expiration date specified in the order by a party other than the protected party, the party who is protected by the order shall be given notice, pursuant to subdivision (b) of Section 1005, of the proceeding by personal service or, if the protected party has satisfied the requirements of Chapter 3.1 (commencing with Section 6205) of Division 7 of Title 1 of the Government Code, by service on the Secretary of State. If the party who is protected by the order cannot be notified prior to the hearing for modification or termination of the protective order, the court shall deny the motion to modify or terminate the order without prejudice or continue the hearing until the party who is protected can be properly noticed and may, upon a showing of good cause, specify another method for service of process that is reasonably designed to afford actual notice to the protected party. The protected party may waive his or her right to notice if he or she is physically present in court and does not challenge the sufficiency of the notice.

(l) This section does not preclude either party from representation by private counsel or from appearing on his or her own behalf.

(m) Upon filing of a petition under this section, the respondent shall be personally served with a copy of the petition, temporary restraining order, if any, and notice of hearing of the petition. Service shall be made at least five days before the hearing. The court may, for good cause, on motion of the petitioner or on its own motion, shorten the time for service on the respondent.

(n) A notice of hearing under this section shall notify the respondent that, if he or she does not attend the hearing, the court may make orders against him or her that could last up to three years.

(o) The respondent shall be entitled, as a matter of course, to one continuance, for a reasonable period, to respond to the petition.

(p)

(1) Either party may request a continuance of the hearing, which the court shall grant on a showing of good cause. The request may be made in writing before or at the hearing or orally at the hearing. The court may also grant a continuance on its own motion.

(2) If the court grants a continuance, any temporary restraining order that has been granted shall remain in effect until the end of the continued hearing, unless otherwise ordered by the court. In granting a continuance, the court may modify or terminate a temporary restraining order.

(q)

(1) If a respondent, named in a restraining order issued under this section after a hearing, has not been served personally with the order but has received actual notice of the existence and substance of the order through personal appearance in court to hear the terms of the order from the court, no additional proof of service is required for enforcement of the order.

(2) If the respondent named in a temporary restraining order is personally served with the order and notice of hearing with respect to a restraining order or protective order based on the temporary restraining order, but the person does not appear at the hearing, either personally or by an attorney, and the terms and conditions of the restraining order or protective order issued at the hearing are identical to the temporary restraining order, except for the duration of the order, then the restraining order or protective order issued at the hearing may be served on the person by first-class mail sent to that person at the most current address for the person available to the court.

(3) The Judicial Council form for temporary orders issued pursuant to this subdivision shall contain a statement in substantially the following form: "If you have been personally served with this temporary restraining order and notice of hearing, but you do not appear at the hearing either in person or by a lawyer, and a restraining order that is the same as this restraining order except for the expiration date is issued at the hearing, a copy of the order will be served on you by mail at the following address: ____.

If that address is not correct or you wish to verify that the temporary restraining order was converted to a restraining order at the hearing without substantive change and to find out the duration of that order, contact the clerk of the court."

(r)

(1) Information on a temporary restraining order or order after hearing relating to workplace violence issued by a court pursuant to this section shall be transmitted to the Department of Justice in accordance with either paragraph (2) or (3).

(2) The court shall order the petitioner or the attorney for the petitioner to deliver a copy of any order issued under this section, or a reissuance, extension, modification, or termination of the order, and any subsequent proof of service, by the close of the business day on which the order, reissuance, extension, modification, or termination was made, to each law enforcement agency having jurisdiction over the residence of the petitioner and to any additional law enforcement agencies within the court's discretion as are requested by the petitioner.

(3) Alternatively, the court or its designee shall transmit, within one business day, to law enforcement personnel all information required under subdivision (b) of Section 6380 of the Family Code regarding any order issued under this section, or a reissuance, extension, modification, or termination of the order, and any subsequent proof of service, by either one of the following methods:

(A) Transmitting a physical copy of the order or proof of service to a local law enforcement agency authorized by the Department of Justice to enter orders into the California Law Enforcement Telecommunications System (CLETS).

(B) With the approval of the Department of Justice, entering the order or proof of service into CLETS directly.

(4) Each appropriate law enforcement agency shall make available information as to the existence and current status of these orders to law enforcement officers responding to the scene of reported unlawful violence or a credible threat of violence.

(5) At the request of the petitioner, an order issued under this section shall be served on the respondent, regardless of whether the respondent has been taken into custody, by any law enforcement officer who is present at the scene of reported unlawful violence or a credible threat of violence involving the parties to the proceedings. The petitioner shall provide the officer with an endorsed copy of the order and proof of service that the officer shall complete and send to the issuing court.

(6) Upon receiving information at the scene of an incident of unlawful violence or a credible threat of violence that a protective order has been issued under this section, or that a person who has been taken into custody is the subject of an order, if the petitioner or the protected person cannot produce an endorsed copy of the order, a law enforcement officer shall immediately attempt to verify the existence of the order.

(7) If the law enforcement officer determines that a protective order has been issued but not served, the officer shall immediately notify the respondent of the terms of the order and obtain the respondent's address. The law enforcement officer shall at that time also enforce the order, but may not arrest or take the respondent into custody for acts in violation of the order that were committed prior to the verbal notice of the terms and conditions of the order. The law enforcement officer's verbal notice of the terms of the order shall constitute service of the order and constitutes sufficient notice for the purposes of this section and for the purposes of Section 29825 of the Penal Code. The petitioner shall mail an endorsed copy of the order to the respondent's mailing address provided to the law enforcement officer within one business day of the reported incident of unlawful violence or a credible threat of violence at which a verbal notice of the terms of the order was provided by a law enforcement officer.

(s)

(1) A person subject to a protective order issued under this section shall not own, possess, purchase, receive, or attempt to purchase or receive a firearm or ammunition while the protective order is in effect.

(2) The court shall order a person subject to a protective order issued under this section to relinquish any firearms he or she owns or possesses pursuant to Section 527.9.

(3) Every person who owns, possesses, purchases or receives, or attempts to purchase or receive a firearm or ammunition while the protective order is in effect is punishable pursuant to Section 29825 of the Penal Code.

(t) Any intentional disobedience of any temporary restraining order or order after hearing granted under this section is punishable pursuant to Section 273.6 of the Penal Code.

(u) This section shall not be construed as expanding, diminishing, altering, or modifying the duty, if any, of an employer to provide a safe workplace for employees and other persons.

(v)

(1) The Judicial Council shall develop forms, instructions, and rules for relating to matters governed by this section. The forms for the petition and response shall be simple and concise, and their use by parties in actions brought pursuant to this section shall be mandatory.

(2) A temporary restraining order or order after hearing relating to unlawful violence or a credible threat of violence issued by a court pursuant to this section shall be issued on forms adopted by the Judicial Council of California and that have been approved by the Department of Justice pursuant to subdivision (i) of Section 6380 of the Family Code. However, the fact that an order issued by a court pursuant to this section was not issued on forms adopted by the Judicial Council and approved by the Department of Justice shall not, in and of itself, make the order unenforceable.

(w) There is no filing fee for a petition that alleges that a person has inflicted or threatened violence against an employee of the petitioner, or stalked the employee, or acted or spoken in any other manner that has placed the employee in reasonable fear of violence, and that seeks a protective or restraining order restraining stalking or future violence or threats of violence, in any action brought pursuant to this section. No fee shall be paid for a subpoena filed in connection with a petition alleging these acts. No fee shall be paid for filing a response to a petition alleging these acts.

(x)

(1) Subject to paragraph (4) of subdivision (b) of Section 6103.2 of the Government Code, there shall be no fee for the service of process by a sheriff or marshal of a temporary restraining order or order after hearing to be issued pursuant to this section if either of the following conditions applies:

(A) The temporary restraining order or order after hearing issued pursuant to this section is based upon stalking, as prohibited by Section 646.9 of the Penal Code.

(B) The temporary restraining order or order after hearing issued pursuant to this section is based on unlawful violence or a credible threat of violence.

(2) The Judicial Council shall prepare and develop forms for persons who wish to avail themselves of the services described in this subdivision.

Amended by Stats 2015 ch 411 (AB 1081),s 2, eff. 1/1/2016.
Amended by Stats 2012 ch 162 (SB 1171),s 13, eff. 1/1/2013.
Amended by Stats 2011 ch 285 (AB 1402),s 2, eff. 1/1/2012, op. 1/1/2012.
Amended by Stats 2011 ch 101 (AB 454),s 2, eff. 1/1/2012.
Amended by Stats 2010 ch 572 (AB 1596),s 2, eff. 1/1/2011, op. 1/1/2012.
Amended by Stats 2010 ch 178 (SB 1115),s 21, eff. 1/1/2011, op. 1/1/2012.
Amended by Stats 2006 ch 476 (AB 2695),s 2, eff. 1/1/2007.
Amended by Stats 2005 ch 467 (AB 429),s 1, eff. 1/1/2006
Amended by Stats 2003 ch 498 (SB 226),s 3, eff. 1/1/2004.
Amended by Stats 2002 ch 1008 (AB 3028),s 3, eff. 1/1/2003.
Amended by Stats 2000 ch 688 (AB 1669), s 6, eff. 1/1/2001.
Previously Amended Octo ber 10, 1999 (Bill Number: AB 825) (Chapter 661).

Section 527.85 - Restraining order on behalf of students of postsecondary education institution suffering threat of violence made off campus

(a) Any chief administrative officer of a postsecondary educational institution, or an officer or employee designated by the chief administrative officer to maintain order on the school campus or facility, a student of which has suffered a credible threat of violence made off the school campus or facility from any individual which can reasonably be construed to be carried out or to have been carried out at the school campus or facility, may, with the written consent of the student, seek a temporary restraining order and an order after hearing on behalf of the student and, at the discretion of the court, any number of other students at the campus or facility who are similarly situated.

(b) For purposes of this section, the following definitions apply:

(1) "Chief administrative officer" means the principal, president, or highest ranking official of the postsecondary educational institution.

(2) "Course of conduct" means a pattern of conduct composed of a series of acts over a period of time, however short, evidencing a continuity of purpose, including any of the following:

(A) Following or stalking a student to or from school.

(B) Entering the school campus or facility.

(C) Following a student during school hours.

(D) Making telephone calls to a student.

(E) Sending correspondence to a student by any means, including, but not limited to, the use of the public or private mails, interoffice mail, facsimile, or computer email.

(3) "Credible threat of violence" means a knowing and willful statement or course of conduct that would place a reasonable person in fear for his or her safety, or the safety of his or her immediate family, and that serves no legitimate purpose.

(4) "Petitioner" means the chief administrative officer, or his or her designee, who petitions under subdivision (a) for a temporary restraining order and order after hearing.

(5) "Postsecondary educational institution" means a private institution of vocational, professional, or postsecondary education.

(6) "Respondent" means the person against whom the temporary restraining order and order after hearing are sought and, if the petition is granted, the restrained person.

(7) "Student" means an adult currently enrolled in or applying for admission to a postsecondary educational institution.

(8) "Temporary restraining order" and "order after hearing" mean orders that include any of the following restraining orders, whether issued ex parte, or after notice and hearing:

(A) An order enjoining a party from harassing, intimidating, molesting, attacking, striking, stalking, threatening, sexually assaulting, battering, abusing, telephoning, including, but not limited to, making annoying telephone calls as described in Section 653m of the Penal Code, destroying personal property, contacting, either directly or indirectly, by mail or otherwise, or coming within a specified distance of, or disturbing the peace of, the student.

(B) An order enjoining a party from specified behavior that the court determines is necessary to effectuate orders described in subparagraph (A).

(9) "Unlawful violence" means any assault or battery, or stalking as prohibited in Section 646.9 of the Penal Code, but shall not include lawful acts of self-defense or defense of others.

(c) This section does not permit a court to issue a temporary restraining order or order after hearing prohibiting speech or other activities that are constitutionally protected, or otherwise protected by Section 527.3 or any other provision of law.

(d) In the discretion of the court, on a showing of good cause, a temporary restraining order or order after hearing issued under this section may include other named family or household members of the student, or other students at the campus or facility.

(e) Upon filing a petition under this section, the petitioner may obtain a temporary restraining order in accordance with subdivision (a) of Section 527, if the petitioner also files a declaration that, to the satisfaction of the court, shows reasonable proof that a student has suffered a credible threat of violence made off the school campus or facility by the respondent, and that great or irreparable harm would result to the student. The temporary restraining order may include any of the protective orders described in paragraph (8) of subdivision (b).

(f) A request for the issuance of a temporary restraining order without notice under this section shall be granted or denied on the same day that the petition is submitted to the court, unless the petition is filed too late in the day to permit effective review, in which case the order shall be granted or denied on the next day of judicial business in sufficient time for the order to be filed that day with the clerk of the court.

(g) A temporary restraining order granted under this section shall remain in effect, at the court's discretion, for a period not to exceed 21 days, or if the court extends the time for hearing under subdivision (h), not to exceed 25 days, unless otherwise modified or terminated by the court.

(h) Within 21 days, or if good cause appears to the court, within 25 days, from the date that a petition for a temporary order is granted or denied, a hearing shall be held on the petition. If no request for temporary orders is made, the hearing shall be held within 21 days, or if good cause appears to the court, 25 days, from the date the petition is filed.

(i) The respondent may file a response that explains, excuses, justifies, or denies the alleged credible threats of violence.

(j) At the hearing, the judge shall receive any testimony that is relevant and may make an independent inquiry. Moreover, if the respondent is a current student of the entity requesting the order, the judge shall receive evidence concerning the decision of the postsecondary educational institution decision to retain, terminate, or otherwise discipline the respondent. If the judge finds by clear and convincing evidence that the respondent made a credible threat of violence off the school campus or facility, an order shall be issued prohibiting further threats of violence.

(k)

(1) In the discretion of the court, an order issued after notice and hearing under this section may have a duration of not more than three years, subject to termination or modification by further order of the court either on written stipulation filed with the court or on the motion of a party. These orders may be renewed, upon the request of a party, for a duration of not more than three years, without a showing of any further violence or threats of violence since the issuance of the original order, subject to termination or modification by further order of the court either on written stipulation filed with the court or on the motion of a party. The request for renewal may be brought at any time within the three months before the expiration of the order.

(2) The failure to state the expiration date on the face of the form creates an order with a duration of three years from the date of issuance.

(3) If an action is filed for the purpose of terminating or modifying a protective order prior to the expiration date specified in the order by a party other than the protected party, the party who is protected by the order shall be given notice, pursuant to subdivision (b) of Section 1005, of the proceeding by personal service or, if the protected party has satisfied the requirements of Chapter 3.1 (commencing with Section 6205) of Division 7 of Title 1 of the Government Code, by service on the Secretary of State. If the party who is protected by the order cannot be notified prior to the hearing for modification or termination of the protective order, the court shall deny the motion to modify or terminate the order without prejudice or continue the hearing until the party who is protected can be properly noticed and may, upon a showing of good cause, specify another method for service of process that is reasonably designed to afford actual notice to the protected party. The protected party may waive his or her right to notice if he or she is physically present in court and does not challenge the sufficiency of the notice.

(l) This section does not preclude either party from representation by private counsel or from appearing on his or her own behalf.

(m) Upon filing of a petition under this section, the respondent shall be personally served with a copy of the petition, temporary restraining order, if any, and notice of hearing of the petition. Service shall be made at least five days before the hearing. The court may, for good cause, on motion of the petitioner or on its own motion, shorten the time for service on the respondent.

(n) A notice of hearing under this section shall notify the respondent that if he or she does not attend the hearing, the court may make orders against him or her that could last up to three years.

(o) The respondent shall be entitled, as a matter of course, to one continuance, for a reasonable period, to respond to the petition.

(p)

(1) Either party may request a continuance of the hearing, which the court shall grant on a showing of good cause. The request may be made in writing before or at the hearing or orally at the hearing. The court may also grant a continuance on its own motion.

(2) If the court grants a continuance, any temporary restraining order that has been granted shall remain in effect until the end of the continued hearing, unless otherwise ordered by the court. In granting a continuance, the court may modify or terminate a temporary restraining order.

(q)

(1) If a respondent, named in an order issued under this section after a hearing, has not been served personally with the order but has received actual notice of the existence and substance of the order through personal appearance in court to hear the terms of the order from the court, no additional proof of service is required for enforcement of the order.

(2) If the respondent named in a temporary restraining order is personally served with the order and notice of hearing with respect to a restraining order or protective order based on the temporary restraining order, but the respondent does not appear at the hearing, either personally or by an attorney, and the terms and conditions of the restraining order or protective order issued at the hearing are identical to the temporary restraining order, except for the duration of the order, then the restraining order or protective order issued at the hearing may be served on the respondent by first-class mail sent to that person at the most current address for the respondent available to the court.

(3) The Judicial Council form for temporary orders issued pursuant to this subdivision shall contain a statement in substantially the following form: "If you have been personally served with a temporary restraining order and notice of hearing, but you do not appear at the hearing either in person or by a lawyer, and a restraining order that is the same as this temporary restraining order except for the expiration date is issued at the hearing, a copy of the order will be served on you by mail at the following address:____.
If that address is not correct or you wish to verify that the temporary restraining order was converted to a restraining order at the hearing without substantive change and to find out the duration of that order, contact the clerk of the court."

(r)

(1) Information on a temporary restraining order or order after hearing relating to schoolsite violence issued by a court pursuant to this section shall be transmitted to the Department of Justice in accordance with either paragraph (2) or (3).

(2) The court shall order the petitioner or the attorney for the petitioner to deliver a copy of any order issued under this section, or a reissuance, extension, modification, or termination of the order, and any subsequent proof of service, by the close of the business day on which the order, reissuance, or termination of the order, and any proof of service, was made, to each law enforcement agency having jurisdiction over the residence of the petition and to any additional law enforcement agencies within the court's discretion as are requested by the petitioner.

(3) Alternatively, the court or its designee shall transmit, within one business day, to law enforcement personnel all information required under subdivision (b) of Section 6380 of the Family Code regarding any order issued under this section, or a reissuance, extension, modification, or termination of the order, and any subsequent proof of service, by either one of the following methods:

      (A) Transmitting a physical copy of the order or proof of service to a local law enforcement agency authorized by the Department of Justice to enter orders into the California Law Enforcement Telecommunications System (CLETS).
      (B) With the approval of the Department of Justice, entering the order of proof of service into CLETS directly.
    (4) Each appropriate law enforcement agency shall make available information as to the existence and current status of these orders to law enforcement officers responding to the scene of reported unlawful violence or a credible threat of violence.
    (5) At the request of the petitioner, an order issued under this section shall be served on the respondent, regardless of whether the respondent has been taken into custody, by any law enforcement officer who is present at the scene of reported unlawful violence or a credible threat of violence involving the parties to the proceedings. The petitioner shall provide the officer with an endorsed copy of the order and proof of service that the officer shall complete and send to the issuing court.
    (6) Upon receiving information at the scene of an incident of unlawful violence or a credible threat of violence that a protective order has been issued under this section, or that a person who has been taken into custody is the subject of an order, if the petitioner or the protected person cannot produce an endorsed copy of the order, a law enforcement officer shall immediately attempt to verify the existence of the order.
    (7) If the law enforcement officer determines that a protective order has been issued but not served, the officer shall immediately notify the respondent of the terms of the order and obtain the respondent's address. The law enforcement officer shall at that time also enforce the order, but may not arrest or take the respondent into custody for acts in violation of the order that were committed prior to the verbal notice of the terms and conditions of the order. The law enforcement officer's verbal notice of the terms of the order shall constitute service of the order and constitutes sufficient notice for the purposes of this section, and Section 29825 of the Penal Code. The petitioner shall mail an endorsed copy of the order to the respondent's mailing address provided to the law enforcement officer within one business day of the reported incident of unlawful violence or a credible threat of violence at which a verbal notice of the terms of the order was provided by a law enforcement officer.
(s)
    (1) A person subject to a protective order issued under this section shall not own, possess, purchase, receive, or attempt to purchase or receive a firearm or ammunition while the protective order is in effect.
    (2) The court shall order a person subject to a protective order issued under this section to relinquish any firearms he or she owns or possesses pursuant to Section 527.9.
    (3) Every person who owns, possesses, purchases, or receives, or attempts to purchase or receive a firearm or ammunition while the protective order is in effect is punishable pursuant to Section 29825 of the Penal Code.
(t) Any intentional disobedience of any temporary restraining order or order after hearing granted under this section is punishable pursuant to Section 273.6 of the Penal Code.
(u) This section shall not be construed as expanding, diminishing, altering, or modifying the duty, if any, of a postsecondary educational institution to provide a safe environment for students and other persons.
(v)
    (1) The Judicial Council shall develop forms, instructions, and rules relating to matters governed by this section. The forms for the petition and response shall be simple and concise, and their use by parties in actions brought pursuant to this section shall be mandatory.
    (2) A temporary restraining order or order after hearing relating to unlawful violence or a credible threat of violence issued by a court pursuant to this section shall be issued on forms adopted by the Judicial Council that have been approved by the Department of Justice pursuant to subdivision (i) of Section 6380 of the Family Code. However, the fact that an order issued by a court pursuant to this section was not issued on forms adopted by the Judicial Council and approved by the Department of Justice shall not, in and of itself, make the order unenforceable.
(w) There is no filing fee for a petition that alleges that a person has threatened violence against a student of the petitioner, or stalked the student, or acted or spoken in any other manner that has placed the student in reasonable fear of violence, and that seeks a protective or restraining order restraining stalking or future threats of violence, in any action brought pursuant to this section. No fee shall be paid for a subpoena filed in connection with a petition alleging these acts. No fee shall be paid for filing a response to a petition alleging these acts.
(x)
    (1) Subject to paragraph (4) of subdivision (b) of Section 6103.2 of the Government Code, there shall be no fee for the service of process by a sheriff or marshal of a temporary restraining order or order after hearing to be issued pursuant to this section if either of the following conditions applies:
      (A) The temporary restraining order or order after hearing issued pursuant to this section is based upon stalking, as prohibited by Section 646.9 of the Penal Code.
      (B) The temporary restraining order or order after hearing issued pursuant to this section is based upon a credible threat of violence.
    (2) The Judicial Council shall prepare and develop forms for persons who wish to avail themselves of the services described in this subdivision.
Amended by Stats 2015 ch 411 (AB 1081),s 3, eff. 1/1/2016.
Amended by Stats 2012 ch 162 (SB 1171),s 14, eff. 1/1/2013.
Amended by Stats 2011 ch 285 (AB 1402),s 3, eff. 1/1/2012, op. 1/1/2012.
Amended by Stats 2011 ch 101 (AB 454),s 3, eff. 1/1/2012.
Amended by Stats 2010 ch 572 (AB 1596),s 4, eff. 1/1/2011, op. 1/1/2012.
Amended by Stats 2010 ch 178 (SB 1115),s 22, eff. 1/1/2011, op. 1/1/2012.
Added by Stats 2009 ch 566 (SB 188),s 1, eff. 1/1/2010.

Section 527.9 - Relinquishment of firearms by persons subject to temporary restraining orders or injunctions

(a) A person subject to a temporary restraining order or injunction issued pursuant to Section 527.6, 527.8, or 527.85 or subject to a restraining order issued pursuant to Section 136.2 of the Penal Code, or Section 15657.03 of the Welfare and Institutions Code, shall relinquish the firearm pursuant to this section.
(b) Upon the issuance of a protective order against a person pursuant to subdivision (a), the court shall order that person to relinquish any firearm in that person's immediate possession or control, or subject to that person's immediate possession or control, within 24 hours of being served with the order, either by surrendering the firearm to the control of local law enforcement officials, or by selling the firearm to a licensed gun dealer, as specified in Article 1 (commencing with Section 26700) and Article 2 (commencing with Section 26800) of Chapter 2 of Division 6 of Title 4 of Part 6 of the Penal Code. A person ordered to relinquish any firearm pursuant to this subdivision shall file with the court a receipt showing the firearm was surrendered to the local law enforcement agency or sold to a licensed gun dealer within 48 hours after receiving the order. In the event that it is necessary to continue the date of any hearing due to a request for a relinquishment order pursuant to this section, the court shall ensure that all applicable protective orders described in Section 6218 of the Family Code remain in effect or bifurcate the issues and grant the permanent restraining order pending the date of the hearing.
(c) A local law enforcement agency may charge the person subject to the order or injunction a fee for the storage of any firearm relinquished pursuant to this section. The fee shall not exceed the actual cost incurred by the local law enforcement agency for the storage of the firearm. For purposes of this subdivision, "actual cost" means expenses directly related to taking possession of a firearm, storing the firearm, and surrendering possession of the firearm to a licensed dealer as defined in Section 26700 of the Penal Code or to the person relinquishing the firearm.

(d) The restraining order requiring a person to relinquish a firearm pursuant to subdivision (b) shall state on its face that the respondent is prohibited from owning, possessing, purchasing, or receiving a firearm while the protective order is in effect and that the firearm shall be relinquished to the local law enforcement agency for that jurisdiction or sold to a licensed gun dealer, and that proof of surrender or sale shall be filed with the court within a specified period of receipt of the order. The order shall also state on its face the expiration date for relinquishment. Nothing in this section shall limit a respondent's right under existing law to petition the court at a later date for modification of the order.
(e) The restraining order requiring a person to relinquish a firearm pursuant to subdivision (b) shall prohibit the person from possessing or controlling any firearm for the duration of the order. At the expiration of the order, the local law enforcement agency shall return possession of any surrendered firearm to the respondent, within five days after the expiration of the relinquishment order, unless the local law enforcement agency determines that (1) the firearm has been stolen, (2) the respondent is prohibited from possessing a firearm because the respondent is in any prohibited class for the possession of firearms, as defined in Chapter 2 (commencing with Section 29800) and Chapter 3 (commencing with Section 29900) of Division 9 of Title 4 of Part 6 of the Penal Code and Sections 8100 and 8103 of the Welfare and Institutions Code, or (3) another successive restraining order is issued against the respondent under this section. If the local law enforcement agency determines that the respondent is the legal owner of any firearm deposited with the local law enforcement agency and is prohibited from possessing any firearm, the respondent shall be entitled to sell or transfer the firearm to a licensed dealer as defined in Section 26700 of the Penal Code. If the firearm has been stolen, the firearm shall be restored to the lawful owner upon his or her identification of the firearm and proof of ownership.
(f) The court may, as part of the relinquishment order, grant an exemption from the relinquishment requirements of this section for a particular firearm if the respondent can show that a particular firearm is necessary as a condition of continued employment and that the current employer is unable to reassign the respondent to another position where a firearm is unnecessary. If an exemption is granted pursuant to this subdivision, the order shall provide that the firearm shall be in the physical possession of the respondent only during scheduled work hours and during travel to and from his or her place of employment. In any case involving a peace officer who as a condition of employment and whose personal safety depends on the ability to carry a firearm, a court may allow the peace officer to continue to carry a firearm, either on duty or off duty, if the court finds by a preponderance of the evidence that the officer does not pose a threat of harm. Prior to making this finding, the court shall require a mandatory psychological evaluation of the peace officer and may require the peace officer to enter into counseling or other remedial treatment program to deal with any propensity for domestic violence.
(g) During the period of the relinquishment order, a respondent is entitled to make one sale of all firearms that are in the possession of a local law enforcement agency pursuant to this section. A licensed gun dealer, who presents a local law enforcement agency with a bill of sale indicating that all firearms owned by the respondent that are in the possession of the local law enforcement agency have been sold by the respondent to the licensed gun dealer, shall be given possession of those firearms, at the location where a respondent's firearms are stored, within five days of presenting the local law enforcement agency with a bill of sale.
Amended by Stats 2011 ch 285 (AB 1402),s 4, eff. 1/1/2012, op. 1/1/2012.
Amended by Stats 2010 ch 572 (AB 1596),s 5, eff. 1/1/2011, op. 1/1/2012.
Amended by Stats 2006 ch 474 (AB 2129),s 1, eff. 1/1/2007.
Added by Stats 2003 ch 498 (SB 226),s 4, eff. 1/1/2004.
Section 527.10 - Prohibition from obtaining addresses or locations of protected persons
(a) The court shall order that any party enjoined pursuant to Section 527.6, 527.8, or 527.85 be prohibited from taking any action to obtain the address or location of any protected person, unless there is good cause not to make that order.
(b) The Judicial Council shall develop forms necessary to effectuate this section.
Amended by Stats 2010 ch 572 (AB 1596),s 3, eff. 1/1/2011, op. 1/1/2012.
Added by Stats 2005 ch 472 (AB 978),s 1, eff. 1/1/2006.
Section 527.11 - [Repealed]
Added by Stats 2014 ch 666 (AB 1513),s 2, eff. 1/1/2015.
Section 527.12 - [Repealed]
Added by Stats 2014 ch 666 (AB 1513),s 3, eff. 1/1/2015.
Section 528 - Allowing injunction after defendant has answered
An injunction cannot be allowed after the defendant has answered, unless upon notice, or upon an order to show cause; but in such case the defendant may be restrained until the decision of the Court or Judge granting or refusing the injunction.
Enacted 1872.
Section 529 - Undertaking required on granting injunction
(a) On granting an injunction, the court or judge must require an undertaking on the part of the applicant to the effect that the applicant will pay to the party enjoined any damages, not exceeding an amount to be specified, the party may sustain by reason of the injunction, if the court finally decides that the applicant was not entitled to the injunction. Within five days after the service of the injunction, the person enjoined may object to the undertaking. If the court determines that the applicant's undertaking is insufficient and a sufficient undertaking is not filed within the time required by statute, the order granting the injunction must be dissolved.
(b) This section does not apply to any of the following persons:
    (1) Either spouse against the other in a proceeding for legal separation or dissolution of marriage.
    (2) The applicant for an order described in Division 10 (commencing with Section 6200) of the Family Code.
    (3) A public entity or officer described in Section 995.220.
    (4) An applicant requesting an injunction under subdivision (d) of Section 1708.85 of the Civil Code.
Amended by Stats 2021 ch 518 (AB 514),s 2, eff. 1/1/2022.
Amended by Stats. 1993, Ch. 219, Sec. 63.7. Effective January 1, 1994.
Section 529.1 - Undertaking by plaintiff in action enjoining construction project
(a) In all actions in which the court has granted an injunction sought by any plaintiff to enjoin a construction project which has received all legally required licenses and permits, the defendant may apply to the court by noticed motion for an order requiring the plaintiff to furnish an undertaking as security for costs and any damages that may be incurred by the defendant by the conclusion of the action or proceeding as the result of a delay in the construction of the project. The motion shall be made on the grounds that there is no reasonable possibility that the plaintiff will obtain a judgment against the moving defendant and that the plaintiff will not suffer undue economic hardship by filing the undertaking.
(b) If the court, after hearing, determines that the grounds for the motion have been established, the court shall order that the plaintiff file the undertaking in an amount specified in the court's order as security for costs and damages of the defendant. The liability of the plaintiff pursuant to this section for the costs and damages of the defendant shall not exceed five hundred thousand dollars ($500,000).
(c) As used in this section, a construction project includes, but is not restricted to, the construction, surveying, design, specifications, alteration, repair, improvement, maintenance, removal, or demolition of any building, highway, road, parking facility, bridge, railroad, airport, pier or dock, excavation or other structure, development or other improvement to real or personal property.
Amended by Stats 2004 ch 193 (SB 111),s 11, eff. 1/1/2005
Section 529.2 - Undertaking by plaintiff in action challenging housing project

(a) In all civil actions, including, but not limited to, actions brought pursuant to Section 21167 of the Public Resources Code, brought by any plaintiff to challenge a housing project which is a development project, as defined by Section 65928 of the Government Code, and which meets or exceeds the requirements for low- or moderate-income housing as set forth in Section 65915 of the Government Code, a defendant may, if the bringing of the action or the seeking by the plaintiff of particular relief including, but not limited to, injunctions, has the effect of preventing or delaying the project from being carried out, apply to the court by noticed motion for an order requiring the plaintiff to furnish an undertaking as security for costs and any damages that may be incurred by the defendant by the conclusion of the action or proceeding as the result of a delay in carrying out the development project. The motion shall be made on the grounds that:

(1) the action was brought in bad faith, vexatiously, for the purpose of delay, or to thwart the low- or moderate-income nature of the housing development project, and

(2) the plaintiff will not suffer undue economic hardship by filing the undertaking.

(b) If the court, after hearing, determines that the grounds for the motion have been established, the court shall order that the plaintiff file the undertaking in an amount specified in the court's order as security for costs and damages of the defendant. The liability of the plaintiff pursuant to this section for the costs and damages of the defendant shall not exceed five hundred thousand dollars ($500,000).

(c) If at any time after the plaintiff has filed an undertaking the housing development plan is changed by the developer in bad faith so that it fails to meet or exceed the requirements for low- or moderate-income housing as set forth in Section 65915 of the Government Code, the developer shall be liable to the plaintiff for the cost of obtaining the undertaking.

Amended by Stats. 1982, Ch. 517, Sec. 124.5.

Section 530 - Notice of application to prevent diversion, diminution or increase of flow of water

In all actions which may be hereafter brought when an injunction or restraining order may be applied for to prevent the diversion, diminution or increase of the flow of water in its natural channels, to the ordinary flow of which the plaintiff claims to be entitled, the court shall first require due notice of the application to be served upon the defendant, unless it shall appear from the verified complaint or affidavits upon which the application therefor is made, that, within ten days prior to the time of such application, the plaintiff has been in the peaceable possession of the flow of such water, and that, within such time, said plaintiff has been deprived of the flow thereof by the wrongful diversion of such flow by the defendant, or that the plaintiff, at the time of such application, is, and for ten days prior thereto, has been, in possession of the flow of said water, and that the defendant threatens to divert the flow of such water; and if such notice of such application be given and upon the hearing thereof, it be made to appear to the court that plaintiff is entitled to the injunction, but that the issuance thereof pending the litigation will entail great damage upon defendant, and that plaintiff will not be greatly damaged by the acts complained of pending the litigation, and can be fully compensated for such damage as he may suffer, the court may refuse the injunction upon the defendant giving a bond such as is provided for in section five hundred and thirty-two; and upon the trial the same proceedings shall be had, and with the same effect as in said section provided.

Amended by Stats. 1911, Ch. 733.

Section 531 - Notice of application to suspend business of corporation

An injunction to suspend the general and ordinary business of a corporation can not be granted without due notice of the application therefor to the proper officers or managing agent of the corporation, except when the people of this state are a party to the proceeding.

Amended by Stats. 1907, Ch. 272.

Section 532 - Dissolution or modification

(a) If an injunction is granted without notice to the person enjoined, the person may apply, upon reasonable notice to the judge who granted the injunction, or to the court in which the action was brought, to dissolve or modify the injunction. The application may be made upon the complaint or the affidavit on which the injunction was granted, or upon affidavit on the part of the person enjoined, with or without the answer. If the application is made upon affidavits on the part of the person enjoined, but not otherwise, the person against whom the application is made may oppose the application by affidavits or other evidence in addition to that on which the injunction was granted.

(b) In all actions in which an injunction or restraining order has been or may be granted or applied for, to prevent the diversion, pending the litigation, of water used, or to be used, for irrigation or domestic purposes only, if it is made to appear to the court that great damage will be suffered by the person enjoined, in case the injunction is continued, and that the person in whose behalf it issued can be fully compensated for any damages suffered by reason of the continuance of the acts enjoined during the pendency of the litigation, the court in its discretion, may dissolve or modify the injunction. The dissolution or modification shall be subject to the person enjoined giving a bond in such amount as may be fixed by the court or judge, conditioned that the enjoined person will pay all damages which the person in whose behalf the injunction issued may suffer by reason of the continuance, during the litigation, of the acts complained of. Upon the trial the amount of the damages must be ascertained, and in case judgment is rendered for the person in whose behalf the injunction was granted, the amount fixed as damages must be included in the judgment, together with reasonable attorney's fees. In any proceedings to enforce the liability on the bond, the amount of the damages as fixed in the judgment is conclusive.

Amended by Stats. 1982, Ch. 517, Sec. 125.

Section 533 - Material change in facts upon which order granted

In any action, the court may on notice modify or dissolve an injunction or temporary restraining order upon a showing that there has been a material change in the facts upon which the injunction or temporary restraining order was granted, that the law upon which the injunction or temporary restraining order was granted has changed, or that the ends of justice would be served by the modification or dissolution of the injunction or temporary restraining order.

Repealed and added by Stats. 1995, Ch. 796, Sec. 8. Effective January 1, 1996.

Section 534 - Defendant's answer in action by riparian owner to enjoin diversion or use of water appropriated

In any action brought by a riparian owner to enjoin the diversion of water appropriated or proposed to be appropriated, or the use thereof, against any person or persons appropriating or proposing to appropriate such waters, the defendant may set up in his answer that the water diverted or proposed to be diverted is for the irrigation of land or other public use, and, in such case, he shall also in such answer set forth the quantity of water desired to be taken and necessary to such irrigation of land or the public use, the nature of such use, the place where the same is used or proposed to be used, the duration and extent of the diversion or the proposed diversion, including the stages of the flow of the stream at and during the time in which the water is to be diverted, and that the same may be diverted without interfering with the actual and necessary beneficial uses of the plaintiff, and that such defendant so answering desires that the court shall ascertain and fix the damages, if any, that will result to the plaintiff or to his riparian lands from the appropriation of the water so appropriated or intended to be appropriated by defendant. The plaintiff may serve and file a reply to the defendant's answer stating plaintiff's rights to the water and the damage plaintiff will suffer by the defendant's taking of the water, and plaintiff may implead as parties to the action all persons necessary to a full determination of the rights of plaintiff to the water and the damages plaintiff will suffer by the proposed taking by defendant, and the court shall have jurisdiction to hear and determine all the rights to water of the plaintiff and other parties to the action, and said parties shall have a right to state and prove their rights, and shall be bound by the judgment rendered the same as though made parties plaintiff at the commencement of the action.

Upon the trial of the case the court shall receive and hear evidence on behalf of the respective parties, and if the court finds that the allegations of such answer are true as to the aforesaid matters, and that the appropriation and diversion of such waters is for irrigation of land or other public use and that, after allowing sufficient water for the actual and necessary beneficial uses of the plaintiff and other parties, there is water available to be beneficially appropriated by such defendant so answering, the court shall fix the time and manner and extent of such appropriation and the actual damages, if any, resulting to the plaintiff or other parties on account of the same, and in fixing such damages the court shall be guided by Article 5 (commencing with Section 1263.410) of Chapter 9 of Title 7 of Part 3, and if, upon the ascertainment and fixing of such damages the defendant, within the time allowed in Section 1268.010 for the payment of damages in proceedings in eminent domain, shall pay into court the amount of damages fixed and the costs adjudged to be paid by such defendant, or give a good and sufficient bond to pay the same upon the final settlement of the case, the injunction prayed for by the plaintiff shall be denied to the extent of the amount the defendant is permitted to appropriate, as aforesaid, and the temporary injunction, if any has been granted, shall be vacated to the extent aforesaid; provided, that any of the parties may appeal from such judgment as in other cases; and provided, further, that if such judgment is in favor of the defendant and if he upon and pending such appeal shall keep on deposit with the clerk of said court the amount of such damages and costs, or the bond, if it be given, so awarded to be paid to the plaintiff or other parties in the event such judgment shall be affirmed, no injunction against the appropriation of the amount the defendant is permitted to appropriate as aforesaid shall be granted or enforced pending such appeal, and, upon the acceptance by the plaintiff or other parties of such amount so awarded or upon the affirmation of such decision on appeal so that such judgment shall become final, the defendant shall have the right to divert and appropriate from such stream, against such plaintiff or other parties and his successors in interest, the quantity of water therein adjudged and allowed. Upon the filing of such answer as is herein provided for, the parties plaintiff or other parties and defendant shall be entitled to a jury trial upon the issues as to damages so raised, as provided in Title 7 (commencing with Section 1230.010) of Part 3, applying to proceedings in eminent domain.

Amended by Stats. 1975, Ch. 1240.

Chapter 5 - RECEIVERS

Section 564 - Cases in which receiver may be appointed

(a) A receiver may be appointed, in the manner provided in this chapter, by the court in which an action or proceeding is pending in any case in which the court is empowered by law to appoint a receiver.

(b) A receiver may be appointed by the court in which an action or proceeding is pending, or by a judge of that court, in the following cases:

(1) In an action by a vendor to vacate a fraudulent purchase of property, or by a creditor to subject any property or fund to the creditor's claim, or between partners or others jointly owning or interested in any property or fund, on the application of the plaintiff, or of any party whose right to or interest in the property or fund, or the proceeds of the property or fund, is probable, and where it is shown that the property or fund is in danger of being lost, removed, or materially injured.

(2) In an action by a secured lender for the foreclosure of a deed of trust or mortgage and sale of property upon which there is a lien under a deed of trust or mortgage, where it appears that the property is in danger of being lost, removed, or materially injured, or that the condition of the deed of trust or mortgage has not been performed, and that the property is probably insufficient to discharge the deed of trust or mortgage debt.

(3) After judgment, to carry the judgment into effect.

(4) After judgment, to dispose of the property according to the judgment, or to preserve it during the pendency of an appeal, or pursuant to the Enforcement of Judgments Law (Title 9 (commencing with Section 680.010)), or after sale of real property pursuant to a decree of foreclosure, during the redemption period, to collect, expend, and disburse rents as directed by the court or otherwise provided by law.

(5) Where a corporation has been dissolved, as provided in Section 565.

(6) Where a corporation is insolvent, or in imminent danger of insolvency, or has forfeited its corporate rights.

(7) In an action of unlawful detainer.

(8) At the request of the Public Utilities Commission pursuant to Section 1825 or 1826 of the Public Utilities Code.

(9) In all other cases where necessary to preserve the property or rights of any party.

(10) At the request of the Office of Statewide Health Planning and Development, or the Attorney General, pursuant to Section 129173 of the Health and Safety Code.

(11) In an action by a secured lender for specific performance of an assignment of rents provision in a deed of trust, mortgage, or separate assignment document. The appointment may be continued after entry of a judgment for specific performance if appropriate to protect, operate, or maintain real property encumbered by a deed of trust or mortgage or to collect rents therefrom while a pending nonjudicial foreclosure under power of sale in a deed of trust or mortgage is being completed.

(12) In a case brought by an assignee under an assignment of leases, rents, issues, or profits pursuant to subdivision (g) of Section 2938 of the Civil Code.

(c) A receiver may be appointed, in the manner provided in this chapter, including, but not limited to, Section 566, by the superior court in an action brought by a secured lender to enforce the rights provided in Section 2929.5 of the Civil Code, to enable the secured lender to enter and inspect the real property security for the purpose of determining the existence, location, nature, and magnitude of any past or present release or threatened release of any hazardous substance into, onto, beneath, or from the real property security. The secured lender shall not abuse the right of entry and inspection or use it to harass the borrower or tenant of the property. Except in case of an emergency, when the borrower or tenant of the property has abandoned the premises, or if it is impracticable to do so, the secured lender shall give the borrower or tenant of the property reasonable notice of the secured lender's intent to enter and shall enter only during the borrower's or tenant's normal business hours. Twenty-four hours' notice shall be presumed to be reasonable notice in the absence of evidence to the contrary.

(d) Any action by a secured lender to appoint a receiver pursuant to this section shall not constitute an action within the meaning of subdivision (a) of Section 726.

(e) For purposes of this section:

(1) "Borrower" means the trustor under a deed of trust, or a mortgagor under a mortgage, where the deed of trust or mortgage encumbers real property security and secures the performance of the trustor or mortgagor under a loan, extension of credit, guaranty, or other obligation. The term includes any successor in interest of the trustor or mortgagor to the real property security before the deed of trust or mortgage has been discharged, reconveyed, or foreclosed upon.

(2) "Hazardous substance" means any of the following:

(A) Any "hazardous substance" as defined in subdivision (h) of Section 25281 of the Health and Safety Code.

(B) Any "waste" as defined in subdivision (d) of Section 13050 of the Water Code.

(C) Petroleum including crude oil or any fraction thereof, natural gas, natural gas liquids, liquefied natural gas, or synthetic gas usable for fuel, or any mixture thereof.

(3) "Real property security" means any real property and improvements, other than a separate interest and any related interest in the common area of a residential common interest development, as the terms "separate interest," "common area," and "common interest development" are defined in Sections 4095, 4100, and 4185 of the Civil Code, or real property consisting of one acre or less that contains 1 to 15 dwelling units.

(4) "Release" means any spilling, leaking, pumping, pouring, emitting, emptying, discharging, injecting, escaping, leaching, dumping, or disposing into the environment, including continuing migration, of hazardous substances into, onto, or through soil, surface water, or groundwater.

(5) "Secured lender" means the beneficiary under a deed of trust against the real property security, or the mortgagee under a mortgage against the real property security, and any successor in interest of the beneficiary or mortgagee to the deed of trust or mortgage.

Amended by Stats 2020 ch 27 (SB 350),s 1, eff. 1/1/2021.

Amended by Stats 2012 ch 181 (AB 806),s 44, eff. 1/1/2013, op. 1/1/2014.

Amended by Stats 2002 ch 999 (AB 2481),s 3, eff. 1/1/2003.
Amended by Stats 2001 ch 44 (SB 562), s 4, eff. 1/1/2002.

Section 565 - Appointment of receivers or trustees upon dissolution of corporation

Upon the dissolution of any corporation, the Superior Court of the county in which the corporation carries on its business or has its principal place of business, on application of any creditor of the corporation, or of any stockholder or member thereof, may appoint one or more persons to be receivers or trustees of the corporation, to take charge of the estate and effects thereof, and to collect the debts and property due and belonging to the corporation, and to pay the outstanding debts thereof, and to divide the moneys and other property that shall remain over among the stockholders or members.

Amended by Code Amendments 1880, Ch. 15.

Section 566 - When consent of parties required for appointment; undertaking if receiver appointed upon ex parte application

(a) No party, or attorney of a party, or person interested in an action, or related to any judge of the court by consanguinity or affinity within the third degree, can be appointed receiver therein without the written consent of the parties, filed with the clerk.

(b) If a receiver is appointed upon an ex parte application, the court, before making the order, must require from the applicant an undertaking in an amount to be fixed by the court, to the effect that the applicant will pay to the defendant all damages the defendant may sustain by reason of the appointment of the receiver and the entry by the receiver upon the duties, in case the applicant shall have procured the appointment wrongfully, maliciously, or without sufficient cause.

Amended by Stats. 1982, Ch. 517, Sec. 127.

Section 567 - Oath and undertaking before entering upon duties

Before entering upon the duties of a receiver:

(a) The receiver must be sworn to perform the duties faithfully.

(b) The receiver shall give an undertaking to the State of California, in such sum as the court or judge may direct, to the effect that the receiver will faithfully discharge the duties of receiver in the action and obey the orders of the court therein. The receiver shall be allowed the cost of the undertaking.

Amended by Stats. 1982, Ch. 517, Sec. 128.

Section 568 - Powers

The receiver has, under the control of the Court, power to bring and defend actions in his own name, as receiver; to take and keep possession of the property, to receive rents, collect debts, to compound for and compromise the same, to make transfers, and generally to do such acts respecting the property as the Court may authorize.

Enacted 1872.

Section 568.1 - Deposit of securities under control of receiver

Any securities in the hands of a receiver may, under the control of the court, be deposited by the receiver in a securities depository, as defined in Section 30004 of the Financial Code, which is licensed under Section 30200 of the Financial Code or exempted from licensing thereunder by Section 30005 or 30006 of the Financial Code, and such securities may be held by such securities depository in the manner authorized by Section 775 of the Financial Code.

Added by Stats. 1972, Ch. 1057.

Section 568.2 - Notice of substandard or unsafe condition concerning rental housing

(a) A receiver of real property containing rental housing shall notify the court of the existence of any order or notice to correct any substandard or unsafe condition, as defined in Section 17920.3 or 17920.10 of the Health and Safety Code, with which the receiver cannot comply within the time provided by the order or notice.

(b) The notice shall be filed within 30 days after the receiver's appointment or, if the substandard condition occurs subsequently, within 15 days of its occurrence.

(c) The notice shall inform the court of all of the following:

(1) The substandard conditions that exist.

(2) The threat or danger that the substandard conditions pose to any occupant of the property or the public.

(3) The approximate cost and time involved in abating the conditions. If more time is needed to approximate the cost, then the notice shall provide the date on which the approximate cost will be filed with the court and that date shall be within 10 days of the filing.

(4) Whether the receivership estate is likely to contain sufficient funds to abate the conditions.

(d) If the receivership estate does not contain sufficient funds to abate the conditions, the receiver shall request further instructions or orders from the court.

(e) The court, upon receipt of a notice pursuant to subdivision (d), shall consider appropriate orders or instructions to enable the receiver to correct the substandard conditions or to terminate or limit the period of receivership.

Amended by Stats 2005 ch 595 (SB 253),s 3, eff. 1/1/2006
Added by Stats 2001 ch 414 (AB 472), s 1, eff. 1/1/2002.

Section 568.3 - Motion for purpose of receiving further instructions or orders

Any tenant of real property that is subject to receivership, a tenant association or organization, or any federal, state, or local enforcement agency, may file a motion in a receivership action for the purpose of seeking further instructions or orders from the court, if either of the following is true:

(a) Substandard conditions exist, as defined by Section 17920.3 or 17920.10 of the Health and Safety Code.

(b) A dispute or controversy exists concerning the powers or duties of the receiver affecting a tenant or the public.

Amended by Stats 2005 ch 595 (SB 253),s 4, eff. 1/1/2006
Added by Stats 2001 ch 414 (AB 472), s 2, eff. 1/1/2002.

Section 568.5 - Sale of property

A receiver may, pursuant to an order of the court, sell real or personal property in the receiver's possession upon the notice and in the manner prescribed by Article 6 (commencing with Section 701.510) of Chapter 3 of Division 2 of Title 9. The sale is not final until confirmed by the court.

Amended by Stats. 1982, Ch. 497, Sec. 35. Operative July 1, 1983, by Sec. 185 of Ch. 497.

Section 568.6 - Receiver appointed by PUC

A receiver appointed at the request of the Public Utilities Commission pursuant to Section 1825 of the Public Utilities Code shall control and operate Pacific Gas and Electric Company upon such terms and conditions as the court prescribes.

Added by Stats 2020 ch 27 (SB 350),s 2, eff. 1/1/2021.

Section 569 - Deposit of funds in interest bearing accounts

Funds in the hands of a receiver may be deposited in one or more interest bearing accounts in the name and for the benefit of the receivership estate with one or more financial institutions, provided that all of the following conditions are satisfied:

(a) The deposits are fully guaranteed or insured under federal law.

(b) The financial institution in which the funds are deposited is not a party to the action in which the receiver was appointed.

(c) The receiver does not own 1 percent or more in value of the outstanding stock of the financial institution, is not an officer, director, or employee of the financial institution, and is not a sibling, whether by the whole or half-blood, spouse, aunt, uncle, nephew, niece, ancestor, or lineal descendant of an owner, officer, employee, or director.
Amended by Stats. 1998, Ch. 932, Sec. 16. Effective January 1, 1999.

Section 570 - Notice of funds belonging to persons whose whereabouts unknown before receiver discharged

A receiver having any funds in his hands belonging to a person whose whereabouts are unknown to him, shall, before receiving his discharge as such receiver, publish a notice, in one or more newspapers published in the county, at least once a week for four consecutive weeks, setting forth the name of the owner of any unclaimed funds, the last known place of residence or post office address of such owner and the amount of such unclaimed funds. Any funds remaining in his hands unclaimed for 30 days after the date of the last publication of such notice, shall be reported to the court, and upon order of the court, all such funds must be paid into the State Treasury accompanied with a copy of the order, which must set forth the facts required in the notice herein provided. Such funds shall be deemed to have been received by the State under Chapter 7 (commencing with Section 1500) of Title 10 of Part 3 of this code and may be recovered in the manner prescribed therein.
All costs and expenses connected with such advertising shall be paid out of the funds the whereabouts of whose owners are unknown.
Amended by Stats. 1963, Ch. 1762.

Chapter 5A - UNDERTAKING OF PERSONS HANDLING PRIVATE PROPERTY OR FUNDS

Section 571 - Referee or commissioner appointed by court

If a referee or commissioner is appointed by a court and the duties of the referee or commissioner will, or are reasonably anticipated to, involve the custody of personal property or the receipt or disbursement of moneys, the order of appointment shall provide that before entering upon the duties, the referee or commissioner shall execute an undertaking to the State of California, to the effect that the referee or commissioner will faithfully discharge the duties of referee or commissioner, as the case may be, and obey the orders of the court therein. The order of appointment shall specify the amount of the undertaking, but a failure to so specify shall not invalidate the order.
Amended by Stats. 1982, Ch. 517, Sec. 129.

Chapter 6 - DEPOSIT IN COURT

Section 572 - Generally

When it is admitted by the pleadings, or shown upon the examination of a party to the action, that he or she has in his or her possession, or under his or her control, any money or other thing capable of delivery, which, being the subject of litigation, is held by him or her as trustee for another party, or which belongs or which is due to another party or which should, under the circumstances of the case be held by the court pending final disposition of the action, the court may order the same, upon motion, to be deposited in court or delivered to such party, upon those conditions that may be just, subject to the further direction of the court.
Amended by Stats. 1986, Ch. 540, Sec. 6.

Section 573 - Deposit with court's treasury

Whenever money is paid into or deposited in the court under this chapter, it shall be deposited with the court's treasury as provided in Section 68084 of the Government Code.
Added by Stats 2005 ch 75 (AB 145),s 35, eff. 7/19/2005, op. 1/1/2006.
Repealed by Stats 2005 ch 75 (AB 145),s 34, eff. 7/19/2005, op. 1/1/2006.

Section 574 - Order requiring sheriff or marshal to take money or thing

Whenever, in the exercise of its authority, a court has ordered the deposit or delivery of money, or other thing, and the order is disobeyed, the court, beside punishing the disobedience, may make an order requiring the sheriff or marshal to take the money, or thing, and deposit or deliver it in conformity with the direction of the court.
Amended by Stats. 1996, Ch. 872, Sec. 15. Effective January 1, 1997.

Title 7a - PRETRIAL CONFERENCES

Section 575 - Promulgation of rules

The Judicial Council may promulgate rules governing pretrial conferences, and the time, manner and nature thereof, in civil cases at issue, or in one or more classes thereof, in the superior courts.
Amended by Stats 2002 ch 784 (SB 1316),s 61, eff. 1/1/2003.

Section 575.1 - Adoption of local rules

(a) The presiding judge of each superior court may prepare, with the assistance of appropriate committees of the court, proposed local rules designed to expedite and facilitate the business of the court. The rules need not be limited to those actions on the civil active list, but may provide for the supervision and judicial management of actions from the date they are filed. Rules prepared pursuant to this section shall be submitted for consideration to the judges of the court and, upon approval by a majority of the judges, the judges shall have the proposed rules published and submitted to the local bar and others, as specified by the Judicial Council, for consideration and recommendations.
(b) After a majority of the judges have officially adopted the rules, they shall be filed with the Judicial Council as required by Section 68071 of the Government Code and as specified in rules adopted by the Judicial Council. The Judicial Council shall prescribe rules to ensure that a complete current set of local rules and amendments, for each county in the state, is made available for public examination in each county. The local rules shall also be published for general distribution in accordance with rules adopted by the Judicial Council. Each court shall make its local rules available for inspection and copying in every location of the court that generally accepts filing of papers. The court may impose a reasonable charge for copying the rules and may impose a reasonable page limit on copying. The rules shall be accompanied by a notice indicating where a full set of the rules may be purchased.
(c) If a judge of a court adopts a rule that applies solely to cases in that judge's courtroom, or a particular branch or district of a court adopts a rule that applies solely to cases in that particular branch or district of a court, the court shall publish these rules as part of the general publication of rules required by the California Rules of Court. The court shall organize the rules so that rules on a common subject, whether individual, branch, district, or courtwide appear sequentially. Individual judges' rules and branch and district rules are local rules of court for purposes of this section and for purposes of the adoption, publication, comment, and filing requirements set forth in the Judicial Council rules applicable to local court rules.
Amended by Stats 2003 ch 149 (SB 79),s 9, eff. 1/1/2004.

Section 575.2 - Failure to comply with local rules

(a) Local rules promulgated pursuant to Section 575.1 may provide that if any counsel, a party represented by counsel, or a party if in pro se, fails to comply with any of the requirements thereof, the court on motion of a party or on its own motion may strike out all or any part of any pleading of that party, or, dismiss the action or proceeding or any part thereof, or enter a judgment by default against that party, or impose other penalties of a lesser nature as otherwise provided by law, and may order that party or his or her counsel to pay to the moving party the reasonable expenses in making the motion, including reasonable attorney fees. No penalty may be imposed under this section without prior notice to, and an opportunity to be heard by, the party against whom the penalty is sought to be imposed.
(b) It is the intent of the Legislature that if a failure to comply with these rules is the responsibility of counsel and not of the party, any penalty shall be imposed on counsel and shall not adversely affect the party's cause of action or defense thereto.

Amended by Stats 2002 ch 806 (AB 3027),s 14, eff. 1/1/2003.

Section 575.5 - [Repealed]

Repealed by Stats 2007 ch 268 (AB 500),s 2, eff. 1/1/2008.

Section 575.6 - [Repealed]

Repealed by Stats 2007 ch 268 (AB 500),s 3, eff. 1/1/2008.

Section 576 - Amendment of pleading or pretrial conference order

Any judge, at any time before or after commencement of trial, in the furtherance of justice, and upon such terms as may be proper, may allow the amendment of any pleading or pretrial conference order.

Added by Stats. 1963, Ch. 882.

Title 8 - OF THE TRIAL AND JUDGMENT IN CIVIL ACTIONS

Chapter 1 - JUDGMENT IN GENERAL

Section 577 - Definition

A judgment is the final determination of the rights of the parties in an action or proceeding.

Enacted 1872.

Section 577.5 - Computation of amount

In any judgment, or execution upon such judgment, the amount shall be computed and stated in dollars and cents, rejecting fractions.

Added by Stats. 1951, Ch. 655.

Section 578 - Given for or against one or more of several plaintiffs or defendants

Judgment may be given for or against one or more of several plaintiffs, and for or against one or more of several defendants; and it may, when the justice of the case requires it, determine the ultimate rights of the parties on each side, as between themselves.

Enacted 1872.

Section 579 - Judgment against one or more defendants leaving action to proceed against others

In an action against several defendants, the Court may, in its discretion, render judgment against one or more of them, leaving the action to proceed against the others, whenever a several judgment is proper.

Enacted 1872.

Section 580 - Relief grant to plaintiff

(a) The relief granted to the plaintiff, if there is no answer, cannot exceed that demanded in the complaint, in the statement required by Section 425.11, or in the statement provided for by Section 425.115; but in any other case, the court may grant the plaintiff any relief consistent with the case made by the complaint and embraced within the issue. The court may impose liability, regardless of whether the theory upon which liability is sought to be imposed involves legal or equitable principles.

(b) Notwithstanding subdivision (a), the following types of relief may not be granted in a limited civil case:

(1) Relief exceeding the maximum amount in controversy for a limited civil case as provided in Section 85, exclusive of attorney's fees, interest, and costs.

(2) A permanent injunction, except as otherwise authorized by statute.

(3) A determination of title to real property.

(4) Declaratory relief, except as authorized by Section 86.

Amended by Stats 2007 ch 43 (SB 649),s 5, eff. 1/1/2008.

Amended by Stats 2006 ch 86 (AB 2126),s 1, eff. 1/1/2007.

Section 580a - Money judgment sought for balance due upon obligation following exercise of power of sale in deed of trust or mortgage

Whenever a money judgment is sought for the balance due upon an obligation for the payment of which a deed of trust or mortgage with power of sale upon real property or any interest therein was given as security, following the exercise of the power of sale in such deed of trust or mortgage, the plaintiff shall set forth in his or her complaint the entire amount of the indebtedness which was secured by the deed of trust or mortgage at the time of sale, the amount for which the real property or interest therein was sold and the fair market value thereof at the date of sale and the date of that sale. Upon the application of either party made at least 10 days before the time of trial the court shall, and upon its own motion the court at any time may, appoint one of the probate referees provided for by law to appraise the property or the interest therein sold as of the time of sale. The referee shall file his or her appraisal with the clerk and that appraisal shall be admissible in evidence. The referee shall take and subscribe an oath to be attached to the appraisal that he or she has truly, honestly and impartially appraised the property to the best of his or her knowledge and ability. Any referee so appointed may be called and examined as a witness by any party or by the court itself. The court must fix the compensation of the referee in an amount as determined by the court to be reasonable, but those fees shall not exceed similar fees for similar services in the community where the services are rendered, which may be taxed and allowed in like manner as other costs. Before rendering any judgment the court shall find the fair market value of the real property, or interest therein sold, at the time of sale. The court may render judgment for not more than the amount by which the entire amount of the indebtedness due at the time of sale exceeded the fair market value of the real property or interest therein sold at the time of sale with interest thereon from the date of the sale; provided, however, that in no event shall the amount of the judgment, exclusive of interest after the date of sale, exceed the difference between the amount for which the property was sold and the entire amount of the indebtedness secured by the deed of trust or mortgage. Any such action must be brought within three months of the time of sale under the deed of trust or mortgage. No judgment shall be rendered in any such action until the real property or interest therein has first been sold pursuant to the terms of the deed of trust or mortgage, unless the real property or interest therein has become valueless.

Amended by Stats. 1988, Ch. 1199, Sec. 6. Operative July 1, 1989, by Sec. 119 of Ch. 1199.

Section 580b - No deficiency judgment owed or collected exception

(a) Except as provided in subdivision (c), no deficiency shall be owed or collected, and no deficiency judgment shall lie, for any of the following:

(1) After a sale of real property or an estate for years therein for failure of the purchaser to complete his or her contract of sale.

(2) Under a deed of trust or mortgage given to the vendor to secure payment of the balance of the purchase price of that real property or estate for years therein.

(3) Under a deed of trust or mortgage on a dwelling for not more than four families given to a lender to secure repayment of a loan that was used to pay all or part of the purchase price of that dwelling, occupied entirely or in part by the purchaser. For purposes of subdivision (b), a loan described in this paragraph is a "purchase money loan."

(b) No deficiency shall be owed or collected, and no deficiency judgment shall lie, on a loan, refinance, or other credit transaction (collectively, a "credit transaction") that is used to refinance a purchase money loan, or subsequent refinances of a purchase money loan, except to the extent that in a credit transaction the lender or creditor advances new principal (hereafter "new advance") that is not applied to an obligation owed or to be owed under the purchase money loan, or to fees, costs, or related expenses of the credit transaction. A new credit transaction shall be deemed to be a purchase money loan except as to the principal amount of a new advance. For purposes of this section, any payment of principal shall be deemed to be applied first to the principal balance of the purchase money loan, and then to the principal balance of a new advance, and interest payments shall be applied to any interest due and owing. This subdivision applies only to credit transactions that are executed on or after January 1, 2013.

(c) The fact that no deficiency shall be owed or collected under the circumstances set forth in subdivisions (a) and (b) does not affect the liability that a guarantor, pledgor, or other surety might otherwise have with respect to the deficiency, or that might otherwise be satisfied in whole or in part from other collateral pledged to secure the obligation that is the subject of the deficiency.

(d) When both a chattel mortgage and a deed of trust or mortgage have been given to secure payment of the balance of the combined purchase price of both real and personal property, no deficiency judgment shall lie under any one thereof if no deficiency judgment would lie under the deed of trust or mortgage on the real property or estate for years therein.

Amended by Stats 2014 ch 71 (SB 1304),s 18, eff. 1/1/2015.
Amended by Stats 2013 ch 65 (SB 426),s 2, eff. 1/1/2014.
Amended by Stats 2012 ch 64 (SB 1069),s 1, eff. 1/1/2013.

Section 580c - Trustee's or attorney's fees for processing judicial foreclosure of deed of trust or mortgage

In all cases where existing deeds of trust or mortgages are judicially foreclosed, unless a different amount is set up in the mortgage or deed of trust, and in all cases of mortgages and deeds of trust executed after this act takes effect, the mortgagor or trustor may be required to pay only such amount as trustee's or attorney's fees for processing the judicial foreclosure as the court may find reasonable and also the actual cost of publishing, recording, mailing and posting notices, litigation guarantee, and litigation cost of suit.

Amended by Stats. 1984, Ch. 1730, Sec. 6.

Section 580d - No deficiency collected or owed on note secured by deed of trust or mortgage, exception

(a)Except as provided in subdivision (b), no deficiency shall be owed or collected, and no deficiency judgment shall be rendered for a deficiency on a note secured by a deed of trust or mortgage on real property or an estate for years therein executed in any case in which the real property or estate for years therein has been sold by the mortgagee or trustee under power of sale contained in the mortgage or deed of trust.

(b)The fact that no deficiency shall be owed or collected under the circumstances set forth in subdivision (a) does not affect the liability that a guarantor, pledgor, or other surety might otherwise have with respect to the deficiency, or that might otherwise be satisfied in whole or in part from other collateral pledged to secure the obligation that is the subject of the deficiency.

(c)This section does not apply to a deed of trust, mortgage, or other lien given to secure the payment of bonds or other evidences of indebtedness authorized or permitted to be issued by the Commissioner of Financial Protection and Innovation or which is made by a public utility subject to the Public Utilities Act (Part 1 (commencing with Section 201) of Division 1 of the Public Utilities Code).

Amended by Stats 2022 ch 452 (SB 1498),s 38, eff. 1/1/2023.
Amended by Stats 2014 ch 401 (AB 2763),s 14, eff. 1/1/2015.
Amended by Stats 2014 ch 71 (SB 1304),s 19, eff. 1/1/2015.
Amended by Stats 2013 ch 65 (SB 426),s 3, eff. 1/1/2014.

Section 580e - No deficiency owed or collected upon note secured by deed of trust or mortgage for dwelling of not more than four units

(a)

(1)No deficiency shall be owed or collected, and no deficiency judgment shall be requested or rendered for any deficiency upon a note secured solely by a deed of trust or mortgage for a dwelling of not more than four units, in any case in which the trustor or mortgagor sells the dwelling for a sale price less than the remaining amount of the indebtedness outstanding at the time of sale, in accordance with the written consent of the holder of the deed of trust or mortgage, provided that both of the following have occurred:

(A)Title has been voluntarily transferred to a buyer by grant deed or by other document of conveyance that has been recorded in the county where all or part of the real property is located.

(B)The proceeds of the sale have been tendered to the mortgagee, beneficiary, or the agent of the mortgagee or beneficiary, in accordance with the parties' agreement.

(2)In circumstances not described in paragraph (1), when a note is not secured solely by a deed of trust or mortgage for a dwelling of not more than four units, no judgment shall be rendered for any deficiency upon a note secured by a deed of trust or mortgage for a dwelling of not more than four units, if the trustor or mortgagor sells the dwelling for a sale price less than the remaining amount of the indebtedness outstanding at the time of sale, in accordance with the written consent of the holder of the deed of trust or mortgage. Following the sale, in accordance with the holder's written consent, the voluntary transfer of title to a buyer by grant deed or by other document of conveyance recorded in the county where all or part of the real property is located, and the tender to the mortgagee, beneficiary, or the agent of the mortgagee or beneficiary of the sale proceeds, as agreed, the rights, remedies, and obligations of any holder, beneficiary, mortgagee, trustor, mortgagor, obligor, obligee, or guarantor of the note, deed of trust, or mortgage, and with respect to any other property that secures the note, shall be treated and determined as if the dwelling had been sold through foreclosure under a power of sale contained in the deed of trust or mortgage for a price equal to the sale proceeds received by the holder, in the manner contemplated by Section 580d.

(b)A holder of a note shall not require the trustor, mortgagor, or maker of the note to pay any additional compensation, aside from the proceeds of the sale, in exchange for the written consent to the sale.

(c)If the trustor or mortgagor commits either fraud with respect to the sale of, or waste with respect to, the real property that secures the deed of trust or mortgage, this section shall not limit the ability of the holder of the deed of trust or mortgage to seek damages and use existing rights and remedies against the trustor or mortgagor or any third party for fraud or waste.

(d)

(1)This section shall not apply if the trustor or mortgagor is a corporation, limited liability company, limited partnership, or political subdivision of the state.

(2)This section shall not apply to any deed of trust, mortgage, or other lien given to secure the payment of bonds or other evidence of indebtedness authorized, or permitted to be issued, by the Commissioner of Financial Protection and Innovation, or that is made by a public utility subject to the Public Utilities Act (Part 1 (commencing with Section 201) of Division 1 of the Public Utilities Code).

(e)Any purported waiver of subdivision (a) or (b) shall be void and against public policy.

Amended by Stats 2022 ch 452 (SB 1498),s 39, eff. 1/1/2023.
Amended by Stats 2019 ch 143 (SB 251),s 19, eff. 1/1/2020.
Amended by Stats 2011 ch 82 (SB 458),s 1, eff. 7/11/2011.
Added by Stats 2010 ch 701 (SB 931),s 1, eff. 1/1/2011.

Section 580.5 - Obligation secured by mortgage or deed of trust and also supported by letter of credit

(a) For purposes of this section:

(1) "Beneficiary" means a "beneficiary" as defined in paragraph (3) of subdivision (a) of Section 5102 of the Commercial Code.

(2) "Issuer" means an "issuer" as defined in paragraph (9) of subdivision (a) of Section 5102 of the Commercial Code.

(3) "Letter of credit" means a "letter of credit" as defined in paragraph (10) of subdivision (a) of Section 5102 of the Commercial Code whether or not the engagement is governed by Division 5 (commencing with Section 5101) of the Commercial Code.

(b) With respect to an obligation which is secured by a mortgage or a deed of trust upon real property or an estate for years therein and which is also supported by a letter of credit, neither the presentment, receipt of payment, or enforcement of a draft or demand for payment under the letter of credit by the beneficiary of the letter of credit nor the honor or payment of, or the demand for reimbursement, receipt of reimbursement or enforcement of any contractual, statutory or other reimbursement obligation relating to, the letter of credit by the issuer of the letter of credit shall, whether done before or after the judicial or nonjudicial foreclosure of the mortgage or deed of trust or conveyance in lieu thereof, constitute any of the following:

(1) An action within the meaning of subdivision (a) of Section 726, or a failure to comply with any other statutory or judicial requirement to proceed first against security.

(2) A money judgment for a deficiency or a deficiency judgment within the meaning of Section 580a, 580b, or 580d, or subdivision (b) of Section 726, or the functional equivalent of any such judgment.

(3) A violation of Section 580a, 580b, 580d, or 726.

Amended by Stats. 1996, Ch. 176, Sec. 2. Effective January 1, 1997.

Section 580.7 - Circumstances in which letter of credit not enforceable in loan transaction

(a) For purposes of this section:

(1) "Beneficiary" means a "beneficiary" as defined in paragraph (3) of subdivision (a) of Section 5102 of the Commercial Code.

(2) "Customer" means an "applicant" as defined in paragraph (2) of subdivision (a) of Section 5102 of the Commercial Code.

(3) "Letter of credit" means a "letter of credit" as defined in paragraph (10) of subdivision (a) of Section 5102 of the Commercial Code whether or not the engagement is governed by Division 5 (commencing with Section 5101) of the Commercial Code.

(b) No letter of credit shall be enforceable by any party thereto in a loan transaction in which all of the following circumstances exist:

(1) The customer is a natural person.

(2) The letter of credit is issued to the beneficiary to avoid a default of the existing loan.

(3) The existing loan is secured by a purchase money deed of trust or purchase money mortgage on real property containing one to four residential units, at least one of which is owned and occupied, or was intended at the time the existing loan was made, to be occupied by the customer.

(4) The letter of credit is issued after the effective date of this section.

Amended by Stats. 1996, Ch. 176, Sec. 3. Effective January 1, 1997.

Section 581 - Dismissal of action

(a) As used in this section:

(1) "Action" means any civil action or special proceeding.

(2) "Complaint" means a complaint and a cross-complaint.

(3) "Court" means the court in which the action is pending.

(4) "Defendant" includes a cross-defendant.

(5) "Plaintiff" includes a cross-complainant.

(6) "Trial." A trial shall be deemed to actually commence at the beginning of the opening statement or argument of any party or his or her counsel, or if there is no opening statement, then at the time of the administering of the oath or affirmation to the first witness, or the introduction of any evidence.

(b) An action may be dismissed in any of the following instances:

(1) With or without prejudice, upon written request of the plaintiff to the clerk, filed with papers in the case, or by oral or written request to the court at any time before the actual commencement of trial, upon payment of the costs, if any.

(2) With or without prejudice, by any party upon the written consent of all other parties.

(3) By the court, without prejudice, when no party appears for trial following 30 days' notice of time and place of trial.

(4) By the court, without prejudice, when dismissal is made pursuant to the applicable provisions of Chapter 1.5 (commencing with Section 583.110).

(5) By the court, without prejudice, when either party fails to appear on the trial and the other party appears and asks for dismissal.

(c) A plaintiff may dismiss his or her complaint, or any cause of action asserted in it, in its entirety, or as to any defendant or defendants, with or without prejudice prior to the actual commencement of trial.

(d) Except as otherwise provided in subdivision (e), the court shall dismiss the complaint, or any cause of action asserted in it, in its entirety or as to any defendant, with prejudice, when upon the trial and before the final submission of the case, the plaintiff abandons it.

(e) After the actual commencement of trial, the court shall dismiss the complaint, or any causes of action asserted in it, in its entirety or as to any defendants, with prejudice, if the plaintiff requests a dismissal, unless all affected parties to the trial consent to dismissal without prejudice or by order of the court dismissing the same without prejudice on a showing of good cause.

(f) The court may dismiss the complaint as to that defendant when:

(1) Except where Section 597 applies, after a demurrer to the complaint is sustained without leave to amend and either party moves for dismissal.

(2) Except where Section 597 applies, after a demurrer to the complaint is sustained with leave to amend, the plaintiff fails to amend it within the time allowed by the court and either party moves for dismissal.

(3) After a motion to strike the whole of a complaint is granted without leave to amend and either party moves for dismissal.

(4) After a motion to strike the whole of a complaint or portion thereof is granted with leave to amend the plaintiff fails to amend it within the time allowed by the court and either party moves for dismissal.

(g) The court may dismiss without prejudice the complaint in whole, or as to that defendant, when dismissal is made under the applicable provisions of Chapter 1.5 (commencing with Section 583.110).

(h) The court may dismiss without prejudice the complaint in whole, or as to that defendant, when dismissal is made pursuant to Section 418.10.

(i) No dismissal of an action may be made or entered, or both, under paragraph (1) of subdivision (b) where affirmative relief has been sought by the cross-complaint of a defendant or if there is a motion pending for an order transferring the action to another court under the provisions of Section 396b.

(j) No dismissal may be made or entered, or both, under paragraph (1) or (2) of subdivision (b) except upon the written consent of the attorney for the party or parties applying therefor, or if consent of the attorney is not obtained, upon order of dismissal by the court after notice to the attorney.

(k) No action may be dismissed which has been determined to be a class action under the provisions of this code unless and until notice that the court deems adequate has been given and the court orders the dismissal.

(l) The court may dismiss, without prejudice, the complaint in whole, or as to that defendant when either party fails to appear at the trial and the other party appears and asks for the dismissal.

(m) The provisions of this section shall not be deemed to be an exclusive enumeration of the court's power to dismiss an action or dismiss a complaint as to a defendant.

Amended by Stats. 1993, Ch. 456, Sec. 9. Effective January 1, 1994.

Section 581.5 - Dismissal of consumer debt in which plaintiff debt buyer fails to appear or not prepared to proceed

In a case involving consumer debt, as defined in Section 1788.2 of the Civil Code, and as regulated under Title 1.6C.5 (commencing with Section 1788.50) of Part 4 of Division 3 of the Civil Code, if the defendant debtor appears for trial on the scheduled trial date, and the plaintiff debt buyer

either fails to appear or is not prepared to proceed to trial, and the court does not find a good cause for continuance, the court may, in its discretion, dismiss the action with or without prejudice. Notwithstanding any other law, in this instance, the court may award the defendant debtor's costs of preparing for trial, including, but not limited to, lost wages and transportation expenses.
Added by Stats 2013 ch 64 (SB 233),s 3, eff. 1/1/2014.

Section 581c - Motion for judgment or nonsuit by defendant
(a) Only after, and not before, the plaintiff has completed his or her opening statement, or after the presentation of his or her evidence in a trial by jury, the defendant, without waiving his or her right to offer evidence in the event the motion is not granted, may move for a judgment of nonsuit.
(b) If it appears that the evidence presented, or to be presented, supports the granting of the motion as to some but not all of the issues involved in the action, the court shall grant the motion as to those issues and the action shall proceed as to the issues remaining. Despite the granting of the motion, no final judgment shall be entered prior to the termination of the action, but the final judgment in the action shall, in addition to any matters determined in the trial, award judgment as determined by the motion herein provided for.
(c) If the motion is granted, unless the court in its order for judgment otherwise specifies, the judgment of nonsuit operates as an adjudication upon the merits.
(d) In actions which arise out of an injury to the person or to property, when a motion for judgment of nonsuit was granted on the basis that the defendant was without fault, no other defendant during trial, over plaintiff's objection, may attempt to attribute fault to or comment on the absence or involvement of the defendant who was granted the motion.
Amended by Stats. 1998, Ch. 200, Sec. 1. Effective January 1, 1999.

Section 581d - Dismissal entered in clerk's register; form or order of dismissal
A written dismissal of an action shall be entered in the clerk's register and is effective for all purposes when so entered.
All dismissals ordered by the court shall be in the form of a written order signed by the court and filed in the action and those orders when so filed shall constitute judgments and be effective for all purposes, and the clerk shall note those judgments in the register of actions in the case.
Amended by Stats. 1998, Ch. 931, Sec. 79. Effective September 28, 1998.

Section 582 - Judgment rendered on merits
In all other cases judgment shall be rendered on the merits.
Amended by Stats. 1947, Ch. 990.

Section 582.5 - Payment of judgment or order by defendant in limited civil case
In a limited civil case in which the defendant has appeared, if the judgment or order is for the payment of money by the defendant, the defendant shall pay the judgment immediately or at any time and upon terms and conditions, including installment payments, that the court may prescribe. The court may amend the terms and conditions for payment of the judgment or order at any time to provide for installment payments for good cause upon motion by a party and notice to all affected parties, regardless of the nature of the underlying debt and regardless of whether the moving party appeared before entry of the judgment or order. In any determination regarding the imposition of terms and conditions upon the payment of the judgment, the court shall consider any factors that would be relevant to the determination of a claim for exemption pursuant to Chapter 4 (commencing with Section 703.010) of Division 2 of Title 9 of Part 2 or the examination of a debtor pursuant to Article 2 (commencing with Section 708.110) of Chapter 6 of Division 2 of Title 9.
Added by Stats. 1998, Ch. 931, Sec. 80. Effective September 28, 1998.

Chapter 1.5 - DISMISSAL FOR DELAY IN PROSECUTION
Article 1 - DEFINITIONS AND GENERAL PROVISIONS

Section 583.110 - Definitions
As used in this chapter, unless the provision or context otherwise requires:
(a) "Action" includes an action commenced by cross-complaint or other pleading that asserts a cause of action or claim for relief.
(b) "Complaint" includes a cross-complaint or other initial pleading.
(c) "Court" means the court in which the action is pending.
(d) "Defendant" includes a cross-defendant or other person against whom an action is commenced.
(e) "Plaintiff" includes a cross-complainant or other person by whom an action is commenced.
(f) "Service" includes return of summons.
Added by Stats. 1984, Ch. 1705, Sec. 5.

Section 583.120 - Applicability of chapter; special proceedings
(a) This chapter applies to a civil action and does not apply to a special proceeding except to the extent incorporated by reference in the special proceeding.
(b) Notwithstanding subdivision (a), the court may, by rule or otherwise under inherent authority of the court, apply this chapter to a special proceeding or part of a special proceeding except to the extent such application would be inconsistent with the character of the special proceeding or the statute governing the special proceeding.
Added by Stats. 1984, Ch. 1705, Sec. 5.

Section 583.130 - Policy of state
It is the policy of the state that a plaintiff shall proceed with reasonable diligence in the prosecution of an action but that all parties shall cooperate in bringing the action to trial or other disposition. Except as otherwise provided by statute or by rule of court adopted pursuant to statute, the policy favoring the right of parties to make stipulations in their own interests and the policy favoring trial or other disposition of an action on the merits are generally to be preferred over the policy that requires dismissal for failure to proceed with reasonable diligence in the prosecution of an action in construing the provisions of this chapter.
Added by Stats. 1984, Ch. 1705, Sec. 5.

Section 583.140 - Waiver and estoppel not affected
Nothing in this chapter abrogates or otherwise affects the principles of waiver and estoppel.
Added by Stats. 1984, Ch. 1705, Sec. 5.

Section 583.150 - Dismissal or sanctions imposed under rule of court
This chapter does not limit or affect the authority of a court to dismiss an action or impose other sanctions under a rule adopted by the court pursuant to Section 575.1 or by the Judicial Council pursuant to statute, or otherwise under inherent authority of the court.
Added by Stats. 1984, Ch. 1705, Sec. 5.

Section 583.160 - Applicability to motion in action commenced on or before effective date of chapter, exceptions
This chapter applies to a motion for dismissal made in an action commenced before, on, or after the effective date of this chapter, except that in the case of an action commenced before the effective date of this chapter:
(a) A motion for dismissal made pursuant to notice given before, on, or within one year after the effective date of this chapter is governed by the applicable law in effect immediately before the effective date and for this purpose the law in effect immediately before the effective date continues in effect.
(b) This chapter does not affect an order dismissing an action made before the effective date of this chapter.

Added by Stats. 1984, Ch. 1705, Sec. 5.

Section 583.161 - Dismissal of petition filed pursuant to sections 299, 2250, 2330 or 7600, Family Code

A petition filed pursuant to Section 299, 2250, 2330, or 7600 of the Family Code shall not be dismissed pursuant to this chapter if any of the following conditions exist:

(a) An order for child support or an order regarding child custody or visitation has been issued in connection with the proceeding and the order has not been (1) terminated by the court or (2) terminated by operation of law pursuant to Sections 3022, 3900, 3901, 4007, and 4013 of the Family Code.

(b) An order for spousal support has been issued in connection with the proceeding and the order has not been terminated by the court.

(c) A personal conduct restraining order has been issued pursuant to the Domestic Violence Prevention Act (Division 10 (commencing with Section 6200) of the Family Code) and the order has not been terminated by operation of law or by the court.

(d) An issue in the case has been bifurcated and one of the following has occurred:

(1) A separate trial has been conducted pursuant to Section 2337 of the Family Code.

(2) A separate trial has been conducted pursuant to the California Rules of Court.

Amended by Stats 2013 ch 40 (AB 522),s 1, eff. 1/1/2014.

Article 2 - MANDATORY TIME FOR SERVICE OF SUMMONS

Section 583.210 - Service within 3 years after commencement of action against defendant; proof of service

(a) The summons and complaint shall be served upon a defendant within three years after the action is commenced against the defendant. For the purpose of this subdivision, an action is commenced at the time the complaint is filed.

(b) Proof of service of the summons shall be filed within 60 days after the time the summons and complaint must be served upon a defendant.

Amended by Stats 2005 ch 300 (AB 496),s 4, eff. 1/1/2006

Section 583.220 - Stipulation in writing by defendant or another act constitutes general appearance

The time within which service must be made pursuant to this article does not apply if the defendant enters into a stipulation in writing or does another act that constitutes a general appearance in the action. For the purpose of this section none of the following constitutes a general appearance in the action:

(a) A stipulation pursuant to Section 583.230 extending the time within which service must be made.

(b) A motion to dismiss made pursuant to this chapter, whether joined with a motion to quash service or a motion to set aside a default judgment, or otherwise.

(c) An extension of time to plead after a motion to dismiss made pursuant to this chapter.

Added by Stats. 1984, Ch. 1705, Sec. 5.

Section 583.230 - Extension of time

The parties may extend the time within which service must be made pursuant to this article by the following means:

(a) By written stipulation. The stipulation need not be filed but, if it is not filed, the stipulation shall be brought to the attention of the court if relevant to a motion for dismissal.

(b) By oral agreement made in open court, if entered in the minutes of the court or a transcript is made.

Added by Stats. 1984, Ch. 1705, Sec. 5.

Section 583.240 - Exclusions when computing time

In computing the time within which service must be made pursuant to this article, there shall be excluded the time during which any of the following conditions existed:

(a) The defendant was not amenable to the process of the court.

(b) The prosecution of the action or proceedings in the action was stayed and the stay affected service.

(c) The validity of service was the subject of litigation by the parties.

(d) Service, for any other reason, was impossible, impracticable, or futile due to causes beyond the plaintiff's control. Failure to discover relevant facts or evidence is not a cause beyond the plaintiff's control for the purpose of this subdivision.

Added by Stats. 1984, Ch. 1705, Sec. 5.

Section 583.250 - Consequences if service not timely made

(a) If service is not made in an action within the time prescribed in this article:

(1) The action shall not be further prosecuted and no further proceedings shall be held in the action.

(2) The action shall be dismissed by the court on its own motion or on motion of any person interested in the action, whether named as a party or not, after notice to the parties.

(b) The requirements of this article are mandatory and are not subject to extension, excuse, or exception except as expressly provided by statute.

Added by Stats. 1984, Ch. 1705, Sec. 5.

Article 3 - MANDATORY TIME FOR BRINGING ACTION TO TRIAL OR NEW TRIAL

Section 583.310 - Generally

An action shall be brought to trial within five years after the action is commenced against the defendant.

Added by Stats. 1984, Ch. 1705, Sec. 5.

Section 583.320 - New trial granted

(a) If a new trial is granted in the action the action shall again be brought to trial within the following times:

(1) If a trial is commenced but no judgment is entered because of a mistrial or because a jury is unable to reach a decision, within three years after the order of the court declaring the mistrial or the disagreement of the jury is entered.

(2) If after judgment a new trial is granted and no appeal is taken, within three years after the order granting the new trial is entered.

(3) If on appeal an order granting a new trial is affirmed or a judgment is reversed and the action remanded for a new trial, within three years after the remittitur is filed by the clerk of the trial court.

(b) Nothing in this section requires that an action again be brought to trial before expiration of the time prescribed in Section 583.310.

Added by Stats. 1984, Ch. 1705, Sec. 5.

Section 583.330 - Extension of time

The parties may extend the time within which an action must be brought to trial pursuant to this article by the following means:

(a) By written stipulation. The stipulation need not be filed but, if it is not filed, the stipulation shall be brought to the attention of the court if relevant to a motion for dismissal.

(b) By oral agreement made in open court, if entered in the minutes of the court or a transcript is made.

Added by Stats. 1984, Ch. 1705, Sec. 5.

Section 583.340 - Exclusions when computing time

In computing the time within which an action must be brought to trial pursuant to this article, there shall be excluded the time during which any of the following conditions existed:

(a) The jurisdiction of the court to try the action was suspended.

(b) Prosecution or trial of the action was stayed or enjoined.

(c) Bringing the action to trial, for any other reason, was impossible, impracticable, or futile.

Added by Stats. 1984, Ch. 1705, Sec. 5.

Section 583.350 - At end of period of tolling or extension less than 6 months remain within which action must be brought

If the time within which an action must be brought to trial pursuant to this article is tolled or otherwise extended pursuant to statute with the result that at the end of the period of tolling or extension less than six months remains within which the action must be brought to trial, the action shall not be dismissed pursuant to this article if the action is brought to trial within six months after the end of the period of tolling or extension.

Added by Stats. 1984, Ch. 1705, Sec. 5.

Section 583.360 - Dismissal by court or on motion of defendant if action not timely brought for trial

(a) An action shall be dismissed by the court on its own motion or on motion of the defendant, after notice to the parties, if the action is not brought to trial within the time prescribed in this article.

(b) The requirements of this article are mandatory and are not subject to extension, excuse, or exception except as expressly provided by statute.

Added by Stats. 1984, Ch. 1705, Sec. 5.

Article 4 - DISCRETIONARY DISMISSAL FOR DELAY

Section 583.410 - Generally

(a) The court may in its discretion dismiss an action for delay in prosecution pursuant to this article on its own motion or on motion of the defendant if to do so appears to the court appropriate under the circumstances of the case.

(b) Dismissal shall be pursuant to the procedure and in accordance with the criteria prescribed by rules adopted by the Judicial Council.

Added by Stats. 1984, Ch. 1705, Sec. 5.

Section 583.420 - Conditions required for dismissal

(a) The court may not dismiss an action pursuant to this article for delay in prosecution except after one of the following conditions has occurred:

(1) Service is not made within two years after the action is commenced against the defendant.

(2) The action is not brought to trial within the following times:

(A) Three years after the action is commenced against the defendant unless otherwise prescribed by rule under subparagraph (B).

(B) Two years after the action is commenced against the defendant if the Judicial Council by rule adopted pursuant to Section 583.410 so prescribes for the court because of the condition of the court calendar or for other reasons affecting the conduct of litigation or the administration of justice.

(3) A new trial is granted and the action is not again brought to trial within the following times:

(A) If a trial is commenced but no judgment is entered because of a mistrial or because a jury is unable to reach a decision, within two years after the order of the court declaring the mistrial or the disagreement of the jury is entered.

(B) If after judgment a new trial is granted and no appeal is taken, within two years after the order granting the new trial is entered.

(C) If on appeal an order granting a new trial is affirmed or a judgment is reversed and the action remanded for a new trial, within two years after the remittitur is filed by the clerk of the trial court.

(b) The times provided in subdivision (a) shall be computed in the manner provided for computation of the comparable times under Articles 2 (commencing with Section 583.210) and 3 (commencing with Section 583.310).

Added by Stats. 1984, Ch. 1705, Sec. 5.

Section 583.430 - Compliance with terms as condition of granting or denying dismissal

(a) In a proceeding for dismissal of an action pursuant to this article for delay in prosecution the court in its discretion may require as a condition of granting or denial of dismissal that the parties comply with such terms as appear to the court proper to effectuate substantial justice.

(b) The court may make any order necessary to effectuate the authority provided in this section, including, but not limited to, provisional and conditional orders.

Added by Stats. 1984, Ch. 1705, Sec. 5.

Chapter 2 - JUDGMENT UPON FAILURE TO ANSWER

Section 585 - Generally

Judgment may be had, if the defendant fails to answer the complaint, as follows:

(a) In an action arising upon contract or judgment for the recovery of money or damages only, if the defendant has, or if more than one defendant, if any of the defendants have, been served, other than by publication, and no answer, demurrer, notice of motion to strike of the character specified in subdivision (f), notice of motion to transfer pursuant to Section 396b, notice of motion to dismiss pursuant to Article 2 (commencing with Section 583.210) of Chapter 1.5 of Title 8, notice of motion to quash service of summons or to stay or dismiss the action pursuant to Section 418.10, or notice of the filing of a petition for writ of mandate as provided in Section 418.10 has been filed with the clerk of the court within the time specified in the summons, or within further time as may be allowed, the clerk, upon written application of the plaintiff, and proof of the service of summons, shall enter the default of the defendant or defendants, so served, and immediately thereafter enter judgment for the principal amount demanded in the complaint, in the statement required by Section 425.11, or in the statement provided for in Section 425.115, or a lesser amount if credit has been acknowledged, together with interest allowed by law or in accordance with the terms of the contract, and the costs against the defendant, or defendants, or against one or more of the defendants. If, by rule of court, a schedule of attorneys' fees to be allowed has been adopted, the clerk may include in the judgment attorneys' fees in accordance with the schedule (1) if the contract provides that attorneys' fees shall be allowed in the event of an action thereon, or (2) if the action is one in which the plaintiff is entitled by statute to recover attorneys' fees in addition to money or damages. The plaintiff shall file a written request at the time of application for entry of the default of the defendant or defendants, to have attorneys' fees fixed by the court, whereupon, after the entry of the default, the court shall hear the application for determination of the attorneys' fees and shall render judgment for the attorneys' fees and for the other relief demanded in the complaint, in the statement required by Section 425.11, or in the statement provided for in Section 425.115, or a lesser amount if credit has been acknowledged, and the costs against the defendant, or defendants, or against one or more of the defendants.

(b) In other actions, if the defendant has been served, other than by publication, and no answer, demurrer, notice of motion to strike of the character specified in subdivision (f), notice of motion to transfer pursuant to Section 396b, notice of motion to dismiss pursuant to Article 2 (commencing with Section 583.210) of Chapter 1.5 of Title 8, notice of motion to quash service of summons or to stay or dismiss the action pursuant to Section 418.10 or notice of the filing of a petition for writ of mandate as provided in Section 418.10 has been filed with the clerk of the court within the time specified in the summons, or within further time as may be allowed, the clerk, upon written application of the plaintiff, shall enter the default of the defendant. The plaintiff thereafter may apply to the court for the relief demanded in the complaint. The court shall hear the evidence offered by the plaintiff, and shall render judgment in the plaintiff's favor for that relief, not exceeding the amount stated in the complaint, in the statement required by Section 425.11, or in the statement provided for by Section 425.115, as appears by the evidence to be just. If the taking of an account, or the proof of any fact, is necessary to enable the court to give judgment or to carry the judgment into effect, the court may take the account or hear the proof, or may, in its discretion, order a reference for that purpose. If the action is for the recovery of damages, in whole or in part, the court may order the damages to be assessed by a jury; or if, to determine the amount of damages, the examination of a long account is involved, by a reference as above provided.

(c) In all actions where the service of the summons was by publication, upon the expiration of the time for answering, and upon proof of the publication and that no answer, demurrer, notice of motion to strike of the character specified in subdivision (f), notice of motion to transfer pursuant to Section 396b, notice of motion to dismiss pursuant to Article 2 (commencing with Section 583.210) of Chapter 1.5 of Title 8, notice of motion to quash service of summons or to stay or dismiss the action pursuant to Section 418.10, or notice of the filing of a petition for writ of mandate as provided in Section 418.10 has been filed, the clerk, upon written application of the plaintiff, shall enter the default of the defendant. The plaintiff thereafter may apply to the court for the relief demanded in the complaint; and the court shall hear the evidence offered by the plaintiff, and shall render judgment in the plaintiff's favor for that relief, not exceeding the amount stated in the complaint, in the statement required by Section 425.11, or in the statement provided for in Section 425.115, as appears by the evidence to be just. If the defendant is not a resident of the state, the court shall require the plaintiff, or the plaintiff's agent, to be examined, on oath, respecting any payments that have been made to the plaintiff, or to anyone for the plaintiff's use, on account of any demand mentioned in the complaint, in the statement required by Section 425.11, or in the statement provided for in Section 425.115, and may render judgment for the amount that the plaintiff is entitled to recover. In all cases affecting the title to or possession of real property, where the service of the summons was by publication and the defendant has failed to answer, no judgment shall be rendered upon proof of mere occupancy, unless the occupancy has continued for the time and has been of the character necessary to confer title by prescription. In all cases where the plaintiff bases a claim upon a paper title, the court shall require evidence establishing the plaintiff's equitable right to judgment before rendering judgment. In actions involving only the possession of real property where the complaint is verified and shows by proper allegations that no party to the action claims title to the real property involved, either by prescription, accession, transfer, will, or succession, but only the possession thereof, the court may render judgment upon proof of occupancy by plaintiff and ouster by defendant.

(d) In the cases referred to in subdivisions (b) and (c), or upon an application to have attorneys' fees fixed by the court pursuant to subdivision (a), the court in its discretion may permit the use of affidavits, in lieu of personal testimony, as to all or any part of the evidence or proof required or permitted to be offered, received, or heard in those cases. The facts stated in the affidavit or affidavits shall be within the personal knowledge of the affiant and shall be set forth with particularity, and each affidavit shall show affirmatively that the affiant, if sworn as a witness, can testify competently thereto.

(e) If a defendant files a cross-complaint against another defendant or the plaintiff, a default may be entered against that party on that cross-complaint if the plaintiff or that cross-defendant has been served with that cross-complaint and has failed to file an answer, demurrer, notice of motion to strike of the character specified in subdivision (f), notice of motion to transfer pursuant to Section 396b, notice of motion to dismiss pursuant to Article 2 (commencing with Section 583.210) of Chapter 1.5 of Title 8, notice of motion to quash service of summons or to stay or dismiss the action pursuant to Section 418.10, or notice of the filing of a petition for a writ of mandate as provided in Section 418.10 within the time specified in the summons, or within another time period as may be allowed. However, no judgment may separately be entered on that cross-complaint unless a separate judgment may, in fact, be properly awarded on that cross-complaint and the court finds that a separate judgment on that cross-complaint would not substantially delay the final disposition of the action between the parties.

(f) A notice of motion to strike within the meaning of this section is a notice of motion to strike the whole or any part of a pleading filed within the time which the moving party is required otherwise to plead to that pleading. The notice of motion to strike shall specify a hearing date set in accordance with Section 1005. The filing of a notice of motion does not extend the time within which to demur.

Amended by Stats 2007 ch 263 (AB 310),s 6, eff. 1/1/2008.

Section 585.5 - affidavit to accompany application to enter default; motion to set aside default

(a) Every application to enter default under subdivision (a) of Section 585 shall include, or be accompanied by, an affidavit stating facts showing that the action is or is not subject to Section 1812.10 or 2984.4 of the Civil Code or subdivision (b) of Section 395.

(b) When a default or default judgment has been entered without full compliance with Section 1812.10 or 2984.4 of the Civil Code, or subdivision (b) of Section 395, the defendant may serve and file a notice of motion to set aside the default or default judgment and for leave to defend the action in the proper court. The notice of motion shall be served and filed within 60 days after the defendant first receives notice of levy under a writ of execution, or notice of any other procedure for enforcing, the default judgment.

(c) A notice of motion to set aside a default or default judgment and for leave to defend the action in the proper court shall designate as the time for making the motion a date prescribed by subdivision (b) of Section 1005, and it shall be accompanied by an affidavit showing under oath that the action was not commenced in the proper court according to Section 1812.10 or 2984.4 of the Civil Code or subdivision (b) of Section 395. The party shall serve and file with the notice a copy of the answer, motion, or other pleading proposed to be filed in the action.

(d) Upon a finding by the court that the motion was made within the period permitted by subdivision (b) and that the action was not commenced in the proper court, it shall set aside the default or default judgment on such terms as may be just and shall allow such a party to defend the action in the proper court.

(e) Unless the plaintiff can show that the plaintiff used reasonable diligence to avoid filing the action in the improper court, upon a finding that the action was commenced in the improper court the court shall award the defendant actual damages and costs, including reasonable attorney's fees.

Amended by Stats. 1991, Ch. 1090, Sec. 3.

Section 586 - Judgment rendered as if defendant failed to answer

(a) In the following cases the same proceedings shall be had, and judgment shall be rendered in the same manner, as if the defendant had failed to answer:

(1) If the complaint has been amended, and the defendant fails to answer it, as amended, or demur thereto, or file a notice of motion to strike, of the character specified in Section 585, within 30 days after service thereof or within the time allowed by the court.

(2) If the demurrer to the complaint is overruled and a motion to strike, of the character specified in Section 585, is denied, or where only one thereof is filed, if the demurrer is overruled or the motion to strike is denied, and the defendant fails to answer the complaint within the time allowed by the court.

(3) If a motion to strike, of the character specified in Section 585, is granted in whole or in part, and the defendant fails to answer the unstricken portion of the complaint within the time allowed by the court, no demurrer having been sustained or being then pending.

(4) If a motion to quash service of summons or to stay or dismiss the action has been filed, or writ of mandate sought and notice thereof given, as provided in Section 418.10, and upon denial of the motion or writ, the defendant fails to respond to the complaint within the time provided in that section or as otherwise provided by law.

(5) If the demurrer to the answer is sustained and the defendant fails to amend the answer within the time allowed by the court.

(6)

(A) If a motion to transfer pursuant to Section 396b is denied and the defendant fails to respond to the complaint within the time allowed by the court pursuant to subdivision (e) of Section 396b or within the time provided in subparagraph (C).

(B) If a motion to transfer pursuant to Section 396b is granted and the defendant fails to respond to the complaint within 30 days of the mailing of notice of the filing and case number by the clerk of the court to which the action or proceeding is transferred or within the time provided in subparagraph (C).

(C) If the order granting or denying a motion to transfer pursuant to Section 396a or 396b is the subject of an appeal pursuant to Section 904.2 in which a stay is granted or of a mandate proceeding pursuant to Section 400, the court having jurisdiction over the trial, upon application or on its own motion after the appeal or mandate proceeding becomes final or upon earlier termination of a stay, shall allow the defendant a reasonable time to respond to the complaint. Notice of the order allowing the defendant further time to respond to the complaint shall be promptly served by the party who obtained the order or by the clerk if the order is made on the court's own motion.

(7) If a motion to strike the answer in whole, of the character specified in Section 585, is granted without leave to amend, or if a motion to strike the answer in whole or in part, of the character specified in Section 585, is granted with leave to amend and the defendant fails to amend the answer within the time allowed by the court.

(8) If a motion to dismiss pursuant to Section 583.250 is denied and the defendant fails to respond within the time allowed by the court.
(b) For the purposes of this section, "respond" means to answer, to demur, or to move to strike.
Amended by Stats 2007 ch 43 (SB 649),s 6, eff. 1/1/2008.

Section 587 - Affidavit that application mail to defendant's attorney or defendant
An application by a plaintiff for entry of default under subdivision (a), (b), or (c) of Section 585 or Section 586 shall include an affidavit stating that a copy of the application has been mailed to the defendant's attorney of record or, if none, to the defendant at his or her last known address and the date on which the copy was mailed. If no such address of the defendant is known to the plaintiff or plaintiff's attorney, the affidavit shall state that fact.

No default under subdivision (a), (b), or (c) of Section 585 or Section 586 shall be entered, unless the affidavit is filed. The nonreceipt of the notice shall not invalidate or constitute ground for setting aside any judgment.
Amended by Stats. 1995, Ch. 796, Sec. 12. Effective January 1, 1996.

Section 587.5 - Construction of terms
As used in this chapter, unless the context otherwise specifically requires, the following terms apply:
(a) "Complaint" includes a cross-complaint.
(b) "Defendant" includes a cross-defendant.
(c) "Plaintiff" includes a cross-complainant.
Added by Stats. 1986, Ch. 540, Sec. 10.

Chapter 3 - ISSUES-THE MODE OF TRIAL AND POSTPONEMENTS

Section 588 - Kinds of issues
Issues arise upon the pleadings when a fact or a conclusion of law is maintained by the one party and is controverted by the other. They are of two kinds:
1. Of law; and,
2. Of fact.
Enacted 1872.

Section 589 - Issue of law
An issue of law arises:
(a) Upon a demurrer to the complaint, cross-complaint, or answer, or to some part thereof.
(b) Upon a motion to strike made pursuant to Section 435, 436, or 473.
Amended by Stats. 1983, Ch. 1167, Sec. 8.

Section 590 - Issue of fact
An issue of fact arises:
1. Upon a material allegation in the complaint controverted by the answer; and,
2. Upon new matters in the answer, except an issue of law is joined thereon.
Enacted 1872.

Section 591 - Issue of law tried by court
An issue of law must be tried by the court, unless it is referred upon consent; provided, however, that failure on the part of any person filing any demurrer to prosecute the same may be construed as a waiver of such demurrer, except as otherwise provided in Section 430.80 of this code.
Amended by Stats. 1982, Ch. 704, Sec. 9.

Section 592 - Issue of fact tried by jury
Section Five Hundred and Ninety-two. In actions for the recovery of specific, real, or personal property, with or without damages, or for money claimed as due upon contract, or as damages for breach of contract, or for injuries, an issue of fact must be tried by a jury, unless a jury trial is waived, or a reference is ordered, as provided in this Code. Where in these cases there are issues both of law and fact, the issue of law must be first disposed of. In other cases, issues of fact must be tried by the Court, subject to its power to order any such issue to be tried by a jury, or to be referred to a referee, as provided in this Code.
Amended by Code Amendments 1873-74, Ch. 383.

Section 594 - Taking dismissal, verdict or judgment in absence of adverse party
(a) In superior courts either party may bring an issue to trial or to a hearing, and, in the absence of the adverse party, unless the court, for good cause, otherwise directs, may proceed with the case and take a dismissal of the action, or a verdict, or judgment, as the case may require; provided, however, if the issue to be tried is an issue of fact, proof shall first be made to the satisfaction of the court that the adverse party has had 15 days' notice of such trial or five days' notice of the trial in an unlawful detainer action as specified in subdivision (b). If the adverse party has served notice of trial upon the party seeking the dismissal, verdict, or judgment at least five days prior to the trial, the adverse party shall be deemed to have had notice.
(b) The notice to the adverse party required by subdivision (a) shall be served by mail on all the parties by the clerk of the court not less than 20 days prior to the date set for trial. In an unlawful detainer action where notice is served by mail that service shall be mailed not less than 10 days prior to the date set for trial. If notice is not served by the clerk as required by this subdivision, it may be served by mail by any party on the adverse party not less than 15 days prior to the date set for trial, and in an unlawful detainer action where notice is served by mail that service shall be mailed not less than 10 days prior to the date set for trial. The time provisions of Section 1013 shall not serve to extend the notice of trial requirements under this subdivision for unlawful detainer actions. If notice is served by the clerk, proof thereof may be made by introduction into evidence of the clerk's certificate pursuant to subdivision (3) of Section 1013a or other competent evidence. If notice is served by a party, proof may be made by introduction into evidence of an affidavit or certificate pursuant to subdivision (1) or (2) of Section 1013a or other competent evidence. The provisions of this subdivision are exclusive.
Amended by Stats 2002 ch 784 (SB 1316),s 62, eff. 1/1/2003.

Section 594a - Postponement of trial if court engaged in another trial or proceeding
The court may, of its own motion, postpone the trial, if at the time fixed for the trial the court is engaged in the trial of another action; or if, as provided in section 473 of this code, an amendment of the pleadings, or the allowance of time to make such amendment, or to plead, renders a postponement necessary.
Added by Stats. 1933, Ch. 744.

Section 595 - Postponement if member of Legislature participant in action or proceeding and Legislature in session

The trial of any civil action, or proceeding in a court, or of any administrative proceeding before a state board or commission or officer, irrespective of the date of the filing thereof or when it became at issue, or the hearing of any motion, demurrer, or other proceeding, shall be postponed to a date certain when it appears to the court, board, commission, or officer before which such action or proceeding is pending that either a party thereto, or any attorney of record therein (whether he became an attorney of record before or after the commencement of a legislative session or before or after his appointment to a legislative committee), or a principal witness, is a Member of the Legislature of this state and that the Legislature is in session or in recess (not exceeding a recess of forty (40) days) or that a legislative interim committee of which he is a duly appointed member is meeting, or is to meet within a period which the court finds does not exceed the time reasonably necessary to enable the member to reach the committee meeting by the ordinary mode of travel. When the Legislature is in session or in recess such action or proceeding shall not, without the consent of the attorney of record therein, be brought on for trial or hearing before the expiration of thirty (30) days next following final adjournment of the Legislature or the commencement of a recess of more than forty (40) days. If a date is available during recess, continuance shall be given if possible to such earlier date. When a legislative committee is meeting or is to meet within a period which the court finds does not exceed the time reasonably necessary to enable the member to reach the committee meeting by the ordinary mode of travel, such action or proceeding shall not, without the consent of the attorney of record therein, be brought on for trial or hearing before the expiration of such period necessary following the adjournment or recess of the committee meeting as the court finds is reasonably necessary to enable the member to reach the place of trial or hearing by the ordinary mode of travel from the place of the committee meeting, unless at the expiration of that period the Legislature is to be in session; and in that case the action or proceeding shall not, without such consent, be brought on for trial or hearing before the expiration of thirty (30) days next following final adjournment or the commencement of a recess of more than forty (40) days. If a date is available during the recess, continuance shall be given to such earlier date. However, any postponement granted under the provisions of this paragraph shall suspend for the same period of time as the postponement, the running of any period of time for any ruling or proceeding by a court, board, commission, or officer, or for the performance by any party of any act affected by said postponement.

Granting of a continuance pursuant to this section is mandatory unless the court determines that such continuance would defeat or abridge a right to relief pendente lite in a paternity action or a right to invoke a provisional remedy such as pendente lite support in a domestic relations controversy, attachment and sale of perishable goods, receivership of a failing business, and temporary restraining order or preliminary injunction, and that the continuance should not be granted.

Amended by Stats. 1968, Ch. 698.

Section 595.1 - Proceeding in a court construed

The term "proceeding in a court" as it is used in Section 595 shall include any discovery proceeding, pretrial conference, deposition, interrogatory, or any other proceeding arising out of a pending civil action.

The enactment of this section at the 1965 Regular Session of the Legislature does not constitute a change in, but is declaratory of, the preexisting law.

Added by Stats. 1965, Ch. 1890.

Section 595.2 - Agreement by attorneys of record to postponement

In all cases, the court shall postpone a trial, or the hearing of any motion or demurrer, for a period not to exceed thirty (30) days, when all attorneys of record of parties who have appeared in the action agree in writing to such postponement.

Added by Stats. 1965, Ch. 1989.

Section 595.3 - Postponement in actions involving mining claims

In actions involving the title to mining claims, or involving trespass for damage upon mining claims, if it be made to appear to the satisfaction of the court that, in order that justice may be done and the action fairly tried on its merits, it is necessary that further developments should be made, underground or upon the surface of the mining claims involved in such action, the court shall grant the postponement of the trial of the action, giving the party a reasonable time in which to prepare for trial and to do said development work.

Added by Stats. 1965, Ch. 1989.

Section 595.4 - Motion to postpone on ground of absence of evidence

A motion to postpone a trial on the ground of the absence of evidence can only be made upon affidavit showing the materiality of the evidence expected to be obtained, and that due diligence has been used to procure it. The court may require the moving party, where application is made on account of the absence of a material witness, to state upon affidavit the evidence which he expects to obtain; and if the adverse party thereupon admits that such evidence would be given, and that it be considered as actually given on the trial, or offered and overruled as improper, the trial must not be postponed.

Added by Stats. 1965, Ch. 1989.

Section 596 - Testimony of adverse party's witness taken by deposition

The party obtaining a postponement of a trial, if required by the adverse party, must consent that the testimony of any witness of such adverse party, who is in attendance, be then taken by deposition before a judge or clerk of the court in which the case is pending, or before such notary public as the court may indicate, which must accordingly be done; and the testimony so taken may be read on the trial, with the same effect, and subject to the same objections, as if the witnesses were produced.

Amended by Stats. 1951, Ch. 1737.

Section 597 - Proceeding to trial of special defenses constituting bar or abatement prior to trial of other issues

When the answer pleads that the action is barred by the statute of limitations, or by a prior judgment, or that another action is pending upon the same cause of action, or sets up any other defense not involving the merits of the plaintiff's cause of action but constituting a bar or ground of abatement to the prosecution thereof, the court may, either upon its own motion or upon the motion of any party, proceed to the trial of the special defense or defenses before the trial of any other issue in the case, and if the decision of the court, or the verdict of the jury, upon any special defense so tried (other than the defense of another action pending) is in favor of the defendant pleading the same, judgment for the defendant shall thereupon be entered and no trial of other issues in the action shall be had unless that judgment shall be reversed on appeal or otherwise set aside or vacated; and where the defense of another action pending or a demurrer based upon subdivision (c) of Section 430.10 is sustained (and no other special defense is sustained) an interlocutory judgment shall be entered in favor of the defendant pleading the same to the effect that no trial of other issues shall be had until the final determination of that other action, and the plaintiff may appeal from the interlocutory judgment in the same manner and within the same time as is now or may be hereafter provided by law for appeals from judgments. If the decision of the court, or the verdict of the jury, upon the special defense or defenses so tried is in favor of the plaintiff, trial of the other issues shall thereafter be had either upon the court's own motion or upon the motion of any party, and judgment shall be entered thereon in the same manner and with the same effect as if all the issues in the case had been tried at one time. In such an event any and all decisions or verdicts upon the special defense or defenses, and all rulings on the trial thereof shall be deemed excepted to and may be reviewed on motion for a new trial or upon appeal from the judgment.

This section also applies to the trial of special defenses pleaded in an answer to a cross-complaint or a demurrer based upon subdivision (c) of Section 430.10, and if the decision of the court or the verdict of the jury upon the special defense or defenses is in favor of the cross-defendant, no further trial shall be had upon the issues raised by the cross-complaint, but trial of the other issues in the action shall thereafter be had either upon the court's own motion or upon the motion of any party, and after the trial thereof the judgment shall be entered in the action as is justified by the decision or verdict on such other issues, considered in connection with the decision or verdict upon the trial of such an affirmative defense raised in the answer to the cross-complaint.

Amended by Stats. 1986, Ch. 540, Sec. 11.

Section 597.5 - Bar of statute of limitations tried separately and before other issues in action against health care provider for professional negligence

In an action against a physician or surgeon, dentist, registered nurse, dispensing optician, optometrist, registered physical therapist, podiatrist, licensed psychologist, osteopathic physician and surgeon, chiropractor, clinical laboratory bioanalyst, clinical laboratory technologist, veterinarian, or a licensed hospital as the employer of any such person, based upon the person's alleged professional negligence, or for rendering professional services without consent, or for error or omission in the person's practice, if the answer pleads that the action is barred by the statute of limitations, and if any party so moves or the court upon its own motion requires, the issues raised thereby must be tried separately and before any other issues in the case are tried. If the issue raised by the statute of limitations is finally determined in favor of the plaintiff, the remaining issues shall then be tried.

Amended by Stats. 1993, Ch. 226, Sec. 5. Effective January 1, 1994.

Section 598 - Order that trial of issue shall precede trial of other issues

The court may, when the convenience of witnesses, the ends of justice, or the economy and efficiency of handling the litigation would be promoted thereby, on motion of a party, after notice and hearing, make an order, no later than the close of pretrial conference in cases in which such pretrial conference is to be held, or, in other cases, no later than 30 days before the trial date, that the trial of any issue or any part thereof shall precede the trial of any other issue or any part thereof in the case, except for special defenses which may be tried first pursuant to Sections 597 and 597.5. The court, on its own motion, may make such an order at any time. Where trial of the issue of liability as to all causes of action precedes the trial of other issues or parts thereof, and the decision of the court, or the verdict of the jury upon such issue so tried is in favor of any party on whom liability is sought to be imposed, judgment in favor of such party shall thereupon be entered and no trial of other issues in the action as against such party shall be had unless such judgment shall be reversed upon appeal or otherwise set aside or vacated.

If the decision of the court, or the verdict of the jury upon the issue of liability so tried shall be against any party on whom liability is sought to be imposed, or if the decision of the court or the verdict of the jury upon any other issue or part thereof so tried does not result in a judgment being entered pursuant to this chapter, then the trial of the other issues or parts thereof shall thereafter be had at such time, and if a jury trial, before the same or another jury, as ordered by the court either upon its own motion or upon the motion of any party, and judgment shall be entered in the same manner and with the same effect as if all the issues in the case had been tried at one time.

Amended by Stats. 1979, Ch. 349.

Section 599 - Extension of deadlines during state of emergency

(a) Notwithstanding any other law and unless ordered otherwise by a court or otherwise agreed to by the parties, a continuance or postponement of a trial or arbitration date extends any deadlines that have not already passed as of March 19, 2020, applicable to discovery, including the exchange of expert witness information, mandatory settlement conferences, and summary judgment motions in the same matter. The deadlines are extended for the same length of time as the continuance or postponement of the trial date.

(b) This section shall remain in effect only during the state of emergency proclaimed by the Governor on March 4, 2020, related to the COVID-19 pandemic and 180 days after the end, pursuant to Section 8629 of the Government Code, of that state of emergency and is repealed on that date.

Amended by Stats 2021 ch 214 (SB 241),s 6, eff. 1/1/2022.
Added by Stats 2020 ch 112 (SB 1146),s 1, eff. 9/18/2020.

Chapter 4 - TRIAL BY JURY
Article 2 - CONDUCT OF THE TRIAL

Section 607 - Order in which trial must proceed when jury sworn

When the jury has been sworn, the trial must proceed in the following order, unless the court, for special reasons otherwise directs:
1. The plaintiff may state the issue and his case;
2. The defendant may then state his defense, if he so wishes, or wait until after plaintiff has produced his evidence;
3. The plaintiff must then produce the evidence on his part;
4. The defendant may then open his defense, if he has not done so previously;
5. The defendant may then produce the evidence on his part;
6. The parties may then respectively offer rebutting evidence only, unless the court, for good reason, in furtherance of justice, permit them to offer evidence upon their original case;
7. When the evidence is concluded, unless the case is submitted to the jury on either side or on both sides without argument, the plaintiff must commence and may conclude the argument;
8. If several defendants having separate defenses, appear by different counsel, the court must determine their relative order in the evidence and argument;
9. The court may then charge the jury.

Amended by Stats. 1965, Ch. 841.

Section 607a - Delivery to judge and service upon opposing counsel Instructions to jury

In every case which is being tried before the court with a jury, it shall be the duty of counsel for the respective parties, before the first witness is sworn, to deliver to the judge presiding at the trial and serve upon opposing counsel, all proposed instructions to the jury covering the law as disclosed by the pleadings. Thereafter, and before the commencement of the argument, counsel may deliver to such judge, and serve upon opposing counsel, additional proposed instructions to the jury upon questions of law developed by the evidence and not disclosed by the pleadings. All proposed instructions shall be typewritten, each on a separate sheet of paper. Before the commencement of the argument, the court, on request of counsel, must:

(1) decide whether to give, refuse, or modify the proposed instructions;
(2) decide which instructions shall be given in addition to those proposed, if any; and
(3) advise counsel of all instructions to be given. However, if, during the argument, issues are raised which have not been covered by instructions given or refused, the court may, on request of counsel, give additional instructions on the subject matter thereof.

Amended by Stats. 1957, Ch. 1698.

Section 608 - Charging jury

In charging the jury the Court may state to them all matters of law which it thinks necessary for their information in giving their verdict; and, if it state the testimony of the case, it must inform the jury that they are the exclusive judges of all questions of fact. The Court must furnish to either party, at the time, upon request, a statement in writing of the points of law contained in the charge, or sign, at the time, a statement of such points prepared and submitted by the counsel of either party.

Enacted 1872.

Section 609 - Special instructions given jury

Where either party asks special instructions to be given to the jury, the Court must either give such instruction, as requested, or refuse to do so, or give the instruction with a modification, in such manner that it may distinctly appear what instructions were given in whole or in part.
Enacted 1872.

Section 611 - Admonishment to jury by court if jury separates during trial or after case submitted

If the jury are permitted to separate, either during the trial or after the case is submitted to them, they shall be admonished by the court that it is their duty not to conduct research, disseminate information, or converse with, or permit themselves to be addressed by, any other person on any subject of the trial, and that it is their duty not to form or express an opinion thereon until the case is finally submitted to them. The court shall clearly explain, as part of the admonishment, that the prohibition on research, dissemination of information, and conversation applies to all forms of electronic and wireless communication.
Amended by Stats 2011 ch 181 (AB 141),s 1, eff. 1/1/2012.

Section 612 - Jury taking papers and exhibits upon retiring for deliberations

Upon retiring for deliberation the jury may take with them all papers which have been received as evidence in the cause, except depositions, or copies of such papers as ought not, in the opinion of the court, to be taken from the person having them in possession; and they may also take with them any exhibits which the court may deem proper, notes of the testimony or other proceedings on the trial, taken by themselves or any of them, but none taken by any other person.
Amended by Stats. 1939, Ch. 753.

Section 612.5 - Copy of written instructions provided jury upon retiring for deliberation

Upon the jury retiring for deliberation, the court shall advise the jury of the availability of a written copy of the jury instructions. The court may, at its discretion, provide the jury with a copy of the written instructions given. However, if the jury requests the court to supply a copy of the written instructions, the court shall supply the jury with a copy.
Amended by Stats. 1986, Ch. 1045, Sec. 1.

Section 613 - Jury deciding to retire for deliberation

When the case is finally submitted to the jury, they may decide in court or retire for deliberation. If they retire, they must be kept together in some convenient place, under charge of an officer, until at least three-fourths of them agree upon a verdict or are discharged by the court. Unless by order of the court, the officer having them under his or her charge shall not permit any communication to be made to them, including any form of electronic or wireless communication, or make any himself or herself, except to ask them if they or three-fourths of them are agreed upon a verdict. The officer shall not, before their verdict is rendered, communicate to any person the state of their deliberations, or the verdict agreed upon.
Amended by Stats 2011 ch 181 (AB 141),s 2, eff. 1/1/2012.

Section 614 - Disagreement as to testimony or desire to be informed of point of law arising in case

After the jury have retired for deliberation, if there be a disagreement between them as to any part of the testimony, or if they desire to be informed of any point of law arising in the cause, they may require the officer to conduct them into Court. Upon their being brought into Court, the information required must be given in the presence of, or after notice to, the parties or counsel.
Enacted 1872.

Section 614.5 - Judge's presence not required while testimony previously receive read to jury

Except for good cause shown, the judge in his or her discretion need not be present in the court while testimony previously received in evidence is read to the jury.
Added by Stats. 1987, Ch. 88, Sec. 1. Effective July 2, 1987.

Section 616 - Trial after jury discharged without rendering verdict or prevented from giving verdict

In all cases where the jury are discharged without having rendered a verdict, or are prevented from giving a verdict, by reason of accident or other cause, during the progress of the trial, or after the cause is submitted to them, except as provided in Section 630, the action may be again tried immediately, or at a future time, as the court may direct.
Amended by Stats. 1947, Ch. 984.

Section 617 - Adjournment while jury absent

While the jury are absent the Court may adjourn from time to time, in respect to other business; but it is nevertheless open for every purpose connected with the cause submitted to the jury, until a verdict is rendered or the jury discharged. The Court may direct the jury to bring in a sealed verdict, at the opening of the Court, in case of an agreement during a recess or adjournment for the day.
Amended by Code Amendments 1880, Ch. 21.

Section 618 - Verdict

When the jury, or three-fourths of them, have agreed upon a verdict, they must be conducted into court and the verdict rendered by their foreperson. The verdict must be in writing, signed by the foreperson, and must be read to the jury by the clerk, and the inquiry made whether it is their verdict. Either party may require the jury to be polled, which is done by the court or clerk, asking each juror if it is the juror's verdict. If upon inquiry or polling, more than one-fourth of the jurors disagree thereto, the jury must be sent out again, but if no disagreement is expressed, the verdict is complete and the jury discharged from the case.
Amended by Stats 2007 ch 263 (AB 310),s 7, eff. 1/1/2008.

Section 619 - Correction of verdict under advice of court

When the verdict is announced, if it is informal or insufficient, in not covering the issue submitted, it may be corrected by the jury under the advice of the Court, or the jury may be again sent out.
Enacted 1872.

Article 3 - THE VERDICT

Section 624 - General and special verdict

The verdict of a jury is either general or special. A general verdict is that by which they pronounce generally upon all or any of the issues, either in favor of the plaintiff or defendant; a special verdict is that by which the jury find the facts only, leaving the judgment to the Court. The special verdict must present the conclusions of fact as established by the evidence, and not the evidence to prove them; and those conclusions of fact must be so presented as that nothing shall remain to the Court but to draw from them conclusions of law.
Enacted 1872.

Section 625 - Special verdict or finding

In all cases the court may direct the jury to find a special verdict in writing, upon all, or any of the issues, and in all cases may instruct them, if they render a general verdict, to find upon particular questions of fact, to be stated in writing, and may direct a written finding thereon. In all cases in which the issue of punitive damages is presented to the jury the court shall direct the jury to find a special verdict in writing separating punitive damages from compensatory damages. The special verdict or finding must be filed with the clerk and entered upon the minutes. Where a special finding of facts is inconsistent with the general verdict, the former controls the latter, and the court must give judgment accordingly.
Amended by Stats. 1983, Ch. 176, Sec. 2.

Section 626 - Action for recovery of money

When a verdict is found for the plaintiff in an action for the recovery of money, or for the cross-complainant when a cross-complaint for the recovery of money is established, the jury must also find the amount of the recovery.
Amended by Stats. 1971, Ch. 244.

Section 627 - Action for recovery of specific personal property
Section Six Hundred and Twenty-seven. In an action for the recovery of specific personal property, if the property has not been delivered to the plaintiff, or the defendant, by his answer, claim a return thereof, the jury, if their verdict be in favor of the plaintiff, or, if being in favor of defendant, they also find that he is entitled to a return thereof, must find the value of the property, and, if so instructed, the value of specific portions thereof, and may at the same time assess the damages, if any are claimed in the complaint or answer, which the prevailing party has sustained by reason of the taking or detention of such property.
Amended by Code Amendments 1873-74, Ch. 383.

Section 628 - Entry in minutes of court upon receipt of verdict
In superior courts upon receipt of a verdict, an entry must be made in the minutes of the court, specifying the time of trial, the names of the jurors and witnesses, and setting out the verdict at length; and where a special verdict is found, either the judgment rendered thereon, or if the case be reserved for argument or further consideration, the order thus reserving it.
Amended by Stats 2002 ch 784 (SB 1316),s 63, eff. 1/1/2003.

Section 629 - Motion for judgment notwithstanding verdict
(a) The court, before the expiration of its power to rule on a motion for a new trial, either of its own motion, after five days' notice, or on motion of a party against whom a verdict has been rendered, shall render judgment in favor of the aggrieved party notwithstanding the verdict whenever a motion for a directed verdict for the aggrieved party should have been granted had a previous motion been made.
(b) A motion for judgment notwithstanding the verdict shall be made within the period specified by Section 659 for the filing and service of a notice of intention to move for a new trial. The moving, opposing, and reply briefs and any accompanying documents shall be filed and served within the periods specified by Section 659a, and the hearing on the motion shall be set in the same manner as the hearing on a motion for new trial under Section 660. The making of a motion for judgment notwithstanding the verdict shall not extend the time within which a party may file and serve notice of intention to move for a new trial. The court shall not rule upon the motion for judgment notwithstanding the verdict until the expiration of the time within which a motion for a new trial must be served and filed, and if a motion for a new trial has been filed with the court by the aggrieved party, the court shall rule upon both motions at the same time. The power of the court to rule on a motion for judgment notwithstanding the verdict shall not extend beyond the last date upon which it has the power to rule on a motion for a new trial. If a motion for judgment notwithstanding the verdict is not determined before that date, the effect shall be a denial of that motion without further order of the court.
(c) If the motion for judgment notwithstanding the verdict is denied and if a new trial is denied, the appellate court shall, if it appears that the motion for judgment notwithstanding the verdict should have been granted, order judgment to be so entered on appeal from the judgment or from the order denying the motion for judgment notwithstanding the verdict.
(d) If a new trial is granted to the party moving for judgment notwithstanding the verdict, and the motion for judgment notwithstanding the verdict is denied, the order denying the motion for judgment notwithstanding the verdict shall nevertheless be reviewable on appeal from that order by the aggrieved party. If the court grants the motion for judgment notwithstanding the verdict or of its own motion directs the entry of judgment notwithstanding the verdict and likewise grants the motion for a new trial, the order granting the new trial shall be effective only if, on appeal, the judgment notwithstanding the verdict is reversed, and the order granting a new trial is not appealed from or, if appealed from, is affirmed.
Amended by Stats 2015 ch 303 (AB 731),s 40, eff. 1/1/2016.
Amended by Stats 2014 ch 93 (AB 1659),s 1, eff. 1/1/2015.

Section 630 - Motion for directed verdict
(a) Unless the court specified an earlier time for making a motion for directed verdict, after all parties have completed the presentation of all of their evidence in a trial by jury, any party may, without waiving his or her right to trial by jury in the event the motion is not granted, move for an order directing entry of a verdict in its favor.
(b) If it appears that the evidence presented supports the granting of the motion as to some, but not all, of the issues involved in the action, the court shall grant the motion as to those issues and the action shall proceed on any remaining issues. Despite the granting of such a motion, no final judgment shall be entered prior to the termination of the action, but the final judgment, in addition to any matter determined in the trial, shall reflect the verdict ordered by the court as determined by the motion for directed verdict.
(c) If the motion is granted, unless the court in its order directing entry of the verdict specifies otherwise, it shall operate as an adjudication upon the merits.
(d) In actions which arise out of an injury to a person or property, when a motion for directed verdict was granted on the basis that a defendant was without fault, no other defendant during trial, over plaintiff's objection, shall attempt to attribute fault to or comment on the absence or involvement of the defendant who was granted the motion.
(e) The order of the court granting the motion for directed verdict is effective without any assent of the jury.
(f) When the jury for any reason has been discharged without having rendered a verdict, the court on its own motion or upon motion of a party, notice of which was given within 10 days after discharge of the jury, may order judgment to be entered in favor of a party whenever a motion for directed verdict for that party should have been granted had a previous motion been made. Except as otherwise provided in Section 12a, the power of the court to act under the provisions of this section shall expire 30 days after the day upon which the jury was discharged, and if judgment has not been ordered within that time the effect shall be the denial of any motion for judgment without further order of the court.
Amended by Stats. 1986, Ch. 540, Sec. 12.

Article 4.5 - VOLUNTARY EXPEDITED JURY TRIALS

Section 630.01 - Definitions
For purposes of this chapter:
(a) "Expedited jury trial" means a consensual, binding jury trial before a reduced jury panel and a judicial officer.
(b) "High/low agreement" means a written agreement entered into by the parties that specifies a minimum amount of damages that a plaintiff is guaranteed to receive from the defendant, and a maximum amount of damages that the defendant will be liable for, regardless of the ultimate verdict returned by the jury. Neither the existence of, nor the amounts contained in, any high/low agreements may be disclosed to the jury.
(c) "Post-trial motions" does not include motions relating to costs and attorney's fees, motions to correct a judgment for a clerical error, and motions to enforce a judgment.
Amended by Stats 2015 ch 330 (AB 555),s 1, eff. 1/1/2016.
Amended by Stats 2011 ch 296 (AB 1023),s 37, eff. 1/1/2012.
Added by Stats 2010 ch 674 (AB 2284),s 2, eff. 1/1/2011.

Section 630.02 - Rules and procedures
The rules and procedures applicable to expedited jury trials are as follows:

(a) The procedures in this chapter and in the implementing rules of court shall apply to expedited jury trials, unless the parties agree otherwise, as permitted under subparagraph (E) of paragraph (1) of subdivision (e) of Section 630.03, and the court so orders.

(b) Any matters not expressly addressed in this chapter, in the implementing rules of court, or in a consent order authorized by this chapter and the implementing rules, are governed by applicable statutes and rules governing civil actions.

Added by Stats 2010 ch 674 (AB 2284),s 2, eff. 1/1/2011.

Section 630.03 - Agreement to participate

(a) All parties agreeing to participate in an expedited jury trial and, if represented, their counsel, shall sign a proposed consent order granting an expedited jury trial.

(b) Except as provided in subdivision (d), the agreement to participate in the expedited jury trial process is binding upon the parties, unless either of the following occurs:

(1) All parties stipulate to end the agreement to participate.

(2) The court, on its own motion or at the request of a party by noticed motion, finds that good cause exists for the action not to proceed under the rules of this chapter.

(c) Any agreement to participate in an expedited jury trial under this chapter may be entered into only after a dispute has arisen and an action has been filed.

(d) The court shall approve the use of an expedited jury trial and any high/low agreements or other stipulations for an expedited jury trial involving either of the following:

(1) A self-represented litigant.

(2) A minor, an incompetent person, or a person for whom a conservator has been appointed.

(e) The proposed consent order submitted to the court shall include all of the following:

(1) A preliminary statement that each named party and any insurance carrier responsible for providing coverage or defense on behalf of that party, individually identified in the proposed consent order, have been informed of the rules and procedures for an expedited jury trial and provided with a Judicial Council information sheet regarding expedited jury trials, have agreed to take part in or, in the case of a responsible insurance carrier, not object to, the expedited jury trial process, and have agreed to all the specific provisions set forth in the consent order.

(2) The parties' agreement to all of the following:

(A) That all parties waive all rights to appeal and to move for directed verdict or make any post-trial motions, except as provided in Sections 630.08 and 630.09.

(B) That each side shall have up to five hours in which to complete voir dire and to present its case.

(C) That the jury shall be composed of eight or fewer jurors with no alternates.

(D) That each side shall be limited to three peremptory challenges, unless the court permits an additional challenge in cases with more than two sides as provided in Section 630.04.

(E) That the trial and pretrial matters will proceed under subparagraphs (A) to (D), inclusive, and, unless the parties expressly agree otherwise in the proposed consent order, under all other provisions in this chapter and in the implementing rules of court.

(f) The court shall issue the consent order as proposed by the parties, unless the court finds good cause why the action should not proceed through the expedited jury trial process, in which case the court shall deny the proposed consent order in its entirety.

Amended by Stats 2015 ch 330 (AB 555),s 2, eff. 1/1/2016.

Added by Stats 2010 ch 674 (AB 2284),s 2, eff. 1/1/2011.

Section 630.04 - Number of jurors; peremptory challenges

(a) Juries in expedited jury trial cases shall be composed of eight jurors, unless the parties have agreed to fewer. No alternates shall be selected.

(b) The court shall allow each side three peremptory challenges. If there are more than two parties in a case and more than two sides, as determined by the court under subdivision (c) of Section 231, the parties may request one additional peremptory challenge each, which is to be granted by the court as the interests of justice may require.

Added by Stats 2010 ch 674 (AB 2284),s 2, eff. 1/1/2011.

Section 630.05 - Deliberations as long as needed

Nothing in this chapter is intended to preclude a jury from deliberating as long as needed.

Added by Stats 2010 ch 674 (AB 2284),s 2, eff. 1/1/2011.

Section 630.06 - Rules of evidence; issuance of subpoenas and notices to appear

(a) The rules of evidence apply in expedited jury trials, unless the parties stipulate otherwise.

(b) Any stipulation by the parties to use relaxed rules of evidence may not be construed to eliminate, or in any way affect, the right of a witness or party to invoke any applicable privilege or other law protecting confidentiality.

(c) The right to issue subpoenas and notices to appear to secure the attendance of witnesses or the production of documents at trial shall be in accordance with this code.

Added by Stats 2010 ch 674 (AB 2284),s 2, eff. 1/1/2011.

Section 630.07 - Verdict

(a) The verdict in an expedited jury trial case is binding, subject to any written high/low agreement or other stipulations concerning the amount of the award agreed upon by the parties.

(b) A vote of six of the eight jurors is required for a verdict, unless the parties stipulate otherwise.

Added by Stats 2010 ch 674 (AB 2284),s 2, eff. 1/1/2011.

Section 630.08 - Waiver of motions for directed verdict, to set aside verdict or judgment

(a) By agreeing to participate in the expedited jury trial process, the parties agree to waive any motions for directed verdict, motions to set aside the verdict or any judgment rendered by the jury, or motions for a new trial on the basis of inadequate or excessive damages.

(b) The court shall not set aside any verdict or any judgment, shall not direct that judgment be entered in favor of a party entitled to judgment as a matter of law, and shall not order a new trial, except on the grounds stated in Section 630.09.

Amended by Stats 2011 ch 296 (AB 1023),s 38, eff. 1/1/2012.

Added by Stats 2010 ch 674 (AB 2284),s 2, eff. 1/1/2011.

Section 630.09 - Motion for new trial or appeal

(a) By agreeing to participate in the expedited jury trial process, the parties agree to waive the right to bring post-trial motions or to appeal from the determination of the matter, except as provided in this section. The only grounds on which a party may move for a new trial or appeal are any of the following:

(1) Judicial misconduct that materially affected the substantial rights of a party.

(2) Misconduct of the jury.

(3) Corruption, fraud, or other undue means employed in the proceedings of the court, jury, or adverse party that prevented a party from having a fair trial.

(b) Within 10 court days of the entry of a jury verdict, a party may file with the clerk and serve on each adverse party a notice of the intention to move for a new trial on any of the grounds specified in subdivision (a). The notice shall be deemed to be a motion for a new trial.

(c) Except as provided in subdivision (b), parties to an expedited jury trial shall not make any post-trial motions except for motions relating to costs and attorney's fees, motions to correct a judgment for clerical error, and motions to enforce a judgment.

(d) Before filing an appeal, a party shall make a motion for a new trial under subdivision (b). If the motion for a new trial is denied, the party may appeal the judgment to the appropriate court with appellate jurisdiction and seek a new trial on any of the grounds specified in subdivision (a). Parties to an expedited jury trial may not appeal on any other ground.

Added by Stats 2010 ch 674 (AB 2284),s 2, eff. 1/1/2011.

Section 630.10 - Costs and attorney's fees

All statutes and rules governing costs and attorney's fees shall apply in expedited jury trials, unless the parties agree otherwise in the consent order.

Added by Stats 2010 ch 674 (AB 2284),s 2, eff. 1/1/2011.

Section 630.11 - Adoption of rules and forms to establish uniform procedures

The Judicial Council shall, on or before July 1, 2016, update rules and forms to establish uniform procedures implementing the provisions of this chapter, including, but not limited to, rules for all of the following:

(a) Additional content of proposed consent orders.

(b) Pretrial exchanges and submissions.

(c) Pretrial conferences.

(d) Presentation of evidence and testimony.

(e) Any other procedures necessary to implement the provisions of this chapter.

Amended by Stats 2015 ch 330 (AB 555),s 3, eff. 1/1/2016.

Added by Stats 2010 ch 674 (AB 2284),s 2, eff. 1/1/2011.

Section 630.12 - [Repealed]

Repealed by Stats 2015 ch 330 (AB 555),s 4, eff. 1/1/2016.

Added by Stats 2010 ch 674 (AB 2284),s 2, eff. 1/1/2011.

Chapter 4.6 - MANDATORY EXPEDITED JURY TRIALS IN LIMITED CIVIL CASES

Section 630.20 - Mandated expedited jury trials in limited civil cases

(a) Except as provided in subdivisions (b) and (c), an action or special proceeding treated as a limited civil case pursuant to Article 1 (commencing with Section 85) of Chapter 5.1 of Title 1 of Part 1, including an action or special proceeding initially filed as a limited civil case or remanded as one thereafter, shall be conducted as a mandatory expedited jury trial pursuant to this chapter.

(b) Either party may opt out of the mandatory expedited jury trial procedures if any of the following criteria is met:

(1) Punitive damages are sought.

(2) Damages in excess of insurance policy limits are sought.

(3) A party's insurer is providing a legal defense subject to a reservation of rights.

(4) The case involves a claim reportable to a governmental entity.

(5) The case involves a claim of moral turpitude that may affect an individual's professional licensing.

(6) The case involves claims of intentional conduct.

(7) The case has been reclassified as unlimited pursuant to Section 403.020.

(8) The complaint contains a demand for attorney's fees, unless those fees are sought pursuant to Section 1717 of the Civil Code.

(9) The judge finds good cause exists for the action not to proceed under the rules of this chapter. Good cause includes, but is not limited to, a showing that a party needs more than five hours to present or defend the action and that the parties have been unable to stipulate to additional time.

(c) This chapter does not apply to a proceeding in forcible entry or forcible or unlawful detainer.

(d) A judgment in a limited civil case conducted as a mandatory expedited jury trial may be appealed to the appellate division of the superior court in which the case was tried.

Added by Stats 2015 ch 330 (AB 555),s 5, eff. 1/1/2016.

Section 630.21 - Definitions

For purposes of this chapter:

(a) "Mandatory expedited jury trial" means a jury trial before a reduced jury panel and a judge, conducted pursuant to this chapter.

(b) "High/low agreement" means a written agreement entered into by the parties that specifies a minimum amount of damages that a plaintiff is guaranteed to receive from the defendant, and a maximum amount of damages that the defendant will be liable for, regardless of the ultimate verdict returned by the jury. Neither the existence of, nor the amounts contained in, any high/low agreements may be disclosed to the jury.

Added by Stats 2015 ch 330 (AB 555),s 5, eff. 1/1/2016.

Section 630.22 - Applicability

(a) The procedures in this chapter and in the implementing rules of court shall apply to mandatory expedited jury trials conducted in limited civil cases, unless the parties agree otherwise, as permitted under subdivision (d) of Section 630.23, and the court so orders.

(b) Any matters not expressly addressed in this chapter, in the implementing rules of court, or in an agreement authorized by this chapter and the implementing rules, are governed by applicable statutes and rules governing civil actions.

Added by Stats 2015 ch 330 (AB 555),s 5, eff. 1/1/2016.

Section 630.23 - Rules and procedures

The following rules and procedures apply to mandatory expedited jury trials conducted pursuant to this chapter:

(a) Each side shall have up to five hours in which to complete voir dire and to present its case.

(b) The jury shall be composed of eight jurors and one alternate, unless the parties have agreed to fewer jurors.

(c) Each side shall be limited to four peremptory challenges, unless the court permits an additional challenge in cases with more than two sides. If there are more than two parties in a case and more than two sides, as determined by the court under subdivision (c) of Section 231, the parties may request one additional peremptory challenge each, which is to be granted by the court as the interests of justice may require.

(d) The parties may agree to modify the rules and procedures specified in this chapter and the implementing rules of court, subject to the court's approval.

Added by Stats 2015 ch 330 (AB 555),s 5, eff. 1/1/2016.

Section 630.24 - Jury deliberation

Nothing in this chapter is intended to preclude a jury from deliberating as long as needed.

Added by Stats 2015 ch 330 (AB 555),s 5, eff. 1/1/2016.

Section 630.25 - Rules of evidence

(a) The rules of evidence apply to mandatory expedited jury trials conducted in limited civil cases, unless the parties stipulate otherwise.

(b) Any stipulation by the parties to use relaxed rules of evidence shall not be construed to eliminate, or in any way affect, the right of a witness or party to invoke any applicable privilege or other law protecting confidentiality.

(c) The right to issue subpoenas and notices to appear to secure the attendance of witnesses or the production of documents at trial shall be in accordance with this code.
Added by Stats 2015 ch 330 (AB 555),s 5, eff. 1/1/2016.
Section 630.26 - Votes required for verdict
(a) A vote of six of the eight jurors is required for a verdict, unless the parties stipulate otherwise.
(b) The verdict in a limited civil case following a mandatory expedited jury trial case shall be appealable under subdivision (d) of Section 630.20 and subject to any written high/low agreement or other stipulations concerning the amount of the award agreed upon by the parties.
Added by Stats 2015 ch 330 (AB 555),s 5, eff. 1/1/2016.
Section 630.27 - Attorney fees
All statutes and rules governing costs and attorney's fees shall apply in limited civil cases that are conducted as mandatory expedited jury trials, unless the parties stipulate otherwise.
Added by Stats 2015 ch 330 (AB 555),s 5, eff. 1/1/2016.
Section 630.28 - Adoption of rules
The Judicial Council shall, on or before July 1, 2016, adopt rules and forms to establish uniform procedures implementing the provisions of this chapter, including, rules for the following:
(a) Pretrial exchanges and submissions.
(b) Pretrial conferences.
(c) Opt-out procedures pursuant to subdivision (b) of Section 630.20.
(d) Presentation of evidence and testimony.
(e) Any other procedures necessary to implement the provisions of this chapter.
Added by Stats 2015 ch 330 (AB 555),s 5, eff. 1/1/2016.
Section 630.29 - Operative date
Sections 630.20 to 630.27, inclusive, shall become operative on July 1, 2016.
Added by Stats 2015 ch 330 (AB 555),s 5, eff. 1/1/2016.
Section 630.30 - [Repealed]
Repealed by Stats 2018 ch 776 (AB 3250),s 7, eff. 1/1/2019.
Added by Stats 2015 ch 330 (AB 555),s 5, eff. 1/1/2016.
Chapter 5 - TRIAL BY THE COURT
Section 631 - Fee paid by party demanding jury; deposit by party demanding jury trial; waiver of jury trial
(a) The right to a trial by jury as declared by Section 16 of Article I of the California Constitution shall be preserved to the parties inviolate. In civil cases, a jury may only be waived pursuant to subdivision (f).
(b) At least one party demanding a jury on each side of a civil case shall pay a nonrefundable fee of one hundred fifty dollars ($150), unless the fee has been paid by another party on the same side of the case. The fee shall offset the costs to the state of providing juries in civil cases. If there are more than two parties to the case, for purposes of this section only, all plaintiffs shall be considered one side of the case, and all other parties shall be considered the other side of the case. Payment of the fee by a party on one side of the case shall not relieve parties on the other side of the case from waiver pursuant to subdivision (f).
(c) The fee described in subdivision (b) shall be due on or before the date scheduled for the initial case management conference in the action, except as follows:
    (1) In unlawful detainer actions, the fees shall be due at least five days before the date set for trial.
    (2) If no case management conference is scheduled in a civil action, or the initial case management conference occurred before June 28, 2012, and the initial complaint was filed on or after July 1, 2011, the fee shall be due no later than 365 calendar days after the filing of the initial complaint.
    (3) If the initial case management conference occurred before June 28, 2012, and the initial complaint in the case was filed before July 1, 2011, the fee shall be due at least 25 calendar days before the date initially set for trial.
    (4) If the party requesting a jury has not appeared before the initial case management conference, or first appeared more than 365 calendar days after the filing of the initial complaint, the fee shall be due at least 25 calendar days before the date initially set for trial.
(d) If a party failed to timely pay the fee described in subdivision (b) that was due between June 27, 2012, and November 30, 2012, the party will be relieved of a jury waiver on that basis only if the party pays the fee on or before December 31, 2012, or 25 calendar days before the date initially set for trial, whichever is earlier.
(e) The parties demanding a jury trial shall deposit with the clerk or judge, at the beginning of the second and each succeeding day's session, a sum equal to that day's fees and mileage of the jury, including the fees and mileage for the trial jury panel if the trial jury has not yet been selected and sworn. If more than one party has demanded a jury, the respective amount to be paid daily by each party demanding a jury shall be determined by stipulation of the parties or by order of the court.
(f) A party waives trial by jury in any of the following ways:
    (1) By failing to appear at the trial.
    (2) By written consent filed with the clerk or judge.
    (3) By oral consent, in open court, entered in the minutes.
    (4) By failing to announce that a jury is required, at the time the cause is first set for trial, if it is set upon notice or stipulation, or within five days after notice of setting if it is set without notice or stipulation.
    (5) By failing to timely pay the fee described in subdivision (b), unless another party on the same side of the case has paid that fee.
    (6) By failing to deposit with the clerk or judge, at the beginning of the second and each succeeding day's session, the sum provided in subdivision (e).
(g) The court may, in its discretion upon just terms, allow a trial by jury although there may have been a waiver of a trial by jury.
(h) The court shall transmit the fee described in subdivision (b) to the State Treasury for deposit in the Trial Court Trust Fund within 45 calendar days after the end of the month in which the fee is paid to the court.
Amended by Stats 2012 ch 342 (AB 1481),s 1, eff. 9/17/2012.
Amended by Stats 2012 ch 41 (SB 1021),s 3, eff. 6/27/2012.
Amended by Stats 2002 ch 806 (AB 3027),s 15, eff. 1/1/2003.
Amended by Stats 2000 ch 127 (AB 2866), s 2, eff. 7/8/2000.
Previously Amended July 12, 1999 (Bill Number: SB 966) (Chapter 83).
Section 631.1 - [Repealed]
Repealed by Stats 2012 ch 470 (AB 1529),s 5, eff. 1/1/2013.
Section 631.2 - Payment of jury fees from general funds of court
(a) Notwithstanding any other provision of law, the superior court may pay jury fees in civil cases from general funds of the court available therefor. Nothing in this section shall be construed to change the requirements for the deposit of jury fees in any civil case by the appropriate

party to the litigation at the time and in the manner otherwise provided by law. Nothing in this section shall preclude the right of the superior court to be reimbursed by the party to the litigation liable therefor for any payment of jury fees pursuant to this section. Nothing in this section shall preclude the right of the county to be reimbursed by the party to the litigation liable therefor for any payment of jury fees pursuant to this section as it read in Section 4 of Chapter 10 of the Statutes of 1988, or pursuant to former Section 631.1 as it read in Section 1 of Chapter 144 of the Statutes of 1971.

(b) The party who has demanded trial by jury shall reimburse the superior court for the fees and mileage of all jurors appearing for voir dire examination, except those jurors who are excused and subsequently on the same day are called for voir dire examination in another case.
Amended by Stats 2012 ch 470 (AB 1529),s 6, eff. 1/1/2013.

Section 631.3 - Deposited fees not refunded; deposit of fees in Trial Court Trust Fund

(a) Notwithstanding any other law, when a party to the litigation has deposited jury fees with the judge or clerk and that party waives a jury or obtains a continuance of the trial, or the case is settled, none of the deposit shall be refunded if the court finds there has been insufficient time to notify the jurors that the trial would not proceed at the time set. If the jury fees so deposited are not refunded for any of these reasons, or if a refund of jury fees deposited with the judge or clerk has not been requested, in writing, by the depositing party within 20 business days from the date on which the jury is waived or the action is settled, dismissed, or a continuance thereof granted, the fees shall be transmitted to the Controller for deposit into the Trial Court Trust Fund.

(b) All jury fees and mileage fees that may accrue by reason of a juror serving on more than one case in the same day shall be transmitted to the Controller for deposit into the Trial Court Trust Fund. All jury fees that were deposited with the court in advance of trial pursuant to Section 631 prior to January 1, 1999, and that remain on deposit in cases that were settled, dismissed, or otherwise disposed of, and three years have passed since the date the case was settled, dismissed, or otherwise disposed of, shall be transmitted to the Controller for deposit into the Trial Court Trust Fund.

(c) The fee described in subdivision (b) of Section 631 shall be nonrefundable and is not subject to this section.
Amended by Stats 2012 ch 342 (AB 1481),s 2, eff. 9/17/2012.
Amended by Stats 2012 ch 41 (SB 1021),s 4, eff. 6/27/2012.
Amended by Stats 2000 ch 447 (SB 1533), s 2, eff. 1/1/2001.
Amended by Stats 2001 ch 824 (AB 1700), s 9, eff. 1/1/2002.

Section 631.5 - Deposit in cases of eminent domain

In all cases of eminent domain the deposits of jury fees and mileage provided for in section 631 of this code shall be made by the party seeking condemnation regardless of which party shall have demanded a jury trial, and the trial shall not proceed until such deposits are made.
Added by Stats. 1939, Ch. 806.

Section 631.7 - Order of trial without jury

Ordinarily, unless the court otherwise directs, the trial of a civil action tried by the court without a jury shall proceed in the order specified in Section 607.
Added by Stats. 1965, Ch. 299.

Section 631.8 - Motion for judgment by other party after party completes presentation of evidence

(a) After a party has completed his presentation of evidence in a trial by the court, the other party, without waiving his right to offer evidence in support of his defense or in rebuttal in the event the motion is not granted, may move for a judgment. The court as trier of the facts shall weigh the evidence and may render a judgment in favor of the moving party, in which case the court shall make a statement of decision as provided in Sections 632 and 634, or may decline to render any judgment until the close of all the evidence. The court may consider all evidence received, provided, however, that the party against whom the motion for judgment has been made shall have had an opportunity to present additional evidence to rebut evidence received during the presentation of evidence deemed by the presenting party to have been adverse to him, and to rehabilitate the testimony of a witness whose credibility has been attacked by the moving party. Such motion may also be made and granted as to any cross-complaint.

(b) If it appears that the evidence presented supports the granting of the motion as to some but not all the issues involved in the action, the court shall grant the motion as to those issues and the action shall proceed as to the issues remaining. Despite the granting of such a motion, no final judgment shall be entered prior to the termination of the action, but the final judgment in such action shall, in addition to any matters determined in the trial, award judgment as determined by the motion herein provided for.

(c) If the motion is granted, unless the court in its order for judgment otherwise specifies, such judgment operates as an adjudication upon the merits.
Amended by Stats. 1986, Ch. 540, Sec. 13.

Section 632 - Written findings of fact and conclusions of law; statement of decision

In superior courts, upon the trial of a question of fact by the court, written findings of fact and conclusions of law shall not be required. The court shall issue a statement of decision explaining the factual and legal basis for its decision as to each of the principal controverted issues at trial upon the request of any party appearing at the trial. The request must be made within 10 days after the court announces a tentative decision unless the trial is concluded within one calendar day or in less than eight hours over more than one day in which event the request must be made prior to the submission of the matter for decision. The request for a statement of decision shall specify those controverted issues as to which the party is requesting a statement of decision. After a party has requested the statement, any party may make proposals as to the content of the statement of decision.

The statement of decision shall be in writing, unless the parties appearing at trial agree otherwise; however, when the trial is concluded within one calendar day or in less than 8 hours over more than one day, the statement of decision may be made orally on the record in the presence of the parties.
Amended by Stats 2002 ch 784 (SB 1316),s 64, eff. 1/1/2003.

Section 634 - Inference when issue not resolved by statement of decision or statement ambiguous

When a statement of decision does not resolve a controverted issue, or if the statement is ambiguous and the record shows that the omission or ambiguity was brought to the attention of the trial court either prior to entry of judgment or in conjunction with a motion under Section 657 or 663, it shall not be inferred on appeal or upon a motion under Section 657 or 663 that the trial court decided in favor of the prevailing party as to those facts or on that issue.
Amended by Stats. 1981, Ch. 900, Sec. 2.

Section 635 - Formal judgment or order conforming to minutes signed by presiding judge of court

In all cases where the decision of the court has been entered in its minutes, and when the judge who heard or tried the case is unavailable, the formal judgment or order conforming to the minutes may be signed by the presiding judge of the court or by a judge designated by the presiding judge.
Amended by Stats. 1992, Ch. 876, Sec. 5. Effective January 1, 1993.

Section 636 - Failure of defendant to answer; reference ordered

On a judgment for the plaintiff upon an issue of law, he may proceed in the manner prescribed by the first two subdivisions of Section 585, upon the failure of the defendant to answer. If judgment be for the defendant upon an issue of law, and the taking of an account, or the proof of any fact, be necessary to enable the Court to complete the judgment, a reference may be ordered, as in that section provided.
Enacted 1872.

Chapter 6 - OF REFERENCES AND TRIALS BY REFEREES

Section 638 - Appointment upon agreement of parties or upon motion of party to contract or lease

A referee may be appointed upon the agreement of the parties filed with the clerk, or judge, or entered in the minutes, or upon the motion of a party to a written contract or lease that provides that any controversy arising therefrom shall be heard by a referee if the court finds a reference agreement exists between the parties:

(a) To hear and determine any or all of the issues in an action or proceeding, whether of fact or of law, and to report a statement of decision.

(b) To ascertain a fact necessary to enable the court to determine an action or proceeding.

(c) In any matter in which a referee is appointed pursuant to this section, a copy of the order shall be forwarded to the office of the presiding judge. The Judicial Council shall, by rule, collect information on the use of these referees. The Judicial Council shall also collect information on fees paid by the parties for the use of referees to the extent that information regarding those fees is reported to the court. The Judicial Council shall report thereon to the Legislature by July 1, 2003. This subdivision shall become inoperative on January 1, 2004.

Amended by Stats 2002 ch 1008 (AB 3028),s 4, eff. 1/1/2003.
Amended by Stats 2001 ch 44 (SB 562), s 5, eff. 1/1/2002.
Amended by Stats 2000 ch 644 (AB 2912), s 1, eff. 1/1/2001.

Section 639 - Appointment when parties do not agree

(a) When the parties do not consent, the court may, upon the written motion of any party, or of its own motion, appoint a referee in the following cases pursuant to the provisions of subdivision (b) of Section 640:

(1) When the trial of an issue of fact requires the examination of a long account on either side; in which case the referees may be directed to hear and decide the whole issue, or report upon any specific question of fact involved therein.

(2) When the taking of an account is necessary for the information of the court before judgment, or for carrying a judgment or order into effect.

(3) When a question of fact, other than upon the pleadings, arises upon motion or otherwise, in any stage of the action.

(4) When it is necessary for the information of the court in a special proceeding.

(5) When the court in any pending action determines that it is necessary for the court to appoint a referee to hear and determine any and all discovery motions and disputes relevant to discovery in the action and to report findings and make a recommendation thereon.

(b) In a discovery matter, a motion to disqualify an appointed referee pursuant to Section 170.6 shall be made to the court by a party either:

(A) Within 10 days after notice of the appointment, or if the party has not yet appeared in the action, a motion shall be made within 10 days after the appearance, if a discovery referee has been appointed for all discovery purposes.

(B) At least five days before the date set for hearing, if the referee assigned is known at least 10 days before the date set for hearing and the discovery referee has been assigned only for limited discovery purposes.

(c) When a referee is appointed pursuant to paragraph (5) of subdivision (a), the order shall indicate whether the referee is being appointed for all discovery purposes in the action.

(d) All appointments of referees pursuant to this section shall be by written order and shall include the following:

(1) When the referee is appointed pursuant to paragraph (1), (2), (3), or (4) of subdivision (a), a statement of the reason the referee is being appointed.

(2) When the referee is appointed pursuant to paragraph (5) of subdivision (a), the exceptional circumstances requiring the reference, which must be specific to the circumstances of the particular case.

(3) The subject matter or matters included in the reference.

(4) The name, business address, and telephone number of the referee.

(5) The maximum hourly rate the referee may charge and, at the request of any party, the maximum number of hours for which the referee may charge. Upon the written application of any party or the referee, the court may, for good cause shown, modify the maximum number of hours subject to any findings as set forth in paragraph (6).

(6)

(A) Either a finding that no party has established an economic inability to pay a pro rata share of the referee's fee or a finding that one or more parties has established an economic inability to pay a pro rata share of the referee's fees and that another party has agreed voluntarily to pay that additional share of the referee's fee. A court shall not appoint a referee at a cost to the parties if neither of these findings is made.

(B) In determining whether a party has established an inability to pay the referee's fees under subparagraph (A), the court shall consider only the ability of the party, not the party's counsel, to pay these fees. If a party is proceeding in forma pauperis, the party shall be deemed by the court to have an economic inability to pay the referee's fees. However, a determination of economic inability to pay the fees shall not be limited to parties that proceed in forma pauperis. For those parties who are not proceeding in forma pauperis, the court, in determining whether a party has established an inability to pay the fees, shall consider, among other things, the estimated cost of the referral and the impact of the proposed fees on the party's ability to proceed with the litigation.

(e) In any matter in which a referee is appointed pursuant to paragraph (5) of subdivision (a), a copy of the order appointing the referee shall be forwarded to the office of the presiding judge of the court. The Judicial Council shall, by rule, collect information on the use of these references and the reference fees charged to litigants, and shall report thereon to the Legislature by July 1, 2003. This subdivision shall become inoperative on January 1, 2004.

Amended by Stats 2000 ch 644 (AB 2912), s 2.5, eff. 1/1/2001.
Amended by Stats 2001 ch 362 (SB 475), s 1, eff. 1/1/2002.
See Stats 2000 ch 644 (AB 2912), s 13.

Section 640 - Appointment of person agreed upon by parties as referee; person appointed if parties do not agree

(a) The court shall appoint as referee or referees the person or persons, not exceeding three, agreed upon by the parties.

(b) If the parties do not agree on the selection of the referee or referees, each party shall submit to the court up to three nominees for appointment as referee and the court shall appoint one or more referees, not exceeding three, from among the nominees against whom there is no legal objection. If no nominations are received from any of the parties, the court shall appoint one or more referees, not exceeding three, against whom there is no legal objection, or the court may appoint a court commissioner of the county where the cause is pending as a referee.

(c) Participation in the referee selection procedure pursuant to this section does not constitute a waiver of grounds for objection to the appointment of a referee under Section 641 or 641.2.

Amended by Stats 2000 ch 644 (AB 2912), s 3, eff. 1/1/2001.

Section 640.5 - Collection of data on use of referees in discovery matters

It is the intent of the Legislature that the practice and cost of referring discovery disputes to outside referees be thoroughly reviewed. Therefore, in addition to the requirements of subdivision (e) of Section 639, the Judicial Council shall collect information from the trial courts on the use of

referees in discovery matters pursuant to either Sections 638 and 639. The collected data shall include information on the number of referees, the cost to the parties, and the time spent by the discovery referee. The Judicial Council shall report thereon to the Legislature by July 1, 2003.
Added by Stats 2001 ch 362 (SB 475), s 2, eff. 1/1/2002.

Section 641 - Grounds for objecting to person appointed as referee
A party may object to the appointment of any person as referee, on one or more of the following grounds:

(a) A want of any of the qualifications prescribed by statute to render a person competent as a juror, except a requirement of residence within a particular county in the state.

(b) Consanguinity or affinity, within the third degree, to either party, or to an officer of a corporation which is a party, or to any judge of the court in which the appointment shall be made.

(c) Standing in the relation of guardian and ward, conservator and conservatee, master and servant, employer and clerk, or principal and agent, to either party; or being a member of the family of either party; or a partner in business with either party; or security on any bond or obligation for either party.

(d) Having served as a juror or been a witness on any trial between the same parties.

(e) Interest on the part of the person in the event of the action, or in the main question involved in the action.

(f) Having formed or expressed an unqualified opinion or belief as to the merits of the action.

(g) The existence of a state of mind in the potential referee evincing enmity against or bias toward either party.
Amended by Stats 2000 ch 644 (AB 2912), s 4, eff. 1/1/2001.

Section 641.2 - Person not technically qualified with respect to subject matter
In any action brought under Article 8 (commencing with Section 12600) of Chapter 6, Part 2, Division 3, Title 3 of the Government Code, a party may object to the appointment of any person as referee on the ground that the person is not technically qualified with respect to the particular subject matter of the proceeding.
Amended by Stats 2000 ch 644 (AB 2912), s 5, eff. 1/1/2001.

Section 642 - Objections in writing and heard by court
Objections, if any, to a reference or to the referee or referees appointed by the court shall be made in writing, and must be heard and disposed of by the court, not by the referee.
Added by Stats 2000 ch 644 (AB 2912), s 7, eff. 1/1/2001.

Section 643 - Report of statement of decision to court
(a) Unless otherwise directed by the court, the referees or commissioner must report their statement of decision in writing to the court within 20 days after the hearing, if any, has been concluded and the matter has been submitted.

(b) A referee appointed pursuant to Section 638 shall report as agreed by the parties and approved by the court.

(c) A referee appointed pursuant to Section 639 shall file with the court a report that includes a recommendation on the merits of any disputed issue, a statement of the total hours spent and the total fees charged by the referee, and the referee's recommended allocation of payment. The referee shall serve the report on all parties. Any party may file an objection to the referee's report or recommendations within 10 days after the referee serves and files the report, or within another time as the court may direct. The objection shall be served on the referee and all other parties. Responses to the objections shall be filed with the court and served on the referee and all other parties within 10 days after the objection is served. The court shall review any objections to the report and any responses submitted to those objections and shall thereafter enter appropriate orders. Nothing in this section is intended to deprive the court of its power to change the terms of the referee's appointment or to modify or disregard the referee's recommendations, and this overriding power may be exercised at any time, either on the motion of any party for good cause shown or on the court's own motion.
Amended by Stats 2000 ch 644 (AB 2912), s 8, eff. 1/1/2001.

Section 644 - Judgment entered on statement of decision
(a) In the case of a consensual general reference pursuant to Section 638, the decision of the referee or commissioner upon the whole issue must stand as the decision of the court, and upon filing of the statement of decision with the clerk of the court, judgment may be entered thereon in the same manner as if the action had been tried by the court.

(b) In the case of all other references, the decision of the referee or commissioner is only advisory. The court may adopt the referee's recommendations, in whole or in part, after independently considering the referee's findings and any objections and responses thereto filed with the court.
Amended by Stats 2007 ch 263 (AB 310),s 8, eff. 1/1/2008.
Amended by Stats 2000 ch 644 (AB 2912), s 9, eff. 1/1/2001.

Section 645 - Decision excepted to and reviewed as if made by court
The decision of the referee appointed pursuant to Section 638 or commissioner may be excepted to and reviewed in like manner as if made by the court. When the reference is to report the facts, the decision reported has the effect of a special verdict.
Amended by Stats 2000 ch 644 (AB 2912), s 10, eff. 1/1/2001.

Section 645.1 - Payment of referee's fees
(a) When a referee is appointed pursuant to Section 638, the referee's fees shall be paid as agreed by the parties. If the parties do not agree on the payment of fees and request the matter to be resolved by the court, the court may order the parties to pay the referee's fees as set forth in subdivision (b).

(b) When a referee is appointed pursuant to Section 639, at any time after a determination of ability to pay is made as specified in paragraph (6) of subdivision (d) of Section 639, the court may order the parties to pay the fees of referees who are not employees or officers of the court at the time of appointment, as fixed pursuant to Section 1023, in any manner determined by the court to be fair and reasonable, including an apportionment of the fees among the parties. For purposes of this section, the term "parties" does not include parties' counsel.
Amended by Stats 2000 ch 644 (AB 2912), s 11, eff. 1/1/2001.
Amended by Stats 2001 ch 159 (SB 662), s 38.5, eff. 1/1/2002.

Section 645.2 - Adoption of rules of court
The Judicial Council shall adopt all rules of court necessary to implement this chapter.
Added by Stats 2000 ch 644 (AB 2912), s 12, eff. 1/1/2001.

Chapter 7 - PROVISIONS RELATING TO TRIALS IN GENERAL
Article 1 - EXCEPTIONS

Section 646 - Definition
An exception is an objection upon a matter of law to a decision made, either before or after judgment, by a Court, tribunal, Judge, or other judicial officer, in an action or proceeding. The exception must be taken at the time the decision is made, except as provided in section six hundred and forty-seven.
Amended by Code Amendments 1875-76, Ch. 517.

Section 647 - Deemed excepted to

All of the following are deemed excepted to: the verdict of the jury; the final decision in an action or proceeding; an interlocutory order or decision, finally determining the rights of the parties, or some of them; an order or decision from which an appeal may be taken; an order sustaining or overruling a demurrer, allowing or refusing to allow an amendment to a pleading, striking out or refusing to strike out a pleading or a portion thereof, or refusing a continuance; an order made upon ex parte application, giving an instruction, refusing to give an instruction, or modifying an instruction requested; an order or decision made in the absence of the party or an order granting or denying a nonsuit or a motion to strike out evidence or testimony; a ruling sustaining or overruling an objection to evidence; and any statement or other action of the court in commenting upon or in summarizing the evidence. If the party, at the time when the order, ruling, action or decision is sought or made, or within a reasonable time thereafter, makes known his position thereon, by objection or otherwise, all other orders, rulings, actions or decisions are deemed to have been excepted to.
Amended by Stats. 1963, Ch. 99.

Article 1.5 - VIEW BY TRIER OF FACT

Section 651 - Generally
(a) On its own motion or on the motion of a party, where the court finds that such a view would be proper and would aid the trier of fact in its determination of the case, the court may order a view of any of the following:

(1) The property which is the subject of litigation.

(2) The place where any relevant event occurred.

(3) Any object, demonstration, or experiment, a view of which is relevant and admissible in evidence in the case and which cannot with reasonable convenience be viewed in the courtroom.

(b) On such occasion, the entire court, including the judge, jury, if any, court reporter, if any, and any necessary officers, shall proceed to the place, property, object, demonstration, or experiment to be viewed. The court shall be in session throughout the view. At the view, the court may permit testimony of witnesses. The proceedings at the view shall be recorded to the same extent as the proceedings in the courtroom.
Added by Stats. 1975, Ch. 301.

Article 2 - NEW TRIALS

Section 655 - [Repealed]
Repealed by Stats 2002 ch 784 (SB 1316),s 65, eff. 1/1/2003.

Section 656 - Definition
A new trial is a re-examination of an issue of fact in the same court after a trial and decision by a jury, court, or referee.
Amended by Stats. 1907, Ch. 380.

Section 657 - Causes for which new or further trial granted
The verdict may be vacated and any other decision may be modified or vacated, in whole or in part, and a new or further trial granted on all or part of the issues, on the application of the party aggrieved, for any of the following causes, materially affecting the substantial rights of such party:

1. Irregularity in the proceedings of the court, jury or adverse party, or any order of the court or abuse of discretion by which either party was prevented from having a fair trial.

2. Misconduct of the jury; and whenever any one or more of the jurors have been induced to assent to any general or special verdict, or to a finding on any question submitted to them by the court, by a resort to the determination of chance, such misconduct may be proved by the affidavit of any one of the jurors.

3. Accident or surprise, which ordinary prudence could not have guarded against.

4. Newly discovered evidence, material for the party making the application, which he could not, with reasonable diligence, have discovered and produced at the trial.

5. Excessive or inadequate damages.

6. Insufficiency of the evidence to justify the verdict or other decision, or the verdict or other decision is against law.

7. Error in law, occurring at the trial and excepted to by the party making the application. When a new trial is granted, on all or part of the issues, the court shall specify the ground or grounds upon which it is granted and the court's reason or reasons for granting the new trial upon each ground stated.

A new trial shall not be granted upon the ground of insufficiency of the evidence to justify the verdict or other decision, nor upon the ground of excessive or inadequate damages, unless after weighing the evidence the court is convinced from the entire record, including reasonable inferences therefrom, that the court or jury clearly should have reached a different verdict or decision.

The order passing upon and determining the motion must be made and entered as provided in Section 660 and if the motion is granted must state the ground or grounds relied upon by the court, and may contain the specification of reasons. If an order granting such motion does not contain such specification of reasons, the court must, within 10 days after filing such order, prepare, sign and file such specification of reasons in writing with the clerk. The court shall not direct the attorney for a party to prepare either or both said order and said specification of reasons.

On appeal from an order granting a new trial the order shall be affirmed if it should have been granted upon any ground stated in the motion, whether or not specified in the order or specification of reasons, except that (a) the order shall not be affirmed upon the ground of the insufficiency of the evidence to justify the verdict or other decision, or upon the ground of excessive or inadequate damages, unless such ground is stated in the order granting the motion and (b) on appeal from an order granting a new trial upon the ground of the insufficiency of the evidence to justify the verdict or other decision, or upon the ground of excessive or inadequate damages, it shall be conclusively presumed that said order as to such ground was made only for the reasons specified in said order or said specification of reasons, and such order shall be reversed as to such ground only if there is no substantial basis in the record for any of such reasons.
Amended by Stats. 1967, Ch. 72.

Section 657.1 - Granted as provided in section 914
A new trial may also be granted as provided in Section 914 of this code.
Added by Stats. 1968, Ch. 387.

Section 658 - Application made upon affidavits or on minutes of court
When the application is made for a cause mentioned in the first, second, third and fourth subdivisions of Section 657, it must be made upon affidavits; otherwise it must be made on the minutes of the court.
Amended by Stats. 1983, Ch. 1167, Sec. 9.

Section 659 - Notice of intention to move for new trial
(a) The party intending to move for a new trial shall file with the clerk and serve upon each adverse party a notice of his or her intention to move for a new trial, designating the grounds upon which the motion will be made and whether the same will be made upon affidavits or the minutes of the court, or both, either:

(1) After the decision is rendered and before the entry of judgment.

(2) Within 15 days of the date of mailing notice of entry of judgment by the clerk of the court pursuant to Section 664.5, or service upon him or her by any party of written notice of entry of judgment, or within 180 days after the entry of judgment, whichever is earliest; provided, that

upon the filing of the first notice of intention to move for a new trial by a party, each other party shall have 15 days after the service of that notice upon him or her to file and serve a notice of intention to move for a new trial.

(b) That notice of intention to move for a new trial shall be deemed to be a motion for a new trial on all the grounds stated in the notice. The times specified in paragraphs (1) and (2) of subdivision (a) shall not be extended by order or stipulation or by those provisions of Section 1013 that extend the time for exercising a right or doing an act where service is by mail.

Amended by Stats 2012 ch 83 (AB 2106),s 1, eff. 1/1/2013.

Section 659a - Time for serving affidavits after filing notice; counter-affidavits

Within 10 days of filing the notice, the moving party shall serve upon all other parties and file any brief and accompanying documents, including affidavits in support of the motion. The other parties shall have 10 days after that service within which to serve upon the moving party and file any opposing briefs and accompanying documents, including counter-affidavits. The moving party shall have five days after that service to file any reply brief and accompanying documents. These deadlines may, for good cause shown by affidavit or by written stipulation of the parties, be extended by any judge for an additional period not to exceed 10 days.

Amended by Stats 2014 ch 93 (AB 1659),s 2, eff. 1/1/2015.

Section 660 - Hearing and disposition of motion

(a) On the hearing of the motion, reference may be had in all cases to the pleadings and orders of the court on file, and when the motion is made on the minutes, reference may also be had to any depositions and documentary evidence offered at the trial and to the report of the proceedings on the trial taken by the phonographic reporter, or to any certified transcript of the report or if there be no such report or certified transcript, to proceedings occurring at the trial that are within the recollection of the judge; when the proceedings at the trial have been phonographically reported, but the reporter's notes have not been transcribed, the reporter shall, upon request of the court or either party, attend the hearing of the motion and read his or her notes, or such parts thereof as the court, or either party, may require.

(b) The hearing and determination of the motion for a new trial shall have precedence over all other matters except criminal cases, probate matters, and cases actually on trial, and it shall be the duty of the court to determine the motion at the earliest possible moment.

(c) Except as otherwise provided in Section 12a of this code, the power of the court to rule on a motion for a new trial shall expire 75 days after the mailing of notice of entry of judgment by the clerk of the court pursuant to Section 664.5 or 75 days after service on the moving party by any party of written notice of entry of judgment, whichever is earlier, or if that notice has not been given, 75 days after the filing of the first notice of intention to move for a new trial. If the motion is not determined within the 75-day period, or within that period as extended, the effect shall be a denial of the motion without further order of the court. A motion for a new trial is not determined within the meaning of this section until an order ruling on the motion is entered in the permanent minutes of the court or signed by the judge and filed with the clerk. The entry of a new trial order in the permanent minutes of the court shall constitute a determination of the motion even though that minute order, as entered, expressly directs that a written order be prepared, signed, and filed. The minute entry shall in all cases show the date on which the order is entered in the permanent minutes, but failure to comply with this direction shall not impair the validity or effectiveness of the order.

Amended by Stats 2018 ch 317 (AB 2230),s 1, eff. 1/1/2019.

Section 661 - Judge to hear and determine motion; oral argument

The motion for a new trial shall be heard and determined by the judge who presided at the trial; provided, however, that in case of the inability of such judge or if at the time noticed for hearing thereon he is absent from the county where the trial was had, the same shall be heard and determined by any other judge of the same court. Upon the expiration of the time to file counter affidavits the clerk forthwith shall call the motion to the attention of the judge who presided at the trial, or the judge acting in his place, as the case may be, and such judge thereupon shall designate the time for oral argument, if any, to be had on said motion. Five (5) days' notice by mail shall be given of such oral argument, if any, by the clerk to the respective parties. Such motion, if heard by a judge other than the trial judge shall be argued orally or shall be submitted without oral argument, as the judge may direct, not later than ten (10) days before the expiration of the time within which the court has power to pass on the same.

Amended by Stats. 1933, Ch. 744.

Section 662 - Ruling by court

In ruling on such motion, in a cause tried without a jury, the court may, on such terms as may be just, change or add to the statement of decision, modify the judgment, in whole or in part, vacate the judgment, in whole or in part, and grant a new trial on all or part of the issues, or, in lieu of granting a new trial, may vacate and set aside the statement of decision and judgment and reopen the case for further proceedings and the introduction of additional evidence with the same effect as if the case had been reopened after the submission thereof and before a decision had been filed or judgment rendered. Any judgment thereafter entered shall be subject to the provisions of sections 657 and 659.

Amended by Stats. 1981, Ch. 900, Sec. 4.

Section 662.5 - Conditional orders where new trial limited to issue of damages

(a) In any civil action where after trial by jury an order granting a new trial limited to the issue of damages would be proper, the trial court may in its discretion:

(1) If the ground for granting a new trial is inadequate damages, issue a conditional order granting the new trial unless the party against whom the verdict has been rendered consents to the addition of damages in an amount the court in its independent judgment determines from the evidence to be fair and reasonable.

(2) If the ground for granting a new trial is excessive damages, issue a conditional order granting the new trial unless the party in whose favor the verdict has been rendered consents to the reduction of so much thereof as the court in its independent judgment determines from the evidence to be fair and reasonable.

(b) If a deadline for acceptance or rejection of the addition or reduction of damages is not set forth in the conditional order, the deadline is 30 days from the date the conditional order is served by the clerk of the court. Failure to respond to the order in accordance with this section shall be deemed a rejection of the addition or reduction of damages and a new trial limited to the issue of damages shall be granted automatically.

(c) A party filing and serving an acceptance of a conditionally ordered addition or reduction of damages shall concurrently serve and submit to the court a proposed amended judgment reflecting the modified judgment amount, as well as any other uncontested judgment awards.

Amended by Stats 2011 ch 409 (AB 1403),s 2, eff. 1/1/2012.

Section 663 - Setting aside and vacating judgment and another or different judgment entered

A judgment or decree, when based upon a decision by the court, or the special verdict of a jury, may, upon motion of the party aggrieved, be set aside and vacated by the same court, and another and different judgment entered, for either of the following causes, materially affecting the substantial rights of the party and entitling the party to a different judgment:

1. Incorrect or erroneous legal basis for the decision, not consistent with or not supported by the facts; and in such case when the judgment is set aside, the statement of decision shall be amended and corrected.

2. A judgment or decree not consistent with or not supported by the special verdict.

Amended by Stats. 1981, Ch. 900, Sec. 5.

Section 663a - Motion to set aside and vacate judgment

(a) A party intending to make a motion to set aside and vacate a judgment, as described in Section 663, shall file with the clerk and serve upon the adverse party a notice of his or her intention, designating the grounds upon which the motion will be made, and specifying the particulars in which the legal basis for the decision is not consistent with or supported by the facts, or in which the judgment or decree is not consistent with the special verdict, either:

(1) After the decision is rendered and before the entry of judgment.

(2) Within 15 days of the date of mailing of notice of entry of judgment by the clerk of the court pursuant to Section 664.5, or service upon him or her by any party of written notice of entry of judgment, or within 180 days after the entry of judgment, whichever is earliest.

(b) Except as otherwise provided in Section 12a, the power of the court to rule on a motion to set aside and vacate a judgment shall expire 75 days from the mailing of notice of entry of judgment by the clerk of the court pursuant to Section 664.5, or 75 days after service upon the moving party by any party of written notice of entry of the judgment, whichever is earlier, or if that notice has not been given, 75 days after the filing of the first notice of intention to move to set aside and vacate the judgment. If that motion is not determined within the 75-day period, or within that period as extended, the effect shall be a denial of the motion without further order of the court. A motion to set aside and vacate a judgment is not determined within the meaning of this section until an order ruling on the motion is entered in the permanent minutes of the court, or signed by the judge and filed with the clerk. The entry of an order to set aside and vacate the judgment in the permanent minutes of the court shall constitute a determination of the motion even though that minute order, as entered, expressly directs that a written order be prepared, signed, and filed. The minute entry shall, in all cases, show the date on which the order is entered in the permanent minutes, but failure to comply with this direction shall not impair the validity or effectiveness of the order.

(c) The provisions of Section 1013 extending the time for exercising a right or doing an act where service is by mail shall not apply to extend the times specified in paragraphs (1) and (2) of subdivision (a).

(d) The moving, opposing, and reply briefs and any accompanying documents shall be filed and served within the periods specified by Section 659a and the hearing on the motion shall be set in the same manner as the hearing on a motion for new trial under Section 660.

(e) An order of the court granting a motion may be reviewed on appeal in the same manner as a special order made after final judgment.

Amended by Stats 2018 ch 317 (AB 2230),s 2, eff. 1/1/2019.

Amended by Stats 2014 ch 93 (AB 1659),s 3, eff. 1/1/2015.

Amended by Stats 2012 ch 83 (AB 2106),s 2, eff. 1/1/2013.

Section 663.1 - Motion for new trial upon loss or destruction of records

The court may grant a new trial of any action or proceeding when all of the following conditions exist:

(a) Any proposed bill of exceptions or statement of the case on motion for a new trial is lost or destroyed by reason of conflagration or other public calamity.

(b) No other record of the proceedings upon the trial thereof can be obtained.

(c) Such action or proceeding is subject to review by motion for new trial pending at the time of such loss or destruction.

(d) The court in which such action or proceeding is pending deems it impossible or impracticable to restore such proceedings and to settle a bill of exceptions or statement of the case containing such proceedings, so as to enable the court to review the judgment or order therein by motion for new trial.

(e) At the time of such loss or destruction a motion for new trial was pending. In order to grant such new trial, it shall be unnecessary to have any bill of exceptions or statement of the case settled, but upon the facts recited in this section being shown to the satisfaction of the court by affidavit or otherwise, the court may grant such new trial.

Added by Stats. 1953, Ch. 52.

Section 663.2 - Extension of time for preparing, serving and presenting bill of exceptions

Pending the hearing of a motion pursuant to Section 663.1 to grant a new trial, the time within which a bill of exceptions may be prepared, served, or presented for settlement shall be extended and shall not commence to run until the decision upon the motion. The motion must be made within 30 days after the loss or destruction of the records.

Added by Stats. 1953, Ch. 52.

Chapter 8 - THE MANNER OF GIVING AND ENTERING JUDGMENT

Section 664 - Trial by jury had

When trial by jury has been had, judgment must be entered by the clerk, in conformity to the verdict within 24 hours after the rendition of the verdict, whether or not a motion for judgment notwithstanding the verdict be pending, unless the court order the case to be reserved for argument or further consideration, or grant a stay of proceedings. If the trial has been had by the court, judgment must be entered by the clerk, in conformity to the decision of the court, immediately upon the filing of such decision. In no case is a judgment effectual for any purpose until entered.

Amended by Stats. 1977, Ch. 1257.

Section 664.5 - Contested action or special proceeding in which prevailing party not represented by counsel

(a) In any contested action or special proceeding other than a small claims action or an action or proceeding in which a prevailing party is not represented by counsel, the party submitting an order or judgment for entry shall prepare and serve, a copy of the notice of entry of judgment to all parties who have appeared in the action or proceeding and shall file with the court the original notice of entry of judgment together with the proof of service. This subdivision does not apply in a proceeding for dissolution of marriage, for nullity of marriage, or for legal separation.

(b) Promptly upon entry of judgment in a contested action or special proceeding in which a prevailing party is not represented by counsel, the clerk of the court shall serve notice of entry of judgment to all parties who have appeared in the action or special proceeding and shall execute a certificate of service and place it in the court's file in the cause.

(c) For purposes of this section, "judgment" includes any judgment, decree, or signed order from which an appeal lies.

(d) Upon order of the court in any action or special proceeding, the clerk shall serve notice of entry of any judgment or ruling, whether or not appealable.

(e) The Judicial Council shall provide by rule of court that, upon entry of judgment in a contested action or special proceeding in which a state statute or regulation has been declared unconstitutional by the court, the Attorney General is promptly notified of the judgment and that a certificate of that service is placed in the court's file in the cause.

Amended by Stats 2017 ch 319 (AB 976),s 1, eff. 1/1/2018.

Amended by Stats 2016 ch 703 (AB 2881),s 8, eff. 1/1/2017.

Section 664.6 - Judgment entered pursuant to terms of stipulated settlement

(a) If parties to pending litigation stipulate, in a writing signed by the parties outside of the presence of the court or orally before the court, for settlement of the case, or part thereof, the court, upon motion, may enter judgment pursuant to the terms of the settlement. If requested by the parties, the court may retain jurisdiction over the parties to enforce the settlement until performance in full of the terms of the settlement.

(b) For purposes of this section, a writing is signed by a party if it is signed by any of the following:

(1) The party.

(2) An attorney who represents the party.

(3) If the party is an insurer, an agent who is authorized in writing by the insurer to sign on the insurer's behalf.

(c) Paragraphs (2) and (3) of subdivision (b) do not apply in a civil harassment action, an action brought pursuant to the Family Code, an action brought pursuant to the Probate Code, or a matter that is being adjudicated in a juvenile court or a dependency court.

(d) In addition to any available civil remedies, an attorney who signs a writing on behalf of a party pursuant to subdivision (b) without the party's express authorization shall, absent good cause, be subject to professional discipline.

Amended by Stats 2020 ch 290 (AB 2723),s 1, eff. 1/1/2021.

Section 664.7 - Judgment entered upon term of stipulated settlement in construction defect action

(a) Notwithstanding Section 664.6, if parties to a pending construction defect action stipulate personally or, where a party's contribution is paid on its behalf pursuant to a policy of insurance, the parties stipulate through their respective counsel, in a writing signed by the parties outside the presence of the court or orally before the court, for settlement of the case, or part thereof, the court, upon motion, may enter judgment pursuant to the terms of the settlement. If requested by the parties, the court may retain jurisdiction over the parties to enforce the settlement until performance in full of the terms of the settlement.

(b) It is the intent of the Legislature that this section modify the holding of Levy v. Superior Court (1995), 10 Cal. 4th 578, regarding the authority of counsel in a construction defect action to bind a party to a settlement.

(c) For purposes of this section, "construction defect action" shall mean any civil action that seeks monetary recovery against a developer, builder, design professional, general contractor, material supplier, or subcontractor of any residential dwelling based upon a claim for alleged defects in the design or construction of the residential dwelling unit.

Added by Stats. 1998, Ch. 856, Sec. 1. Effective January 1, 1999.

Section 665 - Case reserved for argument or further consideration

When the case is reserved for argument or further consideration, as mentioned in the last section, it may be brought by either party before the Court for argument.

Enacted 1872.

Section 666 - Judgment for party asserting cross-complaint

If a claim asserted in a cross-complaint is established at the trial and the amount so established exceeds the demand established by the party against whom the cross-complaint is asserted, judgment for the party asserting the cross-complaint must be given for the excess; or if it appears that the party asserting the cross-complaint is entitled to any other affirmative relief, judgment must be given accordingly.

When the amount found due to either party exceeds the sum for which the court is authorized to enter judgment, such party may remit the excess, and judgment may be rendered for the residue.

Amended by Stats. 1971, Ch. 244.

Section 667 - Judgment in action to recover personal property

In an action to recover the possession of personal property, judgment for the plaintiff may be for the possession or the value thereof, in case a delivery cannot be had, and damages for the detention. If the property has been delivered to the plaintiff, and the defendant claim a return thereof judgment for the defendant may be for a return of the property or the value thereof, in case a return cannot be had, and damages for taking and withholding the same.

Amended by Stats. 1982, Ch. 497, Sec. 37. Operative July 1, 1983, by Sec. 185 of Ch. 497.

Section 667.7 - Judgment ordering payment of future damages by periodic payments in action against health care provider

(a) In any action for injury or damages against a provider of health care services, a superior court shall, at the request of either party, enter a judgment ordering that money damages or its equivalent for future damages of the judgment creditor be paid in whole or in part by periodic payments rather than by a lump-sum payment if the award equals or exceeds two hundred fifty thousand dollars ($250,000) in future damages. In entering a judgment ordering the payment of future damages by periodic payments, the court shall make a specific finding as to the dollar amount of periodic payments which will compensate the judgment creditor for such future damages. As a condition to authorizing periodic payments of future damages, the court shall require the judgment debtor who is not adequately insured to post security adequate to assure full payment of such damages awarded by the judgment. Upon termination of periodic payments of future damages, the court shall order the return of this security, or so much as remains, to the judgment debtor.

(b)

(1) The judgment ordering the payment of future damages by periodic payments shall specify the recipient or recipients of the payments, the dollar amount of the payments, the interval between payments, and the number of payments or the period of time over which payments shall be made. Such payments shall only be subject to modification in the event of the death of the judgment creditor.

(2) In the event that the court finds that the judgment debtor has exhibited a continuing pattern of failing to make the payments, as specified in paragraph (1), the court shall find the judgment debtor in contempt of court and, in addition to the required periodic payments, shall order the judgment debtor to pay the judgment creditor all damages caused by the failure to make such periodic payments, including court costs and attorney's fees.

(c) However, money damages awarded for loss of future earnings shall not be reduced or payments terminated by reason of the death of the judgment creditor, but shall be paid to persons to whom the judgment creditor owed a duty of support, as provided by law, immediately prior to their death. In such cases the court which rendered the original judgment, may, upon petition of any party in interest, modify the judgment to award and apportion the unpaid future damages in accordance with this subdivision.

(d) Following the occurrence or expiration of all obligations specified in the periodic payment judgment, any obligation of the judgment debtor to make further payments shall cease and any security given, pursuant to subdivision (a) shall revert to the judgment debtor.

(e) As used in this section:

(1) "Future damages" includes damages for future medical treatment, care or custody, loss of future earnings, loss of bodily function, or future pain and suffering of the judgment creditor.

(2) "Periodic payments" means the payment of money or delivery of other property to the judgment creditor at regular intervals.

(3) "Health care provider" means any person licensed or certified pursuant to Division 2 (commencing with Section 500) of the Business and Professions Code, or licensed pursuant to the Osteopathic Initiative Act, or the Chiropractic Initiative Act, or licensed pursuant to Chapter 2.5 (commencing with Section 1440) of Division 2 of the Health and Safety Code; and any clinic, health dispensary, or health facility, licensed pursuant to Division 2 (commencing with Section 1200) of the Health and Safety Code. "Health care provider" includes the legal representatives of a health care provider.

(4) "Professional negligence" means a negligent act or omission to act by a health care provider in the rendering of professional services, which act or omission is the proximate cause of a personal injury or wrongful death, provided that such services are within the scope of services for which the provider is licensed and which are not within any restriction imposed by the licensing agency or licensed hospital.

(f) It is the intent of the Legislature in enacting this section to authorize the entry of judgments in malpractice actions against health care providers which provide for the payment of future damages through periodic payments rather than lump-sum payments. By authorizing periodic payment judgments, it is the further intent of the Legislature that the courts will utilize such judgments to provide compensation sufficient to meet the needs of an injured plaintiff and those persons who are dependent on the plaintiff for whatever period is necessary while eliminating the potential windfall from a lump-sum recovery which was intended to provide for the care of an injured plaintiff over an extended period who then dies shortly after the judgment is paid, leaving the balance of the judgment award to persons and purposes for which it was not intended. It is also the intent of the Legislature that all elements of the periodic payment program be specified with certainty in the judgment ordering such payments and that the judgment not be subject to modification at some future time which might alter the specifications of the original judgment.

Amended by Stats 2022 ch 17 (AB 35),s 4, eff. 1/1/2023.
Amended by Stats. 1975, 2nd Ex. Sess., Ch. 2.
Section 668 - Judgment book
Except as provided in Section 668.5, the clerk of the superior court, must keep, with the records of the court, a book called the "judgment book," in which judgments must be entered.
Amended by Stats 2002 ch 784 (SB 1316),s 66, eff. 1/1/2003.
Section 668.5 - Date of filing judgment with clerk constitutes date of entry
In those counties where the clerk of the court places individual judgments in the file of actions and either a microfilm copy of the individual judgment is made, or the judgment is entered in the register of actions, or into the court's electronic data-processing system, prior to placement of the judgment in the file of actions, the clerk shall not be required to enter judgments in a judgment book, and the date of filing the judgment with the clerk shall constitute the date of its entry.
Amended by Stats. 1983, Ch. 464, Sec. 1.
Section 669 - Death of party after trial
If a party dies after trial and submission of the case to a judge sitting without a jury for decision or after a verdict upon any issue of fact, and before judgment, the court may nevertheless render judgment thereon.
Amended by Stats. 1980, Ch. 124, Sec. 2.
Section 670 - Papers constituting judgment roll
In superior courts the following papers, without being attached together, shall constitute the judgment roll:
(a) In case the complaint is not answered by any defendant, the summons, with the affidavit or proof of service; the complaint; the request for entry of default with a memorandum indorsed thereon that the default of the defendant in not answering was entered, and a copy of the judgment; if defendant has appeared by demurrer, and the demurrer has been overruled, then notice of the overruling thereof served on defendant's attorney, together with proof of the service; and in case the service so made is by publication, the affidavit for publication of summons, and the order directing the publication of summons.
(b) In all other cases, the pleadings, all orders striking out any pleading in whole or in part, a copy of the verdict of the jury, the statement of decision of the court, or finding of the referee, and a copy of any order made on demurrer, or relating to a change of parties, and a copy of the judgment; if there are two or more defendants in the action, and any one of them has allowed judgment to pass against him or her by default, the summons, with proof of its service, on the defendant, and if the service on the defaulting defendant be by publication, then the affidavit for publication, and the order directing the publication of the summons.
Amended by Stats 2002 ch 784 (SB 1316),s 67, eff. 1/1/2003.
Section 673 - Acknowledgment of assignment of judgment
(a) An assignee of a right represented by a judgment may become an assignee of record by filing with the clerk of the court which entered the judgment an acknowledgment of assignment of judgment.
(b) An acknowledgment of assignment of judgment shall contain all of the following:
    (1) The title of the court where the judgment is entered and the cause and number of the action.
    (2) The date of entry of the judgment and of any renewals of the judgment and where entered in the records of the court.
    (3) The name and address of the judgment creditor and name and last known address of the judgment debtor.
    (4) A statement describing the right represented by the judgment that is assigned to the assignee.
    (5) The name and address of the assignee.
(c) The acknowledgment of assignment of judgment shall be:
    (1) Made in the manner of an acknowledgment of a conveyance of real property.
    (2) Executed and acknowledged by the judgment creditor or by the prior assignee of record if there is one.
(d)
    (1) If an acknowledgment of assignment of judgment purports to be executed or acknowledged by an authorized agent of the judgment creditor or an authorized agent of a prior assignee of record, then documentation sufficient to evidence that authorization shall be filed together with the acknowledgment of assignment of judgment.
    (2) Notwithstanding paragraph (1), an assignee of a right represented by a judgment may also become an assignee of record by filing with the clerk of the court that entered judgment a court order or other documentation that evidences assignment of judgment by operation of law.
Amended by Stats 2020 ch 36 (AB 3364),s 22, eff. 1/1/2021.
Section 674 - Abstract of judgment requiring payment of money
(a) Except as otherwise provided in Section 4506 of the Family Code, an abstract of a judgment or decree requiring the payment of money shall be certified by the clerk of the court where the judgment or decree was entered and shall contain all of the following:
    (1) The title of the court where the judgment or decree is entered and cause and number of the action.
    (2) The date of entry of the judgment or decree and of any renewals of the judgment or decree and where entered in the records of the court.
    (3) The name and last known address of the judgment debtor and the address at which the summons was either personally served or mailed to the judgment debtor or the judgment debtor's attorney of record.
    (4) The name and address of the judgment creditor.
    (5) The amount of the judgment or decree as entered or as last renewed.
    (6) The last four digits of the social security number and driver's license number of the judgment debtor if they are known to the judgment creditor. If either or both of those sets of numbers are not known to the judgment creditor, that fact shall be indicated on the abstract of judgment.
    (7) Whether a stay of enforcement has been ordered by the court and, if so, the date the stay ends.
    (8) The date of issuance of the abstract.
(b) An abstract of judgment, recorded after January 1, 1979, that does not list the social security number and driver's license number of the judgment debtor, or either of them, as required by subdivision (a) or by Section 4506 of the Family Code, may be amended by the recording of a document entitled "Amendment to Abstract of Judgment." The Amendment to Abstract of Judgment shall contain all of the information required by this section or by Section 4506 of the Family Code, and shall set forth the date of recording and the book and page location in the records of the county recorder of the original abstract of judgment. A recorded Amendment to Abstract of Judgment shall have priority as of the date of recordation of the original abstract of judgment, except as to any purchaser, encumbrancer, or lessee who obtained their interest after the recordation of the original abstract of judgment but prior to the recordation of the Amendment to Abstract of Judgment without actual notice of the original abstract of judgment. The purchaser, encumbrancer, or lessee without actual notice may assert as a defense against enforcement of the abstract of judgment the failure to comply with this section or Section 4506 of the Family Code regarding the contents of the original abstract of judgment notwithstanding the subsequent recordation of an Amendment to Abstract of Judgment. With respect to an abstract of judgment recorded between January 1, 1979, and July 10, 1985, the defense against enforcement for failure to comply with this section or Section 4506 of the Family Code may not be asserted by the holder of another abstract of judgment or involuntary lien, recorded without actual notice of the prior abstract, unless refusal to allow the defense would result in prejudice and substantial injury as used in Section 475. The recordation of an Amendment to Abstract of Judgment does not extend or otherwise alter the computation of time as provided in Section 697.310.

(c)

(1) The abstract of judgment shall be certified in the name of the judgment debtor as listed on the judgment and may also include the additional name or names by which the judgment debtor is known as set forth in the affidavit of identity, as defined in Section 680.135, filed by the judgment creditor with the application for issuance of the abstract of judgment. Prior to the clerk of the court certifying an abstract of judgment containing any additional name or names by which the judgment debtor is known that are not listed on the judgment, the court shall approve the affidavit of identity. If the court determines, without a hearing or a notice, that the affidavit of identity states sufficient facts upon which the judgment creditor has identified the additional names of the judgment debtor, the court shall authorize the certification of the abstract of judgment with the additional name or names.

(2) The remedies provided in Section 697.410 apply to a recorded abstract of a money judgment based upon an affidavit of identity that appears to create a judgment lien on real property of a person who is not the judgment debtor.

Amended by Stats 2007 ch 189 (SB 644),s 1, eff. 1/1/2008.
Amended by Stats 2000 ch 639 (AB 2405), s 1, eff. 1/1/2001.
Amended by Stats 2001 ch 159 (SB 662), s 39, eff. 1/1/2002.

Title 8.5 - UNIFORM FOREIGN-MONEY CLAIMS ACT

Section 676 - Title of act
This title shall be known and may be cited as the Uniform Foreign-Money Claims Act.
Added by Stats. 1991, Ch. 932, Sec. 1.

Section 676.1 - Definitions
As used in this title:

(1) "Action" means a judicial proceeding or arbitration in which a payment in money may be awarded or enforced with respect to a foreign-money claim.

(2) "Bank-offered spot rate" means the spot rate of exchange at which a bank will sell foreign money at a spot rate.

(3) "Conversion date" means the banking day next preceding the date on which money, in accordance with this title, is (i) paid to a claimant in an action or distribution proceeding, (ii) paid to the official designated by law to enforce a judgment or award on behalf of a claimant, or (iii) used to recoup, setoff, or counterclaim in different moneys in an action or distribution proceeding.

(4) "Distribution proceeding" means a judicial or nonjudicial proceeding for the distribution of a fund in which one or more foreign-money claims is asserted and includes an accounting, an assignment for the benefit of creditors, a foreclosure, the liquidation or rehabilitation of a corporation or other entity, and the distribution of an estate, trust, or other fund.

(5) "Foreign money" means money other than money of the United States of America.

(6) "Foreign-money claim" means a claim upon an obligation to pay, or a claim for recovery of a loss, expressed in or measured by a foreign money.

(7) "Money" means a medium of exchange for the payment of obligations or a store of value authorized or adopted by a government or by intergovernmental agreement.

(8) "Money of the claim" means the money determined as proper pursuant to Section 676.4.

(9) "Person" means an individual, a corporation, government or governmental subdivision or agency, business trust, estate, trust, joint venture, partnership, association, two or more persons having a joint or common interest, or any other legal or commercial entity.

(10) "Rate of exchange" means the rate at which money of one country may be converted into money of another country in a free financial market convenient to or reasonably usable by a person obligated to pay or to state a rate of conversion. If separate rates of exchange apply to different kinds of transactions, the term means the rate applicable to the particular transaction giving rise to the foreign-money claim.

(11) "Spot rate" means the rate of exchange at which foreign money is sold by a bank or other dealer in foreign exchange for immediate or next day availability or for settlement by immediate payment in cash or equivalent, by charge to an account, or by an agreed delayed settlement not exceeding two days.

(12) "State" means a State of the United States, the District of Columbia, the Commonwealth of Puerto Rico, or a territory or insular possession subject to the jurisdiction of the United States.

Added by Stats. 1991, Ch. 932, Sec. 1.

Section 676.2 - Applicability of title
(a) This title applies only to a foreign-money claim in an action or distribution proceeding.

(b) This title applies to foreign-money issues even if other law under the conflict-of-laws rules of this state applies to other issues in the action or distribution proceeding.

Added by Stats. 1991, Ch. 932, Sec. 1.

Section 676.3 - Agreement varying effect of title; agreement as to money used in transaction
(a) The effect of this title may be varied by agreement of the parties made before or after commencement of an action or distribution proceeding or the entry of judgment.

(b) Parties to a transaction may agree upon the money to be used in a transaction giving rise to a foreign-money claim and may agree to use different moneys for different aspects of the transaction. Stating the price in a foreign money for one aspect of a transaction does not alone require the use of that money for other aspects of the transaction.

Added by Stats. 1991, Ch. 932, Sec. 1.

Section 676.4 - Proper money of claim
(a) The money in which the parties to a transaction have agreed that payment is to be made is the proper money of the claim for payment.

(b) If the parties to a transaction have not otherwise agreed, the proper money of the claim, as in each case may be appropriate, is one of the following:

(1) The money regularly used between the parties as a matter of usage or course of dealing.

(2) The money used at the time of a transaction in international trade, by trade usage or common practice, for valuing or settling transactions in the particular commodity or service involved.

(3) The money in which the loss was ultimately felt or will be incurred by the party claimant.

Added by Stats. 1991, Ch. 932, Sec. 1.

Section 676.5 - Amount paid determined on conversion date
(a) If an amount contracted to be paid in a foreign money is measured by a specified amount of a different money, the amount to be paid is determined on the conversion date.

(b) If an amount contracted to be paid in a foreign money is to be measured by a different money at the rate of exchange prevailing on a date before default, that rate of exchange applies only to payments made within a reasonable time after default, not exceeding 30 days. Thereafter, conversion is made at the bank-offered spot rate on the conversion date.

(c) A monetary claim is neither usurious nor unconscionable because the agreement on which it is based provides that the amount of the debtor's obligation to be paid in the debtor's money, when received by the creditor, shall equal a specified amount of the foreign money of the country of

the creditor. If, because of unexcused delay in payment of a judgment or award, the amount received by the creditor does not equal the amount of the foreign money specified in the agreement, the court or arbitrator shall amend the judgment or award accordingly.
Added by Stats. 1991, Ch. 932, Sec. 1.

Section 676.6 - Proper money of claim question of law
(a) A person may assert a claim in a specified foreign money. If a foreign-money claim is not asserted, the claimant makes the claim in United States dollars.
(b) An opposing party may allege and prove that a claim, in whole or in part, is in a different money than that asserted by the claimant.
(c) A person may assert a defense, setoff, recoupment, or counterclaim in any money without regard to the money of other claims.
(d) The determination of the proper money of the claim is a question of law.
Added by Stats. 1991, Ch. 932, Sec. 1.

Section 676.7 - Judgment or award
(a) Except as provided in subdivision (c), a judgment or award on a foreign-money claim shall be stated in an amount of the money of the claim.
(b) A judgment or award on a foreign-money claim is payable in that foreign money or, at the option of the debtor, in the amount of United States dollars which will purchase that foreign money on the conversion date at a bank-offered spot rate.
(c) Assessed costs shall be entered in United States dollars.
(d) Each payment in United States dollars shall be accepted and credited on a judgment or award on a foreign-money claim in the amount of the foreign money that could be purchased by the dollars at a bank-offered spot rate of exchange at or near the close of business on the conversion date for that payment.
(e) A judgment or award made in an action or distribution proceeding on both (1) a defense, setoff, recoupment, or counterclaim and (2) the adverse party's claim, shall be netted by converting the money of the smaller into the money of the larger, and by subtracting the smaller from the larger, and specify the rates of exchange used.
(f) A judgment substantially in the following form complies with subdivision (a): "IT IS ADJUDGED AND ORDERED, that Defendant (insert name) pay to Plaintiff (insert name) the sum of (insert amount in the foreign money) plus interest on that sum at the rate of (insert rate--see Section 676.9) percent a year or, at the option of the judgment debtor, the number of United States dollars which will purchase the (insert name of foreign money) with interest due, at a bank-offered spot rate at or near the close of business on the banking day next before the day of payment, together with assessed costs of (insert amount) United States dollars.'
(g) If a contract claim is of the type covered by subdivision (a) or (b) of Section 676.5, the judgment or award shall be entered for the amount of money stated to measure the obligation to be paid in the money specified for payment or, at the option of the debtor, the number of United States dollars which will purchase the computed amount of the money of payment on the conversion date at a bank-offered spot rate.
(h) A judgment shall be entered in foreign money in the same manner, and has the same effect as a lien, as other judgments. It may be discharged by payment.
Added by Stats. 1991, Ch. 932, Sec. 1.

Section 676.8 - Rate of exchange
The rate of exchange prevailing at or near the close of business on the day the distribution proceeding is initiated governs all exchanges of foreign money in a distribution proceeding. A foreign-money claimant in a distribution proceeding shall assert its claim in the named foreign money and show the amount of United States dollars resulting from a conversion as of the date the proceeding was initiated.
Added by Stats. 1991, Ch. 932, Sec. 1.

Section 676.9 - Prejudgment or pre-award interest
(a) With respect to a foreign-money claim, recovery of prejudgment or pre-award interest and the rate of interest to be applied in the action or distribution proceeding, except as provided in subdivision (b), are matters of the substantive law governing the right to recovery under the conflict-of-laws rules of this state.
(b) The court or arbitrator shall increase or decrease the amount of prejudgment or pre-award interest otherwise payable in a judgment or award in foreign money to the extent required by the law of this state governing a failure to make or accept an offer of settlement or offer of judgment, or conduct by a party or its attorney causing undue delay or expense.
(c) A judgment or award on a foreign-money claim bears interest at the rate applicable to judgments of this state.
Added by Stats. 1991, Ch. 932, Sec. 1.

Section 676.10 - Enforcement of foreign judgment
(a) If an action is brought to enforce a judgment of another jurisdiction expressed in a foreign money and the judgment is recognized in this state as enforceable, the enforcing judgment shall be entered as provided in Section 676.7, whether or not the foreign judgment confers an option to pay in an equivalent amount of United States dollars.
(b) A foreign judgment may be enforced in accordance with Title 11 (commencing with Section 1710.10) of Part 3.
(c) A satisfaction or partial payment made upon the foreign judgment, on proof thereof, shall be credited against the amount of foreign money specified in the judgment, notwithstanding the entry of judgment in this state.
(d) A judgment entered on a foreign-money claim only in United States dollars in another state shall be enforced in this state in United States dollars only.
Added by Stats. 1991, Ch. 932, Sec. 1.

Section 676.11 - Computation of United States dollar equivalent of money of judgment
(a) Computations under this section are for the limited purposes of the section and do not affect computation of the United States dollar equivalent of the money of the judgment for the purpose of payment.
(b) For the limited purpose of facilitating the enforcement of provisional remedies in an action, the value in United States dollars of assets to be seized or restrained pursuant to a writ of attachment, garnishment, execution, or other legal process, the amount of United States dollars at issue for assessing costs, or the amount of United States dollars involved for a surety bond or other court-required undertaking, shall be ascertained as provided in subdivisions (c) and (d).
(c) A party seeking process, costs, bond, or other undertaking under subdivision (b) shall compute in United States dollars the amount of the foreign money claimed from a bank-offered spot rate prevailing at or near the close of business on the banking day next preceding the filing of a request or application for the issuance of process or for the determination of costs, or an application for a bond or other court-required undertaking.
(d) A party seeking the process, costs, bond, or other undertaking under subdivision (b) shall file with each request or application an affidavit or certificate executed in good faith by its counsel or a bank officer, stating the market quotation used and how it was obtained, and setting forth the calculation. Affected court officials incur no liability, after a filing of the affidavit or certificate, for acting as if the judgment were in the amount of United States dollars stated in the affidavit or certificate.
Added by Stats. 1991, Ch. 932, Sec. 1.

Section 676.12 - Substitution of new money in place of money obligation expressed or loss incurred

(a) If, after an obligation is expressed or a loss is incurred in a foreign money, the country issuing or adopting that money substitutes a new money in place of that money, the obligation or the loss is treated as if expressed or incurred in the new money at the rate of conversion the issuing country establishes for the payment of like obligations or losses denominated in the former money.
(b) If substitution under subdivision (a) occurs after a judgment or award is entered on a foreign-money claim, the court or arbitrator shall amend the judgment or award by a like conversion of the former money.
Added by Stats. 1991, Ch. 932, Sec. 1.

Section 676.13 - Principles of law and equity
Unless displaced by particular provisions of this title, the principles of law and equity, including the law merchant, and the law relative to capacity to contract, principal and agent, estoppel, fraud, misrepresentation, duress, coercion, mistake, bankruptcy, or other validating or invalidating causes supplement its provisions.
Added by Stats. 1991, Ch. 932, Sec. 1.

Section 676.14 - Construction and application of title
This title shall be applied and construed to effectuate its general purpose to make uniform the law with respect to the subject of this title among states enacting it.
Added by Stats. 1991, Ch. 932, Sec. 1.

Section 676.15 - Severability of provisions
If any provision of this title or its application to any person or circumstance is held invalid, that invalidity does not affect other provisions or applications of this title which can be given effect without the invalid provision or application, and to this end the provisions of this title are severable.
Added by Stats. 1991, Ch. 932, Sec. 1.

Section 676.16 - Effective date of title
This title applies to actions and distribution proceedings commenced on or after January 1, 1992.
Added by Stats. 1991, Ch. 932, Sec. 1.

Title 9 - ENFORCEMENT OF JUDGMENTS
Division 1 - DEFINITIONS AND GENERAL PROVISIONS
Chapter 1 - DEFINITIONS AND GENERAL PROVISIONS

Section 680.010 - Title of law
This title shall be known and may be cited as the Enforcement of Judgments Law.
Added by Stats. 1982, Ch. 1364, Sec. 2. Operative July 1, 1983, by Sec. 3 of Ch. 1364.

Section 680.110 - Definitions govern construction
Unless the provision or context otherwise requires, the definitions in this chapter govern the construction of this title.
Added by Stats. 1982, Ch. 1364, Sec. 2. Operative July 1, 1983, by Sec. 3 of Ch. 1364.

Section 680.120 - Account debtor
"Account debtor" means "account debtor" as defined in paragraph (3) of subdivision (a) of Section 9102 of the Commercial Code.
EFFECTIVE 7/1/2001. Amended October 10, 1999 (Bill Number: SB 45) (Chapter 991).

Section 680.130 - Account receivable or account
"Account receivable" means "account" as defined in paragraph (2) of subdivision (a) of Section 9102 of the Commercial Code.
EFFECTIVE 7/1/2001. Amended October 10, 1999 (Bill Number: SB 45) (Chapter 991).

Section 680.135 - Affidavit of identity
"Affidavit of Identity" means an affidavit or declaration executed by a judgment creditor, under penalty of perjury, that is filed with the clerk of the court in which the judgment is entered at the time the judgment creditor files for a writ of execution or an abstract of judgment. The affidavit of identity shall set forth the case name and number, the name of the judgment debtor stated in the judgment, the additional name or names by which the judgment debtor is known, and the facts upon which the judgment creditor has relied in obtaining the judgment debtor's additional name or names. The affidavit of identity shall not include the name or names of persons, including any corporations, partnerships, or any legal entities not separately named in the judgment in which the judgment debtor is a partner, shareholder, or member, other than the judgment debtor.
Added by Stats 2000 ch 639 (AB 2405), s 2, eff. 1/1/2001.

Section 680.140 - Chattel paper
"Chattel paper" means "chattel paper" as defined in paragraph (11) of subdivision (a) of Section 9102 of the Commercial Code.
EFFECTIVE 7/1/2001. Amended October 10, 1999 (Bill Number: SB 45) (Chapter 991).

Section 680.145 - Child support
"Child support" includes family support.
Added by Stats. 1992, Ch. 163, Sec. 29. Effective January 1, 1993. Operative January 1, 1994, by Sec. 161 of Ch. 163.

Section 680.150 - Costs
"Costs" means costs and disbursements, including but not limited to statutory fees, charges, commissions, and expenses.
Added by Stats. 1982, Ch. 1364, Sec. 2. Operative July 1, 1983, by Sec. 3 of Ch. 1364.

Section 680.160 - Court
"Court" means the court where the judgment sought to be enforced was entered.
Added by Stats. 1982, Ch. 1364, Sec. 2. Operative July 1, 1983, by Sec. 3 of Ch. 1364.

Section 680.170 - Deposit account
"Deposit account" means "deposit account" as defined in paragraph (29) of subdivision (a) of Section 9102 of the Commercial Code.
EFFECTIVE 7/1/2001. Amended October 10, 1999 (Bill Number: SB 45) (Chapter 991).

Section 680.180 - Document of title
"Document of title" means "document" as defined in paragraph (30) of subdivision (a) of Section 9102 of the Commercial Code. A document of title is negotiable if it is negotiable within the meaning of Section 7104 of the Commercial Code.
EFFECTIVE 7/1/2001. Amended October 10, 1999 (Bill Number: SB 45) (Chapter 991).

Section 680.190 - Equity
"Equity" means the fair market value of the interest of the judgment debtor in property, or in the case of community property the fair market value of the interest of the judgment debtor and the spouse of the judgment debtor in the property, over and above all liens and encumbrances on the interest superior to the judgment creditor's lien.
Added by Stats. 1982, Ch. 1364, Sec. 2. Operative July 1, 1983, by Sec. 3 of Ch. 1364.

Section 680.200 - Financial institution
"Financial institution" means a state or national bank, state or federal savings and loan association or credit union, or like organization, and includes a corporation engaged in a safe deposit business.
Added by Stats. 1982, Ch. 1364, Sec. 2. Operative July 1, 1983, by Sec. 3 of Ch. 1364.

Section 680.210 - General intangibles
"General intangibles" means "general intangibles," as defined in paragraph (42) of subdivision (a) of Section 9102 of the Commercial Code, consisting of rights to payment.
EFFECTIVE 7/1/2001. Amended October 10, 1999 (Bill Number: SB 45) (Chapter 991).

Section 680.220 - Instrument
"Instrument" means "instrument", as defined in paragraph (47) of subdivision (a) of Section 9102 of the Commercial Code.
EFFECTIVE 7/1/2001. Amended October 10, 1999 (Bill Number: SB 45) (Chapter 991).

Section 680.230 - Judgment
"Judgment" means a judgment, order, or decree entered in a court of this state.
Added by Stats. 1982, Ch. 1364, Sec. 2. Operative July 1, 1983, by Sec. 3 of Ch. 1364.

Section 680.240 - Judgment creditor
"Judgment creditor" means the person in whose favor a judgment is rendered or, if there is an assignee of record, means the assignee of record. Unless the context otherwise requires, the term also includes the guardian or conservator of the estate, personal representative, or other successor in interest of the judgment creditor or assignee of record.
Added by Stats. 1982, Ch. 1364, Sec. 2. Operative July 1, 1983, by Sec. 3 of Ch. 1364.

Section 680.250 - Judgment debtor
"Judgment debtor" means the person against whom a judgment is rendered.
Added by Stats. 1982, Ch. 1364, Sec. 2. Operative July 1, 1983, by Sec. 3 of Ch. 1364.

Section 680.260 - Levying officer
"Levying officer" means the sheriff or marshal.
Amended by Stats. 1996, Ch. 872, Sec. 16. Effective January 1, 1997.

Section 680.270 - Money judgment
"Money judgment" means that part of a judgment that requires the payment of money.
Added by Stats. 1982, Ch. 1364, Sec. 2. Operative July 1, 1983, by Sec. 3 of Ch. 1364.

Section 680.280 - Person
"Person" includes a natural person, a corporation, a partnership or other unincorporated association, a general partner of a partnership, a limited liability company, and a public entity.
Amended by Stats. 1994, Ch. 1010, Sec. 60. Effective January 1, 1995.

Section 680.290 - Personal property
"Personal property" includes both tangible and intangible personal property.
Added by Stats. 1982, Ch. 1364, Sec. 2. Operative July 1, 1983, by Sec. 3 of Ch. 1364.

Section 680.300 - Principal amount of the judgment
"Principal amount of the judgment" means the total amount of the judgment as entered or as last renewed, together with the costs thereafter added to the judgment pursuant to Section 685.090, reduced by any partial satisfactions of such amount and costs and by any amounts no longer enforceable.
Added by Stats. 1982, Ch. 1364, Sec. 2. Operative July 1, 1983, by Sec. 3 of Ch. 1364.

Section 680.310 - Property
"Property" includes real and personal property and any interest therein.
Added by Stats. 1982, Ch. 1364, Sec. 2. Operative July 1, 1983, by Sec. 3 of Ch. 1364.

Section 680.320 - Real property
"Real property" includes any right in real property, including but not limited to a leasehold interest in real property.
Added by Stats. 1982, Ch. 1364, Sec. 2. Operative July 1, 1983, by Sec. 3 of Ch. 1364.

Section 680.330 - Registered process server
"Registered process server" means a person registered as a process server pursuant to Chapter 16 (commencing with Section 22350) of Division 8 of the Business and Professions Code.
Added by Stats. 1982, Ch. 1364, Sec. 2. Operative July 1, 1983, by Sec. 3 of Ch. 1364.

Section 680.340 - Secured party
"Secured party" means "secured party" as defined in paragraph (73) of subdivision (a) of Section 9102 of the Commercial Code.
Amended by Stats 2013 ch 531 (AB 502),s 4, eff. 1/1/2014, op. 7/1/2014.
EFFECTIVE 7/01/2001. Amended October 10, 1999 (Bill Number: SB 45) (Chapter 991).

Section 680.345 - Security
"Security" means a "security" as defined in Section 8102 of the Commercial Code.
Added by Stats. 1982, Ch. 1364, Sec. 2. Operative July 1, 1983, by Sec. 3 of Ch. 1364.

Section 680.350 - Security agreement
"Security agreement" means "security agreement" as defined in paragraph (74) of subdivision (a) of Section 9102 of the Commercial Code.
Amended by Stats 2013 ch 531 (AB 502),s 5, eff. 1/1/2014, op. 7/1/2014.
EFFECTIVE 7/01/2001. Amended October 10, 1999 (Bill Number: SB 45) (Chapter 991).

Section 680.360 - Security interest
"Security interest" means "security interest" as defined in Section 1201 of the Commercial Code.
Added by Stats. 1982, Ch. 1364, Sec. 2. Operative July 1, 1983, by Sec. 3 of Ch. 1364.

Section 680.365 - Spousal support
"Spousal support" includes support for a former spouse.
Added by Stats. 1982, Ch. 1364, Sec. 2. Operative July 1, 1983, by Sec. 3 of Ch. 1364.

Section 680.370 - Tangible personal property
"Tangible personal property" includes chattel paper, documents of title, instruments, securities, and money.
Added by Stats. 1982, Ch. 1364, Sec. 2. Operative July 1, 1983, by Sec. 3 of Ch. 1364.

Section 680.380 - Writ
"Writ" includes a writ of execution, a writ of possession of personal property, a writ of possession of real property, and a writ of sale.
Added by Stats. 1982, Ch. 1364, Sec. 2. Operative July 1, 1983, by Sec. 3 of Ch. 1364.

Chapter 2 - GENERAL PROVISIONS

Section 681.010 - Laws governing enforcement of judgments
Except as otherwise provided by statute:
(a) A money judgment is enforceable as provided in Division 2 (commencing with Section 695.010).
(b) A judgment for possession of personal property is enforceable as provided in Chapter 2 (commencing with Section 714.010) of Division 3.
(c) A judgment for possession of real property is enforceable as provided in Chapter 3 (commencing with Section 715.010) of Division 3.

(d) A judgment for sale of real or personal property is enforceable as provided in Chapter 4 (commencing with Section 716.010) of Division 3.
(e) A judgment requiring performance of an act not described in subdivisions (a) to (d), inclusive, or requiring forbearance from performing an act, is enforceable as provided in Chapter 5 (commencing with Section 717.010) of Division 3.
Added by Stats. 1982, Ch. 1364, Sec. 2. Operative July 1, 1983, by Sec. 3 of Ch. 1364.

Section 681.020 - Acknowledgment of assignment of judgment
An assignee of a judgment is not entitled to enforce the judgment under this title unless an acknowledgment of assignment of judgment to that assignee has been filed or the assignee has otherwise become an assignee of record under Section 673.
Amended by Stats 2020 ch 36 (AB 3364),s 23, eff. 1/1/2021.

Section 681.030 - Rule providing for practice and procedure; forms
(a) The Judicial Council may provide by rule for the practice and procedure in proceedings under this title.
(b) The Judicial Council may prescribe the form of the applications, notices, orders, writs, and other papers to be used under this title. The Judicial Council may prescribe forms in languages other than English. The timely completion and return of a Judicial Council form prescribed in a language other than English has the same force and effect as the timely completion and return of an English language form.
(c) The Judicial Council shall prepare a form containing all of the following:
(1) A list of each of the federal and this state's exemptions from enforcement of a money judgment against a natural person.
(2) A citation to the relevant statute of the United States or this state which creates each of the exemptions.
(3) Information on how to obtain the list of exemption amounts published pursuant to subdivision (d) of Section 703.150.
Amended by Stats 2003 ch 379 (AB 182),s 1, eff. 1/1/2004.

Section 681.035 - Review and recommendations by California Law Revision Commission
The California Law Revision Commission is authorized to maintain a continuing review of and submit recommendations to the Governor and the Legislature concerning enforcement of judgments.
Added by Stats 2013 ch 15 (AB 567),s 1, eff. 1/1/2014.

Section 681.040 - Paper filed when received by levying officer
If a paper is required or permitted to be filed with a levying officer under this title, the paper is considered filed when it is actually received by the levying officer.
Added by Stats. 1982, Ch. 1364, Sec. 2. Operative July 1, 1983, by Sec. 3 of Ch. 1364.

Section 681.050 - Severability
If any provision or clause of this title or application thereof to any person or circumstances is held invalid, the invalidity does not affect other provisions or applications of this title which can be given effect without the invalid provision or application, and to this end the provisions of this title are severable.
Added by Stats. 1982, Ch. 1364, Sec. 2. Operative July 1, 1983, by Sec. 3 of Ch. 1364.

Chapter 3 - PERIOD FOR ENFORCEMENT AND RENEWAL OF JUDGMENTS
Article 1 - PERIOD FOR ENFORCEMENT OF JUDGMENTS

Section 683.010 - Enforceable upon entry
Except as otherwise provided by statute or in the judgment, a judgment is enforceable under this title upon entry.
Added by Stats. 1982, Ch. 1364, Sec. 2. Operative July 1, 1983, by Sec. 3 of Ch. 1364.

Section 683.020 - Period of enforceability
Except as otherwise provided by statute, upon the expiration of 10 years after the date of entry of a money judgment or a judgment for possession or sale of property:
(a) The judgment may not be enforced.
(b) All enforcement procedures pursuant to the judgment or to a writ or order issued pursuant to the judgment shall cease.
(c) Any lien created by an enforcement procedure pursuant to the judgment is extinguished.
Added by Stats. 1982, Ch. 1364, Sec. 2. Operative July 1, 1983, by Sec. 3 of Ch. 1364.

Section 683.030 - Money judgment payable in installments
If a money judgment is payable in installments, the 10-year period of enforceability prescribed by Section 683.020 runs as to each installment from the date the installment becomes due and runs as to costs from the date the costs are added to the judgment pursuant to Section 685.090.
Added by Stats. 1982, Ch. 1364, Sec. 2. Operative July 1, 1983, by Sec. 3 of Ch. 1364.

Section 683.040 - Affidavit stating that issuance of writ sought in application not barred
If the judgment creditor applies for a writ for the enforcement of a judgment and the application is made more than 10 years after the date the judgment was entered or renewed, the application shall be accompanied by an affidavit of a person having knowledge of the facts stating facts showing that the issuance of the writ sought in the application is not barred under this chapter. A copy of the affidavit shall be attached to the writ when issued.
Added by Stats. 1982, Ch. 1364, Sec. 2. Operative July 1, 1983, by Sec. 3 of Ch. 1364.

Section 683.050 - Period for commencing enforcement action by judgment creditor
(a) Except as provided in subdivision (b), nothing in this chapter limits any right the judgment creditor may have to bring an action on a judgment, but any such action shall be commenced within the period prescribed by Section 337.5.
(b) Notwithstanding subdivision (a), no action on a judgment may be brought on a judgment identified in subdivision (c) of Section 683.110.
Amended by Stats 2022 ch 883 (SB 1200),s 1, eff. 1/1/2023.
Added by Stats. 1982, Ch. 1364, Sec. 2. Operative July 1, 1983, by Sec. 3 of Ch. 1364.

Article 2 - RENEWAL OF JUDGMENTS

Section 683.110 - Generally
(a) The period of enforceability of a money judgment or a judgment for possession or sale of property may be extended by renewal of the judgment as provided in this article.
(b) A judgment shall not be renewed under this article if the application for renewal is filed within five years from the time the judgment was previously renewed under this article.
(c) Notwithstanding subdivision (a), a judgment creditor may renew the period of enforceability of the following types of money judgments only once pursuant to subdivision (c) of Section 683.120:
(1) A judgment on a claim related to medical expenses if the principal amount of the money judgment remaining unsatisfied against a debtor is under two hundred thousand dollars ($200,000).
(2) A judgment on a claim related to personal debt if the principal amount of the money judgment remaining unsatisfied against a debtor is under fifty thousand dollars ($50,000).
(d) For purposes of this section, the following definitions apply:
(1) "Debtor" means a natural person from whom money is due or owing or alleged to be due or owing.

(2) "Due or owing" does not include debts incurred due to, or obtained by tortious or fraudulent conduct or judgments for unpaid wages, damages, or penalties owed to an employee.

(3) "Personal debt" means money due or owing or alleged to be due or owing from a natural person arising out of a transaction in which the money, property, insurance, or services which are the subject of the transaction are primarily for the debtor's personal, family, or household purposes.

Amended by Stats 2022 ch 883 (SB 1200),s 2, eff. 1/1/2023.

Added by Stats. 1982, Ch. 1364, Sec. 2. Operative July 1, 1983, by Sec. 3 of Ch. 1364.

Section 683.120 - Application for renewal

(a) The judgment creditor may renew a judgment by filing an application for renewal of the judgment with the court in which the judgment was entered.

(b) Except as otherwise provided in this article, the filing of the application renews the judgment in the amount determined under Section 683.150 and extends the period of enforceability of the judgment as renewed for a period of 10 years from the date the application is filed.

(c) Notwithstanding subdivisions (a) and (b), for a judgment identified in subdivision (c) of Section 683.110, a judgment creditor may renew the judgment only once. The filing of the application under this subdivision renews the judgment in the amount determined under Section 683.150 and extends the period of enforceability of the judgment as renewed for a period of five years from the date the application is filed. No application may be filed if the judgment was renewed on or before December 31, 2022.

(d) In the case of a money judgment payable in installments, for the purposes of enforcement and of any later renewal, the amount of the judgment as renewed shall be treated as a lump-sum money judgment entered on the date the application is filed.

Amended by Stats 2022 ch 883 (SB 1200),s 3, eff. 1/1/2023.

Added by Stats. 1982, Ch. 1364, Sec. 2. Operative July 1, 1983, by Sec. 3 of Ch. 1364.

Section 683.130 - Time for filing application

(a) In the case of a lump-sum money judgment or a judgment for possession or sale of property, the application for renewal of the judgment may be filed at any time before the expiration of the 10-year period of enforceability provided by Section 683.020 or, if the judgment is a renewed judgment, at any time before the expiration of the 10-year period of enforceability of the renewed judgment provided by Section 683.120.

(b) In the case of a money judgment payable in installments, the application for renewal of the judgment may be filed:

(1) If the judgment has not previously been renewed, at any time as to past due amounts that at the time of filing are not barred by the expiration of the 10-year period of enforceability provided by Sections 683.020 and 683.030.

(2) If the judgment has previously been renewed, within the time specified by subdivision (a) as to the amount of the judgment as previously renewed and, as to any past due amounts that became due and payable after the previous renewal, at any time before the expiration of the 10-year period of enforceability provided by Sections 683.020 and 683.030.

Amended by Stats 2000 ch 808 (AB 1358), s 4, eff. 9/28/2000.

Section 683.140 - Application requirements

The application for renewal of the judgment shall be executed under oath and shall include all of the following:

(a) The title of the court where the judgment is entered and the cause and number of the action.

(b) The date of entry of the judgment and of any renewals of the judgment and where entered in the records of the court.

(c) The name and address of the judgment creditor and the name and last known address of the judgment debtor. However, the judgment creditor shall omit the name of a judgment debtor from the application for a writ of execution if the liability of that judgment debtor has ceased with regard to the judgment, including either of the following occurrences:

(1) The judgment debtor has obtained a discharge of the judgment pursuant to Title 11 of the United States Code and notice thereof has been filed with the court.

(2) The judgment creditor files an acknowledgment of satisfaction of judgment with regard to the judgment debtor pursuant to Chapter 1 (commencing with Section 724.010) of Division 5.

(d) In the case of a money judgment, the information necessary to compute the amount of the judgment as renewed. In the case of a judgment for possession or sale of property, a description of the performance remaining due.

Amended by Stats 2013 ch 176 (SB 551),s 1, eff. 1/1/2014.

Section 683.150 - Entry of renewal on court records; filing fee; amount of judgment as renewed

(a) Upon the filing of the application, the court clerk shall enter the renewal of the judgment in the court records.

(b) The fee for filing an application for renewal of judgment is as provided in subdivision (b) of Section 70626 of the Government Code.

(c) In the case of a money judgment, the entry of renewal shall show the amount of the judgment as renewed. Except as provided in subdivisions (d) and (e), this amount is the amount required to satisfy the judgment on the date of the filing of the application for renewal and includes the fee for the filing of the application for renewal.

(d) In the case of a money judgment payable in installments not previously renewed, the amount of the judgment as renewed is the total of the past due installments, the costs added to the judgment pursuant to Section 685.090, and the accrued interest, which remains unsatisfied and is enforceable on the date of the filing of the application for renewal and includes the fee for the filing of the application for renewal.

(e) In the case of a money judgment payable in installments previously renewed, the amount of the judgment as renewed under the latest renewal is the total of the following which remains unsatisfied and is enforceable on the date of the filing of the application for the latest renewal:

(1) The amount of the judgment as renewed under the previous renewal.

(2) The past due installments that became due and payable after the previous renewal.

(3) The costs that have been added to the judgment pursuant to Section 685.090 after the previous renewal.

(4) The interest that has accrued on the amounts described in paragraphs (1), (2), and (3) since the last renewal.

(5) The fee for filing the application for renewal.

(f) In the case of a judgment for possession or sale of property, the entry of renewal shall describe the performance remaining due.

Amended by Stats 2005 ch 75 (AB 145),s 36, eff. 7/19/2005, op. 1/1/2006

Section 683.160 - Service of notice of renewal

(a) The judgment creditor shall serve a notice of renewal of the judgment on the judgment debtor. Service shall be made personally or by first-class mail and proof of service shall be filed with the court clerk. The notice shall be in a form prescribed by the Judicial Council and shall inform the judgment debtor that the judgment debtor has 60 days within which to make a motion to vacate or modify the renewal.

(b) Until proof of service is filed pursuant to subdivision (a), no writ may be issued, nor may any enforcement proceedings be commenced to enforce the judgment, except to the extent that the judgment would be enforceable had it not been renewed.

Amended by Stats 2022 ch 883 (SB 1200),s 4, eff. 1/1/2023.

Amended by Stats. 1988, Ch. 900, Sec. 5.

Section 683.170 - Vacating renewal

(a) The renewal of a judgment pursuant to this article may be vacated on any ground that would be a defense to an action on the judgment, including the ground that the amount of the renewed judgment as entered pursuant to this article is incorrect, and shall be vacated if the application for renewal was filed within five years from the time the judgment was previously renewed under this article.

(b) Not later than 60 days after service of the notice of renewal pursuant to Section 683.160, the judgment debtor may apply by noticed motion under this section for an order of the court vacating the renewal of the judgment. The notice of motion shall be served on the judgment creditor. Service shall be made personally or by mail.

(c) Upon the hearing of the motion, the renewal may be ordered vacated upon any ground provided in subdivision (a), and another and different renewal may be entered, including, but not limited to, the renewal of the judgment in a different amount if the decision of the court is that the judgment creditor is entitled to renewal in a different amount.

Amended by Stats 2022 ch 883 (SB 1200),s 5, eff. 1/1/2023.
Added by Stats. 1982, Ch. 1364, Sec. 2. Operative July 1, 1983, by Sec. 3 of Ch. 1364.

Section 683.180 - Extension of judgment lien

(a) If a judgment lien on an interest in real property has been created pursuant to a money judgment and the judgment is renewed pursuant to this article, the duration of the judgment lien is extended until 10 years from the date of the filing of the application for renewal if, before the expiration of the judgment lien, a certified copy of the application for renewal is recorded with the county recorder of the county where the real property subject to the judgment lien is located.

(b) A judgment lien on an interest in real property that has been transferred subject to the lien is not extended pursuant to subdivision (a) if the transfer was recorded before the application for renewal was filed unless both of the following requirements are satisfied:

(1) A copy of the application for renewal is personally served on the transferee.

(2) Proof of such service is filed with the court clerk within 90 days after the filing of the application for renewal.

Amended by Stats. 1983, Ch. 155, Sec. 9.5. Effective June 30, 1983. Operative July 1, 1983, by Sec. 32 of Ch. 155.

Section 683.190 - Extension of lien other than judgment lien

If a lien (other than a judgment lien on an interest in real property or an execution lien) has been created by an enforcement procedure pursuant to a judgment and the judgment is renewed pursuant to this article, the duration of the lien is extended, subject to any other limitations on its duration under this title, until 10 years from the date of the filing of the application for renewal of the judgment if, before the expiration of the lien, a certified copy of the application for renewal is served on or filed with the same person and in the same manner as the notice or order that created the lien.

Added by Stats. 1982, Ch. 1364, Sec. 2. Operative July 1, 1983, by Sec. 3 of Ch. 1364.

Section 683.200 - Enforcement proceeding continued

If a judgment is renewed pursuant to this article, any enforcement proceeding previously commenced pursuant to the judgment or to a writ or order issued pursuant to the judgment that would have ceased pursuant to Section 683.020 had the judgment not been renewed may be continued, subject to any other limitations provided in this title, if, before the expiration of the prior 10-year period of enforceability, a certified copy of the application for renewal of the judgment is filed with the levying officer, receiver, or other officer acting pursuant to such writ or order or, in other cases, is filed in the enforcement proceeding.

Added by Stats. 1982, Ch. 1364, Sec. 2. Operative July 1, 1983, by Sec. 3 of Ch. 1364.

Section 683.210 - Stay of enforcement not affected renewal

A judgment may be renewed notwithstanding any stay of enforcement of the judgment, but the renewal of the judgment does not affect the stay of enforcement.

Added by Stats. 1982, Ch. 1364, Sec. 2. Operative July 1, 1983, by Sec. 3 of Ch. 1364.

Section 683.220 - Date for commencing action on renewed judgment

If a judgment is renewed pursuant to this article, the date of the filing of the application for renewal shall be deemed to be the date that the period for commencing an action on the renewed judgment commences to run under Section 337.5.

Added by Stats. 1982, Ch. 1364, Sec. 2. Operative July 1, 1983, by Sec. 3 of Ch. 1364.

Article 3 - APPLICATION OF CHAPTER

Section 683.310 - Inapplicability Family Code judgment or order

Except as otherwise provided in the Family Code, this chapter does not apply to a judgment or order made or entered pursuant to the Family Code.

Amended by Stats 2000 ch 808 (AB 1358), s 5, eff. 9/28/2000.

Section 683.320 - Inapplicable to money judgment against public entity

This chapter does not apply to a money judgment against a public entity that is subject to Section 965.5 or 970.1 of the Government Code.
Added by Stats. 1982, Ch. 1364, Sec. 2. Operative July 1, 1983, by Sec. 3 of Ch. 1364.

Chapter 4 - MANNER OF SERVICE OF WRITS, NOTICES, AND OTHER PAPERS

Article 1 - SERVICE ON ATTORNEY OF CREDITOR OR DEBTOR

Section 684.010 - Service on judgment creditor's attorney of record

Subject to Chapter 1 (commencing with Section 283) of Title 5 of Part 1 of this code and Section 215 of the Family Code, when a notice, order, or other paper is required to be served under this title on the judgment creditor, it shall be served on the judgment creditor's attorney of record rather than on the judgment creditor if the judgment creditor has an attorney of record.

Amended by Stats. 1992, Ch. 163, Sec. 32. Effective January 1, 1993. Operative January 1, 1994, by Sec. 161 of Ch. 163.

Section 684.020 - Service on judgment debtor; service on attorney specified by judgment debtor

(a) Except as provided in subdivision (b), when a writ, notice, order, or other paper is required to be served under this title on the judgment debtor, it shall be served on the judgment debtor instead of the attorney for the judgment debtor.

(b) The writ, notice, order, or other paper shall be served on the attorney specified by the judgment debtor rather than on the judgment debtor if all of the following requirements are satisfied:

(1) The judgment debtor has filed with the court and served on the judgment creditor a request that service on the judgment debtor under this title be made by serving the attorney specified in the request. Service on the judgment creditor of the request shall be made personally or by mail. The request shall include a consent, signed by the attorney, to receive service under this title on behalf of the judgment debtor.

(2) The request has not been revoked by the judgment debtor.

(3) The consent to receive service has not been revoked by the attorney.

(c) A request or consent under subdivision (b) may be revoked by filing with the court a notice revoking the request or consent. A copy of the notice revoking the request or consent shall be served on the judgment creditor. Service shall be made personally or by mail. The judgment creditor is not bound by the revocation until the judgment creditor has received a copy of the notice revoking the request or consent.

Added by Stats. 1982, Ch. 1364, Sec. 2. Operative July 1, 1983, by Sec. 3 of Ch. 1364.

Section 684.030 - Inapplicability to subpoena or other process and contempt

Sections 684.010 and 684.020 do not apply to either of the following:

(a) A subpoena or other process to require the attendance of a party.

(b) A paper to bring a party into contempt.

Added by Stats. 1982, Ch. 1364, Sec. 2. Operative July 1, 1983, by Sec. 3 of Ch. 1364.

Section 684.040 - Manner of making service on attorney
If service on an attorney is required under this article, service on the attorney shall be made in any of the following ways:
(a) By personal delivery to the attorney.
(b) By service in the manner provided in subdivision (1) of Section 1011.
(c) By mail in the manner provided in Section 684.120.
Added by Stats. 1982, Ch. 1364, Sec. 2. Operative July 1, 1983, by Sec. 3 of Ch. 1364.

Section 684.050 - Service pursuant to article constitutes service on judgment creditor or judgment debtor
Service on the attorney for the judgment creditor or the judgment debtor pursuant to the provisions of this article constitutes service on the judgment creditor or judgment debtor for the purposes of this title.
Added by Stats. 1982, Ch. 1364, Sec. 2. Operative July 1, 1983, by Sec. 3 of Ch. 1364.

Article 2 - MANNER OF SERVICE GENERALLY

Section 684.110 - Legal process required to be personally served; service on attorney required; service on financial institution or insurer
(a)
(1) Subject to subdivisions (b), (c), and (d), if legal process is required to be personally served under this title, service shall be made in the same manner as a summons is served under Chapter 4 (commencing with Section 413.10) of Title 5.
(2) For purposes of this title, the term "legal process" shall refer to each and all of the writs, notices, orders, or other papers required or permitted to be served pursuant to this title.
(b) If the legal process is required to be personally served under this title and service on an attorney is required under Article 1 (commencing with Section 684.010), service shall be made on the attorney in the manner provided in Section 684.040.
(c) If the legal process is required to be personally served on (1) a financial institution in connection with a deposit account or with property held for safekeeping, as collateral for an obligation owed to the financial institution or in a safe-deposit box, (2) a title insurer (as defined in Section 12340.4 of the Insurance Code) or underwritten title company (as defined in Section 12340.5 of the Insurance Code), or (3) an industrial loan company (as defined in Section 18003 of the Financial Code), service shall be made at the office or branch that has actual possession of the property levied upon or at which a deposit account levied upon is carried and shall be made upon the officer, manager, or other person in charge of the office or branch at the time of service. For purposes of this section, the office or branch at which a deposit account levied upon is carried shall mean the branch, office, or other location where the financial institution maintains the account.
(d) Notwithstanding subdivision (c), with respect to legal process served on a financial institution, if the financial institution has designated a central location for service of legal process pursuant to Section 684.115, unless the financial institution elects to treat legal process served at a branch or office as effective, that legal process so served on the branch or office will not reach those accounts or property and need not be reported on the financial institution's garnishee memorandum.
(e) Notwithstanding subdivision (c), a financial institution, title insurer, or industrial loan company, in its discretion and without violating any obligation to its customer, may act upon service of legal process at any of its offices or branches, whether or not the office or branch is the location wherein accounts or property that may be reached by the process is or are maintained or located.
Amended by Stats 2012 ch 484 (AB 2364),s 6, eff. 1/1/2013.

Section 684.115 - Central location for service on financial institution
(a)A financial institution may, and if it has more than nine branches or offices at which it conducts its business within this state shall, designate one or more central locations for service of legal process within this state. Each designated location shall be referred to as a "central location." If a financial institution elects or is required to designate a central location for service of legal process, the financial institution shall file a notice of its designation with the Department of Financial Protection and Innovation which filing shall be effective upon filing and shall contain all of the following:
(1)The physical address of the central location.
(2)The days and hours during which service will be accepted at the central location.
(3)If the central location will not accept service of legal process directed at deposit accounts maintained or property held at all of the financial institution's branches or offices within this state, or if the service accepted at the central location will not apply to safe-deposit boxes or other property of the judgment debtor held by or for the judgment debtor, the filing shall also contain sufficient information to permit a determination of the limitation or limitations, including, in the case of a limitation applicable to certain branches or offices, an identification of the branches or offices as to which service at the central location will not apply and the nature of the limitation applicable to those branches or offices. If the limitation will apply to all branches or offices of the financial institution within this state, the filing may indicate the nature of the limitation and that it applies to all branches or offices, in lieu of an identification of branches or offices as to which the limitation applies. To the extent that a financial institution's designation of a central location for service of legal process covers the process directed at deposit accounts, safe-deposit boxes, or other property of the judgment debtor held by or for the judgment debtor at a particular branch or office located within this state, the branch or office shall be a branch or office covered by central process.
(b)Should a financial institution required to designate a central location fail to do so, each branch of that institution located in this state shall be deemed to be a central location at which service of legal process may be made, and all of the institution's branches or offices located within this state shall be deemed to be a branch or office covered by central process.
(c)Subject to any limitation noted pursuant to paragraph (3) of subdivision (a), service of legal process at a central location of a financial institution shall be effective against all deposit accounts and all property held for safekeeping, as collateral for an obligation owed to the financial institution or in a safe-deposit box if the same is described in the legal process and held by the financial institution at any branch or office covered by central process and located within this state. However, while service of legal process at the central location will establish a lien on all property, if any property other than deposit accounts is physically held by the financial institution in a county other than that in which the designated central location is located, the financial institution shall include in its garnishee's memorandum the location or locations of the property, and the judgment creditor shall obtain a writ of execution covering the property and directed to the levying officer in that county to accomplish the turnover of the property and shall forward the writ and related required documentation to the levying officer in the county in which the property is held.
(d)A financial institution may modify or revoke any designation made pursuant to subdivision (a) by filing the modification or revocation with the Department of Financial Protection and Innovation. The modification or revocation shall be effective when the Department of Financial Protection and Innovation's records have been updated to reflect the modification or revocation, provided that the judgment creditor may rely upon the superseded designation during the 30-day period following the effective date of the revocation or modification.
(e)
(1) The Department of Financial Protection and Innovation shall update its online records to reflect a filing by a financial institution pursuant to subdivision (a) or a modification or revocation filed by a financial institution pursuant to subdivision (d) within 10 business days following the filing by the financial institution. The Department of Financial Protection and Innovation's internet website shall reflect the date its online records for each financial institution have most recently been updated.
(2)The Department of Financial Protection and Innovation shall provide any person requesting it with a copy of each current filing made by a financial institution pursuant to subdivision (a). The Department of Financial Protection and Innovation may satisfy its obligation under this

subdivision by posting all current designations of a financial institution, or the pertinent information therein, on an internet website available to the public without charge, and if that information is made available, the Department of Financial Protection and Innovation may impose a reasonable fee for furnishing that information in any other manner.

(f) As to deposit accounts maintained or property held for safekeeping, as collateral for an obligation owed to the financial institution or in a safe-deposit box at a branch or office covered by central process, service of legal process at a location other than a central location designated by the financial institution shall not be effective unless the financial institution, in its absolute discretion, elects to act upon the process at that location as if it were effective. In the absence of an election, the financial institution may respond to the legal process by mailing or delivery of the garnishee's memorandum to the levying officer within the time otherwise provided therefor, with a statement on the garnishee's memorandum that the legal process was not properly served at the financial institution's designated location for receiving legal process, and, therefore, was not processed, and the address at which the financial institution is to receive legal process.

(g) If any legal process is served at a central location of a financial institution pursuant to this section, all related papers to be served on the financial institution shall be served at that location, unless agreed to the contrary between the serving party and the financial institution.

(h) This subdivision shall apply whenever a financial institution operates within this state at least one branch or office in addition to its head office or main office, as applicable, or a financial institution headquartered in another state operates more than one branch or office within this state, and no central location has been designated or deemed to have been designated by the institution for service of legal process relating to deposit accounts maintained at the financial institution's head office or main office, as applicable, and branches located within this state. If a judgment creditor reasonably believes that, pursuant to Section 700.140 and, if applicable, Section 700.160, any act of enforcement would be effective against a specific deposit account maintained at a financial institution described in this subdivision, the judgment creditor may file with the financial institution a written request that the financial institution identify the branch or office within this state at which a specified account might be maintained by the financial institution. The written request shall contain the following statements or information:

(1) The name of the person reasonably believed by the judgment creditor to be a person in whose name the specified deposit account stands.

(2) If the name of the person reasonably believed by the judgment creditor to be a person in whose name the specified deposit account stands is not a judgment debtor identified in the writ of execution, a statement that a person reasonably believed by the judgment creditor to be a person in whose name the specified deposit account stands will be appropriately identified in the legal process to be served pursuant to Section 700.160, including any supplementary papers, such as a court order or affidavit if the same will be required by Section 700.160.

(3) The specific identifying number of the account reasonably believed to be maintained with the financial institution and standing in the name of the judgment debtor or other person.

(4) The address of the requesting party.

(5) An affidavit by the judgment creditor or the judgment creditor's counsel stating substantially the following: "I hereby declare that this deposit account location request complies with Section 684.115 of the Code of Civil Procedure, that the account or accounts of the judgment debtor or other person or persons appropriately identified in the legal process and specified herein are subject to a valid writ of execution, or court order, that I have a reasonable belief, formed after an inquiry reasonable under the circumstances, that the financial institution receiving this deposit account location request has an account standing in the name of the judgment debtor or other person or persons appropriately identified in the legal process, and that information pertaining to the location of the account will assist the judgment creditor in enforcing the judgment."

(i) The affidavit contemplated by subdivision (h) shall be signed by the judgment creditor or the judgment creditor's counsel and filed at the financial institution's head office located within this state or, if the financial institution's head office is in another state, at one of its branches or offices within this state. Failure to comply with the requirements of subdivision (h) and this subdivision shall be sufficient basis for the financial institution to refuse to produce the information that would otherwise be required by subdivision (j).

(j) Within 10 banking days following receipt by a financial institution at the applicable location specified in subdivision (i) of a request contemplated by subdivision (h), as to each specific deposit account identified in the request contemplated by subdivision (h), the financial institution shall respond by mailing, by first-class mail with postage prepaid, to the requester's address as specified in the request a response indicating the branch or office location of the financial institution at which the specified deposit account might be maintained, or, if the specified deposit account, if it exists, would not be maintained at a specific location, at least one place within this state at which legal process relating to the deposit account should or may be served. The response to be furnished pursuant to this subdivision shall not require the financial institution to determine whether an account exists or, if an account does exist, whether it would be reached by the legal process, rather, the branch or office location shall be determined and reported by the financial institution based solely upon its determination that an account with the identifying number provided by the requester would be maintained at that branch if an account did exist, and the response shall not contain any information about the name in which the account stands or any other information concerning the account, if it exists. If more than one account number is specified in the request, the financial institution's responses as to some or all of those account numbers may be combined in a single writing.

(k) A response furnished in good faith by the financial institution pursuant to subdivision (j) shall not be deemed to violate the privacy of any person in whose name the specified deposit account stands nor the privacy of any other person, and shall not require the consent of the person in whose name the account stands nor that of any other person.

(l) A financial institution shall not notify the person in whose name the specified deposit account stands or any other person related to the specified account of the receipt of any request made pursuant to subdivision (h) and affecting that person's or persons' accounts at the financial institution, provided that the financial institution shall have no liability for its failure to comply with the provisions of this subdivision.

Amended by Stats 2022 ch 452 (SB 1498),s 40, eff. 1/1/2023.
Amended by Stats 2014 ch 401 (AB 2763),s 15, eff. 1/1/2015.
Amended by Stats 2013 ch 76 (AB 383),s 23, eff. 1/1/2014.
Added by Stats 2012 ch 484 (AB 2364),s 7, eff. 1/1/2013.

Section 684.120 - Service by mail

(a) Except as otherwise provided in this title, if a writ, notice, order, or other paper is to be served by mail under this title, it shall be sent by first-class mail (unless some other type of mail is specifically required) and shall be deposited in a post office, mailbox, sub-post office, substation, mail chute, or other like facility regularly maintained by the United States Postal Service, in a sealed envelope, with postage paid, addressed as follows:

(1) If an attorney is being served in place of the judgment creditor or judgment debtor as provided in Section 684.010 or 684.020, to the attorney at the last address given by the attorney on any paper filed in the proceeding and served on the party making the service.

(2) If any other person is being served, to such person at the person's current mailing address if known or, if unknown, at the address last given by the person on any paper filed in the proceeding and served on the party making the service.

(3) If the mailing cannot be made as provided in paragraph (1) or (2), to the person at the person's last known address.

(b) Service by mail is complete at the time of deposit; but, unless the court prescribes a shorter period of time, any prescribed period of notice and any right or duty to do any act or make any response within any prescribed period or on a date certain after a paper is served by mail is extended:

(1) Five days if the place of address is within the State of California.
(2) Ten days if the place of address is outside the State of California but within the United States.
(3) Twenty days if the place of address is outside the United States.

(c) The writ, notice, order, or other paper served by mail under this section shall bear a notation of the date and place of mailing or be accompanied by an unsigned copy of the affidavit or certificate of mailing. This subdivision is directory only.
Added by Stats. 1982, Ch. 1364, Sec. 2. Operative July 1, 1983, by Sec. 3 of Ch. 1364.

Section 684.130 - Correct name and address included in instructions to levying officer
(a) If the levying officer is required by any provision of this title to serve any writ, order, notice, or other paper on any person, the judgment creditor shall include in the instructions to the levying officer the correct name and address of the person. The judgment creditor shall use reasonable diligence to ascertain the correct name and address of the person.
(b) Unless the levying officer has actual knowledge that the name or address included in the instructions is incorrect, the levying officer shall rely on the instructions in serving the writ, order, notice, or other paper on the person.
Added by Stats. 1982, Ch. 1364, Sec. 2. Operative July 1, 1983, by Sec. 3 of Ch. 1364.

Section 684.140 - Personal service of paper running in favor of particular person made by person or person's agent
If a provision of this title provides for service by the levying officer of an order, notice, or other paper that runs in favor of a particular person, personal service of the paper may be made by the person or the person's agent if the levying officer gives permission. The levying officer's permission may be evidenced by a certificate signed by the levying officer. This section does not authorize the levying officer to give permission to serve a writ or notice of levy. If service is made by a person or the person's agent pursuant to this section, the cost of the service is not a recoverable cost. Nothing in this section limits the authority of a registered process server provided in this title.
Added by Stats. 1982, Ch. 1364, Sec. 2. Operative July 1, 1983, by Sec. 3 of Ch. 1364.

Article 3 - PROOF OF SERVICE

Section 684.210 - Service of notice of court hearing
If service of notice of a court hearing is required under this title, proof of service of the notice shall be made at or before the hearing to the satisfaction of the court.
Added by Stats. 1982, Ch. 1364, Sec. 2. Operative July 1, 1983, by Sec. 3 of Ch. 1364.

Section 684.220 - Means of making proof of service or publication
Proof of service or of posting or publication under this title may be made by, but is not limited to, the following means:
(a) If service is made in the same manner as a summons is served under Chapter 4 (commencing with Section 413.10) of Title 5, proof of service may be made in the manner provided in Article 5 (commencing with Section 417.10) of that chapter.
(b) If service is made in the same manner as a summons is served under Section 415.10 or 415.20, proof of service may be made by affidavit of the person making the service showing the time, place, and manner of service and the facts showing that the service was made in accordance with the applicable statutory provisions. The affidavit shall recite or in other manner show the name of the person to whom the papers served were delivered and, if appropriate, the title of the person or the capacity in which the person was served.
(c) Proof of service by mail as provided in Section 684.120 may be made in the manner prescribed in Section 1013a.
(d) Proof of posting may be made by the affidavit of the person who posted the notice, showing the time and place of posting.
(e) Proof of publication may be made by the affidavit of the publisher or printer, or the foreman or principal clerk of the publisher or printer, showing the time and place of publication.
(f) Proof of service may be made by the written admission of the person served.
(g) Proof of service however made, or of posting or publication, may be made by testimonial evidence.
Added by Stats. 1982, Ch. 1364, Sec. 2. Operative July 1, 1983, by Sec. 3 of Ch. 1364.

Article 4 - APPLICATION OF CHAPTER

Section 684.310 - Inapplicability to wage garnishment
Except for Sections 684.130 and 684.140, the provisions of Article 1 (commencing with Section 684.010) and Article 2 (commencing with Section 684.110) do not apply to service under Chapter 5 (commencing with Section 706.010) of Division 2 (wage garnishment).
Added by Stats. 1982, Ch. 1364, Sec. 2. Operative July 1, 1983, by Sec. 3 of Ch. 1364.

Chapter 5 - INTEREST AND COSTS

Section 685.010 - Rate of interest
(a)
　(1) Except as provided in paragraph (2), interest accrues at the rate of 10 percent per annum on the principal amount of a money judgment remaining unsatisfied.
　(2)
　　(A) For judgments entered on or after January 1, 2023, or where an application for renewal of judgment is filed on or after January 1, 2023, interest accrues at the rate of 5 percent per annum on the principal amount of a money judgment remaining unsatisfied in the following cases:
　　　(i) The principal amount of a money judgment of under two hundred thousand dollars ($200,000) remaining unsatisfied against a debtor for a claim related to medical expenses.
　　　(ii) The principal amount of a money judgment of under fifty thousand dollars ($50,000) remaining unsatisfied against a debtor for a claim related to personal debt.
　　(B) The claims specified in subparagraph (A) include, but are not limited to, a claim based on any of the following transactions:
　　　(i) An agreement governing the use of a credit card as defined in subdivision (a) of Section 1747.02 of the Civil Code.
　　　(ii) A conditional sale contract as defined in subdivision (a) of Section 2981 of the Civil Code.
　　　(iii) A deferred deposit transaction as defined in subdivision (a) of Section 23001 of the Financial Code.
　　(C) For purposes of this paragraph, the following definitions apply:
　　　(i) "Debtor" means a natural person from whom money is due or owing or alleged to be due or owing.
　　　(ii) "Due or owing" does not include debts incurred due to, or obtained by tortious or fraudulent conduct or judgments for unpaid wages, damages, or penalties owed to an employee.
　　　(iii) "Personal debt" means money due or owing or alleged to be due or owing from a natural person arising out of a transaction in which the money, property, insurance, or services which are the subject of the transaction are primarily for the debtor's personal, family, or household purposes.
(b) The Legislature reserves the right to change the rate of interest provided in subdivision (a) at any time, regardless of the date of entry of the judgment or the date any obligation upon which the judgment is based was incurred. A change in the rate of interest may be made applicable only to the interest that accrues after the operative date of the statute that changes the rate.
Amended by Stats 2022 ch 883 (SB 1200),s 6, eff. 1/1/2023.
Repealed and added by Stats. 1982, Ch. 1364, Sec. 2. Operative July 1, 1983, by Sec. 3 of Ch. 1364.

Section 685.020 - When interest commences to accrue
(a) Except as provided in subdivision (b), interest commences to accrue on a money judgment on the date of entry of the judgment.

(b) Unless the judgment otherwise provides, if a money judgment is payable in installments, interest commences to accrue as to each installment on the date the installment becomes due.

Amended by Stats. 1983, Ch. 155, Sec. 10. Effective June 30, 1983. Operative July 1, 1983, by Sec. 32 of Ch. 155.

Section 685.030 - When interest ceases to accrue when money judgment satisfied in full

(a) If a money judgment is satisfied in full pursuant to a writ under this title, interest ceases to accrue on the judgment:

(1) If the proceeds of collection are paid in a lump sum, on the date of levy.

(2) If the money judgment is satisfied pursuant to an earnings withholding order, on the date and in the manner provided in Section 706.024 or Section 706.028.

(3) In any other case, on the date the proceeds of sale or collection are actually received by the levying officer.

(b) If a money judgment is satisfied in full other than pursuant to a writ under this title, interest ceases to accrue on the date the judgment is satisfied in full.

(c) If a money judgment is partially satisfied pursuant to a writ under this title or is otherwise partially satisfied, interest ceases to accrue as to the part satisfied on the date the part is satisfied.

(d) For the purposes of subdivisions (b) and (c), the date a money judgment is satisfied in full or in part is the earliest of the following times:

(1) The date satisfaction is actually received by the judgment creditor.

(2) The date satisfaction is tendered to the judgment creditor or deposited in court for the judgment creditor.

(3) The date of any other performance that has the effect of satisfaction.

(e) The clerk of a court may enter in the Register of Actions a writ of execution on a money judgment as returned wholly satisfied when the judgment amount, as specified on the writ, is fully collected and only an interest deficit of no more than ten dollars ($10) exists, due to automation of the continual daily interest accrual calculation.

Amended by Stats 2001 ch 812 (AB 223), s 4, eff. 1/1/2002.

Section 685.040 - Costs of enforcing judgment; attorney's fees

The judgment creditor is entitled to the reasonable and necessary costs of enforcing a judgment. Attorney's fees incurred in enforcing a judgment are not included in costs collectible under this title unless otherwise provided by law. Attorney's fees incurred in enforcing a judgment are included as costs collectible under this title if the underlying judgment includes an award of attorney's fees to the judgment creditor pursuant to subparagraph (A) of paragraph (10) of subdivision (a) of Section 1033.5.

Amended by Stats. 1992, Ch. 1348, Sec. 3. Effective January 1, 1993.

Section 685.050 - Costs and interest to be satisfied in levy under writ

(a) If a writ is issued pursuant to this title to enforce a judgment, the costs and interest to be satisfied in a levy under the writ are the following:

(1) The statutory fee for issuance of the writ.

(2) The amount of interest that has accrued from the date of entry or renewal of the judgment to the date of issuance of the writ, as adjusted for partial satisfactions, if the judgment creditor has filed an affidavit with the court clerk stating such amount.

(3) The amount of interest that accrues on the principal amount of the judgment remaining unsatisfied from the date of issuance of the writ until the date interest ceases to accrue.

(4) The levying officer's statutory costs for performing the duties under the writ.

(b) In a levy under the writ, the levying officer shall do all of the following:

(1) Collect the amount of costs and interest entered on the writ pursuant to paragraphs (1) and (2) of subdivision (a).

(2) Compute and collect the amount of additional interest to be collected by paragraph (3) of subdivision (a) by reference to the daily interest entered on the writ. If amounts collected periodically do not fully satisfy the money judgment, the levying officer shall adjust the amount of daily interest to reflect the partial satisfactions, and make later collections by reference to the adjusted amount of daily interest.

(3) Determine and collect the amount of additional costs pursuant to paragraph (4) of subdivision (a).

Amended by Stats 2010 ch 4 (AB 680),s 1, eff. 1/1/2011.

Section 685.070 - Costs judgment creditor may claim in enforcing judgment

(a) The judgment creditor may claim under this section the following costs of enforcing a judgment:

(1) Statutory fees for preparing and issuing, and recording and indexing, an abstract of judgment or a certified copy of a judgment.

(2) Statutory fees for filing a notice of judgment lien on personal property.

(3) Statutory fees for issuing a writ for the enforcement of the judgment to the extent that the fees are not satisfied pursuant to Section 685.050.

(4) Statutory costs of the levying officer for performing the duties under a writ to the extent that the costs are not satisfied pursuant to Section 685.050 and the statutory fee of the levying officer for performing the duties under the Wage Garnishment Law to the extent that the fee has not been satisfied pursuant to the wage garnishment.

(5) Costs incurred in connection with any proceeding under Chapter 6 (commencing with Section 708.010) of Division 2 that have been approved as to amount, reasonableness, and necessity by the judge or referee conducting the proceeding.

(6) Attorney's fees, if allowed by Section 685.040.

(b) Before the judgment is fully satisfied but not later than two years after the costs have been incurred, the judgment creditor claiming costs under this section shall file a memorandum of costs with the court clerk and serve a copy on the judgment debtor. Service shall be made personally or by mail. The memorandum of costs shall be executed under oath by a person who has knowledge of the facts and shall state that to the person's best knowledge and belief the costs are correct, are reasonable and necessary, and have not been satisfied.

(c) Within 10 days after the memorandum of costs is served on the judgment debtor, the judgment debtor may apply to the court on noticed motion to have the costs taxed by the court. The notice of motion shall be served on the judgment creditor. Service shall be made personally or by mail. The court shall make an order allowing or disallowing the costs to the extent justified under the circumstances of the case.

(d) If no motion to tax costs is made within the time provided in subdivision (c), the costs claimed in the memorandum are allowed.

(e) If a memorandum of costs for the costs specified in subdivision (a) is filed at the same time as an application for a writ of execution, these statutory costs not already allowed by the court in an amount not to exceed one hundred dollars ($100) in the aggregate may be included in the amount specified in the writ of execution, subject to subsequent disallowance as ordered by the court pursuant to a motion to tax if filed by the debtor. The memorandum of costs shall contain the following statement: "The fees sought under this memorandum may be disallowed by a court upon a motion to tax filed by the debtor notwithstanding the fees having been included in the writ of execution." The inclusion of the above costs in the writ of execution or the pendency of the motion to tax on these costs shall not be cause for the clerk of the court to delay issuing the writ of execution or for the levying officer to delay enforcing the writ of execution.

(f) Section 1013, extending the time within which a right may be exercised or an act may be done, applies to this section.

Amended by Stats. 1996, Ch. 60, Sec. 2. Effective January 1, 1997.

Section 685.080 - Notice motion by creditor claiming costs

(a) The judgment creditor may claim costs authorized by Section 685.040 by noticed motion. The motion shall be made before the judgment is satisfied in full, but not later than two years after the costs have been incurred. The costs claimed under this section may include, but are not limited to, costs that may be claimed under Section 685.070 and costs incurred but not approved by the court or referee in a proceeding under Chapter 6 (commencing with Section 708.010) of Division 2.

(b) The notice of motion shall describe the costs claimed, shall state their amount, and shall be supported by an affidavit of a person who has knowledge of the facts stating that to the person's best knowledge and belief the costs are correct, are reasonable and necessary, and have not been satisfied. The notice of motion shall be served on the judgment debtor. Service shall be made personally or by mail.

(c) The court shall make an order allowing or disallowing the costs to the extent justified under the circumstances of the case.

Added by Stats. 1982, Ch. 1364, Sec. 2. Operative July 1, 1983, by Sec. 3 of Ch. 1364.

Section 685.090 - Costs added to and part of judgment

(a) Costs are added to and become a part of the judgment:

(1) Upon the filing of an order allowing the costs pursuant to this chapter.

(2) If a memorandum of costs is filed pursuant to Section 685.070 and no motion to tax is made, upon the expiration of the time for making the motion.

(3) As specified in Section 685.095.

(b) The costs added to the judgment pursuant to this section are included in the principal amount of the judgment remaining unsatisfied.

(c) If a writ or earnings withholding order is outstanding at the time the costs are added to the judgment pursuant to this section, the levying officer shall add the amount of those costs to the amount to be collected pursuant to the writ or earnings withholding order if the levying officer receives either of the following before the writ or earnings withholding order is returned:

(1) A certified copy of the court order allowing the costs.

(2) A certificate from the clerk of the court that the costs have been added to the judgment where the costs have been added to the judgment after a memorandum of costs has been filed pursuant to Section 685.070 and no motion to tax has been made within the time allowed for making the motion.

(d) The levying officer shall include the costs described in subdivision (c) in the amount of the sale or collection distributed to the judgment creditor only if the levying officer receives the certified copy of the court order or the clerk's certificate before the distribution is made.

Amended by Stats. 1995, Ch. 576, Sec. 3. Effective January 1, 1996.

Section 685.095 - Costs of service by levying officer or registered process server

When a writ is served by a levying officer or registered process server, the costs for that service, as determined pursuant to Section 1033.5, shall be added to and become part of the judgment.

Amended by Stats. 1987, Ch. 1080, Sec. 4.

Section 685.100 - Deposit by judgment creditor as prerequisite to performance by levying officer of duty or taking property

(a) Except as otherwise provided by law:

(1) As a prerequisite to the performance by the levying officer of a duty under this title, the judgment creditor shall deposit a sum of money with the levying officer sufficient to pay the costs of performing the duty.

(2) As a prerequisite to the taking of property into custody by the levying officer, whether by keeper or otherwise, the judgment creditor shall deposit with the levying officer a sum of money sufficient to pay the costs of taking the property and keeping it safely for a period not to exceed 15 days. If continuation of the custody of the property is required, the levying officer shall, from time to time, demand orally or in writing that the judgment creditor deposit additional amounts to cover estimated costs for periods not to exceed 30 days each. A written demand may be mailed or delivered to the judgment creditor. The judgment creditor has not less than three business days after receipt of the demand within which to comply with the demand. If the amount demanded is not paid within the time specified in the oral or written demand, the levying officer shall release the property.

(b) The levying officer is not liable for failure to take or hold property unless the judgment creditor has complied with the provisions of this section.

Added by Stats. 1982, Ch. 1364, Sec. 2. Operative July 1, 1983, by Sec. 3 of Ch. 1364.

Section 685.110 - Law of prejudgment interest not affected

Nothing in this chapter affects the law relating to prejudgment interest.

Added by Stats. 1982, Ch. 1364, Sec. 2. Operative July 1, 1983, by Sec. 3 of Ch. 1364.

Chapter 6 - ENFORCEMENT AFTER DEATH OF JUDGMENT CREDITOR OR JUDGMENT DEBTOR

Section 686.010 - After death of judgment creditor

After the death of the judgment creditor, the judgment may be enforced as provided in this title by the judgment creditor's executor or administrator or successor in interest.

Repealed and added by Stats. 1982, Ch. 1364, Sec. 2. Operative July 1, 1983, by Sec. 3 of Ch. 1364.

Section 686.020 - After death of judgment debtor

After the death of the judgment debtor, enforcement of a judgment against property in the judgment debtor's estate is governed by the Probate Code, and not by this title.

Amended by Stats. 1989, Ch. 1416, Sec. 21.

Chapter 7 - LEVYING OFFICERS

Section 687.010 - Instructions given levying officer by judgment creditor

(a) The judgment creditor shall give the levying officer instructions in writing. The instructions shall be signed by the judgment creditor's attorney of record or, if the judgment creditor does not have an attorney of record, by the judgment creditor. The instructions shall contain the information needed or requested by the levying officer to comply with this title, including, but not limited to, all of the following:

(1) An adequate description of any property to be levied upon.

(2) A statement whether the property is a dwelling.

(3) If the property is a dwelling, whether it is real or personal property.

(4) The name of the judgment debtor. If the judgment debtor is other than a natural person, the type of legal entity shall be stated.

(b) Subject to subdivision (c), the levying officer shall act in accordance with the written instructions to the extent the actions are taken in conformance with the provisions of this title.

(c) Except to the extent the levying officer has actual knowledge that the information is incorrect, the levying officer may rely on any information contained in the written instructions.

(d) The levying officer instructions may be transmitted electronically to the levying officer pursuant to Chapter 2 (commencing with Section 263) of Title 4 of Part 1.

(e) If the instructions directing the levying officer to perform a levy are accompanied by a writ of execution for money, possession, or sale of personal or real property issued by the court as an electronic record, as defined in subdivision (b) of Section 263.1, or a document printed from an electronic record issued by the court, the instructions shall also include all of the following information, as stated in the writ:

(1) The date of issuance of the writ.

(2) The name of each judgment creditor and judgment debtor.

(3) The amount of the total judgment for money, a description of the property subject to a judgment for possession or sale, or both the amount and the description.

(4) A statement indicating that the accompanying writ is either of the following:

(A) An original writ, or a copy of the original writ issued by the court as an electronic record, not already in the possession of the levying officer.

(B) A copy of the original writ already in possession of the levying officer.

(f) Except to the extent the levying officer has actual knowledge that the information in the electronic writ has been altered, the levying officer may proceed in the same manner as if in possession of a paper version of the original writ.

Amended by Stats 2013 ch 156 (AB 1167),s 1, eff. 1/1/2014.

Amended by Stats 2010 ch 680 (AB 2394),s 5, eff. 1/1/2011.

Section 687.020 - Instrument payable to judgment debtor on demand

(a) As used in this section, "instrument" means a check, draft, money order, or other order for the withdrawal of money from a financial institution, the United States, any state, or any public entity within any state.

(b) If an instrument is payable to the judgment debtor on demand and comes into the possession of a levying officer pursuant to this title, the levying officer shall promptly endorse and present the instrument for payment.

(c) The levying officer shall endorse the instrument by writing on the instrument (1) the name of the judgment debtor, (2) the name and official title of the levying officer, (3) the title of the court where the judgment is entered, and (4) the date of entry of the judgment and where entered in the records of the court. The endorsement is as valid as if the instrument were endorsed by the judgment debtor. No financial institution or public entity on which the instrument is drawn is liable to any person for payment of the instrument to the levying officer rather than to the judgment debtor by reason of the endorsement. No levying officer is liable by reason of endorsing, presenting, and obtaining payment of the instrument.

(d) If it appears from the face of the instrument that it has been tendered to the judgment debtor in satisfaction of a claim or demand and that endorsement of the instrument is considered a release and satisfaction by the judgment debtor of the claim or demand, the levying officer shall not endorse the instrument unless the judgment debtor has first endorsed it to the levying officer. If the judgment debtor does not endorse the instrument to the levying officer, the levying officer shall hold the instrument for 30 days and is not liable to the judgment debtor or to any other person for delay in presenting it for payment. At the end of the 30-day holding period, the levying officer shall return the instrument to the maker.

Added by Stats. 1982, Ch. 1364, Sec. 2. Operative July 1, 1983, by Sec. 3 of Ch. 1364.

Section 687.030 - Methods of taking property into custody

Except as otherwise provided by statute, where the method of levy upon property requires that the property be taken into custody or where the levying officer is otherwise directed to take property into custody, the levying officer may do so by any of the following methods:

(a) Removing the property to a place of safekeeping.

(b) Installing a keeper.

(c) Otherwise obtaining possession or control of the property.

Added by Stats. 1982, Ch. 1364, Sec. 2. Operative July 1, 1983, by Sec. 3 of Ch. 1364.

Section 687.040 - Liability for actions taken in conformance with title; loss of personal property by fire, theft, injury or damage

(a) The levying officer or registered process server is not liable for actions taken in conformance with the provisions of this title, including actions taken in conformance with the provisions of this title in reliance on information contained in the written instructions of the judgment creditor, or in reliance on information provided to the levying officer by a registered process server pursuant to subdivision (d) of Section 699.080 or subdivision (e) of Section 706.101 or subdivision (b) of Section 715.040 or other provision, except to the extent the levying officer or registered process server has actual knowledge that the information is incorrect. Nothing in this subdivision limits any liability the judgment creditor may have if the levying officer or registered process server acts on the basis of incorrect information given in the written instructions.

(b) Unless the levying officer is negligent in the care or handling of the property, the levying officer is not liable to either the judgment debtor or the judgment creditor for loss by fire, theft, injury, or damage of any kind to personal property while (1) in the possession of the levying officer either in a warehouse or other storage place or in the custody of a keeper or (2) in transit to or from a warehouse or other storage place.

Amended by Stats. 1983, Ch. 155, Sec. 11. Effective June 30, 1983. Operative July 1, 1983, by Sec. 32 of Ch. 155.

Section 687.050 - Special lien on property levied upon

The levying officer has a special lien, dependent upon possession, on personal property levied upon in the amount of the levying officer's costs for which an advance has not been made.

Added by Stats. 1982, Ch. 1364, Sec. 2. Operative July 1, 1983, by Sec. 3 of Ch. 1364.

Chapter 8 - ENFORCEMENT OF STATE TAX LIABILITY

Article 1 - ENFORCEMENT PURSUANT TO WARRANT OR NOTICE OF LEVY

Section 688.010 - Proceedings limited civil case

A proceeding for the purpose of the remedies provided under this article is a limited civil case if (a) the amount of liability sought to be collected does not exceed the maximum amount in controversy for a limited civil case provided in Section 85, and (b) the legality of the liability being enforced is not contested by the person against whom enforcement is sought.

Amended by Stats 2007 ch 43 (SB 649),s 7, eff. 1/1/2008.

Section 688.020 - Remedies available to state when authorized to issue warrant; proper court for enforcement

(a) Except as otherwise provided by statute, if a warrant may properly be issued by the state, or by a department or agency of the state, pursuant to any provision of the Public Resources Code, Revenue and Taxation Code, or Unemployment Insurance Code, and the warrant may be levied with the same effect as a levy pursuant to a writ of execution, the state or the department or agency of the state authorized to issue the warrant may use any of the remedies available to a judgment creditor, including, but not limited to, those provided in Chapter 6 (commencing with Section 708.010) of Division 2.

(b) The proper court for the enforcement of those remedies is a court of any of the following counties:

(1) The county where the debtor resides.

(2) The county where the property against which enforcement is sought is located.

(3) If the debtor does not reside in this state, any county of this state.

(4) This section shall become operative on January 1, 2014.

Added by Stats 2008 ch 552 (AB 2578),s 2, eff. 1/1/2009.

Section 688.030 - Claim of exemption or third party claim when property levied on pursuant to warrant or notice issued by state

(a) If pursuant to any provision of the Public Resources Code, Revenue and Taxation Code (excluding Sections 3201 to 3204, inclusive), or Unemployment Insurance Code, property is levied upon pursuant to a warrant or notice of levy issued by the state or by a department or agency of the state for the collection of a liability:

(1) If the debtor is a natural person, the debtor is entitled to the same exemptions to which a judgment debtor is entitled. Except as provided in subdivisions (b) and (c), the claim of exemption shall be made, heard, and determined as provided in Chapter 4 (commencing with Section 703.010) of Division 2 in the same manner as if the property were levied upon under a writ of execution.

(2) A third person may claim ownership or the right to possession of the property or a security interest in or lien on the property. Except as provided in subdivisions (b) and (c) or as otherwise provided by statute, the third-party claim shall be made, heard, and determined as provided in Division 4 (commencing with Section 720.010) in the same manner as if the property were levied upon under a writ of execution.

(b) In the case of a levy pursuant to a notice of levy:

(1) The claim of exemption or the third-party claim shall be filed with the state department or agency that issued the notice of levy.

(2) The state department or agency that issued the notice of levy shall perform the duties of the levying officer, except that the state department or agency need not give itself the notices that the levying officer is required to serve on a judgment creditor or creditor or the notices that a judgment creditor or creditor is required to give to the levying officer. The state department or agency in performing the duties of the levying officer under this paragraph has no obligation to search public records or otherwise seek to determine whether any lien or encumbrance exists on property sold or collected.

(c) A claim of exemption or a third-party claim pursuant to this section shall be heard and determined in the superior court in the county where the property levied upon is located.

(d) This section shall become operative on January 1, 2014.

Added by Stats 2008 ch 552 (AB 2578),s 4, eff. 1/1/2009.

Section 688.040 - Definitions

For the purpose of this article, as used in this title:

(a) "Judgment creditor" or "creditor" means the state or the department or agency of the state seeking to collect the liability.

(b) "Judgment debtor" or "debtor" means the debtor from whom the liability is sought to be collected.

Added by Stats. 1982, Ch. 1364, Sec. 2. Operative July 1, 1983, by Sec. 3 of Ch. 1364.

Section 688.050 - Date of creation of tax lien

For the purpose of applying Section 694.080, 703.050, or 703.100, the date of creation of a tax lien is the earliest of the following times:

(a) The time when a notice of state tax lien is recorded or filed pursuant to Chapter 14 (commencing with Section 7150) of Division 7 of Title 1 of the Government Code.

(b) The time when the property is levied upon pursuant to a warrant or notice of levy or notice to withhold issued by the state or by a department or agency of the state.

(c) The time when any other act is performed that creates or perfects a lien on specific property as distinguished from a lien on the debtor's property generally.

Added by Stats. 1982, Ch. 1364, Sec. 2. Operative July 1, 1983, by Sec. 3 of Ch. 1364.

Article 2 - ENFORCEMENT OF JUDGMENT FOR TAXES

Section 688.110 - Generally

Except as otherwise provided by statute, if a judgment is entered on a claim for taxes by a public entity, the judgment is enforceable pursuant to this title in the same manner as any other money judgment.

Added by Stats. 1982, Ch. 1364, Sec. 2. Operative July 1, 1983, by Sec. 3 of Ch. 1364.

Chapter 9 - ENFORCEMENT OF SUPPORT JUDGMENTS

Section 689.010 - Jurisdiction of superior court

For the purpose of the remedies provided under this chapter, jurisdiction is conferred upon the superior court.

Added by Stats. 1996, Ch. 957, Sec. 4. Effective January 1, 1997.

Section 689.020 - Remedies available to local child support agency

(a) Except as otherwise provided by statute, whenever a warrant may properly be issued by a local child support agency pursuant to Section 17522 of the Family Code, and the warrant may be levied with the same effect as a levy pursuant to a writ of execution, the local child support agency may use any of the remedies available to a judgment creditor, including, but not limited to, those provided in Chapter 6 (commencing with Section 708.010) of Division 2.

(b) The proper court for the enforcement of the remedies provided under this chapter is the superior court in the county where the local child support agency enforcing the support obligation is located.

Amended by Stats 2000 ch 808 (AB 1358), s 6, eff. 9/28/2000.

Section 689.030 - Claim of exemption or third party claim

(a) Whenever the local child support agency, pursuant to Section 17522 of the Family Code, levies upon property pursuant to a warrant or notice of levy for the collection of a support obligation:

(1) If the debtor is a natural person, the debtor is entitled to the same exemptions to which a judgment debtor is entitled. Except as provided in subdivisions (b) and (c), the claim of exemption shall be made, heard, and determined as provided in Chapter 4 (commencing with Section 703.010) of Division 2 in the same manner as if the property were levied upon under a writ of execution.

(2) A third person may claim ownership or the right to possession of the property or a security interest in or lien on the property. Except as provided in subdivisions (b) and (c) or as otherwise provided by statute, the third-party claim shall be made, heard, and determined as provided in Division 4 (commencing with Section 720.010) in the same manner as if the property were levied upon under a writ of execution.

(b) In the case of a warrant or notice of levy issued pursuant to Section 17522 of the Family Code, the claim of exemption or the third-party claim shall be filed with the local child support agency that issued the warrant or notice of levy.

(c) A claim of exemption or a third-party claim pursuant to this section shall be heard and determined in the court specified in Section 689.010 in the county where the local child support agency enforcing the support obligation is located.

Amended by Stats 2000 ch 808 (AB 1358), s 7, eff. 9/28/2000.

Section 689.040 - Performance of duties of levying officer; delivery of writ of execution to centralized location

(a) Notwithstanding any other provision of law, in the case of a writ of execution issued by a court of competent jurisdiction pursuant to Chapter 3 (commencing with Section 699.010) and Chapter 5 (commencing with Section 706.010) of Division 2, the local child support agency, when enforcing a support obligation pursuant to Division 17 (commencing with Section 17000) of the Family Code, may perform the duties of the levying officer, except that the local child support agency need not give itself the notices that the levying officer is required to serve on a judgment creditor or creditor or the notices that a judgment creditor or creditor is required to give to the levying officer.

(b) Notwithstanding subdivision (a) of Section 700.140, if the writ of execution is for a deposit or credits or personal property in the possession or under the control of a bank or savings and loan association, the local child support agency may deliver or mail the writ of execution to a centralized location designated by the bank or savings and loan association. If the writ of execution is received at the designated central location, it will apply to all deposits and credits and personal property held by the bank or savings and loan association regardless of the location of that property.

Amended by Stats 2000 ch 808 (AB 1358), s 8, eff. 9/28/2000.

Section 689.050 - Definitions

For the purpose of this chapter:

(a) "Judgment creditor" or "creditor" means the local child support agency seeking to collect a child or spousal support obligation pursuant to a support order.

(b) "Judgment debtor" or "debtor" means the debtor from whom the support obligation is sought to be collected.

Amended by Stats 2000 ch 808 (AB 1358), s 9, eff. 9/28/2000.

Chapter 10 - ENFORCEMENT OF JUDGMENTS BY LABOR COMMISSIONER

Section 690.020 - Jurisdiction

For the purpose of the remedies provided under this chapter, jurisdiction is conferred upon the superior court.

Added by Stats 2015 ch 803 (SB 588),s 1, eff. 1/1/2016.

Section 690.030 - Remedies; venue

(a) Except as otherwise provided by statute, whenever a warrant or notice of levy may properly be issued by the Labor Commissioner pursuant to Section 96.8 of the Labor Code, and the warrant may be levied with the same effect as a levy pursuant to a writ of execution, the Labor Commissioner may use any of the remedies available to a judgment creditor, including, but not limited to, those provided in Chapter 6 (commencing with Section 708.010) of Division 2.

(b) The proper court for the enforcement of the remedies provided under this chapter is the superior court of any of the following counties:

(1) The county where the employee resides.

(2) The county where the judgment debtor resides.

(3) The county where the person against whom the levy or warrant was issued resides.

Added by Stats 2015 ch 803 (SB 588),s 1, eff. 1/1/2016.

Section 690.040 - Warrant or notice of levy; Exemptions

(a) Whenever the Labor Commissioner, pursuant to Section 96.8 of the Labor Code, levies upon property pursuant to a warrant or notice of levy for the collection of an unsatisfied judgment or award:

(1) If the debtor is a natural person, the debtor is entitled to the same exemptions to which a judgment debtor is entitled. Except as provided in subdivisions (b) and (c), the claim of exemption shall be made, heard, and determined as provided in Chapter 4 (commencing with Section 703.010) of Division 2 in the same manner as if the property were levied upon under a writ of execution.

(2) A third person may claim ownership or the right to possession of the property or a security interest in or lien on the property. Except as provided in subdivisions (b) and (c) or as otherwise provided by statute, the third-party claim shall be made, heard, and determined as provided in Division 4 (commencing with Section 720.010) in the same manner as if the property were levied upon under a writ of execution.

(b) In the case of a warrant or notice of levy issued pursuant to Section 96.8 of the Labor Code, the claim of exemption or the third-party claim shall be filed with the Labor Commissioner.

(c) A claim of exemption or a third-party claim pursuant to this section shall be heard and determined in a superior court specified in subdivision (b) of Section 690.030.

Added by Stats 2015 ch 803 (SB 588),s 1, eff. 1/1/2016.

Section 690.050 - Collection of unsatisfied judgment or award

(a) Notwithstanding any other law, in the case of a writ of execution issued by a court of competent jurisdiction pursuant to Chapter 3 (commencing with Section 699.010) and Chapter 5 (commencing with Section 706.010) of Division 2, the Labor Commissioner, when collecting an unsatisfied judgment or award pursuant to Section 96.8 of the Labor Code, may perform the duties of the levying officer, except that the Labor Commissioner need not give himself or herself the notices that the levying officer is required to serve on a judgment creditor or the notices that a judgment creditor is required to give to the levying officer.

(b) Notwithstanding subdivision (a) of Section 700.140 and Sections 700.150, 700.160, and 700.170, if the levy is for a deposit, credits, money, or property in the possession or under the control of a bank or savings and loan association or for an account receivable or other general intangible owed to the judgment debtor by an account debtor, the Labor Commissioner may deliver or mail a notice of levy to a centralized location designated by the bank or savings and loan association or, in the case of an account receivable or other general intangible, to the agent for service of process of the account debtor. If the notice of levy is received at the designated central location for the bank or savings and loan association, the notice of levy will apply to all deposits, credits, money, and personal property held by the bank or savings and loan association regardless of the location of that property. The notice of levy may be issued directly by the Labor Commissioner, whether or not a court has issued a writ of execution, and shall contain all of the information required to be included in a writ of execution under Section 699.520 and in a notice of levy under Section 699.540.

Added by Stats 2015 ch 803 (SB 588),s 1, eff. 1/1/2016.

Chapter 20 - TRANSITIONAL PROVISIONS

Section 694.010 - Definitions

As used in this chapter:

(a) "Operative date" means July 1, 1983.

(b) "Prior law" means the applicable law in effect on June 30, 1983.

Added by Stats. 1982, Ch. 1364, Sec. 2. Operative July 1, 1983, by Sec. 3 of Ch. 1364.

Section 694.020 - Applicability to proceedings commenced prior to operative date

Except as otherwise provided in this chapter, this title on and after its operative date applies to all proceedings commenced prior thereto unless in the opinion of the court application of a particular provision of this title would substantially interfere with the effective conduct of the proceedings or the rights of the parties or other interested persons, in which case the particular provision of this title does not apply and prior law applies.

Added by Stats. 1982, Ch. 1364, Sec. 2. Operative July 1, 1983, by Sec. 3 of Ch. 1364.

Section 694.030 - Period for enforcement of judgment; renewal of judgment

(a) Except for a judgment described in Section 683.310 or 683.320, the period for enforcement of a money judgment or a judgment for possession or sale of property entered prior to the operative date is governed on and after the operative date by Chapter 3 (commencing with Section 683.010).

(b) Notwithstanding subdivision (a), even though a judgment to which subdivision (a) applies is not renewable pursuant to Chapter 3 (commencing with Section 683.010) because the time for filing an application for renewal has expired, the judgment may be renewed under Chapter 3 (commencing with Section 683.010) if the court which entered the judgment determines, on noticed motion filed within two years after the operative date, that authority to enforce the judgment after the 10-year period provided in former Section 681 would have been granted if a motion had been made under former Section 685 and the court, in its discretion, makes an order authorizing the renewal of the judgment. The notice of motion shall be served personally or by mail on the judgment debtor.

Added by Stats. 1982, Ch. 1364, Sec. 2. Operative July 1, 1983, by Sec. 3 of Ch. 1364.

Section 694.040 - Property subject to prior law relating to sale or delivering of possession

(a) Except as provided in subdivision (c), property levied upon or otherwise subjected to process for enforcement of a money judgment or a judgment for possession or sale of property prior to the operative date is subject to prior law relating to sale or delivery of possession.
(b) The duties to be performed in the execution of a writ or order for the enforcement of a money judgment or a judgment for possession or sale of property that is served prior to the operative date are governed by prior law.
(c) The manner of payment at a sale of property pursuant to a writ or order after the operative date is governed by Section 701.590.
Added by Stats. 1982, Ch. 1364, Sec. 2. Operative July 1, 1983, by Sec. 3 of Ch. 1364.

Section 694.050 - Property sold subject to right of redemption of prior law
(a) Except as provided in subdivision (b), property levied upon, or property to be sold upon which foreclosure or other proceedings for sale have been commenced, prior to the operative date that would have been sold subject to the right of redemption under prior law shall be sold subject to the right of redemption and may be redeemed as provided by prior law.
(b) If the judgment creditor and judgment debtor agree in writing, property described in subdivision (a) may be sold as provided in this title rather than subject to the right of redemption.
(c) Property sold prior to the operative date subject to the right of redemption under prior law may be redeemed as provided by prior law.
Added by Stats. 1982, Ch. 1364, Sec. 2. Operative July 1, 1983, by Sec. 3 of Ch. 1364.

Section 694.060 - Time for commencing action after operative date
Notwithstanding Section 708.230, an action may be commenced pursuant to Section 708.210 within one year after the operative date if the action could have been commenced under prior law on the day before the operative date.
Added by Stats. 1982, Ch. 1364, Sec. 2. Operative July 1, 1983, by Sec. 3 of Ch. 1364.

Section 694.070 - Third-party claim
(a) A third-party claim filed prior to the operative date is governed by prior law.
(b) A demand for a third-party claim served on a secured party prior to the operative date is governed by prior law.
Added by Stats. 1982, Ch. 1364, Sec. 2. Operative July 1, 1983, by Sec. 3 of Ch. 1364.

Section 694.080 - Exemptions
The exemptions from enforcement of a money judgment provided by this title do not apply to property levied upon or otherwise subjected to a lien prior to the operative date. Whether such property is exempt is determined by the exemptions provided by law at the time the lien was created.
Added by Stats. 1982, Ch. 1364, Sec. 2. Operative July 1, 1983, by Sec. 3 of Ch. 1364.

Section 694.090 - Declaration of homestead made under prior law
On and after the operative date, a declaration of homestead made under prior law pursuant to Title 5 (commencing with Section 1237) of Part 4 of Division 2 of the Civil Code is effective only to the extent provided in Article 5 (commencing with Section 704.910) of Chapter 4 of Division 2.
Added by Stats. 1982, Ch. 1364, Sec. 2. Operative July 1, 1983, by Sec. 3 of Ch. 1364.

Division 2 - ENFORCEMENT OF MONEY JUDGMENTS
Chapter 1 - GENERAL PROVISIONS
Article 1 - PROPERTY SUBJECT TO ENFORCEMENT OF MONEY JUDGMENT

Section 695.010 - All property subject to enforcement; property attached but transferred before entry of judgment
(a) Except as otherwise provided by law, all property of the judgment debtor is subject to enforcement of a money judgment.
(b) If property of the judgment debtor was attached in the action but was transferred before entry of the money judgment in favor of the judgment creditor, the property is subject to enforcement of the money judgment so long as the attachment lien remains effective.
Amended by Stats. 1984, Ch. 538, Sec. 17.

Section 695.020 - Community property
(a) Community property is subject to enforcement of a money judgment as provided in the Family Code.
(b) Unless the provision or context otherwise requires, if community property that is subject to enforcement of a money judgment is sought to be applied to the satisfaction of a money judgment:
　　(1) Any provision of this division that applies to the property of the judgment debtor or to obligations owed to the judgment debtor also applies to the community property interest of the spouse of the judgment debtor and to obligations owed to the other spouse that are community property.
　　(2) Any provision of this division that applies to property in the possession or under the control of the judgment debtor also applies to community property in the possession or under the control of the spouse of the judgment debtor.
Amended by Stats. 1992, Ch. 163, Sec. 33. Effective January 1, 1993. Operative January 1, 1994, by Sec. 161 of Ch. 163.

Section 695.030 - Property not assignable or transferable not subject to enforcement; property subject to enforcement
(a) Except as otherwise provided by statute, property of the judgment debtor that is not assignable or transferable is not subject to enforcement of a money judgment.
(b) The following property is subject to enforcement of a money judgment:
　　(1) An interest in a trust, to the extent provided by law.
　　(2) A cause of action for money or property that is the subject of a pending action or special proceeding.
Amended by Stats. 1986, Ch. 820, Sec. 17. Operative July 1, 1987, by Sec. 43 of Ch. 820.

Section 695.035 - Lessee's interest in real property
(a) A lessee's interest in real property may be applied to the satisfaction of a money judgment in any of the following circumstances:
　　(1) If the lessee has the right voluntarily to sublet the property or assign the interest in the lease.
　　(2) If the lessee has the right voluntarily to sublet the property or assign the interest in the lease subject to standards or conditions and the purchaser at the execution sale or other assignee agrees to comply with the standards or conditions that would have had to be complied with had the lessee voluntarily sublet the property or assigned the interest in the lease.
　　(3) If the lessee has the right voluntarily to sublet the property or assign the interest in the lease with the consent of the lessor, in which case the obligation of the lessor to consent to the assignment is subject to the same standard that would apply had the lessee voluntarily sublet the property or assigned the interest in the lease.
　　(4) In any other case, if the lessor consents in writing.
(b) A provision in a lease for the termination or modification of the lease upon an involuntary transfer or assignment of the lessee's interest is ineffective to the extent that such provision would prevent the application of the lessee's interest to the satisfaction of the money judgment under subdivision (a).
Added by Stats. 1982, Ch. 1364, Sec. 2. Operative July 1, 1983, by Sec. 3 of Ch. 1364.

Section 695.040 - Property not subject to enforcement not to be levied upon
Property that is not subject to enforcement of a money judgment may not be levied upon or in any other manner applied to the satisfaction of a money judgment. If property that is not subject to enforcement of a money judgment has been levied upon, the property may be released pursuant to the claim of exemption procedure provided in Article 2 (commencing with Section 703.510) of Chapter 4.

Added by Stats. 1982, Ch. 1364, Sec. 2. Operative July 1, 1983, by Sec. 3 of Ch. 1364.

Section 695.050 - Judgment against public entity
A money judgment against a public entity is not enforceable under this division if the money judgment is subject to Chapter 1 (commencing with Section 965) of, or Article 1 (commencing with Section 970) of Chapter 2 of, Part 5 of Division 3.6 of Title 1 of the Government Code.
Added by Stats. 1982, Ch. 1364, Sec. 2. Operative July 1, 1983, by Sec. 3 of Ch. 1364.

Section 695.060 - License to engage in business, profession or activity
Except as provided in Section 708.630, a license issued by a public entity to engage in any business, profession, or activity is not subject to enforcement of a money judgment.
Added by Stats. 1982, Ch. 1364, Sec. 2. Operative July 1, 1983, by Sec. 3 of Ch. 1364.

Section 695.070 - Property subject to lien after transfer or encumbrance
(a) Notwithstanding the transfer or encumbrance of property subject to a lien created under this division, if the property remains subject to the lien after the transfer or encumbrance, the money judgment may be enforced against the property in the same manner and to the same extent as if it had not been transferred or encumbered.

(b) If the judgment debtor dies after the transfer of property that remains subject to a lien created under this division, the money judgment may be enforced against the property as provided in subdivision (a).
Amended by Stats. 1989, Ch. 1416, Sec. 22.

Article 2 - AMOUNT TO SATISFY MONEY JUDGMENT

Section 695.210 - Generally
The amount required to satisfy a money judgment is the total amount of the judgment as entered or renewed with the following additions and subtractions:

(a) The addition of costs added to the judgment pursuant to Section 685.090.

(b) The addition of interest added to the judgment as it accrues pursuant to Sections 685.010 to 685.030, inclusive.

(c) The subtraction of the amount of any partial satisfactions of the judgment.

(d) The subtraction of the amount of any portion of the judgment that is no longer enforceable.
Amended by Stats. 1993, Ch. 876, Sec. 9. Effective October 6, 1993.

Section 695.211 - Notice of interest on arrearages in judgment or order for child support
(a) Every money judgment or order for child support shall provide notice that interest on arrearages accrues at the legal rate.

(b) The notice provisions required by this section shall be incorporated in the appropriate Judicial Council forms.

(c) Upon implementation of the California Child Support Automation System prescribed in Chapter 4 (commencing with Section 10080) of Part 1 of Division 9 of the Welfare and Institutions Code and certification of the California Child Support Automation System by the United States Department of Health and Human Services, whenever a statement of account is issued by the local child support agency in any child support action, the statement shall include a statement of an amount of current support, arrears, and interest due.
Amended by Stats 2000 ch 808 (AB 1358), s 10, eff. 9/28/2000.

Section 695.215 - Effect of payment to satisfy judgment
Payment in satisfaction of a money judgment, including payment of a severable portion of the money judgment, interest thereon, and associated costs, does not constitute a waiver of the right to appeal, except to the extent that the payment is the product of compromise or is coupled with an agreement not to appeal. Payment in satisfaction of a severable portion of a money judgment, interest thereon, and associated costs, does not constitute a waiver of the right to appeal other portions of the money judgment.
Added by Stats 2019 ch 48 (AB 1361),s 1, eff. 1/1/2020.

Section 695.220 - Credit of money received in satisfaction of judgment
Money received in satisfaction of a money judgment, except a money judgment for support, is to be credited as follows:

(a) The money is first to be credited against the amounts described in subdivision (b) of Section 685.050 that are collected by the levying officer.

(b) Any remaining money is next to be credited against any fee due the court pursuant to Section 6103.5 or 68511.3 of the Government Code, which are to be remitted to the court by the levying officer.

(c) Any remaining money is next to be credited against the accrued interest that remains unsatisfied.

(d) Any remaining money is to be credited against the principal amount of the judgment remaining unsatisfied. If the judgment is payable in installments, the remaining money is to be credited against the matured installments in the order in which they matured.
Amended by Stats. 1994, Ch. 75, Sec. 1. Effective May 20, 1994.

Section 695.221 - Credit of satisfaction of judgment for support
Satisfaction of a money judgment for support shall be credited as follows:

(a) The money shall first be credited against the current month's support.

(b) Any remaining money shall next be credited against the principal amount of the judgment remaining unsatisfied. If the judgment is payable in installments, the remaining money shall be credited against the matured installments in the order in which they matured.

(c) Any remaining money shall be credited against the accrued interest that remains unsatisfied.

(d) In cases enforced pursuant to Part D (commencing with Section 651) of Subchapter 4 of Chapter 7 of Title 42 of the United States Code, if a lump-sum payment is collected from a support obligor who has money judgments for support owing to more than one family, effective September 1, 2006, all support collected shall be distributed pursuant to guidelines developed by the Department of Child Support Services.

(e) Support collections received between January 1, 2009, and April 30, 2020, inclusive, shall be distributed by the Department of Child Support Services as follows:

(1) Notwithstanding subdivisions (a), (b), and (c), a collection received as a result of a federal tax refund offset shall first be credited against the principal amount of past due support that has been assigned to the state pursuant to Section 11477 of the Welfare and Institutions Code and federal law and then any interest due on that past due support, prior to the principal amount of any other past due support remaining unsatisfied and then any interest due on that past due support.

(2) The following shall be the order of distribution of child support collections through September 30, 2000, except for federal tax refund offset collections, for child support received for families and children who are former recipients of Aid to Families with Dependent Children (AFDC) program benefits or former recipients of Temporary Assistance for Needy Families (TANF) program benefits:

(A) The money shall first be credited against the current month's support.

(B) Any remaining money shall next be credited against interest that accrued on arrearages owed to the family or children since leaving the AFDC program or the TANF program and then the arrearages.

(C) Any remaining money shall next be credited against interest that accrued on arrearages owed during the time the family or children received benefits under the AFDC program or the TANF program and then the arrearages.

(D) Any remaining money shall next be credited against interest that accrued on arrearages owed to the family or children prior to receiving benefits from the AFDC program or the TANF program and then the arrearages.

(f) Support collections received on or after May 1, 2020, shall be distributed by the Department of Child Support Services in accordance with Section 657(a)(2)(B)(a)(2)(B) of Title 42 of the United States Code, as amended by Section 7301(b)(1)(b)(1) of the federal Deficit Reduction Act of 2005, in such a manner as to distribute all support collections to families first to the maximum extent permitted by federal law.
Amended by Stats 2021 ch 85 (AB 135),s 1, eff. 7/16/2021.
Added by Stats 2004 ch 305 (AB 2669),s 2, eff. 1/1/2009.
Amended by Stats 2004 ch 305 (AB 2669),s 1, eff. 1/1/2005
Repealed by Stats 2004 ch 305 (AB 2669),s 1, eff. 1/1/2005, op. 1/1/2009.
Amended by Stats 2000 ch 808 (AB 1358), s 11, eff. 9/28/2000.
See Stats 2021 ch 85 (AB 135), s 2.

Chapter 2 - LIENS
Article 1 - GENERAL PROVISIONS

Section 697.010 - Generally
Except as otherwise provided by statute, a lien created under this division or under Title 6.5 (commencing with Section 481.010) (attachment) is a lien for the amount required to satisfy the money judgment.
Added by Stats. 1982, Ch. 1364, Sec. 2. Operative July 1, 1983, by Sec. 3 of Ch. 1364.

Section 697.020 - Relation back of priority of later lien created
(a) If a lien is created on property pursuant to Title 6.5 (commencing with Section 481.010) (attachment) and after judgment in the action a lien is created pursuant to this division on the same property under the same claim while the earlier lien is in effect, the priority of the later lien relates back to the date the earlier lien was created.
(b) If a lien is created on property pursuant to this division and a later lien of the same or a different type is created pursuant to this division on the same property under the same judgment while the earlier lien is in effect, the priority of the later lien relates back to the date the earlier lien was created.
(c) Nothing in this section affects priorities or rights of third persons established while the earlier lien was in effect under the law governing the earlier lien.
Added by Stats. 1982, Ch. 1364, Sec. 2. Operative July 1, 1983, by Sec. 3 of Ch. 1364.

Section 697.030 - Lien effective during period of enforceability
Subject to Sections 683.180 to 683.200, inclusive, and to Section 697.040, except where a shorter period is provided by statute, a lien created pursuant to this title is effective during the period of enforceability of the judgment.
Added by Stats. 1982, Ch. 1364, Sec. 2. Operative July 1, 1983, by Sec. 3 of Ch. 1364.

Section 697.040 - Stay of enforcement of judgment
(a) If enforcement of the judgment is stayed on appeal by the giving of a sufficient undertaking under Chapter 2 (commencing with Section 916) of Title 13:
  (1) Existing liens created under this division are extinguished.
  (2) New liens may not be created under this division during the period of the stay.
(b) Unless the court otherwise expressly orders, a stay of enforcement of the judgment under Section 918 does not extinguish or prevent the creation of a lien under Article 2 (commencing with Section 697.310) or Article 3 (commencing with Section 697.510); but, unless the court otherwise expressly orders, no other liens may be created or continued under this division during the period of the stay of enforcement.
(c) Unless the court expressly orders otherwise, if enforcement of the judgment is stayed pursuant to Section 1699 or 1710.50:
  (1) Existing liens created under this division are extinguished.
  (2) New liens may not be created under this division during the period of the stay.
Added by Stats. 1982, Ch. 1364, Sec. 2. Operative July 1, 1983, by Sec. 3 of Ch. 1364.

Section 697.050 - Lien created extinguished
If a lien created pursuant to this division is extinguished, property held subject to the lien shall be released unless the property is to be held under another lien or the property is ordered by the court to be held pending resolution of a dispute concerning its proper disposition.
Added by Stats. 1982, Ch. 1364, Sec. 2. Operative July 1, 1983, by Sec. 3 of Ch. 1364.

Section 697.060 - Judgment of United States court
(a) An abstract or certified copy of a money judgment of a court of the United States that is enforceable in this state may be recorded to create a judgment lien on real property pursuant to Article 2 (commencing with Section 697.310).
(b) A notice of judgment lien based on a money judgment of a court of the United States that is enforceable in this state may be filed to create a judgment lien on personal property pursuant to Article 3 (commencing with Section 697.510).
Added by Stats. 1982, Ch. 1364, Sec. 2. Operative July 1, 1983, by Sec. 3 of Ch. 1364.

Article 2 - JUDGMENT LIEN ON REAL PROPERTY

Section 697.310 - Lien created by recording abstract of judgment; duration of lien; payable in installments
(a) Except as otherwise provided by statute, a judgment lien on real property is created under this section by recording an abstract of a money judgment with the county recorder.
(b) Unless the money judgment is satisfied or the judgment lien is released, subject to Section 683.180 (renewal of judgment), a judgment lien created under this section continues until 10 years from the date of entry of the judgment.
(c) The creation and duration of a judgment lien under a money judgment entered pursuant to Section 117 or 582.5 of this code or Section 16380 of the Vehicle Code or under a similar judgment is governed by this section, notwithstanding that the judgment may be payable in installments.
Amended by Stats. 1998, Ch. 931, Sec. 90. Effective September 28, 1998.

Section 697.320 - Lien created by recording abstract, notice of support judgment, interstate lien form or certified copy of judgment
(a) A judgment lien on real property is created under this section by recording an abstract, a notice of support judgment, an interstate lien form promulgated by the federal Secretary of Health and Human Services pursuant to Section 652(a)(11)(a)(11) of Title 42 of the United States Code, or a certified copy of either of the following money judgments with the county recorder:
  (1) A judgment for child, family, or spousal support payable in installments.
  (2) A judgment entered pursuant to Section 667.7 (judgment against health care provider requiring periodic payments).
(b) Unless the money judgment is satisfied or the judgment lien is released, a judgment lien created under paragraph (1) of subdivision (a) or by recording an interstate lien form, as described in subdivision (a), continues during the period the judgment remains enforceable. Unless the money judgment is satisfied or the judgment lien is released, a judgment lien created under paragraph (2) of subdivision (a) continues for a period of 10 years from the date of its creation. The duration of a judgment lien created under paragraph (2) of subdivision (a) may be extended any number of times by recording, during the time the judgment lien is in existence, a certified copy of the judgment in the manner provided in this section for the initial recording; this rerecording has the effect of extending the duration of the judgment lien created under paragraph (2) of subdivision (a) until 10 years from the date of the rerecording.
Amended by Stats 2002 ch 927 (AB 3032),s 1.5, eff. 1/1/2003.

Section 697.330 - Creation of lien by workers' compensation, judgment, order, decision or award
(a) In the case of a money judgment entered on an order, decision, or award made under Division 4 (commencing with Section 3200) of the Labor Code (workers' compensation):
  (1) If the judgment is for a lump sum, a judgment lien on real property is created by recording an abstract of the judgment as provided in Section 697.310 and, except as otherwise provided in Division 4 (commencing with Section 3200) of the Labor Code, the judgment lien is governed by the provisions applicable to a judgment lien created under Section 697.310.
  (2) If the judgment is for the payment of money in installments, a judgment lien on real property is created by recording a certified copy of the judgment as provided in Section 697.320 and, except as otherwise provided in Division 4 (commencing with Section 3200) of the Labor Code, the lien is governed by the provisions applicable to a judgment lien created under Section 697.320.
(b) Nothing in this section limits or affects any provision of Division 4 (commencing with Section 3200) of the Labor Code.
Added by Stats. 1982, Ch. 1364, Sec. 2. Operative July 1, 1983, by Sec. 3 of Ch. 1364.

Section 697.340 - Lien attaches to all interest in real property in county where lien attaches
Except as provided in Section 704.950:
(a) A judgment lien on real property attaches to all interests in real property in the county where the lien is created (whether present or future, vested or contingent, legal or equitable) that are subject to enforcement of the money judgment against the judgment debtor pursuant to Article 1 (commencing with Section 695.010) of Chapter 1 at the time the lien was created, but does not reach rental payments, a leasehold estate with an unexpired term of less than two years, the interest of a beneficiary under a trust, or real property that is subject to an attachment lien in favor of the creditor and was transferred before judgment.
(b) If any interest in real property in the county on which a judgment lien could be created under subdivision (a) is acquired after the judgment lien was created, the judgment lien attaches to such interest at the time it is acquired.
Amended by Stats. 1984, Ch. 538, Sec. 18.

Section 697.350 - Amount of lien
(a) Except as otherwise provided by statute, a judgment lien on real property is a lien for the amount required to satisfy the money judgment.
(b) A judgment lien on real property created under a money judgment payable in installments pursuant to Section 116.620 or 582.5 of this code or Section 16380 of the Vehicle Code or under a similar judgment is in the full amount required to satisfy the judgment, but the judgment lien may not be enforced for the amount of unmatured installments unless the court so orders.
(c) A judgment lien created pursuant to Section 697.320 is a lien for the amount of the installments as they mature under the terms of the judgment, plus accrued interest and the costs as they are added to the judgment pursuant to Chapter 5 (commencing with Section 685.010) of Division 1, and less the amount of any partial satisfactions, but does not become a lien for any installment until it becomes due and payable under the terms of the judgment.
Amended by Stats 2009 ch 140 (AB 1164),s 39, eff. 1/1/2010.

Section 697.360 - Lien created under judgment thereafter modified
(a) If a judgment lien on real property has been created under a money judgment that is thereafter modified as to its amount, an abstract of the modified judgment or a certified copy of the order modifying the judgment may be recorded in the same manner as an abstract of judgment or a certified copy of the judgment is recorded to create a judgment lien.
(b) If a judgment lien on real property has been created under a money judgment that is thereafter modified to reduce its amount, the judgment lien continues under the terms of the judgment as modified, whether or not the modification is recorded as provided in subdivision (a).
(c) If a judgment lien on real property has been created under a money judgment that is thereafter modified to increase its amount, the judgment lien continues under the terms of the original judgment until such time as the modification is recorded as provided in subdivision (a). Upon such recording, the judgment lien extends to the judgment as modified, but the priority for the additional amount under the judgment as modified dates from the time the modification is recorded.
(d) Notwithstanding subdivision (c), if a judgment lien on real property has been created under a money judgment, by recording of an abstract of support judgment under paragraph (1) of subdivision (a) of Section 697.320, and the support order is thereafter modified to increase its amount, the judgment lien extends to the judgment as modified without the need for recording of another abstract of support judgment, but the priority for the additional amount under the judgment dates from the time the modification is effective.
(e) A support obligee shall respond in a timely manner to (1) a title or escrow company request for a demand statement needed to close an escrow relating to a support judgment lien, or (2) a support obligor who claims an error exists in the amount of alleged arrears.
(f) A support obligor who complies with the procedure specified in Division 5 (commencing with Section 724.010) shall be entitled to the remedies specified therein.
Amended by Stats. 1995, Ch. 583, Sec. 1. Effective January 1, 1996.

Section 697.370 - Release or subordination
(a) The judgment creditor may do either of the following:
  (1) Release from the judgment lien all or a part of the real property subject to the lien.
  (2) Subordinate to another lien or encumbrance the judgment lien on all or a part of the real property subject to the judgment lien.
(b) A release or subordination is sufficient if it is executed by the judgment creditor in the same manner as an acknowledgment of satisfaction of judgment and contains all of the following:
  (1) A description of the real property being released or on which the lien is being subordinated. If the judgment debtor does not have an interest of record in the real property, the release or subordination shall show the name of the record owner. If all of the real property of the judgment debtor in a county in which the lien is recorded is being released from the judgment lien, or if the judgment debtor has no known interest in any real property in that county, the release shall, in lieu of containing a description of the property being released, contain a statement substantially as follows: "This is a release from the judgment lien described herein of all of the interests in real property in ____ County presently owned or hereafter acquired of the herein named judgment debtor subject to the lien."
  (2) The date the judgment lien was created and where in the records of the county the abstract of judgment or certified copy of the judgment was recorded to create the lien.
  (3) The title of the court where the judgment is entered and the cause and number of the action.
  (4) The date of entry of the judgment and of any subsequent renewals and where entered in the records of the court.
  (5) The name and address of the judgment creditor, the judgment creditor's assignee, if any, and the judgment debtor whose interest in real property is released from the judgment lien or with respect to whom the judgment lien is subordinated.
(c) A release or subordination substantially complying with the requirements of this section is effective even though it contains minor errors that are not seriously misleading.
(d) The execution of a release or subordination of a judgment lien pursuant to this section does not release or subordinate the judgment lien as to judgment debtors not named in the release pursuant to paragraph (5) of subdivision (b).
Amended by Stats. 1987, Ch. 254, Sec. 1.

Section 697.380 - Priorities of liens
(a) As used in this section:

(1) "Installment judgment lien" means a judgment lien created under Section 697.320.
(2) "Lump-sum judgment lien" means a judgment lien created under Section 697. 310.
(b) Except as otherwise provided by law, the rules stated in this section govern the priorities of judgment liens on real property.
(c) A lump-sum judgment lien has priority over any other lump-sum judgment lien thereafter created.
(d) A lump-sum judgment lien has priority over an installment judgment lien as to all of the following:
(1) Installments that mature on the installment judgment after the lump-sum judgment lien is created.
(2) Interest that accrues on the installment judgment after the lump-sum judgment lien is created.
(3) Costs that are added to the installment judgment after the lump-sum judgment lien is created.
(e) An installment judgment lien has priority over a lump-sum judgment lien as to all of the following:
(1) Installments that have matured on the installment judgment before the lump-sum judgment lien is created.
(2) Interest that has accrued on the installment judgment before the lump-sum judgment lien is created.
(3) Costs that have been added to the installment judgment before the lump-sum judgment lien is created.
(f) If an installment judgment lien has been created and another installment judgment lien is thereafter created, the first installment judgment lien has priority over the second installment judgment lien as to the installments that have matured on the judgment at the time the second installment judgment lien is created, the interest that has accrued prior to that time on the judgment, and the costs that have been added prior to that time to the judgment pursuant to Chapter 5 (commencing with Section 685.010) of Division 1. Thereafter, priorities are determined by the time at which each installment matures on a judgment, the time the interest accrues on a judgment, and the time costs are added to a judgment pursuant to Chapter 5 (commencing with Section 685.010) of Division 1.
(g) For the purposes of this section, if two judgment liens attach to the same property at the same time under subdivision (b) of Section 697.340 (after-acquired property), the judgment lien that was first created has priority as to all amounts that are due and payable on that judgment at the time the property is acquired.
Added by Stats. 1982, Ch. 1364, Sec. 2. Operative July 1, 1983, by Sec. 3 of Ch. 1364.

Section 697.390 - Interest subject to lien transferred or encumbered without satisfying or extinguishing lien
If an interest in real property that is subject to a judgment lien is transferred or encumbered without satisfying or extinguishing the judgment lien:
(a) The interest transferred or encumbered remains subject to a judgment lien created pursuant to Section 697.310 in the same amount as if the interest had not been transferred or encumbered.
(b) The interest transferred or encumbered remains subject to a judgment lien created pursuant to Section 697.320 in the amount of the lien at the time of transfer or encumbrance plus interest thereafter accruing on such amount.
Amended by Stats. 1984, Ch. 538, Sec. 19.

Section 697.400 - Recordation of acknowledgment of satisfaction
(a) The judgment creditor, judgment debtor, or owner of real property subject to a judgment lien on real property created under Section 697.310, may record in the office of the county recorder an acknowledgment of satisfaction of judgment executed as provided in Section 724.060 or a court clerk's certificate of satisfaction of judgment issued pursuant to Section 724.100. Upon such recording, the judgment lien created under the judgment that has been satisfied is extinguished as a matter of record.
(b) The judgment creditor, judgment debtor, or owner of real property subject to a judgment lien on real property created under Section 697.320, may record in the office of the county recorder an acknowledgment of satisfaction of matured installments under an installment judgment if the acknowledgment is executed as provided in Section 724.250. Upon such recording, the judgment lien is extinguished as a matter of record to the extent of the satisfied installments described in the acknowledgment of satisfaction.
(c) The judgment creditor, the judgment debtor, or the owner of real property subject to a judgment lien, including a property owner described in Section 697.410, may record in the office of the county recorder a release or subordination of a judgment lien on real property if the release or subordination is executed as provided in Section 697.370.
Added by Stats. 1982, Ch. 1364, Sec. 2. Operative July 1, 1983, by Sec. 3 of Ch. 1364.

Section 697.410 - Demand for recordable document releasing lien by erroneously identified property owner
(a) If a recorded abstract of a money judgment or certified copy of a money judgment appears to create a judgment lien on real property of a person who is not the judgment debtor because the name of the property owner is the same as or similar to that of the judgment debtor, the erroneously identified property owner may deliver to the judgment creditor a written demand for a recordable document releasing the lien. The demand shall be accompanied by proof to the satisfaction of the judgment creditor that the property owner is not the judgment debtor and that the property is not subject to enforcement of the judgment against the judgment debtor.
(b) Within 15 days after receipt of the property owner's demand and proof satisfactory to the judgment creditor that the property owner is not the judgment debtor and that the property is not subject to enforcement of the judgment, the judgment creditor shall deliver to the property owner a recordable document releasing the lien on the property of such owner. If the judgment creditor improperly fails to deliver a recordable document releasing the lien within the time allowed, the judgment creditor is liable to the property owner for all damages sustained by reason of such failure and shall also forfeit one hundred dollars ($100) to the property owner.
(c) If the judgment creditor does not deliver a recordable document pursuant to subdivision (b), the property owner may apply to the court on noticed motion for an order releasing the judgment lien on the property of such owner. Notice of motion shall be served on the judgment creditor. Service shall be made personally or by mail. Upon presentation of evidence to the satisfaction of the court that the property owner is not the judgment debtor and that the property is not subject to enforcement of the judgment, the court shall order the judgment creditor to prepare and deliver a recordable document releasing the lien or shall itself order the release of the judgment lien on the property of such owner. The court order may be recorded in the office of the county recorder with the same effect as the recordable document demanded by the property owner.
(d) The court shall award reasonable attorney's fees to the prevailing party in any proceeding maintained pursuant to this section.
(e) The damages provided by this section are not in derogation of any other damages or penalties to which an aggrieved person may be entitled by law.
Added by Stats. 1982, Ch. 1364, Sec. 2. Operative July 1, 1983, by Sec. 3 of Ch. 1364.

Article 3 - JUDGMENT LIEN ON PERSONAL PROPERTY

Section 697.510 - Creation of lien; duration; continuation statement; extinguished; order releasing lien; attorney's fees
(a) A judgment lien on personal property described in Section 697.530 is created by filing a notice of judgment lien in the office of the Secretary of State pursuant to this article. A judgment lien may be created under this article only if the judgment is a money judgment that was first entered in this state after June 30, 1983. Except as provided in subdivision (b) of Section 697.540, a judgment lien may not be created under this article if the money judgment is payable in installments unless all of the installments under the judgment have become due and payable at the time the notice of judgment lien is filed.
(b) Except as otherwise provided in subdivision (c), (e), or (g), the judgment lien continues for five years from the date of filing.
(c) The effectiveness of a filed judgment lien lapses on the expiration of the period described in subdivision (b) unless, before the lapse, a continuation statement is filed pursuant to subdivision (d). Upon lapse, the judgment lien created by the filing of a notice pursuant to subdivision (a) ceases to be effective.

(d) A continuation statement may be filed only within the six-month period prior to the expiration of the five-year period specified in subdivision (b).

(e) A continuation statement that is not filed within the six-month period prescribed by subdivision (d) is ineffective. Upon timely filing of a continuation statement, the effectiveness of the initial notice of judgment lien continues for a period of five years commencing on the day on which the notice of judgment lien would have become ineffective in the absence of the filing. Upon the expiration of the five-year period, the notice of judgment lien lapses in the same manner as provided in subdivision (c), unless, before the lapse, another continuation statement is filed pursuant to subdivision (d). Succeeding continuation statements may be filed in the same manner to continue the effectiveness of the initial notice of judgment lien.

(f) For purposes of this section, "continuation statement" means an amendment of a notice of judgment lien that does both of the following:

(1) Identifies, by its file number, the initial notice of judgment lien to which it relates.

(2) Indicates that it is a continuation statement for, or that it is filed to continue the effectiveness of, the identified notice of judgment lien.

(g)

(1) Notwithstanding any other provision of this section, the lien created by this section is extinguished at the earliest to occur of the following:

(A) The money judgment is satisfied.

(B) The period of enforceability of the judgment, including any extension thereof pursuant to Article 2 (commencing with Section 683.110) of Chapter 3 of Division 1, terminates.

(C) The judgment lien is terminated or released.

(2) If the lien created by this section is extinguished, the judgment creditor shall file a statement of release within 20 days after the judgment creditor receives an authenticated demand from the judgment debtor. For the purposes of this subdivision, "authenticated demand" means either a signed written demand or an executed or otherwise encrypted demand delivered electronically that identifies the judgment debtor and the demand for a statement of release.

(h) If a judgment creditor does not file a statement of release pursuant to subdivision (g), the person who made the demand may apply to the court on noticed motion for an order releasing the judgment lien. Notice of the motion shall be filed in the county where the judgment was rendered and notice of the motion shall be served on the judgment creditor. Service shall be made personally or by mail. Upon presentation of evidence to the satisfaction of the court that the judgment lien has been extinguished pursuant to subdivision (g), the court shall order the judgment creditor to prepare and file the statement of release or shall itself order the release of the judgment lien. The court order may be filed in the office of the Secretary of State and shall have the same effect as the statement of release demanded under subdivision (g).

(i) The court shall award reasonable attorney's fees to the prevailing party in any action or proceeding maintained pursuant to this section.

(j) Nothing in this section is in derogation of any other relief to which an aggrieved person may be entitled by law.

(k) The fees for filing and indexing a record under this section, or for responding to a request for information from the filing office, are as set forth in Section 9525 of the Commercial Code.

(l) The provisions of Sections 9522 and 9523 of the Commercial Code shall apply to a notice of judgment lien to the same extent as to a filed financing statement.

(m) Terms for which definitions are not set forth in Division 1 (commencing with Section 680.010) have the definitions set forth in the Commercial Code.

Amended by Stats 2009 ch 410 (AB 121),s 1, eff. 1/1/2010.

Section 697.520 - Lien created as alternative or in addition to lien credited by levy under writ of execution

A judgment lien on personal property may be created pursuant to this article as an alternative or in addition to a lien created by levy under a writ of execution pursuant to Chapter 3 (commencing with Section 699.010) or by use of an enforcement procedure provided by Chapter 6 (commencing with Section 708.010).

Added by Stats. 1982, Ch. 1364, Sec. 2. Operative July 1, 1983, by Sec. 3 of Ch. 1364.

Section 697.530 - Interests in personal property

(a) A judgment lien on personal property is a lien on all interests in the following personal property that are subject to enforcement of the money judgment against the judgment debtor pursuant to Article 1 (commencing with Section 695.010) of Chapter 1 at the time when the lien is created if the personal property is, at that time, any of the following:

(1) Accounts receivable, and the judgment debtor is located in this state.

(2) Tangible chattel paper, as defined in paragraph (79) of subdivision (a) of Section 9102 of the Commercial Code, and the judgment debtor is located in this state.

(3) Equipment, located within this state.

(4) Farm products, located within this state.

(5) Inventory, located within this state.

(6) Negotiable documents of title, located within this state.

(b) If any interest in personal property on which a judgment lien could be created under subdivision (a) is acquired after the judgment lien was created, the judgment lien attaches to the interest at the time it is acquired.

(c) To the extent provided by Section 697.620, a judgment lien on personal property continues on the proceeds received upon the sale, collection, or other disposition of the property subject to the judgment lien.

(d) Notwithstanding any other provision of this section, the judgment lien does not attach to:

(1) A vehicle or vessel required to be registered with the Department of Motor Vehicles or a mobilehome or commercial coach required to be registered pursuant to the Health and Safety Code.

(2) As-extracted collateral, as defined in paragraph (6) of subdivision (a) of Section 9102 of the Commercial Code, and timber to be cut.

(3) The inventory of a retail merchant held for sale except to the extent that the inventory of the retail merchant consists of durable goods having a unit retail value of at least five hundred dollars ($500). For the purposes of this paragraph, "retail merchant" does not include either of the following:

(A) A person whose sales for resale exceeded 75 percent in dollar volume of the person's total sales of all goods during the 12 months preceding the filing of the notice of judgment lien on personal property.

(B) A cooperative association organized pursuant to Chapter 1 (commencing with Section 54001) of Division 20 of the Food and Agricultural Code (agricultural cooperative associations) or Part 3 (commencing with Section 13200) of Division 3 of Title 1 of the Corporations Code (Fish Marketing Act).

(e) If property subject to a lien under this article becomes a fixture, as defined in paragraph (41) of subdivision (a) of Section 9102 of the Commercial Code, the judgment lien on that property is extinguished.

(f) Notwithstanding the filing of a notice of judgment lien, subject to the provisions of Chapter 6 (commencing with Section 708.010), a person obligated on an account receivable or chattel paper is authorized to pay or compromise the amount without notice to or consent of the judgment creditor unless and until there is a levy pursuant to Chapter 3 (commencing with Section 699.010).

(g) For purposes of this section, whether a person is located in this state is determined in accordance with Section 9307 of the Commercial Code, except that the location of a registered organization, as defined in paragraph (71) of subdivision (a) of Section 9102 of the Commercial Code, that is organized under the law of another state is determined without regard to subdivision (e) of Section 9307 of the Commercial Code.
Amended by Stats 2013 ch 531 (AB 502),s 6, eff. 1/1/2014, op. 7/1/2014.
Amended by Stats 2009 ch 153 (AB 1549),s 1, eff. 1/1/2010.
EFFECTIVE 7/01/2001. Amended October 10, 1999 (Bill Number: SB 45) (Chapter 991).

Section 697.540 - Amount of lien

(a) Except as otherwise provided by statute, a judgment lien on personal property is a lien for the amount required to satisfy the money judgment.
(b) A judgment lien on personal property created under a money judgment payable in installments pursuant to Section 117 or 582.5 of this code or pursuant to Section 16380 of the Vehicle Code is in the full amount required to satisfy the judgment, but the judgment lien may not be enforced for the amount of unmatured installments unless the court so orders.
Amended by Stats. 1998, Ch. 931, Sec. 92. Effective September 28, 1998.

Section 697.550 - Requirements of notice of judgment lien

The notice of judgment lien on personal property shall be executed under oath by the judgment creditor's attorney if the judgment creditor has an attorney of record or, if the judgment creditor does not have an attorney of record, by the judgment creditor and shall contain the following information:
(a) The name and mailing address of the judgment creditor.
(b) The name and last known mailing address of the judgment debtor.
(c) A statement that: "All property subject to enforcement of a money judgment against the judgment debtor to which a judgment lien on personal property may attach under Section 697.530 of the Code of Civil Procedure is subject to this judgment lien."
(d) The title of the court where the judgment is entered and the cause and number of the action.
(e) The date of entry of the judgment and of any subsequent renewals and where entered in the records of the court.
(f) The amount required to satisfy the judgment at the date of the notice.
(g) The date of the notice.
Added by Stats. 1982, Ch. 1364, Sec. 2. Operative July 1, 1983, by Sec. 3 of Ch. 1364.

Section 697.560 - Service of copy of notice on judgment debtor

At the time of filing the notice of judgment lien on personal property or promptly thereafter, the judgment creditor shall serve a copy of the notice of judgment lien on the judgment debtor. Service shall be made personally or by mail. The failure to comply with this requirement does not affect the validity of the judgment lien.
Added by Stats. 1982, Ch. 1364, Sec. 2. Operative July 1, 1983, by Sec. 3 of Ch. 1364.

Section 697.570 - Filing notice

Upon presentation of a notice of judgment lien on personal property for filing and tender of the filing fee to the office of the Secretary of State, the notice of judgment lien shall be filed, marked, and indexed in the same manner as a financing statement. The fee for filing in the office of the Secretary of State is the same as the fee for filing a financing statement in the standard form. A notice shall not be filed if it is presented for filing more than 10 days after the date of the notice.
Added by Stats. 1982, Ch. 1364, Sec. 2. Operative July 1, 1983, by Sec. 3 of Ch. 1364.

Section 697.580 - Certificate issued by Secretary of State

(a) Upon the request of any person, the Secretary of State shall issue a certificate showing whether there is on file in that office on the date and hour stated therein any notice of judgment lien on personal property filed against the property of a particular person named in the request. If a notice of judgment lien is on file, the certificate shall state the date and hour of filing of each such notice and any notice affecting any such notice of judgment lien and the name and address of the judgment creditor.
(b) Upon request, the Secretary of State shall furnish a copy of any notice of judgment lien or notice affecting a notice of judgment lien. The certificate shall be issued as part of a combined certificate pursuant to Section 9528 of the Commercial Code, and the fee for the certificate and copies shall be in accordance with that section.
EFFECTIVE 7/1/2001. Amended October 10, 1999 (Bill Number: SB 45) (Chapter 991).

Section 697.590 - Conflicting interests

(a) As used in this section:
  (1) "Filing" means:
    (A) With respect to a judgment lien on personal property, the filing of a notice of judgment lien in the office of the Secretary of State to create a judgment lien on personal property under this article.
    (B) With respect to a security interest or agricultural lien, as defined in paragraph (5) of subdivision (a) of Section 9102 of the Commercial Code, the filing of a financing statement pursuant to Division 9 (commencing with Section 9101) of the Commercial Code.
  (2) "Perfection" means perfection of a security interest or agricultural lien pursuant to Division 9 (commencing with Section 9101) of the Commercial Code.
  (3) "Personal property" means:
    (A) With respect to a judgment lien on personal property, the property to which a judgment lien has attached pursuant to this article.
    (B) With respect to a security interest, the collateral subject to a security interest pursuant to Division 9 (commencing with Section 9101) of the Commercial Code.
    (C) With respect to an agricultural lien, the farm products subject to an agricultural lien pursuant to Division 9 (commencing with Section 9101) of the Commercial Code.
  (4) "Purchase money security interest" has the same meaning as used in Section 9103 of the Commercial Code.
(b) Except as provided in subdivisions (d), (e), (g), and (h), priority between a judgment lien on personal property and a conflicting security interest or agricultural lien in the same personal property shall be determined according to this subdivision. Conflicting interests rank according to priority in time of filing or perfection. In the case of a judgment lien, priority dates from the time filing is first made covering the personal property. In the case of a security interest or agricultural lien, priority dates from the earlier of the time a filing is first made covering the personal property or the time the security interest or agricultural lien is first perfected, if there is no period thereafter when there is neither filing nor perfection.
(c) For the purposes of subdivision (b), a date of filing or perfection as to personal property is also a date of filing or perfection as to proceeds.
(d) A purchase money security interest has priority over a conflicting judgment lien on the same personal property or its proceeds if the purchase money security interest is perfected at the time the judgment debtor, as a debtor under the security agreement, receives possession of the personal property or within 20 days thereafter.
(e) If a purchase money security interest in inventory has priority over a judgment lien pursuant to subdivision (d) and a conflicting security interest has priority over the purchase money security interest in the same inventory pursuant to Section 9324 of the Commercial Code, the conflicting security interest also has priority over the judgment lien on the inventory subject to the purchase money security interest, notwithstanding that the conflicting security interest would not otherwise have priority over the judgment lien.

(f) A judgment lien that has attached to personal property, and that is also subordinate under subdivision (b) to a security interest in the same personal property, is subordinate to the security interest only to the extent that the security interest secures advances made before the judgment lien attached or within 45 days thereafter or made without knowledge of the judgment lien or pursuant to a commitment entered into without knowledge of the judgment lien. For the purpose of this subdivision, a secured party shall be deemed not to have knowledge of a judgment lien on personal property until (1) the judgment creditor serves a copy of the notice of judgment lien on the secured party personally or by mail and (2) the secured party has knowledge of the judgment lien on personal property, as "knowledge" is defined in Section 1201 of the Commercial Code. If service on the secured party is by mail, it shall be sent to the secured party at the address shown in the financing statement or security agreement.

(g) A perfected agricultural lien on personal property has priority over a judgment lien on the same personal property if the statute creating the agricultural lien so provides.

(h) A security interest in personal property perfected by the filing of a financing statement under the law of a jurisdiction other than this state, or perfected by another method pursuant to the law of a jurisdiction other than this state, has priority over a judgment lien in the same personal property.

Amended by Stats 2009 ch 153 (AB 1549),s 2, eff. 1/1/2010.
EFFECTIVE 7/01/2001. Amended October 10, 1999 (Bill Number: SB 45) (Chapter 991).

Section 697.600 - Priority of lien

(a) A judgment lien on personal property has priority over any other judgment lien thereafter created on the property.

(b) For the purpose of this section, if two or more judgment liens attach to after-acquired property at the same time under subdivision (b) of Section 697.530, the judgment lien first filed has priority.

Added by Stats. 1982, Ch. 1364, Sec. 2. Operative July 1, 1983, by Sec. 3 of Ch. 1364.

Section 697.610 - Continuation of lien notwithstanding sale or exchange of property

Except as provided in Sections 9617 and 9622 of the Commercial Code, a judgment lien on personal property continues notwithstanding the sale, exchange, or other disposition of the property, unless the person receiving the property is one of the following:

(a) A buyer in ordinary course of business (as defined in Section 1201 of the Commercial Code) who, under Section 9320 of the Commercial Code, would take free of a security interest created by the seller.

(b) A lessee in ordinary course of business (as defined in paragraph (15) of subdivision (a) of Section 10103 of the Commercial Code) who, under Section 9321 of the Commercial Code, would take free of a security interest created by the lessor.

(c) A holder to whom a negotiable document of title has been duly negotiated within the meaning of Section 7501 of the Commercial Code.

(d) A purchaser of chattel paper who, under Section 9330 of the Commercial Code, would have priority over another security interest in the chattel paper.

EFFECTIVE 7/1/2001. Amended October 10, 1999 (Bill Number: SB 45) (Chapter 991).

Section 697.620 - Continuation of lien in proceeds

(a) As used in this section:

(1) "Cash proceeds" means money, checks, deposit accounts, and the like.

(2) "Proceeds" means identifiable cash proceeds received upon the sale, exchange, collection, or other disposition of property subject to a judgment lien on personal property.

(b) Except as provided in subdivision (c), the judgment lien on personal property continues in the proceeds with the same priority.

(c) In the event of insolvency proceedings (as defined in Section 1201 of the Commercial Code) instituted by or against the judgment debtor, the judgment lien continues under subdivision (b) only in the following proceeds:

(1) Proceeds in a separate deposit account containing only proceeds.

(2) Proceeds in the form of money which are neither commingled with other money nor deposited in a deposit account prior to the insolvency proceedings.

(3) Proceeds in the form of checks and the like which are not deposited in a deposit account prior to the insolvency proceedings.

Added by Stats. 1982, Ch. 1364, Sec. 2. Operative July 1, 1983, by Sec. 3 of Ch. 1364.

Section 697.640 - Acknowledgment of satisfaction

(a) The judgment creditor, judgment debtor, owner of property subject to a judgment lien on personal property created under the judgment, or a person having a security interest in or a lien on the property subject to the judgment lien, may file in the office of the Secretary of State an acknowledgment of satisfaction of judgment executed as provided in Section 724.060 or a court clerk's certificate of satisfaction of judgment issued pursuant to Section 724.100, together with a statement containing the name of the judgment creditor, the name and address of the judgment debtor, and the file number of the notice of judgment lien. Upon such filing, the judgment lien created under the judgment that has been satisfied is extinguished as a matter of record. The fee for filing the acknowledgment or certificate is the same as the fee for filing a termination statement under Section 9404 of the Commercial Code.

(b) The filing officer shall treat an acknowledgment of satisfaction of judgment, or court clerk's certificate of satisfaction of judgment, and statement filed pursuant to this section in the same manner as a termination statement filed pursuant to Section 9525 of the Commercial Code.

EFFECTIVE 7/1/2001. Amended October 10, 1999 (Bill Number: SB 45) (Chapter 991).

Section 697.650 - Release or subordination

(a) The judgment creditor may by a writing do any of the following:

(1) Release the judgment lien on all the personal property subject to the lien of a sole judgment debtor or of all the judgment debtors.

(2) If the notice of judgment lien names more than one judgment debtor, release the judgment lien on all the personal property subject to the lien of one or more but of less than all the judgment debtors.

(3) Release the judgment lien on all or a part of the personal property subject to the lien.

(4) Subordinate to a security interest or other lien or encumbrance the judgment lien on all or a part of the personal property subject to the judgment lien.

(b) A statement of release or subordination is sufficient if it is signed by the judgment creditor and contains the name and address of the judgment debtor, the file number of the notice of judgment lien, and wording appropriate to bring the statement within one of the paragraphs of subdivision (a). In the case of a release under paragraph (3) of subdivision (a), the statement of release shall also describe the property being released. In the case of a subordination under paragraph (4) of subdivision (a), the statement of subordination shall also describe the property on which the judgment lien is being subordinated and describe the security interest or other lien or encumbrance to which the judgment lien is being subordinated.

(c) The filing officer shall treat the filing of a statement of release pursuant to paragraph (1) of subdivision (a) of this section in the same manner as a termination statement filed pursuant to Sections 9513 and 9519 of the Commercial Code. The filing officer shall treat the filing of a statement of release pursuant to paragraph (2) of subdivision (a) of this section in the same manner as a comparable amendment filed pursuant to Sections 9512 and 9519 of the Commercial Code. The filing officer shall treat the filing of a statement of release pursuant to paragraph (3) of subdivision (a) of this section and the filing of a statement of subordination filed pursuant to paragraph (4) of subdivision (a) of this section in the same manner as a statement of release filed pursuant to Sections 9512 and 9519 of the Commercial Code.

(d) The fee for filing the statement is the same as that provided in Section 9525 of the Commercial Code.
EFFECTIVE 7/1/2001. Amended October 10, 1999 (Bill Number: SB 45) (Chapter 991).

Section 697.660 - Filing statement releasing lien on property of erroneously identified property owner

(a) If a notice of judgment lien on personal property filed in the office of the Secretary of State appears to create a judgment lien on personal property of a person who is not the judgment debtor because the name of the property owner is the same as or similar to that of the judgment debtor, the erroneously identified property owner or a person having a security interest in or a lien on the property may deliver to the judgment creditor a written demand that the judgment creditor file in the office of the Secretary of State a statement releasing the lien as to the property of such owner. The demand shall be accompanied by proof to the satisfaction of the judgment creditor that the property owner is not the judgment debtor and that the property is not subject to enforcement of the judgment against the judgment debtor.
(b) Within 15 days after receipt of the demand and proof satisfactory to the judgment creditor that the property owner is not the judgment debtor and that the property is not subject to enforcement of the judgment, the judgment creditor shall file in the office of the Secretary of State a statement releasing the lien on the property of such owner. If the judgment creditor improperly fails to file the statement of release within the time allowed, the judgment creditor is liable to the person who made the demand for all damages sustained by reason of such failure and shall also forfeit one hundred dollars ($100) to such person.
(c) If the judgment creditor does not file a statement of release pursuant to subdivision (b), the person who made the demand may apply to the court on noticed motion for an order releasing the judgment lien on the property of such owner. Notice of motion shall be served on the judgment creditor. Service shall be made personally or by mail. Upon presentation of evidence to the satisfaction of the court that the property owner is not the judgment debtor and that the property is not subject to enforcement of the judgment, the court shall order the judgment creditor to prepare and file the statement of release or shall itself order the release of the judgment lien on the property of such owner. The court order may be filed in the office of the Secretary of State with the same effect as the statement of release demanded under subdivision (a).
(d) The court shall award reasonable attorney's fees to the prevailing party in any action or proceeding maintained pursuant to this section.
(e) The damages provided by this section are not in derogation of any other damages or penalties to which an aggrieved person may be entitled by law.
(f) The fee for filing a statement of release or court order under this section is the same as that provided in Section 9525 of the Commercial Code.
EFFECTIVE 7/1/2001. Amended October 10, 1999 (Bill Number: SB 45) (Chapter 991).

Section 697.670 - Forms

(a) The Secretary of State may prescribe, provided that a cost-savings would be achieved thereby:
    (1) The forms for the notice of judgment lien on personal property and the statement of continuation, release, or subordination provided for in this article.
    (2) The form for the statement provided for in Section 697.640 and the situations when that form is required or is not required.
(b) A form prescribed by the Secretary of State for a notice or statement pursuant to subdivision (a) is deemed to comply with this article and supersedes any requirements specified in this article for the notice or statement.
Amended by Stats 2009 ch 410 (AB 121),s 2, eff. 1/1/2010.

Article 4 - EXECUTION LIEN

Section 697.710 - Generally

A levy on property under a writ of execution creates an execution lien on the property from the time of levy until the expiration of two years after the date of issuance of the writ unless the judgment is sooner satisfied.
Added by Stats. 1982, Ch. 1364, Sec. 2. Operative July 1, 1983, by Sec. 3 of Ch. 1364.

Section 697.720 - Interest transferred or encumbered subject to lien

Subject to Section 701.630, if an interest in real property subject to an execution lien is transferred or encumbered, the interest transferred or encumbered remains subject to the lien after the transfer or encumbrance.
Added by Stats. 1982, Ch. 1364, Sec. 2. Operative July 1, 1983, by Sec. 3 of Ch. 1364.

Section 697.730 - Tangible personal property subject to lien

(a) Subject to Section 701.630 and except as provided in subdivision (b), if tangible personal property subject to an execution lien is in the custody of a levying officer and is transferred or encumbered, the property remains subject to the lien after the transfer or encumbrance.
(b) If a levy upon tangible personal property of a going business is made by the levying officer placing a keeper in charge of the business, a purchaser or lessee of property subject to the execution lien takes the property free of the execution lien if the purchaser or lessee is one of the following:
    (1) A buyer in ordinary course of business (as defined in Section 1201 of the Commercial Code) who, under Section 9320 of the Commercial Code, would take free of a security interest created by his or her seller.
    (2) A lessee in ordinary course of business (as defined in paragraph (15) of subdivision (a) of Section 10103 of the Commercial Code) who, under Section 9321 of the Commercial Code, would take free of a security interest created by the lessor.
EFFECTIVE 7/1/2001. Amended October 10, 1999 (Bill Number: SB 45) (Chapter 991).

Section 697.740 - Transfer or encumbrance of personal property subject to lien

Except as provided in Sections 9617 and 9622 of the Commercial Code and in Section 701.630, if personal property subject to an execution lien is not in the custody of a levying officer and the property is transferred or encumbered, the property remains subject to the lien after the transfer or encumbrance except where the transfer or encumbrance is made to one of the following persons:
(a) A person who acquires an interest in the property under the law of this state for reasonably equivalent value without knowledge of the lien. For purposes of this subdivision, value is given for a transfer or encumbrance if, in exchange for the transfer or encumbrance, property is transferred or an antecedent debt is secured or satisfied.
(b) A buyer in ordinary course of business (as defined in Section 1201 of the Commercial Code) who, under Section 9320 of the Commercial Code, would take free of a security interest created by the seller or encumbrancer.
(c) A lessee in ordinary course of business (as defined in paragraph (15) of subdivision (a) of Section 10103 of the Commercial Code) or a licensee in the ordinary course of business (as defined in subdivision (a) of Section 9321 of the Commercial Code) who, under Section 9321 of the Commercial Code, would take free of a security interest created by the lessor or the licensor.
(d) A holder in due course (as defined in Section 3302 of the Commercial Code) of a negotiable instrument within the meaning of Section 3104 of the Commercial Code.
(e) A holder to whom a negotiable document of title has been duly negotiated within the meaning of Section 7501 of the Commercial Code.
(f) A protected purchaser (as defined in Section 8303 of the Commercial Code) of a security or a person entitled to the benefits of Section 8502 or 8510 of the Commercial Code.
(g) A purchaser of chattel paper who gives new value and takes possession of the chattel paper in good faith and in the ordinary course of the purchaser's business or a purchaser of an instrument who gives value and takes possession of the instrument in good faith.
(h) A holder of a purchase money security interest (as defined in Section 9103 of the Commercial Code).
(i) A collecting bank holding a security interest in items being collected, accompanying documents and proceeds, pursuant to Section 4210 of the Commercial Code.

(j) A person who acquires any right or interest in letters of credit, advices of credit, or money.

(k) A person who acquires any right or interest in property subject to a certificate of title statute of another jurisdiction under the law of which indication of a security interest on the certificate of title is required as a condition of perfection of the security interest.

EFFECTIVE 7/1/2001. Amended October 10, 1999 (Bill Number: SB 45) (Chapter 991).

Section 697.750 - Transfer or encumbrance of growing crops, timber to be cut or minerals

Notwithstanding Section 697.740, except as provided in Section 9617 of the Commercial Code and in Section 701.630, if (1) growing crops, (2) timber to be cut, or (3) minerals or the like (including oil or gas) to be extracted or accounts receivable resulting from the sale thereof at wellhead or minehead are subject to an execution lien and are transferred or encumbered, the property remains subject to the execution lien after the transfer or encumbrance.

EFFECTIVE 7/1/2001. Amended October 10, 1999 (Bill Number: SB 45) (Chapter 991).

Article 5 - OTHER LIENS CREATED BY ENFORCEMENT PROCESS

Section 697.910 - Applicability of article

This article applies to liens created by any of the following:

(a) An examination proceeding as provided in Section 708.110, 708.120, or 708.205.

(b) A creditor's suit as provided in Section 708.250.

(c) A charging order as provided in Section 708.320.

Added by Stats. 1982, Ch. 1364, Sec. 2. Operative July 1, 1983, by Sec. 3 of Ch. 1364.

Section 697.920 - Transfer or encumbrance of property subject to lien

Except as provided in Section 9617 of the Commercial Code and in Section 701.630, a lien described in Section 697.910 continues on property subject to the lien, notwithstanding the transfer or encumbrance of the property subject to the lien, unless the transfer or encumbrance is made to a person listed in Section 697.740.

EFFECTIVE 7/1/2001. Amended October 10, 1999 (Bill Number: SB 45) (Chapter 991).

Chapter 3 - EXECUTION

Article 1 - GENERAL PROVISIONS

Section 699.010 - Generally

Except as otherwise provided by statute, this chapter governs enforcement of a money judgment by a writ of execution.

Added by Stats. 1982, Ch. 1364, Sec. 2. Operative July 1, 1983, by Sec. 3 of Ch. 1364.

Section 699.020 - Payment of debt to person indebted to judgment debtor

At any time after delivery of a writ of execution to a levying officer and before its return, a person indebted to the judgment debtor may pay to the levying officer the amount of the debt or so much thereof as is necessary to satisfy the money judgment. The levying officer shall give a receipt for the amount paid and such receipt is a discharge for the amount paid.

Added by Stats. 1982, Ch. 1364, Sec. 2. Operative July 1, 1983, by Sec. 3 of Ch. 1364.

Section 699.030 - Personal property located in private place of judgment debtor

If personal property sought to be levied upon is located in a private place of the judgment debtor:

(a) The levying officer making the levy shall demand delivery of the property by the judgment debtor and shall advise the judgment debtor that the judgment debtor may be liable for costs and attorney's fees incurred in any further proceedings to obtain delivery of the property. If the judgment debtor does not deliver the property, the levying officer shall make no further effort to obtain custody of the property and shall promptly notify the judgment creditor of the failure to obtain custody of the property.

(b) The judgment creditor may apply to the court ex parte, or on noticed motion if the court so directs or a court rule so requires, for an order directing the levying officer to seize the property in the private place. The application may be made whether or not a writ has been issued and whether or not demand has been made pursuant to subdivision (a). The application for the order shall describe with particularity both the property sought to be levied upon, and the place where it is to be found, according to the best knowledge, information, and belief of the judgment creditor. The court may not issue the order unless the judgment creditor establishes that there is probable cause to believe that property sought to be levied upon is located in the place described. The levying officer making the levy, at the time delivery of the property pursuant to the order is demanded, shall announce his or her identity, purpose, and authority. If the property is not voluntarily delivered, the levying officer may cause the building or enclosure where the property is believed to be located to be broken open in such manner as the levying officer reasonably believes will cause the least damage, but if the levying officer reasonably believes that entry and seizure of the property will involve a substantial risk of death or serious bodily harm to any person, the levying officer shall refrain from entering and shall promptly make a return to the court setting forth the reasons for believing that the risk exists. In such a case, the court shall make such orders as may be appropriate.

Added by Stats. 1982, Ch. 1364, Sec. 2. Operative July 1, 1983, by Sec. 3 of Ch. 1364.

Section 699.040 - Order directing judgment debtor to transfer to levying officer

(a) If a writ of execution is issued, the judgment creditor may apply to the court ex parte, or on noticed motion if the court so directs or a court rule so requires, for an order directing the judgment debtor to transfer to the levying officer either or both of the following:

(1) Possession of the property sought to be levied upon if the property is sought to be levied upon by taking it into custody.

(2) Possession of documentary evidence of title to property of or a debt owed to the judgment debtor that is sought to be levied upon. An order pursuant to this paragraph may be served when the property or debt is levied upon or thereafter.

(b) The court may issue an order pursuant to this section upon a showing of need for the order.

(c) The order shall be personally served on the judgment debtor and shall contain a notice to the judgment debtor that failure to comply with the order may subject the judgment debtor to arrest and punishment for contempt of court.

Added by Stats. 1982, Ch. 1364, Sec. 2. Operative July 1, 1983, by Sec. 3 of Ch. 1364.

Section 699.060 - Release of property levied upon

(a) The levying officer shall release property levied upon when the levying officer receives a written direction to release the property from the judgment creditor's attorney of record or, if the judgment creditor does not have an attorney of record, from the judgment creditor, or when the levying officer receives a certified copy of a court order for release, or when otherwise required to release the property. The release shall include the signature and name of the attorney or judgment creditor issuing the release. The release extinguishes any execution lien or attachment lien in favor of the judgment creditor on the property released.

(b) If the property to be released has been taken into custody under the levy, it shall be released to the person from whom it was taken unless otherwise ordered by the court. If the person does not claim the property to be released, the levying officer shall retain custody of the property and shall serve on the person a notice of where possession of the property may be obtained. Service shall be made personally or by mail. If the person does not claim the property within 30 days after the notice is served, the levying officer shall sell the property in the manner provided by Article 6 (commencing with Section 701.510), other than cash, which does not have a value exceeding its face value. The levying officer shall deposit the proceeds of sale and cash, after first deducting the levying officer's costs, with the county treasurer of the county where the property is located, payable to the order of the person. If the amount deposited is not claimed by the person, or the legal representative of the person, within five years after the deposit is made by making application to the treasurer or other official designated by the county, it shall be paid into the general fund of the county.

(c) If the property to be released has not been taken into custody under the levy, the levying officer shall release the property by issuing a written notice of release and serving it on the person who was served with a copy of the writ and a notice of levy to create the lien. Service shall be made personally or by mail.

(d) If the property to be released was levied upon by recording or filing a copy of the writ and a notice of levy, the levying officer shall record or file a written notice of release in the same office.

(e) The levying officer is not liable for releasing property in accordance with this section nor is any other person liable for acting in conformity with the release.

(f) The written direction to release property specified in subdivision (a) may be transmitted electronically to the levying officer pursuant to Chapter 2 (commencing with Section 263) of Title 4 of Part 1.

Amended by Stats 2010 ch 680 (AB 2394),s 6, eff. 1/1/2011.

Section 699.070 - Preservation of value of property levied on; perishable property

(a) The court may appoint a receiver or order the levying officer to take any action the court orders that is necessary to preserve the value of property levied upon, including but not limited to selling the property, if the court determines that the property is perishable or will greatly deteriorate or greatly depreciate in value or that for some other reason the interests of the parties will be best served by the order. An order may be made under this subdivision upon application of the judgment creditor, the judgment debtor, or a person who has filed a third-party claim pursuant to Division 4 (commencing with Section 720.010). The application shall be made on noticed motion if the court so directs or a court rule so requires. Otherwise, the application may be made ex parte.

(b) If the levying officer determines that property levied upon is extremely perishable or will greatly deteriorate or greatly depreciate in value before a court order pursuant to subdivision (a) could be obtained, the levying officer may take any action necessary to preserve the value of the property or may sell the property. The levying officer is not liable for a determination made in good faith under this subdivision.

(c) Except as otherwise provided by order of the court, a sale of property pursuant to this section shall be made in the manner provided by Article 6 (commencing with Section 701.510) and the proceeds shall be applied to the satisfaction of the money judgment in the manner provided by Article 7 (commencing with Section 701.810). Notwithstanding subdivisions (b) and (d) of Section 701.530, notice of sale shall be posted and served at a reasonable time before the sale, considering the character and condition of the property.

(d) If a receiver is appointed, the court shall fix the daily fee of the receiver and may order the judgment creditor to pay the fees and expenses of the receiver in advance or may direct that the whole or any part of the fees and expenses be paid from the proceeds of any sale of the property. Except as otherwise provided in this section, the provisions of Chapter 5 (commencing with Section 564) and Chapter 5a (commencing with Section 571) of Title 7 govern the appointment, qualifications, powers, rights, and duties of a receiver appointed under this section.

Added by Stats. 1982, Ch. 1364, Sec. 2. Operative July 1, 1983, by Sec. 3 of Ch. 1364.

Section 699.080 - Types of property levied upon by registered process server

(a) A registered process server may levy under a writ of execution on the following types of property:

(1) Real property, pursuant to Section 700.015.

(2) Growing crops, timber to be cut, or minerals or the like including oil and gas, to be extracted or accounts receivable resulting from the sale thereof at the wellhead or minehead, pursuant to Section 700.020.

(3) Personal property in the custody of a levying officer, pursuant to Section 700.050.

(4) Personal property used as a dwelling, pursuant to subdivision (a) of Section 700.080.

(5) Deposit accounts, pursuant to Section 700.140.

(6) Property in a safe-deposit box, pursuant to Section 700.150.

(7) Accounts receivable or general intangibles, pursuant to Section 700.170.

(8) Final money judgments, pursuant to Section 700.190.

(9) Interest of a judgment debtor in personal property in the estate of a decedent, pursuant to Section 700.200.

(b) Before levying under the writ of execution, the registered process server shall cause to be deposited with the levying officer a copy of the writ and the fee, as provided by Section 26721 of the Government Code.

(c) If a registered process server levies on property pursuant to subdivision (a), the registered process server shall do both of the following:

(1) Comply with the applicable levy, posting, and service provisions of Article 4 (commencing with Section 700.010).

(2) Request any third person served to give a garnishee's memorandum to the levying officer in compliance with Section 701.030 on a form provided by the registered process server.

(d) Within five court days after levy under this section, all of the following shall be filed with the levying officer:

(1) The writ of execution.

(2) A proof of service by the registered process server stating the manner of levy performed.

(3) Proof of service of the copy of the writ and notice of levy on other persons, as required by Article 4 (commencing with Section 700.010).

(4) Instructions in writing, as required by the provisions of Section 687.010.

(e) If the fee provided by Section 26721 of the Government Code has been paid, the levying officer shall perform all other duties under the writ as if the levying officer had levied under the writ and shall return the writ to the court. If the registered process server does not comply with subdivisions (b) and (d), the levy is ineffective and the levying officer shall not be required to perform any duties under the writ, and may issue a release for any property sought to be levied upon.

(f) The fee for services of a registered process server under this section is a recoverable cost pursuant to Section 1033.5.

(g) A registered process server may levy more than once under the same writ of execution, provided that the writ is still valid.

Amended by Stats 2016 ch 102 (AB 2211),s 2, eff. 1/1/2017.

Amended by Stats 2007 ch 15 (AB 859),s 3, eff. 1/1/2008.

Amended by Stats 2002 ch 197 (AB 2493),s 3, eff. 1/1/2003.

Section 699.090 - Liability to third person for levy

If property that is required by law to be registered or recorded in the name of the owner is levied upon under a writ of execution and it appears at the time of the levy that the judgment debtor was the registered or record owner of the property and the judgment creditor caused the levy to be made and the lien maintained in good faith and in reliance upon such registered or recorded ownership, neither the judgment creditor, the levying officer, nor the sureties on an undertaking given by the judgment creditor pursuant to Chapter 2 (commencing with Section 720.110) or Chapter 3 (commencing with Section 720.210) of Division 4 is liable to a third person for the levy itself.

Added by Stats. 1982, Ch. 1364, Sec. 2. Operative July 1, 1983, by Sec. 3 of Ch. 1364.

Article 2 - WRIT OF EXECUTION AND NOTICE OF LEVY

Section 699.510 - Issuance of writ

(a) Subject to subdivision (b), after entry of a money judgment, a writ of execution shall be issued by the clerk of the court, upon application of the judgment creditor, and shall be directed to the levying officer in the county where the levy is to be made and to any registered process server. The clerk of the court shall give priority to the application for, and issuance of, writs of execution on orders or judgments for child support and spousal support. A separate writ shall be issued for each county where a levy is to be made. Writs may be issued successively until the money judgment is satisfied, except that a new writ may not be issued for a county until the expiration of 180 days after the issuance of a prior writ for that county unless the prior writ is first returned.

(b) If the judgment creditor seeks a writ of execution to enforce a judgment made, entered, or enforceable pursuant to the Family Code, in addition to the requirements of this article, the judgment creditor shall satisfy the requirements of any applicable provisions of the Family Code.

(c)

(1) The writ of execution shall be issued in the name of the judgment debtor as listed on the judgment, except that the judgment creditor shall omit the name of a judgment debtor from the application for a writ of execution if the liability of that judgment debtor has ceased with regard to the judgment, including either of the following occurrences:

(A) The judgment debtor has obtained a discharge of the judgment pursuant to Title 11 of the United States Code and notice thereof has been filed with the court.

(B) The judgment creditor files an acknowledgment of satisfaction of judgment with regard to the judgment debtor pursuant to Chapter 1 (commencing with Section 724.010) of Division 5.

(2) The writ of execution shall include the additional name or names, and the type of legal entity, by which the judgment debtor is known, as set forth in the affidavit of identity, as defined in Section 680.135, filed by the judgment creditor with the application for issuance of the writ of execution. Prior to the clerk of the court issuing a writ of execution containing any additional name or names by which the judgment debtor is known that are not listed on the judgment, the court shall approve the affidavit of identity. If the court determines, without a hearing or a notice, that the affidavit of identity states sufficient facts upon which the judgment creditor has identified the additional names of the judgment debtor, the court shall authorize the issuance of the writ of execution with the additional name or names.

(d) In any case where the writ of execution lists any name other than that listed on the judgment, the person in possession or control of the levied property, if other than the judgment debtor, shall not pay to the levying officer the amount or deliver the property being levied upon until being notified to do so by the levying officer. The levying officer may not require the person, if other than the judgment debtor, in possession or control of the levied property to pay the amount or deliver the property levied upon until the expiration of 15 days after service of notice of levy.

(e) If a person who is not the judgment debtor has property erroneously subject to an enforcement of judgment proceeding based upon an affidavit of identity, the person shall be entitled to the recovery of reasonable attorney's fees and costs from the judgment creditor incurred in releasing the person's property from a writ of execution, in addition to any other damages or penalties to which an aggrieved person may be entitled to by law, including Division 4 (commencing with Section 720.010).

Amended by Stats 2013 ch 176 (SB 551),s 2, eff. 1/1/2014.
Amended by Stats 2010 ch 680 (AB 2394),s 7, eff. 1/1/2011.
Amended by Stats 2003 ch 17 (AB 308), eff. 7/1/2003.
Amended by Stats 2001 ch 159 (SB 662), s 40, eff. 1/1/2002.
Amended by Stats 2000 ch 808 (AB 1358), s 12.1, eff. 9/28/2000.
See Stats 2000 ch 808 (AB 1358), s 130.1. .

Section 699.520 - Information included in writ

The writ of execution shall require the levying officer to whom it is directed to enforce the money judgment and shall include the following information:

(a) The date of issuance of the writ.

(b) The title of the court in which the judgment is entered and the cause and number of the action.

(c) Whether the judgment is for wages owed, child support, or spousal support. This subdivision shall become operative on September 1, 2020.

(d) The name and address of the judgment creditor and the name and last known address of the judgment debtor. If the judgment debtor is other than a natural person, the type of legal entity shall be stated.

(e) The date of the entry of the judgment and of any subsequent renewals and where entered in the records of the court.

(f) The total amount of the money judgment as entered or renewed, together with costs thereafter added to the judgment pursuant to Section 685.090 and the accrued interest on the judgment from the date of entry or renewal of the judgment to the date of issuance of the writ, reduced by any partial satisfactions and by any amounts no longer enforceable.

(g) The amount required to satisfy the money judgment on the date the writ is issued.

(h) The amount of interest accruing daily on the principal amount of the judgment from the date the writ is issued.

(i) Whether any person has requested notice of sale under the judgment and, if so, the name and mailing address of that person.

(j) The sum of the fees and costs added to the judgment pursuant to Section 6103.5 or Article 6 (commencing with Section 68630) of Chapter 2 of Title 8 of the Government Code, and which is in addition to the amount owing to the judgment creditor on the judgment.

(k) Whether the writ of execution includes any additional names of the judgment debtor pursuant to an affidavit of identity, as defined in Section 680.135.

(l) A statement indicating whether the case is limited or unlimited.

Amended by Stats 2020 ch 370 (SB 1371),s 36, eff. 1/1/2021.
Amended by Stats 2019 ch 552 (SB 616),s 1, eff. 1/1/2020.
Amended by Stats 2010 ch 680 (AB 2394),s 8, eff. 1/1/2011.
Amended by Stats 2000 ch 639 (AB 2405), s 4, eff. 1/1/2001.

Section 699.530 - Execution of writ

(a) Upon delivery of the writ of execution to the levying officer to whom the writ is directed, together with the written instructions of the judgment creditor, the levying officer shall execute the writ in the manner prescribed by law.

(b) The levying officer may not levy upon any property under the writ after the expiration of 180 days from the date the writ was issued.

Added by Stats. 1982, Ch. 1364, Sec. 2. Operative July 1, 1983, by Sec. 3 of Ch. 1364.

Section 699.540 - Notice of levy

The notice of levy required by Article 4 (commencing with Section 700.010) shall inform the person notified of all of the following:

(a) The capacity in which the person is notified.

(b) The property that is levied upon.

(c) The person's rights under the levy, including all of the following:

(1) The right to claim an exemption pursuant to Chapter 4 (commencing with Section 703.010).

(2) The right to make a third-party claim pursuant to Division 4 (commencing with Section 720.010).

(3) The right to, and the limitations of, the automatic exemption pursuant to Section 704.220. This paragraph shall become operative on September 1, 2020.

(d) The person's duties under the levy.

(e) All names listed in the writ of execution pursuant to an affidavit of identity, as defined in Section 680.135, if any.

Amended by Stats 2019 ch 552 (SB 616),s 2, eff. 1/1/2020.
Amended by Stats 2000 ch 639 (AB 2405), s 5, eff. 1/1/2001.

Section 699.545 - Copy of notice of levy served upon third party served upon debtor or other party
A copy of the original notice of levy which has been served upon a third party holding the property sought to be levied upon and the affidavit of identity, as defined in Section 680.135, if any, if served upon the judgment debtor or any other party, shall suffice as the notice of levy to that person.
Amended by Stats 2000 ch 639 (AB 2405), s 6, eff. 1/1/2001.

Section 699.550 - Lien not affected by failure to post, serve or mail copy of writ and notice
In any case where property has been levied upon and, pursuant to a levy, a copy of the writ of execution and a notice of levy are required by statute to be posted or to be served on or mailed to the judgment debtor or other person, failure to post, serve, or mail the copy of the writ and the notice does not affect the execution lien created by the levy. Failure to serve on or mail to the judgment debtor a list of exemptions does not affect the execution lien created by the levy.
Added by Stats. 1982, Ch. 1364, Sec. 2. Operative July 1, 1983, by Sec. 3 of Ch. 1364.

Section 699.560 - Return
(a) Except as provided in subdivisions (b) and (c), the writ expires and the levying officer to whom the writ of execution is delivered shall return the writ to the court, or store the writ as provided in Section 263.6, and file a return with the court reporting the levying officer's actions and an accounting of amounts collected, and costs incurred, at the earliest of the following times:
(1) Two years from the date of issuance of the writ, unless paragraph (1) of subdivision (a) of Section 706.022 is applicable.
(2) Promptly after all of the duties under the writ are performed.
(3) When return is requested in writing by the judgment creditor.
(4) If no levy takes place under the writ within 180 days after its issuance, promptly after the expiration of the 180-day period.
(5) Upon expiration of the time for enforcement of the money judgment.
(b) If a levy has been made under Section 700.200 upon an interest in personal property in the estate of a decedent, the writ shall be returned within the time prescribed in Section 700.200.
(c) If a levy has been made under Section 5103 of the Family Code on the judgment debtor's right to the payment of benefits from an employee pension benefit plan, the writ shall be returned within the time prescribed in that section.
(d) If a levy has been made under the Wage Garnishment Law (Chapter 5 (commencing with Section 706.010)), and the earnings withholding order remains in effect, the writ of execution shall be returned as provided in subdivision (a) and a supplemental return shall be made as provided in Section 706.033.
(e) Subject to the limitations in subdivision (c) of Section 263, a levying officer may electronically file with the court the return, containing the information required by subdivision (a), pursuant to Chapter 2 (commencing with Section 263) of Title 4 of Part 1.
Amended by Stats 2010 ch 680 (AB 2394),s 9, eff. 1/1/2011.

Article 3 - PROPERTY SUBJECT TO EXECUTION

Section 699.710 - Generally
Except as otherwise provided by law, all property that is subject to enforcement of a money judgment pursuant to Article 1 (commencing with Section 695.010) of Chapter 1 is subject to levy under a writ of execution to satisfy a money judgment.
Added by Stats. 1982, Ch. 1364, Sec. 2. Operative July 1, 1983, by Sec. 3 of Ch. 1364.

Section 699.720 - Property not subject to execution
(a) The following types of property are not subject to execution:
(1) An alcoholic beverage license that is transferable under Article 5 (commencing with Section 24070) of Chapter 6 of Division 9 of the Business and Professions Code.
(2) The interest of a partner in a partnership or member in a limited liability company if the partnership or the limited liability company is not a judgment debtor.
(3) A cause of action that is the subject of a pending action or special proceeding.
(4) A judgment in favor of the judgment debtor prior to the expiration of the time for appeal from the judgment or, if an appeal is filed, prior to the final determination of the appeal.
(5) A debt (other than earnings) owing and unpaid by a public entity.
(6) The loan value of an unmatured life insurance, endowment, or annuity policy.
(7) A franchise granted by a public entity and all the rights and privileges of the franchise.
(8) The interest of a trust beneficiary.
(9) A contingent remainder, executory interest, or other interest in property that is not vested.
(10) Property in a guardianship or conservatorship estate.
(b) Nothing in subdivision (a) affects or limits the right of the judgment creditor to apply property to the satisfaction of a money judgment pursuant to any applicable procedure other than execution.
Amended by Stats. 1996, Ch. 57, Sec. 1. Effective June 6, 1996.

Section 699.730 - Judgment lien based on consumer debt
(a) Notwithstanding any other law, the principal place of residence of a judgment debtor is not subject to sale under execution of a judgment lien based on a consumer debt unless the debt was secured by the debtor's principal place of residence at the time it was incurred. As used in this subdivision, "consumer debt" means debt incurred by an individual primarily for personal, family, or household purposes.
(b) Subdivision (a) does not apply to any of the following types of unpaid debts:
(1) Wages or employment benefits.
(2) Taxes.
(3) Child support.
(4) Spousal support.
(5) Fines and fees owed to governmental units.
(6) Tort judgments.
(7)
(A) Debts, other than student loan debt, owed to a financial institution at the time of execution on the judgment lien, if both of the following requirements are met:
(i) The amount of the original judgment on which the lien is based, when entered, was greater than seventy-five thousand dollars ($75,000), as adjusted pursuant to Section 703.150.
(ii) The amount owed on the outstanding judgment at the time of execution on the judgment lien is greater than seventy-five thousand dollars ($75,000), as adjusted pursuant to Section 703.150.
(B) As used in this paragraph, the following terms have the following meanings:
(i) "Financial institution" means a financial institution, as defined in Section 680.200.

(ii) "Student loan debt" means debt based on any loan made to finance postsecondary education expenses, including tuition, fees, books, supplies, room and board, transportation, and personal expenses. Student loan debt includes debt based on a loan made to refinance a student loan, but does not include debt secured by the debtor's principal place of residence at the time it was incurred.
Added by Stats 2020 ch 218 (AB 2463),s 1, eff. 1/1/2021.

Article 4 - METHODS OF LEVY

Section 700.010 - Service on debtor at time of levy
(a) At the time of levy pursuant to this article or promptly thereafter, the levying officer shall serve a copy of the following on the judgment debtor:
    (1) The writ of execution.
    (2) A notice of levy.
    (3) If the judgment debtor is a natural person, a copy of the form listing exemptions prepared by the Judicial Council pursuant to subdivision (c) of Section 681.030, the list of exemption amounts published pursuant to subdivision (e) of Section 703.150, a copy of the form that the judgment debtor may use to make a claim of exemption pursuant to Section 703.520, and a copy of the form the judgment debtor may use to provide a financial statement pursuant to Section 703.530.
    (4) Any affidavit of identity, as defined in Section 680.135, for names of the debtor listed on the writ of execution.
(b) Service under this section shall be made personally or by mail.
Amended by Stats 2013 ch 64 (SB 233),s 4, eff. 1/1/2014.
Amended by Stats 2003 ch 379 (AB 182),s 2, eff. 1/1/2004.
Amended by Stats 2000 ch 639 (AB 2405), s 7, eff. 1/1/2001.

Section 700.015 - Levy upon real property
(a) To levy upon real property, the levying officer shall record with the recorder of the county where the real property is located a copy of the writ of execution and a notice of levy that describes the property levied upon and states that the judgment debtor's interest in the described property has been levied upon. If the judgment debtor's interest in the real property stands upon the records of the county in the name of a person other than the judgment debtor, the notice of levy shall identify the third person and the recorder shall index the copy of the writ and notice of levy in the names of both the judgment debtor and the third person.
(b) At the time of levy or promptly thereafter, the levying officer shall serve a copy of the writ and a notice of levy on any third person in whose name the judgment debtor's interest in the real property stands upon the records of the county. Service shall be made personally or by mail. If service on the third person is by mail, it shall be sent to the person at the address for such person, if any, shown by the records of the office of the tax assessor of the county where the real property is located or, if no address is so shown, to the person at the address used by the county recorder for the return of the instrument creating the interest of the third person in the property.
(c) At the time of levy or promptly thereafter, the levying officer shall serve a copy of the writ and a notice of levy on one occupant of the real property. Service on the occupant shall be made by leaving the copy of the writ and a notice of levy with the occupant personally or, in the occupant's absence, with a person of suitable age and discretion found upon the real property when service is attempted who is either an employee or agent of the occupant or a member of the occupant's household. If unable to serve such an occupant at the time service is attempted, the levying officer shall post the copy of the writ and the notice of levy in a conspicuous place on the real property. If the real property described in the notice of levy consists of more than one distinct lot, parcel, or governmental subdivision and any of the lots, parcels, or governmental subdivisions lies with relation to any of the others so as to form one or more continuous, unbroken tracts, only one service or posting need be made under this subdivision as to each continuous, unbroken tract.
Added by Stats. 1982, Ch. 1364, Sec. 2. Operative July 1, 1983, by Sec. 3 of Ch. 1364.

Section 700.020 - Levy upon growing crops timber to be cut or minerals
(a) To levy upon (1) growing crops, (2) timber to be cut, or (3) minerals or the like (including oil and gas) to be extracted or accounts receivable resulting from the sale thereof at the wellhead or minehead, the levying officer shall record with the recorder of the county where those crops, timber, or minerals or the like are located a copy of the writ of execution and a notice of levy that describes the property levied upon and states that the judgment debtor's interest in the described property has been levied upon and describes the real property where the crops, timber, or minerals or the like are located. If the judgment debtor's interest in the crops, timber, minerals or the like, or if the real property where the crops, timber, or minerals or the like are located, stands upon the records of the county in the name of a person other than the judgment debtor, the notice of levy shall identify the third person and the recorder shall index the copy of the writ and notice of levy in the names of both the judgment debtor and the third person.
(b) At the time of levy or promptly thereafter, the levying officer shall serve a copy of the writ and a notice of levy personally or by mail on the following persons:
    (1) Any third person in whose name the judgment debtor's interest in the crops, timber, minerals or the like stands upon the records of the county and any third person in whose name the real property stands upon the records of the county. If service on the third person is by mail, it shall be sent to the person at the address for the person, if any, shown by the records of the office of the assessor of the county where the real property is located or, if no address is so shown, to the person at the address used by the county recorder for the return of the instrument creating the interest of the third person in the property.
    (2) Any secured party who has filed a financing statement with respect to the crops, timber, or minerals or the like or the accounts receivable, prior to the date of levy on the property.
(c) At the time of levy or promptly thereafter, the levying officer shall serve a copy of the writ and a notice of levy on one occupant of the real property where the crops, timber, or minerals or the like are located. Service on the occupant shall be made by leaving the copy of the writ and a notice of levy with the occupant personally or, in the occupant's absence, with a person of suitable age and discretion found upon the real property when service is attempted who is either an employee or agent of the occupant or a member of the occupant's household. If he or she is unable to serve an occupant or suitable person at the time service is attempted, the levying officer shall post the copy of the writ and the notice of levy in a conspicuous place on the real property. However, the posting requirement of the preceding sentence shall not apply where the levy is made upon minerals or the like (but not including oil or gas) and no dwelling is located on the real property. If the real property described in the notice of levy consists of more than one distinct lot, parcel, or governmental subdivision and any of the lots, parcels, or governmental subdivisions lies with relation to any of the others so as to form one or more continuous, unbroken tracts, only one service or posting need be made under this subdivision as to each continuous, unbroken tract.
Amended by Stats. 1993, Ch. 1187, Sec. 1.5. Effective January 1, 1994.

Section 700.030 - Levy upon tangible personal property under control of debtor
Unless another method of levy is provided by this article, to levy upon tangible personal property in the possession or under the control of the judgment debtor, the levying officer shall take the property into custody.
Added by Stats. 1982, Ch. 1364, Sec. 2. Operative July 1, 1983, by Sec. 3 of Ch. 1364.

Section 700.040 - Levy upon tangible personal property under control of third person
(a) Unless another method of levy is provided by this article, to levy upon tangible personal property in the possession or under the control of a third person, the levying officer shall personally serve a copy of the writ of execution and a notice of levy on the third person.

(b) If goods are in the possession of a bailee who has issued a negotiable document of title therefor, the goods may not be levied upon but the negotiable document of title may be levied upon in the manner provided by Section 700.120. If goods are in the possession of a bailee other than one who has issued a negotiable document of title therefor, the goods may be levied upon in the manner provided by Section 700.060. As used in this subdivision, "bailee" means "bailee" as defined in Section 7102 of the Commercial Code.
Added by Stats. 1982, Ch. 1364, Sec. 2. Operative July 1, 1983, by Sec. 3 of Ch. 1364.

Section 700.050 - Levy upon person property in custody of levying officer
(a) To levy upon personal property in the custody of a levying officer:
    (1) If the writ of execution is directed to the levying officer having custody of the property, the judgment creditor shall deliver the writ to the levying officer.
    (2) If the writ of execution is directed to a levying officer other than the levying officer having custody of the property, the levying officer to whom the writ is directed shall serve a copy of the writ and a notice of levy on the levying officer having custody. Service shall be made personally or by mail.
(b) The levying officer having custody of the property shall comply with the writs in the order they are received and is not subject to the provisions of Article 5 (commencing with Section 701.010) (duties and liabilities of third persons after levy).
Added by Stats. 1982, Ch. 1364, Sec. 2. Operative July 1, 1983, by Sec. 3 of Ch. 1364.

Section 700.060 - Levy upon goods in possession of bailee
(a) To levy upon goods in the possession of a bailee (as defined in Section 7102 of the Commercial Code) other than one who has issued a negotiable document of title therefor, the levying officer shall personally serve a copy of the writ of execution and a notice of levy on the bailee.
(b) If the goods described in subdivision (a) are subject to a security interest, the levying officer shall, if so instructed by the judgment creditor, serve a copy of the writ of execution and a notice of levy on the secured party. Service shall be made personally or by mail.
Added by Stats. 1982, Ch. 1364, Sec. 2. Operative July 1, 1983, by Sec. 3 of Ch. 1364.

Section 700.070 - Levy upon tangible personal property of going business in possession of debtor
To levy upon tangible personal property of a going business in the possession or under the control of the judgment debtor, the levying officer shall comply with Section 700.030, except to the extent that the judgment creditor instructs that levy be made in the following manner:
(a) The levying officer shall place a keeper in charge of the business for the period requested by the judgment creditor. During the period, the business may continue to operate in the ordinary course of business provided that all sales are final and are for cash or its equivalent. For the purpose of this subdivision, a check is the equivalent of cash. The levying officer is not liable for accepting payment in the form of a cash equivalent. The keeper shall take custody of the proceeds from all sales unless otherwise directed by the judgment creditor.
(b) The levying officer shall take the tangible personal property into exclusive custody at the earliest of the following times:
    (1) At any time the judgment debtor objects to placement of a keeper in charge of the business.
    (2) At any time when requested by the judgment creditor.
    (3) At the end of 10 days from the time the keeper is placed in charge of the business.
(c) Where a keeper is placed in a business for the purpose of taking into custody tangible personal property consisting solely of money or equivalent proceeds of sales, the provisions of subdivision (b) shall not apply, and the levying officer shall take such property into exclusive custody at the end of each daily keeper period.
Amended by Stats. 1996, Ch. 1159, Sec. 11. Effective January 1, 1997.

Section 700.080 - Levy upon personal property used as dwelling
(a) To levy upon personal property used as a dwelling, the levying officer shall serve a copy of the writ of execution and a notice of levy on one occupant of the property. Service on the occupant shall be made by leaving the copy of the writ and the notice of levy with the occupant personally or, in the occupant's absence, with a person of suitable age and discretion found at the property when service is attempted who is a member of the occupant's family or household. If unable to serve the occupant at the time service is attempted, the levying officer shall make the levy by posting the copy of the writ and the notice of levy in a conspicuous place on the property.
(b) If the judgment creditor so instructs, the levying officer shall place a keeper in charge of the property for a period requested by the judgment creditor.
(c) The judgment creditor may apply to the court on noticed motion for an order directing the levying officer to remove the occupants. The notice of motion shall be served on any legal owner and any junior lienholder who was served pursuant to Section 700.090, on the occupant, and, if the judgment debtor is not the occupant, on the judgment debtor. Service shall be made personally or by mail. At the hearing on the motion the court shall determine the occupant's right to possession and shall make an order including terms and conditions that are appropriate under the circumstances of the case.
(d) Personal property used as a dwelling shall include a mobilehome, whether the mobilehome is occupied or unoccupied at the time of the levy.
Amended by Stats. 1995, Ch. 446, Sec. 2. Effective January 1, 1996.

Section 700.090 - Vehicle, vessel, manufactured home, mobilehome or commercial coach levied upon
If a vehicle or vessel is levied upon and a certificate of ownership has been issued by the Department of Motor Vehicles for such vehicle or vessel and the certificate of ownership is still in effect, or if a manufactured home, mobilehome, or commercial coach is levied upon and a permanent title record has been established by the Department of Housing and Community Development for such manufactured home, mobilehome, or commercial coach the levying officer shall determine from the appropriate department the name and address of the legal owner and each junior lienholder of the property levied upon. If the legal owner or junior lienholder is not the judgment debtor and is not in possession of the vehicle, vessel, manufactured home, mobilehome, or commercial coach, the levying officer shall at the time of levy or promptly thereafter serve a copy of the writ of execution and a notice of levy on the legal owner or junior lienholder. Service shall be made personally or by mail.
Amended by Stats. 1983, Ch. 1124, Sec. 10.

Section 700.100 - Levy upon chattel paper
(a) To levy upon chattel paper, the levying officer shall:
    (1) If the chattel paper is in the possession of the judgment debtor, take the chattel paper into custody.
    (2) If the chattel paper is in the possession of a third person, personally serve a copy of the writ of execution and a notice of levy on the third person.
(b) If the levying officer obtains custody of the chattel paper or if pursuant to a security agreement the judgment debtor has liberty to collect or compromise the chattel paper or to accept the return of goods or make repossessions, the levying officer shall, if so instructed by the judgment creditor, serve a copy of the writ of execution and a notice of levy on the account debtor. Service shall be made personally or by mail.
(c) In addition to any other rights created by a levy on chattel paper, the levy creates a lien on the judgment debtor's rights in specific goods subject to the chattel paper.
Added by Stats. 1982, Ch. 1364, Sec. 2. Operative July 1, 1983, by Sec. 3 of Ch. 1364.

Section 700.110 - Levy upon instrument
(a) To levy upon an instrument, the levying officer shall:
    (1) If the instrument is in the possession of the judgment debtor, take the instrument into custody.

(2) If the instrument is in the possession of a third person, personally serve a copy of the writ of execution and a notice of levy on the third person.

(b) If the levying officer obtains custody of the instrument, the levying officer shall, if the judgment creditor so instructs, serve a copy of the writ of execution and a notice of levy on the obligor. Service shall be made personally or by mail.

Added by Stats. 1982, Ch. 1364, Sec. 2. Operative July 1, 1983, by Sec. 3 of Ch. 1364.

Section 700.120 - Levy upon negotiable document of title

To levy upon a negotiable document of title, the levying officer shall:

(a) If the negotiable document of title is in the possession of the judgment debtor, take the negotiable document of title into custody.

(b) If the negotiable document of title is in the possession of a third person, personally serve a copy of the writ of execution and a notice of levy on the third person.

Added by Stats. 1982, Ch. 1364, Sec. 2. Operative July 1, 1983, by Sec. 3 of Ch. 1364.

Section 700.130 - Levy upon security

To levy upon a security, the levying officer shall comply with Section 8112 of the Commercial Code. The legal process referred to in Section 8112 of the Commercial Code means the legal process required by the state in which the chief executive office of the issuer of the security is located and, where that state is California, means personal service by the levying officer of a copy of the writ of execution and notice of levy on the person who is to be served.

Amended by Stats. 1996, Ch. 497, Sec. 3. Effective January 1, 1997.

Section 700.140 - Levy upon deposit account

(a) Subject to Sections 684.115 and 700.160, to levy upon a deposit account, the levying officer shall personally serve a copy of the writ of execution and a notice of levy on the financial institution with which the deposit account is maintained.

(b) The execution lien that arises upon service of a writ of execution and notice of levy reaches only amounts in a deposit account at the time of service on the financial institution, including the amount of any deposit not yet finally collected unless the deposit is returned unpaid to the financial institution.

(c) The levying officer shall serve a copy of the writ of execution and a notice of levy on any third person in whose name any deposit account described therein stands. Service shall be made personally or by mail as follows:

(1) At the time of levy or promptly thereafter, if the party seeking the levy informs the levying officer of the person and his, her, or its residence or business address.

(2) Promptly following the levying officer's receipt of a garnishee's memorandum if service was not accomplished pursuant to paragraph (1) if the garnishee's memorandum identifies the person and his, her, or its residence or business address.

(d) The financial institution shall not honor a withdrawal request or a check or other order for the payment of money from the deposit account if presentment of the withdrawal request or item to the financial institution occurs during the time the execution lien is in effect unless, following the withdrawal or payment, sufficient funds are available to cover the levy. For these purposes, a withdrawal from the deposit account to cover the financial institution's standard fee or charge for processing the levy shall not be considered a payment of money from the account in violation of this subdivision.

(e) During the time the execution lien is in effect, the financial institution is not liable to any person for any of the following:

(1) Performance of the duties of a garnishee under the levy.

(2) Nonpayment of a check or other order for the payment or transfer of money drawn or presented against the deposit account if the nonpayment is pursuant to the requirements of subdivision (d).

(3) Refusal to pay a withdrawal from the deposit account if the refusal is pursuant to the requirements of subdivision (d).

(f) When the amount levied upon pursuant to this section is paid to the levying officer, the execution lien on the deposit account levied upon terminates.

(g) For the purposes of this section, none of the following is a third person in whose name the deposit account stands:

(1) A person who is only a person named as the beneficiary of a Totten trust account.

(2) A person who is only a payee designated in a pay-on-death provision in an account pursuant to Section 18318.5 of the Financial Code or Section 5140 of the Probate Code, or other similar provision.

(3) A person who is only acting in a representative or custodial capacity with respect to benefits paid or payable by the United States government. Rather, accounts maintained by the representative or custodian shall be deemed to stand in the beneficiary's name, and the amounts therein shall be covered by a levy against the beneficiary.

(h) For purposes of this section, final payment of a deposit shall be deemed to have occurred in accordance with Section 4215 or 11210 of the Commercial Code or with automated clearinghouse or Federal Reserve System rule, regulation, operating circular, or similar governing document, as applicable to the deposit. If, for any reason, a deposit is returned by the financial institution upon which it is drawn, the deposit shall not be deemed finally collected for purposes of this subdivision regardless of any later payment by the financial institution upon which the deposit is drawn.

Amended by Stats 2012 ch 484 (AB 2364),s 8, eff. 1/1/2013.
Amended by Stats 2009 ch 153 (AB 1549),s 3, eff. 1/1/2010.
Amended by Stats 2003 ch 110 (AB 690),s 2, eff. 1/1/2004.
Amended by Stats 2002 ch 664 (AB 3034),s 48, eff. 1/1/2003.

Section 700.150 - Levy upon property in safe-deposit box

(a) Subject to Section 700.160, to levy upon property in a safe-deposit box, the levying officer shall personally serve a copy of the writ of execution and a notice of levy on the financial institution with which the safe-deposit box is maintained.

(b) At the time of the levy or promptly thereafter, the levying officer shall serve a copy of the writ of execution and a notice of levy on any third person in whose name the safe-deposit box stands. Service shall be made personally or by mail.

(c) During the time the execution lien is in effect, the financial institution may not permit the removal of any of the contents of the safe-deposit box except as directed by the levying officer.

(d) Upon receipt of a garnishee's memorandum from the financial institution indicating a safe-deposit box is under levy, the levying officer shall promptly mail a written notice to the judgment creditor demanding an additional fee as required by Section 26723 of the Government Code, plus the costs to open the safe-deposit box and seize and store the contents. The levying officer shall release the levy on the safe-deposit box if the judgment creditor does not pay the required fee, plus costs, within three business days plus the extended time period specified in subdivision (a) of Section 1013 for service by mail by the levying officer.

(e) The levying officer may first give the person in whose name the safe-deposit box stands an opportunity to open the safe-deposit box to permit the removal pursuant to the levy of the property levied upon. The financial institution may refuse to permit the forcible opening of the safe-deposit box to permit the removal of the property levied upon unless the levying officer or the judgment creditor pays in advance the cost of forcibly opening the safe-deposit box and of repairing any damage caused thereby.

(f) The levying officer shall give the judgment creditor at least three court days' advance notice of the date and time the levying officer will open the safe-deposit box and seize the contents thereof, and the judgment creditor shall be entitled to be present at that time.

(g) During the time the execution lien is in effect, the financial institution is not liable to any person for any of the following:
- **(1)** Performance of the duties of a garnishee under the levy.
- **(2)** Refusal to permit access to the safe-deposit box by the person in whose name it stands.
- **(3)** Removal of any of the contents of the safe-deposit box pursuant to the levy.

(h) If the levying officer removes any property from the safe-deposit box to satisfy the levy, but allows other property to remain in the safe-deposit box, the execution lien is released automatically with respect to any property that remains in the safe-deposit box.

Amended by Stats 2012 ch 484 (AB 2364),s 9, eff. 1/1/2013.
Amended by Stats 2003 ch 888 (AB 394),s 2, eff. 1/1/2004.

Section 700.160 - Deposit account or safe-deposit box standing in name person other than debtor

(a) Except as provided in subdivision (b), a deposit account or safe-deposit box standing in the name of a person other than the judgment debtor, either alone or together with third persons, is not subject to levy under Section 700.140 or 700.150 unless the legal process served on the third party includes a court order authorizing the levy.

(b) A court order is not required to levy on a deposit account or safe-deposit box standing in the name of any of the following:
- **(1)** The judgment debtor, whether alone or together with third persons.
- **(2)** The judgment debtor's spouse or registered domestic partner, whether alone or together with other persons, provided an affidavit is delivered to the financial institution at the time of levy showing that person is the judgment debtor's spouse or registered domestic partner.
- **(3)** A fictitious business name, provided a copy of an unexpired statement certified in accordance with Section 17926 of the Business and Professions Code is delivered to the financial institution at the time of levy, the fictitious business name statement does not list any person other than the judgment debtor, the judgment debtor's spouse or the judgment debtor's registered domestic partner as the person or persons doing business under the fictitious business name, and, if a person other than the judgment debtor is listed in the statement, an affidavit stating that the other person is the judgment debtor's spouse or registered domestic partner is delivered to the financial institution at the time of the levy.
- **(4)** The additional name of a judgment debtor listed on the legal process pursuant to an affidavit of identity as provided by Section 680.135, whether alone or together with third persons.

(c) In any case where a deposit account in the name of a person other than the judgment debtor, whether alone or together with the judgment debtor, is levied upon, the financial institution shall not pay to the levying officer the amount levied upon until being notified to do so by the levying officer. The levying officer may not require the financial institution to pay the amount levied upon until the expiration of 15 days after service of notice of levy on the third person.

Amended by Stats 2012 ch 484 (AB 2364),s 10, eff. 1/1/2013.
Amended by Stats 2011 ch 308 (SB 647),s 3, eff. 1/1/2012.
Amended by Stats 2000 ch 639 (AB 2405), s 8, eff. 1/1/2001.

Section 700.170 - Levy upon account receivable or general intangible

(a) Unless another method of levy is provided by this article, to levy upon an account receivable or general intangible, the levying officer shall personally serve a copy of the writ of execution and a notice of levy on the account debtor.

(b) If a levy is made under subdivision (a) and payments on the account receivable or general intangible are made to a person other than the judgment debtor (whether pursuant to a security agreement, assignment for collection, or otherwise), the levying officer shall, if so instructed by the judgment creditor, personally serve a copy of the writ of execution and a notice of levy on such third person. Service of the copy of the writ and notice of levy on such third person is a levy on any amounts owed to the judgment debtor by such third person.

Added by Stats. 1982, Ch. 1364, Sec. 2. Operative July 1, 1983, by Sec. 3 of Ch. 1364.

Section 700.180 - Property levied on subject to pending action or special proceeding

(a) The following property may be levied upon pursuant to this article notwithstanding that the property levied upon is the subject of a pending action or special proceeding:
- **(1)** Real property.
- **(2)** Growing crops, timber to be cut, or minerals or the like (including oil and gas) to be extracted or accounts receivable resulting from the sale thereof at the wellhead or minehead.
- **(3)** Tangible personal property in the possession or under the control of the judgment debtor or in the custody of a levying officer.
- **(4)** The interest of a judgment debtor in personal property in the estate of a decedent, whether the interest arises by testate or intestate succession.

(b) Except as provided in subdivision (a), a levy upon property that is the subject of an action or special proceeding pending at the time of the levy is not effective.

(c) If a levy is attempted but is ineffective under subdivision (b) and the levying officer has requested a garnishee's memorandum under Section 701.030 in connection with the ineffective levy, the garnishee's memorandum shall include the following information in addition to that required by Section 701.030:
- **(1)** A statement that the levy on the property is not effective because the property is the subject of a pending action or special proceeding.
- **(2)** The title of the court, cause, and number of the pending action or proceeding.

(d) For the purpose of this section, an action or proceeding is pending from the time the action or proceeding is commenced until judgment has been entered and the time for appeal has expired or, if an appeal is filed, until the appeal has been finally determined.

(e) Nothing in this section affects or limits the right of the judgment creditor to obtain a lien pursuant to Article 5 (commencing with Section 708.410) of Chapter 6.

Added by Stats. 1982, Ch. 1364, Sec. 2. Operative July 1, 1983, by Sec. 3 of Ch. 1364.

Section 700.190 - Levy upon final money judgment

(a) As used in this section, "final money judgment" means a money judgment after the time for appeal from the judgment has expired or, if an appeal is filed, after the appeal has been finally determined.

(b) To levy upon a final money judgment, the levying officer shall file a copy of the writ of execution and a notice of levy with the clerk of the court that entered the final money judgment. The court clerk shall endorse upon the judgment a statement of the existence of the execution lien and the time it was created. If an abstract of the judgment is issued, it shall include a statement of the execution lien in favor of the judgment creditor.

(c) At the time of levy or promptly thereafter, the levying officer shall serve a copy of the writ of execution and a notice of levy on the judgment debtor obligated to pay the final money judgment levied upon. Service shall be made personally or by mail.

Amended by Stats. 1984, Ch. 538, Sec. 25.3.

Section 700.200 - Levy upon debtor's interest in personal property of estate of decedent

(a) To levy upon the interest of the judgment debtor in personal property in the estate of a decedent, whether the interest arises by testate or intestate succession, the levying officer shall personally serve a copy of the writ and a notice of levy on the personal representative of the decedent. The levy does not impair the powers of the representative over the property for the purposes of administration.

(b) The personal representative shall report the levy to the court in which the estate is being administered when any petition for distribution is filed. If a decree orders distribution to the judgment debtor, the court making the decree shall order the property levied upon to be delivered to the levying officer. The property may not be delivered to the levying officer until the decree distributing the property has become final. To the extent the property delivered to the levying officer is not necessary to satisfy the money judgment, it shall be released to the judgment debtor.

(c) Promptly after the property is delivered to the levying officer pursuant to subdivision (b), the levying officer shall serve a notice describing the property on the judgment debtor. Service shall be made personally or by mail. Notwithstanding Section 703.520, a claim of exemption for the property described in the notice may be made within 10 days after the notice was served on the judgment debtor.

(d) Notwithstanding Section 697.710, an execution lien created by a levy pursuant to this section continues for a period of one year after the decree distributing the interest has become final unless the judgment is sooner satisfied.

(e) A writ under which a levy is made pursuant to this section shall be returned not later than one year after the date the decree distributing the interest has become final.

Added by Stats. 1982, Ch. 1364, Sec. 2. Operative July 1, 1983, by Sec. 3 of Ch. 1364.

Article 5 - DUTIES AND LIABILITIES OF THIRD PERSONS AFTER LEVY

Section 701.010 - Duties

(a) Except as otherwise provided by statute, when a levy is made by service of a copy of the writ of execution and a notice of levy on a third person, the third person at the time of levy or promptly thereafter shall comply with this section.

(b) Unless the third person has good cause for failure or refusal to do so:

(1) The third person shall deliver to the levying officer any of the property levied upon that is in the possession or under the control of the third person at the time of levy unless the third person claims the right to possession of the property.

(2) To the extent that the third person does not deny an obligation levied upon, or claim a priority over the judgment creditor's lien, the third person shall pay to the levying officer both of the following:

(A) The amount of the obligation levied upon that is due and payable to the judgment debtor at the time of levy.

(B) Amounts that become due and payable to the judgment debtor on the obligation levied upon during the period of the execution lien.

(3) If the third person makes a delivery or payment to the levying officer pursuant to this section, the third person shall execute and deliver any documents necessary to effect the transfer of the property.

(c) For the purposes of this section, "good cause" includes, but is not limited to, a showing that the third person did not know or have reason to know of the levy from all the facts and circumstances known to the third person.

Added by Stats. 1982, Ch. 1364, Sec. 2. Operative July 1, 1983, by Sec. 3 of Ch. 1364.

Section 701.020 - Liability for failure or refusal to deliver property or make payments

(a) If a third person is required by this article to deliver property to the levying officer or to make payments to the levying officer and the third person fails or refuses without good cause to do so, the third person is liable to the judgment creditor for whichever of the following is the lesser amount:

(1) The value of the judgment debtor's interest in the property or the amount of the payments required to be made.

(2) The amount required to satisfy the judgment pursuant to which the levy is made.

(b) The third person's liability continues until the earliest of the following times:

(1) The time when the property levied upon is delivered to the levying officer or the payments are made to the levying officer.

(2) The time when the property levied upon is released pursuant to Section 699.060.

(3) The time when the judgment is satisfied or discharged.

(c) If the third person's liability is established, the court that determines the liability may, in its discretion, require the third person to pay the costs and reasonable attorney's fees incurred by the judgment creditor in establishing the liability.

Added by Stats. 1982, Ch. 1364, Sec. 2. Operative July 1, 1983, by Sec. 3 of Ch. 1364.

Section 701.030 - Garnishee's memorandum

(a) At the time of service of a copy of the legal process on a third person, the levying officer shall request the third person to give the levying officer a garnishee's memorandum containing the information required by this section. Within 10 days after the legal process is served, the third person shall mail or deliver the garnishee's memorandum to the levying officer whether or not the levy is effective.

(b) The garnishee's memorandum shall be executed under oath and shall contain the following information, as applicable:

(1) A description of any property of the judgment debtor sought to be levied upon that is not delivered to the levying officer and the reason for not delivering the property.

(2) A description of any property of the judgment debtor not sought to be levied upon that is in the possession or under the control of the third person at the time of levy.

(3) A statement of the amount and terms of any obligation to the judgment debtor sought to be levied upon that is due and payable and is not paid to the levying officer, and the reason for not paying the obligation.

(4) A statement of the amount and terms of any obligation to the judgment debtor sought to be levied upon that is not due and payable at the time of levy.

(5) A statement of the amount and terms of any obligation to the judgment debtor at the time of levy not sought to be levied upon.

(6) A description of claims and rights of other persons to the property or obligation levied upon that are known to the third person and the names and addresses of those other persons.

(7) A statement that the garnishee holds neither any property nor any obligations in favor of the judgment debtor.

(c) If a garnishee's memorandum is received from the third person, the levying officer shall retain a copy and promptly mail or deliver a copy of the memorandum to the judgment creditor.

(d) Except as provided in subdivisions (e) and (f), if a third person does not give the levying officer a garnishee's memorandum within the time provided in subdivision (a), or does not provide complete information, the third person may, in the court's discretion, be required to pay the costs and reasonable attorney's fees incurred in any proceedings to obtain the information required in the garnishee's memorandum.

(e) Notwithstanding subdivision (a), when the levy is made upon a deposit account or upon property in a safe-deposit box, the financial institution need not give a garnishee's memorandum to the levying officer if the financial institution fully complies with the levy and, if a garnishee's memorandum is required, the garnishee's memorandum needs to provide information with respect only to property that is carried on the records available at the office or branch where the levy is made provided that if a levy has been served at a central location designated by a financial institution in accordance with Section 684.115, the garnishee's memorandum shall apply to all offices and branches of the financial institution except to the extent acceptance of the levy at those central locations is limited pursuant to paragraph (3) of subdivision (a) of Section 684.115.

(f) Notwithstanding subdivision (a), the third person need not give a garnishee's memorandum to the levying officer if both of the following conditions are satisfied:

(1) The third person has delivered to the levying officer all of the property sought to be levied upon.

(2) The third person has paid to the levying officer the amount due at the time of levy on any obligation to the judgment debtor that was levied upon, and there is no additional amount that thereafter will become payable on the obligation levied upon.

(g) The garnishee may electronically transmit the garnishee's memorandum to the levying officer pursuant to Chapter 2 (commencing with Section 263) of Title 4 of Part 1.

Amended by Stats 2012 ch 484 (AB 2364),s 11, eff. 1/1/2013.

Amended by Stats 2010 ch 680 (AB 2394),s 10, eff. 1/1/2011.

Section 701.035 - Not liable for disclosures in memorandum
A third person who gives a garnishee's memorandum pursuant to this title is not liable to any person for the disclosure in the garnishee's memorandum of any information contained in the garnishee's memorandum.

Added by Stats. 1983, Ch. 155, Sec. 14.6. Effective June 30, 1983. Operative July 1, 1983, by Sec. 32 of Ch. 155.

Section 701.040 - Property levied upon subject to security interest that attached prior to levy
(a) Except as otherwise ordered by the court upon a determination that the judgment creditor's lien has priority over the security interest, if property levied upon is subject to a security interest that attached prior to levy, the property or obligation is subject to enforcement of the security interest without regard to the levy unless the property is in the custody of the levying officer; but, if the execution lien has priority over the security interest, the secured party is liable to the judgment creditor for any proceeds received by the secured party from the property to the extent of the execution lien.

(b) After the security interest is satisfied, the secured party shall deliver any excess property, and pay any excess payments or proceeds of property, remaining in the possession of the secured party to the levying officer for the purposes of the levy, as provided in Section 9615 of the Commercial Code, unless otherwise ordered by the court or directed by the levying officer.

EFFECTIVE 7/1/2001. Amended October 10, 1999 (Bill Number: SB 45) (Chapter 991).

Section 701.050 - Duties of account debtor
After service of a copy of the writ of execution and a notice of levy on an account debtor obligated on an account receivable, chattel paper, or general intangible:

(a) If the account debtor has been making payments or is required to make payments to the judgment debtor, the account debtor shall make payments to the levying officer as they become due unless otherwise directed by court order or by the levying officer. Payments made to the judgment debtor after the account debtor has received notice of the levy do not discharge the obligation of the account debtor to make payments as required by this subdivision.

(b) If the account debtor has been making payments to a third person or is required to make payments to a third person (whether pursuant to a security agreement, assignment for collection, or otherwise), the account debtor shall continue to make such payments to the third person notwithstanding the levy until the account debtor receives notice that the obligation to the third person is satisfied or is otherwise directed by court order or by the third person. After the account debtor receives notice that the obligation to the third person is satisfied, the account debtor shall make payments to the levying officer as they become due unless otherwise directed by court order or by the levying officer.

(c) If pursuant to a security agreement the judgment debtor has liberty to accept the return of goods or make repossessions under the account receivable or chattel paper, the account debtor shall deliver to the levying officer property returnable to the judgment debtor unless otherwise directed by court order or by the levying officer.

Added by Stats. 1982, Ch. 1364, Sec. 2. Operative July 1, 1983, by Sec. 3 of Ch. 1364.

Section 701.060 - Duties of obligor under instrument levied upon
If the levying officer obtains custody of an instrument levied upon and serves the obligor under the instrument pursuant to the levy, the obligor shall make payments to the levying officer as they become due. Payments made to a person other than the levying officer do not discharge the obligation of the obligor to make payments as required by this section if the payments are made after the obligor has received notice of the levy.

Added by Stats. 1982, Ch. 1364, Sec. 2. Operative July 1, 1983, by Sec. 3 of Ch. 1364.

Section 701.070 - Payments if final money judgment levied upon
If a final money judgment has been levied upon and the levying officer has served the judgment debtor under the final money judgment levied upon, the judgment debtor shall make any payments due under the judgment to the levying officer. Payments made to a person other than the levying officer do not discharge the obligation of the judgment debtor under the final money judgment levied upon if the payments are made after the judgment debtor has received notice of the levy.

Added by Stats. 1984, Ch. 538, Sec. 25.5.

Article 6 - SALE AND COLLECTION

Section 701.510 - Property levied on not subject to be sold
Subject to Sections 687.020 and 701.520, the levying officer shall sell all property that has been levied upon except:

(a) Tangible personal property may not be sold until the levying officer obtains custody of the property.

(b) Cash may not be sold unless it has a value exceeding its face value.

Added by Stats. 1982, Ch. 1364, Sec. 2. Operative July 1, 1983, by Sec. 3 of Ch. 1364.

Section 701.520 - Property collected rather sold
(a) Except as provided in this section, any of the following property that has been levied upon shall be collected rather than sold:

(1) Accounts receivable.

(2) Chattel paper.

(3) General intangibles.

(4) Final money judgments.

(5) Instruments that are not customarily transferred in an established market.

(6) Instruments that represent an obligation arising out of the sale or lease of property, a license to use property, the furnishing of services, or the loan of money where the property sold or leased or licensed for use, the services furnished, or the money loaned was used by an individual primarily for personal, family, or household purposes.

(b) At the time of levy on property described in subdivision (a) or thereafter, the judgment creditor may serve a notice of intended sale of the property on the judgment debtor. Service shall be made personally or by mail. A copy of the notice of intended sale and proof of service on the judgment debtor shall be filed with the court and with the levying officer. The notice of intended sale shall describe the property and state that it will be sold at an execution sale unless, within the time allowed after service of the notice of intended sale, the judgment debtor applies to the court on noticed motion for an order that the property be collected rather than sold.

(c) Within 10 days after service of the notice of intended sale, the judgment debtor may apply to the court on noticed motion for an order that the property be collected rather than sold. A judgment debtor who so applies shall, within the time allowed for the application, serve a copy of the notice of motion on the judgment creditor and file a copy of the notice of motion with the levying officer. Service of the copy of the notice of motion on the judgment creditor shall be made personally or by mail. If the copy of the notice of motion is not filed with the levying officer within the time allowed, the levying officer shall proceed to sell the property. If a copy of the notice of motion is filed with the levying officer within the time allowed, the levying officer shall continue to collect the property until otherwise ordered by the court.

(d) At the hearing on the motion, the court may in its discretion order that the property be sold or be collected depending on the equities and circumstances of the particular case. If the court orders that the property be sold, the order may specify terms and conditions of sale. If the court orders that the property be collected, the court may condition its order on an assignment of the property by the judgment debtor to the judgment creditor pursuant to Article 6 (commencing with Section 708.510) of Chapter 6.

Added by Stats. 1982, Ch. 1364, Sec. 2. Operative July 1, 1983, by Sec. 3 of Ch. 1364.

Section 701.530 - Notice of sale of personal property

(a) Notice of sale of personal property shall be in writing, shall state the date, time, and place of sale, and shall describe the property to be sold.
(b) Not less than 10 days before a sale of personal property, notice of sale shall be posted and served on the judgment debtor by the levying officer. Service shall be made personally or by mail.
(c) Posting under this section shall be in three public places in:
(1) The city in which the property is to be sold if it is to be sold in a city.
(2) The county in which the property is to be sold if it is not to be sold in a city.
(d) A sale of personal property of an individual may not take place until the expiration of the time during which the judgment debtor may make a claim of exemption under subdivision (a) of Section 703.520.
Amended by Stats 2002 ch 784 (SB 1316),s 68, eff. 1/1/2003.

Section 701.540 - Notice of sale of interest in real property
(a) Notice of sale of an interest in real property shall be in writing, shall state the date, time, and place of sale, shall describe the interest to be sold, and shall give a legal description of the real property and its street address or other common designation, if any. If the real property has no street address or other common designation, the notice of sale shall include a statement that directions to its location may be obtained from the levying officer upon oral or written request or, in the discretion of the levying officer, the notice of sale may contain directions to its location. Directions are sufficient if information as to the location of the real property is given by reference to the direction and approximate distance from the nearest crossroads, frontage road, or access road. If an accurate legal description of the real property is given, the validity of the notice and sale is not affected by the fact that the street address or other common designation, or directions to its location, are erroneous or omitted.
(b) Not less than 20 days before the date of sale, notice of sale of an interest in real property shall be served, mailed, and posted by the levying officer as provided in subdivisions (c), (d), (e), and (f).
(c) Notice of sale shall be served on the judgment debtor. Service shall be made personally or by mail.
(d) Notice of sale shall be posted in the following places:
(1) One public place in the city in which the interest in the real property is to be sold if it is to be sold in a city or, if not to be sold in a city, one public place in the county in which the interest in the real property is to be sold.
(2) A conspicuous place on the real property.
(e) At the time notice is posted pursuant to paragraph (2) of subdivision (d), notice of sale shall be served or service shall be attempted on one occupant of the real property. Service on the occupant shall be made by leaving the notice with the occupant personally or, in the occupant's absence, with any person of suitable age and discretion found upon the real property at the time service is attempted who is either an employee or agent of the occupant or a member of the occupant's household. If the levying officer is unable to serve an occupant, as specified, at the time service is attempted, the levying officer is not required to make any further attempts to serve an occupant.
(f) If the property described in the notice of sale consists of more than one distinct lot, parcel, or governmental subdivision and any of the lots, parcels, or governmental subdivisions lies with relation to any of the others so as to form one or more continuous, unbroken tracts, only one service pursuant to subdivision (e) and posting pursuant to paragraph (2) of subdivision (d) need be made as to each continuous, unbroken tract.
(g) Notice of sale shall be published pursuant to Section 6063 of the Government Code, with the first publication at least 20 days prior to the time of sale, in a newspaper of general circulation published in the city in which the real property or a part thereof is situated if any part thereof is situated in a city or, if not, in a newspaper of general circulation published in the public notice district in which the real property or a part thereof is situated. If no newspaper of general circulation is published in the city or public notice district, notice of sale shall be published in a newspaper of general circulation in the county in which the real property or a part thereof is situated.
(h) Not earlier than 30 days after the date of levy, the judgment creditor shall determine the names of all persons having liens on the real property on the date of levy that are of record in the office of the county recorder and shall instruct the levying officer to mail notice of sale to each lienholder at the address used by the county recorder for the return of the instrument creating the lien after recording. The levying officer shall mail notice to each lienholder, at the address given in the instructions, not less than 20 days before the date of sale.
(i) For the purposes of this section, publication of notice in a public notice district is governed by Chapter 1.1 (commencing with Section 6080) of Division 7 of Title 1 of the Government Code.
Amended by Stats 2016 ch 703 (AB 2881),s 9, eff. 1/1/2017.
Amended by Stats 2002 ch 784 (SB 1316),s 69, eff. 1/1/2003.

Section 701.545 - Time for giving notice of sale of interest in real property
Notice of sale of an interest in real property, other than a leasehold estate with an unexpired term of less than two years at the time of levy, may not be given pursuant to Section 701.540 until the expiration of 120 days after the date notice of levy on the interest in real property was served on the judgment debtor.
Added by Stats. 1982, Ch. 1364, Sec. 2. Operative July 1, 1983, by Sec. 3 of Ch. 1364.

Section 701.547 - Statement relating to prospective bidders
A notice of sale shall contain the substance of the following statement: "Prospective bidders should refer to Sections 701.510 to 701.680, inclusive, of the Code of Civil Procedure for provisions governing the terms, conditions, and effect of the sale and the liability of defaulting bidders."
Added by Stats. 1982, Ch. 1364, Sec. 2. Operative July 1, 1983, by Sec. 3 of Ch. 1364.

Section 701.550 - Notice of sale to persons requesting notice
(a) In addition to the notice of sale required by this article, the levying officer shall, at the time notice of sale is posted pursuant to Section 701.530 or 701.540, mail notice of sale to any person who has requested notice of the sale pursuant to this section.
(b) A request for notice of sale under this section made prior to the issuance of the writ shall be in writing and shall be filed with the clerk of the court where the judgment is entered. The request shall specify the title of the court, the cause and number of the action in which the judgment was entered, and the date of entry thereof, and shall state the address to which the notice of sale is to be mailed. The name and address of the person requesting notice of sale under this subdivision shall be noted on the writ.
(c) A person who desires notice of sale of particular property that has been levied upon may file a request for notice of sale with the levying officer who will conduct the sale. The request shall contain the information specified by the levying officer as needed in order to comply with the request.
Added by Stats. 1982, Ch. 1364, Sec. 2. Operative July 1, 1983, by Sec. 3 of Ch. 1364.

Section 701.555 - Advertising sale in newspaper or other publication
In addition to the notice of sale required by this article, the judgment creditor may advertise the sale in the classified or other advertising section of a newspaper of general circulation or other publication and may recover reasonable costs of such advertising. The judgment debtor may also advertise the sale at the judgment debtor's own expense.
Added by Stats. 1982, Ch. 1364, Sec. 2. Operative July 1, 1983, by Sec. 3 of Ch. 1364.

Section 701.560 - Failure to give notice of sale
(a) Failure to give notice of sale as required by this article does not invalidate the sale.
(b) A levying officer who sells property without giving the required notice is liable to the judgment creditor and the judgment debtor for actual damages caused by failure to give notice.

Added by Stats. 1982, Ch. 1364, Sec. 2. Operative July 1, 1983, by Sec. 3 of Ch. 1364.

Section 701.570 - Sale procedure

(a) A sale of property shall be held at the date, time, and place specified in the notice of sale, which shall be in the county where the property or a part thereof is situated and between the hours of nine in the morning and five in the afternoon. Subject to subdivision (d), real property consisting of one parcel, or of two or more contiguous parcels, situated in two or more counties may be sold in one county as instructed by the judgment creditor.

(b) The sale shall be made at auction to the highest bidder.

(c) If personal property capable of manual delivery is to be sold, it shall be within the view of those who attend the sale unless, upon application of the judgment creditor or the judgment debtor, the court orders otherwise.

(d) Property shall be sold separately or in such groups or lots as are likely to bring the highest price. The judgment debtor may request that the property be sold separately or together and may request that the property be sold in a particular order. If the judgment debtor is not present at the sale, the request may be made in writing and delivered to the levying officer prior to the sale. The levying officer shall honor the request if, in the opinion of the levying officer, the requested manner of sale is likely to yield an amount at least equal to any other manner of sale or the amount required to satisfy the money judgment. The levying officer is not liable for a decision made in good faith under this subdivision.

(e) After sufficient property has been sold to yield the amount required to satisfy the money judgment, no more shall be sold.

Added by Stats. 1982, Ch. 1364, Sec. 2. Operative July 1, 1983, by Sec. 3 of Ch. 1364.

Section 701.580 - Request to postpone sale

The judgment debtor and judgment creditor together may request in writing that a sale be postponed to an agreed day and hour. The request shall be delivered to the levying officer conducting the sale, and the levying officer shall, by public declaration at the time and place originally fixed for the sale, postpone the sale to the day and hour fixed in the request. Notice of any additional postponements shall be given by public declaration by the levying officer at the time and place last appointed for the sale. No other notice of postponed sale need be given. A postponed sale shall be held at the place originally fixed for the sale.

Added by Stats. 1982, Ch. 1364, Sec. 2. Operative July 1, 1983, by Sec. 3 of Ch. 1364.

Section 701.590 - Payment; bid by judgment creditor; election to treat sale as credit transaction

(a) Except as otherwise provided in this section, the purchaser at a sale shall pay in cash or by certified check or cashier's check.

(b) The judgment creditor may bid by giving the levying officer a written receipt crediting all or part of the amount required to satisfy the judgment, except that the levying officer's costs remaining unsatisfied and the amount of preferred labor claims, exempt proceeds, and any other claim that is required by statute to be satisfied, shall be paid in cash or by certified check or cashier's check.

(c) If the highest bid for an interest in real property sold exceeds five thousand dollars ($5,000), the highest bidder may elect to treat the sale as a credit transaction. A person who makes the election shall deposit at least five thousand dollars ($5,000) or 10 percent of the amount bid, whichever is greater, and within 10 days after the date of the sale shall pay the balance due plus costs accruing with regard to the property sold and interest accruing at the rate on money judgments on the balance of the amount bid from the date of sale until the date of payment.

(d) If the highest bid for an item, group, or lot of personal property sold exceeds two thousand five hundred dollars ($2,500), the highest bidder may elect to treat the sale as a credit transaction. A person who makes the election shall deposit at least two thousand five hundred dollars ($2,500) or 10 percent of the amount bid, whichever is greater, and within 10 days after the date of the sale shall pay the balance due plus costs accruing with regard to the property sold and interest accruing at the rate on money judgments on the balance of the amount bid from the date of sale until the date of payment.

(e) A person who makes the election under subdivision (c) or (d) is not entitled to possession of the property sold until the amount bid, plus accruing costs and interest, have been paid.

Added by Stats. 1982, Ch. 1364, Sec. 2. Operative July 1, 1983, by Sec. 3 of Ch. 1364.

Section 701.600 - Defaulting bidder

If the highest bidder does not pay the amount bid as prescribed by Section 701.590:

(a) The levying officer shall sell the property:

(1) If the default occurs at the sale, either to the next highest bidder at the amount of the next highest bid if such bidder agrees or to the highest bidder at a new sale held immediately.

(2) If the default occurs after the sale to a credit bidder pursuant to subdivision (c) of Section 701.590, to the highest bidder at a new sale.

(b) The levying officer shall apply the amount of any deposit made pursuant to subdivision (c) of Section 701.590 in the following order:

(1) To the satisfaction of costs accruing with regard to the property sold from the date of the sale until the date the property is resold, including costs of resale.

(2) To the satisfaction of interest at the rate on money judgments on the amount bid from the date of the sale until the date the property is resold.

(3) To the amount required to satisfy the money judgment in the order of distribution prescribed by Section 701.810 or Section 704.850, whichever is applicable.

(c) If there is a sale to the next highest bidder or to the highest bidder at a new sale, the defaulting bidder is liable for the following amounts in an action by the judgment creditor or judgment debtor:

(1) The amount bid, less the amount obtained from the resale of the property and the amount of any deposit applied pursuant to subdivision (b). The amount recovered pursuant to this paragraph shall be distributed in the manner prescribed by Section 701.810 or Section 704.850, whichever is applicable.

(2) Any costs accruing with regard to the property sold from the date of sale until the date the property is resold, including costs of resale.

(3) Interest at the rate on money judgments on the amount bid from the date of the sale until the date the property is resold.

(4) Costs and attorney's fees incurred in the action under this subdivision.

(d) The levying officer may, in the levying officer's discretion, reject any subsequent bid of the defaulting bidder.

Added by Stats. 1982, Ch. 1364, Sec. 2. Operative July 1, 1983, by Sec. 3 of Ch. 1364.

Section 701.610 - Levying officer may not be purchaser

The levying officer may not be a purchaser or have an interest in any purchase at a sale.

Added by Stats. 1982, Ch. 1364, Sec. 2. Operative July 1, 1983, by Sec. 3 of Ch. 1364.

Section 701.620 - Minimum bid required

(a) Property may not be sold unless the amount bid exceeds the total of the following amounts:

(1) The amount of all preferred labor claims that are required by Section 1206 to be satisfied from the proceeds.

(2) The amount of any state tax lien (as defined in Section 7162 of the Government Code) that is superior to the judgment creditor's lien.

(3) If the purchaser is not the judgment creditor, the amount of any deposit made pursuant to Section 720.260 with interest thereon at the rate on money judgments from the date of the deposit to the date of the sale.

(b) Property for which a proceeds exemption is provided by Section 704.010 (motor vehicle), 704.020 (household furnishings and other personal effects), or 704.060 (tools of trade), may not be sold unless the amount bid exceeds the sum of any amount under subdivision (a) and the amount of the proceeds exemption.

(c) If a minimum bid required for the sale of property pursuant to this section is not received, the levying officer shall promptly release the property.
Added by Stats. 1982, Ch. 1364, Sec. 2. Operative July 1, 1983, by Sec. 3 of Ch. 1364.

Section 701.630 - Liens extinguished
If property is sold pursuant to this article, the lien under which it is sold, any liens subordinate thereto, and any state tax lien (as defined in Section 7162 of the Government Code) on the property sold are extinguished.
Added by Stats. 1982, Ch. 1364, Sec. 2. Operative July 1, 1983, by Sec. 3 of Ch. 1364.

Section 701.640 - Interest acquired by purchaser
The purchaser of property at an execution sale acquires any interest of the judgment debtor in the property sold (1) that is held on the effective date of the lien under which the property was sold or (2) that is acquired between such effective date and the date of sale.
Added by Stats. 1982, Ch. 1364, Sec. 2. Operative July 1, 1983, by Sec. 3 of Ch. 1364.

Section 701.650 - Personal property or certificate of sale delivered to purchaser upon payment
(a) When the purchaser of personal property pays the amount due:
(1) If the property is capable of manual delivery, the levying officer shall deliver the property to the purchaser and, if the purchaser so requests, shall execute and deliver a certificate of sale to the purchaser.
(2) If the property is not tangible personal property or if it is otherwise not capable of manual delivery, the levying officer shall execute and deliver a certificate of sale to the purchaser.
(b) If property or a certificate is delivered pursuant to subdivision (a), the levying officer shall sign or endorse any document or instrument in the levying officer's possession relating to the title to or the right to possession of the property and deliver it to the purchaser.
Added by Stats. 1982, Ch. 1364, Sec. 2. Operative July 1, 1983, by Sec. 3 of Ch. 1364.

Section 701.660 - Deed of sale delivered upon payment by purchaser of amount due
When the purchaser of an interest in real property pays the amount due to the levying officer, including any amount required to be paid as a documentary transfer tax pursuant to Section 11911 of the Revenue and Taxation Code, the levying officer conducting the sale shall execute and deliver a deed of sale to the purchaser, record a duplicate of the deed of sale in the office of the county recorder, and forward to the county or city and county any documentary transfer tax paid by the purchaser.
Amended by Stats 2010 ch 680 (AB 2394),s 11, eff. 1/1/2011.

Section 701.670 - Requirements of certificate or deed of sale
The certificate of sale or deed of sale shall contain all of the following:
(a) The title of the court where the judgment was entered under which the sale was made and the cause and number of the action.
(b) The date of entry of the judgment and of any subsequent renewals and where entered in the records of the court.
(c) The name and address of the judgment creditor and the name and last known address of the judgment debtor.
(d) A description of the property sold.
(e) The date of sale.
Added by Stats. 1982, Ch. 1364, Sec. 2. Operative July 1, 1983, by Sec. 3 of Ch. 1364.

Section 701.680 - Sale absolute and not set aside; exceptions
(a) Except as provided in paragraph (1) of subdivision (c), a sale of property pursuant to this article is absolute and shall not be set aside for any reason.
(b) If the judgment is reversed, vacated, or otherwise set aside, the judgment debtor may recover from the judgment creditor the proceeds of a sale pursuant to the judgment with interest at the rate on money judgments to the extent the proceeds were applied to the satisfaction of the judgment.
(c) If the sale was improper because of irregularities in the proceedings, because the property sold was not subject to execution, or for any other reason:
(1) The judgment debtor, or the judgment debtor's successor in interest, may commence an action within 90 days after the date of sale to set aside the sale if the purchaser at the sale is the judgment creditor. Subject to paragraph (2), if the sale is set aside, the judgment of the judgment creditor is revived to reflect the amount that was satisfied from the proceeds of the sale and the judgment creditor is entitled to interest on the amount of the judgment as so revived as if the sale had not been made. Any liens extinguished by the sale of the property are revived and reattach to the property with the same priority and effect as if the sale had not been made.
(2) The judgment debtor, or the judgment debtor's successor in interest, may recover damages caused by the impropriety. If damages are recovered against the judgment creditor, they shall be offset against the judgment to the extent the judgment is not satisfied. If damages are recovered against the levying officer, they shall be applied to the judgment to the extent the judgment is not satisfied.
(d) For the purposes of subdivision (c), the purchaser of the property at the sale is not a successor in interest.
(e) This section does not affect, limit, or eliminate a judgment debtor's equitable right of redemption.
Amended by Stats 2014 ch 183 (AB 2317),s 1, eff. 1/1/2015.

Article 7 - DISTRIBUTION OF PROCEEDS OF SALE OR COLLECTION

Section 701.810 - Order of distribution
Except as otherwise provided by statute, the levying officer shall distribute the proceeds of sale or collection in the following order:
(a) To persons having preferred labor claims that are required by Section 1206 to be satisfied from the proceeds, in the amounts required by Section 1206 to be satisfied.
(b) To the state department or agency having a state tax lien (as defined in Section 7162 of the Government Code) that is superior to the judgment creditor's lien, in the amount of the lien.
(c) If a deposit has been made pursuant to Section 720.260 and the purchaser at the sale is not the judgment creditor, to the judgment creditor in the amount required to repay the deposit with interest thereon at the rate on money judgments from the date of the deposit.
(d) To the judgment debtor in the amount of any applicable exemption of proceeds pursuant to Section 704.010 (motor vehicle), 704.020 (household furnishings and other personal effects), or 704.060 (tools of trade), except that such proceeds shall be used to satisfy all of the following in the order of their respective priorities:
(1) Any consensual liens and encumbrances, and any liens for labor or materials, that are subordinate to the judgment creditor's lien.
(2) Subject to Section 688.030, any state tax lien (as defined in Section 7162 of the Government Code) on the property sold if the notice of state tax lien on the property has been recorded or filed pursuant to Section 7171 of the Government Code prior to the time the levying officer received the proceeds of the sale or collection.
(e) To the levying officer for the reimbursement of the levying officer's costs for which an advance has not been made.
(f) To the judgment creditor to satisfy the following, in the following order:
(1) First, any costs and interest accruing on the judgment after issuance of the writ pursuant to which the sale or collection is conducted.
(2) Second, the principal amount due on the judgment with costs and interest, as entered on the writ.
(g) To any other judgment creditors who have delivered writs to the levying officer, accompanied by instructions to levy upon the judgment debtor's property or the proceeds of its sale or collection, or any other persons actually known by the levying officer to have a claim, lien, or other

interest subordinate to the judgment creditor's lien that is extinguished by the sale and that is not otherwise satisfied pursuant to this section, in the amounts to which they are entitled in order of their respective priorities.

(h) To the judgment debtor in the amount remaining.

Amended by Stats 2010 ch 4 (AB 680),s 2, eff. 1/1/2011.

Section 701.820 - Duty of levying officer after sale

(a) Promptly after a sale or collection under this title, the levying officer shall distribute the proceeds to the persons entitled thereto or, in cases covered by Section 701.830, deposit the proceeds with the court.

(b) Except as otherwise provided by statute, the proceeds shall be paid to the persons entitled thereto within 30 days after the proceeds are received by the levying officer.

(c) If the proceeds are not received by the levying officer in one payment, the levying officer may accumulate proceeds received during a 30-day period and the accumulated proceeds shall be paid to the persons entitled thereto not later than 10 days after the expiration of the 30-day period.

(d) When proceeds are received by the levying officer in the form of a check or other form of noncash payment that is to be honored upon presentation by the levying officer for payment, the proceeds are not received for the purposes of this section until the check or other form of noncash payment has actually been honored upon presentation for payment.

(e) The provisions of Section 26680 of the Government Code apply to the levying officer only if all of the following conditions are satisfied:

(1) The levying officer has failed to pay the proceeds or deposit them with the court as provided in this article within the time provided in this section.

(2) Upon such failure, a person entitled to any of the proceeds has filed, in person or by certified mail, with the levying officer a written demand for the payment of the proceeds to the persons entitled thereto.

(3) The levying officer has failed within 10 days after the demand is filed to pay to the person filing the demand the proceeds to which that person is entitled.

(f) If all proceeds have not been received within 10 days after the filing of the demand specified by paragraph (3) of subdivision (e), a judgment creditor may file an ex parte application for an order directing the levying officer to show cause why relief should not be granted pursuant to Section 26680 of the Government Code. The order shall name a date and time for the levying officer to appear not less than 20 and not more than 30 days after filing of the application. If the levying officer pays all proceeds as provided in subdivision (e) of Section 701.810 to the judgment creditor no later than 10 days prior to the hearing, the judgment creditor shall notify the court of full payment no later than three days prior to the hearing and the court shall withdraw the order and vacate the hearing.

(g) An ex parte application filed pursuant to subdivision (f) shall state the date and manner of all of the following:

(1) Delivery of the writ of execution to the levying officer.

(2) Remittance of the proceeds to the levying officer.

(3) Filing of the 10-day demand pursuant to subdivision (e).

(h) If the court finds that the facts alleged in the ex parte application filed pursuant to subdivision (f) to be knowingly false, or made in bad faith, the court may award costs and reasonable attorney fees to the levying officer.

Amended by Stats 2010 ch 4 (AB 680),s 3, eff. 1/1/2011.

Section 701.830 - Conflicting claims; motion for order of distribution

(a) If there are conflicting claims to all or a portion of the proceeds of sale or collection known to the levying officer before the proceeds are distributed, the levying officer may deposit with the court the proceeds that are the subject of the conflicting claims instead of distributing such proceeds under Section 701.810. Any interested person may apply on noticed motion for an order for the distribution of the proceeds deposited with the court. A copy of the notice of motion shall be served on such persons as the court shall by order determine in such manner as the court prescribes. Any interested person may request time for filing a response to the motion for an order for the distribution of the proceeds, for discovery proceedings in connection with the motion, or for other preparation for the hearing on the motion, and the court shall grant a continuance for a reasonable time for any of these purposes.

(b) Except as provided in subdivision (c), at the hearing on the motion the court shall determine the issues presented by the motion and make an order for the distribution of the proceeds deposited with the court.

(c) The court shall not determine the issues presented by the motion and instead shall abate the hearing until the issues presented by the motion can be determined in a civil action in the following cases if:

(1) The court is not the proper court under any other provision of law for the trial of a civil action with respect to the subject matter of the motion and any interested person at or prior to the hearing objects to the determination of the issues presented by the motion by the court.

(2) A civil action is pending with respect to the subject matter of the motion and jurisdiction has been obtained in the court in which the civil action is pending.

(3) The court determines that the matter should be determined in a civil action.

Added by Stats. 1982, Ch. 1364, Sec. 2. Operative July 1, 1983, by Sec. 3 of Ch. 1364.

Chapter 4 - EXEMPTIONS

Article 1 - GENERAL PROVISIONS

Section 703.010 - Generally

Except as otherwise provided by statute:

(a) The exemptions provided by this chapter or by any other statute apply to all procedures for enforcement of a money judgment.

(b) The exemptions provided by this chapter or by any other statute do not apply if the judgment to be enforced is for the foreclosure of a mortgage, deed of trust, or other lien or encumbrance on the property other than a lien created pursuant to this division or pursuant to Title 6.5 (commencing with Section 481.010) (attachment).

Added by Stats. 1982, Ch. 1364, Sec. 2. Operative July 1, 1983, by Sec. 3 of Ch. 1364.

Section 703.020 - Applicable to natural persons only; person who may claim

(a) The exemptions provided by this chapter apply only to property of a natural person.

(b) The exemptions provided in this chapter may be claimed by any of the following persons:

(1) In all cases, by the judgment debtor or a person acting on behalf of the judgment debtor.

(2) In the case of community property, by the spouse of the judgment debtor, whether or not the spouse is also a judgment debtor under the judgment.

(3) In the case of community property, by the domestic partner of the judgment debtor, as defined in Section 297 of the Family Code, whether or not the domestic partner is also a judgment debtor under the judgment.

Amended by Stats 2014 ch 415 (AB 1945),s 1, eff. 1/1/2015.

Section 703.030 - Claiming exemption; waiver if not claimed

(a) An exemption for property that is described in this chapter or in any other statute as exempt may be claimed within the time and in the manner prescribed in the applicable enforcement procedure. If the exemption is not so claimed, the exemption is waived and the property is subject to enforcement of a money judgment.

(b) Except as otherwise specifically provided by statute, property that is described in this chapter or in any other statute as exempt without making a claim is not subject to any procedure for enforcement of a money judgment.

(c) Nothing in this section limits the authority of the court pursuant to Section 473 to relieve a person upon such terms as may be just from failure to claim an exemption within the time and in the manner prescribed in the applicable enforcement procedure.

Added by Stats. 1982, Ch. 1364, Sec. 2. Operative July 1, 1983, by Sec. 3 of Ch. 1364.

Section 703.040 - Contractual or other waiver against public policy and void

A purported contractual or other prior waiver of the exemptions provided by this chapter or by any other statute, other than a waiver by failure to claim an exemption required to be claimed or otherwise made at the time enforcement is sought, is against public policy and void.

Added by Stats. 1982, Ch. 1364, Sec. 2. Operative July 1, 1983, by Sec. 3 of Ch. 1364.

Section 703.050 - Determination whether property exempt or amount of exemption

(a) The determination whether property is exempt or the amount of an exemption shall be made by application of the exemption statutes in effect (1) at the time the judgment creditor's lien on the property was created or (2) if the judgment creditor's lien on the property is the latest in a series of overlapping liens created when an earlier lien on the property in favor of the judgment creditor was in effect, at the time the earliest lien in the series of overlapping liens was created.

(b) This section applies to all judgments, whether based upon tort, contract, or other legal theory or cause of action that arose before or after the operative date of this section, and whether the judgment was entered before or after the operative date of this section.

(c) Notwithstanding subdivision (a), in the case of a levy of execution, the procedures to be followed in levying upon, selling, or releasing property, claiming, processing, opposing, and determining exemptions, and paying exemption proceeds, shall be governed by the law in effect at the time the levy of execution is made on the property.

Added by Stats. 1982, Ch. 1364, Sec. 2. Operative July 1, 1983, by Sec. 3 of Ch. 1364.

Section 703.060 - Power of state to repeal, alter and add to statutes

(a) The Legislature finds and declares that generally persons who enter into contracts do not do so in reliance on an assumption that the exemptions in effect at the time of the contract will govern enforcement of any judgment based on the contract, that liens imposed on property are imposed not as a matter of right but as a matter of privilege granted by statute for purposes of priority, that no vested rights with respect to exemptions are created by the making of a contract or imposition of a lien, that application of exemptions and exemption procedures in effect at the time of enforcement of a judgment is essential to the proper balance between the rights of judgment debtors and judgment creditors and has a minimal effect on the economic stability essential for the maintenance of private and public faith in commercial matters, and that it is the policy of the state to treat all judgment debtors equally with respect to exemptions and exemption procedures in effect at the time of enforcement of a money judgment. To this end, the Legislature reserves the right to repeal, alter, or add to the exemptions and the procedures therefor at any time and intends, unless otherwise provided by statute, that any repeals, alterations, or additions apply upon their operative date to enforcement of all money judgments, whether based upon tort, contract, or other legal theory or cause of action that arose before or after the operative date of the repeals, alterations, or additions, whether the judgment was entered before or after the operative date of the repeals, alterations, or additions.

(b) All contracts shall be deemed to have been made and all liens on property shall be deemed to have been created in recognition of the power of the state to repeal, alter, and add to statutes providing for liens and exemptions from the enforcement of money judgments.

Added by Stats. 1982, Ch. 1364, Sec. 2. Operative July 1, 1983, by Sec. 3 of Ch. 1364.

Section 703.070 - Judgment for child, family or spousal support

Except as otherwise provided by statute:

(a) The exemptions provided by this chapter or by any other statute apply to a judgment for child, family, or spousal support.

(b) If property is exempt without making a claim, the property is not subject to being applied to the satisfaction of a judgment for child, family, or spousal support.

(c) Except as provided in subdivision (b), if property sought to be applied to the satisfaction of a judgment for child, family, or spousal support is shown to be exempt under subdivision (a) in appropriate proceedings, the court shall, upon noticed motion of the judgment creditor, determine the extent to which the exempt property nevertheless shall be applied to the satisfaction of the judgment. In making this determination, the court shall take into account the needs of the judgment creditor, the needs of the judgment debtor and all the persons the judgment debtor is required to support, and all other relevant circumstances. The court shall effectuate its determination by an order specifying the extent to which the otherwise exempt property is to be applied to the satisfaction of the judgment.

Amended by Stats. 1992, Ch. 163, Sec. 37. Effective January 1, 1993. Operative January 1, 1994, by Sec. 161 of Ch. 163.

Section 703.080 - Exempt fund

(a) Subject to any limitation provided in the particular exemption, a fund that is exempt remains exempt to the extent that it can be traced into deposit accounts or in the form of cash or its equivalent.

(b) The exemption claimant has the burden of tracing an exempt fund.

(c) The tracing of exempt funds in a deposit account shall be by application of the lowest intermediate balance principle unless the exemption claimant or the judgment creditor shows that some other method of tracing would better serve the interests of justice and equity under the circumstances of the case.

Added by Stats. 1982, Ch. 1364, Sec. 2. Operative July 1, 1983, by Sec. 3 of Ch. 1364.

Section 703.090 - Recovery of subsequent cost of collection

If a judgment creditor has failed to oppose a claim of exemption within the time allowed by Section 703.550 or if property has been determined by a court to be exempt, and the judgment creditor thereafter levies upon or otherwise seeks to apply the property toward the satisfaction of the same money judgment, the judgment creditor is not entitled to recover the subsequent costs of collection unless the property is applied to satisfaction of the judgment.

Added by Stats. 1982, Ch. 1364, Sec. 2. Operative July 1, 1983, by Sec. 3 of Ch. 1364.

Section 703.100 - Exempt determination circumstances; changes considered

(a) Subject to subdivision (b), the determination whether property is exempt shall be made under the circumstances existing at the earliest of the following times:

    (1) The time of levy on the property.

    (2) The time of the commencement of court proceedings for the application of the property to the satisfaction of the money judgment.

    (3) The time a lien is created under Title 6.5 (commencing with Section 481.010) (attachment) or under this title.

(b) The court, in its discretion, may take into consideration any of the following changes that have occurred between the time of levy or commencement of enforcement proceedings or creation of the lien and the time of the hearing:

    (1) A change in the use of the property if the exemption is based upon the use of property and if the property was used for the exempt purpose at the time of the levy or the commencement of enforcement proceedings or the creation of the lien but is used for a nonexempt purpose at the time of the hearing.

    (2) A change in the value of the property if the exemption is based upon the value of property.

    (3) A change in the financial circumstances of the judgment debtor and spouse and dependents of the judgment debtor if the exemption is based upon their needs.

Added by Stats. 1982, Ch. 1364, Sec. 2. Operative July 1, 1983, by Sec. 3 of Ch. 1364.

Section 703.110 - Judgment debtor married

If the judgment debtor is married:

(a) The exemptions provided by this chapter or by any other statute apply to all property that is subject to enforcement of a money judgment, including the interest of the spouse of the judgment debtor in community property. The fact that one or both spouses are judgment debtors under the judgment or that property sought to be applied to the satisfaction of the judgment is separate or community does not increase or reduce the number or amount of the exemptions. Where the property exempt under a particular exemption is limited to a specified maximum dollar amount, unless the exemption provision specifically provides otherwise, the two spouses together are entitled to one exemption limited to the specified maximum dollar amount, whether one or both of the spouses are judgment debtors under the judgment and whether the property sought to be applied to the satisfaction of the judgment is separate or community.

(b) If an exemption is required by statute to be applied first to property not before the court and then to property before the court, the application of the exemption to property not before the court shall be made to the community property and separate property of both spouses, whether or not such property is subject to enforcement of the money judgment.

(c) If the same exemption is claimed by the judgment debtor and the spouse of the judgment debtor for different property, and the property claimed by one spouse, but not both, is exempt, the exemption shall be applied as the spouses agree. If the spouses are unable to agree, the exemption shall be applied as directed by the court in its discretion.

Amended by Stats. 1983, Ch. 155, Sec. 14.7. Effective June 30, 1983. Operative July 1, 1983, by Sec. 32 of Ch. 155.

Section 703.115 - Determination made based upon needs of debtor and debtor's family

In determining an exemption based upon the needs of the judgment debtor and the spouse and dependents of the judgment debtor or an exemption based upon the needs of the judgment debtor and the family of the judgment debtor, the court shall take into account all property of the judgment debtor and, to the extent the judgment debtor has a spouse and dependents or family, all property of such spouse and dependents or family, including community property and separate property of the spouse, whether or not such property is subject to enforcement of the money judgment.

Added by Stats. 1983, Ch. 155, Sec. 15. Effective June 30, 1983. Operative July 1, 1983, by Sec. 32 of Ch. 155.

Section 703.120 - [Repealed]

Repealed by Stats 2013 ch 15 (AB 567),s 2, eff. 1/1/2014.

Section 703.130 - Exemptions set forth in Bankruptcy Code not authorized in state

Pursuant to the authority of paragraph (2) of subsection (b) of Section 522 of Title 11 of the United States Code, the exemptions set forth in subsection (d) of Section 522 of Title 11 of the United States Code (Bankruptcy) are not authorized in this state.

Amended by Stats 2009 ch 500 (AB 1059),s 14, eff. 1/1/2010.

Section 703.140 - Applicability of exemption in case under Title 11 of United States Code

(a) In a case under Title 11 of the United States Code, all of the exemptions provided by this chapter, including the homestead exemption, other than the provisions of subdivision (b) are applicable regardless of whether there is a money judgment against the debtor or whether a money judgment is being enforced by execution sale or any other procedure, but the exemptions provided by subdivision (b) may be elected in lieu of all other exemptions provided by this chapter, as follows:

(1) If spouses are joined in the petition, they jointly may elect to utilize the applicable exemption provisions of this chapter other than the provisions of subdivision (b), or to utilize the applicable exemptions set forth in subdivision (b), but not both.

(2)

(A) If the petition is filed individually, and not jointly, for a spouse, the exemptions provided by this chapter other than the provisions of subdivision (b) are applicable, except that, if both of the spouses effectively waive in writing the right to claim, during the period the case commenced by filing the petition is pending, the exemptions provided by the applicable exemption provisions of this chapter, other than subdivision (b), in any case commenced by filing a petition for either of them under Title 11 of the United States Code, then they may elect to instead utilize the applicable exemptions set forth in subdivision (b).

(B) Notwithstanding subparagraph (A), a waiver is not required from a debtor who is living separate and apart from their spouse as of the date the petition commencing the case under Title 11 of the United States Code is filed, unless, on the petition date, the debtor and the debtor's spouse shared an ownership interest in property that could be exempted as a homestead under Article 4 of this chapter.

(3) If the petition is filed for an unmarried person, that person may elect to utilize the applicable exemption provisions of this chapter other than subdivision (b), or to utilize the applicable exemptions set forth in subdivision (b), but not both.

(b) The following exemptions may be elected as provided in subdivision (a):

(1) The debtor's aggregate interest, not to exceed twenty-nine thousand two hundred seventy-five dollars ($29,275) in value, in real property or personal property that the debtor or a dependent of the debtor uses as a residence, in a cooperative that owns property that the debtor or a dependent of the debtor uses as a residence.

(2) The debtor's interest, not to exceed seven thousand five hundred dollars ($7,500) in value, in one or more motor vehicles.

(3) The debtor's interest, not to exceed seven hundred twenty-five dollars ($725) in value in any particular item, in household furnishings, household goods, wearing apparel, appliances, books, animals, crops, or musical instruments, that are held primarily for the personal, family, or household use of the debtor or a dependent of the debtor.

(4) The debtor's aggregate interest, not to exceed one thousand seven hundred fifty dollars ($1,750) in value, in jewelry held primarily for the personal, family, or household use of the debtor or a dependent of the debtor.

(5) The debtor's aggregate interest, not to exceed one thousand five hundred fifty dollars ($1,550) in value, plus any unused amount of the exemption provided under paragraph (1), in any property.

(6) The debtor's aggregate interest, not to exceed eight thousand seven hundred twenty-five dollars ($8,725) in value, in any implements, professional books, or tools of the trade of the debtor or the trade of a dependent of the debtor.

(7) Any unmatured life insurance contract owned by the debtor, other than a credit life insurance contract.

(8) The debtor's aggregate interest, not to exceed fifteen thousand six hundred fifty dollars ($15,650) in value, in any accrued dividend or interest under, or loan value of, any unmatured life insurance contract owned by the debtor under which the insured is the debtor or an individual of whom the debtor is a dependent.

(9) Professionally prescribed health aids for the debtor, the debtor's spouse, or a dependent of the debtor, including vehicles converted for use by the debtor, the debtor's spouse, or a dependent of the debtor, who has a disability. Conversion of a vehicle for use by a person who has a disability includes altering the interior, installing steering, a wheelchair lift, or motorized steps, or modifying the operation of the vehicle.

(10) The debtor's right to receive any of the following:

(A) A social security benefit, unemployment compensation, or a local public assistance benefit.

(B) A veterans' benefit.

(C) A disability, illness, or unemployment benefit.

(D) Alimony, support, or separate maintenance, to the extent reasonably necessary for the support of the debtor and any dependent of the debtor.

(E) A payment under a stock bonus, pension, profit-sharing, annuity, or similar plan or contract on account of illness, disability, death, age, or length of service, to the extent reasonably necessary for the support of the debtor and any dependent of the debtor, unless all of the following apply:

    (i) That plan or contract was established by or under the auspices of an insider that employed the debtor at the time the debtor's rights under the plan or contract arose.

    (ii) The payment is on account of age or length of service.

    (iii) That plan or contract does not qualify under Section 401(a), 403(a), 403(b), 408, or 408A of the Internal Revenue Code of 1986.

(F) The aggregate interest, not to exceed seven thousand five hundred dollars ($7,500), in vacation credits or accrued, or unused, vacation pay, sick leave, family leave, or wages, as defined in Section 200 of the Labor Code.

(11) The debtor's right to receive, or property that is traceable to, any of the following:

(A) An award under a crime victim's reparation law.

(B) A payment under a settlement agreement arising out of or regarding the debtor's employment, to the extent reasonably necessary for the support of the debtor, the debtor's spouse, or a dependent of the debtor.

(C) A payment on account of the wrongful death of an individual of whom the debtor was a dependent, to the extent reasonably necessary for the support of the debtor and any dependent of the debtor.

(D) A payment under a life insurance contract that insured the life of an individual of whom the debtor was a spouse or dependent on the date of that individual's death, to the extent reasonably necessary for the support of the debtor and any dependent of the debtor.

(E) A payment, not to exceed twenty-nine thousand two hundred seventy-five dollars ($29,275) on account of personal bodily injury of the debtor, the debtor's spouse, or an individual of whom the debtor is a dependent.

(F) A payment in compensation of loss of future earnings of the debtor or an individual of whom the debtor is or was a spouse or dependent, to the extent reasonably necessary for the support of the debtor and the debtor's spouse or a dependent of the debtor.

(12) Money held in an account owned by the judgment debtor and established pursuant to the Golden State Scholarshare Trust Act (Article 19 (commencing with Section 69980) of Chapter 2 of Part 42 of Division 5 of Title 3 of the Education Code), subject to the following limits:

(A) The amount exempted for contributions to an account during the 365-day period prior to the date of filing of the debtor's petition for bankruptcy, in the aggregate during this period, shall not exceed the amount of the annual gift tax exclusion under Section 2503(b) of the Internal Revenue Code of 1986, as amended, in effect at the time of the filing of the debtor's petition for bankruptcy.

(B) The amount exempted for contributions to an account during the period commencing 730 days prior to and ending 366 days prior to the date of filing of the debtor's petition for bankruptcy, in the aggregate during this period, shall not exceed the amount of the annual gift tax exclusion under Section 2503(b) of the Internal Revenue Code of 1986, as amended, in effect at the time of the filing of the debtor's petition for bankruptcy.

(C) For the purposes of this paragraph, "account" includes all accounts having the same beneficiary.

(D) This paragraph is not subject to the requirements of Section 703.150.

(c) In a case under Title 11 of the United States Code, the value of the property claimed as exempt and the debtor's exemptions provided by this chapter with respect to such property shall be determined as of the date the bankruptcy petition is filed. In a case where the debtor's equity in a residence is less than or equal to the amount of the debtor's allowed homestead exemption as of the date the bankruptcy petition is filed, any appreciation in the value of the debtor's interest in the property during the pendency of the case is exempt.

Amended by Stats 2022 ch 716 (SB 1099),s 2.5, eff. 1/1/2023.
Amended by Stats 2022 ch 25 (SB 956),s 1, eff. 1/1/2023.
Amended by Stats 2021 ch 124 (AB 938),s 10, eff. 1/1/2022.
Amended by Stats 2020 ch 81 (SB 898),s 1, eff. 1/1/2021.
Amended by Stats 2016 ch 50 (SB 1005),s 16, eff. 1/1/2017.
Amended by Stats 2012 ch 678 (AB 929),s 1, eff. 1/1/2013.
Amended by Stats 2003 ch 379 (AB 182),s 3, eff. 1/1/2004.
Amended by Stats 2001 ch 42 (AB 1704), s 1, eff. 1/1/2002.
Amended by Stats 2000 ch 135 (AB 2539), s 15, eff. 1/1/2001.
Previously Amended July 13, 1999 (Bill Number: SB 469) (Chapter 98).

Section 703.150 - Adjustment of dollar amounts of exemptions

(a) On April 1, 2004, and at each three-year interval ending on April 1 thereafter, the dollar amounts of exemptions provided in subdivision (b) of Section 703.140 in effect immediately before that date shall be adjusted as provided in subdivision (e).

(b) On April 1, 2007, and at each three-year interval ending on April 1 thereafter, the dollar amounts of exemptions provided in Article 3 (commencing with Section 704.010) in effect immediately before that date shall be adjusted as provided in subdivision (e).

(c) On April 1, 2022, and at each three-year interval ending on April 1 thereafter, the dollar amount set forth in paragraph (7) of subdivision (b) of Section 699.730 in effect immediately before that date shall be adjusted as provided in subdivision (e).

(d) On April 1, 2013, and at each three-year interval ending on April 1 thereafter, the Judicial Council shall submit to the Legislature the amount by which the dollar amounts of exemptions provided in subdivision (a) of Section 704.730 in effect immediately before that date may be increased as provided in subdivision (e). Those increases shall not take effect unless they are approved by the Legislature.

(e) The Judicial Council shall determine the amount of the adjustment based on the change in the annual California Consumer Price Index for All Urban Consumers, published by the Department of Industrial Relations, Division of Labor Statistics, for the most recent three-year period ending on December 31 preceding the adjustment, with each adjusted amount rounded to the nearest twenty-five dollars ($25).

(f) Beginning April 1, 2004, the Judicial Council shall publish a list of the current dollar amounts of exemptions provided in subdivision (b) of Section 703.140 and in Article 3 (commencing with Section 704.010), and the dollar amount set forth in paragraph (7) of subdivision (b) of Section 699.730, together with the date of the next scheduled adjustment. In any year that the Legislature votes to increase the exemptions provided in subdivision (a) of Section 704.730, the Judicial Council shall publish a list of current dollar amounts of exemptions.

(g) Adjustments made under subdivision (a) do not apply with respect to cases commenced before the date of the adjustment, subject to any contrary rule applicable under the federal Bankruptcy Code. The applicability of adjustments made under subdivisions (b), (c), and (d) is governed by Section 703.050.

Amended by Stats 2020 ch 218 (AB 2463),s 2, eff. 1/1/2021.
Amended by Stats 2012 ch 678 (AB 929),s 2, eff. 1/1/2013.
Amended by Stats 2010 ch 212 (AB 2767),s 1, eff. 1/1/2011.
Amended by Stats 2009 ch 499 (AB 1046),s 1, eff. 1/1/2010.
Added by Stats 2003 ch 379 (AB 182),s 4, eff. 1/1/2004.

Article 2 - PROCEDURE FOR CLAIMING EXEMPTIONS AFTER LEVY

Section 703.510 - Generally

(a) Except as otherwise provided by statute, property that has been levied upon may be claimed to be exempt as provided in this article.

(b) If property that is exempt without making a claim is levied upon, it may be released pursuant to the exemption procedure provided in this article.
Added by Stats. 1982, Ch. 1364, Sec. 2. Operative July 1, 1983, by Sec. 3 of Ch. 1364.

Section 703.520 - Filing claim; time; information included

(a) The claimant may make a claim of exemption by filing with the levying officer, either in person or by mail, a claim of exemption together with a copy of the claim. If the claimant is personally served, the claim shall be made within 15 days after the date the notice of levy on the property claimed to be exempt is served on the judgment debtor. If the claimant is served by mail, the claim shall be made within 20 days after the date the notice of levy on the property claimed to be exempt is served on the judgment debtor. If the claim is filed by mail and assigned a tracking number by the United States Postal Service or another common carrier, the filing shall be deemed complete on the date the claim is postmarked. If the claim is filed by mail and not assigned a tracking number, the filing shall be deemed complete on the date the claim is received by the levying officer.

(b) The claim of exemption shall be executed under oath and shall include all of the following:

(1) The name of the claimant and the mailing address where service of a notice of opposition to the claim may be made upon the claimant.

(2) The name and last known address of the judgment debtor if the claimant is not the judgment debtor.

(3) A description of the property claimed to be exempt. If an exemption is claimed pursuant to Section 704.010 or 704.060, the claimant shall describe all other property of the same type, including exempt proceeds of the property of the same type, owned by the judgment debtor alone or in combination with others on the date of levy and identify the property, whether or not levied upon, to which the exemption is to be applied. If an exemption is claimed pursuant to subdivision (b) of Section 704.100, the claimant shall state the nature and amount of all other property of the same type owned by the judgment debtor or the spouse of the judgment debtor alone or in combination with others on the date of levy.

(4) A financial statement if required by Section 703.530.

(5) A citation of the provision of this chapter or other statute upon which the claim is based.

(6) A statement of the facts necessary to support the claim.

(c) This section shall become operative on September 1, 2020.
Added by Stats 2019 ch 552 (SB 616),s 4, eff. 1/1/2020.

Section 703.530 - Financial statement

(a) If property is claimed as exempt pursuant to a provision exempting property to the extent necessary for the support of the judgment debtor and the spouse and dependents of the judgment debtor, the claim of exemption shall include a financial statement.

(b) The financial statement shall include all of the following information:

(1) The name of the spouse of the judgment debtor.

(2) The name, age, and relationship of all persons dependent upon the judgment debtor or the spouse of the judgment debtor for support.

(3) All sources and the amounts of earnings and other income of the judgment debtor and the spouse and dependents of the judgment debtor.

(4) A list of the assets of the judgment debtor and the spouse and dependents of the judgment debtor and the value of such assets.

(5) All outstanding obligations of the judgment debtor and the spouse and dependents of the judgment debtor.

(c) The financial statement shall be executed under oath by the judgment debtor and, unless the spouses are living separate and apart, by the spouse of the judgment debtor.
Added by Stats. 1982, Ch. 1364, Sec. 2. Operative July 1, 1983, by Sec. 3 of Ch. 1364.

Section 703.540 - Service on judgment creditor

Promptly after the filing of the claim of exemption, the levying officer shall serve both of the following on the judgment creditor personally or by mail:

(a) A copy of the claim of exemption.

(b) A notice of claim of exemption stating that the claim of exemption has been made and that the levying officer will release the property unless, within the time allowed as specified in the notice, both of the following are filed with the levying officer:

(1) A copy of the notice of opposition to the claim of exemption.

(2) A copy of the notice of motion for an order determining the claim of exemption.

Added by Stats. 1982, Ch. 1364, Sec. 2. Operative July 1, 1983, by Sec. 3 of Ch. 1364.

Section 703.550 - Filing notice of opposition to claim

(a) Within 15 days after service of the notice of claim of exemption, a judgment creditor who opposes the claim of exemption shall file with the court a notice of opposition to the claim of exemption and a notice of motion for an order determining the claim of exemption and shall file with the levying officer a copy of the notice of opposition and a copy of the notice of motion. Upon the filing of the copies of the notice of opposition and notice of motion, the levying officer shall promptly file the claim of exemption with the court. If copies of the notice of opposition and notice of motion are not filed with the levying officer within the time allowed, the levying officer shall immediately release the property to the extent it is claimed to be exempt.

(b) This section shall become operative on September 1, 2020.
Added by Stats 2019 ch 552 (SB 616),s 6, eff. 1/1/2020.

Section 703.560 - Requirements of notice of opposition

The notice of opposition to the claim of exemption shall be executed under oath and shall include both of the following:

(a) An allegation either (1) that the property is not exempt under the provision of this chapter or other statute relied upon or (2) that the equity in the property claimed to be exempt is in excess of the amount provided in the applicable exemption.

(b) A statement of the facts necessary to support the allegation.
Added by Stats. 1982, Ch. 1364, Sec. 2. Operative July 1, 1983, by Sec. 3 of Ch. 1364.

Section 703.570 - Time for holding hearing on motion; service of notice of hearing

(a) The hearing on the motion shall be held not later than 30 days from the date the notice of motion was filed with the court unless continued by the court for good cause.

(b) Not less than 10 days prior to the hearing, the judgment creditor shall serve a notice of the hearing and a copy of the notice of opposition to the claim of exemption on the claimant and on the judgment debtor, if other than the claimant. Service shall be made personally or by mail.
Amended by Stats 2012 ch 484 (AB 2364),s 12, eff. 1/1/2013.

Section 703.580 - Claim and notice of opposition constitute pleadings; burden of proof; claim controverted by notice; determination of court

(a) The claim of exemption and notice of opposition to the claim of exemption constitute the pleadings, subject to the power of the court to permit amendments in the interest of justice.

(b) At a hearing under this section, the exemption claimant has the burden of proof.

(c) The claim of exemption is deemed controverted by the notice of opposition to the claim of exemption and both shall be received in evidence. If no other evidence is offered, the court, if satisfied that sufficient facts are shown by the claim of exemption (including the financial statement if one is required) and the notice of opposition, may make its determination thereon. If not satisfied, the court shall order the hearing continued for the production of other evidence, oral or documentary.

(d) At the conclusion of the hearing, the court shall determine by order whether or not the property is exempt in whole or in part. Subject to Section 703.600, the order is determinative of the right of the judgment creditor to apply the property to the satisfaction of the judgment. No findings are required in a proceeding under this section.

(e) The court clerk shall promptly transmit a certified copy of the order to the levying officer. Subject to Section 703.610, the levying officer shall, in compliance with the order, release the property or apply the property to the satisfaction of the money judgment.

(f) Unless otherwise ordered by the court, if an exemption is not determined within the time provided by Section 703.570, the property claimed to be exempt shall be released.

Amended by Stats 2002 ch 68 (SB 1322),s 5, eff. 1/1/2003.

Section 703.590 - service of notice of extension to act

If the court extends the time allowed for an act to be done under this article, written notice of the extension shall be filed with the levying officer and, unless notice is waived, shall be served promptly on the opposing party. Service shall be made personally or by mail.

Added by Stats. 1982, Ch. 1364, Sec. 2. Operative July 1, 1983, by Sec. 3 of Ch. 1364.

Section 703.600 - Appeal

An appeal lies from any order made under this article.

Amended by Stats. 1998, Ch. 931, Sec. 93. Effective September 28, 1998.

Section 703.610 - Disposition of property; orders for disposition; notice of appeal

(a) Except as otherwise provided by statute or ordered by the court, the levying officer shall not release, sell, or otherwise dispose of the property for which an exemption is claimed until an appeal is waived, the time to file an appeal has expired, or the exemption is finally determined.

(b) At any time while the exemption proceedings are pending, upon motion of the judgment creditor or a claimant, or upon its own motion, the court may make any orders for disposition of the property that may be proper under the circumstances of the case. The order may be modified or vacated by the court at any time during the pendency of the exemption proceedings upon any terms that are just.

(c) If an appeal of the determination of a claim of exemption is taken, notice of the appeal shall be given to the levying officer and the levying officer shall hold, release, or dispose of the property in accordance with the provisions governing enforcement and stay of enforcement of money judgments pending appeal.

Amended by Stats 2002 ch 68 (SB 1322),s 6, eff. 1/1/2003.

Article 3 - EXEMPT PROPERTY

Section 704.010 - Motor vehicles, execution sale proceeds and insurance proceeds

(a) Any combination of the following is exempt in the amount of seven thousand five hundred dollars ($7,500):

  (1) The aggregate equity in motor vehicles.

  (2) The proceeds of an execution sale of a motor vehicle.

  (3) The proceeds of insurance or other indemnification for the loss, damage, or destruction of a motor vehicle.

(b) Proceeds exempt under subdivision (a) are exempt for a period of 90 days after the time the proceeds are actually received by the judgment debtor.

(c) For the purpose of determining the equity, the fair market value of a motor vehicle shall be determined by reference to used car price guides customarily used by California automobile dealers unless the motor vehicle is not listed in such price guides.

(d) If the judgment debtor has only one motor vehicle and it is sold at an execution sale, the proceeds of the execution sale are exempt in the amount of seven thousand five hundred dollars ($7,500) without making a claim. The levying officer shall consult and may rely upon the records of the Department of Motor Vehicles in determining whether the judgment debtor has only one motor vehicle. In the case covered by this subdivision, the exemption provided by subdivision (a) is not available.

Amended by Stats 2022 ch 716 (SB 1099),s 3, eff. 1/1/2023.

Amended by Stats 2020 ch 81 (SB 898),s 2, eff. 1/1/2021.

Amended by Stats 2003 ch 379 (AB 182),s 5, eff. 1/1/2004.

Section 704.020 - Household furnishings appliance wearing apparel and other personal effects

(a) Household furnishings, appliances, provisions, wearing apparel, and other personal effects are exempt in the following cases:

  (1) If ordinarily and reasonably necessary to, and personally used or procured for use by, the judgment debtor and members of the judgment debtor's family at the judgment debtor's principal place of residence.

  (2) Where the judgment debtor and the judgment debtor's spouse live separate and apart, if ordinarily and reasonably necessary to, and personally used or procured for use by, the spouse and members of the spouse's family at the spouse's principal place of residence.

(b) In determining whether an item of property is "ordinarily and reasonably necessary" under subdivision (a), the court shall take into account both of the following:

  (1) The extent to which the particular type of item is ordinarily found in a household.

  (2) Whether the particular item has extraordinary value as compared to the value of items of the same type found in other households.

(c) If an item of property for which an exemption is claimed pursuant to this section is an item of the type ordinarily found in a household but is determined not to be exempt because the item has extraordinary value as compared to the value of items of the same type found in other households, the proceeds obtained at an execution sale of the item are exempt in the amount determined by the court to be a reasonable amount sufficient to purchase a replacement of ordinary value if the court determines that a replacement is reasonably necessary. Proceeds exempt under this subdivision are exempt for a period of 90 days after the proceeds are actually received by the judgment debtor.

Added by Stats. 1982, Ch. 1364, Sec. 2. Operative July 1, 1983, by Sec. 3 of Ch. 1364.

Section 704.030 - Material to be applied to repair or improvement of residence

Material that in good faith is about to be applied to the repair or improvement of a residence is exempt if the equity in the material does not exceed three thousand five hundred dollars ($3,500) in the following cases:

(a) If purchased in good faith for use in the repair or improvement of the judgment debtor's principal place of residence.

(b) Where the judgment debtor and the judgment debtor's spouse live separate and apart, if purchased in good faith for use in the repair or improvement of the spouse's principal place of residence.

Amended by Stats 2020 ch 81 (SB 898),s 3, eff. 1/1/2021.

Amended by Stats 2003 ch 379 (AB 182),s 6, eff. 1/1/2004.

Section 704.040 - Jewelry, heirlooms and works of art

Jewelry, heirlooms, and works of art are exempt to the extent that the aggregate equity therein does not exceed eight thousand seven hundred twenty-five dollars ($8,725).

Amended by Stats 2020 ch 81 (SB 898),s 4, eff. 1/1/2021.

Amended by Stats 2003 ch 379 (AB 182),s 7, eff. 1/1/2004.

Section 704.050 - Health aids; vechicles included

(a) Health aids reasonably necessary to enable the judgment debtor or the spouse or a dependent of the judgment debtor to work or sustain health, and prosthetic and orthopedic appliances, are exempt.

(b) Health aids described in subdivision (a) include vehicles converted for use by the debtor, the debtor's spouse, or a dependent of the debtor, who has a disability. Conversion of a vehicle for use by a person who has a disability includes altering the interior, installing steering, a wheelchair lift, or motorized steps, or modifying the operation of the vehicle.
Amended by Stats 2022 ch 716 (SB 1099),s 4, eff. 1/1/2023.
Added by Stats. 1982, Ch. 1364, Sec. 2. Operative July 1, 1983, by Sec. 3 of Ch. 1364.

Section 704.060 - Tolls, implements, materials, uniforms, books, commercial vehicle, vessel and other personal property
(a) Tools, implements, instruments, materials, uniforms, furnishings, books, equipment, one commercial motor vehicle, one vessel, and other personal property are exempt to the extent that the aggregate equity therein does not exceed:

(1) Eight thousand seven hundred twenty-five dollars ($8,725), if reasonably necessary to and actually used by the judgment debtor in the exercise of the trade, business, or profession by which the judgment debtor earns a livelihood.

(2) Eight thousand seven hundred twenty-five dollars ($8,725), if reasonably necessary to and actually used by the spouse of the judgment debtor in the exercise of the trade, business, or profession by which the spouse earns a livelihood.

(3) Twice the amount of the exemption provided in paragraph (1), if reasonably necessary to and actually used by the judgment debtor and by the spouse of the judgment debtor in the exercise of the same trade, business, or profession by which both earn a livelihood. In the case covered by this paragraph, the exemptions provided in paragraphs (1) and (2) are not available.

(b) If property described in subdivision (a) is sold at an execution sale, or if it has been lost, damaged, or destroyed, the proceeds of the execution sale or of insurance or other indemnification are exempt for a period of 90 days after the proceeds are actually received by the judgment debtor or the judgment debtor's spouse. The amount exempt under this subdivision is the amount specified in subdivision (a) that applies to the particular case less the aggregate equity of any other property to which the exemption provided by subdivision (a) for the particular case has been applied.

(c) Notwithstanding subdivision (a), a motor vehicle is not exempt under subdivision (a) if there is a motor vehicle exempt under Section 704.010 which is reasonably adequate for use in the trade, business, or profession for which the exemption is claimed under this section.

(d) Notwithstanding subdivisions (a) and (b):

(1) The amount of the exemption for a commercial motor vehicle under paragraph (1) or (2) of subdivision (a) is limited to four thousand eight hundred fifty dollars ($4,850).

(2) The amount of the exemption for a commercial motor vehicle under paragraph (3) of subdivision (a) is limited to twice the amount of the exemption provided in paragraph (1) of this subdivision.
Amended by Stats 2021 ch 124 (AB 938),s 11, eff. 1/1/2022.
Amended by Stats 2020 ch 81 (SB 898),s 5, eff. 1/1/2021.
Amended by Stats 2003 ch 379 (AB 182),s 8, eff. 1/1/2004.

Section 704.070 - Paid earnings
(a) As used in this section:

(1) "Earnings withholding order" means an earnings withholding order under Chapter 5 (commencing with Section 706.010) (Wage Garnishment Law).

(2) "Paid earnings" means earnings as defined in Section 706.011 that were paid to the employee during the 30-day period ending on the date of the levy. For the purposes of this paragraph, where earnings that have been paid to the employee are sought to be subjected to the enforcement of a money judgment other than by a levy, the date of levy is deemed to be the date the earnings were otherwise subjected to the enforcement of the judgment.

(3) "Earnings assignment order for support" means an earnings assignment order for support as defined in Section 706.011.

(b) Paid earnings that can be traced into deposit accounts or in the form of cash or its equivalent as provided in Section 703.080 are exempt in the following amounts:

(1) All of the paid earnings are exempt if prior to payment to the employee they were subject to an earnings withholding order or an earnings assignment order for support.

(2) Disposable earnings that would otherwise not be subject to levy under Section 706.050 that are levied upon or otherwise sought to be subjected to the enforcement of a money judgment are exempt if prior to payment to the employee they were not subject to an earnings withholding order or an earnings assignment order for support.
Amended by Stats 2019 ch 552 (SB 616),s 7, eff. 1/1/2020.

Section 704.080 - Deposit account
(a) For the purposes of this section:

(1) "Deposit account" means a deposit account in which payments of public benefits or social security benefits are directly deposited by the government or its agent.

(2) "Social security benefits" means payments authorized by the Social Security Administration for regular retirement and survivors' benefits, supplemental security income benefits, coal miners' health benefits, and disability insurance benefits. "Public benefits" means aid payments authorized pursuant to subdivision (a) of Section 11450 of the Welfare and Institutions Code, payments for supportive services as described in Section 11323.2 of the Welfare and Institutions Code, and general assistance payments made pursuant to Section 17000.5 of the Welfare and Institutions Code.

(b) A deposit account is exempt without making a claim in the following amount:

(1) One thousand seven hundred fifty dollars ($1,750) where one depositor is the designated payee of the directly deposited public benefits payments.

(2) Three thousand five hundred dollars ($3,500) where one depositor is the designated payee of directly deposited social security payments.

(3) Two thousand six hundred dollars ($2,600) where two or more depositors are the designated payees of the directly deposited public benefits payments, unless those depositors are joint payees of directly deposited payments that represent a benefit to only one of the depositors, in which case the exemption under paragraph (1) applies.

(4) Five thousand two hundred fifty dollars ($5,250) where two or more depositors are the designated payees of directly deposited social security payments, unless those depositors are joint payees of directly deposited payments that represent a benefit to only one of the depositors, in which case the exemption under paragraph (2) applies.

(c) The amount of a deposit account that exceeds the exemption provided in subdivision (b) is exempt to the extent that it consists of payments of public benefits or social security benefits.

(d) Notwithstanding Article 5 (commencing with Section 701.010) of Chapter 3, when a deposit account is levied upon or otherwise sought to be subjected to the enforcement of a money judgment, the financial institution that holds the deposit account shall either place the amount that exceeds the exemption provided in subdivision (b) in a suspense account or otherwise prohibit withdrawal of that amount pending notification of the failure of the judgment creditor to file the affidavit required by this section or the judicial determination of the exempt status of the amount. Within 10 business days after the levy, the financial institution shall provide the levying officer with a written notice stating (1) that the deposit account is one in which payments of public benefits or social security benefits are directly deposited by the government or its agent and (2) the balance of the deposit account that exceeds the exemption provided by subdivision (b). Promptly upon receipt of the notice, the levying officer shall serve the notice on the judgment creditor. Service shall be made personally or by mail.

(e) Notwithstanding the procedure prescribed in Article 2 (commencing with Section 703.510), whether there is an amount exempt under subdivision (c) shall be determined as follows:

(1) Within five days after the levying officer serves the notice on the judgment creditor under subdivision (d), a judgment creditor who desires to claim that the amount is not exempt shall file with the court an affidavit alleging that the amount is not exempt and file a copy with the levying officer. The affidavit shall be in the form of the notice of opposition provided by Section 703.560, and a hearing shall be set and held, and notice given, as provided by Sections 703.570 and 703.580. For the purpose of this subdivision, the "notice of opposition to the claim of exemption" in Sections 703.570 and 703.580 means the affidavit under this subdivision.

(2) If the judgment creditor does not file the affidavit with the levying officer and give notice of hearing pursuant to Section 703.570 within the time provided in paragraph (1), the levying officer shall release the deposit account and shall notify the financial institution.

(3) The affidavit constitutes the pleading of the judgment creditor, subject to the power of the court to permit amendments in the interest of justice. The affidavit is deemed controverted and no counteraffidavit is required.

(4) At a hearing under this subdivision, the judgment debtor has the burden of proving that the excess amount is exempt.

(5) At the conclusion of the hearing, the court by order shall determine whether or not the amount of the deposit account is exempt pursuant to subdivision (c) in whole or in part and shall make an appropriate order for its prompt disposition. No findings are required in a proceeding under this subdivision.

(6) Upon determining the exemption claim for the deposit account under subdivision (c), the court shall immediately transmit a certified copy of the order of the court to the financial institution and to the levying officer. If the order determines that all or part of the excess is exempt under subdivision (c), with respect to the amount of the excess which is exempt, the financial institution shall transfer the exempt excess from the suspense account or otherwise release any restrictions on its withdrawal by the judgment debtor. The transfer or release shall be effected within three business days of the receipt of the certified copy of the court order by the financial institution.

(f) If the judgment debtor claims that a portion of the amount is exempt other than pursuant to subdivision (c), the claim of exemption shall be made pursuant to Article 2 (commencing with Section 703.510). If the judgment debtor also opposes the judgment creditor's affidavit regarding an amount exempt pursuant to subdivision (c), both exemptions shall be determined at the same hearing, provided the judgment debtor has complied with Article 2 (commencing with Section 703.510).

Amended by Stats 2020 ch 81 (SB 898),s 6, eff. 1/1/2021.

Amended by Stats 2003 ch 379 (AB 182),s 9, eff. 1/1/2004.

Section 704.090 - Funds of imprisoned debtor

(a) The funds of a judgment debtor confined in a prison or facility under the jurisdiction of the Department of Corrections or the Department of the Youth Authority or confined in any county or city jail, road camp, industrial farm, or other local correctional facility, held in trust for or to the credit of the judgment debtor, in an inmate's trust account or similar account by the state, county, or city, or any agency thereof, are exempt without making a claim in the amount of one thousand seven hundred fifty dollars ($1,750). If the judgment debtor is married, each spouse is entitled to a separate exemption under this section or the spouses may combine their exemptions.

(b) Notwithstanding subdivision (a), if the judgment is for a restitution fine or order imposed pursuant to subdivision (a) of Section 13967 of the Government Code, as operative on or before September 28, 1994, or Section 1203.04 of the Penal Code, as operative on or before August 2, 1995, or Section 1202.4 of the Penal Code, the funds held in trust for, or to the credit of, a judgment debtor described in subdivision (a) are exempt in the amount of three hundred twenty-five dollars ($325) without making a claim. The exemption provided in this subdivision is not subject to adjustment under Section 703.150.

Amended by Stats 2020 ch 81 (SB 898),s 7, eff. 1/1/2021.

Amended by Stats 2003 ch 379 (AB 182),s 10, eff. 1/1/2004.

Section 704.100 - Unmatured life insurance policies

(a) Unmatured life insurance policies (including endowment and annuity policies), but not the loan value of such policies, are exempt without making a claim.

(b) The aggregate loan value of unmatured life insurance policies (including endowment and annuity policies) is subject to the enforcement of a money judgment but is exempt in the amount of thirteen thousand nine hundred seventy-five dollars ($13,975). If the judgment debtor is married, each spouse is entitled to a separate exemption under this subdivision, and the exemptions of the spouses may be combined, regardless of whether the policies belong to either or both spouses and regardless of whether the spouse of the judgment debtor is also a judgment debtor under the judgment. The exemption provided by this subdivision shall be first applied to policies other than the policy before the court and then, if the exemption is not exhausted, to the policy before the court.

(c) Benefits from matured life insurance policies (including endowment and annuity policies) are exempt to the extent reasonably necessary for the support of the judgment debtor and the spouse and dependents of the judgment debtor.

Amended by Stats 2020 ch 81 (SB 898),s 8, eff. 1/1/2021.

Amended by Stats 2003 ch 379 (AB 182),s 11, eff. 1/1/2004.

Section 704.105 - Money held in account owned by the judgment debtor and established pursuant to Golden State Scholarshare Trust Act

Money held in an account owned by the judgment debtor and established pursuant to the Golden State Scholarshare Trust Act (Article 19 (commencing with Section 69980) of Chapter 2 of Part 42 of Division 5 of Title 3 of the Education Code) is exempt without making a claim, subject to the following limitations:

(a)The amount exempted for contributions to an account during the 365-day period prior to the date of entry of a money judgment, in the aggregate during this period, shall not exceed the amount of the annual gift tax exclusion under Section 2503(b) of the Internal Revenue Code of 1986, as amended, in effect at the time of entry of the money judgment.

(b)The amount exempted for contributions to an account during the period commencing 730 days prior to and ending 366 days prior to the date of entry of a money judgment, in the aggregate during this period, shall not exceed the amount of the annual gift tax exclusion under Section 2503(b) of the Internal Revenue Code of 1986, as amended, in effect at the time of entry of the money judgment.

(c)For the purposes of this section, "account" includes all accounts having the same beneficiary.

(d)This section is not subject to the requirements of Section 703.150.

Amended by Stats 2022 ch 25 (SB 956),s 2, eff. 1/1/2023.

Added by Stats 2020 ch 81 (SB 898),s 9, eff. 1/1/2021.

Section 704.110 - Rights and benefits under public retirement system

(a) As used in this section:

(1) "Public entity" means the state, or a city, city and county, county, or other political subdivision of the state, or a public trust, public corporation, or public board, or the governing body of any of them, but does not include the United States except where expressly so provided.

(2) "Public retirement benefit" means a pension or an annuity, or a retirement, disability, death, or other benefit, paid or payable by a public retirement system.

(3) "Public retirement system" means a system established pursuant to statute by a public entity for retirement, annuity, or pension purposes or payment of disability or death benefits.

(b) All amounts held, controlled, or in process of distribution by a public entity derived from contributions by the public entity or by an officer or employee of the public entity for public retirement benefit purposes, and all rights and benefits accrued or accruing to any person under a public retirement system, are exempt without making a claim.
(c) Notwithstanding subdivision (b), where an amount described in subdivision (b) becomes payable to a person and is sought to be applied to the satisfaction of a judgment for child, family, or spousal support against that person:

(1) Except as provided in paragraphs (2) and (3), the amount is exempt only to the extent that the court determines under subdivision (c) of Section 703.070.

(2) If the amount sought to be applied to the satisfaction of the judgment is payable periodically, the amount payable is subject to an earnings assignment order for support as defined in Section 706.011, or any other applicable enforcement procedure, but the amount to be withheld pursuant to the assignment order or other procedure shall not exceed the amount permitted to be withheld on an earnings withholding order for support under Section 706.052. The paying entity may deduct from the payment being made to the judgment debtor, for each payment made pursuant to an earnings assignment order under this paragraph, an amount reflecting the actual cost of administration caused by the assignment order of up to two dollars ($2) for each payment.

(3) If the intercept procedure provided for in Section 11357 of the Welfare and Institutions Code is used for benefits that are payable periodically, the amount to be withheld shall not exceed the amount permitted to be withheld on an earnings withholding order for support under Section 706.052.

(4) If the amount sought to be applied to the satisfaction of the judgment is payable as a lump-sum distribution, the amount payable is subject to the intercept procedure provided in Section 11357 of the Welfare and Institutions Code or any other applicable enforcement procedure.
(d) All amounts received by any person, a resident of the state, as a public retirement benefit or as a return of contributions and interest thereon from the United States or a public entity or from a public retirement system are exempt.
Amended by Stats. 1996, Ch. 927, Sec. 1.5. Effective January 1, 1997.

Section 704.111 - Exemption for alimony, support, and separate maintenance

Alimony, support, and separate maintenance, to the extent reasonably necessary for the support of the debtor and any dependent of the debtor, are exempt.
Added by Stats 2022 ch 716 (SB 1099),s 5, eff. 1/1/2023.

Section 704.113 - Vacation credits

(a) As used in this chapter, "vacation credits" means vacation credits accumulated by a state employee pursuant to Section 19858.1 of the Government Code or by any other public employee pursuant to any law for the accumulation of vacation credits applicable to the employee.
(b) The aggregate interest, not to exceed seven thousand five hundred dollars ($7,500), in vacation credits or accrued, or unused, vacation pay, sick leave, or family leave is exempt.
(c) Amounts paid periodically or as a lump sum representing vacation credits are subject to any earnings withholding order served under Chapter 5 (commencing with Section 706.010) or any earnings assignment order for support as defined in Section 706.011 and are exempt to the same extent as earnings of a judgment debtor.
Amended by Stats 2022 ch 716 (SB 1099),s 6, eff. 1/1/2023.
Amended by Stats 2022 ch 28 (SB 1380),s 25, eff. 1/1/2023. Not implemented per s 168.
Amended by Stats. 1992, Ch. 163, Sec. 40. Effective January 1, 1993. Operative January 1, 1994, by Sec. 161 of Ch. 163.

Section 704.114 - Earnings assignment order of support or order or notice to withhold income for child support service on public entity

(a) Notwithstanding any other provision of law, service of an earnings assignment order for support, or an order or notice to withhold income for child support on any public entity described in Section 704.110, other than the United States government, creates a lien on all employee contributions in the amount necessary to satisfy a support judgment as determined under Section 695.210 to the extent that the judgment remains enforceable.
(b) The public entity shall comply with any request for a return of employee contributions by an employee named in the order or notice to withhold by delivering the contributions to the clerk of the court in which the support order was awarded or last registered, unless the entity has received a certified copy of an order or administrative notice terminating the earnings assignment order for support.
(c) Upon receipt of moneys pursuant to this section, the clerk of the court, within 10 days, shall send written notice of the receipt of the deposit to the parties and to the local child support agency enforcing any order pursuant to Section 17400 of the Family Code.
(d) Moneys received pursuant to this section are subject to any procedure available to enforce an order for support, but if no enforcement procedure is commenced after 30 days have elapsed from the date the notice of receipt is sent, the clerk shall, upon request, return the moneys to the public entity that delivered the moneys to the court unless the public entity has informed the court in writing that the moneys shall be released to the employee.
(e) A court shall not directly or indirectly condition the issuance, modification, or termination of, or condition the terms or conditions of, any order for support upon the making of a request for the return of employee contributions by an employee.
Amended by Stats 2000 ch 808 (AB 1358), s 13, eff. 9/28/2000.

Section 704.115 - Private retirement plan

(a) As used in this section, "private retirement plan" means:

(1) Private retirement plans, including, but not limited to, union retirement plans.

(2) Profit-sharing plans designed and used for retirement purposes.

(3) Self-employed retirement plans and individual retirement annuities or accounts provided for in the Internal Revenue Code of 1986, as amended, including individual retirement accounts qualified under Section 408 or 408A of that code, to the extent the amounts held in the plans, annuities, or accounts do not exceed the maximum amounts exempt from federal income taxation under that code.
(b) All amounts held, controlled, or in process of distribution by a private retirement plan, for the payment of benefits as an annuity, pension, retirement allowance, disability payment, or death benefit from a private retirement plan are exempt.
(c) Notwithstanding subdivision (b), where an amount described in subdivision (b) becomes payable to a person and is sought to be applied to the satisfaction of a judgment for child, family, or spousal support against that person:

(1) Except as provided in paragraph (2), the amount is exempt only to the extent that the court determines under subdivision (c) of Section 703.070.

(2) If the amount sought to be applied to the satisfaction of the judgment is payable periodically, the amount payable is subject to an earnings assignment order for support as defined in Section 706.011 or any other applicable enforcement procedure, but the amount to be withheld pursuant to the assignment order or other procedure shall not exceed the amount permitted to be withheld on an earnings withholding order for support under Section 706.052.
(d) After payment, the amounts described in subdivision (b) and all contributions and interest thereon returned to any member of a private retirement plan are exempt.
(e) Notwithstanding subdivisions (b) and (d), except as provided in subdivision (f), the amounts described in paragraph (3) of subdivision (a) are exempt only to the extent necessary to provide for the support of the judgment debtor when the judgment debtor retires and for the support of the spouse and dependents of the judgment debtor, taking into account all resources that are likely to be available for the support of the judgment

debtor when the judgment debtor retires. In determining the amount to be exempt under this subdivision, the court shall allow the judgment debtor such additional amount as is necessary to pay any federal and state income taxes payable as a result of the applying of an amount described in paragraph (3) of subdivision (a) to the satisfaction of the money judgment.

(f) Where the amounts described in paragraph (3) of subdivision (a) are payable periodically, the amount of the periodic payment that may be applied to the satisfaction of a money judgment is the amount that may be withheld from a like amount of earnings under Chapter 5 (commencing with Section 706.010) (Wage Garnishment Law). To the extent a lump-sum distribution from an individual retirement account is treated differently from a periodic distribution under this subdivision, any lump-sum distribution from an account qualified under Section 408A of the Internal Revenue Code shall be treated the same as a lump-sum distribution from an account qualified under Section 408 of the Internal Revenue Code for purposes of determining whether any of that payment may be applied to the satisfaction of a money judgment.

Amended by Stats 2000 ch 135 (AB 2539), s 16, eff. 1/1/2001.
EFFECTIVE 1/1/2000. Amended July 13, 1999 (Bill Number: SB 469) (Chapter 98).

Section 704.120 - Contributions payable to Unemployment Compensation Disability Fund and Unemployment Fund

(a) Contributions by workers payable to the Unemployment Compensation Disability Fund and by employers payable to the Unemployment Fund are exempt without making a claim.

(b) Before payment, amounts held for payment of the following benefits are exempt without making a claim:

(1) Benefits payable under Division 1 (commencing with Section 100) of the Unemployment Insurance Code.

(2) Incentives payable under Division 2 (commencing with Section 5000) of the Unemployment Insurance Code.

(3) Benefits payable under an employer's plan or system to supplement unemployment compensation benefits of the employees generally or for a class or group of employees.

(4) Unemployment benefits payable by a fraternal organization to its bona fide members.

(5) Benefits payable by a union due to a labor dispute.

(c) After payment, the benefits described in subdivision (b) are exempt.

(d) During the payment of benefits described in paragraph (1) of subdivision (b) to a judgment debtor under a support judgment, the judgment creditor may, through the appropriate local child support agency, seek to apply the benefit payment to satisfy the judgment as provided by Section 17518 of the Family Code.

(e) During the payment of benefits described in paragraphs (2) to (5), inclusive, of subdivision (b) to a judgment debtor under a support judgment, the judgment creditor may, directly or through the appropriate local child support agency, seek to apply the benefit payments to satisfy the judgment by an earnings assignment order for support as defined in Section 706.011 or any other applicable enforcement procedure. If the benefit is payable periodically, the amount to be withheld pursuant to the assignment order or other procedure shall be 25 percent of the amount of each periodic payment or any lower amount specified in writing by the judgment creditor or court order, rounded down to the nearest whole dollar. Otherwise the amount to be withheld shall be the amount the court determines under subdivision (c) of Section 703.070. The paying entity may deduct from each payment made pursuant to an assignment order under this subdivision an amount reflecting the actual cost of administration caused by the assignment order up to two dollars ($2) for each payment.

Amended by Stats 2000 ch 808 (AB 1358), s 14, eff. 9/28/2000.

Section 704.130 - Benefits from disability or health insurance policy

(a) Before payment, benefits from a disability or health insurance policy or program are exempt without making a claim. After payment, the benefits are exempt.

(b) Subdivision (a) does not apply to benefits that are paid or payable to cover the cost of health care if the judgment creditor is a provider of health care whose claim is the basis on which the benefits are paid or payable.

(c) During the payment of disability benefits described in subdivision (a) to a judgment debtor under a support judgment, the judgment creditor or local child support agency may seek to apply the benefit payments to satisfy the judgment by an earnings assignment order for support, as defined in Section 706.011, or any other applicable enforcement procedure, but the amount to be withheld pursuant to the earnings assignment order or other procedure shall not exceed the amount permitted to be withheld on an earnings assignment order for support under Section 706.052.

Amended by Stats 2000 ch 808 (AB 1358), s 15, eff. 9/28/2000.

Section 704.140 - Cause of action for personal injury

(a) Except as provided in Article 5 (commencing with Section 708.410) of Chapter 6, a cause of action for personal injury is exempt without making a claim.

(b) Except as provided in subdivisions (c) and (d), an award of damages or a settlement arising out of personal injury is exempt to the extent necessary for the support of the judgment debtor and the spouse and dependents of the judgment debtor.

(c) Subdivision (b) does not apply if the judgment creditor is a provider of health care whose claim is based on the providing of health care for the personal injury for which the award or settlement was made.

(d) Where an award of damages or a settlement arising out of personal injury is payable periodically, the amount of such periodic payment that may be applied to the satisfaction of a money judgment is the amount that may be withheld from a like amount of earnings under Chapter 5 (commencing with Section 706.010) (Wage Garnishment Law).

Added by Stats. 1982, Ch. 1364, Sec. 2. Operative July 1, 1983, by Sec. 3 of Ch. 1364.

Section 704.150 - Cause of action for wrongful death

(a) Except as provided in Article 5 (commencing with Section 708.410) of Chapter 6, a cause of action for wrongful death is exempt without making a claim.

(b) Except as provided in subdivision (c), an award of damages or a settlement arising out of the wrongful death of the judgment debtor's spouse or a person on whom the judgment debtor or the judgment debtor's spouse was dependent is exempt to the extent reasonably necessary for support of the judgment debtor and the spouse and dependents of the judgment debtor.

(c) Where an award of damages or a settlement arising out of the wrongful death of the judgment debtor's spouse or a person on whom the judgment debtor or the judgment debtor's spouse was dependent is payable periodically, the amount of such a periodic payment that may be applied to the satisfaction of a money judgment is the amount that may be withheld from a like amount of earnings under Chapter 5 (commencing with Section 706.010) (Wage Garnishment Law).

Added by Stats. 1982, Ch. 1364, Sec. 2. Operative July 1, 1983, by Sec. 3 of Ch. 1364.

Section 704.160 - Claims for workers' compensation or workers' compensation awarded or adjudged

(a) Except as provided by Chapter 1 (commencing with Section 4900) of Part 3 of Division 4 of the Labor Code, before payment, a claim for workers' compensation or workers' compensation awarded or adjudged is exempt without making a claim. Except as specified in subdivision (b), after payment, the award is exempt.

(b) Notwithstanding any other provision of law, during the payment of workers' compensation temporary disability benefits described in subdivision (a) to a support judgment debtor, the support judgment creditor may, through the appropriate local child support agency, seek to apply the workers' compensation temporary disability benefit payment to satisfy the support judgment as provided by Section 17404 of the Family Code.

(c) Notwithstanding any other provision of law, during the payment of workers' compensation temporary disability benefits described in subdivision (a) to a support judgment debtor under a support judgment, including a judgment for reimbursement of public assistance, the judgment creditor may, directly or through the appropriate local child support agency, seek to apply the temporary disability benefit payments to satisfy the support judgment by an earnings assignment order for support, as defined in Section 5208 of the Family Code, or any other applicable enforcement procedure. The amount to be withheld pursuant to the earnings assignment order for support or other enforcement procedure shall be 25 percent of the amount of each periodic payment or any lower amount specified in writing by the judgment creditor or court order, rounded down to the nearest dollar. Otherwise, the amount to be withheld shall be the amount the court determines under subdivision (c) of Section 703.070. The paying entity may deduct from each payment made pursuant to an order assigning earnings under this subdivision an amount reflecting the actual cost of administration of this assignment, up to two dollars ($2) for each payment.

(d) Unless the provision or context otherwise requires, the following definitions govern the construction of this section.

(1) "Judgment debtor" or "support judgment debtor" means a person who is owing a duty of support.

(2) "Judgment creditor" or "support judgment creditor" means the person to whom support has been ordered to be paid.

(3) "Support" refers to an obligation owing on behalf of a child, spouse, or family; or an amount owing pursuant to Section 17402 of the Family Code. It also includes past due support or arrearage when it exists.

Amended by Stats 2000 ch 808 (AB 1358), s 16, eff. 9/28/2000.

Section 704.170 - Aid provided to charitable organization or fraternal organization society

Before payment, aid provided pursuant to Division 9 (commencing with Section 10000) of the Welfare and Institutions Code or similar aid provided by a charitable organization or a fraternal benefit society as defined in Section 10990 of the Insurance Code, is exempt without making a claim. After payment, the aid is exempt.

Added by Stats. 1982, Ch. 1364, Sec. 2. Operative July 1, 1983, by Sec. 3 of Ch. 1364.

Section 704.180 - Relocation benefits for displacement from dwelling

Before payment, relocation benefits for displacement from a dwelling which are to be paid pursuant to Chapter 16 (commencing with Section 7260) of Division 7 of Title 1 of the Government Code or the federal "Uniform Relocation Assistance and Real Property Acquisition Policies Act of 1970" (42 U.S.C. Sec. 4601 et seq.), as amended, are exempt without making a claim. After payment, the benefits are exempt.

Added by Stats. 1982, Ch. 1364, Sec. 2. Operative July 1, 1983, by Sec. 3 of Ch. 1364.

Section 704.190 - Student financial aid provided by institution of higher education

(a) As used in this section, "institution of higher education" means "institution of higher education" as defined in Section 1141(a)(a) of Title 20 of the United States Code, as amended.

(b) Before payment, financial aid for expenses while attending school provided to a student by an institution of higher education is exempt without making a claim. After payment, the aid is exempt.

Added by Stats. 1982, Ch. 1364, Sec. 2. Operative July 1, 1983, by Sec. 3 of Ch. 1364.

Section 704.200 - Family plot or cemetery plot

(a) As used in this section:

(1) "Cemetery" has the meaning provided by Section 7003 of the Health and Safety Code.

(2) "Family plot" is a plot that satisfies the requirements of Section 8650 of the Health and Safety Code.

(3) "Plot" has the meaning provided by Section 7022 of the Health and Safety Code.

(b) A family plot is exempt without making a claim.

(c) Except as provided in subdivision (d), a cemetery plot for the judgment debtor and the spouse of the judgment debtor is exempt.

(d) Land held for the purpose of sale or disposition as cemetery plots or otherwise is not exempt.

Added by Stats. 1982, Ch. 1364, Sec. 2. Operative July 1, 1983, by Sec. 3 of Ch. 1364.

Section 704.210 - Property not subject to enforcement of money judgment

Property that is not subject to enforcement of a money judgment is exempt without making a claim.

Added by Stats. 1982, Ch. 1364, Sec. 2. Operative July 1, 1983, by Sec. 3 of Ch. 1364.

Section 704.220 - Money exempt from levy; amount equal to or less than the minimum basic standard of adequate care for a family of four for Region 1

(a) Money in the judgment debtor's deposit account in an amount equal to or less than the minimum basic standard of adequate care for a family of four for Region 1, established by Section 11452 of the Welfare and Institutions Code and as annually adjusted by the State Department of Social Services pursuant to Section 11453 of the Welfare and Institutions Code, is exempt without making a claim.

(b)

(1) Subdivision (a) does not preclude or reduce a judgment debtor's right to any other exemption provided by state or federal law.

(2) If the financial institution holding the judgment debtor's deposit account has actual knowledge that the judgment debtor is entitled to one or more exemptions that the financial institution is required to apply pursuant to federal law or state law other than that set forth in subdivision (a), the following shall apply:

(A) If the sum of the amount of money in the deposit account that would be exempt from levy under the additional exemptions is less than or equal to the amount set forth in subdivision (a), the additional exemptions described in this paragraph shall be considered encompassed within the exemption set forth in subdivision (a) and subdivision (a) shall apply.

(B) If the sum of the amount of money in the deposit account that would be exempt from levy under the additional exemptions is greater than the amount set forth in subdivision (a), subdivision (a) shall not apply and instead money in the deposit account equal to or less than the sum of the additional exemptions is exempt without making a claim.

(c) Subdivision (a) does not apply to money levied upon to satisfy any of the following:

(1) A levy to satisfy a judgment for wages owed, child support, or spousal support. For purposes of this paragraph, "wages owed" includes damages and penalties.

(2) A provision of the Public Resources Code, Revenue and Taxation Code, or Unemployment Insurance Code.

(3) A warrant or notice of levy issued by the state, or any department or agency thereof, for the collection of a liability.

(d) A levy against a judgment debtor's deposit account shall include a written description of the requirements of this section.

(e)

(1) The exemption applies per debtor, not per account.

(2) If a judgment debtor holds an interest in multiple accounts at a single financial institution, the judgment creditor or judgment debtor may file an ex parte application in the superior court in which the judgment was entered for a hearing to establish how and to which account the exemption should be applied. Subject to a service of an order issued in that hearing, if any, the financial institution may determine how and to which account the exemption should be applied. This paragraph does not create a cause of action against a judgment creditor who executes a levy or against a financial institution that complies with a levy pursuant to the court's determination.

(3) If a judgment debtor holds an interest in multiple accounts at two or more financial institutions, the judgment creditor shall, and the judgment debtor may, file an ex parte application in the superior court in which the judgment was entered for a hearing to establish how and to which account the exemption should be applied. Subject to a service of an order issued in that hearing, if any, the financial institutions shall

comply with the levy subject to the exemption. This paragraph does not create a cause of action against a judgment creditor who executes a levy or against a financial institution which complies with a levy pursuant to the court's determination.

(f) Subdivision (e) of Section 700.140 applies to a financial institution acting under this section.

(g) The Judicial Council shall amend or adopt all forms necessary to implement this section. The forms shall clearly delineate the amount of funds exempt from levy by a financial institution, including funds exempted by this section.

(h) This section shall become operative on September 1, 2020.

Added by Stats 2019 ch 552 (SB 616),s 8, eff. 1/1/2020.

Section 704.225 - Money necessary for the support of the judgment debtor and the spouse and dependents of the judgment debtor

Money in a judgment debtor's deposit account that is not otherwise exempt under this chapter is exempt to the extent necessary for the support of the judgment debtor and the spouse and dependents of the judgment debtor.

Added by Stats 2019 ch 552 (SB 616),s 9, eff. 1/1/2020.

Section 704.230 - FEMA money

Money provided to the judgment debtor by the Federal Emergency Management Agency (FEMA) is exempt without making a claim.

Added by Stats 2019 ch 552 (SB 616),s 10, eff. 1/1/2020.

Article 4 - HOMESTEAD EXEMPTION

Section 704.710 - Definitions

As used in this article:

(a) "Dwelling" means a place where a person resides and may include but is not limited to the following:

    (1) A house together with the outbuildings and the land upon which they are situated.

    (2) A mobilehome together with the outbuildings and the land upon which they are situated.

    (3) A boat or other waterborne vessel.

    (4) A condominium, as defined in Section 783 of the Civil Code.

    (5) A planned development, as defined in Section 11003 of the Business and Professions Code.

    (6) A stock cooperative, as defined in Section 11003.2 of the Business and Professions Code.

    (7) A community apartment project, as defined in Section 11004 of the Business and Professions Code.

(b) "Family unit" means any of the following:

    (1) The judgment debtor and the judgment debtor's spouse if the spouses reside together in the homestead.

    (2) The judgment debtor and at least one of the following persons who the judgment debtor cares for or maintains in the homestead:

        (A) The minor child or minor grandchild of the judgment debtor or the judgment debtor's spouse or the minor child or grandchild of a deceased spouse or former spouse.

        (B) The minor brother or sister of the judgment debtor or judgment debtor's spouse or the minor child of a deceased brother or sister of either spouse.

        (C) The father, mother, grandfather, or grandmother of the judgment debtor or the judgment debtor's spouse or the father, mother, grandfather, or grandmother of a deceased spouse.

        (D) An unmarried relative described in this paragraph who has attained the age of majority and is unable to take care of or support himself or herself.

    (3) The judgment debtor's spouse and at least one of the persons listed in paragraph (2) who the judgment debtor's spouse cares for or maintains in the homestead.

(c) "Homestead" means the principal dwelling (1) in which the judgment debtor or the judgment debtor's spouse resided on the date the judgment creditor's lien attached to the dwelling, and (2) in which the judgment debtor or the judgment debtor's spouse resided continuously thereafter until the date of the court determination that the dwelling is a homestead. Where exempt proceeds from the sale or damage or destruction of a homestead are used toward the acquisition of a dwelling within the six-month period provided by Section 704.720, "homestead" also means the dwelling so acquired if it is the principal dwelling in which the judgment debtor or the judgment debtor's spouse resided continuously from the date of acquisition until the date of the court determination that the dwelling is a homestead, whether or not an abstract or certified copy of a judgment was recorded to create a judgment lien before the dwelling was acquired.

(d) "Spouse" does not include a married person following entry of a judgment decreeing legal separation of the parties, unless such married persons reside together in the same dwelling.

Amended by Stats. 1983, Ch. 1159, Sec. 11. Operative July 1, 1984, by Sec. 17 of Ch. 1159.

Section 704.720 - Generally

(a) A homestead is exempt from sale under this division to the extent provided in Section 704.800.

(b) If a homestead is sold under this division or is damaged or destroyed or is acquired for public use, the proceeds of sale or of insurance or other indemnification for damage or destruction of the homestead or the proceeds received as compensation for a homestead acquired for public use are exempt in the amount of the homestead exemption provided in Section 704.730. The proceeds are exempt for a period of six months after the time the proceeds are actually received by the judgment debtor, except that, if a homestead exemption is applied to other property of the judgment debtor or the judgment debtor's spouse during that period, the proceeds thereafter are not exempt.

(c) If the judgment debtor and spouse of the judgment debtor reside in separate homesteads, only the homestead of one of the spouses is exempt and only the proceeds of the exempt homestead are exempt.

(d) If a judgment debtor is not currently residing in the homestead, but his or her separated or former spouse continues to reside in or exercise control over possession of the homestead, that judgment debtor continues to be entitled to an exemption under this article until entry of judgment or other legally enforceable agreement dividing the community property between the judgment debtor and the separated or former spouse, or until a later time period as specified by court order. Nothing in this subdivision shall entitle the judgment debtor to more than one exempt homestead. Notwithstanding subdivision (d) of Section 704.710, for purposes of this article, "spouse" may include a separated or former spouse consistent with this subdivision.

Amended by Stats 2007 ch 153 (SB 433),s 1, eff. 1/1/2008.

Section 704.730 - Amount

(a) The amount of the homestead exemption is the greater of the following:

    (1) The countywide median sale price for a single-family home in the calendar year prior to the calendar year in which the judgment debtor claims the exemption, not to exceed six hundred thousand dollars ($600,000).

    (2) Three hundred thousand dollars ($300,000).

(b) The amounts specified in this section shall adjust annually for inflation, beginning on January 1, 2022, based on the change in the annual California Consumer Price Index for All Urban Consumers for the prior fiscal year, published by the Department of Industrial Relations.

Amended by Stats 2020 ch 94 (AB 1885),s 1, eff. 1/1/2021.
Amended by Stats 2012 ch 678 (AB 929),s 3, eff. 1/1/2013.
Amended by Stats 2009 ch 499 (AB 1046),s 2, eff. 1/1/2010.
Amended by Stats 2003 ch 64 (SB 804),s 1, eff. 1/1/2004.

Section 704.740 - Sale of dwelling to enforce money judgment
(a) Except as provided in subdivision (b), the interest of a natural person in a dwelling may not be sold under this division to enforce a money judgment except pursuant to a court order for sale obtained under this article and the dwelling exemption shall be determined under this article.
(b) If the dwelling is personal property or is real property in which the judgment debtor has a leasehold estate with an unexpired term of less than two years at the time of levy:
　(1) A court order for sale is not required and the procedures provided in this article relating to the court order for sale do not apply.
　(2) An exemption claim shall be made and determined as provided in Article 2 (commencing with Section 703.510).
Amended by Stats. 1984, Ch. 538, Sec. 26.

Section 704.750 - Notice served on judgment creditor that dwelling levied on; application by creditor for order of sale
(a) Promptly after a dwelling is levied upon (other than a dwelling described in subdivision (b) of Section 704.740), the levying officer shall serve notice on the judgment creditor that the levy has been made and that the property will be released unless the judgment creditor complies with the requirements of this section. Service shall be made personally or by mail. Within 20 days after service of the notice, the judgment creditor shall apply to the court for an order for sale of the dwelling and shall file a copy of the application with the levying officer. If the judgment creditor does not file the copy of the application for an order for sale of the dwelling within the allowed time, the levying officer shall release the dwelling.
(b) If the dwelling is located in a county other than the county where the judgment was entered:
　(1) The judgment creditor shall apply to the superior court of the county where the dwelling is located.
　(2) The judgment creditor shall file with the application an abstract of judgment in the form prescribed by Section 674 or, in the case of a judgment described in Section 697.320, a certified copy of the judgment.
　(3) The judgment creditor shall pay the filing fee for a motion as provided in subdivision (a) of Section 70617 of the Government Code.
Amended by Stats 2005 ch 75 (AB 145),s 37, eff. 7/19/2005, op. 1/1/2006

Section 704.760 - Requirements of application for order of sale
The judgment creditor's application shall be made under oath, shall describe the dwelling, and shall contain all of the following:
(a) A statement whether or not the records of the county tax assessor indicate that there is a current homeowner's exemption or disabled veteran's exemption for the dwelling and the person or persons who claimed any such exemption.
(b) A statement, which may be based on information and belief, whether the dwelling is a homestead and the amount of the homestead exemption, if any, and a statement whether or not the records of the county recorder indicate that a homestead declaration under Article 5 (commencing with Section 704.910) that describes the dwelling has been recorded by the judgment debtor or the spouse of the judgment debtor.
(c) A statement of the amount of any liens or encumbrances on the dwelling, the name of each person having a lien or encumbrance on the dwelling, and the address of such person used by the county recorder for the return of the instrument creating such person's lien or encumbrance after recording.
(d) A statement that the judgment is based on a consumer debt, as defined in subdivision (a) of Section 699.730, or that the judgment is not based on a consumer debt, and if the judgment is based on a consumer debt, whether the judgment is based on a consumer debt that was secured by the debtor's principal place of residence at the time it was incurred or a statement indicating which of the exemptions listed in subdivision (b) of Section 699.730 are applicable. If the statement indicates that paragraph (7) of subdivision (b) is applicable, the statement shall also provide the dollar amount of the original judgment on which the lien is based. If there is more than one basis, the statement shall indicate all bases that are applicable.
Amended by Stats 2020 ch 218 (AB 2463),s 3, eff. 1/1/2021.

Section 704.770 - Time and place for hearing; service by judgment debtor and each dwelling occupant
(a) Upon the filing of the application by the judgment creditor, the court shall set a time and place for hearing and order the judgment debtor to show cause why an order for sale should not be made in accordance with the application. The time set for hearing shall be not later than 45 days after the application is filed or such later time as the court orders upon a showing of good cause.
(b) Not later than 30 days before the time set for hearing, the judgment creditor shall do both of the following:
　(1) Serve on the judgment debtor a copy of the order to show cause, a copy of the application of the judgment creditor, and a copy of the notice of the hearing in the form prescribed by the Judicial Council. Service shall be made personally or by mail.
　(2) Personally serve a copy of each document listed in paragraph (1) on an occupant of the dwelling or, if there is no occupant present at the time service is attempted, post a copy of each document in a conspicuous place at the dwelling.
Amended by Stats. 1985, Ch. 41, Sec. 7.

Section 704.780 - Burden of proof; determination by court; order of sale
(a) The burden of proof at the hearing is determined in the following manner:
　(1) If the records of the county tax assessor indicate that there is a current homeowner's exemption or disabled veteran's exemption for the dwelling claimed by the judgment debtor or the judgment debtor's spouse, the judgment creditor has the burden of proof that the dwelling is not a homestead. If the records of the county tax assessor indicate that there is not a current homeowner's exemption or disabled veteran's exemption for the dwelling claimed by the judgment debtor or the judgment debtor's spouse, the burden of proof that the dwelling is a homestead is on the person who claims that the dwelling is a homestead.
　(2) If the application states the amount of the homestead exemption, the person claiming the homestead exemption has the burden of proof that the amount of the exemption is other than the amount stated in the application.
(b) The court shall determine whether the dwelling is exempt. If the court determines that the dwelling is exempt, the court shall determine the amount of the homestead exemption and the fair market value of the dwelling. The court shall make an order for sale of the dwelling subject to the homestead exemption, unless the court determines that the sale of the dwelling would not be likely to produce a bid sufficient to satisfy any part of the amount due on the judgment pursuant to Section 704.800. The order for sale of the dwelling subject to the homestead exemption shall specify the amount of the proceeds of the sale that is to be distributed to each person having a lien or encumbrance on the dwelling and shall include the name and address of each such person. Subject to the provisions of this article, the sale is governed by Article 6 (commencing with Section 701.510) of Chapter 3. If the court determines that the dwelling is not exempt, the court shall make an order for sale of the property in the manner provided in Article 6 (commencing with Section 701.510) of Chapter 3.
(c) The court clerk shall transmit a certified copy of the court order (1) to the levying officer and (2) if the court making the order is not the court in which the judgment was entered, to the clerk of the court in which the judgment was entered.
(d) The court may appoint a qualified appraiser to assist the court in determining the fair market value of the dwelling. If the court appoints an appraiser, the court shall fix the compensation of the appraiser in an amount determined by the court to be reasonable, not to exceed similar fees for similar services in the community where the dwelling is located.
Amended by Stats. 1995, Ch. 196, Sec. 8. Effective July 31, 1995.

Section 704.790 - Declaration by judgment debtor that absence from hearing due to mistake, inadvertence, surprise or excusable neglect and debtor wishes to assert exemption
(a) This section applies in any case where the court makes an order for sale of the dwelling upon a hearing at which none of the following appeared:

(1) The judgment debtor.
(2) The judgment debtor's spouse.
(3) The attorney for the judgment debtor.
(4) The attorney for the judgment debtor's spouse.

(b) Not later than 10 days after the date of the order for sale, the judgment creditor shall serve a copy of the order and a notice of the order in the form prescribed by the Judicial Council:
(1) Personally or by mail on the judgment debtor and the judgment debtor's spouse.
(2) Personally on an occupant of the dwelling or, if there is no occupant present at the time service is attempted, post a copy of the order and notice in a conspicuous place at the dwelling.

(c) Proof of service and of any posting shall be filed with the court and with the levying officer. If the judgment creditor fails to comply with this subdivision and with subdivision (b) in any case where this section applies, the dwelling may not be sold under the order for sale.

(d) If, within 10 days after service of notice of the order, the judgment debtor or the judgment debtor's spouse files with the levying officer a declaration that the absence of the judgment debtor and the judgment debtor's spouse or the attorney for the judgment debtor or the judgment debtor's spouse from the hearing was due to mistake, inadvertence, surprise, or excusable neglect and that the judgment debtor or spouse of the judgment debtor wishes to assert the homestead exemption, the levying officer shall transmit the declaration forthwith to the court. Upon receipt of the declaration, the court shall set a time and place for hearing to determine whether the determinations of the court should be modified. The time set for hearing shall be not later than 20 days after receipt of the declaration. The court clerk shall cause notice of the hearing promptly to be given to the parties.

Amended by Stats. 1985, Ch. 41, Sec. 8.

Section 704.800 - Homestead not sold and released

(a) If no bid is received at a sale of a homestead pursuant to a court order for sale that exceeds the amount of the homestead exemption plus any additional amount necessary to satisfy all liens and encumbrances on the property, including but not limited to any attachment or judgment lien, the homestead shall not be sold and shall be released and is not thereafter subject to a court order for sale upon subsequent application by the same judgment creditor for a period of one year.

(b) If no bid is received at the sale of a homestead pursuant to a court order for sale that is 90 percent or more of the fair market value determined pursuant to Section 704.780, the homestead shall not be sold unless the court, upon motion of the judgment creditor, does one of the following:
(1) Grants permission to accept the highest bid that exceeds the amount of the minimum bid required by subdivision (a).
(2) Makes a new order for sale of the homestead.

Added by Stats. 1982, Ch. 1364, Sec. 2. Operative July 1, 1983, by Sec. 3 of Ch. 1364.

Section 704.810 - Amount payable to satisfy lien or encumbrance not to include prepayment penalty

Levy on a homestead that is subject to a lien or encumbrance is not by itself grounds for acceleration of the obligation secured by the lien or encumbrance, notwithstanding any provision of the obligation, lien, or encumbrance and if the homestead is sold pursuant to court order under this article the amount payable to satisfy a lien or encumbrance shall not include any penalty for prepayment.

Added by Stats. 1982, Ch. 1364, Sec. 2. Operative July 1, 1983, by Sec. 3 of Ch. 1364.

Section 704.820 - Dwelling owned by debtor as joint tenant or tenant in common or is leasehold

If the dwelling is owned by the judgment debtor as a joint tenant or tenant in common or if the interest of the judgment debtor in the dwelling is a leasehold or other interest less than a fee interest:

(a) At an execution sale of a dwelling, the interest of the judgment debtor in the dwelling and not the dwelling shall be sold. If there is more than one judgment debtor of the judgment creditor, the interests of the judgment debtors in the dwelling shall be sold together and each of the judgment debtors entitled to a homestead exemption is entitled to apply his or her exemption to his or her own interest.

(b) For the purposes of this section, all references in this article to the "dwelling" or "homestead" are deemed to be references to the interest of the judgment debtor in the dwelling or homestead.

Added by Stats. 1982, Ch. 1364, Sec. 2. Operative July 1, 1983, by Sec. 3 of Ch. 1364.

Section 704.830 - Applicability of sections 703.590 and 703.600

The provisions of Sections 703.590 and 703.600 apply to proceedings under this article.

Added by Stats. 1982, Ch. 1364, Sec. 2. Operative July 1, 1983, by Sec. 3 of Ch. 1364.

Section 704.840 - Recovery of costs

(a) Except as provided in subdivision (b), the judgment creditor is entitled to recover reasonable costs incurred in a proceeding under this article.

(b) If no bid is received at a sale of a homestead pursuant to a court order for sale that exceeds the amount of the homestead exemption plus any additional amount necessary to satisfy all liens and encumbrances on the property, the judgment creditor is not entitled to recover costs incurred in a proceeding under this article or costs of sale.

Added by Stats. 1982, Ch. 1364, Sec. 2. Operative July 1, 1983, by Sec. 3 of Ch. 1364.

Section 704.850 - Order of distribution of proceeds of sale

(a) The levying officer shall distribute the proceeds of sale of a homestead in the following order:
(1) To the discharge of all liens and encumbrances, if any, on the property.
(2) To the judgment debtor in the amount of any applicable exemption of proceeds pursuant to Section 704.720.
(3) To the levying officer for the reimbursement of the levying officer's costs for which an advance has not been made.
(4) To the judgment creditor to satisfy the following:
(A) First, costs and interest accruing after issuance of the writ pursuant to which the sale is conducted.
(B) Second, the amount due on the judgment with costs and interest, as entered on the writ.
(5) To the judgment debtor in the amount remaining.

(b) Sections 701.820 and 701.830 apply to distribution of proceeds under this section.

Added by Stats. 1982, Ch. 1364, Sec. 2. Operative July 1, 1983, by Sec. 3 of Ch. 1364.

Article 5 - DECLARED HOMESTEADS

Section 704.910 - Definitions

As used in this article:

(a) "Declared homestead" means the dwelling described in a homestead declaration.

(b) "Declared homestead owner" includes both of the following:
(1) The owner of an interest in the declared homestead who is named as a declared homestead owner in a homestead declaration recorded pursuant to this article.
(2) The declarant named in a declaration of homestead recorded prior to July 1, 1983, pursuant to former Title 5 (commencing with Section 1237) of Part 4 of Division 2 of the Civil Code and the spouse of such declarant.

(c) "Dwelling" means any interest in real property (whether present or future, vested or contingent, legal or equitable) that is a "dwelling" as defined in Section 704.710, but does not include a leasehold estate with an unexpired term of less than two years or the interest of the beneficiary of a trust.

(d) "Homestead declaration" includes both of the following:

(1) A homestead declaration recorded pursuant to this article.

(2) A declaration of homestead recorded prior to July 1, 1983, pursuant to former Title 5 (commencing with former Section 1237) of Part 4 of Division 2 of the Civil Code.

(e) "Spouse" means a "spouse" as defined in Section 704.710.

Added by Stats. 1982, Ch. 1364, Sec. 2. Operative July 1, 1983, by Sec. 3 of Ch. 1364.

Section 704.920 - Recording homestead declaration

A dwelling in which an owner or spouse of an owner resides may be selected as a declared homestead pursuant to this article by recording a homestead declaration in the office of the county recorder of the county where the dwelling is located. From and after the time of recording, the dwelling is a declared homestead for the purposes of this article.

Added by Stats. 1982, Ch. 1364, Sec. 2. Operative July 1, 1983, by Sec. 3 of Ch. 1364.

Section 704.930 - Information contained in declaration; person who execute and acknowledge; statement of truth of facts

(a) A homestead declaration recorded pursuant to this article shall contain all of the following:

(1) The name of the declared homestead owner. Spouses both may be named as declared homestead owners in the same homestead declaration if each owns an interest in the dwelling selected as the declared homestead.

(2) A description of the declared homestead.

(3) A statement that the declared homestead is the principal dwelling of the declared homestead owner or such person's spouse, and that the declared homestead owner or such person's spouse resides in the declared homestead on the date the homestead declaration is recorded.

(b) The homestead declaration shall be executed and acknowledged in the manner of an acknowledgment of a conveyance of real property by at least one of the following persons:

(1) The declared homestead owner.

(2) The spouse of the declared homestead owner.

(3) The guardian or conservator of the person or estate of either of the persons listed in paragraph (1) or (2). The guardian or conservator may execute, acknowledge, and record a homestead declaration without the need to obtain court authorization.

(4) A person acting under a power of attorney or otherwise authorized to act on behalf of a person listed in paragraph (1) or (2).

(c) The homestead declaration shall include a statement that the facts stated in the homestead declaration are known to be true as of the personal knowledge of the person executing and acknowledging the homestead declaration. If the homestead declaration is executed and acknowledged by a person listed in paragraph (3) or (4) of subdivision (b), it shall also contain a statement that the person has authority to so act on behalf of the declared homestead owner or the spouse of the declared homestead owner and the source of the person's authority.

Amended by Stats 2016 ch 50 (SB 1005),s 17, eff. 1/1/2017.

Section 704.940 - Right to convey or encumber not restricted; prima facie evidence of facts stated

A homestead declaration does not restrict or limit any right to convey or encumber the declared homestead. A homestead declaration, when properly recorded, is prima facie evidence of the facts therein stated, and conclusive evidence thereof in favor of a purchaser or encumbrancer in good faith and for a valuable consideration.

Added by Stats. 1982, Ch. 1364, Sec. 2. Operative July 1, 1983, by Sec. 3 of Ch. 1364.

Section 704.950 - Attachment of judgment lien to declared homestead

(a) Except as provided in subdivisions (b) and (c), a judgment lien on real property created pursuant to Article 2 (commencing with Section 697.310) of Chapter 2 does not attach to a declared homestead if both of the following requirements are satisfied:

(1) A homestead declaration describing the declared homestead was recorded prior to the time the abstract or certified copy of the judgment was recorded to create the judgment lien.

(2) The homestead declaration names the judgment debtor or the spouse of the judgment debtor as a declared homestead owner.

(b) This section does not apply to a judgment lien created under Section 697.320 by recording a certified copy of a judgment for child, family, or spousal support.

(c) A judgment lien attaches to a declared homestead in the amount of any surplus over the total of the following:

(1) All liens and encumbrances on the declared homestead at the time the abstract of judgment or certified copy of the judgment is recorded to create the judgment lien.

(2) The homestead exemption set forth in Section 704.730.

Amended by Stats. 1992, Ch. 163, Sec. 44. Effective January 1, 1993. Operative January 1, 1994, by Sec. 161 of Ch. 163.

Section 704.960 - Proceeds from voluntary sale of homestead

(a) If a declared homestead is voluntarily sold, the proceeds of sale are exempt in the amount provided by Section 704.730 for a period of six months after the date of sale.

(b) If the proceeds of a declared homestead are invested in a new dwelling within six months after the date of a voluntary sale or within six months after proceeds of an execution sale or of insurance or other indemnification for damage or destruction are received, the new dwelling may be selected as a declared homestead by recording a homestead declaration within the applicable six-month period. In such case, the homestead declaration has the same effect as if it had been recorded at the time the prior homestead declaration was recorded.

Added by Stats. 1982, Ch. 1364, Sec. 2. Operative July 1, 1983, by Sec. 3 of Ch. 1364.

Section 704.965 - Amount of exemption when declaration recorded prior to increase in exemption amount

If a homestead declaration is recorded prior to the operative date of an amendment to Section 704.730 which increases the amount of the homestead exemption, the amount of the exemption for the purposes of subdivision (c) of Section 704.950 and Section 704.960 is the increased amount, except that, if the judgment creditor obtained a lien on the declared homestead prior to the operative date of the amendment to Section 704.730, the exemption for the purposes of subdivision (c) of Section 704.950 and Section 704.960 shall be determined as if that amendment to Section 704.730 had not been enacted.

Added by Stats. 1984, Ch. 454, Sec. 2.

Section 704.970 - Effect whether or not homestead declaration recorded

Whether or not a homestead declaration has been recorded:

(a) Nothing in this article affects the right of levy pursuant to a writ of execution.

(b) Any levy pursuant to a writ of execution on a dwelling (as defined in Section 704.710) and the sale pursuant thereto shall be made in compliance with Article 4 (commencing with Section 704.710) and the judgment debtor and the judgment creditor shall have all the rights and benefits provided by that article.

Added by Stats. 1982, Ch. 1364, Sec. 2. Operative July 1, 1983, by Sec. 3 of Ch. 1364.

Section 704.980 - Declaration of abandonment of homestead

(a) A declared homestead may be abandoned by a declaration of abandonment under this section, whether the homestead declaration was recorded pursuant to this article or pursuant to former Title 5 (commencing with former Section 1237) of Part 4 of Division 2 of the Civil Code.

(b) A declaration of abandonment shall be executed and acknowledged in the manner of an acknowledgment of a conveyance of real property. It shall be executed and acknowledged by a declared homestead owner or by a person authorized to act on behalf of a declared homestead owner. If it is executed and acknowledged by a person authorized to act on behalf of a declared homestead owner, the declaration shall contain a statement that the person has authority to act on behalf of the declared homestead owner and the source of the person's authority.

(c) The declaration of abandonment does not affect the declared homestead of any person other than the declared homestead owner named in the declaration of abandonment.

Added by Stats. 1982, Ch. 1364, Sec. 2. Operative July 1, 1983, by Sec. 3 of Ch. 1364.

Section 704.990 - Homestead abandoned by operation of law

(a) A declared homestead is abandoned by operation of law as to a declared homestead owner if the declared homestead owner or a person authorized to act on behalf of the declared homestead owner executes, acknowledges, and records a new homestead declaration for the declared homestead owner on different property. An abandonment under this subdivision does not affect the declared homestead of any person other than the declared homestead owner named in the new homestead declaration.

(b) Notwithstanding subdivision (a), if a homestead declaration is recorded which includes property described in a previously recorded homestead declaration, to the extent that the prior homestead declaration is still valid, the new homestead declaration shall not be considered an abandonment of the prior declared homestead.

Added by Stats. 1982, Ch. 1364, Sec. 2. Operative July 1, 1983, by Sec. 3 of Ch. 1364.

Section 704.995 - Continuation of protection of declared homestead after death of declared home stead owner

(a) The protection of the declared homestead from any creditor having an attachment lien, execution lien, or judgment lien on the dwelling continues after the death of the declared homestead owner if, at the time of the death, the dwelling was the principal dwelling of one or more of the following persons to whom all or part of the interest of the deceased declared homestead owner passes:

(1) The surviving spouse of the decedent.

(2) A member of the family of the decedent.

(b) The protection of the declared homestead provided by subdivision (a) continues regardless of whether the decedent was the sole owner of the declared homestead or owned the declared homestead with the surviving spouse or a member of the decedent's family and regardless of whether the surviving spouse or the member of the decedent's family was a declared homestead owner at the time of the decedent's death.

(c) The amount of the homestead exemption is determined pursuant to Section 704.730 depending on the circumstances of the case at the time the amount is required to be determined.

Added by Stats. 1984, Ch. 538, Sec. 27.

Chapter 5 - WAGE GARNISHMENT

Article 1 - SHORT TITLE; DEFINITIONS

Section 706.010 - Title of law

This chapter shall be known and may be cited as the "Wage Garnishment Law."

Added by Stats. 1982, Ch. 1364, Sec. 2. Operative July 1, 1983, by Sec. 3 of Ch. 1364.

Section 706.011 - Definitions

As used in this chapter:

(a) "Disposable earnings" means the portion of an individual's earnings that remains after deducting all amounts required to be withheld by law.

(b) "Earnings" means compensation payable by an employer to an employee for personal services performed by such employee, whether denominated as wages, salary, commission, bonus, or otherwise.

(c) "Earnings withholding order for elder or dependent adult financial abuse" means an earnings withholding order, made pursuant to Article 5 (commencing with Section 706.100) and based on a money judgment in an action for elder or adult dependent financial abuse under Section 15657.5 of the Welfare and Institutions Code.

(d) "Earnings assignment order for support" means an order, made pursuant to Chapter 8 (commencing with Section 5200) of Part 5 of Division 9 of the Family Code or Section 3088 of the Probate Code, which requires an employer to withhold earnings for support.

(e) "Employee" means a public officer and any individual who performs services subject to the right of the employer to control both what shall be done and how it shall be done.

(f) "Employer" means a person for whom an individual performs services as an employee.

(g) "Judgment creditor," as applied to the state, means the specific state agency seeking to collect a judgment or tax liability.

(h) "Judgment debtor" includes a person from whom the state is seeking to collect a tax liability under Article 4 (commencing with Section 706.070), whether or not a judgment has been obtained on such tax liability.

(i) "Person" includes an individual, a corporation, a partnership or other unincorporated association, a limited liability company, and a public entity.

Amended by Stats 2012 ch 474 (AB 1775),s 1, eff. 1/1/2013, op. 7/1/2013.

Amended by Stats 2010 ch 64 (AB 2619),s 1, eff. 1/1/2011, op. 1/1/2012.

Article 2 - GENERAL PROVISIONS

Section 706.020 - Generally

Except for an earning assignment order for support, the earnings of an employee shall not be required to be withheld by an employer for payment of a debt by means of any judicial procedure other than pursuant to this chapter.

Amended by Stats. 1992, Ch. 163, Sec. 46. Effective January 1, 1993. Operative January 1, 1994, by Sec. 161 of Ch. 163.

Section 706.021 - Levy of execution made by service of earnings withholding order

Notwithstanding any other provision of this title, a levy of execution upon the earnings of an employee shall be made by service of an earnings withholding order upon the employer in accordance with this chapter.

Added by Stats. 1982, Ch. 1364, Sec. 2. Operative July 1, 1983, by Sec. 3 of Ch. 1364.

Section 706.022 - Withholding period defined; withholding for pay period ending during withholding period

(a) As used in this section, "withholding period" means the period which commences on the 10th day after service of an earnings withholding order upon the employer and which continues until the earliest of the following dates:

(1) The date the employer has withheld the full amount required to satisfy the order.

(2) The date of termination specified in a court order served on the employer.

(3) The date of termination specified in a notice of termination served on the employer by the levying officer.

(4) The date of termination of a dormant or suspended earnings withholding order as determined pursuant to Section 706.032.

(b) Except as otherwise provided by statute, an employer shall withhold the amounts required by an earnings withholding order from all earnings of the employee payable for any pay period of the employee which ends during the withholding period.

(c) An employer is not liable for any amounts withheld and paid over to the levying officer pursuant to an earnings withholding order prior to service upon the employer pursuant to paragraph (2) or (3) of subdivision (a).

Amended by Stats. 1992, Ch. 283, Sec. 5. Effective July 21, 1992.

Section 706.023 - Compliance with orders served upon employer

Except as otherwise provided in this chapter:

(a) An employer shall comply with the first earnings withholding order served upon the employer.
(b) If the employer is served with two or more earnings withholding orders on the same day, the employer shall comply with the order issued pursuant to the judgment first entered. If two or more orders served on the same day are based on judgments entered upon the same day, the employer shall comply with whichever one of the orders the employer selects.
(c) If an earnings withholding order is served while an employer is required to comply with another earnings withholding order with respect to the earnings of the same employee, the subsequent order is ineffective and the employer shall not withhold earnings pursuant to the subsequent order, except as provided in subdivision (d).
(d) Notwithstanding any other provisions of this section, a withholding order for elder or dependent adult financial abuse has priority over any other earning withholding order except for a withholding order for support under Section 706.030 and a withholding order for taxes under Section 706.072.
(1) An employer upon whom a withholding order for elder or dependent adult financial abuse is served shall withhold and pay over earnings of the employee pursuant to that order notwithstanding the requirements of another earnings withholding order except as provided in paragraph (2).
(2) An employer shall not withhold earnings of an employee pursuant to an earnings withholding order for elder or dependent adult financial abuse if a withholding order for support or for taxes is in effect or if a prior withholding order for elder or dependent adult financial abuse is in effect. In that case, the subsequent withholding order for elder or dependent financial abuse is ineffective.
(3) When an employer is required to cease withholding earnings pursuant to a prior earnings withholding order, the employer shall notify the levying officer who served the prior earnings withholding order that a supervening earnings withholding order for elder or dependent financial abuse is in effect.
Amended by Stats 2010 ch 64 (AB 2619),s 2, eff. 1/1/2011, op. 1/1/2012.

Section 706.024 - Amount required to satisfy withholding order
(a) The amount required to satisfy an earnings withholding order is the total amount required to satisfy the writ of execution on the date the order is issued, with the following additions and subtractions:
(1) The addition of the statutory fee for service of the order and any other statutory fees for performing duties under the order.
(2) The addition of costs added to the order pursuant to Section 685.090.
(3) The subtraction of the amount of any partial satisfactions.
(4) The addition of daily interest accruing after issuance of the order, as adjusted for partial satisfactions.
(b) From time to time the levying officer, in the levying officer's discretion, may give written notice to the employer of the amount required to satisfy the earnings withholding order and the employer shall determine the total amount to withhold based upon the levying officer's notice, notwithstanding a different amount stated in the order originally served on the employer.
(c) If the full amount required to satisfy the earnings withholding order as stated in the order or in the levying officer's notice under subdivision (b) is withheld from the judgment debtor's earnings, interest ceases to accrue on that amount.
Added by Stats. 1992, Ch. 283, Sec. 6. Effective July 21, 1992.

Section 706.025 - Monthly payments; election to pay more frequently
(a) Except as provided in subdivision (b), the amount required to be withheld pursuant to an earnings withholding order shall be paid monthly to the levying officer not later than the 15th day of each month. The initial monthly payment shall include all amounts required to be withheld from the earnings of the employee during the preceding calendar month up to the close of the employee's pay period ending closest to the last day of that month, and thereafter each monthly payment shall include amounts withheld from the employee's earnings for services rendered in the interim up to the close of the employee's pay period ending closest to the last day of the preceding calendar month.
(b) The employer may elect to pay the amounts withheld to the levying officer more frequently than monthly. If the employer so elects, payment of the amount withheld from the employee's earnings for each pay period shall be made not later than 10 days after the close of the pay period.
Added by Stats. 1982, Ch. 1364, Sec. 2. Operative July 1, 1983, by Sec. 3 of Ch. 1364.

Section 706.026 - Payment of amounts received to person entitled; accounting filed by levying officer
(a) The levying officer shall receive and account for all amounts paid by the employer pursuant to Section 706.025 and shall pay the amounts so received over to the person entitled thereto at least once every 30 days.
(b) At least once every two years, the levying officer shall file an accounting with the court, as provided by Section 699.560, for all amounts collected under the earnings withholding order, including costs and interest added to the amount due. Subject to the limitations in subdivision (c) of Section 263, the levying officer may electronically file the accounting with the court, pursuant to Chapter 2 (commencing with Section 263) of Title 4 of Part 1.
Amended by Stats 2010 ch 680 (AB 2394),s 12, eff. 1/1/2011.

Section 706.027 - Termination of order serving notice of termination
If the judgment pursuant to which the earnings withholding order is issued is satisfied before the order otherwise terminates pursuant to Section 706.022, the judgment creditor shall promptly notify the levying officer who shall promptly terminate the order by serving a notice of termination on the employer.
Added by Stats. 1982, Ch. 1364, Sec. 2. Operative July 1, 1983, by Sec. 3 of Ch. 1364.

Section 706.028 - Final earnings withholding order for costs and interest
(a) "Final earnings withholding order for costs and interest" means an earnings withholding order for the collection only of unsatisfied costs and interest, which is issued after an earlier earnings withholding order has been returned satisfied.
(b) After the amount stated as owing in a prior earnings withholding order is paid, the judgment creditor may obtain a final earnings withholding order for costs and interest to collect amounts of costs and interest that were not collected under the prior earnings withholding order.
(c) A final earnings withholding order for costs and interest shall be enforced in the same manner as other earnings withholding orders.
(d) Satisfaction of the amount stated as owing in a final earnings withholding order for costs and interest is equivalent to satisfaction of the money judgment. For this purpose, interest ceases to accrue on the date of issuance of the final earnings withholding order and no additional costs may be added after that date, except for the statutory fee for service of the order and any other statutory fees for performing duties under the order.
Repealed and added by Stats. 1992, Ch. 283, Sec. 9. Effective July 21, 1992.

Section 706.029 - Lien upon earning created by service of withholding order
Service of an earnings withholding order creates a lien upon the earnings of the judgment debtor that are required to be withheld pursuant to the order and upon all property of the employer subject to the enforcement of a money judgment in the amount required to be withheld pursuant to such order. The lien continues for a period of one year from the date the earnings of the judgment debtor become payable unless the amount required to be withheld pursuant to the order is paid as required by law.
Added by Stats. 1982, Ch. 1364, Sec. 2. Operative July 1, 1983, by Sec. 3 of Ch. 1364.

Section 706.030 - Withholding order for support

(a) A "withholding order for support" is an earnings withholding order issued on a writ of execution to collect delinquent amounts payable under a judgment for the support of a child, or spouse or former spouse, of the judgment debtor. A withholding order for support shall be denoted as such on its face.

(b) The local child support agency may issue a withholding order for support on a notice of levy pursuant to Section 17522 of the Family Code to collect a support obligation.

(1) When the local child support agency issues a withholding order for support, a reference in this chapter to a levying officer is deemed to mean the local child support agency who issues the withholding order for support.

(2) Service of a withholding order for support issued by the local child support agency may be made by first-class mail or in any other manner described in Section 706.101. Service of a withholding order for support issued by the local child support agency is complete when it is received by the employer or a person described in paragraph (1) or (2) of subdivision (a) of Section 706.101, or if service is by first-class mail, service is complete as specified in Section 1013.

(3) The local child support agency shall serve upon the employer the withholding order for support, a copy of the order, and a notice informing the support obligor of the effect of the order and of his or her right to hearings and remedies provided in this chapter and in the Family Code. The notice shall be accompanied by the forms necessary to obtain an administrative review and a judicial hearing and instructions on how to file the forms. Within 10 days from the date of service, the employer shall deliver to the support obligor a copy of the withholding order for support, the forms to obtain an administrative review and judicial hearing, and the notice. If the support obligor is no longer employed by the employer and the employer does not owe the support obligor any earnings, the employer shall inform the local child support agency that the support obligor is no longer employed by the employer.

(4) An employer who fails to comply with paragraph (3) shall be subject to a civil penalty of five hundred dollars ($500) for each occurrence.

(5) The local child support agency shall provide for an administrative review to reconsider or modify the amount to be withheld for arrearages pursuant to the withholding order for support, if the support obligor requests a review at any time after service of the withholding order. The local child support agency shall provide the review in the same manner and timeframes provided for resolution of a complaint pursuant to Section 17800 of the Family Code. The local child support agency shall notify the employer if the review results in any modifications to the withholding order for support. If the local child support agency cannot complete the administrative review within 30 calendar days of receipt of the complaint, the local child support agency shall notify the employer to suspend withholding any disputed amount pending the completion of the review and the determination by the local child support agency.

(6) Nothing in this section prohibits the support obligor from seeking a judicial determination of arrearages pursuant to subdivision (c) of Section 17256 of the Family Code or from filing a motion for equitable division of earnings pursuant to Section 706.052 either prior to or after the administrative review provided by this section. Within five business days after receiving notice of the obligor having filed for judicial relief pursuant to this section, the local child support agency shall notify the employer to suspend withholding any disputed amount pending a determination by the court. The employer shall then adjust the withholding within not more than nine days of receiving the notice from the local child support agency.

(c) Notwithstanding any other provision of this chapter:

(1) An employer shall continue to withhold pursuant to a withholding order for support until the earliest of the dates specified in paragraph (1), (2), or (3) of subdivision (a) of Section 706.022, except that a withholding order for support shall automatically terminate one year after the employment of the employee by the employer terminates.

(2) A withholding order for support has priority over any other earnings withholding order. An employer upon whom a withholding order for support is served shall withhold and pay over earnings of the employee pursuant to that order notwithstanding the requirements of another earnings withholding order.

(3) Subject to paragraph (2) and to Article 3 (commencing with Section 706.050), an employer shall withhold earnings pursuant to both a withholding order for support and another earnings withholding order simultaneously.

(4) An employer who willfully fails to withhold and forward support pursuant to a valid earnings withholding order for support issued and served upon the employer pursuant to this chapter is liable to the support obligee, as defined in Section 5214 of the Family Code, for the amount of support not withheld, forwarded, or otherwise paid to the support obligee.

(5) Notwithstanding any other provision of law, an employer shall send all earnings withheld pursuant to a withholding order for support to the levying officer or the State Disbursement Unit as described in Section 17309 of the Family Code within the time period specified by federal law.

(6) Once the State Disbursement Unit as described in Section 17309 of the Family Code is operational, all support payments made pursuant to an earnings withholding order shall be made to that unit.

(7) Earnings withheld pursuant to an earnings withholding order for support shall be credited toward satisfaction of a support judgment as specified in Section 695.221.

Amended by Stats 2003 ch 387 (AB 739),s 1, eff. 1/1/2004.
Amended by Stats 2001 ch 755 (SB 943), s 1, eff. 10/11/2001.
Amended by Stats 2000 ch 808 (AB 1358), s 17, eff. 9/28/2000.

Section 706.031 - Priority of withholding order for support

(a) Nothing in this chapter affects an earnings assignment order for support.

(b) An earnings assignment order for support shall be given priority over any earnings withholding order. An employer upon whom an earnings assignment order for support is served shall withhold and pay over the earnings of the employee pursuant to the assignment order notwithstanding the requirements of any earnings withholding order. When an employer is required to cease withholding earnings pursuant to an earnings withholding order, the employer shall notify the levying officer who served the earnings withholding order that a supervening earnings assignment order for support is in effect.

(c) Subject to subdivisions (b), (d), and (e), an employer shall withhold earnings of an employee pursuant to both an earnings assignment order for support and an earnings withholding order.

(d) The employer shall withhold pursuant to an earnings withholding order only to the extent that the sum of the amount withheld pursuant to any earnings assignment order for support and the amount withheld pursuant to the earnings withholding order does not exceed the amount that may be withheld under Article 3 (commencing with Section 706.050).

(e) The employer shall withhold pursuant to an earnings withholding order for taxes only to the extent that the sum of the amount withheld pursuant to any earnings assignment order for support and the amount withheld pursuant to the earnings withholding order for taxes does not exceed the amount that may be withheld under Article 4 (commencing with Section 706.070).

Amended by Stats. 1992, Ch. 163, Sec. 47. Effective January 1, 1993. Operative January 1, 1994, by Sec. 161 of Ch. 163.

Section 706.032 - Cessation of withholding because debtor's employment terminated; debtor's earnings subject to assignment with higher priority

(a) Except as otherwise provided by statute:

(1) If withholding under an earnings withholding order ceases because the judgment debtor's employment has terminated, the earnings withholding order terminates at the conclusion of a continuous 180-day period during which no amounts are withheld under the order.

(2) If withholding under an earnings withholding order ceases because the judgment debtor's earnings are subject to an order or assignment with higher priority, the earnings withholding order terminates at the conclusion of a continuous two-year period during which no amounts are withheld under the order.

(b) If an earnings withholding order has terminated pursuant to subdivision (a), the employer shall return the order to the levying officer along with a statement of the reasons for returning the order.

Added by Stats. 1992, Ch. 283, Sec. 11. Effective July 21, 1992.

Section 706.033 - Supplemental return on writ

If the writ is returned before the earnings withholding order terminates, on termination of the earnings withholding order the levying officer shall make a supplemental return on the writ. The supplemental return shall contain the same information as an original return pursuant to Section 699.560.

Added by Stats. 1992, Ch. 283, Sec. 12. Effective July 21, 1992.

Section 706.034 - Deduction by employer from employee's earning for each payment

The employer may deduct from the earnings of the employee the sum of one dollar and fifty cents ($1.50) for each payment made in accordance with an earnings withholding order issued pursuant to this chapter.

Amended by Stats 2004 ch 520 (AB 2530),s 1, eff. 1/1/2005

Article 3 - RESTRICTIONS ON EARNINGS WITHHOLDING

Section 706.050 - [Operative until 9/1/2023] Maximum amount for workweek subject to levy; period other than weekly

(a) Except as otherwise provided in this chapter, the maximum amount of disposable earnings of an individual judgment debtor for any workweek that is subject to levy under an earnings withholding order shall not exceed the lesser of the following:

(1) Twenty-five percent of the individual's disposable earnings for that week.

(2) Fifty percent of the amount by which the individual's disposable earnings for that week exceed 40 times the state minimum hourly wage in effect at the time the earnings are payable. If a judgment debtor works in a location where the local minimum hourly wage is greater than the state minimum hourly wage, the local minimum hourly wage in effect at the time the earnings are payable shall be used for the calculation made pursuant to this paragraph.

(b) For any pay period other than weekly, the following multipliers shall be used to determine the maximum amount of disposable earnings subject to levy under an earnings withholding order that is proportional in effect to the calculation described in paragraph (2) of subdivision (a), except as specified in paragraph (1):

(1) For a daily pay period, the amounts shall be identical to the amounts described in subdivision (a).

(2) For a biweekly pay period, multiply the applicable hourly minimum wage by 80 work hours.

(3) For a semimonthly pay period, multiply the applicable hourly minimum wage by $86^2/_3$ work hours.

(4) For a monthly pay period, multiply the applicable hourly minimum wage by $173^1/_3$ work hours.

(c) This section shall become inoperative on September 1, 2023, and, as of January 1, 2024, is repealed, unless a later enacted statute that becomes operative on or before January 1, 2024, deletes or extends the dates on which it becomes inoperative and is repealed.

Amended by Stats 2022 ch 849 (SB 1477),s 1, eff. 1/1/2023.

Added by Stats 2015 ch 800 (SB 501),s 2, eff. 1/1/2016.

Section 706.050 - [Operative 9/1/2023] Maximum amount for workweek subject to levy; period other than weekly

(a) Except as otherwise provided in this chapter, the maximum amount of disposable earnings of an individual judgment debtor for any workweek that is subject to levy under an earnings withholding order shall not exceed the lesser of the following:

(1) Twenty percent of the individual's disposable earnings for that week.

(2) Forty percent of the amount by which the individual's disposable earnings for that week exceed 48 times the state minimum hourly wage in effect at the time the earnings are payable. If a judgment debtor works in a location where the local minimum hourly wage is greater than the state minimum hourly wage, the local minimum hourly wage in effect at the time the earnings are payable shall be used for the calculation made pursuant to this paragraph.

(b) For any pay period other than weekly, the following multipliers shall be used to determine the maximum amount of disposable earnings subject to levy under an earnings withholding order that is proportional in effect to the calculation described in paragraph (2) of subdivision (a), except as specified in paragraph (1):

(1) For a daily pay period, the amounts shall be identical to the amounts described in subdivision (a).

(2) For a biweekly pay period, multiply the applicable hourly minimum wage by 96 work hours.

(3) For a semimonthly pay period, multiply the applicable hourly minimum wage by 104 work hours.

(4) For a monthly pay period, multiply the applicable hourly minimum wage by 208 work hours.

(c) This section shall become operative on September 1, 2023.

Added by Stats 2022 ch 849 (SB 1477),s 2, eff. 1/1/2023.

Amended by Stats 2022 ch 849 (SB 1477),s 1, eff. 1/1/2023.

Added by Stats 2015 ch 800 (SB 501),s 2, eff. 1/1/2016.

Section 706.051 - Exemption of amount necessary for support of debtor or debtor's family

(a) For the purposes of this section, "family of the judgment debtor" includes the spouse or former spouse of the judgment debtor.

(b) Except as provided in subdivision (c), the portion of the judgment debtor's earnings that the judgment debtor proves is necessary for the support of the judgment debtor or the judgment debtor's family supported in whole or in part by the judgment debtor is exempt from levy under this chapter.

(c) The exemption provided in subdivision (b) is not available if any of the following exceptions applies:

(1) The debt was incurred pursuant to an order or award for the payment of attorney's fees under Section 2030, 3121, or 3557 of the Family Code.

(2) The debt was incurred for personal services rendered by an employee or former employee of the judgment debtor.

(3) The order is a withholding order for support under Section 706.030.

(4) The order is one governed by Article 4 (commencing with Section 706.070) (state tax order).

Amended by Stats 2011 ch 694 (AB 1388),s 1, eff. 1/1/2012.

Section 706.052 - Exemption where withhold order for support

(a) Except as provided in subdivision (b), one-half of the disposable earnings (as defined by Section 1672 of Title 15 of the United States Code) of the judgment debtor, plus any amount withheld from the judgment debtor's earnings pursuant to any earnings assignment order for support, is exempt from levy under this chapter where the earnings withholding order is a withholding order for support under Section 706.030.

(b) Except as provided in subdivision (c), upon motion of any interested party, the court shall make an equitable division of the judgment debtor's earnings that takes into account the needs of all the persons the judgment debtor is required to support and shall effectuate such division by an order determining the amount to be withheld from the judgment debtor's earnings pursuant to the withholding order for support.

(c) An order made under subdivision (b) may not authorize the withholding of an amount in excess of the amount that may be withheld for support under federal law under Section 1673 of Title 15 of the United States Code.

Amended by Stats. 1992, Ch. 163, Sec. 48. Effective January 1, 1993. Operative January 1, 1994, by Sec. 161 of Ch. 163.

Article 4 - EARNINGS WITHHOLDING ORDER FOR TAXES

Section 706.070 - Definitions

As used in this article:

(a) "State" means the State of California and includes any officer, department, board, or agency thereof.

(b) "State tax liability" means an amount for which the state has a state tax lien as defined in Section 7162 of the Government Code excluding a state tax lien created pursuant to the Fish and Game Code.

(c) For purposes of an earnings withholding order for taxes issued by the Franchise Tax Board, "state tax liability" also includes any liability under Part 10 (commencing with Section 17001), Part 10.2 (commencing with Section 18401), or Part 11 (commencing with Section 23001) of Division 2 of the Revenue and Taxation Code that is due and payable within the meaning of subdivision (b) of Section 19221 of the Revenue and Taxation Code, and unpaid. The amendments to this section by the act adding this subdivision shall apply to any amount that is unpaid on or after the effective date of that act, or any amount that first becomes due and payable, and unpaid, after the effective date of that act.

Amended by Stats 2012 ch 37 (SB 1015),s 1, eff. 6/27/2012.

Section 706.071 - Limitations on state's right to collect state tax liability

This chapter does not limit the state's right to collect a state tax liability except that (a) no levy upon earnings of an employee held by an employer is effective unless such levy is made in accordance with the provisions of this chapter and (b) other methods of collection may not be used to require an employer to withhold earnings of an employee in payment of a state tax liability.

Added by Stats. 1982, Ch. 1364, Sec. 2. Operative July 1, 1983, by Sec. 3 of Ch. 1364.

Section 706.072 - Withholding order for taxes defined; requirements for issuing; notice of proposed issuance of withholding order for taxes

(a) A "withholding order for taxes" is an earnings withholding order issued pursuant to this article to collect a state tax liability and shall be denoted as a withholding order for taxes on its face.

(b) A withholding order for taxes may only be issued under one of the following circumstances:

(1) The existence of the state tax liability appears on the face of the taxpayer's return, including a case where such tax liability is disclosed from the taxpayer's return after errors in mathematical computations in the return have been corrected.

(2) The state tax liability has been assessed or determined as provided by statute and the taxpayer had notice of the proposed assessment or determination and had available an opportunity to have the proposed assessment or determination reviewed by appropriate administrative procedures. If the taxpayer makes a timely request for review of the assessment or determination, the state shall not issue a withholding order for taxes until the administrative review procedure is completed. If the taxpayer is given notice of the proposed assessment or determination but does not make a timely request for review, the state may issue a withholding order for taxes.

(c) In any case where a state tax liability has been assessed or determined prior to July 1, 1983, and the state determines that the requirement of subdivision (b) may not have been satisfied, the state may send a "Notice of Proposed Issuance of Withholding Order for Taxes" to the taxpayer at the taxpayer's last known address by first-class mail, postage prepaid. The notice shall advise the taxpayer that the taxpayer may have the assessment or determination reviewed by appropriate administrative procedures and state how such a review may be obtained. If the taxpayer is sent such a notice and requests such a review within 30 days from the date the notice was mailed to the taxpayer, the state shall provide appropriate administrative procedures for review of the assessment or determination and shall not issue the withholding order for taxes until the administrative review procedure is completed. If the taxpayer is sent such a notice and does not request such a review within 30 days from the date the notice was mailed to the taxpayer, the state may issue the withholding order for taxes.

(d) A withholding order for taxes may be issued whether or not the state tax liability has been reduced to judgment.

Added by Stats. 1982, Ch. 1364, Sec. 2. Operative July 1, 1983, by Sec. 3 of Ch. 1364.

Section 706.073 - Chapter governs procedures and proceedings

Except as otherwise provided in this article, the provisions of this chapter govern the procedures and proceedings concerning a withholding order for taxes. For the purposes of this article, a reference in this chapter to a "levying officer" shall be deemed to mean the specific state agency seeking to collect a state tax liability under this article.

Added by Stats. 1982, Ch. 1364, Sec. 2. Operative July 1, 1983, by Sec. 3 of Ch. 1364.

Section 706.074 - State may issue order; amount to be withheld

(a) The state may itself issue a withholding order for taxes under this section to collect a state tax liability. The order shall specify the total amount required to be withheld pursuant to the order (unpaid tax liability including any penalties, accrued interest, and costs).

(b) Unless a lesser amount is specified in the order, the amount to be withheld by the employer each pay period pursuant to an order issued under this section is the amount required to be withheld under Section 1673(a)(a) of Title 15 of the United States Code, and is not subject to the exception provided in Section 1673(b)(b) of Title 15 of the United States Code.

Added by Stats. 1982, Ch. 1364, Sec. 2. Operative July 1, 1983, by Sec. 3 of Ch. 1364.

Section 706.075 - Procedures applicable to withholding order issued under article

(a) This section applies to any withholding order for taxes issued under this article.

(b) Together with the withholding order for taxes, the state shall serve upon the employer an additional copy of the order and a notice informing the taxpayer of the effect of the order and of his right to hearings and remedies provided in this chapter. Within 10 days from the date of service, the employer shall deliver to the taxpayer a copy of the order and the notice, except that immediate delivery shall be made where a jeopardy withholding order for taxes has been served. If the taxpayer is no longer employed by the employer and the employer does not owe the taxpayer any earnings, the employer is not required to make such delivery.

(c) The state shall provide for an administrative hearing to reconsider or modify the amount to be withheld pursuant to the withholding order for taxes, and the taxpayer may request such a hearing at any time after service of the order. If the taxpayer requests a hearing, the hearing shall be provided, and the matter shall be determined, within 15 days after the request is received by the state. The determination of the amount to be withheld is subject to the standard provided in subdivision (b) of Section 706.051. Judicial review of the determination made pursuant to this subdivision by the state may be had only if a petition for a writ of mandate pursuant to Section 1094.5 is filed within 90 days from the date that written notice of the state's determination was delivered or mailed to the taxpayer.

(d) The employer is not subject to any civil liability for failure to comply with subdivision (b). Nothing in this subdivision limits the power of a court to hold the employer in contempt of court for failure to comply with subdivision (b).

Added by Stats. 1982, Ch. 1364, Sec. 2. Operative July 1, 1983, by Sec. 3 of Ch. 1364.

Section 706.076 - Application by state to court for withholding order

(a) A withholding order for taxes may be issued pursuant to this section requiring the employer of the taxpayer to withhold an amount in excess of the amount that may be required to be withheld pursuant to an order issued under Section 706.074.

(b) The state may, at any time, apply to a court of record in the county where the taxpayer was last known to reside for the issuance of a withholding order for taxes under this section to collect a state tax liability.

(c) The application for the order shall include a statement under oath that the state has served upon the taxpayer both of the following:

(1) A copy of the application.

(2) A notice informing the taxpayer of the purpose of the application and the right of the taxpayer to appear at the court hearing on the application.
(d) Upon the filing of the application, the court shall immediately set the matter for hearing and the court clerk shall send a notice of the time and place of the hearing by first-class mail, postage prepaid, to the state and the taxpayer. The notice shall be deposited in the mail at least 10 days before the day set for the hearing.
(e) After hearing, the court shall issue a withholding order for taxes which shall require the taxpayer's employer to withhold and pay over all earnings of the taxpayer other than that amount which the taxpayer proves is exempt under subdivision (b) of Section 706.051, but in no event shall the amount to be withheld be less than that permitted to be withheld under Section 706.050.
(f) The state may issue a temporary earnings holding order, which shall be denoted as such on its face, in any case where the state intends to apply for a withholding order for taxes under this section and has determined that the collection of the state tax liability will be jeopardized in whole or in part if the temporary earnings holding order is not issued. The temporary earnings holding order shall be directed to the taxpayer's employer and shall require the employer to retain in the employer's possession or under the employer's control all or such portion of the earnings of the taxpayer then or thereafter due as is specified in the order. Together with the temporary earnings holding order, the state shall serve upon the employer an additional copy of the order and a notice informing the taxpayer of the effect of the order and of the right to the remedies provided in this chapter. Upon receipt of the order, the employer shall deliver to the taxpayer a copy of the order and notice. If the taxpayer is no longer employed by the employer and the employer does not owe the taxpayer any earnings, the employer is not required to make such delivery. The temporary earnings holding order expires 15 days from the date it is served on the employer unless it is extended by the court on ex parte application for good cause shown. If a temporary earnings holding order is served on an employer, the state may not thereafter, for a period of six months, serve on the same employer another temporary earnings holding order for the same employee unless the court for good cause shown otherwise orders. Sections 706.153 and 706.154 apply to temporary earnings holding orders issued under this section.
Added by Stats. 1982, Ch. 1364, Sec. 2. Operative July 1, 1983, by Sec. 3 of Ch. 1364.

Section 706.077 - Duty of employer to withhold and pay over earnings
(a) Subject to subdivision (b), an employer upon whom a withholding order for taxes is served shall withhold and pay over earnings of the employee pursuant to such order and shall cease to withhold earnings pursuant to any prior earnings withholding order except that a withholding order for support shall be given priority as provided in Section 706.030. When an employer is required to cease withholding earnings pursuant to an earlier earnings withholding order, the employer shall notify the levying officer who served the earlier earnings withholding order that a supervening withholding order for taxes is in effect.
(b) An employer shall not withhold earnings of an employee pursuant to a withholding order for taxes if a prior withholding order for taxes is in effect, and, in such case, the subsequent withholding order for taxes is ineffective.
Added by Stats. 1982, Ch. 1364, Sec. 2. Operative July 1, 1983, by Sec. 3 of Ch. 1364.

Section 706.078 - Jeopardy withholding order for taxes
(a) Except as provided in subdivision (b), the employer shall not withhold pursuant to a withholding order for taxes from earnings of the employee payable for any pay period of such employee that ends prior to the 10th day after service of the order.
(b) A "jeopardy withholding order for taxes," which shall be denoted as such on its face, is a withholding order for taxes that requires that the employer withhold pursuant to the order from earnings due to the employee at the time of service of the order on the employer and from earnings thereafter due. A jeopardy withholding order for taxes may be issued only where the state has determined that the collection of a state tax liability will be jeopardized in whole or in part by delaying the time when withholding from earnings commences.
(c) An employer shall continue to withhold pursuant to a withholding order for taxes until the amount specified in the order has been paid in full or the order is withdrawn, except that the order automatically terminates one year after the employment of the employee by the employer terminates. The state shall promptly serve on the employer a notice terminating the withholding order for taxes if the state tax liability for which the withholding order for taxes was issued is satisfied before the employer has withheld the full amount specified in the order, and the employer shall discontinue withholding in compliance with such notice.
Added by Stats. 1982, Ch. 1364, Sec. 2. Operative July 1, 1983, by Sec. 3 of Ch. 1364.

Section 706.080 - Service of order or any other notice or document
Service of a withholding order for taxes or of any other notice or document required under this chapter in connection with a withholding order for taxes may be made by the state by first-class mail, postage prepaid, or by any authorized state employee. Service of a withholding order for taxes is complete when it is received by the employer or a person described in paragraph (1) or (2) of subdivision (a) of Section 706.101. Service of, or the providing of, any other notice or document required to be served or provided under this chapter in connection with a withholding order for taxes is complete when the notice or document is deposited in the mail addressed to the last known address of the person on whom it is served or to whom it is to be provided.
Added by Stats. 1982, Ch. 1364, Sec. 2. Operative July 1, 1983, by Sec. 3 of Ch. 1364.

Section 706.081 - Forms prescribed by state
Except for the forms referred to in Section 706.076, the state shall prescribe the form of any order, notice, or other document required by this chapter in connection with a withholding order for taxes notwithstanding Sections 706.100 and 706.120, and any form so prescribed is deemed to comply with this chapter.
Added by Stats. 1982, Ch. 1364, Sec. 2. Operative July 1, 1983, by Sec. 3 of Ch. 1364.

Section 706.082 - No review of taxpayer's tax liability
No review of the taxpayer's tax liability shall be permitted in any court proceedings under this chapter.
Added by Stats. 1982, Ch. 1364, Sec. 2. Operative July 1, 1983, by Sec. 3 of Ch. 1364.

Section 706.084 - Warrant, notice of levy or notice or order to withhold served on employer deemed withholding order for taxes
Where a warrant, notice of levy, or notice or order to withhold is served on the employer to enforce a state tax liability of a person who is an employee of that employer, it shall be deemed to be a withholding order for taxes as to any earnings that are subject to the provisions of this chapter if both of the following requirements are satisfied:
(a) The form provides notice on its face that it is to be treated as a withholding order for taxes as to any earnings that are subject to the provisions of this chapter.
(b) The form provides all the information provided in a withholding order for taxes.
Added by Stats. 1982, Ch. 1364, Sec. 2. Operative July 1, 1983, by Sec. 3 of Ch. 1364.

Article 5 - PROCEDURE FOR EARNINGS WITHHOLDING ORDERS AND EXEMPTION CLAIMS

Section 706.100 - Rule for practice and procedure in proceedings
Notwithstanding any other provision of law, the Judicial Council may provide by rule for the practice and procedure in proceedings under this chapter except for the state's administrative hearings provided by Article 4 (commencing with Section 706.070).
Added by Stats. 1982, Ch. 1364, Sec. 2. Operative July 1, 1983, by Sec. 3 of Ch. 1364.

Section 706.101 - Service

(a) An earnings withholding order shall be served by the levying officer upon the employer by delivery of the order to any of the following:

(1) The managing agent or person in charge, at the time of service, of the branch or office where the employee works or the office from which the employee is paid. In the case of a state employee, the office from which the employee is paid does not include the Controller's office unless the employee works directly for the Controller's office.

(2) Any person to whom a copy of the summons and of the complaint may be delivered to make service on the employer under Article 4 (commencing with Section 416.10) of Chapter 4 of Title 5.

(b) Service of an earnings withholding order shall be made by personal delivery as provided in Section 415.10 or 415.20 or by delivery by first-class mail, postage prepaid. When service is made by first-class mail, service is complete at the time of receipt of the earnings withholding order, as indicated in the employer's return, or the date of mailing if the date of receipt is not indicated on the employer's return. If the levying officer attempts service by first-class mail under this subdivision and does not receive the employer's return within 15 days from the date of mailing, the levying officer shall make service as provided in Article 3 (commencing with Section 415.10) of Chapter 4 of Title 5. For purposes of this section, "employer's return" refers to the Judicial Council-issued form specified by Section 706.126.

(c) The state may issue an earnings withholding order directly, without the use of a levying officer, for purposes of collecting overpayments of unemployment compensation or disability benefits pursuant to Article 4 (commencing with Section 1375) of Chapter 5 of Part 1 of, and Article 5 (commencing with Section 2735) of Chapter 2 of Part 2 of, Division 1 of the Unemployment Insurance Code. The earnings withholding order shall be served by registered or certified mail, postage prepaid, with return receipt requested. Service is deemed complete at the time the return receipt is executed by, or on behalf of, the recipient. If the state does not receive a return receipt within 15 days from the date of deposit in the mail of the withholding order, the state shall refer the earnings withholding order to a levying officer for service in accordance with subdivision (b).

(d) Except as provided in subdivision (b) or (c), service of any notice or document under this chapter may be made by first-class mail, postage prepaid. If service is made on the employer after the employer's return has been received by the levying officer, the service shall be made by first-class mail, postage prepaid, on the person designated in the employer's return to receive notices and at the address indicated in the employer's return, whether or not that address is within the county. This subdivision does not preclude service by personal delivery (1) on the employer before the employer's return has been received by the levying officer or (2) on the person designated in the employer's return after its receipt.

(e) Notwithstanding subdivision (b), if the judgment creditor so requests, the levying officer shall make service of the earnings withholding order by personal delivery as provided in Section 415.10 or 415.20.

Amended by Stats 2010 ch 680 (AB 2394),s 13, eff. 1/1/2011.

Amended by Stats 2002 ch 890 (AB 2929),s 1, eff. 1/1/2003.

Section 706.102 - Filing application for issuance of order

(a) If a writ of execution has been issued to the county where the judgment debtor's employer is to be served and the time specified in subdivision (b) of Section 699.530 for levy on property under the writ has not expired, a judgment creditor may apply for the issuance of an earnings withholding order by filing an application with a levying officer in such county who shall promptly issue an earnings withholding order.

(b) This section does not apply where the earnings withholding order is a withholding order for taxes.

Added by Stats. 1982, Ch. 1364, Sec. 2. Operative July 1, 1983, by Sec. 3 of Ch. 1364.

Section 706.103 - Documents served upon designated employer by levying officer

(a) The levying officer shall serve upon the designated employer all of the following:

(1) The original and one copy of the earnings withholding order.

(2) The form for the employer's return.

(3) The notice to employee of earnings withholding order.

(4) A copy of the form that the judgment debtor may use to make a claim of exemption.

(5) A copy of the form the judgment debtor may use to provide a financial statement.

(b) At the time the levying officer makes service pursuant to subdivision (a), the levying officer shall provide the employer with a copy of the employer's instructions referred to in Section 706.127. The Judicial Council may adopt rules prescribing the circumstances when compliance with this subdivision is not required.

(c) No earnings withholding order shall be served upon the employer after the time specified in subdivision (b) of Section 699.530.

Amended by Stats 2013 ch 64 (SB 233),s 5, eff. 1/1/2014.

Section 706.104 - Duties of employer served with order

Any employer who is served with an earnings withholding order shall:

(a) Deliver to the judgment debtor a copy of the earnings withholding order, the notice to employee of earnings withholding, a copy of the form that the judgment debtor may use to make a claim of exemption, and a copy of the form the judgment debtor may use to provide a financial statement within 10 days from the date of service. If the judgment debtor is no longer employed by the employer and the employer does not owe the employee any earnings, the employer is not required to make such delivery. The employer is not subject to any civil liability for failure to comply with this subdivision. Nothing in this subdivision limits the power of a court to hold the employer in contempt of court for failure to comply with this subdivision.

(b) Complete the employer's return on the form provided by the levying officer and mail it by first-class mail, postage prepaid, to the levying officer within 15 days from the date of service. If the earnings withholding order is ineffective, the employer shall state in the employer's return that the order will not be complied with for this reason and shall return the order to the levying officer with the employer's return.

Amended by Stats 2013 ch 64 (SB 233),s 6, eff. 1/1/2014.

Section 706.105 - Filing claim of exemption

(a) A judgment debtor may claim an exemption under Section 706.051 under either of the following circumstances:

(1) No prior hearing has been held with respect to the earnings withholding order.

(2) There has been a material change in circumstances since the time of the last prior hearing on the earnings withholding order.

(b) A claim of exemption shall be made by filing with the levying officer an original and one copy of (1) the judgment debtor's claim of exemption and (2) the judgment debtor's financial statement.

(c) Upon filing of the claim of exemption, the levying officer shall promptly send to the judgment creditor, at the address stated in the application for the earnings withholding order, by first-class mail, postage prepaid, all of the following:

(1) A copy of the claim of exemption.

(2) A copy of the financial statement.

(3) A notice of claim of exemption. The notice shall state that the claim of exemption has been filed and that the earnings withholding order will be terminated, or modified to reflect the amount of earnings claimed to be exempt in the claim of exemption, unless a notice of opposition to the claim of exemption is filed with the levying officer by the judgment creditor within 10 days after the date of the mailing of the notice of claim of exemption.

(d) A judgment creditor who desires to contest a claim of exemption shall, within 10 days after the date of the mailing of the notice of claim of exemption, file with the levying officer a notice of opposition to the claim of exemption.

(e) If a notice of opposition to the claim of exemption is filed with the levying officer within the 10-day period, the judgment creditor is entitled to a hearing on the claim of exemption. If the judgment creditor desires a hearing on the claim of exemption, the judgment creditor shall file a notice of motion for an order determining the claim of exemption with the court within 10 days after the date the levying officer mailed the notice of claim of exemption. If the notice of motion is so filed, the hearing on the motion shall be held not later than 30 days from the date the notice of motion was filed unless continued by the court for good cause. At the time prescribed by subdivision (b) of Section 1005, the judgment creditor shall give written notice of the hearing to the levying officer and shall serve a notice of the hearing and a copy of the notice of opposition to the claim of exemption on the judgment debtor and, if the claim of exemption so requested, on the attorney for the judgment debtor. Service is deemed made when the notice of the hearing and a copy of the notice of opposition to the claim of exemption are deposited in the mail, postage prepaid, addressed to the judgment debtor at the address stated in the claim of exemption and, if service on the attorney for the judgment debtor was requested in the claim of exemption, to the attorney at the address stated in the claim of exemption. The judgment creditor shall file proof of the service with the court. After receiving the notice of the hearing and before the date set for the hearing, the levying officer shall file the claim of exemption and the notice of opposition to the claim of exemption with the court.

(f) If the levying officer does not receive a notice of opposition to the claim of exemption within the 10-day period after the date of mailing of the notice of claim of exemption and a notice of the hearing not later than 10 days after the filing of the notice of opposition to the claim of exemption, the levying officer shall serve on the employer one of the following:

(1) A notice that the earnings withholding order has been terminated if all of the judgment debtor's earnings were claimed to be exempt.

(2) A modified earnings withholding order that reflects the amount of earnings claimed to be exempt in the claim of exemption if only a portion of the judgment debtor's earnings was claimed to be exempt.

(g) If, after hearing, the court orders that the earnings withholding order be modified or terminated, the clerk shall promptly transmit a certified copy of the order to the levying officer who shall promptly serve on the employer of the judgment debtor (1) a copy of the modified earnings withholding order or (2) a notice that the earnings withholding order has been terminated. The court may order that the earnings withholding order be terminated as of a date that precedes the date of hearing. If the court determines that any amount withheld pursuant to the earnings withholding order shall be paid to the judgment debtor, the court shall make an order directing the person who holds that amount to pay it promptly to the judgment debtor.

(h) If the earnings withholding order is terminated by the court, unless the court otherwise orders or unless there is a material change of circumstances since the time of the last prior hearing on the earnings withholding order, the judgment creditor may not apply for another earnings withholding order directed to the same employer with respect to the same judgment debtor for a period of 100 days following the date of service of the earnings withholding order or 60 days after the date of the termination of the order, whichever is later.

(i) If an employer has withheld and paid over amounts pursuant to an earnings withholding order after the date of termination of the order but prior to the receipt of notice of its termination, the judgment debtor may recover those amounts only from the levying officer if the levying officer still holds those amounts or, if those amounts have been paid over to the judgment creditor, from the judgment creditor. If the employer has withheld amounts pursuant to an earnings withholding order after termination of the order but has not paid over those amounts to the levying officer, the employer shall promptly pay those amounts to the judgment debtor.

(j) An appeal lies from any court order under this section denying a claim of exemption or modifying or terminating an earnings withholding order. An appeal by the judgment creditor from an order modifying or terminating the earnings withholding order does not stay the order from which the appeal is taken. Notwithstanding the appeal, until the order modifying or terminating the earnings withholding order is set aside or modified, the order allowing the claim of exemption in whole or in part shall be given the same effect as if the appeal had not been taken.

(k) This section does not apply to a withholding order for support or a withholding order for taxes.

Amended by Stats. 1998, Ch. 931, Sec. 94. Effective September 28, 1998.

Section 706.106 - No findings required

No findings are required in court proceedings under this chapter.

Added by Stats. 1982, Ch. 1364, Sec. 2. Operative July 1, 1983, by Sec. 3 of Ch. 1364.

Section 706.108 - Issuance of order by registered process server

(a) If a writ of execution has been issued to the county where the judgment debtor's employer is to be served and the time specified in subdivision (b) of Section 699.530 for levy on property under the writ has not expired, a judgment creditor may deliver an application for issuance of an earnings withholding order to a registered process server who may then issue an earnings withholding order.

(b) If the registered process server has issued the earnings withholding order, the registered process server, before serving the earnings withholding order, shall cause to be deposited with the levying officer a copy of the writ of execution, the application for issuance of an earnings withholding order, a copy of the earnings withholding order, and the fee, as provided by Section 26750 of the Government Code.

(c) A registered process server may serve an earnings withholding order on an employer whether the earnings withholding order was issued by a levying officer or by a registered process server, but no earnings withholding order may be served after the time specified in subdivision (b) of Section 699.530. In performing this function, the registered process server shall serve upon the designated employer all of the following:

(1) The original and one copy of the earnings withholding order.

(2) The form for the employer's return.

(3) The notice to the employee of the earnings withholding order.

(4) A copy of the form that the judgment debtor may use to make a claim of exemption.

(5) A copy of the form the judgment debtor may use to provide a financial statement.

(6) A copy of the employer's instructions referred to in Section 706.127, except as otherwise prescribed in rules adopted by the Judicial Council.

(d) Within five court days after service under this section, all of the following shall be filed with the levying officer:

(1) The writ of execution, if it is not already in the hands of the levying officer.

(2) Proof of service on the employer of the papers listed in subdivision (c).

(3) Instructions in writing, as required by the provisions of Section 687.010.

(e) If the fee provided by Section 26750 of the Government Code has been paid, the levying officer shall perform all other duties required by this chapter as if the levying officer had served the earnings withholding order. If the registered process server does not comply with subdivisions (b), where applicable, and (d), the service of the earnings withholding order is ineffective and the levying officer shall not be required to perform any duties under the order, and may terminate the order and release any withheld earnings to the judgment debtor.

(f) The fee for services of a registered process server under this section is a recoverable cost pursuant to Section 1033.5.

Amended by Stats 2016 ch 102 (AB 2211),s 3, eff. 1/1/2017.
Amended by Stats 2013 ch 64 (SB 233),s 7, eff. 1/1/2014.
Amended by Stats 2009 ch 54 (SB 544),s 6, eff. 1/1/2010.
Amended by Stats 2002 ch 197 (AB 2493),s 4, eff. 1/1/2003.

Section 706.109 - Issuance of order against earnings of debtor's spouse

An earnings withholding order may not be issued against the earnings of the spouse of the judgment debtor except by court order upon noticed motion.

Added by Stats. 1984, Ch. 1671, Sec. 20.

Article 6 - FORMS; EMPLOYER'S INSTRUCTIONS

Section 706.120 - Judicial Council to prescribe forms

Except as provided in Section 706.081, the Judicial Council shall prescribe the form of the applications, notices, claims of exemption, orders, and other documents required by this chapter as provided in Section 681.030, and only such forms may be used to implement this chapter.

Added by Stats. 1982, Ch. 1364, Sec. 2. Operative July 1, 1983, by Sec. 3 of Ch. 1364.

Section 706.121 - Application for issuance of earnings withholding order

The "application for issuance of earnings withholding order" shall be executed under oath and shall include all of the following:

(a) The name, the last known address, and, if known, the social security number of the judgment debtor.

(b) The name and address of the judgment creditor.

(c) The court where the judgment was entered and the date the judgment was entered.

(d) Whether the judgment is based in whole or in part on a claim for elder or dependent adult financial abuse and, if in part, how much of the judgment arises from that claim.

(e) The date of issuance of a writ of execution to the county where the earnings withholding order is sought.

(f) The total amount required to satisfy the order on the date of issuance (which may not exceed the amount required to satisfy the writ of execution on the date of issuance of the order plus the levying officer's statutory fee for service of the order).

(g) The name and address of the employer to whom the order will be directed.

(h) The name and address of the person to whom the withheld money is to be paid by the levying officer.

Amended by Stats 2010 ch 64 (AB 2619),s 3, eff. 1/1/2011, op. 1/1/2012.

Section 706.122 - Notice to employee of earnings withholding order

The "notice to employee of earnings withholding order" shall contain a statement that informs the employee in simple terms of the nature of a wage garnishment, the right to an exemption, the procedure for claiming an exemption, and any other information the Judicial Council determines would be useful to the employee and appropriate for inclusion in the notice, including all of the following:

(a) The named employer has been ordered to withhold from the earnings of the judgment debtor the amounts required to be withheld under Section 706.050, or such other amounts as are specified in the earnings withholding order, and to pay these amounts over to the levying officer for transmittal to the person specified in the order in payment of the judgment described in the order.

(b) The manner of computing the amounts required to be withheld pursuant to Section 706.050.

(c) The judgment debtor may be able to keep more or all of the judgment debtor's earnings if the judgment debtor proves that the additional earnings are necessary for the support of the judgment debtor or the judgment debtor's family supported in whole or in part by the judgment debtor.

(d) If the judgment debtor wishes a court hearing to prove that amounts should not be withheld from the judgment debtor's earnings because they are necessary for the support of the judgment debtor or the judgment debtor's family supported in whole or in part by the judgment debtor, the judgment debtor shall file with the levying officer an original and one copy of the "judgment debtor's claim of exemption" and an original and one copy of the "judgment debtor's financial statement."

Amended by Stats 2013 ch 64 (SB 233),s 8, eff. 1/1/2014.

Section 706.123 - Judgment debtor's claim of exemption

The "judgment debtor's claim of exemption" shall be executed under oath. The claim of exemption shall indicate how much the judgment debtor believes should be withheld from the judgment debtor's earnings each pay period by the employer pursuant to the earnings withholding order and shall state the judgment debtor's present mailing address.

Added by Stats. 1982, Ch. 1364, Sec. 2. Operative July 1, 1983, by Sec. 3 of Ch. 1364.

Section 706.124 - Judgment debtor's financial statement

The "judgment debtor's financial statement" shall be executed as provided in Section 703.530 and contain all of the information required by that section and the following additional information:

(a) Whether any earnings withholding orders are in effect with respect to the earnings of the judgment debtor or the spouse or dependents of the judgment debtor.

(b) Whether any earnings assignment orders for support are in effect with respect to the earnings of the judgment debtor or the spouse or dependents of the judgment debtor.

Amended by Stats. 1992, Ch. 163, Sec. 49. Effective January 1, 1993. Operative January 1, 1994, by Sec. 161 of Ch. 163.

Section 706.125 - Earnings withholding order

The "earnings withholding order" shall include all of the following:

(a) The name, address, and, if known, the social security number of the judgment debtor.

(b) The name and address of the employer to whom the order is directed.

(c) The court where the judgment was entered, the date the judgment was entered, and the name of the judgment creditor.

(d) Whether the judgment is based in whole or in part on a claim for elder or dependent adult financial abuse and, if in part, how much of the judgment arises from the claim.

(e) The date of issuance of the writ of execution to the county where the earnings withholding order is sought.

(f) The total amount required to satisfy the order on the date of issuance (which may not exceed the amount required to satisfy the writ of execution on the date of issuance of the order plus the levying officer's statutory fee for service of the order).

(g) A description of the withholding period and an order to the employer to withhold from the earnings of the judgment debtor for each pay period the amount required to be withheld under Section 706.050 or the amount specified in the order subject to Section 706.024, as the case may be, for the pay periods ending during the withholding period.

(h) An order to the employer to pay over to the levying officer at a specified address the amount required to be withheld and paid over pursuant to the order in the manner and within the times provided by law.

(i) An order that the employer fill out the "employer's return" and return it by first-class mail, postage prepaid, to the levying officer at a specified address within 15 days after service of the earnings withholding order.

(j) An order that the employer deliver to the judgment debtor a copy of the earnings withholding order and the "notice to employee of earnings withholding order" within 10 days after service of the earnings withholding order; but, if the judgment debtor is no longer employed by the employer and the employer does not owe the employee any earnings, the employer is not required to make the delivery.

(k) The name and address of the levying officer.

Amended by Stats 2010 ch 64 (AB 2619),s 4, eff. 1/1/2011, op. 1/1/2012.

Section 706.126 - Employer's return

(a) The "employer's return" shall be executed under oath. The form for the return provided to the employer shall state all of the following information:

(1) The name and address of the levying officer to whom the form is to be returned.

(2) A direction that the form be mailed to the levying officer by first-class mail, postage prepaid, no later than 15 days after the date of service of the earnings withholding order.

(3) The name, the address, and, if known, the social security number of the judgment debtor.

(b) In addition, the employer's return form shall require the employer to supply all of the following information:

(1) The date the earnings withholding order was served on the employer.

(2) Whether the judgment debtor is employed by the employer or whether the employer otherwise owes earnings to the employee.

(3) If the judgment debtor is employed by the employer or the employer otherwise owes earnings to the employee, the amount of the employee's earnings for the last pay period and the length of this pay period.

(4) Whether the employer was required on the date of service to comply with an earlier earnings withholding order and, if so, the name of the judgment creditor who secured the earlier order, the levying officer who served such order, the date it was issued, the date it was served, the expiration date of such order, and which of the earnings withholding orders the employer is required to comply with under the applicable statutory rules concerning the priority of such orders.

(5) Whether the employer was required on the date of service to comply with an earnings assignment order for support and, if so, the court which issued such assignment order and the date it was issued and any other information the Judicial Council determines is needed to identify the order.

(6) The name and address of the person to whom notices to the employer are to be sent.

Amended by Stats. 1992, Ch. 163, Sec. 50. Effective January 1, 1993. Operative January 1, 1994, by Sec. 161 of Ch. 163.

Section 706.127 - Employer's instructions

(a) The Judicial Council shall prepare "employer's instructions" for employers and revise or supplement these instructions to reflect changes in the law or rules regulating the withholding of earnings.

(b) Except to the extent that they are included in the forms required to be provided by the employer to the levying officer, the Judicial Council shall publish and provide to the levying officers copies of the employer's instructions.

Added by Stats. 1982, Ch. 1364, Sec. 2. Operative July 1, 1983, by Sec. 3 of Ch. 1364.

Section 706.128 - Judgment creditor's notice of opposition to claim of exemption

The "judgment creditor's notice of opposition to the claim of exemption" shall be executed under oath and shall include all of the following:

(a) The name, last known address, and, if known, the social security number of the judgment debtor.

(b) The name and address of the judgment creditor.

(c) The date of mailing of the notice of claim of exemption.

(d) The amount of the judgment debtor's claim of exemption which the judgment creditor claims is not exempt.

(e) The factual and legal grounds for the judgment creditor's opposition to the claim of exemption.

Added by Stats. 1982, Ch. 1364, Sec. 2. Operative July 1, 1983, by Sec. 3 of Ch. 1364.

Section 706.129 - Copies of forms available at levying officer's office

The levying officer shall have copies of the forms for the "judgment debtor's claim of exemption" and "judgment debtor's financial statement" available at the levying officer's office for distribution without charge to a person who desires to make a claim of exemption under Section 706.051.

Added by Stats. 1982, Ch. 1364, Sec. 2. Operative July 1, 1983, by Sec. 3 of Ch. 1364.

Article 7 - ADMINISTRATION AND ENFORCEMENT

Section 706.151 - Acts required by Administrator of the Wage and Hour Division performed by Judicial Council

The Judicial Council may perform all acts required by the Administrator of the Wage and Hour Division of the United States Department of Labor as conditions to exemption of this state from the earnings garnishment provisions of the Consumer Credit Protection Act of 1968 (15 U.S.C. Secs. 1671-1677), including, but not limited to:

(a) Representing and acting on behalf of the state in relation to the Administrator of the Wage and Hour Division and the administrator's representatives with regard to any matter relating to, or arising out of, the application, interpretation, and enforcement of the laws of this state regulating withholding of earnings.

(b) Submitting to the Administrator of the Wage and Hour Division in duplicate and on a current basis, a certified copy of every statute of this state affecting earnings withholding, and a certified copy of any decision in any case involving any of those statutes, made by the Supreme Court of this state.

(c) Submitting to the Administrator of the Wage and Hour Division any information relating to the enforcement of earnings withholding laws of this state which the administrator may request.

Added by Stats. 1982, Ch. 1364, Sec. 2. Operative July 1, 1983, by Sec. 3 of Ch. 1364.

Section 706.152 - Employer's failure to pay earnings over to levying office with intent to defraud

If an employer withholds earnings pursuant to this chapter and, with the intent to defraud either the judgment creditor or the judgment debtor, fails to pay such withheld earnings over to the levying officer, the employer is guilty of a misdemeanor.

Added by Stats. 1982, Ch. 1364, Sec. 2. Operative July 1, 1983, by Sec. 3 of Ch. 1364.

Section 706.153 - Deferral or acceleration of payment with intent to defeat of diminish creditor's rights

(a) No employer shall defer or accelerate any payment of earnings to an employee with the intent to defeat or diminish the judgment creditor's rights under an earnings withholding order issued pursuant to the procedures provided by this chapter.

(b) If an employer violates this section, the judgment creditor may bring a civil action against the employer to recover the amount that would have been withheld and paid over pursuant to this chapter had the employer not violated this section. The remedy provided by this subdivision is not exclusive.

Added by Stats. 1982, Ch. 1364, Sec. 2. Operative July 1, 1983, by Sec. 3 of Ch. 1364.

Section 706.154 - Civil action against employer for failure to pay required amount

(a) If an employer fails to withhold or to pay over the amount the employer is required to withhold and pay over pursuant to this chapter, the judgment creditor may bring a civil action against the employer to recover such amount. The remedy provided by this subdivision is not exclusive.

(b) Notwithstanding subdivision (a), an employer who complies with any written order or written notice which purports to be given or served in accordance with the provisions of this chapter is not subject to any civil or criminal liability for such compliance unless the employer has actively participated in a fraud.

Added by Stats. 1982, Ch. 1364, Sec. 2. Operative July 1, 1983, by Sec. 3 of Ch. 1364.

Chapter 6 - MISCELLANEOUS CREDITORS' REMEDIES

Article 1 - WRITTEN INTERROGATORIES TO JUDGMENT DEBTOR

Section 708.010 - Stay of proceedings

(a) Except as provided in this section and in subdivision (b) of Section 708.020, the procedure in this article may be used at any time a money judgment is enforceable.

(b) If enforcement of the judgment is stayed on appeal by the giving of a sufficient undertaking under Chapter 2 (commencing with Section 916) of Title 13, all proceedings under this article are stayed. In any other case where the enforcement of the judgment is stayed, all proceedings under this article are stayed unless the court otherwise expressly orders.
Added by Stats. 1982, Ch. 1364, Sec. 2. Operative July 1, 1983, by Sec. 3 of Ch. 1364.

Section 708.020 - Interrogatories to aid in enforcement of money judgment
(a) The judgment creditor may propound written interrogatories to the judgment debtor, in the manner provided in Chapter 13 (commencing with Section 2030.010) of Title 4 of Part 4, requesting information to aid in enforcement of the money judgment. The judgment debtor shall answer the interrogatories in the manner and within the time provided by Chapter 13 (commencing with Section 2030.010) of Title 4 of Part 4.
(b) The judgment creditor may not serve interrogatories pursuant to this section within 120 days after the judgment debtor has responded to interrogatories previously served pursuant to this section or within 120 days after the judgment debtor has been examined pursuant to Article 2 (commencing with Section 708.110), and the judgment debtor is not required to respond to any interrogatories so served.
(c) Interrogatories served pursuant to this section may be enforced, to the extent practicable, in the same manner as interrogatories in a civil action.
(d) The limitation provided by Chapter 13 (commencing with Section 2030.010) of Title 4 of Part 4 on the number of interrogatories that may be propounded applies to each set of interrogatories propounded from time to time pursuant to this section, but does not apply cumulatively to interrogatories propounded by the judgment creditor to the judgment debtor.
Amended by Stats 2004 ch 182 (AB 3081),s 11, eff. 7/1/2005

Section 708.030 - Inspection demands
(a) The judgment creditor may demand that any judgment debtor produce and permit the party making the demand, or someone acting on that party's behalf, to inspect and to copy a document that is in the possession, custody, or control of the party on whom the demand is made in the manner provided in Chapter 14 (commencing with Section 2031.010) of Title 4 of Part 4, if the demand requests information to aid in enforcement of the money judgment. The judgment debtor shall respond and comply with the demand in the manner and within the time provided by Chapter 14 (commencing with Section 2031.010) of Title 4 of Part 4.
(b) The judgment creditor may not serve interrogatories or inspection demands pursuant to this section or Section 708.020 within 120 days after the judgment debtor has responded to the interrogatories or demands previously served pursuant to this section or Section 708.020, or within 120 days after the judgment debtor has been examined pursuant to Article 2 (commencing with Section 708.110), and the judgment debtor is not required to respond to any discovery so served.
(c) Inspection demands served pursuant to this section may be enforced to the extent practicable, in the same manner as inspection demands in a civil action.
Amended by Stats 2004 ch 182 (AB 3081),s 12, eff. 7/1/2005

Article 2 - EXAMINATION PROCEEDINGS
Section 708.110 - Order for judgment debtor to appear and furnish information in aid of enforcement
(a) The judgment creditor may apply to the proper court for an order requiring the judgment debtor to appear before the court, or before a referee appointed by the court, at a time and place specified in the order, to furnish information to aid in enforcement of the money judgment.
(b) If the judgment creditor has not caused the judgment debtor to be examined under this section during the preceding 120 days, the court shall make the order upon ex parte application of the judgment creditor.
(c) If the judgment creditor has caused the judgment debtor to be examined under this section during the preceding 120 days, the court shall make the order if the judgment creditor by affidavit or otherwise shows good cause for the order. The application shall be made on noticed motion if the court so directs or a court rule so requires. Otherwise, it may be made ex parte.
(d) The judgment creditor shall personally serve a copy of the order on the judgment debtor not less than 10 days before the date set for the examination. Service shall be made in the manner specified in Section 415.10. Service of the order creates a lien on the personal property of the judgment debtor for a period of one year from the date of the order unless extended or sooner terminated by the court.
(e) The order shall contain the following statement in 14-point boldface type if printed or in capital letters if typed: "NOTICE TO JUDGMENT DEBTOR. If you fail to appear at the time and place specified in this order, you may be subject to arrest and punishment for contempt of court and the court may make an order requiring you to pay the reasonable attorney's fees incurred by the judgment creditor in this proceeding."
Amended by Stats. 1993, Ch. 793, Sec. 1. Effective January 1, 1994.

Section 708.120 - Order directing third person to appear to answer concerning property or debt
(a) Upon ex parte application by a judgment creditor who has a money judgment and proof by the judgment creditor by affidavit or otherwise to the satisfaction of the proper court that a third person has possession or control of property in which the judgment debtor has an interest or is indebted to the judgment debtor in an amount exceeding two hundred fifty dollars ($250), the court shall make an order directing the third person to appear before the court, or before a referee appointed by the court, at a time and place specified in the order, to answer concerning such property or debt. The affidavit in support of the judgment creditor's application may be based on the affiant's information and belief.
(b) Not less than 10 days prior to the date set for the examination, a copy of the order shall be:
  (1) Served personally on the third person.
  (2) Served personally or by mail on the judgment debtor.
(c) If the property in the third person's possession or control in which the judgment debtor has an interest or the debt owed by the third person to the judgment debtor is described in the affidavit or application for an order under subdivision (a) in a manner reasonably adequate to permit it to be identified, service of the order on the third person creates a lien on the judgment debtor's interest in the property or on the debt for a period of one year from the date of the order unless extended or sooner terminated by the court.
(d) The judgment debtor may claim that all or any portion of the property or debt is exempt from enforcement of a money judgment by application to the court on noticed motion, filed with the court and personally served on the judgment creditor not later than three days before the date set for the examination. The judgment debtor shall execute an affidavit in support of the application that includes all of the matters set forth in subdivision (b) of Section 703.520. If a claim of exemption is made pursuant to this section, a notice of opposition to the claim of exemption is not required. The court shall determine any claim of exemption made pursuant to this section. Failure of the judgment debtor to make a claim of exemption does not preclude the judgment debtor from later claiming the exemption unless the property or debt is described in the order in a manner reasonably adequate to permit it to be identified and the judgment debtor receives notice of the examination proceeding at least 10 days before the date set for the examination.
(e) An order made pursuant to subdivision (a) shall contain the following statements in 14-point boldface type if printed or in capital letters if typed:
  (1) "NOTICE TO PERSON SERVED. If you fail to appear at the time and place specified in this order, you may be subject to arrest and punishment for contempt of court and the court may make an order requiring you to pay the reasonable attorney's fees incurred by the judgment creditor in this proceeding."
  (2) "NOTICE TO JUDGMENT DEBTOR. The person in whose favor the judgment was entered in this action claims that the person to be examined pursuant to this order has possession or control of property which is yours or owes you a debt. This property or debt is as follows: (Description of property or debt). If you claim that all or any portion of this property or debt is exempt from enforcement of the money judgment,

you must file your exemption claim in writing with the court and personally serve a copy on the judgment creditor not later than three days before the date set for the examination. You must appear at the time and place set for this examination to establish your claim of exemption or your exemption may be waived."

(f) An order made pursuant to subdivision (a) is not effective unless, at the time it is served on the third person, the person serving the order tenders to the third person fees for the mileage necessary to be traveled from the third person's residence to the place of examination. The mileage fees shall be in the same amount generally provided for witnesses when legally required to attend civil proceedings in the court where the examination proceeding is to be conducted.

Amended by Stats. 1995, Ch. 576, Sec. 3.6. Effective January 1, 1996.

Section 708.130 - Witnesses required to appear and testify

(a) Witnesses may be required to appear and testify before the court or referee in an examination proceeding under this article in the same manner as upon the trial of an issue.

(b) The privilege prescribed by Article 4 (commencing with Section 970) of Chapter 4 of Division 8 of the Evidence Code does not apply in an examination proceeding under this article.

Added by Stats. 1982, Ch. 1364, Sec. 2. Operative July 1, 1983, by Sec. 3 of Ch. 1364.

Section 708.140 - Referee conducting proceedings

(a) The examination proceedings authorized by this article may be conducted by a referee appointed by the court. The referee may issue, modify, or vacate an order authorized by Section 708.205, may make a protective order authorized by Section 708.200, and may issue a warrant authorized by Section 708.170, and has the same power as the court to grant adjournments, to preserve order, and to subpoena witnesses to attend the examination, but only the court that ordered the reference has power to do the following:

   (1) Punish for contempt for disobeying an order of the referee.
   (2) Make an award of attorney's fees pursuant to Section 708.170.
   (3) Determine a contested claim of exemption or determine a third-party claim under Section 708.180.

(b) Only a member of the State Bar of California is eligible for appointment as a referee pursuant to this article. A person who was duly appointed as a referee prior to July 1, 1983, pursuant to the law in operation at the time of appointment, and who is available to perform the duties of a referee on July 1, 1983, shall be exempt from the requirements of this subdivision.

(c) Nothing in subdivision (a) limits the power of a court to appoint a temporary judge pursuant to Section 21 of Article VI of the California Constitution.

Amended by Stats. 1983, Ch. 155, Sec. 19. Effective June 30, 1983. Operative July 1, 1983, by Sec. 32 of Ch. 155.

Section 708.150 - Corporation, partnership, association, trust, other organization ordered to appear

(a)
   (1) If a corporation, partnership, association, trust, limited liability company, or other organization is served with an order to appear for an examination, it shall designate to appear and be examined one or more officers, directors, managing agents, or other persons who are familiar with its property and debts.
   (2) If a corporation, partnership, association, trust, limited liability company, or other organization served with an order to appear for an examination fails to designate a person to appear pursuant to paragraph (1), the order to appear for an examination shall be deemed to have been made to and served upon the individuals designated in the manner described in paragraph (2) of subdivision (c).

(b) If the order to appear for an examination requires the appearance of a specified individual, the specified individual shall appear for the examination and may be accompanied by one or more officers, directors, managing agents, or other persons familiar with the property and debts of the corporation, partnership, association, trust, limited liability company, or other organization.

(c) If the order to appear for the examination does not require the appearance of a specified individual, the order shall advise the corporation, partnership, association, trust, limited liability company, or other organization of all of the following:

   (1) The organization's duty to make a designation under paragraph (1) of subdivision (a).
   (2) That the organization's failure to make a designation under paragraph (1) of subdivision (a) shall result in the order to appear for the examination to be deemed to have been made to, and require the appearance of, the following:

      (A) If the organization is a corporation registered with the Secretary of State, a natural person named as the chief financial officer in the corporation's most recent filing with the Secretary of State. If no one is so named, a natural person named as the chief executive officer in the corporation's most recent filing with the Secretary of State. If no one is so named, a natural person named as the secretary in the corporation's most recent filing with the Secretary of State.
      (B) If the organization is a limited liability company registered with the Secretary of State, the first natural person named as a manager or member in the limited liability company's most recent filing with the Secretary of State.
      (C) If the organization is a limited partnership registered with the Secretary of State, the first natural person named as a general partner in the limited partnership's most recent filing with the Secretary of State.
      (D) If the organization is not registered with the Secretary of State or the organization's filings with the Secretary of State do not identify a natural person as described in subparagraph (A), (B), or (C), a natural person identified by the judgment creditor as being familiar with the property and debts of the organization, together with an affidavit or declaration signed by the judgment creditor that sets forth the factual basis for the identification of the individual. The affidavit or declaration shall be served on the organization together with the order.

   (3) That service of an order to appear for an examination upon an organization by any method permitted under this code or the Corporations Code, including service on the agent of the organization for service of process, shall be deemed effective service of the order to appear upon the individuals identified under subparagraphs (A), (B), (C), and (D) of paragraph (2).

(d) A corporation, partnership, association, trust, limited liability company, or other organization, whether or not a party, may appear at an examination through any authorized officer, director, or employee, whether or not the person is an attorney.

(e) The powers of the court under Section 708.170 extend to natural persons ordered to appear and served pursuant to this section.

(f) This section shall be strictly construed and its requirements may not be varied by local rule or otherwise.

Amended by Stats 2021 ch 30 (AB 1580),s 1, eff. 1/1/2022.
Amended by Stats 2020 ch 36 (AB 3364),s 24, eff. 1/1/2021.

Section 708.160 - Proper court for examination

(a) Except as otherwise provided in this section, the proper court for examination of a person under this article is the court in which the money judgment is entered.

(b) A person sought to be examined may not be required to attend an examination before a court located outside the county in which the person resides or has a place of business unless the distance from the person's place of residence or place of business to the place of examination is less than 150 miles.

(c) If a person sought to be examined does not reside or have a place of business in the county where the judgment is entered, the superior court in the county where the person resides or has a place of business is a proper court for examination of the person.

(d) If the judgment creditor seeks an examination of a person before a court other than the court in which the judgment is entered, the judgment creditor shall file an application that shall include all of the following:

(1) An abstract of judgment in the form prescribed by Section 674.
(2) An affidavit in support of the application stating the place of residence or place of business of the person sought to be examined.
(3) Any necessary affidavit or showing for the examination as required by Section 708.110 or 708.120.
(4) The filing fee for a motion as provided in subdivision (a) of Section 70617 of the Government Code.
Amended by Stats 2005 ch 75 (AB 145),s 38, eff. 7/19/2005, op. 1/1/2006

Section 708.170 - Failure of person to appear when served by sheriff, marshal, specially appointed person, or process server

(a) If an order requiring a person to appear for an examination was served by a sheriff, marshal, a person specially appointed by the court in the order, or a registered process server, and the person fails to appear:
(1) The court may do either of the following:
(A) Pursuant to a warrant, have the person brought before the court to answer for the failure to appear and may punish the person for contempt.
(B) Issue a warrant for the arrest of the person who failed to appear as required by the court order, pursuant to Section 1993.
(2) If the person's failure to appear is without good cause, the judgment creditor shall be awarded reasonable attorney's fees incurred in the examination proceeding. Attorney's fees awarded against the judgment debtor shall be added to and become part of the principal amount of the judgment.
(b) A person who willfully makes an improper service of an order for an examination which subsequently results in the arrest pursuant to subdivision (a) of the person who fails to appear is guilty of a misdemeanor.
Amended by Stats 2006 ch 277 (AB 2369),s 2, eff. 1/1/2007.

Section 708.180 - Determination by court when third person claim interest adverse to debtor or denies debt

(a) Subject to subdivision (b), if a third person examined pursuant to Section 708.120 claims an interest in the property adverse to the judgment debtor or denies the debt, the court may, if the judgment creditor so requests, determine the interests in the property or the existence of the debt. The determination is conclusive as to the parties to the proceeding and the third person, but an appeal may be taken from the determination. The court may grant a continuance for a reasonable time for discovery proceedings, the production of evidence, or other preparation for the hearing.
(b) The court may not make the determination provided in subdivision (a) if the third person's claim is made in good faith and any of the following conditions is satisfied:
(1) The court would not be a proper court for the trial of an independent civil action (including a creditor's suit) for the determination of the interests in the property or the existence of the debt, and the third person objects to the determination of the matter under subdivision (a).
(2) At the time an order for examination pursuant to Section 708.120 is served on the third person a civil action (including a creditor's suit) is pending with respect to the interests in the property or the existence of the debt.
(3) The court determines that the interests in the property or the existence of the debt should be determined in a creditor's suit.
(c) Upon application of the judgment creditor made ex parte, the court may make an order forbidding transfer of the property to the judgment debtor or payment of the debt to the judgment debtor until the interests in the property or the existence of the debt is determined pursuant to subdivision (a) or until a creditor's suit may be commenced and an order obtained pursuant to Section 708.240. An undertaking may be required in the discretion of the court. The court may modify or vacate the order at any time with or without a hearing on such terms as are just.
(d) Upon application of the judgment creditor upon noticed motion, the court may, if it determines that the judgment debtor probably owns an interest in the property or that the debt probably is owed to the judgment debtor, make an order forbidding the transfer or other disposition of the property to any person or forbidding payment of the debt until the interests in the property or the existence of the debt is determined pursuant to subdivision (a) or until a creditor's suit may be commenced and an order obtained pursuant to Section 708.240. The court shall require the judgment creditor to furnish an undertaking as provided in Section 529. The court may modify or vacate the order at any time after notice and hearing on such terms as are just.
Amended by Stats. 1998, Ch. 931, Sec. 95. Effective September 28, 1998.

Section 708.190 - Intervention

The court may permit a person claiming an interest in the property or debt sought to be applied in an examination proceeding to intervene in the proceeding and may determine the person's rights in the property or debt pursuant to Section 708.180.
Added by Stats. 1982, Ch. 1364, Sec. 2. Operative July 1, 1983, by Sec. 3 of Ch. 1364.

Section 708.200 - Protective orders

In any proceeding under this article, the court may, on motion of the person to be examined or on its own motion, make such protective orders as justice may require.
Added by Stats. 1982, Ch. 1364, Sec. 2. Operative July 1, 1983, by Sec. 3 of Ch. 1364.

Section 708.205 - Order creating lien; order forbidding transfer or payment

(a) Except as provided in subdivision (b), at the conclusion of a proceeding pursuant to this article, the court may order the judgment debtor's interest in the property in the possession or under the control of the judgment debtor or the third person or a debt owed by the third person to the judgment debtor to be applied toward the satisfaction of the money judgment if the property is not exempt from enforcement of a money judgment. Such an order creates a lien on the property or debt.
(b) If a third person examined pursuant to Section 708.120 claims an interest in the property adverse to the judgment debtor or denies the debt and the court does not determine the matter as provided in subdivision (a) of Section 708.180, the court may not order the property or debt to be applied toward the satisfaction of the money judgment but may make an order pursuant to subdivision (c) or (d) of Section 708.180 forbidding transfer or payment to the extent authorized by that section.
Added by Stats. 1982, Ch. 1364, Sec. 2. Operative July 1, 1983, by Sec. 3 of Ch. 1364.

Article 3 - CREDITOR'S SUIT

Section 708.210 - Action against third person

If a third person has possession or control of property in which the judgment debtor has an interest or is indebted to the judgment debtor, the judgment creditor may bring an action against the third person to have the interest or debt applied to the satisfaction of the money judgment.
Added by Stats. 1982, Ch. 1364, Sec. 2. Operative July 1, 1983, by Sec. 3 of Ch. 1364.

Section 708.220 - Judgment debtor not indispensable party; debtor's residence considered in venue determination

The judgment debtor shall be joined in an action brought pursuant to this article but is not an indispensable party. The residence of the judgment debtor may not be considered in the determination of proper venue unless otherwise provided by contract between the judgment debtor and the third person.
Added by Stats. 1982, Ch. 1364, Sec. 2. Operative July 1, 1983, by Sec. 3 of Ch. 1364.

Section 708.230 - Time for commencing action

(a) Except as provided in subdivision (b), an action shall be commenced pursuant to this article before the expiration of the later of the following times:
(1) The time when the judgment debtor may bring an action against the third person concerning the property or debt.
(2) One year after creation of a lien on the property or debt pursuant to this title if the lien is created at the time when the judgment debtor may bring an action against the third person concerning the property or debt.

(b) An action may not be commenced pursuant to this article after the period for enforcement of the money judgment has expired.
(c) Notwithstanding Section 683.020, if an action is commenced pursuant to this article within the time permitted in this section, the action may be prosecuted to judgment.
Added by Stats. 1982, Ch. 1364, Sec. 2. Operative July 1, 1983, by Sec. 3 of Ch. 1364.

Section 708.240 - Restraining orders

The judgment creditor may apply to the court in which an action under this article is pending for either or both of the following:
(a) An order restraining the third person from transferring to the judgment debtor the property in which the judgment debtor is claimed to have an interest or from paying to the judgment debtor the alleged debt. The order shall be made on noticed motion if the court so directs or a court rule so requires. Otherwise, the order may be made on ex parte application. The order shall remain in effect until judgment is entered in the action or until such earlier time as the court may provide in the order. An undertaking may be required in the discretion of the court. The court may modify or vacate the order at any time with or without a hearing on such terms as are just.
(b) A temporary restraining order or a preliminary injunction or both, restraining the third person from transferring to any person or otherwise disposing of the property in which the judgment debtor is claimed to have an interest, pursuant to Chapter 3 (commencing with Section 525) of Title 7, and the court may make, dissolve, and modify such orders as provided therein.
Added by Stats. 1982, Ch. 1364, Sec. 2. Operative July 1, 1983, by Sec. 3 of Ch. 1364.

Section 708.250 - Lien created

Service of summons on the third person creates a lien on the interest of the judgment debtor in the property or on the debt owed to the judgment debtor that is the subject of an action under this article.
Added by Stats. 1982, Ch. 1364, Sec. 2. Operative July 1, 1983, by Sec. 3 of Ch. 1364.

Section 708.260 - Claim of exemption

(a) In an action brought pursuant to this article, the judgment debtor may claim that all or any portion of the property or debt is exempt from enforcement of a money judgment. The claim shall be made by application to the court on noticed motion, filed with the court and served on the judgment creditor not later than 30 days before the date set for hearing. Service shall be made personally or by mail. The judgment debtor shall execute an affidavit in support of the application that includes all of the matters set forth in subdivision (b) of Section 703.520. No notice of opposition to the claim of exemption is required. If the judgment debtor has not been named as a party to the action, the judgment debtor may obtain an order under Section 389 that the judgment debtor be made a party. Except as provided in subdivision (b), failure of the judgment debtor to make a claim of exemption is a waiver of the exemption.
(b) Failure of the judgment debtor to make a claim of exemption in an action brought pursuant to this article is not a waiver of the exemption if both of the following conditions are satisfied:
(1) The judgment debtor has not been served with process in the action that contains a description of the property or debt reasonably adequate to permit it to be identified.
(2) The judgment debtor does not have actual notice of the pendency of the action and the identity of the property or the nature of the debt in issue.
Added by Stats. 1982, Ch. 1364, Sec. 2. Operative July 1, 1983, by Sec. 3 of Ch. 1364.

Section 708.270 - No right to jury trial

There is no right to a jury trial in an action under this article.
Added by Stats. 1982, Ch. 1364, Sec. 2. Operative July 1, 1983, by Sec. 3 of Ch. 1364.

Section 708.280 - Determination by court

(a) The court shall determine any exemption claim made in the action. If the judgment debtor establishes to the satisfaction of the court that the property or debt is exempt from enforcement of a money judgment, the court shall so adjudge and may not make the orders referred to in subdivisions (b), (c), and (d).
(b) If the judgment creditor establishes that the third person has property in which the judgment debtor has an interest or is indebted to the judgment debtor, the court shall render judgment accordingly. The property or debt may be applied to the satisfaction of the judgment creditor's judgment against the judgment debtor as ordered by the court.
(c) If the court determines that the third person has property in which the judgment debtor has an interest, the court may order the third person not to transfer the property until it can be levied upon or otherwise applied to the satisfaction of the judgment.
(d) If the court determines that the third person has transferred property that was subject to a lien in favor of the judgment creditor or, contrary to court order of which the third person has notice, has paid the debt to the judgment debtor or has transferred the property, the court shall render judgment against the third person in an amount equal to the lesser of the following:
(1) The value of the judgment debtor's interest in the property or the amount of the debt.
(2) The amount of the judgment creditor's judgment against the judgment debtor remaining unsatisfied.
Added by Stats. 1982, Ch. 1364, Sec. 2. Operative July 1, 1983, by Sec. 3 of Ch. 1364.

Section 708.290 - Costs not recovered against judgment debtor

Costs incurred by or taxed against the judgment creditor in an action under this article may not be recovered from the judgment debtor as a cost of enforcing the judgment.
Added by Stats. 1982, Ch. 1364, Sec. 2. Operative July 1, 1983, by Sec. 3 of Ch. 1364.

Article 4 - CHARGING ORDERS

Section 708.310 - Judgment rendered against partner or member of limited liability company

If a money judgment is rendered against a partner or member but not against the partnership or limited liability company, the judgment debtor's interest in the partnership or limited liability company may be applied toward the satisfaction of the judgment by an order charging the judgment debtor's interest pursuant to Section 15907.03, 16504, or 17705.03 of the Corporations Code.
Amended by Stats 2021 ch 124 (AB 938),s 12, eff. 1/1/2022.
Amended by Stats 2012 ch 419 (SB 323),s 4, eff. 1/1/2013, op. 1/1/2014.
Amended by Stats 2002 ch 451 (AB 2355),s 1, eff. 1/1/2003.

Section 708.320 - Lien created

(a) A lien on a judgment debtor's interest in a partnership or limited liability company is created by service of a notice of motion for a charging order on the judgment debtor and on either of the following:
(1) All partners or the partnership.
(2) All members or the limited liability company.
(b) If a charging order is issued, the lien created pursuant to subdivision (a) continues under the terms of the order. If issuance of the charging order is denied, the lien is extinguished.
Amended by Stats 2002 ch 451 (AB 2355),s 2, eff. 1/1/2003.

Article 5 - LIEN IN PENDING ACTION OR PROCEEDING

Section 708.410 - When judgment creditor may obtain lien; filing notice of lien and abstract or copy of judgment

(a) A judgment creditor who has a money judgment against a judgment debtor who is a party to a pending action or special proceeding may obtain a lien under this article, to the extent required to satisfy the judgment creditor's money judgment, on both of the following:

(1) Any cause of action of such judgment debtor for money or property that is the subject of the action or proceeding.

(2) The rights of such judgment debtor to money or property under any judgment subsequently procured in the action or proceeding.

(b) To obtain a lien under this article, the judgment creditor shall file a notice of lien and an abstract or certified copy of the judgment creditor's money judgment in the pending action or special proceeding.

(c) At the time of the filing under subdivision (b) or promptly thereafter, the judgment creditor shall serve on all parties who, prior thereto, have made an appearance in the action or special proceeding a copy of the notice of lien and a statement of the date when the notice of lien was filed in the action or special proceeding. Service shall be made personally or by mail. Failure to serve all parties as required by this subdivision does not affect the lien created by the filing under subdivision (b), but the rights of a party are not affected by the lien until the party has notice of the lien.

(d) For the purpose of this article, an action or special proceeding is pending until the time for appeal from the judgment has expired or, if an appeal is filed, until the appeal has been finally determined.

Added by Stats. 1982, Ch. 1364, Sec. 2. Operative July 1, 1983, by Sec. 3 of Ch. 1364.

Section 708.420 - Requirements of notice of lien

The notice of lien under Section 708.410 shall contain all of the following:

(a) A statement that a lien has been created under this article and the title of the court and the cause and number of the pending action or proceeding in which the notice of lien is filed.

(b) The name and last known address of the judgment debtor.

(c) The name and address of the judgment creditor.

(d) The title of the court where the judgment creditor's money judgment is entered and the cause and number of the action, the date of entry of the judgment, and the date of any subsequent renewals, and where entered in the records of the court.

(e) The amount required to satisfy the judgment creditor's money judgment at the time the notice of lien is filed in the action or proceeding.

(f) A statement that the lien attaches to any cause of action of the judgment debtor that is the subject of the action or proceeding and to the judgment debtor's rights to money or property under any judgment subsequently procured in the action or proceeding.

(g) A statement that no compromise, dismissal, settlement, or satisfaction of the pending action or proceeding or any of the judgment debtor's rights to money or property under any judgment procured therein may be entered into by or on behalf of the judgment debtor, and that the judgment debtor may not enforce the judgment debtor's rights to money or property under any judgment procured in the action or proceeding by a writ or otherwise, unless one of the following requirements is satisfied:

(1) The prior approval by order of the court in which the action or proceeding is pending has been obtained.

(2) The written consent of the judgment creditor has been obtained or the judgment creditor has released the lien.

(3) The money judgment of the judgment creditor has been satisfied.

(h) A statement that the judgment debtor may claim an exemption for all or any portion of the money or property within 30 days after the judgment debtor has notice of the creation of the lien and a statement that, if the exemption is not claimed within the time allowed, the exemption is waived.

Added by Stats. 1982, Ch. 1364, Sec. 2. Operative July 1, 1983, by Sec. 3 of Ch. 1364.

Section 708.430 - Intervention in proceeding by judgment creditor

(a) The court in which the action or special proceeding is pending may permit a judgment creditor who has obtained a lien under this article to intervene in the action or proceeding pursuant to Section 387.

(b) For the purposes of Sections 708.450 and 708.470, a judgment creditor shall be deemed to be a party to the action or special proceeding even though the judgment creditor has not become a party to the action or proceeding under subdivision (a).

Added by Stats. 1982, Ch. 1364, Sec. 2. Operative July 1, 1983, by Sec. 3 of Ch. 1364.

Section 708.440 - Consent of judgment creditor or court order for judgment debtor to enforce judgment

(a) Except as provided in subdivision (c) of Section 708.410, unless the judgment creditor's money judgment is first satisfied or the lien is released, the judgment recovered in the action or special proceeding in favor of the judgment debtor may not be enforced by a writ or otherwise, and no compromise, dismissal, settlement, or satisfaction of the pending action or special proceeding or the judgment procured therein may be entered into by or on behalf of the judgment debtor, without the written consent of the judgment creditor or authorization by order of the court obtained under subdivision (b).

(b) Upon application by the judgment debtor, the court in which the action or special proceeding is pending or the judgment procured therein is entered may, in its discretion, after a hearing, make an order described in subdivision (a) that may include such terms and conditions as the court deems necessary. The application for an order under this subdivision shall be made on noticed motion. The notice of motion shall be served on the judgment creditor. Service shall be made personally or by mail.

Added by Stats. 1982, Ch. 1364, Sec. 2. Operative July 1, 1983, by Sec. 3 of Ch. 1364.

Section 708.450 - Claim of exemption

(a) If a lien is created under this article, the judgment debtor may claim that all or any portion of the money or property that the judgment debtor may recover in the action or special proceeding is exempt from enforcement of a money judgment. The claim shall be made by application on noticed motion to the court in which the action or special proceeding is pending, filed and served on the judgment creditor not later than 30 days after the judgment debtor has notice of the creation of the lien. Service shall be made personally or by mail. The judgment debtor shall execute an affidavit in support of the application that includes all the matters set forth in subdivision (b) of Section 703.520. No notice of opposition to the claim of exemption is required. The failure of the judgment debtor to make a claim of exemption under this section constitutes a waiver of the exemption.

(b) The court may determine the exemption claim at any time prior to the entry of judgment in the action or special proceeding or may consolidate the exemption hearing with the hearing on a motion pursuant to Section 708.470.

(c) If the judgment debtor establishes to the satisfaction of the court that the right of the judgment debtor to money or property under the judgment in the action or special proceeding is all or partially exempt from enforcement of a money judgment, the court shall order the termination of the lien created under this article on the exempt portion of the money or property.

Amended by Stats. 1984, Ch. 538, Sec. 31.

Section 708.460 - Statement or existence of lien endorsed upon judgment

(a) If a lien is created pursuant to this article, the court clerk shall endorse upon the judgment recovered in the action or special proceeding a statement of the existence of the lien and the time it was created.

(b) Any abstract issued upon the judgment shall include a statement of the lien in favor of the judgment creditor.

Added by Stats. 1982, Ch. 1364, Sec. 2. Operative July 1, 1983, by Sec. 3 of Ch. 1364.

Section 708.470 - Application for order to apply judgment debtor's rights under judgment to satisfy lien

(a) If the judgment debtor is entitled to money or property under the judgment in the action or special proceeding and a lien created under this article exists, upon application of any party to the action or special proceeding, the court may order that the judgment debtor's rights to money or property under the judgment be applied to the satisfaction of the lien created under this article as ordered by the court. Application for an order under this section shall be on noticed motion. The notice of motion shall be served on all other parties. Service shall be made personally or by mail.

(b) If the judgment determines that the judgment debtor has an interest in property, the court may order the party having custody or control of the property not to transfer the property until it can be levied upon or otherwise applied to the satisfaction of the lien created under this article.

(c) If the court determines that a party (other than the judgment debtor) having notice of the lien created under this article has transferred property that was subject to the lien or has paid an amount to the judgment debtor that was subject to the lien, the court shall render judgment against the party in an amount equal to the lesser of the following:

(1) The value of the judgment debtor's interest in the property or the amount paid the judgment debtor.

(2) The amount of the judgment creditor's lien created under this article.

Added by Stats. 1982, Ch. 1364, Sec. 2. Operative July 1, 1983, by Sec. 3 of Ch. 1364.

Section 708.480 - Enforcement of lien

A lien created under this article may be enforced by any applicable procedure:

(a) After the judgment subject to the lien is entered and the time for appeal from the judgment has expired.

(b) If an appeal is filed from the judgment subject to the lien, after the appeal is finally determined.

Added by Stats. 1982, Ch. 1364, Sec. 2. Operative July 1, 1983, by Sec. 3 of Ch. 1364.

Article 6 - ASSIGNMENT ORDER

Section 708.510 - Generally

(a) Except as otherwise provided by law, upon application of the judgment creditor on noticed motion, the court may order the judgment debtor to assign to the judgment creditor or to a receiver appointed pursuant to Article 7 (commencing with Section 708.610) all or part of a right to payment due or to become due, whether or not the right is conditioned on future developments, including but not limited to the following types of payments:

(1) Wages due from the federal government that are not subject to withholding under an earnings withholding order.

(2) Rents.

(3) Commissions.

(4) Royalties.

(5) Payments due from a patent or copyright.

(6) Insurance policy loan value.

(b) The notice of the motion shall be served on the judgment debtor. Service shall be made personally or by mail.

(c) Subject to subdivisions (d), (e), and (f), in determining whether to order an assignment or the amount of an assignment pursuant to subdivision (a), the court may take into consideration all relevant factors, including the following:

(1) The reasonable requirements of a judgment debtor who is a natural person and of persons supported in whole or in part by the judgment debtor.

(2) Payments the judgment debtor is required to make or that are deducted in satisfaction of other judgments and wage assignments, including earnings assignment orders for support.

(3) The amount remaining due on the money judgment.

(4) The amount being or to be received in satisfaction of the right to payment that may be assigned.

(d) A right to payment may be assigned pursuant to this article only to the extent necessary to satisfy the money judgment.

(e) When earnings or periodic payments pursuant to a pension or retirement plan are assigned pursuant to subdivision (a), the amount of the earnings or the periodic payments assigned shall not exceed the amount that may be withheld from a like amount of earnings under Chapter 5 (commencing with Section 706.010) (Wage Garnishment Law).

(f) Where a specific amount of the payment or payments to be assigned is exempt by another statutory provision, the amount of the payment or payments to be assigned pursuant to subdivision (a) shall not exceed the amount by which the payment or payments exceed the exempt amount.

Amended by Stats. 1992, Ch. 163, Sec. 51. Effective January 1, 1993. Operative January 1, 1994, by Sec. 161 of Ch. 163.

Section 708.520 - Application for order restraining debtor from assigning or disposing of right of payment

(a) When an application is made pursuant to Section 708.510 or thereafter, the judgment creditor may apply to the court for an order restraining the judgment debtor from assigning or otherwise disposing of the right to payment that is sought to be assigned. The application shall be made on noticed motion if the court so directs or a court rule so requires. Otherwise, it may be made ex parte.

(b) The court may issue an order pursuant to this section upon a showing of need for the order. The court, in its discretion, may require the judgment creditor to provide an undertaking.

(c) The court may modify or vacate the order at any time with or without a hearing on such terms as are just.

(d) The order shall be personally served upon the judgment debtor and shall contain a notice to the judgment debtor that failure to comply with the order may subject the judgment debtor to being held in contempt of court.

Added by Stats. 1982, Ch. 1364, Sec. 2. Operative July 1, 1983, by Sec. 3 of Ch. 1364.

Section 708.530 - Effect and priority of order; assignment of right to future rent

(a) Except as provided in subdivision (b), the effect and priority of an assignment ordered pursuant to this article is governed by Section 955.1 of the Civil Code. For the purpose of priority, an assignee of a right to payment pursuant to this article shall be deemed to be a bona fide assignee for value under the terms of Section 955.1 of the Civil Code.

(b) An assignment of the right to future rent ordered under this article is recordable as an instrument affecting real property and the priority of such an assignment is governed by Section 1214 of the Civil Code.

Amended by Stats. 1984, Ch. 538, Sec. 32.

Section 708.540 - Obligor's rights not affected until notice of order received

The rights of an obligor are not affected by an order assigning the right to payment until notice of the order is received by the obligor. For the purpose of this section, "obligor" means the person who is obligated to make payments to the judgment debtor or who may become obligated to make payments to the judgment debtor depending upon future developments.

Added by Stats. 1982, Ch. 1364, Sec. 2. Operative July 1, 1983, by Sec. 3 of Ch. 1364.

Section 708.550 - Claim of exemption

(a) The judgment debtor may claim that all or a portion of the right to payment is exempt from enforcement of a money judgment by application to the court on noticed motion filed not later than three days before the date set for the hearing on the judgment creditor's application for an assignment order. The judgment debtor shall execute an affidavit in support of the application that includes all of the matters set forth in subdivision (b) of Section 703.520. Failure of the judgment debtor to make a claim of exemption is a waiver of the exemption.

(b) The notice of the motion shall be personally served on the judgment creditor not later than three days before the date set for the hearing.

(c) The court shall determine any claim of exemption made pursuant to this section at the hearing on issuance of the assignment order.

Added by Stats. 1982, Ch. 1364, Sec. 2. Operative July 1, 1983, by Sec. 3 of Ch. 1364.

Section 708.560 - Notice motion for order to modify or set aside order

(a) Either the judgment creditor or the judgment debtor may apply to the court on noticed motion for an order to modify or set aside the assignment order. The notice of motion shall be served on the other party. Service shall be made personally or by mail.
(b) The court shall make an order modifying or setting aside the assignment order upon a showing that there has been a material change in circumstances since the time of the previous hearing on the assignment order. The court may order a reassignment of the right to payments as necessary. The order shall state whether and to what extent it applies to payments already made.
Added by Stats. 1982, Ch. 1364, Sec. 2. Operative July 1, 1983, by Sec. 3 of Ch. 1364.

Article 7 - RECEIVER TO ENFORCE JUDGMENT

Section 708.610 - Generally
The provisions of Chapter 5 (commencing with Section 564) and Chapter 5a (commencing with Section 571) of Title 7 govern the appointment, qualifications, powers, rights, and duties of a receiver appointed under this article.
Added by Stats. 1982, Ch. 1364, Sec. 2. Operative July 1, 1983, by Sec. 3 of Ch. 1364.

Section 708.620 - When court may appoint receiver
The court may appoint a receiver to enforce the judgment where the judgment creditor shows that, considering the interests of both the judgment creditor and the judgment debtor, the appointment of a receiver is a reasonable method to obtain the fair and orderly satisfaction of the judgment.
Added by Stats. 1982, Ch. 1364, Sec. 2. Operative July 1, 1983, by Sec. 3 of Ch. 1364.

Section 708.630 - Receiver appointed for purpose of transferring debtor's interest in alcoholic beverage license
(a) The judgment debtor's interest in an alcoholic beverage license may be applied to the satisfaction of a money judgment only as provided in this section.
(b) The court may appoint a receiver for the purpose of transferring the judgment debtor's interest in an alcoholic beverage license that is transferable under Article 5 (commencing with Section 24070) of Chapter 6 of Division 9 of the Business and Professions Code, unless the judgment debtor shows in the proceeding to appoint a receiver that the amount of delinquent taxes described in Section 24049 of the Business and Professions Code and claims of creditors with priority over the judgment creditor pursuant to Section 24074 of the Business and Professions Code exceed the probable sale price of the license.
(c) The receiver may exercise the powers of the licensee as necessary and in exercising such powers shall comply with the applicable provisions of Division 9 (commencing with Section 23000) of the Business and Professions Code and applicable regulations of the Department of Alcoholic Beverage Control. An application shall be filed to transfer the license to the receiver and a temporary retail permit shall be obtained during the pendency of the transfer.
Added by Stats. 1982, Ch. 1364, Sec. 2. Operative July 1, 1983, by Sec. 3 of Ch. 1364.

Article 8 - COLLECTION OF JUDGMENT WHERE JUDGMENT DEBTOR IS CREDITOR OF PUBLIC ENTITY

Section 708.710 - Definitions
As used in this article:
(a) "Local public entity" means any public entity other than the state.
(b) "Public entity" means the state, a county, city, district, public authority, public agency, and any other political subdivision in the state.
(c) "State" means the State of California.
(d) "State agency" means a state office, officer, department, division, bureau, board, commission or agency claims against which are paid by warrants drawn by the Controller.
Added by Stats. 1982, Ch. 1364, Sec. 2. Operative July 1, 1983, by Sec. 3 of Ch. 1364.

Section 708.720 - Application of public entity's obligation to satisfaction of judgment; withholding public officer's or employee's earning; obligation subject of pending action or proceeding
(a) If a public entity owes money to the judgment debtor, the obligation of the public entity may be applied to the satisfaction of the money judgment against the judgment debtor only in the manner provided by (1) this article, (2) Chapter 5 (commencing with Section 706.010) (wage garnishment), or (3) Article 5 (commencing with Section 708.410) (lien in pending action or proceeding).
(b) The earnings of a public officer or employee shall not be withheld pursuant to this article. Except as expressly provided by law, the earnings of a public officer or employee may be withheld for the payment of a money judgment only pursuant to Chapter 5 (commencing with Section 706.010).
(c) If the obligation of a public entity to pay money to the judgment debtor is the subject of a pending action or special proceeding, the procedure in this article does not apply. The payment of the obligation that is the subject of the pending action or special proceeding may be applied to the satisfaction of the money judgment against the judgment debtor only in the manner provided in Article 5 (commencing with Section 708.410).
Added by Stats. 1982, Ch. 1364, Sec. 2. Operative July 1, 1983, by Sec. 3 of Ch. 1364.

Section 708.730 - Abstract or copy of judgment and affidavit stating creditor desires relief provided by article; service of notice of filing
(a) If money is owing and unpaid to the judgment debtor by a public entity, the judgment creditor may file, in the manner provided in this article, an abstract of the money judgment or a certified copy of the money judgment, together with an affidavit that states that the judgment creditor desires the relief provided by this article and states the exact amount then required to satisfy the judgment. The judgment creditor may state in the affidavit any fact tending to establish the identity of the judgment debtor.
(b) Promptly after filing the abstract or certified copy of the judgment and the affidavit with the public entity, the judgment creditor shall serve notice of the filing on the judgment debtor. Service shall be made personally or by mail.
(c) If the judgment is for support and related costs and money is owing and unpaid to the judgment debtor by a state agency, including, but not limited to, money owing and unpaid to the judgment debtor by a state agency on a claim for refund from the Franchise Tax Board under the Personal Income Tax Law, Part 10 (commencing with Section 17001) of Division 2 of the Revenue and Taxation Code, or the Bank and Corporation Tax Law, Part 11 (commencing with Section 23001) of Division 2 of the Revenue and Taxation Code or as a result of the judgment debtor's winnings in the California State Lottery, and the local child support agency is enforcing the support obligation pursuant to Section 17400 of the Family Code, the claim may be submitted as follows: The local child support agency may file the affidavit referred to in subdivision (a) without filing an abstract or certified copy of the judgment. In lieu thereof, the affidavit shall also state that an abstract of the judgment could be obtained. Where there is more than one judgment debtor, the local child support agency may include all the judgment debtors in a single affidavit. Separate affidavits need not be submitted for each judgment debtor. The affidavit need not on its face separately identify each judgment debtor or the exact amount required to satisfy the judgment, so long as it incorporates by reference forms or other automated data transmittals, as required by the Department of Child Support Services, which contain this information. Affidavits submitted pursuant to this subdivision by the local child support agency shall meet the standards and procedures prescribed by the state agency to which the affidavit is submitted, except that those affidavits submitted with respect to moneys owed and unpaid to the judgment debtor as a result of a claim for refund from the Franchise Tax Board under the Personal Income Tax Law, Part 10 (commencing with Section 17001) of Division 2 of the Revenue and Taxation Code, or the Bank and Corporation Tax Law, Part 11 (commencing with Section 23001) of Division 2 of the Revenue and Taxation Code, shall meet the standards and procedures prescribed by the Franchise Tax Board. In serving the notice required by subdivision (b), the Director of the

Department of Child Support Services or his or her designee may act in lieu of the judgment creditor as to judgments enforced under this division.

(d) If the judgment is for child, spousal, or family support and related costs and money is owing and unpaid to the judgment debtor by a state agency on a claim for refund from the Franchise Tax Board under the Personal Income Tax Law, Part 10 (commencing with Section 17001) of Division 2 of the Revenue and Taxation Code, or the Bank and Corporation Tax Law, Part 11 (commencing with Section 23001) of Division 2 of the Revenue and Taxation Code, or as a result of the judgment debtor's winnings in the California State Lottery, the judgment creditor may file with the court an abstract or a certified copy of the judgment ordering the payment of child, spousal, or family support, together with a request that the court issue a Notice of Support Arrearage, as provided in Section 708.780, to which any personal income tax refunds and lottery winnings owed the judgment debtor by the State of California will be subject. The request shall be accompanied by an affidavit, signed under penalty of perjury, which shall state that the judgment creditor desires the relief provided by this subdivision and shall state the exact amount then required to satisfy the judgment. In addition, the affidavit shall specify the beginning and ending dates of all periods during which the arrearage for support occurred, specify the arrearage for each month, and state that the support is at least 90 days overdue or is overdue in an amount equal to 90 days of support. It shall also certify that the child or children are not recipients, and during the period for which payment is requested, were not recipients, of Aid to Families with Dependent Children and there was no assignment to a state or county agency of support and shall certify on information and belief that there is not current or past action by a district attorney pending for support or support enforcement on the judgment creditor's behalf. The request shall have attached a proof of service showing that copies of the request, the affidavit, and the abstract or certified copy of the judgment ordering the payment of support have been served on the judgment debtor and the district attorney of the county in which the support judgment is entered. Service shall be by certified mail, postage prepaid, return receipt requested, to the last known address of the party to be served, or by personal service.

This subdivision does not apply in any instance in which a district attorney initiated or participated as counsel in the action for support or if support is required to be paid through a district attorney's office.

The Department of Child Support Services shall, upon request, inform the Legislature of the use and effect of this subdivision on or before December 31, 2000.

This subdivision shall become operative on January 1, 1996, and shall become inoperative on December 31, 2000.

(e) For purposes of this section, "support" means an obligation owing on behalf of a child, spouse, or family, or combination thereof.
Amended by Stats 2000 ch 808 (AB 1358), s 18, eff. 9/28/2000.

Section 708.740 - Filing abstract or copy of judgment and affidavit with state agency owing money

(a) Except as provided in subdivision (e), if money is owing and unpaid to the judgment debtor by a state agency, the judgment creditor shall file the abstract or certified copy of the judgment and the affidavit with the state agency owing the money to the judgment debtor prior to the time the state agency presents the claim of the judgment debtor to the Controller. Where the affidavit is prepared under subdivision (c) of Section 708.730, the affidavit shall be filed with the Department of Child Support Services, and no abstract need be filed. Filing of the affidavit with the department shall be sufficient to require the Controller to transfer the funds claimed by the judgment debtor, notwithstanding that the claim of the judgment debtor has been filed with another state agency.

(b) When presenting the claim of the judgment debtor to the Controller, the state agency shall do all of the following:

    (1) Note the fact of the filing of the abstract or certified copy of the judgment and the affidavit.

    (2) State the amount required to satisfy the judgment as shown by the affidavit.

    (3) State any amounts advanced to the judgment debtor by the state, or owed by the judgment debtor to the state, for expenses or for any other purpose.

(c) Except as provided in subdivisions (d) and (e), to discharge the claim of the judgment debtor, the Controller shall (1) deposit with the court, by a warrant or check payable to the court, the amount due the judgment debtor (after deducting an amount sufficient to reimburse the state for any amounts advanced to the judgment debtor or owed by the judgment debtor to the state) required to satisfy the money judgment as shown by the affidavit in full or to the greatest extent and (2) pay the balance thereof, if any, to the judgment debtor.

(d) Where an affidavit stating the existence of a judgment for support has been submitted to the Department of Child Support Services, pursuant to subdivision (c) of Section 708.730, to discharge the claim of a judgment debtor, the Controller shall direct payment to the county agency designated by the local child support agency in his or her affidavit.

(e) Where the judgment is for support and the money owed is for lottery winnings or a refund of overpayment of tax, penalty, interest, or interest allowable with respect to an overpayment under Part 10 (commencing with Section 17001) of Division 2 of the Revenue and Taxation Code, and the support obligation is not being enforced pursuant to Section 17400 of the Family Code, the judgment creditor may file the abstract or certified copy of the judgment with the local child support agency of the county in which the support judgment is entered or registered. The local child support agency shall then file the claim of the judgment creditor pursuant to subdivision (c) of Section 708.730. When funds are received by the local child support agency, it shall discharge any claim of the judgment debtor by forwarding those sums to the clerk of the court pursuant to subdivision (c) of this section. Any and all notices otherwise required of a judgment creditor or the clerk of the court, and any litigation to enforce rights under this subdivision shall be the responsibility of the judgment creditor, the same as if service had been directly on the Controller without the intervention of the local child support agency.

(f) Where the claim of the judgment debtor is less than ten dollars ($10) and the claim of the judgment creditor arises under an affidavit filed pursuant to subdivision (c) of Section 708.730, the Controller may disregard the claim of the judgment creditor and forward any and all sums due to the judgment debtor. In the event that there is more than one claimant for a refund, the Franchise Tax Board shall have discretion in allocating the overpayment among claimants.

(g) Should two or more local child support agencies submit claims on behalf of a judgment creditor, the Controller in his or her discretion may select which claim or claims he or she shall honor.

(h) Any claims which are honored in behalf of a judgment creditor shall be considered as refunds of tax overpayments to the judgment debtor.

(i) For purposes of this section, "support" means an obligation owing on behalf of a child, spouse, or family, or combination thereof.
Amended by Stats 2000 ch 808 (AB 1358), s 19, eff. 9/28/2000.

Section 708.750 - Filing abstract or copy of judgment and affidavit with auditor of public entity

If money is owing and unpaid to the judgment debtor by a public entity other than a state agency, the judgment creditor shall file the abstract or certified copy of the judgment and the affidavit with the auditor of the public entity or, if there is no auditor, with the official whose duty corresponds to that of auditor. To discharge the claim of the judgment debtor, the auditor or other official shall (1) deposit with the court by a warrant or check payable to the court, the amount due the judgment debtor (after deducting an amount sufficient to reimburse the public entity for any amounts advanced to the judgment debtor or owed by the judgment debtor to the public entity) required to satisfy the money judgment as shown by the affidavit in full or to the greatest extent and (2) pay the balance thereof, if any, to the judgment debtor.
Added by Stats. 1982, Ch. 1364, Sec. 2. Operative July 1, 1983, by Sec. 3 of Ch. 1364.

Section 708.755 - Lien created against lottery prize

(a) Upon compliance with this section, the lien of a judgment creditor pursuant to this article is created against a lottery prize to be paid in annual installments and shall continue in force and effect until the judgment is paid or expires, whichever occurs first. For the lien to continue in effect, the judgment creditor shall do all of the following:

(1) Commencing with the second installment against which the judgment lien creditor asserts its lien, annually file with the lottery an affidavit stating that the judgment has not been satisfied and the amount of the remaining unsatisfied judgment, including interest and costs, if any. This affidavit shall be filed with the lottery not less than 45 days, nor more than 90 days, before the annual payment due date on the prize that is the subject of the judgment lien.

(2) If the judgment lien is renewed, file with the lottery a certified copy of the renewal application, as authorized in this code not less than 45 days, nor more than 90 days, before the annual payment due date on the prize that is the subject of the judgment lien, in order for the judgment lien to be effective in continuing the existing judgment lien against the annual lottery prize payments.

(b) If the judgment lien creditor fails to file the annual statement, renewal of judgment, or renewal of abstract, the lien shall expire. Expiration of a lien for failure to comply with this section shall not preclude the judgment creditor from commencing a new procedure under this article to enforce the judgment, to the extent that the judgment otherwise continues to be enforceable under applicable law.

Added by renumbering Section 708.750 (as added by Stats. 1995, Ch. 363) by Stats. 1996, Ch. 124, Sec. 14. Effective January 1, 1997.

Section 708.760 - Contract price deemed owing and unpaid of debtor is contractor upon public work

(a) If the judgment debtor named in the abstract or certified copy of the judgment filed pursuant to this article is a contractor upon a public work, the cost of which is to be paid out of public moneys voted, appropriated, or otherwise set apart for such purpose, only so much of the contract price shall be deemed owing and unpaid within the meaning of Section 708.740 or 708.750 as may remain payable under the terms of the contractor's contract, upon the completion thereof, after deducting sums due and to become due to persons described in Section 9100 of the Civil Code. In ascertaining the sums due or to become due to such persons, only claims which are filed against the moneys due or to become due to the judgment debtor in accordance with Chapter 4 (commencing with Section 9350) of Title 3 of Part 6 of Division 4 of the Civil Code shall be considered.

(b) The Controller, auditor, or other public disbursing officer whose duty it is to make payments under the provisions of the contract may not deposit an amount with the court pursuant to this article until the contract is completed, but may deposit an amount with the court to satisfy the claim of the judgment debtor before the payments specified in subdivision (a) are made so long as a sufficient amount is retained for the satisfaction of the claims of persons described in Section 9100 of the Civil Code.

Amended by Stats 2010 ch 697 (SB 189),s 23, eff. 1/1/2011, op. 7/1/2012.

Section 708.770 - Service of notice of deposit with court

(a) Except as provided in subdivision (g), promptly after deposit with the court by the public entity, the court clerk shall cause a notice of deposit to be served on the judgment debtor. Service shall be made personally or by mail.

(b) Within 10 days after service of the notice of deposit pursuant to subdivision (a), the judgment debtor who claims an exemption shall do both of the following:

(1) File with the court a claim of exemption and a notice of motion for an order determining the claim of exemption. The claim of exemption shall include all of the matters set forth in subdivision (b) of Section 703.520.

(2) Serve on the judgment creditor a copy of the notice of motion, a copy of the claim of exemption, and a notice of hearing on the motion. Service shall be made personally or by mail.

(c) The hearing on the motion shall be held not later than 30 days from the date the notice of motion was filed with the court unless continued by the court for good cause.

(d) Within 10 days after the judgment creditor is served under subdivision (b), the judgment creditor who opposes the motion shall do both of the following:

(1) File with the court a notice of opposition to the claim of exemption. The notice of opposition to the claim of exemption shall be executed under oath and shall include all of the matters set forth in Section 703.560.

(2) Serve on the judgment debtor a copy of the notice of opposition to the claim of exemption. Service shall be made personally or by mail.

(e) Subdivisions (a) to (d), inclusive, of Section 703.580 and Sections 703.590 and 703.600 apply to a claim of exemption made pursuant to this section.

(f) The failure of the judgment debtor to make a claim of exemption under this section constitutes a waiver of the exemption.

(g) In lieu of service of the notice of deposit described herein, where a state agency has been served with an affidavit pursuant to subdivision (c) of Section 708.730 and has presented the claim of the judgment creditor to the Controller pursuant to subdivision (a) of Section 708.740, the state agency shall cause a notice of deposit to be sent to the judgment debtor instructing the judgment debtor to file any and all requests for relief with the district attorney who filed the affidavit, or the court clerk if the seizure arises under subdivision (e) of Section 708.740. Except in those cases arising under subdivision (e) of Section 708.740, the judgment debtor shall file the request for relief with the district attorney within 15 days after service of notice from the public agency, or the judgment debtor shall be deemed to have waived any claim he or she might otherwise have. If the matter cannot be resolved with the district attorney, the district attorney shall so advise the judgment debtor and the judgment debtor shall then be authorized to commence proceedings under this section or any other appropriate provision of law. The notice from the district attorney shall for any limitation have the same effect as a notice of deposit under subdivision (a). Service of any notice or request under this subdivision shall be made personally or by mail. Claims arising from the filing of an abstract or certified copy of a judgment, under subdivision (e) of Section 708.740 shall be governed by the procedure and limitations set forth in subdivisions (a) through (f).

Amended by Stats. 1983, Ch. 1010, Sec. 3.

Section 708.775 - Payment of portion of deposit to which creditor entitled

After the expiration of the period allowed for claiming an exemption under Section 708.770 if no exemption has been claimed, or after the determination of the claim of exemption if an exemption is claimed within the period allowed for claiming the exemption under Section 708.770, the court shall pay the nonexempt portion of the money deposited to which the judgment creditor is entitled to the judgment creditor and the balance thereof, if any, to the judgment debtor, unless some other disposition is required by law.

Added by Stats. 1982, Ch. 1364, Sec. 2. Operative July 1, 1983, by Sec. 3 of Ch. 1364.

Section 708.780 - Lien credited upon filing; filing applicable to income tax refunds; notice of support arrearage

(a) Filing of the abstract or certified copy of the judgment and the affidavit pursuant to this article creates a lien on the money owing and unpaid to the judgment debtor by the public entity in an amount equal to that which may properly be applied to the satisfaction of the money judgment under this article.

(b) When an affidavit is filed pursuant to subdivision (c) of Section 708.730, it shall apply to all claims for refund from the Franchise Tax Board under the Personal Income Tax Law, Part 10 (commencing with Section 17001) of Division 2 of the Revenue and Taxation Code, or the Bank and Corporation Tax Law, Part 11 (commencing with Section 23001) of Division 2 of the Revenue and Taxation Code, which the judgment debtor subsequently claims during a period one year after filing of the affidavit, or October 1 of the year following the filing of the affidavit, whichever occurs later, the same as if claims for these overpayments were filed by the judgment debtor with the appropriate state agency on the date the affidavit was filed.

(c) When a request is filed pursuant to subdivision (d) of Section 708.730 with the court, the clerk of the court shall issue a Notice of Support Arrearage. The clerk of the court shall issue the notice 30 days after the request was filed pursuant to subdivision (d) of Section 708.730 without a hearing if no objection has been raised by the judgment debtor pursuant to this subdivision. If an objection has been raised, the notice shall not be ordered until after a hearing. The notice shall contain the name of the person ordered to pay support and his or her social security number; the amount of the arrearage determined by the court; whether the arrearage is for child, spousal, or family support and the specific combination thereof; a statement of how the recipient may challenge the statement of arrearage; and the name, address, and social security number of the person to whom the arrearage is owed. Upon the clerk of the court issuing the Notice of Support Arrearage, a copy of the request, the affidavit, and the notice shall be served by the party who requested the court to issue the Notice of Support Arrearage upon the person ordered to pay support and the Controller. Service may be personal, in accordance with Section 1011, or by mail, in accordance with Section 1013. Service upon the Controller shall be at the Controller's office in Sacramento. The judgment debtor may object to the request or affidavit upon any of the following grounds:

(1) there is an error in the amount of the arrearage stated in the affidavit;

(2) the alleged judgment debtor is not the judgment debtor from whom the support is due;

(3) the amount to be intercepted exceeds that allowable under federal law;

(4) a default in payment of the support for 30 days has not occurred; or

(5) other necessary factual allegations contained in the affidavit are erroneous. Upon receipt of the Notice of Support Arrearage, the Controller shall take reasonable measures to deduct from any personal income tax refunds and lottery winnings owed and processed for payment to the judgment debtor and deposit with the court a warrant, subject to Sections 708.770 and 708.775, with service of a copy of the warrant upon the local child support agency of the county in which the support judgment is entered, payable to the court, the amount due the judgment creditor (after deducting an amount sufficient to reimburse the state for any amounts advanced to the judgment debtor or owed by the judgment debtor to the state) required to satisfy the money judgment as shown by the affidavit in full or to the greatest extent, and pay the balance thereof, if any, to the judgment debtor. At any hearing pursuant to Section 708.770, the judgment debtor may challenge the distribution of these funds on exemption or other grounds, including, but not limited to, an allegation that the judgment has been satisfied or that service was improper. The notice shall not apply to any money which is exempt by law from execution. The Controller shall determine the cost of enforcing the notice and may establish a notice filing fee not to exceed five dollars ($5).

Service of the Notice of Support Arrearage and of the request and affidavit pursuant to this subdivision creates a lien on the money owing and unpaid to the judgment debtor which shall become effective 30 days following service upon the Controller. This notice shall remain in effect for four years from the date of its issuance or until the arrearage for which the notice was issued is satisfied, whichever occurs first.

Any person who files a request with the court to issue a Notice of Support Arrearage pursuant to subdivision (d) of Section 708.730 shall notify the court and the Controller of any satisfaction of the arrearage after the Notice of Support Arrearage has been issued by the clerk of the court. The notice to the court and the Controller shall be filed with the court and the Controller and served upon the local child support agency of the county in which the support judgment is entered within 30 days of the satisfaction or discharge and shall show a partial or full satisfaction of the arrearage or any other resolution of the arrearage.

Upon filing and service, the Notice of Support Arrearage shall be of no force and effect.

The State Department of Social Services shall, upon request, inform the Legislature of the use and effect of this subdivision on or before December 31, 2001.

This subdivision shall become operative on January 1, 1996, and shall become inoperative on December 31, 2001.

(d) For purposes of this section, "support" means an obligation owing on behalf of a child, spouse, or family, or combination thereof.

Amended 10/10/1999 (Bill Number: SB 240) (Chapter 652).

Section 708.785 - Filing fee

(a) The judgment creditor upon filing the abstract or certified copy of the judgment and the affidavit shall pay a fee of six dollars ($6) to the public entity with which it is filed.

(b) Fees received by the state under this section shall be deposited to the credit of the fund from which payments were, or would be, made on account of collection under this article.

Added by Stats. 1982, Ch. 1364, Sec. 2. Operative July 1, 1983, by Sec. 3 of Ch. 1364.

Section 708.790 - Liability of public officer or employee for failure to perform duty

No public officer or employee is liable for failure to perform a duty imposed by this article unless sufficient information is furnished by the abstract or certified copy of the judgment together with the affidavit to enable the officer or employee in the exercise of reasonable diligence to ascertain the identity of the judgment debtor therefrom and from the papers and records on file in the office in which the officer or employee works. The word "office" as used in this section does not include any branch or subordinate office located in a different city.

Added by Stats. 1982, Ch. 1364, Sec. 2. Operative July 1, 1983, by Sec. 3 of Ch. 1364.

Section 708.795 - Filing against overpayment of tax, penalty or interest

Except as to sums due and unpaid under a judgment for support, nothing in this article authorizes the filing against an overpayment of tax, penalty, or interest, or interest allowable with respect to an overpayment, under Part 10 (commencing with Section 17001), or Part 11 (commencing with Section 23001) of Division 2 of the Revenue and Taxation Code or under Division 6 (commencing with Section 13000) of the Unemployment Insurance Code.

Amended by Stats. 1984, Ch. 1007, Sec. 3.

Article 9 - ENFORCEMENT AGAINST FRANCHISE

Section 708.910 - Franchise defined

As used in this article, "franchise" means a franchise granted by a public entity and all the rights and privileges thereof, other than the franchise of being a corporation.

Added by Stats. 1982, Ch. 1364, Sec. 2. Operative July 1, 1983, by Sec. 3 of Ch. 1364.

Section 708.920 - Generally

(a) The court may, in its discretion, order a franchise applied to the satisfaction of a money judgment upon application by the judgment creditor made on noticed motion. The notice of motion shall be served on the judgment debtor and the public entity that granted the franchise. Service shall be made personally or by mail. In exercising its discretion, the court shall determine whether application of the franchise to the satisfaction of the judgment is proper taking into account all the circumstances of the case, including but not limited to the nature of the franchise, whether the franchise is by its terms transferable, and the likelihood that application of the franchise to the satisfaction of the judgment will yield a substantial amount.

(b) If the court orders application of the franchise to the satisfaction of the judgment, application shall be by such means as appears proper to the court, including but not limited to sale of the franchise, assignment of the franchise or proceeds of the franchise, or appointment of a receiver. The court may include in its order, or make additional orders containing, provisions to effectuate the application of the franchise to the satisfaction of the judgment, including but not limited to provisions relating to the place of sale of the franchise, possession of the property of the judgment debtor necessary for the exercise of the franchise, receipt of proceeds of the franchise, recovery of penalties imposed by law and recoverable for injury to the franchise or for damages or other cause, and the judgment debtor's powers, duties, and liability for penalties and forfeitures.

Added by Stats. 1982, Ch. 1364, Sec. 2. Operative July 1, 1983, by Sec. 3 of Ch. 1364.

Section 708.930 - Order subject to laws governing sale, transfer or other actions concerning franchise

Notwithstanding any other provision of this article, an order for application of a franchise to the satisfaction of a money judgment is subject to all applicable laws governing sale, transfer, or other actions concerning the franchise, including but not limited to any necessary approvals by the Public Utilities Commission or local public entities and compliance with statutory or administrative regulations.
Added by Stats. 1982, Ch. 1364, Sec. 2. Operative July 1, 1983, by Sec. 3 of Ch. 1364.

Article 10 - OTHER ENFORCEMENT PROCEDURES

Section 709.010 - Debtor's interest as beneficiary of trust

(a) As used in this section, "trust" has the meaning provided in Section 82 of the Probate Code.

(b) The judgment debtor's interest as a beneficiary of a trust is subject to enforcement of a money judgment only upon petition under this section by a judgment creditor to a court having jurisdiction over administration of the trust as prescribed in Part 5 (commencing with Section 17000) of Division 9 of the Probate Code. The judgment debtor's interest in the trust may be applied to the satisfaction of the money judgment by such means as the court, in its discretion, determines are proper, including but not limited to imposition of a lien on or sale of the judgment debtor's interest, collection of trust income, and liquidation and transfer of trust property by the trustee.

(c) Nothing in this section affects the limitations on the enforcement of a money judgment against the judgment debtor's interest in a trust under Chapter 2 (commencing with Section 15300) of Part 2 of Division 9 of the Probate Code, and the provisions of this section are subject to the limitations of that chapter.
Amended by Stats. 1986, Ch. 820, Sec. 18. Operative July 1, 1987, by Sec. 43 of Ch. 820.

Section 709.020 - Contingent remainder executory interest or other interest in property not vested in judgment debtor

The judgment creditor may apply to the court on noticed motion for an order applying to the satisfaction of a money judgment a contingent remainder, executory interest, or other interest of the judgment debtor in property that is not vested in the judgment debtor. The interest of the judgment debtor may be applied to the satisfaction of the money judgment by such means as the court, in its discretion, determines are proper to protect the interests of both the judgment debtor and judgment creditor, including but not limited to the imposition of a lien on or the sale of the judgment debtor's interest.
Added by Stats. 1982, Ch. 1364, Sec. 2. Operative July 1, 1983, by Sec. 3 of Ch. 1364.

Section 709.030 - Property in guardianship or conservatorship estate

Property in a guardianship or conservatorship estate is not subject to enforcement of a money judgment by a procedure provided in this division, but the judgment creditor may apply to the court in which the guardianship or conservatorship proceeding is pending under Division 4 (commencing with Section 1400) of the Probate Code for an order requiring payment of the judgment.
Added by Stats. 1982, Ch. 1364, Sec. 2. Operative July 1, 1983, by Sec. 3 of Ch. 1364.

Division 3 - ENFORCEMENT OF NONMONEY JUDGMENTS

Chapter 1 - GENERAL PROVISIONS

Section 712.010 - Application for writ of possession or sale

After entry of a judgment for possession or sale of property, a writ of possession or sale shall be issued by the clerk of the court upon application of the judgment creditor and shall be directed to the levying officer in the county where the judgment is to be enforced. The application shall include a declaration under penalty of perjury stating the daily rental value of the property as of the date the complaint for unlawful detainer was filed. A separate writ shall be issued for each county where the judgment is to be enforced. Writs may be issued successively until the judgment is satisfied, except that a new writ may not be issued for a county until the expiration of 180 days after the issuance of a prior writ for that county unless the prior writ is first returned.
Amended by Stats. 1988, Ch. 1405, Sec. 1.

Section 712.020 - Information included in writ

A writ of possession or sale issued pursuant to this division shall require the levying officer to whom it is directed to enforce the judgment and shall include the following information:

(a) The date of issuance of the writ.

(b) The title of the court where the judgment for possession or sale is entered and the cause and number of the action.

(c) The name and address of the creditor and the name and last known address of the judgment debtor. If the judgment debtor is other than a natural person, the type of legal entity shall be stated.

(d) The date the judgment was entered, and the date of any subsequent renewals, and where entered in the records of the court.

(e) If the judgment for possession or sale includes a money judgment, the amount required to satisfy the money judgment on the date the writ is issued, and the amount of interest accruing daily on the principal amount of the judgment from the date the writ is issued may be included on the writ at the option of the creditor.

(f) Whether any person has requested notice of sale under the judgment and, if so, the name and address of that person.

(g) Any other information required to be included in the particular writ.

(h) A statement indicating whether the case is limited or unlimited.
Amended by Stats 2010 ch 680 (AB 2394),s 14, eff. 1/1/2011.

Section 712.030 - Execution of writ by levying officer

(a) Upon delivery of the writ of possession or sale to the levying officer to whom the writ is directed, together with the written instructions of the judgment creditor, the levying officer shall execute the writ in the manner prescribed by law.

(b) The levying officer may not levy upon or otherwise seize property under the writ after the expiration of 180 days from the date the writ was issued.
Added by Stats. 1982, Ch. 1364, Sec. 2. Operative July 1, 1983, by Sec. 3 of Ch. 1364.

Section 712.040 - Writ of execution; remedies provided in Chapter 5 or Chapter 6

(a) A writ of possession or sale may be enforced as a writ of execution to satisfy any money judgment included in the judgment for possession or sale. If amounts due under the judgment are not satisfied pursuant to the writ of possession or sale, the judgment creditor may use a writ of execution to satisfy any money judgment included in the judgment after the writ of possession or sale has been returned or 180 days after its issuance, whichever is earlier. If the judgment creditor does not desire issuance of a writ of possession or sale (because possession has been voluntarily surrendered, the secured obligation has been voluntarily satisfied, or other reason), a writ of execution may be issued to satisfy any money judgment included in the judgment.

(b) Whether or not a writ of possession or sale has been issued, enforced, or returned, the judgment creditor may use any available remedies provided by Chapter 5 (commencing with Section 706.010) or Chapter 6 (commencing with Section 708.010) of Division 2 to satisfy any money judgment included in the judgment.

(c) Notwithstanding subdivisions (a) and (b), if so ordered in a judgment for sale, a money judgment included in the judgment may only be enforced as ordered by the court.
Added by Stats. 1982, Ch. 1364, Sec. 2. Operative July 1, 1983, by Sec. 3 of Ch. 1364.

Section 712.050 - Return of writ of possession or sale

The return of a writ of possession or sale is governed by Section 699.560 (return of writ of execution).

Added by Stats. 1982, Ch. 1364, Sec. 2. Operative July 1, 1983, by Sec. 3 of Ch. 1364.

Section 712.060 - Appointment of receiver

The court may appoint a receiver pursuant to Article 7 (commencing with Section 708.610) of Chapter 6 of Division 2 to enforce a judgment for possession or sale of property.

Added by Stats. 1982, Ch. 1364, Sec. 2. Operative July 1, 1983, by Sec. 3 of Ch. 1364.

Section 712.070 - Judgment against public entity

Except as provided in Section 695.050, a judgment against a public entity is enforceable under this division.

Added by Stats. 1982, Ch. 1364, Sec. 2. Operative July 1, 1983, by Sec. 3 of Ch. 1364.

Chapter 2 - JUDGMENT FOR POSSESSION OF PERSONAL PROPERTY

Section 714.010 - Writ of possession of personal property

(a) A judgment for possession of personal property may be enforced by a writ of possession of personal property issued pursuant to Section 712.010.

(b) In addition to the information required by Section 712.020, the writ of possession of personal property shall contain the following:

(1) A description of the property to be delivered to the judgment creditor in satisfaction of the judgment.

(2) The value of the property if specified in the judgment or a supplemental order.

Added by Stats. 1982, Ch. 1364, Sec. 2. Operative July 1, 1983, by Sec. 3 of Ch. 1364.

Section 714.020 - Execution of writ

(a) To execute the writ of possession of personal property, the levying officer shall search for the property specified in the writ and, if the property is in the possession of the judgment debtor or an agent of the judgment debtor, take custody of the property in the same manner as a levy under a writ of execution on such property in the possession of the judgment debtor. Custody of personal property used as a dwelling shall be taken as provided by Section 700.080. Custody of property in a private place shall be taken as provided by Section 699.030. If the levying officer obtains possession of the property specified in the writ of possession, the levying officer shall deliver the property to the judgment creditor in satisfaction of the judgment.

(b) If the property specified in the writ of possession cannot be taken into custody, the levying officer shall make a demand upon the judgment debtor for the property if the judgment debtor can be located. If custody of the property is not then obtained, the levying officer shall so state in the return. Thereafter the judgment for the possession of the property may be enforced in the same manner as a money judgment for the value of the property as specified in the judgment or a supplemental order.

(c) The writ of possession of personal property may, under the circumstances described in subdivision (b), be treated as a writ of execution.

Added by Stats. 1982, Ch. 1364, Sec. 2. Operative July 1, 1983, by Sec. 3 of Ch. 1364.

Section 714.030 - Order directing judgment debtor to transfer possession

(a) After entry of a judgment for possession of personal property, and whether or not a writ of possession of personal property has been issued, the judgment creditor may apply to the court for an order directing the judgment debtor to transfer possession of the property or documentary evidence of title to the property or both to the judgment creditor. The application shall be made on noticed motion if the court so directs or a court rule so requires. Otherwise, the application may be made ex parte.

(b) The court may issue an order pursuant to this section upon a showing of need for the order.

(c) The order shall be personally served on the judgment debtor and shall contain a notice to the judgment debtor that failure to comply with the order may subject the judgment debtor to being held in contempt of court.

Added by Stats. 1982, Ch. 1364, Sec. 2. Operative July 1, 1983, by Sec. 3 of Ch. 1364.

Chapter 3 - JUDGMENT FOR POSSESSION OF REAL PROPERTY

Section 715.010 - Writ of possession of real property

(a) A judgment for possession of real property may be enforced by a writ of possession of real property issued pursuant to Section 712.010. The application for the writ shall provide a place to indicate that the writ applies to all tenants, subtenants, if any, name of claimants, if any, and any other occupants of the premises.

(b) In addition to the information required by Section 712.020, the writ of possession of real property shall contain the following:

(1) A description of the real property, possession of which is to be delivered to the judgment creditor in satisfaction of the judgment.

(2) A statement that if the real property is not vacated within five days from the date of service of a copy of the writ on the occupant or, if the copy of the writ is posted, within five days from the date a copy of the writ is served on the judgment debtor, the levying officer will remove the occupants from the real property and place the judgment creditor in possession.

(3) A statement that any personal property, except a mobilehome, remaining on the real property after the judgment creditor has been placed in possession will be sold or otherwise disposed of in accordance with Section 1174 unless the judgment debtor or other owner pays the judgment creditor the reasonable cost of storage and takes possession of the personal property not later than 15 days after the time the judgment creditor takes possession of the real property.

(4) The date the complaint was filed in the action that resulted in the judgment of possession.

(5) The date or dates on which the court will hear objections to enforcement of a judgment of possession that are filed pursuant to Section 1174.3, unless a summons, complaint, and prejudgment claim of right to possession were served upon the occupants in accordance with Section 415.46.

(6) The daily rental value of the property as of the date the complaint for unlawful detainer was filed unless a summons, complaint, and prejudgment claim of right of possession were served upon the occupants in accordance with Section 415.46.

(7) If a summons, complaint, and prejudgment claim of right to possession were served upon the occupants in accordance with Section 415.46, a statement that the writ applies to all tenants, subtenants, if any, named claimants, if any, and any other occupants of the premises.

(c) At the time the writ of possession is served or posted, the levying officer shall also serve or post a copy of the form for a claim of right to possession, unless a summons, complaint, and prejudgment claim of right to possession were served upon the occupants in accordance with Section 415.46.

Amended by Stats. 2004, Ch. 183, Sec. 43. Effective January 1, 2005.

Section 715.020 - Execution of writ

To execute the writ of possession of real property:

(a) The levying officer shall serve a copy of the writ of possession on one occupant of the property. Service on the occupant shall be made by leaving the copy of the writ with the occupant personally or, in the occupant's absence, with a person of suitable age and discretion found upon the property when service is attempted who is either an employee or agent of the occupant or a member of the occupant's household.

(b) If unable to serve an occupant described in subdivision (a) at the time service is attempted, the levying officer shall execute the writ of possession by posting a copy of the writ in a conspicuous place on the property and serving a copy of the writ of possession on the judgment debtor. Service shall be made personally or by mail. If the judgment debtor's address is not known, the copy of the writ may be served by mailing it to the address of the property.

(c) If the judgment debtor, members of the judgment debtor's household, and any other occupants holding under the judgment debtor do not vacate the property within five days from the date of service on an occupant pursuant to subdivision (a) or on the judgment debtor pursuant to subdivision (b), the levying officer shall remove the occupants from the property and place the judgment creditor in possession. The provisions of Section 684.120 extending time do not apply to the five-day period specified in this subdivision.

(d) Notwithstanding subdivision (c), unless the person is named in the writ, the levying officer may not remove any person from the property who claims a right to possession of the property accruing prior to the commencement of the unlawful detainer action or who claims to have been in possession of the property on the date of the filing of the unlawful detainer action. However, if the summons, complaint, and prejudgment claim of right to possession were served upon the occupants in accordance with Section 415.46, no occupant of the premises, whether or not the occupant is named in the judgment for possession, may object to the enforcement of the judgment as prescribed in Section 1174.3.

Amended by Stats. 1991, Ch. 57, Sec. 4. Effective June 17, 1991.

Section 715.030 - Disposition of personal property remaining on real property

The disposition of personal property remaining on the real property after the judgment creditor is placed in possession thereof pursuant to the writ of possession is governed by subdivisions (e) to (m), inclusive, of Section 1174. For this purpose, references in Section 1174 and in provisions incorporated by reference in Section 1174 to the "landlord" shall be deemed to be references to the judgment creditor and references to the "tenant" shall be deemed to be references to the judgment debtor or other occupant.

Added by Stats. 1982, Ch. 1364, Sec. 2. Operative July 1, 1983, by Sec. 3 of Ch. 1364.

Section 715.040 - Execution of writ by registered process server

(a) A registered process server may execute the writ of possession of real property as provided in subdivisions (a) and (b) of Section 715.020 if a proper writ of possession is delivered to the sheriff or marshal and that officer does not execute the writ as provided in subdivisions (a) and (b) of Section 715.020 within three days (Saturday, Sunday, and legal holidays excluded) from the day the writ is delivered to that officer. If the writ is not executed within that time, the levying officer shall upon request give the writ to the judgment creditor or to a registered process server designated by the judgment creditor.

(b) Within five days after executing the writ under this section, all of the following shall be filed with the levying officer:

(1) The writ of possession of real property.

(2) An affidavit of the registered process server stating the manner in which the writ was executed.

(3) Proof of service of the writ.

(4) Instructions in writing, as required by the provisions of Section 687.010.

(c) If the writ is executed by a registered process server, the levying officer shall perform all other duties under the writ and shall return the writ to the court.

(d) The fee for services of a registered process server under this section may, in the court's discretion, be allowed as a recoverable cost upon a motion pursuant to Section 685.080. If allowed, the amount of the fee to be allowed is governed by Section 1033.5.

Amended by Stats. 1996, Ch. 872, Sec. 18. Effective January 1, 1997.

Section 715.050 - Writ of possession issued pursuant to judgment for possession unlawful detainer action

Except with respect to enforcement of a judgment for money, a writ of possession issued pursuant to a judgment for possession in an unlawful detainer action shall be enforced pursuant to this chapter without delay, notwithstanding receipt of notice of the filing by the defendant of a bankruptcy proceeding.

This section does not apply to a writ of possession issued for possession of a mobilehome or manufactured home, as those terms are defined in subdivision (a) of Section 1161a, and does not apply to a writ of possession issued for possession of real property in a mobilehome park subject to the Mobilehome Residency Law (Chapter 2.5 (commencing with Section 798) of Title 2 of Part 2 of Division 2 of the Civil Code), or to a manufactured housing community, as defined in Section 18801 of the Health and Safety Code.

Added by Stats. 1994, Ch. 898, Sec. 2. Effective January 1, 1995.

Chapter 4 - JUDGMENT FOR SALE OF PROPERTY

Section 716.010 - Writ of sale

(a) A judgment for sale of real or personal property may be enforced by a writ of sale issued pursuant to Section 712.010.

(b) In addition to the information required by Section 712.020, the writ of sale shall contain a description of the property to be sold in satisfaction of the judgment for sale.

(c) The writ of sale delivered to the levying officer shall be accompanied by a certified copy of the judgment for sale.

Added by Stats. 1982, Ch. 1364, Sec. 2. Operative July 1, 1983, by Sec. 3 of Ch. 1364.

Section 716.020 - Execution of writ

To execute the writ of sale, the levying officer shall:

(a) Levy upon the property described in the writ of sale in the manner prescribed by Article 4 (commencing with Section 700.010) of Chapter 3 of Division 2 for levy under a writ of execution.

(b) Except as otherwise ordered by the court, give notice of sale and sell the property described in the writ of sale in the manner prescribed by Article 6 (commencing with Section 701.510) of Chapter 3 of Division 2 for giving notice and selling under a writ of execution.

(c) Apply the proceeds of the sale of the property in conformity with the judgment for sale.

Added by Stats. 1982, Ch. 1364, Sec. 2. Operative July 1, 1983, by Sec. 3 of Ch. 1364.

Section 716.030 - Order directing judgment debtor to transfer possession

(a) If a writ of sale is issued, the judgment creditor may apply to the court ex parte, or on noticed motion if the court so directs or a court rule so requires, for an order directing the judgment debtor to transfer to the levying officer:

(1) Possession of the property to be sold if the prescribed method of levy is by taking the property into custody.

(2) Possession of any documentary evidence of title to property to be sold. An order pursuant to this paragraph may be served when the property is levied upon or thereafter.

(b) The court may issue an order pursuant to this section upon a showing of need for the order.

(c) The order shall be personally served on the judgment debtor and shall contain a notice to the judgment debtor that failure to comply with the order may subject the judgment debtor to being held in contempt of court.

Added by Stats. 1982, Ch. 1364, Sec. 2. Operative July 1, 1983, by Sec. 3 of Ch. 1364.

Chapter 5 - OTHER JUDGMENTS

Section 717.010 - Generally

A judgment not otherwise enforceable pursuant to this title may be enforced by personally serving a certified copy of the judgment on the person required to obey it and invoking the power of the court to punish for contempt.

Added by Stats. 1982, Ch. 1364, Sec. 2. Operative July 1, 1983, by Sec. 3 of Ch. 1364.

Division 4 - THIRD-PARTY CLAIMS AND RELATED PROCEDURES
Chapter 1 - DEFINITIONS
Section 720.010 - Generally
Unless the provision or context otherwise requires, the definitions in this chapter govern the construction of this division.
Added by Stats. 1982, Ch. 1364, Sec. 2. Operative July 1, 1983, by Sec. 3 of Ch. 1364.
Section 720.020 - Creditor
"Creditor" means the judgment creditor or, in the case of a levy under a writ of attachment or prejudgment writ of possession of personal property, the plaintiff.
Added by Stats. 1982, Ch. 1364, Sec. 2. Operative July 1, 1983, by Sec. 3 of Ch. 1364.
Section 720.030 - Debtor
"Debtor" means the judgment debtor or, in the case of a levy under a writ of attachment or prejudgment writ of possession of personal property, the defendant.
Added by Stats. 1982, Ch. 1364, Sec. 2. Operative July 1, 1983, by Sec. 3 of Ch. 1364.
Chapter 2 - THIRD-PARTY CLAIMS OF OWNERSHIP AND POSSESSION
Section 720.110 - Cases in which claim allowed
A third person claiming ownership or the right to possession of property may make a third-party claim under this chapter in any of the following cases if the interest claimed is superior to the creditor's lien on the property:
(a) Where real property has been levied upon under a writ of attachment or a writ of execution.
(b) Where personal property has been levied upon under a writ of attachment, a writ of execution, a prejudgment or postjudgment writ of possession, or a writ of sale.
Added by Stats. 1982, Ch. 1364, Sec. 2. Operative July 1, 1983, by Sec. 3 of Ch. 1364.
Section 720.120 - Time for filing claim
A person making a third-party claim under this chapter shall file the claim with the levying officer, together with two copies of the claim, after levy on the property but before the levying officer does any of the following:
(a) Sells the property.
(b) Delivers possession of the property to the creditor.
(c) Pays proceeds of collection to the creditor.
Added by Stats. 1982, Ch. 1364, Sec. 2. Operative July 1, 1983, by Sec. 3 of Ch. 1364.
Section 720.130 - Information required in claim; copy of writing upon which claim based attached
(a) The third-party claim shall be executed under oath and shall contain all of the following:
   (1) The name of the third person and an address in this state where service by mail may be made on the third person.
   (2) A description of the property in which an interest is claimed.
   (3) A description of the interest claimed, including a statement of the facts upon which the claim is based.
   (4) An estimate of the market value of the interest claimed.
(b) A copy of any writing upon which the claim is based shall be attached to the third-party claim. At a hearing on the third-party claim, the court in its discretion may exclude from evidence any writing a copy of which was not attached to the third-party claim.
Added by Stats. 1982, Ch. 1364, Sec. 2. Operative July 1, 1983, by Sec. 3 of Ch. 1364.
Section 720.140 - Service on creditor; time for objecting to undertaking or filing undertaking
(a) Not later than five days after the third-party claim is filed with the levying officer, the levying officer shall serve the following personally or by mail on the creditor:
   (1) A copy of the third-party claim.
   (2) A statement whether the third person has filed an undertaking to release the property pursuant to Chapter 6 (commencing with Section 720.610).
   (3) If the third person has filed an undertaking to release the property, a notice that the property will be released unless, within the time allowed as specified in the notice, the creditor objects to the undertaking.
   (4) If the third person has not filed an undertaking to release the property, a notice that the property will be released unless, within the time allowed as specified in the notice, the creditor files with the levying officer an undertaking that satisfies the requirements of Section 720.160.
(b) The time allowed the creditor for objecting to the third person's undertaking to release the property or for filing an undertaking is 10 days after service under subdivision (a).
(c) Within the time allowed for service on the creditor under subdivision (a), the levying officer shall serve a copy of the papers specified in subdivision (a) on the debtor. Service shall be made personally or by mail.
(d) The levying officer may serve the copy of the third-party claim and the statement and notice pursuant to this section notwithstanding any defect, informality, or insufficiency of the claim.
Added by Stats. 1982, Ch. 1364, Sec. 2. Operative July 1, 1983, by Sec. 3 of Ch. 1364.
Section 720.150 - Sale or delivering of property to creditor prohibited if claim timely filed; third person's interest not affected for failure to file
(a) Except as otherwise provided by statute, if a third-party claim is timely filed, the levying officer may not do any of the following with respect to the property in which an interest is claimed:
   (1) Sell the property.
   (2) Deliver possession of the property to the creditor.
   (3) Pay proceeds of collection to the creditor.
(b) The interest of the third person in the property levied upon is not affected by the third person's failure to file a third-party claim under this chapter.
Added by Stats. 1982, Ch. 1364, Sec. 2. Operative July 1, 1983, by Sec. 3 of Ch. 1364.
Section 720.160 - Undertaking filed by creditor
(a) If the creditor files with the levying officer an undertaking that satisfies the requirements of this section within the time allowed under subdivision (b) of Section 720.140:
   (1) The levying officer shall execute the writ in the manner provided by law unless the third person files an undertaking to release the property pursuant to Chapter 6 (commencing with Section 720.610).
   (2) After sale, payment, or delivery of the property pursuant to the writ, the property is free of all claims of the third person for which the creditor has given the undertaking.
(b) Subject to Sections 720.770 and 996.010, unless the creditor elects to file an undertaking in a larger amount, the amount of the undertaking filed by the creditor under this section shall be in the amount of ten thousand dollars ($10,000), or twice the amount of the execution lien as of the date of levy or other enforcement lien as of the date it was created, whichever is the lesser amount.

(c) An undertaking given by the creditor under this chapter shall:
(1) Be made in favor of the third person.
(2) Indemnify the third person against any loss, liability, damages, costs, and attorney's fees, incurred by reason of the enforcement proceedings.
(3) Be conditioned on a final judgment that the third person owns or has the right of possession of the property.
(d) If the creditor is a public entity exempt from giving an undertaking, the public entity shall, in lieu of filing the undertaking, file with the levying officer a notice stating that the public entity opposes the claim of the third person. When so filed, the notice is deemed to satisfy the requirement of this section that an undertaking be filed.
Amended by Stats 2001 ch 812 (AB 223), s 5, eff. 1/1/2002.

Section 720.170 - Release of property
(a) In a case where the third person has not filed with the levying officer an undertaking to release the property pursuant to Chapter 6 (commencing with Section 720.610), if the creditor does not within the time allowed under subdivision (b) of Section 720.140 file with the levying officer an undertaking (or file a notice if the creditor is a public entity) that satisfies the requirements of Section 720.160, the levying officer shall release the property unless it is to be held under another lien or unless otherwise ordered by the court.
(b) Except as otherwise provided in this section, release is governed by Section 699.060.
(c) If personal property that has been taken into custody is to be released to the debtor pursuant to Section 699.060 and the debtor has not claimed the property within 10 days after notice was served pursuant to Section 699.060, the levying officer shall release the property to the third person making the claim.
(d) A hearing may be had on the third-party claim pursuant to Chapter 4 (commencing with Section 720.310) notwithstanding the release of the property pursuant to this section.
Added by Stats. 1982, Ch. 1364, Sec. 2. Operative July 1, 1983, by Sec. 3 of Ch. 1364.

Chapter 3 - THIRD-PARTY CLAIM OF SECURITY INTEREST OR LIEN

Section 720.210 - Generally
(a) Where personal property has been levied upon under a writ of attachment, a writ of execution, a prejudgment or postjudgment writ of possession, or a writ of sale, a third person claiming a security interest in or lien on the personal property may make a third-party claim under this chapter if the security interest or lien claimed is superior to the creditor's lien on the property.
(b) A secured party claiming a security interest in fixtures may make a third-party claim pursuant to this chapter if the security interest claimed is superior to the creditor's lien on the property. For this purpose, references in this division to "personal property" shall be deemed references to fixtures.
Added by Stats. 1982, Ch. 1364, Sec. 2. Operative July 1, 1983, by Sec. 3 of Ch. 1364.

Section 720.220 - Time for filing claim
A person making a third-party claim under this chapter shall file the claim with the levying officer, together with two copies of the claim, after levy on the personal property but before the levying officer does any of the following:
(a) Sells the property.
(b) Delivers possession of the property to the creditor.
(c) Pays proceeds of collection to the creditor.
Added by Stats. 1982, Ch. 1364, Sec. 2. Operative July 1, 1983, by Sec. 3 of Ch. 1364.

Section 720.230 - Information included in claim; copy of security agreement and financing statement attached
(a) The third-party claim shall be executed under oath and shall contain all of the following:
(1) The name of the secured party or lienholder and an address in this state where service by mail may be made on the secured party or lienholder.
(2) A description of the personal property in which a security interest or lien is claimed.
(3) A detailed description of the security interest or lien claimed, including a statement of the facts upon which it is based.
(4) A statement of the total amount of sums due or to accrue under the security interest or lien and the applicable rate of interest on amounts due.
(b) In the case of a security interest, a copy of the security agreement and any financing statement shall be attached to the third-party claim. In the case of a lien, a copy of any writing upon which the claim is based shall be attached to the third-party claim. At a hearing on the third-party claim, the court in its discretion may exclude from evidence any writing a copy of which was not attached to the third-party claim.
Added by Stats. 1982, Ch. 1364, Sec. 2. Operative July 1, 1983, by Sec. 3 of Ch. 1364.

Section 720.240 - Service on creditor; time for objecting to undertaking or filing undertaking
(a) Not later than five days after the third-party claim is filed with the levying officer, the levying officer shall serve the following personally or by mail on the creditor:
(1) A copy of the third-party claim.
(2) A statement whether the third person has filed an undertaking to release the property pursuant to Chapter 6 (commencing with Section 720.610).
(3) If the third person has filed an undertaking to release the property, a notice that the property will be released unless, within the time allowed as specified in the notice, the creditor objects to the undertaking.
(4) If the third person has not filed an undertaking to release the property, a notice that the property will be released unless, within the time allowed as specified in the notice, the creditor does one of the following:
(A) Files with the levying officer an undertaking that satisfies the requirements of Section 720.260 and a statement under Section 720.280.
(B) Deposits with the levying officer the amount claimed plus interest at the applicable rate to the estimated date of tender to the secured party or lienholder.
(b) The time allowed the creditor for objecting to the third person's undertaking to release the property or for filing an undertaking and statement or making a deposit pursuant to subdivision (a) is 10 days after service under subdivision (a).
(c) Within the time allowed for service on the creditor under subdivision (a), the levying officer shall serve a copy of the papers specified in subdivision (a) on the debtor. Service shall be made personally or by mail.
(d) The levying officer may serve the copy of the third-party claim and the statement and notice pursuant to this section notwithstanding any defect, informality, or insufficiency of the claim.
Added by Stats. 1982, Ch. 1364, Sec. 2. Operative July 1, 1983, by Sec. 3 of Ch. 1364.

Section 720.250 - Sale or delivery of possession to creditor prohibited if claim timely filed
(a) Except as otherwise provided by statute, if a third-party claim is timely filed, the levying officer may not do any of the following with respect to the personal property in which the security interest or lien is claimed:
(1) Sell the property.
(2) Deliver possession of the property to the creditor.
(3) Pay proceeds of collection to the creditor.

(b) The interest of a secured party or lienholder in the property levied upon is not affected by the failure of the secured party or lienholder to file a third-party claim under this chapter.
Added by Stats. 1982, Ch. 1364, Sec. 2. Operative July 1, 1983, by Sec. 3 of Ch. 1364.

Section 720.260 - Undertaking timely filed by creditor
(a) If the creditor within the time allowed under subdivision (b) of Section 720.240 either files with the levying officer an undertaking that satisfies the requirements of this section and a statement that satisfies the requirements of Section 720.280 or makes a deposit with the levying officer of the amount claimed under Section 720.230:

(1) The levying officer shall execute the writ in the manner provided by law unless, in a case where the creditor has filed an undertaking, the secured party or lienholder files an undertaking to release the property pursuant to Chapter 6 (commencing with Section 720.610).

(2) After sale, payment, or delivery of the property pursuant to the writ, the property is free of all claims or liens of the secured party or lienholder for which the creditor has given the undertaking or made the deposit.

(b) Subject to Sections 720.770 and 996.010, unless the creditor elects to file an undertaking in a larger amount, the amount of the undertaking filed by the creditor under this section shall be in the amount of ten thousand dollars ($10,000) or twice the amount of the execution lien as of the date of levy or other enforcement lien as of the date it was created, whichever is the lesser amount.

(c) An undertaking given by the creditor under this chapter shall:

(1) Be made in favor of the secured party or lienholder.

(2) Indemnify the secured party or lienholder against any loss, liability, damages, costs, and attorney's fees, incurred by reason of the enforcement proceedings.

(3) Be conditioned on a final judgment that the security interest or lien of the third person is entitled to priority over the creditor's lien.

(d) If the creditor is a public entity exempt from giving an undertaking, the public entity shall, in lieu of filing the undertaking, file with the levying officer a notice stating that the public entity opposes the claim of the third person. When so filed, the notice is deemed to satisfy the requirement of this section that an undertaking be filed.
Amended by Stats 2001 ch 812 (AB 223), s 6, eff. 1/1/2002.

Section 720.270 - Release of property
(a) In a case where the third person has not filed with the levying officer an undertaking to release the property pursuant to Chapter 6 (commencing with Section 720.610), if the creditor does not within the time allowed under subdivision (b) of Section 720.240 file with the levying officer an undertaking (or file a notice if the creditor is a public entity) that satisfies the requirements of Section 720.260 and a statement under Section 720.280, or deposit with the levying officer the amount claimed under Section 720.230, the levying officer shall release the personal property unless it is to be held under another lien or unless otherwise ordered by the court.

(b) Except as otherwise provided in this section, release is governed by Section 699.060.

(c) If property that has been taken into custody is to be released to the debtor pursuant to Section 699.060 and the debtor has not claimed the property within 10 days after notice was served pursuant to Section 699.060, the levying officer shall release the property to the secured party or lienholder making the claim.

(d) A hearing may be had on the third-party claim pursuant to Chapter 4 (commencing with Section 720.310) notwithstanding the release of the property pursuant to this section.
Added by Stats. 1982, Ch. 1364, Sec. 2. Operative July 1, 1983, by Sec. 3 of Ch. 1364.

Section 720.280 - Statement filed by creditor at time of filing undertaking
At the time the creditor files an undertaking with the levying officer in response to a third-party claim by a secured party, the creditor shall do all of the following:

(a) File with the levying officer a statement executed under oath that the security interest is invalid, that the security interest is not entitled to priority over the creditor's lien, or that the amount demanded in the claim exceeds the amount to which the secured party is entitled, for the reasons specified therein.

(b) Serve a copy of the statement on the secured party. Service shall be made personally or by mail.

(c) Serve a copy of the statement on the debtor. Service shall be made personally or by mail.
Added by Stats. 1982, Ch. 1364, Sec. 2. Operative July 1, 1983, by Sec. 3 of Ch. 1364.

Section 720.290 - Payment of deposit to secured party or lienholder
(a) If the levying officer receives a sufficient deposit from the creditor, the levying officer shall promptly tender or pay the deposit to the secured party or lienholder who made the third-party claim except that, if the deposit is made by personal check, the levying officer is allowed a reasonable time for the check to clear.

(b) If the tender is accepted, the interest of the secured party or lienholder in the property for which deposit is made passes to the creditor making the deposit and, on distribution of any proceeds under Section 701.810, the creditor who makes the deposit shall be entitled to the proceeds to the extent of the deposit in the priority of the interest for which the deposit is made.

(c) If the tender is refused, the amount of the deposit shall be deposited with the county treasurer payable to the order of the secured party or lienholder.
Added by Stats. 1982, Ch. 1364, Sec. 2. Operative July 1, 1983, by Sec. 3 of Ch. 1364.

Chapter 4 - HEARING ON THIRD-PARTY CLAIM

Section 720.310 - Time for filing petition for hearing; time for holding
(a) Not later than 15 days after the third-party claim is filed with the levying officer pursuant to Section 720.120 or 720.220, or 15 days after filing an undertaking pursuant to Section 720.610, either the creditor or the third person may petition the court for a hearing to determine the validity of the third-party claim and the proper disposition of the property that is the subject of the claim.

(b) The hearing may be held whether or not an undertaking has been filed but not if a deposit has been made pursuant to Section 720.260.

(c) The hearing shall be held within 20 days after the filing of the petition unless continued by the court for good cause shown.
Amended by Stats. 1986, Ch. 672, Sec. 1.

Section 720.320 - Notice of hearing
(a) At the time prescribed in subdivision (b) of Section 1005, the petitioner shall do both of the following:

(1) Serve notice of the time and place of the hearing on the creditor or the third person (whichever person is not the petitioner) and on the debtor. Service shall be made personally or by mail.

(2) File a copy of the notice of hearing with the levying officer.

(b) The notice of the hearing shall include a statement that the purpose of the hearing is to determine the validity of the third-party claim and the proper disposition of the property that is the subject of the third-party claim.
Amended by Stats. 1989, Ch. 693, Sec. 4.

Section 720.330 - Papers filed with court after receipt of notice
Promptly after receipt of the notice of the hearing on the third-party claim, the levying officer shall file the following papers with the court:

(a) The third-party claim that was filed with the levying officer pursuant to Section 720.120 or 720.220.

(b) Any statement filed by the creditor with the levying officer pursuant to Section 720.280 in opposition to the third-party claim of a secured party.
(c) Any undertaking of the creditor filed with the levying officer pursuant to Section 720.160 or Section 720.260.
(d) Any undertaking to release filed by a third person pursuant to Chapter 6 (commencing with section 720.610).
(e) Any notice filed by a public entity pursuant to Section 720.160 or 720.260.
Added by Stats. 1982, Ch. 1364, Sec. 2. Operative July 1, 1983, by Sec. 3 of Ch. 1364.

Section 720.340 - Statement filed by creditor if creditor has not filed statement in opposition to claim

If the creditor has not filed a statement with the levying officer pursuant to Section 720.280 in opposition to a third-party claim by a secured party:
(a) In a case where the creditor petitions for a hearing on the third-party claim, the creditor shall file the statement with the court at the time the petition is filed and shall serve a copy thereof on the secured party with notice of the hearing served pursuant to Section 720.320.
(b) In a case where the secured party has petitioned for a hearing on the third-party claim, the creditor shall file the statement with the court and serve a copy of the statement on the secured party not later than five days before the date set for the hearing. Service shall be made personally or by mail.
Added by Stats. 1982, Ch. 1364, Sec. 2. Operative July 1, 1983, by Sec. 3 of Ch. 1364.

Section 720.350 - Pleadings

(a) Subject to the power of the court to permit an amendment in the interest of justice:
(1) The third-party claim constitutes the pleading of the third person.
(2) In the case of a third-party claim by a secured party, the creditor's statement constitutes the pleading of the creditor.
(b) A third-party claim of ownership, right to possession, or a lien, shall be deemed controverted by the creditor.
Added by Stats. 1982, Ch. 1364, Sec. 2. Operative July 1, 1983, by Sec. 3 of Ch. 1364.

Section 720.360 - Burden of proof

At a hearing on a third-party claim, the third person has the burden of proof.
Added by Stats. 1982, Ch. 1364, Sec. 2. Operative July 1, 1983, by Sec. 3 of Ch. 1364.

Section 720.370 - Consent required to dismiss proceedings

If the petition for a hearing was made by the third person, neither the petition nor the proceedings pursuant thereto may be dismissed without the consent of the creditor. If the petition for a hearing was made by the creditor, neither the petition nor the proceedings pursuant thereto may be dismissed without the consent of the third person.
Added by Stats. 1982, Ch. 1364, Sec. 2. Operative July 1, 1983, by Sec. 3 of Ch. 1364.

Section 720.380 - Staying sale or enjoining transfer or other disposition of property

(a) Notwithstanding any other provision of this title, the court may make an order staying the sale of the property under a writ or enjoining any transfer or other disposition of the property levied upon under a writ until proceedings for the determination of the rights of a third person can be commenced and prosecuted to termination and may require such undertaking as it considers necessary as a condition for making the order.
(b) After the filing of a third-party claim, notwithstanding Sections 720.160 and 720.260, the creditor, the debtor, or the third person may apply to the court for an order staying the sale of the property under a writ or enjoining any transfer or other disposition of the property until proceedings under this article can be commenced and prosecuted to termination. The application shall be made on noticed motion if the court so directs or a court rule otherwise so requires. Otherwise, the application may be made ex parte.
(c) An order made pursuant to this section may be modified or vacated by the court at any time prior to the termination of the proceedings upon such terms as are just.
Added by Stats. 1982, Ch. 1364, Sec. 2. Operative July 1, 1983, by Sec. 3 of Ch. 1364.

Section 720.390 - Judgment of court

At the conclusion of the hearing, the court shall give judgment determining the validity of the third-party claim and may order the disposition of the property or its proceeds in accordance with the respective interests of the parties. Subject to Section 720.420, the judgment is conclusive between the parties to the proceeding.
Added by Stats. 1982, Ch. 1364, Sec. 2. Operative July 1, 1983, by Sec. 3 of Ch. 1364.

Section 720.400 - No findings required

No findings are required in proceedings under this chapter.
Added by Stats. 1982, Ch. 1364, Sec. 2. Operative July 1, 1983, by Sec. 3 of Ch. 1364.

Section 720.410 - No right to jury trial

There is no right to a jury trial in a proceeding pursuant to this chapter.
Added by Stats. 1982, Ch. 1364, Sec. 2. Operative July 1, 1983, by Sec. 3 of Ch. 1364.

Section 720.420 - Appeal

An appeal may be taken from a judgment given pursuant to Section 720.390.
Amended by Stats. 1998, Ch. 931, Sec. 98. Effective September 28, 1998.

Section 720.430 - Levy upon or application of property released to satisfaction of judgment

If property has been released pursuant to Section 720.170, 720.270, or 720.660, it may be levied upon or otherwise sought to be applied to the satisfaction of the judgment only if it is determined in the hearing on the third-party claim that the debtor has an interest in the property that may be levied upon or otherwise applied to the satisfaction of the judgment.
Added by Stats. 1982, Ch. 1364, Sec. 2. Operative July 1, 1983, by Sec. 3 of Ch. 1364.

Chapter 5 - CREDITOR'S DEMAND FOR THIRD-PARTY CLAIM BY SECURED PARTY OR LIENHOLDER

Section 720.510 - Generally

A creditor may make a demand as provided in this chapter that a secured party or lienholder file a third-party claim to personal property that has been levied upon under a writ of attachment or a writ of execution.
Added by Stats. 1982, Ch. 1364, Sec. 2. Operative July 1, 1983, by Sec. 3 of Ch. 1364.

Section 720.520 - Filing and service of demand

(a) The creditor's demand for a third-party claim by the secured party or lienholder, together with a copy of the demand, shall be filed with the levying officer after levy on the personal property but before the levying officer sells the property or pays proceeds of collection to the creditor.
(b) Promptly after the demand and a copy thereof are filed, the levying officer shall personally serve the demand on the secured party or lienholder. Service of the demand on the secured party or lienholder shall be attested by the certificate of the levying officer and the certificate shall be filed in the action promptly after service.
(c) The demand shall be served by the levying officer who levied on the property or by any other levying officer whose office is closer to the place of service. If service is made by another levying officer, such levying officer's costs shall be paid out of the costs prepaid to the levying officer who levied on the property.

Added by Stats. 1982, Ch. 1364, Sec. 2. Operative July 1, 1983, by Sec. 3 of Ch. 1364.

Section 720.530 - Information included

The demand for a third-party claim served on a secured party or lienholder shall contain all of the following:

(a) The name and address of the secured party or lienholder.

(b) The name and address of the creditor.

(c) A detailed description of the personal property levied upon and the date of levy.

(d) A statement that if the secured party or lienholder does not file a third-party claim pursuant to Chapter 3 (commencing with Section 720.210) within 30 days after service of the demand, the secured party or lienholder shall be deemed to have waived any priority the security interest or lien may have over the creditor's lien on the property levied upon unless the property levied upon is released from the creditor's lien.

(e) A statement that if any priority of the security interest or lien is waived, the secured party or lienholder may have a right to share in any excess proceeds of an execution sale of the property as provided in Section 701.810.

Added by Stats. 1982, Ch. 1364, Sec. 2. Operative July 1, 1983, by Sec. 3 of Ch. 1364.

Section 720.540 - Release, sale or disposal property described in demand

Except as otherwise provided by statute, the levying officer may not release, sell, or otherwise dispose of the personal property described in the demand before the expiration of 30 days after service of the demand on the secured party or lienholder.

Added by Stats. 1982, Ch. 1364, Sec. 2. Operative July 1, 1983, by Sec. 3 of Ch. 1364.

Section 720.550 - Waiver of priority of security interest or lien

(a) If the secured party or lienholder does not file a third-party claim with the levying officer pursuant to Chapter 3 (commencing with Section 720.210) within 30 days after service of the demand, the secured party or lienholder shall be deemed to have waived any priority the security interest or lien may have over the creditor's lien on the personal property levied upon and the property may be applied toward the satisfaction of the judgment free of the security interest or lien.

(b) If the secured party or lienholder is deemed to have waived any priority over the creditor's lien pursuant to subdivision (a) and the creditor's lien on the personal property is released, the security interest or lien is restored to its former position of priority.

Added by Stats. 1982, Ch. 1364, Sec. 2. Operative July 1, 1983, by Sec. 3 of Ch. 1364.

Chapter 6 - THIRD-PARTY UNDERTAKING TO RELEASE PROPERTY

Section 720.610 - Cases in which undertaking allowed

A third person may give an undertaking to release property pursuant to this chapter in the following cases:

(a) Where the third person claims ownership or the right to possession of real property that has been levied upon under a writ of attachment or a writ of execution.

(b) Where the third person claims ownership or the right to possession of personal property that has been levied upon under a writ of attachment, a writ of execution, or a writ of sale.

(c) Where the third person claims a security interest in or a lien on personal property that has been levied upon under a writ of attachment, a writ of execution, or a writ of sale.

Added by Stats. 1982, Ch. 1364, Sec. 2. Operative July 1, 1983, by Sec. 3 of Ch. 1364.

Section 720.620 - Time for filing undertaking

The third person shall file the undertaking to release property with the levying officer, together with two copies of the undertaking:

(a) At the time the third person files a third-party claim pursuant to Chapter 2 (commencing with Section 720.110) or Chapter 3 (commencing with Section 720.210).

(b) If the third person has previously filed a third-party claim to the property, at any time before the levying officer does any of the following:

(1) Sells the property.

(2) Delivers possession of the property to the creditor.

(3) Pays proceeds of collection to the creditor.

Added by Stats. 1982, Ch. 1364, Sec. 2. Operative July 1, 1983, by Sec. 3 of Ch. 1364.

Section 720.630 - Requirements

(a) The undertaking to release property shall contain a description of the property to be released and shall describe the interest of the third person.

(b) The undertaking shall be made in favor of the creditor and shall provide that, if the debtor is finally adjudged to have an interest in the property levied upon, the third person shall pay to the creditor the lesser of the following:

(1) The amount required to satisfy the judgment against the debtor of the creditor who had the lien on the property.

(2) A sum equal to the market value of the debtor's interest in the property levied upon.

(c) Except as provided in subdivision (d) and unless the third person elects to file an undertaking in a larger amount, the amount of the undertaking shall be the lesser of the following amounts:

(1) Twice the market value of the property sought to be released.

(2) Twice the amount of the creditor's lien on the property sought to be released.

(d) If the creditor has given an undertaking in response to the third person's claim regarding the property pursuant to Section 720.160 or 720.260, the third person's undertaking shall be in the amount of the creditor's undertaking.

Added by Stats. 1982, Ch. 1364, Sec. 2. Operative July 1, 1983, by Sec. 3 of Ch. 1364.

Section 720.640 - Service of copy

(a) If the undertaking to release property is filed with the levying officer at the time the third-party claim is filed, the levying officer shall serve a copy of the undertaking on the creditor and on the debtor with the notice of the filing of the third-party claim served pursuant to Section 720.140 or 720.240.

(b) If the undertaking to release property is filed with the levying officer after the third-party claim is filed, not later than five days after the undertaking is filed, the levying officer shall serve a copy of the undertaking on the creditor and on the debtor with a notice that the property will be released unless, within the time allowed as specified in the notice, the creditor objects to the undertaking. Service shall be made personally or by mail.

Added by Stats. 1982, Ch. 1364, Sec. 2. Operative July 1, 1983, by Sec. 3 of Ch. 1364.

Section 720.650 - When undertaking becomes effective

The third person's undertaking becomes effective when the property described therein is released pursuant to this chapter.

Added by Stats. 1982, Ch. 1364, Sec. 2. Operative July 1, 1983, by Sec. 3 of Ch. 1364.

Section 720.660 - Release of property

The levying officer shall release the property described in the third person's undertaking in the manner provided by Section 720.170 promptly after the expiration of the time allowed for objecting to the undertaking, unless the creditor has objected to the undertaking, and filed with the levying officer a copy of the notice of motion as required by Section 720.760, prior to the expiration of that time.

Amended by Stats. 1985, Ch. 41, Sec. 12.

Chapter 7 - UNDERTAKINGS

Section 720.710 - Applicability of Bond and Undertaking Law

The Bond and Undertaking Law (Chapter 2 (commencing with Section 995. 010) of Title 14) applies to a bond given pursuant to this title, except to the extent this title prescribes a different rule or is inconsistent.

Added by Stats. 1985, Ch. 41, Sec. 13.

Section 720.760 - Filing copy of notice of motion objection to undertaking

A copy of a notice of motion objecting to an undertaking shall be filed with the levying officer.

Amended by Stats. 1983, Ch. 18, Sec. 14. Effective April 21, 1983. Operative July 1, 1983, by Sec. 40 of Ch. 18.

Section 720.770 - Time for holding hearing on objection; order deceasing amount

Unless the parties otherwise agree, the hearing on an objection to an undertaking shall be held not less than 10 nor more than 15 days after service of the notice of motion. The court may order the amount of the undertaking decreased below the amount prescribed by Section 720.160 or 720.260 if the court determines the amount prescribed exceeds the probable recovery of the beneficiary if the beneficiary ultimately prevails in proceedings to enforce the liability on the undertaking.

Amended by Stats. 1983, Ch. 18, Sec. 15. Effective April 21, 1983. Operative July 1, 1983, by Sec. 40 of Ch. 18.

Section 720.800 - Filing undertaking with court at time writ returned

If an undertaking has been filed with a levying officer pursuant to this division, and the undertaking remains in the levying officer's possession when the writ is to be returned, the levying officer shall file the undertaking with the court at the time the writ is returned.

Added by Stats. 1982, Ch. 1364, Sec. 2. Operative July 1, 1983, by Sec. 3 of Ch. 1364.

Division 5 - SATISFACTION OF JUDGMENT

Chapter 1 - SATISFACTION OF JUDGMENT

Section 724.010 - Payment of full or lesser amount; acknowledgment of satisfaction

(a) A money judgment may be satisfied by payment of the full amount required to satisfy the judgment or by acceptance by the judgment creditor of a lesser sum in full satisfaction of the judgment.

(b) Where a money judgment is satisfied by levy, the obligation of the judgment creditor to give or file an acknowledgment of satisfaction arises only when the judgment creditor has received the full amount required to satisfy the judgment from the levying officer.

(c) Where a money judgment is satisfied by payment to the judgment creditor by check or other form of noncash payment that is to be honored upon presentation by the judgment creditor for payment, the obligation of the judgment creditor to give or file an acknowledgment of satisfaction of judgment arises only when the check or other form of noncash payment has actually been honored upon presentation for payment.

Added by Stats. 1982, Ch. 1364, Sec. 2. Operative July 1, 1983, by Sec. 3 of Ch. 1364.

Section 724.020 - When satisfaction entered in register of actions

The court clerk shall enter satisfaction of a money judgment in the register of actions when the following occur:

(a) A writ is returned satisfied for the full amount of a lump-sum judgment.

(b) An acknowledgment of satisfaction of judgment is filed with the court.

(c) The court orders entry of satisfaction of judgment.

Added by Stats. 1982, Ch. 1364, Sec. 2. Operative July 1, 1983, by Sec. 3 of Ch. 1364.

Section 724.030 - Filing acknowledgment with court

When a money judgment is satisfied, the judgment creditor immediately shall file with the court an acknowledgment of satisfaction of judgment. This section does not apply where the judgment is satisfied in full pursuant to a writ.

Added by Stats. 1982, Ch. 1364, Sec. 2. Operative July 1, 1983, by Sec. 3 of Ch. 1364.

Section 724.040 - Filing and serving acknowledgment when abstract recorded

If an abstract of a money judgment has been recorded with the recorder of any county and the judgment is satisfied, the judgment creditor shall immediately do both of the following:

(a) File an acknowledgment of satisfaction of judgment with the court.

(b) Serve an acknowledgment of satisfaction of judgment on the judgment debtor. Service shall be made personally or by mail.

Added by Stats. 1982, Ch. 1364, Sec. 2. Operative July 1, 1983, by Sec. 3 of Ch. 1364.

Section 724.050 - Demand that creditor file acknowledgment or execute, acknowledge and deliver acknowledgment

(a) If a money judgment has been satisfied, the judgment debtor, the owner of real or personal property subject to a judgment lien created under the judgment, or a person having a security interest in or a lien on personal property subject to a judgment lien created under the judgment may serve personally or by mail on the judgment creditor a demand in writing that the judgment creditor do one or both of the following:

(1) File an acknowledgment of satisfaction of judgment with the court.

(2) Execute, acknowledge, and deliver an acknowledgment of satisfaction of judgment to the person who made the demand.

(b) The demand shall include the following statement: "Important warning. If this judgment has been satisfied, the law requires that you comply with this demand not later than 15 days after you receive it. If a court proceeding is necessary to compel you to comply with this demand, you will be required to pay my reasonable attorney's fees in the proceeding if the court determines that the judgment has been satisfied and that you failed to comply with the demand. In addition, if the court determines that you failed without just cause to comply with this demand within the 15 days allowed, you will be liable for all damages I sustain by reason of such failure and will also forfeit one hundred dollars to me."

(c) If the judgment has been satisfied, the judgment creditor shall comply with the demand not later than 15 days after actual receipt of the demand.

(d) If the judgment creditor does not comply with the demand within the time allowed, the person making the demand may apply to the court on noticed motion for an order requiring the judgment creditor to comply with the demand. The notice of motion shall be served on the judgment creditor. Service shall be made personally or by mail. If the court determines that the judgment has been satisfied and that the judgment creditor has not complied with the demand, the court shall either (1) order the judgment creditor to comply with the demand or (2) order the court clerk to enter satisfaction of the judgment.

(e) If the judgment has been satisfied and the judgment creditor fails without just cause to comply with the demand within the time allowed, the judgment creditor is liable to the person who made the demand for all damages sustained by reason of such failure and shall also forfeit one hundred dollars ($100) to such person. Liability under this subdivision may be determined in the proceedings on the motion pursuant to subdivision (d) or in an action.

Added by Stats. 1982, Ch. 1364, Sec. 2. Operative July 1, 1983, by Sec. 3 of Ch. 1364.

Section 724.060 - Information included in acknowledgment

(a) An acknowledgment of satisfaction of judgment shall contain the following information:

(1) The title of the court.

(2) The cause and number of the action.

(3) The names and addresses of the judgment creditor, the judgment debtor, and the assignee of record if any. If an abstract of the judgment has been recorded in any county, the judgment debtor's name shall appear on the acknowledgment of satisfaction of judgment as it appears on the abstract of judgment.

(4) The date of entry of judgment and of any renewals of the judgment and where entered in the records of the court.

(5) A statement either that the judgment is satisfied in full or that the judgment creditor has accepted payment or performance other than that specified in the judgment in full satisfaction of the judgment.

(6) A statement whether an abstract of the judgment has been recorded in any county and, if so, a statement of each county where the abstract has been recorded and the book and page of the county records where the abstract has been recorded, and a notice that the acknowledgment of satisfaction of judgment (or a court clerk's certificate of satisfaction of judgment) will have to be recorded with the county recorder of each county where the abstract of judgment has been recorded in order to release the judgment lien on real property in that county.

(7) A statement whether a notice of judgment lien has been filed in the office of the Secretary of State and, if such a notice has been filed, a statement of the file number of such notice, and a notice that the acknowledgment of satisfaction of judgment (or a court clerk's certificate of satisfaction of judgment) will have to be filed in that office in order to terminate the judgment lien on personal property.

(b) The acknowledgment of satisfaction of judgment shall be made in the manner of an acknowledgment of a conveyance of real property.

(c) The acknowledgment of satisfaction of judgment shall be executed and acknowledged by one of the following:

(1) The judgment creditor.

(2) The assignee of record.

(3) The attorney for the judgment creditor or assignee of record unless a revocation of the attorney's authority is filed.

(4) The local child support agency director or his or her designee, if the local child support agency has been providing child support services pursuant to Section 17400 of the Family Code. The acknowledgment of satisfaction of judgment may be recorded by the local child support agency pursuant to Section 27282 of the Government Code.

Amended by Stats 2004 ch 339 (AB 1704),s 1, eff. 1/1/2005

Section 724.070 - Liability for conditioning acknowledgment upon performance of act or payment of amount in excess to which creditor entitled

(a) If a judgment creditor intentionally conditions delivery of an acknowledgment of satisfaction of judgment upon the performance of any act or the payment of an amount in excess of that to which the judgment creditor is entitled under the judgment, the judgment creditor is liable to the judgment debtor for all damages sustained by reason of such action or two hundred fifty dollars ($250), whichever is the greater amount.

(b) Subdivision (a) does not apply if the judgment creditor has agreed to deliver an acknowledgment of satisfaction of judgment to the judgment debtor prior to full satisfaction of the judgment in consideration for the judgment debtor's agreement either to furnish security or to execute a promissory note, or both, the principal amount of which does not exceed the amount to which the judgment creditor is entitled under the judgment.

Added by Stats. 1982, Ch. 1364, Sec. 2. Operative July 1, 1983, by Sec. 3 of Ch. 1364.

Section 724.080 - Attorney's fees

In an action or proceeding maintained pursuant to this chapter, the court shall award reasonable attorney's fees to the prevailing party.

Added by Stats. 1982, Ch. 1364, Sec. 2. Operative July 1, 1983, by Sec. 3 of Ch. 1364.

Section 724.090 - Damages

The damages recoverable pursuant to this chapter are not in derogation of any other damages or penalties to which an aggrieved person may be entitled by law.

Added by Stats. 1982, Ch. 1364, Sec. 2. Operative July 1, 1983, by Sec. 3 of Ch. 1364.

Section 724.100 - Certificate of satisfaction of judgment

(a) If satisfaction of a judgment has been entered in the register of actions, the court clerk shall issue a certificate of satisfaction of judgment upon application therefor and payment of the fee as provided in subdivision (a) of Section 70626 of the Government Code.

(b) The certificate of satisfaction of judgment shall contain the following information:

(1) The title of the court.

(2) The cause and number of the action.

(3) The names of the judgment creditor and the judgment debtor.

(4) The date of entry of judgment and of any renewals of the judgment and where entered in the records of the court.

(5) The date of entry of satisfaction of judgment and where it was entered in the register of actions.

Amended by Stats 2005 ch 75 (AB 145),s 39, eff. 7/19/2005, op. 1/1/2006

Chapter 2 - ACKNOWLEDGMENT OF PARTIAL SATISFACTION OF JUDGMENT

Section 724.110 - Demand that creditor execute and deliver acknowledgment

(a) The judgment debtor or the owner of real or personal property subject to a judgment lien created under a money judgment may serve on the judgment creditor a demand in writing that the judgment creditor execute, acknowledge, and deliver an acknowledgment of partial satisfaction of judgment to the person who made the demand. Service shall be made personally or by mail. If the judgment has been partially satisfied, the judgment creditor shall comply with the demand not later than 15 days after actual receipt of the demand.

(b) If the judgment creditor does not comply with the demand within the time allowed, the judgment debtor or the owner of the real or personal property subject to a judgment lien created under the judgment may apply to the court on noticed motion for an order requiring the judgment creditor to comply with the demand. The notice of motion shall be served on the judgment creditor. Service shall be made personally or by mail. If the court determines that the judgment has been partially satisfied and that the judgment creditor has not complied with the demand, the court shall make an order determining the amount of the partial satisfaction and may make an order requiring the judgment creditor to comply with the demand.

Added by Stats. 1982, Ch. 1364, Sec. 2. Operative July 1, 1983, by Sec. 3 of Ch. 1364.

Section 724.120 - Information included in acknowledgment

An acknowledgment of partial satisfaction of judgment shall be made in the same manner and by the same person as an acknowledgment of satisfaction of judgment and shall contain the following information:

(a) The title of the court.

(b) The cause and number of the action.

(c) The names and addresses of the judgment creditor, the judgment debtor, and the assignee of record if any. If an abstract of the judgment has been recorded in any county, the judgment debtor's name shall appear on the acknowledgment of partial satisfaction of judgment as it appears on the abstract of judgment.

(d) The date of entry of judgment and of any renewals of the judgment and where entered in the records of the court.

(e) A statement of the amount received by the judgment creditor in partial satisfaction of the judgment.

(f) A statement whether an abstract of judgment has been recorded in any county and, if so, a statement of each county where the abstract has been recorded and the book and page of the county records where the abstract has been recorded.

(g) A statement whether a notice of judgment lien has been filed in the office of the Secretary of State and, if so, the file number of the notice.

Added by Stats. 1982, Ch. 1364, Sec. 2. Operative July 1, 1983, by Sec. 3 of Ch. 1364.

Chapter 3 - ACKNOWLEDGMENT OF SATISFACTION OF MATURED INSTALLMENTS UNDER INSTALLMENT JUDGMENT

Section 724.210 - Definitions

As used in this chapter:

(a) "Installment judgment" means a money judgment under which a lien may be created on an interest in real property under Section 697.320.

(b) "Matured installments" means the sum of all of the following:

(1) All amounts and installments that have matured under an installment judgment on or before the date specified in the demand for an acknowledgment of satisfaction of matured installments under an installment judgment.

(2) The interest that has accrued on the installment judgment on the date specified in the demand.

(3) The costs that have been added to the installment judgment on or before the date specified in the demand pursuant to Chapter 5 (commencing with Section 685.010) of Division 1.

Added by Stats. 1982, Ch. 1364, Sec. 2. Operative July 1, 1983, by Sec. 3 of Ch. 1364.

Section 724.220 - Demand that judgment creditor execute and deliver acknowledgment

(a) If real property is subject to a judgment lien created under an installment judgment, the judgment debtor or the owner of real property subject to the judgment lien may serve on the judgment creditor a demand in writing that the judgment creditor execute, acknowledge, and deliver to the person who made the demand an acknowledgment of satisfaction of matured installments under an installment judgment. Service shall be made personally or by mail.

(b) The demand shall include the following statement: "Important warning. If the matured installments on this judgment have been satisfied as of date specified in this demand, the law requires that you comply with this demand not later than 15 days after you receive it. (The 'matured installments' are all amounts and installments that are due and payable on or before the date specified in this demand together with the accrued interest to that date and costs added to the judgment on or before that date.) If a court proceeding is necessary to compel you to comply with this demand, you will be required to pay my reasonable attorney's fees in the proceeding if the court determines that the matured installments have been satisfied and that you failed to comply with the demand. In addition, if the court determines that you failed without just cause to comply with this demand within the 15 days allowed, you will be liable for all damages I sustain by reason of such failure and will also forfeit one hundred dollars to me."

(c) If the matured installments have been satisfied as of the date specified in the demand, the judgment creditor shall comply with the demand not later than 15 days after actual receipt of the demand.

Added by Stats. 1982, Ch. 1364, Sec. 2. Operative July 1, 1983, by Sec. 3 of Ch. 1364.

Section 724.230 - Notice motion for order that judgment creditor comply with demand

If the judgment creditor does not comply with the demand within the time allowed, the judgment debtor or the owner of the real property subject to a judgment lien created under the installment judgment may apply to the court on noticed motion for an order requiring the judgment creditor to comply with the demand. The notice of motion shall be served on the judgment creditor. Service shall be made personally or by mail. If the court determines that the matured installments have been satisfied as of the date specified in the demand and that the judgment creditor has not complied with the demand, the court shall either (1) order the judgment creditor to comply with the demand or (2) make an order determining that the matured installments as of the date specified in the demand have been satisfied.

Added by Stats. 1982, Ch. 1364, Sec. 2. Operative July 1, 1983, by Sec. 3 of Ch. 1364.

Section 724.240 - Liability for failure to comply with demand

(a) If the matured installments under the installment judgment have been satisfied as of the date specified in the demand and the judgment creditor fails without just cause to comply with the demand within the time allowed, the judgment creditor is liable to the person who made the demand for all damages sustained by reason of such failure and shall also forfeit one hundred dollars ($100) to such person. Liability under this subdivision may be determined in the proceedings on a motion pursuant to Section 724.230 or in an action.

(b) The damages recoverable pursuant to subdivision (a) are not in derogation of any other damages or penalties to which an aggrieved person may be entitled by law.

Added by Stats. 1982, Ch. 1364, Sec. 2. Operative July 1, 1983, by Sec. 3 of Ch. 1364.

Section 724.250 - Information included in acknowledgment

(a) An acknowledgment of satisfaction of matured installments under an installment judgment shall be made in the same manner and by the same person as an acknowledgment of satisfaction of judgment and shall contain the following information:

(1) The title of the court.

(2) The cause and number of the action.

(3) The names and addresses of the judgment creditor, the judgment debtor, and the assignee of record if any. The judgment debtor's name shall appear on the acknowledgment of satisfaction of matured installments as it appears on the certified copy of the judgment that was recorded to create the judgment lien.

(4) The date of entry of the judgment and of any renewals of the judgment and where entered in the records of the court.

(5) A statement that the matured installments under the installment judgment had been satisfied as of a specified date.

(6) A statement whether a certified copy or abstract of the judgment has been recorded in any county and, if so, a statement of each county where the certified or abstract copy has been recorded and the book and page of the county records where the certified copy or abstract of the judgment has been recorded.

(b) If any amount of child or spousal support provided in a support order has been directed to be made to an officer designated by statute or by the court pursuant to Article 4 (commencing with Section 4200) of Chapter 2 of Part 2 of Division 9 of the Family Code or Chapter 4 (commencing with Section 4350) of Part 3 of Division 9 of the Family Code or any other provision of law and the directive is set forth in the certified copy or abstract of the judgment that was recorded to create the judgment lien on real property, or in a similarly recorded certified copy or abstract of an amended or supplemental order, the acknowledgment of satisfaction of matured installments under the installment judgment is not effective and does not affect the judgment lien unless the acknowledgment is executed by or approved in writing by the designated officer.

Amended by Stats. 1992, Ch. 163, Sec. 53. Effective January 1, 1993. Operative January 1, 1994, by Sec. 161 of Ch. 163.

Section 724.260 - Attorney's fees

In an action or proceeding maintained pursuant to this chapter, the court shall award reasonable attorney's fees to the prevailing party.

Added by Stats. 1982, Ch. 1364, Sec. 2.3 (Sec. 2). Operative July 1, 1983, by Sec. 3 of Ch. 1364.

Title 10 - ACTIONS IN PARTICULAR CASES

Chapter 1 - ACTIONS FOR THE FORECLOSURE OF MORTGAGES

Section 725a - Right to bring suit

The beneficiary or trustee named in a deed of trust or mortgagee named in a mortgage with power of sale upon real property or any interest therein to secure a debt or other obligation, or if there be a successor or successors in interest of such beneficiary, trustee or mortgagee, then such successor or successors in interest, shall have the right to bring suit to foreclose the same in the manner and subject to the provisions, rights and remedies relating to the foreclosure of a mortgage upon such property.

Amended by Stats. 1982, Ch. 497, Sec. 45. Operative July 1, 1983, by Sec. 185 of Ch. 497.

Section 726 - One form of action; judgment of court; decree for foreclosure

(a) There can be but one form of action for the recovery of any debt or the enforcement of any right secured by mortgage upon real property or an estate for years therein, which action shall be in accordance with the provisions of this chapter. In the action the court may, by its judgment, direct the sale of the encumbered real property or estate for years therein (or so much of the real property or estate for years as may be necessary), and the application of the proceeds of the sale to the payment of the costs of court, the expenses of levy and sale, and the amount due plaintiff, including, where the mortgage provides for the payment of attorney's fees, the sum for attorney's fees as the court shall find reasonable, not exceeding the amount named in the mortgage.

(b) The decree for the foreclosure of a mortgage or deed of trust secured by real property or estate for years therein shall declare the amount of the indebtedness or right so secured and, unless judgment for any deficiency there may be between the sale price and the amount due with costs is waived by the judgment creditor or a deficiency judgment is prohibited by Section 580b, shall determine the personal liability of any defendant for the payment of the debt secured by the mortgage or deed of trust and shall name the defendants against whom a deficiency judgment may be ordered following the proceedings prescribed in this section. In the event of waiver, or if the prohibition of Section 580b is applicable, the decree shall so declare and there shall be no judgment for a deficiency. In the event that a deficiency is not waived or prohibited and it is decreed that any defendant is personally liable for the debt, then upon application of the plaintiff filed at any time within three months of the date of the foreclosure sale and after a hearing thereon at which the court shall take evidence and at which hearing either party may present evidence as to the fair value of the real property or estate for years therein sold as of the date of sale, the court shall render a money judgment against the defendant or defendants for the amount by which the amount of the indebtedness with interest and costs of levy and sale and of action exceeds the fair value of the real property or estate for years therein sold as of the date of sale. In no event shall the amount of the judgment, exclusive of interest from the date of sale and of costs exceed the difference between the amount for which the real property or estate for years therein was sold and the entire amount of the indebtedness secured by the mortgage or deed of trust. Notice of the hearing shall be served upon all defendants who have appeared in the action and against whom a deficiency judgment is sought, or upon their attorneys of record, at least 15 days before the date set for the hearing. Upon application of any party made at least 10 days before the date set for the hearing the court shall, and upon its own motion the court at any time may, appoint one of the probate referees provided for by law to appraise the real property or estate for years therein sold as of the time of sale. The probate referee shall file the appraisal with the clerk and the appraisal is admissible in evidence. The probate referee shall take and subscribe an oath to be attached to the appraisal that the referee has truly, honestly and impartially appraised the real property or estate for years therein to the best of the referee's knowledge and ability. Any probate referee so appointed may be called and examined as a witness by any party or by the court itself. The court shall fix the compensation, in an amount as determined by the court to be reasonable, but the fees shall not exceed similar fees for similar services in the community where the services are rendered, which may be taxed and allowed in like manner as other costs.

(c) No person holding a conveyance from or under the mortgagor of real property or estate for years therein, or having a lien thereon, which conveyance or lien does not appear of record in the proper office at the time of the commencement of the action need be made a party to the action, and the judgment therein rendered, and the proceedings therein had, are as conclusive against the person holding the unrecorded conveyance or lien as if the person had been a party to the action. Notwithstanding Section 701.630, the sale of the encumbered real property or estate for years therein does not affect the interest of a person who holds a conveyance from or under the mortgagor of the real property or estate for years therein mortgaged, or has a lien thereon, if the conveyance or lien appears of record in the proper office at the time of the commencement of the action and the person holding the recorded conveyance or lien is not made a party to the action.

(d) If the real property or estate for years therein mortgaged consists of a single parcel, or two or more parcels, situated in two or more counties, the court may, in its judgment, direct the whole thereof to be sold in one of the counties, and upon these proceedings, and with like effect, as if the whole of the property were situated in that county.

(e) If a deficiency judgment is waived or prohibited, the real property or estate for years therein shall be sold as provided in Section 716.020. If a deficiency judgment is not waived or prohibited, the real property or estate for years therein shall be sold subject to the right of redemption as provided in Sections 729.010 to 729.090, inclusive.

(f) Notwithstanding this section or any other provision of law to the contrary, any person authorized by this state to make or arrange loans secured by real property or any successor in interest thereto, that originates, acquires, or purchases, in whole or in part, any loan secured directly or collaterally, in whole or in part, by a mortgage or deed of trust on real property or an estate for years therein, may bring an action for recovery of damages, including exemplary damages not to exceed 50 percent of the actual damages, against a borrower where the action is based on fraud under Section 1572 of the Civil Code and the fraudulent conduct by the borrower induced the original lender to make that loan.

(g) Subdivision (f) does not apply to loans secured by single-family, owner-occupied residential real property, when the property is actually occupied by the borrower as represented to the lender in order to obtain the loan and the loan is for an amount of one hundred fifty thousand dollars ($150,000) or less, as adjusted annually, commencing on January 1, 1987, to the Consumer Price Index as published by the United States Department of Labor.

(h) Any action maintained pursuant to subdivision (f) for damages shall not constitute a money judgment for deficiency, or a deficiency judgment within the meaning of Section 580a, 580b, or 580d of the Code of Civil Procedure.

Amended by Stats. 1992, Ch. 1095, Sec. 4. Effective January 1, 1993.

Section 726.5 - [Operative Until 1/1/2024] Rights and remedies where property environmentally impaired and borrower's obligations in default

(a) Notwithstanding subdivision (a) of Section 726 or any other provision of law, except subdivision (d) of this section, a secured lender may elect between the following where the real property security is environmentally impaired and the borrower's obligations to the secured lender are in default:

(1)
　(A) Waiver of its lien against (i) any parcel of real property security that is environmentally impaired or is an affected parcel, and (ii) all or any portion of the fixtures and personal property attached to the parcels; and
　(B) Exercise of (i) the rights and remedies of an unsecured creditor, including reduction of its claim against the borrower to judgment, and (ii) any other rights and remedies permitted by law.

(2) Exercise of (i) the rights and remedies of a creditor secured by a deed of trust or mortgage and, if applicable, a lien against fixtures or personal property attached to the real property security, and (ii) any other rights and remedies permitted by law.

(b) Before the secured lender may waive its lien against any parcel of real property security pursuant to paragraph (1) of subdivision (a) on the basis of the environmental impairment contemplated by paragraph (3) of subdivision (e), (i) the secured lender shall provide written notice of the default to the borrower, and (ii) the value of the subject real property security shall be established and its environmentally impaired status shall be confirmed by an order of a court of competent jurisdiction in an action brought by the secured lender against the borrower. The complaint for a valuation and confirmation action may include causes of action for a money judgment for all or part of the secured obligation, in which case the waiver of the secured lender's liens under paragraph (1) of subdivision (a) shall result only if and when a final money judgment is obtained against the borrower.

(c) If a secured lender elects the rights and remedies permitted by paragraph (1) of subdivision (a) and the borrower's obligations are also secured by other real property security, fixtures, or personal property, the secured lender shall first foreclose against the additional collateral to the extent required by applicable law in which case the amount of the judgment of the secured lender pursuant to paragraph (1) of subdivision (a) shall be limited to the extent Section 580a or 580d, or subdivision (b) of Section 726 apply to the foreclosures of additional real property security. The borrower may waive or modify the foreclosure requirements of this subdivision provided that the waiver or modification is in writing and signed by the borrower after default.

(d) Subdivision (a) shall be inapplicable if all of the following are true:

(1) The release or threatened release was not knowingly or negligently caused or contributed to, or knowingly or willfully permitted or acquiesced to, by any of the following:

(A) The borrower or any related party.

(B) Any affiliate or agent of the borrower or any related party.

(2) In conjunction with the making, renewal, or modification of the loan, extension of credit, guaranty, or other obligation secured by the real property security, neither the borrower, any related party, nor any affiliate or agent of either the borrower or any related party had actual knowledge or notice of the release or threatened release, or if a person had knowledge or notice of the release or threatened release, the borrower made written disclosure thereof to the secured lender after the secured lender's written request for information concerning the environmental condition of the real property security, or the secured lender otherwise obtained actual knowledge thereof, prior to the making, renewal, or modification of the obligation.

(e) For purposes of this section:

(1) "Affected parcel" means any portion of a parcel of real property security that is (A) contiguous to the environmentally impaired parcel, even if separated by roads, streets, utility easements, or railroad rights-of-way, (B) part of an approved or proposed subdivision within the meaning of Section 66424 of the Government Code, of which the environmentally impaired parcel is also a part, or (C) within 2,000 feet of the environmentally impaired parcel.

(2) "Borrower" means the trustor under a deed of trust, or a mortgagor under a mortgage, where the deed of trust or mortgage encumbers real property security and secures the performance of the trustor or mortgagor under a loan, extension of credit, guaranty, or other obligation. The term includes any successor-in-interest of the trustor or mortgagor to the real property security before the deed of trust or mortgage has been discharged, reconveyed, or foreclosed upon.

(3) "Environmentally impaired" means that the estimated costs to clean up and remediate a past or present release or threatened release of any hazardous substance into, onto, beneath, or from the real property security, not disclosed in writing to, or otherwise actually known by, the secured lender prior to the making of the loan or extension of credit secured by the real property security, exceeds 25 percent of the higher of the aggregate fair market value of all security for the loan or extension of credit (A) at the time of the making of the loan or extension of credit, or (B) at the time of the discovery of the release or threatened release by the secured lender. For the purposes of this definition, the estimated cost to clean up and remediate the contamination caused by the release or threatened release shall include only those costs that would be incurred reasonably and in good faith, and fair market value shall be determined without giving consideration to the release or threatened release, and shall be exclusive of the amount of all liens and encumbrances against the security that are senior in priority to the lien of the secured lender. Notwithstanding the foregoing, the real property security for any loan or extension of credit secured by a single parcel of real property which is included in the National Priorities List pursuant to Section 9605 of Title 42 of the United States Code, or in any list published by the Department of Toxic Substances Control pursuant to subdivision (b) of Section 25356 of the Health and Safety Code, shall be deemed to be environmentally impaired.

(4) "Hazardous substance" means any of the following:

(A) Any "hazardous substance" as defined in subdivision (h) of Section 25281 of the Health and Safety Code.

(B) Any "waste" as defined in subdivision (d) of Section 13050 of the Water Code.

(C) Petroleum, including crude oil or any fraction thereof, natural gas, natural gas liquids, liquefied natural gas, or synthetic gas usable for fuel, or any mixture thereof.

(5) "Real property security" means any real property and improvements, other than a separate interest and any related interest in the common area of a residential common interest development, as the terms "separate interest," "common area," and "common interest development" are defined in Sections 4095, 4100, and 4185 of the Civil Code, or real property which contains only 1 to 15 dwelling units, which in either case (A) is solely used (i) for residential purposes, or (ii) if reasonably contemplated by the parties to the deed of trust or mortgage, for residential purposes as well as limited agricultural or commercial purposes incidental thereto, and (B) is the subject of an issued certificate of occupancy unless the dwelling is to be owned and occupied by the borrower.

(6) "Related party" means any person who shares an ownership interest with the borrower in the real property security, or is a partner or joint venturer with the borrower in a partnership or joint venture, the business of which includes the acquisition, development, use, lease, or sale of the real property security.

(7) "Release" means any spilling, leaking, pumping, pouring, emitting, emptying, discharging, injecting, escaping, leaching, dumping, or disposing into the environment, including continuing migration, of hazardous substances into, onto, or through soil, surface water, or groundwater. The term does not include actions directly relating to the incorporation in a lawful manner of building materials into a permanent improvement to the real property security.

(8) "Secured lender" means the beneficiary under a deed of trust against the real property security, or the mortgagee under a mortgage against the real property security, and any successor-in-interest of the beneficiary or mortgagee to the deed of trust or mortgage.

(f) This section shall not be construed to invalidate or otherwise affect in any manner any rights or obligations arising under contract in connection with a loan or extension of credit, including, without limitation, provisions limiting recourse.

(g) This section shall only apply to loans, extensions of credit, guaranties, or other obligations secured by real property security made, renewed, or modified on or after January 1, 1992.

Amended by Stats 2012 ch 181 (AB 806),s 45, eff. 1/1/2013, op. 1/1/2014.

Amended by Stats 2002 ch 999 (AB 2481),s 4, eff. 1/1/2003.

Previously Amended July 6, 1999 (Bill Number: SB 328) (Chapter 60).

This section is set out more than once due to postponed, multiple, or conflicting amendments.

Section 726.5 - [Operative 1/1/2024] Rights and remedies where property environmentally impaired and borrower's obligations in default

(a)Notwithstanding subdivision (a) of Section 726 or any other provision of law, except subdivision (d) of this section, a secured lender may elect between the following where the real property security is environmentally impaired and the borrower's obligations to the secured lender are in default:

(1)

(A) Waiver of its lien against (i) any parcel of real property security that is environmentally impaired or is an affected parcel, and (ii) all or any portion of the fixtures and personal property attached to the parcels; and

(B) Exercise of (i) the rights and remedies of an unsecured creditor, including reduction of its claim against the borrower to judgment, and (ii) any other rights and remedies permitted by law.

(2) Exercise of (i) the rights and remedies of a creditor secured by a deed of trust or mortgage and, if applicable, a lien against fixtures or personal property attached to the real property security, and (ii) any other rights and remedies permitted by law.

(b) Before the secured lender may waive its lien against any parcel of real property security pursuant to paragraph (1) of subdivision (a) on the basis of the environmental impairment contemplated by paragraph (3) of subdivision (e), (i) the secured lender shall provide written notice of the default to the borrower, and (ii) the value of the subject real property security shall be established and its environmentally impaired status shall be confirmed by an order of a court of competent jurisdiction in an action brought by the secured lender against the borrower. The complaint for a valuation and confirmation action may include causes of action for a money judgment for all or part of the secured obligation, in which case the waiver of the secured lender's liens under paragraph (1) of subdivision (a) shall result only if and when a final money judgment is obtained against the borrower.

(c) If a secured lender elects the rights and remedies permitted by paragraph (1) of subdivision (a) and the borrower's obligations are also secured by other real property security, fixtures, or personal property, the secured lender shall first foreclose against the additional collateral to the extent required by applicable law in which case the amount of the judgment of the secured lender pursuant to paragraph (1) of subdivision (a) shall be limited to the extent Section 580a or 580d, or subdivision (b) of Section 726 apply to the foreclosures of additional real property security. The borrower may waive or modify the foreclosure requirements of this subdivision provided that the waiver or modification is in writing and signed by the borrower after default.

(d) Subdivision (a) shall be inapplicable if all of the following are true:

(1) The release or threatened release was not knowingly or negligently caused or contributed to, or knowingly or willfully permitted or acquiesced to, by any of the following:

(A) The borrower or any related party.

(B) Any affiliate or agent of the borrower or any related party.

(2) In conjunction with the making, renewal, or modification of the loan, extension of credit, guaranty, or other obligation secured by the real property security, neither the borrower, any related party, nor any affiliate or agent of either the borrower or any related party had actual knowledge or notice of the release or threatened release, or if a person had knowledge or notice of the release or threatened release, the borrower made written disclosure thereof to the secured lender after the secured lender's written request for information concerning the environmental condition of the real property security, or the secured lender otherwise obtained actual knowledge thereof, prior to the making, renewal, or modification of the obligation.

(e) For purposes of this section:

(1) "Affected parcel" means any portion of a parcel of real property security that is (A) contiguous to the environmentally impaired parcel, even if separated by roads, streets, utility easements, or railroad rights-of-way, (B) part of an approved or proposed subdivision within the meaning of Section 66424 of the Government Code, of which the environmentally impaired parcel is also a part, or (C) within 2,000 feet of the environmentally impaired parcel.

(2) "Borrower" means the trustor under a deed of trust, or a mortgagor under a mortgage, where the deed of trust or mortgage encumbers real property security and secures the performance of the trustor or mortgagor under a loan, extension of credit, guaranty, or other obligation. The term includes any successor-in-interest of the trustor or mortgagor to the real property security before the deed of trust or mortgage has been discharged, reconveyed, or foreclosed upon.

(3) "Environmentally impaired" means that the estimated costs to clean up and remediate a past or present release or threatened release of any hazardous substance into, onto, beneath, or from the real property security, not disclosed in writing to, or otherwise actually known by, the secured lender prior to the making of the loan or extension of credit secured by the real property security, exceeds 25 percent of the higher of the aggregate fair market value of all security for the loan or extension of credit (A) at the time of the making of the loan or extension of credit, or (B) at the time of the discovery of the release or threatened release by the secured lender. For purposes of this definition, the estimated cost to clean up and remediate the contamination caused by the release or threatened release shall include only those costs that would be incurred reasonably and in good faith, and fair market value shall be determined without giving consideration to the release or threatened release, and shall be exclusive of the amount of all liens and encumbrances against the security that are senior in priority to the lien of the secured lender. Notwithstanding the foregoing, the real property security for any loan or extension of credit secured by a single parcel of real property which is included in the National Priorities List pursuant to Section 9605 of Title 42 of the United States Code, or in any list published by the Department of Toxic Substances Control pursuant to Section 78760 of the Health and Safety Code, shall be deemed to be environmentally impaired.

(4) "Hazardous substance" means any of the following:

(A) Any "hazardous substance" as defined in subdivision (h) of Section 25281 of the Health and Safety Code.

(B) Any "waste" as defined in subdivision (d) of Section 13050 of the Water Code.

(C) Petroleum, including crude oil or any fraction thereof, natural gas, natural gas liquids, liquefied natural gas, or synthetic gas usable for fuel, or any mixture thereof.

(5) "Real property security" means any real property and improvements, other than a separate interest and any related interest in the common area of a residential common interest development, as the terms "separate interest," "common area," and "common interest development" are defined in Sections 4095, 4100, and 4185 of the Civil Code, or real property which contains only 1 to 15 dwelling units, which in either case (A) is solely used (i) for residential purposes, or (ii) if reasonably contemplated by the parties to the deed of trust or mortgage, for residential purposes as well as limited agricultural or commercial purposes incidental thereto, and (B) is the subject of an issued certificate of occupancy unless the dwelling is to be owned and occupied by the borrower.

(6) "Related party" means any person who shares an ownership interest with the borrower in the real property security, or is a partner or joint venturer with the borrower in a partnership or joint venture, the business of which includes the acquisition, development, use, lease, or sale of the real property security.

(7) "Release" means any spilling, leaking, pumping, pouring, emitting, emptying, discharging, injecting, escaping, leaching, dumping, or disposing into the environment, including continuing migration, of hazardous substances into, onto, or through soil, surface water, or groundwater. The term does not include actions directly relating to the incorporation in a lawful manner of building materials into a permanent improvement to the real property security.

(8) "Secured lender" means the beneficiary under a deed of trust against the real property security, or the mortgagee under a mortgage against the real property security, and any successor-in-interest of the beneficiary or mortgagee to the deed of trust or mortgage.

(f) This section shall not be construed to invalidate or otherwise affect in any manner any rights or obligations arising under contract in connection with a loan or extension of credit, including, without limitation, provisions limiting recourse.

(g) This section shall only apply to loans, extensions of credit, guaranties, or other obligations secured by real property security made, renewed, or modified on or after January 1, 1992.

Amended by Stats 2022 ch 258 (AB 2327),s 8, eff. 1/1/2023, op. 1/1/2024.

Amended by Stats 2012 ch 181 (AB 806),s 45, eff. 1/1/2013, op. 1/1/2014.
Amended by Stats 2002 ch 999 (AB 2481),s 4, eff. 1/1/2003.
Previously Amended July 6, 1999 (Bill Number: SB 328) (Chapter 60).
This section is set out more than once due to postponed, multiple, or conflicting amendments.

Section 727 - Surplus money remaining after payment of amount due
If there be surplus money remaining, after payment of the amount due on the mortgage, lien, or incumbrance, with costs, the Court may cause the same to be paid to the person entitled to it, and in the meantime may direct it to be deposited in Court.
Enacted 1872.

Section 728 - Sale of property in portions
If the debt for which the mortgage, lien, or incumbrance is held is not all due, so soon as sufficient of the property has been sold to pay the amount due, with costs, the sale must cease; and afterwards, as often as more becomes due, for principal or interest, the Court may, on motion, order more to be sold. But if the property cannot be sold in portions, without injury to the parties, the whole may be ordered to be sold in the first instance, and the entire debt and costs paid, there being a rebate of interest where such rebate is proper.
Enacted 1872.

Section 729.010 - Sale of property subject to right of redemption
(a) If the decree of foreclosure of a mortgage or deed of trust on real property pursuant to Section 726 determines that a deficiency judgment may be ordered against the defendant, the real property (other than a leasehold estate with an unexpired term of less than two years at the time of levy) shall be sold subject to the right of redemption.
(b) If the property is to be sold subject to the right of redemption, the sale is governed by Section 716.020, except that:
(1) The notice of sale of the property shall state that the property will be sold subject to the right of redemption and shall state the amount of the secured indebtedness with interest and costs.
(2) Notice of sale may be given upon entry of the judgment for sale of the property and the provision of Section 701.545 delaying notice of sale does not apply.
(3) Notice of sale may be given to persons having liens on the property upon entry of the judgment for sale of the property and the provision of subdivision (h) of Section 701.540 delaying such notice does not apply.
Added by Stats. 1982, Ch. 497, Sec. 48. Operative July 1, 1983, by Sec. 185 of Ch. 497.

Section 729.020 - Property redeemed by judgment debtor or successor
Property sold subject to the right of redemption may be redeemed only by the judgment debtor or the judgment debtor's successor in interest. For the purpose of this article, the purchaser of the property at the foreclosure sale is not a successor in interest.
Added by Stats. 1982, Ch. 497, Sec. 49. Operative July 1, 1983, by Sec. 185 of Ch. 497.

Section 729.030 - End of redemption period
The redemption period during which property may be redeemed from a foreclosure sale under this chapter ends:
(a) Three months after the date of sale if the proceeds of the sale are sufficient to satisfy the secured indebtedness with interest and costs of action and of sale.
(b) One year after the date of sale if the proceeds of the sale are not sufficient to satisfy the secured indebtedness with interest and costs of action and of sale.
Added by Stats. 1982, Ch. 497, Sec. 50. Operative July 1, 1983, by Sec. 185 of Ch. 497.

Section 729.035 - Sale of separate interest in common interest development subject to redemption
Notwithstanding any provision of law to the contrary, the sale of a separate interest in a common interest development is subject to the right of redemption within 90 days after the sale if the sale arises from a foreclosure by the association of a common interest development pursuant to Sections 5700, 5710, and 5735 of the Civil Code, subject to the conditions of Sections 5705, 5715, and 5720 of the Civil Code.
Amended by Stats 2012 ch 181 (AB 806),s 46, eff. 1/1/2013, op. 1/1/2014.
Added by Stats 2005 ch 452 (SB 137),s 8, eff. 1/1/2006.

Section 729.040 - Certificate sale
(a) Notwithstanding Section 701.660, when the purchaser of an interest in real property sold subject to the right of redemption pays the amount due, the levying officer conducting the sale shall execute and deliver a certificate of sale to the purchaser and record a duplicate of the certificate of sale in the office of the county recorder.
(b) The certificate of sale shall contain either:
(1) In the case of a judicial foreclosure, the information required by Section 701.670.
(2) In the case of a nonjudicial foreclosure, all of the information required by subdivisions (c), (d), and (e) of Section 701.670.
(c) In addition to the information required by subdivision (b), the certificate of sale shall also contain the following:
(1) The price paid for each distinct lot or parcel of real property sold subject to the right of redemption.
(2) The total price paid.
(3) A statement that the property is subject to the right of redemption, indicating the applicable redemption period.
Amended by Stats 2006 ch 575 (AB 2624),s 6, eff. 1/1/2007.

Section 729.050 - Service of notice of right of redemption
If property is sold subject to the right of redemption, promptly after the sale the levying officer or trustee who conducted the sale shall serve notice of the right of redemption on the judgment debtor. Service shall be made personally or by mail. The notice of the right of redemption shall indicate the applicable redemption period.
Amended by Stats 2006 ch 575 (AB 2624),s 7, eff. 1/1/2007.

Section 729.060 - Deposit of redemption price
(a) A person who seeks to redeem the property shall deposit the redemption price with the levying officer who conducted the sale before the expiration of the redemption period. If a successor in interest to the judgment debtor seeks to redeem the property, the successor in interest shall, at the time the redemption price is deposited, file with the levying officer either (1) a certified copy of a recorded conveyance or (2) a copy of an assignment or any other evidence of the interest verified by an affidavit of the successor in interest or of a subscribing witness thereto.
(b) The redemption price is the total of the following amounts, less any offset allowed under subdivision (c).
(1) The purchase price at the sale.
(2) The amount of any assessments or taxes and reasonable amounts for fire insurance, maintenance, upkeep, and repair of improvements on the property.
(3) Any amount paid by the purchaser on a prior obligation secured by the property to the extent that the payment was necessary for the protection of the purchaser's interest.
(4) Interest on the amounts described in paragraphs (1), (2), and (3) at the rate of interest on money judgments from the time such amount was paid until the date the deposit is made.
(5) If the purchaser at the sale has any liens subordinate to the lien under which the property was sold, the amount of the purchaser's lien, plus interest at the rate of interest on money judgments from the date of the sale until the date the deposit is made.

(c) Rents and profits from the property paid to the purchaser or the value of the use and occupation of the property to the purchaser may be offset against the amounts described in subdivision (b).
Amended by Stats. 1984, Ch. 538, Sec. 32.5.

Section 729.070 - Petition for court order determining redemption price or if person entitled to redeem
(a) If the purchaser and the person seeking to redeem the property disagree on the redemption price or as to whether the person is entitled to redeem the property, or if the purchaser refuses the tender of the redemption price pursuant to Section 729.080, the person seeking to redeem may file a petition with the court for an order determining the redemption price or whether the person is entitled to redeem the property. The petition shall be filed before the expiration of the redemption period. At the time the petition is filed, the petitioner shall deposit the undisputed amount of the redemption price with the levying officer, if deposit has not previously been made, and give written notice to the levying officer or trustee of the filing of the petition.
(b) The petition shall be in writing and shall include the following statements:
(1) The amounts demanded to which the person seeking to redeem objects and the reasons for the objection.
(2) Any amounts offset to which the purchaser objects and the justification for the offset.
(3) The status of the petitioner that qualifies the petitioner to redeem the property. A copy of the papers required by subdivision (a) of Section 729.060 shall be filed with the petition.
(c) The hearing on the petition shall be held not later than 20 days after the date the petition was filed unless continued by the court for good cause.
(d) Not less than 10 days before the hearing, the person seeking to redeem the property shall personally serve on the purchaser a copy of the petition together with a notice of the time and place of the hearing.
(e) At the hearing on the petition, the person seeking to redeem the property has the burden of proof.
(f) At the conclusion of the hearing, the court shall determine by order the amount required to redeem the property. The determination shall be made upon affidavit or evidence satisfactory to the court.
(g) If an amount in addition to that deposited with the levying officer is required to redeem the property, the person seeking to redeem shall, within 10 days after the issuance of the order, pay the additional amount to the levying officer.
Amended by Stats 2006 ch 575 (AB 2624),s 8, eff. 1/1/2007.

Section 729.080 - Execution and delivery of certificate of sale; certificate of redemption
(a) If the redemption price is not deposited pursuant to Section 729.060 before the expiration of the redemption period, or if no additional deposit is made pursuant to subdivision (g) of Section 729.070 before the expiration of the time provided, the levying officer who conducted the sale shall promptly execute and deliver to the purchaser a deed of sale that complies with the requirements of Section 701.670, or the nonjudicial foreclosure trustee pursuant to Section 729.035 shall deliver an executed trustee's deed and comply with the requirements of Section 2924j of the Civil Code.
(b) If the person seeking to redeem the property deposits the redemption price pursuant to Section 729.060 or 729.070 during the redemption period, the levying officer shall tender the deposit to the purchaser. If the purchaser accepts the tender or if the redemption price determined by court order is tendered, the levying officer or trustee shall promptly execute and deliver a certificate of redemption to the person seeking to redeem and shall immediately record a duplicate of the certificate in the office of the recorder of the county where the property is located.
(c) Tender of the redemption price determined by court order or agreed upon by the purchaser and the person seeking to redeem the property is equivalent to payment. If the tender is refused, the levying officer shall deposit the amount tendered with the county treasurer of the county where the property is located, payable to the order of the purchaser. If the amount deposited is not claimed by the purchaser, or the legal representative of the purchaser, within five years after the deposit is made, by making application to the treasurer or other official designated by the county, it shall be paid into the general fund of the county.
(d) Except as provided in subdivision (e), upon redemption the effect of the sale is terminated and the person who redeemed the property is restored to the estate therein sold at the sale.
(e) Liens extinguished by the sale, as provided in Section 701.630, do not reattach to the property after redemption, and the property that was subject to the extinguished lien may not be applied to the satisfaction of the claim or judgment under which the lien was created.
Amended by Stats 2006 ch 575 (AB 2624),s 9, eff. 1/1/2007.

Section 729.090 - Rents or profits from property
(a) From the time of the sale until a redemption, the purchaser is entitled to receive from the person in possession the rents and profits from the property or the value of the use and occupation of the property.
(b) Notwithstanding subdivision (a), the purchaser is liable to the person who redeems for any rents or profits that have been received by the purchaser pursuant to subdivision (a).
(c) The purchaser, from the time of sale until redemption, is entitled to enter the property during reasonable hours to repair and maintain the premises and is entitled to an order restraining waste on the property from the court. Such order may be granted with or without notice in the discretion of the court.
Added by Stats. 1982, Ch. 497, Sec. 56. Operative July 1, 1983, by Sec. 185 of Ch. 497.

Section 730 - Attorney's fees
In all cases of foreclosure of mortgage the attorney's fee shall be fixed by the court in which the proceedings are had, any stipulation in the mortgage to the contrary notwithstanding.
Added by Stats. 1953, Ch. 52.

Section 730.5 - Inapplicability to security interest in personal property
Except as otherwise provided by Section 9604 of the Commercial Code, none of the provisions of this chapter or of Section 580a, 580b, 580c, or 580d applies to any security interest in personal property or fixtures governed by the Commercial Code.
EFFECTIVE 7/1/2001. Amended October 10, 1999 (Bill Number: SB 45) (Chapter 991).

Chapter 2 - ACTIONS FOR NUISANCE, WASTE, AND WILLFUL TRESPASS, IN CERTAIN CASES, ON REAL PROPERTY

Section 731 - Action by person whose property affected; civil action in name of people of state
An action may be brought by any person whose property is injuriously affected, or whose personal enjoyment is lessened by a nuisance, as defined in Section 3479 of the Civil Code, and by the judgment in that action the nuisance may be enjoined or abated as well as damages recovered therefor. A civil action may be brought in the name of the people of the State of California to abate a public nuisance, as defined in Section 3480 of the Civil Code, by the district attorney or county counsel of any county in which the nuisance exists, or by the city attorney of any town or city in which the nuisance exists. Each of those officers shall have concurrent right to bring an action for a public nuisance existing within a town or city. The district attorney, county counsel, or city attorney of any county or city in which the nuisance exists shall bring an action whenever directed by the board of supervisors of the county, or whenever directed by the legislative authority of the town or city.
Amended by Stats 2010 ch 570 (AB 1502),s 2, eff. 1/1/2011.

Section 731a - Zones or districts wherein manufacturing or commercial or airport uses permitted

Whenever any city, city and county, or county shall have established zones or districts under authority of law wherein certain manufacturing or commercial or airport uses are expressly permitted, except in an action to abate a public nuisance brought in the name of the people of the State of California, no person or persons, firm or corporation shall be enjoined or restrained by the injunctive process from the reasonable and necessary operation in any such industrial or commercial zone or airport of any use expressly permitted therein, nor shall such use be deemed a nuisance without evidence of the employment of unnecessary and injurious methods of operation. Nothing in this act shall be deemed to apply to the regulation and working hours of canneries, fertilizing plants, refineries and other similar establishments whose operation produce offensive odors.

Amended by Stats. 1959, Ch. 795.

Section 731b - Rebuttable presumption that airport operation not nuisance

In any action or proceeding to abate the use of an airport or an airpark, proof that the airport or airpark has been in existence for three years constitutes a rebuttable presumption which shall be prima facie evidence that the operation of the airport or airpark does not constitute a nuisance.

Added by Stats. 1953, Ch. 52.

Section 731c - Secondary recovery operations causing injury to oil or gas formations or wells

Injury to formations bearing oil or gas or to oil or gas wells caused by the subsurface migration of any substance as a result of secondary recovery operations for oil or gas conducted in accordance with good oilfield practices shall not be grounds for enjoining the secondary recovery operations if an undertaking is given for the payment of any compensable damages to which the owners of interests in the formations or wells may be entitled resulting from the injury. Any benefit to the injured property from the secondary recovery operation shall be considered in mitigation of damages for the injury.

Amended by Stats. 1982, Ch. 517, Sec. 154.

Section 731.5 - Unlawful closure of public trail

Whenever any person unlawfully closes any public trail, any person who uses such trail or would use such trail, and any association, corporation or other entity whose membership as a whole is adversely affected by such closure may bring an action to enjoin such closure.

The prevailing party in such action shall be entitled to recover reasonable attorney's fees, in addition to court costs.

As used in this section, a public trail is any trail to which the public in general has a right of access, which right is established pursuant to a recorded document conveying to a political corporation or governmental agency, specifying the nature of such public trail, specifically describing the location thereof, and naming the record owners of the real property over which such trail exists if created by a license, permit or easement. It includes, but is not limited to, pedestrian, equestrian, and boating trails, but does not include any public street, road, or highway.

Added by Stats. 1979, Ch. 682.

Section 732 - Action by person aggrieved by waste

If a guardian, conservator, tenant for life or years, joint tenant, or tenant in common of real property, commit waste thereon, any person aggrieved by the waste may bring an action against him therefor, in which action there may be judgment for treble damages.

Amended by Stats. 1979, Ch. 730.

Section 733 - Injuries to trees or timber

Any person who cuts down or carries off any wood or underwood, tree, or timber, or girdles or otherwise injures any tree or timber on the land of another person, or on the street or highway in front of any person's house, village, or city lot, or cultivated grounds; or on the commons or public grounds of any city or town, or on the street or highway in front thereof, without lawful authority, is liable to the owner of such land, or to such city or town, for treble the amount of damages which may be assessed therefor, in a civil action, in any Court having jurisdiction.

Enacted 1872.

Section 734 - Recovery of just value of timber taken

Nothing in the last section authorizes the recovery of more than the just value of the timber taken from uncultivated woodland for the repair of a public highway or bridge upon the land, or adjoining it.

Enacted 1872.

Section 735 - Damages for forcible or unlawful entry or detention of building or cultivated property

If a person recover damages for a forcible or unlawful entry in or upon, or detention of any building or any cultivated real property, judgment may be entered for three times the amount at which the actual damages are assessed.

Enacted 1872.

Section 736 - Action by secured lender for breach of environmental provision by borrower

(a) Notwithstanding any other provision of law, a secured lender may bring an action for breach of contract against a borrower for breach of any environmental provision made by the borrower relating to the real property security, for the recovery of damages, and for the enforcement of the environmental provision, and that action or failure to foreclose first against collateral shall not constitute an action within the meaning of subdivision (a) of Section 726, or constitute a money judgment for a deficiency or a deficiency judgment within the meaning of Section 580a, 580b, or 580d, or subdivision (b) of Section 726. No injunction for the enforcement of an environmental provision may be issued after (1) the obligation secured by the real property security has been fully satisfied, or (2) all of the borrower's rights, title, and interest in and to the real property security has been transferred in a bona fide transaction to an unaffiliated third party for fair value.

(b) The damages a secured lender may recover pursuant to subdivision (a) shall be limited to reimbursement or indemnification of the following:

(1) If not pursuant to an order of any federal, state, or local governmental agency relating to the cleanup, remediation, or other response action required by applicable law, those costs relating to a reasonable and good faith cleanup, remediation, or other response action concerning a release or threatened release of hazardous substances which is anticipated by the environmental provision.

(2) If pursuant to an order of any federal, state, or local governmental agency relating to the cleanup, remediation, or other response action required by applicable law which is anticipated by the environmental provision, all amounts reasonably advanced in good faith by the secured lender in connection therewith, provided that the secured lender negotiated, or attempted to negotiate, in good faith to minimize the amounts it was required to advance under the order.

(3) Indemnification against all liabilities of the secured lender to any third party relating to the breach and not arising from acts, omissions, or other conduct which occur after the borrower is no longer an owner or operator of the real property security, and provided the secured lender is not responsible for the environmentally impaired condition of the real property security in accordance with the standards set forth in subdivision (d) of Section 726.5. For purposes of this paragraph, the term "owner or operator" means those persons described in Section 101(20)(A)(20)(A) of the Comprehensive Environmental Response, Compensation, and Liability Act of 1980, as amended (42 U.S.C. Sec. 9601, et seq.).

(4) Attorneys' fees and costs incurred by the secured lender relating to the breach. The damages a secured lender may recover pursuant to subdivision (a) shall not include (i) any part of the principal amount or accrued interest of the secured obligation, except for any amounts advanced by the secured lender to cure or mitigate the breach of the environmental provision that are added to the principal amount, and contractual interest thereon, or (ii) amounts which relate to a release which was knowingly permitted, caused, or contributed to by the secured lender or any affiliate or agent of the secured lender.

(c) A secured lender may not recover damages against a borrower pursuant to subdivision (a) for amounts advanced or obligations incurred for the cleanup or other remediation of real property security, and related attorneys' fees and costs, if all of the following are true:

(1) The original principal amount of, or commitment for, the loan or other obligation secured by the real property security did not exceed two hundred thousand dollars ($200,000).

(2) In conjunction with the secured lender's acceptance of the environmental provision, the secured lender agreed in writing to accept the real property security on the basis of a completed environmental site assessment and other relevant information from the borrower.

(3) The borrower did not permit, cause, or contribute to the release or threatened release.

(4) The deed of trust or mortgage covering the real property security has not been discharged, reconveyed, or foreclosed upon.

(d) This section is not intended to establish, abrogate, modify, limit, or otherwise affect any cause of action other than that provided by subdivision (a) that a secured lender may have against a borrower under an environmental provision.

(e) This section shall apply only to environmental provisions contracted in conjunction with loans, extensions of credit, guaranties, or other obligations made, renewed, or modified on or after January 1, 1992. Notwithstanding the foregoing, this section shall not be construed to validate, invalidate, or otherwise affect in any manner the rights and obligations of the parties to, or the enforcement of, environmental provisions contracted before January 1, 1992.

(f) For purposes of this section:

(1) "Borrower" means the trustor under a deed of trust, or a mortgagor under a mortgage, where the deed of trust or mortgage encumbers real property security and secures the performance of the trustor or mortgagor under a loan, extension of credit, guaranty, or other obligation. The term includes any successor-in-interest of the trustor or mortgagor to the real property security before the deed of trust or mortgage has been discharged, reconveyed, or foreclosed upon.

(2) "Environmental provision" means any written representation, warranty, indemnity, promise, or covenant relating to the existence, location, nature, use, generation, manufacture, storage, disposal, handling, or past, present, or future release or threatened release, of any hazardous substance into, onto, beneath, or from the real property security, or to past, present, or future compliance with any law relating thereto, made by a borrower in conjunction with the making, renewal, or modification of a loan, extension of credit, guaranty, or other obligation involving the borrower, whether or not the representation, warranty, indemnity, promise, or covenant is or was contained in or secured by the deed of trust or mortgage, and whether or not the deed of trust or mortgage has been discharged, reconveyed, or foreclosed upon.

(3) "Hazardous substance" means any of the following:

(A) Any "hazardous substance" as defined in subdivision (h) of Section 25281 of the Health and Safety Code.

(B) Any "waste" as defined in subdivision (d) of Section 13050 of the Water Code.

(C) Petroleum, including crude oil or any fraction thereof, natural gas, natural gas liquids, liquefied natural gas, or synthetic gas usable for fuel, or any mixture thereof.

(4) "Real property security" means any real property and improvements, other than a separate interest and any related interest in the common area of a residential common interest development, as the terms "separate interest," "common area," and "common interest development" are defined in Sections 4095, 4100, and 4185 of the Civil Code, or real property which contains only 1 to 15 dwelling units, which in either case (A) is solely used (i) for residential purposes, or (ii) if reasonably contemplated by the parties to the deed of trust or mortgage, for residential purposes as well as limited agricultural or commercial purposes incidental thereto, and (B) is the subject of an issued certificate of occupancy unless the dwelling is to be owned and occupied by the borrower.

(5) "Release" means any spilling, leaking, pumping, pouring, emitting, emptying, discharging, injecting, escaping, leaching, dumping, or disposing into the environment, including continuing migration, of hazardous substances into, onto, or through soil, surface water, or groundwater. The term does not include actions directly relating to the incorporation in a lawful manner of building materials into a permanent improvement to the real property security.

(6) "Secured lender" means the beneficiary under a deed of trust against the real property security, or the mortgagee under a mortgage against the real property security, and any successor-in-interest of the beneficiary or mortgagee to the deed of trust or mortgage.

Amended by Stats 2012 ch 181 (AB 806),s 47, eff. 1/1/2013, op. 1/1/2014.
Amended by Stats 2002 ch 999 (AB 2481),s 5, eff. 1/1/2003.
Previously Amended July 6, 1999 (Bill Number: SB 328) (Chapter 60).

Chapter 3 - ACTIONS FOR THE RECOVERY OF REAL PROPERTY, AND OTHER PROVISIONS RELATING TO ACTIONS CONCERNING REAL PROPERTY

Section 740 - Damages in action for recovery where right to recover terminated during pendency of action

In an action for the recovery of property, where the plaintiff shows a right to recover at the time the action was commenced, but it appears that his right has terminated during the pendency of the action, the verdict and judgment must be according to the fact, and the plaintiff may recover damages for withholding the property.
Amended by Stats. 1907, Ch. 363.

Section 741 - Improvements made as good faith improver

(a) As used in this section, "good faith improver" has the meaning given that term by Section 871.1.

(b) When damages are claimed for withholding the property recovered, and improvements have been made on the property by a defendant or his predecessor in interest as a good faith improver, the amount by which such improvements enhance the value of the land must be allowed as a setoff against such damages.
Amended by Stats. 1968, Ch. 150.

Section 742 - Order allowing right to enter and make survey or measurement

The Court in which an action is pending for the recovery of real property, or for damages for an injury thereto, or a Judge thereof may, on motion, upon notice by either party for good cause shown, grant an order allowing to such party the right to enter upon the property and make survey and measurement thereof, and of any tunnels, shafts, or drifts therein, for the purpose of the action, even though entry for such purpose has to be made through other lands belonging to parties to the action.
Amended by Code Amendments 1880, Ch. 22.

Section 743 - Unnecessary injury done by surveyors and assistants

The order must describe the property, and a copy thereof must be served on the owner or occupant; and thereupon such party may enter upon the property, with necessary surveyors and assistants, and make such survey and measurement; but if any unnecessary injury be done to the property he is liable therefor.
Enacted 1872.

Section 744 - Mortgage not deemed conveyance enabling owner to recover possession without foreclosure and sale

A mortgage of real property shall not be deemed a conveyance, whatever its terms, so as to enable the owner of the mortgage to recover possession of the real property without a foreclosure and sale.
Enacted 1872.

Section 745 - Injunction restraining injury to property by party in possession

The court may, by injunction, on good cause shown, restrain the party in possession from doing any act to the injury of real property:

(a) During the foreclosure of a mortgage on the property.

(b) After levy on the property and before the possession of the property is transferred pursuant to sale under the levy.
Amended by Stats. 1982, Ch. 497, Sec. 57. Operative July 1, 1983, by Sec. 185 of Ch. 497.

Section 746 - Recovery of damages by purchaser for injury caused by person after levy and before possession
When real property has been sold pursuant to a levy, the purchaser of the property, or any person who has succeeded to the interest of the purchaser, may recover damages from the person causing the injury for injury to the property after levy and before possession is delivered to the purchaser or the person who has succeeded to the interest of the purchaser.
Amended by Stats. 1982, Ch. 497, Sec. 58. Operative July 1, 1983, by Sec. 185 of Ch. 497.

Section 747 - Action not prejudiced by alienation made by person in possession
An action for the recovery of real property against a person in possession cannot be prejudiced by any alienation made by such person, either before or after the commencement of the action.
Enacted 1872.

Section 748 - Customs, usages or regulations in actions respecting mining claims
In actions respecting mining claims, proof must be admitted of the customs, usages, or regulations established and in force at the bar or diggings embracing such claim; and such customs, usages, or regulations, when not in conflict with the laws of this State, must govern the decision of the action.
Enacted 1872.

Section 749 - Damages in action by homeowner against beneficiary of trust deed where trust deed forged by beneficiary
(a) In an action for damages by a homeowner or trustor against a beneficiary of a trust deed on real property consisting of a single-family residence containing not more than four dwelling units, or against an assignee or successor in interest thereof, wherein it is established the trust deed was forged in whole or in part by the beneficiary, judgment may be entered for three times the amount at which the actual damages are assessed.
(b) An assignee or successor in interest of a beneficiary or a transferee of a prior assignee or of a prior successor in interest shall not be subject to treble damages unless it is established that the person purchased or obtained the deed of trust with actual knowledge of the forgery of the deed of trust.
(c) This section shall not apply to any person who does not purchase and sell four or more deeds of trust in any calendar year.
(d) This section shall not limit or affect the availability of punitive damages, if any, to the injured party.
(e) This section shall apply to any action filed on or after July 1, 1983, provided that any action filed prior to the effective date of this section is pending at that time in the court of original jurisdiction.
Added by Stats. 1984, Ch. 1397, Sec. 1.

Section 749.5 - Damages in action by assignee or successor in interest against beneficiary of trust deed
(a) In an action for damages by an assignee or a successor in interest against a beneficiary of a trust deed on real property consisting of a single-family residence containing not more than four dwelling units, wherein it is established the trust deed was forged in whole or in part by the beneficiary, judgment may be entered for three times the amount at which the actual damages are assessed.
(b) This section shall not apply to any person who does not purchase and sell four or more deeds of trust in any calendar year.
(c) This section shall not limit or affect the availability of punitive damages, if any, to the injured party.
(d) This section shall apply to any action filed on or after January 1, 1984.
Added by Stats. 1984, Ch. 1397, Sec. 2.

Chapter 3.5 - ACTIONS TO RE-ESTABLISH DESTROYED LAND RECORDS

Section 751.01 - Title of law
This chapter may be cited as the Destroyed Land Records Relief Law.
Added by Stats. 1953, Ch. 52.

Section 751.02 - Persons who may bring action; venue
Whenever the public records in the office of the county recorder of any county are lost or destroyed in whole or in any material part by flood, fire, earthquake, enemy attack, or from any other cause, any person who claims an estate of inheritance or for life in, and who is by himself, or his tenant or other person holding under him in the actual and peaceable possession of, any real property in the county may bring and maintain an action in rem against all the world, in the superior court for the county in which such real property is situate, to establish his title to such property and to determine all adverse claims thereto.
Such action may also be brought in the county in which the real property is situate if any real property is in another county, but was formerly in the county of which all or a material part of the records were so lost or destroyed, and if the lost or destroyed records included all or a material part of the public records in the office of the county recorder covering all or a material part of the time when the real property was in the county whose records were so lost or destroyed.
Added by Stats. 1953, Ch. 52.

Section 751.03 - Any number of parcels included in action
Any number of separate parcels of land claimed by the plaintiff may be included in the same action.
Added by Stats. 1953, Ch. 52.

Section 751.04 - Complaint commencing action; plaintiff and defendants
The action shall be commenced by the filing of a verified complaint. The party commencing the action shall be named as plaintiff, and the defendants shall be described as "all persons claiming any interest in, or lien upon, the real property herein described, or any part thereof." The complaint shall contain a statement of the facts enumerated in Section 751.02, a particular description of the real property, and a specification of the estate, title, or interest of the plaintiff in the property.
Added by Stats. 1953, Ch. 52.

Section 751.05 - Summons issued upon filing complaint
Upon the filing of the complaint, a summons shall be issued under the seal of the court. The summons shall contain the name of the court and county in which the action is brought, and the name of the plaintiff and a particular description of the real property involved, and shall be directed to "all persons claiming any interest in, or lien upon, the real property herein described, or any part thereof," as defendants, and shall be substantially in the following form:

"IN THE SUPERIOR COURT OF THE STATE OF CALIFORNIA IN ANDFOR THE COUNTY (OR CITY AND COUNTY) OF

_____

_____,		Action No. _____
Plaintiff,	
vs.	
All Persons Claiming Any Interest in, or	
Lien Upon, the Real Property Herein	
Described or Any Part thereof,	

Defendants.

The people of the State of California, to all persons claiming any interest in, or lien upon, the real property herein described, or any part thereof, defendants, greeting:

You are hereby required to appear and answer the complaint of _____, plaintiff, filed with the clerk of the above-entitled court and county, within three months after the first publication of this summons, and to set forth what interest or lien, if any, you have in or upon that certain real property or any part thereof, situated in the County (or City and County) of _____, State of California, particularly described as follows: (here insert description.)

And you are hereby notified that, unless you so appear and answer, the plaintiff will apply to the court for the relief demanded in the complaint, to wit: (here insert a statement of the relief so demanded.)

Witness my hand and the seal of said court, this _____ day of _____, A.D. _____.

(SEAL)

_____, Clerk."

Added by Stats. 1953, Ch. 52.

Section 751.06 - Publication of summons

The summons shall be published in a newspaper of general circulation published in the county in which the action is brought. The newspaper in which publication is to be made shall be designated by an order of the court or a judge thereof to be signed and filed with the clerk. No other order for the publication of the summons shall be necessary, nor shall any affidavit therefor be required, nor need any copy of the complaint be served, except as required by this chapter. The summons shall be published pursuant to Section 6065 of the Government Code, and to each publication thereof shall be appended a memorandum in substance as follows:

"The first publication of this summons was made in ____ (here insert name) newspaper on the ____ day of ____ A.D. ____," (inserting the date).

Added by Stats. 1953, Ch. 52.

Section 751.07 - Memorandum attached to summons stating persons claiming interest adverse to plaintiff

If the affidavit provided for in Section 751.09 discloses the name of any person claiming an interest in the property or a lien thereon adverse to the plaintiff, that fact and the name and address, if given, of the person shall be stated in a memorandum to be appended to the summons in substance as follows:

"The following persons are said to claim an interest in, or lien upon, said property adverse to plaintiff," (giving their names and addresses as above provided).

Added by Stats. 1953, Ch. 52.

Section 751.08 - Posting copy of summons and memorandum

A copy of the summons and a copy of the memorandum shall be posted in a conspicuous place on each separate parcel of the property described in the complaint within 15 days after the first publication of the summons.

Added by Stats. 1953, Ch. 52.

Section 751.09 - Affidavit filed at time of filing complaint

At the time of filing the complaint the plaintiff shall file with it his affidavit fully and explicitly setting forth and showing:

(a) The character of the plaintiff's estate, right, title, interest, or claim in, and possession of, the property, the period it has existed, and from whom obtained.

(b) Whether or not the plaintiff has ever made any conveyance of all or any part of the property, or any interest therein, and if so when and to whom, and a statement of any and all subsisting mortgages, deeds of trust, and other liens thereon.

(c) That the plaintiff does not know and has never been informed of any other person who claims or who may claim any interest in or lien upon all or any part of the property adversely to the plaintiff, or if the plaintiff does know or has been informed of any such person, the name and address of such person. If the plaintiff is unable to state any of the required matters, the plaintiff shall set forth and show fully and explicitly the reasons for such inability. Such affidavit shall constitute a part of the judgment-roll. If the plaintiff is a corporation, the affidavit shall be made by an officer thereof. If the plaintiff is a person under guardianship or conservatorship, the affidavit shall be made by the guardian or conservator.

Amended by Stats. 1979, Ch. 730.

Section 751.10 - Service upon persons claiming interest adverse to plaintiff

If the affidavit discloses the name of any person claiming any interest in or lien upon the property adverse to the plaintiff, a copy of the summons and complaint and affidavit shall also be served upon such person, if he can be found, in the manner provided by law for the service of a summons in a civil action, other than by publication. Service shall be made during the period of the publication of the summons. A copy of the memorandum provided for in Section 751.07 shall be appended to the copy of the summons served upon any such person.

If such person cannot, with reasonable diligence, be served as provided above within the period of publication of the summons, a copy of the summons, memorandum, complaint, and affidavit shall be mailed, postage prepaid, addressed to him at the address given in the affidavit, or, if no address is given, at his last address known to the plaintiff, or, if none, at the county seat of the county in which the action is brought, forthwith upon the expiration of the period of publication.

Amended by Stats. 1969, Ch. 1611.

Section 751.11 - Complete jurisdiction of court over plaintiff and property and person claiming interest

Upon the completion of the publication and posting of the summons and its service or mailing as provided for in Section 751.10, the court has complete jurisdiction over the plaintiff and the property and the person of everyone having or claiming any estate, right, title, or interest in or to, or lien upon, all or any part of the property, and shall be deemed to have obtained the possession and control of the property for the purposes of the action with complete jurisdiction to render the judgment provided for in this chapter.

Amended by Stats. 1969, Ch. 1611.

Section 751.12 - Answer to complaint

At any time within three months after the first publication of the summons, or such further time not exceeding 30 days as the court for good cause may grant, any person having or claiming any estate, right, title, or interest in or to, or lien upon, all or any part of the property may appear and make himself a party to the action by pleading to the complaint. All answers must be verified and must specifically set forth the estate, right, title, interest, or lien so claimed.

Added by Stats. 1953, Ch. 52.

Section 751.13 - Recording notice of pendency of action

At the time of filing the complaint the plaintiff, and at the time of filing his or her answer every defendant claiming any affirmative relief, shall record in the office of the recorder of the county in which the property is situated a notice of the pendency of the action containing the object of the action or defense, and a particular description of the property affected by it. The recorder shall record the notice in the same manner as provided in Section 409.

Amended by Stats. 1982, Ch. 843, Sec. 1.

Section 751.14 - Judgment by default not given

Judgment in any such action shall not be given by default, but the court must require proof of the facts alleged in the complaint and other pleadings.
Added by Stats. 1953, Ch. 52.

Section 751.15 - Judgment
The judgment shall determine all estates, rights, titles, interests, and claims in and to such property and every part thereof, whether legal or equitable, present or future, vested or contingent, or whether they consist of mortgages or liens of any description. It shall be conclusive upon every person who at the commencement of the action had or claimed any estate, right, title, or interest in or to all or any part of such property and upon every person claiming under him by title subsequent to the commencement of the action.
Added by Stats. 1953, Ch. 52.

Section 751.16 - Recording certified copy of judgment
A certified copy of the judgment shall be recorded in the office of the recorder of the county in which the action was commenced. Any party or the successor in interest of any party to the action may file the entire judgment roll for record in the office of the county recorder.
Added by Stats. 1953, Ch. 52.

Section 751.17 - Applicability of rules and law relating to civil actions
Except as otherwise provided in this chapter, all rules of law relating to evidence, pleading, practice, new trials, and appeals applicable to other civil actions shall apply to actions authorized by this chapter.
Added by Stats. 1953, Ch. 52.

Section 751.18 - Depositions
At any time after the issuance of summons, any party to the action may take depositions in conformity to law upon notice to the adverse party sought to be bound by such depositions and who has appeared in the action and upon notice filed with the clerk. The depositions may be used by any party against any other party giving or receiving the notice, subject to all just exceptions.
Added by Stats. 1953, Ch. 52.

Section 751.19 - Actions numbered, index and register
The clerk shall number all actions authorized by this chapter consecutively in a distinct series and shall keep an index and register devoted exclusively to such actions.
Added by Stats. 1953, Ch. 52.

Section 751.20 - Other action relative to same property after entry of judgment
Whenever judgment in an action authorized by this chapter has been entered as to any real property, no other action relative to all or any part of the same property shall be tried until proof has first been made to the court that all persons who appeared in the first action or their successors in interest have been personally served pursuant to this chapter either within or without the State more than one month before the time to plead expired.
Added by Stats. 1953, Ch. 52.

Section 751.21 - Person holding possession of property in right of another as plaintiff
An executor, administrator, guardian, conservator, or other person holding the possession of property in the right of another may maintain as plaintiff, and may appear and defend in, any action provided for by this chapter.
Amended by Stats. 1979, Ch. 730.

Section 751.22 - Remedies cumulative
The remedies provided for by this chapter are cumulative and in addition to any other remedy provided by law for quieting or establishing title to real property.
Added by Stats. 1953, Ch. 52.

Section 751.23 - Notice of ownership and claim to real property under the destroyed records relief law
Where the title to real property may be established or quieted pursuant to this chapter, any person who is or claims to be the owner of such real property or of any interest therein or lien thereon, by himself or by his agent duly authorized by letter of attorney theretofore recorded in the office of the county recorder of the county where the property is situated, may sign, verify, and file for record in the office of the county recorder a notice in substantially the following form:
"Notice of Ownership and Claim to Real Property Under the Destroyed Records Relief Law
"Notice is hereby given that ____ (here insert name of claimant) ____, whose residence is at ____ (here insert street and number, city or town, county and state of residence), is the owner of an interest in the real property situated in the ____ (here insert name of city if the property be located in a city) ____, county of ____ (here insert name of county or city and county in which property is located) ____, State of California, described as follows: ____ (here insert a particular description of real property) ____.
"The character of the interest in the real property owned by the claimant is ____ (here insert description of the character of interest in or lien upon the real property) ____ and the interest was obtained from ____ (here insert the name of the party from whom the interest was obtained) ____, and at the time and in the manner following ____ (here insert time at which and manner in which the interest was acquired) ____."
Added by Stats. 1953, Ch. 52.

Section 751.24 - Notice signed and verified
The notice shall be signed by the claimant or by his agent and shall be verified by the oath of the party signing it, to the effect that all of the statements therein contained are true to his knowledge.
Added by Stats. 1953, Ch. 52.

Section 751.25 - Recording notice
Upon the filing of the notice for recordation the recorder shall record the notice in the same manner as provided in Section 409.
Amended by Stats. 1982, Ch. 843, Sec. 2.

Section 751.26 - Notice of facts stated in notice of ownership
After three days after the notice has been filed for record, all persons who may begin actions pursuant to this chapter shall be deemed to have notice of the facts stated in the notice. Neither the filing of the notice for record nor its recordation constitute constructive notice to any other person or for any other purpose. The original of the notice shall be returned to the party requesting the recordation as provided in Section 27321 of the Government Code.
Amended by Stats. 1982, Ch. 843, Sec. 3.

Section 751.27 - Affidavit and memorandum pended to summons naming claimant or successor in interest; service
After three days after the filing of the notice for record, any person who begins an action pursuant to this chapter to perfect or establish his title to the real property described in the notice, or any interest therein, must name, in the affidavit and memorandum appended to the summons, the claimant in the notice, or any person who is a successor in interest of such claimant under a subsequently duly recorded written instrument, judgment, or decree, as a party who claims an interest in or lien upon the property adverse to the plaintiff. He must cause such claimant, or successor in interest, to be served with summons in the action. Otherwise neither the action nor any judgment or decree made therein shall affect the title or interest in the property described in the notice and owned by the claimant at the time of the filing of the notice, or by any such successor in interest prior to the commencement of the action. The failure to name such claimant or successor in interest in the affidavit or

memorandum or to serve such claimant or such successor in interest shall not affect the validity of the judgment or decree rendered in such action as to any other persons, but such judgment or decree shall be valid and binding upon all persons except such claimant or successor in interest.
Added by Stats. 1953, Ch. 52.

Section 751.28 - Person holding possession in right of another filing notice and affidavit
An executor, administrator, guardian, conservator, or other person holding the possession of property in the right of another, may make, sign, verify, and file for record the notice and affidavit provided for in this chapter on behalf of the estate or interest which he represents.
Amended by Stats. 1979, Ch. 730.

Chapter 3.6 - CULLEN EARTHQUAKE ACT

Section 751.50 - Action to equitably reestablish boundaries and to quiet title
If the boundaries of land owned either by public or by private entities have been disturbed by earth movements such as, but not limited to, slides, subsidence, lateral or vertical displacements or similar disasters caused by man, or by earthquake or other acts of God, so that such lands are in a location different from that at which they were located prior to the disaster, an action in rem may be brought to equitably reestablish boundaries and to quiet title to land within the boundaries so reestablished.
Added by Stats. 1972, Ch. 936.

Section 751.51 - Entities or persons allowed to commence action; plaintiffs; unknown entities designated in caption and complaint
(a) An action authorized by this chapter may be commenced by:
　(1) A county in which lands were affected by a disaster described in Section 751.50 with or without the joinder of a city or cities included in the county and within the area so affected.
　(2) A city, if the disaster has affected land in the city.
　(3) Any other entity or person owning or having an interest in or lien upon land affected by the disaster if granted permission by the court to bring the action, and if the county in which the land is located is made a party to the action.
(b) In an action authorized by this chapter every entity in actual and peaceable possession of, or having an estate or interest in or lien upon any of the land affected by the action, whose possession or evidence of estate or interest is either recorded or known to the plaintiffs, the city, if the land is within a city, the county in which the land is located, and the State of California must be designated in the complaint of the action, and given notice in the manner required by this chapter.
(c) All unknown entities, including owners, lien or interest claimants, heirs, devisees, legatees or assigns, may be described in the caption and complaint as "all entities claiming any interest in or lien upon, the real property herein described or any part of it."
Added by Stats. 1972, Ch. 936.

Section 751.52 - Separate action by permissive plaintiff with respect to separate portions of disaster area
An entity which is a permissive plaintiff under this chapter, may bring a separate action with respect to separate portions of the disaster area of sufficient size to equitably reestablish boundaries without harm to other areas of the common disaster, its decision regarding the desirability of the separate action, and regarding the area to be dealt with in each action to be approved by the court.
Added by Stats. 1972, Ch. 936.

Section 751.53 - Requirements of complaint
The complaint shall substantially include:
(a) A statement of the facts which make the provisions of this chapter applicable.
(b) A description of the exterior boundaries of the real property area sought to be affected by the action.
(c) A specification of the estate, title, interest or claim owned, and in the actual possession of the plaintiff or plaintiffs in described parts of the entire real property sought to be affected by the action.
(d) A specification of the estate, title, interest, or claim, so far as they are known to the plaintiffs or either of them, and so far as they are capable of being discovered by reasonably diligent search by the plaintiff or plaintiffs, in each separate part of the entire real property sought to be affected by the action.
(e) A specification of the street areas sought to be vacated or offered by the plaintiff, or plaintiffs, to be vacated in whole or in part for judicial equitable allocation to landowners for the mitigation of the losses inflicted upon the landowners by the particular disaster or disasters to which this chapter is applicable.
(f) A proposed replatting of the entire real property sought to be affected by the action, embodying the land boundaries as fixed by the disaster, except as these boundaries have been equitably and judicially readjusted, or as liberalized by judicially directed use of the vacated lands.
Amended by Stats. 1984, Ch. 193, Sec. 10.

Section 751.54 - Summons, publication of notice, posting and related matters
Summons, publication of notice, posting and related matters and procedures shall be governed by the provisions of Sections 751.05 through 751.10, inclusive, of the Code of Civil Procedure.
Added by Stats. 1972, Ch. 936.

Section 751.55 - Complete jurisdiction of court
Upon the completion of the service, publication and posting of the summons, as may be required by this chapter, the court has complete jurisdiction over the parties plaintiff or plaintiffs and the entire real property described in the complaint as intended to be affected by the action, and over every entity having or claiming an estate, right, title or interest in or to, or lien upon, all or any part of the property, and shall be considered to have obtained the possession and control of the property for the purposes of the action with complete jurisdiction to render the judgment provided for in this chapter.
Added by Stats. 1972, Ch. 936.

Section 751.56 - Answer to complaint
(a) An answer to the complaint must be served within 90 days after the first publication of the notice, or such further time not exceeding 30 days, as the court for good cause may grant.
(b) An answer must:
　(1) Specifically set out the particulars in which the claimant's estate, right, title, or interest in or to, or lien upon all or any part of the property is different from, or greater than, the interest of the claimant as it is described in the complaint.
　(2) Be confined to rights based on events occurring at the time of, or since the time of the disaster.
(c) To whatever extent, if at all, the answering party has rights against anyone whatsoever, based upon facts or events which occurred before the disaster, the claims shall remain unaffected by the action brought under this chapter and shall be assertable subsequent to the conclusion of the action at any time and in any manner permitted by law, notwithstanding the judgment granted in this action, recognizing however the finality of this judgment as to the consequences, with respect to land boundaries as applicable to land in the disaster area.
Added by Stats. 1972, Ch. 936.

Section 751.57 - Filing notice of pendency of action
A party to an action authorized by this chapter may file a notice of the pendency of the action in the form and at the place and with the effects specified by law.
Added by Stats. 1972, Ch. 936.

Section 751.58 - Vacating of streets, highways or other public ways

The vacating of streets, highways or other public ways within or abutting the area affected by the disaster, in whole or in part, by the voluntary action of the governmental agency under whose jurisdiction the streets, highways, or ways are vested, for the purpose of making it possible for the court to mitigate the hardships suffered by entities because of the change in land boundaries caused by the disaster can be accomplished by the affected governmental agency expressing the offer in the proceedings followed by the court's acceptance thereof in an action authorized by this chapter, without complying with any other formalities of law.
Added by Stats. 1972, Ch. 936.

Section 751.59 - Judgment not given by default

In an action of the type authorized by this chapter, judgment shall not be given by default, but the court must require proof of the facts alleged in the complaint and other pleadings.
Added by Stats. 1972, Ch. 936.

Section 751.60 - Judgment generally

The judgment shall:
(a) Determine the land boundaries of each parcel of land located within the entire area of real property sought to be affected by the action, whether owned publicly or privately, as fixed by the disaster, except as these boundaries have been judicially and equitably readjusted and as liberalized by judicial equitable allocation of lands voluntarily vacated by a city, county or the state under this act.
(b) Determine the entity or entities having estates, rights, titles, interests and claims in and to each parcel, whether legal or equitable, present or future, vested or contingent, or whether they consist of mortgages or liens of any description.
(c) Approve and direct the proper filing of an official map covering the entire area of real property sought to be affected by the action, as a substitute for the plat maps previously filed, but rendered inaccurate by the disaster.
Added by Stats. 1972, Ch. 936.

Section 751.61 - Reaching conclusion

In reaching the conclusions called for by Section 751.60, the court shall give effect to the changes in land boundaries caused by the disaster, mitigated, however, so far as can equitably be done by adjustment of land boundaries and by allocating to contiguous lots parts of the land released by a city, county or the state by its voluntary vacation of areas formerly constituting public ways, which vacatings of streets shall be approved by the judgment.
Added by Stats. 1972, Ch. 936.

Section 751.62 - judgment conclusive

The judgment shall be conclusive with respect to land boundaries upon every entity who at the commencement of the action had or claimed an estate, right, title or interest in or to or lien upon a part of the entire area of real property described in the complaint as intended to be affected by the action, and upon every entity claiming under any such person by title subsequent to the commencement of the action.
Added by Stats. 1972, Ch. 936.

Section 751.63 - Recording certified copy of judgment

A certified copy of the judgment shall be recorded, at the expense of the plaintiff or plaintiffs in the action, in the office of the recorder of the county in which the affected land is situated and shall constitute constructive notice of the findings therein and of the official plat or plats referred to therein, which findings and plats shall supersede and control all prior plats, maps and documents to the extent inconsistent therewith.
Added by Stats. 1972, Ch. 936.

Section 751.64 - Remedies cumulative

The remedies provided for by this chapter are cumulative and in addition to any other remedy provided by law for quieting or establishing title to real property or the boundaries of it.
Added by Stats. 1972, Ch. 936.

Section 751.65 - Title of act

This chapter may be cited as the Cullen Earthquake Act.
Added by Stats. 1972, Ch. 936.

Chapter 4 - QUIET TITLE

Article 1 - GENERAL PROVISIONS

Section 760.010 - Definitions

As used in this chapter:
(a) "Claim" includes a legal or equitable right, title, estate, lien, or interest in property or cloud upon title.
(b) "Property" includes real property, and to the extent applicable, personal property.
Added by Stats. 1980, Ch. 44, Sec. 15.

Section 760.020 - Action to establish title against adverse claims; actions by parties to agreements pursuant to section 6307 or 6357, Public Resources Code

(a) An action may be brought under this chapter to establish title against adverse claims to real or personal property or any interest therein.
(b) An action may be brought under this chapter by parties to an agreement entered into pursuant to Section 6307 or 6357 of the Public Resources Code to confirm the validity of the agreement.
(c) Nothing in this section shall be construed to limit the right of members of the public to bring or participate in actions challenging the validity of agreements entered into pursuant to Section 6307 or 6357 of the Public Resources Code.
Amended by Stats. 1989, Ch. 1045, Sec. 1.

Section 760.030 - Remedy cumulative; requiring issue be resolve pursuant to chapter

(a) The remedy provided in this chapter is cumulative and not exclusive of any other remedy, form or right of action, or proceeding provided by law for establishing or quieting title to property.
(b) In an action or proceeding in which establishing or quieting title to property is in issue the court in its discretion may, upon motion of any party, require that the issue be resolved pursuant to the provisions of this chapter to the extent practicable.
Added by Stats. 1980, Ch. 44, Sec. 15.

Section 760.040 - Superior court jurisdiction

(a) The superior court has jurisdiction of actions under this chapter.
(b) The court has complete jurisdiction over the parties to the action and the property described in the complaint and is deemed to have obtained possession and control of the property for the purposes of the action with complete jurisdiction to render the judgment provided for in this chapter.
(c) Nothing in this chapter limits any authority the court may have to grant such equitable relief as may be proper under the circumstances of the case.
Added by Stats. 1980, Ch. 44, Sec. 15.

Section 760.050 - Venue

Subject to the power of the court to transfer actions, the proper county for the trial of an action under this chapter is:

(a) Where the subject of the action is real property or real and personal property, the county in which the real property, or some part thereof, is located.

(b) Where the subject of the action is personal property, the county in which the personal property is principally located at the commencement of the action or in which the defendants, or any of them, reside at the commencement of the action.

Added by Stats. 1980, Ch. 44, Sec. 15.

Section 760.060 - Applicability of statutes and rules governing practice in civil actions

The statutes and rules governing practice in civil actions generally apply to actions under this chapter except where they are inconsistent with the provisions of this chapter.

Added by Stats. 1980, Ch. 44, Sec. 15.

Article 2 - COMMENCEMENT OF ACTION

Section 761.010 - Commenced by filing complaint; notice of pendency of action

(a) An action under this chapter is commenced by filing a complaint with the court.

(b) Immediately upon commencement of the action, the plaintiff shall file a notice of the pendency of the action in the office of the county recorder of each county in which any real property described in the complaint is located.

Added by Stats. 1980, Ch. 44, Sec. 15.

Section 761.020 - Requirements of complaint

The complaint shall be verified and shall include all of the following:

(a) A description of the property that is the subject of the action. In the case of tangible personal property, the description shall include its usual location. In the case of real property, the description shall include both its legal description and its street address or common designation, if any.

(b) The title of the plaintiff as to which a determination under this chapter is sought and the basis of the title. If the title is based upon adverse possession, the complaint shall allege the specific facts constituting the adverse possession.

(c) The adverse claims to the title of the plaintiff against which a determination is sought.

(d) The date as of which the determination is sought. If the determination is sought as of a date other than the date the complaint is filed, the complaint shall include a statement of the reasons why a determination as of that date is sought.

(e) A prayer for the determination of the title of the plaintiff against the adverse claims.

Added by Stats. 1980, Ch. 44, Sec. 15.

Section 761.030 - Answer

(a) The answer shall be verified and shall set forth:

(1) Any claim the defendant has.

(2) Any facts tending to controvert such material allegations of the complaint as the defendant does not wish to be taken as true.

(3) A statement of any new matter constituting a defense.

(b) If the defendant disclaims in the answer any claim, or suffers judgment to be taken without answer, the plaintiff shall not recover costs.

Added by Stats. 1980, Ch. 44, Sec. 15.

Section 761.040 - Cross-complaint

(a) The defendant may by cross-complaint seek affirmative relief in the action.

(b) If the defendant seeks a determination of title as of a date other than the date specified in the complaint, the cross-complaint shall include the date and a statement of the reasons why a determination as of that date is sought.

Added by Stats. 1980, Ch. 44, Sec. 15.

Article 3 - DEFENDANTS

Section 762.010 - Generally

The plaintiff shall name as defendants in the action the persons having adverse claims to the title of the plaintiff against which a determination is sought.

Added by Stats. 1980, Ch. 44, Sec. 15.

Section 762.020 - Unknown parties; unknown, uncertain or contingent claims

(a) If the name of a person required to be named as a defendant is not known to the plaintiff, the plaintiff shall so state in the complaint and shall name as parties all persons unknown in the manner provided in Section 762.060.

(b) If the claim or the share or quantity of the claim of a person required to be named as a defendant is unknown, uncertain, or contingent, the plaintiff shall so state in the complaint. If the lack of knowledge, uncertainty, or contingency is caused by a transfer to an unborn or unascertained person or class member, or by a transfer in the form of a contingent remainder, vested remainder subject to defeasance, executory interest, or similar disposition, the plaintiff shall also state in the complaint, so far as is known to the plaintiff, the name, age, and legal disability (if any) of the person in being who would be entitled to the claim had the contingency upon which the claim depends occurred prior to the commencement of the action.

Added by Stats. 1980, Ch. 44, Sec. 15.

Section 762.030 - Defendant dead or believed to be dead

(a) If a person required to be named as a defendant is dead and the plaintiff knows of a personal representative, the plaintiff shall join the personal representative as a defendant.

(b) If a person required to be named as a defendant is dead, or is believed by the plaintiff to be dead, and the plaintiff knows of no personal representative:

(1) The plaintiff shall state these facts in an affidavit filed with the complaint.

(2) Where it is stated in the affidvit that such person is dead, the plaintiff may join as defendants "the testate and intestate successors of ____ (naming the deceased person), deceased, and all persons claiming by, through, or under such decedent," naming them in that manner.

(3) Where it is stated in the affidavit that such person is believed to be dead, the plaintiff may join the person as a defendant, and may also join "the testate and intestate successors of ____ (naming the person) believed to be deceased, and all persons claiming by, through, or under such person," naming them in that manner.

Added by Stats. 1980, Ch. 44, Sec. 15.

Section 762.040 - Joinder of additional parties; requiring plaintiff to obtain title report

The court upon its own motion may, and upon motion of any party shall, make such orders as appear appropriate:

(a) For joinder of such additional parties as are necessary or proper.

(b) Requiring the plaintiff to procure a title report and designate a place where it shall be kept for inspection, use, and copying by the parties.

Added by Stats. 1980, Ch. 44, Sec. 15.

Section 762.050 - Appearance of any person claiming property described in complaint

Any person who has a claim to the property described in the complaint may appear in the proceeding. Whether or not the person is named as a defendant in the complaint, the person shall appear as a defendant.

Added by Stats. 1980, Ch. 44, Sec. 15.

Section 762.060 - Naming as defendants all persons unknown claiming interest

(a) In addition to the persons required to be named as defendants in the action, the plaintiff may name as defendants "all persons unknown, claiming any legal or equitable right, title, estate, lien, or interest in the property described in the complaint adverse to plaintiff's title, or any cloud upon plaintiff's title thereto," naming them in that manner.

(b) In an action under this section, the plaintiff shall name as defendants the persons having adverse claims that are of record or known to the plaintiff or reasonably apparent from an inspection of the property.

(c) If the plaintiff admits the validity of any adverse claim, the complaint shall so state.

Added by Stats. 1980, Ch. 44, Sec. 15.

Section 762.070 - Rights of person named and served as unknown defendant

A person named and served as an unknown defendant has the same rights as are provided by law in cases of all other defendants named and served, and the action shall proceed against unknown defendants in the same manner as against other defendants named and served, and with the same effect.

Added by Stats. 1980, Ch. 44, Sec. 15.

Section 762.080 - Appointment of guardians ad litem

The court upon its own motion may, and upon motion of any party shall, make such orders for appointment of guardians ad litem as appear necessary to protect the interest of any party.

Added by Stats. 1980, Ch. 44, Sec. 15.

Section 762.090 - Joinder of state

(a) The state may be joined as a party to an action under this chapter.

(b) This section does not constitute a change in, but is declaratory of, existing law.

Added by Stats. 1980, Ch. 44, Sec. 15.

Article 4 - SERVICE OF PROCESS

Section 763.010 - Same as in civil actions; service by publication

(a) The form, content, and manner of the service of summons shall be the same as in civil actions generally.

(b) If upon affidavit it appears to the satisfaction of the court that the plaintiff has used reasonable diligence to ascertain the identity and residence of and to serve summons on the persons named as unknown defendants and persons joined as testate or intestate successors of a person known or believed to be dead, the court shall order service by publication pursuant to Section 415.50 and the provisions of this article. The court may, in its discretion, appoint a referee to investigate whether the plaintiff has used reasonable diligence to ascertain the identity and residence of persons sought to be served by publication, and the court may rely on the report of the referee instead of the affidavit of the plaintiff in making the order for service by publication.

(c) Nothing in this section authorizes service by publication upon any person named as an unknown defendant who is in open and actual possession of the property.

Added by Stats. 1980, Ch. 44, Sec. 15.

Section 763.020 - Conditions of order of service by publication

Whenever the court orders service by publication, the order is subject to the following conditions:

(a) The plaintiff shall post, not later than 10 days after the date the order is made, a copy of the summons and complaint in a conspicuous place on the real property that is the subject of the action.

(b) The plaintiff shall record, if not already recorded, a notice of the pendency of the action.

(c) The publication shall describe the property that is the subject of the action. In addition to particularly describing the property, the publication shall describe the property by giving its street address, if any, or other common designation, if any; but, if a legal description of the property is given, the validity of the publication shall not be affected by the fact that the street address or other common designation recited is erroneous or that the street address or other common designation is omitted.

Added by Stats. 1980, Ch. 44, Sec. 15.

Section 763.030 - Defendants named and property described in publication

(a) Whenever the court orders service by publication, the publication may:

(1) Name only the defendants to be served thereby.

(2) Describe only the property in which the defendants to be served thereby claim interests.

(b) Judgment against a defendant who fails to appear and answer following service under this section shall be conclusive against the defendant named in respect only to property described in the publication.

Added by Stats. 1980, Ch. 44, Sec. 15.

Section 763.040 - Proof summons served and notice of pendency of action filed

Whenever the court orders service by publication, the court before hearing the case shall require proof that the summons has been served, posted, published as required, and that the notice of pendency of action has been filed.

Added by Stats. 1980, Ch. 44, Sec. 15.

Article 5 - JUDGMENT

Section 764.010 - Judgment by default not entered

The court shall examine into and determine the plaintiff's title against the claims of all the defendants. The court shall not enter judgment by default but shall in all cases require evidence of plaintiff's title and hear such evidence as may be offered respecting the claims of any of the defendants, other than claims the validity of which is admitted by the plaintiff in the complaint. The court shall render judgment in accordance with the evidence and the law.

Added by Stats. 1980, Ch. 44, Sec. 15.

Section 764.020 - Validity or interpretation of gift, devise, bequest or trust under will

(a) If in an action under this chapter the validity or interpretation of a gift, devise, bequest, or trust, under a will or instrument purporting to be a will, whether admitted to probate or not, is involved:

(1) The will or instrument purporting to be a will is admissible in evidence.

(2) All questions concerning the validity of the gift, devise, bequest, or trust shall be finally determined in the action.

(3) If the will has been admitted to probate and the gift, devise, bequest, or trust has been interpreted by a final decree of the probate court, the interpretation is conclusive as to the proper construction thereof.

(b) Nothing in this section deprives a party of the right to a jury trial in any case where, by law, the right is now given.

Added by Stats. 1980, Ch. 44, Sec. 15.

Section 764.030 - Persons judgment binding and conclusive on

The judgment in the action is binding and conclusive on all of the following persons, regardless of any legal disability:

(a) All persons known and unknown who were parties to the action and who have any claim to the property, whether present or future, vested or contingent, legal or equitable, several or undivided.
(b) Except as provided in Section 764.045, all persons who were not parties to the action and who have any claim to the property which was not of record at the time the lis pendens was filed or, if none was filed, at the time the judgment was recorded.
Amended by Stats. 1984, Ch. 20, Sec. 1.

Section 764.045 - Claim in property of person not party to action
Except to the extent provided in Section 1908, the judgment does not affect a claim in the property or part thereof of any person who was not a party to the action if any of the following conditions is satisfied:
(a) The claim was of record at the time the lis pendens was filed or, if none was filed, at the time the judgment was recorded.
(b) The claim was actually known to the plaintiff or would have been reasonably apparent from an inspection of the property at the time the lis pendens was filed or, if none was filed, at the time the judgment was entered. Nothing in this subdivision shall be construed to impair the rights of a bona fide purchaser or encumbrancer for value dealing with the plaintiff or the plaintiff's successors in interest.
Added by Stats. 1984, Ch. 20, Sec. 3.

Section 764.060 - Rights of purchaser or encumbrancer for value
The relief granted in an action or proceeding directly or collaterally attacking the judgment in the action, whether based on lack of actual notice to a party or otherwise, shall not impair the rights of a purchaser or encumbrancer for value of the property acting in reliance on the judgment without knowledge of any defects or irregularities in the judgment or the proceedings.
Added by Stats. 1980, Ch. 44, Sec. 15.

Section 764.070 - Judgment not binding or conclusive upon state or United States unless joined
Notwithstanding any other provision of this chapter, the judgment in the action is not binding or conclusive on the following:
(a) The state, unless individually joined as a party to the action.
(b) The United States, unless the United States is individually joined as a party to the action and federal law authorizes judgment in the action to be binding or conclusive as to its interests.
Amended by Stats. 1986, Ch. 271, Sec. 2.

Section 764.080 - Action brought to quiet title to land subject to agreement pursuant to sections 6307 or 6357, Public Resources Code
(a) In any action brought to quiet title to land that has been subject to an agreement entered into pursuant to Section 6307 or 6357 of the Public Resources Code, at the time set for trial the court shall, at the request of any party, receive evidence on the nature of the agreement. After receiving that evidence, the court shall render a statement of decision. In the case of an agreement pursuant to Section 6357, the statement of decision shall include a recitation of the underlying facts and a determination whether the agreement meets the criteria of Section 6357 and other law applicable to the validity of boundary line agreements. In the case of an agreement pursuant to Section 6307, the statement of decision shall recite the relevant facts and shall contain a determination whether the requirements of Section 6307 of the Public Resources Code, Sections 3 and 4 of Article 10 of the California Constitution, and other applicable law have been met. If the court finds the agreement to be valid, the judgment in the action shall quiet title in the parties named in the agreement in accordance with the agreement. If the judgment is entered prior to the effective date of the agreement, the judgment shall provide that, upon the effective date, title is quieted in the parties in accordance with the agreements. However, no action may be brought pursuant to this section until the State Lands Commission has approved the agreement following a public hearing. All such actions shall be set on the trial calendar within one year from the filing of a memorandum to set, unless the court extends this time for good cause.
(b) Nothing in this section shall be construed to limit the right of members of the public to bring or participate in actions challenging the validity of agreements entered into pursuant to Section 6307 or 6357 of the Public Resources Code. Any action brought by a member of the public shall be set on the trial calendar within one year from the filing of a memorandum to set, unless the court extends this time for good cause.
Added by Stats. 1989, Ch. 1045, Sec. 2.

Article 6 - LIENS AND ENCUMBRANCES

Section 765.010 - Use of lien or lis pendens to harass of hinder duties of public officer or employee
(a) For purposes of this section:
　(1) "Harass" means engage in knowing and willful conduct that serves no legitimate purpose.
　(2) "Entity" includes both governmental and private entities.
(b) A person shall not file or record, or direct another to file or record, a lawsuit, lien, or other encumbrance, including a notice of lis pendens, against another person or entity knowing it is false, with the intent to harass the person or entity or to influence or hinder the person in discharging his or her official duties if the person is a public officer or employee.
(c)
　(1) A person or entity whose property is subject to a lien or encumbrance in violation of this section may petition the superior court of the county in which the person or entity resides or in which the property is located for an order, which may be granted ex parte, directing the lien or other encumbrance claimant to appear at a hearing before the court and show cause why the lien or other encumbrance should not be stricken and other relief provided by this article should not be granted.
　(2) The court shall schedule the hearing no earlier than 14 days after the date of the order. The scheduled date of the hearing shall allow adequate time for notice of the hearing.
Added by Stats 2015 ch 208 (AB 1267),s 2, eff. 1/1/2016.

Section 765.020 - Requirements of petition
A petition under this article shall state the grounds upon which relief is requested, and shall be supported by the affidavit of the petitioner or the petitioner's attorney setting forth a concise statement of the facts upon which the motion is based.
The petition and affidavit shall be in substantially the form prescribed by the Judicial Council.
Added by Stats. 1998, Ch. 779, Sec. 2. Effective January 1, 1999.

Section 765.030 - Order if court determines lien in violation of section 6223
If the court determines that the lien or other encumbrance is in violation of Section 765.010, the court shall issue an order striking and releasing the lien or other encumbrance and may award costs and reasonable attorney's fees to the petitioner to be paid by the lien or other encumbrance claimant. If the court determines that the lien or other encumbrance is valid, the court shall issue an order so stating and may award costs and reasonable attorney's fees to the encumbrance claimant to be paid by the petitioner. The court may direct that an order issued pursuant to this section be recorded.
Amended by Stats 2016 ch 86 (SB 1171),s 25, eff. 1/1/2017.
Amended by Stats 2015 ch 208 (AB 1267),s 3, eff. 1/1/2016.

Section 765.040 - Liability of claimant filing or recording lien in violation of section 6223
Any lien or encumbrance claimant who records or files, or directs another to record or file, a lawsuit, lien, or other encumbrance in violation of Section 765.010 shall be liable to the person subject to the lawsuit or the owner of the property bound by the lien or other encumbrance for a civil penalty of up to five thousand dollars ($5,000).
Amended by Stats 2015 ch 208 (AB 1267),s 4, eff. 1/1/2016.

Section 765.050 - Inapplicability to claim of encumbrance by financial institution
This article does not apply to a document which acts as a claim of encumbrance by a financial institution, as defined in subdivision (a) of Section 14161 of the Penal Code or Section 481.113 of this code, or a public entity, as defined in Section 481.200 of this code.
Added by Stats. 1998, Ch. 779, Sec. 2. Effective January 1, 1999.

Section 765.060 - Counsel provided public officer or employee
If a lien or other encumbrance is recorded or filed against a public officer or employee in violation of Section 765.010, the state or local agency that employs the public officer or employee may provide counsel for the public officer or employee in an action brought pursuant to that section.
Amended by Stats 2015 ch 208 (AB 1267),s 5, eff. 1/1/2016.

Chapter 4.5 - SPECIAL ACTIONS AND PROCEEDINGS TO CLEAR TITLE
Article 1 - IDENTITY OF PERSON IN CHAIN OF TITLE

Section 770.010 - Definitions
As used in this article:
(a) "Acquired" means received or taken by conveyance, judgment, decree, or otherwise.
(b) "Property" means any right, title, or interest in or lien upon real property or part thereof.
(c) "Subsequent owner" means the person to whom property is transferred whether as owner, part owner, or otherwise, or the successors in interest of the person, and includes a distributee of the estate of a decedent.
(d) "Transfer" means voluntary or involuntary transfer and includes a conveyance, reconveyance, satisfaction of a lien, or divestment by judgment, decree, or otherwise. The probate of the estate of a decedent and entry of the decree of distribution is a transfer within the meaning of this subdivision.
Added by Stats. 1980, Ch. 44, Sec. 16.

Section 770.020 - Property transferred under name other than name in which property acquired or stands of record
If property is acquired or stands of record in the name of a person who heretofore or hereafter transfers the property under a name other than or different from the name in which the property is acquired or stands of record, a proceeding is authorized to adjudicate and determine the identity of the person in whose name the property is acquired or stands of record and the person who transfers the property.
Added by Stats. 1980, Ch. 44, Sec. 16.

Section 770.030 - Venue
The proceeding shall be brought in the superior court of the county in which the property or any part thereof is situated.
Added by Stats. 1980, Ch. 44, Sec. 16.

Section 770.040 - Proceeding brought by filing petition; answer
(a) The proceeding may be brought by a subsequent owner of the property by filing a petition with the court.
(b) At any time before the date fixed for the hearing of the petition, any person interested in the property may answer the petition and deny any of the matters contained therein.
Added by Stats. 1980, Ch. 44, Sec. 16.

Section 770.050 - Verified petition; information included; joinder
(a) The petition shall be verified in the manner provided for verification of a complaint.
(b) The petition may be substantially entitled, "In the matter of the determination of the identity of ____" (naming all the persons sought to be identified), and may set forth:
   (1) A statement of petitioner's interest in the property as subsequent owner.
   (2) A particular description of the property.
   (3) The name or names of the person or persons sought to be identified, setting out the name and a reference to the record of the transaction under which the property was acquired or stands of record and the name and a reference to the record of the transaction under which the property was transferred or stands of record, that the names are the names of the same person, and that the transfers affect the petitioner's title to the real property.
   (4) A prayer that the identity of such persons be established.
(c) As many persons sought to be identified as appear of record in the chain of title to the property may be joined in one petition or proceeding.
Added by Stats. 1980, Ch. 44, Sec. 16.

Section 770.060 - Setting petition for hearing; notice
(a) Upon the filing of the petition, the clerk shall set the petition for hearing by the court.
(b) The petitioner shall give notice of the hearing by causing notices of the time and place of hearing to be posted at the courthouse of the county where the proceeding is pending and in a conspicuous place on the real property described in the petition, at least 10 days before the hearing.
(c) The special notice shall be substantially in the following form: (Title of court and cause)
Notice is hereby given that ____ has filed a petition herein claiming to be the owner (or distributee) of the following described lands ____ (description) and praying that the identity of the following-named persons, in former conveyances (or judgments or decrees) to said lands or in decrees of distribution of said lands in probate be determined, to wit: _____ (names as J. Doe and John Doe); and that the time and place of hearing said petition has been set for ____ the ____ day of ____, 19__, at the hour of ____, __m. of said day at the courtroom of said court in the City of ____, County of ____, State of California.

_____ Clerk

Added by Stats. 1980, Ch. 44, Sec. 16.

Section 770.070 - Decree; appeal
(a) At the time fixed for the hearing or such time thereafter as may be fixed by the court, the court shall hear the proofs offered by the petitioner and by any persons answering the petition, and shall make and enter a decree determining the identity of the person or persons set out in the petition in accordance with the proofs.
(b) An appeal may be taken by any party aggrieved.
Added by Stats. 1980, Ch. 44, Sec. 16.

Section 770.080 - Effect of decree on becoming final; recording
(a) After the decree has become final it constitutes prima facie evidence of the matters thereby determined and it is presumed that the identity of the person or persons described in the decree is such as is stated in the decree.
(b) A certified copy of the decree shall be recorded in the office of the county recorder of every county in which any part of the property is situated.
Added by Stats. 1980, Ch. 44, Sec. 16.

Article 2 - LAND DEDICATED FOR PUBLIC IMPROVEMENT
Section 771.010 - Presumption proposed dedication not accepted

If a proposal is heretofore or hereafter made to dedicate real property for public improvement, there is a conclusive presumption that the proposed dedication was not accepted if all of the following conditions are satisfied:
(a) The proposal was made by filing a map only.
(b) No acceptance of the dedication was made and recorded within 25 years after the map was filed.
(c) The real property was not used for the purpose for which the dedication was proposed within 25 years after the map was filed.
(d) The real property was sold to a third person after the map was filed and used as if free of the dedication.
Added by Stats. 1980, Ch. 44, Sec. 16.

Section 771.020 - Action to clear title if proposed dedication presumed not accepted
(a) An action is authorized to clear title to real property of a proposal to dedicate the property for public improvement if there is a conclusive presumption pursuant to Section 771.010 that the proposed dedication was not accepted.
(b) The action shall be pursuant to Chapter 4 (commencing with Section 760.010) and shall have the following features:
   (1) The public entity to which the dedication was proposed shall be named as defendant.
   (2) The judgment in the action shall clear the title of the proposed dedication and remove the cloud created by the proposed dedication.
Added by Stats. 1980, Ch. 44, Sec. 16.

Article 3 - RIGHT OF ENTRY OR OCCUPATION OF SURFACE LANDS UNDER OIL OR GAS LEASE

Section 772.010 - Applicability of article
This article applies only to lands within a city in any county with a population exceeding 4,000,000, or with a population of more than 700,000 and less than 710,000 as determined by the 1960 Federal Decennial Census.
Added by Stats. 1980, Ch. 44, Sec. 16.

Section 772.020 - Definitions
As used in this article:
(a) "Surface zone" means the zone which lies above a plane which is 500 feet below the surface of the land.
(b) "Subject land" means that area occupied by the particular described surface and surface zone for which plaintiff seeks to terminate the leasehold right of entry and occupation.
(c) "Lease facilities" means storage tanks, wash tanks, separators, heaters, and other facilities reasonably necessary for the production of oil or gas, including secondary recovery operations.
Added by Stats. 1980, Ch. 44, Sec. 16.

Section 772.030 - Action to terminate mining or oil and gas lessee's right of entry or occupation
(a) If a mining rights lease, including a community lease, exists for the production of oil, gas, or other hydrocarbons, and a right of entry or occupation provided by the lease encumbers all or part of the surface or surface zone of the leasehold lands, any person who owns a fee interest in the surface of the leasehold lands may bring an action in the superior court to terminate the right of entry or occupation as to all or some described portion of the surface and surface zone of the leasehold lands in which the person owns an interest.
(b) No judgment rendered pursuant to this article shall change or affect the terms or operation of any valid unit agreement or valid operating agreement which comes within the provisions of Section 3301 or 3321 of the Public Resources Code.
Added by Stats. 1980, Ch. 44, Sec. 16.

Section 772.040 - Evidence required for judgment terminating lessee's right of entry or occupation
The court may render a judgment terminating the lessee's right of entry or occupation of the surface and surface zone, subject to such conditions as the court deems fair and equitable, if the evidence shows each of the following:
(a) The document that created the leasehold interest was originally executed more than 20 years prior to filing the action under this article regardless of any amendments to the document. However, if any amendment was entered into expressly for the purpose of waiving, limiting, or rearranging surface rights of entry and occupation by the lessee, the 20-year period shall be computed as if the document were originally executed on the date of execution of the amendment.
(b) The subject land is not presently occupied by any of the following:
   (1) A producing oil or gas well or well bore.
   (2) A well or well bore being utilized for injection of water, gas, or other substance into geologic substrata as an aid to oil or gas production or to ameliorating subsidence.
   (3) A well or well bore being utilized for the disposal injection of waste oil well brine and byproducts.
   (4) A well or well bore being utilized for the production of water for use in oil field injection, waterflood, and pressure maintenance programs.
(c) Termination of the right of entry or occupation within the subject land in the manner requested by the plaintiff, or subject to such conditions as the court may impose pursuant to this section, will not significantly interfere with the right of the lessee, under the lease, to continue to conduct operations for the continued production of oil from leasehold strata beneath the surface zone in a practical and economic manner, utilizing such production techniques as will be appropriate to the leasehold area, consistent with good oilfield practice, and to gather, transport, and market the oil.
Added by Stats. 1980, Ch. 44, Sec. 16.

Section 772.050 - Judgment qualified to provide limited surface and surface zone easement; judgment conditioned on relocation of pipelines, roadways, etc.
(a) The court may qualify the judgment terminating the surface and surface zone right of entry or occupation so as to provide for limited surface and surface zone easements that the lessee may continue to enjoy within the subject land.
(b) A judgment may be conditioned upon the relocation of pipelines, roadways, equipment, or lease facilities in such manner as will most effectively free the subject land for surface use while safeguarding continued oil and gas operations in a practical and economic manner. Any such condition of the judgment shall require the plaintiff to pay the costs of the relocation. However, the plaintiff shall be entitled to a setoff against the costs to the extent of any benefit to the lessee resulting from the installation of new equipment or material. The plaintiff has the burden of proving any benefit accruing to the lessee.
Added by Stats. 1980, Ch. 44, Sec. 16.

Section 772.060 - Waiver of rights created by article
It is against public policy for any oil or gas lease, at its inception, to provide for the waiver of any rights created by this article, or for such rights to be waived by amendment to any oil or gas lease within 20 years of the date of its execution by a plaintiff or the plaintiff's predecessor in interest.
Added by Stats. 1980, Ch. 44, Sec. 16.

Chapter 4.6 - ACTIONS CONCERNING REAL PROPERTY TITLES AFFECTED BY PUBLIC IMPROVEMENT ASSESSMENTS

Section 801.1 - Action to determine adverse interests upon title arising out of assessment or bond
An action may be brought to determine adverse interests in, liens or clouds upon title to real property arising out of any public improvement assessment or any bond issued to represent such assessment where the lien of such assessment or bond is presumed to have been extinguished under the provisions of Section 2911 of the Civil Code, or to determine adverse interests in, liens or clouds upon title to real property by reason of any certificate issued on sale made to satisfy any public improvement assessment or bond where such sale was made more than four years prior to the commencement of the action and no deed pursuant thereto has been issued prior to the commencement of the action or prior to January 1, 1951, whichever is the later.
Added by Stats. 1949, Ch. 1108.

Section 801.2 - Action brought as separate action or joined with other causes
The action may be brought as a separate action or joined as a cause with other causes of action to determine adverse claims to and clouds upon title to real property, but the complaint shall aver the pertinent matters stated in the preceding section and shall be verified.
Added by Stats. 1949, Ch. 1108.

Section 801.3 - Defendants to action
The complaint shall include as defendants to the action (a) all persons known to the plaintiff owning or claiming an interest under such public improvement assessment, bond or certificate of sale; (b) the payee, as shown by the bond representing the assessment, if any; (c) the owner of the special assessment or certificate of sale, if any, and any person claiming an interest therein, as shown by the records of the treasurer, street superintendent or other public official who is the custodian of the funds to be collected thereon or who issued such certificate of sale, and (d) such treasurer, street superintendent or other public official. If any person owning or claiming an interest under such assessment, bond or certificate of sale is known to be dead, the heirs and devisees of such person may be sued as: "the heirs and devisees of" said person, naming him, or if such person is believed to be dead and such belief is alleged in the complaint on information and belief then the heirs and devisees of such person may also be sued as "the heirs and devisees" of said person, naming him, provided that such person is also named as a defendant.
Amended by Stats. 1951, Ch. 521.

Section 801.4 - Unknown persons included as defendants
The complaint shall also include, as defendants, unknown persons owning or claiming an interest in such bond, special assessment or certificate of sale and they may be described in the complaint as: "Also the owner or any person claiming an interest (here describe the bond, special assessment or certificate of sale as it is described in the office in which it was issued)."
Added by Stats. 1949, Ch. 1108.

Section 801.5 - Notice of pendency of action
Within ten days after the filing of the complaint, plaintiff shall file or cause to be filed in the office of the recorder of the county where the property is situated, a notice of the pendency of the action, containing the title and object of the action and a description of the property in that county affected thereby. From the time of filing such notice of record only, shall all persons have constructive notice thereof.
Added by Stats. 1949, Ch. 1108.

Section 801.6 - Summons
Within three years after the filing of the complaint, a summons shall be issued which shall contain the matters required by Section 412.20, designating the defendants as in the complaint, and in addition, a description of the property and a statement of the object of the action.
Amended by Stats. 1969, Ch. 1611.

Section 801.7 - Posting copy of summons on property
Within thirty days after the issuance of the summons, the plaintiff shall post, or cause to be posted, a copy thereof in a conspicuous place on the property.
Added by Stats. 1949, Ch. 1108.

Section 801.8 - Service on defendants
All known defendants shall be served in the manner provided by law for the service of a summons in a civil action. All unknown defendants shall be served by publication as provided in Section 750.
Amended by Stats. 1969, Ch. 1611.

Section 801.9 - Reasonable diligence to ascertain identity and addresses of unknown defendants to appear in affidavit
In addition to the matters required to be set forth in the affidavit by the plaintiff for publication of summons, it shall appear by the affidavit that the plaintiff used reasonable diligence to ascertain the identity and residence of the unknown defendants and of any persons sued as heirs and devisees.
Amended by Stats. 1969, Ch. 1611.

Section 801.10 - Rights of unknown defendants; judgment conclusive against unknown defendants
All unknown defendants, including the heirs and devisees designated in the complaint, shall have the same rights as are provided by law for other defendants upon whom summons is served, and the action shall proceed against them in the same manner. Regardless of any legal disability, any unknown defendant, including any heir or devisee designated in the complaint, who has been served, and anyone claiming under him, shall be concluded by a judgment in the action as if the action were brought against and personal service made upon that person by his or her name.
Amended by Stats. 1969, Ch. 1611.

Section 801.11 - Presumption that certificate issued on sale made to satisfy assessment or bond paid and redeemed
On the trial of the action, the court shall determine the rights of all the parties thereto and shall require proof of the facts alleged. Any certificate issued on sale made to satisfy any public improvement assessment or any bond issued to represent such assessment shall be presumed to have been paid and redeemed where no deed pursuant thereto has been issued and such sale was made more than four years prior to the commencement of the action.
The presumption herein mentioned shall become and be conclusive if no deed pursuant to such sale is issued within four years after the date of sale or prior to January 1, 1953, whichever is the later; and no public official shall thereafter execute or issue any deed pursuant to such sale.
Amended by Stats. 1951, Ch. 521.

Section 801.12 - Decree
If the court determines that none of the defendants have any right, title, interest, lien or estate in the property, it shall render its final decree quieting the plaintiff's title. If the court determines that any of the defendants have any right, title, interest, lien or estate in the property, it shall render its decree establishing these rights and may order the sale of the property or partition thereof. The decree shall direct the public officer having the record of the assessment, bond or certificate of sale to cancel the record thereof.
Added by Stats. 1949, Ch. 1108.

Section 801.13 - Sale or partition ordered
If the court orders a sale of the property or a partition thereof, the same shall be made in accordance with the provisions of Title 10.5 (commencing with Section 872.010) of Part 2, except that proceeds of sale belonging to unknown defendants or defendants whose identities or

whereabouts are unascertained shall be paid to the public officer who is the custodian of the funds collected on such public improvement assessments, bonds or certificates of sale, to be held by him as in like instances of collection.
Amended by Stats. 1976, Ch. 73.

Section 801.14 - Decree conclusive upon becoming final
The decree, after it has become final, is conclusive against all persons named in the complaint who have been served and all unknown persons and the heirs and devisees of deceased persons designated in the complaint and served as hereinbefore provided.
Added by Stats. 1949, Ch. 1108.

Section 801.15 - Filing and recording certified copy of judgment
After the judgment has become final, a certified copy thereof shall be delivered to the public officer having the record of the assessment, bond or certificate of sale in his office and he shall thereupon mark the record of the assessment, bond or certificate of sale as follows: "Canceled by judgment of court, superior court case number (here give number)."
Added by Stats. 1949, Ch. 1108.

Chapter 5 - ACTIONS FOR THE USURPATION OF AN OFFICE OR FRANCHISE

Section 802 - Sire facies abolished
The writ of sire facies is abolished.
Amended by Code Amendments 1880, Ch. 22.

Section 803 - Action brought by Attorney General
An action may be brought by the attorney-general, in the name of the people of this state, upon his own information, or upon a complaint of a private party, against any person who usurps, intrudes into, or unlawfully holds or exercises any public office, civil or military, or any franchise, or against any corporation, either de jure or de facto, which usurps, intrudes into, or unlawfully holds or exercises any franchise, within this state. And the attorney-general must bring the action, whenever he has reason to believe that any such office or franchise has been usurped, intruded into, or unlawfully held or exercised by any person, or when he is directed to do so by the governor.
Amended by Stats. 1907, Ch. 324.

Section 804 - Name of person rightly entitled to office included in complaint
Whenever such action is brought, the Attorney General, in addition to the statement of the cause of action, may also set forth in the complaint the name of the person rightly entitled to the office, with a statement of his right thereto.
Amended by Stats. 1973, Ch. 20.

Section 805 - Judgment generally
In every such action judgment may be rendered upon the right of the defendant, and also upon the right of the party so alleged to be entitled, or only upon the right of the defendant, as justice may require.
Enacted 1872.

Section 806 - Judgment rendered upon right of person alleged to be entitled
If the judgment be rendered upon the right of the person so alleged to be entitled, and the same be in favor of such person, he will be entitled, after taking the oath of office and executing such official bond as may be required by law, to take upon himself the execution of the office.
Enacted 1872.

Section 807 - Damages recovered by person alleged to be entitled
If judgment be rendered upon the right of the person so alleged to be entitled, in favor of such person, he may recover, by action, the damages which he may have sustained by reason of the usurpation of the office by the defendant.
Enacted 1872.

Section 808 - Several persons claiming to be entitled
When several persons claim to be entitled to the same office or franchise, one action may be brought against all such persons, in order to try their respective rights to such office or franchise.
Enacted 1872.

Section 809 - Defendant guilty of usurping or intruding or unlawfully holding office, franchise or privilege
When a defendant, against whom such action has been brought, is adjudged guilty of usurping or intruding into, or unlawfully holding any office, franchise, or privilege, judgment must be rendered that such defendant be excluded from the office, franchise, or privilege, and that he pay the costs of the action. The Court may also, in its discretion, impose upon the defendant a fine not exceeding five thousand dollars, which fine, when collected, must be paid into the Treasury of the State.
Enacted 1872.

Section 810 - Undertaking when action brought upon information or application of private party
If the action is brought upon the information or application of a private party, the Attorney General may require that party to enter into an undertaking, with sureties to be approved by the Attorney General, conditioned on the party or the sureties paying any judgment for costs or damages recovered against the plaintiff, and all the costs and expenses incurred in prosecuting the action.
Amended by Stats 2017 ch 561 (AB 1516),s 23, eff. 1/1/2018.

Section 811 - Action maintained by board of supervisors or governing body of municipal corporation
The action provided for in this chapter may be maintained by the board of supervisors of any county or city and county or the legislative body of any municipal corporation, respectively, in the name of such county, city and county or municipal corporation against any person who usurps, intrudes into or unlawfully holds or exercises any franchise, or portion thereof, within the respective territorial limits of such county, city and county or municipal corporation and which is of a kind that is within the jurisdiction of such board or body to grant or withhold.
Added by Stats. 1937, Ch. 575.

Chapter 7 - ACTIONS RELATING TO GROUNDWATER RIGHTS
Article 1 - GENERAL PROVISIONS

Section 830 - Purpose and applicability of chapter
(a) This chapter establishes methods and procedures for a comprehensive adjudication.
(b) This chapter shall be applied and interpreted consistently with all of the following:
　　(1) Protecting water rights consistent with Section 2 of Article X of the California Constitution.
　　(2) Conducting a comprehensive adjudication in a manner that promotes efficiency, reduces unnecessary delays, and provides due process.
　　(3) Encouraging the compromise and settlement of comprehensive adjudications.
　　(4) Conducting a comprehensive adjudication in a manner that is consistent with the achievement of groundwater sustainability within the timeframes of the Sustainable Groundwater Management Act.
　　(5) Establishing procedures by which courts may conduct comprehensive determinations of all rights and priorities to groundwater in a basin.
　　(6) Providing for the conduct of a comprehensive adjudication consistent with Winters v. United States (1908) 207 U.S. 564, the McCarran Amendment (codified at 43 U.S.C. Sec. 666), and any other federal laws regarding the determination of federal or tribal water rights, as applicable.

(7) Providing notice and due process sufficient to enable a court in a comprehensive adjudication conducted pursuant to this chapter to determine and establish the priority for unexercised water rights. The court may consider applying the principles established in In re Waters of Long Valley Creek Stream System (1979) 25 Cal.3d 339. Except as provided in this paragraph, this chapter shall not alter groundwater rights or the law concerning groundwater rights.

(c) The other provisions of this code apply to procedures in a comprehensive adjudication to the extent they do not conflict with the provisions of this chapter.

Added by Stats 2015 ch 672 (AB 1390),s 1, eff. 1/1/2016.

Section 831 - Court fees and costs

Article 6 (commencing with Section 68630) of Chapter 2 of Title 8 of the Government Code applies to a comprehensive adjudication conducted pursuant to this chapter.

Added by Stats 2015 ch 672 (AB 1390),s 1, eff. 1/1/2016.

Section 832 - Definitions

For purposes of this chapter, the following definitions apply:

(a) "Basin" has the same meaning as defined in Section 10721 of the Water Code.

(b) "Complaint" means a complaint filed in superior court to determine rights to extract groundwater and includes any cross-complaint that initiates a comprehensive adjudication in response to a plaintiff's complaint or other cross-complaint.

(c) "Comprehensive adjudication" means an action filed in superior court to comprehensively determine rights to extract groundwater in a basin.

(d) "Condition of long-term overdraft" means the condition of a groundwater basin where the average annual amount of water extracted for a long-term period, generally 10 years or more, exceeds the long-term average annual supply of water to the basin, plus any temporary surplus. Overdraft during a period of drought is not sufficient to establish a condition of long-term overdraft if extractions and recharge are managed as necessary to ensure that reductions in groundwater levels or storage during a period of drought are offset by increases in groundwater levels or storage during other periods.

(e) "Department" means the Department of Water Resources.

(f) "Expert witness" means a witness qualified pursuant to Section 720 of the Evidence Code.

(g) "Groundwater" means water beneath the surface of the earth within the zone below the water table in which the soil is completely saturated with water, but does not include water that flows in known and definite channels.

(h) "Groundwater extraction facility" means a device or method for extracting groundwater in a basin.

(i) "Groundwater recharge" means the augmentation of groundwater, by natural or artificial means.

(j) "Person" includes, but is not limited to, counties, local agencies, state agencies, federal agencies, tribes, business entities, and individuals.

(k) "Plaintiff" means the person filing the complaint initiating a comprehensive adjudication and includes a cross-complainant who initiates a comprehensive adjudication by cross-complaint.

(l) "Public water system" has the same meaning as defined in Section 116275 of the Health and Safety Code.

(m) "State small water system" has the same meaning as defined in Section 116275 of the Health and Safety Code.

(n) "Sustainable Groundwater Management Act" means Part 2.74 (commencing with Section 10720) of Division 6 of the Water Code.

Amended by Stats 2016 ch 86 (SB 1171),s 26, eff. 1/1/2017.

Added by Stats 2015 ch 672 (AB 1390),s 1, eff. 1/1/2016.

Article 2 - SCOPE OF ACTION

Section 833 - Applicability to actions determining rights to extract groundwater in a basin

(a) Except as provided in subdivision (b), this chapter applies to actions that would comprehensively determine rights to extract groundwater in a basin, whether based on appropriation, overlying right, or other basis of right.

(b) This chapter does not apply to any of the following:

(1) An action that concerns only allegations that a groundwater extraction facility, or group of facilities, is interfering with another groundwater extraction facility or facilities and does not involve a comprehensive allocation of the basin's groundwater supply.

(2) An action that concerns only claims to extract, or to prevent interference with extractions of, a specific source of groundwater recharge and does not involve a comprehensive allocation of the basin's groundwater supply.

(3) An action that can be resolved among a limited number of parties and does not involve a comprehensive determination of rights to extract groundwater within the basin.

(4) An adjudicated area described in subdivisions (a) to (d), inclusive, of Section 10720.8 of the Water Code, unless a court with jurisdiction over a proposed expansion of the adjudicated area orders that the proceeding be conducted in accordance with this chapter.

(c) If the court finds that including an interconnected surface water body or subterranean stream flowing through known and definite channels is necessary for the fair and effective determination of the groundwater rights in a basin, the court may require the joinder of persons who claim rights to divert and use water from that surface water body or subterranean stream in a comprehensive adjudication conducted pursuant to this chapter.

(d) If the court finds that claims of right to extract or divert only minor quantities of water, not to exceed five acre-feet of water per year, would not have a material effect on the groundwater rights of other parties, the court may exempt those claimants with respect to those claims for only minor quantities of water, but a person who is exempted may elect to continue as a party to the comprehensive adjudication.

Added by Stats 2015 ch 672 (AB 1390),s 1, eff. 1/1/2016.

Section 834 - Scope of adjudication

(a) In a comprehensive adjudication conducted pursuant to this chapter, the court may determine all groundwater rights of a basin, whether based on appropriation, overlying right, or other basis of right, and use of storage space in the basin.

(b) The court's final judgment in a comprehensive adjudication, for the groundwater rights of each party, may declare the priority, amount, purposes of use, extraction location, place of use of the water, and use of storage space in the basin, together with appropriate injunctive relief, subject to terms adopted by the court to implement a physical solution in the comprehensive adjudication.

Added by Stats 2015 ch 672 (AB 1390),s 1, eff. 1/1/2016.

Article 3 - NOTICE AND SERVICE OF COMPLAINT

Section 835 - Notice

(a) The plaintiff shall provide notice of the comprehensive adjudication to all of the following:

(1) A groundwater sustainability agency that overlies the basin or a portion of the basin.

(2) A city, county, or city and county that overlies the basin or a portion of the basin.

(3) A district with authority to manage or replenish groundwater resources of the basin in whole or in part.

(4) The operator of a public water system or state small water system that uses groundwater from the basin to supply water service.

(5) A California Native American tribe that is on the contact list maintained by the Native American Heritage Commission.

(6) The Attorney General, the State Water Resources Control Board, the department, and the Department of Fish and Wildlife.

(7) A federal department or agency that manages a federal reservation that overlies the basin or a portion of the basin.

(8) A person identified under Section 836.5 who is not a party to the comprehensive adjudication.
(9) A person who is on a list, maintained by a groundwater management agency, of interested parties that have requested notice under the Sustainable Groundwater Management Act.
(b) The plaintiff may provide notice under this section by first class mail or electronic mail.
(c)
  (1) Except as provided in paragraph (2), the plaintiff shall provide notice under this section as follows:
    (A) To any person entitled to notice under paragraphs (1) to (7), inclusive, of subdivision (a) within 15 days of the filing of the complaint.
    (B) To any person entitled to notice under paragraphs (8) and (9) of subdivision (a) within 30 days of receipt of the name and address of the person entitled to notice.
  (2) The plaintiff may take additional time as is reasonably necessary before providing notice under this section if the plaintiff determines that additional time is necessary to identify a person entitled to notice under this section, confirm the accuracy of the name or address of a person, or to determine if the conditions requiring notice have been satisfied.
(d) The plaintiff is not required to provide notice under this section to a person who has already been served or intervened in the action.
Amended by Stats 2016 ch 86 (SB 1171),s 27, eff. 1/1/2017.
Added by Stats 2015 ch 672 (AB 1390),s 1, eff. 1/1/2016.

Section 836 - Draft notice and answer

(a) When the plaintiff files the complaint, the plaintiff shall also lodge with the court both of the following:
  (1)
    (A) A draft notice titled "NOTICE OF COMMENCEMENT OF GROUNDWATER BASIN ADJUDICATION" in no less than 20-point font and the following text printed immediately below the draft notice title in no less than 14-point font: "THIS NOTICE IS IMPORTANT. ANY RIGHTS YOU CLAIM TO PUMP OR STORE GROUNDWATER FROM THE BASIN IDENTIFIED IN THIS NOTICE MAY BE AFFECTED BY A LAWSUIT INITIATED BY THE COMPLAINT SUMMARIZED BELOW.
A copy of the complaint may be obtained by contacting the plaintiff or the plaintiff's attorney identified in this notice. If you claim rights to pump or store groundwater within the basin, either now or in the future, you may become a party to this lawsuit by filing an answer to the lawsuit on or before the deadline specified in this notice. You may file an answer by completing the attached form answer, filing it with the court indicated in this notice, and sending a copy of the form answer to the plaintiff or the plaintiff's attorney.
Failing to participate in this lawsuit could have a significant adverse effect on any right to pump or store groundwater that you may have. You may seek the advice of an attorney in relation to this lawsuit. Such attorney should be consulted promptly. A case management conference in this groundwater basin adjudication proceeding shall occur on the date specified in this notice. If you intend to participate in the groundwater adjudication proceeding to which this notice applies, you are advised to attend the initial case management conference in person or have an attorney represent you at the initial case management conference.
Participation requires the production of all information regarding your groundwater use. You must provide this information by the date identified in this notice.
A form answer is provided for your convenience. You may fill out the form answer and file it with the court. Should you choose to file the form answer, it will serve as an answer to all complaints and cross-complaints filed in this case."
    (B) The following information shall be provided immediately following the text described in subparagraph (A):
      (i) The name of the basin that is the subject of the comprehensive adjudication and a link to the Internet Web site address where the department has posted a map of the basin.
      (ii) A space to be completed with the case number assigned to the comprehensive adjudication, and the name and address of the court and department to which the action is assigned.
      (iii) The name, address, telephone number, and email address of the plaintiff, or plaintiff's attorney, from whom the complaint may be obtained and to whom a copy of the form answer should be sent.
      (iv) A summary of the causes of action alleged in the complaint and the relief sought. The summary shall not exceed 25 lines.
      (v) A date by which persons receiving the notice must appear in the comprehensive adjudication.
  (2)
    (A) A draft form answer titled "ANSWER TO ADJUDICATION COMPLAINT" in no less than 20-point font and the following text printed immediately below the draft form answer title in no less than 14-point font: "The undersigned denies all material allegations in the complaint or cross-complaint in this action that seeks to adjudicate rights in the groundwater basin and asserts all applicable affirmative defenses to that complaint."
    (B) Notwithstanding any other law, the filing of an answer in the form described in subparagraph (A) in a comprehensive adjudication is sufficient to put at issue all material allegations and applicable affirmative defenses to the complaint in the comprehensive adjudication. If a party intends to seek adjustment of the basin's boundaries, it shall disclose that intention in the form answer described in subparagraph (A).
(b) Within 30 days of the assignment of a judge by the Chairperson of the Judicial Council, the plaintiff shall file a motion for approval of the draft notice and draft form answer filed pursuant to subdivision (a). The plaintiff's motion shall include a copy of the draft notice and draft form answer filed pursuant to subdivision (a).
(c) Once the court approves the draft notice, service of that notice in accordance with this section shall substitute for the summons otherwise provided for in civil actions pursuant to Section 412.20.
(d)
  (1) Following a court order approving the notice and form answer and authorizing service of landowners pursuant to this section, the plaintiff shall do all of the following:
    (A) Identify the assessor parcel numbers and physical addresses of all real property in the basin and the names and addresses of all holders of fee title to real property in the basin using the records of the assessor or assessors of the county or counties in which the basin to be adjudicated lies. The plaintiff shall provide the court and all parties with notice of its acquisition of, or sufficient access to, this information.
    (B) Mail, by registered mail or certified mail, return receipt requested, the notice, complaint, and form answer to all holders of fee title to real property in the basin. If the physical address of the real property differs from the address of the holder of fee title, the notice, complaint, and form answer shall be mailed by registered or certified mail, return receipt requested, to the physical address of the real property and the address of the holder of fee title.
    (C) If return receipt is not received for a parcel of real property, the plaintiff shall post a copy of the notice, complaint, and form answer in a conspicuous place on the real property.
    (D) Within 20 days of the court order, publish the notice at least once per week for four consecutive weeks in one or more newspapers of general circulation in each county overlying the basin in whole or in part.
  (2) Service pursuant to this subdivision is not required if the real property is owned by a person in a class of water users that are otherwise noticed in accordance with this chapter. If the owner is part of a class of water users proposed for certification, service is not required until the court acts on the proposal for certification.
(e) After completing the mailing pursuant to subdivision (d), the plaintiff shall file with the court a notice of the completion of the mailing.

(f) A property owner who has received notice of the comprehensive adjudication and transfers property during the pendency of the comprehensive adjudication shall disclose, on the Real Estate Transfer Disclosure Statement, that the property is subject to a comprehensive adjudication and shall attach the court-approved notice to the Real Estate Transfer Disclosure Statement.

(g) Following a court order authorizing service of landowners pursuant to this section, the plaintiff shall serve any known person that pumps groundwater who would not otherwise be served pursuant to subdivision (d) of this section, except those who have been exempted by the court pursuant to subdivision (d) of Section 833 or those who are part of a class certified pursuant to paragraph (2) of subdivision (d) of this section. Service pursuant to this subdivision shall be by personal delivery or by mail in the manner prescribed by Article 3 (commencing with Section 415.10) of Chapter 4 of Title 5.

(h) Service on the United States shall be made in accordance with Section 666 of Title 43 of the United States Code.

(i) The court may authorize any other procedures it finds appropriate and necessary to provide notice to persons who may hold groundwater rights in the basin.

(j) Compliance with the service and notice provisions of this chapter shall be deemed effective service of process of the complaint and notice on all interested parties of the comprehensive adjudication for purposes of establishing in rem jurisdiction and the comprehensive effect of the comprehensive adjudication.

(k) Whenever proceedings are instituted under this chapter, it shall be the duty of all claimants interested in the proceedings and having notice of the proceedings pursuant to this chapter to appear in the proceedings and to submit proof of their claims at the time, and in the manner, required by this chapter.

(l) The court may require notice to be made available in languages other than English.

(m) Within 15 days of the court order approving the notice and form answer, the plaintiff shall provide the notice and form answer to the department and each county and groundwater sustainability agency that overlies the basin or a portion of the basin. The department, and each county and groundwater sustainability agency that overlies the basin or a portion of the basin and has an Internet Web site shall do all of the following:

(1) Within 15 days of receiving the notice and form answer, post those documents on its Internet Web site.

(2) Provide a link to the notice and form answer on the home page of its Internet Web site.

(3) Maintain the posting and link described in paragraphs (1) and (2) for the entire time the comprehensive adjudication is pending. The plaintiff shall notify the department and each county and groundwater sustainability agency when the comprehensive adjudication is no longer pending.

Added by Stats 2015 ch 672 (AB 1390),s 1, eff. 1/1/2016.

Section 836.5 - Requests for information regarding persons reporting extractions within basin

(a) Within 15 days of the court order approving the notice and form answer under Section 836, the plaintiff shall request from the following entities the names and addresses of persons reporting extractions within the basin under the Sustainable Groundwater Management Act, or Part 5 (commencing with Section 4999) or Part 5.2 (commencing with Section 5200) of Division 2 of the Water Code:

(1) The State Water Resources Control Board.

(2) A local agency designated under Section 5009 of the Water Code as the local agency for a board-designated local area that includes the basin or a portion of the basin.

(3) A groundwater sustainability agency for the basin or a portion of the basin.

(b) The entities described in paragraphs (1) to (3), inclusive, of subdivision (a) shall provide the plaintiff with the names, mailing addresses, and email addresses, if available, within 45 days of the plaintiff's request. The State Water Resources Control Board shall also provide the mailing address and email addresses, if available, of any person known to the board who holds a permit or license authorizing underground storage in the basin or who claims a right to divert water for underground storage in the basin.

(c) Upon request, the plaintiff shall reimburse the reasonable costs incurred under this section by an entity described in paragraphs (1) to (3), inclusive, of subdivision (a).

(d) An entity shall not be held civilly liable for complying with this section.

Added by Stats 2015 ch 672 (AB 1390),s 1, eff. 1/1/2016.

Article 4 - INTERVENTION

Section 837 - Intervention

(a) A groundwater sustainability agency for the basin or a portion of the basin may intervene in a comprehensive adjudication conducted pursuant to this chapter.

(b) A city, county, or city and county that overlies the basin or a portion of the basin may intervene in a comprehensive adjudication conducted pursuant to this chapter.

(c) The court shall allow any person to intervene in a comprehensive adjudication conducted pursuant to this chapter upon an ex parte application that demonstrates that the person holds fee simple ownership in a parcel in the basin, or extracts or stores water in the basin. A person filing an ex parte application pursuant to this subdivision shall give notice to the plaintiff consistent with the California Rules of Court.

(d) A person may apply to intervene in a comprehensive adjudication conducted pursuant to this chapter pursuant to Section 387.

Added by Stats 2015 ch 672 (AB 1390),s 1, eff. 1/1/2016.

Section 837.5 - State intervention

(a) The state may intervene in a comprehensive adjudication conducted pursuant to this chapter.

(b) This section does not affect substantive law.

Added by Stats 2015 ch 676 (SB 226),s 1, eff. 1/1/2016.

Article 5 - JUDGE

Section 838 - Assignment of judge

(a)

(1) In a comprehensive adjudication conducted pursuant to this chapter, a judge of a superior court of a county that overlies the basin or any portion of the basin shall be disqualified. The Chairperson of the Judicial Council shall assign a judge to preside in all proceedings in the comprehensive adjudication.

(2) A judge of the superior court in which an action is filed may, on the court's own motion or the motion of a party, determine if the action is a comprehensive adjudication under Section 833. A motion for a determination pursuant to this paragraph shall receive calendar preference within the action and shall be resolved before other procedural or dispositive motions.

(b) A comprehensive adjudication is presumed to be a complex action under Rule 3.400 of the California Rules of Court.

(c) Sections 170.6 and 394 shall not apply in a comprehensive adjudication.

(d) Notwithstanding subdivision (b) of Section 10726.6 of the Water Code, an action against a groundwater sustainability agency that is located in a basin that is being adjudicated pursuant to this chapter shall be subject to transfer, coordination, and consolidation with the comprehensive adjudication, as appropriate, if the action concerns the adoption, substance, or implementation of a groundwater sustainability plan, or the groundwater sustainability agency's compliance with the timelines in the Sustainable Groundwater Management Act.

(e) The judge assigned by the Chairperson of the Judicial Council pursuant to subdivision (a) shall determine if transfer, coordination, or consolidation is appropriate.
Added by Stats 2015 ch 672 (AB 1390),s 1, eff. 1/1/2016.

Article 6 - ELECTRONIC SERVICE

Section 839 - Service of pleadings and papers; electronic service system
Service of pleadings and papers in a comprehensive adjudication, other than the complaint initiating a comprehensive adjudication, shall occur electronically to the greatest extent possible. The court may provide, or authorize the use of, an electronic service system. If an electronic service system is not provided or authorized by the court, the court and the parties shall serve documents by email or other equivalent electronic means to the greatest extent possible. To enable electronic service of pleadings and papers, the attorneys of record or parties representing themselves shall include an email address for service in the captions of all pleadings they file in the comprehensive adjudication.
Added by Stats 2015 ch 672 (AB 1390),s 1, eff. 1/1/2016.

Article 7 - CASE MANAGEMENT

Section 840 - Case management conference
(a) In managing a comprehensive adjudication, the court shall convene a case management conference as provided by the California Rules of Court.
(b) In an initial case management conference, or as soon as practicable, the court may consider the following in addition to other matters:
 (1) Determining whether to seek adjustment of the basin boundaries pursuant to Section 841.
 (2) Staying the action pursuant to Section 848.
 (3) Appointing a special master pursuant to Section 845.
 (4) Scheduling a hearing on a preliminary injunction pursuant to Section 847.
 (5) Dividing the case into phases to resolve legal and factual issues.
 (6) Issuing orders to ensure that issues resolved in one phase are not relitigated in another phase.
 (7) Limiting discovery to correspond to the phases.
 (8) Scheduling early resolution of claims to prescriptive rights.
 (9) Forming a class or classes of overlying groundwater rights holders pursuant to the criteria specified in Section 382.
Added by Stats 2015 ch 672 (AB 1390),s 1, eff. 1/1/2016.

Article 8 - BASIN BOUNDARIES

Section 841 - Boundaries
(a) Except as otherwise provided in this section, the boundaries of the area subject to a comprehensive adjudication shall be consistent with the boundaries of a basin.
(b) If the department revises the boundaries of a basin pursuant to Section 10722.2, or subdivision (b) of Section 12924, of the Water Code after a comprehensive adjudication has been initiated, the court may revise the boundaries of the area subject to the comprehensive adjudication as the interests of justice and the objectives of this chapter require.
(c) Upon a showing that a revision of the basin boundaries would further a fair and effective determination of water rights, the court may direct any of the following to submit a request to the department pursuant to Section 10722.2 of the Water Code to revise the basin boundaries:
 (1) A party to the comprehensive adjudication.
 (2) The State Water Resources Control Board, if the court has made a reference pursuant to Part 3 (commencing with Section 2000) of Division 2 of the Water Code.
 (3) A special master, if one has been appointed.
(d) A determination of the department on a submission made pursuant to subdivision (c) is subject to judicial review pursuant to Section 1085. Venue shall be in the court with jurisdiction over the comprehensive adjudication and the case shall be coordinated with the comprehensive adjudication.
Added by Stats 2015 ch 672 (AB 1390),s 1, eff. 1/1/2016.

Article 9 - INITIAL DISCLOSURES

Section 842 - Service of initial disclosure
(a) Except as otherwise stipulated by the parties or ordered by the court, within six months of appearing in a comprehensive adjudication, a party shall serve on the other parties and the special master, if one is appointed, an initial disclosure that includes all of the following information:
 (1) The name, address, telephone number, and email address of the party and, if applicable, the party's attorney.
 (2) The quantity of any groundwater extracted from the basin by the party and the method of measurement used by the party or the party's predecessor in interest for each of the previous 10 years preceding the filing of the complaint.
 (3) The type of water right or rights claimed by the party for the extraction of groundwater.
 (4) A general description of the purpose to which the groundwater has been put.
 (5) The location of each well or other source through which groundwater has been extracted.
 (6) The area in which the groundwater has been used.
 (7) Any claims for increased or future use of groundwater.
 (8) The quantity of any beneficial use of any alternative water use that the party claims as its use of groundwater under any applicable law, including, but not limited to, Section 1005.1, 1005.2, or 1005.4 of the Water Code.
 (9) Identification of all surface water rights and contracts that the party claims provides the basis for its water right claims in the comprehensive adjudication.
 (10) The quantity of any replenishment of water to the basin that augmented the basin's native water supply, resulting from the intentional storage of imported or non-native water in the basin, managed recharge of surface water, or return flows resulting from the use of imported water or non-native water on lands overlying the basin by the party, or the party's representative or agent, during each of the 10 calendar years immediately preceding the filing of the complaint.
 (11) The names, addresses, telephone numbers, and email addresses of all persons possessing information that supports the party's disclosures.
 (12) Any other facts that tend to prove the party's claimed water right.
(b) The Judicial Council may develop a form for initial disclosures made pursuant to subdivision (a) to facilitate the consistent, independent, impartial, and accessible administration of comprehensive adjudications. The Judicial Council may coordinate with the department in developing the form.
(c) A party shall make its initial disclosures based on the information then reasonably available to it. A party is not excused from making its initial disclosures because it has not fully investigated the case, because it challenges the sufficiency of another party's disclosures, or because another party has not made its disclosures.

(d) A party that has made its initial disclosures, as described in subdivision (a), or that has responded to another party's discovery request, shall supplement or correct a disclosure or response in all of the following situations:

    (1) In a timely manner if the party learns that in some material respect the disclosure or response is incomplete or incorrect and the additional or corrective information has not otherwise been made known to the other parties during the disclosure or discovery process.

    (2) If the party extracts groundwater from the basin after the complaint is filed. A supplement filed pursuant to this paragraph shall report the quantity of water extracted and be filed within 90 days after the end of the calendar year.

    (3) As ordered by the court.

(e) To the greatest extent possible, a party shall serve his or her initial disclosures electronically. If it is not possible for the party to serve his or her disclosures electronically, he or she shall serve the disclosures in an electronic format saved on a portable storage media device such as a compact disc or flash drive.

(f) A party's obligations under this section may be enforced by a court on its own motion or the motion of a party to compel disclosure.

(g) A party's disclosures under this section shall be verified under penalty of perjury as being true and correct to the best of the party's knowledge.
Added by Stats 2015 ch 672 (AB 1390),s 1, eff. 1/1/2016.

Article 10 - EXPERT WITNESSES

Section 843 - Disclosure of expert witnesses

(a) In addition to all other disclosures required by this chapter, a party shall disclose to the other parties the identity of any expert witness it may use at trial to present evidence.

(b) Unless otherwise stipulated by the parties or ordered by the court, the disclosure made pursuant to subdivision (a) shall be accompanied by a written report prepared and signed by the expert witness if the witness is retained or specially employed by the party offering the expert witness to testify as an expert in the action, or if the expert witness's duties as the party's employee regularly involves giving expert testimony. The report shall include all of the following:

    (1) A complete statement of all opinions the witness will express and the basis and reasons for those opinions.

    (2) The facts or data considered by the witness in forming his or her opinions.

    (3) Any exhibits the witness will use to summarize or support his or her opinions.

    (4) The witness's qualifications, including a list of all publications authored by the witness in the previous 10 years.

    (5) A list of all other cases in which the witness testified as an expert at trial or by deposition in the last five years.

    (6) A statement of the compensation to be paid for the witness's work and testimony in the comprehensive adjudication.

(c) If subdivision (b) does not apply to an expert witness because of a stipulation by the parties or an order of the court, the witness's disclosure shall include both of the following:

    (1) The subject matter on which the witness is expected to present evidence.

    (2) A summary of the witness's opinions, and the facts or data considered by the witness in forming his or her opinions.

(d) Unless otherwise stipulated by the parties, a party shall make the disclosures of any expert witness it intends to present at trial, except for an expert witness presented solely for purposes of impeachment or rebuttal, at the times and in the sequence ordered by the court. If there is no stipulation or court order, the disclosures of an expert witness shall be made as follows:

    (1) At least 30 days after the court's entry of an order establishing the scope of the relevant phase of the comprehensive adjudication.

    (2) Except for a supplemental expert witness described in paragraph (3), at least 60 days before the date set for trial of the relevant phase of the comprehensive adjudication.

    (3) For a supplemental expert witness who will express an opinion on a subject to be covered by another expert witness designated by an adverse party that was not among the subjects covered by an expert witness initially disclosed by the party offering the supplemental expert witness, no more than 20 days after the initial expert witness disclosure date.

(e) The court may modify the disclosure requirements of subdivisions (b) to (d), inclusive, for expert witnesses presented solely for purposes of impeachment or rebuttal. In modifying the disclosure requirements, the court shall adopt disclosure requirements that expedite the court's consideration of the issues presented and shall ensure that expert testimony presented solely for purposes of impeachment or rebuttal is strictly limited to the scope of the testimony that it intends to impeach or rebut.

(f)

    (1) A party whose expert witness has made a disclosure pursuant to this section shall promptly supplement or correct the expert witness's disclosure in either of the following instances:

        (A) In a timely manner if the party learns that in some material respect the disclosure is incomplete or incorrect, if the additional or corrective information has not otherwise been made known to the other parties during the disclosure or discovery process.

        (B) As ordered by the court.

    (2) A party's duty to supplement or correct its expert witness's disclosure includes the information included in the report and the information given during the expert witness's deposition. Unless otherwise stipulated by the parties or ordered by the court, any supplementation or correction shall occur at least 14 days before trial of the applicable phase of the comprehensive adjudication.

    (3) The court may authorize a supplemental deposition of an expert witness based on a supplemental disclosure made pursuant to this subdivision. The court shall appropriately condition the authorization of a supplemental deposition of an expert witness to ensure the expeditious completion of the applicable phase of the comprehensive adjudication. The court may require the party whose expert makes the supplemental disclosure to pay some or all of the costs associated with the supplemental deposition.

(g) To the greatest extent possible, the parties shall serve expert witness disclosures electronically through an electronic service system, an electronic document repository, email, or another method of electronic transmission. If it is not possible for the party to serve his or her expert witness disclosures electronically, he or she shall serve the expert witness disclosures in an electronic format saved on a portable storage media device such as a compact disc or flash drive.
Added by Stats 2015 ch 672 (AB 1390),s 1, eff. 1/1/2016.

Article 11 - WRITTEN TESTIMONY

Section 844 - Submission of written testimony in lieu of live

(a) A court may require the parties in a comprehensive adjudication to submit written testimony of relevant witnesses in the forms of affidavits or declarations under penalty of perjury in lieu of presenting live testimony. The required written testimony may include, but is not limited to, expert witness opinions and testimony that authenticates documentary evidence. The court may order that the written testimony constitutes the entirety of the witness's direct testimony, require the written testimony to include any exhibits offered in support of the written testimony, and, in the case of written testimony of an expert witness, require a statement of the witness's qualifications.

(b) If the court requires the submission of written testimony pursuant to subdivision (a), a complete copy of the direct testimony shall be served at least 21 days before trial. A complete copy of any rebuttal testimony shall be served no later than the first day of trial.

(c) If the contents of the written testimony would have been admissible if the witness testified orally, the written testimony shall be received by the court as a documentary exhibit if the witness whose written testimony is being offered is made available for cross-examination by all parties.
Added by Stats 2015 ch 672 (AB 1390),s 1, eff. 1/1/2016.

Article 12 - SPECIAL MASTER

Section 845 - Appointment of special master

(a) The court may appoint one or more special masters whose duties may include the following:

(1) Investigating technical and legal issues, as directed by the court. The special master shall compile a report of findings in accordance with Section 846.

(2) Conducting joint factfinding with the parties, their designees, or both.

(3) Investigating the need for, and developing a proposal for, a preliminary injunction pursuant to Article 13 (commencing with Section 847).

(4) Performing other tasks the court may deem appropriate.

(b) The court shall fix the special master's compensation on the basis and terms stated in the appointing order, and the court may set a new basis and new terms after giving the parties notice and an opportunity to be heard. The court shall allocate payment of the special master's compensation among the parties in an amount and a manner that the court deems equitable. The court may waive a party's obligations to pay the special master's compensation upon a showing of good cause.

(c) The court may request the State Water Resources Control Board or the department to recommend candidates for appointment as a special master or to review the qualifications of candidates.

(d) This section does not limit the authority of the court to make a reference pursuant to Chapter 1 (commencing with Section 2000) of Part 3 of Division 2 of the Water Code.

(e) This section does not limit the authority to appoint a watermaster pursuant to Chapter 3 (commencing with Section 4050) of Part 4 of Division 2 of the Water Code or any other law.

Added by Stats 2015 ch 672 (AB 1390),s 1, eff. 1/1/2016.

Section 846 - Draft report

(a) The special master shall make a draft report available to the parties and provide at least 60 days for the parties to submit written objections to the draft report.

(b) An objection to the draft report shall identify the specific grounds and evidence on which the objection is based.

(c) The special master may notice and hold hearings, as he or she deems appropriate, to gather information or address issues raised in the objections to the draft report.

(d) The special master shall consider the objections to the draft report and develop a final report that shall be filed with the court, together with supporting evidence.

Added by Stats 2015 ch 672 (AB 1390),s 1, eff. 1/1/2016.

Article 13 - PRELIMINARY INJUNCTION

Section 847 - Issuance of preliminary injunction

(a) Upon a showing that the basin is in a condition of long-term overdraft, the court may, upon notice and hearing, issue a preliminary injunction.

(b) Bulletins and other reports of the department, and a report of a special master indicating that a condition of long-term overdraft exists in the basin, shall be admissible as evidence of a condition of long-term overdraft. This subdivision does not limit the admissibility of other relevant evidence.

(c) The preliminary injunction may include any of the following terms:

(1) A moratorium on new or increased appropriations of water.

(2) A limitation on, or reduction in, the diversion or extraction of water.

(3) An allocation among the parties establishing amounts of extraction allowed during the pendency of the comprehensive adjudication.

(4) Procedures for voluntary transfers.

(d) The court shall issue a preliminary injunction upon determining all of the following:

(1) The basin is in a condition of long-term overdraft.

(2) The basin has been designated as a probationary basin or the planning deadlines in subdivision (a) of Section 10720.7 of the Water Code are not being complied with.

(3) There is no interim plan in effect under Section 10735.8 of the Water Code.

(e) The court may provide a schedule for further reductions in extractions over a period of years if it finds that doing so appears reasonably necessary to achieve groundwater sustainability within the timelines provided in subdivision (b) of Section 10727.2 of the Water Code.

(f) The terms of a preliminary injunction shall not determine the rights in a final judgment of the comprehensive adjudication.

(g) A bond or undertaking shall not be required for the issuance of a preliminary injunction pursuant to this section.

(h) The court may appoint a watermaster to oversee enforcement of the preliminary injunction.

Added by Stats 2015 ch 672 (AB 1390),s 1, eff. 1/1/2016.

Article 14 - STAY

Section 848 - Stay

(a) Upon the court's own motion or the motion of any party to a comprehensive adjudication, a court may stay a comprehensive adjudication for a period of up to one year, subject to renewal in the court's discretion upon a showing of good cause, in order to facilitate any of the following:

(1) Adoption of a groundwater sustainability plan that provides for a physical solution or otherwise addresses issues in the comprehensive adjudication.

(2) The development of technical studies that may be useful to the parties in the comprehensive adjudication.

(3) Voluntary mediation or participation in a settlement conference on all, or a portion of, the subject matters or legal questions identified in the comprehensive adjudication.

(4) Compromise and settlement of the comprehensive adjudication or issues in the comprehensive adjudication.

(b) Before renewing a stay granted pursuant to subdivision (a), the parties shall report on the progress being made on the issues that were identified as the reasons for the stay.

(c) A stay pursuant to this section shall not stay, or otherwise delay, the parties' obligations to provide initial disclosures pursuant to Section 842 unless the court determines the initial disclosures will not benefit resolution of the comprehensive adjudication.

Added by Stats 2015 ch 672 (AB 1390),s 1, eff. 1/1/2016.

Article 15 - PHYSICAL SOLUTION

Section 849 - Authority

(a) The court shall have the authority and the duty to impose a physical solution on the parties in a comprehensive adjudication where necessary and consistent with Article 2 of Section X of the California Constitution.

(b) Before adopting a physical solution, the court shall consider any existing groundwater sustainability plan or program.

Added by Stats 2015 ch 672 (AB 1390),s 1, eff. 1/1/2016.

Article 16 - JUDGMENT

Section 850 - Entry of judgment

(a) The court may enter a judgment in a comprehensive adjudication if the court finds that the judgment meets all of the following criteria:

(1) It is consistent with Section 2 of Article X of the California Constitution.

(2) It is consistent with the water right priorities of all non-stipulating parties and any persons who have claims that are exempted pursuant to Section 833 in the basin.

(3) It treats all objecting parties and any persons who have claims that are exempted pursuant to Section 833 equitably as compared to the stipulating parties.

(b) If a party or group of parties submits a proposed stipulated judgment that is supported by more than 50 percent of all parties who are groundwater extractors in the basin or use the basin for groundwater storage and is supported by groundwater extractors responsible for at least 75 percent of the groundwater extracted in the basin during the five calendar years before the filing of the complaint, the court may adopt the proposed stipulated judgment, as applied to the stipulating parties, if the proposed stipulated judgment meets the criteria described in subdivision (a). A party objecting to a proposed stipulated judgment shall demonstrate, by a preponderance of evidence, that the proposed stipulated judgment does not satisfy one or more criteria described in subdivision (a) or that it substantially violates the water rights of the objecting party. If the objecting party is unable to make this showing, the court may impose the proposed stipulated judgment on the objecting party. An objecting party may be subject to a preliminary injunction issued pursuant to Section 847 while his or her objections are being resolved.

Amended by Stats 2016 ch 86 (SB 1171),s 28, eff. 1/1/2017.

Added by Stats 2015 ch 672 (AB 1390),s 1, eff. 1/1/2016.

Article 17 - JUDGMENT BINDING ON SUCCESSORS

Section 851 - Judgment binding on successors

The judgment in a comprehensive adjudication conducted pursuant to this chapter shall be binding on the parties to the comprehensive adjudication and all their successors in interest, including, but not limited to, heirs, executors, administrators, assigns, lessees, licensees, the agents and employees of the parties to the comprehensive adjudication and all their successors in interest, and all landowners or other persons claiming rights to extract groundwater from the basin whose claims have not been exempted and are covered by the notice provided in the comprehensive adjudication.

Amended by Stats 2016 ch 86 (SB 1171),s 31, eff. 1/1/2017.

Added by Stats 2015 ch 672 (AB 1390),s 1, eff. 1/1/2016.

Article 18 - CONTINUING JURISDICTION

Section 852 - Continuing jurisdiction

The court shall have continuing jurisdiction to modify or amend a final judgment in a comprehensive adjudication in response to new information, changed circumstances, the interests of justice, or to ensure that the criteria of subdivision (a) of Section 850 are met. If feasible, the judge who heard the original comprehensive adjudication shall preside over actions or motions to modify or amend the final judgment.

Amended by Stats 2016 ch 86 (SB 1171),s 33, eff. 1/1/2017.

Added by Stats 2015 ch 672 (AB 1390),s 1, eff. 1/1/2016.

Chapter 8 - ACTIONS AGAINST COOWNERS OF MINES

Section 853 - Notice of co-owner's failure to contribute proportionate share of taxes for period of five years

Upon the failure of a coowner of a mine or mining claim to contribute his proportionate share of the taxes that have been levied and assessed upon the mine or mining claim for the period of five years, a coowner who has paid that share may, at the expiration of the five years, serve upon the delinquent coowner notice thereof.

Renumbered from Ca. Civ. Proc. Code § 850 by Stats 2016 ch 86 (SB 1171),s 29, eff. 1/1/2017.

Chapter heading amended by Stats 2016 ch 86 (SB 1171),s 30, eff. 1/1/2017.

Section 854 - Service of notice

The notice shall be served in the manner provided by law for the service of a summons in a civil action, but where service is by publication, the publication shall be in a newspaper of general circulation published in the county in which the mine or mining claim is situated or if there is no such newspaper, in such a newspaper in an adjoining county, and the publication shall be at least once a week for 90 days.

Renumbered from Ca. Civ. Proc. Code § 851 by Stats 2016 ch 86 (SB 1171),s 32, eff. 1/1/2017.

Section 855 - Filing petition upon delinquent's failure or refusal to contribute

If before the expiration of 90 days from the service the delinquent fails or refuses to contribute his proportionate share of the taxes, the coowner contributing such share may file in the superior court of the county in which the mine or mining claim is situated a verified petition setting forth the facts and particularly describing the mine or mining claim.

Renumbered from Ca. Civ. Proc. Code § 852 by Stats 2016 ch 86 (SB 1171),s 34, eff. 1/1/2017.

Section 856 - Place of filing if mine or claim situated in more than one county

If the mine or mining claim is situated in more than one county, the petition may be filed in the superior court of either county.

Renumbered from Ca. Civ. Proc. Code § 853 by Stats 2016 ch 86 (SB 1171),s 35, eff. 1/1/2017.

Section 857 - Setting petition for hearing, notice

The clerk shall set the petition for hearing by the court and give notice of the hearing by causing a notice of the time and place of the hearing to be posted at the county courthouse at least 10 days before the hearing. The court may order such further notice as it deems proper.

Renumbered from Ca. Civ. Proc. Code § 854 and amended by Stats 2016 ch 86 (SB 1171),s 36, eff. 1/1/2017.

Section 858 - Judgment vesting interest of delinquent

The court shall hear evidence for or against the petition and may order judgment on the petition vesting the interest of the delinquent in the mine or mining claim in the petitioner.

Renumbered from Ca. Civ. Proc. Code § 855 and amended by Stats 2016 ch 86 (SB 1171),s 37, eff. 1/1/2017.

Section 859 - Recording certified copy of decree

A certified copy of the decree may be recorded in the office of the recorder of each county in which any part of the mine or mining claim is situated.

Renumbered from Ca. Civ. Proc. Code § 856 and amended by Stats 2016 ch 86 (SB 1171),s 38, eff. 1/1/2017.

Chapter 9 - VALIDATING PROCEEDINGS

Section 860 - Action by public agency to determine validity of matter

A public agency may upon the existence of any matter which under any other law is authorized to be determined pursuant to this chapter, and for 60 days thereafter, bring an action in the superior court of the county in which the principal office of the public agency is located to determine the validity of such matter. The action shall be in the nature of a proceeding in rem.

Added by Stats. 1961, Ch. 1479.

Section 861 - Jurisdiction of interested parties had by publication of summons

Jurisdiction of all interested parties may be had by publication of summons pursuant to Section 6063 of the Government Code in a newspaper of general circulation designated by the court, published in the county where the action is pending and whenever possible within the boundaries of

the public agency, and in such other counties as may be ordered by the court, and if there be no such newspaper in any such county or counties then in some adjoining county. In addition, prior to completion of such publication, the agency shall, to the extent which the court finds reasonably practicable, give notice of the pendency of the proceeding by mail or other means ordered by the court.
Added by Stats. 1961, Ch. 1479.

Section 861.1 - Requirements of summons
The summons shall be directed to "all persons interested in the matter of [specifying the matter]," and shall contain a notice to all persons interested in the matter that they may contest the legality or validity of the matter by appearing and filing a written answer to the complaint not later than the date specified in the summons, which date shall be 10 or more days after the completion of publication of the summons. The summons shall provide a detailed summary of the matter the public agency or other person seeks to validate. The summons shall also state that persons who contest the legality or validity of the matter will not be subject to punitive action, such as wage garnishment or seizure of their real or personal property. Except as otherwise specified in this section the summons shall be in the form prescribed in Section 412.20.
Amended by Stats. 1998, Ch. 529, Sec. 1. Effective January 1, 1999.

Section 862 - Jurisdiction complete after specified date in summons
Jurisdiction shall be complete after the date specified in the summons. Any party interested may, not later than the date specified in the summons, appear and contest the legality or validity of the matter sought to be determined.
Amended by Stats. 1965, Ch. 894.

Section 863 - Interested person bringing action if no proceedings brought by public agency
If no proceedings have been brought by the public agency pursuant to this chapter, any interested person may bring an action within the time and in the court specified by Section 860 to determine the validity of such matter. The public agency shall be a defendant and shall be served with the summons and complaint in the action in the manner provided by law for the service of a summons in a civil action. In any such action the summons shall be in the form prescribed in Section 861.1 except that in addition to being directed to "all persons interested in the matter of [specifying the matter]," it shall also be directed to the public agency. If the interested person bringing such action fails to complete the publication and such other notice as may be prescribed by the court in accordance with Section 861 and to file proof thereof in the action within 60 days from the filing of his complaint, the action shall be forthwith dismissed on the motion of the public agency unless good cause for such failure is shown by the interested person.
Amended by Stats. 1969, Ch. 1611.

Section 864 - Bonds, warrants, contracts, obligations, etc. deemed in existence upon authorization
For purposes of this chapter, bonds, warrants, contracts, obligations, and evidences of indebtedness shall be deemed to be in existence upon their authorization. Bonds and warrants shall be deemed authorized as of the date of adoption by the governing body of the public agency of a resolution or ordinance authorizing their issuance, and contracts shall be deemed authorized as of the date of adoption by the governing body of the public agency of a resolution or ordinance approving the contract and authorizing its execution.
Added by Stats. 1961, Ch. 1479.

Section 865 - Consolidation of actions
If more than one action is pending concerning similar contests which may be brought under this chapter, they shall be consolidated for trial.
Added by Stats. 1961, Ch. 1479.

Section 866 - Error, irregularity, omission not affecting substantial rights disregarded
The court hearing the action shall disregard any error, irregularity, or omission which does not affect the substantial rights of the parties.
Added by Stats. 1961, Ch. 1479.

Section 867 - Actions given preference
Actions brought pursuant to this chapter shall be given preference over all other civil actions before the court in the matter of setting the same for hearing or trial, and in hearing the same, to the end that such actions shall be speedily heard and determined.
Added by Stats. 1961, Ch. 1479.

Section 867.5 - Action by party answering after dismissal by public agency
(a) In the event that an action is brought by a public agency pursuant to this chapter, and that public agency later dismisses the action after any party has answered, then, notwithstanding Section 863, the party that answered may file an action pursuant to this chapter within 30 days after the public agency's dismissal was filed by the court.
(b) Subdivision (a) is not applicable to a case in which a public agency has by formal act rescinded the action on the matter subject to validation.
Added by Stats 2000 ch 723 (AB 2300), s 2, eff. 1/1/2001.

Section 868 - Costs of proceeding
The costs of any proceeding or action pursuant to this chapter may be allowed and apportioned between the parties or taxed to the losing party in the discretion of the court.
Added by Stats. 1961, Ch. 1479.

Section 869 - Mandamus or other remedy not precluded
No contest except by the public agency or its officer or agent of any thing or matter under this chapter shall be made other than within the time and the manner herein specified. The availability to any public agency, including any local agency, or to its officers or agents, of the remedy provided by this chapter, shall not be construed to preclude the use by such public agency or its officers or agents, of mandamus or any other remedy to determine the validity of any thing or matter.
Amended by Stats. 1963, Ch. 1865.

Section 870 - Judgment binding and conclusive; time for filing notice of appeal
(a) The judgment, if no appeal is taken, or if taken and the judgment is affirmed, shall, notwithstanding any other provision of law including, without limitation, Sections 473 and 473.5, thereupon become and thereafter be forever binding and conclusive, as to all matters therein adjudicated or which at that time could have been adjudicated, against the agency and against all other persons, and the judgment shall permanently enjoin the institution by any person of any action or proceeding raising any issue as to which the judgment is binding and conclusive.
(b) Notwithstanding any other provision of law including, without limitation, Section 901 and any rule of court, no appeal shall be allowed from any judgment entered pursuant to this chapter unless a notice of appeal is filed within 30 days after the notice of entry of the judgment, or, within 30 days after the entry of the judgment if there is no answering party. If there is no answering party, only issues related to the jurisdiction of the court to enter a judgment in the action pursuant to this chapter may be raised on appeal.
Amended by Stats. 1994, Ch. 242, Sec. 1. Effective July 21, 1994.

Section 870.5 - Notice to public agency imposing taxes pledged as security at time of filing action
Any local public agency that pledges sales or retail transaction and use tax revenues received from taxes imposed by another public agency for bond payments or payment of other security obligations shall, in any validation action it files involving those bonds or other obligations, provide written notice thereof to the public agency imposing the taxes pledged as security for the bonds or other obligations at the time it files the validation action.
Added by Stats. 1998, Ch. 360, Sec. 1. Effective January 1, 1999.

Chapter 10 - GOOD FAITH IMPROVER OF PROPERTY OWNED BY ANOTHER

Section 871.1 - Good faith improver defined
as used in this chapter, "good faith improver" means:
(a) A person who makes an improvement to land in good faith and under the erroneous belief, because of a mistake of law or fact, that he is the owner of the land.
(b) A successor in interest of a person described in subdivision (a).
Added by Stats. 1968, Ch. 150.

Section 871.2 - Person includes unincorporated association
As used in this chapter, "person" includes an unincorporated association.
Amended by Stats. 1971, Ch. 244.

Section 871.3 - Action treated as unlimited civil case; cross-complaint treated as limited civil case; burden
(a) An action for relief under this chapter shall be treated as an unlimited civil case, regardless of the amount in controversy and regardless of whether a defendant cross-complains for relief under this chapter. Any other case in which a defendant cross-complains for relief under this chapter shall be treated as a limited civil case if the cross-complaint is defensive and the case otherwise satisfies the amount in controversy and other requirements of Section 85.
(b) In every case, the burden is on the good faith improver to establish that the good faith improver is entitled to relief under this chapter, and the degree of negligence of the good faith improver should be taken into account by the court in determining whether the improver acted in good faith and in determining the relief, if any, that is consistent with substantial justice to the parties under the circumstances of the particular case.
Amended by Stats 2000 ch 688 (AB 1669), s 7, eff. 1/1/2001.
Previously Amended September 7, 1999 (Bill Number: SB 210) (Chapter 344).

Section 871.4 - Removal of improvement would result in substantial justice to parties
The court shall not grant relief under this chapter if the court determines that exercise of the good faith improver's right of setoff under Section 741 of the Code of Civil Procedure or right to remove the improvement under Section 1013.5 of the Civil Code would result in substantial justice to the parties under the circumstances of the particular case. In determining whether removal of the improvement would result in substantial justice to the parties under the circumstances of the particular case, the court shall take into consideration any plans the owner of the land may have for the use or development of the land upon which the improvement was made and his need for the land upon which the improvement was made in connection with the use or development of other property owned by him.
Added by Stats. 1968, Ch. 150.

Section 871.5 - Adjustment of rights, equities and interests
When an action or cross-complaint is brought pursuant to Section 871.3, the court may, subject to Section 871.4, effect such an adjustment of the rights, equities, and interests of the good faith improver, the owner of the land, and other interested parties (including, but not limited to, lessees, lienholders, and encumbrancers) as is consistent with substantial justice to the parties under the circumstances of the particular case. The relief granted shall protect the owner of the land upon which the improvement was constructed against any pecuniary loss but shall avoid, insofar as possible, enriching him unjustly at the expense of the good faith improver. In protecting the owner of the land against pecuniary loss, the court shall take into consideration the expenses the owner of the land has incurred in the action in which relief under this chapter is sought, including but not limited to reasonable attorney fees. In determining the appropriate form of relief under this section, the court shall take into consideration any plans the owner of the land may have for the use or development of the land upon which the improvement was made and his need for the land upon which the improvement was made in connection with the use or development of other property owned by him.
Amended by Stats. 1974, Ch. 244.

Section 871.6 - Relief granted for encroachment not affected
Nothing in this chapter affects the rules of law which determine the relief, if any, to be granted when a person constructs on his own land an improvement which encroaches on adjoining land.
Added by Stats. 1968, Ch. 150.

Section 871.7 - Inapplicability if improver public entity or improvement on public entity's land
(a) This chapter does not apply where the improver is a public entity or where the improvement is made to land owned or possessed by a public entity. As used in this section, "public entity" includes the United States, a state, county, city and county, city, district, public authority, public agency, or any other political subdivision or public corporation.
(b) This chapter does not apply where the owner of the land upon which the improvement is constructed has appropriated the land to a public use and could have acquired the land for that use by exercising the power of eminent domain.
Added by Stats. 1968, Ch. 150.

Chapter 11 - ACTIONS TO RECOVER COVID-19 RENTAL DEBT

Section 871.10 - [Effective until 10/1/2027] General provisions
(a) In any action seeking recovery of COVID-19 rental debt, as defined in Section 1179.02, the plaintiff shall, in addition to any other requirements provided by law, attach to the complaint documentation showing that the plaintiff has made a good faith effort to investigate whether governmental rental assistance is available to the tenant, seek governmental rental assistance for the tenant, or cooperate with the tenant's efforts to obtain rental assistance from any governmental entity, or other third party pursuant to paragraph (3) of subdivision (a) of Section 1947.3 of the Civil Code.
(b) In an action subject to subdivision (a), the court may reduce the damages awarded for any amount of COVID-19 rental debt, as defined in Section 1179.02, sought if the court determines that the landlord refused to obtain rental assistance from the state rental assistance program created pursuant to Chapter 17 (commencing with Section 50897) of Part 2 of Division 31 of the Health and Safety Code, if the tenant met the eligibility requirements and funding was available.
(c) An action to recover COVID-19 rental debt, as defined in Section 1179.02, that is subject to this section shall not be commenced before November 1, 2021.
(d) Subdivisions (a) through (c), inclusive, shall not apply to an action to recover COVID-19 rental debt, as defined in Section 1179.02, that was pending before the court as of January 29, 2021.
(e) Except as provided in subdivision (g), any action to recover COVID-19 rental debt, as defined in Section 1179.02, that is subject to this section and is pending before the court as of January 29, 2021, shall be stayed until November 1, 2021.
(f) This section shall not apply to any unlawful detainer action to recover possession pursuant to Section 1161.
(g)
    (1) Actions for breach of contract to recover rental debt that were filed before October 1, 2020, shall not be stayed and may proceed.
    (2) This subdivision does not apply to actions filed against any person who would have qualified under the rental assistance funding provided through the Secretary of the Treasury pursuant to Section 501 of Subtitle A of Title V of Division N of the federal Consolidated Appropriations Act, 2021 (Public Law 116-260) if the person's household income is at or below 80 percent of the area median income for the 2020 or 2021 calendar year.

Amended by Stats 2021 ch 27 (AB 832),s 8, eff. 6/28/2021.
Amended by Stats 2021 ch 5 (AB 81),s 7, eff. 2/23/2021.
Added by Stats 2021 ch 2 (SB 91),s 10, eff. 1/29/2021.

Section 871.11 - [Effective until 10/1/2027] Attorneys' fees

(a) Notwithstanding any other law, in any action to recover COVID-19 rental debt, as defined in Section 1179.02, brought as a limited or unlimited civil case, the court shall not, under ordinary circumstances, award reasonable attorneys' fees to a prevailing party that exceed the following amounts:

    (1) If the matter is uncontested, five hundred dollars ($500).

    (2) If the matter is contested, one thousand dollars ($1,000).

(b) In determining whether a case was litigated under ordinary circumstances, the court may consider the following:

    (1) The number and complexity of pretrial and posttrial motions.

    (2) The nature and extent of any discovery performed.

    (3) Whether the case was tried by jury or by the court.

    (4) The length of the trial.

    (5) Any other factor the court, in its discretion, finds relevant, including whether the tenant or the landlord, or both the tenant and the landlord, would have been eligible to receive a rental assistance payment from the governmental entity, or other third party pursuant to paragraph (3) of subdivision (a) of Section 1947.3 of the Civil Code.

(c) Nothing in this section shall be interpreted to entitle the prevailing party to an award of reasonable attorneys' fees if that award is not otherwise provided for by law or agreement.

(d) This section shall remain in effect until October 1, 2025, and as of that date is repealed.

Amended by Stats 2021 ch 27 (AB 832),s 9, eff. 6/28/2021.
Added by Stats 2021 ch 2 (SB 91),s 10, eff. 1/29/2021.

Section 871.12 - [Effective until 10/1/2027] Repealer

This chapter shall remain in effect until October 1, 2027, and as of the date is repealed.

Amended by Stats 2021 ch 27 (AB 832),s 10, eff. 6/28/2021.
Added by Stats 2021 ch 2 (SB 91),s 10, eff. 1/29/2021.

Title 10.5 - PARTITION OF REAL AND PERSONAL PROPERTY

Chapter 1 - GENERAL PROVISIONS

Article 1 - PRELIMINARY PROVISIONS

Section 872.010 - Definitions

As used in this title:

(a) "Action" means an action for partition under this title.

(b) "Lien" means a mortgage, deed of trust, or other security interest in property whether arising from contract, statute, common law, or equity.

(c) "Property" includes real and personal property.

(d) "Remainder" includes reversion, reversionary interest, right of entry, and executory interest.

(e) "Title report" includes a preliminary report, guarantee, binder, or policy of title insurance.

Amended by Stats. 1979, Ch. 730.

Section 872.020 - Title governs actions for partition

This title governs actions for partition of real property and, except to the extent not applicable, actions for partition of personal property.

Amended by Stats 2022 ch 82 (AB 2245),s 1, eff. 1/1/2023.
Amended by Stats 2021 ch 119 (AB 633),s 1, eff. 1/1/2022.
Added by Stats. 1976, Ch. 73.

Section 872.030 - Applicability of statutes and rules governing practice in civil actions

The statutes and rules governing practice in civil actions generally apply to actions under this title except where they are inconsistent with the provisions of this title.

Added by Stats. 1976, Ch. 73.

Section 872.040 - Compliance with laws regulations ordinances governing division sale or transfer of property

Nothing in this title excuses compliance with any applicable laws, regulations, or ordinances governing the division, sale, or transfer of property.

Added by Stats. 1976, Ch. 73.

Article 2 - POWERS OF COURT

Section 872.110 - Superior court jurisdiction; venue

(a) The superior court has jurisdiction of actions under this title.

(b) Subject to the power of the court to transfer actions, the proper county for the trial of actions under this title is:

    (1) Where the subject of the action is real property or real and personal property, the county in which the real property, or some part thereof, is situated.

    (2) Where the subject of the action is personal property, the county in which the personal property is principally located at the commencement of the action or in which the defendants, or any of them, reside at the commencement of the action.

Added by Stats. 1976, Ch. 73.

Section 872.120 - Powers of court in conducting action

In the conduct of the action, the court may hear and determine all motions, reports, and accounts and may make any decrees and orders necessary or incidental to carrying out the purposes of this title and to effectuating its decrees and orders.

Added by Stats. 1976, Ch. 73.

Section 872.130 - Temporary restraining orders and injunctions

In the conduct of the action, the court may issue temporary restraining orders and injunctions, with or without bond, for the purpose of:

(a) Preventing waste.

(b) Protecting the property or title thereto.

(c) Restraining unlawful interference with a partition of the property ordered by the court.

Added by Stats. 1976, Ch. 73.

Section 872.140 - Ordering allowance, accounting, contribution, other compensatory adjustment,

The court may, in all cases, order allowance, accounting, contribution, or other compensatory adjustment among the parties according to the principles of equity.

Added by Stats. 1976, Ch. 73.

Chapter 2 - COMMENCEMENT OF ACTION
Article 1 - COMPLAINT AND LIS PENDENS

Section 872.210 - Persons who may commence;; action relating to community property not commenced under title

(a) A partition action may be commenced and maintained by any of the following persons:

(1) A coowner of personal property.

(2) An owner of an estate of inheritance, an estate for life, or an estate for years in real property where such property or estate therein is owned by several persons concurrently or in successive estates.

(b) Notwithstanding subdivision (a), an action between spouses or putative spouses for partition of their community or quasi-community property or their quasi-marital interest in property may not be commenced or maintained under this title.

Added by Stats. 1976, Ch. 73.

Section 872.220 - Title report

If it is necessary to have a title report:

(a) The plaintiff may, prior to commencing the action, procure a title report and shall in the complaint indicate this has been done and designate a place where it will be kept for inspection, use, and copying by the parties.

(b) The court may, upon application of a party, authorize the party to procure a title report and shall designate a place where it shall be kept for inspection, use, and copying by the parties.

Added by Stats. 1976, Ch. 73.

Section 872.230 - Requirements of complaint

The complaint shall set forth:

(a) A description of the property that is the subject of the action. In the case of tangible personal property, the description shall include its usual location. In the case of real property, the description shall include both its legal description and its street address or common designation, if any.

(b) All interests the plaintiff has or claims in the property.

(c) All interests of record or actually known to the plaintiff that persons other than the plaintiff have or claim in the property and that the plaintiff reasonably believes will be materially affected by the action, whether the names of such persons are known or unknown to the plaintiff.

(d) The estate as to which partition is sought and a prayer for partition of the interests therein.

(e) Where the plaintiff seeks sale of the property, an allegation of the facts justifying such relief in ordinary and concise language.

Added by Stats. 1976, Ch. 73.

Section 872.240 - Real and personal property partitioned in one action

Real and personal property may be partitioned in one action.

Added by Stats. 1976, Ch. 73.

Section 872.250 - Recordation of notice of pendency of action; supplemental notice

(a) Immediately upon filing the complaint, the plaintiff shall record a notice of the pendency of the action in the office of the county recorder of each county in which any real property described in the complaint is located.

(b) If, thereafter, partition of other real property is sought in the same action, the plaintiff or other person seeking such relief shall immediately record a supplemental notice.

(c) If the notice is not recorded, the court, upon its own motion or upon the motion of any party at any time, shall order the plaintiff or person seeking partition of the property, or another party on behalf of the plaintiff or other person, to record the notice and shall stay the action until the notice is recorded. The expense of recordation shall be allowed to the party incurring it.

(d) From the time of filing the notice for record, all persons shall be deemed to have notice of the pendency of the action as to the property described in the notice.

Added by Stats. 1976, Ch. 73.

Article 2 - SUMMONS

Section 872.310 - Form, content, and service

(a) The form, content, and manner of service of summons shall be as in civil actions generally.

(b) Service on persons named as parties pursuant to Sections 872.530(b)(b) and 872.550, and on other persons named as unknown defendants, shall be by publication pursuant to Section 415.50 and the provisions of this article.

Added by Stats. 1976, Ch. 73.

Section 872.320 - Conditions for ordering service by publication

Where the court orders service by publication, such order shall be subject to the following conditions:

(a) The plaintiff shall post, not later than 10 days after the date the order is made, a copy of the summons and complaint on the real property that is the subject of the action.

(b) The plaintiff shall record, if not already recorded, a notice of the pendency of the action.

(c) The publication shall describe the property that is the subject of the action. In addition to particularly describing the property, the publication shall describe the property by giving its street address, if any, or other common designation, if any; but, if a legal description of the property is given, the validity of the publication shall not be affected by the fact that the street address or other common designation recited is erroneous or that the street address or other common designation is omitted.

Added by Stats. 1976, Ch. 73.

Section 872.330 - Information included in publication; judgment based on failure to appear and answer following service

(a) Where the court orders service by publication, the publication may:

(1) Name only the defendants to be served thereby.

(2) Describe only the property in which the defendants to be served thereby have or claim interests.

(b) Judgment based on failure to appear and answer following service under this section shall be conclusive against the defendants named in respect only to property described in the publication.

Added by Stats. 1976, Ch. 73.

Article 3 - ANSWER

Section 872.410 - Requirements

The answer shall set forth:

(a) Any interest the defendant has or claims in the property.

(b) Any facts tending to controvert such material allegations of the complaint as the defendant does not wish to be taken as true.

(c) Where the defendant seeks sale of the property, an allegation of the facts justifying such relief in ordinary and concise language.

Added by Stats. 1976, Ch. 73.

Section 872.420 - Lien claimed on property

Where the defendant has or claims a lien on the property, the answer shall set forth the date and character of the lien and the amount remaining due thereon.

Added by Stats. 1976, Ch. 73.

Section 872.430 - Claim for contribution or other compensatory adjustment

The answer may set forth any claim the defendant has for contribution or other compensatory adjustment.

Added by Stats. 1976, Ch. 73.

Article 4 - PARTIES

Section 872.510 - Defendants joined in action

The plaintiff shall join as defendants in the action all persons having or claiming interests of record or actually known to the plaintiff or reasonably apparent from an inspection of the property, in the estate as to which partition is sought.

Added by Stats. 1976, Ch. 73.

Section 872.520 - Unknown parties; ownership or interest unknown, uncertain or contingent

(a) If the name of a person described in Section 872.510 is not known to the plaintiff, the plaintiff shall so state in the complaint and shall name as parties all persons unknown in the manner provided in Section 872.550.

(b) If the ownership or the share or quantity of the interest of a person described in Section 872.510 is unknown, uncertain, or contingent, the plaintiff shall so state in the complaint. If the lack of knowledge, uncertainty, or contingency is caused by a transfer to an unborn or unascertained person or class member, or by a transfer in the form of a contingent remainder, vested remainder subject to defeasance, executory interest, or similar disposition, the plaintiff shall also state in the complaint, so far as is known to the plaintiff, the name, age, and legal disability (if any) of the person in being who would be entitled to ownership of the interest had the contingency upon which the right of such person depends occurred prior to the commencement of the action.

(c) The court shall upon its own motion or upon motion of any party make such orders for joinder of additional parties and for appointment of guardians ad litem pursuant to Sections 372, 373, and 373.5 as are necessary or proper.

Added by Stats. 1976, Ch. 73.

Section 872.530 - Defendant dead or believed to be dead

(a) If a person described in Section 872.510 is dead and the plaintiff knows of a personal representative, the plaintiff shall join such personal representative as a defendant.

(b) If a person described in Section 872.510 is dead, or is believed by the plaintiff to be dead, and the plaintiff knows of no personal representative:

(1) The plaintiff shall state these facts in an affidavit filed with the complaint.

(2) Where it is stated in the affidavit that such person is dead, the plaintiff may join as defendants "the testate and intestate successors of ____ (naming such deceased person), deceased, and all persons claiming by, through, or under said decedent," naming them in that manner.

(3) Where it is stated in the affidavit that such person is believed to be dead, the plaintiff may join such person as a defendant, and he may also join "the testate and intestate successors of ____ (naming such person) believed to be deceased, and all persons claiming by, through, or under such person," naming them in that manner.

Added by Stats. 1976, Ch. 73.

Section 872.540 - Property subject to lease, community lease, unit agreement, other pooling arrangement with respect to oil or gas

Where property is subject to a lease, community lease, unit agreement, or other pooling arrangement with respect to oil or gas or both, the plaintiff need not join as defendants persons whose only interest in the property is that of a lessee, royalty-owner, lessor-owner of other real property in the community, unit, or pooled area, or working interest owner, or persons claiming under them, and the judgment shall not affect the interests of such persons not joined as defendants.

Added by Stats. 1976, Ch. 73.

Section 872.550 - Joiner of all persons unknown claiming interest

Where partition is sought as to all interests in the property, the plaintiff may join as defendants "all persons unknown claiming any interest in the property," naming them in that manner.

Added by Stats. 1976, Ch. 73.

Chapter 3 - TRIAL

Article 1 - DETERMINATION OF INTERESTS OF PARTIES

Section 872.610 - Generally

The interests of the parties, plaintiff as well as defendant, may be put in issue, tried, and determined in the action.

Added by Stats. 1976, Ch. 73.

Section 872.620 - Duty of court to ascertain state of title

To the extent necessary to grant the relief sought or other appropriate relief, the court shall upon adequate proof ascertain the state of the title to the property.

Added by Stats. 1976, Ch. 73.

Section 872.630 - Duty to determine status and priority of liens; appointment of referee

(a) To the extent necessary to grant the relief sought or other appropriate relief, the court shall determine the status and priority of all liens upon the property.

(b) The court may appoint a referee to ascertain the facts necessary for the determination required by this section. Upon application of the referee or a lienholder, the court shall direct the issuance of process to compel attendance of witnesses, the production of books, documents, or things, and the filing of verified claims. The report of the referee thereon shall be made in writing to the court and shall be confirmed, modified, or set aside and a new reference ordered, as the justice of the case may require.

Added by Stats. 1976, Ch. 73.

Section 872.640 - Consideration of interest of unknown parties

Where two or more parties are unknown, the court may consider their interests together in the action and not as between each other.

Added by Stats. 1976, Ch. 73.

Article 2 - DETERMINATION OF RIGHT TO PARTITION

Section 872.710 - Partition as to concurrent interests; successive interests

(a) At the trial, the court shall determine whether the plaintiff has the right to partition.

(b) Except as provided in Section 872.730, partition as to concurrent interests in the property shall be as of right unless barred by a valid waiver.

(c) Partition as to successive estates in the property shall be allowed if it is in the best interest of all the parties. The court shall consider whether the possessory interest has become unduly burdensome by reason of taxes or other charges, expense of ordinary or extraordinary repairs, character of the property and change in the character of the property since creation of the estates, circumstances under which the estates were

created and change in the circumstances since creation of the estates, and all other factors that would be considered by a court of equity having in mind the intent of the creator of the successive estates and the interests and needs of the successive owners.
Added by Stats. 1976, Ch. 73.

Section 872.720 - Interlocutory judgment determining interests; impracticable or inconvenient to make single judgment
(a) If the court finds that the plaintiff is entitled to partition, it shall make an interlocutory judgment that determines the interests of the parties in the property and orders the partition of the property and, unless it is to be later determined, the manner of partition.
(b) If the court determines that it is impracticable or highly inconvenient to make a single interlocutory judgment that determines, in the first instance, the interests of all the parties in the property, the court may first ascertain the interests of the original concurrent or successive owners and thereupon make an interlocutory judgment as if such persons were the sole parties in interest and the only parties to the action. Thereafter, the court may proceed in like manner as between the original concurrent or successive owners and the parties claiming under them or may allow the interests to remain without further partition if the parties so desire.
Added by Stats. 1976, Ch. 73.

Section 872.730 - Partnerships
To the extent that the court determines that the provisions of this title are a suitable remedy, such provisions may be applied in a proceeding for partnership accounting and dissolution, or in an action for partition of partnership property, where the rights of unsecured creditors of the partnership will not be prejudiced.
Added by Stats. 1976, Ch. 73.

Article 3 - DETERMINATION OF MANNER OF PARTITION

Section 872.810 - Property divided in accordance with parties' interests
The court shall order that the property be divided among the parties in accordance with their interests in the property as determined in the interlocutory judgment.
Added by Stats. 1976, Ch. 73.

Section 872.820 - Property ordered sold and proceeds divided among parties
Notwithstanding Section 872.810, the court shall order that the property be sold and the proceeds be divided among the parties in accordance with their interests in the property as determined in the interlocutory judgment in the following situations:
(a) The parties agree to such relief, by their pleadings or otherwise.
(b) The court determines that, under the circumstances, sale and division of the proceeds would be more equitable than division of the property. For the purpose of making the determination, the court may appoint a referee and take into account his report.
Added by Stats. 1976, Ch. 73.

Section 872.830 - Ordering sale of part of property and remainder divided
If, in making a determination whether sale would be more equitable than division of the property, the court finds that sale and division of proceeds for part of the property would be more equitable than division of the whole property, the court may order that such part be sold and the remainder divided.
Added by Stats. 1976, Ch. 73.

Section 872.840 - Sale of property subject to express trust
(a) Where the property or an interest therein is subject to an express trust, the court may, in its discretion, order that the property be sold.
(b) Upon division or sale of such property, the property or proceeds of sale allotted to the trustee of the express trust shall be held by him upon the trust therein stated, and no further action by the court pursuant to Section 873.840 is required.
Added by Stats. 1976, Ch. 73.

Chapter 4 - REFEREES
Article 1 - GENERAL PROVISIONS

Section 873.010 - Appointment by court, powers of court
(a) The court shall appoint a referee to divide or sell the property as ordered by the court.
(b) The court may:
  (1) Determine whether a referee's bond is necessary and fix the amount of the bond.
  (2) Instruct the referee.
  (3) Fix the reasonable compensation for the services of the referee and provide for payment of the referee's reasonable expenses.
  (4) Provide for the date of commencement of the lien of the referee allowed by law.
  (5) Require the filing of interim or final accounts of the referee, settle the accounts of the referee, and discharge the referee.
  (6) Remove the referee.
  (7) Appoint a new referee.
Added by Stats. 1976, Ch. 73.

Section 873.020 - Appointment of referee for sale and referee for division or single referee
The court in its discretion may appoint a referee for sale and a referee for division, or may appoint a single referee for both.
Added by Stats. 1976, Ch. 73.

Section 873.030 - Three referees appointed to divide and sell
(a) The court may, with the consent of the parties, appoint three referees to divide or sell the property as ordered by the court.
(b) The three referees so appointed shall have all the powers and may perform all the duties required of one referee.
Added by Stats. 1976, Ch. 73.

Section 873.040 - Consent to person appointed
(a) The court shall appoint as referee under this title any person or persons to whose appointment all parties have consented.
(b) In the case of a minor party or a party for whom a conservator of the estate has been appointed, the guardian or conservator of the estate of the party may so consent.
Amended by Stats. 1979, Ch. 730.

Section 873.050 - Persons not to be appointed
None of the following persons shall be appointed a referee under this title:
(a) A clerk or deputy clerk of the court.
(b) A former or present partner or employee of the judge.
(c) A relative within the third degree of the judge or the judge's spouse or the spouse of such a relative.
(d) An owner of any interest in the property that is the subject of the action.
Added by Stats. 1976, Ch. 73.

Section 873.060 - Powers generally
The referee may perform any acts necessary to exercise the authority conferred by this title or by order of the court.
Added by Stats. 1976, Ch. 73.

Section 873.070 - Petition for instructions

The referee or any party may, on noticed motion, petition the court for instructions concerning the referee's duties under this title.
Added by Stats. 1976, Ch. 73.

Section 873.080 - Designation of property as public or private way, road or street; closure of roads on property

(a) In selling or dividing the property, the referee may, if it will be for the advantage of those interested, designate a portion of the property as a public or private way, road, or street. In connection therewith, the referee may also recommend the closure of any or all other roads on the property and allocation of the portion of the property occupied by such roads to the parties.

(b) Upon making such a designation and recommendation that is adequate to accommodate public and private needs, the referee shall report that fact to the court.

(c) Upon confirmation of the referee's report by the court, subject to any necessary action by the appropriate public entities:

(1) The portion of the property designated as a public way, road, or street shall not be allocated to any of the parties or sold but shall be an open and public way, road, or street.

(2) The property designated as a private way, road, or street shall be a private way for the use of the parties interested.

(3) The roads recommended to be closed shall be deemed abandoned upon the terms stated in the order of confirmation.

Added by Stats. 1976, Ch. 73.

Article 2 - CONTRACTS OF REFEREE

Section 873.110 - Powers of court

Subject to the limitations of this article, the court may:

(a) Authorize or approve contracts of the referee for the services and expenses of surveyors, engineers, appraisers, attorneys, real estate brokers, auctioneers, and others.

(b) Allow and direct payment of or reject claims under such contracts.

(c) Provide for the date of commencement of any lien provided by law or contract for such claims.

Added by Stats. 1976, Ch. 73.

Section 873.120 - Employment of attorney

(a) The referee may employ an attorney only with the approval of the court pursuant to Section 873.110.

(b) The application for approval shall be in writing and shall include the name of the attorney whom the referee wishes to employ and the necessity for the employment.

(c) The attorney so employed may not be attorney for, or associated with or employed by an attorney for, any party to the action except with the written consent of all the parties to the action.

(d) Any claim for compensation for the attorney shall detail the services performed by the attorney.

Added by Stats. 1976, Ch. 73.

Section 873.130 - Employment of surveyor

The referee may, with the approval of the court pursuant to Section 873.110, employ a surveyor with the necessary assistants to aid in making a sale or division of property.

Added by Stats. 1976, Ch. 73.

Section 873.140 - Employment of auctioneer

The referee may, with the approval of the court pursuant to Section 873.110, employ an auctioneer, authorized to act as such in the locality, to conduct a public auction and to secure purchasers by such method for any property to be sold at public auction.

Added by Stats. 1976, Ch. 73.

Section 873.150 - Contract providing for accrual of interest

A contract for the services of an attorney, surveyor, auctioneer, or other third person may provide for the accrual of interest at a rate not in excess of the legal rate for amounts due under the contract that are not paid within three months after the time they become due and payable.

Added by Stats. 1976, Ch. 73.

Section 873.160 - Liability on contracts made

The referee is not personally liable on contracts made, or for expenses incurred, except as such liability is expressly assumed by the referee in writing.

Added by Stats. 1976, Ch. 73.

Chapter 5 - DIVISION OF THE PROPERTY

Section 873.210 - Duty of referee appointed to divide property

The referee appointed by the court to make a division of the property shall divide the property and allot the several portions to the parties, quality and quantity relatively considered, according to their interests in the property as determined in the interlocutory judgment.

Added by Stats. 1976, Ch. 73.

Section 873.220 - Allotment of portion of property embracing improvements made by party

As far as practical, and to the extent it can be done without material injury to the rights of the other parties, the property shall be so divided as to allot to a party any portion that embraces improvements made by that party or that party's predecessor in interest. In such division and allotment, the value of such improvements shall be excluded.

Added by Stats. 1976, Ch. 73.

Section 873.230 - Allotment of portion of property to purchaser prior to commencement of action

Where prior to the commencement of the action a party has executed a deed purporting to convey to a purchaser a portion of the property to be divided, to the extent it can be done without material injury to the rights of the other parties, the property shall be so divided as to allot that portion to the purchaser, the purchaser's heirs or assigns, or such other action taken as to make the deed effectual as a conveyance of that portion of the property.

Added by Stats. 1976, Ch. 73.

Section 873.240 - Property consisting of more than one distinct lot or parcel

Where real property consists of more than one distinct lot or parcel, the property shall be divided by such lots or parcels without other internal division to the extent that it can be done without material injury to the rights of the parties.

Added by Stats. 1976, Ch. 73.

Section 873.250 - Compensation required where division cannot be made equally

(a) Where division cannot be made equally among the parties according to their interests without prejudice to the rights of some, compensation may be required to be made by one party to another to correct the inequality.

(b) No compensation shall be required to be made to others by unknown owners or by minors unless it appears that a minor has personal property sufficient for that purpose and the minor's interest will be promoted thereby.

Added by Stats. 1976, Ch. 73.

Section 873.260 - Lien on undivided interest of party

Where a lien is on an undivided interest of a party, the lien shall, upon division of the property, become a charge only on the share allotted to that party.
Added by Stats. 1976, Ch. 73.

Section 873.270 - Interests of two or more unknown parties undivided
Where the court has determined the combined interests of two or more unknown parties, the entire portion of the property allocated to such parties shall remain undivided.
Added by Stats. 1976, Ch. 73.

Section 873.280 - Report of referee's proceedings, notice of filing
(a) The referee shall file with the court a report of the referee's proceedings and give written notice of filing to each party who has appeared in the action.
(b) The report shall include all of the following:
(1) A specification of the manner in which the referee has executed the referee's trust.
(2) A description of the property divided and of the share allotted to each party, along with any recommendation as to owelty.
(3) Any recommendation as to opening and closing public and private ways, roads, streets, and easements.
Added by Stats. 1976, Ch. 73.

Section 873.290 - Motion to confirm, modify or set aside report
(a) Any party, upon notice to the other parties who have appeared, may move the court to confirm, modify, or set aside the report.
(b) At the hearing, the court may either confirm the report as filed or as the court may modify and enter judgment of partition accordingly or set aside the report and order preparation of a new report and, if necessary, appoint a new referee for this purpose.
(c) The division is effective and title vests in accordance therewith upon entry of judgment of partition.
Added by Stats. 1976, Ch. 73.

Chapter 6 - SALE OF THE PROPERTY
Article 1 - MANNER OF SALE

Section 873.510 - Duty of referee
The referee appointed by the court to make a sale of the property shall sell the property in the manner and following the procedures provided in this chapter.
Added by Stats. 1976, Ch. 73.

Section 873.520 - Property sold at public auction or private sale as determined by court
The property shall be sold at public auction or private sale as the court determines will be more beneficial to the parties. For the purpose of making this determination, the court may refer the matter to the referee and take into account the referee's report.
Added by Stats. 1976, Ch. 73.

Section 873.530 - Part sold at public auction and part sold at private sale
Part of the property may be sold at public auction and part at private sale if it appears that to do so will be more beneficial to the parties.
Added by Stats. 1976, Ch. 73.

Article 2 - SALES PROCEDURES

Section 873.600 - Sale as agreed to by parties
Notwithstanding any other provision of this title, the court shall order sale by such methods and upon such terms as are expressly agreed to in writing by all the parties to the action.
Added by Stats. 1976, Ch. 73.

Section 873.610 - Court power to prescribe manner, terms and conditions; matter referred to referee for recommendation
(a) The court may, at the time of trial or thereafter, prescribe such manner, terms, and conditions of sale not inconsistent with the provisions of this chapter as it deems proper for the particular property or sale.
(b) The court may refer the manner, terms, and conditions of sale to the referee for recommendation but shall not approve the referee's report except following a hearing upon noticed motion.
Added by Stats. 1976, Ch. 73.

Section 873.620 - Distinct lots or parcels sold separately; real and personal property sold as unit
(a) Unless the interests and rights of the parties will be materially prejudiced thereby, the court shall order that distinct lots or parcels of real property be sold separately.
(b) The court may order that the real and personal property or any portion thereof be sold as a unit.
Added by Stats. 1976, Ch. 73.

Section 873.630 - Sale on credit
The court may:
(a) Direct a sale on credit for the property or any part thereof.
(b) Prescribe such terms of credit as may be appropriate.
(c) Approve or prescribe the terms of security to be taken upon the sale, including the manner in which title to the security is to be taken, whether in a single instrument or several instruments, according to the interests of the parties.
Added by Stats. 1976, Ch. 73.

Section 873.640 - Notice of sale
(a) Notice of the sale of real or personal property shall be given in the manner required for notice of sale of like property upon execution. Such notice shall also be given to every party who has appeared in the action and to such other interested persons as may have in writing requested the referee for special notice.
(b) Where real and personal property are to be sold as a unit, notice of the sale may be in the manner required for notice of sale of real property alone.
(c) The court may order such additional notice as it deems proper.
(d) Where the court orders a new sale of property pursuant to Section 873.730 or Section 873.740, notice of sale shall be as provided in this section.
Added by Stats. 1976, Ch. 73.

Section 873.650 - Contents of notice
(a) The court shall prescribe the contents of the notice of sale, which shall include a description of the property, the time and place of sale, and a statement of the principal terms of sale. In place of the principal terms of sale, the notice may refer to an order of the court or to a written statement containing such information which may be inspected at the place of business of the referee or the referee's attorney.
(b) A notice of private sale shall state a place where bids or offers will be received and a day on or after which the sale will be made.
Added by Stats. 1976, Ch. 73.

Section 873.660 - Sale of securities and perishable property

(a) The court may order securities listed on an established stock or bond exchange, and personal property that is perishable, that will depreciate in value if not promptly disposed of, or that will incur loss or expense by being kept, to be sold upon such notice and conditions as may be appropriate.
(b) Unless otherwise ordered by the court, title to property sold pursuant to this section passes without court confirmation. The referee is responsible for the actual value of the property until, after return and proper showing, the court approves the sale.
Added by Stats. 1976, Ch. 73.

Section 873.670 - Sale at public auction
(a) A sale at public auction to the highest bidder shall be held in the county in which the action is pending or such other place as may be specified by the court.
(b) Unless otherwise ordered by the court, personal property shall be present at the sale.
(c) The sale may be postponed by the referee by public declaration as provided for sales upon execution.
Added by Stats. 1976, Ch. 73.

Section 873.680 - Sale at private sale
(a) A sale at private sale shall not be made before the day specified in the notice of sale but shall be made within one year thereafter.
(b) The bids or offers shall be in writing and left at the place designated in the notice at any time after the first publication or, if none, the posting of the notice.
Added by Stats. 1976, Ch. 73.

Section 873.690 - Persons prohibited from purchasing property sold
(a) The following persons shall not purchase property sold in the action directly or indirectly:
  (1) The referee.
  (2) The attorney of a party.
  (3) The guardian or conservator of a party, unless for the benefit of the ward or conservatee.
(b) All sales contrary to this section are void except that a sale to a bona fide purchaser following a sale contrary to this section shall not be disturbed.
Amended by Stats. 1979, Ch. 730.

Article 3 - CONSUMMATION OF SALE

Section 873.710 - Referee's report upon making sale
(a) Upon making a sale of property, the referee shall report the sale to the court.
(b) The referee's report shall contain, in addition to such other information as may be appropriate, all of the following information:
  (1) A description of the property sold to each purchaser.
  (2) The name of the purchaser.
  (3) The sale price.
  (4) The terms and conditions of the sale and the security, if any, taken.
  (5) Any amounts payable to lienholders.
  (6) A statement as to contractual or other arrangements or conditions as to agents' commissions.
  (7) Any determination and recommendation as to opening and closing public and private ways, roads, streets, and easements.
  (8) Other material facts relevant to the sale and the confirmation proceeding.
Added by Stats. 1976, Ch. 73.

Section 873.720 - Motion to confirm or set aside sale
(a) A purchaser, the referee, or any party may move the court to confirm or set aside the sale.
(b) The moving party shall give not less than 10 days' notice of motion to:
  (1) The purchaser if the purchaser is not the moving party; and
  (2) All other parties who have appeared in the action.
Added by Stats. 1976, Ch. 73.

Section 873.730 - Hearing; confirmation notwithstanding variance; vacating sale and directing new sale
(a) At the hearing, the court shall examine the report and witnesses in relation to the report.
(b) The court may confirm the sale notwithstanding a variance from the prescribed terms of sale if to do so will be beneficial to the parties and will not result in substantial prejudice to persons interested in the sale.
(c) The court may vacate the sale and direct that a new sale be made if it determines any of the following:
  (1) The proceedings were unfair or notice of sale was not properly given. If there is no finding at the hearing of unfairness or improper notice, the sale may thereafter not be attacked on such grounds.
  (2) The sale price is disproportionate to the value of the property.
  (3) It appears that a new sale will yield a sum that exceeds the sale price by at least 10 percent on the first ten thousand dollars ($10,000) and 5 percent on the amount in excess thereof, determined after a reasonable allowance for the expenses of a new sale.
Added by Stats. 1976, Ch. 73.

Section 873.740 - Written increased offer made at hearing
(a) If at the hearing under Section 873.730 a responsible bidder makes a written increased offer that exceeds the sale price by at least 10 percent on the first ten thousand dollars ($10,000) and 5 percent on the amount in excess thereof, the court in its discretion may do either of the following:
  (1) Vacate the sale and direct that a new sale be made.
  (2) Vacate the sale, accept the increased offer, and confirm the sale to the offerer.
(b) Except as provided in subdivision (c), the amount by which an increased offer exceeds the sale price is determined on the basis of the gross amount of the increased offer including any commission on the increased offer to which an agent may be entitled.
(c) Where in advance of sale the court has so ordered or the parties have so agreed, if an increased offer is made by a party to the action who is not represented by an agent, the amount by which an increased offer of a nonparty exceeds the sale price is determined on the basis of the net amount of the increased offer excluding any commission on the increased offer to which an agent may be entitled.
Added by Stats. 1976, Ch. 73.

Section 873.745 - Amount of agents' commissions
The amount of agents' commissions on the sale, if any, shall be fixed by the court and divided or limited in the manner provided for private sales of real property in decedents' estates.
Added by Stats. 1976, Ch. 73.

Section 873.750 - Order upon confirmation of sale
(a) Upon confirmation of a sale, the court shall order the referee to execute a conveyance or other instrument of transfer, to collect the proceeds, take security, and perform other acts required to consummate the sale.
(b) The order may direct the referee concerning the distribution, deposit, or securing of sale deposits and sale proceeds.

Added by Stats. 1976, Ch. 73.

Section 873.760 - Failure of purchaser to pay sale price

If the purchaser, after the confirmation of the sale, fails to pay the sale price, the purchaser is subject to the court's jurisdiction and to further proceedings in the action. Upon such failure, a party, or the referee, may upon notice move the court to order either of the following forms of relief:

(a) Resale of the property upon notice as provided in this chapter. If any loss is occasioned thereby, the referee may recover the amount of such loss and costs and expenses incurred, including a reasonable attorney's fee, from the purchaser who failed to pay.

(b) Maintenance by the referee of an action against the purchaser for the amount of the sale price. If the referee recovers judgment, the referee shall be awarded a reasonable attorney's fee against the purchaser.

Added by Stats. 1976, Ch. 73.

Section 873.770 - Purchaser party or lienholder entitles to share of proceeds

Where the purchaser is a party or lienholder entitled to a share of the proceeds of sale, the referee may:

(a) Take the purchaser's receipt for so much of the proceeds of sale as belongs to the purchaser.

(b) Take security, or other arrangement satisfactory to the referee, for payment of amounts which are or may become due from the purchaser on account of the expenses of sale, general costs of the action, and costs of the reference.

Added by Stats. 1976, Ch. 73.

Section 873.780 - Orders relating to closing of sale after confirmation

The court may make orders relating to the closing of a sale after confirmation, including escrow and closing provisions and, if the referee and purchaser so agree and the court upon noticed motion determines it will not result in substantial prejudice to the parties, may make adjustments varying the terms of sale based on after-discovered defects.

Added by Stats. 1976, Ch. 73.

Section 873.790 - Execution of conveyance or other instrument of transfer

(a) Upon fulfillment of the terms of sale, the referee shall execute a conveyance or other instrument of transfer to the purchaser.

(b) The conveyance or transfer of real property and the order authorizing such conveyance or transfer shall be recorded in each county in which the property is located.

Added by Stats. 1976, Ch. 73.

Article 4 - DISPOSITION OF PROCEEDS OF SALE

Section 873.810 - Generally

The court shall order the proceeds of sale and any security therefor to be paid, transferred, deposited in court, placed in trust, or invested in State of California or United States government obligations or interest-bearing accounts in an institution whose accounts are insured by an agency of the federal government, to or for the benefit of the persons in interest entitled thereto, as may be appropriate or as specifically provided in this article.

Added by Stats. 1976, Ch. 73.

Section 873.820 - Order of application of proceeds

The proceeds of sale for any property sold shall be applied in the following order:

(a) Payment of the expenses of sale.

(b) Payment of the other costs of partition in whole or in part or to secure any cost of partition later allowed.

(c) Payment of any liens on the property in their order of priority except liens which under the terms of sale are to remain on the property.

(d) Distribution of the residue among the parties in proportion to their shares as determined by the court.

Added by Stats. 1976, Ch. 73.

Section 873.830 - Rights of tenant for life or years where only part of property sold

Where a part only of the property is sold, a tenant for life or years in an undivided share of the whole property may have his estate equitably set off in any part of the property not sold by way of complete or partial satisfaction of his share of the proceeds.

Added by Stats. 1976, Ch. 73.

Section 873.840 - Tenant for life or years; future right or estate; estate fir life or defeasible estate with remainder over

(a) The court shall ascertain the proportion of the proceeds of sale that will be a just and reasonable sum for the satisfaction of the estate of a tenant for life or years and shall order such amount distributed to him or held for his benefit.

(b) The court shall ascertain the proportional value of any vested or contingent future right or estate in the property and shall direct such proportion of the proceeds of sale to be distributed, secured, or held in such a manner as to protect the rights and interests of the parties.

(c) Notwithstanding any other provision of this section, in the case of an estate for life or defeasible estate with remainder over, the court may direct that the entire proceeds of sale be placed in trust as provided in this section upon a showing that the establishment of such a trust is economically feasible and will serve the best interests of the parties. The court shall appoint a trustee, upon security satisfactory to the court, who under court supervision shall invest and reinvest the proceeds, pay the income of the investments, if any, to the life tenant or owner of the defeasible interest, and upon termination of the life or defeasible estate, deliver or pay the corpus of the trust estate to the remainderman. The court shall retain jurisdiction over the settlement of the accounts of the trustee and in all matters necessary for the proper administration of the trust and the final distribution of the trust fund.

Added by Stats. 1976, Ch. 73.

Section 873.850 - Continuance of action where proceeds not allocated

When the proceeds of the sale belonging to persons who are parties to the action, whether known or unknown, have not been allocated among such parties, the action may be continued as between such parties, for the determination of their respective claims thereto, which must be ascertained and adjudged by the court. Further testimony may be taken in court, or by a referee, at the discretion of the court, and the court may, if necessary, require such parties to present the facts or law in controversy, by pleadings, as in an original action.

Added by Stats. 1976, Ch. 73.

Chapter 7 - PARTITION BY APPRAISAL

Section 873.910 - Agreement of parties

When the interests of all parties are undisputed or have been adjudicated, the parties may agree upon a partition by appraisal pursuant to this chapter.

Added by Stats. 1976, Ch. 73.

Section 873.920 - Included in agreement

The agreement shall be in writing filed with the clerk of court and shall include:

(a) A description of the property.

(b) The names of the parties and their interests.

(c) The names of the parties who are willing to acquire the interests.

(d) The name or names of a person or persons to whose appointment as referee or referees the parties consent.

(e) The date or dates as of which the interests to be acquired are to be appraised.
(f) Other terms mutually agreed upon which may include, but are not limited to, provisions relating to abandonment of the action if the appraised value of the interest to be acquired exceeds a stated amount, required deposits on account of purchase price, terms of any credit, title and objections to title, and payment of the expenses of the procedure authorized by this chapter and of costs of the action.
Added by Stats. 1976, Ch. 73.

Section 873.930 - Approval of agreement
(a) Any party to the agreement may, upon noticed motion, apply to the court for approval of the agreement.
(b) If the court determines that the agreement complies with Section 873.920 and that the terms and conditions are equitable, it shall approve the agreement and stay any pending division or sale of the property.
Added by Stats. 1976, Ch. 73.

Section 873.940 - Appointment of referee or referees to appraise property; report
The court shall appoint one referee or, if provided in the agreement, three referees to appraise the property and the interests involved. The referee shall report the valuations and other findings to the court in writing filed with the clerk.
Added by Stats. 1976, Ch. 73.

Section 873.950 - Motion to confirm, modify or set aside report
Any party to the agreement or the referee, upon 10 days' notice to the referee if the referee is not the moving party and to the other parties to the agreement, may move the court to confirm, modify, or set aside the report.
Added by Stats. 1976, Ch. 73.

Section 873.960 - Hearing; court determination
At the hearing, the court shall examine the report and witnesses. If the court determines that the proceedings have been regularly conducted, that transfer of title to the interests may regularly be made, and that no facts appear which would make such transfer inequitable, it shall confirm the report and order the interests transferred to the acquiring parties in proportion to their respective interests, or in such other proportion as is set out in the agreement. The order shall be conditioned upon payment of the amounts fixed as the purchase price and any other amounts required by the agreement, the giving of any required security, and payment by the parties of the expenses of the procedure authorized by this chapter and of the general costs of the partition or an appropriate share thereof. Thereafter the court, upon motion of a party to the agreement or of the referee, made upon not less than 10 days' notice to the parties who have appeared, shall determine whether the conditions have been fulfilled and, if so, shall enter judgment confirming the transfer; otherwise, upon such further proceedings as may be ordered, the action or proceeding shall be ordered terminated.
Added by Stats. 1976, Ch. 73.

Section 873.970 - Binding effect of agreement; specific enforcement upon default
The agreement binds the heirs, executors, administrators, successors, and assigns of the parties. In the event of default, the aggrieved parties may specifically enforce the agreement by further proceedings in the action or may pursue any other remedy they may have at law or in equity.
Added by Stats. 1976, Ch. 73.

Section 873.980 - Other rights and remedies
The provisions of this chapter are cumulative and if, for default or other cause, interests are not transferred and acquired pursuant to this chapter, the parties may pursue their other rights of partition, subject to Section 873.970.
Added by Stats. 1976, Ch. 73.

Chapter 8 - COSTS OF PARTITION
Article 1 - ALLOWANCE AND APPORTIONMENT OF COSTS OF PARTITION

Section 874.010 - Included in costs
The costs of partition include:
(a) Reasonable attorney's fees incurred or paid by a party for the common benefit.
(b) The fee and expenses of the referee.
(c) The compensation provided by contract for services of a surveyor or other person employed by the referee in the action.
(d) The reasonable costs of a title report procured pursuant to Section 872.220 with interest thereon at the legal rate from the time of payment or, if paid before commencement of the action, from the time of commencement of the action.
(e) Other disbursements or expenses determined by the court to have been incurred or paid for the common benefit.
Added by Stats. 1976, Ch. 73.

Section 874.020 - Expenses incurred in prosecuting or defending other actions or proceedings
The costs of partition include reasonable expenses, including attorney's fees, necessarily incurred by a party for the common benefit in prosecuting or defending other actions or other proceedings for the protection, confirmation, or perfection of title, setting the boundaries, or making a survey of the property, with interest thereon at the legal rate from the time of making the expenditures.
Added by Stats. 1976, Ch. 73.

Section 874.030 - Interest allowed from time of making disbursements
Where disbursements have been made by a party under the direction of the court, interest at the legal rate shall be allowed thereon from the time of making such disbursements.
Added by Stats. 1976, Ch. 73.

Section 874.040 - Apportionment of costs
Except as otherwise provided in this article, the court shall apportion the costs of partition among the parties in proportion to their interests or make such other apportionment as may be equitable.
Added by Stats. 1976, Ch. 73.

Section 874.050 - Payment of costs apportioned to future interest
(a) The court may order that the share of the costs apportioned to a future interest be paid by other parties to the action or by the persons who are then the presumptive owners of the future interest.
(b) Where the court orders payment pursuant to this section, such payment is subject to a right of reimbursement, with interest at the legal rate, secured by a charge upon the future interest.
Added by Stats. 1976, Ch. 73.

Article 2 - PAYMENT OF COSTS OF PARTITION

Section 874.110 - Payment in whole or in part prior to judgment
(a) The costs of partition as apportioned by the court may be ordered paid in whole or in part prior to judgment.
(b) Any costs that remain unpaid shall be included and specified in the judgment.
Added by Stats. 1976, Ch. 73.

Section 874.120 - Lien on share of party
(a) The costs shall be a lien on the share of the party specified.

(b) A lien imposed by this section has priority over any other lien on the share except those imposed under this section.
Added by Stats. 1976, Ch. 73.

Section 874.130 - Sale of property for benefit of lien
Upon application of a person entitled to a lien imposed under this article and upon a showing of good cause, the court may order a sale of all or a portion of the property before or after judgment for the benefit of all such lien claimants without priority among them.
Added by Stats. 1976, Ch. 73.

Section 874.140 - Enforcement of judgment for unpaid costs
A judgment for unpaid costs of partition may be enforced by the person entitled to the costs in the manner provided for enforcement of money judgments generally against the share of the party specified in the judgment or against other property of the party.
Amended by Stats. 1982, Ch. 497, Sec. 60. Operative July 1, 1983, by Sec. 185 of Ch. 497.

Chapter 9 - JUDGMENT

Section 874.210 - Binding and conclusive
The judgment in the action is binding and conclusive on all of the following:
(a) All persons known and unknown who were parties to the action and who have or claim any interest in the property, whether present or future, vested or contingent, legal or beneficial, several or undivided.
(b) All persons not in being or not ascertainable at the time the judgment is entered who have any remainder interest in the property, or any part thereof, after the determination of a particular estate therein and who by any contingency may be entitled to a beneficial interest in the property, provided the judge shall make appropriate provision for the protection of such interests.
(c) Except as provided in Section 874.225, all persons who were not parties to the action and who have or claim any interest in the property which was not of record at the time the lis pendens was filed, or if none was filed, at the time the judgment was recorded.
Amended by Stats. 1984, Ch. 20, Sec. 5.

Section 874.225 - Effect on person not party to action
Except to the extent provided in Section 1908, the judgment does not affect a claim in the property or part thereof of any person who was not a party to the action if any of the following conditions is satisfied:
(a) The claim was of record at the time the lis pendens was filed or, if none was filed, at the time the judgment was recorded.
(b) The claim was actually known to the plaintiff or would have been reasonably apparent from an inspection of the property at the time the lis pendens was filed or, if none was filed, at the time the judgment was entered. For the purpose of this subdivision, a "claim in the property or part thereof" of any person means the interest of the person in the portion of the property or proceeds of sale thereof allocated to the plaintiff. Nothing in this subdivision shall be construed to impair the rights of a bona fide purchaser or encumbrancer for value dealing with the plaintiff or the plaintiff's successors in interest.
Added by Stats. 1984, Ch. 20, Sec. 7.

Section 874.240 - Conveyance or transfer binding and conclusive
A conveyance or transfer pursuant to Sections 873.750 and 873.790 or Section 873.960 is binding and conclusive, in the same manner as a judgment.
Added by Stats. 1976, Ch. 73.

Chapter 10 - PARTITION OF REAL PROPERTY ACT

Section 874.311 - Title; applicability
(a) This act shall be known, and may be cited, as the Partition of Real Property Act.
(b) This act applies to real property held in tenancy in common where there is no agreement in a record binding all the cotenants which governs the partition of the property.
(c) This act applies to actions for partition of real property filed on or after January 1, 2023.
Amended by Stats 2022 ch 82 (AB 2245),s 3, eff. 1/1/2023.
Amended by Stats 2022 ch 82 (AB 2245),s 2, eff. 1/1/2023(amends chapter heading).
Added by Stats 2021 ch 119 (AB 633),s 2, eff. 1/1/2022.

Section 874.312 - Definitions
For purposes of this chapter, the following definitions apply:
(a) "Determination of value" means a court order determining the fair market value of the property under Section 874.316 or 874.320 or adopting the valuation of the property agreed to by all cotenants.
(b) "Partition by sale" means a court-ordered sale of the entire property, whether by auction, sealed bids, or open-market sale conducted under Section 874.320.
(c) "Partition in kind" means the division of property into physically distinct and separately titled parcels.
(d) "Record" means information that is inscribed on a tangible medium or that is stored in an electronic or other medium and is retrievable in perceivable form.
Amended by Stats 2022 ch 82 (AB 2245),s 4, eff. 1/1/2023.
Added by Stats 2021 ch 119 (AB 633),s 2, eff. 1/1/2022.

Section 874.313 - Property to be partitioned under this chapter; exceptions
(a) In an action to partition real property, the property shall be partitioned under this chapter unless all of the cotenants otherwise agree in a record.
(b) This chapter supplements the other provisions of this title and, if an action is governed by this chapter, this chapter shall control over any provisions of this title that are inconsistent with this chapter.
Amended by Stats 2022 ch 82 (AB 2245),s 5, eff. 1/1/2023.
Added by Stats 2021 ch 119 (AB 633),s 2, eff. 1/1/2022.

Section 874.314 - Method of service of complaint not limited or affected; signage
(a) This act does not limit or affect the method by which service of a complaint in a partition action may be made.
(b) If the plaintiff in a partition action seeks an order of notice by publication, the plaintiff, not later than 10 days after the court's determination, shall post and maintain while the action is pending a conspicuous sign on the property that is the subject of the action. The sign shall state that the action has commenced and identify the name and address of the court and the common designation by which the property is known. The court may require the plaintiff to publish on the sign the name of the plaintiff and the known defendants.
Amended by Stats 2022 ch 82 (AB 2245),s 6, eff. 1/1/2023.
Added by Stats 2021 ch 119 (AB 633),s 2, eff. 1/1/2022.

Section 874.315 - Court appointed referees
If the court appoints referees pursuant to Section 873.010, each referee, in addition to any other requirements and disqualifications applicable to referees, shall be disinterested and impartial and not a party to or a participant in the action.
Added by Stats 2021 ch 119 (AB 633),s 2, eff. 1/1/2022.

Section 874.316 - Fair market value of property
(a) Except as otherwise provided in subdivisions (b) and (c), the court shall determine the fair market value of the property by ordering an appraisal pursuant to subdivision (d).
(b) If all cotenants have agreed to the value of the property or to another method of valuation, the court shall adopt that value or the value produced by the agreed method of valuation.
(c) If the court determines that the evidentiary value of an appraisal is outweighed by the cost of the appraisal, the court, after an evidentiary hearing, shall determine the fair market value of the property and send notice to the parties of the value.
(d) If the court orders an appraisal, the court shall appoint a disinterested real estate appraiser licensed in the State of California to determine the fair market value of the property assuming sole ownership of the fee simple estate. On completion of the appraisal, the appraiser shall file a sworn or verified appraisal with the court.
(e) If an appraisal is conducted pursuant to subdivision (d), not later than 10 days after the appraisal is filed, the court shall send notice to each party with a known address, stating all of the following:
  (1) The appraised fair market value of the property.
  (2) That the appraisal is available at the court clerk's office.
  (3) That a party may file with the court an objection to the appraisal not later than 30 days after the notice is sent, stating the grounds for the objection.
(f) If an appraisal is filed with the court pursuant to subdivision (d), the court shall conduct a hearing to determine the fair market value of the property not sooner than 30 days after a copy of the notice of the appraisal is sent to each party under subdivision (e), whether or not an objection to the appraisal is filed under paragraph (3) of subdivision (e). In addition to the court-ordered appraisal, the court may consider any other evidence of value offered by a party.
(g) After a hearing under subdivision (f), but before considering the merits of the partition action, the court shall determine the fair market value of the property and send notice to the parties of the value.
Amended by Stats 2022 ch 82 (AB 2245),s 7, eff. 1/1/2023.
Added by Stats 2021 ch 119 (AB 633),s 2, eff. 1/1/2022.

Section 874.317 - Notice of cotenant requested partition; purchase price
(a) If any cotenant requested partition by sale, the court shall, after the determination of value under Section 874.316, send notice to the parties that any cotenant except a cotenant that requested partition by sale may buy all the interests of the cotenants that requested partition by sale.
(b) Not later than 45 days after the notice is sent under subdivision (a), any cotenant except a cotenant that requested partition by sale may give notice to the court that it elects to buy all the interests of the cotenants that requested partition by sale.
(c) The purchase price for each of the interests of a cotenant that requested partition by sale is the value of the entire parcel determined under Section 874.316 multiplied by the cotenant's fractional ownership of the entire parcel.
(d) After expiration of the period described in subdivision (b), the following rules apply:
  (1) If only one cotenant elects to buy all the interests of the cotenants that requested partition by sale, the court shall notify all the parties of that fact.
  (2) If more than one cotenant elects to buy all the interests of the cotenants that requested partition by sale, the court shall allocate the right to buy those interests among the electing cotenants based on each electing cotenant's existing fractional ownership of the entire parcel divided by the total existing fractional ownership of all cotenants electing to buy and send notice to all the parties of that fact and of the price to be paid by each electing cotenant.
  (3) If no cotenant elects to buy all the interests of the cotenants that requested partition by sale, the court shall send notice to all the parties of that fact and resolve the partition action under paragraphs (a) and (b) of Section 874.318.
(e) If the court sends notice to the parties under paragraph (1) or (2) of subdivision (d), the court shall set a date, not sooner than 60 days after the date the notice was sent, by which electing cotenants shall pay their apportioned price into the court. After this date, the following rules apply:
  (1) If all electing cotenants timely pay their apportioned price into court, the court shall issue an order reallocating all the interests of the cotenants and disburse the amounts held by the court to the persons entitled to them.
  (2) If no electing cotenant timely pays its apportioned price, the court shall resolve the partition action under paragraphs (a) and (b) of Section 874.318 as if the interests of the cotenants that requested partition by sale were not purchased.
  (3) If one or more but not all of the electing cotenants fail to pay their apportioned price on time, the court, on motion, shall give notice to the electing cotenants that paid their apportioned price of the interest remaining and the price for all that interest.
(f) Not later than 20 days after the court gives notice pursuant to paragraph (3) of subdivision (e), any cotenant that paid may elect to purchase all of the remaining interest by paying the entire price into the court. After the 20-day period, the following rules apply:
  (1) If only one cotenant pays the entire price for the remaining interest, the court shall issue an order reallocating the remaining interest to that cotenant. The court shall promptly issue an order reallocating the interests of all of the cotenants and disburse the amounts held by it to the persons entitled to them.
  (2) If no cotenant pays the entire price for the remaining interest, the court shall resolve the partition action under paragraphs (a) and (b) of Section 874.318 as if the interests of the cotenants that requested partition by sale were not purchased.
  (3) If more than one cotenant pays the entire price for the remaining interest, the court shall reapportion the remaining interest among those paying cotenants, based on each paying cotenant's original fractional ownership of the entire parcel divided by the total original fractional ownership of all cotenants that paid the entire price for the remaining interest. The court shall issue promptly an order reallocating all of the cotenants' interests, disburse the amounts held by it to the persons entitled to them, and promptly refund any excess payment held by the court.
(g) Not later than 45 days after the court sends notice to the parties pursuant to subdivision (a), any cotenant entitled to buy an interest under this section may request the court to authorize the sale as part of the pending action of the interests of cotenants named as defendants and served with the complaint but that did not appear in the action.
(h) If the court receives a timely request under subdivision (g), the court, after a hearing, may deny the request or authorize the requested additional sale on such terms as the court determines are fair and reasonable, subject to the following limitations:
  (1) A sale authorized under this subdivision may occur only after the purchase prices for all interests subject to sale under subdivisions (a) to (f), inclusive, have been paid into court and those interests have been reallocated among the cotenants as provided in those subdivisions.
  (2) The purchase price for the interest of a nonappearing cotenant is based on the court's determination of value under Section 874.316.
Added by Stats 2021 ch 119 (AB 633),s 2, eff. 1/1/2022.

Section 874.318 - Court ordered partition in kind
(a) If all the interests of all cotenants that requested partition by sale are not purchased by other cotenants pursuant to Section 874.317, or if after conclusion of the buyout under Section 874.317 a cotenant remains that has requested partition in kind, the court shall order partition in kind unless the court, after consideration of the factors listed in Section 874.319, finds that partition in kind will result in great prejudice to the cotenants as a group. In considering whether to order partition in kind, the court shall approve a request by two or more parties to have their individual interests aggregated.

(b) If the court does not order partition in kind under subdivision (a), the court shall order partition by sale pursuant to Section 874.320 or, if no cotenant requested partition by sale, the court shall dismiss the action.

(c) If the court orders partition in kind pursuant to subdivision (a), the court may require that one or more cotenants pay one or more other cotenants amounts so that the payments, taken together with the value of the in-kind distributions to the cotenants, will make the partition in kind just and proportionate in value to the fractional interests held.

(d) If the court orders partition in kind, the court shall allocate to the cotenants that are unknown, unlocatable, or the subject of a default judgment, if their interests were not bought out, a part of the property representing the combined interests of these cotenants as determined by the court.

Added by Stats 2021 ch 119 (AB 633),s 2, eff. 1/1/2022.

Section 874.319 - Factors to consider for partition in kind

(a)In determining whether partition in kind would result in great prejudice to the cotenants as a group, the court shall consider the following:

(1)Whether the property practicably can be divided among the cotenants.

(2)Whether partition in kind would apportion the property in such a way that the aggregate fair market value of the parcels resulting from the division would be materially less than the value of the property if it were sold as a whole, taking into account the condition under which a court-ordered sale likely would occur.

(3)Evidence of the collective duration of ownership or possession of the property by a cotenant and one or more predecessors in title or predecessors in possession to the cotenant who are or were relatives of the cotenant or each other.

(4)A cotenant's sentimental attachment to the property, including any attachment arising because the property has ancestral or other unique or special value to the cotenant.

(5)The lawful use being made of the property by a cotenant and the degree to which the cotenant would be harmed if the cotenant could not continue the same use of the property.

(6)The degree to which the cotenants have contributed their pro rata share of the property taxes, insurance, and other expenses associated with maintaining ownership of the property or have contributed to the physical improvement, maintenance, or upkeep of the property.

(7)Any other relevant factor.

(b)The court shall not consider any one factor in subdivision (a) to be dispositive without weighing the totality of all relevant factors and circumstances.

Amended by Stats 2022 ch 82 (AB 2245),s 8, eff. 1/1/2023.

Added by Stats 2021 ch 119 (AB 633),s 2, eff. 1/1/2022.

Section 874.320 - Court ordered sale of property to be an open-market sale

(a)If the court orders a sale of property, the sale shall be an open-market sale unless the court finds that a sale by sealed bids or an auction would be more economically advantageous and in the best interest of the cotenants as a group.

(b)If the court orders an open-market sale and the parties, not later than 10 days after the entry of the order, agree on a real estate broker licensed in the State of California to offer the property for sale, the court shall appoint the broker and establish a reasonable commission. If the parties do not agree on a broker, the court shall appoint a disinterested real estate broker licensed in the State of California to offer the property for sale and shall establish a reasonable commission. The broker shall offer the property for sale in a commercially reasonable manner at a price no lower than the determination of value and on the terms and conditions established by the court.

(c)If the broker appointed under subdivision (b) obtains within a reasonable time an offer to purchase the property for at least the determination of value, the following requirements apply:

(1)The broker shall comply with the reporting requirements in Section 874.321.

(2)The sale shall be completed in accordance with state law.

(d)If the broker appointed under subdivision (b) does not obtain an offer to purchase the property for at least the determination of value within a reasonable time, the court, after a hearing, may do any of the following:

(1)Approve the highest outstanding offer, if any.

(2)Redetermine the value of the property and order that the property continue to be offered for an additional time.

(3)Order that the property be sold by sealed bids or at an auction.

(e)If the court orders a sale by sealed bids or an auction, the court shall set terms and conditions of the sale. If the court orders an auction, the auction shall be conducted under Chapter 6 (commencing with Section 873.510).

(f)If a purchaser is entitled to a share of the proceeds of the sale, the purchaser is entitled to a credit against the price in an amount equal to the purchaser's share of the proceeds.

Amended by Stats 2022 ch 82 (AB 2245),s 9, eff. 1/1/2023.

Added by Stats 2021 ch 119 (AB 633),s 2, eff. 1/1/2022.

Section 874.321 - Broker shall file report with the court; contents

(a)A broker appointed to offer property for open-market sale shall file a report with the court not later than seven days after receiving an offer to purchase the property for at least the value determined under Section 874.316 or 874.320.

(b)The report required by subdivision (a) shall contain the following information:

(1)A description of the property to be sold to each buyer.

(2)The name of each buyer.

(3)The proposed purchase price.

(4)The terms and conditions of the proposed sale, including the terms of any owner financing.

(5)The amounts to be paid to lienholders.

(6)A statement of contractual or other arrangements or conditions of the broker's commission.

(7)Other material facts relevant to the sale.

Amended by Stats 2022 ch 82 (AB 2245),s 10, eff. 1/1/2023.

Added by Stats 2021 ch 119 (AB 633),s 2, eff. 1/1/2022.

Section 874.321.5 - Court may apportion the costs of partition

874.321.5.In an action for partition of property, the court may apportion the costs of partition, including an appraisal fee, pursuant to Section 874.040, except that the court shall not apportion the costs of partition to any party that opposes the partition unless doing so is equitable and consistent with the purposes of this chapter.

Amended by Stats 2022 ch 82 (AB 2245),s 11, eff. 1/1/2023.

Added by Stats 2021 ch 119 (AB 633),s 2, eff. 1/1/2022.

Section 874.322 - [Repealed]

Repealed by Stats 2022 ch 82 (AB 2245),s 12, eff. 1/1/2023.

Added by Stats 2021 ch 119 (AB 633),s 2, eff. 1/1/2022.

Section 874.323 - Supersedes the Electronic Signatures in Global and National Commerce Act; exceptions

This act modifies, limits, and supersedes the Electronic Signatures in Global and National Commerce Act (15 U.S.C. Sec. 7001 et seq.), but does not modify, limit, or supersede Section 101(c)(c) of that act (15 U.S.C. Section 7001(c)), or authorize electronic delivery of any of the notices described in Section 103(b)(b) of that act (15 U.S.C. Section 7003(b)).

Added by Stats 2021 ch 119 (AB 633),s 2, eff. 1/1/2022.

Title 11 - CONTRIBUTION AMONG JOINT JUDGMENT DEBTORS
Chapter 1 - RELEASES FROM AND CONTRIBUTION AMONG JOINT TORTFEASORS

Section 875 - Right of contribution

(a) Where a money judgment has been rendered jointly against two or more defendants in a tort action there shall be a right of contribution among them as hereinafter provided.

(b) Such right of contribution shall be administered in accordance with the principles of equity.

(c) Such right of contribution may be enforced only after one tortfeasor has, by payment, discharged the joint judgment or has paid more than his pro rata share thereof. It shall be limited to the excess so paid over the pro rata share of the person so paying and in no event shall any tortfeasor be compelled to make contribution beyond his own pro rata share of the entire judgment.

(d) There shall be no right of contribution in favor of any tortfeasor who has intentionally injured the injured person.

(e) A liability insurer who by payment has discharged the liability of a tortfeasor judgment debtor shall be subrogated to his right of contribution.

(f) This title shall not impair any right of indemnity under existing law, and where one tortfeasor judgment debtor is entitled to indemnity from another there shall be no right of contribution between them.

(g) This title shall not impair the right of a plaintiff to satisfy a judgment in full as against any tortfeasor judgment debtor.

Added by Stats. 1957, Ch. 1700.

Section 876 - Pro rata share of each tortfeasor judgment debtor

(a) The pro rata share of each tortfeasor judgment debtor shall be determined by dividing the entire judgment equally among all of them.

(b) Where one or more persons are held liable solely for the tort of one of them or of another, as in the case of the liability of a master for the tort of his servant, they shall contribute a single pro rata share, as to which there may be indemnity between them.

Added by Stats. 1957, Ch. 1700.

Section 877 - Effect of release, dismissal or covenant not to sue or enforce judgment to one or more of joint tortfeasors

Where a release, dismissal with or without prejudice, or a covenant not to sue or not to enforce judgment is given in good faith before verdict or judgment to one or more of a number of tortfeasors claimed to be liable for the same tort, or to one or more other co-obligors mutually subject to contribution rights, it shall have the following effect:

(a) It shall not discharge any other such party from liability unless its terms so provide, but it shall reduce the claims against the others in the amount stipulated by the release, the dismissal or the covenant, or in the amount of the consideration paid for it, whichever is the greater.

(b) It shall discharge the party to whom it is given from all liability for any contribution to any other parties.

(c) This section shall not apply to co-obligors who have expressly agreed in writing to an apportionment of liability for losses or claims among themselves.

(d) This section shall not apply to a release, dismissal with or without prejudice, or a covenant not to sue or not to enforce judgment given to a co-obligor on an alleged contract debt where the contract was made prior to January 1, 1988.

Amended by Stats 2011 ch 296 (AB 1023),s 39, eff. 1/1/2012.

Section 877.5 - Sliding scale recovery agreement between one or more tortfeasors

(a) Where an agreement or covenant is made which provides for a sliding scale recovery agreement between one or more, but not all, alleged defendant tortfeasors and the plaintiff or plaintiffs:

  (1) The parties entering into any such agreement or covenant shall promptly inform the court in which the action is pending of the existence of the agreement or covenant and its terms and provisions.

  (2) If the action is tried before a jury, and a defendant party to the agreement is called as a witness at trial, the court shall, upon motion of a party, disclose to the jury the existence and content of the agreement or covenant, unless the court finds that this disclosure will create substantial danger of undue prejudice, of confusing the issues, or of misleading the jury. The jury disclosure herein required shall be no more than necessary to inform the jury of the possibility that the agreement may bias the testimony of the witness.

(b) As used in this section, a "sliding scale recovery agreement" means an agreement or covenant between a plaintiff or plaintiffs and one or more, but not all, alleged tortfeasor defendants, which limits the liability of the agreeing tortfeasor defendants to an amount which is dependent upon the amount of recovery which the plaintiff is able to recover from the nonagreeing defendant or defendants. This includes, but is not limited to, agreements within the scope of Section 877, and agreements in the form of a loan from the agreeing tortfeasor defendant or defendants to the plaintiff or plaintiffs which is repayable in whole or in part from the recovery against the nonagreeing tortfeasor defendant or defendants.

(c) No sliding scale recovery agreement is effective unless, at least 72 hours prior to entering into the agreement, a notice of intent to enter into an agreement has been served on all nonsignatory alleged defendant tortfeasors. However, upon a showing of good cause, the court or a judge thereof may allow a shorter time. The failure to comply with the notice requirements of this subdivision shall not constitute good cause to delay commencement of trial.

Amended by Stats. 1990, Ch. 17, Sec. 1.

Section 877.6 - Determination of good faith settlement

(a)

  (1) Any party to an action in which it is alleged that two or more parties are joint tortfeasors or co-obligors on a contract debt shall be entitled to a hearing on the issue of the good faith of a settlement entered into by the plaintiff or other claimant and one or more alleged tortfeasors or co-obligors, upon giving notice in the manner provided in subdivision (b) of Section 1005. Upon a showing of good cause, the court may shorten the time for giving the required notice to permit the determination of the issue to be made before the commencement of the trial of the action, or before the verdict or judgment if settlement is made after the trial has commenced.

  (2) In the alternative, a settling party may give notice of settlement to all parties and to the court, together with an application for determination of good faith settlement and a proposed order. The application shall indicate the settling parties, and the basis, terms, and amount of the settlement. The notice, application, and proposed order shall be given by certified mail, return receipt requested, or by personal service. Proof of service shall be filed with the court. Within 25 days of the mailing of the notice, application, and proposed order, or within 20 days of personal service, a nonsettling party may file a notice of motion to contest the good faith of the settlement. If none of the nonsettling parties files a motion within 25 days of mailing of the notice, application, and proposed order, or within 20 days of personal service, the court may approve the settlement. The notice by a nonsettling party shall be given in the manner provided in subdivision (b) of Section 1005. However, this paragraph shall not apply to settlements in which a confidentiality agreement has been entered into regarding the case or the terms of the settlement.

(b) The issue of the good faith of a settlement may be determined by the court on the basis of affidavits served with the notice of hearing, and any counteraffidavits filed in response, or the court may, in its discretion, receive other evidence at the hearing.

(c) A determination by the court that the settlement was made in good faith shall bar any other joint tortfeasor or co-obligor from any further claims against the settling tortfeasor or co-obligor for equitable comparative contribution, or partial or comparative indemnity, based on comparative negligence or comparative fault.
(d) The party asserting the lack of good faith shall have the burden of proof on that issue.
(e) When a determination of the good faith or lack of good faith of a settlement is made, any party aggrieved by the determination may petition the proper court to review the determination by writ of mandate. The petition for writ of mandate shall be filed within 20 days after service of written notice of the determination, or within any additional time not exceeding 20 days as the trial court may allow.

(1) The court shall, within 30 days of the receipt of all materials to be filed by the parties, determine whether or not the court will hear the writ and notify the parties of its determination.

(2) If the court grants a hearing on the writ, the hearing shall be given special precedence over all other civil matters on the calendar of the court except those matters to which equal or greater precedence on the calendar is granted by law.

(3) The running of any period of time after which an action would be subject to dismissal pursuant to the applicable provisions of Chapter 1.5 (commencing with Section 583.110) of Title 8 of Part 2 shall be tolled during the period of review of a determination pursuant to this subdivision.
Amended by Stats 2017 ch 64 (SB 543),s 1, eff. 1/1/2018.
Amended by Stats 2001 ch 812 (AB 223), s 7, eff. 1/1/2002.

Section 878 - Motion for judgment for contribution; notice
Judgment for contribution may be entered by one tortfeasor judgment debtor against other tortfeasor judgment debtors by motion upon notice. Notice of such motion shall be given to all parties in the action, including the plaintiff or plaintiffs, at least 10 days before the hearing thereon. Such notice shall be accompanied by an affidavit setting forth any information which the moving party may have as to the assets of defendants available for satisfaction of the judgment or claim for contribution.
Added by Stats. 1957, Ch. 1700.

Section 879 - Severability of provisions
If any provision of this title or the application thereof to any person is held invalid, such invalidity shall not affect other provisions or applications of the title which can be given effect without the invalid provision or application and to this end the provisions of this title are declared to be severable.
Added by Stats. 1957, Ch. 1700.

Section 880 - Effective date of title
This title shall become effective as to causes of action accruing on or after January 1, 1958.
Added by Stats. 1957, Ch. 1700.

Chapter 2 - CONTRIBUTION AMONG OTHER JUDGMENT DEBTORS

Section 881 - Generally
This chapter governs contribution among joint judgment debtors other than joint tortfeasors.
Added by Stats. 1982, Ch. 497, Sec. 63. Operative July 1, 1983, by Sec. 185 of Ch. 497.

Section 882 - Compelling contribution or repayment
If two or more judgment debtors are jointly liable on a money judgment:
(a) A judgment debtor who has satisfied more than his or her due proportion of the judgment, whether voluntarily or through enforcement procedures, may compel contribution from another judgment debtor who has satisfied less than his or her due proportion of the judgment.
(b) If the judgment is based upon an obligation of one judgment debtor as surety for another and the surety satisfies the judgment or any part thereof, whether voluntarily or through enforcement procedures, the surety may compel repayment from the principal.
Added by Stats. 1982, Ch. 497, Sec. 63. Operative July 1, 1983, by Sec. 185 of Ch. 497.

Section 883 - Motion for order determining liability for contribution or repayment
(a) A judgment debtor entitled to compel contribution or repayment pursuant to this chapter may apply on noticed motion to the court that entered the judgment for an order determining liability for contribution or repayment. The application shall be made at any time before the judgment is satisfied in full or within 30 days thereafter.
(b) The order determining liability for contribution or repayment entitles the judgment debtor to the benefit of the judgment to enforce the liability, including every remedy that the judgment creditor has against the persons liable, to the extent of the liability.
(c) Nothing in this section limits any other remedy that a judgment debtor entitled to contribution or repayment may have.
Amended by Stats. 1998, Ch. 77, Sec. 1. Effective January 1, 1999.

Title 13 - APPEALS IN CIVIL ACTIONS

Chapter 1 - APPEALS IN GENERAL

Section 901 - Generally
A judgment or order in a civil action or proceeding may be reviewed as prescribed in this title. The Judicial Council shall prescribe rules for the practice and procedure on appeal not inconsistent with the provisions of this title.
Added by Stats. 1968, Ch. 385.

Section 902 - Parties
Any party aggrieved may appeal in the cases prescribed in this title. A party appealing is known as an appellant, and an adverse party as a respondent.
Added by Stats. 1968, Ch. 385.

Section 902.1 - Right of Attorney General to intervene and participate
In any case in which a notice was required pursuant to subdivision (e) of Section 664.5, the Attorney General shall have the right to intervene and participate in any appeal taken therefrom. These rights shall apply regardless of whether the Attorney General participated in the case in the trial court. However, the Attorney General has no direct right to appeal. If the Attorney General elects not to intervene and participate in the appeal, he or she shall file a statement with the Legislature and the Judicial Council stating the reason or reasons for the decision not to intervene and participate in the appeal. This statement may be in the form of an annual report to the Legislature and Judicial Council and that report shall be a matter of public record.
Added by Stats. 1997, Ch. 259, Sec. 2. Effective January 1, 1998.

Section 903 - Death of person with right of appeal
In the event of the death of any person who would, if still alive, have a right of appeal, either the attorney of record representing the decedent in the court in which the judgment was rendered, or the executor or administrator of the estate of the decedent, may file a notice of appeal therefrom within the time within which the decedent could have filed such a notice if he had survived.
Added by Stats. 1968, Ch. 385.

Section 904 - How appeal taken
An appeal may be taken in a civil action or proceeding as provided in Sections 904.1, 904.2, 904.3, and 904.5.
Amended by Stats 2007 ch 263 (AB 310),s 9.5, eff. 1/1/2008.

Section 904.1 - Appeal to court of appeal
(a) An appeal, other than in a limited civil case, is to the court of appeal. An appeal, other than in a limited civil case, may be taken from any of the following:
　(1) From a judgment, except an interlocutory judgment, other than as provided in paragraphs (8), (9), and (11), or a judgment of contempt that is made final and conclusive by Section 1222.
　(2) From an order made after a judgment made appealable by paragraph (1).
　(3) From an order granting a motion to quash service of summons or granting a motion to stay the action on the ground of inconvenient forum, or from a written order of dismissal under Section 581d following an order granting a motion to dismiss the action on the ground of inconvenient forum.
　(4) From an order granting a new trial or denying a motion for judgment notwithstanding the verdict.
　(5) From an order discharging or refusing to discharge an attachment or granting a right to attach order.
　(6) From an order granting or dissolving an injunction, or refusing to grant or dissolve an injunction.
　(7) From an order appointing a receiver.
　(8) From an interlocutory judgment, order, or decree, made or entered in an action to redeem real or personal property from a mortgage thereof, or a lien thereon, determining the right to redeem and directing an accounting.
　(9) From an interlocutory judgment in an action for partition determining the rights and interests of the respective parties and directing partition to be made.
　(10) From an order made appealable by the Probate Code or the Family Code.
　(11) From an interlocutory judgment directing payment of monetary sanctions by a party or an attorney for a party if the amount exceeds five thousand dollars ($5,000).
　(12) From an order directing payment of monetary sanctions by a party or an attorney for a party if the amount exceeds five thousand dollars ($5,000).
　(13) From an order granting or denying a special motion to strike under Section 425.16.
　(14) From a final order or judgment in a bifurcated proceeding regarding child custody or visitation rights.
(b) Sanction orders or judgments of five thousand dollars ($5,000) or less against a party or an attorney for a party may be reviewed on an appeal by that party after entry of final judgment in the main action, or, at the discretion of the court of appeal, may be reviewed upon petition for an extraordinary writ.
Amended by Stats 2017 ch 41 (AB 369),s 1, eff. 1/1/2018.
Amended by Stats 2007 ch 43 (SB 649),s 9, eff. 1/1/2008.
Amended by Stats 2006 ch 567 (AB 2303),s 8, eff. 1/1/2007.
Effective October 10, 1999 (Bill Number: AB 1675) (Chapter 960).

Section 904.2 - Appeal to appellate division of superior court
An appeal of a ruling by a superior court judge or other judicial officer in a limited civil case is to the appellate division of the superior court. An appeal of a ruling by a superior court judge or other judicial officer in a limited civil case may be taken from any of the following:
(a) From a judgment, except (1) an interlocutory judgment, or (2) a judgment of contempt that is made final and conclusive by Section 1222.
(b) From an order made after a judgment made appealable by subdivision (a).
(c) From an order changing or refusing to change the place of trial.
(d) From an order granting a motion to quash service of summons or granting a motion to stay the action on the ground of inconvenient forum, or from a written order of dismissal under Section 581d following an order granting a motion to dismiss the action on the ground of inconvenient forum.
(e) From an order granting a new trial or denying a motion for judgment notwithstanding the verdict.
(f) From an order discharging or refusing to discharge an attachment or granting a right to attach order.
(g) From an order granting or dissolving an injunction, or refusing to grant or dissolve an injunction.
(h) From an order appointing a receiver.
Amended by Stats 2007 ch 43 (SB 649),s 10, eff. 1/1/2008.
Amended by Stats 2006 ch 567 (AB 2303),s 9, eff. 1/1/2007.

Section 904.3 - Judgment of appellate division granting or denying petition for issuance of writ of mandamus or prohibition
An appeal shall not be taken from a judgment of the appellate division of a superior court granting or denying a petition for issuance of a writ of mandamus or prohibition directed to the superior court, or a judge thereof, in a limited civil case or a misdemeanor or infraction case. An appellate court may, in its discretion, upon petition for extraordinary writ, review the judgment.
Added by Stats 2007 ch 43 (SB 649),s 11, eff. 1/1/2008.

Section 904.5 - Appeals from small claims division of superior court
Appeals from the small claims division of a superior court shall be governed by the Small Claims Act (Chapter 5.5 (commencing with Section 116.110) of Title 1 of Part 1).
Amended by Stats 2002 ch 784 (SB 1316),s 70, eff. 1/1/2003.

Section 906 - Review by reviewing court upon appeal taken pursuant to sections 904.1 and 904.2
Upon an appeal pursuant to Section 904.1 or 904.2, the reviewing court may review the verdict or decision and any intermediate ruling, proceeding, order or decision which involves the merits or necessarily affects the judgment or order appealed from or which substantially affects the rights of a party, including, on any appeal from the judgment, any order on motion for a new trial, and may affirm, reverse or modify any judgment or order appealed from and may direct the proper judgment or order to be entered, and may, if necessary or proper, direct a new trial or further proceedings to be had. The respondent, or party in whose favor the judgment was given, may, without appealing from such judgment, request the reviewing court to and it may review any of the foregoing matters for the purpose of determining whether or not the appellant was prejudiced by the error or errors upon which he relies for reversal or modification of the judgment from which the appeal is taken. The provisions of this section do not authorize the reviewing court to review any decision or order from which an appeal might have been taken.
Amended by Stats. 1976, Ch. 1288.

Section 907 - Frivolous appeal or appeal taken for delay
When it appears to the reviewing court that the appeal was frivolous or taken solely for delay, it may add to the costs on appeal such damages as may be just.
Added by Stats. 1968, Ch. 385.

Section 908 - Judgment or order reversed or modified
When the judgment or order is reversed or modified, the reviewing court may direct that the parties be returned so far as possible to the positions they occupied before the enforcement of or execution on the judgment or order. In doing so, the reviewing court may order restitution on reasonable terms and conditions of all property and rights lost by the erroneous judgment or order, so far as such restitution is consistent with rights of third parties and may direct the entry of a money judgment sufficient to compensate for property or rights not restored. The reviewing court may take evidence and make findings concerning such matters or may, by order, refer such matters to the trial court for determination.

Added by Stats. 1968, Ch. 385.

Section 909 - Factual determinations contrary to or in addition to those made by trial court

In all cases where trial by jury is not a matter of right or where trial by jury has been waived, the reviewing court may make factual determinations contrary to or in addition to those made by the trial court. The factual determinations may be based on the evidence adduced before the trial court either with or without the taking of evidence by the reviewing court. The reviewing court may for the purpose of making the factual determinations or for any other purpose in the interests of justice, take additional evidence of or concerning facts occurring at any time prior to the decision of the appeal, and may give or direct the entry of any judgment or order and may make any further or other order as the case may require. This section shall be liberally construed to the end among others that, where feasible, causes may be finally disposed of by a single appeal and without further proceedings in the trial court except where in the interests of justice a new trial is required on some or all of the issues.
Amended by Stats. 1981, Ch. 900, Sec. 7.

Section 911 - Transfer of case on appeal to court of appeal

A court of appeal may order any case on appeal to a superior court in its district transferred to it for hearing and decision as provided by rules of the Judicial Council when the superior court certifies, or the court of appeal determines, that the transfer appears necessary to secure uniformity of decision or to settle important questions of law.

No case in which there is a right on appeal to a trial anew in the superior court shall be transferred pursuant to this section before a decision in the case becomes final therein.

A court to which any case is transferred pursuant to this section shall have similar power to review any matter and make orders and judgments as the appellate division of the superior court would have in the case, except that if the case was tried anew in the superior court, the court of appeal shall have similar power to review any matter and make orders and judgments as it has in a case appealed pursuant to Section 904.1.
Amended by Stats. 1998, Ch. 931, Sec. 103. Effective September 28, 1998.

Section 912 - Duty of clerk upon receiving certified copy of final judgment or order of reviewing court

Upon final determination of an appeal by the reviewing court, the clerk of the court shall remit to the trial court a certified copy of the judgment or order of the reviewing court and of its opinion, if any. The clerk of the trial court shall file the certified copy of the judgment and opinion of the reviewing court, shall attach that copy to the judgment roll if the appeal was from a judgment, and shall enter a note of the judgment of the reviewing court stating whether the judgment or order appealed from has been affirmed, reversed or modified, in the margin of the original entry of the judgment or order, and also in the register of actions.
Amended by Stats 2002 ch 664 (AB 3034),s 49, eff. 1/1/2003.
Amended by Stats 2001 ch 44 (SB 562), s 6, eff. 1/1/2002.

Section 913 - Dismissal with prejudice to right to file another appeal, exception

The dismissal of an appeal shall be with prejudice to the right to file another appeal within the time permitted, unless the dismissal is expressly made without prejudice to another appeal.
Added by Stats. 1968, Ch. 385.

Section 914 - New trial ordered when no photographic report of trial transcribed or lost or destroyed

When the right to a phonographic report has not been waived and when it shall be impossible to have a phonographic report of the trial transcribed by a stenographic reporter as provided by law or by rule, because of the death or disability of a reporter who participated as a stenographic reporter at the trial or because of the loss or destruction, in whole or in substantial part, of the notes of such reporter, the trial court or a judge thereof, or the reviewing court shall have power to set aside and vacate the judgment, order or decree from which an appeal has been taken or is to be taken and to order a new trial of the action or proceeding.
Added by Stats. 1968, Ch. 385.

Chapter 2 - STAY OF ENFORCEMENT AND OTHER PROCEEDINGS

Section 916 - Proceedings in trial court stayed upon perfection of appeal; trial court jurisdiction when stay other than enforcement of judgment

(a) Except as provided in Sections 917.1 to 917.9, inclusive, and in Section 116.810, the perfecting of an appeal stays proceedings in the trial court upon the judgment or order appealed from or upon the matters embraced therein or affected thereby, including enforcement of the judgment or order, but the trial court may proceed upon any other matter embraced in the action and not affected by the judgment or order.

(b) When there is a stay of proceedings other than the enforcement of the judgment, the trial court shall have jurisdiction of proceedings related to the enforcement of the judgment as well as any other matter embraced in the action and not affected by the judgment or order appealed from.
Amended by Stats. 1990, Ch. 1305, Sec. 8.

Section 917.1 - Undertaking required to stay enforcement of judgment or order

(a) Unless an undertaking is given, the perfecting of an appeal shall not stay enforcement of the judgment or order in the trial court if the judgment or order is for any of the following:

(1) Money or the payment of money, whether consisting of a special fund or not, and whether payable by the appellant or another party to the action.

(2) Costs awarded pursuant to Section 998 which otherwise would not have been awarded as costs pursuant to Section 1033.5.

(3) Costs awarded pursuant to Section 1141.21 which otherwise would not have been awarded as costs pursuant to Section 1033.5.

(b) The undertaking shall be on condition that if the judgment or order or any part of it is affirmed or the appeal is withdrawn or dismissed, the party ordered to pay shall pay the amount of the judgment or order, or the part of it as to which the judgment or order is affirmed, as entered after the receipt of the remittitur, together with any interest which may have accrued pending the appeal and entry of the remittitur, and costs which may be awarded against the appellant on appeal. This section shall not apply in cases where the money to be paid is in the actual or constructive custody of the court; and such cases shall be governed, instead, by the provisions of Section 917.2. The undertaking shall be for double the amount of the judgment or order unless given by an admitted surety insurer in which event it shall be for one and one-half times the amount of the judgment or order. The liability on the undertaking may be enforced if the party ordered to pay does not make the payment within 30 days after the filing of the remittitur from the reviewing court.

(c) If a surety on the undertaking pays the judgment, either with or without action, after the judgment is affirmed, the surety is substituted to the rights of the creditor and is entitled to control, enforce, and satisfy the judgment, in all respects as if the surety had recovered the judgment.

(d) Costs awarded by the trial court under Chapter 6 (commencing with Section 1021) of Title 14 shall be included in the amount of the judgment or order for the purpose of applying paragraph (1) of subdivision (a) and subdivision (b). However, no undertaking shall be required pursuant to this section solely for costs awarded under Chapter 6 (commencing with Section 1021) of Title 14.
Amended by Stats. 1993, Ch. 456, Sec. 13. Effective January 1, 1994.

Section 917.15 - [Operative Until 1/1/2024] Enforcement not stayed as to certain Health and Safety Code orders

The perfecting of an appeal shall not stay enforcement of the judgment or order in the trial court if the judgment or order appealed from, or the administrative order which is the subject of the trial court proceeding, was issued pursuant to either of the following:

(a) Subdivision (a) of Section 25358.3 of the Health and Safety Code and ordered a responsible party to take appropriate removal or remedial actions in response to a release or a threatened release of a hazardous substance.

(b) Section 25181 of the Health and Safety Code and ordered the party to comply with Chapter 6.5 (commencing with Section 25100) of Division 20 of the Health and Safety Code or any rule, regulation, permit, covenant, standard, requirement, or order issued, adopted or executed pursuant to that Chapter 6.5.

Added by Stats. 1985, Ch. 1492, Sec. 1.

This section is set out more than once due to postponed, multiple, or conflicting amendments.

Section 917.15 - [Operative 1/1/2024] Enforcement not stayed as to certain Health and Safety Code orders

The perfecting of an appeal shall not stay enforcement of the judgment or order in the trial court if the judgment or order appealed from, or the administrative order which is the subject of the trial court proceeding, was issued pursuant to either of the following:

(a) Section 78870 of the Health and Safety Code and ordered a responsible party to take appropriate removal or remedial actions in response to a release or a threatened release of a hazardous substance.

(b) Section 25181 of the Health and Safety Code and ordered the party to comply with Chapter 6.5 (commencing with Section 25100) of Division 20 of the Health and Safety Code or any rule, regulation, permit, covenant, standard, requirement, or order issued, adopted or executed pursuant to that Chapter 6.5.

Amended by Stats 2022 ch 258 (AB 2327),s 9, eff. 1/1/2023, op. 1/1/2024.

Added by Stats. 1985, Ch. 1492, Sec. 1.

This section is set out more than once due to postponed, multiple, or conflicting amendments.

Section 917.2 - Judgment or order directing assignment or delivery of personal property or sale of personal property upon foreclosure

The perfecting of an appeal shall not stay enforcement of the judgment or order of the trial court if the judgment or order appealed from directs the assignment or delivery of personal property, including documents, whether by the appellant or another party to the action, or the sale of personal property upon the foreclosure of a mortgage, or other lien thereon, unless an undertaking in a sum and upon conditions fixed by the trial court, is given that the appellant or party ordered to assign or deliver the property will obey and satisfy the order of the reviewing court, and will not commit or suffer to be committed any damage to the property, and that if the judgment or order appealed from is affirmed, or the appeal is withdrawn or dismissed, the appellant shall pay the damage suffered to such property and the value of the use of such property for the period of the delay caused by the appeal. The appellant may cause the property to be placed in the custody of an officer designated by the court to abide the order of the reviewing court, and such fact shall be considered by the court in fixing the amount of the undertaking. If the judgment or order appealed from directs the sale of perishable property the trial court may order such property to be sold and the proceeds thereof to be deposited with the clerk of the trial court to abide the order of the reviewing court; such fact shall be considered by the court in fixing the amount of the undertaking.

Amended by Stats. 1972, Ch. 546.

Section 917.3 - Judgment or order directing execution of one or more instruments

The perfecting of an appeal shall not stay enforcement of the judgment or order in the trial court if the judgment or order appealed from directs the execution of one or more instruments unless the instrument or instruments are executed and deposited in the office of the clerk of the court where the original judgment or order is entered to abide the order of the reviewing court.

Added by Stats. 1968, Ch. 385.

Section 917.4 - Judgment or order directing sale, conveyance or delivery of real property

The perfecting of an appeal shall not stay enforcement of the judgment or order in the trial court if the judgment or order appealed from directs the sale, conveyance or delivery of possession of real property which is in the possession or control of the appellant or the party ordered to sell, convey or deliver possession of the property, unless an undertaking in a sum fixed by the trial court is given that the appellant or party ordered to sell, convey or deliver possession of the property will not commit or suffer to be committed any waste thereon and that if the judgment or order appealed from is affirmed, or the appeal is withdrawn or dismissed, the appellant shall pay the damage suffered by the waste and the value of the use and occupancy of the property, or the part of it as to which the judgment or order is affirmed, from the time of the taking of the appeal until the delivery of the possession of the property. If the judgment or order directs the sale of mortgaged real property and the payment of any deficiency, the undertaking shall also provide for the payment of any deficiency.

Amended by Stats. 1982, Ch. 517, Sec. 156.

Section 917.5 - Judgment or order appointing receiver

The perfecting of an appeal shall not stay enforcement of the judgment or order in the trial court if the judgment or order appealed from appoints a receiver, unless an undertaking in a sum fixed by the trial court is given on condition that if the judgment or order is affirmed or the appeal is withdrawn, or dismissed, the appellant will pay all damages which the respondent may sustain by reason of the stay in the enforcement of the judgment.

Amended by Stats. 1982, Ch. 517, Sec. 157.

Section 917.6 - Judgment or order directing performance of acts specified in sections 917.1 through 915.5

The perfecting of an appeal shall not stay enforcement of the judgment or order in the trial court if the judgment or order appealed from directs the performance of two or more of the acts specified in Sections 917.1 through 917.5, unless the appellant complies with the requirements of each applicable section.

Added by Stats. 1968, Ch. 385.

Section 917.65 - Enforcement of right to attach order

The perfecting of an appeal shall not stay enforcement of a right to attach order unless an undertaking is given. The undertaking shall be in the amount specified in the right to attach order as the amount to be secured by the attachment. The undertaking shall be on condition that if the right to attach order is not reversed and the plaintiff recovers judgment in the action in which the right to attach order was issued, the appellant shall pay the amount of the judgment, together with any interest which may have accrued. The liability on the undertaking may be enforced if the judgment is not paid within 30 days after it becomes final. If a surety on the undertaking pays the judgment, either with or without action, the surety is substituted to the rights of the creditor and is entitled to control, enforce, and satisfy the judgment, in all respects as if the surety had recovered the judgment.

Added by Stats. 1983, Ch. 155, Sec. 22.5. Effective June 30, 1983. Operative July 1, 1983, by Sec. 32 of Ch. 155.

Section 917.7 - Judgment or order awarding, changing or affecting custody of minor child

The perfecting of an appeal shall not stay proceedings as to those provisions of a judgment or order which award, change, or otherwise affect the custody, including the right of visitation, of a minor child in any civil action, in an action filed under the Juvenile Court Law, or in a special proceeding, or the provisions of a judgment or order for the temporary exclusion of a party from a dwelling, as provided in the Family Code. However, the trial court may in its discretion stay execution of these provisions pending review on appeal or for any other period or periods that it may deem appropriate. Further, in the absence of a writ or order of a reviewing court providing otherwise, the provisions of the judgment or order allowing, or eliminating restrictions against, removal of the minor child from the state are stayed by operation of law for a period of seven calendar days from the entry of the judgment or order by a juvenile court in a dependency hearing, or for a period of 30 calendar days from the entry of judgment or order by any other trial court. The periods during which these provisions allowing, or eliminating restrictions against, removal of the minor child from the state are stayed, are subject to further stays as ordered by the trial court or by the juvenile court pursuant to this section. An order directing the return of a child to a sister state or country, including any order effectuating that return, made in a proceeding

brought pursuant to the Uniform Child Custody Jurisdiction and Enforcement Act (Part 3 (commencing with Section 3400) of Division 8 of the Family Code), the Parental Kidnapping Prevention Act of 1980 (28 U.S.C. Sec. 1738A), or the Hague Convention on the Civil Aspects of International Child Abduction (implemented pursuant to the International Child Abduction Remedies Act (22 U.S.C. Secs. 9001-9011)) is not a judgment or order which awards, changes, or otherwise affects the custody of a minor child within the meaning of this section, and therefore is not subject to the automatic stay provisions of this section.
Amended by Stats 2021 ch 124 (AB 938),s 13, eff. 1/1/2022.
Amended by Stats 2001 ch 48 (SB 1151), s 1, eff. 1/1/2002.
Previously Amended September 7, 1999 (Bill Number: SB 518) (Chapter 346).

Section 917.8 - Proceedings not stayed in absence of order of trial court or writ of supersedeas

The perfecting of an appeal does not stay proceedings, in the absence of an order of the trial court providing otherwise or of a writ of supersedeas, under any of the following circumstances:

(a) If a party to the proceeding has been adjudged guilty of usurping, or intruding into, or unlawfully holding a public office, civil or military, within this state.

(b) If the judgment or order directs a corporation, or any of its officers or agents, to give to a person adjudged to be a director, stockholder, or member of that corporation a reasonable opportunity to inspect or make copies of the books, papers, or documents of the corporation as the trial court finds that the director, stockholder, or member is entitled by law to inspect or copy.

(c) If a judgment or order adjudges a building or place to be a nuisance and, as part of that judgment or order, directs the closing or discontinuance of any specific use of the building or place for any period of time.

(d) If a judgment or order, including, but not limited to, a temporary restraining order or preliminary injunction, grants relief in an action brought by a governmental agency under the provisions of Article 2 (commencing with Section 11225) of Chapter 3 of Title 1 of Part 4 of the Penal Code or Article 3 (commencing with Section 11570) of Chapter 10 of Division 10 of the Health and Safety Code.
Amended by Stats 2003 ch 31 (AB 1639),s 1, eff. 1/1/2004.

Section 917.9 - Judgment or order in cases not provided for in sections 917.1 to 917.8

(a) The perfecting of an appeal shall not stay enforcement of the judgment or order in cases not provided for in Sections 917.1 to 917.8, inclusive, if the trial court, in its discretion, requires an undertaking and the undertaking is not given, in any of the following cases:

    (1) Appellant was found to possess money or other property belonging to respondent.

    (2) Appellant is required to perform an act for respondent's benefit pursuant to judgment or order under appeal.

    (3) The judgment against appellant is solely for costs awarded to the respondent by the trial court pursuant to Chapter 6 (commencing with Section 1021) of Title 14.

(b) The undertaking shall be in a sum fixed by the court and shall be in an amount sufficient to cover all damages which the respondent may sustain by reason of the stay in the enforcement of the judgment or order.

(c) The undertaking shall be in the sum fixed by the court. The undertaking shall be conditioned upon the performance of the judgment or order appealed from or payment of the sums required by the judgment or order appealed from, if the judgment or order is affirmed or the appeal is withdrawn or dismissed, and it shall provide that if the judgment or order appealed from or any part of it is affirmed, or the appeal is withdrawn or dismissed, the appellant will pay all damages which the respondent may sustain by reason of the stay in the enforcement of the judgment.

(d) For the purpose of this section, "damages" means either of the following:

    (1) Reasonable compensation for the loss of use of the money or property.

    (2) Payment of the amounts specified in paragraph (3) of subdivision (a).
Amended by Stats. 1994, Ch. 493, Sec. 3. Effective September 12, 1994.

Section 917.75 - Appeal from proceeding under family code

The perfecting of an appeal shall not stay enforcement of the judgment or order of the trial court awarding attorney's fees or costs, or both, if the judgment or order appealed from was rendered in a proceeding under the Family Code, unless an undertaking is given in a sum and upon conditions fixed by the trial court.
Added by Stats 2014 ch 95 (AB 2154),s 1, eff. 1/1/2015.

Section 918 - Trial court's power to stay enforcement; exception

(a) Subject to subdivision (b), the trial court may stay the enforcement of any judgment or order.

(b) If the enforcement of the judgment or order would be stayed on appeal only by the giving of an undertaking, a trial court shall not have power, without the consent of the adverse party, to stay the enforcement thereof pursuant to this section for a period which extends for more than 10 days beyond the last date on which a notice of appeal could be filed.

(c) This section applies whether or not an appeal will be taken from the judgment or order and whether or not a notice of appeal has been filed.
Amended by Stats. 1982, Ch. 497, Sec. 65. Operative July 1, 1983, by Sec. 185 of Ch. 497.

Section 918.5 - Trial court's discretion to stay enforcement of judgment debtor has another action pending on disputed claim

(a) The trial court may, in its discretion, stay the enforcement of a judgment or order if the judgment debtor has another action pending on a disputed claim against the judgment creditor.

(b) In exercising its discretion under this section, the court shall consider all of the following:

    (1) The likelihood of the judgment debtor prevailing in the other action.

    (2) The amount of the judgment of the judgment creditor as compared to the amount of the probable recovery of the judgment debtor in the action on the disputed claim.

    (3) The financial ability of the judgment creditor to satisfy the judgment if a judgment is rendered against the judgment creditor in the action on the disputed claim.
Added by Stats. 1982, Ch. 497, Sec. 66. Operative July 1, 1983, by Sec. 185 of Ch. 497.

Section 919 - Trial court's discretion to dispense with or limit security required

The trial court may, in its discretion, dispense with or limit the security required by any section in this chapter, when the appellant is an executor, administrator, trustee, guardian, conservator or other person acting in another's right.
Added by Stats. 1968, Ch. 385.

Section 921 - Undertaking required to continue in force attachment

An appeal by a party who has levied an attachment shall not continue in force the attachment, unless an undertaking is executed and filed on the part of the appellant that the appellant will pay all costs and damages which the respondent may sustain by reason of the attachment, in case the order of the court below is sustained in favor of the respondent; and unless, within five days after written notice of the entry of the order appealed from, the appeal is perfected. The amount of the undertaking on appeal required by this section shall be such amount as is fixed by the trial court on motion of the respondent as provided in Section 489.410 and if no such order has been made, the undertaking shall be in double the amount of the debt claimed by the appellant. If the respondent is not satisfied with the undertaking in double the amount of the debt or the amount fixed by order under Section 489.410, the trial court upon motion of the respondent made within 60 days after perfecting the appeal may order an increase in the amount of the undertaking in such amount as is justified by the detriment reasonably to be anticipated by continuing the attachment. If such an order is made, the attachment shall be discharged and the property released therefrom, unless the undertaking is executed and filed within 10 days after the order is made.

Amended by Stats. 1982, Ch. 517, Sec. 160.

Section 922 - Determination that undertaking insufficient and sufficient undertaking not given in time provided by statute

If an undertaking required or permitted by this title is objected to by the respondent and the court determines the undertaking is insufficient and a sufficient undertaking is not given within the time provided by statute, enforcement of the judgment or order appealed from is no longer stayed and property which has been levied upon under execution issued upon such judgment shall not be released from levy.

Amended by Stats. 1982, Ch. 517, Sec. 161.

Section 923 - Power of reviewing court or judge not limited

The provisions of this chapter shall not limit the power of a reviewing court or of a judge thereof to stay proceedings during the pendency of an appeal or to issue a writ of supersedeas or to suspend or modify an injunction during the pendency of an appeal or to make any order appropriate to preserve the status quo, the effectiveness of the judgment subsequently to be entered, or otherwise in aid of its jurisdiction.

Added by Stats. 1968, Ch. 385.

Section 936.1 - Notice of appeal in civil commitment or other proceeding wherein appellant entitled to appointment of counsel on appeal

An appeal from any judgment or order in any civil commitment or other proceeding wherein the appellant would be entitled to the appointment of counsel on appeal if indigent shall be initiated by the filing of a notice of appeal in conformity with the requirements of Section 1240.1 of the Penal Code.

Added by Stats. 1978, Ch. 1385. Note: Termination clause in Sec. 3.5 of Ch. 1385 was deleted by Stats. 1980, Ch. 369.

Title 14 - OF MISCELLANEOUS PROVISIONS

Chapter 1 - PROCEEDINGS AGAINST JOINT DEBTORS

Section 989 - Joint debtors not originally served with summons summoned to appear

When a judgment is recovered against one or more of several persons, jointly indebted upon an obligation, by proceeding as provided in Section 410.70, those who were not originally served with the summons, and did not appear in the action, may be summoned to appear before the court in which such judgment is entered to show cause why they should not be bound by the judgment, in the same manner as though they had been originally served with the summons.

Amended by Stats. 1969, Ch. 1611.

Section 990 - Requirements of summons

The summons specified in Section 989 shall be issued by the clerk upon presentation of the affidavit specified in Section 991. The summons must describe the judgment, and require the person summoned to show cause why the person should not be bound by it, and must be served in the same manner, and returnable no later than ninety (90) days after the time specified for the return of the original summons. It is not necessary to file a new complaint.

Amended by Stats 2007 ch 263 (AB 310),s 10, eff. 1/1/2008.

Section 991 - Affidavit to accompany summons

The summons must be accompanied by an affidavit of the plaintiff, his agent, representative, or attorney, that the judgment, or some part thereof, remains unsatisfied, and must specify the amount due thereon.

Enacted 1872.

Section 992 - Answer

Upon such summons, the defendant may answer within the time specified therein, denying the judgment, or setting up any defense which may have arisen subsequently; or he may deny his liability on the obligation upon which the judgment was recovered, by reason of any defense existing at the commencement of the action.

Amended by Stats. 1907, Ch. 325.

Section 993 - Allegations

If the defendant, in his answer, denies the judgment, or sets up any defense which may have arisen subsequently, the summons, with the affidavit annexed, and the answer, constitute the written allegations in the case; if he denies his liability on the obligation upon which the judgment was recovered, a copy of the original complaint and judgment, the summons, with the affidavit annexed, and the answer, constitute such written allegations, subject to the right of the parties to amend their pleadings as in other cases.

Amended by Stats. 1907, Ch. 325.

Section 994 - Issues tried as other cases

The issues formed may be tried as in other cases; but when the defendant denies, in his answer, any liability on the obligation upon which the judgment was rendered, if a verdict be found against him, it must be for not exceeding the amount remaining unsatisfied on such original judgment, with interest thereon.

Enacted 1872.

Chapter 2 - BONDS AND UNDERTAKINGS

Article 1 - PRELIMINARY PROVISIONS AND DEFINITIONS

Section 995.010 - Title of law

This chapter shall be known and may be cited as the Bond and Undertaking Law.

Added by Stats. 1982, Ch. 998, Sec. 1.

Section 995.020 - Applicability of chapter; effective date

(a) The provisions of this chapter apply to a bond or undertaking executed, filed, posted, furnished, or otherwise given as security pursuant to any statute of this state, except to the extent the statute prescribes a different rule or is inconsistent.

(b) The provisions of this chapter apply to a bond or undertaking given at any of the following times:

(1) On or after January 1, 1983.

(2) Before January 1, 1983, to the extent another surety is substituted for the original surety on or after January 1, 1983, or to the extent the principal gives a new, additional, or supplemental bond or undertaking on or after January 1, 1983. Except to the extent provided in this section, the law governing a bond or undertaking given before January 1, 1983, is the law applicable to the bond or undertaking immediately before January 1, 1983, pursuant to Section 414 of Chapter 517 of the Statutes of 1982.

(c) The provisions of this chapter do not apply to a bail bond or an undertaking of bail.

Amended by Stats. 1983, Ch. 18, Sec. 18.2. Effective April 21, 1983.

Section 995.030 - Manner of making service

If service of a notice, paper, or other document is required under this chapter, service shall be made in the same manner as service of process in civil actions generally.

Added by Stats. 1982, Ch. 998, Sec. 1.

Section 995.040 - Standards for affidavits

An affidavit made under this chapter shall conform to the standards prescribed for an affidavit made pursuant to Section 437c.
Added by Stats. 1982, Ch. 998, Sec. 1.

Section 995.050 - Extension of time
The times provided in this chapter, or in any other statute relating to a bond given in an action or proceeding, may be extended pursuant to Sections 1054 and 1054.1.
Added by Stats. 1982, Ch. 998, Sec. 1.

Section 995.110 - Definitions govern construction
Unless the provision or context otherwise requires, the definitions in this article govern the construction of this chapter.
Added by Stats. 1982, Ch. 998, Sec. 1.

Section 995.120 - Admitted surety insurer
(a) "Admitted surety insurer" means a corporate insurer or a reciprocal or interinsurance exchange to which the Insurance Commissioner has issued a certificate of authority to transact surety insurance in this state, as defined in Section 105 of the Insurance Code.
(b) For the purpose of application of this chapter to a bond given pursuant to any statute of this state, the phrases "admitted surety insurer," "authorized surety company," "bonding company," "corporate surety," and comparable phrases used in the statute mean "admitted surety insurer" as defined in this section.
Added by Stats. 1982, Ch. 998, Sec. 1.

Section 995.130 - Beneficiary
(a) "Beneficiary" means the person for whose benefit a bond is given, whether executed to, in favor of, in the name of, or payable to the person as an obligee.
(b) If a bond is given for the benefit of the State of California or the people of the state, "beneficiary" means the court, officer, or other person required to determine the sufficiency of the sureties or to approve the bond.
(c) For the purpose of application of this chapter to a bond given pursuant to any statute of this state, the terms "beneficiary," "obligee," and comparable terms used in the statute mean "beneficiary" as defined in this section.
Added by Stats. 1982, Ch. 998, Sec. 1.

Section 995.140 - Bond
(a) "Bond" includes both of the following:
   (1) A surety, indemnity, fiduciary, or like bond executed by both the principal and sureties.
   (2) A surety, indemnity, fiduciary, or like undertaking executed by the sureties alone.
(b) A bond provided for or given "in an action or proceeding" does not include a bond provided for, or given as, a condition of a license or permit.
Added by Stats. 1982, Ch. 998, Sec. 1.

Section 995.150 - Court
"Court" means, if a bond is given in an action or proceeding, the court in which the action or proceeding is pending.
Added by Stats. 1982, Ch. 998, Sec. 1.

Section 995.160 - Officer
"Officer" means the sheriff, marshal, clerk of court, judge or magistrate (if there is no clerk), board, commission, department, or other public official or entity to whom the bond is given or with whom a copy of the bond is filed or who is required to determine the sufficiency of the sureties or to approve the bond.
Amended by Stats. 1996, Ch. 872, Sec. 19. Effective January 1, 1997.

Section 995.170 - Principal
(a) "Principal" means the person who gives a bond.
(b) For the purpose of application of this chapter to a bond given pursuant to any statute of this state, the terms "obligor," "principal," and comparable terms used in the statute mean "principal" as defined in this section.
Added by Stats. 1982, Ch. 998, Sec. 1.

Section 995.180 - Statute
"Statute" includes administrative regulation promulgated pursuant to statute.
Added by Stats. 1982, Ch. 998, Sec. 1.

Section 995.185 - Surety
(a) "Surety" has the meaning provided in Section 2787 of the Civil Code and includes personal surety and admitted surety insurer.
(b) For the purpose of application of this chapter to a bond given pursuant to any statute of this state, the terms "bail," "guarantor," "bondsman," "surety," and comparable terms used in the statute mean "surety" as defined in this section.
Added by Stats. 1982, Ch. 998, Sec. 1.

Section 995.190 - Undertaking
"Undertaking" means a surety, indemnity, fiduciary, or like undertaking executed by the sureties alone.
Added by Stats. 1982, Ch. 998, Sec. 1.

Article 2 - GENERAL PROVISIONS

Section 995.210 - Undertaking given in place of bond; bond given in place of undertaking
Unless the provision or context otherwise requires:
(a) If a statute provides for a bond, an undertaking that otherwise satisfies the requirements for the bond may be given in its place with the same effect as if a bond were given, and references in the statute to the bond shall be deemed to be references to the undertaking.
(b) If a statute provides for an undertaking, a bond that otherwise satisfies the requirements for the undertaking may be given in its place with the same effect as if an undertaking were given, and references in the statute to the undertaking shall be deemed to be references to the bond.
Added by Stats. 1982, Ch. 998, Sec. 1.

Section 995.220 - Public entities and officers not required to give bond
Notwithstanding any other statute, if a statute provides for a bond in an action or proceeding, including but not limited to a bond for issuance of a restraining order or injunction, appointment of a receiver, or stay of enforcement of a judgment on appeal, the following public entities and officers are not required to give the bond and shall have the same rights, remedies, and benefits as if the bond were given:
(a) The State of California or the people of the state, a state agency, department, division, commission, board, or other entity of the state, or a state officer in an official capacity or on behalf of the state.
(b) A county, city, or district, or public authority, public agency, or other political subdivision in the state, or an officer of the local public entity in an official capacity or on behalf of the local public entity.
(c) The United States or an instrumentality or agency of the United States, or a federal officer in an official capacity or on behalf of the United States or instrumentality or agency.
Added by Stats. 1982, Ch. 998, Sec. 1.

Section 995.230 - Consent to bond in amount less than required amount

The beneficiary of a bond given in an action or proceeding may in writing consent to the bond in an amount less than the amount required by statute or may waive the bond.
Added by Stats. 1982, Ch. 998, Sec. 1.

Section 995.240 - Waiver of provision of bond in action or proceeding
The court may, in its discretion, waive a provision for a bond in an action or proceeding and make such orders as may be appropriate as if the bond were given, if the court determines that the principal is unable to give the bond because the principal is indigent and is unable to obtain sufficient sureties, whether personal or admitted surety insurers. In exercising its discretion the court shall take into consideration all factors it deems relevant, including but not limited to the character of the action or proceeding, the nature of the beneficiary, whether public or private, and the potential harm to the beneficiary if the provision for the bond is waived.
Added by Stats. 1982, Ch. 998, Sec. 1.

Section 995.250 - Costs include premium on bond paid by party
If a statute allows costs to a party in an action or proceeding, the costs shall include all of the following:
(a) The premium on a bond reasonably paid by the party pursuant to a statute that provides for the bond in the action or proceeding.
(b) The premium on a bond reasonably paid by the party in connection with the action or proceeding, unless the court determines that the bond was unnecessary.
Added by Stats. 1982, Ch. 998, Sec. 1.

Section 995.260 - Certified copy of recorded bond admitted in evidence
If a bond is recorded pursuant to statute, a certified copy of the record of the bond with all affidavits, acknowledgments, endorsements, and attachments may be admitted in evidence in an action or proceeding with the same effect as the original, without further proof.
Added by Stats. 1982, Ch. 998, Sec. 1.

Article 3 - EXECUTION AND FILING

Section 995.310 - execution by personal sureties or admitted surety insurers
Unless the statute providing for the bond requires execution by an admitted surety insurer, a bond shall be executed by two or more sufficient personal sureties or by one sufficient admitted surety insurer or by any combination of sufficient personal sureties and admitted surety insurers.
Added by Stats. 1982, Ch. 998, Sec. 1.

Section 995.311 - Execution of bond required on public works contract
(a) Notwithstanding any other provision of law, any bond required on a public works contract, as defined in Section 1101 of the Public Contract Code, shall be executed by an admitted surety insurer. A public agency approving the bond on a public works contract shall have a duty to verify that the bond is being executed by an admitted surety insurer.
(b) A public agency may fulfill its duty under subdivision (a) by verifying the status of the party executing the bond in one of the following ways:
  (1) Printing out information from the website of the Department of Insurance confirming the surety is an admitted surety insurer and attaching it to the bond.
  (2) Obtaining a certificate from the county clerk that confirms the surety is an admitted insurer and attaching it to the bond.
Added by Stats 2001 ch 181 (AB 263), s 1, eff. 1/1/2002.

Section 995.320 - Information required in bond
(a) A bond shall be in writing signed by the sureties under oath and shall include all of the following:
  (1) A statement that the sureties are jointly and severally liable on the obligations of the statute providing for the bond.
  (2) The address at which the principal and sureties may be served with notices, papers, and other documents under this chapter.
  (3) If the amount of the bond is based upon the value of property or an interest in property, a description of the property or interest, and the principal's estimate of the value of the property or interest, or if given pursuant to the estimate of the beneficiary or court, the value as so estimated.
(b) The sureties signing the bond are jointly and severally liable on the obligations of the bond, the provisions of this chapter, and the statute providing for the bond.
Added by Stats. 1982, Ch. 998, Sec. 1.

Section 995.330 - Form
A bond or undertaking given in an action or proceeding may be in the following form:
"(Title of court. Title of cause.)
Whereas the ... desires to give (a bond) (an undertaking) for (state what) as provided by (state sections of code requiring bond or undertaking); now, therefore, the undersigned (principal and) (sureties) (surety) hereby (obligate ourselves, jointly and severally) (obligates itself) to (name who) under the statutory obligations, in the amount of ... dollars."
Added by Stats. 1982, Ch. 998, Sec. 1.

Section 995.340 - Filing
If a bond is given in an action or proceeding:
(a) The bond shall be filed with the court unless the statute providing for the bond requires that the bond be given to another person.
(b) If the statute providing for the bond requires that the bond be given to an officer, the officer shall file the bond with the court unless the statute providing for the bond otherwise provides.
(c) A bond filed with the court shall be preserved in the office of the clerk of the court.
Added by Stats. 1982, Ch. 998, Sec. 1.

Section 995.350 - Information entered in register of action upon filing
(a) Upon the filing of a bond with the court in an action or proceeding, the clerk shall enter in the register of actions the following information:
  (1) The date and amount of the bond.
  (2) The names of the sureties on the bond.
(b) In the event of the loss of the bond, the entries in the register of actions are prima facie evidence of the giving of the bond in the manner required by statute.
Added by Stats. 1982, Ch. 998, Sec. 1.

Section 995.360 - Withdrawal from file and return to principal on order of court
A bond given in an action or proceeding may be withdrawn from the file and returned to the principal on order of the court only if one of the following conditions is satisfied:
(a) The beneficiary so stipulates.
(b) The bond is no longer in force and effect and the time during which the liability on the bond may be enforced has expired.
Added by Stats. 1982, Ch. 998, Sec. 1.

Section 995.370 - Service of copy of bond on beneficiary
At the time a bond is given, the principal shall serve a copy of the bond on the beneficiary. An affidavit of service shall be given and filed with the bond.
Added by Stats. 1982, Ch. 998, Sec. 1.

Section 995.380 - Defects in bond or its giving or filing
(a) If a bond does not contain the substantial matter or conditions required by this chapter or by the statute providing for the bond, or if there are any defects in the giving or filing of the bond, the bond is not void so as to release the principal and sureties from liability.
(b) The beneficiary may, in proceedings to enforce the liability on the bond, suggest the defect in the bond, or its giving or filing, and enforce the liability against the principal and the persons who intended to become and were included as sureties on the bond.
Added by Stats. 1982, Ch. 998, Sec. 1.

Article 4 - APPROVAL AND EFFECT

Section 995.410 - Statute requiring approval of bond
(a) A bond becomes effective without approval unless the statute providing for the bond requires that the bond be approved by the court or officer.
(b) If the statute providing for a bond requires that the bond be approved, the court or officer may approve or disapprove the bond on the basis of the affidavit or certificate of the sureties or may require the attendance of witnesses and the production of evidence and may examine the sureties under oath touching their qualifications.
(c) Nothing shall be construed to preclude approval of a bond in an amount greater than that required by statute.
Added by Stats. 1982, Ch. 998, Sec. 1.

Section 995.420 - Time bond becomes effective
(a) Unless the statute providing for a bond provides that the bond becomes effective at a different time, a bond is effective at the time it is given or, if the statute requires that the bond be approved, at the time it is approved.
(b) If the statute providing for a bond provides that the bond becomes effective at a time other than the time it is given or approved, the bond is effective at the time provided unless an objection is made to the bond before that time. If an objection is made to a bond before the time provided, the bond becomes effective when the court makes an order determining the sufficiency of the bond.
Added by Stats. 1982, Ch. 998, Sec. 1.

Section 995.430 - Events terminating force and effect of bond
A bond remains in force and effect until the earliest of the following events:
(a) The sureties withdraw from or cancel the bond or a new bond is given in place of the original bond.
(b) The purpose for which the bond was given is satisfied or the purpose is abandoned without any liability having been incurred.
(c) A judgment of liability on the bond that exhausts the amount of the bond is satisfied.
(d) The term of the bond expires. Unless the statute providing for the bond prescribes a fixed term, the bond is continuous.
Added by Stats. 1982, Ch. 998, Sec. 1.

Section 995.440 - Bond given as condition of license or permit
A bond given as a condition of a license or permit shall be continuous in form, remain in full force and effect, and run concurrently with the license or permit period and any and all renewals, or until cancellation or withdrawal of the surety from the bond.
Added by Stats. 1982, Ch. 998, Sec. 1.

Article 5 - PERSONAL SURETIES

Section 995.510 - Personal surety sufficient
(a) A personal surety on a bond is sufficient if all of the following conditions are satisfied:
   (1) The surety is a person other than the principal. No officer of the court or member of the State Bar shall act as a surety.
   (2) The surety is a resident, and either an owner of real property or householder, within the state.
   (3) The surety is worth the amount of the bond in real or personal property, or both, situated in this state, over and above all debts and liabilities, exclusive of property exempt from enforcement of a money judgment.
(b) If the amount of a bond exceeds ten thousand dollars ($10,000) and is executed by more than two personal sureties, the worth of a personal surety may be less than the amount of the bond, so long as the aggregate worth of all sureties executing the bond is twice the amount of the bond.
Added by Stats. 1982, Ch. 998, Sec. 1.

Section 995.520 - Affidavit of qualification
(a) A bond executed by personal sureties shall be accompanied by an affidavit of qualifications of each surety.
(b) The affidavit shall contain all of the following information:
   (1) The name, occupation, residence address, and business address (if any) of the surety.
   (2) A statement that the surety is a resident, and either an owner of real property or householder, within the state.
   (3) A statement that the surety is worth the amount of the bond in real or personal property, or both, situated in this state, over and above all debts and liabilities, exclusive of property exempt from enforcement of a money judgment.
(c) If the amount of the bond exceeds five thousand dollars ($5,000), the affidavit shall contain, in addition to the information required by subdivision (b), all of the following information:
   (1) A description sufficient for identification of real and personal property of the surety situated in this state and the nature of the surety's interest therein that qualifies the surety on the bond.
   (2) The surety's best estimate of the fair market value of each item of property.
   (3) A statement of any charge or lien and its amount, known to the surety, whether of public record or not, against any item of property.
   (4) Any other impediment or cloud known to the surety on the free right of possession, use, benefit, or enjoyment of the property.
(d) If the amount of the bond exceeds ten thousand dollars ($10,000) and is executed by more than two sureties, the affidavit may state that the surety is worth less than the amount of the bond and the bond may stipulate that the liability of the surety is limited to the worth of the surety stated in the affidavit, so long as the aggregate worth of all sureties executing the bond is twice the amount of the bond.
Added by Stats. 1982, Ch. 998, Sec. 1.

Article 6 - ADMITTED SURETY INSURERS

Section 995.610 - Accepted as sole surety on bond; rights and liabilities
(a) If a statute provides for a bond with any number of sureties, one sufficient admitted surety insurer may become and shall be accepted as sole surety on the bond.
(b) The admitted surety insurer is subject to all the liabilities and entitled to all the rights of personal sureties.
Added by Stats. 1982, Ch. 998, Sec. 1.

Section 995.620 - Two or more admitted surety insurers on bond; joint and several liability
Two or more admitted surety insurers may be sureties on a bond by executing the same or separate bonds for amounts aggregating the required amount of the bond. Each admitted surety insurer is jointly and severally liable to the extent of the amount of the liability assumed by it.
Added by Stats. 1982, Ch. 998, Sec. 1.

Section 995.630 - Acceptance or approval by court as surety without further acknowledgment

An admitted surety insurer shall be accepted or approved by the court or officer as surety on a bond without further acknowledgment if the bond is executed in the name of the surety insurer under penalty of perjury or the fact of execution of the bond is duly acknowledged before an officer authorized to take and certify acknowledgments, and either one of the following conditions, at the option of the surety insurer, is satisfied:
(a) A copy of the transcript or record of the unrevoked appointment, power of attorney, bylaws, or other instrument, duly certified by the proper authority and attested by the seal of the insurer entitling or authorizing the person who executed the bond to do so for and in behalf of the insurer, is filed in the office of the clerk of the county in which the court or officer is located.
(b) A copy of a power of attorney is attached to the bond.
Amended by Stats. 1992, Ch. 380, Sec. 1. Effective January 1, 1993.

Section 995.640 - Certificate stating whether surety admitted
Upon review of the Internet Web site of the Department of Insurance, the county clerk of any county shall, upon request of any person, do any of the following:
(a) Issue a certificate stating whether a surety is admitted or if the certificate of authority of an admitted surety insurer issued by the Insurance Commissioner authorizing the insurer to transact surety insurance has been surrendered, revoked, canceled, annulled, or suspended, and, in the event that it has, whether renewed authority has been granted. The county clerk in issuing the certificate shall rely solely upon the information furnished by the Insurance Commissioner pursuant to Article 2 (commencing with Section 12070) of Chapter 1 of Part 4 of Division 2 of the Insurance Code.
(b) Issue a certificate stating whether a copy of the transcript or record of the unrevoked appointment, power of attorney, bylaws, or other instrument, duly certified by the proper authority and attested by the seal of an admitted surety insurer entitling or authorizing the person who executed a bond to do so for and on behalf of the insurer, is filed in the office of the clerk.
Amended by Stats 2008 ch 351 (SB 1279),s 1, eff. 1/1/2009.
Amended by Stats 2005 ch 22 (SB 1108),s 19, eff. 1/1/2006

Section 995.650 - Attachment required to objection made to sufficiency of admitted surety insurer
If an objection is made to the sufficiency of an admitted surety insurer, the person making the objection shall attach to and incorporate in the objection one or both of the following:
(a) The certificate of the county clerk of the county in which the court is located stating that the insurer is not listed as an admitted surety insurer on the department's Internet Web site or that the certificate of authority of the insurer has been surrendered, revoked, canceled, annulled, or suspended and has not been renewed.
(b) An affidavit stating facts that establish the insufficiency of the insurer.
Amended by Stats 2008 ch 351 (SB 1279),s 2, eff. 1/1/2009.

Section 995.660 - Documents submitted by insurer if objection made to sufficiency or approval of bond required
(a) If an objection is made to the sufficiency of an admitted surety insurer on a bond or if the bond is required to be approved, the insurer shall submit to the court or officer the following documents:
(1) The original, or a certified copy, of the unrevoked appointment, power of attorney, bylaws, or other instrument entitling or authorizing the person who executed the bond to do so, within 10 calendar days of the insurer's receipt of a request to submit the instrument.
(2) A certified copy of the certificate of authority of the insurer issued by the Insurance Commissioner, within 10 calendar days of the insurer's receipt of a request to submit the copy.
(3) A certificate from the clerk of the county in which the court or officer is located that the certificate of authority of the insurer has not been surrendered, revoked, canceled, annulled, or suspended or, in the event that it has, that renewed authority has been granted, within 10 calendar days of the insurer's receipt of the certificate.
(4) Copies of the insurer's most recent annual statement and quarterly statement filed with the Department of Insurance pursuant to Article 10 (commencing with Section 900) of Chapter 1 of Part 2 of Division 1 of the Insurance Code, within 10 calendar days of the insurer's receipt of a request to submit the statements.
(b) If the admitted surety insurer complies with subdivision (a), and if it appears that the bond was duly executed, that the insurer is authorized to transact surety insurance in the state, and that its assets exceed its liabilities in an amount equal to or in excess of the amount of the bond, the insurer is sufficient and shall be accepted or approved as surety on the bond, subject to Section 12090 of the Insurance Code.
Amended by Stats. 1994, Ch. 487, Sec. 1. Effective January 1, 1995.

Section 995.670 - Public agency requiring compliance with requirements other than those stated in section 995.660 prohibited
(a) This section applies to a bond executed, filed, posted, furnished, or otherwise given as security pursuant to any statute of this state or any law or ordinance of a public agency. No public agency shall require an admitted surety insurer to comply with any requirements other than those in Section 995.660 whenever an objection is made to the sufficiency of the admitted surety insurer on the bond or if the bond is required to be approved.
(b) For the purposes of this section, "public agency" means the state, any agency or authority, any city, county, city and county, district, municipal or public corporation, or any instrumentality thereof.
Amended by Stats. 1994, Ch. 487, Sec. 2. Effective January 1, 1995.

Section 995.675 - Listing in Circular 570 required to comply with Resource Conservation and Recovery Act of 1976
Notwithstanding Sections 995.660 and 995.670, the California Integrated Waste Management Board, the State Water Resources Control Board, and the Department of Toxic Substances Control may require, in order to comply with Subtitle C or Subtitle D of the federal Resource Conservation and Recovery Act of 1976, as amended (42 U.S.C. Sec. 6901 et seq.), an admitted surety insurer to be listed in Circular 570 issued by the United States Treasury.
Added by Stats. 1998, Ch. 477, Sec. 1. Effective January 1, 1999.

Article 7 - DEPOSIT IN LIEU OF BOND

Section 995.710 - Deposits allowed, exceptions
(a)Except as provided in subdivision (e) or to the extent the statute providing for a bond precludes a deposit in lieu of bond or limits the form of deposit, the principal may, without prior court approval, instead of giving a bond, deposit with the officer any of the following:
(1)Lawful money of the United States or a cashier's check, made payable to the officer, issued by a bank, savings association, or credit union authorized to do business in this state. The money shall be held in trust by the officer in interest-bearing deposit or share accounts.
(2)Bonds or notes, including bearer bonds and bearer notes, of the United States or the State of California. The deposit of a bond or note pursuant to this section shall be accomplished by filing with the court, and serving upon all parties and the appropriate officer of the bank holding the bond or note, instructions executed by the person or entity holding title to the bond or note that the treasurer of the county where the judgment was entered is the custodian of that account for the purpose of staying enforcement of the judgment, and that the title holder assigns to the treasurer the right to collect, sell, or otherwise apply the bond or note to enforce the judgment debtor's liability pursuant to Section 995.760.
(3)Certificates of deposit payable to the officer, not exceeding the federally insured amount, issued by banks or savings associations authorized to do business in this state and insured by the Federal Deposit Insurance Corporation.
(4)Savings accounts assigned to the officer, not exceeding the federally insured amount, together with evidence of the deposit in the savings accounts with banks authorized to do business in this state and insured by the Federal Deposit Insurance Corporation.

(5) Investment certificates or share accounts assigned to the officer, not exceeding the federally insured amount, issued by savings associations authorized to do business in this state and insured by the Federal Deposit Insurance Corporation.

(6) Share certificates payable to the officer, not exceeding the guaranteed or insured amount, issued by a credit union, as defined in Section 14002 of the Financial Code, whose share accounts are insured by the National Credit Union Administration or guaranteed or insured by any other agency that the Commissioner of Financial Protection and Innovation has not deemed to be unsatisfactory.

(b) The deposit shall be in an amount or have a face value, or, in the case of bonds or notes, have a market value, equal to or in excess of the amount that would be required to be secured by the bond if the bond were given by an admitted surety insurer. Notwithstanding any other provision of this chapter, in the case of a deposit of bonds or notes other than in an action or proceeding, the officer may, in the officer's discretion, require that the amount of the deposit be determined not by the market value of the bonds or notes but by a formula based on the principal amount of the bonds or notes.

(c) The deposit shall be accompanied by an agreement executed by the principal authorizing the officer to collect, sell, or otherwise apply the deposit to enforce the liability of the principal on the deposit. The agreement shall include the address at which the principal may be served with notices, papers, and other documents under this chapter.

(d) The officer may prescribe terms and conditions to implement this section.

(e) This section does not apply to deposits with the Secretary of State.

Amended by Stats 2022 ch 452 (SB 1498),s 41, eff. 1/1/2023.
Amended by Stats 2014 ch 305 (AB 1856),s 1, eff. 1/1/2015.
Amended October 10, 1999 (Bill Number: AB 1672) (Chapter 892).

Section 995.720 - Market value of bearer bonds and notes

(a) The market value of bonds or notes, including bearer bonds and bearer notes, shall be agreed upon by stipulation of the principal and beneficiary or, if the bonds or notes are given in an action or proceeding and the principal and beneficiary are unable to agree, the market value shall be determined by court order in the manner prescribed in this section. A certified copy of the stipulation or court order shall be delivered to the officer at the time of the deposit of the bonds or notes.

(b) If the bonds or notes are given in an action or proceeding, the principal may file a written application with the court to determine the market value of the bonds or notes. The application shall be served upon the beneficiary and proof of service shall be filed with the application. The application shall contain all of the following:

(1) A specific description of the bonds or notes.

(2) A statement of the current market value of the bonds or notes as of the date of the filing of the application.

(3) A statement of the amount of the bonds or notes that the principal believes would be equal to the required amount of the deposit.

(c) The application pursuant to subdivision (b) shall be heard by the court not less than five days or more than 10 days after service of the application. If at the time of the hearing no objection is made to the current market value of the bonds or notes alleged in the application, the court shall fix the amount of the bonds or notes on the basis of the market value alleged in the application. If the beneficiary contends that the current market value of the bonds or notes is less than alleged in the application, the principal shall offer evidence in support of the application, and the beneficiary may offer evidence in opposition. At the conclusion of the hearing, the court shall make an order determining the market value of the bonds or notes and shall fix and determine the amount of the bonds or notes to be deposited by the principal.

Amended by Stats 2014 ch 305 (AB 1856),s 2, eff. 1/1/2015.

Section 995.730 - Force and effect of deposit

A deposit given instead of a bond has the same force and effect, is treated the same, and is subject to the same conditions, liability, and statutory provisions, including provisions for increase and decrease of amount, as the bond.

Added by Stats. 1982, Ch. 998, Sec. 1.

Section 995.740 - Payment of interest or delivery of interest coupons upon demand

If no proceedings are pending to enforce the liability of the principal on the deposit, the officer shall:

(a) Pay quarterly, on demand, any interest on the deposit, when earned in accordance with the terms of the account or certificate, to the principal.

(b) Deliver to the principal, on demand, any interest coupons attached to bonds or notes, including bearer bonds and bearer notes, as the interest coupons become due and payable, or pay annually any interest payable on the bonds or notes.

Amended by Stats 2014 ch 305 (AB 1856),s 3, eff. 1/1/2015.

Section 995.750 - Time for payment of liability on deposit

(a) The principal shall pay the amount of the liability on the deposit within 30 days after the date on which the judgment of liability becomes final.

(b) If the deposit was given to stay enforcement of a judgment on appeal, the principal shall pay the amount of the liability on the deposit, including damages and costs awarded against the principal on appeal, within 30 days after the filing of the remittitur from the appellate court in the court from which the appeal is taken.

Added by Stats. 1982, Ch. 998, Sec. 1.

Section 995.760 - Failure to timely pay amount of liability

(a) If the principal does not pay the amount of the liability on the deposit within the time prescribed in Section 995.750, the deposit shall be collected, sold, or otherwise applied to the liability upon order of the court that entered the judgment of liability, made upon five days' notice to the parties.

(b) Bonds or notes, including bearer bonds and bearer notes, without a prevailing market price shall be sold at public auction. Notice of sale shall be served on the principal. Bonds or notes having a prevailing market price may be sold at private sale at a price not lower than the prevailing market price.

(c) The deposit shall be distributed in the following order:

(1) First, to pay the cost of collection, sale, or other application of the deposit.

(2) Second, to pay the judgment of liability of the principal on the deposit.

(3) Third, the remainder, if any, shall be returned to the principal.

Amended by Stats 2014 ch 305 (AB 1856),s 4, eff. 1/1/2015.

Section 995.770 - Return of deposit to principal

A deposit given pursuant to this article shall be returned to the principal at the earliest of the following times:

(a) Upon substitution of a sufficient bond for the deposit. The bond shall be in full force and effect for all liabilities incurred, and for acts, omissions, or causes existing or which arose, during the period the deposit was in effect.

(b) The time provided by Section 995.360 for return of a bond.

(c) The time provided by statute for return of the deposit.

Added by Stats. 1982, Ch. 998, Sec. 1.

Article 8 - BONDS TO THE STATE OF CALIFORNIA

Section 995.810 - Generally

The provisions of this article apply to a bond executed to, in favor of, in the name of, or payable to the State of California or the people of the state, including but not limited to an official bond.

Added by Stats. 1982, Ch. 998, Sec. 1.

Section 995.820 - Bond given by officer of court

Except as otherwise provided by statute, a bond given by an officer of the court for the faithful discharge of the officer's duties and obedience to the orders of the court shall be to the State of California.

Added by Stats. 1982, Ch. 998, Sec. 1.

Section 995.830 - Statute or court order not specifying beneficiary of bond

If a statute or court order pursuant thereto providing for a bond does not specify the beneficiary of the bond, the bond shall be to the State of California.

Added by Stats. 1982, Ch. 998, Sec. 1.

Section 995.840 - Approval by court; objection

If a bond under this article is given in an action or proceeding:

(a) The bond shall be approved by the court.

(b) Any party for whose benefit the bond is given may object to the bond.

Added by Stats. 1982, Ch. 998, Sec. 1.

Section 995.850 - Enforcement of liability on bond

(a) The liability on a bond under this article may be enforced by or for the benefit of, and in the name of, any and all persons for whose benefit the bond is given who are damaged by breach of the condition of the bond.

(b) A person described in subdivision (a) may, in addition to any other remedy the person has, enforce the liability on the bond in the person's own name, without assignment of the bond.

Added by Stats. 1982, Ch. 998, Sec. 1.

Article 9 - OBJECTIONS TO BONDS

Section 995.910 - Generally

This article governs objections to a bond given in an action or proceeding.

Added by Stats. 1982, Ch. 998, Sec. 1.

Section 995.920 - Grounds

The beneficiary may object to a bond on any of the following grounds:

(a) The sureties are insufficient.

(b) The amount of the bond is insufficient.

(c) The bond, from any other cause, is insufficient.

Added by Stats. 1982, Ch. 998, Sec. 1.

Section 995.930 - Notice of motion; time for making; waiver

(a) An objection shall be in writing and shall be made by noticed motion. The notice of motion shall specify the precise grounds for the objection. If a ground for the objection is that the amount of the bond is insufficient, the notice of motion shall state the reason for the insufficiency and shall include an estimate of the amount that would be sufficient.

(b) The objection shall be made within 10 days after service of a copy of the bond on the beneficiary or such other time as is required by the statute providing for the bond.

(c) If no objection is made within the time required by statute, the beneficiary is deemed to have waived all objections except upon a showing of good cause for failure to make the objection within the time required by statute or of changed circumstances.

Amended by Stats. 1984, Ch. 538, Sec. 33.

Section 995.940 - Value of property exceeds value estimated in bond

If a ground for the objection is that the value of property or an interest in property on which the amount of the bond is based exceeds the value estimated in the bond:

(a) The objection shall state the beneficiary's estimate of the market value of the property or interest in property.

(b) The principal may accept the beneficiary's estimate of the market value of the property or interest in property and immediately file an increased bond based on the estimate. In such case, no hearing shall be held on that ground for the objection, and the beneficiary is bound by the estimate of the market value of the property or interest in property.

Added by Stats. 1982, Ch. 998, Sec. 1.

Section 995.950 - Hearing

(a) Unless the parties otherwise agree, the hearing on an objection shall be held not less than two or more than five days after service of the notice of motion.

(b) The hearing shall be conducted in such manner as the court determines is proper. The court may permit witnesses to attend and testify and evidence to be procured and introduced in the same manner as in the trial of a civil case.

(c) If the value of property or an interest in property is a ground for the objection, the court shall estimate its value. The court may appoint one or more disinterested persons to appraise property or an interest in property for the purpose of estimating its value.

Added by Stats. 1982, Ch. 998, Sec. 1.

Section 995.960 - Order determining sufficiency or insufficiency

(a) Upon the hearing, the court shall make an order determining the sufficiency or insufficiency of the bond.

(b) If the court determines that the bond is insufficient:

(1) The court shall specify in what respect the bond is insufficient and shall order that a bond with sufficient sureties and in a sufficient amount be given within five days. If a sufficient bond is not given within the time required by the court order, all rights obtained by giving the bond immediately cease and the court shall upon ex parte motion so order.

(2) If a bond is in effect, the bond remains in effect until a bond with sufficient sureties and in a sufficient amount is given in its place, or the time in which to give the bond has expired, whichever first occurs. If the time in which to give a sufficient bond expires, the original bond remains in full force and effect for all liabilities incurred before, and for acts, omissions, or causes existing or which arose before, expiration.

(c) If the court determines that a bond is sufficient, no future objection to the bond may be made except upon a showing of changed circumstances.

Added by Stats. 1982, Ch. 998, Sec. 1.

Article 10 - INSUFFICIENT AND EXCESSIVE BONDS

Section 996.010 - Court determination bond insufficient

(a) If a bond is given in an action or proceeding, the court may determine that the bond is or has from any cause become insufficient because the sureties are insufficient or because the amount of the bond is insufficient.

(b) The court determination shall be upon motion supported by affidavit or upon the court's own motion. The motion shall be deemed to be an objection to the bond. The motion shall be heard and notice of motion shall be given in the same manner as an objection to the bond.

(c) Upon the determination the court shall order that a sufficient new, additional, or supplemental bond be given within a reasonable time not less than five days. The court order is subject to any limitations in the statute providing for the bond.

(d) If a sufficient bond is not given within the time required by the court order, all rights obtained by giving the original bond immediately cease and the court shall upon ex parte motion so order.

Added by Stats. 1982, Ch. 998, Sec. 1.

Section 996.020 - Order by officer served on principal to appear and show cause

(a) If a bond is given other than in an action or proceeding and it is shown by affidavit of a credible witness or it otherwise comes to the attention of the officer that the bond is or has from any cause become insufficient because the sureties are insufficient or because the amount of the bond is insufficient, the officer may serve an order on the principal to appear and show cause why the officer should not make a determination that the bond is insufficient. The order shall name a day not less than three or more than 10 days after service.

(b) If the principal fails to appear or show good cause on the day named why a determination that the bond is insufficient should not be made, the officer may determine that the bond is insufficient and order a sufficient new, additional, or supplemental bond to be given.

(c) If a sufficient bond is not given within 10 days after the order, the officer shall make an order vacating the rights obtained by giving the original bond, including declaring vacant any office and suspending or revoking any license or certificate for which the bond was given. Any office vacated, license suspended or revoked, or any other rights lost, for failure to give a new, additional, or supplemental bond, shall not be reinstated until a new, additional, or supplemental bond is given.

Added by Stats. 1982, Ch. 998, Sec. 1.

Section 996.030 - Determination bond excessive

(a) The court if a bond is given or ordered in an action or proceeding, or the officer if a bond is given or ordered other than in an action or proceeding, may determine that the amount of the bond is excessive and order the amount reduced to an amount that in the discretion of the court or officer appears proper under the circumstances. The order is subject to any limitations in the statute providing for the bond.

(b) The determination shall be made upon motion or affidavit of the principal in the same manner as a motion or affidavit for a determination under this article that a bond is insufficient. The notice of motion or the order to show cause made pursuant to affidavit shall be served on the beneficiary. The determination shall be made in the same manner and pursuant to the same procedures as a determination under this article that the bond is insufficient.

(c) The principal may give a new bond for the reduced amount. The sureties may be the same sureties as on the original bond.

Amended by Stats. 1988, Ch. 309, Sec. 1.

Article 11 - RELEASE OR SUBSTITUTION OF SURETIES ON BOND GIVEN IN ACTION OR PROCEEDING

Section 996.110 - Application for order that surety be released; application for order that another surety be substituted

(a) A surety on a bond given in an action or proceeding may at any time apply to the court for an order that the surety be released from liability on the bond.

(b) The principal on a bond may, if a surety applies for release from liability on a bond, apply to the court for an order that another surety be substituted for the original surety.

(c) The applicant shall serve on the principal or surety (other than the applicant) and on the beneficiary a copy of the application and a notice of hearing on the application. Service shall be made not less than 15 days before the date set for hearing.

Added by Stats. 1982, Ch. 998, Sec. 1.

Section 996.120 - Determination upon hearing

Upon the hearing of the application, the court shall determine whether injury to the beneficiary would result from substitution or release of the surety. If the court determines that release would not reduce the amount of the bond or the number of sureties below the minimum required by the statute providing for the bond, substitution of a sufficient surety is not necessary and the court shall order the release of the surety. If the court determines that no injury would result from substitution of the surety, the court shall order the substitution of a sufficient surety within such time as appears reasonable.

Added by Stats. 1982, Ch. 998, Sec. 1.

Section 996.130 - Substitute surety given

(a) If a substitute surety is given, the substitute surety is subject to all the provisions of this chapter, including but not limited to the provisions governing insufficient and excessive bonds.

(b) Upon the substitution of a sufficient surety, the court shall order the release of the original surety from liability on the bond.

Added by Stats. 1982, Ch. 998, Sec. 1.

Section 996.140 - Sufficient substitute surety not timely given by principal

If the principal does not give a sufficient substitute surety within the time ordered by the court or such longer time as the surety consents to, all rights obtained by giving the original bond immediately cease and the court shall upon ex parte motion so order.

Added by Stats. 1982, Ch. 998, Sec. 1.

Section 996.150 - Surety ordered released from liability

If a surety is ordered released from liability on a bond:

(a) The bond remains in full force and effect for all liabilities incurred before, and for acts, omissions, or causes existing or which arose before, the release. Legal proceedings may be had therefor in all respects as though there had been no release.

(b) The surety is not liable for any act, default, or misconduct of the principal or other breach of the condition of the bond that occurs after, or for any liabilities on the bond that arise after, the release.

(c) The release does not affect the bond as to the remaining sureties, or alter or change their liability in any respect.

Added by Stats. 1982, Ch. 998, Sec. 1.

Article 12 - NEW, ADDITIONAL, AND SUPPLEMENTAL BONDS

Section 996.210 - Generally

(a) The principal shall give a new, additional, or supplemental bond if the court or officer orders that a new, additional, or supplemental bond be given.

(b) The principal may give a new bond if a surety withdraws from or cancels the original bond or to obtain the release of sureties from liability on the original bond.

Added by Stats. 1982, Ch. 998, Sec. 1.

Section 996.220 - Form and obligation; supplemental bond requirements

(a) A new, additional, or supplemental bond shall be in the same form and have the same obligation as the original bond and shall be in all other respects the same as the original bond, and shall be in such amount as is necessary for the purpose for which the new, additional, or supplemental bond is given.

(b) A supplemental bond shall, in addition to any other requirements, recite the names of the remaining original sureties, the name of the new surety, and the amount for which the new surety is liable. The supplemental bond shall be for the amount for which the original surety was liable on the original bond.

Added by Stats. 1982, Ch. 998, Sec. 1.

Section 996.230 - Subject to provisions applicable to original bond and chapter

A new, additional, or supplemental bond is subject to all the provisions applicable to the original bond and to the provisions of this chapter, including but not limited to the provisions governing giving and objecting to a bond and liabilities and enforcement procedures.

Added by Stats. 1982, Ch. 998, Sec. 1.

Section 996.240 - New bond given

If a new bond is given in place of the original bond:

(a) The original bond remains in full force and effect for all liabilities incurred before, and for acts, omissions, or causes existing or which arose before, the new bond became effective.

(b) The sureties on the original bond are not liable for any act, default, or misconduct of the principal or other breach of the condition of the bond that occurs after or for any liabilities on the bond that arise after, the new bond becomes effective.

Added by Stats. 1982, Ch. 998, Sec. 1.

Section 996.250 - Additional or supplemental bond

(a) An additional or supplemental bond does not discharge or affect the original bond. The original bond remains in full force and effect as if the additional or supplemental bond had not been given.

(b) After an additional or supplemental bond is given, the principal and sureties are liable upon either or both bonds for injury caused by breach of any condition of the bonds. Subject to subdivision (c), the beneficiary may enforce the liability on either bond, or may enforce the liability separately on both bonds and recover separate judgments of liability on both.

(c) If the beneficiary recovers separate judgments of liability on both bonds for the same cause of action, the beneficiary may enforce both judgments. The beneficiary may collect, by execution or otherwise, the costs of both proceedings to enforce the liability and the amount actually awarded to the beneficiary on the same cause of action in only one of the proceedings, and no double recovery shall be allowed.

(d) If the sureties on either bond have been compelled to pay any sum of money on account of the principal, they are entitled to recover from the sureties on the remaining bond a distributive part of the sum paid, in the proportion the amounts of the bonds bear one to the other and to the sums paid.

Added by Stats. 1982, Ch. 998, Sec. 1.

Article 13 - CANCELLATION OF BOND OR WITHDRAWAL OF SURETIES

Section 996.310 - Generally

This article governs cancellation of or withdrawal of a surety from a bond given other than in an action or proceeding.

Added by Stats. 1982, Ch. 998, Sec. 1.

Section 996.320 - Notice of cancellation or withdrawal

A surety may cancel or withdraw from a bond by giving a notice of cancellation or withdrawal to the officer to whom the bond was given in the same manner the bond was given, notwithstanding Section 995.030. The surety shall at the same time mail or deliver a copy of the notice of cancellation or withdrawal to the principal.

Added by Stats. 1982, Ch. 998, Sec. 1.

Section 996.330 - Effective date of cancellation or withdrawal

Cancellation or withdrawal of a surety is effective at the earliest of the following times:

(a) Thirty days after notice of cancellation or withdrawal is given.

(b) If a new surety is substituted for the original surety, the date the substitution becomes effective.

(c) If a new bond is given, the date the new bond becomes effective.

Added by Stats. 1982, Ch. 998, Sec. 1.

Section 996.340 - New bond not timely given after notice; license or registration suspended

(a) If the principal does not give a new bond within 30 days after notice of cancellation or withdrawal is given, all rights obtained by giving the original bond immediately cease, any office for which the bond is given is vacant, any commission for which the bond is given is revoked, and any license or registration for which the bond is given is suspended.

(b) A person whose license or registration is suspended shall not operate or carry on business pursuant to the license or registration during the period of suspension. A license or registration that is suspended may be revived only by the giving of a new bond during the license or registration period in which the cancellation or withdrawal occurred.

Amended by Stats. 1983, Ch. 18, Sec. 19. Effective April 21, 1983.

Section 996.350 - Effect of withdrawal of surety

If the withdrawal of a surety does not reduce the amount of the bond or the number of sureties below the minimum required by the statute providing for the bond, no new bond is required or necessary to maintain the original bond in effect.

Added by Stats. 1982, Ch. 998, Sec. 1.

Section 996.360 - Surety cancels or withdraws from bond

If a surety cancels or withdraws from a bond:

(a) The bond remains in full force and effect for all liabilities incurred before, and for acts, omissions, or causes existing or which arose before, the cancellation or withdrawal. Legal proceedings may be had therefor in all respects as though there had been no cancellation or withdrawal.

(b) The surety is not liable for any act, default, or misconduct of the principal or other breach of the condition of the bond that occurs after, or for any liabilities on the bond that arise after, the cancellation or withdrawal.

(c) The cancellation or withdrawal does not affect the bond as to the remaining sureties, or alter or change their liability in any respect.

Added by Stats. 1982, Ch. 998, Sec. 1.

Article 14 - LIABILITY OF PRINCIPAL AND SURETIES

Section 996.410 - Beneficiary may enforce; beneficiary class of persons

(a) The beneficiary may enforce the liability on a bond against both the principal and sureties.

(b) If the beneficiary is a class of persons, any person in the class may enforce the liability on a bond in the person's own name, without assignment of the bond.

Added by Stats. 1982, Ch. 998, Sec. 1.

Section 996.420 - Surety submits to jurisdiction of court

(a) A surety on a bond given in an action or proceeding submits itself to the jurisdiction of the court in all matters affecting its liability on the bond.

(b) This section does not apply to a bond of a public officer or fiduciary.

Added by Stats. 1982, Ch. 998, Sec. 1.

Section 996.430 - Enforced by civil action; principal and sureties joined as parties; venue; transfer or assignment of action

(a) The liability on a bond may be enforced by civil action. Both the principal and the sureties shall be joined as parties to the action.

(b) If the bond was given in an action or proceeding, the action shall be commenced in the court in which the action or proceeding was pending. If the bond was given other than in an action or proceeding, the action shall be commenced in any court of competent jurisdiction, and the amount of damage claimed in the action, not the amount of the bond, determines the jurisdictional classification of the case.

(c) A cause of action on a bond may be transferred and assigned as other causes of action.

Amended by Stats. 1998, Ch. 931, Sec. 105. Effective September 28, 1998.

Section 996.440 - Enforcement of bond in action or proceeding by motion

(a) If a bond is given in an action or proceeding, the liability on the bond may be enforced on motion made in the court without the necessity of an independent action.

(b) The motion shall not be made until after entry of the final judgment in the action or proceeding in which the bond is given and the time for appeal has expired or, if an appeal is taken, until the appeal is finally determined. The motion shall not be made or notice of motion served more than one year after the later of the preceding dates.

(c) Notice of motion shall be served on the principal and sureties at least 30 days before the time set for hearing of the motion. The notice shall state the amount of the claim and shall be supported by affidavits setting forth the facts on which the claim is based. The notice and affidavits shall be served in accordance with any procedure authorized by Chapter 5 (commencing with Section 1010).

(d) Judgment shall be entered against the principal and sureties in accordance with the motion unless the principal or sureties serve and file affidavits in opposition to the motion showing such facts as may be deemed by the judge hearing the motion sufficient to present a triable issue of fact. If such a showing is made, the issues to be tried shall be specified by the court. Trial shall be by the court and shall be set for the earliest date convenient to the court, allowing sufficient time for such discovery proceedings as may be requested.

(e) The principal and sureties shall not obtain a stay of the proceedings pending determination of any conflicting claims among beneficiaries.

Added by Stats. 1982, Ch. 998, Sec. 1.

Section 996.450 - Contract provision shortening period for commencing action invalid

No provision in a bond is valid that attempts by contract to shorten the period prescribed by Section 337 or other statute for the commencement of an action on the bond or the period prescribed by Section 996.440 for a motion to enforce a bond. This section does not apply if the principal, beneficiary, and surety accept a provision for a shorter period in a bond.

Added by Stats. 1982, Ch. 998, Sec. 1.

Section 996.460 - Judgment of liability on bond

(a) Notwithstanding Section 2845 of the Civil Code, a judgment of liability on a bond shall be in favor of the beneficiary and against the principal and sureties and shall obligate each of them jointly and severally.

(b) The judgment shall be in an amount determined by the court.

(c) A judgment that does not exhaust the full amount of the bond decreases the amount of the bond but does not discharge the bond. The liability on the bond may be enforced thereafter from time to time until the amount of the bond is exhausted.

(d) The judgment may be enforced by the beneficiary directly against the sureties. Nothing in this section affects any right of subrogation of a surety against the principal or any right of a surety to compel the principal to satisfy the judgment.

Added by Stats. 1982, Ch. 998, Sec. 1.

Section 996.470 - Liability of surety on bond

(a) Notwithstanding any other statute other than Section 996.480, the aggregate liability of a surety to all persons for all breaches of the condition of a bond is limited to the amount of the bond. Except as otherwise provided by statute, the liability of the principal is not limited to the amount of the bond.

(b) If a bond is given in an amount greater than the amount required by statute or by order of the court or officer pursuant to statute, the liability of the surety on the bond is limited to the amount required by statute or by order of the court or officer, unless the amount of the bond has been increased voluntarily or by agreement of the parties to satisfy an objection to the bond made in an action or proceeding.

(c) The liability of a surety is limited to the amount stipulated in any of the following circumstances:

(1) The bond contains a stipulation pursuant to Section 995.520 that the liability of a personal surety is limited to the worth of the surety.

(2) The bond contains a stipulation that the liability of a surety is an amount less than the amount of the bond pursuant to a statute that provides that the liability of sureties in the aggregate need not exceed the amount of the bond.

Amended by Stats. 1993, Ch. 527, Sec. 2. Effective January 1, 1994.

Section 996.475 - Liability of surety pursuant to other statute not limited by chapter

Nothing in this chapter is intended to limit the liability of a surety pursuant to any other statute. This section is declaratory of, and not a change in, existing law.

Added by Stats. 1984, Ch. 538, Sec. 33.3.

Section 996.480 - Payment on bond if liability of principal established by final judgment

(a) If the nature and extent of the liability of the principal is established by final judgment of a court and the time for appeal has expired or, if an appeal is taken, the appeal is finally determined and the judgment is affirmed:

(1) A surety may make payment on a bond without awaiting enforcement of the bond. The amount of the bond is reduced to the extent of any payment made by the surety in good faith.

(2) If the beneficiary makes a claim for payment on a bond given in an action or proceeding after the liability of the principal is so established and the surety fails to make payment, the surety is liable for costs incurred in obtaining a judgment against the surety, including a reasonable attorney's fee, and interest on the judgment from the date of the claim, notwithstanding Section 996.470.

(b) Partial payment of a claim by a surety shall not be considered satisfaction of the claim and the beneficiary may enforce the liability on the bond. If a right is affected or a license is suspended or revoked until payment of a claim, the right continues to be affected and the license continues to be suspended or revoked until the claim is satisfied in full.

Added by Stats. 1982, Ch. 998, Sec. 1.

Section 996.490 - Payment by surety constitutes discharge; contribution to cosureties

(a) Payment by a surety of the amount of a bond constitutes a full discharge of all the liability of the surety on the bond.

(b) Each surety is liable to contribution to cosureties who have made payment in proportion to the amount for which each surety is liable.

Added by Stats. 1982, Ch. 998, Sec. 1.

Section 996.495 - Enforcement of judgment of liability on bond

A judgment of liability on a bond may be enforced in the same manner and to the same extent as other money judgments.

Added by Stats. 1982, Ch. 998, Sec. 1.

Article 15 - ENFORCEMENT LIEN

Section 996.510 - Applicability to proceedings to enforce liability on bond executed in favor of state

This article applies to proceedings for the benefit of the state to enforce the liability on a bond executed to, in favor of, or payable to the state or the people of the state, including but not limited to an official bond.

Added by Stats. 1982, Ch. 998, Sec. 1.

Section 996.520 - Affidavit by person enforcing liability
The person enforcing the liability may file with the court in the proceedings an affidavit stating the following:
(a) The bond was executed by the defendant or one or more of the defendants (designating whom).
(b) The bond is one to which this article applies.
(c) The defendant or defendants have real property or an interest in real property (designating the county or counties in which the real property is situated).
(d) The liability is being enforced for the benefit of the state.
Added by Stats. 1982, Ch. 998, Sec. 1.

Section 996.530 - Certification by clerk receiving affidavit
The clerk receiving the affidavit shall certify to the recorder of the county in which the real property is situated all of the following:
(a) The names of the parties.
(b) The court in which the proceedings are pending.
(c) The amount claimed.
(d) The date of commencement of the proceedings.
Added by Stats. 1982, Ch. 998, Sec. 1.

Section 996.540 - Filing and recording certificate
(a) Upon receiving the certificate the county recorder shall endorse upon it the time of its receipt.
(b) The certificate shall be filed and recorded in the same manner as notice of the pendency of an action affecting real property.
Added by Stats. 1982, Ch. 998, Sec. 1.

Section 996.550 - Lien
(a) Any judgment recovered is a lien upon all real property belonging to the defendant situated in any county in which the certificate is filed, from the filing of the certificate.
(b) The lien is for the amount for which the owner of the real property is liable upon the judgment.
Added by Stats. 1982, Ch. 998, Sec. 1.

Section 996.560 - Purchaser entitled to specific performance of agreement to sell real property
If an agreement to sell real property affected by the lien created by the filing of a certificate was made before the filing of the certificate and the purchase price under the agreement was not due until after the filing of the certificate, and the purchaser is otherwise entitled to specific performance of the agreement:
(a) The court in an action to compel specific performance of the agreement shall order the purchaser to pay the purchase price, or so much of the purchase price as may be due, to the State Treasurer, and to take the State Treasurer's receipt for payment.
(b) Upon payment, the purchaser is entitled to enforcement of specific performance of the agreement. The purchaser takes the real property free from the lien created by the filing of the certificate.
(c) The State Treasurer shall hold the payment pending the proceedings referred to in the certificate. The payment is subject to the lien created by the filing of the certificate.
Added by Stats. 1982, Ch. 998, Sec. 1.

Chapter 3 - OFFERS BY A PARTY TO COMPROMISE

Section 998 - Offer served prior to resolution of dispute by arbitration
(a) The costs allowed under Sections 1031 and 1032 shall be withheld or augmented as provided in this section.
(b) Not less than 10 days prior to commencement of trial or arbitration (as provided in Section 1281 or 1295) of a dispute to be resolved by arbitration, any party may serve an offer in writing upon any other party to the action to allow judgment to be taken or an award to be entered in accordance with the terms and conditions stated at that time. The written offer shall include a statement of the offer, containing the terms and conditions of the judgment or award, and a provision that allows the accepting party to indicate acceptance of the offer by signing a statement that the offer is accepted. Any acceptance of the offer, whether made on the document containing the offer or on a separate document of acceptance, shall be in writing and shall be signed by counsel for the accepting party or, if not represented by counsel, by the accepting party.
(1) If the offer is accepted, the offer with proof of acceptance shall be filed and the clerk or the judge shall enter judgment accordingly. In the case of an arbitration, the offer with proof of acceptance shall be filed with the arbitrator or arbitrators who shall promptly render an award accordingly.
(2) If the offer is not accepted prior to trial or arbitration or within 30 days after it is made, whichever occurs first, it shall be deemed withdrawn, and cannot be given in evidence upon the trial or arbitration.
(3) For purposes of this subdivision, a trial or arbitration shall be deemed to be actually commenced at the beginning of the opening statement of the plaintiff or counsel, or, if there is no opening statement, at the time of the administering of the oath or affirmation to the first witness, or the introduction of any evidence.
(c)
(1) If an offer made by a defendant is not accepted and the plaintiff fails to obtain a more favorable judgment or award, the plaintiff shall not recover his or her postoffer costs and shall pay the defendant's costs from the time of the offer. In addition, in any action or proceeding other than an eminent domain action, the court or arbitrator, in its discretion, may require the plaintiff to pay a reasonable sum to cover postoffer costs of the services of expert witnesses, who are not regular employees of any party, actually incurred and reasonably necessary in either, or both, preparation for trial or arbitration, or during trial or arbitration, of the case by the defendant.
(2)
(A) In determining whether the plaintiff obtains a more favorable judgment, the court or arbitrator shall exclude the postoffer costs.
(B) It is the intent of the Legislature in enacting subparagraph (A) to supersede the holding in Encinitas Plaza Real v. Knight, 209 Cal.App.3d 996, that attorney's fees awarded to the prevailing party were not costs for purposes of this section but were part of the judgment.
(d) If an offer made by a plaintiff is not accepted and the defendant fails to obtain a more favorable judgment or award in any action or proceeding other than an eminent domain action, the court or arbitrator, in its discretion, may require the defendant to pay a reasonable sum to cover postoffer costs of the services of expert witnesses, who are not regular employees of any party, actually incurred and reasonably necessary in either, or both, preparation for trial or arbitration, or during trial or arbitration, of the case by the plaintiff, in addition to plaintiff's costs.
(e) If an offer made by a defendant is not accepted and the plaintiff fails to obtain a more favorable judgment or award, the costs under this section, from the time of the offer, shall be deducted from any damages awarded in favor of the plaintiff. If the costs awarded under this section exceed the amount of the damages awarded to the plaintiff the net amount shall be awarded to the defendant and judgment or award shall be entered accordingly.
(f) Police officers shall be deemed to be expert witnesses for the purposes of this section. For purposes of this section, "plaintiff" includes a cross-complainant and "defendant" includes a cross-defendant. Any judgment or award entered pursuant to this section shall be deemed to be a compromise settlement.
(g) This chapter does not apply to either of the following:

(1) An offer that is made by a plaintiff in an eminent domain action.

(2) Any enforcement action brought in the name of the people of the State of California by the Attorney General, a district attorney, or a city attorney, acting as a public prosecutor.

(h) The costs for services of expert witnesses for trial under subdivisions (c) and (d) shall not exceed those specified in Section 68092.5 of the Government Code.

(i) This section shall not apply to labor arbitrations filed pursuant to memoranda of understanding under the Ralph C. Dills Act (Chapter 10.3 (commencing with Section 3512) of Division 4 of Title 1 of the Government Code).

Amended by Stats 2015 ch 345 (AB 1141),s 2, eff. 1/1/2016.
Amended by Stats 2005 ch 706 (AB 1742),s 13, eff. 1/1/2006
Amended by Stats 2001 ch 153 (AB 732), s 1, eff. 1/1/2002.
Previously Amended September 7, 1999 (Bill Number: SB 1161) (Chapter 353).

Chapter 3.2 - TIME-LIMITED DEMANDS

Section 999 - Public policy; definitions

(a) It is declared to be the public policy of the State of California that prompt settlements of civil actions and claims are encouraged as beneficial to claimants, policyholders, and insurers.

(b) For purposes of this section, the following definitions apply:

(1) "Extracontractual damages" means any amount of damage that exceeds the total available limit of liability insurance for all of a liability insurer's liability insurance policies applicable to a claim for property damage, personal injury, bodily injury, or wrongful death.

(2) "Time-limited demand" means an offer prior to the filing of the complaint or demand for arbitration to settle any cause of action or a claim for personal injury, property damage, bodily injury, or wrongful death made by or on behalf of a claimant to a tortfeasor with a liability insurance policy for purposes of settling the claim against the tortfeasor within the insurer's limit of liability insurance, which by its terms must be accepted within a specified period of time.

Added by Stats 2022 ch 719 (SB 1155),s 1, eff. 1/1/2023.

Section 999.1 - Requirements for time-limited demand to settle any claim

A time-limited demand to settle any claim shall be in writing, be labeled as a time-limited demand or reference this section, and contain material terms, which include the following:

(a) The time period within which the demand must be accepted shall be not fewer than 30 days from date of transmission of the demand, if transmission is by email, facsimile, or certified mail, or not fewer than 33 days, if transmission is by mail.

(b) A clear and unequivocal offer to settle all claims within policy limits, including the satisfaction of all liens.

(c) An offer for a complete release from the claimant for the liability insurer's insureds from all present and future liability for the occurrence.

(d) The date and location of the loss.

(e) The claim number, if known.

(f) A description of all known injuries sustained by the claimant.

(g) Reasonable proof, which may include, if applicable, medical records or bills, sufficient to support the claim.

Added by Stats 2022 ch 719 (SB 1155),s 1, eff. 1/1/2023.

Section 999.2 - Where demands should be sent; address to be posted

(a) A claimant shall send their time-limited demand to either of the following:

(1) The email address or physical address designated by the liability insurer for receipt of time-limited demands for purposes of this chapter, if an address has been provided by the liability insurer to the Department of Insurance and the Department of Insurance has made the address publicly available.

(2) The insurance representative assigned to handle the claim, if known.

(b) To implement this section, the Department of Insurance shall post on its internet website the email address or physical address designated by a liability insurer for receipt of time-limited demands for purposes of this chapter.

(c) An act by the Department of Insurance pursuant to this section is a discretionary act for purposes of Section 820.2 of the Government Code.

Added by Stats 2022 ch 719 (SB 1155),s 1, eff. 1/1/2023.

Section 999.3 - Acceptance

(a) The recipients of a time-limited demand may accept the demand by providing written acceptance of the material terms outlined in Section 999.1 in their entirety.

(b) Upon receipt of a time-limited demand, an attempt to seek clarification or additional information or a request for an extension due to the need for further information or investigation, made during the time within which to accept a time-limited demand, shall not, in and of itself, be deemed a counteroffer or rejection of the demand.

(c) If, for any reason, an insurer does not accept a time-limited demand, the insurer shall notify the claimant, in writing, of its decision and the basis for its decision. This notification shall be sent prior to the expiration of the time-limited demand, including any extension agreed to by the parties, and shall be relevant in any lawsuit alleging extracontractual damages against the tortfeasor's liability insurer.

Added by Stats 2022 ch 719 (SB 1155),s 1, eff. 1/1/2023.

Section 999.4 - Compliance; claimant needs counsel; conflict with Civil Discovery Act

(a) In any lawsuit filed by a claimant, or by a claimant as an assignee of the tortfeasor or by the tortfeasor for the benefit of the claimant, a time-limited demand that does not substantially comply with the terms of this chapter shall not be considered to be a reasonable offer to settle the claims against the tortfeasor for an amount within the insurance policy limits for purposes of any lawsuit alleging extracontractual damages against the tortfeasor's liability insurer.

(b) This section shall not apply to a claimant that is not represented by counsel.

(c) In the event a court determines that this chapter conflicts with the Civil Discovery Act, (Title 4 (commencing with Section 2016.010) of Part 4), the Civil Discovery Act shall prevail.

Added by Stats 2022 ch 719 (SB 1155),s 1, eff. 1/1/2023.

Section 999.5 - Applicability; construction with existing law

(a) This chapter shall only apply to causes of action and claims covered under automobile, motor vehicle, homeowner, or commercial premises liability insurance policies for property damage, personal or bodily injury, and wrongful death claims.

(b) Except as provided in this chapter, nothing shall alter existing law, including law relating to claims, damages, and defenses, that may be asserted in litigation seeking extracontractual damages.

(c) This chapter shall apply to time-limited demands transmitted on or after January 1, 2023.

Added by Stats 2022 ch 719 (SB 1155),s 1, eff. 1/1/2023.

Chapter 3.5 - CONFIDENTIAL SETTLEMENT AGREEMENTS

Section 1001 - Provisions preventing disclosure of facts related to claim in administrative action prohibited

(a) Notwithstanding any other law, a provision within a settlement agreement that prevents or restricts the disclosure of factual information related to a claim filed in a civil action or a complaint filed in an administrative action, regarding any of the following, is prohibited:

(1) An act of sexual assault that is not governed by subdivision (a) of Section 1002.

(2) An act of sexual harassment, as defined in Section 51.9 of the Civil Code.

(3) An act of workplace harassment or discrimination, failure to prevent an act of workplace harassment or discrimination, or an act of retaliation against a person for reporting or opposing harassment or discrimination, as described in subdivisions (a), (h), (i), (j), and (k) of Section 12940 of the Government Code.

(4) An act of harassment or discrimination, or an act of retaliation against a person for reporting harassment or discrimination by the owner of a housing accommodation, as described in Section 12955 of the Government Code.

(b) Notwithstanding any other law, in a civil matter described in paragraphs (1) to (4), inclusive, of subdivision (a), a court shall not enter, by stipulation or otherwise, an order that restricts the disclosure of information in a manner that conflicts with subdivision (a).

(c) Notwithstanding subdivisions (a) and (b), a provision that shields the identity of the claimant and all facts that could lead to the discovery of the claimant's identity, including pleadings filed in court, may be included within a settlement agreement at the request of the claimant. This subdivision does not apply if a government agency or public official is a party to the settlement agreement.

(d) Except as authorized by subdivision (c), a provision within a settlement agreement that prevents or restricts the disclosure of factual information related to the claim described in subdivision (a) that is entered into on or after January 1, 2019, is void as a matter of law and against public policy.

(e) This section does not prohibit the entry or enforcement of a provision in any agreement that precludes the disclosure of the amount paid in settlement of a claim.

(f) In determining the factual foundation of a cause of action for civil damages under subdivision (a), a court may consider the pleadings and other papers in the record, or any other findings of the court.

(g) The amendments made to paragraphs (3) and (4) of subdivision (a) by Senate Bill 331 of the 2021-22 Regular Session apply only to agreements entered into on or after January 1, 2022. All other amendments made to this section by Senate Bill 331 of the 2021-22 Regular Session shall not be construed as substantive changes, but instead as merely clarifying existing law.

Amended by Stats 2022 ch 28 (SB 1380),s 26, eff. 1/1/2023.
Amended by Stats 2021 ch 638 (SB 331),s 1, eff. 1/1/2022.
Added by Stats 2018 ch 953 (SB 820),s 1, eff. 1/1/2019.

Section 1002 - Prohibited in civil action for act that may be prosecuted as felony sex offense

(a) Notwithstanding any other law, a provision within a settlement agreement that prevents the disclosure of factual information related to the action is prohibited in any civil action the factual foundation for which establishes a cause of action for civil damages for any of the following:

(1) An act that may be prosecuted as a felony sex offense.

(2) An act of childhood sexual assault, as defined in Section 340.1.

(3) An act of sexual exploitation of a minor, as defined in Section 11165.1 of the Penal Code, or conduct prohibited with respect to a minor pursuant to Section 311.1, 311.5, or 311.6 of the Penal Code.

(4) An act of sexual assault, as defined in paragraphs (1) to (9), inclusive, of subdivision (e) of Section 15610.63 of the Welfare and Institutions Code, against an elder or dependent adult, as defined in Sections 15610.23 and 15610.27 of the Welfare and Institutions Code.

(b) Notwithstanding any other law, in a civil action described in paragraphs (1) to (4), inclusive, of subdivision (a), a court shall not enter, by stipulation or otherwise, an order that restricts the disclosure of information in a manner that conflicts with subdivision (a).

(c) Subdivisions (a) and (b) do not preclude an agreement preventing the disclosure of any medical information or personal identifying information, as defined in subdivision (b) of Section 530.55 of the Penal Code, regarding the victim of the offense listed in subdivision (a) or of any information revealing the nature of the relationship between the victim and the defendant. This subdivision shall not be construed to limit the right of a crime victim to disclose this information.

(d) Except as authorized by subdivision (c), a provision within a settlement agreement that prevents the disclosure of factual information related to the action described in subdivision (a) that is entered into on or after January 1, 2017, is void as a matter of law and against public policy.

(e) An attorney's failure to comply with the requirements of this section by demanding that a provision be included in a settlement agreement that prevents the disclosure of factual information related to the action described in subdivision (a) that is not otherwise authorized by subdivision (c) as a condition of settlement, or advising a client to sign an agreement that includes such a provision, may be grounds for professional discipline and the State Bar of California shall investigate and take appropriate action in any such case brought to its attention.

Amended by Stats 2019 ch 861 (AB 218),s 2, eff. 1/1/2020.
Amended by Stats 2017 ch 561 (AB 1516),s 24, eff. 1/1/2018.
Amended by Stats 2016 ch 876 (AB 1682),s 1, eff. 1/1/2017.
Added by Stats 2006 ch 151 (AB 2875),s 1, eff. 1/1/2007.

Chapter 3.6 - AGREEMENTS SETTLING EMPLOYMENT DISPUTES

Section 1002.5 - Generally

(a) An agreement to settle an employment dispute shall not contain a provision prohibiting, preventing, or otherwise restricting a settling party that is an aggrieved person from obtaining future employment with the employer against which the aggrieved person has filed a claim, or any parent company, subsidiary, division, affiliate, or contractor of the employer. A provision in an agreement entered into on or after January 1, 2020, that violates this section is void as a matter of law and against public policy.

(b) Nothing in subdivision (a) does any of the following:

(1) Preclude the employer and aggrieved person from making an agreement to do either of the following:

(A) End a current employment relationship.

(B) Prohibit or otherwise restrict the settling aggrieved person from obtaining future employment with the settling employer, if the employer has made and documented a good faith determination, before the aggrieved person filed the claim that the aggrieved person engaged in sexual harassment, sexual assault, or any criminal conduct.

(2) Require an employer to continue to employ or rehire a person if there is a legitimate non-discriminatory or non-retaliatory reason for terminating the employment relationship or refusing to rehire the person.

(c) For purposes of this section:

(1) "Aggrieved person" means a person who, in good faith, has filed a claim against the person's employer in court, before an administrative agency, in an alternative dispute resolution forum, or through the employer's internal complaint process.

(2) "Sexual assault" means conduct that would constitute a crime under Section 243.3, 261, 262, 264.1, 286, 287, or 289 of the Penal Code, assault with the intent to commit any of those crimes, or an attempt to commit any of those crimes.

(3) "Sexual harassment" has the same meaning as in subdivision (j) of Section 12940 of the Government Code.

Amended by Stats 2020 ch 73 (AB 2143),s 1, eff. 1/1/2021.
Amended by Stats 2020 ch 370 (SB 1371),s 37, eff. 1/1/2021.
Added by Stats 2019 ch 808 (AB 749),s 1, eff. 1/1/2020.

Chapter 3.7 - ENROLLMENT AGREEMENTS

Section 1002.7 - Enrollment Agreements

(a) The Legislature finds and declares that it is unconscionable for a parent, on behalf of the parent's minor child, to be required to waive a legal right, remedy, forum, proceeding, or procedure, including the right to file and pursue a civil action, belonging to that minor child with respect to claims arising out of a criminal sexual assault or criminal sexual battery as a condition of enrollment in an educational institution.

(b) Notwithstanding Chapter 2 (commencing with Section 6710) of Part 3 of Division 11 of the Family Code, a provision in an educational institution's enrollment agreement that purports to waive a legal right, remedy, forum, proceeding, or procedure may be disaffirmed by the minor, regardless of whether a parent or legal guardian has signed the enrollment agreement on the minor's behalf, to the extent that the provision is construed to require the minor to waive a legal right, remedy, forum, proceeding, or procedure arising out of a criminal sexual assault or criminal sexual battery on that minor.

(c) The fact that a provision in an enrollment agreement has been disaffirmed by the minor pursuant to this section does not affect the validity or enforceability of any other provision of the enrollment agreement.

(d) For purposes of this section, the following definitions apply:

(1) "Criminal sexual assault" means an act that was perpetrated against a person under 18 years of age and that would be a crime under Section 261.5, 286, 287, 288, 288.7, or 289 of the Penal Code, or any predecessor statute.

(2) "Criminal sexual battery" means an act that was perpetrated against a person under 18 years of age and that would be a crime under Section 243.4 of the Penal Code.

(3) "Educational institution" means a public or private school maintaining a kindergarten or any of grades 1 through 12.

(4) "Enrollment agreement" means a written contract between a student and institution concerning an educational program.

Added by Stats 2021 ch 146 (AB 272),s 1, eff. 1/1/2022.

Chapter 4 - MOTIONS AND ORDERS

Section 1003 - Direction of court denominated order; application for order is motion

Every direction of a court or judge, made or entered in writing, and not included in a judgment, is denominated an order. An application for an order is a motion.

Amended by Stats. 1951, Ch. 1737.

Section 1004 - Venue for making motions

Except as provided in section 166 of this code, motions must be made in the court in which the action is pending.

Amended by Stats. 1933, Ch. 744.

Section 1005 - Motions for which written notice required

(a) Written notice shall be given, as prescribed in subdivisions (b) and (c), for the following motions:

(1) Notice of Application and Hearing for Writ of Attachment under Section 484.040.

(2) Notice of Application and Hearing for Claim and Delivery under Section 512.030.

(3) Notice of Hearing for Claim of Exemption under Section 706.105.

(4) Motion to Quash Summons pursuant to subdivision (b) of Section 418.10.

(5) Motion for Determination of Good Faith Settlement pursuant to Section 877.6.

(6) Hearing for Discovery of Peace Officer Personnel Records in a civil action pursuant to Section 1043 of the Evidence Code.

(7) Notice of Hearing of Third-Party Claim pursuant to Section 720.320.

(8) Motion for an Order to Attend Deposition more than 150 miles from deponent's residence pursuant to Section 2025.260.

(9) Notice of Hearing of Application for Relief pursuant to Section 946.6 of the Government Code.

(10) Motion to Set Aside Default or Default Judgment and for Leave to Defend Actions pursuant to Section 473.5.

(11) Motion to Expunge Notice of Pendency of Action pursuant to Section 405.30.

(12) Motion to Set Aside Default and for Leave to Amend pursuant to Section 585.5.

(13) Any other proceeding under this code in which notice is required, and no other time or method is prescribed by law or by court or judge.

(b) Unless otherwise ordered or specifically provided by law, all moving and supporting papers shall be served and filed at least 16 court days before the hearing. The moving and supporting papers served shall be a copy of the papers filed or to be filed with the court. However, if the notice is served by mail, the required 16-day period of notice before the hearing shall be increased by five calendar days if the place of mailing and the place of address are within the State of California, 10 calendar days if either the place of mailing or the place of address is outside the State of California but within the United States, 12 calendar days if the place of address is the Secretary of State's address confidentiality program (Chapter 3.1 (commencing with Section 6205) of Division 7 of Title 1 of the Government Code), and 20 calendar days if either the place of mailing or the place of address is outside the United States, and if the notice is served by facsimile transmission, express mail, or another method of delivery providing for overnight delivery, the required 16-day period of notice before the hearing shall be increased by two calendar days. Section 1013, which extends the time within which a right may be exercised or an act may be done, does not apply to a notice of motion, papers opposing a motion, or reply papers governed by this section. All papers opposing a motion so noticed shall be filed with the court and a copy served on each party at least nine court days, and all reply papers at least five court days before the hearing. The court, or a judge thereof, may prescribe a shorter time.

(c) Notwithstanding any other provision of this section, all papers opposing a motion and all reply papers shall be served by personal delivery, facsimile transmission, express mail, or other means consistent with Sections 1010, 1011, 1012, and 1013, and reasonably calculated to ensure delivery to the other party or parties not later than the close of the next business day after the time the opposing papers or reply papers, as applicable, are filed. This subdivision applies to the service of opposition and reply papers regarding motions for summary judgment or summary adjudication, in addition to the motions listed in subdivision (a). The court, or a judge thereof, may prescribe a shorter time.

Amended by Stats 2022 ch 686 (AB 1726),s 1, eff. 1/1/2023.
Amended by Stats 2019 ch 585 (AB 1600),s 1, eff. 1/1/2020.
Amended by Stats 2005 ch 294 (AB 333),s 3, eff. 1/1/2006
Amended by Stats 2004 ch 182 (AB 3081),s 13, eff. 7/1/2005
Amended by Stats 2004 ch 171 (AB 3078),s 3, eff. 1/1/2005
Amended by Stats 2002 ch 806 (AB 3027),s 16, eff. 1/1/2003.

Section 1005.5 - Motion deemed made and pending upon service and filing

A motion upon all the grounds stated in the written notice thereof is deemed to have been made and to be pending before the court for all purposes, upon the due service and filing of the notice of motion, but this shall not deprive a party of a hearing of the motion to which he is otherwise entitled. Procedure upon a motion for new trial shall be as otherwise provided.

Added by Stats. 1953, Ch. 909.

Section 1006 - Transfer of matter to some other judge

When a notice of motion is given, or an order to show cause is made returnable before a judge out of court, and at the time fixed for the motion, or on the return day of the order, the judge is unable to hear the parties, the matter may be transferred by his order to some other judge, before whom it might originally have been brought.
Amended by Stats. 1951, Ch. 1737.

Section 1006.5 - [Repealed]
Repealed by Stats 2007 ch 268 (AB 500),s 4, eff. 1/1/2008.

Section 1008 - Motion to reconsider matter and modify, amend or revoke prior order
(a) When an application for an order has been made to a judge, or to a court, and refused in whole or in part, or granted, or granted conditionally, or on terms, any party affected by the order may, within 10 days after service upon the party of written notice of entry of the order and based upon new or different facts, circumstances, or law, make application to the same judge or court that made the order, to reconsider the matter and modify, amend, or revoke the prior order. The party making the application shall state by affidavit what application was made before, when and to what judge, what order or decisions were made, and what new or different facts, circumstances, or law are claimed to be shown.

(b) A party who originally made an application for an order which was refused in whole or part, or granted conditionally or on terms, may make a subsequent application for the same order upon new or different facts, circumstances, or law, in which case it shall be shown by affidavit what application was made before, when and to what judge, what order or decisions were made, and what new or different facts, circumstances, or law are claimed to be shown. For a failure to comply with this subdivision, any order made on a subsequent application may be revoked or set aside on ex parte motion.

(c) If a court at any time determines that there has been a change of law that warrants it to reconsider a prior order it entered, it may do so on its own motion and enter a different order.

(d) A violation of this section may be punished as a contempt and with sanctions as allowed by Section 128.7. In addition, an order made contrary to this section may be revoked by the judge or commissioner who made it, or vacated by a judge of the court in which the action or proceeding is pending.

(e) This section specifies the court's jurisdiction with regard to applications for reconsideration of its orders and renewals of previous motions, and applies to all applications to reconsider any order of a judge or court, or for the renewal of a previous motion, whether the order deciding the previous matter or motion is interim or final. No application to reconsider any order or for the renewal of a previous motion may be considered by any judge or court unless made according to this section.

(f) For the purposes of this section, an alleged new or different law shall not include a later enacted statute without a retroactive application.

(g) An order denying a motion for reconsideration made pursuant to subdivision (a) is not separately appealable. However, if the order that was the subject of a motion for reconsideration is appealable, the denial of the motion for reconsideration is reviewable as part of an appeal from that order.

(h) This section applies to all applications for interim orders.
Amended by Stats 2011 ch 78 (AB 1067),s 1, eff. 1/1/2012.

Chapter 5 - NOTICES, AND FILING AND SERVICE OF PAPERS

Section 1010 - Requirements of notices; service of notices and other papers
Notices must be in writing, and the notice of a motion, other than for a new trial, must state when, and the grounds upon which it will be made, and the papers, if any, upon which it is to be based. If any such paper has not previously been served upon the party to be notified and was not filed by him, a copy of such paper must accompany the notice. Notices and other papers may be served upon the party or attorney in the manner prescribed in this chapter, when not otherwise provided by this code. No bill of exceptions, notice of appeal, or other notice or paper, other than amendments to the pleadings, or an amended pleading, need be served upon any party whose default has been duly entered or who has not appeared in the action or proceeding.
Amended by Stats. 1935, Ch. 722.

Section 1010.5 - Facsimile filing of papers
The Judicial Council may adopt rules permitting the filing of papers by facsimile transmission, both directly with the courts and through third parties. Notwithstanding any other provision of law, the rules may provide that the facsimile transmitted document shall constitute an original document, and that notwithstanding Section 6159 of the Government Code or Title 1.3 (commencing with Section 1747) of Part 4 of Division 3 of the Civil Code, any court authorized to accept a credit card as payment pursuant to this section may add a surcharge to the amount of the transaction to be borne by the litigant to cover charges imposed on credit card transactions regarding fax filings between a litigant and the court. If the Judicial Council adopts rules permitting the filing of papers by facsimile transmission, the consent of the Judicial Council shall not be necessary to permit the use of credit cards to pay fees for the filing of papers by facsimile transmission directly with the court, provided that the court charges a processing fee to the filing party sufficient to cover the cost to the court of processing payment by credit card.
Amended by Stats 2001 ch 824 (AB 1700), s 10, eff. 1/1/2002.

Section 1010.6 - Electronic service of document
(a) A document may be served electronically in an action filed with the court as provided in this section, in accordance with rules adopted pursuant to subdivision (h).

(1) For purposes of this section:

(A) "Electronic service" means service of a document, on a person, by either electronic transmission or electronic notification. Electronic service may be performed directly by a person, including a party, by a person's agent, including the person's attorney, or through an electronic filing service provider, and by a court.

(B) "Electronic transmission" means the transmission of a document by electronic means to the electronic service address at or through which a person receives electronic service.

(C) "Electronic notification" means the notification of the person that a document is served by sending an electronic message to the electronic address at or through which the person receives electronic service, specifying the exact name of the document served, and providing a hyperlink at which the served document may be viewed and downloaded.

(D) "Electronic filing" means the electronic transmission to a court of a document presented for filing in electronic form. For purposes of this section, this definition of electronic filing concerns the activity of filing and does not include the processing and review of the document and its entry into the court's records, which are necessary for a document to be officially filed.

(2) If a document is required to be served by certified or registered mail, electronic service of the document is not authorized.

(3)
(A) If a document may be served by mail, express mail, overnight delivery, or facsimile transmission, electronic service of that document is deemed complete at the time of the electronic transmission of the document or at the time that the electronic notification of service of the document is sent.

(B) Any period of notice, or any right or duty to do any act or make any response within any period or on a date certain after the service of the document, which time period or date is prescribed by statute or rule of court, shall be extended after service by electronic means by two court days, but the extension shall not apply to extend the time for filing any of the following:

(i) A notice of intention to move for new trial.

(ii)A notice of intention to move to vacate judgment under Section 663a.
(iii)A notice of appeal.
(C)This extension applies in the absence of a specific exception provided by any other statute or rule of court.
(4)Any document that is served electronically between 12:00 a.m. and 11:59:59 p.m. on a court day shall be deemed served on that court day. Any document that is served electronically on a noncourt day shall be deemed served on the next court day.
(5)Confidential or sealed records shall be electronically served through encrypted methods to ensure that the documents are not improperly disclosed.
(b)
(1)This subdivision applies to mandatory electronic service. The court may order electronic service on a person represented by counsel who has appeared in an action or proceeding.
(2)A person represented by counsel, who has appeared in an action or proceeding, shall accept electronic service of a notice or document that may be served by mail, express mail, overnight delivery, or facsimile transmission.
(3)Before first serving a represented person electronically, the person effecting service shall confirm the appropriate electronic service address for the counsel being served.
(4)A person represented by counsel shall, upon the request of any person who has appeared in an action or proceeding and who provides an electronic service address, electronically serve the requesting person with any notice or document that may be served by mail, express mail, overnight delivery, or facsimile transmission.
(c)
(1)This subdivision applies to electronic service by consent of an unrepresented person in a civil action.
(2)An unrepresented party may consent to receive electronic service.
(3)Express consent to electronic service may be given by either of the following:
(i)Serving a notice on all parties and filing the notice with the court.
(ii)Manifesting affirmative consent through electronic means with the court or the court's electronic filing service provider, and concurrently providing the party's electronic address with that consent for the purpose of receiving electronic service. The act of electronic filing shall not be construed as express consent.
(4)A person who has provided express consent to accept service electronically may withdraw consent at any time by completing and filing with the court the appropriate Judicial Council form.
(5)Consent, or the withdrawal of consent, to receive electronic service may only be completed by a person entitled to service.
(d) On and after July 1, 2024, in any action in which a party or other person is subject to mandatory electronic service under subdivision (b) or has consented to electronic service under subdivision (c), the court shall electronically transmit, to a person subject to mandatory electronic service or who consented to electronic service, any document issued by the court that the court is required to transmit, deliver, or serve. The electronic service of documents by the court shall have the same legal effect as service by mail, except as provided in paragraph (3) of subdivision (a).
(e)A trial court may adopt local rules permitting electronic filing of documents, subject to rules adopted by the Judicial Council pursuant to subdivision (h) and the following conditions:
(1)A document that is filed electronically shall have the same legal effect as an original paper document.
(2)
(A)When a document to be filed requires the signature of any person, not under penalty of perjury, the document shall be deemed to have been signed by that person if filed electronically and if either of the following conditions is satisfied:
(i)The filer is the signer.
(ii)The person has signed the document pursuant to the procedure set forth in the California Rules of Court.
(B)When a document to be filed requires the signature, under penalty of perjury, of any person, the document shall be deemed to have been signed by that person if filed electronically and if either of the following conditions is satisfied:
(i)The person has signed a printed form of the document before, or on the same day as, the date of filing. The attorney or other person filing the document represents, by the act of filing, that the declarant has complied with this section. The attorney or other person filing the document shall maintain the printed form of the document bearing the original signature until final disposition of the case, as defined in subdivision (c) of Section 68151 of the Government Code, and make it available for review and copying upon the request of the court or any party to the action or proceeding in which it is filed.
(ii)The person has signed the document using a computer or other technology pursuant to the procedure set forth in a rule of court adopted by the Judicial Council by January 1, 2019.
(3)Any document received electronically by the court between 12:00 a.m. and 11:59:59 p.m. on a court day shall be deemed filed on that court day. Any document that is received electronically on a noncourt day shall be deemed filed on the next court day.
(4)
(A)Whichever of a court, an electronic filing service provider, or an electronic filing manager is the first to receive a document submitted for electronic filing shall promptly send a confirmation of receipt of the document indicating the date and time of receipt to the party or person who submitted the document.
(B)If a document received by the court under subparagraph (A) complies with filing requirements and all required filing fees have been paid, the court shall promptly send confirmation that the document has been filed to the party or person who submitted the document.
(C)If the clerk of the court does not file a document received by the court under subparagraph (A) because the document does not comply with applicable filing requirements or the required filing fee has not been paid, the court shall promptly send notice of the rejection of the document for filing to the party or person who submitted the document. The notice of rejection shall state the reasons that the document was rejected for filing and include the date the clerk of the court sent the notice.
(D)If the court utilizes an electronic filing service provider or electronic filing manager to send the notice of rejection described in subparagraph (C), the electronic filing service provider or electronic filing manager shall promptly send the notice of rejection to the party or person who submitted the document. A notice of rejection sent pursuant to this subparagraph shall include the date the electronic filing service provider or electronic filing manager sent the notice.
(E)If the clerk of the court does not file a complaint or cross complaint because the complaint or cross complaint does not comply with applicable filing requirements or the required filing fee has not been paid, any statute of limitations applicable to the causes of action alleged in the complaint or cross complaint shall be tolled for the period beginning on the date on which the court received the document and as shown on the confirmation of receipt described in subparagraph (A), through the later of either the date on which the clerk of the court sent the notice of rejection described in subparagraph (C) or the date on which the electronic filing service provider or electronic filing manager sent the notice of rejection as described in subparagraph (D), plus one additional day if the complaint or cross complaint is subsequently submitted in a form that corrects the errors which caused the document to be rejected. The party filing the complaint or cross complaint shall not make any change to the complaint or cross complaint other than those required to correct the errors which caused the document to be rejected.
(5)Upon electronic filing of a complaint, petition, or other document that must be served with a summons, a trial court, upon request of the party filing the action, shall issue a summons with the court seal and the case number. The court shall keep the summons in its records and shall

electronically transmit a copy of the summons to the requesting party. Personal service of a printed form of the electronic summons shall have the same legal effect as personal service of an original summons.

(6)The court shall permit a party or attorney to file an application for waiver of court fees and costs, in lieu of requiring the payment of the filing fee, as part of the process involving the electronic filing of a document. The court shall consider and determine the application in accordance with Article 6 (commencing with Section 68630) of Chapter 2 of Title 8 of the Government Code and shall not require the party or attorney to submit any documentation other than that set forth in Article 6 (commencing with Section 68630) of Chapter 2 of Title 8 of the Government Code. The court, an electronic filing service provider, or an electronic filing manager shall waive any fees charged to a party or the party's attorney if the party has been granted a waiver of court fees pursuant to Section 68631 of the Government Code or if the party is indigent or being represented by the public defender or court-appointed counsel. The electronic filing manager or electronic filing service provider shall not seek payment from the court of any fee waived by the court. This section does not require the court to waive a filing fee that is not otherwise waivable.

(7)If a party electronically files a filing that is exempt from the payment of filing fees under any other law, including a filing described in Section 212 of the Welfare and Institutions Code or Section 6103.9, subdivision (b) of Section 70617, or Section 70672 of the Government Code, the party shall not be required to pay any court fees associated with the electronic filing. An electronic filing service provider or an electronic filing manager shall not seek payment of these fees from the court.

(8)A fee, if any, charged by the court, an electronic filing service provider, or an electronic filing manager to process a payment for filing fees and other court fees shall not exceed the costs incurred in processing the payment.

(9)The court shall not charge fees for electronic filing and service of documents that are more than the court's actual cost of electronic filing and service of the documents.

(f)

(1)Except as provided in paragraph (2), if a trial court adopts rules conforming to subdivision (e), it may provide by order, subject to the requirements and conditions stated in paragraphs (2) to (4), inclusive, of subdivision (g), and the rules adopted by the Judicial Council under subdivision (i), that all parties to an action file documents electronically in a class action, a consolidated action, a group of actions, a coordinated action, or an action that is deemed complex under Judicial Council rules, provided that the trial court's order does not cause undue hardship or significant prejudice to any party in the action.

(2)Unrepresented persons are exempt from any mandatory electronic filing imposed pursuant to this subdivision.

(g)A trial court may, by local rule, require electronic filing in civil actions, subject to the requirements and conditions stated in subdivision (e), the rules adopted by the Judicial Council under subdivision (i), and the following conditions:

(1)The court shall have the ability to maintain the official court record in electronic format for all cases where electronic filing is required.

(2)The court and the parties shall have access to more than one electronic filing service provider capable of electronically filing documents with the court or to electronic filing access directly through the court. Any fees charged by an electronic filing service provider shall be reasonable. An electronic filing manager or an electronic filing service provider shall waive any fees charged if the court deems a waiver appropriate, including in instances where a party has received a fee waiver.

(3)The court shall have a procedure for the filing of nonelectronic documents in order to prevent the program from causing undue hardship or significant prejudice to any party in an action, including, but not limited to, unrepresented parties. The Judicial Council shall make a form available to allow a party to seek an exemption from mandatory electronic filing and service on the grounds provided in this paragraph.

(4)Unrepresented persons are exempt from mandatory electronic filing imposed pursuant to this subdivision.

(5)Until January 1, 2021, a local child support agency, as defined in subdivision (h) of Section 17000 of the Family Code, is exempt from a trial court's mandatory electronic filing and service requirements, unless the Department of Child Support Services and the local child support agency determine it has the capacity and functionality to comply with the trial court's mandatory electronic filing and service requirements.

(h)The Judicial Council shall adopt uniform rules for the electronic filing and service of documents in the trial courts of the state, which shall include statewide policies on vendor contracts, privacy, and access to public records, and rules relating to the integrity of electronic service. These rules shall conform to the conditions set forth in this section, as amended from time to time.

(i)The Judicial Council shall adopt uniform rules to permit the mandatory electronic filing and service of documents for specified civil actions in the trial courts of the state, which shall include statewide policies on vendor contracts, privacy, access to public records, unrepresented parties, parties with fee waivers, hardships, reasonable exceptions to electronic filing, and rules relating to the integrity of electronic service. These rules shall conform to the conditions set forth in this section, as amended from time to time.

(j)

(1)Any system for the electronic filing and service of documents, including any information technology applications, internet websites and web-based applications, used by an electronic service provider or any other vendor or contractor that provides an electronic filing and service system to a trial court, regardless of the case management system used by the trial court, shall satisfy both of the following requirements:

(A)The system shall be accessible to individuals with disabilities, including parties and attorneys with disabilities, in accordance with Section 508 of the federal Rehabilitation Act of 1973 (29 U.S.C. Sec. 794d), as amended, the regulations implementing that act set forth in Part 1194 of Title 36 of the Code of Federal Regulations and Appendices A, C, and D of that part, and the federal Americans with Disabilities Act of 1990 (42 U.S.C. Sec. 12101 et seq.).

(B)The system shall comply with the Web Content Accessibility Guidelines 2.0 at a Level AA success criteria.

(2)Commencing on June 27, 2017, the vendor or contractor shall provide an accommodation to an individual with a disability in accordance with subparagraph (D) of paragraph (3).

(3)A trial court that contracts with an entity for the provision of a system for electronic filing and service of documents shall require the entity, in the trial court's contract with the entity, to do all of the following:

(A)Test and verify that the entity's system complies with this subdivision and provide the verification to the Judicial Council no later than June 30, 2019.

(B)Respond to, and resolve, any complaints regarding the accessibility of the system that are brought to the attention of the entity.

(C)Designate a lead individual to whom any complaints concerning accessibility may be addressed and post the individual's name and contact information on the entity's internet website.

(D)Provide to an individual with a disability, upon request, an accommodation to enable the individual to file and serve documents electronically at no additional charge for any time period that the entity is not compliant with paragraph (1). Exempting an individual with a disability from mandatory electronic filing and service of documents shall not be deemed an accommodation unless the person chooses that as an accommodation. The vendor or contractor shall clearly state on its internet website that an individual with a disability may request an accommodation and the process for submitting a request for an accommodation.

(4)A trial court that provides electronic filing and service of documents directly to the public shall comply with this subdivision to the same extent as a vendor or contractor that provides electronic filing and services to a trial court.

(5)

(A) The Judicial Council shall submit four reports to the appropriate committees of the Legislature relating to the trial courts that have implemented a system of electronic filing and service of documents. The first report is due by June 30, 2018; the second report is due by December 31, 2019; the third report is due by December 31, 2021; and the fourth report is due by December 31, 2023.

(B) The Judicial Council's reports shall include all of the following information:

(i) The name of each court that has implemented a system of electronic filing and service of documents.

(ii) A description of the system of electronic filing and service.

(iii) The name of the entity or entities providing the system.

(iv) A statement as to whether the system complies with this subdivision and, if the system is not fully compliant, a description of the actions that have been taken to make the system compliant.

(6) An entity that contracts with a trial court to provide a system for electronic filing and service of documents shall cooperate with the Judicial Council by providing all information, and by permitting all testing, necessary for the Judicial Council to prepare its reports to the Legislature in a complete and timely manner.

Amended by Stats 2022 ch 215 (AB 2961),s 1, eff. 1/1/2023.
Amended by Stats 2021 ch 214 (SB 241),s 7, eff. 1/1/2022.
Amended by Stats 2021 ch 124 (AB 938),s 14, eff. 1/1/2022.
Amended by Stats 2020 ch 215 (AB 2165),s 1.5, eff. 1/1/2021.
Amended by Stats 2020 ch 112 (SB 1146),s 2, eff. 9/18/2020.
Amended by Stats 2018 ch 504 (AB 3248),s 1, eff. 1/1/2019.
Amended by Stats 2017 ch 319 (AB 976),s 2, eff. 1/1/2018.
Amended by Stats 2017 ch 17 (AB 103),s 5, eff. 6/27/2017.
Amended by Stats 2016 ch 461 (AB 2244),s 1, eff. 1/1/2017.
Amended by Stats 2012 ch 320 (AB 2073),s 1, eff. 1/1/2013.
Amended by Stats 2011 ch 296 (AB 1023),s 40, eff. 1/1/2012.
Amended by Stats 2010 ch 156 (SB 1274),s 1, eff. 1/1/2011.
Amended by Stats 2005 ch 300 (AB 496),s 5, eff. 1/1/2006.
Amended by Stats 2001 ch 824 (AB 1700), s 10.5, eff. 1/1/2002.
Added September 27, 1999 (Bill Number: SB 367) (Chapter 514).

Section 1011 - Manner of service

The service may be personal, by delivery to the party or attorney on whom the service is required to be made, or it may be as follows:

(a) If upon an attorney, service may be made at the attorney's office, by leaving the notice or other papers in an envelope or package clearly labeled to identify the attorney being served, with a receptionist or with a person having charge thereof. If there is no person in the office with whom the notice or papers may be left for purposes of this subdivision at the time service is to be effected, service may be made by leaving them between the hours of 9 a.m. and 5 p.m., in a conspicuous place in the office, or, if the attorney's office is not open so as to admit of that service, then service may be made by leaving the notice or papers at the attorney's residence, with some person of not less than 18 years of age, if the attorney's residence is in the same county with his or her office, and, if the attorney's residence is not known or is not in the same county with his or her office, or, being in the same county, it is not open, or a person 18 years of age or older cannot be found at the attorney's residence, then service may be made by putting the notice or papers, enclosed in a sealed envelope, into the post office or a mail box, subpost office, substation, or mail chute or other like facility regularly maintained by the Government of the United States directed to the attorney at his or her office, if known, and otherwise to the attorney's residence, if known. If neither the attorney's office nor residence is known, service may be made by delivering the notice or papers to the address of the attorney or party of record as designated on the court papers, or by delivering the notice or papers to the clerk of the court, for the attorney.

(b) If upon a party, service shall be made in the manner specifically provided in particular cases, or, if no specific provision is made, service may be made by leaving the notice or other paper at the party's residence with some person 18 years of age or older.

(1) Any attempt of service upon a party at the party's residence shall be made between the hours of 8 a.m. and 8 p.m.

(2) If, at the time of service, as provided in paragraph (1), a person 18 years of age or older cannot be found at the party's residence, the notice or papers may be served by mail.

(3) If the party's residence is not known, any attempt of service pursuant to this subdivision may be made by delivering the notice or papers to the clerk of the court, for that party.

(c) If service is made by electronic service, it shall be made pursuant to Section 1010.6 and applicable rules on electric service in the California Rules of Court.

Amended by Stats 2018 ch 212 (AB 2286),s 1, eff. 1/1/2019.
Amended by Stats 2017 ch 319 (AB 976),s 3, eff. 1/1/2018.
Amended by Stats 2007 ch 263 (AB 310),s 11, eff. 1/1/2008.

Section 1012 - Mail service

Service by mail may be made where the person on whom it is to be made resides or has his office at a place where there is a delivery service by mail, or where the person making the service and the person on whom it is to be made reside or have their offices in different places between which there is a regular communication by mail.

Amended by Stats. 1931, Ch. 739.

Section 1012.5 - [Repealed]

Repealed by Stats 2001 ch 115 (SB 153), s 3, eff. 1/1/2002.

Section 1013 - Requirements for service by mail

(a) In case of service by mail, the notice or other paper shall be deposited in a post office, mailbox, subpost office, substation, or mail chute, or other like facility regularly maintained by the United States Postal Service, in a sealed envelope, with postage paid, addressed to the person on whom it is to be served, at the office address as last given by that person on any document filed in the cause and served on the party making service by mail; otherwise at that party's place of residence. Service is complete at the time of the deposit, but any period of notice and any right or duty to do any act or make any response within any period or on a date certain after service of the document, which time period or date is prescribed by statute or rule of court, shall be extended five calendar days, upon service by mail, if the place of address and the place of mailing is within the State of California, 10 calendar days if either the place of mailing or the place of address is outside the State of California but within the United States, 12 calendar days if the place of address is the Secretary of State's address confidentiality program (Chapter 3.1 (commencing with Section 6205) of Division 7 of Title 1 of the Government Code), and 20 calendar days if either the place of mailing or the place of address is outside the United States, but the extension shall not apply to extend the time for filing notice of intention to move for new trial, notice of intention to move to vacate judgment pursuant to Section 663a, or notice of appeal. This extension applies in the absence of a specific exception provided for by this section or other statute or rule of court.

(b) The copy of the notice or other paper served by mail pursuant to this chapter shall bear a notation of the date and place of mailing or be accompanied by an unsigned copy of the affidavit or certificate of mailing.

(c) In case of service by Express Mail, the notice or other paper shall be deposited in a post office, mailbox, subpost office, substation, or mail chute, or other like facility regularly maintained by the United States Postal Service for receipt of Express Mail, in a sealed envelope, with Express Mail postage paid, addressed to the person on whom it is to be served, at the office address as last given by that person on any document filed in the cause and served on the party making service by Express Mail; otherwise at that party's place of residence. In case of service by another method of delivery providing for overnight delivery, the notice or other paper shall be deposited in a box or other facility regularly maintained by the express service carrier, or delivered to an authorized courier or driver authorized by the express service carrier to receive documents, in an envelope or package designated by the express service carrier with delivery fees paid or provided for, addressed to the person on whom it is to be served, at the office address as last given by that person on any document filed in the cause and served on the party making service; otherwise at that party's place of residence. Service is complete at the time of the deposit, but any period of notice and any right or duty to do any act or make any response within any period or on a date certain after service of the document served by Express Mail or other method of delivery providing for overnight delivery shall be extended by two court days. The extension shall not apply to extend the time for filing notice of intention to move for new trial, notice of intention to move to vacate judgment pursuant to Section 663a, or notice of appeal. This extension applies in the absence of a specific exception provided for by this section or other statute or rule of court.

(d) The copy of the notice or other paper served by Express Mail or another means of delivery providing for overnight delivery pursuant to this chapter shall bear a notation of the date and place of deposit or be accompanied by an unsigned copy of the affidavit or certificate of deposit.

(e) Service by facsimile transmission shall be permitted only where the parties agree and a written confirmation of that agreement is made. The Judicial Council may adopt rules implementing the service of documents by facsimile transmission and may provide a form for the confirmation of the agreement required by this subdivision. In case of service by facsimile transmission, the notice or other paper shall be transmitted to a facsimile machine maintained by the person on whom it is served at the facsimile machine telephone number as last given by that person on any document which they have filed in the cause and served on the party making the service. Service is complete at the time of transmission, but any period of notice and any right or duty to do any act or make any response within any period or on a date certain after service of the document, which time period or date is prescribed by statute or rule of court, shall be extended, after service by facsimile transmission, by two court days, but the extension shall not apply to extend the time for filing notice of intention to move for new trial, notice of intention to move to vacate judgment pursuant to Section 663a, or notice of appeal. This extension applies in the absence of a specific exception provided for by this section or other statute or rule of court.

(f) The copy of the notice or other paper served by facsimile transmission pursuant to this chapter shall bear a notation of the date and place of transmission and the facsimile telephone number to which transmitted, or to be accompanied by an unsigned copy of the affidavit or certificate of transmission which shall contain the facsimile telephone number to which the notice or other paper was transmitted.

(g) Electronic service shall be permitted pursuant to Section 1010.6 and the rules on electronic service in the California Rules of Court.

(h) Subdivisions (b), (d), and (f) are directory.

Amended by Stats 2022 ch 686 (AB 1726),s 2, eff. 1/1/2023.
Amended by Stats 2010 ch 156 (SB 1274),s 2, eff. 1/1/2011.
Amended by Stats 2001 ch 812 (AB 223), s 8, eff. 1/1/2002.

Section 1013a - Proof of mail service

Proof of service by mail may be made by one of the following methods:

(1) An affidavit setting forth the exact title of the document served and filed in the cause, showing the name and residence or business address of the person making the service, showing that he or she is a resident of or employed in the county where the mailing occurs, that he or she is over the age of 18 years and not a party to the cause, and showing the date and place of deposit in the mail, the name and address of the person served as shown on the envelope, and also showing that the envelope was sealed and deposited in the mail with the postage thereon fully prepaid.

(2) A certificate setting forth the exact title of the document served and filed in the cause, showing the name and business address of the person making the service, showing that he or she is an active member of the State Bar of California and is not a party to the cause, and showing the date and place of deposit in the mail, the name and address of the person served as shown on the envelope, and also showing that the envelope was sealed and deposited in the mail with the postage thereon fully prepaid.

(3) An affidavit setting forth the exact title of the document served and filed in the cause, showing (A) the name and residence or business address of the person making the service, (B) that he or she is a resident of, or employed in, the county where the mailing occurs, (C) that he or she is over the age of 18 years and not a party to the cause, (D) that he or she is readily familiar with the business' practice for collection and processing of correspondence for mailing with the United States Postal Service, (E) that the correspondence would be deposited with the United States Postal Service that same day in the ordinary course of business, (F) the name and address of the person served as shown on the envelope, and the date and place of business where the correspondence was placed for deposit in the United States Postal Service, and (G) that the envelope was sealed and placed for collection and mailing on that date following ordinary business practices. Service made pursuant to this paragraph, upon motion of a party served, shall be presumed invalid if the postal cancellation date or postage meter date on the envelope is more than one day after the date of deposit for mailing contained in the affidavit.

(4) In case of service by the clerk of a court of record, a certificate by that clerk setting forth the exact title of the document served and filed in the cause, showing the name of the clerk and the name of the court of which he or she is the clerk, and that he or she is not a party to the cause, and showing the date and place of deposit in the mail, the name and address of the person served as shown on the envelope, and also showing that the envelope was sealed and deposited in the mail with the postage thereon fully prepaid. This form of proof is sufficient for service of process in which the clerk or deputy clerk signing the certificate places the document for collection and mailing on the date shown thereon, so as to cause it to be mailed in an envelope so sealed and so addressed on that date following standard court practices. Service made pursuant to this paragraph, upon motion of a party served and a finding of good cause by the court, shall be deemed to have occurred on the date of postage cancellation or postage meter imprint as shown on the envelope if that date is more than one day after the date of deposit for mailing contained in the certificate.

Amended by Stats. 1995, Ch. 576, Sec. 4. Effective January 1, 1996.

Section 1013b - Proof of electronic service

(a) Proof of electronic service may be made by any of the following methods:

  (1) An affidavit setting forth the exact title of the document served and filed in the cause, showing the name and residence or business address of the person making the service, showing that the person is a resident of or employed in the county where the electronic service occurs, and that the person is over 18 years of age.

  (2) A certificate setting forth the exact title of the document served and filed in the cause, showing the name and business address of the person making the service, and showing that the person is an active member of the State Bar of California.

  (3) An affidavit setting forth the exact title of the document served and filed in the cause, showing all of the following:

   (A) The name and residence or business address of the person making the service.
   (B) That the person is a resident of, or employed in, the county where the electronic service occurs.
   (C) That the person is over 18 years of age.
   (D) That the person is readily familiar with the business' practice for filing electronically.
   (E) That the document would be electronically served that same day in the ordinary course of business following ordinary business practices.

(4) In case of service by the clerk of a court of record, a certificate by that clerk setting forth the exact title of the document served and filed in the cause, showing the name of the clerk and the name of the court of which they are the clerk.
(b) Proof of electronic service shall include all of the following:
    (1) The electronic service address and the residence or business address of the person making the electronic service.
    (2) The date of electronic service.
    (3) The name and electronic service address of the person served.
    (4) A statement that the document was served electronically.
(c) Proof of electronic service shall be signed as provided in subparagraph (B) of paragraph (2) of subdivision (e) of Section 1010.6.
(d) Proof of electronic service may be in electronic form and may be filed electronically with the court.
Amended by Stats 2022 ch 215 (AB 2961),s 2, eff. 1/1/2023.
Amended by Stats 2018 ch 776 (AB 3250),s 8, eff. 1/1/2019.
Added by Stats 2017 ch 319 (AB 976),s 4, eff. 1/1/2018.

Section 1014 - When defendant appears in action

A defendant appears in an action when the defendant answers, demurs, files a notice of motion to strike, files a notice of motion to transfer pursuant to Section 396b, moves for reclassification pursuant to Section 403.040, gives the plaintiff written notice of appearance, or when an attorney gives notice of appearance for the defendant. After appearance, a defendant or the defendant's attorney is entitled to notice of all subsequent proceedings of which notice is required to be given. Where a defendant has not appeared, service of notice or papers need not be made upon the defendant.
Amended 9/7/1999 (Bill Number: SB 210) (Chapter 344).

Section 1015 - Service upon party residing out of state

When a plaintiff or a defendant, who has appeared, resides out of the state, and has no attorney in the action or proceeding, the service may be made on the clerk of the court, for that party. But in all cases where a party has an attorney in the action or proceeding, the service of papers, when required, must be upon the attorney instead of the party, except service of subpoenas, of writs, and other process issued in the suit, and of papers to bring the party into contempt. If the sole attorney for a party is removed or suspended from practice, then the party has no attorney within the meaning of this section. If the party's sole attorney has no known office in this state, notices and papers may be served by leaving a copy thereof with the clerk of the court, unless the attorney has filed in the cause an address of a place at which notices and papers may be served on the attorney, in which event they may be served at that place.
Amended by Stats 2007 ch 263 (AB 310),s 12, eff. 1/1/2008.

Section 1016 - Inapplicability to contempt

The foregoing provisions of this Chapter do not apply to the sevice of a summons or other process, or of any paper to bring a party into contempt.
Enacted 1872.

Section 1017 - Service transmitted by telegraph

Any summons, writ, or order in any civil suit or proceeding, and all other papers requiring service, may be transmitted by telegraph for service in any place, and the telegraphic copy of such writ, or order, or paper so transmitted, may be served or executed by the officer or person to whom it is sent for that purpose, and returned by him, if any return be requisite, in the same manner, and with the same force and effect in all respects, as the original thereof might be if delivered to him, and the officer or person serving or executing the same has the same authority, and is subject to the same liabilities, as if the copy were the original. The original, when a writ or order, must also be filed in the Court from which it was issued, and a certified copy thereof must be preserved in the telegraph office from which it was sent. In sending it, either the original or the certified copy may be used by the operator for that purpose. Whenever any document to be sent by telegraph bears a seal, either private or official, it is not necessary for the operator, in sending the same, to telegraph a description of the seal, or any words or device thereon, but the same may be expressed in the telegraphic copy of the letters "L. S.," or by the word "seal."
Enacted 1872.

Section 1018 - [Repealed]

Repealed 10/10/1999 (Bill Number: SB 284) (Chapter 1000).

Section 1019 - Size of type required determined by conventional customs and practices of printing industry

Whenever any notice or publication is required by a provision in this code or any other code or statute of this state to be provided in a specified size of type or printing which is to be measured by points, the size required, unless otherwise specifically defined, shall be determined by the conventional customs and practices of the printing industry and within the tolerances permitted by conventional custom and practice in that industry, except that the provisions of this section shall not be used for purposes of evasion of any requirement for notice or publication.
Added by Stats. 1980, Ch. 199, Sec. 1.

Section 1019.5 - Notice when motion granted or denied

(a) When a motion is granted or denied, unless the court otherwise orders, notice of the court's decision or order shall be given by the prevailing party to all other parties or their attorneys, in the manner provided in this chapter, unless notice is waived by all parties in open court and is entered in the minutes.
(b) When a motion is granted or denied on the court's own motion, notice of the court's order shall be given by the court in the manner provided in this chapter, unless notice is waived by all parties in open court and is entered in the minutes.
Amended by Stats. 1992, Ch. 1348, Sec. 6. Effective January 1, 1993.

Section 1020 - Service by mail of notice not governed by chapter

(a) Any notice required by law, other than those required to be given to a party to an action or to his attorney, the service of which is not governed by the other sections of this chapter and which is not otherwise specifically provided for by law, may be given by sending the same by registered mail with proper postage prepaid addressed to the addressee's last known address with request for return receipt, and the production of a returned receipt purporting to be signed by the addressee shall create a disputable presumption that such notice was received by the person to whom the notice was required to be sent.
(b) Electronic service is not authorized for a notice that requires certified or registered mail.
Amended by Stats 2017 ch 319 (AB 976),s 4.5, eff. 1/1/2018.

Chapter 6 - OF COSTS

Section 1021 - Measure and mode of attorney's compensation left to agreement

Except as attorney's fees are specifically provided for by statute, the measure and mode of compensation of attorneys and counselors at law is left to the agreement, express or implied, of the parties; but parties to actions or proceedings are entitled to their costs, as hereinafter provided.
Amended by Stats. 1986, Ch. 377, Sec. 2.

Section 1021.4 - Attorney's fees against defendant convicted of felony for which action based

In an action for damages against a defendant based upon that defendant's commission of a felony offense for which that defendant has been convicted, the court may, upon motion, award reasonable attorney's fees to a prevailing plaintiff against the defendant who has been convicted of the felony.
Added by Stats. 1983, Ch. 938, Sec. 3. Effective September 20, 1983.

Section 1021.5 - Attorney's fees in action resulting in enforcement of important right affecting public interest

Upon motion, a court may award attorneys' fees to a successful party against one or more opposing parties in any action which has resulted in the enforcement of an important right affecting the public interest if:

(a) a significant benefit, whether pecuniary or nonpecuniary, has been conferred on the general public or a large class of persons,

(b) the necessity and financial burden of private enforcement, or of enforcement by one public entity against another public entity, are such as to make the award appropriate, and

(c) such fees should not in the interest of justice be paid out of the recovery, if any. With respect to actions involving public entities, this section applies to allowances against, but not in favor of, public entities, and no claim shall be required to be filed therefor, unless one or more successful parties and one or more opposing parties are public entities, in which case no claim shall be required to be filed therefor under Part 3 (commencing with Section 900) of Division 3.6 of Title 1 of the Government Code. Attorneys' fees awarded to a public entity pursuant to this section shall not be increased or decreased by a multiplier based upon extrinsic circumstances, as discussed in Serrano v. Priest, 20 Cal. 3d 25, 49.

Amended by Stats. 1993, Ch. 645, Sec. 2. Effective January 1, 1994.

Section 1021.6 - Attorney's fees awarded on claim of implied indemnity

Upon motion, a court after reviewing the evidence in the principal case may award attorney's fees to a person who prevails on a claim for implied indemnity if the court finds (a) that the indemnitee through the tort of the indemnitor has been required to act in the protection of the indemnitee's interest by bringing an action against or defending an action by a third person and (b) if that indemnitor was properly notified of the demand to bring the action or provide the defense and did not avail itself of the opportunity to do so, and (c) that the trier of fact determined that the indemnitee was without fault in the principal case which is the basis for the action in indemnity or that the indemnitee had a final judgment entered in his or her favor granting a summary judgment, a nonsuit, or a directed verdict.

Amended by Stats. 1982, Ch. 1383, Sec. 1.

Section 1021.7 - Attorney's fees in action against peace officer or for libel and slander not filed in good faith and with reasonable cause

In any action for damages arising out of the performance of a peace officer's duties, brought against a peace officer, as defined in Chapter 4.5 (commencing with Section 830) of Title 3 of Part 2 of the Penal Code, or against a public entity employing a peace officer or in an action for libel or slander brought pursuant to Section 45 or 46 of the Civil Code, the court may, in its discretion, award reasonable attorney's fees to the defendant or defendants as part of the costs, upon a finding by the court that the action was not filed or maintained in good faith and with reasonable cause.

Added by Stats. 1981, Ch. 980, Sec. 1.

Section 1021.8 - Costs of investigating and prosecuting certain actions awarded to Attorney General

(a) Whenever the Attorney General prevails in a civil action to enforce Section 17537.3, 22445, 22446.5, 22958, 22962, or 22963 of the Business and Professions Code, Section 52, 52.1, 55.1, or 3494 of the Civil Code, the Corporate Securities Law of 1968 (Division 1 (commencing with Section 25000) of Title 4 of the Corporations Code) or the California Commodity Law of 1990 (Division 4.5 (commencing with Section 29500) of Title 4 of the Corporations Code), Section 1615, 2014, or 5650.1 of the Fish and Game Code, Section 4458, 12598, 12606, 12607, 12989.3, 16147, 66640, 66641, or 66641.7 of the Government Code, Section 13009, 13009.1, 19958.5, 25299, 39674, 41513, 42402, 42402.1, 42402.2, 42402.3, 42402.4, 43016, 43017, 43154, 104557, or 118950 of the Health and Safety Code, Section 308.1 or 308.3 of the Penal Code, Section 2774.1, 4601.1, 4603, 4605, 30820, 30821.6, 30822, 42847, or 48023 of the Public Resources Code, Section 30101.7 of the Revenue and Taxation Code, or Section 275, 1052, 1845, 13261, 13262, 13264, 13265, 13268, 13304, 13331, 13350, or 13385, or Part 1 (commencing with Section 6000) of Division 3, of the Water Code, the court shall award to the Attorney General all costs of investigating and prosecuting the action, including expert fees, reasonable attorney's fees, and costs. Awards under this section shall be paid to the Public Rights Law Enforcement Special Fund established by Section 12530 of the Government Code.

(b) This section applies to any action pending on the effective date of this section and to any action filed thereafter.

(c) The amendments made to this section by Chapter 227 of the Statutes of 2004 shall apply to any action pending on the effective date of these amendments and to any action filed thereafter.

Amended by Stats 2023 ch 51 (SB 122),s 3, eff. 7/10/2023.
Amended by Stats 2006 ch 538 (SB 1852),s 65, eff. 1/1/2007.
Amended by Stats 2004 ch 702 (AB 2104),s 1, eff. 9/23/2004.
Amended by Stats 2004 ch 227 (SB 1102),s 12, eff. 8/16/2004.
Added by Stats 2003 ch 159 (AB 1759), eff. 8/2/2003.

Section 1021.9 - Attorney's fees in action for damages resulting from trespassing upon lands under cultivation or used for raising livestock

In any action to recover damages to personal or real property resulting from trespassing on lands either under cultivation or intended or used for the raising of livestock, the prevailing plaintiff shall be entitled to reasonable attorney's fees in addition to other costs, and in addition to any liability for damages imposed by law.

Added by Stats. 1986, Ch. 1381, Sec. 1.

Section 1021.10 - Fees and costs in action for failure to comply with Jenkins Act

Notwithstanding any other provision of law, in an action brought in the name of the people of the State of California against any person for failure to comply with Chapter 10A (commencing with Section 375) of Title 15 of the United States Code, otherwise known as the "Jenkins Act," the court, to the extent not expressly prohibited by federal law, shall award fees and costs, including reasonable attorney's fees, to the people if the people succeed on any claim to enforce the Jenkins Act. Any attorney's fees awarded under this section shall be in addition to any other remedies or penalties available under all other laws of this state.

Added by Stats 2002 ch 686 (SB 1766),s 2, eff. 1/1/2003.

Section 1021.11 - Attorney's fees and costs of prevailing party to be paid

(a) Notwithstanding any other law, any person, including an entity, attorney, or law firm, who seeks declaratory or injunctive relief to prevent this state, a political subdivision, a governmental entity or public official in this state, or a person in this state from enforcing any statute, ordinance, rule, regulation, or any other type of law that regulates or restricts firearms, or that represents any litigant seeking that relief, is jointly and severally liable to pay the attorney's fees and costs of the prevailing party.

(b) For purposes of this section, a party is considered a prevailing party if a court does either of the following:

(1) Dismisses any claim or cause of action brought by the party seeking the declaratory or injunctive relief described by subdivision (a), regardless of the reason for the dismissal.

(2) Enters judgment in favor of the party opposing the declaratory or injunctive relief described by subdivision (a), on any claim or cause of action.

(c) Regardless of whether a prevailing party sought to recover attorney's fees or costs in the underlying action, a prevailing party under this section may bring a civil action to recover attorney's fees and costs against a person, including an entity, attorney, or law firm, that sought declaratory or injunctive relief described by subdivision (a) not later than the third anniversary of the date on which, as applicable:

(1) The dismissal or judgment described by subdivision (b) becomes final upon the conclusion of appellate review.

(2) The time for seeking appellate review expires.

(d) None of the following are a defense to an action brought under subdivision (c):

    (1) A prevailing party under this section failed to seek recovery of attorney's fees or costs in the underlying action.

    (2) The court in the underlying action declined to recognize or enforce the requirements of this section.

    (3) The court in the underlying action held that any provision of this section is invalid, unconstitutional, or preempted by federal law, notwithstanding the doctrines of issue or claim preclusion.

(e) Any person, including an entity, attorney, or law firm, who seeks declaratory or injunctive relief as described in subdivision (a), shall not be deemed a prevailing party under this section or any other provision of this chapter.

Added by Stats 2022 ch 146 (SB 1327),s 2, eff. 1/1/2023.

See Stats 2022 ch 146 (SB 1327), s 3.

Section 1022 - Costs awarded to plaintiff when several actions brought

When several actions are brought on one bond, undertaking, promissory note, bill of exchange, or other instrument in writing, or in any other case for the same cause of action, against several parties who might have been joined as defendants in the same action, no costs can be allowed to the plaintiff in more than one of such actions, which may be at his election, if the party proceeded against in the other actions were, at the commencement of the previous action, openly within this State; but the disbursements of the plaintiff must be allowed to him in each action.

Added by renumbering Section 1023 by Stats. 1933, Ch. 744.

Section 1023 - Fees of referees

The fees of referees are such reasonable sum as the court may fix for the time spent in the business of the reference; but the parties may agree, in writing, upon any other rate of compensation, and thereupon such rates shall be allowed.

Amended by Stats. 1953, Ch. 795.

Section 1024 - Expenses occasioned by postponement of trial

When an application is made to the court or referee to postpone a trial, the payment of the expenses occasioned by the postponement may be imposed, in the discretion of the court or referee, as a condition of granting the same.

Amended by Stats. 1986, Ch. 377, Sec. 3.

Section 1025 - Deposit in court by defendant upon allegation that full amount tendered to plaintiff

When, in an action for the recovery of money only, the defendant alleges in his answer that before the commencement of the action he tendered to the plaintiff the full amount to which he was entitled, and thereupon deposits in court, for plaintiff, the amount so tendered, and the allegation is found to be true, the plaintiff can not recover costs, but must pay costs to the defendant.

Added by renumbering Section 1030 by Stats. 1933, Ch. 744.

Section 1026 - Action prosecuted or defended by personal representative, trustee, guardian, etc.

(a) Except as provided in subdivision (b), in an action prosecuted or defended by a personal representative, trustee of an express trust, guardian, conservator, or a person expressly authorized by statute, costs may be recovered as in an action by or against a person prosecuting or defending in the person's own right.

(b) Costs allowed under subdivision (a) shall, by the judgment, be made chargeable only upon the estate, fund, or party represented, unless the court directs the costs to be paid by the fiduciary personally for mismanagement or bad faith in the action or defense.

Amended by Stats. 1988, Ch. 1199, Sec. 8. Operative July 1, 1989, by Sec. 119 of Ch. 1199.

Section 1027 - Costs when decision of court of inferior jurisdiction in special proceeding brought before court of higher jurisdiction for review

When the decision of a court of inferior jurisdiction in a special proceeding is brought before a court of higher jurisdiction for a review, in any other way than by appeal, the same costs must be allowed as in cases on appeal, and may be collected in the manner provided for enforcement of money judgments generally, or in such manner as the court may direct, according to the nature of the case.

Amended by Stats. 1982, Ch. 497, Sec. 68. Operative July 1, 1983, by Sec. 185 of Ch. 497.

Section 1028 - Costs when state party

Notwithstanding any other provisions of law, when the State is a party, costs shall be awarded against it on the same basis as against any other party and, when awarded, must be paid out of the appropriation for the support of the agency on whose behalf the State appeared.

Amended by Stats. 1943, Ch. 165.

Section 1028.5 - Reasonable litigation expenses in action between small business or licensee and state agency

(a) In any civil action between a small business or a licensee and a state regulatory agency, involving the regulatory functions of a state agency as applied to a small business or a licensee, if the small business or licensee prevails, and if the court determines that the action of the agency was undertaken without substantial justification, the small business or licensee may, in the discretion of the court, be awarded reasonable litigation expenses in addition to other costs. Funds for such expenses and costs shall be paid from funds in the regular operating budget of the state regulatory agency where the appropriation therefor encompasses the payment of such costs and expenses, and not from unappropriated money in the General Fund.

(b) "Reasonable litigation expenses" means any expenses not in excess of seven thousand five hundred dollars ($7,500) which the judge finds were reasonably incurred in opposing the agency action, including court costs, expenses incurred in administrative proceedings, attorney's fees, witness fees of all necessary witnesses, and such other expenses as were reasonably incurred.

(c) "Small business" means a business activity that is all of the following:

    (1) Independently owned and operated.

    (2) Not dominant in its field of operation.

    (3) Not exceeding the following annual gross receipts or other criteria in the categories of:

        (A) Agriculture, one million dollars ($1,000,000).

        (B) General construction, nine million five hundred thousand dollars ($9,500,000).

        (C) Special trade construction, five million dollars ($5,000,000).

        (D) Retail trade, two million dollars ($2,000,000).

        (E) Wholesale trade, nine million five hundred thousand dollars ($9,500,000).

        (F) Services, two million dollars ($2,000,000).

        (G) Transportation and warehousing, one million five hundred thousand dollars ($1,500,000).

        (H) A manufacturing enterprise not exceeding 250 employees.

        (I) A health care facility not exceeding 150 beds or one million five hundred thousand dollars ($1,500,000) in annual gross receipts.

        (J) Generating and transmitting electric power not exceeding 4,500 megawatt hours annually.

(d) "Licensee" means any person licensed by a state agency who does not qualify as a small business, but whose annual gross receipts from the use of such license do not exceed one million dollars ($1,000,000).

(e) A small business or a licensee shall be deemed to prevail in any action in which there is no adjudication, stipulation, or acceptance of liability on the part of the small business or licensee.

(f) A small business or licensee shall not be deemed to have prevailed in actions commenced at the instance of, or on the basis of a complaint filed by, a person who is not an officer, employee, or other agent of the state regulatory agency if the action is dismissed by the agency upon a finding of no cause for the action, or is settled by the agency and small business or licensee without a finding of fault.
(g) Section 800 of the Government Code shall not apply to actions which are subject to the provisions of this section.
(h) Every state regulatory agency against which litigation expenses have been awarded under this section shall, at the time of submission of its proposed budget pursuant to Section 13320 of the Government Code, submit a report to the Department of Finance and the Legislature as to the amount of those expenses awarded and paid during the fiscal year.
(i) This section shall be known and may be cited as the Carpenter-Katz Small Business Equal Access to Justice Act of 1981.
Amended by Stats. 1983, Ch. 445, Sec. 1.

Section 1029 - Costs when county, city, public agency or entity party
When any county, city, district, or other public agency or entity, or any officer thereof in his official capacity, is a party, costs shall be awarded against it on the same basis as against any other party and, when awarded, must be paid out of the treasury thereof.
Amended by Stats. 1945, Ch. 217.

Section 1029.5 - Professional negligence in creation and preparation of plans, specifications designs, reports or surveys
(a) Whenever a complaint for damages is filed against any architect, landscape architect, engineer, building designer, or land surveyor, duly licensed as such under the laws of this state, in an action for error, omission, or professional negligence in the creation and preparation of plans, specifications, designs, reports or surveys which are the basis for work performed or agreed to be performed on real property, any such defendant may, within 30 days after service of summons, move the court for an order, upon notice and hearing, requiring the plaintiff to file an undertaking in a sum not to exceed five hundred dollars ($500) as security for the costs of defense as provided in subdivision (d), which may be awarded against the plaintiff. The motion shall be supported by affidavit showing that the claim against the defendant is frivolous. At the hearing upon the motion, the court shall order the plaintiff to file the undertaking if the defendant shows to the satisfaction of the court that (i) the plaintiff would not suffer undue economic hardship in filing the undertaking, and (ii) there is no reasonable possibility that the plaintiff has a cause of action against each named defendant with respect to whom the plaintiff would otherwise be required to file the undertaking. No appeal shall be taken from any order made pursuant to this subdivision to file or not to file the undertaking.
A determination by the court that the undertaking either shall or shall not be filed or shall be filed as to one or more defendants and not as to others, shall not be deemed a determination of any one or more issues in the action or of the merits thereof. If the court, upon any such motion, makes a determination that an undertaking be filed by the plaintiff as to any one or more defendants, the action shall be dismissed as to the defendant or defendants, unless the undertaking required by the court has been filed within such reasonable time as may be fixed by the court.
(b) This section does not apply to a complaint for bodily injury or for wrongful death, nor to an action commenced in a small claims court.
(c) Whenever more than one such defendant is named, the undertaking shall be increased to the extent of not to exceed five hundred dollars ($500) for each additional defendant in whose favor the undertaking is ordered not to exceed the total of three thousand dollars ($3,000).
(d) In any action requiring an undertaking as provided in this section, upon the dismissal of the action or the award of judgment to the defendant, the court shall require the plaintiff to pay the defendant's costs of defense authorized by law. Any sureties shall be liable for such costs in an amount not to exceed the sum of five hundred dollars ($500) or the amount of the undertaking, whichever is lesser, for each defendant with respect to whom the sureties have executed an undertaking.
Amended by Stats. 1982, Ch. 517, Sec. 162.

Section 1029.6 - Negligence in performance of professional services by health care providers
(a) Whenever a complaint for damages for personal injuries is filed against a physician and surgeon, dentist, registered nurse, dispensing optician, optometrist, pharmacist, registered physical therapist, podiatrist, licensed psychologist, osteopathic physician and surgeon, chiropractor, clinical laboratory bioanalyst, clinical laboratory technologist, or veterinarian, duly licensed as such under the laws of this state, or a licensed hospital as the employer of any such person, in an action for error, omission, or negligence in the performance of professional services, or performance of professional services without consent, any such defendant may, within six months after service of summons, move the court for an order, upon notice to plaintiff and all defendants having appeared in the action, and hearing, requiring the plaintiff to file an undertaking in a sum not to exceed five hundred dollars ($500) as security for the costs of defense as provided in subdivision (d), which may be awarded against the plaintiff. The motion shall be supported by affidavit showing that the claim against the defendant is frivolous. Any defendant having appeared in the action and within 30 days after receipt of notice may join with the moving party requesting an order under this section as to the additional defendant. The failure of any defendant to join with the moving party shall preclude that defendant from subsequently requesting an order under this section. At the hearing upon the motion, the court shall order the plaintiff to file the undertaking if the defendant shows to the satisfaction of the court that:

  (i) the plaintiff would not suffer undue economic hardship in filing the undertaking and

  (ii) there is no reasonable possibility that the plaintiff has a cause of action against each named defendant with respect to whom the plaintiff would otherwise be required to file the undertaking. A determination by the court that an undertaking either shall or shall not be filed or shall be filed as to one or more defendants and not as to others, shall not be deemed a determination of any one or more issues in the action or of the merits thereof. If the court, upon any such motion, makes a determination that an undertaking be filed by the plaintiff as to any one or more defendants, the action shall be dismissed as to that defendant or defendants, unless the undertaking required by the court shall have been filed within the reasonable time as may be fixed by the court.
(b) This section does not apply to a complaint in an action commenced in a small claims court.
(c) Whenever more than one defendant is named, the undertaking shall be increased to the extent of not to exceed five hundred dollars ($500) for each additional defendant in whose favor the undertaking is ordered, not to exceed the total of one thousand dollars ($1,000).
(d) In any action requiring an undertaking as provided in this section, upon the dismissal of the action or the award of judgment to the defendant, the court shall require the plaintiff to pay the defendant's court costs. Any sureties shall be liable for those costs in an amount not to exceed the sum of five hundred dollars ($500) or the amount of the undertaking, whichever is lesser, for each defendant with respect to whom the sureties have executed an undertaking. If the plaintiff prevails in the action against any defendant with respect to whom an undertaking has been filed, the defendant shall pay the costs to plaintiff incurred in defending the motion for dismissal authorized by this section.
(e) Any defendant filing a motion under this section or joining with a moving party under this section is precluded from subsequently filing a motion for summary judgment.
(f) Any defendant filing a motion for summary judgment is precluded from subsequently filing a motion, or joining with a moving party, under this section.
Amended by Stats. 1993, Ch. 226, Sec. 6. Effective January 1, 1994.

Section 1029.8 - Unlicensed person providing goods or services for which license required
(a) Any unlicensed person who causes injury or damage to another person as a result of providing goods or performing services for which a license is required under Division 2 (commencing with Section 500) or any initiative act referred to therein, Division 3 (commencing with Section 5000), or Chapter 2 (commencing with Section 18600) or Chapter 3 (commencing with Section 19000) of Division 8, of the Business and Professions Code, or Chapter 2 (commencing with Section 25210) or Chapter 3 (commencing with Section 25230) of Part 3 of Division 1 of Title

4 of the Corporations Code, shall be liable to the injured person for treble the amount of damages assessed in a civil action in any court having proper jurisdiction. The court may, in its discretion, award all costs and attorney's fees to the injured person if that person prevails in the action.

(b) This section shall not be construed to confer an additional cause of action or to affect or limit any other remedy, including, but not limited to, a claim for exemplary damages.

(c) The additional damages provided for in subdivision (a) shall not exceed ten thousand dollars ($10,000).

(d) For the purposes of this section, the term "unlicensed person" shall not apply to any of the following:

(1) Any person, partnership, corporation, or other entity providing goods or services under the good faith belief that they are properly licensed and acting within the proper scope of that licensure.

(2) Any person, partnership, corporation, or other entity whose license has expired for nonpayment of license renewal fees, but who is eligible to renew that license without the necessity of applying and qualifying for an original license.

(3) Any person, partnership, or corporation licensed under Chapter 6 (commencing with Section 2700) or Chapter 6.5 (commencing with Section 2840) of the Business and Professions Code, who provides professional nursing services under an existing license, if the action arises from a claim that the licensee exceeded the scope of practice authorized by his or her license.

(e) This section shall not apply to any action for unfair trade practices brought against an unlicensed person under Chapter 4 (commencing with Section 17000) of Part 2 of Division 7 of the Business and Professions Code, by a person who holds a license that is required, or closely related to the license that is required, to engage in those activities performed by the unlicensed person.

Amended by Stats 2004 ch 575 (AB 2167),s 1, eff. 1/1/2005

Section 1030 - Motion for plaintiff residing out of state or foreign corporation to file undertaking securing costs in special proceeding

(a) When the plaintiff in an action or special proceeding resides out of the state, or is a foreign corporation, the defendant may at any time apply to the court by noticed motion for an order requiring the plaintiff to file an undertaking to secure an award of costs and attorney's fees which may be awarded in the action or special proceeding. For the purposes of this section, "attorney's fees" means reasonable attorney's fees a party may be authorized to recover by a statute apart from this section or by contract.

(b) The motion shall be made on the grounds that the plaintiff resides out of the state or is a foreign corporation and that there is a reasonable possibility that the moving defendant will obtain judgment in the action or special proceeding. The motion shall be accompanied by an affidavit in support of the grounds for the motion and by a memorandum of points and authorities. The affidavit shall set forth the nature and amount of the costs and attorney's fees the defendant has incurred and expects to incur by the conclusion of the action or special proceeding.

(c) If the court, after hearing, determines that the grounds for the motion have been established, the court shall order that the plaintiff file the undertaking in an amount specified in the court's order as security for costs and attorney's fees.

(d) The plaintiff shall file the undertaking not later than 30 days after service of the court's order requiring it or within a greater time allowed by the court. If the plaintiff fails to file the undertaking within the time allowed, the plaintiff's action or special proceeding shall be dismissed as to the defendant in whose favor the order requiring the undertaking was made.

(e) If the defendant's motion for an order requiring an undertaking is filed not later than 30 days after service of summons on the defendant, further proceedings may be stayed in the discretion of the court upon application to the court by the defendant by noticed motion for the stay until 10 days after the motion for the undertaking is denied or, if granted, until 10 days after the required undertaking has been filed and the defendant has been served with a copy of the undertaking. The hearing on the application for the stay shall be held not later than 60 days after service of the summons. If the defendant files a motion for an order requiring an undertaking, which is granted but the defendant objects to the undertaking, the court may in its discretion stay the proceedings not longer than 10 days after a sufficient undertaking has been filed and the defendant has been served with a copy of the undertaking.

(f) The determinations of the court under this section have no effect on the determination of any issues on the merits of the action or special proceeding and may not be given in evidence nor referred to in the trial of the action or proceeding.

(g) An order granting or denying a motion for an undertaking under this section is not appealable.

Amended by Stats. 1988, Ch. 189, Sec. 1.

Section 1031 - Actions for recovery of wages for labor performed

In actions for the recovery of wages for labor performed, where the amount of the demand, exclusive of interest, does not exceed three hundred dollars ($300), the court shall add, as part of the cost, in any judgment recovered by the plaintiff or cross-complainant, an attorney's fee not exceeding 20 percent of the amount recovered.

Amended by Stats. 1986, Ch. 377, Sec. 4.

Section 1032 - Right of prevailing party to recover costs

(a) As used in this section, unless the context clearly requires otherwise:

(1) "Complaint" includes a cross-complaint.

(2) "Defendant" includes a cross-defendant, a person against whom a complaint is filed, or a party who files an answer in intervention.

(3) "Plaintiff" includes a cross-complainant or a party who files a complaint in intervention.

(4) "Prevailing party" includes the party with a net monetary recovery, a defendant in whose favor a dismissal is entered, a defendant where neither plaintiff nor defendant obtains any relief, and a defendant as against those plaintiffs who do not recover any relief against that defendant. If any party recovers other than monetary relief and in situations other than as specified, the "prevailing party" shall be as determined by the court, and under those circumstances, the court, in its discretion, may allow costs or not and, if allowed, may apportion costs between the parties on the same or adverse sides pursuant to rules adopted under Section 1034.

(b) Except as otherwise expressly provided by statute, a prevailing party is entitled as a matter of right to recover costs in any action or proceeding.

(c) Nothing in this section shall prohibit parties from stipulating to alternative procedures for awarding costs in the litigation pursuant to rules adopted under Section 1034.

Amended by Stats 2017 ch 131 (AB 1693),s 2, eff. 1/1/2018.

Section 1033 - Limited civil cases

(a) Costs or any portion of claimed costs shall be as determined by the court in its discretion in a case other than a limited civil case in accordance with Section 1034 where the prevailing party recovers a judgment that could have been rendered in a limited civil case.

(b) When a prevailing plaintiff in a limited civil case recovers less than the amount prescribed by law as the maximum limitation upon the jurisdiction of the small claims court, the following shall apply:

(1) When the party could have brought the action in the small claims division but did not do so, the court may, in its discretion, allow or deny costs to the prevailing party, or may allow costs in part in any amount as it deems proper.

(2) When the party could not have brought the action in the small claims court, costs and necessary disbursements shall be limited to the actual cost of the filing fee, the actual cost of service of process, and, when otherwise specifically allowed by law, reasonable attorneys' fees. However, those costs shall only be awarded to the plaintiff if the court is satisfied that prior to the commencement of the action, the plaintiff informed the defendant in writing of the intended legal action against the defendant and that legal action could result in a judgment against the defendant that would include the costs and necessary disbursements allowed by this paragraph.

Amended by Stats. 1998, Ch. 931, Sec. 107. Effective September 28, 1998.

Section 1033.5 - Items allowable as costs

(a) The following items are allowable as costs under Section 1032:

(1) Filing, motion, and jury fees.

(2) Juror food and lodging while they are kept together during trial and after the jury retires for deliberation.

(3)

(A) Taking, video recording, and transcribing necessary depositions, including an original and one copy of those taken by the claimant and one copy of depositions taken by the party against whom costs are allowed.

(B) Fees of a certified or registered interpreter for the deposition of a party or witness who does not proficiently speak or understand the English language.

(C) Travel expenses to attend depositions.

(4) Service of process by a public officer, registered process server, or other means, as follows:

(A) When service is by a public officer, the recoverable cost is the fee authorized by law at the time of service.

(B) If service is by a process server registered pursuant to Chapter 16 (commencing with Section 22350) of Division 8 of the Business and Professions Code, the recoverable cost is the amount actually incurred in effecting service, including, but not limited to, a stakeout or other means employed in locating the person to be served, unless those charges are successfully challenged by a party to the action.

(C) When service is by publication, the recoverable cost is the sum actually incurred in effecting service.

(D) When service is by a means other than that set forth in subparagraph (A), (B), or (C), the recoverable cost is the lesser of the sum actually incurred, or the amount allowed to a public officer in this state for that service, except that the court may allow the sum actually incurred in effecting service upon application pursuant to paragraph (4) of subdivision (c).

(5) Expenses of attachment including keeper's fees.

(6) Premiums on necessary surety bonds.

(7) Ordinary witness fees pursuant to Section 68093 of the Government Code.

(8) Fees of expert witnesses ordered by the court.

(9) Transcripts of court proceedings ordered by the court.

(10) Attorney's fees, when authorized by any of the following:

(A) Contract.

(B) Statute.

(C) Law.

(11) Court reporter fees as established by statute.

(12) Court interpreter fees for a qualified court interpreter authorized by the court for an indigent person represented by a qualified legal services project, as defined in Section 6213 of the Business and Professions Code, or a pro bono attorney, as defined in Section 8030.4 of the Business and Professions Code.

(13) Models, the enlargements of exhibits and photocopies of exhibits, and the electronic presentation of exhibits, including costs of rental equipment and electronic formatting, may be allowed if they were reasonably helpful to aid the trier of fact.

(14) Fees for the electronic filing or service of documents through an electronic filing service provider if a court requires or orders electronic filing or service of documents.

(15) Fees for the hosting of electronic documents if a court requires or orders a party to have documents hosted by an electronic filing service provider. This paragraph shall become inoperative on January 1, 2022.

(16) Any other item that is required to be awarded to the prevailing party pursuant to statute as an incident to prevailing in the action at trial or on appeal.

(b) The following items are not allowable as costs, except when expressly authorized by law:

(1) Fees of experts not ordered by the court.

(2) Investigation expenses in preparing the case for trial.

(3) Postage, telephone, and photocopying charges, except for exhibits.

(4) Costs in investigation of jurors or in preparation for voir dire.

(5) Transcripts of court proceedings not ordered by the court.

(c) An award of costs shall be subject to the following:

(1) Costs are allowable if incurred, whether or not paid.

(2) Allowable costs shall be reasonably necessary to the conduct of the litigation rather than merely convenient or beneficial to its preparation.

(3) Allowable costs shall be reasonable in amount.

(4) Items not mentioned in this section and items assessed upon application may be allowed or denied in the court's discretion.

(5)

(A) If a statute of this state refers to the award of "costs and attorney's fees," attorney's fees are an item and component of the costs to be awarded and are allowable as costs pursuant to subparagraph (B) of paragraph (10) of subdivision (a). A claim not based upon the court's established schedule of attorney's fees for actions on a contract shall bear the burden of proof. Attorney's fees allowable as costs pursuant to subparagraph (B) of paragraph (10) of subdivision (a) may be fixed as follows:

(i) upon a noticed motion,

(ii) at the time a statement of decision is rendered,

(iii) upon application supported by affidavit made concurrently with a claim for other costs, or

(iv) upon entry of default judgment. Attorney's fees allowable as costs pursuant to subparagraph (A) or (C) of paragraph (10) of subdivision (a) shall be fixed either upon a noticed motion or upon entry of a default judgment, unless otherwise provided by stipulation of the parties.

(B) Attorney's fees awarded pursuant to Section 1717 of the Civil Code are allowable costs under Section 1032 as authorized by subparagraph (A) of paragraph (10) of subdivision (a).

Amended by Stats 2017 ch 583 (AB 828),s 1, eff. 1/1/2018.
Amended by Stats 2016 ch 461 (AB 2244),s 2, eff. 1/1/2017.
Amended by Stats 2015 ch 90 (AB 1002),s 1, eff. 1/1/2016.
Amended by Stats 2012 ch 758 (AB 2684),s 2, eff. 1/1/2013.
Amended by Stats 2011 ch 409 (AB 1403),s 3, eff. 1/1/2012.
Amended by Stats 2009 ch 88 (AB 176),s 17, eff. 1/1/2010.

Section 1034 - Prejudgment costs

(a) Prejudgment costs allowable under this chapter shall be claimed and contested in accordance with rules adopted by the Judicial Council.

(b) The Judicial Council shall establish by rule allowable costs on appeal and the procedure for claiming those costs.

Repealed and added by Stats. 1986, Ch. 377, Sec. 15.

Section 1034.5 - Plaintiff recovering judgment for possession in unlawful detainer proceedings

In unlawful detainer proceedings, the plaintiff who recovers judgment for possession of premises, and who advances or pays to the sheriff or marshal the expenses required for the eviction of any persons in possession or occupancy of the premises and the personal property of such persons, shall, after being advised by the sheriff or marshal of the exact amount necessarily used and expended to effect the eviction, be allowed to file a request for the same pursuant to rules adopted by the Judicial Council.
Amended by Stats. 1986, Ch. 377, Sec. 16.

Section 1036 - Inverse condemnation proceeding
In any inverse condemnation proceeding, the court rendering judgment for the plaintiff by awarding compensation, or the attorney representing the public entity who effects a settlement of that proceeding, shall determine and award or allow to the plaintiff, as a part of that judgment or settlement, a sum that will, in the opinion of the court, reimburse the plaintiff's reasonable costs, disbursements, and expenses, including reasonable attorney, appraisal, and engineering fees, actually incurred because of that proceeding in the trial court or in any appellate proceeding in which the plaintiff prevails on any issue in that proceeding.
Amended by Stats. 1995, Ch. 181, Sec. 1. Effective January 1, 1996.

Section 1038 - Reasonable cause and good faith belief as to justifiable controversy determination in Government Claims Act proceedings
(a) In any civil proceeding under the Government Claims Act (Division 3.6 (commencing with Section 810) of Title 1 of the Government Code) or for express or implied indemnity or for contribution in any civil action, the court, upon motion of the defendant or cross-defendant, shall, at the time of the granting of any summary judgment, motion for directed verdict, motion for judgment under Section 631.8, or any nonsuit dismissing the moving party other than the plaintiff, petitioner, cross-complainant, or intervenor, or at a later time set forth by rule of the Judicial Council adopted under Section 1034, determine whether or not the plaintiff, petitioner, cross-complainant, or intervenor brought the proceeding with reasonable cause and in the good faith belief that there was a justifiable controversy under the facts and law which warranted the filing of the complaint, petition, cross-complaint, or complaint or answer in intervention. If the court should determine that the proceeding was not brought in good faith and with reasonable cause, an additional issue shall be decided as to the defense costs reasonably and necessarily incurred by the party or parties opposing the proceeding, and the court shall render judgment in favor of that party in the amount of all reasonable and necessary defense costs, in addition to those costs normally awarded to the prevailing party. An award of defense costs under this section shall not be made except on notice contained in a party's papers and an opportunity to be heard.
(b) "Defense costs," as used in this section, shall include reasonable attorney's fees, expert witness fees, the expense of services of experts, advisers, and consultants in defense of the proceeding, and where reasonably and necessarily incurred in defending the proceeding.
(c) This section shall be applicable only on motion made before the discharge of the jury or entry of judgment, and any party requesting the relief pursuant to this section waives any right to seek damages for malicious prosecution. Failure to make the motion shall not be deemed a waiver of the right to pursue a malicious prosecution action.
(d) This section shall only apply if the defendant or cross-defendant has made a motion for summary judgment, judgment under Section 631.8, directed verdict, or nonsuit and the motion is granted.
Amended by Stats 2017 ch 131 (AB 1693),s 3, eff. 1/1/2018.
Amended by Stats 2012 ch 759 (AB 2690),s 2, eff. 1/1/2013.

Chapter 7 - GENERAL PROVISIONS

Section 1045 - Original pleading or paper lost
If an original pleading or paper be lost, the Court may authorize a copy thereof to be filed and used instead of the original.
Enacted 1872.

Section 1046 - Affidavit, notice, other paper without tile of action or without defective title
An affidavit, notice, or other paper, without the title of the action or proceeding in which it is made, or with a defective title, is as valid and effectual for any purpose as if duly entitled, if it intelligibly refers to the action or proceeding.
Amended by Stats. 1981, Ch. 714, Sec. 71.

Section 1046a - Force and effect of papers filed in quiet title action lost or destroyed by flood, fire, earthquake
In all cases brought under the provisions of any act providing for the establishment and quieting of title to real property in cases where the public records in the office of the county recorder have been, or shall hereafter be, lost or destroyed, in whole or in any material part by flood, fire or earthquake, all papers filed under order of court nunc pro tunc as of the date when they should have been filed, shall have the same force and effect as if filed on the date when they should have been filed.
Added by Stats. 1909, Ch. 686.

Section 1047 - Successive actions upon same contract or transaction
Successive actions may be maintained upon the same contract or transaction, whenever, after the former action, a new cause of action arises therefrom.
Enacted 1872.

Section 1048 - Joint hearing ordered; separate trial ordered
(a) When actions involving a common question of law or fact are pending before the court, it may order a joint hearing or trial of any or all the matters in issue in the actions; it may order all the actions consolidated and it may make such orders concerning proceedings therein as may tend to avoid unnecessary costs or delay.
(b) The court, in furtherance of convenience or to avoid prejudice, or when separate trials will be conducive to expedition and economy, may order a separate trial of any cause of action, including a cause of action asserted in a cross-complaint, or of any separate issue or of any number of causes of action or issues, preserving the right of trial by jury required by the Constitution or a statute of this state or of the United States.
Amended by Stats. 1971, Ch. 244.

Section 1049 - Action deemed to be pending
An action is deemed to be pending from the time of its commencement until its final determination upon appeal, or until the time for appeal has passed, unless the judgment is sooner satisfied.
Enacted 1872.

Section 1050 - Action against one person to determine adverse claim and against two or more to compel one to satisfy debt due other
An action may be brought by one person against another for the purpose of determining an adverse claim, which the latter makes against the former for money or property upon an alleged obligation; and also against two or more persons, for the purpose of compelling one to satisfy a debt due to the other, for which plaintiff is bound as a surety.
Enacted 1872.

Section 1052 - [Repealed]
Repealed by Stats 2002 ch 784 (SB 1316),s 71, eff. 1/1/2003.

Section 1052.5 - [Repealed]
Repealed by Stats 2002 ch 784 (SB 1316),s 72, eff. 1/1/2003.

Section 1053 - Authority of two of three referees to do any act
When there are three referees all must meet, but two of them may do any act which might be done by all.
Amended by Stats. 1961, Ch. 461.

Section 1054 - Extension of time allowed to do act
(a) When an act to be done, as provided in this code, relates to the pleadings in the action, or the preparation of bills of exceptions, or of amendments thereto, or to the service of notices other than of appeal and of intention to move for a new trial, the time allowed therefor, unless otherwise expressly provided, may be extended, upon good cause shown, by the judge of the court in which the action is pending, or by the judge who presided at the trial of the action; but the extension so allowed shall not exceed 30 days, without the consent of the adverse party.
(b) In all cases in which the court or judge is authorized by this section to grant an extension of time, the extension of time shall be granted when all attorneys of record of parties who have appeared in the action agree in writing to the extension of time, and any extension of time previously granted by stipulation of all attorneys of record of parties who have appeared in the action shall not be included in the computation of the 30-day limitation upon extensions of time allowed by the court or judge.
Amended by Stats. 1982, Ch. 517, Sec. 168.

Section 1054.1 - Extension of time allowed to do act in action or proceeding in state court or before state administrative agency
(a) When an act to be done in any action or proceeding in any court of this state or before any state administrative agency, as provided by law or rule, relates to the pleadings in the action, or the preparation of bills of exceptions, or of amendments thereto, or to the service of notices (other than of appeal, of intention to move for a new trial, and of intention to move to vacate a judgment), and such act is not a motion for a judgment notwithstanding the verdict, the time allowed therefor, unless otherwise expressly provided, shall be extended to a date certain by the judges of the court or by the agency in which the action or proceeding is pending, or by the judge who presided at the trial of the action, when it appears to the judge of any court or to the agency to whom the application is made that an attorney of record for the party applying for the extension is a Member of the Legislature of this state, and that the Legislature is in session or in recess not exceeding a recess of 40 days or that a legislative committee of which the attorney is a duly appointed member is meeting or is to meet within a period which the court or agency finds does not exceed the time reasonably necessary to enable the member to reach the committee meeting by the ordinary mode of travel. When the Legislature is in session or in recess, extension shall be to a date not less than 30 days next following the final adjournment of the Legislature or the commencement of a recess of more than 40 days. If a date is available during recess, extension shall be to such earlier date. When a legislative committee is meeting or is to meet within a period which the court or agency finds does not exceed the time reasonably necessary to enable the member to reach the committee meeting by the ordinary mode of travel, extension shall be for such period as the court or agency finds will be reasonably necessary to enable the member to perform the act to be done in the action or proceeding, unless the extension would expire when the Legislature is to be in session; and in that case the extension shall be to a date not less than 30 days following the final adjournment of the Legislature or the commencement of a recess of more than 40 days. If the act may be reasonably done by the member within the recess, continuance shall be to such earlier date. However, any postponement granted under the provisions of this section shall suspend for the same period of time as the postponement, the running of any period of time for any ruling or proceeding by a court, board, commission, or officer, or for the performance by any party of any act affected by the postponement.
(b) Extension of time pursuant to this section is mandatory unless the court determines that the extension would defeat or abridge a right to relief pendente lite in a paternity action or a right to invoke a provisional remedy such as pendente lite support in a domestic relations controversy, attachment and sale of perishable goods, receivership of a failing business, and temporary restraining order or preliminary injunction, and that the continuance should not be granted.
Amended by Stats. 1982, Ch. 517, Sec. 169.

Section 1055 - Judgment against persons executing bond or covenant of indemnity
If an action is brought against any officer or person for an act for the doing of which he had theretofore received any valid bond or convenant of indemnity, and he gives seasonable notice thereof in writing to the persons who executed such bond or covenant, and permits them to conduct the defense of such action, the judgment recovered therein is conclusive evidence against the persons so notified; and the court may, on motion of the defendant, upon notice of five days, and upon proof of such bond or covenant, and of such notice and permission, enter judgment against them for the amount so recovered and costs.
Amended by Stats. 1907, Ch. 246.

Chapter 8 - DECLARATORY RELIEF

Section 1060 - Generally
Any person interested under a written instrument, excluding a will or a trust, or under a contract, or who desires a declaration of his or her rights or duties with respect to another, or in respect to, in, over or upon property, or with respect to the location of the natural channel of a watercourse, may, in cases of actual controversy relating to the legal rights and duties of the respective parties, bring an original action or cross-complaint in the superior court for a declaration of his or her rights and duties in the premises, including a determination of any question of construction or validity arising under the instrument or contract. He or she may ask for a declaration of rights or duties, either alone or with other relief; and the court may make a binding declaration of these rights or duties, whether or not further relief is or could be claimed at the time. The declaration may be either affirmative or negative in form and effect, and the declaration shall have the force of a final judgment. The declaration may be had before there has been any breach of the obligation in respect to which said declaration is sought.
Amended by Stats 2002 ch 784 (SB 1316),s 73, eff. 1/1/2003.

Section 1060.5 - Action against Franchise tax Board to determine residence for purposes of Personal Income Tax Law
Any individual claiming to be a nonresident of the State of California for the purposes of the Personal Income Tax Law may commence an action in the Superior Court in the County of Sacramento, or in the County of Los Angeles, or in the City and County of San Francisco, against the Franchise Tax Board to determine the fact of his or her residence in this state under the conditions and circumstances set forth in Section 19381 of the Revenue and Taxation Code.
Amended by Stats. 1996, Ch. 952, Sec. 1. Effective January 1, 1997.

Section 1061 - Declaration or determinations not necessary or proper
The court may refuse to exercise the power granted by this chapter in any case where its declaration or determination is not necessary or proper at the time under all the circumstances.
Added by Stats. 1921, Ch. 463.

Section 1062 - Remedies cumulative
The remedies provided by this chapter are cumulative, and shall not be construed as restricting any remedy, provisional or otherwise, provided by law for the benefit of any party to such action, and no judgment under this chapter shall preclude any party from obtaining additional relief based upon the same facts.
Added by Stats. 1921, Ch. 463.

Section 1062.3 - Precedence of actions
(a) Except as provided in subdivision (b), actions brought under the provisions of this chapter shall be set for trial at the earliest possible date and shall take precedence over all other cases, except older matters of the same character and matters to which special precedence may be given by law.
(b) Any action brought under the provisions of this chapter in which the plaintiff seeks any relief, in addition to a declaration of rights and duties, shall take such precedence only upon noticed motion and a showing that the action requires a speedy trial.
Added by renumbering Section 1062a by Stats. 1980, Ch. 676, Sec. 66.

Section 1062.5 - Action by insurer issuing policies of professional liability insurance to health care providers

Any insurer who issues policies of professional liability insurance to health care providers for professional negligence, as defined in Chapter 1 as amended by Chapter 2, Statutes of 1975, Second Extraordinary Session, any health care provider covered by such a policy, or any potentially aggrieved person, may bring an action in the superior court for a declaration of its, his, or her rights, duties, and obligations under Chapter 1 as amended by Chapter 2, Statutes of 1975, Second Extraordinary Session.

The court shall permit any of the following persons to intervene in the action:

(1) The Attorney General.

(2) Any other person whose appearance is determined by the court to be essential to a complete determination or settlement of any issues in the action. The action shall be commenced in the superior court in the county in which the Attorney General is required to reside and keep his office pursuant to Section 1060 of the Government Code.

The action shall be set for trial at the earliest possible date and shall take precedence over all cases other than those in which the state is a party. The court may make a binding declaration of the rights, duties, and obligations of the insurer, whether or not further relief is or could be claimed at the time. The declaration may be affirmative or negative in form and effect and shall have the force and effect of a final judgment.

If the declaration is appealed, the appeal shall be given precedence in the court of appeal and Supreme Court and placed on the calendar in the order of its date of issue immediately following cases in which the state is a party.

The remedy established by this section is cumulative, and shall not be construed as restricting any remedy established for the benefit of any party to the action by any other provision of law. No declaration under this section shall preclude any party from obtaining additional relief based upon the same facts.

Added by Stats. 1979, Ch. 373.

Chapter 9 - ACTIONS TO ENFORCE REAL PROPERTY AND MOBILEHOME SALES AGREEMENTS

Section 1062.10 - Recording of agreement required to maintain action

No person or legal entity may maintain an action in any court in this state to enforce the terms of a real property sales contract as defined in Section 2985 of the Civil Code or a conditional sale contract on a mobilehome subject to local property taxation and subject to Division 13 (commencing with Section 18000) of Part 2 of the Health and Safety Code, providing for a change in ownership of real property or of a mobilehome subject to local property taxation until the agreement is duly recorded by the county recorder or the change-in-ownership statement required by Section 480 of the Revenue and Taxation Code is filed as provided in that section.

This section shall apply to the enforcement of those agreements which are alleged to have transferred ownership of real property or of a mobilehome subject to property taxation which are entered into after January 1, 1986.

Amended by Stats. 1986, Ch. 62, Sec. 1. Effective April 23, 1986.

Chapter 10 - COMPUTER ASSISTANCE

Section 1062.20 - Interactive computer system to assist pro per litigant

(a) In accordance with rules and policy of the Judicial Council, each court may establish and operate an interactive computer system to enable and assist a pro per litigant to prepare standardized pro per court documents for use in the following civil actions:

   (1) Enforcement of court orders, including orders for visitation, child custody, and property division.

   (2) Landlord and tenant actions.

   (3) Uncontested dissolution of marriage.

   (4) Probate of a will.

(b) The computer system may also provide standardized information to users, including, but not limited to, information regarding calculations for child and spousal support payments that meet the requirements described in Section 3830 of the Family Code, court procedures, rights and responsibilities of landlords and tenants, and alternative dispute resolution.

(c) The court may contract with a private entity to establish and operate the program and collect any fees described in subdivision (d).

(d) The court may establish and collect fees from the program not to exceed the reasonable costs to establish and operate the program.

Added by Stats. 1995, Ch. 507, Sec. 1. Effective January 1, 1996.

Part 3 - OF SPECIAL PROCEEDINGS OF A CIVIL NATURE

Title - PRELIMINARY PROVISIONS

Section 1063 - Parties

The party prosecuting a special proceeding may be known as the plaintiff, and the adverse party as the defendant.

Section 1064 - Judgment; motion and order

A judgment in a special proceeding is the final determination of the rights of the parties therein. The definitions of a motion and an order in a civil action are applicable to similar acts in a special proceeding.

Title 1 - OF WRITS OF REVIEW, MANDATE, AND PROHIBITION

Chapter 1 - WRIT OF REVIEW

Section 1067 - Writ of certiorari denominated writ of review

Section Ten Hundred and Sixty-seven. The writ of certiorari may be denominated the writ of review.

Amended by Code Amendments 1873-74, Ch. 383.

Section 1068 - When writ of review granted

(a) A writ of review may be granted by any court when an inferior tribunal, board, or officer, exercising judicial functions, has exceeded the jurisdiction of such tribunal, board, or officer, and there is no appeal, nor, in the judgment of the court, any plain, speedy, and adequate remedy.

(b) The appellate division of the superior court may grant a writ of review directed to the superior court in a limited civil case or in a misdemeanor or infraction case. Where the appellate division grants a writ of review directed to the superior court, the superior court is an inferior tribunal for purposes of this chapter.

Amended by Stats 2002 ch 784 (SB 1316),s 74, eff. 1/1/2003.

Previously Amended September 7, 1999 (Bill Number: SB 210) (Chapter 344).

Section 1069 - Application, notice, granting writ without notice

The application must be made on the verified petition of the party beneficially interested, and the court may require a notice of the application to be given to the adverse party, or may grant an order to show cause why it should not be allowed, or may grant the writ without notice.

Amended by Stats. 1907, Ch. 328.

Section 1069.1 - Return by demurrer or answer

The provisions of Section 1089 as to a return by demurrer or answer apply to a proceeding pursuant to this chapter.

Added by Stats. 1971, Ch. 1475.

Section 1070 - To whom writ directed

The writ may be directed to the inferior tribunal, Board, or officer, or to any other person having the custody of the record or proceedings to be certified. When directed to a tribunal, the Clerk, if there be one, must return the writ with the transcript required.
Enacted 1872.

Section 1071 - Command of writ
The writ of review must command the party to whom it is directed to certify fully to the court issuing the writ at a time and place then or thereafter specified by court order a transcript of the record and proceedings (describing or referring to them with convenient certainty), that the same may be reviewed by the court; and requiring the party, in the meantime, to desist from further proceedings in the matter to be reviewed.
Amended by Stats. 1963, Ch. 461.

Section 1072 - Words requiring stay
If a stay of proceedings be not intended, the words requiring the stay must be omitted from the writ; these words may be inserted or omitted, in the sound discretion of the Court, but if omitted, the power of the inferior Court or officer is not suspended or the proceedings stayed.
Enacted 1872.

Section 1073 - Service of writ
The writ must be served in the same manner as a summons in civil action, except when otherwise expressly directed by the Court.
Enacted 1872.

Section 1074 - Review upon writ
The review upon this writ cannot be extended further than to determine whether the inferior tribunal, Board, or officer has regularly pursued the authority of such tribunal, Board, or officer.
Enacted 1872.

Section 1075 - Return of writ
If the return of the writ be defective, the Court may order a further return to be made. When a full return has been made, the Court must hear the parties, or such of them as may attend for that purpose, and may thereupon give judgment, either affirming or annulling, or modifying the proceedings below.
Enacted 1872.

Section 1076 - Transmission of copy of judgment
A copy of the judgment, signed by the Clerk, must be transmitted to the inferior tribunal, Board, or officer having the custody of the record or proceeding certified up.
Enacted 1872.

Section 1077 - Judgment roll
A copy of the judgment, signed by the Clerk, entered upon or attached to the writ and return, constitute the judgment roll.
Enacted 1872.

Chapter 2 - WRIT OF MANDATE

Section 1084 - Denominated writ of mandate
The writ of mandamus may be denominated a writ of mandate.
Amended by Stats 2016 ch 86 (SB 1171),s 39, eff. 1/1/2017.

Section 1085 - When writ may be issued
(a) A writ of mandate may be issued by any court to any inferior tribunal, corporation, board, or person, to compel the performance of an act which the law specially enjoins, as a duty resulting from an office, trust, or station, or to compel the admission of a party to the use and enjoyment of a right or office to which the party is entitled, and from which the party is unlawfully precluded by that inferior tribunal, corporation, board, or person.
(b) The appellate division of the superior court may grant a writ of mandate directed to the superior court in a limited civil case or in a misdemeanor or infraction case. Where the appellate division grants a writ of mandate directed to the superior court, the superior court is an inferior tribunal for purposes of this chapter.
Amended by Stats 2010 ch 212 (AB 2767),s 2, eff. 1/1/2011.
Amended by Stats 2002 ch 784 (SB 1316),s 75, eff. 1/1/2003.
Previously Amended September 7, 1999 (Bill Number: SB 210) (Chapter 344).

Section 1085.5 - Action or proceeding attacking activity of Director of Food and Agriculture
Notwithstanding this chapter, in any action or proceeding to attack, review, set aside, void, or annul the activity of the Director of Food and Agriculture under Division 4 (commencing with Section 5001) or Division 5 (commencing with Section 9101) of the Food and Agricultural Code, the procedure for issuance of a writ of mandate shall be in accordance with Chapter 1.5 (commencing with Section 5051) of Part 1 of Division 4 of that code.
Amended by Stats. 1987, Ch. 1284, Sec. 1.

Section 1086 - Cases in which writ must issue; issued upon verified petition of party beneficially interested
The writ must be issued in all cases where there is not a plain, speedy, and adequate remedy, in the ordinary course of law. It must be issued upon the verified petition of the party beneficially interested.
Amended by Stats. 1907, Ch. 244.

Section 1087 - Writ either alternative or peremptory
The writ may be either alternative or peremptory. The alternative writ must command the party to whom it is directed immediately after the receipt of the writ, or at some other specified time, to do the act required to be performed, or to show cause before the court at a time and place then or thereafter specified by court order why he has not done so. The peremptory writ must be in a similar form, except that the words requiring the party to show cause why he has not done as commanded must be omitted.
Amended by Stats. 1963, Ch. 461.

Section 1088 - Application made without notice and writ allowed; application upon due notice and writ allowed
When the application to the court is made without notice to the adverse party, and the writ is allowed, the alternative must be first issued; but if the application is upon due notice and the writ is allowed, the peremptory may be issued in the first instance. With the alternative writ and also with any notice of an intention to apply for the writ, there must be served on each person against whom the writ is sought a copy of the petition. The notice of the application, when given, must be at least ten days. The writ cannot be granted by default. The case must be heard by the court, whether the adverse party appears or not.
Amended by Stats. 1907, Ch. 244.

Section 1088.5 - Proof of service of copy of petition if no alternative writ sought
In a trial court, if no alternative writ is sought, proof of service of a copy of the petition need not accompany the application for a writ at the time of filing, but proof of service of a copy of the filed petition must be lodged with the court prior to a hearing or any action by the court.
Amended by Stats. 1983, Ch. 818, Sec. 1.

Section 1089 - Return by demurrer, verified answer or both

On the date for return of the alternative writ, or on which the application for the writ is noticed, or, if the Judicial Council shall adopt rules relating to the return and answer, then at the time provided by those rules, the party upon whom the writ or notice has been served may make a return by demurrer, verified answer or both. If the return is by demurrer alone, the court may allow an answer to be filed within such time as it may designate. Nothing in this section affects rules of the Judicial Council governing original writ proceedings in reviewing courts.
Amended by Stats. 1971, Ch. 1475.

Section 1089.5 - Time to answer or otherwise respond
Where a petition for writ of mandate is filed in the trial court pursuant to Section 1088.5, and where a record of the proceedings to be reviewed has been filed with the petition or where no record of a proceeding is required, the respondent shall answer or otherwise respond within 30 days after service of the petition. However, where a record of the proceeding to be reviewed has been requested pursuant to Section 11523 of the Government Code, or otherwise, and has not been filed with the petition, the party upon whom the petition has been served, including any real party in interest, shall answer or otherwise respond within 30 days following receipt of a copy of the record.
Amended by Stats. 1983, Ch. 818, Sec. 2.

Section 1090 - Question of fact ordered tried before jury
If a return be made, which raises a question as to a matter of fact essential to the determination of the motion, and affecting the substantial rights of the parties, and upon the supposed truth of the allegation of which the application for the writ is based, the court may, in its discretion, order the question to be tried before a jury, and postpone the argument until such trial can be had, and the verdict certified to the court. The question to be tried must be distinctly stated in the order for trial, and the county must be designated in which the same shall be had. The order may also direct the jury to assess any damages which the applicant may have sustained, in case they find for him.
Amended by Stats. 1971, Ch. 1475.

Section 1091 - Objection to sufficiency of return
On the trial, the applicant is not precluded by the return from any valid objection to its sufficiency, and may countervail it by proof either in direct denial or by way of avoidance.
Amended by Stats. 1971, Ch. 1475.

Section 1092 - Proper court for making motion for new trial
The motion for new trial must be made in the Court in which the issue of fact is tried.
Enacted 1872.

Section 1093 - Certified copy of verdict or denial
If no notice of a motion for a new trial be given, or if given, the motion be denied, the Clerk, within five days after rendition of the verdict or denial of the motion, must transmit to the Court in which the application for the writ is pending, a certified copy of the verdict attached to the order of trial; after which either party may bring on the argument of the application, upon reasonable notice to the adverse party.
Enacted 1872.

Section 1094 - Case heard on papers of applicant if no return made; case determined by notice motion
If no return be made, the case may be heard on the papers of the applicant. If the return raises only questions of law, or puts in issue immaterial statements, not affecting the substantial rights of the parties, the court must proceed to hear or fix a day for hearing the argument of the case.
If a petition for a writ of mandate filed pursuant to Section 1088.5 presents no triable issue of fact or is based solely on an administrative record, the matter may be determined by the court by noticed motion of any party for a judgment on the peremptory writ.
Amended by Stats. 1982, Ch. 193, Sec. 3. Effective May 5, 1982.

Section 1094.5 - Writ issued for purpose of inquiring into validity of final administrative order or decision made in proceeding requiring hearing
(a) Where the writ is issued for the purpose of inquiring into the validity of any final administrative order or decision made as the result of a proceeding in which by law a hearing is required to be given, evidence is required to be taken, and discretion in the determination of facts is vested in the inferior tribunal, corporation, board, or officer, the case shall be heard by the court sitting without a jury. All or part of the record of the proceedings before the inferior tribunal, corporation, board, or officer may be filed with the petition, may be filed with respondent's points and authorities, or may be ordered to be filed by the court. Except when otherwise prescribed by statute, the cost of preparing the record shall be borne by the petitioner. Where the petitioner has proceeded pursuant to Article 6 (commencing with Section 68630) of Chapter 2 of Title 8 of the Government Code and the Rules of Court implementing that section and where the transcript is necessary to a proper review of the administrative proceedings, the cost of preparing the transcript shall be borne by the respondent. Where the party seeking the writ has proceeded pursuant to Section 1088.5, the administrative record shall be filed as expeditiously as possible, and may be filed with the petition, or by the respondent after payment of the costs by the petitioner, where required, or as otherwise directed by the court. If the expense of preparing all or any part of the record has been borne by the prevailing party, the expense shall be taxable as costs.
(b) The inquiry in such a case shall extend to the questions whether the respondent has proceeded without, or in excess of, jurisdiction; whether there was a fair trial; and whether there was any prejudicial abuse of discretion. Abuse of discretion is established if the respondent has not proceeded in the manner required by law, the order or decision is not supported by the findings, or the findings are not supported by the evidence.
(c) Where it is claimed that the findings are not supported by the evidence, in cases in which the court is authorized by law to exercise its independent judgment on the evidence, abuse of discretion is established if the court determines that the findings are not supported by the weight of the evidence. In all other cases, abuse of discretion is established if the court determines that the findings are not supported by substantial evidence in the light of the whole record.
(d) Notwithstanding subdivision (c), in cases arising from private hospital boards or boards of directors of districts organized pursuant to the Local Health Care District Law (Chapter 1 (commencing with Section 32000) of Division 23 of the Health and Safety Code) or governing bodies of municipal hospitals formed pursuant to Article 7 (commencing with Section 37600) or Article 8 (commencing with Section 37650) of Chapter 5 of Part 2 of Division 3 of Title 4 of the Government Code, abuse of discretion is established if the court determines that the findings are not supported by substantial evidence in the light of the whole record. However, in all cases in which the petition alleges discriminatory actions prohibited by Section 1316 of the Health and Safety Code, and the plaintiff makes a preliminary showing of substantial evidence in support of that allegation, the court shall exercise its independent judgment on the evidence and abuse of discretion shall be established if the court determines that the findings are not supported by the weight of the evidence.
(e) Where the court finds that there is relevant evidence that, in the exercise of reasonable diligence, could not have been produced or that was improperly excluded at the hearing before respondent, it may enter judgment as provided in subdivision (f) remanding the case to be reconsidered in the light of that evidence; or, in cases in which the court is authorized by law to exercise its independent judgment on the evidence, the court may admit the evidence at the hearing on the writ without remanding the case.
(f) The court shall enter judgment either commanding respondent to set aside the order or decision, or denying the writ. Where the judgment commands that the order or decision be set aside, it may order the reconsideration of the case in light of the court's opinion and judgment and may order respondent to take such further action as is specially enjoined upon it by law, but the judgment shall not limit or control in any way the discretion legally vested in the respondent.
(g) Except as provided in subdivision (h), the court in which proceedings under this section are instituted may stay the operation of the administrative order or decision pending the judgment of the court, or until the filing of a notice of appeal from the judgment or until the

expiration of the time for filing the notice, whichever occurs first. However, no such stay shall be imposed or continued if the court is satisfied that it is against the public interest. The application for the stay shall be accompanied by proof of service of a copy of the application on the respondent. Service shall be made in the manner provided by Title 4.5 (commencing with Section 405) of Part 2 or Chapter 5 (commencing with Section 1010) of Title 14 of Part 2. If an appeal is taken from a denial of the writ, the order or decision of the agency shall not be stayed except upon the order of the court to which the appeal is taken. However, in cases where a stay is in effect at the time of filing the notice of appeal, the stay shall be continued by operation of law for a period of 20 days from the filing of the notice. If an appeal is taken from the granting of the writ, the order or decision of the agency is stayed pending the determination of the appeal unless the court to which the appeal is taken shall otherwise order. Where any final administrative order or decision is the subject of proceedings under this section, if the petition shall have been filed while the penalty imposed is in full force and effect, the determination shall not be considered to have become moot in cases where the penalty imposed by the administrative agency has been completed or complied with during the pendency of the proceedings.

(h)

(1) The court in which proceedings under this section are instituted may stay the operation of the administrative order or decision of any licensed hospital or any state agency made after a hearing required by statute to be conducted under the Administrative Procedure Act, as set forth in Chapter 5 (commencing with Section 11500) of Part 1 of Division 3 of Title 2 of the Government Code, conducted by the agency itself or an administrative law judge on the staff of the Office of Administrative Hearings pending the judgment of the court, or until the filing of a notice of appeal from the judgment or until the expiration of the time for filing the notice, whichever occurs first. However, the stay shall not be imposed or continued unless the court is satisfied that the public interest will not suffer and that the licensed hospital or agency is unlikely to prevail ultimately on the merits. The application for the stay shall be accompanied by proof of service of a copy of the application on the respondent. Service shall be made in the manner provided by Title 4.5 (commencing with Section 405) of Part 2 or Chapter 5 (commencing with Section 1010) of Title 14 of Part 2.

(2) The standard set forth in this subdivision for obtaining a stay shall apply to any administrative order or decision of an agency that issues licenses pursuant to Division 2 (commencing with Section 500) of the Business and Professions Code or pursuant to the Osteopathic Initiative Act or the Chiropractic Initiative Act. With respect to orders or decisions of other state agencies, the standard in this subdivision shall apply only when the agency has adopted the proposed decision of the administrative law judge in its entirety or has adopted the proposed decision but reduced the proposed penalty pursuant to subdivision (c) of Section 11517 of the Government Code; otherwise the standard in subdivision (g) shall apply.

(3) If an appeal is taken from a denial of the writ, the order or decision of the hospital or agency shall not be stayed except upon the order of the court to which the appeal is taken. However, in cases where a stay is in effect at the time of filing the notice of appeal, the stay shall be continued by operation of law for a period of 20 days from the filing of the notice. If an appeal is taken from the granting of the writ, the order or decision of the hospital or agency is stayed pending the determination of the appeal unless the court to which the appeal is taken shall otherwise order. Where any final administrative order or decision is the subject of proceedings under this section, if the petition shall have been filed while the penalty imposed is in full force and effect, the determination shall not be considered to have become moot in cases where the penalty imposed by the administrative agency has been completed or complied with during the pendency of the proceedings.

(i) Any administrative record received for filing by the clerk of the court may be disposed of as provided in Sections 1952, 1952.2, and 1952.3.

(j) Effective January 1, 1996, this subdivision shall apply to state employees in State Bargaining Unit 5. For purposes of this section, the court is not authorized to review any disciplinary decisions reached pursuant to Section 19576.1 of the Government Code.

Amended by Stats 2011 ch 296 (AB 1023),s 41, eff. 1/1/2012.
Amended by Stats 2008 ch 150 (AB 3042),s 1, eff. 1/1/2009.
Amended by Stats 2000 ch 402 (AB 649), s 1, eff. 9/11/2000.
Amended September 21, 1999 (Bill Number: AB 1013) (Chapter 446).

Section 1094.6 - Judicial review of local agency other than school district

(a) Judicial review of any decision of a local agency, other than school district, as the term local agency is defined in Section 54951 of the Government Code, or of any commission, board, officer or agent thereof, may be had pursuant to Section 1094.5 of this code only if the petition for writ of mandate pursuant to such section is filed within the time limits specified in this section.

(b) Any such petition shall be filed not later than the 90th day following the date on which the decision becomes final. If there is no provision for reconsideration of the decision, or for a written decision or written findings supporting the decision, in any applicable provision of any statute, charter, or rule, for the purposes of this section, the decision is final on the date it is announced. If the decision is not announced at the close of the hearing, the date, time, and place of the announcement of the decision shall be announced at the hearing. If there is a provision for reconsideration, the decision is final for purposes of this section upon the expiration of the period during which such reconsideration can be sought; provided, that if reconsideration is sought pursuant to any such provision the decision is final for the purposes of this section on the date that reconsideration is rejected. If there is a provision for a written decision or written findings, the decision is final for purposes of this section upon the date it is mailed by first-class mail, postage prepaid, including a copy of the affidavit or certificate of mailing, to the party seeking the writ. Subdivision (a) of Section 1013 does not apply to extend the time, following deposit in the mail of the decision or findings, within which a petition shall be filed.

(c) The complete record of the proceedings shall be prepared by the local agency or its commission, board, officer, or agent which made the decision and shall be delivered to the petitioner within 190 days after he has filed a written request therefor. The local agency may recover from the petitioner its actual costs for transcribing or otherwise preparing the record. Such record shall include the transcript of the proceedings, all pleadings, all notices and orders, any proposed decision by a hearing officer, the final decision, all admitted exhibits, all rejected exhibits in the possession of the local agency or its commission, board, officer, or agent, all written evidence, and any other papers in the case.

(d) If the petitioner files a request for the record as specified in subdivision (c) within 10 days after the date the decision becomes final as provided in subdivision (b), the time within which a petition pursuant to Section 1094.5 may be filed shall be extended to not later than the 30th day following the date on which the record is either personally delivered or mailed to the petitioner or his attorney of record, if he has one.

(e) As used in this section, decision means a decision subject to review pursuant to Section 1094.5, suspending, demoting, or dismissing an officer or employee, revoking, denying an application for a permit, license, or other entitlement, imposing a civil or administrative penalty, fine, charge, or cost, or denying an application for any retirement benefit or allowance.

(f) In making a final decision as defined in subdivision (e), the local agency shall provide notice to the party that the time within which judicial review must be sought is governed by this section. As used in this subdivision, "party" means an officer or employee who has been suspended, demoted or dismissed; a person whose permit, license, or other entitlement has been revoked or suspended, or whose application for a permit, license, or other entitlement has been denied; or a person whose application for a retirement benefit or allowance has been denied.

(g) This section shall prevail over any conflicting provision in any otherwise applicable law relating to the subject matter, unless the conflicting provision is a state or federal law which provides a shorter statute of limitations, in which case the shorter statute of limitations shall apply.

Amended by Stats. 1995, Ch. 898, Sec. 1. Effective January 1, 1996.

Section 1094.7 - [Repealed]

Repealed 9/21/1999 (Bill Number: AB 1013) (Chapter 446).

Section 1094.8 - Issuance, revocation, suspension or denial of permit or other entitlement for constitutionally protected expressive conduct

(a) Notwithstanding anything to the contrary in this chapter, an action or proceeding to review the issuance, revocation, suspension, or denial of a permit or other entitlement for expressive conduct protected by the First Amendment to the United States Constitution shall be conducted in accordance with subdivision (d).

(b) For purposes of this section, the following definitions shall apply:

(1) The terms "permit" and "entitlement" are used interchangeably.

(2) The term "permit applicant" means both an applicant for a permit and a permitholder.

(3) The term "public agency" means a city, county, city and county, a joint powers authority or similar public entity formed pursuant to Section 65850.4 of the Government Code, or any other public entity authorized by law to issue permits for expressive conduct protected by the First Amendment to the United States Constitution.

(c) A public agency may, if it so chooses, designate the permits or entitlements to which this section applies by adopting an ordinance or resolution which contains a specific listing or other description of the permits or entitlements issued by the public agency which are eligible for expedited judicial review pursuant to this section because the permits regulate expressive conduct protected by the First Amendment to the United States Constitution.

(d) The procedure set forth in this subdivision, when applicable, shall supersede anything to the contrary set forth in this chapter.

(1) Within five court days after receipt of written notification from a permit applicant that the permit applicant will seek judicial review of a public agency's action on the permit, the public agency shall prepare, certify, and make available the administrative record to the permit applicant.

(2) Either the public agency or the permit applicant may bring an action in accordance with the procedure set forth in this section. If the permit applicant brings the action, the action shall be in the form of a petition for writ of mandate pursuant to Section 1085 or 1094.5, as appropriate.

(3) The party bringing the action pursuant to this section shall file and serve the petition on the respondent no later than 21 calendar days following the public agency's final decision on the permit. The title page of the petition shall contain the following language in 18-point type: "ATTENTION: THIS MATTER IS ENTITLED TO PRIORITY AND SUBJECT TO THE EXPEDITED HEARING AND REVIEW PROCEDURES CONTAINED IN SECTION 1094.8 OF THE CODE OF CIVIL PROCEDURE."

(4) The clerk of the court shall set a hearing for review of the petition no later than 25 calendar days from the date the petition is filed. Moving, opposition, and reply papers shall be filed as provided in the California Rules of Court. The petitioner shall lodge the administrative record with the court no later than 10 calendar days in advance of the hearing date.

(5) Following the conclusion of the hearing, the court shall render its decision in an expeditious manner consistent with constitutional requirements in view of the particular facts and circumstances. In no event shall the decision be rendered later than 20 calendar days after the matter is submitted or 50 calendar days after the date the petition is filed pursuant to paragraph (4), whichever is earlier.

(e) If the presiding judge of the court in which the action is filed determines that, as a result of either the press of other court business or other factors, the court will be unable to meet any one or more of the deadlines provided within this section, the presiding judge shall request the temporary assignment of a judicial officer to hear the petition and render a decision within the time limits contained herein, pursuant to Section 68543.8 of the Government Code. Given the short time period involved, the request shall be entitled to priority.

(f) In any action challenging the issuance, revocation, suspension, or denial of a permit or entitlement, the parties to the action shall be permitted to jointly waive the time limits provided for herein.

Added by Stats. 1999, Ch. 49, Sec. 1. Effective June 28, 1999.

Section 1095 - Recovery of damages and costs

If judgment be given for the applicant, the applicant may recover the damages which the applicant has sustained, as found by the jury, or as may be determined by the court or referee, upon a reference to be ordered, together with costs; and a peremptory mandate must also be awarded without delay. Damages and costs may be enforced in the manner provided for money judgments generally. In all cases where the respondent is an officer of a public entity, all damages and costs, or either, which may be recovered or awarded, shall be recovered and awarded against the public entity represented by the officer, and not against the officer so appearing in the proceeding, and are a proper claim against the public entity for which the officer appeared and shall be paid as other claims against the public entity are paid; but in all such cases, the court shall first determine that the officer appeared and made defense in the proceeding in good faith. For the purpose of this section, "public entity" includes the state, a county, city, district or other public agency or public corporation. For the purpose of this section, "officer" includes officer, agent or employee.

Amended by Stats. 1982, Ch. 497, Sec. 73. Operative July 1, 1983, by Sec. 185 of Ch. 497.

Section 1096 - Service of writ

The writ must be served in the same manner as a summons in a civil action, except when otherwise expressly directed by order of the Court. Service upon a majority of the members of any Board or body, is service upon the Board or body, whether at the time of the service the Board or body was in session or not.

Enacted 1872.

Section 1097 - Refusal or neglect to obey peremptory mandate

If a peremptory mandate has been issued and directed to an inferior tribunal, corporation, board, or person, and it appears to the court that a member of the tribunal, corporation, or board, or the person upon whom the writ has been personally served, has, without just excuse, refused or neglected to obey the writ, the court may, upon motion, impose a fine not exceeding one thousand dollars. In case of persistence in a refusal of obedience, the court may order the party to be imprisoned until the writ is obeyed, and may make any orders necessary and proper for the complete enforcement of the writ.

Amended by Stats 2016 ch 86 (SB 1171),s 40, eff. 1/1/2017.

Chapter 3 - WRIT OF PROHIBITION

Section 1102 - Writ arrests proceedings

The writ of prohibition arrests the proceedings of any tribunal, corporation, board, or person exercising judicial functions, when such proceedings are without or in excess of the jurisdiction of such tribunal, corporation, board, or person.

Amended by Stats. 1955, Ch. 971.

Section 1103 - When writ may issue or be granted

(a) A writ of prohibition may be issued by any court to an inferior tribunal or to a corporation, board, or person, in all cases where there is not a plain, speedy, and adequate remedy in the ordinary course of law. It is issued upon the verified petition of the person beneficially interested.

(b) The appellate division of the superior court may grant a writ of prohibition directed to the superior court in a limited civil case or in a misdemeanor or infraction case. Where the appellate division grants a writ of prohibition directed to the superior court, the superior court is an inferior tribunal for purposes of this chapter.

Amended by Stats 2010 ch 212 (AB 2767),s 3, eff. 1/1/2011.

Amended by Stats 2002 ch 784 (SB 1316),s 76, eff. 1/1/2003.

Previously Amended September 7, 1999 (Bill Number: SB 210) (Chapter 344).

Section 1104 - Writ alternative or peremptory
The writ must be either alternative or peremptory. The alternative writ must command the party to whom it is directed to desist or refrain from further proceedings in the action or matter specified therein, until the further order of the court from which it is issued, and to show cause before such court at a time and place then or thereafter specified by court order why such party should not be absolutely restrained from any further proceedings in such action or matter. The peremptory writ must be in a similar form, except that the words requiring the party to show cause why he should not be absolutely restrained must be omitted.
Amended by Stats. 1963, Ch. 461.

Section 1105 - Applicability of provisions of preceding chapter
The provisions of the preceding Chapter, except of the first four sections thereof, apply to this proceeding.
Enacted 1872.

Chapter 4 - WRITS OF REVIEW, MANDATE, AND PROHIBITION MAY ISSUE AND BE HEARD AT CHAMBERS

Section 1107 - Generally
When an application is filed for the issuance of any prerogative writ, the application shall be accompanied by proof of service of a copy thereof upon the respondent and the real party in interest named in such application. The provisions of Chapter 5 (commencing with Section 1010) of Title 14 of Part 2 shall apply to the service of the application. However, when a writ of mandate is sought pursuant to the provisions of Section 1088.5, the action may be filed and served in the same manner as an ordinary action under Part 2 (commencing with Section 307). Where the real party in respondent's interest is a board or commission, the service shall be made upon the presiding officer, or upon the secretary, or upon a majority of the members, of the board or commission. Within five days after service and filing of the application, the real party in interest or the respondent or both may serve upon the applicant and file with the court points and authorities in opposition to the granting of the writ.
The court in which the application is filed, in its discretion and for good cause, may grant the application ex parte, without notice or service of the application as herein provided.
The provisions of this section shall not be applicable to applications for the writ of habeas corpus, or to applications for writs of review of the Industrial Accident or Public Utilities Commissions.
Amended by Stats. 1982, Ch. 812, Sec. 4.

Section 1108 - Writ returnable and heard in discretion of court
Writs of review, mandate, and prohibition issued by the Supreme Court, a court of appeal, or a superior court, may, in the discretion of the court issuing the writ, be made returnable, and a hearing thereon be had at any time.
Amended by Stats. 1967, Ch. 17.

Chapter 5 - RULES OF PRACTICE AND APPEALS

Section 1109 - Generally
Except as otherwise provided in this Title, the provisions of Part II of the Code are applicable to and constitute the rules of practice in the proceedings mentioned in this Title.
Enacted 1872.

Section 1110 - Applicability of provisions of Part II relative to new trials and appeals
The provisions of Part II of this Code relative to new trials and appeals, except in so far as they are inconsistent with the provisions of this Title, apply to the proceedings mentioned in this Title.
Enacted 1872.

Section 1110a - Order or judgment commanding person to deliver water for irrigation purposes not stayed by appeal
If an appeal be taken from an order or judgment directing the issuance of a writ of mandate commanding a party to deliver water, for irrigation purposes, such appeal shall not stay the operation of the order, judgment or writ as to the delivery of such water, but such water must until the final determination of said appeal be delivered as commanded by said writ; provided, that if any expense is necessary to be incurred by the defendant in connecting the water supply with the land to be irrigated, said defendant shall not be obliged to furnish water unless the plaintiff shall provide a bond in such sum as the court may fix, conditioned that in the event of the judgment being reversed, plaintiff will pay defendant the amount of the expense so incurred not exceeding the amount of said bond.
Added by Stats. 1919, Ch. 358.

Section 1110b - When appeal directed not to operate as stay of order or judgment granting writ of mandate
If an appeal be taken from an order or judgment granting a writ of mandate the court granting the writ, or the appellate court, may direct that the appeal shall not operate as a stay of execution if it is satisfied upon the showing made by the petitioner that he will suffer irreparable damage in his business or profession if the execution is stayed.
Added by Stats. 1941, Ch. 330.

Title 3 - OF SUMMARY PROCEEDINGS

Chapter 1 - CONFESSION OF JUDGMENT WITHOUT ACTION

Section 1132 - Judgment by confession unenforceable; applicability
(a) A judgment by confession is unenforceable and may not be entered in any superior court.
(b) This section does not apply to a judgment by confession obtained or entered before January 1, 2023.
Amended by Stats 2022 ch 851 (SB 688),s 1, eff. 1/1/2023.
Amended by Stats 2002 ch 784 (SB 1316),s 77, eff. 1/1/2003.

Section 1133 - [Repealed]
Repealed by Stats 2022 ch 851 (SB 688),s 2, eff. 1/1/2023.
Enacted 1872.

Section 1134 - [Repealed]
Repealed by Stats 2022 ch 851 (SB 688),s 3, eff. 1/1/2023.
Amended by Stats 2005 ch 75 (AB 145),s 40, eff. 7/19/2005, op. 1/1/2006
Amended by Stats 2001 ch 812 (AB 223), s 9, eff. 1/1/2002.

Chapter 2 - SUBMITTING A CONTROVERSY WITHOUT ACTION

Section 1138 - Generally
Parties to a question in difference, which might be the subject of a civil action, may, without action, agree upon a case containing the facts upon which the controversy depends, and present a submission of the same to any Court which would have jurisdiction if an action had been brought; but it must appear, by affidavit, that the controversy is real and the proceedings in good faith, to determine the rights of the parties. The Court must thereupon hear and determine the case, and render judgment thereon, as if an action were depending.
Enacted 1872.

Section 1139 - Judgment; judgment roll

Judgment must be entered as in other cases, but without costs for any proceeding prior to the trial. The case, the submission, and a copy of the judgment constitute the judgment roll.

Amended by Stats. 1933, Ch. 745.

Section 1140 - Enforcement of judgment

The judgment may be enforced in the same manner as if it had been rendered in an action of the same jurisdictional classification in the same court, and is in the same manner subject to appeal.

Amended by Stats. 1998, Ch. 931, Sec. 115. Effective September 28, 1998.

Chapter 2.5 - JUDICIAL ARBITRATION

Section 1141.10 - Legislative findings and declaration; legislative intent

(a) The Legislature finds and declares that litigation involving small civil cases can be so costly and complex that efficiently resolving these civil cases is difficult, and that the resulting delays and expenses may deny parties their right to a timely resolution of minor civil disputes. The Legislature further finds and declares that arbitration has proven to be an efficient and equitable method for resolving small civil cases, and that courts should encourage or require the use of arbitration for those actions whenever possible.

(b) It is the intent of the Legislature that:

(1) Arbitration hearings held pursuant to this chapter shall provide parties with a simplified and economical procedure for obtaining prompt and equitable resolution of their disputes.

(2) Arbitration hearings shall be as informal as possible and shall provide the parties themselves maximum opportunity to participate directly in the resolution of their disputes, and shall be held during nonjudicial hours whenever possible.

(3) Members of the State Bar selected to serve as arbitrators should have experience with cases of the type under dispute and are urged to volunteer their services without compensation whenever possible.

Amended by Stats 2003 ch 449 (AB 1712),s 9, eff. 1/1/2004.

Section 1141.11 - Unlimited civil cases submitted to arbitration; limited civil cases; motor vehicle collisions

(a) In each superior court with 18 or more judges, all nonexempt unlimited civil cases shall be submitted to arbitration under this chapter if the amount in controversy, in the opinion of the court, will not exceed fifty thousand dollars ($50,000) for each plaintiff.

(b) In each superior court with fewer than 18 judges, the court may provide by local rule, when it determines that it is in the best interests of justice, that all nonexempt, unlimited civil cases shall be submitted to arbitration under this chapter if the amount in controversy, in the opinion of the court, will not exceed fifty thousand dollars ($50,000) for each plaintiff.

(c) Each superior court may provide by local rule, when it is determined to be in the best interests of justice, that all nonexempt, limited civil cases shall be submitted to arbitration under this chapter. This section does not apply to any action in small claims court, or to any action maintained pursuant to Section 1781 of the Civil Code or Section 1161.

(d)

(1) In each court that has adopted judicial arbitration pursuant to subdivision (c), all limited civil cases that involve a claim for money damages against a single defendant as a result of a motor vehicle collision, except those heard in the small claims division, shall be submitted to arbitration within 120 days of the filing of the defendant's answer to the complaint (except as may be extended by the court for good cause) before an arbitrator selected by the court.

(2) The court may provide by local rule for the voluntary or mandatory use of case questionnaires, established under Section 93, in any proceeding subject to these provisions. Where local rules provide for the use of case questionnaires, the questionnaires shall be exchanged by the parties upon the defendant's answer and completed and returned within 60 days.

(3) For the purposes of this subdivision, the term "single defendant" means any of the following:

(A) An individual defendant, whether a person or an entity.

(B) Two or more persons covered by the same insurance policy applicable to the motor vehicle collision.

(C) Two or more persons residing in the same household when no insurance policy exists that is applicable to the motor vehicle collision.

(4) The naming of one or more cross-defendants, not a plaintiff, shall constitute a multiple-defendant case not subject to the provisions of this subdivision.

Amended by Stats 2003 ch 449 (AB 1712),s 10, eff. 1/1/2004.

Amended by Stats 2002 ch 784 (SB 1316),s 78, eff. 1/1/2003.

Section 1141.12 - Uniform system provided by rule

In all superior courts, the Judicial Council shall provide by rule for a uniform system of arbitration of the following causes:

(a) Any cause, regardless of the amount in controversy, upon stipulation of the parties.

(b) Upon filing of an election by the plaintiff, any cause in which the plaintiff agrees that the arbitration award shall not exceed the amount in controversy as specified in Section 1141.11.

Amended by Stats 2003 ch 449 (AB 1712),s 11, eff. 1/1/2004.

Amended by Stats 2002 ch 784 (SB 1316),s 79, eff. 1/1/2003.

Section 1141.13 - Prayer for equitable relief

This chapter shall not apply to any civil action which includes a prayer for equitable relief, except that if the prayer for equitable relief is frivolous or insubstantial, this chapter shall be applicable.

Added by Stats. 1978, Ch. 743.

Section 1141.14 - Rules for practice and procedure

Notwithstanding any other provision of law except the provisions of this chapter, the Judicial Council shall provide by rule for practice and procedure for all actions submitted to arbitration under this chapter. The Judicial Council rules shall provide for and conform with the provisions of this chapter.

Added by Stats. 1978, Ch. 743.

Section 1141.15 - Exception provided by rules

The Judicial Council rules shall provide exceptions for cause to arbitration pursuant to subdivision (a), (b), or (c) of Section 1141.11. In providing for such exceptions, the Judicial Council shall take into consideration whether the civil action might not be amenable to arbitration.

Added by Stats. 1978, Ch. 743.

Section 1141.16 - Determination of amount in controversy

(a) The determination of the amount in controversy, under subdivision (a) or (b) of Section 1141.11, shall be made by the court and the case referred to arbitration after all named parties have appeared or defaulted. The determination shall be made at a case management conference or based upon review of the written submissions of the parties, as provided in rules adopted by the Judicial Council. The determination shall be based on the total amount of damages, and the judge may not consider questions of liability or comparative negligence or any other defense. At that time the court shall also make a determination whether any prayer for equitable relief is frivolous or insubstantial. The determination of the amount in controversy and whether any prayer for equitable relief is frivolous or insubstantial may not be appealable. No determination pursuant to this section shall be made if all parties stipulate in writing that the amount in controversy exceeds the amount specified in Section 1141.11.

(b) The determination and any stipulation of the amount in controversy shall be without prejudice to any finding on the value of the case by an arbitrator or in a subsequent trial de novo.
(c) Except as provided in this section, the arbitration hearing may not be held until 210 days after the filing of the complaint, or 240 days after the filing of a complaint if the parties have stipulated to a continuance pursuant to subdivision (d) of Section 68616 of the Government Code. A case shall be submitted to arbitration at an earlier time upon any of the following:
   (1) The stipulation of the parties to an earlier arbitration hearing.
   (2) The written request of all plaintiffs, subject to a motion by a defendant for good cause shown to delay the arbitration hearing.
   (3) An order of the court if the parties have stipulated, or the court has ordered under Section 1141.24, that discovery other than that permitted under Chapter 18 (commencing with Section 2034.010) of Title 4 of Part 4 will be permitted after the arbitration award is rendered.
Amended by Stats 2004 ch 182 (AB 3081),s 14, eff. 7/1/2005
Amended by Stats 2003 ch 449 (AB 1712),s 12, eff. 1/1/2004.

Section 1141.17 - Running of time periods not suspended
(a) Submission of an action to arbitration pursuant to this chapter shall not suspend the running of the time periods specified in Chapter 1.5 (commencing with Section 583.110) of Title 8 of Part 2, except as provided in this section.
(b) If an action is or remains submitted to arbitration pursuant to this chapter more than four years and six months after the plaintiff has filed the action, then the time beginning on the date four years and six months after the plaintiff has filed the action and ending on the date on which a request for a de novo trial is filed under Section 1141.20 shall not be included in computing the five-year period specified in Section 583.310.
Amended by Stats. 1984, Ch. 1705, Sec. 6.

Section 1141.18 - Who may serve as arbitrators; compensation; assignment of arbitrator; disqualification
(a) Arbitrators shall be retired judges, retired court commissioners who were licensed to practice law prior to their appointment as a commissioner, or members of the State Bar, and shall sit individually. A judge may also serve as an arbitrator without compensation. People who are not attorneys may serve as arbitrators upon the stipulation of all parties.
(b) The Judicial Council rules shall provide for the compensation, if any, of arbitrators. Compensation for arbitrators may not be less than one hundred fifty dollars ($150) per case, or one hundred fifty dollars ($150) per day, whichever is greater. A superior court may set a higher level of compensation for that court. Arbitrators may waive compensation in whole or in part. No compensation shall be paid before the filing of the award by the arbitrator, or before the settlement of the case by the parties.
(c) In cases submitted to arbitration under Section 1141.11 or 1141.12, an arbitrator shall be assigned within 30 days from the time of submission to arbitration.
(d) Any party may request the disqualification of the arbitrator selected for his or her case on the grounds and by the procedures specified in Section 170.1 or 170.6. A request for disqualification of an arbitrator on grounds specified in Section 170.6 shall be made within five days of the naming of the arbitrator. An arbitrator shall disqualify himself or herself, upon demand of any party to the arbitration made before the conclusion of the arbitration proceedings on any of the grounds specified in Section 170.1.
Amended by Stats 2003 ch 449 (AB 1712),s 13, eff. 1/1/2004.

Section 1141.19 - Arbitrator's powers
Arbitrators approved pursuant to this chapter shall have the powers necessary to perform duties pursuant to this chapter as prescribed by the Judicial Council.
Added by Stats. 1978, Ch. 743.

Section 1141.19.5 - Pretrial discovery
In any arbitration proceeding under this chapter, no party may require the production of evidence specified in subdivision (a) of Section 3295 of the Civil Code at the arbitration, unless the court enters an order permitting pretrial discovery of that evidence pursuant to subdivision (c) of Section 3295 of the Civil Code.
Amended by Stats. 1994, Ch. 327, Sec. 1. Effective January 1, 1995.

Section 1141.20 - Award final unless de novo trial or dismissal requested;; de novo trial
(a) An arbitration award shall be final unless a request for a de novo trial or a request for dismissal in the form required by the Judicial Council is filed within 60 days after the date the arbitrator files the award with the court.
(b) Any party may elect to have a de novo trial, by court or jury, both as to law and facts. Such trial shall be calendared, insofar as possible, so that the trial shall be given the same place on the active list as it had prior to arbitration, or shall receive civil priority on the next setting calendar.
Amended by Stats 2011 ch 49 (SB 731),s 3, eff. 1/1/2012.

Section 1141.21 - Costs and fees if judgment upon trial de novo not more favorable than arbitration award
(a)
   (1) If the judgment upon the trial de novo is not more favorable in either the amount of damages awarded or the type of relief granted for the party electing the trial de novo than the arbitration award, the court shall order that party to pay the following nonrefundable costs and fees, unless the court finds in writing and upon motion that the imposition of these costs and fees would create such a substantial economic hardship as not to be in the interest of justice:
      (A) To the court, the compensation actually paid to the arbitrator, less any amount paid pursuant to subparagraph (D).
      (B) To the other party or parties, all costs specified in Section 1033.5, and the party electing the trial de novo shall not recover his or her costs.
      (C) To the other party or parties, the reasonable costs of the services of expert witnesses, who are not regular employees of any party, actually incurred or reasonably necessary in the preparation or trial of the case.
      (D) To the other party or parties, the compensation paid by the other party or parties to the arbitrator, pursuant to subdivision (b) of Section 1141.28.
   (2) Those costs and fees, other than the compensation of the arbitrator, shall include only those incurred from the time of election of the trial de novo.
(b) If the party electing the trial de novo has proceeded in the action in forma pauperis and has failed to obtain a more favorable judgment, the costs and fees under subparagraphs (B) and (C) of paragraph (1) of subdivision (a) shall be imposed only as an offset against any damages awarded in favor of that party.
(c) If the party electing the trial de novo has proceeded in the action in forma pauperis and has failed to obtain a more favorable judgment, the costs under subparagraph (A) of paragraph (1) of subdivision (a) shall be imposed only to the extent that there remains a sufficient amount in the judgment after the amount offset under subdivision (b) has been deducted from the judgment.
Amended by Stats 2006 ch 538 (SB 1852),s 66, eff. 1/1/2007.
Amended by Stats 2005 ch 706 (AB 1742),s 14, eff. 1/1/2006

Section 1141.22 - Rules to specify grounds for correction, modification or vacation of award
The Judicial Council rules shall specify the grounds upon which the arbitrator or the court, or both, may correct, modify or vacate an award.
Added by Stats. 1978, Ch. 743.

Section 1141.23 - Requirements of award; entry in judgment book; force and effect of award

The arbitration award shall be in writing, signed by the arbitrator and filed in the court in which the action is pending. If there is no request for a de novo trial or a request for dismissal in the form required by the Judicial Council and the award is not vacated, the award shall be entered in the judgment book in the amount of the award. Such award shall have the same force and effect as a judgment in any civil action or proceeding, except that it is not subject to appeal and it may not be attacked or set aside except as provided by Section 473, 1286.2, or Judicial Council rule.
Amended by Stats 2011 ch 49 (SB 731),s 4, eff. 1/1/2012.

Section 1141.24 - Discovery after award
In cases ordered to arbitration pursuant to Section 1141.11, no discovery other than that permitted by Chapter 18 (commencing with Section 2034.010) of Title 4 of Part 4 is permissible after an arbitration award except by stipulation of the parties or by leave of court upon a showing of good cause.
Amended by Stats 2004 ch 182 (AB 3081),s 15, eff. 7/1/2005
Amended by Stats 2003 ch 449 (AB 1712),s 14, eff. 1/1/2004.

Section 1141.25 - Reference to arbitration proceedings and award in subsequent trial constitutes irregularity
Any reference to the arbitration proceedings or arbitration award during any subsequent trial shall constitute an irregularity in the proceedings of the trial for the purposes of Section 657.
Added by Stats. 1978, Ch. 743.

Section 1141.26 - Award or judgment in excess of amount in controversy
Nothing in this act shall prohibit an arbitration award in excess of the amount in controversy as specified in Section 1141.11. No party electing a trial de novo after such award shall be subject to the provisions of Section 1141.21 if the judgment upon the trial de novo is in excess of the amount in controversy as specified in Section 1141.11.
Amended by Stats. 1981, Ch. 1110, Sec. 4.

Section 1141.27 - Applicability to public agency or public entity
This chapter shall apply to any civil action otherwise within the scope of this chapter in which a party to the action is a public agency or public entity.
Added by Stats. 1978, Ch. 743.

Section 1141.28 - Administrative costs; actual costs of compensation of arbitrators
(a) All administrative costs of arbitration, including compensation of arbitrators, shall be paid for by the court in which the arbitration costs are incurred, except as otherwise provided in subdivision (b) and in Section 1141.21.
(b) The actual costs of compensation of arbitrators in any proceeding which would not otherwise be subject to the provisions of this chapter but in which arbitration is conducted pursuant to this chapter solely because of the stipulation of the parties, shall be paid for in equal shares by the parties. If the imposition of these costs would create such a substantial economic hardship for any party as not to be in the interest of justice, as determined by the arbitrator, that party's share of costs shall be paid for by the court in which the arbitration costs are incurred. The determination as to substantial economic hardship may be reviewed by the court.
Amended by Stats 2000 ch 447 (SB 1533), s 3, eff. 1/1/2001.

Section 1141.29 - [Repealed]
Repealed by Stats 2002 ch 784 (SB 1316),s 80, eff. 1/1/2003.

Section 1141.30 - Construction of chapter
This chapter shall not be construed in derogation of Title 9 (commencing with Section 1280) of Part 3, and, to that extent, this chapter and that title, other than Section 1280.1, are mutually exclusive and independent of each other.
Amended (as added by Stats. 1978, Ch. 743) by Stats. 1990, Ch. 817, Sec. 1.

Section 1141.31 - Effective date
The provisions of this chapter shall become operative July 1, 1979, except that the Judicial Council shall adopt the arbitration rules for practice and procedures on or before March 31, 1979.
Added by Stats. 1978, Ch. 743.

Chapter 4 - SUMMARY PROCEEDINGS FOR OBTAINING POSSESSION OF REAL PROPERTY IN CERTAIN CASES

Section 1159 - When person guilty of forcible entry
(a) Every person is guilty of a forcible entry who either:
 (1) By breaking open doors, windows, or other parts of a house, or by any kind of violence or circumstance of terror enters upon or into any real property.
 (2) Who, after entering peaceably upon real property, turns out by force, threats, or menacing conduct, the party in possession.
(b) For purposes of this section, "party in possession" means any person who hires real property and includes a boarder or lodger, except those persons whose occupancy is described in subdivision (b) of Section 1940 of the Civil Code.
Amended by Stats 2018 ch 92 (SB 1289),s 42, eff. 1/1/2019.

Section 1160 - When person guilty of forcible detainer
(a) Every person is guilty of a forcible detainer who either:
 (1) By force, or by menaces and threats of violence, unlawfully holds and keeps the possession of any real property, whether the same was acquired peaceably or otherwise.
 (2) Who, in the night-time, or during the absence of the occupant of any lands, unlawfully enters upon real property, and who, after demand made for the surrender thereof, for the period of five days, refuses to surrender the same to such former occupant.
(b) The occupant of real property, within the meaning of this section is one who, within five days preceding such unlawful entry, was in the peaceable and undisturbed possession of such lands.
Amended by Stats 2018 ch 92 (SB 1289),s 43, eff. 1/1/2019.

Section 1161 - [Effective until 2/1/2025] When tenant for term less than life guilty of unlawful detainer
A tenant of real property, for a term less than life, or the executor or administrator of the tenant's estate heretofore qualified and now acting or hereafter to be qualified and act, is guilty of unlawful detainer:
1. When the tenant continues in possession, in person or by subtenant, of the property, or any part thereof, after the expiration of the term for which it is let to the tenant; provided the expiration is of a nondefault nature however brought about without the permission of the landlord, or the successor in estate of the landlord, if applicable; including the case where the person to be removed became the occupant of the premises as a servant, employee, agent, or licensee and the relation of master and servant, or employer and employee, or principal and agent, or licensor and licensee, has been lawfully terminated or the time fixed for occupancy by the agreement between the parties has expired; but nothing in this subdivision shall be construed as preventing the removal of the occupant in any other lawful manner; but in case of a tenancy at will, it shall first be terminated by notice, as prescribed in the Civil Code.
2. When the tenant continues in possession, in person or by subtenant, without the permission of the landlord, or the successor in estate of the landlord, if applicable, after default in the payment of rent, pursuant to the lease or agreement under which the property is held, and three days'

notice, excluding Saturdays and Sundays and other judicial holidays, in writing, requiring its payment, stating the amount that is due, the name, telephone number, and address of the person to whom the rent payment shall be made, and, if payment may be made personally, the usual days and hours that person will be available to receive the payment (provided that, if the address does not allow for personal delivery, then it shall be conclusively presumed that upon the mailing of any rent or notice to the owner by the tenant to the name and address provided, the notice or rent is deemed received by the owner on the date posted, if the tenant can show proof of mailing to the name and address provided by the owner), or the number of an account in a financial institution into which the rental payment may be made, and the name and street address of the institution (provided that the institution is located within five miles of the rental property), or if an electronic funds transfer procedure has been previously established, that payment may be made pursuant to that procedure, or possession of the property, shall have been served upon the tenant and if there is a subtenant in actual occupation of the premises, also upon the subtenant. The notice may be served at any time within one year after the rent becomes due. In all cases of tenancy upon agricultural lands, if the tenant has held over and retained possession for more than 60 days after the expiration of the term without any demand of possession or notice to quit by the landlord or the successor in estate of the landlord, if applicable, the tenant shall be deemed to be holding by permission of the landlord or successor in estate of the landlord, if applicable, and shall be entitled to hold under the terms of the lease for another full year, and shall not be guilty of an unlawful detainer during that year, and the holding over for that period shall be taken and construed as a consent on the part of a tenant to hold for another year.

An unlawful detainer action under this paragraph shall be subject to the COVID-19 Tenant Relief Act of 2020 (Chapter 5 (commencing with Section 1179.01)) if the default in the payment of rent is based upon the COVID-19 rental debt.

3. When the tenant continues in possession, in person or by subtenant, after a neglect or failure to perform other conditions or covenants of the lease or agreement under which the property is held, including any covenant not to assign or sublet, than the one for the payment of rent, and three days' notice, excluding Saturdays and Sundays and other judicial holidays, in writing, requiring the performance of those conditions or covenants, or the possession of the property, shall have been served upon the tenant, and if there is a subtenant in actual occupation of the premises, also, upon the subtenant. Within three days, excluding Saturdays and Sundays and other judicial holidays, after the service of the notice, the tenant, or any subtenant in actual occupation of the premises, or any mortgagee of the term, or other person interested in its continuance, may perform the conditions or covenants of the lease or pay the stipulated rent, as the case may be, and thereby save the lease from forfeiture; provided, if the conditions and covenants of the lease, violated by the lessee, cannot afterward be performed, then no notice, as last prescribed herein, need be given to the lessee or the subtenant, demanding the performance of the violated conditions or covenants of the lease. A tenant may take proceedings, similar to those prescribed in this chapter, to obtain possession of the premises let to a subtenant or held by a servant, employee, agent, or licensee, in case of that person's unlawful detention of the premises underlet to or held by that person.

An unlawful detainer action under this paragraph shall be subject to the COVID-19 Tenant Relief Act of 2020 (Chapter 5 (commencing with Section 1179.01)) if the neglect or failure to perform other conditions or covenants of the lease or agreement is based upon the COVID-19 rental debt.

4. Any tenant, subtenant, or executor or administrator of that person's estate heretofore qualified and now acting, or hereafter to be qualified and act, assigning or subletting or committing waste upon the demised premises, contrary to the conditions or covenants of the lease, or maintaining, committing, or permitting the maintenance or commission of a nuisance upon the demised premises or using the premises for an unlawful purpose, thereby terminates the lease, and the landlord, or the landlord's successor in estate, shall upon service of three days' notice to quit upon the person or persons in possession, be entitled to restitution of possession of the demised premises under this chapter. For purposes of this subdivision, a person who commits or maintains a public nuisance as described in Section 3482.8 of the Civil Code, or who commits an offense described in subdivision (c) of Section 3485 of the Civil Code, or subdivision (c) of Section 3486 of the Civil Code, or uses the premises to further the purpose of that offense shall be deemed to have committed a nuisance upon the premises.

5. When the tenant gives written notice as provided in Section 1946 of the Civil Code of the tenant's intention to terminate the hiring of the real property, or makes a written offer to surrender which is accepted in writing by the landlord, but fails to deliver possession at the time specified in that written notice, without the permission of the landlord, or the successor in estate of the landlord, if applicable.

6. As used in this section: "COVID-19 rental debt" has the same meaning as defined in Section 1179.02.

"Tenant" includes any person who hires real property except those persons whose occupancy is described in subdivision (b) of Section 1940 of the Civil Code.

7. This section shall remain in effect until February 1, 2025, and as of that date is repealed.

Amended by Stats 2020 ch 37 (AB 3088),s 15, eff. 8/31/2020.
Amended by Stats 2018 ch 260 (AB 2343),s 1, eff. 1/1/2019.
Amended by Stats 2011 ch 128 (SB 426),s 2, eff. 1/1/2012.
Amended by Stats 2009 ch 244 (AB 530),s 5, eff. 1/1/2010.
Added by Stats 2008 ch 440 (AB 2052),s 3, eff. 9/27/2008.

Section 1161 - [Operative 2/1/2025] When tenant for term less than life guilty of unlawful detainer

A tenant of real property, for a term less than life, or the executor or administrator of the tenant's estate heretofore qualified and now acting or hereafter to be qualified and act, is guilty of unlawful detainer:

1. When the tenant continues in possession, in person or by subtenant, of the property, or any part thereof, after the expiration of the term for which it is let to the tenant; provided the expiration is of a nondefault nature however brought about without the permission of the landlord, or the successor in estate of the landlord, if applicable; including the case where the person to be removed became the occupant of the premises as a servant, employee, agent, or licensee and the relation of master and servant, or employer and employee, or principal and agent, or licensor and licensee, has been lawfully terminated or the time fixed for occupancy by the agreement between the parties has expired; but nothing in this subdivision shall be construed as preventing the removal of the occupant in any other lawful manner; but in case of a tenancy at will, it shall first be terminated by notice, as prescribed in the Civil Code.

2. When the tenant continues in possession, in person or by subtenant, without the permission of the landlord, or the successor in estate of the landlord, if applicable, after default in the payment of rent, pursuant to the lease or agreement under which the property is held, and three days' notice, excluding Saturdays and Sundays and other judicial holidays, in writing, requiring its payment, stating the amount that is due, the name, telephone number, and address of the person to whom the rent payment shall be made, and, if payment may be made personally, the usual days and hours that person will be available to receive the payment (provided that, if the address does not allow for personal delivery, then it shall be conclusively presumed that upon the mailing of any rent or notice to the owner by the tenant to the name and address provided, the notice or rent is deemed received by the owner on the date posted, if the tenant can show proof of mailing to the name and address provided by the owner), or the number of an account in a financial institution into which the rental payment may be made, and the name and street address of the institution (provided that the institution is located within five miles of the rental property), or if an electronic funds transfer procedure has been previously established, that payment may be made pursuant to that procedure, or possession of the property, shall have been served upon the tenant and if there is a subtenant in actual occupation of the premises, also upon the subtenant. The notice may be served at any time within one year after the rent becomes due. In all cases of tenancy upon agricultural lands, if the tenant has held over and retained possession for more than 60 days after the expiration of the term without any demand of possession or notice to quit by the landlord or the successor in estate of the landlord, if applicable, the tenant shall be deemed to be holding by permission of the landlord or successor in estate of the landlord, if applicable, and shall be entitled to hold under the terms of the lease for another full year, and shall not be guilty of an unlawful detainer during that year, and the holding over for that period shall be taken and construed as a consent on the part of a tenant to hold for another year.

3. When the tenant continues in possession, in person or by subtenant, after a neglect or failure to perform other conditions or covenants of the lease or agreement under which the property is held, including any covenant not to assign or sublet, than the one for the payment of rent, and three days' notice, excluding Saturdays and Sundays and other judicial holidays, in writing, requiring the performance of those conditions or covenants, or the possession of the property, shall have been served upon the tenant, and if there is a subtenant in actual occupation of the premises, also, upon the subtenant. Within three days, excluding Saturdays and Sundays and other judicial holidays, after the service of the notice, the tenant, or any subtenant in actual occupation of the premises, or any mortgagee of the term, or other person interested in its continuance, may perform the conditions or covenants of the lease or pay the stipulated rent, as the case may be, and thereby save the lease from forfeiture; provided, if the conditions and covenants of the lease, violated by the lessee, cannot afterward be performed, then no notice, as last prescribed herein, need be given to the lessee or the subtenant, demanding the performance of the violated conditions or covenants of the lease. A tenant may take proceedings, similar to those prescribed in this chapter, to obtain possession of the premises let to a subtenant or held by a servant, employee, agent, or licensee, in case of that person's unlawful detention of the premises underlet to or held by that person.

4. Any tenant, subtenant, or executor or administrator of that person's estate heretofore qualified and now acting, or hereafter to be qualified and act, assigning or subletting or committing waste upon the demised premises, contrary to the conditions or covenants of the lease, or maintaining, committing, or permitting the maintenance or commission of a nuisance upon the demised premises or using the premises for an unlawful purpose, thereby terminates the lease, and the landlord, or the landlord's successor in estate, shall upon service of three days' notice to quit upon the person or persons in possession, be entitled to restitution of possession of the demised premises under this chapter. For purposes of this subdivision, a person who commits or maintains a public nuisance as described in Section 3482.8 of the Civil Code, or who commits an offense described in subdivision (c) of Section 3485 of the Civil Code, or subdivision (c) of Section 3486 of the Civil Code, or uses the premises to further the purpose of that offense shall be deemed to have committed a nuisance upon the premises.

5. When the tenant gives written notice as provided in Section 1946 of the Civil Code of the tenant's intention to terminate the hiring of the real property, or makes a written offer to surrender which is accepted in writing by the landlord, but fails to deliver possession at the time specified in that written notice, without the permission of the landlord, or the successor in estate of the landlord, if applicable.

6. As used in this section, "tenant" includes any person who hires real property except those persons whose occupancy is described in subdivision (b) of Section 1940 of the Civil Code.

7. This section shall become operative on February 1, 2025.

Added by Stats 2020 ch 37 (AB 3088),s 16, eff. 8/31/2020.

Section 1161.1 - Cases of possession of commercial property after default in payment of rent

With respect to application of Section 1161 in cases of possession of commercial real property after default in the payment of rent:

(a) If the amount stated in the notice provided to the tenant pursuant to subdivision (2) of Section 1161 is clearly identified by the notice as an estimate and the amount claimed is not in fact correct, but it is determined upon the trial or other judicial determination that rent was owing, and the amount claimed in the notice was reasonably estimated, the tenant shall be subject to judgment for possession and the actual amount of rent and other sums found to be due. However, if (1) upon receipt of such a notice claiming an amount identified by the notice as an estimate, the tenant tenders to the landlord within the time for payment required by the notice, the amount which the tenant has reasonably estimated to be due and (2) if at trial it is determined that the amount of rent then due was the amount tendered by the tenant or a lesser amount, the tenant shall be deemed the prevailing party for all purposes. If the court determines that the amount so tendered by the tenant was less than the amount due, but was reasonably estimated, the tenant shall retain the right to possession if the tenant pays to the landlord within five days of the effective date of the judgment (1) the amount previously tendered if it had not been previously accepted, (2) the difference between the amount tendered and the amount determined by the court to be due, and (3) any other sums as ordered by the court.

(b) If the landlord accepts a partial payment of rent, including any payment pursuant to subdivision (a), after serving notice pursuant to Section 1161, the landlord, without any further notice to the tenant, may commence and pursue an action under this chapter to recover the difference between the amount demanded in that notice and the payment actually received, and this shall be specified in the complaint.

(c) If the landlord accepts a partial payment of rent after filing the complaint pursuant to Section 1166, the landlord's acceptance of the partial payment is evidence only of that payment, without waiver of any rights or defenses of any of the parties. The landlord shall be entitled to amend the complaint to reflect the partial payment without creating a necessity for the filing of an additional answer or other responsive pleading by the tenant, and without prior leave of court, and such an amendment shall not delay the matter from proceeding. However, this subdivision shall apply only if the landlord provides actual notice to the tenant that acceptance of the partial rent payment does not constitute a waiver of any rights, including any right the landlord may have to recover possession of the property.

(d) "Commercial real property" as used in this section, means all real property in this state except dwelling units made subject to Chapter 2 (commencing with Section 1940) of Title 5 of Part 4 of Division 3 of the Civil Code, mobilehomes as defined in Section 798.3 of the Civil Code, or recreational vehicles as defined in Section 799.24 of the Civil Code.

(e) For the purposes of this section, there is a presumption affecting the burden of proof that the amount of rent claimed or tendered is reasonably estimated if, in relation to the amount determined to be due upon the trial or other judicial determination of that issue, the amount claimed or tendered was no more than 20 percent more or less than the amount determined to be due. However, if the rent due is contingent upon information primarily within the knowledge of the one party to the lease and that information has not been furnished to, or has not accurately been furnished to, the other party, the court shall consider that fact in determining the reasonableness of the amount of rent claimed or tendered pursuant to subdivision (a).

Added by Stats. 1990, Ch. 890, Sec. 1.

Section 1161.2 - Access to limited civil case records filed under chapter

(a)

(1) The clerk shall allow access to limited civil case records filed under this chapter, including the court file, index, and register of actions, only as follows:

(A) To a party to the action, including a party's attorney.

(B) To a person who provides the clerk with the names of at least one plaintiff and one defendant and the address of the premises, including the apartment or unit number, if any.

(C) To a resident of the premises who provides the clerk with the name of one of the parties or the case number and shows proof of residency.

(D) To a person by order of the court, which may be granted ex parte, on a showing of good cause.

(E) Except as provided in subparagraph (G), to any person by order of the court if judgment is entered for the plaintiff after trial more than 60 days since the filing of the complaint. The court shall issue the order upon issuing judgment for the plaintiff.

(F) Except as provided in subparagraph (G), to any other person 60 days after the complaint has been filed if judgment against all defendants has been entered for the plaintiff within 60 days of the filing of the complaint, in which case the clerk shall allow access to any court records in the action. If a default or default judgment is set aside more than 60 days after the complaint has been filed, this section shall apply as if the complaint had been filed on the date the default or default judgment is set aside.

(G)

(i) In the case of a complaint involving residential property based on Section 1161a as indicated in the caption of the complaint, as required in subdivision (c) of Section 1166, to any other person, if 60 days have elapsed since the complaint was filed with the court, and, as of that date, judgment against all defendants has been entered for the plaintiff, after a trial.

(ii) Subparagraphs (E) and (F) shall not apply if the plaintiff filed the action between March 4, 2020, and September 30, 2021, and the action is based on an alleged default in the payment of rent.

(2) This section shall not be construed to prohibit the court from issuing an order that bars access to the court record in an action filed under this chapter if the parties to the action so stipulate.

(b)

(1) For purposes of this section, "good cause" includes, but is not limited to, both of the following:

(A) The gathering of newsworthy facts by a person described in Section 1070 of the Evidence Code.

(B) The gathering of evidence by a party to an unlawful detainer action solely for the purpose of making a request for judicial notice pursuant to subdivision (d) of Section 452 of the Evidence Code.

(2) It is the intent of the Legislature that a simple procedure be established to request the ex parte order described in subparagraph (D) of paragraph (1) of subdivision (a).

(c) Upon the filing of a case so restricted, the court clerk shall mail notice to each defendant named in the action. The notice shall be mailed to the address provided in the complaint. The notice shall contain a statement that an unlawful detainer complaint (eviction action) has been filed naming that party as a defendant, and that access to the court file will be delayed for 60 days except to a party, an attorney for one of the parties, or any other person who (1) provides to the clerk the names of at least one plaintiff and one defendant in the action and provides to the clerk the address, including any applicable apartment, unit, or space number, of the subject premises, or (2) provides to the clerk the name of one of the parties in the action or the case number and can establish through proper identification that the person lives at the subject premises. The notice shall also contain a statement that access to the court index, register of actions, or other records is not permitted until 60 days after the complaint is filed, except pursuant to an order upon a showing of good cause for access. The notice shall contain on its face the following information:

(1) The name and telephone number of the county bar association.

(2) The name and telephone number of any entity that requests inclusion on the notice and demonstrates to the satisfaction of the court that it has been certified by the State Bar of California as a lawyer referral service and maintains a panel of attorneys qualified in the practice of landlord-tenant law pursuant to the minimum standards for a lawyer referral service established by the State Bar of California and Section 6155 of the Business and Professions Code.

(3) The following statement: "The State Bar of California certifies lawyer referral services in California and publishes a list of certified lawyer referral services organized by county. To locate a lawyer referral service in your county, go to the State Bar's internet website at www.calbar.ca.gov or call 1-866-442-2529."

(4) The name and telephone number of an office or offices funded by the federal Legal Services Corporation or qualified legal services projects that receive funds distributed pursuant to Section 6216 of the Business and Professions Code that provide legal services to low-income persons in the county in which the action is filed. The notice shall state that these telephone numbers may be called for legal advice regarding the case. The notice shall be issued between 24 and 48 hours of the filing of the complaint, excluding weekends and holidays. One copy of the notice shall be addressed to "all occupants" and mailed separately to the subject premises. The notice shall not constitute service of the summons and complaint.

(5) The following statement, for a notice sent out pursuant to this section between October 1, 2021 and March 31, 2022: "IMPORTANT NOTICE FROM THE STATE OF CALIFORNIA - YOU MUST TAKE ACTION TO AVOID AN EVICTION: As part of the state's COVID-19 relief plan, money has been set aside to help renters who have fallen behind on rent or utility payments.

If you are behind on rent or utility payments, YOU SHOULD COMPLETE A RENTAL ASSISTANCE APPLICATION IMMEDIATELY! It is free and simple to apply. Citizenship or immigration status does not matter.

You can find out how to start your application by calling 1-833-430-2122 or visiting http://housingiskey.com right away."

(d) Notwithstanding any other law, the court shall charge an additional fee of fifteen dollars ($15) for filing a first appearance by the plaintiff. This fee shall be added to the uniform filing fee for actions filed under this chapter.

(e) This section does not apply to a case that seeks to terminate a mobilehome park tenancy if the statement of the character of the proceeding in the caption of the complaint clearly indicates that the complaint seeks termination of a mobilehome park tenancy.

(f) This section does not alter any provision of the Evidence Code.

Amended by Stats 2021 ch 360 (AB 1584),s 7, eff. 1/1/2022.
Amended by Stats 2021 ch 27 (AB 832),s 11, eff. 6/28/2021.
Amended by Stats 2021 ch 2 (SB 91),s 11, eff. 1/29/2021.
Amended by Stats 2020 ch 37 (AB 3088),s 17, eff. 8/31/2020.
Amended by Stats 2020 ch 36 (AB 3364),s 25, eff. 1/1/2021.
Amended by Stats 2016 ch 336 (AB 2819),s 3, eff. 1/1/2017.
Amended by Stats 2012 ch 241 (AB 1865),s 1, eff. 1/1/2013.
Amended by Stats 2010 ch 641 (SB 1149),s 1, eff. 1/1/2011.
Amended by Stats 2005 ch 610 (AB 664),s 2, eff. 1/1/2006
Amended by Stats 2005 ch 75 (AB 145),s 41, eff. 7/19/2005, op. 1/1/2006
Amended by Stats 2004 ch 568 (SB 1145),s 6, eff. 1/1/2005
Amended by Stats 2003 ch 449 (AB 1712),s 15, eff. 1/1/2004.
Amended by Stats 2003 ch 787 (SB 345),s 2, eff. 1/1/2004.
Amended by Stats 2001 ch 824 (AB 1700), s 11, eff. 1/1/2002.

Section 1161.2.5 - Access to civil case records for actions seeking recovery of COVID-19 rental debt

(a)

(1) Except as provided in Section 1161.2, the clerk shall allow access to civil case records for actions seeking recovery of COVID-19 rental debt, as defined in Section 1179.02, including the court file, index, and register of actions, only as follows:

(A) To a party to the action, including a party's attorney.

(B) To a person who provides the clerk with the names of at least one plaintiff and one defendant.

(C) To a resident of the premises for which the COVID-19 rental debt is owed who provides the clerk with the name of one of the parties or the case number and shows proof of residency.

(D) To a person by order of the court, which may be granted ex parte, on a showing of good cause.

(2) To give the court notice that access to the records in an action is limited, any complaint or responsive pleading in a case subject to this section shall include on either the first page of the pleading or a cover page, the phrase "ACTION FOR RECOVERY OF COVID-19 RENTAL DEBT AS DEFINED UNDER SECTION 1179.02" in bold, capital letters, in 12 point or larger font.

(3) The Judicial Council shall develop forms for parties to utilize in actions brought pursuant to Section 116.223 and in civil actions for recovery of COVID-19 rental debt as defined in Section 1179.02. The forms shall provide prominent notice on the first page that access to the records in the case is limited pursuant to this section.

(b)

(1) For purposes of this section, "good cause" includes, but is not limited to, both of the following:

(A) The gathering of newsworthy facts by a person described in Section 1070 of the Evidence Code.

(B) The gathering of evidence by a party to a civil action solely for the purpose of making a request for judicial notice pursuant to subdivision (d) of Section 452 of the Evidence Code.

(2) It is the intent of the Legislature that a simple procedure be established to request the ex parte order described in subparagraph (D) of paragraph (1) of subdivision (a).

(c) This section does not alter any provision of the Evidence Code.

Amended by Stats 2021 ch 27 (AB 832),s 13, eff. 6/28/2021.
Amended by Stats 2021 ch 2 (SB 91),s 13, eff. 1/29/2021.
Added by Stats 2020 ch 37 (AB 3088),s 19, eff. 8/31/2020.

Section 1161.3 - Acts against tenant or tenant's household member constituting domestic violence

(a) For purposes of this section:

(1) "Abuse or violence" means domestic violence as defined in Section 6211 of the Family Code, sexual assault as defined in Section 1219, stalking as defined in Section 1708.7 of the Civil Code or Section 646.9 of the Penal Code, human trafficking as defined in Section 236.1 of the Penal Code, abuse of an elder or a dependent adult as defined in Section 15610.07 of the Welfare and Institutions Code, or any act described in paragraphs (6) to (8), inclusive, of subdivision (a) of Section 1946.7 of the Civil Code.

(2) "Documentation evidencing abuse or violence against the tenant, the tenant's immediate family member, or the tenant's household member" means any of the following:

(A) A temporary restraining order, emergency protective order, or protective order lawfully issued within the last 180 days pursuant to Section 527.6, Part 3 (commencing with Section 6240), Part 4 (commencing with Section 6300), or Part 5 (commencing with Section 6400) of Division 10 of the Family Code, Section 136.2 of the Penal Code, or Section 213.5 or 15657.03 of the Welfare and Institutions Code that protects the tenant, the tenant's immediate family member, or the tenant's household member from abuse or violence.

(B) A copy of a written report, written within the last 180 days, by a peace officer employed by a state or local law enforcement agency acting in the officer's official capacity, stating that the tenant, the tenant's immediate family member, or the tenant's household member has filed a report alleging that they are a victim of abuse or violence.

(C)

(i) Documentation from a qualified third party based on information received by that third party while acting in their professional capacity to indicate that the tenant, the tenant's immediate family member, or the tenant's household member is seeking assistance for physical or mental injuries or abuse resulting from an act of abuse or violence, which shall contain, in substantially the same form, the following:

Tenant Statement and Qualified Third Party Statement under Code of Civil Procedure Section 1161.3

Part I. Statement By Tenant

I, [insert name of tenant], state as follows:

I, my immediate family member, or a member of my household, have been a victim of:

[insert one or more of the following: domestic violence, sexual assault, stalking, human trafficking, elder abuse, dependent adult abuse, a crime that caused bodily injury or death, a crime that included the exhibition, drawing, brandishing, or use of a firearm or other deadly weapon or instrument, or a crime that included the use or threat of force against the victim.]

The most recent incident(s) happened on or about:

[insert date or dates.]

The incident(s) was/were committed by the following person(s), with these physical description(s), if known and safe to provide:

[if known and safe to provide, insert name(s) and physical description(s).]

(signature of tenant)(date)

Part II. Qualified Third Party Statement

I, [insert name of qualified third party], state as follows:

My business address and phone number are:

[insert business address and phone number.]

Check and complete one of the following:

_____ I meet the requirements for a sexual assault counselor provided in Section 1035.2 of the Evidence Code and I am either engaged in an office, hospital, institution, or center commonly known as a rape crisis center described in that section or employed by an organization providing the programs specified in Section 13835.2 of the Penal Code.

_____ I meet the requirements for a domestic violence counselor provided in Section 1037.1 of the Evidence Code and I am employed, whether financially compensated or not, by a domestic violence victim service organization, as defined in that section.

_____ I meet the requirements for a human trafficking caseworker provided in Section 1038.2 of the Evidence Code and I am employed, whether financially compensated or not, by an organization that provides programs specified in Section 18294 of the Welfare and Institutions Code or in Section 13835.2 of the Penal Code.

_____ I meet the definition of "victim of violent crime advocate" provided in Section 1946.7 of the Civil Code and I am employed, whether financially compensated or not, by an agency or organization that has a documented record of providing services to victims of violent crime or provides those services under the auspices or supervision of a court or a law enforcement or prosecution agency.

_____ I am licensed by the State of California as a:

[insert one of the following: physician and surgeon, osteopathic physician and surgeon, registered nurse, psychiatrist, psychologist, licensed clinical social worker, licensed marriage and family therapist, or licensed professional clinical counselor.] and I am licensed by, and my license number is:

[insert name of state licensing entity and license number.]

The person who signed the Statement By Tenant above stated to me that they, a member of their immediate family, or a member of their household is a victim of:

[insert one or more of the following: domestic violence, sexual assault, stalking, human trafficking, elder abuse, dependent adult abuse, a crime that caused bodily injury or death, a crime that included the exhibition, drawing, brandishing, or use of a firearm or other deadly weapon or instrument, or a crime that included the use or threat of force against the victim.]

The person further stated to me the incident(s) occurred on or about the date(s) stated above.

(signature of qualified third party)(date)

(ii)The documentation may be signed by a person who meets the requirements for a sexual assault counselor, domestic violence counselor, a human trafficking caseworker, or a victim of violent crime advocate only if the documentation displays the letterhead of the office, hospital, institution, center, or organization, as appropriate, that engages or employs, whether financially compensated or not, this counselor, caseworker, or advocate.

(D)Any other form of documentation or evidence that reasonably verifies that the abuse or violence occurred.

(3)"Health practitioner" means a physician and surgeon, osteopathic physician and surgeon, psychiatrist, psychologist, registered nurse, licensed clinical social worker, licensed marriage and family therapist, or licensed professional clinical counselor.

(4)"Immediate family member" has the same meaning as defined in Section 1946.7 of the Civil Code.

(5)"Perpetrator of abuse or violence" means any of the following:

(A)The person against whom an order described in subparagraph (A) of paragraph (1) of subdivision (a) has been issued.

(B)The person who was named or referred to as causing the abuse or violence in the report described in subparagraph (B) of paragraph (1) of subdivision (a).

(C)The person who was named or referred to as causing the abuse or violence in the documentation described in subparagraph (C) of paragraph (1) of subdivision (a).

(D)The person who was named or referred to as causing the abuse or violence in the documentation described in subparagraph (D) of paragraph (1) of subdivision (a).

(6)"Qualified third party" means a health practitioner, domestic violence counselor, as defined in Section 1037.1 of the Evidence Code, a sexual assault counselor, as defined in Section 1035.2 of the Evidence Code, a human trafficking caseworker, as defined in Section 1038.2 of the Evidence Code, or a victim of violent crime advocate.

(7)"Tenant" means tenant, subtenant, lessee, or sublessee.

(8)"Tenant in residence" means a tenant who is currently residing in the unit and has full physical and legal access to the unit.

(9)"Victim of violent crime advocate" has the same meaning as defined in Section 1946.7 of the Civil Code.

(b)

(1)A landlord shall not terminate a tenancy or fail to renew a tenancy based on an act of abuse or violence against a tenant, a tenant's immediate family member, or a tenant's household member if the landlord has received documentation evidencing abuse or violence against the tenant, the tenant's immediate family member, or the tenant's household member.

(2)Notwithstanding paragraph (1), a landlord may terminate a tenancy or fail to renew a tenancy based on an act of abuse or violence against a tenant, a tenant's immediate family member, or a tenant's household member even after receiving documentation of abuse or violence against the tenant, the tenant's immediate family member, or the tenant's household member if either of the following apply:

(A)The perpetrator of abuse or violence is a tenant in residence of the same dwelling unit as the tenant, the tenant's immediate family member, or household member.

(B)Both of the following apply:

(i)The perpetrator of abuse or violence's words or actions have threatened the physical safety of other tenants, guests, invitees, or licensees.

(ii)After expiration of a three-day notice requiring the tenant not to voluntarily permit or consent to the presence of the perpetrator of abuse or violence on the premises, the tenant continues to do so.

(c)Notwithstanding any provision in a lease to the contrary, a landlord shall not be liable to any other tenants for any action that arises due to the landlord's compliance with this section.

(d)A violation of subdivision (b) by the landlord shall be an affirmative defense to a cause of action for unlawful detainer that is based on an act of abuse or violence against a tenant, a tenant's immediate family member, or a tenant's household member as follows:

(1)If the perpetrator of the abuse or violence is not a tenant in residence of the same dwelling unit as the tenant, the tenant's immediate family member, or household member, then the defendant shall have a complete defense as to that cause of action, unless each clause of subparagraph (B) of paragraph (2) of subdivision (b) applies.

(2)If the perpetrator of the abuse or violence is a tenant in residence of the same dwelling unit as the tenant, the tenant's immediate family member, or household member, the court shall proceed in accordance with Section 1174.27.

(e)

(1)A landlord shall not disclose any information provided by a tenant under this section to a third party unless either of the following is true:

(A)The tenant has consented in writing to the disclosure.

(B)The disclosure is required by law or court order.

(2)A landlord's communication with the qualified third party who provides documentation in order to verify the contents of that documentation is not a disclosure for purposes of this subdivision.

(f)The Judicial Council shall review its forms that may be used by a party to assert in the responsive pleading the grounds set forth in this section as an affirmative defense to an unlawful detainer action and, by January 1, 2024, make any changes to those forms that the Judicial Council deems necessary to conform them to this section.

Amended by Stats 2022 ch 558 (SB 1017),s 2, eff. 1/1/2023.
Amended by Stats 2018 ch 190 (AB 2413),s 2, eff. 1/1/2019.
Amended by Stats 2013 ch 130 (SB 612),s 3, eff. 1/1/2014.
Amended by Stats 2012 ch 516 (SB 1403),s 2, eff. 1/1/2013.
Added by Stats 2010 ch 626 (SB 782),s 4, eff. 1/1/2011.

Section 1161.4 - Causing tenant to quit involuntarily or bring action to recover possession because of immigration or citizenship status prohibited

(a) A landlord shall not cause a tenant or occupant to quit involuntarily or bring an action to recover possession because of the immigration or citizenship status of a tenant, occupant, or other person known to the landlord to be associated with a tenant or occupant, unless the landlord is complying with any legal obligation under any federal government program that provides for rent limitations or rental assistance to a qualified tenant.

(b) In an unlawful detainer action, a tenant or occupant may raise, as an affirmative defense, that the landlord violated subdivision (a).

(c) It is a rebuttable presumption that a tenant or occupant has established an affirmative defense under this section in an unlawful detainer action if the landlord did both of the following:

(1) Approved the tenant or occupant to take possession of the unit before filing the unlawful detainer action.

(2) Included in the unlawful detainer action a claim based on one of the following:

(A) The failure at any time of a previously approved tenant or occupant to provide a valid social security number.

(B) The failure at any time of a previously approved tenant or occupant to provide information required to obtain a consumer credit report under Section 1785.11 of the Civil Code.

(C) The failure at any time of a previously approved tenant or occupant to provide a form of identification deemed acceptable by the landlord.

(d) This section does not create a rebuttable presumption that a tenant or occupant has established an affirmative defense under this section if a landlord has requested the information described in paragraph (2) of subdivision (c) for the purpose of complying with any legal obligation under any federal government program that provides for rent limitations or rental assistance to a qualified tenant, or any other federal law, or a subpoena, warrant, or other order issued by a court.
(e) The rebuttable presumption in this section does not limit paragraph (2) of subdivision (c) of Section 1940.3 of the Civil Code.
(f) No affirmative defense is established under subdivision (b) if a landlord files an unlawful detainer action for the purpose of complying with any legal obligation under any federal government program that provides for rent limitations or rental assistance to a qualified tenant.
(g) For purposes of this section, "immigration or citizenship status" includes a perception that the person has a particular immigration status or citizenship status, or that the person is associated with a person who has, or is perceived to have, a particular immigration status or citizenship status.
Added by Stats 2017 ch 489 (AB 291),s 8, eff. 1/1/2018.

Section 1161.5 - Declaration of forfeiture nullified upon timely performance after notice or waiver of breach
When the notice required by Section 1161 states that the lessor or the landlord may elect to declare the forfeiture of the lease or rental agreement, that declaration shall be nullified and the lease or rental agreement shall remain in effect if the lessee or tenant performs within three days after service of the notice or if the breach is waived by the lessor or the landlord after service of the notice.
Added by Stats. 1984, Ch. 174, Sec. 1.

Section 1161a - Removal of persons holding over and continuing in possession of manufactured home, mobilehome, floating home or real property after three-day notice
(a) As used in this section:

(1) "Manufactured home" has the same meaning as provided in Section 18007 of the Health and Safety Code.

(2) "Mobilehome" has the same meaning as provided in Section 18008 of the Health and Safety Code.

(3) "Floating home" has the same meaning as provided in subdivision (d) of Section 18075.55 of the Health and Safety Code.

(b) In any of the following cases, a person who holds over and continues in possession of a manufactured home, mobilehome, floating home, or real property after a three-day written notice to quit the property has been served upon the person, or if there is a subtenant in actual occupation of the premises, also upon such subtenant, as prescribed in Section 1162, may be removed therefrom as prescribed in this chapter:

(1) Where the property has been sold pursuant to a writ of execution against such person, or a person under whom such person claims, and the title under the sale has been duly perfected.

(2) Where the property has been sold pursuant to a writ of sale, upon the foreclosure by proceedings taken as prescribed in this code of a mortgage, or under an express power of sale contained therein, executed by such person, or a person under whom such person claims, and the title under the foreclosure has been duly perfected.

(3) Where the property has been sold in accordance with Section 2924 of the Civil Code, under a power of sale contained in a deed of trust executed by such person, or a person under whom such person claims, and the title under the sale has been duly perfected.

(4) Where the property has been sold by such person, or a person under whom such person claims, and the title under the sale has been duly perfected.

(5) Where the property has been sold in accordance with Section 18037.5 of the Health and Safety Code under the default provisions of a conditional sale contract or security agreement executed by such person, or a person under whom such person claims, and the title under the sale has been duly perfected.

(c) Notwithstanding the provisions of subdivision (b), a tenant or subtenant in possession of a rental housing unit which has been sold by reason of any of the causes enumerated in subdivision (b), who rents or leases the rental housing unit either on a periodic basis from week to week, month to month, or other interval, or for a fixed period of time, shall be given written notice to quit pursuant to Section 1162, at least as long as the term of hiring itself but not exceeding 30 days, before the tenant or subtenant may be removed therefrom as prescribed in this chapter.
(d) For the purpose of subdivision (c), "rental housing unit" means any structure or any part thereof which is rented or offered for rent for residential occupancy in this state.
Amended by Stats. 1991, Ch. 942, Sec. 11.

Section 1161b - Tenant or subtenant in possession of rental housing unit at time property sold in foreclosure
(a) Notwithstanding Section 1161a, a tenant or subtenant in possession of a rental housing unit under a month-to-month lease or periodic tenancy at the time the property is sold in foreclosure shall be given 90 days' written notice to quit pursuant to Section 1162 before the tenant or subtenant may be removed from the property as prescribed in this chapter.
(b) In addition to the rights set forth in subdivision (a), tenants or subtenants holding possession of a rental housing unit under a fixed-term residential lease entered into before transfer of title at the foreclosure sale shall have the right to possession until the end of the lease term, and all rights and obligations under the lease shall survive foreclosure, except that the tenancy may be terminated upon 90 days' written notice to quit pursuant to subdivision (a) if any of the following conditions apply:

(1) The purchaser or successor in interest will occupy the housing unit as a primary residence.

(2) The lessee is the mortgagor or the child, spouse, or parent of the mortgagor.

(3) The lease was not the result of an arms' length transaction.

(4) The lease requires the receipt of rent that is substantially less than fair market rent for the property, except when rent is reduced or subsidized due to a federal, state, or local subsidy or law.

(c) The purchaser or successor in interest shall bear the burden of proof in establishing that a fixed-term residential lease is not entitled to protection under subdivision (b).
(d) This section shall not apply if any party to the note remains in the property as a tenant, subtenant, or occupant.
(e) Nothing in this section is intended to affect any local just cause eviction ordinance. This section does not, and shall not be construed to, affect the authority of a public entity that otherwise exists to regulate or monitor the basis for eviction.
Amended by Stats 2019 ch 134 (SB 18),s 3, eff. 1/1/2020.
Amended by Stats 2012 ch 562 (AB 2610),s 3, eff. 1/1/2013.
Added by Stats 2008 ch 69 (SB 1137),s 6, eff. 7/8/2008.

Section 1161c - [Repealed]
Amended by Stats 2012 ch 210 (SB 825),s 1, eff. 1/1/2013.
Added by Stats 2010 ch 641 (SB 1149),s 2, eff. 1/1/2011.

Section 1162 - Service of required notices
(a) Except as provided in subdivision (b), the notices required by Sections 1161 and 1161a may be served by any of the following methods:

(1) By delivering a copy to the tenant personally.

(2) If he or she is absent from his or her place of residence, and from his or her usual place of business, by leaving a copy with some person of suitable age and discretion at either place, and sending a copy through the mail addressed to the tenant at his or her place of residence.

(3) If such place of residence and business cannot be ascertained, or a person of suitable age or discretion there can not be found, then by affixing a copy in a conspicuous place on the property, and also delivering a copy to a person there residing, if such person can be found; and also

sending a copy through the mail addressed to the tenant at the place where the property is situated. Service upon a subtenant may be made in the same manner.

(b) The notices required by Section 1161 may be served upon a commercial tenant by any of the following methods:

(1) By delivering a copy to the tenant personally.

(2) If he or she is absent from the commercial rental property, by leaving a copy with some person of suitable age and discretion at the property, and sending a copy through the mail addressed to the tenant at the address where the property is situated.

(3) If, at the time of attempted service, a person of suitable age or discretion is not found at the rental property through the exercise of reasonable diligence, then by affixing a copy in a conspicuous place on the property, and also sending a copy through the mail addressed to the tenant at the address where the property is situated. Service upon a subtenant may be made in the same manner.

(c) For purposes of subdivision (b), "commercial tenant" means a person or entity that hires any real property in this state that is not a dwelling unit, as defined in subdivision (c) of Section 1940 of the Civil Code, or a mobilehome, as defined in Section 798.3 of the Civil Code.

Amended by Stats 2010 ch 144 (AB 1263),s 1, eff. 1/1/2011.

Amended by Stats 2002 ch 664 (AB 3034),s 49.5, eff. 1/1/2003.

Section 1162a - Service of copy of receiver's or levying officer's deed

In any case in which service or exhibition of a receiver's or levying officer's deed is required, in lieu thereof service of a copy or copies of the deed may be made as provided in Section 1162.

Amended by Stats. 1982, Ch. 497, Sec. 75. Operative July 1, 1983, by Sec. 185 of Ch. 497.

Section 1164 - Parties defendants

No person other than the tenant of the premises and subtenant, if there be one, in the actual occupation of the premises when the complaint is filed, need be made parties defendant in the proceeding, nor shall any proceeding abate, nor the plaintiff be nonsuited for the nonjoinder of any person who might have been made party defendant, but when it appears that any of the parties served with process, or appearing in the proceeding, are guilty of the offense charged, judgment must be rendered against him or her. In case a defendant has become a subtenant of the premises in controversy, after the service of the notice provided for by subdivision 2 of Section 1161 of this code, upon the tenant of the premises, the fact that such notice was not served on each subtenant shall constitute no defense to the action. All persons who enter the premises under the tenant, after the commencement of the suit, shall be bound by the judgment, the same as if he or they had been made party to the action.

Amended by Stats. 1975, Ch. 1241.

Section 1165 - Applicability of procedures relating to civil actions

Except as provided in the preceding section, the provisions of Part II of this Code, relating to parties to civil actions, are applicable to this proceeding.

Enacted 1872.

Section 1166 - Complaint requirements

(a) The complaint shall:

(1) Be verified and include the typed or printed name of the person verifying the complaint.

(2) Set forth the facts on which the plaintiff seeks to recover.

(3) Describe the premises with reasonable certainty.

(4) If the action is based on paragraph (2) of Section 1161, state the amount of rent in default.

(5) State specifically the method used to serve the defendant with the notice or notices of termination upon which the complaint is based. This requirement may be satisfied by using and completing all items relating to service of the notice or notices in an appropriate Judicial Council form complaint, or by attaching a proof of service of the notice or notices of termination served on the defendant.

(b) The complaint may set forth any circumstances of fraud, force, or violence that may have accompanied the alleged forcible entry or forcible or unlawful detainer, and claim damages therefor.

(c) In an action regarding residential real property based on Section 1161a, the plaintiff shall state in the caption of the complaint "Action based on Code of Civil Procedure Section 1161a."

(d)

(1) In an action regarding residential property, the plaintiff shall attach to the complaint the following:

(A) A copy of the notice or notices of termination served on the defendant upon which the complaint is based.

(B) A copy of any written lease or rental agreement regarding the premises. Any addenda or attachments to the lease or written agreement that form the basis of the complaint shall also be attached. The documents required by this subparagraph are not required to be attached if the complaint alleges any of the following:

(i) The lease or rental agreement is oral.

(ii) A written lease or rental agreement regarding the premises is not in the possession of the landlord or any agent or employee of the landlord.

(iii) An action based solely on subdivision (2) of Section 1161.

(2) If the plaintiff fails to attach the documents required by this subdivision, the court shall grant leave to amend the complaint for a five-day period in order to include the required attachments.

(e) Upon filing the complaint, a summons shall be issued thereon.

Amended by Stats 2010 ch 641 (SB 1149),s 3, eff. 1/1/2011.

Added by Stats 2003 ch 787 (SB 345),s 4, eff. 1/1/2004 op. 1/1/2005.

Former §1166 repealed by Stats 2003 ch 787 (SB 345),s 3, eff. 1/1/2004

Section 1166a - Immediate possession upon motion by writ of possession

(a) Upon filing the complaint, the plaintiff may, upon motion, have immediate possession of the premises by a writ of possession of a manufactured home, mobilehome, or real property issued by the court and directed to the sheriff of the county or marshal, for execution, where it appears to the satisfaction of the court, after a hearing on the motion, from the verified complaint and from any affidavits filed or oral testimony given by or on behalf of the parties, that the defendant resides out of state, has departed from the state, cannot, after due diligence, be found within the state, or has concealed himself or herself to avoid the service of summons. The motion shall indicate that the writ applies to all tenants, subtenants, if any, named claimants, if any, and any other occupants of the premises.

(b) Written notice of the hearing on the motion shall be served on the defendant by the plaintiff in accordance with the provisions of Section 1011, and shall inform the defendant as follows: "You may file affidavits on your own behalf with the court and may appear and present testimony on your own behalf. However, if you fail to appear, the plaintiff will apply to the court for a writ of possession of a manufactured home, mobilehome, or real property."

(c) The plaintiff shall file an undertaking in a sum that shall be fixed and determined by the judge, to the effect that, if the plaintiff fails to recover judgment against the defendant for the possession of the premises or if the suit is dismissed, the plaintiff will pay to the defendant those damages, not to exceed the amount fixed in the undertaking, as may be sustained by the defendant by reason of that dispossession under the writ of possession of a manufactured home, mobilehome, or real property.

(d) If, at the hearing on the motion, the findings of the court are in favor of the plaintiff and against the defendant, an order shall be entered for the immediate possession of the premises.
(e) The order for the immediate possession of the premises may be enforced as provided in Division 3 (commencing with Section 712.010) of Title 9 of Part 2.
(f) For the purposes of this section, references in Division 3 (commencing with Section 712.010) of Title 9 of Part 2 and in subdivisions (e) to (m), inclusive, of Section 1174, to the "judgment debtor" shall be deemed references to the defendant, to the "judgment creditor" shall be deemed references to the plaintiff, and to the "judgment of possession or sale of property" shall be deemed references to an order for the immediate possession of the premises.
Amended by Stats. 1996, Ch. 872, Sec. 20. Effective January 1, 1997.

Section 1167 - Summons; defendant's response
(a) The summons shall be in the form specified in Section 412.20 except that when the defendant is served, the defendant's response shall be filed within five days, excluding Saturdays and Sundays and other judicial holidays, after the complaint is served upon the defendant.
(b) If service is completed by mail or in person through the Secretary of State's address confidentiality program under Chapter 3.1 (commencing with Section 6205) of Division 7 of Title 1 of the Government Code, the defendant shall have an additional five court days to file a response.
(c) In all other respects the summons shall be issued and served and returned in the same manner as a summons in a civil action.
Amended by Stats 2022 ch 686 (AB 1726),s 3, eff. 1/1/2023.
Amended by Stats 2018 ch 260 (AB 2343),s 2, eff. 1/1/2019.

Section 1167.1 - Dismissal for failure to file proof of service
If proof of service of the summons has not been filed within 60 days of the complaint's filing, the court may dismiss the action without prejudice.
Added by Stats 2016 ch 336 (AB 2819),s 4, eff. 1/1/2017.

Section 1167.25 - [Repealed]
Repealed by Stats 2001 ch 115 (SB 153), s 4, eff. 1/1/2002.

Section 1167.3 - Time allowed defendant to answer
In any action under this chapter, unless otherwise ordered by the court for good cause shown, the time allowed the defendant to answer the complaint, answer the complaint, if amended, or amend the answer under paragraph (2), (3), (5), (6), or (7) of subdivision (a) of Section 586 shall not exceed five days.
EFFECTIVE 1/1/2000. Amended September 7, 1999 (Bill Number: SB 210) (Chapter 344).
Amended July 12, 1999 (Bill Number: SB 966) (Chapter 83).

Section 1167.4 - Notice of motion as provided for in section 418.10(a) filed by defendant
Notwithstanding any other provision of law, in any action under this chapter:
(a) Where the defendant files a notice of motion as provided for in subdivision (a) of Section 418.10, the time for making the motion shall be not less than three days nor more than seven days after the filing of the notice.
(b) The service and filing of a notice of motion under subdivision (a) shall extend the defendant's time to plead until five days after service upon him of the written notice of entry of an order denying his motion, except that for good cause shown the court may extend the defendant's time to plead for an additional period not exceeding 15 days.
Added by Stats. 1971, Ch. 1332.

Section 1167.5 - Number of days allowed in extension of time
Unless otherwise ordered by the court for good cause shown, no extension of time allowed in any action under this chapter for the causes specified in Section 1054 shall exceed 10 days without the consent of the adverse party.
Added by Stats. 1971, Ch. 849.

Section 1169 - Default judgment
If, at the time appointed, any defendant served with a summons does not appear and defend, the clerk, upon written application of the plaintiff and proof of the service of summons and complaint, shall enter the default of any defendant so served, and, if requested by the plaintiff, immediately shall enter judgment for restitution of the premises and shall issue a writ of execution thereon. The application for default judgment and the default judgment shall include a place to indicate that the judgment includes tenants, subtenants, if any, named claimants, if any, and any other occupants of the premises. Thereafter, the plaintiff may apply to the court for any other relief demanded in the complaint, including the costs, against the defendant, or defendants, or against one or more of the defendants.
Amended by Stats 2007 ch 263 (AB 310),s 13, eff. 1/1/2008.

Section 1170 - Appearance by defendant
On or before the day fixed for his appearance, the defendant may appear and answer or demur.
Enacted 1872.

Section 1170.5 - Trial of proceeding
(a) If the defendant appears pursuant to Section 1170, trial of the proceeding shall be held not later than the 20th day following the date that the request to set the time of the trial is made. Judgment shall be entered thereon and, if the plaintiff prevails, a writ of execution shall be issued immediately by the court upon the request of the plaintiff.
(b) The court may extend the period for trial upon the agreement of all of the parties. No other extension of the time for trial of an action under this chapter may be granted unless the court, upon its own motion or on motion of any party, holds a hearing and renders a decision thereon as specified in subdivision (c).
(c) If trial is not held within the time specified in this section, the court, upon finding that there is a reasonable probability that the plaintiff will prevail in the action, shall determine the amount of damages, if any, to be suffered by the plaintiff by reason of the extension, and shall issue an order requiring the defendant to pay that amount into court as the rent would have otherwise become due and payable or into an escrow designated by the court for so long as the defendant remains in possession pending the termination of the action. The determination of the amount of the payment shall be based on the plaintiff's verified statement of the contract rent for rental payment, any verified objection thereto filed by the defendant, and the oral or demonstrative evidence presented at the hearing. The court's determination of the amount of damages shall include consideration of any evidence, presented by the parties, embracing the issue of diminution of value or any set off permitted by law.
(d) If the defendant fails to make a payment ordered by the court, trial of the action shall be held within 15 days of the date payment was due.
(e) Any cost for administration of an escrow account pursuant to this section shall be recoverable by the prevailing party as part of any recoverable cost in the action.
(f) After trial of the action, the court shall determine the distribution of the payment made into court or the escrow designated by the court.
(g) Where payments into court or the escrow designated by the court are made pursuant to this section, the court may order that the payments be invested in an insured interest-bearing account. Interest on the account shall be allocated to the parties in the same proportions as the original funds are allocated.
(h) If any provision of this section or the application thereof to any person or circumstances is held invalid, such invalidity shall not affect other provisions or applications of the section which can be given effect without the invalid provision or application, and to this end the provisions of this section are severable.

(i) Nothing in this section shall be construed to abrogate or interfere with the precedence given to the trial of criminal cases over the trial of civil matters by Section 1050 of the Penal Code.
Added by Stats. 1982, Ch. 1620, Sec. 2.

Section 1170.7 - Motion for summary judgment
A motion for summary judgment may be made at any time after the answer is filed upon giving five days notice. Summary judgment shall be granted or denied on the same basis as a motion under Section 437c.
Added by Stats. 1982, Ch. 1620, Sec. 3.

Section 1170.8 - Discovery motion
In any action under this chapter, a discovery motion may be made at any time upon giving five days' notice.
Added by Stats 2007 ch 113 (AB 1126),s 1, eff. 1/1/2008.

Section 1170.9 - Rules prescribing time for filing and serving opposition and reply papers
The Judicial Council shall adopt rules, not inconsistent with statute, prescribing the time for filing and serving opposition and reply papers, if any, relating to a motion under Section 1167.4, 1170.7, or 1170.8.
Added by Stats 2007 ch 113 (AB 1126),s 2, eff. 1/1/2008.

Section 1171 - Issue of fact tried by jury
Whenever an issue of fact is presented by the pleadings, it must be tried by a jury, unless such jury be waived as in other cases. The jury shall be formed in the same manner as other trial juries in an action of the same jurisdictional classification in the Court in which the action is pending.
Amended by Stats. 1998, Ch. 931, Sec. 120. Effective September 28, 1998.

Section 1172 - Showing required by plaintiff in proceeding for forcible entry or forcible detainer; defendant's showing in defense
On the trial of any proceeding for any forcible entry or forcible detainer, the plaintiff shall only be required to show, in addition to the forcible entry or forcible detainer complained of, that he was peaceably in the actual possession at the time of the forcible entry, or was entitled to the possession at the time of the forcible detainer. The defendant may show in his defense that he or his ancestors, or those whose interest in such premises he claims, have been in the quiet possession thereof for the space of one whole year together next before the commencement of the proceedings, and that his interest therein is not then ended or determined; and such showing is a bar to the proceedings.
Enacted 1872.

Section 1173 - Amendment of complaint when evidence shows defendant guilty of offense other than charged in complaint
When, upon the trial of any proceeding under this chapter, it appears from the evidence that the defendant has been guilty of either a forcible entry or a forcible or unlawful detainer, and other than the offense charged in the complaint, the Judge must order that such complaint be forthwith amended to conform to such proofs; such amendment must be made without any imposition of terms. No continuance shall be permitted upon account of such amendment unless the defendant, by affidavit filed, shows to the satisfaction of the Court good cause therefor.
Amended by Stats. 1885, Ch. 121.

Section 1174 - Judgment if verdict or findings of court in favor of plaintiff; action brought by petroleum distributor against gasoline dealer
(a) If upon the trial, the verdict of the jury, or, if the case be tried without a jury, the findings of the court be in favor of the plaintiff and against the defendant, judgment shall be entered for the possession of the premises; and if the proceedings be for an unlawful detainer after neglect, or failure to perform the conditions or covenants of the lease or agreement under which the property is held, or after default in the payment of rent, the judgment shall also declare the forfeiture of that lease or agreement if the notice required by Section 1161 states the election of the landlord to declare the forfeiture thereof, but if that notice does not so state that election, the lease or agreement shall not be forfeited. Except as provided in Section 1166a, in any action for unlawful detainer brought by a petroleum distributor against a gasoline dealer, possession shall not be restored to the petroleum distributor unless the court in the unlawful detainer action determines that the petroleum distributor had good cause under Section 20999.1 of the Business and Professions Code to terminate, cancel, or refuse to renew the franchise of the gasoline dealer.
In any action for unlawful detainer brought by a petroleum distributor against the gasoline dealer, the court may, at the time of request of either party, require the tenant to make rental payments into the court, for the lessor, at the contract rate, pending the resolution of the action.
(b) The jury or the court, if the proceedings be tried without a jury, shall also assess the damages occasioned to the plaintiff by any forcible entry, or by any forcible or unlawful detainer, alleged in the complaint and proved on the trial, and find the amount of any rent due, if the alleged unlawful detainer be after default in the payment of rent. If the defendant is found guilty of forcible entry, or forcible or unlawful detainer, and malice is shown, the plaintiff may be awarded statutory damages of up to six hundred dollars ($600), in addition to actual damages, including rent found due. The trier of fact shall determine whether actual damages, statutory damages, or both, shall be awarded, and judgment shall be entered accordingly.
(c) When the proceeding is for an unlawful detainer after default in the payment of rent, and the lease or agreement under which the rent is payable has not by its terms expired, and the notice required by Section 1161 has not stated the election of the landlord to declare the forfeiture thereof, the court may, and, if the lease or agreement is in writing, is for a term of more than one year, and does not contain a forfeiture clause, shall order that a writ shall not be issued to enforce the judgment until the expiration of five days after the entry of the judgment, within which time the tenant, or any subtenant, or any mortgagee of the term, or any other party interested in its continuance, may pay into the court, for the landlord, the amount found due as rent, with interest thereon, and the amount of the damages found by the jury or the court for the unlawful detainer, and the costs of the proceedings, and thereupon the judgment shall be satisfied and the tenant be restored to the tenant's estate. If payment as provided in this subdivision is not made within five days, the judgment may be enforced for its full amount and for the possession of the premises. In all other cases the judgment may be enforced immediately.
(d) Subject to subdivision (c), the judgment for possession of the premises may be enforced as provided in Division 3 (commencing with Section 712.010) of Title 9 of Part 2.
(e) Personal property remaining on the premises which the landlord reasonably believes to have been lost shall be disposed of pursuant to Article 1 (commencing with Section 2080) of Chapter 4 of Title 6 of Part 4 of Division 3 of the Civil Code. The landlord is not liable to the owner of any property which is disposed of in this manner. If the appropriate police or sheriff's department refuses to accept that property, it shall be deemed not to have been lost for the purposes of this subdivision.
(f) The landlord shall give notice pursuant to Section 1983 of the Civil Code to any person (other than the tenant) reasonably believed by the landlord to be the owner of personal property remaining on the premises unless the procedure for surrender of property under Section 1965 of the Civil Code has been initiated or completed.
(g) The landlord shall store the personal property in a place of safekeeping until it is either released pursuant to subdivision (h) or disposed of pursuant to subdivision (i).
(h) The landlord shall release the personal property pursuant to Section 1965 of the Civil Code or shall release it to the tenant or, at the landlord's option, to a person reasonably believed by the landlord to be its owner if the tenant or other person pays the costs of storage as provided in Section 1990 of the Civil Code and claims the property not later than the date specified in the writ of possession before which the tenant must make his or her claim or the date specified in the notice before which a person other than the tenant must make his or her claim.
(i) Personal property not released pursuant to subdivision (h) shall be disposed of pursuant to Section 1988 of the Civil Code.

(j) Where the landlord releases personal property to the tenant pursuant to subdivision (h), the landlord is not liable with respect to that property to any person.

(k) Where the landlord releases personal property pursuant to subdivision (h) to a person (other than the tenant) reasonably believed by the landlord to be its owner, the landlord is not liable with respect to that property to:

(1) The tenant or to any person to whom notice was given pursuant to subdivision (f); or

(2) Any other person, unless that person proves that, prior to releasing the property, the landlord believed or reasonably should have believed that the person had an interest in the property and also that the landlord knew or should have known upon reasonable investigation the address of that person.

(l) Where personal property is disposed of pursuant to Section 1988 of the Civil Code, the landlord is not liable with respect to that property to:

(1) The tenant or to any person to whom notice was given pursuant to subdivision (f); or

(2) Any other person, unless that person proves that, prior to disposing of the property pursuant to Section 1988 of the Civil Code, the landlord believed or reasonably should have believed that the person had an interest in the property and also that the landlord knew or should have known upon reasonable investigation the address of that person.

(m) For the purposes of subdivisions (e), (f), (h), (k), and (l), the terms "owner," "premises," and "reasonable belief" have the same meaning as provided in Section 1980 of the Civil Code.

Amended by Stats. 1993, Ch. 755, Sec. 2. Effective January 1, 1994.

Section 1174.2 - Affirmative defense of breach of landlord's obligations or warranty of habitability raised in unlawful detainer proceeding

(a) In an unlawful detainer proceeding involving residential premises after default in payment of rent and in which the tenant has raised as an affirmative defense a breach of the landlord's obligations under Section 1941 of the Civil Code or of any warranty of habitability, the court shall determine whether a substantial breach of these obligations has occurred. If the court finds that a substantial breach has occurred, the court (1) shall determine the reasonable rental value of the premises in its untenantable state to the date of trial, (2) shall deny possession to the landlord and adjudge the tenant to be the prevailing party, conditioned upon the payment by the tenant of the rent that has accrued to the date of the trial as adjusted pursuant to this subdivision within a reasonable period of time not exceeding five days, from the date of the court's judgment or, if service of the court's judgment is made by mail, the payment shall be made within the time set forth in Section 1013, (3) may order the landlord to make repairs and correct the conditions which constitute a breach of the landlord's obligations, (4) shall order that the monthly rent be limited to the reasonable rental value of the premises as determined pursuant to this subdivision until repairs are completed, and (5) except as otherwise provided in subdivision (b), shall award the tenant costs and attorneys' fees if provided by, and pursuant to, any statute or the contract of the parties. If the court orders repairs or corrections, or both, pursuant to paragraph (3), the court's jurisdiction continues over the matter for the purpose of ensuring compliance. The court shall, however, award possession of the premises to the landlord if the tenant fails to pay all rent accrued to the date of trial, as determined due in the judgment, within the period prescribed by the court pursuant to this subdivision. The tenant shall, however, retain any rights conferred by Section 1174.

(b) If the court determines that there has been no substantial breach of Section 1941 of the Civil Code or of any warranty of habitability by the landlord or if the tenant fails to pay all rent accrued to the date of trial, as required by the court pursuant to subdivision (a), then judgment shall be entered in favor of the landlord, and the landlord shall be the prevailing party for the purposes of awarding costs or attorneys' fees pursuant to any statute or the contract of the parties.

(c) As used in this section, "substantial breach" means the failure of the landlord to comply with applicable building and housing code standards which materially affect health and safety.

(d) Nothing in this section is intended to deny the tenant the right to a trial by jury. Nothing in this section shall limit or supersede any provision of Chapter 12.75 (commencing with Section 7060) of Division 7 of Title 1 of the Government Code.

Amended by Stats. 1993, Ch. 589, Sec. 28. Effective January 1, 1994.

Section 1174.21 - Landlord's liability for attorney's fees and costs

A landlord who institutes an unlawful detainer proceeding based upon a tenant's nonpayment of rent, and who is liable for a violation of Section 1942.4 of the Civil Code, shall be liable to the tenant or lessee for reasonable attorneys' fees and costs of the suit, in an amount to be fixed by the court.

Added by Stats 2003 ch 109 (AB 647),s 2, eff. 1/1/2004.

Section 1174.25 - Claim filed as prescribed by section 415.46 when occupant served with prejudgment claim of right of possession

(a)

(1) Except as provided in paragraph (2), an occupant who is served with a prejudgment claim of right to possession in accordance with Section 415.46 may file a claim as prescribed in Section 415.46, with the court within 10 days of the date of service of the prejudgment claim of right to possession as shown on the return of service, which period shall include Saturday and Sunday but exclude all other judicial holidays. If the last day for filing the claim falls on a Saturday or Sunday, the filing period shall be extended to and including the next court day. Filing the prejudgment claim of right to possession shall constitute a general appearance for which a fee shall be collected as provided in Section 70614 of the Government Code. Section 68511.3 of the Government Code applies to the prejudgment claim of right to possession.

(2) In an action as described in paragraph (2) of subdivision (e) of Section 415.46, an occupant may file a prejudgment claim of right to possession at any time before judgment is entered.

(b) At the time of filing, the claimant shall be added as a defendant in the action for unlawful detainer and the clerk shall notify the plaintiff that the claimant has been added as a defendant in the action by mailing a copy of the claim filed with the court to the plaintiff with a notation so indicating. The claimant shall answer or otherwise respond to the summons and complaint within five days, including Saturdays and Sundays, but excluding all other judicial holidays, after filing the prejudgment claim of possession. Thereafter, the name of the claimant shall be added to any pleading, filing or form filed in the action for unlawful detainer.

Amended by Stats 2014 ch 913 (AB 2747),s 8, eff. 1/1/2015.

Amended by Stats 2005 ch 75 (AB 145),s 42, eff. 7/19/2005, op. 1/1/2006

Section 1174.27 - Unlawful detainer proceeding; documentation evidencing abuse or violence; affirmative defense

(a)This section shall apply to an unlawful detainer proceeding in which all of the following are true:

(1)The proceeding involves a residential premises.

(2)The complaint includes a cause of action based on an act of abuse or violence against a tenant, a tenant's immediate family member, or a tenant's household member.

(3)A defendant has invoked paragraph (2) of subdivision (d) of Section 1161.3 as an affirmative defense to the cause of action described in paragraph (2).

(b)For the purposes of this section, the definitions in subdivision (a) of Section 1161.3 apply.

(c)The court shall determine whether there is documentation evidencing abuse or violence against the tenant, the tenant's immediate family member, or the tenant's household member.

(d)If the court determines there is not documentation evidencing abuse or violence against the tenant, the court shall deny the affirmative defense.

(e) If the court determines that there is documentation evidencing abuse or violence against the tenant, the tenant's immediate family member, or the tenant's household member, and the court does not find the defendant raising the affirmative defense guilty of an unlawful detainer on any other grounds, then both of the following:

(1) The defendant raising the affirmative defense and any other occupant not found guilty of an unlawful detainer shall not be guilty of an unlawful detainer and shall not be named in any judgment in favor of the landlord.

(2) The defendant raising the affirmative defense and any other occupant not found guilty of an unlawful detainer shall not be held liable to the landlord for any amount related to the unlawful detainer, including, but not limited to, holdover damages, court costs, lease termination fees, or attorney's fees.

(f)

(1) If the court makes the determination described in subdivision (e), upon a showing that any other defendant was the perpetrator of the abuse or violence on which the affirmative defense was based and is guilty of an unlawful detainer, the court shall do both of the following:

(A) Issue a partial eviction ordering the removal of the perpetrator of abuse or violence and ordering that person be immediately removed and barred from the dwelling unit, but the court shall not order the tenancy terminated.

(B) Order the landlord to change the locks and to provide the remaining occupants with the new key.

(2) If a court issues a partial eviction order as described in subparagraph (A) of paragraph (1), then only a defendant found guilty of an unlawful detainer may be liable for holdover damages, court costs, lease termination fees, or attorney's fees, as applicable.

(3) If the court makes the determination described in subdivision (e), the court may, upon a showing that any other defendant was the perpetrator of the abuse or violence on which the affirmative defense was based and is guilty of an unlawful detainer, do any of the following:

(A) Permanently bar the perpetrator of abuse or violence from entering any portion of the residential premises.

(B) Order as an express condition of the tenancy that the remaining occupants shall not give permission to or invite the perpetrator of abuse or violence to live in the dwelling unit.

(4) In exercising its discretion under this subdivision, the court shall take into account custody or visitation orders or arrangements and any other factor that may necessitate the temporary reentry of the perpetrator of abuse or violence.

(g) The Judicial Council shall develop a judgment form for use in a ruling pursuant to subdivision (e) or (f).

(h) Notwithstanding any other law, a determination that a person is a perpetrator of abuse or violence under subdivision (e) or (f) shall not constitute a finding that the person is a perpetrator of abuse or violence for any other purposes and shall not be admissible as evidence that the person committed a crime or is a perpetrator of abuse or violence in any other proceeding, including, but not limited to, a civil action or proceeding, a criminal action or proceeding, and a proceeding involving a juvenile for a criminal offense.

Added by Stats 2022 ch 558 (SB 1017),s 3, eff. 1/1/2023.

Section 1174.3 - Claim of possession filed by occupant not named in judgment for possession

(a)

(1) Except as provided in paragraph (2), unless a prejudgment claim of right to possession has been served upon occupants in accordance with Section 415.46, any occupant not named in the judgment for possession who occupied the premises on the date of the filing of the action may object to enforcement of the judgment against that occupant by filing a claim of right to possession as prescribed in this section. A claim of right to possession may be filed at any time after service or posting of the writ of possession pursuant to subdivision (a) or (b) of Section 715.020, up to and including the time at which the levying officer returns to effect the eviction of those named in the judgment of possession. Filing the claim of right to possession shall constitute a general appearance for which a fee shall be collected as provided in Section 70614 of the Government Code. Section 68511.3 of the Government Code applies to the claim of right to possession. An occupant or tenant who is named in the action shall not be required to file a claim of right to possession to protect that occupant's right to possession of the premises.

(2) In an action as described in paragraph (2) of subdivision (e) of Section 415.46, an occupant may file a claim of right to possession at any time up to and including the time at which the levying officer returns to effect the eviction of those named in the judgment of possession, without regard to whether a prejudgment claim of right to possession has been served upon the occupant.

(b) The court issuing the writ of possession of real property shall set a date or dates when the court will hold a hearing to determine the validity of objections to enforcement of the judgment specified in subdivision (a). An occupant of the real property for which the writ is issued may make an objection to eviction to the levying officer at the office of the levying officer or at the premises at the time of the eviction. If a claim of right to possession is completed and presented to the sheriff, marshal, or other levying officer, the officer shall forthwith (1) stop the eviction of occupants at the premises, and (2) provide a receipt or copy of the completed claim of right of possession to the claimant indicating the date and time the completed form was received, and (3) deliver the original completed claim of right to possession to the court issuing the writ of possession of real property.

(c) A claim of right to possession is effected by any of the following:

(1) Presenting a completed claim form in person with identification to the sheriff, marshal, or other levying officer as prescribed in this section, and delivering to the court within two court days after its presentation, an amount equal to 15 days' rent together with the appropriate fee or form for proceeding in forma pauperis. Upon receipt of a claim of right to possession, the sheriff, marshal, or other levying officer shall indicate thereon the date and time of its receipt and forthwith deliver the original to the issuing court and a receipt or copy of the claim to the claimant and notify the plaintiff of that fact. Immediately upon receipt of an amount equal to 15 days' rent and the appropriate fee or form for proceeding in forma pauperis, the court shall file the claim of right to possession and serve an endorsed copy with the notice of the hearing date on the plaintiff and the claimant by first-class mail. The court issuing the writ of possession shall set and hold a hearing on the claim not less than five nor more than 15 days after the claim is filed with the court.

(2) Presenting a completed claim form in person with identification to the sheriff, marshal, or other levying officer as prescribed in this section, and delivering to the court within two court days after its presentation, the appropriate fee or form for proceeding in forma pauperis without delivering the amount equivalent to 15 days' rent. In this case, the court shall immediately set a hearing on the claim to be held on the fifth day after the filing is completed. The court shall notify the claimant of the hearing date at the time the claimant completes the filing by delivering to the court the appropriate fee or form for proceeding in forma pauperis, and shall notify the plaintiff of the hearing date by first-class mail. Upon receipt of a claim of right to possession, the sheriff, marshal, or other levying officer shall indicate thereon the date and time of its receipt and forthwith deliver the original to the issuing court and a receipt or copy of the claim to the claimant and notify the plaintiff of that fact.

(d) At the hearing, the court shall determine whether there is a valid claim of possession by the claimant who filed the claim, and the court shall consider all evidence produced at the hearing, including, but not limited to, the information set forth in the claim. The court may determine the claim to be valid or invalid based upon the evidence presented at the hearing. The court shall determine the claim to be invalid if the court determines that the claimant is an invitee, licensee, guest, or trespasser. If the court determines the claim is invalid, the court shall order the return to the claimant of the amount of the 15 days' rent paid by the claimant, if that amount was paid pursuant to paragraph (1) or (3) of subdivision (c), less a pro rata amount for each day that enforcement of the judgment was delayed by reason of making the claim of right to possession, which pro rata amount shall be paid to the landlord. If the court determines the claim is valid, the amount equal to 15 days' rent paid by the claimant shall be returned immediately to the claimant.

(e) If, upon hearing, the court determines that the claim is valid, then the court shall order further proceedings as follows:

(1) If the unlawful detainer is based upon a curable breach, and the claimant was not previously served with a proper notice, if any notice is required, then the required notice may at the plaintiff's discretion be served on the claimant at the hearing or thereafter. If the claimant does not cure the breach within the required time, then a supplemental complaint may be filed and served on the claimant as defendant if the plaintiff proceeds against the claimant in the same action. For the purposes of this section only, service of the required notice, if any notice is required, and of the supplemental complaint may be made by first-class mail addressed to the claimant at the subject premises or upon his or her attorney of record and, in either case, Section 1013 shall otherwise apply. Further proceedings on the merits of the claimant's continued right to possession after service of the Summons and Supplemental Complaint as prescribed by this subdivision shall be conducted pursuant to this chapter.

(2) In all other cases, the court shall deem the unlawful detainer Summons and Complaint to be amended on their faces to include the claimant as defendant, service of the Summons and Complaint, as thus amended, may at the plaintiff's discretion be made at the hearing or thereafter, and the claimant thus named and served as a defendant in the action shall answer or otherwise respond within five days thereafter.

(f) If a claim is made without delivery to the court of the appropriate filing fee or a form for proceeding in forma pauperis, as prescribed in this section, the claim shall be immediately deemed denied and the court shall so order. Upon the denial of the claim, the court shall immediately deliver an endorsed copy of the order to the levying officer and shall serve an endorsed copy of the order on the plaintiff and claimant by first-class mail.

(g) If the claim of right to possession is denied pursuant to subdivision (f), or if the claimant fails to appear at the hearing or, upon hearing, if the court determines that there are no valid claims, or if the claimant does not prevail at a trial on the merits of the unlawful detainer action, the court shall order the levying officer to proceed with enforcement of the original writ of possession of real property as deemed amended to include the claimant, which shall be effected within a reasonable time not to exceed five days. Upon receipt of the court's order, the levying officer shall enforce the writ of possession of real property against any occupant or occupants.

(h) The claim of right to possession shall be made on the following form: [SEE PRINTED VERSION OF THE BILL]

Amended by Stats 2014 ch 913 (AB 2747),s 9, eff. 1/1/2015.
Amended by Stats 2005 ch 75 (AB 145),s 43, eff. 7/19/2005, op. 1/1/2006
Amended by Stats 2002 ch 664 (AB 3034),s 50, eff. 1/1/2003.
Amended by Stats 2001 ch 115 (SB 153), s 5, eff. 1/1/2002.

Section 1174.5 - Lessee not relieved from liability upon judgment declaring forfeiture of lease or agreement

A judgment in unlawful detainer declaring the forfeiture of the lease or agreement under which real property is held shall not relieve the lessee from liability pursuant to Section 1951.2 of the Civil Code.

Added by Stats. 1982, Ch. 488, Sec. 1.

Section 1176 - Stay of judgment pending appeal

(a) An appeal taken by the defendant shall not automatically stay proceedings upon the judgment. Petition for stay of the judgment pending appeal shall first be directed to the judge before whom it was rendered. Stay of judgment shall be granted when the court finds that the moving party will suffer extreme hardship in the absence of a stay and that the nonmoving party will not be irreparably injured by its issuance. If the stay is denied by the trial court, the defendant may forthwith file a petition for an extraordinary writ with the appropriate appeals court. If the trial or appellate court stays enforcement of the judgment, the court may condition the stay on whatever conditions the court deems just, but in any case it shall order the payment of the reasonable monthly rental value to the court monthly in advance as rent would otherwise become due as a condition of issuing the stay of enforcement. As used in this subdivision, "reasonable rental value" means the contract rent unless the rental value has been modified by the trial court in which case that modified rental value shall be used.

(b) A new cause of action on the same agreement for the rental of real property shall not be barred because of an appeal by any party.

Amended by Stats. 1985, Ch. 1279, Sec. 3.

Section 1177 - Applicability of Part II of Code

Except as otherwise provided in this Chapter the provisions of Part II of this Code are applicable to, and constitute the rules of practice in the proceedings mentioned in this Chapter.

Enacted 1872.

Section 1178 - Applicability of Part 2 relative to new trials and appeals

The provisions of Part 2 of this code, relative to new trials and appeals, except insofar as they are inconsistent with the provisions of this chapter or with rules adopted by the Judicial Council, apply to the proceedings mentioned in this chapter.

Amended by Stats. 1945, Ch. 40.

Section 1179 - Relief against forfeiture in case of hardship

The court may relieve a tenant against a forfeiture of a lease or rental agreement, whether written or oral, and whether or not the tenancy has terminated, and restore him or her to his or her former estate or tenancy, in case of hardship, as provided in Section 1174. The court has the discretion to relieve any person against forfeiture on its own motion.

An application for relief against forfeiture may be made at any time prior to restoration of the premises to the landlord. The application may be made by a tenant or subtenant, or a mortgagee of the term, or any person interested in the continuance of the term. It must be made upon petition, setting forth the facts upon which the relief is sought, and be verified by the applicant. Notice of the application, with a copy of the petition, must be served at least five days prior to the hearing on the plaintiff in the judgment, who may appear and contest the application. Alternatively, a person appearing without an attorney may make the application orally, if the plaintiff either is present and has an opportunity to contest the application, or has been given ex parte notice of the hearing and the purpose of the oral application. In no case shall the application or motion be granted except on condition that full payment of rent due, or full performance of conditions or covenants stipulated, so far as the same is practicable, be made.

Amended by Stats 2002 ch 301 (SB 1403),s 4, eff. 1/1/2003.

Section 1179a - Precedence of actions

In all proceedings brought to recover the possession of real property pursuant to the provisions of this chapter all courts, wherein such actions are or may hereafter be pending, shall give such actions precedence over all other civil actions therein, except actions to which special precedence is given by law, in the matter of the setting the same for hearing or trial, and in hearing the same, to the end that all such actions shall be quickly heard and determined.

Added by Stats. 1931, Ch. 885.

Chapter 5 - COVID-19 TENANT RELIEF ACT

Section 1179.01 - [Effective until 10/1/2025] Short title

This chapter is known, and may be cited, as the COVID-19 Tenant Relief Act.

Amended by Stats 2021 ch 2 (SB 91),s 15, eff. 1/29/2021.
Chapter heading amended by Stats 2021 ch 2 (SB 91),s 14, eff. 1/29/2021.
Added by Stats 2020 ch 37 (AB 3088),s 20, eff. 8/31/2020.

Section 1179.01.5 - [Effective until 10/1/2025] Legislative intent; prohibited acts by court; unlawful detainer cover sheet

(a) It is the intent of the Legislature that the Judicial Council and the courts have adequate time to prepare to implement the new procedures resulting from this chapter, including educating and training judicial officers and staff.

(b) Notwithstanding any other law, before October 5, 2020, a court shall not do any of the following:

(1) Issue a summons on a complaint for unlawful detainer in any action that seeks possession of residential real property and that is based, in whole or in part, on nonpayment of rent or other charges.

(2) Enter a default or a default judgment for restitution in an unlawful detainer action that seeks possession of residential real property and that is based, in whole or in part, on nonpayment of rent or other charges.

(c)

(1) A plaintiff in an unlawful detainer action shall file a cover sheet in the form specified in paragraph (2) that indicates both of the following:

(A) Whether the action seeks possession of residential real property.

(B) If the action seeks possession of residential real property, whether the action is based, in whole or part, on an alleged default in payment of rent or other charges.

(2) The cover sheet specified in paragraph (1) shall be in the following form: "UNLAWFUL DETAINER SUPPLEMENTAL COVER SHEET

1. This action seeks possession of real property that is:

    a. [ ] Residential

    b. [ ] Commercial

2. (Complete only if paragraph 1(a) is checked) This action is based, in whole or in part, on an alleged default in payment of rent or other charges.

    a. [ ] Yes

    b. [ ] No Date:_____

_____

Type Or Print Name Signature Of Party Or Attorney For Party"

(3) The cover sheet required by this subdivision shall be in addition to any civil case cover sheet or other form required by law, the California Rules of Court, or a local court rule.

(4) The Judicial Council may develop a form for mandatory use that includes the information in paragraph (2).

(d) This section does not prevent a court from issuing a summons or entering default in an unlawful detainer action that seeks possession of residential real property and that is not based, in whole or in part, on nonpayment of rent or other charges.

Added by Stats 2020 ch 37 (AB 3088),s 20, eff. 8/31/2020.

Section 1179.02 - [Effective until 10/1/2025] Definitions

For purposes of this chapter:

(a) "Covered time period" means the time period between March 1, 2020, and September 30, 2021.

(b) "COVID-19-related financial distress" means any of the following:

(1) Loss of income caused by the COVID-19 pandemic.

(2) Increased out-of-pocket expenses directly related to performing essential work during the COVID-19 pandemic.

(3) Increased expenses directly related to the health impact of the COVID-19 pandemic.

(4) Childcare responsibilities or responsibilities to care for an elderly, disabled, or sick family member directly related to the COVID-19 pandemic that limit a tenant's ability to earn income.

(5) Increased costs for childcare or attending to an elderly, disabled, or sick family member directly related to the COVID-19 pandemic.

(6) Other circumstances related to the COVID-19 pandemic that have reduced a tenant's income or increased a tenant's expenses.

(c) "COVID-19 rental debt" means unpaid rent or any other unpaid financial obligation of a tenant under the tenancy that came due during the covered time period.

(d) "Declaration of COVID-19-related financial distress" means the following written statement: I am currently unable to pay my rent or other financial obligations under the lease in full because of one or more of the following:

1. Loss of income caused by the COVID-19 pandemic.

2. Increased out-of-pocket expenses directly related to performing essential work during the COVID-19 pandemic.

3. Increased expenses directly related to health impacts of the COVID-19 pandemic.

4. Childcare responsibilities or responsibilities to care for an elderly, disabled, or sick family member directly related to the COVID-19 pandemic that limit my ability to earn income.

5. Increased costs for childcare or attending to an elderly, disabled, or sick family member directly related to the COVID-19 pandemic.

6. Other circumstances related to the COVID-19 pandemic that have reduced my income or increased my expenses. Any public assistance, including unemployment insurance, pandemic unemployment assistance, state disability insurance (SDI), or paid family leave, that I have received since the start of the COVID-19 pandemic does not fully make up for my loss of income and/or increased expenses.

Signed under penalty of perjury:

Dated:

(e) "Landlord" includes all of the following or the agent of any of the following:

(1) An owner of residential real property.

(2) An owner of a residential rental unit.

(3) An owner of a mobilehome park.

(4) An owner of a mobilehome park space or lot.

(f) "Protected time period" means the time period between March 1, 2020, and August 31, 2020.

(g) "Rental payment" means rent or any other financial obligation of a tenant under the tenancy.

(h) "Tenant" means any natural person who hires real property except any of the following:

(1) Tenants of commercial property, as defined in subdivision (c) of Section 1162 of the Civil Code.

(2) Those persons whose occupancy is described in subdivision (b) of Section 1940 of the Civil Code.

(i) "Transition time period" means the time period between September 1, 2020, and September 30, 2021.

Amended by Stats 2021 ch 27 (AB 832),s 14, eff. 6/28/2021.

Amended by Stats 2021 ch 2 (SB 91),s 16, eff. 1/29/2021.

Added by Stats 2020 ch 37 (AB 3088),s 20, eff. 8/31/2020.

Section 1179.02.5 - [Effective until 10/1/2025] Serving notice to high income tenant

(a) For purposes of this section:

(1)

(A) "High-income tenant" means a tenant with an annual household income of 130 percent of the median income, as published by the Department of Housing and Community Development in the Official State Income Limits for 2020, for the county in which the residential rental property is located.

(B) For purposes of this paragraph, all lawful occupants of the residential rental unit, including minor children, shall be considered in determining household size.

(C) "High-income tenant" shall not include a tenant with a household income of less than one hundred thousand dollars ($100,000).

(2) "Proof of income" means any of the following:

(A) A tax return.

(B) A W-2.

(C) A written statement from a tenant's employer that specifies the tenant's income.

(D) Pay stubs.

(E) Documentation showing regular distributions from a trust, annuity, 401k, pension, or other financial instrument.

(F) Documentation of court-ordered payments, including, but not limited to, spousal support or child support.

(G) Documentation from a government agency showing receipt of public assistance benefits, including, but not limited to, social security, unemployment insurance, disability insurance, or paid family leave.

(H) A written statement signed by the tenant that states the tenant's income, including, but not limited to, a rental application.

(b)

(1) This section shall apply only if the landlord has proof of income in the landlord's possession before the service of the notice showing that the tenant is a high-income tenant.

(2) This section does not do any of the following:

(A) Authorize a landlord to demand proof of income from the tenant.

(B) Require the tenant to provide proof of income for the purposes of determining whether the tenant is a high-income tenant.

(C)

(i) Entitle a landlord to obtain, or authorize a landlord to attempt to obtain, confidential financial records from a tenant's employer, a government agency, financial institution, or any other source.

(ii) Confidential information described in clause (i) shall not constitute valid proof of income unless it was lawfully obtained by the landlord with the tenant's consent during the tenant screening process.

(3) Paragraph (2) does not alter a party's rights under Title 4 (commencing with Section 2016.010), Chapter 4 (commencing with Section 708.010) of Title 9, or any other law.

(c) A landlord may require a high-income tenant that is served a notice pursuant to subdivision (b) or (c) of Section 1179.03 to submit, in addition to and together with a declaration of COVID-19-related financial distress, documentation supporting the claim that the tenant has suffered COVID-19-related financial distress. Any form of objectively verifiable documentation that demonstrates the COVID-19-related financial distress the tenant has experienced is sufficient to satisfy the requirements of this subdivision, including the proof of income, as defined in subparagraphs (A) to (G), inclusive, of paragraph (2) of subdivision (a), a letter from an employer, or an unemployment insurance record.

(d) A high-income tenant is required to comply with the requirements of subdivision (c) only if the landlord has included the following language on the notice served pursuant to subdivision (b) or (c) of Section 1179.03 in at least 12-point font: "Proof of income on file with your landlord indicates that your household makes at least 130 percent of the median income for the county where the rental property is located, as published by the Department of Housing and Community Development in the Official State Income Limits for 2020. As a result, if you claim that you are unable to pay the amount demanded by this notice because you have suffered COVID-19-related financial distress, you are required to submit to your landlord documentation supporting your claim together with the completed declaration of COVID-19-related financial distress provided with this notice. If you fail to submit this documentation together with your declaration of COVID-19-related financial distress, and you do not either pay the amount demanded in this notice or deliver possession of the premises back to your landlord as required by this notice, you will not be covered by the eviction protections enacted by the California Legislature as a result of the COVID-19 pandemic, and your landlord can begin eviction proceedings against you as soon as this 15-day notice expires."

(e) A high-income tenant that fails to comply with subdivision (c) shall not be subject to the protections of subdivision (g) of Section 1179.03.

(f)

(1) A landlord shall be required to plead compliance with this section in any unlawful detainer action based upon a notice that alleges that the tenant is a high-income tenant. If that allegation is contested, the landlord shall be required to submit to the court the proof of income upon which the landlord relied at the trial or other hearing, and the tenant shall be entitled to submit rebuttal evidence.

(2) If the court in an unlawful detainer action based upon a notice that alleges that the tenant is a high-income tenant determines that at the time the notice was served the landlord did not have proof of income establishing that the tenant is a high-income tenant, the court shall award attorney's fees to the prevailing tenant.

Added by Stats 2020 ch 37 (AB 3088),s 20, eff. 8/31/2020.

Section 1179.03 - [Effective until 10/1/2025] Modification of notice demanding payment

(a)

(1) Any notice that demands payment of COVID-19 rental debt served pursuant to subdivision (e) of Section 798.56 of the Civil Code or paragraph (2) or (3) of Section 1161 shall be modified as required by this section. A notice which does not meet the requirements of this section, regardless of when the notice was issued, shall not be sufficient to establish a cause of action for unlawful detainer or a basis for default judgment.

(2) Any case based solely on a notice that demands payment of COVID-19 rental debt served pursuant to subdivision (e) of Section 798.56 of the Civil Code or paragraph (2) or (3) of Section 1161 may be dismissed if the notice does not meet the requirements of this section, regardless of when the notice was issued.

(3) Notwithstanding paragraphs (1) and (2), this section shall have no effect if the landlord lawfully regained possession of the property or obtained a judgment for possession of the property before the operative date of this section.

(b) If the notice demands payment of rent that came due during the protected time period, as defined in Section 1179.02, the notice shall comply with all of the following:

(1) The time period in which the tenant may pay the amount due or deliver possession of the property shall be no shorter than 15 days, excluding Saturdays, Sundays, and other judicial holidays.

(2) The notice shall set forth the amount of rent demanded and the date each amount became due.

(3) The notice shall advise the tenant that the tenant cannot be evicted for failure to comply with the notice if the tenant delivers a signed declaration of COVID-19-related financial distress to the landlord on or before the date that the notice to pay rent or quit or notice to perform covenants or quit expires, by any of the methods specified in subdivision (f).

(4) The notice shall include the following text in at least 12-point font: "NOTICE FROM THE STATE OF CALIFORNIA: If you are unable to pay the amount demanded in this notice, and have decreased income or increased expenses due to COVID-19, your landlord will not be able to evict you for this missed payment if you sign and deliver the declaration form included with your notice to your landlord within 15 days, excluding Saturdays, Sundays, and other judicial holidays, but you will still owe this money to your landlord. If you do not sign and deliver the declaration within this time period, you may lose the eviction protections available to you. You must return this form to be protected. You should keep a copy or picture of the signed form for your records.

You will still owe this money to your landlord and can be sued for the money, but you cannot be evicted from your home if you comply with these requirements. You should keep careful track of what you have paid and any amount you still owe to protect your rights and avoid future disputes. Failure to respond to this notice may result in an unlawful detainer action (eviction) being filed against you.

For information about legal resources that may be available to you, visit lawhelpca.org."

(c) If the notice demands payment of rent that came due during the transition time period, as defined in Section 1179.02, the notice shall comply with all of the following:

(1) The time period in which the tenant may pay the amount due or deliver possession of the property shall be no shorter than 15 days, excluding Saturdays, Sundays, and other judicial holidays.

(2) The notice shall set forth the amount of rent demanded and the date each amount became due.

(3) The notice shall advise the tenant that the tenant will not be evicted for failure to comply with the notice, except as allowed by this chapter, if the tenant delivers a signed declaration of COVID-19-related financial distress to the landlord on or before the date the notice to pay rent or quit or notice to perform covenants or quit expires, by any of the methods specified in subdivision (f).

(4) For notices served before February 1, 2021, the notice shall include the following text in at least 12-point type: "NOTICE FROM THE STATE OF CALIFORNIA: If you are unable to pay the amount demanded in this notice, and have decreased income or increased expenses due to COVID-19, you may sign and deliver the declaration form included with your notice to your landlord within 15 days, excluding Saturdays, Sundays, and other judicial holidays, and your landlord will not be able to evict you for this missed payment so long as you make the minimum payment (see below). You will still owe this money to your landlord. You should keep a copy or picture of the signed form for your records.

If you provide the declaration form to your landlord as described above AND, on or before January 31, 2021, you pay an amount that equals at least 25 percent of each rental payment that came due or will come due during the period between September 1, 2020, and January 31, 2021, that you were unable to pay as a result of decreased income or increased expenses due to COVID-19, your landlord cannot evict you. Your landlord may require you to submit a new declaration form for each rental payment that you do not pay that comes due between September 1, 2020, and January 31, 2021.

For example, if you provided a declaration form to your landlord regarding your decreased income or increased expenses due to COVID-19 that prevented you from making your rental payment in September and October of 2020, your landlord could not evict you if, on or before January 31, 2021, you made a payment equal to 25 percent of September's and October's rental payment (i.e., half a month's rent). If you were unable to pay any of the rental payments that came due between September 1, 2020, and January 31, 2021, and you provided your landlord with the declarations in response to each 15-day notice your landlord sent to you during that time period, your landlord could not evict you if, on or before January 31, 2021, you paid your landlord an amount equal to 25 percent of all the rental payments due from September through January (i.e., one and a quarter month's rent).

You will still owe the full amount of the rent to your landlord, but you cannot be evicted from your home if you comply with these requirements. You should keep careful track of what you have paid and any amount you still owe to protect your rights and avoid future disputes. Failure to respond to this notice may result in an unlawful detainer action (eviction) being filed against you.

For information about legal resources that may be available to you, visit lawhelpca.org."

(5) For notices served on or after February 1, 2021, and before July 1, 2021, the notice shall include the following text in at least 12-point type: "NOTICE FROM THE STATE OF CALIFORNIA: If you are unable to pay the amount demanded in this notice, and have decreased income or increased expenses due to COVID-19, you may sign and deliver the declaration form included with your notice to your landlord within 15 days, excluding Saturdays, Sundays, and other judicial holidays, and your landlord will not be able to evict you for this missed payment so long as you make the minimum payment (see below). You will still owe this money to your landlord. You should keep a copy or picture of the signed form for your records.

If you provide the declaration form to your landlord as described above AND, on or before June 30, 2021, you pay an amount that equals at least 25 percent of each rental payment that came due or will come due during the period between September 1, 2020, and June 30, 2021, that you were unable to pay as a result of decreased income or increased expenses due to COVID-19, your landlord cannot evict you. Your landlord may require you to submit a new declaration form for each rental payment that you do not pay that comes due between September 1, 2020, and June 30, 2021.

If you were unable to pay any of the rental payments that came due between September 1, 2020, and June 30, 2021, and you provided your landlord with the declarations in response to each 15-day notice your landlord sent to you during that time period, your landlord could not evict you if, on or before June 30, 2021, you paid your landlord an amount equal to 25 percent of all the rental payments due from September 2020 through June 2021.

You will still owe the full amount of the rent to your landlord, but you cannot be evicted from your home if you comply with these requirements. You should keep careful track of what you have paid and any amount you still owe to protect your rights and avoid future disputes. Failure to respond to this notice may result in an unlawful detainer action (eviction) being filed against you.

YOU MAY QUALIFY FOR RENTAL ASSISTANCE. In addition to extending these eviction protections, the State of California, in partnership with federal and local governments, has created an emergency rental assistance program to assist renters who have been unable to pay their rent and utility bills as a result of the COVID-19 pandemic. This program may be able to help you get caught up with past-due rent. Additionally, depending on the availability of funds, the program may also be able to assist you with making future rental payments.

While not everyone will qualify for this assistance, you can apply for it regardless of your citizenship or immigration status. There is no charge to apply for or receive this assistance.

Additional information about the extension of the COVID-19 Tenant Relief Act and new state or local rental assistance programs, including more information about how to qualify for assistance, can be found by visiting http://housingiskey.com or by calling 1-833-422-4255."

(6) For notices served on or after July 1, 2021, and before April 1, 2022, the notice shall include the following text in at least 12-point type: "NOTICE FROM THE STATE OF CALIFORNIA - YOU MUST TAKE ACTION TO AVOID EVICTION. If you are unable to pay the amount demanded in this notice because of the COVID-19 pandemic, you should take action right away.

IMMEDIATELY: Sign and return the declaration form included with your notice to your landlord within 15 days, excluding Saturdays, Sundays, and other judicial holidays. Sign and return the declaration even if you have done this before. You should keep a copy or a picture of the signed form for your records.

BEFORE SEPTEMBER 30, 2021: Pay your landlord at least 25 percent of any rent you missed between September 1, 2020, and September 30, 2021. If you need help paying that amount, apply for rental assistance. You will still owe the rest of the rent to your landlord, but as long as you pay 25 percent by September 30, 2021, your landlord will not be able to evict you for failing to pay the rest of the rent. You should keep careful track of what you have paid and any amount you still owe to protect your rights and avoid future disputes.

AS SOON AS POSSIBLE: Apply for rental assistance! As part of California's COVID-19 relief plan, money has been set aside to help renters who have fallen behind on rent or utility payments. If you are behind on rent or utility payments, YOU SHOULD COMPLETE A RENTAL ASSISTANCE APPLICATION IMMEDIATELY! It is free and simple to apply. Citizenship or immigration status does not matter. You can find out how to start your application by calling 1-833-430-2122 or visiting http://housingiskey.com right away."

(7) For notices served on or after April 1, 2022, and before July 1, 2022, the notice shall include the following text in at least 12-point type: "NOTICE FROM THE STATE OF CALIFORNIA:

If:

(1)Before October 1, 2021, you paid your landlord at least 25 percent of any rent you missed between September 1, 2020, and September 30, 2021, and you signed and returned on time any and all declarations of COVID-19 related financial distress that your landlord gave to you, or

(2)You completed an application for government rental assistance on or before March 31, 2022, You may have protections against eviction.

For information about legal resources that may be available to you, visit lawhelpca.org."

(d)An unsigned copy of a declaration of COVID-19-related financial distress shall accompany each notice delivered to a tenant to which subdivision (b) or (c) is applicable. If the landlord was required, pursuant to Section 1632 of the Civil Code, to provide a translation of the rental contract or agreement in the language in which the contract or agreement was negotiated, the landlord shall also provide the unsigned copy of a declaration of COVID-19-related financial distress to the tenant in the language in which the contract or agreement was negotiated. The Department of Housing and Community Development shall make available an official translation of the text required by paragraph (4) of subdivision (b) and paragraphs (4) to (6), inclusive, of subdivision (c) in the languages specified in Section 1632 of the Civil Code by no later than July 15, 2021.

(e)If a tenant owes a COVID-19 rental debt to which both subdivisions (b) and (c) apply, the landlord shall serve two separate notices that comply with subdivisions (b) and (c), respectively.

(f)A tenant may deliver the declaration of COVID-19-related financial distress to the landlord by any of the following methods:

(1)In person, if the landlord indicates in the notice an address at which the declaration may be delivered in person.

(2)By electronic transmission, if the landlord indicates an email address in the notice to which the declaration may be delivered.

(3)Through United States mail to the address indicated by the landlord in the notice. If the landlord does not provide an address pursuant to subparagraph (1), then it shall be conclusively presumed that upon the mailing of the declaration by the tenant to the address provided by the landlord, the declaration is deemed received by the landlord on the date posted, if the tenant can show proof of mailing to the address provided by the landlord.

(4)Through any of the same methods that the tenant can use to deliver the payment pursuant to the notice if delivery of the declaration by that method is possible.

(g)Except as provided in Section 1179.02.5, the following shall apply to a tenant who, within 15 days of service of the notice specified in subdivision (b) or (c), excluding Saturdays, Sundays, and other judicial holidays, demanding payment of COVID-19 rental debt delivers a declaration of COVID-19-related financial distress to the landlord by any of the methods provided in subdivision (f):

(1)With respect to a notice served pursuant to subdivision (b), the tenant shall not then or thereafter be deemed to be in default with regard to that COVID-19 rental debt for purposes of subdivision (e) of Section 798.56 of the Civil Code or paragraphs (2) and (3) of Section 1161.

(2)With respect to a notice served pursuant to subdivision (c), the following shall apply:

(A)Except as provided by subparagraph (B), the landlord may not initiate an unlawful detainer action before October 1, 2021.

(B)A tenant shall not be guilty of unlawful detainer, now or in the future, based upon nonpayment of COVID-19 rental debt that came due during the transition period if, on or before September 30, 2021, the tenant tenders one or more payments that, when taken together, are of an amount equal to or not less than 25 percent of each transition period rental payment demanded in one or more notices served pursuant to subdivision (c) and for which the tenant complied with this subdivision by timely delivering a declaration of COVID-19-related financial distress to the landlord.

(h)

(1)

(A)Within the time prescribed in Section 1167, a tenant shall be permitted to file a signed declaration of COVID-19-related financial distress with the court.

(B)If the tenant files a signed declaration of COVID-19-related financial distress with the court pursuant to this subdivision, the court shall dismiss the case, pursuant to paragraph (2), if the court finds, after a noticed hearing on the matter, that the tenant's failure to return a declaration of COVID-19-related financial distress within the time required by subdivision (g) was the result of mistake, inadvertence, surprise, or excusable neglect, as those terms have been interpreted under subdivision (b) of Section 473.

(C)The noticed hearing required by this paragraph shall be held with not less than five days' notice and not more than 10 days' notice, to be given by the court, and may be held separately or in conjunction with any regularly noticed hearing in the case, other than a trial.

(2)If the court dismisses the case pursuant to paragraph (1), that dismissal shall be without prejudice as follows:

(A)If the case was based in whole or in part upon a notice served pursuant to subdivision (b), the court shall dismiss any cause of action based on the notice served pursuant to subdivision (b).

(B)Before October 1, 2021, if the case is based in whole or in part on a notice served pursuant to subdivision (c), the court shall dismiss any cause of action based on the notice served pursuant to subdivision (c).

(C)On or after October 1, 2021, if the case is based in whole or in part on a notice served pursuant to subdivision (c), the court shall dismiss any cause of action based upon the notice served pursuant to subdivision (c) if the tenant, within five days of the court's order to do so, makes the payment required by subparagraph (B) of paragraph (2) of subdivision (g), provided that if the fifth day falls on a Saturday, Sunday, or judicial holiday the last day to pay shall be extended to the next court day.

(3)If the court dismisses the case pursuant to this subdivision, the tenant shall not be considered the prevailing party for purposes of Section 1032, any attorney's fee provision appearing in contract or statute, or any other law.

(i)Notwithstanding any other law, a notice which is served pursuant to subdivision (b) or (c) that complies with the requirements of this chapter and subdivision (e) of Section 798.56 of the Civil Code or paragraphs (2) and (3) of Section 1161, as applicable, need not include specific language required by any ordinance, resolution, regulation, or administrative action adopted by a city, county, or city and county.

Amended by Stats 2022 ch 13 (AB 2179),s 1, eff. 3/31/2022.
Amended by Stats 2021 ch 27 (AB 832),s 15, eff. 6/28/2021.
Amended by Stats 2021 ch 5 (AB 81),s 8, eff. 2/23/2021.
Amended by Stats 2021 ch 2 (SB 91),s 17, eff. 1/29/2021.
Added by Stats 2020 ch 37 (AB 3088),s 20, eff. 8/31/2020.

Section 1179.03.5 - [Effective until 10/1/2025] Conditions for court to find tenant guilty of unlawful detainer

(a) Before October 1, 2021, a court may not find a tenant guilty of an unlawful detainer unless it finds that one of the following applies:

(1) The tenant was guilty of the unlawful detainer before March 1, 2020.

(2) In response to service of a notice demanding payment of COVID-19 rental debt pursuant to subdivision (e) of Section 798.56 of the Civil Code or paragraph (2) or (3) of Section 1161, the tenant failed to comply with the requirements of Section 1179.03.

(3)

(A) The unlawful detainer arises because of a termination of tenancy for any of the following:

(i) An at-fault just cause, as defined in paragraph (1) of subdivision (b) of Section 1946.2 of the Civil Code.

(ii)

(I) A no-fault just cause, as defined in paragraph (2) of subdivision (b) of Section 1946.2 of the Civil Code, other than intent to demolish or to substantially remodel the residential real property, as defined in subparagraph (D) of paragraph (2) of subdivision (b) of Section 1946.2.

(II) Notwithstanding subclause (I), termination of a tenancy based on intent to demolish or to substantially remodel the residential real property shall be permitted if necessary to maintain compliance with the requirements of Section 1941.1 of the Civil Code, Section 17920.3 or 17920.10 of the Health and Safety Code, or any other applicable law governing the habitability of residential rental units.

(iii) The owner of the property has entered into a contract for the sale of that property with a buyer who intends to occupy the property, and all the requirements of paragraph (8) of subdivision (e) of Section 1946.2 of the Civil Code have been satisfied.

(B) In an action under this paragraph, other than an action to which paragraph (2) also applies, the landlord shall be precluded from recovering COVID-19 rental debt in connection with any award of damages.

(b)

(1) This section does not require a landlord to assist the tenant to relocate through the payment of relocation costs if the landlord would not otherwise be required to do so pursuant to Section 1946.2 of the Civil Code or any other law.

(2) A landlord who is required to assist the tenant to relocate pursuant to Section 1946.2 of the Civil Code or any other law, may offset the tenant's COVID-19 rental debt against their obligation to assist the tenant to relocate.

Amended by Stats 2021 ch 27 (AB 832),s 16, eff. 6/28/2021.
Amended by Stats 2021 ch 2 (SB 91),s 18, eff. 1/29/2021.
Added by Stats 2020 ch 37 (AB 3088),s 20, eff. 8/31/2020.

Section 1179.04 - [Effective until 10/1/2025] Notice to tenants

(a)On or before September 30, 2020, a landlord shall provide, in at least 12-point type, the following notice to tenants who, as of September 1, 2020, have not paid one or more rental payments that came due during the protected time period: "NOTICE FROM THE STATE OF CALIFORNIA: The California Legislature has enacted the COVID-19 Tenant Relief Act of 2020 which protects renters who have experienced COVID-19-related financial distress from being evicted for failing to make rental payments due between March 1, 2020, and January 31, 2021. "COVID-19-related financial distress" means any of the following:

1. Loss of income caused by the COVID-19 pandemic.

2. Increased out-of-pocket expenses directly related to performing essential work during the COVID-19 pandemic.

3. Increased expenses directly related to the health impact of the COVID-19 pandemic.

4. Childcare responsibilities or responsibilities to care for an elderly, disabled, or sick family member directly related to the COVID-19 pandemic that limit your ability to earn income.

5. Increased costs for childcare or attending to an elderly, disabled, or sick family member directly related to the COVID-19 pandemic.

6. Other circumstances related to the COVID-19 pandemic that have reduced your income or increased your expenses.This law gives you the following protections:

1. If you failed to make rental payments due between March 1, 2020, and August 31, 2020, because you had decreased income or increased expenses due to the COVID-19 pandemic, as described above, you cannot be evicted based on this nonpayment.

2. If you are unable to pay rental payments that come due between September 1, 2020, and January 31, 2021, because of decreased income or increased expenses due to the COVID-19 pandemic, as described above, you cannot be evicted if you pay 25 percent of the rental payments missed during that time period on or before January 31, 2021. You must provide, to your landlord, a declaration under penalty of perjury of your COVID-19-related financial distress attesting to the decreased income or increased expenses due to the COVID-19 pandemic to be protected by the eviction limitations described above. Before your landlord can seek to evict you for failing to make a payment that came due between March 1, 2020, and January 31, 2021, your landlord will be required to give you a 15-day notice that informs you of the amounts owed and includes a blank declaration form you can use to comply with this requirement.

If your landlord has proof of income on file which indicates that your household makes at least 130 percent of the median income for the county where the rental property is located, as published by the Department of Housing and Community Development in the Official State Income Limits for 2020, your landlord may also require you to provide documentation which shows that you have experienced a decrease in income or increase in expenses due to the COVID-19 pandemic. Your landlord must tell you in the 15-day notice whether your landlord is requiring that documentation. Any form of objectively verifiable documentation that demonstrates the financial impact you have experienced is sufficient, including a letter from your employer, an unemployment insurance record, or medical bills, and may be provided to satisfy the documentation requirement.

It is very important you do not ignore a 15-day notice to pay rent or quit or a notice to perform covenants or quit from your landlord. If you are served with a 15-day notice and do not provide the declaration form to your landlord before the 15-day notice expires, you could be evicted. You could also be evicted beginning February 1, 2021, if you owe rental payments due between September 1, 2020, and January 31, 2021, and you do not pay an amount equal to at least 25 percent of the payments missed for that time period.

For information about legal resources that may be available to you, visit lawhelpca.org."

(b)On or before February 28, 2021, a landlord shall provide, in at least 12-point type, the following notice to tenants who, as of February 1, 2021, have not paid one or more rental payments that came due during the covered time period: "NOTICE FROM THE STATE OF CALIFORNIA: The California Legislature has enacted the COVID-19 Tenant Relief Act which protects renters who have experienced COVID-19-related financial distress from being evicted for failing to make rental payments due between March 1, 2020, and June 30, 2021. "COVID-19-related financial distress" means any of the following:

1. Loss of income caused by the COVID-19 pandemic.

2. Increased out-of-pocket expenses directly related to performing essential work during the COVID-19 pandemic.

3. Increased expenses directly related to the health impact of the COVID-19 pandemic.

4. Childcare responsibilities or responsibilities to care for an elderly, disabled, or sick family member directly related to the COVID-19 pandemic that limit your ability to earn income.

5. Increased costs for childcare or attending to an elderly, disabled, or sick family member directly related to the COVID-19 pandemic.

6. Other circumstances related to the COVID-19 pandemic that have reduced your income or increased your expenses.This law gives you the following protections:

1. If you failed to make rental payments due between March 1, 2020, and August 31, 2020, because you had decreased income or increased expenses due to the COVID-19 pandemic, as described above, you cannot be evicted based on this nonpayment.

2. If you are unable to pay rental payments that come due between September 1, 2020, and June 30, 2021, because of decreased income or increased expenses due to the COVID-19 pandemic, as described above, you cannot be evicted if you pay 25 percent of the rental payments missed during that time period on or before June 30, 2021. You must provide, to your landlord, a declaration under penalty of perjury of your COVID-19-related financial distress attesting to the decreased income or increased expenses due to the COVID-19 pandemic to be protected by the eviction limitations described above. Before your landlord can seek to evict you for failing to make a payment that came due between March 1, 2020, and June 30, 2021, your landlord will be required to give you a 15-day notice that informs you of the amounts owed and includes a blank declaration form you can use to comply with this requirement.

If your landlord has proof of income on file which indicates that your household makes at least 130 percent of the median income for the county where the rental property is located, as published by the Department of Housing and Community Development in the Official State Income Limits for 2020, your landlord may also require you to provide documentation which shows that you have experienced a decrease in income or increase in expenses due to the COVID-19 pandemic. Your landlord must tell you in the 15-day notice whether your landlord is requiring that documentation. Any form of objectively verifiable documentation that demonstrates the financial impact you have experienced is sufficient, including a letter from your employer, an unemployment insurance record, or medical bills, and may be provided to satisfy the documentation requirement.

It is very important you do not ignore a 15-day notice to pay rent or quit or a notice to perform covenants or quit from your landlord. If you are served with a 15-day notice and do not provide the declaration form to your landlord before the 15-day notice expires, you could be evicted. You could also be evicted beginning July 1, 2021, if you owe rental payments due between September 1, 2020, and June 30, 2021, and you do not pay an amount equal to at least 25 percent of the payments missed for that time period.

YOU MAY QUALIFY FOR RENTAL ASSISTANCE. In addition to extending these eviction protections, the State of California, in partnership with federal and local governments, has created an emergency rental assistance program to assist renters who have been unable to pay their rent and utility bills as a result of the COVID-19 pandemic. This program may be able to help you get caught up with past-due rent. Additionally, depending on the availability of funds, the program may also be able to assist you with making future rental payments.

While not everyone will qualify for this assistance, you can apply for it regardless of your citizenship or immigration status. There is no charge to apply for or receive this assistance.

Additional information about the extension of the COVID-19 Tenant Relief Act and new state or local rental assistance programs, including more information about how to qualify for assistance, can be found by visiting http://housingiskey.com or by calling 1-833-422-4255."

(c) On or before July 31, 2021, a landlord shall provide, in at least 12-point type, the following notice to tenants who, as of July 1, 2021, have not paid one or more rental payments that came due during the covered time period: "NOTICE FROM THE STATE OF CALIFORNIA: The California Legislature has extended the COVID-19 Tenant Relief Act. The law now protects renters who have experienced COVID-19-related financial distress from being evicted for failing to make rental payments due between March 1, 2020, and September 30, 2021.

"COVID-19-related financial distress" means any of the following:

   1. Loss of income caused by the COVID-19 pandemic.

   2. Increased out-of-pocket expenses directly related to performing essential work during the COVID-19 pandemic.

   3. Increased expenses directly related to the health impact of the COVID-19 pandemic.

   4. Childcare responsibilities or responsibilities to care for an elderly, disabled, or sick family member directly related to the COVID-19 pandemic that limit your ability to earn income.

   5. Increased costs for childcare or attending to an elderly, disabled, or sick family member directly related to the COVID-19 pandemic.

   6. Other circumstances related to the COVID-19 pandemic that have reduced your income or increased your expenses. This law gives you the following protections:

   1. If you failed to make rental payments due between March 1, 2020, and August 31, 2020, because you had decreased income or increased expenses due to the COVID-19 pandemic, as described above, you cannot be evicted based on this nonpayment.

   2. If you are unable to pay rental payments that come due between September 1, 2020, and September 30, 2021, because of decreased income or increased expenses due to the COVID-19 pandemic, as described above, you cannot be evicted if you pay 25 percent of the rental payments missed during that time period on or before September 30, 2021. You must provide, to your landlord, a declaration under penalty of perjury of your COVID-19-related financial distress attesting to the decreased income or increased expenses due to the COVID-19 pandemic to be protected by the eviction limitations described above. Before your landlord can seek to evict you for failing to make a payment that came due between March 1, 2020, and September 30, 2021, your landlord will be required to give you a 15-day notice that informs you of the amounts owed and includes a blank declaration form you can use to comply with this requirement.

If your landlord has proof of income on file that indicates that your household makes at least 130 percent of the median income for the county where the rental property is located, as published by the Department of Housing and Community Development in the Official State Income Limits for 2020, your landlord may also require you to provide documentation that shows that you have experienced a decrease in income or increase in expenses due to the COVID-19 pandemic. Your landlord must tell you in the 15-day notice whether your landlord is requiring that documentation. Any form of objectively verifiable documentation that demonstrates the financial impact you have experienced is sufficient, including a letter from your employer, an unemployment insurance record, or medical bills, and may be provided to satisfy the documentation requirement.

It is very important you do not ignore a 15-day notice to pay rent or quit or a notice to perform covenants or quit from your landlord. If you are served with a 15-day notice and do not provide the declaration form to your landlord before the 15-day notice expires, you could be evicted. You could also be evicted beginning October 1, 2021, if you owe rental payments due between September 1, 2020, and September 30, 2021, and you do not pay an amount equal to at least 25 percent of the payments missed for that time period.

YOU MAY QUALIFY FOR RENTAL ASSISTANCE. In addition to extending these eviction protections, the State of California, in partnership with federal and local governments, has created an emergency rental assistance program to assist renters who have been unable to pay their rent and utility bills as a result of the COVID-19 pandemic. This program may be able to help you get caught up with past-due rent. Additionally, depending on the availability of funds, the program may also be able to assist you with making future rental payments.

While not everyone will qualify for this assistance, you can apply for it regardless of your citizenship or immigration status. There is no charge to apply for or receive this assistance.

Additional information about the extension of the COVID-19 Tenant Relief Act and new state or local rental assistance programs, including more information about how to qualify for assistance, can be found by visiting http://housingiskey.com or by calling 1-833-430-2122."

(d) The landlord may provide the notice required by subdivisions (a) to (c), inclusive, as applicable, in the manner prescribed by Section 1162 or by mail.

(e)

   (1) A landlord may not serve a notice pursuant to subdivision (b) or (c) of Section 1179.03 before the landlord has provided the notice required by subdivisions (a) to (c), inclusive, as applicable.

   (2) The notice required by subdivision (a) may be provided to a tenant concurrently with a notice pursuant to subdivision (b) or (c) of Section 1179.03 that is served on or before September 30, 2020.

   (3) The notice required by subdivision (b) may be provided to a tenant concurrently with a notice pursuant to subdivision (b) or (c) of Section 1179.03 that is served on or before February 28, 2021.

   (4) The notice required by subdivision (c) may be provided to a tenant concurrently with a notice pursuant to subdivision (b) or (c) of Section 1179.03 that is served on or before September 30, 2021.

Amended by Stats 2022 ch 28 (SB 1380),s 27, eff. 1/1/2023.
Amended by Stats 2021 ch 27 (AB 832),s 17, eff. 6/28/2021.
Amended by Stats 2021 ch 2 (SB 91),s 19, eff. 1/29/2021.
Added by Stats 2020 ch 37 (AB 3088),s 20, eff. 8/31/2020.

Section 1179.04.5 - [Effective until 10/1/2025] Application of security deposit or rental payments to COVID-19 rental debt without tenant's consent prohibited

Notwithstanding Sections 1470, 1947, and 1950 of the Civil Code, or any other law, for the duration of any tenancy that existed during the covered time period, the landlord shall not do either of the following:

(a) Apply a security deposit to satisfy COVID-19 rental debt, unless the tenant has agreed, in writing, to allow the deposit to be so applied. Nothing in this subdivision shall prohibit a landlord from applying a security deposit to satisfy COVID-19 rental debt after the tenancy ends, in accordance with Section 1950.5 of the Civil Code.

(b) Apply a monthly rental payment to any COVID-19 rental debt other than the prospective month's rent, unless the tenant has agreed, in writing, to allow the payment to be so applied.

Renumbered from Ca. Civ. Code § Civ. 1179.04.5 and amended by Stats 2021 ch 124 (AB 938),s 3, eff. 1/1/2022.
Renumbered from Ca. Civ. Code § Civ. 1179.04.5 and amended by Stats 2021 ch 5 (AB 81),s 2, eff. 2/23/2021.
Added by Stats 2021 ch 2 (SB 91),s 20, eff. 1/29/2021.

Section 1179.05 - [Effective until 10/1/2025] Laws or regulations adopted in response to pandemic to protect tenants

(a) Any ordinance, resolution, regulation, or administrative action adopted by a city, county, or city and county in response to the COVID-19 pandemic to protect tenants from eviction is subject to all of the following:

(1) Any extension, expansion, renewal, reenactment, or new adoption of a measure, however delineated, that occurs between August 19, 2020, and June 30, 2022, shall have no effect before July 1, 2022.

(2) Any provision which allows a tenant a specified period of time in which to repay COVID-19 rental debt shall be subject to all of the following:

(A) If the provision in effect on August 19, 2020, required the repayment period to commence on a specific date on or before August 1, 2022, any extension of that date made after August 19, 2020, shall have no effect.

(B) If the provision in effect on August 19, 2020, required the repayment period to commence on a specific date after August 1, 2022, or conditioned commencement of the repayment period on the termination of a proclamation of state of emergency or local emergency, the repayment period is deemed to begin on August 1, 2022.

(C) The specified period of time during which a tenant is permitted to repay COVID-19 rental debt may not extend beyond the period that was in effect on August 19, 2020. In addition, a provision may not permit a tenant a period of time that extends beyond August 31, 2023, to repay COVID-19 rental debt.

(b) This section does not alter a city, county, or city and county's authority to extend, expand, renew, reenact, or newly adopt an ordinance that requires just cause for termination of a residential tenancy or amend existing ordinances that require just cause for termination of a residential tenancy, consistent with subdivision (g) of Section 1946.2, provided that a provision enacted or amended after August 19, 2020, shall not apply to rental payments that came due between March 1, 2020, and June 30, 2022.

(c) The one-year limitation provided in subdivision (2) of Section 1161 is tolled during any time period that a landlord is or was prohibited by any ordinance, resolution, regulation, or administrative action adopted by a city, county, or city and county in response to the COVID-19 pandemic to protect tenants from eviction based on nonpayment of rental payments from serving a notice that demands payment of COVID-19 rental debt pursuant to subdivision (e) of Section 798.56 of the Civil Code or paragraph (2) of Section 1161.

(d) It is the intent of the Legislature that this section be applied retroactively to August 19, 2020.

(e) The Legislature finds and declares that this section addresses a matter of statewide concern rather than a municipal affair as that term is used in Section 5 of Article XI of the California Constitution. Therefore, this section applies to all cities, including charter cities.

(f) It is the intent of the Legislature that the purpose of this section is to protect individuals negatively impacted by the COVID-19 pandemic, and that this section does not provide the Legislature's understanding of the legal validity on any specific ordinance, resolution, regulation, or administrative action adopted by a city, county, or city and county in response to the COVID-19 pandemic to protect tenants from eviction.

Amended by Stats 2022 ch 13 (AB 2179),s 2, eff. 3/31/2022.
Amended by Stats 2021 ch 27 (AB 832),s 18, eff. 6/28/2021.
Amended by Stats 2021 ch 5 (AB 81),s 9, eff. 2/23/2021.
Amended by Stats 2021 ch 2 (SB 91),s 21, eff. 1/29/2021.
Added by Stats 2020 ch 37 (AB 3088),s 20, eff. 8/31/2020.

Section 1179.06 - [Effective until 10/1/2025] Waiver void

Any provision of a stipulation, settlement agreement, or other agreement entered into on or after the effective date of this chapter, including a lease agreement, that purports to waive the provisions of this chapter is prohibited and is void as contrary to public policy.

Added by Stats 2020 ch 37 (AB 3088),s 20, eff. 8/31/2020.

Section 1179.07 - [Effective until 10/1/2025] Repealer

This chapter shall remain in effect until October 1, 2025, and as of that date is repealed.

Amended by Stats 2021 ch 27 (AB 832),s 19, eff. 6/28/2021.
Amended by Stats 2021 ch 2 (SB 91),s 22, eff. 1/29/2021.
Added by Stats 2020 ch 37 (AB 3088),s 20, eff. 8/31/2020.

Chapter 6 - COVID-19 RENTAL HOUSING RECOVERY ACT

Section 1179.08 - [Effective until 9/30/2024] Title

This chapter shall be known, and may be cited, as the COVID-19 Rental Housing Recovery Act.

Added by Stats 2021 ch 27 (AB 832),s 20, eff. 6/28/2021.

Section 1179.09 - [Effective until 9/30/2024] Definitions

For purposes of this chapter:

(a) "Approved application" means an application for which a government rental assistance program has verified applicant eligibility, and the requested funds have been obligated to the applicant for payment.

(b) "COVID-19 recovery period rental debt" means a rental debt of a tenant under a tenancy that came due between October 1, 2021, and March 31, 2022.

(c) "COVID-19 rental debt" has the same meaning as defined in Section 1179.02.

(d)

(1) "Final decision" means either of the following determinations by a government rental assistance program regarding an application for rental assistance:

(A) The application is an approved application.

(B) The application is denied for any of the following reasons:

(i) The tenant is not eligible for government rental assistance.

(ii) The government rental assistance program no longer has sufficient rental assistance funds to approve the application.

(iii) The application for government rental assistance remains incomplete 15 days, excluding Saturdays, Sundays, and other judicial holidays, after the landlord properly completed the portion of the application that is the responsibility of the landlord because of failure on the part of the tenant to properly complete the portion of the application that is the responsibility of the tenant.

(2) "Final decision" does not include any of the following:

(A) The rejection of an application as incomplete or improperly completed by a landlord.

(B) Notification that an application is temporarily pending further action by the government rental assistance program or the applicant.

(C) Notification that the landlord or tenant applied to the wrong government rental assistance program for the property or rental debt at issue.

(e) "Government rental assistance program" means any rental assistance program authorized pursuant to Chapter 17 (commencing with Section 50897) of Part 2 of Division 31 of the Health and Safety Code.

(f) "Pertinent government rental assistance program" means a government rental assistance program for the city, county, or city and county in which the property at issue is located.

(g) "Rental debt" means an unpaid rent or other unpaid financial obligation of a tenant under the tenancy that has come due.

(h)

(1) "Rental debt that accumulated due to COVID-19 hardship" means COVID-19 rental debt, COVID-19 recovery period rental debt, or a combination of both, if it accumulated during a tenancy initially established before October 1, 2021.

(2)

(A) For purposes of this subdivision, a tenancy is initially established when the tenants first lawfully occupy the premises.

(B) Any of the following do not initially establish a tenancy:

(i) The renewal of a periodic tenancy.

(ii) The extension of an existing lease or rental agreement.

(iii) The execution of a new lease or rental agreement with one or more individuals who already lawfully occupy the premises.

Added by Stats 2021 ch 27 (AB 832),s 20, eff. 6/28/2021.

Section 1179.10 - [Effective until 9/30/2024] Modification of notice demanding payment

(a) Before April 1, 2022, a notice for a residential rental property that demands payment of COVID-19 recovery period rental debt and that is served pursuant to subdivision (e) of Section 798.56 of the Civil Code or paragraph (2) or (3) of Section 1161 shall be modified as follows:

(1) The time period in which the tenant may pay the amount due or deliver possession of the property shall be no shorter than three days, excluding Saturdays, Sundays, and other judicial holidays.

(2) The notice shall include all of the following:

(A) The amount of rent demanded and the date each amount became due.

(B) The telephone number and internet website address of the pertinent government rental assistance program.

(C) The following bold text in at least 12-point font: "IMPORTANT NOTICE FROM THE STATE OF CALIFORNIA - YOU MUST TAKE ACTION TO AVOID AN EVICTION: As part of the state's COVID-19 relief plan, money has been set aside to help renters who have fallen behind on rent or utility payments.

If you cannot pay the amount demanded in this notice, YOU SHOULD COMPLETE A RENTAL ASSISTANCE APPLICATION IMMEDIATELY! It is free and simple to apply. Citizenship or immigration status does not matter.

DO NOT DELAY! IF YOU DO NOT COMPLETE YOUR APPLICATION FOR RENTAL ASSISTANCE WITHIN 15 BUSINESS DAYS, YOUR LANDLORD MAY BE ABLE TO SUE TO OBTAIN A COURT ORDER FOR YOUR EVICTION.

You can start your application by calling 1-833-430-2122 or visiting http://housingiskey.com."

(D) If the landlord was required, pursuant to Section 1632 of the Civil Code, to provide a translation of the rental contract or agreement in the language in which the contract or agreement was negotiated, the landlord shall also provide the text of the notice in subparagraph (C) to the tenant in the language in which the contract or agreement was negotiated. The Business, Consumer Services, and Housing Agency shall make available on the http://housingiskey.com internet website an official translation of the text required by subparagraph (C) in the languages specified in Section 1632 of the Civil Code by no later than September 15, 2021.

(b) On or after April 1, 2022, and before July 1, 2022, a notice for a residential rental property that demands payment of COVID-19 recovery period rental debt and that is served pursuant to subdivision (e) of Section 798.56 of the Civil Code or paragraph (2) or (3) of Section 1161 shall be modified as follows: "NOTICE FROM THE STATE OF CALIFORNIA:

If you completed an application for government rental assistance on or before March 31, 2022, you may have protections against eviction. For information about legal resources that may be available to you, visit lawhelpca.org."

(c)

(1) A notice that demands payment of COVID-19 recovery period rental debt that does not meet the requirements of this section is not sufficient to establish a cause of action for unlawful detainer or a basis for default judgment.

(2) The court, upon its own motion or upon a motion by a defendant in the case, shall dismiss a cause of action for unlawful detainer that is based on a notice that demands payment of COVID-19 recovery period rental debt if the notice does not meet the requirements of this section.

(3) A defendant may raise the insufficiency of a notice pursuant to this section as a complete defense to an unlawful detainer.

Amended by Stats 2022 ch 13 (AB 2179),s 3, eff. 3/31/2022.

Added by Stats 2021 ch 27 (AB 832),s 20, eff. 6/28/2021.

Section 1179.11 - [Effective until 9/30/2024] Procedures for unlawful detainer actions

On or after October 1, 2021, and before July 1, 2022, in an unlawful detainer action pertaining to residential real property and based, in whole or in part, on nonpayment of rental debt that accumulated due to COVID-19 hardship, all of the following shall apply:

(a) A court shall not issue a summons on a complaint for unlawful detainer that seeks possession of residential real property based on nonpayment of rental debt that accumulated due to COVID-19 hardship unless the plaintiff, in addition to any other requirements provided by law, also files any of the following:

(1) Both of the following:

(A) A statement verifying, under penalty of perjury, that before filing the complaint, the landlord completed an application for government rental assistance to cover the rental debt demanded from the defendants in the case, but the application was denied.

(B) A copy of a final decision from the pertinent government rental assistance program denying a rental assistance application for the property at issue in the case.

(2) A statement, under penalty of perjury, verifying that all of the following are true:

(A) Before filing the complaint, the landlord submitted a completed application, as defined in Section 50897 of the Health and Safety Code, for rental assistance to the pertinent government rental assistance program to cover the rental debt demanded from the defendants in the case.

(B) Twenty days have passed since the later of the following:

(i) The date that the landlord submitted the application as described in subparagraph (A).

(ii) The date that the landlord served the tenant with the three-day notice underlying the complaint.

(C) The landlord has not received notice or obtained verification from the pertinent government rental assistance program indicating that the tenant has submitted a completed application for rental assistance to cover the rental debt demanded from the defendants in the case.

(D) The landlord has received no communication from the tenant that the tenant has applied for government rental assistance to cover the unpaid rental debt demanded from the defendants in the case.

(3) A statement, under penalty of perjury, that the rental debt demanded from the defendant in the complaint accumulated under a tenancy that was initially established, as described in paragraph (2) of subdivision (h) of Section 1179.09, on or after October 1, 2021.

(4) A statement, under penalty of perjury, that a determination is not pending on an application, filed prior to April 1, 2022, for government rental assistance to cover any part of the rental debt demanded from the defendants in the case.

(b) A statement under penalty of perjury described in subdivision (a) shall be made on a form developed or revised by the Judicial Council for this purpose if the Judicial Council determines that this requirement is necessary to accomplish the purpose of the statement.

(c)

(1) In an action filed before April 1, 2022, judgment or default judgment shall not issue in favor of the plaintiff unless the court finds, upon review of the pleadings and any other evidence brought before it, that both of the following are true:

(A) Before filing the complaint, the plaintiff completed an application to the pertinent government rental assistance program for rental assistance to cover the rental debt demanded in the complaint.

(B) The plaintiff's application for rental assistance was denied because of lack of eligibility, lack of funding, or the application remained incomplete due to the tenant's failure to properly complete the portion of the application that is the responsibility of the tenant for 15 days, excluding Saturdays, Sundays, and other judicial holidays, after the landlord properly completed the portion of the application that is responsibility of the landlord.

(2) In an action filed on or after April 1, 2022, and before July 1, 2022, a judgment or default judgment shall not issue in favor of the plaintiff unless the court finds, upon review of the pleadings and any other evidence brought before it, that one of the following is true:

(A) Both of the following:

(i) Before April 1, 2022, the plaintiff completed an application to the pertinent government rental assistance program for rental assistance to cover that portion of the rental debt demanded in the complaint that constitutes rental debt that accumulated due to COVID-19 hardship.

(ii) The plaintiff's application for rental assistance was denied because lack of eligibility, lack of funding, or the application remained incomplete due to the tenant's failure to properly complete the portion of the application that is the responsibility of the tenant for 15 days, excluding Saturdays, Sundays, and other judicial holidays, after the landlord properly completed the portion of the application that is responsibility of the landlord.

(B) A determination is not pending on an application, filed prior to April 1, 2022, for government rental assistance to cover any part of the rental debt demanded from the defendants in the case.

(3) In making its findings pursuant to this paragraph, the court may take judicial notice of information available to the court pursuant to Section 1179.12.

(d) In addition to the summons, the complaint, and any other required document, the plaintiff shall serve the defendant with copies of the statement and final decision filed with the court pursuant to subdivision (a). The absence of these copies shall be sufficient grounds to grant a motion to quash service of the summons.

(e) If the defendant contests whether the plaintiff has met the requirements of subdivision (c), the plaintiff shall bear the burden of proving to the court that the plaintiff has met those requirements.

(f) The Legislature finds and declares all of the following:

(1) For rental debt that accumulated due to COVID-19 hardship that was incurred on or after October 1, 2021, and before April 1, 2022, a landlord must be compensated for all of the unpaid rent demanded in the notice that forms the basis of the complaint in order to prevent an unlawful detainer judgment based on that complaint.

(2) That for rental debt that accumulated due to COVID-19 hardship that was incurred on or after September 1, 2020, and before September 30, 2021, a landlord must be provided 25 percent of the unpaid rent demanded in the notice that forms the basis of the complaint before October 1, 2021, in order to prevent an unlawful detainer judgment based on that complaint.

(g) A summons on a complaint issued pursuant to paragraph (3) of subdivision (a) shall not be construed to subject the complaint to the requirements of this chapter.

Amended by Stats 2022 ch 13 (AB 2179),s 4, eff. 3/31/2022.

Added by Stats 2021 ch 27 (AB 832),s 20, eff. 6/28/2021.

Section 1179.12 - [Effective until 9/30/2024] Requirements for government rental assistance program; noncompliance; privacy

(a) Each government rental assistance program shall, by no later than September 15, 2021, develop mechanisms, including, but not limited to, telephone or online access, through which landlords, tenants, and the court may do both of the following:

(1) Verify the status of an application for rental assistance based upon the property address and a unique application number.

(2) Obtain copies of any determination on an application for rental assistance. A determination shall indicate all of the following:

(A) The name of the tenant that is the subject of the application.

(B) The address of the property that is the subject of the application.

(C) Whether the application has been approved or denied.

(D) If the application has been approved, then the amount of the payment that has been approved and the period and type of rental debt to which the amount corresponds.

(E) If the application has been denied, the reason for the denial, which shall be any of the following:

(i) The tenant is ineligible for government rental assistance.

(ii) The government rental assistance program no longer has sufficient funds to approve the application.

(iii) The application remained incomplete 15 days, excluding Saturdays, Sundays, and other judicial holidays, after it was initially submitted because of failure on the part of the tenant to provide required information.

(b) A government rental assistance program that does not comply with this section shall be deemed ineligible to receive further block grant allocations pursuant to Section 50897.2 or 50897.2.1 of the Health and Safety Code.

(c) It shall be unlawful for a person to access or use any information available pursuant to subdivision (a) for any purpose other than to determine the status of an application for assistance.

Amended by Stats 2022 ch 28 (SB 1380),s 28, eff. 1/1/2023.

Added by Stats 2021 ch 27 (AB 832),s 20, eff. 6/28/2021.

Section 1179.13 - [Effective until 9/30/2024] Application for relief due to COVID-10 financial hardship

(a) A court shall prevent the forfeiture of a lease or rental agreement, whether written or oral, and whether or not the tenancy has terminated, and restore the tenant to the former estate or tenancy, if necessary, if all of the following apply:

(1) The complaint for unlawful detainer is based on a demand for payment of rental debt that accumulated due to COVID-19 financial hardship.

(2)

(A) The tenant submits verification to the court that a government rental assistance program has approved an application for rental assistance corresponding to part or all of the rental debt demanded in the complaint.

(B) The verification described in this paragraph shall be in the form of either of the following:

(i) A copy of a final decision from the government rental assistance program showing the property address, the amount of payment approved, and the time period for which assistance was provided.

(ii) The property address and a unique application number to enable the court to obtain confirmation of the final decision, the corresponding property address, the amount of the payment approved, and the time period for which assistance was provided.

(3) The approved payment from the rental assistance program, together with any additional payments made by the tenant, constitute full payment of the rental debt demanded in the complaint.

(b) An application pursuant to this section may be made only at any time before restoration of the premises to the landlord.

(c)

(1) An application pursuant to this section shall consist of verification that a government rental assistance program has approved an application for rental assistance corresponding to the rental debt demanded in the complaint.

(2) The verification described in this subdivision shall consist of either of the following:

(A) A copy of the final decision from the government rental assistance program approving the application, showing the property address, and indicating the amount of payment approved.

(B) A property address and unique application number to enable the court to obtain confirmation of the final decision, the corresponding property address, and the amount of the payment approved.

(3)

(A) Except as provided in subparagraph (B), a tenant shall not be required to file any documentation not described in paragraph (1) or pleading with the court in order to apply for relief pursuant to this section.

(B) The verification required by this subdivision shall be provided on or accompanied by a form developed or revised by the Judicial Council for this purpose if the Judicial Council determines that this requirement is necessary to accomplish the purpose of the verification.

(d) Upon the filing of an application for relief pursuant to this section, the court shall do both of the following:

(1) Set a hearing on the matter on not less than 5 days' notice and not more than 10 days' notice to the parties, to be given by the court, and to be held separately or in conjunction with any regularly noticed hearing or trial in the case.

(2) Stay the action if no judgment has been entered in the case, immediately stay execution of any writ of possession issued in the case through the date of the hearing, and notify the sheriff accordingly.

(e)

(1) At the hearing set pursuant to paragraph (1) of subdivision (d), the court shall rule upon the application for relief pursuant to this section in one of the following ways:

(A) If the tenant does not qualify for relief pursuant to subdivision (a), the court shall deny the application. A denial pursuant to this subparagraph may be used as evidence in an unlawful detainer action between the parties.

(B) If the tenant qualifies for relief pursuant to subdivision (a), and the plaintiff has received all of the payments described in paragraph (3) of subdivision (a), then the court shall grant the application, set aside any judgment issued in the case, and dismiss the case.

(C) If the tenant qualifies for relief pursuant to subdivision (a), and the plaintiff has not received all of the payments described in paragraph (3) of subdivision (a), the court shall do all of the following:

(i) Set a followup hearing to be held within 15 days, excluding Saturdays, Sundays, and other judicial holidays.

(ii) Extend the stay of the action through the date of that followup hearing.

(iii) Extend the stay of execution of any writ of possession in the case through the date of that followup hearing.

(D) At any followup hearing pursuant to subparagraph (C), the court shall issue one of the following orders:

(i) If the government rental assistance program has withdrawn the approval of rental assistance, then the court shall deny the application.

(ii) If the plaintiff has received all of the payments described in paragraph (3) of subdivision (a), then the court shall grant the application, set aside any judgment issued in the case, and dismiss the case.

(iii) If the government rental assistance program has not withdrawn the approval of rental assistance, but the landlord has not received all of the payments described in paragraph (3) of subdivision (a) because the rental assistance program has not yet issued its part of the payment, then the court shall order another followup hearing in accordance with this subparagraph.

(iv) If the government rental assistance program has not withdrawn the approval of rental assistance, but the landlord has not received all of the payments described in paragraph (3) of subdivision (a) because the tenant has not yet paid the tenant's part of the payment, then the court shall deny the application with prejudice.

(2) If a court grants an application for relief pursuant to this section, the tenant shall not be considered the prevailing party for purposes of Section 1032, any attorney's fee provision appearing in contract or statute, or any other law.

Added by Stats 2021 ch 27 (AB 832),s 20, eff. 6/28/2021.

Section 1179.14 - [Effective until 9/30/2024] 60 day time period

If the criteria for issuance of a summons pursuant to subdivision (a) of Section 1179.11 have not been satisfied within 60 days of the complaint's filing, the court shall dismiss the action without prejudice.

Added by Stats 2021 ch 27 (AB 832),s 20, eff. 6/28/2021.

Section 1179.15 - [Effective until 9/30/2024] Repealer

This chapter shall remain in effect until September 30, 2024, and as of that date is repealed.

Added by Stats 2021 ch 27 (AB 832),s 20, eff. 6/28/2021.

Title 4 - OF THE ENFORCEMENT OF LIENS

Chapter 1 - LIENS IN GENERAL

Section 1180 - Lien defined

A lien is a charge imposed upon specific property, by which it is made security for the performance of an act.

Enacted 1872.

Chapter 2.5 - OIL AND GAS LIENS

Section 1203.50 - Title of act

This chapter shall be known and may be cited as the Oil and Gas Lien Act.

Added by Stats. 1959, Ch. 2020.

Section 1203.51 - Definitions

Unless the context otherwise requires, the definitions set forth in this section shall govern the construction of this chapter.

(a) "Person" means an individual, corporation, firm, partnership, limited liability company, or association.

(b) "Owner" means a person holding any interest in the legal or equitable title or both to any leasehold for oil or gas purposes, or his or her agent and shall include purchasers under executory contract, receivers, and trustees.

(c) "Contract" means a contract, written or oral, express or implied, or partly express and partly implied, or executory or executed, or partly executory and partly executed.

(d) "Material" means any material, machinery, appliances, buildings, structures, casing, tanks, pipelines, tools, bits, or other equipment or supplies but does not include rigs or hoists or their integral component parts except wire lines.

(e) "Labor" means work performed in return for wages.

(f) "Services" means work performed exclusive of labor, including the hauling of material, whether or not involving the furnishing of material.

(g) "Furnish" means sell or rent.

(h) "Drilling" means drilling, digging, shooting, torpedoing, perforating, fracturing, testing, logging, acidizing, cementing, completing or repairing.

(i) "Operating" means all operations conducted on the lease in connection with or necessary to the production of oil or gas, either in the development thereof or in working thereon by the subtractive process.

(j) "Construction" means construction, maintenance, operation, or repair, either in the development thereof or in working thereon by the subtractive process.

(k) "Original contractor" means any person for whose benefit a lien is prescribed under Section 1203.52.

Amended by Stats. 1994, Ch. 1010, Sec. 62. Effective January 1, 1995.

Section 1203.52 - Persons entitled to lien under chapter

Any person who shall, under contract with the owner of any leasehold for oil or gas purposes perform any labor or furnish any material or services used or employed, or furnished to be used or employed in the drilling or operating of any oil or gas well upon such leasehold, or in the constructing, putting together, or repairing of any material so used or employed, or furnished to be so used or employed, shall be entitled to a lien under this chapter, whether or not a producing well is obtained and whether or not such material is incorporated in or becomes a part of the completed oil or gas well, for the amount due him for any such labor performed, or materials or services furnished, within six months prior to the date of recording the statement of lien as provided in Section 1203.58, including, without limitation, shipping and mileage charges connected therewith, and interest from the date the same was due.

Added by Stats. 1959, Ch. 2020.

Section 1203.53 - Lien extends to leasehold and appurtenances materials and fixtures and wells located on leasehold

Liens created under Section 1203.52 shall extend to:

(a) The leasehold for oil or gas purposes to which the materials or services were furnished, or for which the labor was performed, and the appurtenances thereunto belonging, exclusive of any and all royalty interest, overriding interests and production payments created by an instrument recorded prior to the date such materials or services were first furnished or such labor was first performed for which lien is claimed; and

(b) All materials and fixtures owned by the owner or owners of such leasehold and used or employed, or furnished to be used or employed in the drilling or operating of any oil or gas well located thereon; and

(c) All oil or gas wells located on such leasehold, and the oil or gas produced therefrom, and the proceeds thereof, except the interest therein owned by the owners of royalty interests, overriding royalty interests and production payments created by an instrument recorded prior to the date such materials or services were first furnished or such labor was first performed for which the lien is claimed.

Added by Stats. 1959, Ch. 2020.

Section 1203.54 - Subcontractors entitled to lien

Any person who shall, under contract, perform any labor or furnish any material or services as a subcontractor under an original contractor or for or to an original contractor or a subcontractor under an original contractor, shall be entitled to a lien upon all the property upon which the lien of an original contactor may attach to the same extent as an original contractor, and the lien provided for in this section shall further extend and attach to all materials and fixtures owned by such original contractor or subcontractor to or for whom the labor is performed or material or services furnished and used or employed, or furnished to be used or employed in the drilling or operating of such oil or gas wells.

Added by Stats. 1959, Ch. 2020.

Section 1203.55 - Forfeiture of estate; failure of equitable or contingent interest to ripen into legal interest

When a lien provided for in this chapter shall have attached to a leasehold estate, forfeiture of such estate shall not impair any lien as to material, appurtenances and fixtures located thereon and to which such lien has attached prior to forfeiture. If a lien provided for in this chapter attaches to an equitable interest or to a legal interest contingent upon the happening of a condition subsequent, failure of such interest to ripen into legal title or such condition subsequent to be fulfilled, shall not impair any such lien as to material, appurtenances and fixtures located thereon and to which said lien had attached prior to such failure.

Added by Stats. 1959, Ch. 2020.

Section 1203.56 - Date lien arises; preference

The lien provided for in this chapter arises on the date of the furnishing of the first item of material or services or the date of performance of the first labor for which a lien is claimed under the provisions of this chapter. Upon compliance with the provisions of Section 1203.58, such lien shall be preferred to all other titles, charges, liens or encumbrances which may attach to or upon any of the property upon which a lien is given by this chapter subsequent to the date the lien herein provided for arises.

Added by Stats. 1959, Ch. 2020.

Section 1203.57 - Liens arising upon same property

All liens arising by virtue of this chapter upon the same property shall be of equal standing except that liens of persons for the performance of labor shall be preferred to all other liens arising by virtue of this chapter.

Added by Stats. 1959, Ch. 2020.

Section 1203.58 - Statement recorded by persons claiming liens

Every person claiming a lien under this chapter, shall record in the office of the county recorder for the county in which such leasehold, or some part thereof, is situated, a verified statement setting forth the amount claimed and the items thereof, the dates on which labor was performed or material or services furnished, the name of the owner of the leasehold, if known, the name of the claimant and his mailing address, a description of the leasehold, and if the claimant be a claimant under Section 1203.54, the name of the person for whom the labor was immediately performed or the material or services were immediately furnished. The statement of lien must be recorded within six months after the date on which the claimant's labor was performed or his materials or services were furnished to be effective as to such labor, materials, or services.

Added by Stats. 1959, Ch. 2020.

Section 1203.59 - Notice of lien

Anything in this chapter to the contrary notwithstanding, any lien claimed by virtue of this chapter, insofar as it may extend to oil or gas or the proceeds of the sale of oil or gas, shall not be effective against any purchaser of such oil or gas until written notice of such claim has been delivered to such purchaser. Such notice shall state the name of the claimant, his address, the amount for which the lien is claimed, and a description of the leasehold upon which the lien is claimed. Such notice shall be delivered personally to the purchaser or by registered letter or

certified mail. Upon receipt of such notice the purchaser shall withhold payments for such oil or gas runs to the extent of the lien amount claimed until delivery of notice in writing that the claim has been paid. The funds so withheld by the purchaser shall be used in payment of the lien judgment upon foreclosure. The lien claimant shall within 10 days give notice in writing that the claim has been paid.
Added by Stats. 1959, Ch. 2020.

Section 1203.60 - Bond given by lessor or owner or contractor or subcontractor

(a) Whenever any lien or liens shall be claimed or recorded under the provisions of this chapter then the lessor or owner of the property on which the lien or liens are claimed or the contractor or subcontractor through whom such lien or liens are claimed, or either of them, may record a bond with the county recorder of the county in which the property is located as herein provided. Such bond shall describe the property on which lien or liens are claimed, shall refer to the lien or liens claimed in manner sufficient to identify them and shall be in an amount equal to 150 percent of the amount of the claimed lien or liens referred to and shall be payable to the party or parties claiming same. Such bond shall be executed by the party recording same as principal and by a corporate surety authorized to execute such bonds as surety and shall be conditioned substantially that the principal and surety will pay to the obligees named or their assigns the amounts of the liens so claimed by them with all costs in the event same shall be proven to be liens on such property.

(b) Such bond, when recorded, shall take the place of the property against which any claim for lien referred to in such bond is asserted. At any time within the period of time provided in Section 1203.61, any person claiming such lien may sue upon such bond but no action shall be brought upon such bond after the expiration of such period. One action upon such bond shall not exhaust the remedies thereon but each obligee or assignee of an obligee named therein may maintain a separate suit thereon in any court having jurisdiction.
Added by Stats. 1959, Ch. 2020.

Section 1203.61 - Action to enforce lien

(a) Any lien provided for by this chapter shall be enforced in the same manner as provided in Chapter 4 (commencing with Section 8400) of Title 2 of Part 6 of Division 4 of the Civil Code. The action shall be filed within 180 days from the time of the recording of the lien. If a credit is given and notice of the fact and terms of the credit is filed in the office of the county recorder subsequent to the filing of the lien and prior to the expiration of the 180-day period, then the lien continues in force until 180 days after the expiration of the credit, but no lien continues in force by reason of any agreement to give credit for a longer time than one year from the time the work is completed. If the proceedings to enforce the lien are not prosecuted to trial within two years after commencement, the court may in its discretion dismiss the action for want of prosecution, and in all cases the dismissal of the action (unless it is expressly stated that it is without prejudice) or a judgment in the action that no lien exists is equivalent to the cancellation and removal from the record of the lien.

(b) As against any purchaser or encumbrancer for value and in good faith whose rights are acquired subsequent to the expiration of the 180-day period following the filing of the lien, no giving of credit or extension of the lien or time to enforce the lien shall be effective unless evidenced by a notice or agreement filed for record in the office of the county recorder prior to the acquisition of the rights of the purchaser or encumbrancer.
Amended by Stats 2010 ch 697 (SB 189),s 24, eff. 1/1/2011, op. 7/1/2012.

Section 1203.62 - Personal action to whom debt due for work performed or materials and services furnished

Nothing in this chapter shall be construed to impair or affect the right of any person to whom any debt may be due for work performed or materials or services furnished to maintain a personal action against the person liable for such debt.
Added by Stats. 1959, Ch. 2020.

Section 1203.63 - Waiver of lien

The taking of any note or any additional security by any person given a lien by this chapter shall not constitute a waiver of the lien given by this chapter unless made a waiver by express agreement of the parties in writing. The claiming of a lien under this chapter shall not constitute a waiver of any other right or security held by the claimant unless made a waiver by express agreement of the parties in writing.
Added by Stats. 1959, Ch. 2020.

Section 1203.64 - Claims and actions assignable

All claims for liens and likewise all actions to recover therefor under this chapter shall be assignable upon compliance with the provisions of Section 1203.58 so as to vest in the assignee all rights and remedies herein given subject to all defenses thereto that might be raised if such assignments had not been made.
Added by Stats. 1959, Ch. 2020.

Section 1203.65 - Subsequent perfection of unperfected lien arising prior to effective date of chapter

All liens granted by this chapter shall be perfected and enforced in accordance with the provisions hereof whether such liens arise before or after the effective date of this chapter; provided, however, that any unperfected lien granted under any statute in effect prior to the effective date of this chapter and which could be subsequently perfected in accordance with such prior statute were it not for the existence of this chapter may be perfected and enforced in accordance with the provisions of this chapter if the statement of lien required to be recorded under Section 1203.58 is recorded within the time therein required or within two months after the effective date of this chapter, whichever period is longer; and provided further, that the validity of any lien perfected prior to the effective date of this chapter in accordance with the requirements of any statute in effect prior to such effective date shall be determined on the basis of such prior statute but the enforcement thereof shall insofar as possible be governed by the provisions of this chapter.
Added by Stats. 1959, Ch. 2020.

Section 1203.66 - Liberal construction

This chapter shall be given liberal construction in favor of all persons entitled to any lien under it.
Added by Stats. 1959, Ch. 2020.

Chapter 3 - CERTAIN LIENS AND PRIORITIES FOR SALARIES, WAGES AND CONSUMER DEBTS

Section 1204 - Priority of claims when assignment made for benefit of creditors or assignor

When any assignment, whether voluntary or involuntary, and whether formal or informal, is made for the benefit of creditors of the assignor, or results from any proceeding in insolvency or receivership commenced against him or her, or when any property is turned over to the creditors of a person, firm, association or corporation, or to a receiver or trustee for the benefit of creditors, the following claims have priority in the following order:

(a) Allowed unsecured claims, but only to the extent of four thousand three hundred dollars ($4,300) for each individual or corporation, as the case may be, earned within 90 days before the date of the making of such assignment or the taking over of the property or the commencement of the court proceeding or the date of the cessation of the debtor's business, whichever occurs first, for either of the following:

(1) Wages, salaries, or commissions, including vacation, severance and sick leave pay earned by an individual.

(2) Sales commissions earned by an individual, or by a corporation with only one employee, acting as an independent contractor in the sale of goods or services of the debtor in the ordinary course of the debtor's business if, and only if, during the 12 months preceding the date of the making of the assignment or the taking over of the property or the commencement of the proceeding or the date of the cessation of the debtor's business, whichever occurs first, at least 75 percent of the amount that the individual or corporation earned by acting as an independent contractor in the sale of goods or services was earned from the debtor.

(b) Allowed unsecured claims for contributions to employee benefit plans arising from services rendered within 180 days before the date of the making of the assignment or the taking over of the property or the commencement of the court proceeding or the date of the cessation of the debtor's business, whichever occurs first; but only for each employee benefit plan, to the extent of the number of employees covered by the plan multiplied by four thousand three hundred dollars ($4,300), less the aggregate amount paid to the employees under subdivision (a), plus the aggregate amount paid by the estate on behalf of the employees to any other employee benefit plan.

(c) The above claims shall be paid by the trustee, assignee or receiver before the claim of any other creditor of the assignor, insolvent, or debtor whose property is so turned over, and shall be paid as soon as the money with which to pay same becomes available. If there is insufficient money to pay all the labor claims in full, the money available shall be distributed among the claimants in proportion to the amount of their respective claims. The trustee, receiver or assignee for the benefit of creditors shall have the right to require sworn claims to be presented and shall have the right to refuse to pay any such preferred claim, either in whole or in part, if he or she has reasonable cause to believe that a claim is not valid but shall pay any part thereof that is not disputed, without prejudice to the claimant's rights, as to the balance of his or her claim, and withheld sufficient money to cover the disputed portion until the claimant in question has a reasonable opportunity to establish the validity of his or her claim by court action, either in his or her own name or through an assignee.

(d) This section is binding upon all the courts of this state and in all receivership actions the court shall order the receiver to pay promptly out of the first receipts and earnings of the receivership, after paying the current operating expenses, such preferred labor claims.

EFFECTIVE 1/1/2000. Amended July 28, 1999 (Bill Number: SB 219) (Chapter 202).

Section 1204.5 - Claims having priority but subordinate to priorities of labor claims

In any general assignment for the benefit of creditors, the following claims shall have priority, subordinate to the priorities for labor claims under Section 1204, but prior to all other unsecured claims: allowed unsecured claims of individuals, to the extent of nine hundred dollars ($900) for each such individual, arising from the deposit, before the commencement of the case, of money in connection with the purchase, lease, or rental of property, or the purchase of services, for the personal, family, or household use of such individuals, that were not delivered or provided. The priority granted by this section shall be subordinate to that granted by Sections 18933 and 26312 of the Revenue and Taxation Code.

Amended by Stats. 1980, Ch. 135, Sec. 5.

Section 1205 - Unpaid wages preferred claims and liens upon sale or transfer of business not in ordinary and regular course of business

Upon the sale or transfer of any business or the stock in trade, in bulk, or a substantial part thereof, not in the ordinary and regular course of business or trade, unpaid wages of employees of the seller or transferor earned within ninety (90) days prior to the sale, transfer, or opening of an escrow for the sale thereof, shall constitute preferred claims and liens thereon as between creditors of the seller or transferor and must be paid first from the proceeds of the sale or transfer.

Added by Stats. 1961, Ch. 1083.

Section 1206 - Statement of claim filed by persons performing work or rendering services upon levy under writ of attachment or execution

(a) Upon the levy under a writ of attachment or execution not founded upon a claim for labor, any miner, mechanic, salesman, servant, clerk, laborer or other person who has performed work or rendered personal services for the defendant within 90 days prior to the levy may file a verified statement of the claim with the officer executing the writ, file a copy with the court that issued the writ, and give copies, containing his or her address, to the plaintiff and the defendant, or any attorney, clerk or agent representing them, or mail copies to them by registered mail at their last known address, return of which by the post office undelivered shall be deemed a sufficient service if no better address is available, and that claim, not exceeding nine hundred dollars ($900), unless disputed, shall be paid by the officer, immediately upon the expiration of the time for dispute of the claim as prescribed in Section 1207, from the proceeds of the levy remaining in the officer's hands at the time of the filing of the statement or collectible by the officer on the basis of the writ.

(b) The court issuing the writ shall make a notation in the register of actions of every preferred labor claim of which it receives a copy and shall endorse on any writ of execution or abstract of judgment issued subsequently in the case that it is issued subject to the rights of a preferred labor claimant or claimants and giving the names and amounts of all preferred labor claims of which it has notice. In levying under any writ of execution the officer making the levy shall include in the amount due under the execution all preferred labor claims that have been filed in the action and of which the officer has notice, except any claims that may have been finally disallowed by the court under this procedure and of which disallowance the officer has actual notice. The amount due on preferred labor claims that have not been finally disallowed by the court shall be considered a part of the sum due under any writ of attachment or execution in augmentation of that amount and any person, firm, association, or corporation on whom a writ of attachment or execution is levied shall immediately pay to the levying officer the amount of the preferred labor claims, out of any money belonging to the defendant in the action, before paying the principal sum called for in the writ.

(c) If any claim is disputed within the time, and in the manner prescribed in Section 1207, and a copy of the dispute is mailed by registered mail to the claimant or the claimant's attorney at the address given in the statement of claim and the registry receipt is attached to the original of the dispute when it is filed with the levying officer, or is handed to the claimant or the claimant's attorney, the claimant, or the claimant's assignee, must within 10 days after the copy is deposited in the mail or is handed to the claimant or the claimant's attorney, petition the court having jurisdiction of the action on which the writ is based, for a hearing before it to determine the claim for priority, or the claim to priority is barred. If more than one attachment or execution is involved, the petition shall be filed in the court having jurisdiction over the senior attachment or execution. The hearing shall be held within 20 days from the filing of the petition, unless the court continues it for good cause. Ten days' notice of the hearing shall be given by the petitioner to the plaintiff, the defendant, and all parties claiming an interest in the property, or their attorneys. The notice may be informal and need specify only the name of the court, the names of the principal parties to the senior attachment or execution, and the name of the wage claimant or claimants on whose behalf it is filed but shall specify that the hearing is for the purpose of determining the claim for priority. The plaintiff, the defendant, or any other party claiming an interest may contest the amount or validity of the claim in spite of any confession of judgment or failure to appear or to contest the claim on the part of any other person.

(d) There shall be no cost for filing or hearing the petition. The hearing on the petition shall be informal but all parties testifying shall be sworn. Any claimant may appear on the claimant's own behalf at the hearing and may call and examine witnesses to substantiate his or her claim. An appeal may be taken from a judgment in a proceeding under this section in the manner provided for appeals from judgments of the court where the proceeding occurred, in an action of the same jurisdictional classification.

(e) The officer shall keep, until the determination of the claim for priority, any amount of the proceeds of the writ necessary to satisfy the claim. If the claim for priority is allowed, the officer shall pay the amount due, including the claimant's cost of suit, from those proceeds, immediately after the order allowing the claim becomes final.

Amended by Stats 2002 ch 664 (AB 3034),s 51, eff. 1/1/2003.

Amended by Stats 2001 ch 44 (SB 562), s 7, eff. 1/1/2002.

Section 1207 - Sworn statement denying that claim due

Within five days after receiving a copy of the statement provided for in the next preceding section, either the plaintiff or the defendant in the action in which the writ issued may file with the officer a sworn statement denying that any part of such claim is due for services rendered within ninety days next preceding the levy of the writ, or denying that any part of such claim, beyond a sum specified, is so due. Such sworn statement can not be made on information and belief unless the party swearing to same has actual information and belief that the wage claim, or the portion thereof that is contested, is not justly due, and in such case the nature and source of the information must be given. If a part of the claim is

admitted to be due, and the claimant nevertheless files a petition for hearing and the court does not allow more than the amount so admitted, he can not recover costs but the costs must be adjudged against him, and the amount thereof deducted from the sum found due him.
Amended by Stats. 1935, Ch. 557.

Section 1208 - Distribution of proceeds of writ; right to proceed directly against money or property; notice of request to release original attachment or execution

If the claims presented under Section 1206 and not disputed, or, if disputed, established by judgment, exceed the proceeds of the writ not disposed of before their presentation, such proceeds shall be distributed among the claimants in proportion to the amount of their respective claims after the costs incurred by the senior attaching plaintiff or judgment creditor in such action have first been taken care of.

If sufficient money to pay in full all preferred labor claims filed under an attachment or execution does not become available immediately upon the expiration of the time for dispute of such claims under Section 1207, any of the claimants, or their assignees, have the right to proceed directly against the money or other property levied on in individual or joint actions by themselves or their assignees against the defendant, and the attachment or execution under which the preferred claims were filed shall be considered set aside as far as such claimants, or their assignees, are concerned so as to enable them, or any of them, or any of their assignees, to proceed directly against any or all of the money or other property in question by means of their own attachments or executions; provided, however, that any money collected on behalf of any such labor claimant, or his or her assignee, on the basis of such new attachment or execution shall be shared in by the other preferred labor claimants who have filed claims that have not been disputed, or, if disputed, established by judgment, in proportion to the amount of their respective claims, deducting only the costs in the action brought by the said labor claimant, or his or her assignee, and the costs in the original action brought by the senior attaching plaintiff or judgment creditor.

If such senior attaching plaintiff or judgment creditor requests a release of his or her original attachment or execution, and the preferred labor claims filed under same are not released, the officer who levied the writ must first mail notices of such request to release to each of the labor claimants who have filed claims, or their attorneys, which notices must specify that unless the claimants bring attachment actions of their own and levy on the money or property in question within five days from the date thereof the money or property will be released from the attachment or execution; provided, however, that such officer may instead collect sufficient money on the basis of the original writ to pay off the preferred labor claims in full and then release the attachment or execution, but in no case shall the officer release the attachment or execution without first taking care of the labor claims until the five-day period has expired, unless the officer's costs, keepers' fees or storage charges have not been immediately taken care of by some of the parties involved. In any case it shall be lawful for a garnishee to pay over to the officer levying the writ any money held by the garnishee without waiting for execution to be levied and the officer's receipt for the money shall be a sufficient quittance, and the officer shall collect such money and immediately pay off the established preferred labor claims in all cases where it is possible to do so without additional court proceedings on the officer's part.
Amended by Stats. 1982, Ch. 497, Sec. 78. Operative July 1, 1983, by Sec. 185 of Ch. 497.

Chapter 4 - CERTAIN LIENS UPON ANIMALS

Section 1208.5 - Satisfaction of lien

A person having a lien upon an animal or animals under the provisions of Section 597a or 597.1 of the Penal Code may satisfy the lien in any of the following ways:

(a) If the lien is not discharged and satisfied, by the person responsible, within three days after the obligation becomes due, the person holding the lien may resort to the proper court to satisfy the claim.

(b) Three days after the charges against the property become due, sell the property, or an undivided fraction thereof as may become necessary, to defray the amount due and costs of sale, by giving three days' notice of the sale by advertising in some newspaper published in the county, or city and county, in which the lien has attached to the property.

(c) If there is no newspaper published in the county, by posting notices of the sale in three of the most public places in the town or county for three days previous to the sale. The notices shall contain an accurate description of the property to be sold, together with the terms of sale, which shall be for cash, payable on the consummation of the sale. The proceeds of the sale shall be applied to the discharge of the lien and the costs of sale; the remainder, if any, shall be paid over to the owner, if known, and if not known shall be paid into the treasury of the humane society of the county, or city and county, where the sale takes place. If there is no humane society in the county, then the remainder shall be paid into the county treasury.
Amended by Stats 2019 ch 256 (SB 781),s 2, eff. 1/1/2020.
Amended by Stats 2003 ch 62 (SB 600),s 25, eff. 1/1/2004.
Amended by Stats 2002 ch 784 (SB 1316),s 81, eff. 1/1/2003.

Chapter 5 - LIENS ON AIRCRAFT

Section 1208.61 - Lien for making repairs, performing labor or furnishing supplies and materials

Subject to the limitations set forth in this chapter, every person has a lien dependent upon possession for the compensation to which he is legally entitled for making repairs or performing labor upon, and furnishing supplies or materials for, and for the storage, repair, or safekeeping of, any aircraft, also for reasonable charges for the use of any landing aid furnished such aircraft and reasonable landing fees.
Added by Stats. 1953, Ch. 52.

Section 1208.62 - Notice and consent prior to commencing work or service

That portion of such lien in excess of two hundred fifty dollars ($250) for work or services rendered or performed at the request of any person other than the holder of the legal title is invalid, unless prior to commencing such work or service the person claiming the lien gives actual notice to the legal owner and the mortgagee, if any, of the aircraft, and the written consent of the legal owner and the mortgagee of the aircraft is obtained before such work or services are performed. For the purposes of this chapter the person named in the federal aircraft registration certificate issued by the Administrator of Civil Aeronautics shall be deemed to be the legal owner.
Added by Stats. 1953, Ch. 52.

Section 1208.63 - Assignment of lien for labor and materials

Any lien for labor or materials provided for in this chapter may be assigned by written instrument accompanied by delivery of possession of the aircraft subject to the lien and the assignee may exercise the rights of a lienholder pursuant to this chapter. Any lienholder assigning a lien shall at the time of the assignment give written notice, either by personal delivery or by registered mail with return receipt requested, to the legal owner of the property covered by the lien, including the name and address of the person to whom the lien is assigned.
Added by Stats. 1953, Ch. 52.

Section 1208.64 - Lien lost by reason of possession revived upon repossession by lienholder

Whenever the lien upon any aircraft is lost by reason of the loss of possession through trick, fraud, or device, the repossession of such aircraft by the lienholder revives the lien, but the lien so revived is subordinate to any right, title, or interest of any person under any sale, transfer, encumbrance, lien, or other interest acquired or secured in good faith and for value between the time of the loss of possession and the time of repossession.
Added by Stats. 1953, Ch. 52.

Section 1208.65 - Sale of property to satisfy lien

If the lienholder is not paid the amount due within 10 days after it becomes due, the lienholder may proceed to sell the property, or so much thereof as is necessary to satisfy the lien and costs of sale, at public auction.
Added by Stats. 1953, Ch. 52.

Section 1208.66 - Notice of sale
Prior to any such sale the lienholder shall publish a notice of the sale pursuant to Section 6062 of the Government Code in a newspaper published in the county in which the aircraft is situated, or if there is no such newspaper, by posting notice of sale in three of the most public places in the city or place where such aircraft is to be sold for 10 days previous to the date of the sale. Prior to the sale of any aircraft to satisfy any such lien, 20 days' notice by registered mail shall be given to the legal owner as it appears in the registration certificate.
Amended by Stats. 1957, Ch. 452.

Section 1208.67 - Application of proceeds of sale
The proceeds of the sale must be applied to the discharge of the lien and the cost of keeping and selling the property. The remainder, if any, shall be paid to the legal owner.
Added by Stats. 1953, Ch. 52.

Section 1208.68 - Redemption of sold aircraft
Within 20 days after the sale, the legal owner may redeem the aircraft so sold upon the payment of the amount of the lien, all costs and expenses of sale, and interest on such sum at the rate of 12 percent a year from the date it became due or the date when the amounts were advanced until the repayment.
Added by Stats. 1953, Ch. 52.

Section 1208.69 - Obtaining possession of aircraft through trick, fraud or device perpetrated upon lienholder
It is a misdemeanor for any person to obtain possession of all or any part of any aircraft subject to a lien under this chapter through surreptitious removal or by trick, fraud, or device perpetrated upon the lienholder.
Added by Stats. 1953, Ch. 52.

Section 1208.70 - Inapplicability to aircraft operated by air carrier or foreign aircraft
This chapter shall not apply to aircraft operated exclusively by an air carrier or a foreign air carrier, as defined in subdivisions (2) and (19) of Section 1 of Chapter 601 of the Statutes of the Seventy-fifth United States Congress, Second Session (1938), engaged in air transportation as defined in subdivision (10) of the same section while there is in force a certificate by, or a foreign air carrier permit of, the Civil Aeronautics Board of the United States, or its successor, authorizing such air carrier to engage in such transportation.
Added by Stats. 1953, Ch. 52.

Title 5 - OF CONTEMPTS

Section 1209 - Acts or omissions deemed contempt upon authority of court
(a) The following acts or omissions in respect to a court of justice, or proceedings therein, are contempts of the authority of the court:

(1) Disorderly, contemptuous, or insolent behavior toward the judge while holding the court, tending to interrupt the due course of a trial or other judicial proceeding.

(2) A breach of the peace, boisterous conduct, or violent disturbance, tending to interrupt the due course of a trial or other judicial proceeding.

(3) Misbehavior in office, or other willful neglect or violation of duty by an attorney, counsel, clerk, sheriff, coroner, or other person, appointed or elected to perform a judicial or ministerial service.

(4) Abuse of the process or proceedings of the court, or falsely pretending to act under authority of an order or process of the court.

(5) Disobedience of any lawful judgment, order, or process of the court.

(6) Willful disobedience by a juror of a court admonishment related to the prohibition on any form of communication or research about the case, including all forms of electronic or wireless communication or research.

(7) Rescuing any person or property in the custody of an officer by virtue of an order or process of that court.

(8) Unlawfully detaining a witness or party to an action while going to, remaining at, or returning from the court where the action is on the calendar for trial.

(9) Any other unlawful interference with the process or proceedings of a court.

(10) Disobedience of a subpoena duly served, or refusing to be sworn or answer as a witness.

(11) When summoned as a juror in a court, neglecting to attend or serve as a juror, or improperly conversing with a party to an action to be tried at the court, or with any other person, in relation to the merits of the action, or receiving a communication from a party or other person in respect to the action, without immediately disclosing the communication to the court.

(12) Disobedience by an inferior tribunal or judicial officer of the lawful judgment, order, or process of a superior court, or proceeding in an action or special proceeding contrary to law, after the action or special proceeding is removed from the jurisdiction of the inferior tribunal or judicial officer.

(b) A speech or publication reflecting upon or concerning a court or an officer thereof shall not be treated or punished as a contempt of the court unless made in the immediate presence of the court while in session and in such a manner as to actually interfere with its proceedings.

(c) Notwithstanding Section 1211 or any other law, if an order of contempt is made affecting an attorney, his or her agent, investigator, or any person acting under the attorney's direction, in the preparation and conduct of an action or proceeding, the execution of any sentence shall be stayed pending the filing within three judicial days of a petition for extraordinary relief testing the lawfulness of the court's order, the violation of which is the basis of the contempt, except for conduct proscribed by subdivision (b) of Section 6068 of the Business and Professions Code, relating to an attorney's duty to maintain respect due to the courts and judicial officers.

(d) Notwithstanding Section 1211 or any other law, if an order of contempt is made affecting a public safety employee acting within the scope of employment for reason of the employee's failure to comply with a duly issued subpoena or subpoena duces tecum, the execution of any sentence shall be stayed pending the filing within three judicial days of a petition for extraordinary relief testing the lawfulness of the court's order, a violation of which is the basis for the contempt. As used in this subdivision, "public safety employee" includes any peace officer, firefighter, paramedic, or any other employee of a public law enforcement agency whose duty is either to maintain official records or to analyze or present evidence for investigative or prosecutorial purposes.
Amended by Stats 2011 ch 181 (AB 141),s 3, eff. 1/1/2012.

Section 1209.5 - Parent not in compliance with order compelling parent to furnish support for child
When a court of competent jurisdiction makes an order compelling a parent to furnish support or necessary food, clothing, shelter, medical attendance, or other remedial care for his or her child, proof that the order was made, filed, and served on the parent or proof that the parent was present in court at the time the order was pronounced and proof that the parent did not comply with the order is prima facie evidence of a contempt of court.
Amended by Stats. 1992, Ch. 163, Sec. 57. Effective January 1, 1993. Operative January 1, 1994, by Sec. 161 of Ch. 163.

Section 1210 - Reentry upon or taking possession of property after person dispossessed or ejected
Every person dispossessed or ejected from any real property by the judgment or process of any court of competent jurisdiction, who, not having right so to do, reenters into or upon or takes possession of the real property, or induces or procures any person not having right so to do, or aids or

abets such a person therein, is guilty of a contempt of the court by which the judgment was rendered or from which the process issued. Upon a conviction for contempt the court must immediately issue an alias process, directed to the proper officer, and requiring the officer to restore possession to the party entitled under the original judgment or process, or to the party's lessee, grantee, or successor in interest. No appeal from the order directing the issuance of an alias writ of possession stays the execution of the writ, unless an undertaking is executed on the part of the appellant to the effect that the appellant will not commit or suffer to be committed any waste on the property, and if the order is affirmed, or the appeal dismissed, the appellant will pay the value of the use and occupation of the property from the time of the unlawful reentry until the delivery of the possession of the property, pursuant to the judgment or order, not exceeding a sum to be fixed by the judge of the court by which the order for the alias writ was made.

Amended by Stats. 1982, Ch. 517, Sec. 179.

Section 1211 - Contempt committed in immediate view and presence of judge; contempt not committed in immediate view or presence of judge

(a) When a contempt is committed in the immediate view and presence of the court, or of the judge at chambers, it may be punished summarily; for which an order must be made, reciting the facts as occurring in such immediate view and presence, adjudging that the person proceeded against is thereby guilty of a contempt, and that he or she be punished as therein prescribed. When the contempt is not committed in the immediate view and presence of the court, or of the judge at chambers, an affidavit shall be presented to the court or judge of the facts constituting the contempt, or a statement of the facts by the referees or arbitrators, or other judicial officers.

(b) In family law matters, filing of the Judicial Council form entitled "Order to Show Cause and Affidavit for Contempt (Family Law)" shall constitute compliance with this section.

Amended by Stats 2001 ch 754 (AB 1697), s 1, eff. 1/1/2002.

Section 1211.5 - Construction, amendment and review of affidavit or statement of facts

At all stages of all proceedings, the affidavit or statement of facts, as the case may be, required by Section 1211 shall be construed, amended, and reviewed according to the followings rules:

(a) If no objection is made to the sufficiency of such affidavit or statement during the hearing on the charges contained therein, jurisdiction of the subject matter shall not depend on the averments of such affidavit or statement, but may be established by the facts found by the trial court to have been proved at such hearing, and the court shall cause the affidavit or statement to be amended to conform to proof.

(b) The court may order or permit amendment of such affidavit or statement for any defect or insufficiency at any stage of the proceedings, and the trial of the person accused of contempt shall continue as if the affidavit or statement had been originally filed as amended, unless substantial rights of such person accused would be prejudiced thereby, in which event a reasonable postponement, not longer than the ends of justice require, may be granted.

(c) No such affidavit or statement is insufficient, nor can the trial, order, judgment, or other proceeding thereon be affected by reason of any defect or imperfection in matter of form which does not prejudice a substantial right of the person accused on the merits. No order or judgment of conviction of contempt shall be set aside, nor new trial granted, for any error as to any matter of pleading in such affidavit or statement, unless, after an examination of the entire cause, including the evidence, the court shall be of the opinion that the error complained of has resulted in a miscarriage of justice.

Added by Stats. 1970, Ch. 1264.

Section 1212 - Issuance of warrant of attachment and warrant of commitment

When the contempt is not committed in the immediate view and presence of the court or judge, a warrant of attachment may be issued to bring the person charged to answer, or, without a previous arrest, a warrant of commitment may, upon notice, or upon an order to show cause, be granted; and no warrant of commitment can be issued without such previous attachment to answer, or such notice or order to show cause.

Amended by Stats. 1951, Ch. 1737.

Section 1213 - Undertaking for person's appearance

Whenever a warrant of attachment is issued pursuant to this title the court or judge must direct, by an endorsement on the warrant, that the person charged may give an undertaking for the person's appearance in an amount to be specified in such endorsement.

Amended by Stats. 1982, Ch. 517, Sec. 179.5.

Section 1214 - Execution of warrant of attachment

Upon executing the warrant of attachment, the officer executing the warrant must keep the person in custody, bring him before the court or judge, and detain him until an order be made in the premises, unless the person arrested entitle himself to be discharged, as provided in the next section.

Amended by Stats. 1951, Ch. 1737.

Section 1215 - Discharge of person arrested upon executing and delivering undertaking

The person arrested must be discharged from the arrest upon executing and delivering to the officer, at any time before the return day of the warrant, an undertaking to the effect that the person arrested will appear on the return of the warrant and abide the order of the court or judge thereupon.

Amended by Stats. 1982, Ch. 517, Sec. 180.

Section 1216 - Return of warrant and undertaking

The officer must return the warrant of arrest and undertaking, if any, received by him from the person arrested, by the return day specified therein.

Enacted 1872.

Section 1217 - Investigation of charge and hearing on answer

When the person arrested has been brought up or appeared, the court or judge must proceed to investigate the charge, and must hear any answer which the person arrested may make to the same, and may examine witnesses for or against him, for which an adjournment may be had from time to time if necessary.

Amended by Stats. 1951, Ch. 1737.

Section 1218 - Finding that person guilty of contempt

(a) Upon the answer and evidence taken, the court or judge shall determine whether the person proceeded against is guilty of the contempt charged, and if it be adjudged that the person is guilty of the contempt, a fine may be imposed on the person not exceeding one thousand dollars ($1,000), payable to the court, or the person may be imprisoned not exceeding five days, or both. In addition, a person who is subject to a court order as a party to the action, or any agent of this person, who is adjudged guilty of contempt for violating that court order may be ordered to pay to the party initiating the contempt proceeding the reasonable attorney's fees and costs incurred by this party in connection with the contempt proceeding.

(b) Any party, who is in contempt of a court order or judgment in a dissolution of marriage, dissolution of domestic partnership, or legal separation action, shall not be permitted to enforce such an order or judgment, by way of execution or otherwise, either in the same action or by way of a separate action, against the other party. This restriction shall not affect nor apply to the enforcement of child or spousal support orders.

(c)

(1) In any court action in which a party is found in contempt of court for failure to comply with a court order pursuant to the Family Code, the court shall, subject to the sentencing option provided in paragraph (2), order the following:

(A) Upon a first finding of contempt, the court shall order the contemner to perform community service of up to 120 hours, or to be imprisoned up to 120 hours, for each count of contempt.

(B) Upon the second finding of contempt, the court shall order the contemner to perform community service of up to 120 hours, in addition to ordering imprisonment of the contemner up to 120 hours, for each count of contempt.

(C) Upon the third or any subsequent finding of contempt, the court shall order that the contemner serve a term of imprisonment of up to 240 hours and perform community service of up to 240 hours, for each count of contempt. The court shall also order the contemner to pay an administrative fee, not to exceed the actual cost of the contemner's administration and supervision, while assigned to a community service program pursuant to this paragraph.

(D) The court shall take parties' employment schedules into consideration when ordering either community service or imprisonment, or both.

(2) In lieu of an order of imprisonment, community service, or both, as set forth in paragraph (1), the court may grant probation or a conditional sentence for a period not to exceed one year upon a first finding of contempt, a period not to exceed two years upon a second finding of contempt, and a period not to exceed three years upon a third or any subsequent finding of contempt.

(3) For purposes of this subdivision, "probation" and "conditional sentence" shall have the meanings set forth in subdivision (a) of Section 1203 of the Penal Code.

(d) Pursuant to Section 1211 and this section, a district attorney or city attorney may initiate and pursue a court action for contempt against a party for failing to comply with a court order entered pursuant to the Domestic Violence Protection Act (Division 10 (commencing with Section 6200) of the Family Code). Any attorney's fees and costs ordered by the court pursuant to subdivision (a) against a party who is adjudged guilty of contempt under this subdivision shall be paid to the Office of Emergency Services' account established for the purpose of funding domestic violence shelter service providers pursuant to subdivision (f) of Section 13823.15 of the Penal Code.

Amended by Stats 2020 ch 283 (AB 2338),s 1, eff. 1/1/2021.
Amended by Stats 2013 ch 352 (AB 1317),s 56, eff. 9/26/2013, op. 7/1/2013.
Amended by Stats 2010 ch 618 (AB 2791),s 3, eff. 1/1/2011.
Amended by Stats 2005 ch 631 (SB 720),s 1, eff. 1/1/2006
Amended by Stats 2005 ch 75 (AB 145),s 44, eff. 7/19/2005, op. 1/1/2006
Amended by Stats 2000 ch 808 (AB 1358), s 20, eff. 9/28/2000.

Section 1218.5 - Contempt alleged for failure to pay support

(a) If the contempt alleged is for failure to pay child, family, or spousal support, each month for which payment has not been made in full may be alleged as a separate count of contempt and punishment imposed for each count proven.

(b) If the contempt alleged is the failure to pay child, family, or spousal support, the period of limitations for commencing a contempt action is three years from the date that the payment was due. If the action before the court is enforcement of another order under the Family Code, the period of limitations for commencing a contempt action is two years from the time that the alleged contempt occurred.

Added by Stats. 1994, Ch. 1269, Sec. 3.5. Effective January 1, 1995.

Section 1219 - Imprisonment until person performs act; refusal of victim to testify concerning sexual assault or domestic violence

(a) Except as provided in subdivisions (b) and (c), if the contempt consists of the omission to perform an act which is yet in the power of the person to perform, he or she may be imprisoned until he or she has performed it, and in that case the act shall be specified in the warrant of commitment.

(b) Notwithstanding any other law, a court shall not imprison or otherwise confine or place in custody the victim of a sexual assault or domestic violence crime for contempt if the contempt consists of refusing to testify concerning that sexual assault or domestic violence crime. Before finding a victim of a domestic violence crime in contempt as described in this section, the court may refer the victim for consultation with a domestic violence counselor. All communications between the victim and the domestic violence counselor that occur as a result of that referral shall remain confidential under Section 1037.2 of the Evidence Code.

(c) Notwithstanding any other law, a court shall not imprison, hold in physical confinement, or otherwise confine or place in custody a minor for contempt if the contempt consists of the minor's failure to comply with a court order pursuant to subdivision (b) of Section 601 of, or Section 727 of, the Welfare and Institutions Code, if the minor was adjudged a ward of the court on the ground that he or she is a person described in subdivision (b) of Section 601 of the Welfare and Institutions Code. Upon a finding of contempt of court, the court may issue any other lawful order, as necessary, to secure the minor's attendance at school.

(d) As used in this section, the following terms have the following meanings:

(1) "Sexual assault" means any act made punishable by Section 261, 262, 264.1, 285, 286, 287, 288, or 289 of, or former Section 288a of, the Penal Code.

(2) "Domestic violence" means "domestic violence" as defined in Section 6211 of the Family Code.

(3) "Domestic violence counselor" means "domestic violence counselor" as defined in subdivision (a) of Section 1037.1 of the Evidence Code.

(4) "Physical confinement" has the same meaning as defined in subdivision (d) of Section 726 of the Welfare and Institutions Code.

Amended by Stats 2018 ch 423 (SB 1494),s 9, eff. 1/1/2019.
Amended by Stats 2014 ch 70 (SB 1296),s 1, eff. 1/1/2015.
Amended by Stats 2012 ch 510 (AB 2051),s 1, eff. 1/1/2013.
Amended by Stats 2009 ch 35 (SB 174),s 3, eff. 1/1/2010.
Amended by Stats 2008 ch 49 (SB 1356),s 1, eff. 1/1/2009.

Section 1219.5 - Refusal of minor 16 years of age to take oath and testify

(a) Except as provided in subdivision (d), in any case in which a contempt consists of the refusal of a minor under 16 years of age to take the oath or to testify, before imposing any sanction for the contempt, the court shall first refer the matter to the probation officer in charge of matters coming before the juvenile court for a report and recommendation as to the appropriateness of the imposition of a sanction. The probation officer shall prepare and file the report and recommendation within the time directed by the court. In making the report and recommendation, the probation officer shall consider factors such as the maturity of the minor, the reasons for the minor's refusal to take the oath or to testify, the probability that available sanctions will affect the decision of the minor not to take the oath or not to testify, the potential impact on the minor of his or her testimony, the potential impact on the pending litigation of the minor's unavailability as a witness, and the appropriateness of the various available sanctions in the minor's case. The court shall consider the report and recommendation in imposing a sanction in the case.

(b) A victim of a sex crime who is subject to subdivision (a) shall meet with a victim advocate, as defined in Section 679.04 of the Penal Code, unless the court, for good cause, finds that it is not in the best interest of the victim.

(c) In any case in which the court orders the minor to be placed outside of his or her home, the placement shall be in the least restrictive setting available. Except as provided in subdivision (e), the court shall not order the minor to be placed in a secure facility unless other placements have been made and the minor has fled the custody and control of the person under the control of whom he or she has been placed or has persistently refused to obey the reasonable and proper orders or directions of the person under the control of whom he or she has been placed.

(d) The court may impose a sanction for contempt prior to receipt of the report and recommendation required by subdivision (a) if the court enters a finding, supported by specific facts stated on the record, that the minor would be likely to flee if released before the receipt of the report and recommendation.

(e) The court may order the minor placed in a secure facility without first attempting the nonsecure placement required by subdivision (c) if the court enters a finding, supported by specific facts stated on the record, that the minor would be likely to flee if released to nonsecure placement as a prerequisite to secure confinement.

Amended by Stats 2012 ch 223 (SB 1248),s 1, eff. 1/1/2013.

Section 1220 - Failure of person arrested to appear on return day

When the warrant of arrest has been returned served, if the person arrested does not appear on the return day, the court or judge may issue another warrant of arrest or may order the undertaking to be enforced, or both. If the undertaking is enforced, the measure of damages is the extent of the loss or injury sustained by the aggrieved party by reason of the misconduct for which the warrant was issued.

Amended by Stats. 1982, Ch. 517, Sec. 181.

Section 1221 - Inability from illness or otherwise of officer to bring person confined before court or judge

Whenever, by the provisions of this title, an officer is required to keep a person arrested on a warrant of attachment in custody, and to bring him before a court or judge, the inability, from illness or otherwise, of the person to attend, is a sufficient excuse for not bringing him up; and the officer must not confine a person arrested upon the warrant in a prison, or otherwise restrain him of personal liberty, except so far as may be necessary to secure his personal attendance.

Amended by Stats. 1951, Ch. 1737.

Section 1222 - Judgment or orders final and conclusive

The judgment and orders of the court or judge, made in cases of contempt, are final and conclusive.

Amended by Stats. 1951, Ch. 1737.

Title 7 - EMINENT DOMAIN LAW
Chapter 1 - GENERAL PROVISIONS

Section 1230.010 - Title of law

This title shall be known and may be cited as the Eminent Domain Law.

Added by Stats. 1975, Ch. 1275.

Section 1230.020 - Generally

Except as otherwise specifically provided by statute, the power of eminent domain may be exercised only as provided in this title.

Added by Stats. 1975, Ch. 1275.

Section 1230.030 - Exercise of power not required by title; discretion of person authorized to acquire property

Nothing in this title requires that the power of eminent domain be exercised to acquire property necessary for public use. Whether property necessary for public use is to be acquired by purchase or other means or by eminent domain is a decision left to the discretion of the person authorized to acquire the property.

Added by Stats. 1975, Ch. 1275.

Section 1230.040 - Applicability of rules of practice governing civil actions

Except as otherwise provided in this title, the rules of practice that govern civil actions generally are the rules of practice for eminent domain proceedings.

Added by Stats. 1975, Ch. 1275.

Section 1230.050 - Power of court to determine right to possession and enforce orders for possession

The court in which a proceeding in eminent domain is brought has the power to:

(a) Determine the right to possession of the property, as between the plaintiff and the defendant, in accordance with this title.

(b) Enforce any of its orders for possession by appropriate process. The plaintiff is entitled to enforcement of an order for possession as a matter of right.

Added by Stats. 1975, Ch. 1275.

Section 1230.060 - Title not to affect proceedings to Public Utilities Commission

Nothing in this title affects any other statute granting jurisdiction over any issue in eminent domain proceedings to the Public Utilities Commission.

Added by Stats. 1975, Ch. 1275.

Section 1230.065 - Effective date

(a) This title becomes operative July 1, 1976.

(b) This title does not apply to an eminent domain proceeding commenced prior to January 1, 1976. Subject to subdivisions (c) and (d), in the case of an eminent domain proceeding which is commenced on or after January 1, 1976, but prior to the operative date, this title upon the operative date applies to the proceeding to the fullest extent practicable with respect to issues to be tried or retried.

(c) Chapter 3 (commencing with Section 1240.010), Chapter 4 (commencing with Section 1245.010), and Chapter 5 (commencing with Section 1250.010) do not apply to a proceeding commenced prior to the operative date.

(d) If, on the operative date, an appeal, motion to modify or vacate the verdict or judgment, or motion for new trial is pending, the law applicable thereto prior to the operative date governs the determination of the appeal or motion.

Added by Stats. 1975, Ch. 1275.

Section 1230.070 - Judgments prior to operative date not affected

No judgment rendered prior to the operative date of this title in a proceeding to enforce the right of eminent domain is affected by the enactment of this title and the repeal of former Title 7 of this part.

Added by Stats. 1975, Ch. 1275.

Chapter 2 - PRINCIPLES OF CONSTRUCTION; DEFINITIONS
Article 1 - CONSTRUCTION

Section 1235.010 - Generally

Unless the provision or context otherwise requires, these preliminary provisions and rules of construction shall govern the construction of this title.

Added by Stats. 1975, Ch. 1275.

Section 1235.020 - Headings not to affect scope, meaning or intent

Chapter, article, and section headings do not in any manner affect the scope, meaning, or intent of the provisions of this title.

Added by Stats. 1975, Ch. 1275.

Section 1235.030 - References to title applicable to amendments and additions

Whenever any reference is made to any portion of this title or to any other statute, such reference shall apply to all amendments and additions heretofore or hereafter made.
Added by Stats. 1975, Ch. 1275.

Section 1235.040 - Definitions
Unless otherwise expressly stated:
(a) "Chapter" means a chapter of this title.
(b) "Article" means an article of the chapter in which that term occurs.
(c) "Section" means a section of this code.
(d) "Subdivision" means a subdivision of the section in which that term occurs.
(e) "Paragraph" means a paragraph of the subdivision in which that term occurs.
Added by Stats. 1975, Ch. 1275.

Section 1235.050 - Present tense
The present tense includes the past and future tenses; and the future, the present.
Added by Stats. 1975, Ch. 1275.

Section 1235.060 - Shall and may
"Shall" is mandatory and "may" is permissive.
Added by Stats. 1975, Ch. 1275.

Section 1235.070 - Severability of provisions
If any provision or clause of this title or application thereof to any person or circumstances is held invalid, the invalidity does not affect other provisions or applications of the title that can be given effect without the invalid provision or application, and to this end the provisions of this title are severable.
Added by Stats. 1975, Ch. 1275.

Article 2 - WORDS AND PHRASES DEFINED

Section 1235.110 - Generally
Unless the provision or context otherwise requires, these definitions govern the construction of this title.
Added by Stats. 1975, Ch. 1275.

Section 1235.120 - Final judgment
"Final judgment" means a judgment with respect to which all possibility of direct attack by way of appeal, motion for a new trial, or motion under Section 663 to vacate the judgment has been exhausted.
Added by Stats. 1975, Ch. 1275.

Section 1235.125 - Interest
When used with reference to property, "interest" includes any right, title, or estate in property.
Added by Stats. 1975, Ch. 1275.

Section 1235.130 - Judgment
"Judgment" means the judgment determining the right to take the property by eminent domain and fixing the amount of compensation to be paid by the plaintiff.
Added by Stats. 1975, Ch. 1275.

Section 1235.140 - Litigation expenses
"Litigation expenses" includes both of the following:
(a) All expenses reasonably and necessarily incurred in the proceeding in preparing for trial, during trial, and in any subsequent judicial proceedings.
(b) Reasonable attorney's fees, appraisal fees, and fees for the services of other experts where such fees were reasonably and necessarily incurred to protect the defendant's interests in the proceeding in preparing for trial, during trial, and in any subsequent judicial proceedings whether such fees were incurred for services rendered before or after the filing of the complaint.
Added by Stats. 1975, Ch. 1275.

Section 1235.150 - Local public entity
"Local public entity" means any public entity other than the state.
Added by Stats. 1975, Ch. 1275.

Section 1235.155 - Nonprofit special use property
"Nonprofit, special use property" means property which is operated for a special nonprofit, tax-exempt use such as a school, church, cemetery, hospital, or similar property. "Nonprofit, special use property" does not include property owned by a public entity.
Added by Stats. 1992, Ch. 7, Sec. 1. Effective January 1, 1993.

Section 1235.160 - Person
"Person" includes any public entity, individual, association, organization, partnership, trust, limited liability company, or corporation.
Amended by Stats. 1994, Ch. 1010, Sec. 63. Effective January 1, 1995.

Section 1235.165 - Proceeding
"Proceeding" means an eminent domain proceeding under this title.
Added by Stats. 1975, Ch. 1275.

Section 1235.170 - Property
"Property" includes real and personal property and any interest therein.
Added by Stats. 1975, Ch. 1275.

Section 1235.180 - Property appropriated to public use
"Property appropriated to public use" means property either already in use for a public purpose or set aside for a specific public purpose with the intention of using it for such purpose within a reasonable time.
Added by Stats. 1975, Ch. 1275.

Section 1235.190 - Public entity
"Public entity" includes the state, a county, city, district, public authority, public agency, and any other political subdivision in the state.
Added by Stats. 1975, Ch. 1275.

Section 1235.193 - Electric, gas or water utility property
"Electric, gas, or water public utility property" means property appropriated to a public use by a public utility, as defined in Section 218, 222, or 241 of the Public Utilities Code.
Added by Stats. 1992, Ch. 812, Sec. 1. Effective January 1, 1993.

Section 1235.195 - Resolution
"Resolution" includes ordinance.
Added by Stats. 1975, Ch. 1275.

Section 1235.200 - State
"State" means the State of California and includes the Regents of the University of California.
Added by Stats. 1975, Ch. 1275.

Section 1235.210 - Statute
"Statute" means a constitutional provision or statute, but does not include a charter provision or ordinance.
Added by Stats. 1975, Ch. 1275.

Chapter 3 - THE RIGHT TO TAKE
Article 1 - GENERAL LIMITATIONS ON EXERCISE OF POWER OF EMINENT DOMAIN

Section 1240.010 - Power exercised to acquire property for public use; legislative declaration as to public use
The power of eminent domain may be exercised to acquire property only for a public use. Where the Legislature provides by statute that a use, purpose, object, or function is one for which the power of eminent domain may be exercised, such action is deemed to be a declaration by the Legislature that such use, purpose, object, or function is a public use.
Added by Stats. 1975, Ch. 1275.

Section 1240.020 - Exercise of power to acquire property for particular use
The power of eminent domain may be exercised to acquire property for a particular use only by a person authorized by statute to exercise the power of eminent domain to acquire such property for that use.
Added by Stats. 1975, Ch. 1275.

Section 1240.030 - Exercise of power to acquire property for proposed use
The power of eminent domain may be exercised to acquire property for a proposed project only if all of the following are established:
(a) The public interest and necessity require the project.
(b) The project is planned or located in the manner that will be most compatible with the greatest public good and the least private injury.
(c) The property sought to be acquired is necessary for the project.
Added by Stats. 1975, Ch. 1275.

Section 1240.040 - Adoption of resolution by public entity required to exercise power
A public entity may exercise the power of eminent domain only if it has adopted a resolution of necessity that meets the requirements of Article 2 (commencing with Section 1245.210) of Chapter 4.
Added by Stats. 1975, Ch. 1275.

Section 1240.050 - Acquisition of property within territorial limits, exception
A local public entity may acquire by eminent domain only property within its territorial limits except where the power to acquire by eminent domain property outside its limits is expressly granted by statute or necessarily implied as an incident of one of its other statutory powers.
Added by Stats. 1975, Ch 1275.

Section 1240.055 - Acquisition of property subject to conservation easement
(a) As used in this section, the following terms have the following meanings:
   (1) "Conservation easement" means a conservation easement as defined in Section 815.1 of the Civil Code and recorded as required by Section 815.5 of the Civil Code.
   (2) "Holder of a conservation easement" means the entity or organization that holds the conservation easement on the property that is proposed for acquisition and that is authorized to acquire and hold conservation easements pursuant to Section 815.3 of the Civil Code.
   (3) "Property appropriated to public use," as used in Article 6 (commencing with Section 1240.510) and Article 7 (commencing with Section 1240.610), includes a conservation easement if any of the following applies:
      (A) The conservation easement is held by a public entity.
      (B) A public entity provided funds, not including the value of a charitable contribution for federal or state income tax purposes but including the California Natural Heritage Preservation Tax Credit, for the acquisition of that easement.
      (C) A public entity imposed conditions on approval or permitting of a project that were satisfied, in whole or in part, by the conservation easement.
(b) A person authorized to acquire property for public use by eminent domain shall exercise the power of eminent domain to acquire property that is subject to a conservation easement only as provided in this section.
(c) Not later than 105 days prior to the hearing held pursuant to Section 1245.235, or at the time of the offer made to the owner or owners of record pursuant to Section 7267.2 of the Government Code, whichever occurs earlier, the person seeking to acquire property subject to a conservation easement shall give notice to the holder of the conservation easement as provided in this subdivision. If the person is not required to hold a hearing pursuant to Section 1245.235, then the notice shall be given 105 days prior to the time of the offer made to the owner or owners of record pursuant to Section 7267.2 of the Government Code.
   (1) The notice required by subdivision (c) shall be sent by first-class mail and shall state all of the following:
      (A) A general description, in text or by diagram, of the property subject to a conservation easement that the person proposes to acquire by eminent domain.
      (B) A description of the public use or improvement that the person is considering for the property subject to a conservation easement.
      (C) That written comments on the acquisition may be submitted in accordance with paragraph (3) no later than 45 days from the date the person seeking to acquire the property mailed the notice to the holder of the conservation easement.
      (D) That the holder of the conservation easement, within 15 days of receipt of the notice required by subdivision (c), is required, under certain circumstances, to do all of the following:
         (i) Send a copy of the notice by first-class mail to each public entity that provided funds for the purchase of the easement or that imposed conditions on approval or permitting of a project that were satisfied, in whole or in part, by the creation of the conservation easement.
         (ii) Inform the public entity that written comments on the acquisition may be submitted in accordance with paragraph (3).
         (iii) Notify the person seeking to acquire the property of the name and address of any public entity that was sent a copy of the notice pursuant to this paragraph.
   (2)
      (A) The holder of the conservation easement, within 15 days of receipt of the notice required by subdivision (c), shall do all of the following:
         (i) Send a copy of the notice by first-class mail to each public entity that provided funds for the purchase of the easement or that imposed conditions on approval or permitting of a project that were satisfied, in whole or in part, by the creation of the conservation easement.
         (ii) Inform the public entity that written comments on the acquisition may be submitted in accordance with paragraph (3).
         (iii) Notify the person seeking to acquire the property of the name and address of any public entity that was sent a copy of the notice pursuant to this paragraph.
      (B) Subparagraph (A) shall apply only if one of the following applies:

(i) The holder of the easement is the original grantee of the conservation easement and there is a public entity as described in subparagraph (A).

(ii) The holder of the easement has actual knowledge of a public entity as described in subparagraph (A).

(iii) Recorded documents evidence the identity of a public entity as described in subparagraph (A).

(3) The holder of the conservation easement or the public entity receiving notice, or both, may provide to the person seeking to acquire the property written comments on the acquisition, including identifying any potential conflict between the public use proposed for the property and the purposes and terms of the conservation easement. Written comments on the acquisition may be submitted no later than 45 days from the date the person seeking to acquire the property mailed the notice to the holder of the conservation easement.

(d) The person seeking to acquire the property subject to a conservation easement, within 30 days after receipt of written comments from the holder of the conservation easement or from a public entity described in paragraph (2) of subdivision (c), shall respond in writing to the comments. The response to the comments shall be mailed by first-class mail to each easement holder or public entity that filed comments.

(e) The notice of the hearing on the resolution of necessity, pursuant to Section 1245.235, shall be sent by first-class mail to the holder of any conservation easement and to any public entity whose name and address are provided as described in paragraph (2) of subdivision (c) and shall state that they have the right to appear and be heard on the matters referred to in Sections 1240.030, 1240.510, and 1240.610. The notice shall state that, pursuant to paragraph (3) of subdivision (b) of Section 1245.235, failure to file a written request to appear and be heard within 15 days after the notice was mailed will result in waiver of the right to appear and be heard. The resolution of necessity to acquire property subject to a conservation easement shall refer specifically either to Section 1240.510 or 1240.610 as authority for the acquisition of the property.

(f) In any eminent domain proceeding to acquire property subject to a conservation easement, the holder of the conservation easement:

(1) Shall be named as a defendant, as set forth in Section 1250.220.

(2) May appear in the proceedings, as set forth in Section 1250.230.

(3) Shall have all the same rights and obligations as any other defendant in the eminent domain proceeding.

(g)

(1) The holder of the conservation easement is an owner of property entitled to compensation determined pursuant to Section 1260.220 and Chapter 9 (commencing with Section 1263.010) and in accordance with all of the following:

(A) The total compensation for the acquisition of all interests in property encumbered by a conservation easement shall not be less than, and shall not exceed, the fair market value of the fee simple interest of the property as if it were not encumbered by the conservation easement.

(B) If the acquisition does not damage the conservation easement, the total compensation shall be assessed by determining the value of all interests in the property as encumbered by the conservation easement.

(C) If the acquisition damages the conservation easement in whole or in part, compensation shall be determined consistent with Section 1260.220 and the value of the fee simple interest of the property shall be assessed as if it were not encumbered by the conservation easement.

(2) This subdivision shall not apply if the requirements of Section 10261 of the Public Resources Code apply.

(h) This section shall not apply if the requirements of Section 1348.3 of the Fish and Game Code apply.

Added by Stats 2011 ch 589 (SB 328),s 2, eff. 1/1/2012.

Article 2 - RIGHTS INCLUDED IN GRANT OF EMINENT DOMAIN AUTHORITY

Section 1240.110 - Acquisition of interest in property necessary for particular use

(a) Except to the extent limited by statute, any person authorized to acquire property for a particular use by eminent domain may exercise the power of eminent domain to acquire any interest in property necessary for that use including, but not limited to, submerged lands, rights of any nature in water, subsurface rights, airspace rights, flowage or flooding easements, aircraft noise or operation easements, right of temporary occupancy, public utility facilities and franchises, and franchises to collect tolls on a bridge or highway.

(b) Where a statute authorizes the acquisition by eminent domain only of specified interests in or types of property, this section does not expand the scope of the authority so granted.

Added by Stats. 1975, Ch. 1275.

Section 1240.120 - Acquisition of property necessary to carry out and make effective principal purpose

(a) Subject to any other statute relating to the acquisition of property, any person authorized to acquire property for a particular use by eminent domain may exercise the power of eminent domain to acquire property necessary to carry out and make effective the principal purpose involved including but not limited to property to be used for the protection or preservation of the attractiveness, safety, and usefulness of the project.

(b) Subject to any applicable procedures governing the disposition of property, a person may acquire property under subdivision (a) with the intent to sell, lease, exchange, or otherwise dispose of the property, or an interest therein, subject to such reservations or restrictions as are necessary to protect or preserve the attractiveness, safety, and usefulness of the project.

Added by Stats. 1975, Ch. 1275.

Section 1240.125 - Purposes for which local public entity may acquire property outside territorial limits

Except as otherwise expressly provided by statute and subject to any limitations imposed by statute, a local public entity may acquire property by eminent domain outside its territorial limits for water, gas, or electric supply purposes or for airports, drainage or sewer purposes if it is authorized to acquire property by eminent domain for the purposes for which the property is to be acquired.

Added by Stats. 1975, Ch. 1275.

Section 1240.130 - Acquisition of property for particular use by purchase, lease, gift, etc.

Subject to any other statute relating to the acquisition of property, any public entity authorized to acquire property for a particular use by eminent domain may also acquire such property for such use by grant, purchase, lease, gift, devise, contract, or other means.

Added by Stats. 1975, Ch. 1275.

Section 1240.140 - Agreement for joint exercise of power by two or more public agencies

(a) As used in this section, "public agencies" includes all those agencies included within the definition of "public agency" in Section 6500 of the Government Code.

(b) Two or more public agencies may enter into an agreement for the joint exercise of their respective powers of eminent domain, whether or not possessed in common, for the acquisition of property as a single parcel. Such agreement shall be entered into and performed pursuant to the provisions of Chapter 5 (commencing with Section 6500) of Division 7 of Title 1 of the Government Code.

Added by Stats. 1975, Ch. 1275.

Section 1240.150 - Acquisition of remainder of property

Whenever a part of a larger parcel of property is to be acquired by a public entity for public use and the remainder, or a portion of the remainder, will be left in such size, shape, or condition as to be of little value to its owner or to give rise to a claim for severance or other damages, the public entity may acquire the remainder, or portion of the remainder, by any means (including eminent domain) expressly consented to by the owner.

Added by Stats. 1975, Ch. 1275.

Section 1240.160 - Provisions distinct and separate authorization

(a) None of the provisions of this article is intended to limit, or shall limit, any other provision of this article, each of which is a distinct and separate authorization.

(b) None of the provisions of Article 2 (commencing with Section 1240.110), Article 3 (commencing with Section 1240.210), Article 4 (commencing with Section 1240.310), Article 5 (commencing with Section 1240.410), Article 6 (commencing with Section 1240.510), or Article 7 (commencing with Section 1240.610) is intended to limit, or shall limit, the provisions of any other of the articles, each of which articles is a distinct and separate authorization.
Added by Stats. 1975, Ch. 1275.

Article 3 - FUTURE USE

Section 1240.210 - Date of use of property taken for public use
For the purposes of this article, the "date of use" of property taken for public use is the date when the property is devoted to that use or when construction is started on the project for which the property is taken with the intent to complete the project within a reasonable time. In determining the "date of use," periods of delay caused by extraordinary litigation or by failure to obtain from any public entity any agreement or permit necessary for construction shall not be included.
Added by Stats. 1975, Ch. 1275.

Section 1240.220 - Generally
(a) Any person authorized to acquire property for a particular use by eminent domain may exercise the power of eminent domain to acquire property to be used in the future for that use, but property may be taken for future use only if there is a reasonable probability that its date of use will be within seven years from the date the complaint is filed or within such longer period as is reasonable.
(b) Unless the plaintiff plans that the date of use of property taken will be within seven years from the date the complaint is filed, the complaint, and the resolution of necessity if one is required, shall refer specifically to this section and shall state the estimated date of use.
Added by Stats. 1975, Ch. 1275.

Section 1240.230 - Burden of proof if defendant objects to taking for future use
(a) If the defendant objects to a taking for future use, the burden of proof is as prescribed in this section.
(b) Unless the complaint states an estimated date of use that is not within seven years from the date the complaint is filed, the defendant has the burden of proof that there is no reasonable probability that the date of use will be within seven years from the date the complaint is filed.
(c) If the defendant proves that there is no reasonable probability that the date of use will be within seven years from the date the complaint is filed, or if the complaint states an estimated date of use that is not within seven years from the date the complaint is filed, the plaintiff has the burden of proof that a taking for future use satisfies the requirements of this article.
Added by Stats. 1975, Ch. 1275.

Section 1240.240 - Acquisition of property by any means consented to by owner
Notwithstanding any other provision of this article, any public entity authorized to acquire property for a particular use by eminent domain may acquire property to be used in the future for that use by any means (including eminent domain) expressly consented to by its owner.
Added by Stats. 1975, Ch. 1275.

Section 1240.250 - Property taken pursuant to Federal Aid Highway Act of 1973
Notwithstanding any other provision of this article, where property is taken pursuant to the Federal Aid Highway Act of 1973:
(a) A date of use within 10 years from the date the complaint is filed shall be deemed reasonable.
(b) The resolution of necessity and the complaint shall indicate that the taking is pursuant to the Federal Aid Highway Act of 1973 and shall state the estimated date of use.
(c) If the defendant objects to the taking, the defendant has the burden of proof that there is no reasonable probability that the date of use will be within 10 years from the date the complaint is filed. If the defendant proves that there is no reasonable probability that the date of use will be within 10 years from the date the complaint is filed, the plaintiff has the burden of proof that the taking satisfies the requirements of this article.
Added by Stats. 1975, Ch. 1275.

Article 4 - SUBSTITUTE CONDEMNATION

Section 1240.310 - Definitions
As used in this article:
(a) "Necessary property" means property to be used for a public use for which the public entity is authorized to acquire property by eminent domain.
(b) "Substitute property" means property to be exchanged for necessary property.
Added by Stats. 1975, Ch. 1275.

Section 1240.320 - Generally
(a) Any public entity authorized to exercise the power of eminent domain to acquire property for a particular use may exercise the power of eminent domain to acquire for that use substitute property if all of the following are established:
　(1) The owner of the necessary property has agreed in writing to the exchange.
　(2) The necessary property is devoted to or held for some public use and the substitute property will be devoted to or held for the same public use by the owner of the necessary property.
　(3) The owner of the necessary property is authorized to exercise the power of eminent domain to acquire the substitute property for such use.
(b) Where property is sought to be acquired pursuant to this section, the resolution of necessity and the complaint filed pursuant to such resolution shall specifically refer to this section and shall include a statement that the property is necessary for the purpose specified in this section. The determination in the resolution that the taking of the substitute property is necessary has the effect prescribed in Section 1245.250.
Added by Stats. 1975, Ch. 1275.

Section 1240.330 - Acquisition of substitute property relocation of public use to substitute property and conveyance of substitute property to owner of necessary property
(a) Where necessary property is devoted to public use, any public entity authorized to exercise the power of eminent domain to acquire such property for a particular use may exercise the power of eminent domain to acquire substitute property in its own name, relocate on such substitute property the public use to which necessary property is devoted, and thereafter convey the substitute property to the owner of the necessary property if all of the following are established:
　(1) The public entity is required by court order or judgment in an eminent domain proceeding, or by agreement with the owner of the necessary property, to relocate the public use to which the necessary property is devoted and thereafter to convey the property upon which the public use has been relocated to the owner of the necessary property.
　(2) The substitute property is necessary for compliance with the court order or judgment or agreement.
　(3) The owner of the necessary property will devote the substitute property to the public use being displaced from the necessary property.
(b) Where property is sought to be acquired pursuant to this section, the resolution of necessity and the complaint filed pursuant to such resolution shall specifically refer to this section and shall include a statement that the property is necessary for the purpose specified in this section. The determination in the resolution that the taking of the substitute property is necessary has the effect prescribed in Section 1245.250.
Added by Stats. 1975, Ch. 1275.

Section 1240.350 - Acquisition of additional property as appears necessary

(a) Whenever a public entity acquires property for a public use and exercises or could have exercised the power of eminent domain to acquire such property for such use, the public entity may exercise the power of eminent domain to acquire such additional property as appears reasonably necessary and appropriate (after taking into account any hardship to the owner of the additional property) to provide utility service to, or access to a public road from, any property that is not acquired for such public use but which is cut off from utility service or access to a public road as a result of the acquisition by the public entity.

(b) Where property is sought to be acquired pursuant to this section, the resolution of necessity and the complaint filed pursuant to such resolution shall specifically refer to this section and shall include a statement that the property is necessary for the purpose specified in this section. The determination in the resolution that the taking of the substitute property is necessary has the effect prescribed in Section 1245.250.
Added by Stats. 1975, Ch. 1275.

Article 5 - EXCESS CONDEMNATION

Section 1240.410 - Acquisition of remnant

(a) As used in this section, "remnant" means a remainder or portion thereof that will be left in such size, shape, or condition as to be of little market value.

(b) Whenever the acquisition by a public entity by eminent domain of part of a larger parcel of property will leave a remnant, the public entity may exercise the power of eminent domain to acquire the remnant in accordance with this article.

(c) Property may not be acquired under this section if the defendant proves that the public entity has a reasonable, practicable, and economically sound means to prevent the property from becoming a remnant.
Added by Stats. 1975, Ch. 1275.

Section 1240.420 - Resolution and complaint

When property is sought to be acquired pursuant to Section 1240.410, the resolution of necessity and the complaint filed pursuant to such resolution shall specifically refer to that section. It shall be presumed from the adoption of the resolution that the taking of the property is authorized under Section 1240.410. This presumption is a presumption affecting the burden of producing evidence.
Added by Stats. 1975, Ch. 1275.

Section 1240.430 - Sale, lease or exchange of property taken

A public entity may sell, lease, exchange, or otherwise dispose of property taken under this article and may credit the proceeds to the fund or funds available for acquisition of the property being acquired for the public work or improvement. Nothing in this section relieves a public entity from complying with any applicable statutory procedures governing the disposition of property.
Added by Stats. 1975, Ch. 1275.

Article 6 - CONDEMNATION FOR COMPATIBLE USE

Section 1240.510 - Acquisition of property appropriated to public use

Any person authorized to acquire property for a particular use by eminent domain may exercise the power of eminent domain to acquire for that use property appropriated to public use if the proposed use will not unreasonably interfere with or impair the continuance of the public use as it then exists or may reasonably be expected to exist in the future. Where property is sought to be acquired pursuant to this section, the complaint, and the resolution of necessity if one is required, shall refer specifically to this section.
Added by Stats. 1975, Ch. 1275.

Section 1240.520 - Burden proof

If the defendant objects to a taking under Section 1240.510, the defendant has the burden of proof that his property is appropriated to public use. If it is established that the property is appropriated to public use, the plaintiff has the burden of proof that its proposed use satisfies the requirements of Section 1240.510.
Added by Stats. 1975, Ch. 1275.

Section 1240.530 - Agreement by parties determining terms and conditions; court fixing terms and conditions

(a) Where property is taken under Section 1240.510, the parties shall make an agreement determining the terms and conditions upon which the property is taken and the manner and extent of its use by each of the parties. Except as otherwise provided by statute, if the parties are unable to agree, the court shall fix the terms and conditions upon which the property is taken and the manner and extent of its use by each of the parties.

(b) If the court determines that the use in the manner proposed by the plaintiff would not satisfy the requirements of Section 1240.510, the court shall further determine whether the requirements of Section 1240.510 could be satisfied by fixing terms and conditions upon which the property may be taken. If the court determines that the requirements of Section 1240.510 could be so satisfied, the court shall permit the plaintiff to take the property upon such terms and conditions and shall prescribe the manner and extent of its use by each of the parties.

(c) Where property is taken under this article, the court may order any necessary removal or relocation of structures or improvements if such removal or relocation would not require any significant alteration of the use to which the property is appropriated. Unless otherwise provided by statute, all costs and damages that result from the relocation or removal shall be paid by the plaintiff.
Added by Stats. 1975, Ch. 1275.

Article 7 - CONDEMNATION FOR MORE NECESSARY PUBLIC USE

Section 1240.610 - Generally

Any person authorized to acquire property for a particular use by eminent domain may exercise the power of eminent domain to acquire for that use property appropriated to public use if the use for which the property is sought to be taken is a more necessary public use than the use to which the property is appropriated. Where property is sought to be acquired pursuant to this section, the complaint, and the resolution of necessity if one is required, shall refer specifically to this section.
Added by Stats. 1975, Ch. 1275.

Section 1240.620 - Burden of proof

If the defendant objects to a taking under Section 1240.610, the defendant has the burden of proof that his property is appropriated to public use. If it is established that the property is appropriated to public use, the plaintiff has the burden of proof that its use satisfies the requirements of Section 1240.610.
Added by Stats. 1975, Ch. 1275.

Section 1240.630 - Defendant entitled to continue public use

(a) Where property is sought to be taken under Section 1240.610, the defendant is entitled to continue the public use to which the property is appropriated if the continuance of such use will not unreasonably interfere with or impair, or require a significant alteration of, the more necessary public use as it is then planned or exists or may reasonably be expected to exist in the future.

(b) If the defendant objects to a taking under this article on the ground that he is entitled under subdivision (a) to continue the public use to which the property is appropriated, upon motion of either party, the court shall determine whether the defendant is entitled under subdivision (a) to continue the use to which the property is appropriated; and, if the court determines that the defendant is so entitled, the parties shall make an agreement determining the terms and conditions upon which the defendant may continue the public use to which the property is appropriated, the terms and conditions upon which the property is taken by the plaintiff is acquired, and the manner and extent of the use of the property by each of

the parties. Except as otherwise provided by statute, if the parties are unable to agree, the court shall fix such terms and conditions and the manner and extent of the use of the property by each of the parties.
Added by Stats. 1975, Ch. 1275.

Section 1240.640 - Presumption that use by state more necessary use

(a) Where property has been appropriated to public use by any person other than the state, the use thereof by the state for the same use or any other public use is presumed to be a more necessary use than the use to which such property has already been appropriated.

(b) Where property has been appropriated to public use by the state, the use thereof by the state is presumed to be a more necessary use than any use to which such property might be put by any other person.

(c) The presumptions established by this section are presumptions affecting the burden of proof.
Added by Stats. 1975, Ch. 1275.

Section 1240.650 - Use by public entity more necessary use

(a) Where property has been appropriated to public use by any person other than a public entity, the use thereof by a public entity for the same use or any other public use is a more necessary use than the use to which such property has already been appropriated.

(b) Where property has been appropriated to public use by a public entity, the use thereof by the public entity is a more necessary use than any use to which such property might be put by any person other than a public entity.

(c) Where property which has been appropriated to a public use is electric, gas, or water public utility property which the public entity intends to put to the same use, the presumption of a more necessary use established by subdivision (a) is a rebuttable presumption affecting the burden of proof, unless the acquiring public entity is a sanitary district exercising the powers of a county water district pursuant to Section 6512.7 of the Health and Safety Code.
Amended by Stats. 1992, Ch. 812, Sec. 2. Effective January 1, 1993.

Section 1240.655 - Action by Golden State Energy to acquire PG&E

(a) If Golden State Energy commences an eminent domain action to acquire Pacific Gas and Electric Company property, including any franchise rights and stock, pursuant to Section 713 of the Public Utilities Code, that acquisition is for a more necessary public use pursuant to Section 1240.610. Golden State Energy may exclude from the acquisition only property not directly related to providing electrical or gas service.

(b) For purposes of this section, the following definitions apply:

(1) "Golden State Energy" has the same meaning as defined in Section 222.5 of the Public Utilities Code.

(2) "Pacific Gas and Electric Company" means Pacific Gas and Electric Company, PG&E Corporation, any subsidiary or affiliate of the foregoing holding any assets related to the provision of electrical or gas service within Pacific Gas and Electric Company's service territory, and any successor to any of the foregoing.
Added by Stats 2020 ch 27 (SB 350),s 3, eff. 1/1/2021.

Section 1240.660 - Presumption use by local public entity more necessary use

Where property has been appropriated to public use by a local public entity, the use thereof by the local public entity is presumed to be a more necessary use than any use to which such property might be put by any other local public entity. The presumption established by this section is a presumption affecting the burden of proof.
Added by Stats. 1975, Ch. 1275.

Section 1240.670 - Presumption property appropriated for best and most necessary public use

(a) Subject to Section 1240.690, notwithstanding any other provision of law, property is presumed to have been appropriated for the best and most necessary public use if all of the following are established:

(1) The property is owned by a nonprofit organization contributions to which are deductible for state and federal income tax purposes under the laws of this state and of the United States and having the primary purpose of preserving areas in their natural condition.

(2) The property is open to the public subject to reasonable restrictions and is appropriated, and used exclusively, for the preservation of native plants or native animals including, but not limited to, mammals, birds, and marine life, or biotic communities, or geological or geographical formations of scientific or educational interest.

(3) The property is irrevocably dedicated to such uses so that, upon liquidation, dissolution, or abandonment of or by the owner, such property will be distributed only to a fund, foundation, or corporation whose property is likewise irrevocably dedicated to such uses, or to a governmental agency holding land for such uses.

(b) The presumption established by this section is a presumption affecting the burden of proof.
Added by Stats. 1975, Ch. 1275.

Section 1240.680 - Presumption property appropriated for best and most necessary public use

(a) Subject to Sections 1240.690 and 1240.700, notwithstanding any other provision of law, property is presumed to have been appropriated for the best and most necessary public use if the property is appropriated to public use as any of the following:

(1) A state, regional, county, or city park, open space, or recreation area.

(2) A wildlife or waterfowl management area established by the Department of Fish and Game pursuant to Section 1525 of the Fish and Game Code.

(3) A historic site included in the National Register of Historic Places or state-registered landmarks.

(4) An ecological reserve as provided for in Article 4 (commencing with Section 1580) of Chapter 5 of Division 2 of the Fish and Game Code.

(b) The presumption established by this section is a presumption affecting the burden of proof.
Added by Stats. 1975, Ch. 1275, Sec. 3.

Section 1240.690 - Action for declaratory relief by public entity or nonprofit organization where property sought to be acquired for highway purposes

(a) When property described in Section 1240.670 or 1240.680 is sought to be acquired for state highway purposes, and the property was dedicated or devoted to a use described in those sections prior to the initiation of highway route location studies, an action for declaratory relief may be brought by the public entity or nonprofit organization owning the property in the superior court to determine the question of which public use is the best and most necessary public use for the property.

(b) The action for declaratory relief shall be filed and served within 120 days after the California Transportation Commission has published in a newspaper of general circulation pursuant to Section 6061 of the Government Code, and delivered to the public entity or nonprofit organization owning the property a written notice that a proposed route or an adopted route includes the property. In the case of nonprofit organizations, the written notice need only be given to nonprofit organizations that are on file with the Registrar of Charitable Trusts of this state.

(c) In the declaratory relief action, the resolution of the California Transportation Commission is not conclusive evidence of the matters set forth in Section 1240.030.

(d) With respect to property described in Section 1240.670 or 1240.680 which is sought to be acquired for state highway purposes:

(1) If an action for declaratory relief is not filed and served within the 120-day period established by subdivision (b), the right to bring the action is waived and Sections 1240.670 and 1240.680 do not apply.

(2) When a declaratory relief action may not be brought pursuant to this section, Sections 1240.670 and 1240.680 do not apply.

Amended by Stats. 1982, Ch. 681, Sec. 2.

Section 1240.700 - Action for declaratory relief where property sought to be acquired for city or county road street or highway purposes
(a) When property described in Section 1240.680 is sought to be acquired for city or county road, street, or highway purposes, and such property was dedicated or devoted to regional park, recreational, or open-space purposes prior to the initiation of road, street, or highway route location studies, an action for declaratory relief may be brought in the superior court by the regional park district which operates the park, recreational, or open-space area to determine the question of which public use is the best and most necessary public use for such property.
(b) The action for declaratory relief shall be filed and served within 120 days after the city or county, as the case may be, has published in a newspaper of general circulation pursuant to Section 6061 of the Government Code, and delivered to the regional park district, a written notice that a proposed route or site or an adopted route includes such property.
(c) With respect to property dedicated or devoted to regionl park, recreational, or open-space purposes which is sought to be acquired for city or county road, street, or highway purposes:
  (1) If an action for declaratory relief is not filed and served within the 120-day period established by subdivision (b), the right to bring such action is waived and the provisions of Section 1240.680 do not apply.
  (2) When a declaratory relief action may not be brought pursuant to this section, the provisions of Section 1240.680 do not apply.
Added by Stats. 1975, Ch. 1275.

Chapter 4 - PRECONDEMNATION ACTIVITIES
Article 1 - PRELIMINARY LOCATION, SURVEY, AND TESTS

Section 1245.010 - Right to enter property to make photographs, studies, surveys, etc.
Subject to requirements of this article, any person authorized to acquire property for a particular use by eminent domain may enter upon property to make photographs, studies, surveys, examinations, tests, soundings, borings, samplings, or appraisals or to engage in similar activities reasonably related to acquisition or use of the property for that use.
Added by Stats. 1975, Ch. 1275.

Section 1245.020 - Duty to secure consent before entry
In any case in which the entry and activities mentioned in Section 1245.010 will subject the person having the power of eminent domain to liability under Section 1245.060, before making that entry and undertaking those activities, the person shall secure at least one of the following:
(a) The written consent of the owner to enter upon the owner's property and to undertake those activities.
(b) An order for entry from the superior court in accordance with Section 1245. 030.
Amended by Stats 2021 ch 401 (AB 1578),s 3, eff. 1/1/2022.
Added by Stats. 1975, Ch. 1275.

Section 1245.030 - Petition seeking entry
(a) The person seeking to enter upon the property may petition the court for an order permitting the entry and shall give such prior notice to the owner of the property as the court determines is appropriate under the circumstances of the particular case.
(b) Upon such petition and after such notice has been given, the court shall determine the purpose for the entry, the nature and scope of the activities reasonably necessary to accomplish such purpose, and the probable amount of compensation to be paid to the owner of the property for the actual damage to the property and interference with its possession and use.
(c) After such determination, the court may issue its order permitting the entry. The order shall prescribe the purpose for the entry and the nature and scope of the activities to be undertaken and shall require the person seeking to enter to deposit with the court the probable amount of compensation.
Added by Stats. 1975, Ch. 1275.

Section 1245.040 - Modification of order; amount of deposit increased by order of modification
(a) The court, after notice and hearing, may modify any of the provisions of an order made under Section 1245.030.
(b) If the amount required to be deposited is increased by an order of modification, the court shall specify the time within which the additional amount shall be deposited and may direct that any further entry or that specified activities under the order as modified be stayed until the additional amount has been deposited.
Added by Stats. 1975, Ch. 1275.

Section 1245.050 - Period of retention of amount deposited; deposit made in Condemnation Deposits Fund
(a) Unless sooner disbursed by court order, the amount deposited under this article shall be retained on deposit for six months following the termination of the entry. The period of retention may be extended by the court for good cause.
(b) The deposit shall be made in the Condemnation Deposits Fund in the State Treasury or, upon written request of the plaintiff filed with the deposit, in the county treasury. If made in the State Treasury, the deposit shall be held, invested, deposited, and disbursed in accordance with Article 10 (commencing with Section 16429) of Chapter 2 of Part 2 of Division 4 of Title 2 of the Government Code.
Added by Stats. 1975, Ch. 1275.

Section 1245.060 - Action for damage or interference with possession caused by entry and activities
(a) If the entry and activities upon property cause actual damage to or substantial interference with the possession or use of the property, whether or not a claim has been presented in compliance with Part 3 (commencing with Section 900) of Division 3.6 of Title 1 of the Government Code, the owner may recover for that damage or interference in a civil action, as a defendant in an eminent domain action affecting the property, or by application to the court under subdivision (c).
(b) The prevailing claimant in an action or proceeding under this section shall be awarded the claimant's costs and, if the court finds that any of the following occurred, the claimant's litigation expenses incurred in proceedings under this article:
  (1) The entry was unlawful.
  (2) The entry was lawful but the activities upon the property were abusive or lacking in due regard for the interests of the owner.
  (3) There was a failure substantially to comply with the terms of an order made under Section 1245.030 or 1245.040.
(c) If funds are on deposit under this article, upon application of the owner, the court shall determine and award the amount the owner is entitled to recover under this section and shall order that amount paid out of the funds on deposit. If the funds on deposit are insufficient to pay the full amount of the award, the court shall enter judgment for the unpaid portion. In a proceeding under this subdivision, the owner has a right to a jury trial, unless waived, on the amount of compensation for actual damage or substantial interference with the possession or use of the property.
(d) Nothing in this section affects the availability of any other remedy the owner may have for the damaging of the owner's property.
Amended by Stats 2021 ch 401 (AB 1578),s 4, eff. 1/1/2022.
Added by Stats. 1975, Ch. 1275.

Article 2 - RESOLUTION OF NECESSITY

Section 1245.210 - "Governing body" defined
As used in this article, "governing body" means:
(a) In the case of a taking by a local public entity, the legislative body of the local public entity.
(b) In the case of a taking by the Sacramento and San Joaquin Drainage District, the Central Valley Flood Protection Board.

(c) In the case of a taking by the State Public Works Board pursuant to the Property Acquisition Law (Part 11 (commencing with Section 15850) of Division 3 of Title 2 of the Government Code), the State Public Works Board.
(d) In the case of a taking by the Department of Fish and Wildlife pursuant to Section 1348 of the Fish and Game Code, the Wildlife Conservation Board.
(e) In the case of a taking by the Department of Transportation (other than a taking pursuant to Section 21633 of the Public Utilities Code or Section 30100 of the Streets and Highways Code), the California Transportation Commission.
(f) In the case of a taking by the Department of Transportation pursuant to Section 21633 of the Public Utilities Code, the California Transportation Commission.
(g) In the case of a taking by the Department of Transportation pursuant to Section 30100 of the Streets and Highways Code, the California Transportation Commission.
(h) In the case of a taking by the Department of Water Resources, the California Water Commission.
(i) In the case of a taking by the University of California, the Regents of the University of California.
(j) In the case of a taking by the State Lands Commission, the State Lands Commission.
(k) In the case of a taking by the college named in Section 92200 of the Education Code, the board of directors of that college.
(l) In the case of a taking by the High-Speed Rail Authority, the State Public Works Board.
Amended by Stats 2022 ch 478 (AB 1936),s 3, eff. 1/1/2023.
Amended by Stats 2018 ch 790 (SB 1172),s 1, eff. 1/1/2019.

Section 1245.220 - Adoption of resolution required
A public entity may not commence an eminent domain proceeding until its governing body has adopted a resolution of necessity that meets the requirements of this article.
Added by Stats. 1975, Ch. 1275.

Section 1245.230 - Requirements of resolution
In addition to other requirements imposed by law, the resolution of necessity shall contain all of the following:
(a) A general statement of the public use for which the property is to be taken and a reference to the statute that authorizes the public entity to acquire the property by eminent domain.
(b) A description of the general location and extent of the property to be taken, with sufficient detail for reasonable identification.
(c) A declaration that the governing body of the public entity has found and determined each of the following:
(1) The public interest and necessity require the proposed project.
(2) The proposed project is planned or located in the manner that will be most compatible with the greatest public good and the least private injury.
(3) The property described in the resolution is necessary for the proposed project.
(4) That either the offer required by Section 7267.2 of the Government Code has been made to the owner or owners of record, or the offer has not been made because the owner cannot be located with reasonable diligence. If at the time the governing body of a public entity is requested to adopt a resolution of necessity and the project for which the property is needed has been determined by the public entity to be an emergency project, which project is necessary either to protect or preserve health, safety, welfare, or property, the requirements of Section 7267.2 of the Government Code need not be a prerequisite to the adoption of an authorizing resolution at the time. However, in those cases the provisions of Section 7267.2 of the Government Code shall be implemented by the public entity within a reasonable time thereafter but in any event, not later than 90 days after adoption of the resolution of necessity.
Amended by Stats. 1983, Ch. 1079, Sec. 1.

Section 1245.235 - Notice and hearing prior to adoption of resolution
(a) The governing body of the public entity may adopt a resolution of necessity only after the governing body has given each person whose property is to be acquired by eminent domain and whose name and address appears on the last equalized county assessment roll notice and a reasonable opportunity to appear and be heard on the matters referred to in Section 1240.030.
(b) The notice required by subdivision (a) shall be sent by first-class mail to each person described in subdivision (a) and shall state all of the following:
(1) The intent of the governing body to adopt the resolution.
(2) The right of such person to appear and be heard on the matters referred to in Section 1240.030.
(3) Failure to file a written request to appear and be heard within 15 days after the notice was mailed will result in waiver of the right to appear and be heard.
(c) The governing body, or a committee of not less than 11 members thereof designated by the governing body if the governing body has more than 40 members, shall hold a hearing at which all persons described in subdivision (a) who filed a written request within the time specified in the notice may appear and be heard on the matters referred to in Section 1240.030. Such a committee shall be reasonably representative of the various geographical areas within the public entity's jurisdiction. The governing body need not give an opportunity to appear and be heard to any person who fails to so file a written request within the time specified in the notice. If a committee is designated by the governing body pursuant to this subdivision to hold the hearing, the committee, subsequent to the hearing, shall provide the governing body and any person described in subdivision (a) who has appeared before the committee with a written summary of the hearing and a written recommendation as to whether to adopt the resolution of necessity. Any person described in subdivision (a) who has appeared before the committee shall also be given an opportunity to appear and be heard before the governing body on the matters referred to in Section 1240.030.
(d) Notwithstanding subdivision (b), the governing body may satisfy the requirements of this section through any other procedure that has given each person described in subdivision (a) reasonable written personal notice and a reasonable opportunity to appear and be heard on the matters referred to in Section 1240.030.
Amended by Stats. 1986, Ch. 358, Sec. 1.

Section 1245.240 - Vote required to adopt resolution
Unless a greater vote is required by statute, charter, or ordinance, the resolution shall be adopted by a vote of two-thirds of all the members of the governing body of the public entity.
Added by Stats. 1975, Ch. 1275.

Section 1245.245 - Property used for public use stated in resolution; sale of property not used for stated use; acquisition subject to requirements
(a) Property acquired by a public entity by any means set forth in subdivision (e) that is subject to a resolution of necessity adopted pursuant to this article shall only be used for the public use stated in the resolution unless the governing body of the public entity adopts a resolution authorizing a different use of the property by a vote of at least two-thirds of all members of the governing body of the public entity, or a greater vote as required by statute, charter, or ordinance. The resolution shall contain all of the following:
(1) A general statement of the new public use that is proposed for the property and a reference to the statute that would have authorized the public entity to acquire the property by eminent domain for that use.

(2) A description of the general location and extent of the property proposed to be used for the new use, with sufficient detail for reasonable identification.

(3) A declaration that the governing body has found and determined each of the following:

(A) The public interest and necessity require the proposed use.

(B) The proposed use is planned and located in the manner that will be most compatible with the greatest public good and least private injury.

(C) The property described in the resolution is necessary for the proposed use.

(b) Property acquired by a public entity by any means set forth in subdivision (e) that is subject to a resolution of necessity pursuant to this article, and is not used for the public use stated in the resolution of necessity within 10 years of the adoption of the resolution of necessity, shall be sold in accordance with the terms of subdivisions (f) and (g), unless the governing body adopts a resolution according to the terms of subdivision (a) or a resolution according to the terms of this subdivision reauthorizing the existing stated public use of the property by a vote of at least two-thirds of all members of the governing body of the public entity or a greater vote as required by statute, charter, or ordinance. A reauthorization resolution under this subdivision shall contain all of the following:

(1) A general statement of the public use that is proposed to be reauthorized for the property and a reference to the statute that authorized the public entity to acquire the property by eminent domain for that use.

(2) A description of the general location and extent of the property proposed to be used for the public use, but not yet in use for the public use, with sufficient detail for reasonable identification.

(3) A declaration that the governing body has found and determined each of the following:

(A) The public interest and necessity require the proposed use.

(B) The proposed use is planned and located in the manner that will be most compatible with the greatest public good and least private injury.

(C) The property described in the resolution is necessary for the proposed use.

(c) In addition to any notice required by law, the notice required for a new or reauthorization resolution sought pursuant to subdivision (a) or (b) shall comply with Section 1245.235 and shall be sent to each person who was given notice required by Section 1245.235 in connection with the original acquisition of the property by the public entity.

(d) Judicial review of an action pursuant to subdivision (a) or (b) may be obtained by a person who had an interest in the property described in the resolution at the time that the property was acquired by the public entity, and shall be governed by Section 1085.

(e) The following property acquisitions are subject to the requirements of this section:

(1) Any acquisition by a public entity pursuant to eminent domain.

(2) Any acquisition by a public entity following adoption of a resolution of necessity pursuant to this article for the property.

(3) Any acquisition by a public entity prior to the adoption of a resolution of necessity pursuant to this article for the property, but subsequent to a written notice that the public entity may take the property by eminent domain.

(f) If the public entity fails to adopt either a new resolution pursuant to subdivision (a) or a reauthorization resolution pursuant to subdivision (b), as required by this section, and that property was not used for the public use stated in a resolution of necessity adopted pursuant to this article or a resolution adopted pursuant to subdivision (a) or (b) between the time of its acquisition and the time of the public entity's failure to adopt a resolution pursuant to subdivision (a) or (b), the public entity shall offer the person or persons from whom the property was acquired the right of first refusal to purchase the property pursuant to this section, as follows:

(1) At the present market value, as determined by independent licensed appraisers.

(2) For property that was a single-family residence at the time of acquisition, at an affordable price, which price shall not be greater than the price paid by the agency for the original acquisition, adjusted for inflation, and shall not be greater than fair market value, if the following requirements are met:

(A) The person or persons from whom the property was acquired certify their income to the public entity as persons or families of low or moderate income.

(B) If the single-family residence is offered at a price that is less than fair market value, the public entity may verify the certifications of income in accordance with procedures used for verification of incomes of purchasers and occupants of housing financed by the California Housing Finance Agency.

(C) If the single-family residence is offered at a price that is less than fair market value, the public entity shall impose terms, conditions, and restrictions to ensure that the residence will either:

(i) Remain owner-occupied by the person or persons from whom the property was acquired for at least five years.

(ii) Remain available to persons or families of low or moderate income and households with incomes no greater than the incomes of the present occupants in proportion to the area median income for the longest feasible time, but for not less than 55 years for rental units and 45 years for home ownership units.

(D) The Department of Housing and Community Development shall provide to the public entity recommendations of standards and criteria for those prices, terms, conditions, and restrictions.

(g) If after a diligent effort the public entity is unable to locate the person from whom the property was acquired, if the person from whom the property was acquired does not choose to purchase the property as provided in subdivision (f), or if the public entity fails to adopt a resolution as required pursuant to subdivision (a) or (b) but is not required to offer a right of first refusal pursuant to subdivision (f), the public entity shall sell the property as surplus property pursuant to Article 8 (commencing with Section 54220) of Chapter 5 of Part 1 of Division 2 of Title 5 of the Government Code.

(h) If residential property acquired by a public entity by any means set forth in subdivision (e) is sold as surplus property pursuant to subdivision (g), and that property was not used for the public use stated in a resolution of necessity adopted pursuant to this article or a resolution adopted pursuant to subdivision (a) or (b) between the time of its acquisition and the time of its sale as surplus property, the public entity shall pay to the person or persons from whom the public entity acquired the property the sum of any financial gain between the original acquisition price, adjusted for inflation, and the final sale price.

(i) Upon completion of any acquisition described in subdivision (e) or upon the adoption of a resolution of necessity pursuant to this section, whichever is later, the public entity shall give written notice to the person or persons from whom the property was acquired as described in subdivision (e) stating that the notice, right of first refusal, and return of financial gain rights discussed in this section may accrue.

(j) At least 60 days before selling the property pursuant to subdivision (g), the public entity shall make a diligent effort to locate the person from whom the property was acquired. At any time before the proposed sale, the person from whom the property was acquired may exercise the rights provided by this section. As used in this section, "diligent effort" means that the public entity has done all of the following:

(1) Mailed the notice of the proposed sale by certified mail, return receipt requested, to the last known address of the person from whom the property was acquired.

(2) Mailed the notice of the proposed sale by certified mail, return receipt requested, to each person with the same name as the person from whom the property was acquired at any other address on the last equalized assessment roll.

(3) Published the notice of the proposed sale pursuant to Section 6061 of the Government Code in at least one newspaper of general circulation within the city or county in which the property is located.

(4) Posted the notice of the proposed sale in at least three public places within the city or county in which the property is located.

(5) Posted the notice of the proposed sale on the property proposed to be sold.

(k) For purposes of this section, "adjusted for inflation" means the original acquisition price increased to reflect the proportional increase in the Consumer Price Index for all items for the State of California, as determined by the United States Bureau of Labor Statistics, for the period from the date of acquisition to the date the property is offered for sale.

Amended by Stats 2007 ch 130 (AB 299),s 36, eff. 1/1/2008.

Added by Stats 2006 ch 602 (SB 1650),s 1, eff. 1/1/2007.

Section 1245.250 - Resolution conclusively establishes matters referred to in section 1240.030

(a) Except as otherwise provided by statute, a resolution of necessity adopted by the governing body of the public entity pursuant to this article conclusively establishes the matters referred to in Section 1240.030.

(b) If the taking is by a local public entity, other than a sanitary district exercising the powers of a county water district pursuant to Section 6512.7 of the Health and Safety Code, and the property is electric, gas, or water public utility property, the resolution of necessity creates a rebuttable presumption that the matters referred to in Section 1240.030 are true. This presumption is a presumption affecting the burden of proof.

(c) If the taking is by a local public entity and the property described in the resolution is not located entirely within the boundaries of the local public entity, the resolution of necessity creates a presumption that the matters referred to in Section 1240.030 are true. This presumption is a presumption affecting the burden of producing evidence.

(d) For the purposes of subdivision (b), a taking by the State Reclamation Board for the Sacramento and San Joaquin Drainage District is not a taking by a local public entity.

Amended by Stats. 1992, Ch. 812, Sec. 3. Effective January 1, 1993.

Section 1245.255 - Judicial review of validity of resolution

(a) A person having an interest in the property described in a resolution of necessity adopted by the governing body of the public entity pursuant to this article may obtain judicial review of the validity of the resolution:

(1) Before the commencement of the eminent domain proceeding, by petition for a writ of mandate pursuant to Section 1085. The court having jurisdiction of the writ of mandate action, upon motion of any party, shall order the writ of mandate action dismissed without prejudice upon commencement of the eminent domain proceeding unless the court determines that dismissal will not be in the interest of justice.

(2) After the commencement of the eminent domain proceeding, by objection to the right to take pursuant to this title.

(b) A resolution of necessity does not have the effect prescribed in Section 1245.250 to the extent that its adoption or contents were influenced or affected by gross abuse of discretion by the governing body.

(c) Nothing in this section precludes a public entity from rescinding a resolution of necessity and adopting a new resolution as to the same property subject, after the commencement of an eminent domain proceeding, to the same consequences as a conditional dismissal of the proceeding under Section 1260.120.

Amended by Stats. 1978, Ch. 286.

Section 1245.260 - Inverse condemnation

(a) If a public entity has adopted a resolution of necessity but has not commenced an eminent domain proceeding to acquire the property within six months after the date of adoption of the resolution, or has commenced such proceeding but has not within six months after the commencement of such proceeding attempted diligently to serve the complaint and the summons relating to such proceeding, the property owner may, by an action in inverse condemnation, do either or both of the following:

(1) Require the public entity to take the property and pay compensation therefor.

(2) Recover damages from the public entity for any interference with the possession and use of the property resulting from adoption of the resolution. Service by mail pursuant to Section 415.30 shall constitute a diligent attempt at service within the meaning of this section.

(b) No claim need be presented against a public entity under Part 3 (commencing with Section 900) of Division 3.6 of Title 1 of the Government Code as a prerequisite to commencement or maintenance of an action under subdivision (a), but any such action shall be commenced within one year and six months after the date the public entity adopted the resolution of necessity.

(c) A public entity may commence an eminent domain proceeding or rescind a resolution of necessity as a matter of right at any time before the property owner commences an action under this section. If the public entity commences an eminent domain proceeding or rescinds the resolution of necessity before the property owner commences an action under this section, the property owner may not thereafter bring an action under this section.

(d) After a property owner has commenced an action under this section, the public entity may rescind the resolution of necessity and abandon the taking of the property only under the same circumstances and subject to the same conditions and consequences as abandonment of an eminent domain proceeding.

(e) Commencement of an action under this section does not affect any authority a public entity may have to commence an eminent domain proceeding, take possession of the property pursuant to Article 3 (commencing with Section 1255.410) of Chapter 6, or abandon the eminent domain proceeding.

(f) In lieu of bringing an action under subdivision (a) or if the limitations period provided in subdivision (b) has run, the property owner may obtain a writ of mandate to compel the public entity, within such time as the court deems appropriate, to rescind the resolution of necessity or to commence an eminent domain proceeding to acquire the property.

Amended by Stats. 1978, Ch. 411.

Section 1245.270 - Member voting in favor of resolution receive or agreed to receive bribe

(a) A resolution of necessity does not meet the requirements of this article if the defendant establishes by a preponderance of the evidence both of the following:

(1) A member of the governing body who voted in favor of the resolution received or agreed to receive a bribe (as that term is defined in subdivision 6 of Section 7 of the Penal Code) involving adoption of the resolution.

(2) But for the conduct described in paragraph (1), the resolution would not otherwise have been adopted.

(b) Where there has been a prior criminal prosecution of the member for the conduct described in paragraph (1) of subdivision (a), proof of conviction shall be conclusive evidence that the requirement of paragraph (1) of subdivision (a) is satisfied, and proof of acquittal or other dismissal of the prosecution shall be conclusive evidence that the requirement of paragraph (1) of subdivision (a) is not satisfied. Where there is a pending criminal prosecution of the member for the conduct described in paragraph (1) of subdivision (a), the court may take such action as is just under the circumstances of the case.

(c) Nothing in this section precludes a public entity from rescinding a resolution of necessity and adopting a new resolution as to the same property, subject to the same consequences as a conditional dismissal of the proceeding under Section 1260.120.

Added by Stats. 1975, Ch. 1275.

Article 3 - RESOLUTION CONSENTING TO EMINENT DOMAIN PROCEEDING BY QUASI-PUBLIC ENTITY

Section 1245.310 - Legislative body defined
As used in this article, "legislative body" means both of the following:
(a) The legislative body of each city within whose boundaries property sought to be taken by the quasi-public entity by eminent domain is located.
(b) If property sought to be taken by the quasi-public entity is not located within city boundaries, the legislative body of each county within whose boundaries such property is located.
Added by Stats. 1975, Ch. 1275.

Section 1245.320 - Quasi-public entity
As used in this article, "quasi-public entity" means:
(a) An educational institution of collegiate grade not conducted for profit that seeks to take property by eminent domain under Section 94500 of the Education Code.
(b) A nonprofit hospital that seeks to take property by eminent domain under Section 1260 of the Health and Safety Code.
(c) A cemetery authority that seeks to take property by eminent domain under Section 8501 of the Health and Safety Code.
(d) A limited-dividend housing corporation that seeks to take property by eminent domain under Section 34874 of the Health and Safety Code.
(e) A land-chest corporation that seeks to take property by eminent domain under former Section 35167 of the Health and Safety Code.
(f) A mutual water company that seeks to take property by eminent domain under Section 2729 of the Public Utilities Code.
Amended by Stats 2006 ch 538 (SB 1852),s 67, eff. 1/1/2007.

Section 1245.325 - Owner of property seeking to acquire appurtenant easement; requirements of resolution
Where an owner of real property seeks to acquire an appurtenant easement by eminent domain pursuant to Section 1001 of the Civil Code:
(a) The person seeking to exercise the power of eminent domain shall be deemed to be a "quasi-public entity" for the purposes of this article.
(b) In lieu of the requirements of subdivision (c) of Section 1245.340, the resolution required by this article shall contain a declaration that the legislative body has found and determined each of the following:
   (1) There is a great necessity for the taking.
   (2) The location of the easement affords the most reasonable service to the property to which it is appurtenant, consistent with the least damage to the burdened property.
   (3) The hardship to the owner of the appurtenant property, if the taking is not permitted, clearly outweighs any hardship to the owner of the burdened property.
Added by Stats. 1976, Ch. 994.

Section 1245.326 - Owner of property seeks to acquire temporary right of entry; requirements of resolution
Where an owner of real property seeks to acquire by eminent domain a temporary right of entry pursuant to Section 1002 of the Civil Code:
(a) The person seeking to exercise the power of eminent domain shall be deemed to be a "quasi-public entity" for the purposes of this article.
(b) In lieu of the requirements of subdivision (c) of Section 1245.340, the resolution required by this article shall contain a declaration that the legislative body has found and determined that each of the conditions required by Section 1002 of the Civil Code appears to exist.
Added by Stats. 1982, Ch. 1239, Sec. 2.

Section 1245.330 - Adoption of resolution required
Notwithstanding any other provision of law, a quasi-public entity may not commence an eminent domain proceeding to acquire any property until the legislative body has adopted a resolution consenting to the acquisition of such property by eminent domain.
Added by Stats. 1975, Ch. 1275.

Section 1245.340 - Information required in resolution
The resolution required by this article shall contain all of the following:
(a) A general statement of the public use for which the property is to be taken and a reference to the statute that authorizes the quasi-public entity to acquire the property by eminent domain.
(b) A description of the general location and extent of the property to be taken, with sufficient detail for reasonable identification.
(c) A declaration that the legislative body has found and determined each of the following:
   (1) The public interest and necessity require the proposed project.
   (2) The proposed project is planned or located in the manner that will be most compatible with the greatest good and least private injury.
   (3) The property described in the resolution is necessary for the proposed project.
   (4) The hardship to the quasi-public entity if the acquisition of the property by eminent domain is not permitted outweighs any hardship to the owners of such property.
Added by Stats. 1975, Ch. 1275.

Section 1245.350 - Hearing; notice
(a) The legislative body may refuse to consent to the acquisition with or without a hearing, but it may adopt the resolution required by this article only after the legislative body has held a hearing at which persons whose property is to be acquired by eminent domain have had a reasonable opportunity to appear and be heard.
(b) Notice of the hearing shall be sent by first-class mail to each person whose property is to be acquired by eminent domain if the name and address of the person appears on the last equalized county assessment roll (including the roll of state-assessed property). The notice shall state the time, place, and subject of the hearing and shall be mailed at least 15 days prior to the date of the hearing.
Added by Stats. 1975, Ch. 1275.

Section 1245.360 - Vote required to adopt resolution
The resolution required by this article shall be adopted by a vote of two-thirds of all the members of the legislative body.
Added by Stats. 1975, Ch. 1275.

Section 1245.370 - Payment of costs incurred by legislative body; deposit securing costs
The legislative body may require that the quasi-public entity pay all of the costs reasonably incurred by the legislative body under this article. The legislative body may require that such costs be secured by payment or deposit or other satisfactory security in advance of any action by the legislative body under this article.
Added by Stats. 1975, Ch. 1275.

Section 1245.380 - Requirements in addition to other requirements
The requirement of this article is in addition to any other requirements imposed by law. Nothing in this article relieves the quasi-public entity from satisfying the requirements of Section 1240.030 or any other requirements imposed by law.
Added by Stats. 1975, Ch. 1275.

Section 1245.390 - City or county not liable for damages caused by acquisition or by project

The adoption of a resolution pursuant to this article does not make the city or county liable for any damages caused by the acquisition of the property or by the project for which it is acquired.
Added by Stats. 1975, Ch. 1275.

Chapter 5 - COMMENCEMENT OF PROCEEDING

Article 1 - JURISDICTION AND VENUE

Section 1250.010 - Superior court jurisdiction
Except as otherwise provided in Section 1230.060 and in Chapter 12 (commencing with Section 1273.010), all eminent domain proceedings shall be commenced and prosecuted in the superior court.
Added by Stats. 1975, Ch. 1275.

Section 1250.020 - Venue
(a) Except as provided in subdivision (b), the proceeding shall be commenced in the county in which the property sought to be taken is located.
(b) When property sought to be taken is situated in more than one county, the plaintiff may commence the proceeding in any one of such counties.
Added by Stats. 1975, Ch. 1275.

Section 1250.030 - Proper county
(a) Except as provided in subdivision (b), the county in which the proceeding is commenced pursuant to Section 1250.020 is the proper county for trial of the proceeding.
(b) Where the court changes the place of trial pursuant to Section 1250.040, the county to which the proceeding is transferred is the proper county for trial of the proceeding.
Added by Stats. 1975, Ch. 1275.

Section 1250.040 - Change of place of trial
The provisions of the Code of Civil Procedure for the change of place of trial of actions apply to eminent domain proceedings.
Added by Stats. 1975, Ch. 1275.

Article 2 - COMMENCEMENT OF PROCEEDING GENERALLY

Section 1250.110 - Commenced by filing complaint
An eminent domain proceeding is commenced by filing a complaint with the court.
Added by Stats. 1975, Ch. 1275.

Section 1250.120 - Form and contents of summons; process served by publication
(a) Except as provided in subdivision (b), the form and contents of the summons shall be as in civil actions generally.
(b) Where process is served by publication, in addition to the summons, the publication shall describe the property sought to be taken in a manner reasonably calculated to give persons with an interest in the property actual notice of the pending proceeding.
Added by Stats. 1975, Ch. 1275.

Section 1250.125 - Defendants named and property described in summons served by publication; failure to appear and answer
(a) Where summons is served by publication, the publication may name only the defendants to be served thereby and describe only the property in which the defendants to be served thereby have or claim interests.
(b) Judgment based on failure to appear and answer following service under this section shall be conclusive against the defendants named in respect only to property described in the publication.
(c) Notwithstanding subdivision (b), a defendant who did not receive the offer required by Section 7267.2 of the Government Code because the owner could not be located with reasonable diligence, who was served by publication, and who failed to appear, may contest the amount of compensation within one year of the judgment and for good cause shown, whereupon that issue shall be litigated according to the provisions of this title.
Amended by Stats. 1983, Ch. 1079, Sec. 2.

Section 1250.130 - Plaintiff required to post copy of summons and record notice of pendency of proceeding
Where the court orders service by publication, it shall also order the plaintiff (1) to post a copy of the summons and complaint on the property sought to be taken and (2), if not already recorded, to record a notice of the pendency of the proceeding in the manner provided by Section 1250.150. Such posting and recording shall be done not later than 10 days after the date the order is made.
Added by Stats. 1975, Ch. 1275.

Section 1250.140 - Service where state defendant
Where the state is a defendant, the summons and the complaint shall be served on the Attorney General.
Added by Stats. 1975, Ch. 1275.

Section 1250.150 - Recording and serving notice of pendency of proceeding
The plaintiff, at the time of the commencement of the proceeding, shall record a notice of the pendency of the proceeding in the office of the county recorder of any county in which property described in the complaint is located. A copy of the notice shall be served with the summons and complaint.
Amended by Stats. 1983, Ch. 78, Sec. 2.

Article 3 - PARTIES; JOINDER OF PROPERTY

Section 1250.210 - Persons named as plaintiffs
Each person seeking to take property by eminent domain shall be named as a plaintiff.
Added by Stats. 1975, Ch. 1275.

Section 1250.220 - Persons named as defendants by plaintiff
(a) The plaintiff shall name as defendants, by their real names, those persons who appear of record or are known by the plaintiff to have or claim an interest in the property described in the complaint.
(b) If a person described in subdivision (a) is dead and the plaintiff knows of a duly qualified and acting personal representative of the estate of such person, the plaintiff shall name such personal representative as a defendant. If a person described in subdivision (a) is dead or is believed by the plaintiff to be dead and if plaintiff knows of no duly qualified and acting personal representative of the estate of such person and states these facts in an affidavit filed with the complaint, plaintiff may name as defendants "the heirs and devisees of ____ (naming such deceased person), deceased, and all persons claiming by, through, or under said decedent," naming them in that manner and, where it is stated in the affidavit that such person is believed by the plaintiff to be dead, such person also may be named as a defendant.
(c) In addition to those persons described in subdivision (a), the plaintiff may name as defendants "all persons unknown claiming an interest in the property," naming them in that manner.
(d) A judgment rendered in a proceeding under this title is binding and conclusive upon all persons named as defendants as provided in this section and properly served.
Added by Stats. 1975, Ch. 1275.

Section 1250.230 - Appearance by persons claiming legal or equitable interest
Any person who claims a legal or equitable interest in the property described in the complaint may appear in the proceeding. Whether or not such person is named as a defendant in the complaint, he shall appear as a defendant.
Added by Stats. 1975, Ch. 1275.

Section 1250.240 - Joinder of property in one complaint
The plaintiff may join in one complaint all property located within the same county which is sought to be acquired for the same project.
Added by Stats. 1975, Ch. 1275.

Section 1250.250 - Naming holder of lien as defendant
(a) If the only interest of the county or other taxing agency in the property described in the complaint is a lien for ad valorem taxes, the county or other taxing agency need not be named as a defendant.
(b) The holder of a lien that secures a special assessment or a bond representing the special assessment shall be named as a defendant, regardless of the nature of the special assessment and the manner of collection of the special assessment. The holder of the lien may, instead of an answer, certify to the court within 30 days after service of the summons and complaint on the holder all of the following information:
    (1) A complete description of the lien.
    (2) A description of the property encumbered by the lien.
    (3) The amount remaining due on the lien as of the date of the certificate.
    (4) The date upon which each installment payable on the lien is due and the amount of each installment.
(c) A copy of the certification shall be sent by first-class mail to all parties to the proceeding at the time it is provided to the court. The filing of the certification or answer shall be considered as a general appearance.
Amended by Stats. 1981, Ch. 139, Sec. 1.

Article 4 - PLEADINGS

Section 1250.310 - Requirements of complaint
The complaint shall contain all of the following:
(a) The names of all plaintiffs and defendants.
(b) A description of the property sought to be taken. The description may, but is not required to, indicate the nature or extent of the interest of the defendant in the property.
(c) If the plaintiff claims an interest in the property sought to be taken, the nature and extent of such interest.
(d) A statement of the right of the plaintiff to take by eminent domain the property described in the complaint. The statement shall include:
    (1) A general statement of the public use for which the property is to be taken.
    (2) An allegation of the necessity for the taking as required by Section 1240.030; where the plaintiff is a public entity, a reference to its resolution of necessity; where the plaintiff is a quasi-public entity within the meaning of Section 1245.320, a reference to the resolution adopted pursuant to Article 3 (commencing with Section 1245.310) of Chapter 4; where the plaintiff is a nonprofit hospital, a reference to the certificate required by Section 1260 of the Health and Safety Code; where the plaintiff is a public utility and relies on a certification of the State Energy Resources Conservation and Development Commission or a requirement of that commission that development rights be acquired, a reference to such certification or requirement.
    (3) A reference to the statute that authorizes the plaintiff to acquire the property by eminent domain. Specification of the statutory authority may be in the alternative and may be inconsistent.
(e) A map or diagram portraying as far as practicable the property described in the complaint and showing its location in relation to the project for which it is to be taken.
Amended by Stats. 1975, Ch. 1275.

Section 1250.320 - Answer
(a) The answer shall include a statement of the nature and extent of the interest the defendant claims in the property described in the complaint.
(b) If the defendant seeks compensation provided in Article 6 (commencing with Section 1263.510) (goodwill) of Chapter 9, the answer shall include a statement that the defendant claims compensation under Section 1263.510, but the answer need not specify the amount of that compensation.
(c) If the defendant seeks compensation as provided in Article 1 (commencing with Section 1245.010) of Chapter 4, the answer shall include a statement that the defendant claims compensation under Section 1245.060, but need not specify the amount of that compensation.
(d) If the defendant seeks compensation for losses caused by the plaintiff's unreasonable conduct prior to commencing the eminent domain proceeding, the answer shall include a statement that the defendant claims compensation for that loss, but need not specify the amount of the compensation.
Amended by Stats 2021 ch 401 (AB 1578),s 5, eff. 1/1/2022.
Added by Stats. 1975, Ch. 1275.

Section 1250.325 - Disclaimer
(a) A defendant may file a disclaimer at any time, whether or not he is in default, and the disclaimer supersedes an answer previously filed by the defendant. The disclaimer need not be in any particular form. It shall contain a statement that the defendant claims no interest in the property or in the compensation that may be awarded. Notwithstanding Section 1250.330, the disclaimer shall be signed by the defendant.
(b) Subject to subdivision (c), a defendant who has filed a disclaimer has no right to participate in further proceedings or to share in the compensation awarded.
(c) The court may implement the disclaimer by appropriate orders including, where justified, awarding costs and litigation expenses.
Added by Stats. 1975, Ch. 1275.

Section 1250.330 - Pleadings signed by attorney representing party
Where a party is represented by an attorney, his pleading need not be verified but shall be signed by the attorney for the party. The signature of the attorney constitutes a certificate by him that he has read the pleading and that to the best of his knowledge, information, and belief there is ground to support it. If the pleading is not signed or is signed with intent to defeat the purposes of this section, it may be stricken.
Added by Stats. 1975, Ch. 1275.

Section 1250.340 - Amendment or supplement to pleading
(a) Subject to subdivisions (b) and (c), the court may allow upon such terms and conditions as may be just an amendment or supplement to any pleading. In the case of an amendment or supplement to the complaint, such terms and conditions may include a change in the applicable date of valuation for the proceeding and an award of costs and litigation expenses which would not have been incurred had the proceeding as originally commenced been the same as the proceeding following such amendment or supplement.
(b) A public entity may add to the property sought to be taken only if it has adopted a resolution of necessity that satisfies the requirements of Article 2 (commencing with Section 1245.210) of Chapter 4 for the property to be added.
(c) Property previously sought to be taken may be deleted from the complaint only if the plaintiff has followed the procedure for partial abandonment of the proceeding as to that property.
Added by Stats. 1975, Ch. 1275.

Section 1250.345 - Waiver of objection to complaint
Subject to the power of the court to permit an amendment of the answer, if the defendant fails to object to the complaint, either by demurrer or answer, he is deemed to have waived the objection.
Added by Stats. 1975, Ch. 1275.

Article 5 - OBJECTIONS TO RIGHT TO TAKE

Section 1250.350 - Demurrer or answer
A defendant may object to the plaintiff's right to take, by demurrer or answer as provided in Section 430.30, on any ground authorized by Section 1250.360 or Section 1250.370. The demurrer or answer shall state the specific ground upon which the objection is taken and, if the objection is taken by answer, the specific facts upon which the objection is based. An objection may be taken on more than one ground, and the grounds may be inconsistent.
Added by Stats. 1975, Ch. 1275.

Section 1250.360 - Grounds regardless of whether plaintiff adopted resolution
Grounds for objection to the right to take, regardless of whether the plaintiff has adopted a resolution of necessity that satisfies the requirements of Article 2 (commencing with Section 1245.210) of Chapter 4, include:
(a) The plaintiff is not authorized by statute to exercise the power of eminent domain for the purpose stated in the complaint.
(b) The stated purpose is not a public use.
(c) The plaintiff does not intend to devote the property described in the complaint to the stated purpose.
(d) There is no reasonable probability that the plaintiff will devote the described property to the stated purpose within (1) seven years, or (2) 10 years where the property is taken pursuant to the Federal Aid Highway Act of 1973, or (3) such longer period as is reasonable.
(e) The described property is not subject to acquisition by the power of eminent domain for the stated purpose.
(f) The described property is sought to be acquired pursuant to Section 1240.410 (excess condemnation), 1240.510 (condemnation for compatible use), or 1240.610 (condemnation for more necessary public use), but the acquisition does not satisfy the requirements of those provisions.
(g) The described property is sought to be acquired pursuant to Section 1240.610 (condemnation for more necessary public use), but the defendant has the right under Section 1240.630 to continue the public use to which the property is appropriated as a joint use.
(h) Any other ground provided by law.
Added by Stats. 1975, Ch. 1275.

Section 1250.370 - Grounds where plaintiff has not adopted resolution
In addition to the grounds listed in Section 1250.360, grounds for objection to the right to take where the plaintiff has not adopted a resolution of necessity that conclusively establishes the matters referred to in Section 1240.030 include:
(a) The plaintiff is a public entity and has not adopted a resolution of necessity that satisfies the requirements of Article 2 (commencing with Section 1245.210) of Chapter 4.
(b) The public interest and necessity do not require the proposed project.
(c) The proposed project is not planned or located in the manner that will be most compatible with the greatest public good and the least private injury.
(d) The property described in the complaint is not necessary for the proposed project.
(e) The plaintiff is a quasi-public entity within the meaning of Section 1245.320 and has not satisfied the requirements of Article 3 (commencing with Section 1245.310) of Chapter 4.
Added by Stats. 1975, Ch. 1275.

Article 6 - SETTLEMENT OFFERS AND ALTERNATIVE DISPUTE RESOLUTION

Section 1250.410 - Offer of compensation served on defendant; demand for compensation served on plaintiff; litigation expenses
(a) At least 20 days prior to the date of the trial on issues relating to compensation, the plaintiff shall file with the court and serve on the defendant its final offer of compensation in the proceeding and the defendant shall file and serve on the plaintiff its final demand for compensation in the proceeding. The offer and the demand shall include all compensation required pursuant to this title, including compensation for loss of goodwill, if any, and shall state whether interest and costs are included. These offers and demands shall be the only offers and demands considered by the court in determining the entitlement, if any, to litigation expenses. Service shall be in the manner prescribed by Chapter 5 (commencing with Section 1010) of Title 14 of Part 2.
(b) If the court, on motion of the defendant made within 30 days after entry of judgment, finds that the offer of the plaintiff was unreasonable and that the demand of the defendant was reasonable viewed in the light of the evidence admitted and the compensation awarded in the proceeding, the costs allowed pursuant to Section 1268.710 shall include the defendant's litigation expenses.
(c) In determining the amount of litigation expenses allowed under this section, the court shall consider the offer required to be made by the plaintiff pursuant to Section 7267.2 of the Government Code, any deposit made by the plaintiff pursuant to Chapter 6 (commencing with Section 1255.010), and any other written offers and demands filed and served before or during the trial.
(d) If timely made, the offers and demands as provided in subdivision (a) shall be considered by the court on the issue of determining an entitlement to litigation expenses.
(e) As used in this section, "litigation expenses" means the party's reasonable attorney's fees and costs, including reasonable expert witness and appraiser fees.
Amended by Stats 2006 ch 594 (SB 1210),s 1, eff. 1/1/2007.
Amended by Stats 2002 ch 295 (AB 1770),s 1, eff. 1/1/2003.
Article heading amended by Stats 2001 ch 428 (AB 237), ss 1, 2 eff. 1/1/2002.
Previously Amended July 13, 1999 (Bill Number: SB 634) (Chapter 102).

Section 1250.420 - Resolution of dispute by mediation or binding arbitration
The parties may by agreement refer a dispute that is the subject of an eminent domain proceeding for resolution by any of the following means:
(a) Mediation by a neutral mediator.
(b) Binding arbitration by a neutral arbitrator. The arbitration is subject to Chapter 12 (commencing with Section 1273.010).
(c) Nonbinding arbitration by a neutral arbitrator. The arbitrator's decision in a nonbinding arbitration is final unless within 30 days after service of the arbitrator's decision a party moves the court for a trial of the eminent domain proceeding. If the judgment in the eminent domain proceeding is not more favorable to the moving party, the court shall order that party to pay to the other parties the following nonrefundable costs and fees, unless the court finds in writing and on motion that the imposition of costs and fees would create such a substantial economic hardship as not to be in the interest of justice:
(1) All costs specified in Section 1033.5, limited to those incurred from the time of election of the trial de novo. Nothing in this subdivision affects the right of a defendant to recover costs otherwise allowable pursuant to Section 1268.710, incurred before election of a trial de novo, except that a defendant may recover the costs of determining the apportionment of the award made pursuant to subdivision (b) of Section 1260.220 whenever incurred.

(2) The reasonable costs of the services of expert witnesses who are not regular employees of any party, actually incurred and reasonably necessary in the preparation or trial of the case, limited to those incurred from the time of election of the trial de novo.

(3) The compensation paid by the parties to the arbitrator.

Added by Stats 2001 ch 428 (AB 237), s 3, eff. 1/1/2002.

Section 1250.430 - Motion to postpone date of trial

Notwithstanding any other statute or rule of court governing the date of trial of an eminent domain proceeding, on motion of a party the court may postpone the date of trial for a period that appears adequate to enable resolution of a dispute pursuant to alternative resolution procedures, if it is demonstrated to the satisfaction of the court that all of the following conditions are satisfied:

(a) The parties are actively engaged in alternative resolution of the dispute pursuant to Section 1250.420.

(b) The parties appear to be making progress toward resolution of the dispute without the need for a trial of the matter.

(c) The parties agree that additional time for the purpose of alternative dispute resolution is desirable.

Added by Stats 2001 ch 428 (AB 237), s 4, eff. 1/1/2002.

Chapter 6 - DEPOSIT AND WITHDRAWAL OF PROBABLE COMPENSATION; POSSESSION PRIOR TO JUDGMENT

Article 1 - DEPOSIT OF PROBABLE COMPENSATION

Section 1255.010 - Appraisal upon which deposit made; deposit without appraisal

(a) At any time before entry of judgment, the plaintiff may deposit with the State Treasury the probable amount of compensation, based on an appraisal, that will be awarded in the proceeding. The appraisal upon which the deposit is based shall be one that satisfies the requirements of subdivision (b). The deposit may be made whether or not the plaintiff applies for an order for possession or intends to do so.

(b) Before making a deposit under this section, the plaintiff shall have an expert qualified to express an opinion as to the value of the property (1) make an appraisal of the property and (2) prepare a written statement of, or summary of the basis for, the appraisal. The statement or summary shall contain detail sufficient to indicate clearly the basis for the appraisal, including, but not limited to, all of the following information:

(A) The date of valuation, highest and best use, and applicable zoning of the property.

(B) The principal transactions, reproduction or replacement cost analysis, or capitalization analysis, supporting the appraisal.

(C) If the appraisal includes compensation for damages to the remainder, the compensation for the property and for damages to the remainder separately stated, and the calculations and a narrative explanation supporting the compensation, including any offsetting benefits.

(c) On noticed motion, or upon ex parte application in an emergency, the court may permit the plaintiff to make a deposit without prior compliance with subdivision (b) if the plaintiff presents facts by affidavit showing that (1) good cause exists for permitting an immediate deposit to be made, (2) an adequate appraisal has not been completed and cannot reasonably be prepared before making the deposit, and (3) the amount of the deposit to be made is not less than the probable amount of compensation that the plaintiff, in good faith, estimates will be awarded in the proceeding. In its order, the court shall require that the plaintiff comply with subdivision (b) within a reasonable time, to be specified in the order, and also that any additional amount of compensation shown by the appraisal required by subdivision (b) be deposited within that time.

Amended by Stats 2001 ch 428 (AB 237), s 5, eff. 1/1/2002.

Section 1255.020 - Notice of deposit; statement of summary of basis of appraisal

(a) On making a deposit pursuant to Section 1255.010, the plaintiff shall serve a notice of deposit on all parties who have appeared in the proceeding and file with the court a proof of service together with the notice of deposit. The plaintiff shall so serve parties who appear thereafter on their appearance. The notice of deposit shall state that a deposit has been made and the date and the amount of the deposit. Service of the notice of deposit shall be made in the manner provided in Section 1255.450 for service of an order for possession.

(b) The notice of deposit shall be accompanied by a written statement or summary of the basis for the appraisal referred to in Section 1255.010.

(c) If the plaintiff has obtained an order under Section 1255.010 deferring completion of the written statement or summary, the plaintiff:

(1) On making the deposit, shall comply with subdivision (a) and include with the notice a copy of all affidavits on which the order was based.

(2) Upon completion of the written statement or summary, shall comply with subdivision (b).

Amended by Stats. 1990, Ch. 1491, Sec. 10.

Section 1255.030 - Whether deposit probable amount of compensation determination

(a) At any time after a deposit has been made pursuant to this article, the court shall, upon motion of the plaintiff or of any party having an interest in the property for which the deposit was made, determine or redetermine whether the amount deposited is the probable amount of compensation that will be awarded in the proceeding. The motion shall be supported with detail sufficient to indicate clearly the basis for the motion, including, but not limited to, the following information to the extent relevant to the motion:

(1) The date of valuation, highest and best use, and applicable zoning of the property.

(2) The principal transactions, reproduction or replacement cost analysis, or capitalization analysis, supporting the motion.

(3) The compensation for the property and for damages to the remainder separately stated, and the calculations and a narrative explanation supporting the compensation, including any offsetting benefits.

(b) If the plaintiff has not taken possession of the property and the court determines that the probable amount of compensation exceeds the amount deposited, the court may order the plaintiff to increase the deposit or may deny the plaintiff possession of the property until the amount deposited has been increased to the amount specified in the order.

(c) If the plaintiff has taken possession of the property and the court determines that the probable amount of compensation exceeds the amount deposited, the court shall order the amount deposited to be increased to the amount determined to be the probable amount of compensation. If the amount on deposit is not increased accordingly within 30 days from the date of the court's order, or any longer time as the court may have allowed at the time of making the order, the defendant may serve on the plaintiff a notice of election to treat that failure as an abandonment of the proceeding. If the plaintiff does not cure its failure within 10 days after receipt of such notice, the court shall, upon motion of the defendant, enter judgment dismissing the proceeding and awarding the defendant his or her litigation expenses and damages as provided in Sections 1268.610 and 1268.620.

(d) After any amount deposited pursuant to this article has been withdrawn by a defendant, the court may not determine or redetermine the probable amount of compensation to be less than the total amount already withdrawn. Nothing in this subdivision precludes the court from making a determination or redetermination that probable compensation is greater than the amount withdrawn.

(e) If the court determines that the amount deposited exceeds the probable amount of compensation, it may permit the plaintiff to withdraw the excess not already withdrawn by the defendant.

(f) The plaintiff may at any time increase the amount deposited without making a motion under this section. In that case, notice of the increase shall be served as provided in subdivision (a) of Section 1255.020.

Amended by Stats 2001 ch 428 (AB 237), s 6, eff. 1/1/2002.

Section 1255.040 - Deposit where property includes dwelling occupied by defendant as residence

(a) If the plaintiff has not made a deposit that satisfies the requirements of this article and the property includes a dwelling containing not more than two residential units and the dwelling or one of its units is occupied as his or her residence by a defendant, the defendant may serve notice on the plaintiff requiring a deposit of the probable amount of compensation that will be awarded in the proceeding. The notice shall specify the date by which the defendant desires the deposit to be made. The date shall not be earlier than 30 days after the date of service of the notice and may be any later date.

(b) If the plaintiff deposits the probable amount of compensation, determined or redetermined as provided in this article, on or before the date specified by the defendant, the plaintiff may obtain an order for possession that authorizes the plaintiff to take possession of the property 30 days after the date for the deposit specified by the defendant or any later date as the plaintiff may request.

(c) Notwithstanding Section 1268.310, if the deposit is not made on or before the date specified by the defendant or such later date as the court specifies on motion and good cause shown by the plaintiff, the compensation awarded to the defendant in the proceeding shall draw legal interest from that date. The defendant is entitled to the full amount of such interest without offset for rents or other income received by him or her or the value of his or her continued possession of the property.

(d) If the proceeding is abandoned by the plaintiff, the interest under subdivision (c) may be recovered as costs in the proceeding in the manner provided for the recovery of litigation expenses under Section 1268.610. If, in the proceeding, the court or a jury verdict eventually determines the compensation that would have been awarded to the defendant, then the interest shall be computed on the amount of the award. If no determination is ever made, then the interest shall be computed on the probable amount of compensation as determined by the court.

(e) The serving of a notice pursuant to this section constitutes a waiver by operation of law, conditioned upon subsequent deposit by the plaintiff of the probable amount of compensation, of all claims and defenses in favor of the defendant except his or her claim for greater compensation.

(f) Notice of a deposit made under this section shall be served as provided by subdivision (a) of Section 1255.020. The defendant may withdraw the deposit as provided in Article 2 (commencing with Section 1255.210).

(g) No notice may be served by a defendant under subdivision (a) after entry of judgment unless the judgment is reversed, vacated, or set aside and no other judgment has been entered at the time the notice is served.

Amended by Stats 2006 ch 594 (SB 1210),s 2, eff. 1/1/2007.

Section 1255.050 - Deposit where property to be taken subject to leasehold interest

If the property to be taken is subject to a leasehold interest and the plaintiff has not made a deposit that satisfies the requirements of this article, the lessor may serve notice on the plaintiff requiring a deposit of the probable amount of compensation that will be awarded in the proceeding in the same manner and subject to the same procedures and conditions as a motion pursuant to Section 1255.040 except that, if the plaintiff fails to make the deposit, the interest awarded shall be offset by the lessor's net rental profits on the property.

Added by Stats. 1975, Ch. 1275.

Section 1255.060 - Trial of issue of compensation

(a) The amount deposited or withdrawn pursuant to this chapter may not be given in evidence or referred to in the trial of the issue of compensation.

(b) In the trial of the issue of compensation, an appraisal report, written statement and summary of an appraisal, or other statement made in connection with a deposit or withdrawal pursuant to this chapter may not be considered to be an admission of any party.

(c) Upon objection of the party at whose request an appraisal report, written statement and summary of the appraisal, or other statement was made in connection with a deposit or withdrawal pursuant to this chapter, the person who made the report or statement and summary or other statement may not be called at the trial on the issue of compensation by any other party to give an opinion as to compensation. If the person who prepared the report, statement and summary, or other statement is called at trial to give an opinion as to compensation, the report, statement and summary, or other statement may be used for impeachment of the witness.

Amended by Stats 2002 ch 295 (AB 1770),s 2, eff. 1/1/2003.

Section 1255.070 - Deposit in county treasury in lieu of state treasury; investment of money deposited in state treasury

In lieu of depositing the money with the State Treasury as provided in Section 1255.010, upon written request of the plaintiff, the court shall order the money be deposited in the county treasury. If money is deposited in the State Treasury pursuant to Section 1255.010, it shall be held, invested, deposited, and disbursed in the manner specified in Article 10 (commencing with Section 16429) of Chapter 2 of Part 2 of Division 4 of Title 2 of the Government Code, and interest earned or other increment derived from its investment shall be apportioned and disbursed in the manner specified in that article. As between the parties to the proceeding, money deposited pursuant to this article shall remain at the risk of the plaintiff until paid or made payable to the defendant by order of the court.

Amended by Stats. 1990, Ch. 1491, Sec. 11.

Section 1255.075 - Motion to invest deposit for benefit of defendants

(a) Prior to entry of judgment, a defendant who has an interest in the property for which a deposit has been made under this chapter may, upon notice to the other parties to the proceeding, move the court to have all of such deposit invested for the benefit of the defendants.

(b) At the hearing on the motion, the court shall consider the interests of the parties and the effect that investment would have upon them. The court may, in its discretion, if it finds that the interests of justice will be served, grant the motion subject to such terms and conditions as are appropriate under the circumstances of the case.

(c) An investment under this section shall be specified by the court and shall be limited to United States government obligations or interest-bearing accounts in an institution whose accounts are insured by an agency of the federal government.

(d) The investment of the deposit has the same consequences as if the deposit has been withdrawn under this chapter.

Added by Stats. 1975, Ch. 1275.

Section 1255.080 - Rights not waived by plaintiff

By depositing the probable compensation pursuant to this article, the plaintiff does not waive the right to appeal from the judgment, the right to move to abandon, or the right to request a new trial.

Added by Stats. 1975, Ch. 1275.

Article 2 - WITHDRAWAL OF DEPOSIT

Section 1255.210 - Application to court by defendant

Prior to entry of judgment, any defendant may apply to the court for the withdrawal of all or any portion of the amount deposited. The application shall be verified, set forth the applicant's interest in the property, and request withdrawal of a stated amount. The applicant shall serve a copy of the application on the plaintiff.

Added by Stats. 1975, Ch. 1275.

Section 1255.220 - Court order for payment to applicant

Subject to the requirements of this article, the court shall order the amount requested in the application, or such portion of that amount as the applicant is entitled to receive, to be paid to the applicant.

Added by Stats. 1975, Ch. 1275.

Section 1255.230 - Objections to withdrawal

(a) No withdrawal may be ordered until 20 days after service on the plaintiff of a copy of the application or until the time for all objections has expired, whichever is later.

(b) Within the 20-day period, the plaintiff may file objections to withdrawal on any one or more of the following grounds:

(1) Other parties to the proceeding are known or believed to have interests in the property.

(2) An undertaking should be filed by the applicant as provided in Section 1255.240 or 1255.250.
(3) The amount of an undertaking filed by the applicant under this chapter or the sureties thereon are insufficient.
(c) If an objection is filed on the ground that other parties are known or believed to have interests in the property, the plaintiff shall serve or attempt to serve on such other parties a notice that they may appear within 10 days after such service and object to the withdrawal. The notice shall advise such parties that their failure to object will result in waiver of any rights against the plaintiff to the extent of the amount withdrawn. The notice shall be served in the manner provided in Section 1255.450 for service of an order for possession. The plaintiff shall file, and serve on the applicant, a report setting forth (1) the names of the parties upon whom the notice was served and the dates of service and (2) the names and last known addresses of the other parties who are known or believed to have interests in the property but who were not so served. The applicant may serve parties whom the plaintiff has been unable to serve. Parties served in the manner provided in Section 1255.450 shall have no claim against the plaintiff for compensation to the extent of the amount withdrawn by all applicants. The plaintiff shall remain liable to parties having an interest of record who are not so served but, if such liability is enforced, the plaintiff shall be subrogated to the rights of such parties under Section 1255.280.
(d) If any party objects to the withdrawal, or if the plaintiff so requests, the court shall determine, upon hearing, the amounts to be withdrawn, if any, and by whom.
Added by Stats. 1975, Ch. 1275.

Section 1255.240 - Undertaking required of defendant prior to withdrawal
(a) If the court determines that an applicant is entitled to withdraw any portion of a deposit that another party claims or to which another person may be entitled, the court may require the applicant, before withdrawing such portion, to file an undertaking. The undertaking shall secure payment to such party or person of any amount withdrawn that exceeds the amount to which the applicant is entitled as finally determined in the proceeding, together with interest as provided in Section 1255.280. If withdrawal is permitted notwithstanding the lack of personal service of the application for withdrawal upon any party to the proceeding, the court may also require that the undertaking indemnify the plaintiff against any liability it may incur under Section 1255.230. The undertaking shall be in such amount as is fixed by the court, but if executed by an admitted surety insurer the amount shall not exceed the portion claimed by the adverse claimant or appearing to belong to another person. If executed by two or more sufficient sureties, the amount shall not exceed double such portion.
(b) If the undertaking is required primarily because of an issue as to title between the applicant and another party or person, the applicant filing the undertaking is not entitled to recover the premium reasonably paid for the undertaking as a part of the recoverable costs in the eminent domain proceeding.
Amended by Stats. 1982, Ch. 517, Sec. 182.

Section 1255.250 - Undertaking if amount withdrawn exceeds amount of original deposit
(a) If the amount originally deposited is increased pursuant to Section 1255.030 and the total amount sought to be withdrawn exceeds the amount of the original deposit, the applicant, or each applicant if there are two or more, shall file an undertaking. The undertaking shall be in favor of the plaintiff and shall secure repayment of any amount withdrawn that exceeds the amount to which the applicant is entitled as finally determined in the eminent domain proceeding, together with interest as provided in Section 1255.280. If the undertaking is executed by an admitted surety insurer, the undertaking shall be in the amount by which the total amount to be withdrawn exceeds the amount originally deposited. If the undertaking is executed by two or more sufficient sureties, the undertaking shall be in double such amount, but the maximum amount that may be recovered from such sureties is the amount by which the total amount to be withdrawn exceeds the amount originally deposited.
(b) If there are two or more applicants, the applicants, in lieu of filing separate undertakings, may jointly file a single undertaking in the amount required by subdivision (a).
Amended by Stats. 1982, Ch. 517, Sec. 183.

Section 1255.260 - Waiver of claims and defenses
If any portion of the money deposited pursuant to this chapter is withdrawn, the receipt of any such money shall constitute a waiver by operation of law of all claims and defenses in favor of the persons receiving such payment except a claim for greater compensation.
Added by Stats. 1975, Ch. 1275.

Section 1255.280 - Withdrawal in amount in excess of amount party entitled
(a) Any amount withdrawn by a party pursuant to this article in excess of the amount to which he is entitled as finally determined in the eminent domain proceeding shall be paid to the parties entitled thereto. The court shall enter judgment accordingly.
(b) The judgment so entered shall not include interest except in the following cases:
(1) Any amount that is to be paid to a defendant shall include legal interest from the date of its withdrawal by another defendant.
(2) If the amount originally deposited by a plaintiff was increased pursuant to Section 1255.030 on motion of a party obligated to pay under this section, any amount that is attributable to such increase and that is to be repaid to the plaintiff shall include legal interest from the date of its withdrawal.
(c) If the judgment so entered is not paid within 30 days after its entry, the court may, on motion, enter judgment against the sureties, if any, for the amount of such judgment.
(d) The court may, in its discretion and with such security, if any, as it deems appropriate, grant a party obligated to pay under this section a stay of execution for any amount to be paid to a plaintiff. Such stay of execution shall not exceed one year following entry of judgment under this section.
Added by Stats. 1975, Ch. 1275.

Article 3 - POSSESSION PRIOR TO JUDGMENT

Section 1255.410 - Motion for possession
(a) At the time of filing the complaint or at any time after filing the complaint and prior to entry of judgment, the plaintiff may move the court for an order for possession under this article, demonstrating that the plaintiff is entitled to take the property by eminent domain and has deposited pursuant to Article 1 (commencing with Section 1255.010) an amount that satisfies the requirements of that article. The motion shall describe the property of which the plaintiff is seeking to take possession, which description may be by reference to the complaint, and shall state the date after which the plaintiff is seeking to take possession of the property. The motion shall include a statement substantially in the following form: "You have the right to oppose this motion for an order of possession of your property. If you oppose this motion you must serve the plaintiff and file with the court a written opposition to the motion within 30 days from the date you were served with this motion." If the written opposition asserts a hardship, it shall be supported by a declaration signed under penalty of perjury stating facts supporting the hardship.
(b) The plaintiff shall serve a copy of the motion on the record owner of the property and on the occupants, if any. The plaintiff shall set the court hearing on the motion not less than 60 days after service of the notice of motion on the record owner of unoccupied property. If the property is lawfully occupied by a person dwelling thereon or by a farm or business operation, service of the notice of motion shall be made not less than 90 days prior to the hearing on the motion.
(c) Not later than 30 days after service of the plaintiff's motion seeking to take possession of the property, any defendant or occupant of the property may oppose the motion in writing by serving the plaintiff and filing with the court the opposition. If the written opposition asserts a hardship, it shall be supported by a declaration signed under penalty of perjury stating facts supporting the hardship. The plaintiff shall serve and file any reply to the opposition not less than 15 days before the hearing.

(d)

(1) If the motion is not opposed within 30 days of service on each defendant and occupant of the property, the court shall make an order for possession of the property if the court finds each of the following:

(A) The plaintiff is entitled to take the property by eminent domain.

(B) The plaintiff has deposited pursuant to Article 1 (commencing with Section 1255.010) an amount that satisfies the requirements of that article.

(2) If the motion is opposed by a defendant or occupant within 30 days of service, the court may make an order for possession of the property upon consideration of the relevant facts and any opposition, and upon completion of a hearing on the motion, if the court finds each of the following:

(A) The plaintiff is entitled to take the property by eminent domain.

(B) The plaintiff has deposited pursuant to Article 1 (commencing with Section 1255.010) an amount that satisfies the requirements of that article.

(C) There is an overriding need for the plaintiff to possess the property prior to the issuance of final judgment in the case, and the plaintiff will suffer a substantial hardship if the application for possession is denied or limited.

(D) The hardship that the plaintiff will suffer if possession is denied or limited outweighs any hardship on the defendant or occupant that would be caused by the granting of the order of possession.

(e)

(1) Notwithstanding the time limits for notice prescribed by this section and Section 1255.450, a court may issue an order of possession upon an ex parte application by a water, wastewater, gas, electric, or telephone utility, as the court deems appropriate under the circumstances of the case, if the court finds each of the following:

(A) An emergency exists and as a consequence the utility has an urgent need for possession of the property. For purposes of this section, an emergency is defined to include, but is not limited to, a utility's urgent need to protect the public's health and safety or the reliability of utility service.

(B) An emergency order of possession will not displace or unreasonably affect any person in actual and lawful possession of the property to be taken or the larger parcel of which it is a part.

(2) Not later than 30 days after service of the order authorizing the plaintiff to take possession of the property, any defendant or occupant of the property may move for relief from an emergency order of possession that has been issued under this subdivision. The court may modify, stay, or vacate the order upon consideration of the relevant facts and any objections raised, and upon completion of a hearing if requested.

Amended by Stats 2007 ch 436 (SB 698),s 1, eff. 1/1/2008.
Amended by Stats 2006 ch 594 (SB 1210),s 3, eff. 1/1/2007.

Section 1255.420 - [Repealed]
Repealed by Stats 2006 ch 594 (SB 1210),s 4, eff. 1/1/2007.

Section 1255.430 - [Repealed]
Repealed by Stats 2006 ch 594 (SB 1210),s 5, eff. 1/1/2007.

Section 1255.440 - Conditions specified in order not satisfied
If an order has been made under Section 1255.410 authorizing the plaintiff to take possession of property and the court subsequently determines that the conditions specified in Section 1255.410 for issuance of the order are not satisfied, the court shall vacate the order.
Added by Stats. 1975, Ch. 1275.

Section 1255.450 - Service of copy of order
(a) As used in this section, "record owner" means the owner of the legal or equitable title to the fee or any lesser interest in property as shown by recorded deeds or other recorded instruments.

(b) The plaintiff shall serve a copy of the order for possession issued under Section 1255.410 on the record owner of the property and on the occupants, if any. If the property is lawfully occupied by a person dwelling thereon or by a farm or business operation, service shall be made not less than 30 days prior to the time possession is to be taken pursuant to the order. In all other cases, service shall be made not less than 10 days prior to the time possession is to be taken pursuant to the order. Service may be made with or following service of summons.

(c) At least 30 days prior to the time possession is taken pursuant to an order for possession made pursuant to Section 1255.040, 1255.050, or 1255.460, the plaintiff shall serve a copy of the order on the record owner of the property and on the occupants, if any.

(d) Service of the order shall be made by personal service except that:

(1) If the person on whom service is to be made has previously appeared in the proceeding or been served with summons in the proceeding, service of the order may be made by mail upon that person and his or her attorney of record, if any.

(2) If the person on whom service is to be made resides out of the state, or has departed from the state or cannot with due diligence be found within the state, service of the order may be made by registered or certified mail addressed to that person at his or her last known address.

(e) When the record owner cannot be located, the court may, for good cause shown on ex parte application, authorize the plaintiff to take possession of unoccupied property without serving a copy of the order for possession upon a record owner.

(f) A single service upon or mailing to one of several persons having a common business or residence address is sufficient.

Amended by Stats 2006 ch 594 (SB 1210),s 6, eff. 1/1/2007.

Section 1255.460 - Requirements of order of possession
An order for possession issued pursuant to Section 1255.410 shall:

(a) Recite that it has been made under this section.

(b) Describe the property to be acquired, which description may be by reference to the complaint.

(c) State the date after which plaintiff is authorized to take possession of the property.

Amended by Stats 2006 ch 594 (SB 1210),s 7, eff. 1/1/2007.

Section 1255.470 - Rights not waived
By taking possession pursuant to this chapter, the plaintiff does not waive the right to appeal from the judgment, the right to move to abandon, or the right to request a new trial.
Added by Stats. 1975, Ch. 1275.

Section 1255.480 - Right of public entity to exercise police power
Nothing in this article limits the right of a public entity to exercise its police power in emergency situations.
Added by Stats. 1975, Ch. 1275.

Chapter 7 - DISCOVERY; EXCHANGE OF VALUATION DATA
Article 1 - DISCOVERY

Section 1258.010 - Provisions supplemental
The provisions of this chapter supplement but do not replace, restrict, or prevent the use of discovery procedures or limit the matters that are discoverable in eminent domain proceedings.

Added by Stats. 1975, Ch. 1275.

Section 1258.020 - Discovery after time of exchange; order to protect from annoyance, embarrassment or oppression

(a) Notwithstanding any other statute or any court rule relating to discovery, proceedings pursuant to subdivision (b) may be had without requirement of court order and may proceed until not later than 20 days prior to the day set for trial of the issue of compensation.

(b) A party to an exchange of lists of expert witnesses and statements of valuation data pursuant to Article 2 (commencing with Section 1258.210) or pursuant to court rule as provided in Section 1258.300 may after the time of the exchange obtain discovery from the other party to the exchange and from any person listed by him as an expert witness.

(c) The court, upon noticed motion by the person subjected to discovery pursuant to subdivision (b), may make any order that justice requires to protect such person from annoyance, embarrassment, or oppression.

Amended by Stats. 1992, Ch. 876, Sec. 8. Effective January 1, 1993.

Section 1258.030 - Evidence not otherwise admissible not admissible

Nothing in this chapter makes admissible any evidence that is not otherwise admissible or permits a witness to base an opinion on any matter that is not a proper basis for such an opinion.

Added by Stats. 1975, Ch. 1275.

Article 2 - EXCHANGE OF VALUATION DATA

Section 1258.210 - Demand to exchange lists of expert witnesses and statement of valuation data

(a) Not later than the 10th day after the trial date is selected, any party may file and serve on any other party a demand to exchange lists of expert witnesses and statements of valuation data. Thereafter, the court may, upon noticed motion and a showing of good cause, permit any party to serve such a demand upon any other party.

(b) The demand shall:

(1) Describe the property to which it relates, which description may be by reference to the complaint.

(2) Include a statement in substantially the following form: "You are required to serve and deposit with the clerk of court a list of expert witnesses and statements of valuation data in compliance with Article 2 (commencing with Section 1258.210) of Chapter 7 of Title 7 of Part 3 of the Code of Civil Procedure not later than the date of exchange to be set in accordance with that article. Except as otherwise provided in that article, your failure to do so will constitute a waiver of your right to call unlisted expert witnesses during your case in chief and of your right to introduce on direct examination during your case in chief any matter that is required to be, but is not, set forth in your statements of valuation data."

Added by Stats. 1975, Ch. 1275.

Section 1258.220 - Date of exchange

(a) For the purposes of this article, the "date of exchange" is the date agreed to for the exchange of their lists of expert witnesses and statements of valuation data by the party who served a demand and the party on whom the demand was served or, failing agreement, a date 90 days prior to commencement of the trial on the issue of compensation or the date set by the court on noticed motion of either party establishing good cause therefor.

(b) Notwithstanding subdivision (a), unless otherwise agreed to by the parties, the date of exchange shall not be earlier than nine months after the date of commencement of the proceeding.

Amended by Stats 2001 ch 428 (AB 237), s 7, eff. 1/1/2002.

Previously Amended July 13, 1999 (Bill Number: SB 634) (Chapter 102).

Section 1258.230 - Duties of parties not later than date of exchange

(a) Not later than the date of exchange:

(1) Each party who served a demand and each party upon whom a demand was served shall deposit with the clerk of the court a list of expert witnesses and statements of valuation data.

(2) A party who served a demand shall serve his list and statements upon each party on whom he served his demand.

(3) Each party on whom a demand was served shall serve his list and statements upon the party who served the demand.

(b) The clerk of the court shall make an entry in the register of actions for each list of expert witnesses and statement of valuation data deposited with him pursuant to this article. The lists and statements shall not be filed in the proceeding, but the clerk shall make them available to the court at the commencement of the trial for the limited purpose of enabling the court to apply the provisions of this article. Unless the court otherwise orders, the clerk shall, at the conclusion of the trial, return all lists and statements to the attorneys for the parties who deposited them. Lists or statements ordered by the court to be retained may thereafter be destroyed or otherwise disposed of in accordance with the provisions of law governing the destruction or disposition of exhibits introduced in the trial.

Added by Stats. 1975, Ch. 1275.

Section 1258.240 - Information included in lists of expert witnesses

The list of expert witnesses shall include the name, business or residence address, and business, occupation, or profession of each person intended to be called as an expert witness by the party and a statement of the subject matter to which his testimony relates.

Added by Stats. 1975, Ch. 1275.

Section 1258.250 - Statement of valuation data exchanged for each person party intents to call as witness

A statement of valuation data shall be exchanged for each person the party intends to call as a witness to testify to his opinion as to any of the following matters:

(a) The value of the property being taken.

(b) The amount of the damage, if any, to the remainder of the larger parcel from which such property is taken.

(c) The amount of the benefit, if any, to the remainder of the larger parcel from which such property is taken.

(d) The amount of any other compensation required to be paid by Chapter 9 (commencing with Section 1263.010) or Chapter 10 (commencing with Section 1265.010).

Added by Stats. 1975, Ch. 1275.

Section 1258.260 - Information included in state of valuation data

(a) The statement of valuation data shall give the name and business or residence address of the witness and shall include a statement whether the witness will testify to an opinion as to any of the matters listed in Section 1258.250 and, as to each matter upon which the witness will give an opinion, what that opinion is and the following items to the extent that the opinion is based on them:

(1) The interest being valued.

(2) The date of valuation used by the witness.

(3) The highest and best use of the property.

(4) The applicable zoning and the opinion of the witness as to the probability of any change in zoning.

(5) The sales, contracts to sell and purchase, and leases supporting the opinion.

(6) The cost of reproduction or replacement of the existing improvements on the property, the depreciation or obsolescence the improvements have suffered, and the method of calculation used to determine depreciation.

(7) The gross income from the property, the deductions from gross income, and the resulting net income; the reasonable net rental value attributable to the land and existing improvements, and the estimated gross rental income and deductions upon which the reasonable net rental value is computed; the rate of capitalization used; and the value indicated by the capitalization.

(8) If the property is a portion of a larger parcel, a description of the larger parcel and its value.

(9) If the opinion concerns loss of goodwill, the method used to determine the loss, and a summary of the data supporting the opinion.

(b) With respect to each sale, contract, or lease listed under paragraph (5) of subdivision (a), the statement of valuation data shall give:

(1) The names and business or residence addresses, if known, of the parties to the transaction.

(2) The location of the property subject to the transaction.

(3) The date of the transaction.

(4) If recorded, the date of recording and the volume and page or other identification of the record of the transaction.

(5) The price and other terms and circumstances of the transaction. In lieu of stating the terms contained in any contract, lease, or other document, the statement may, if the document is available for inspection by the adverse party, state the place where and the times when it is available for inspection.

(6) The total area and shape of the property subject to the transaction.

(c) If any opinion referred to in Section 1258.250 is based in whole or in substantial part upon the opinion of another person, the statement of valuation data shall include the name and business or residence address of that other person, his business, occupation, or profession, and a statement as to the subject matter to which his or her opinion relates.

(d) Except when an appraisal report is used as a statement of valuation data as permitted by subdivision (e), the statement of valuation data shall include a statement, signed by the witness, that the witness has read the statement of valuation data and that it fairly and correctly states his or her opinions and knowledge as to the matters therein stated.

(e) An appraisal report that has been prepared by the witness which includes the information required to be included in a statement of valuation data may be used as a statement of valuation data under this article.

Amended by Stats 2001 ch 428 (AB 237), s 8, eff. 1/1/2002.

Section 1258.270 - Notice to parties upon whom lists and statements served required

(a) A party who is required to exchange lists of expert witnesses and statements of valuation data shall diligently give notice to the parties upon whom his list and statements were served if, after service of his list and statements, he:

(1) Determines to call an expert witness not included in his list of expert witnesses to testify on direct examination during his case in chief;

(2) Determines to have a witness called by him testify on direct examination during his case in chief to any opinion or data required to be listed in the statement of valuation data for that witness but which was not so listed; or

(3) Discovers any data required to be listed in a statement of valuation data but which was not so listed.

(b) The notice required by subdivision (a) shall include the information specified in Sections 1258.240 and 1258.260 and shall be in writing; but such notice is not required to be in writing if it is given after the commencement of the trial.

Added by Stats. 1975, Ch. 1275.

Section 1258.280 - Objection of party who has served list and statement

Except as provided in Section 1258.290, upon objection of a party who has served his list of expert witnesses and statements of valuation data in compliance with Section 1258.230:

(a) No party required to serve a list of expert witnesses on the objecting party may call an expert witness to testify on direct examination during his case in chief unless the information required by Section 1258.240 for such witness is included in the list served.

(b) No party required to serve statements of valuation data on the objecting party may call a witness to testify on direct examination during his case in chief to his opinion on any matter listed in Section 1258.250 unless a statement of valuation data for such witness was served.

(c) No witness called by a party required to serve statements of valuation data on the objecting party may testify on direct examination during the case in chief of the party who called him to any opinion or data required to be listed in the statement of valuation data for such witness unless such opinion or data is listed in the statement served except that testimony that is merely an explanation or elaboration of data so listed is not inadmissible under this subdivision.

Added by Stats. 1975, Ch. 1275.

Section 1258.290 - Witness, opinion or data not included in party's list or statement

(a) The court may, upon such terms as may be just (including but not limited to continuing the trial for a reasonable period of time and awarding costs and litigation expenses), permit a party to call a witness, or permit a witness called by a party to testify to an opinion or data on direct examination, during the party's case in chief where such witness, opinion, or data is required to be, but is not, included in such party's list of expert witnesses or statements of valuation data if the court finds that such party has made a good faith effort to comply with Sections 1258.210 to 1258.260, inclusive, that he has complied with Section 1258.270, and that by the date of exchange he:

(1) Would not in the exercise of reasonable diligence have determined to call such witness or discovered or listed such opinion or data; or

(2) Failed to determine to call such witness or to discover or list such opinion or data through mistake, inadvertence, surprise, or excusable neglect.

(b) In making a determination under this section, the court shall take into account the extent to which the opposing party has relied upon the list of expert witnesses and statements of valuation data and will be prejudiced if the witness is called or the testimony concerning such opinion or data is given.

Added by Stats. 1975, Ch. 1275.

Section 1258.300 - Court rule providing for exchange of valuation data in lieu of procedure provided for in article

The superior court in any county may provide by court rule a procedure for the exchange of valuation data which shall be used in lieu of the procedure provided by this article if the Judicial Council finds that such procedure serves the same purpose and is an adequate substitute for the procedure provided by this article.

Added by Stats. 1975, Ch. 1275.

Chapter 8 - PROCEDURES FOR DETERMINING RIGHT TO TAKE AND COMPENSATION

Article 1 - GENERAL PROVISIONS

Section 1260.010 - Precedence over other civil actions

Proceedings under this title take precedence over all other civil actions in the matter of setting the same for hearing or trial in order that such proceedings shall be quickly heard and determined.

Added by Stats. 1975, Ch. 1275.

Section 1260.020 - Determination whether public uses comparable if proceedings to acquire same property consolidated

(a) If proceedings to acquire the same property are consolidated, the court shall first determine whether the public uses for which the property is sought are compatible within the meaning of Article 6 (commencing with Section 1240.510) of Chapter 3. If the court determines that the uses are compatible, it shall permit the proceeding to continue with the plaintiffs acting jointly. The court shall apportion the obligation to pay any award in the proceeding in proportion to the use, damage, and benefits attributable to each plaintiff.

(b) If the court determines pursuant to subdivision (a) that the uses are not all compatible, it shall further determine which of the uses is the more necessary public use within the meaning of Article 7 (commencing with Section 1240.610) of Chapter 3. The court shall permit the plaintiff alleging the more necessary public use, along with any other plaintiffs alleging compatible public uses under subdivision (a), to continue the proceeding. The court shall dismiss the proceeding as to the other plaintiffs.
Added by Stats. 1975, Ch. 1275.

Section 1260.030 - Determination as to whether property improvement pertaining to realty
(a) If there is a dispute between plaintiff and defendant whether particular property is an improvement pertaining to the realty, either party may, not later than 30 days prior to the date specified in an order for possession of the property, move the court for a determination whether the property is an improvement pertaining to the realty.
(b) A motion under this section shall be heard not sooner than 10 days and not later than 20 days after service of notice of the motion. At the hearing, the court may consider any relevant evidence, including a view of the premises and property, in making its determinations.
Added by Stats. 1975, Ch. 1275.

Section 1260.040 - Motion for ruling on issue of compensation
(a) If there is a dispute between plaintiff and defendant over an evidentiary or other legal issue affecting the determination of compensation, either party may move the court for a ruling on the issue. The motion shall be made not later than 60 days before commencement of trial on the issue of compensation. The motion shall be heard by the judge assigned for trial of the case.
(b) Notwithstanding any other statute or rule of court governing the date of final offers and demands of the parties and the date of trial of an eminent domain proceeding, the court may postpone those dates for a period sufficient to enable the parties to engage in further proceedings before trial in response to its ruling on the motion.
(c) This section supplements, and does not replace any other pretrial or trial procedure otherwise available to resolve an evidentiary or other legal issue affecting the determination of compensation.
Added by Stats 2001 ch 428 (AB 237), s 9, eff. 1/1/2002.

Article 2 - CONTESTING RIGHT TO TAKE

Section 1260.110 - Hearing objections
(a) Where objections to the right to take are raised, unless the court orders otherwise, they shall be heard and determined prior to the determination of the issue of compensation.
(b) The court may, on motion of any party, after notice and hearing, specially set such objections for trial.
Added by Stats. 1975, Ch. 1275.

Section 1260.120 - Orders upon hearing and determining objections
(a) The court shall hear and determine all objections to the right to take.
(b) If the court determines that the plaintiff has the right to acquire by eminent domain the property described in the complaint, the court shall so order.
(c) If the court determines that the plaintiff does not have the right to acquire by eminent domain any property described in the complaint, it shall order either of the following:
  (1) Immediate dismissal of the proceeding as to that property.
  (2) Conditional dismissal of the proceeding as to that property unless such corrective and remedial action as the court may prescribe has been taken within the period prescribed by the court in the order. An order made under this paragraph may impose such limitations and conditions as the court determines to be just under the circumstances of the particular case including the requirement that the plaintiff pay to the defendant all or part of the reasonable litigation expenses necessarily incurred by the defendant because of the plaintiff's failure or omission which constituted the basis of the objection to the right to take.
Added by Stats. 1975, Ch. 1275.

Article 3 - PROCEDURES RELATING TO DETERMINATION OF COMPENSATION

Section 1260.210 - Generally
(a) The defendant shall present his evidence on the issue of compensation first and shall commence and conclude the argument.
(b) Except as otherwise provided by statute, neither the plaintiff nor the defendant has the burden of proof on the issue of compensation.
Added by Stats. 1975, Ch. 1275.

Section 1260.220 - Divided interests in property acquired
(a) Except as provided in subdivision (b), where there are divided interests in property acquired by eminent domain, the value of each interest and the injury, if any, to the remainder of such interest shall be separately assessed and compensation awarded therefor.
(b) The plaintiff may require that the amount of compensation be first determined as between plaintiff and all defendants claiming an interest in the property. Thereafter, in the same proceeding, the trier of fact shall determine the respective rights of the defendants in and to the amount of compensation awarded and shall apportion the award accordingly. Nothing in this subdivision limits the right of a defendant to present during the first stage of the proceeding evidence of the value of, or injury to, the property or the defendant's interest in the property; and the right of a defendant to present evidence during the second stage of the proceeding is not affected by the failure to exercise the right to present evidence during the first stage of the proceeding.
Amended by Stats. 1978, Ch. 294.

Section 1260.230 - Issues separately assessed by trier of fact
As far as practicable, the trier of fact shall assess separately each of the following:
(a) Compensation for the property taken as required by Article 4 (commencing with Section 1263.310) of Chapter 9.
(b) When the property acquired is part of a larger parcel:
  (1) The amount of the damage, if any, to the remainder as required by Article 5 (commencing with Section 1263.410) of Chapter 9.
  (2) The amount of the benefit, if any, to the remainder as required by Article 5 (commencing with Section 1263.410) of Chapter 9.
(c) Compensation for loss of goodwill, if any, as required by Article 6 (commencing with Section 1263.510) of Chapter 9.
(d) Compensation claimed under subdivision (c) of Section 1250.320.
(e) Compensation claimed under subdivision (d) of Section 1250.320.
Amended by Stats 2021 ch 401 (AB 1578),s 6, eff. 1/1/2022.
Added by Stats. 1975, Ch. 1275.

Section 1260.240 - Determination when unknown persons or deceased persons properly joined as defendants
Where any persons unknown or any deceased persons or the heirs and devisees of any deceased persons have been properly joined as defendants but have not appeared either personally or by a personal representative, the court shall determine the extent of the interests of such defendants in the property taken or in the remainder if the property taken is part of a larger parcel and the compensation to be awarded for such interests. The court may determine the extent and value of the interests of all such defendants in the aggregate without apportionment between the respective defendants. In any event, in the case of deceased persons, the court shall determine only the extent and value of the interest of the decedent and shall not determine the extent and value of the separate interests of the heirs and devisees in such decedent's interest.

Added by Stats. 1975, Ch. 1275.

Section 1260.250 - Court order directing county auditor and tax collector to certify information; information required to be certified

(a) In a county where both the auditor and the tax collector are elected officials, the court shall by order give the auditor or tax collector the legal description of the property sought to be taken and direct the auditor or tax collector to certify to the court the information required by subdivision (c), and the auditor or tax collector shall promptly certify the required information to the court. In all other counties, the court shall by order give the tax collector the legal description of the property sought to be taken and direct the tax collector to certify to the court the information required by subdivision (c), and the tax collector shall promptly certify the required information to the court.

(b) The court order shall be made on or before the earliest of the following dates:

(1) The date the court makes an order for possession.

(2) The date set for trial.

(3) The date of entry of judgment.

(c) The court order shall require certification of the following information:

(1) The current assessed value of the property together with its assessed identification number.

(2) All unpaid taxes on the property, and any penalties and costs that have accrued thereon while on the secured roll, levied for prior tax years that constitute a lien on the property.

(3) All unpaid taxes on the property, and any penalties and costs that have accrued thereon while on the secured roll, levied for the current tax year that constitute a lien on the property prorated to, but not including, the date of apportionment determined pursuant to Section 5082 of the Revenue and Taxation Code or the date of trial, whichever is earlier. If the amount of the current taxes is not ascertainable at the time of proration, the amount shall be estimated and computed based on the assessed value for the current assessment year and the tax rate levied on the property for the immediately prior tax year.

(4) The actual or estimated amount of taxes on the property that are or will become a lien on the property in the next succeeding tax year prorated to, but not including, the date of apportionment determined pursuant to Section 5082 of the Revenue and Taxation Code or the date of trial, whichever is earlier. Any estimated amount of taxes shall be computed based on the assessed value of the property for the current assessment year and the tax rate levied on the property for the current tax year.

(5) The amount of the taxes, penalties, and costs allocable to one day of the current tax year, and where applicable, the amount allocable to one day of the next succeeding tax year, hereinafter referred to as the "daily prorate."

(6) The total of paragraphs (2), (3), and (4).

(d) If the property sought to be taken does not have a separate valuation on the assessment roll, the information required by this section shall be for the larger parcel of which the property is a part.

(e) The court, as part of the judgment, shall separately state the amount certified pursuant to this section and order that the amount be paid to the tax collector from the award. If the amount so certified is prorated to the date of trial, the order shall include, in addition to the amount so certified, an amount equal to the applicable daily prorate multiplied by the number of days commencing on the date of trial and ending on and including the day before the date of apportionment determined pursuant to Section 5082 of the Revenue and Taxation Code.

(f) Notwithstanding any other provision of this section, if the board of supervisors provides the procedure set forth in Section 5087 of the Revenue and Taxation Code, the court shall make no award of taxes in the judgment.

Amended 10/10/1999 (Bill Number: AB 1672) (Chapter 892).

Chapter 9 - COMPENSATION

Article 1 - GENERAL PROVISIONS

Section 1263.010 - Owner of property acquired entitled to compensation

(a) The owner of property acquired by eminent domain is entitled to compensation as provided in this chapter.

(b) Nothing in this chapter affects any rights the owner of property acquired by eminent domain may have under any other statute. In any case where two or more statutes provide compensation for the same loss, the person entitled to compensation may be paid only once for that loss.

Added by Stats. 1975, Ch. 1275.

Section 1263.015 - Agreement with owner specifying manner of payment

At the request of an owner of property acquired by eminent domain, the public entity may enter into an agreement with the owner specifying the manner of payment of compensation to which the owner is entitled as the result of the acquisition. The agreement may provide that the compensation shall be paid by the public entity to the owner over a period not to exceed 10 years from the date the owner's right to compensation accrues. The agreement may also provide for the payment of interest by the public entity; however, the rate of interest agreed upon may not exceed the maximum rate authorized by Section 16731 or 53531 of the Government Code, as applicable, in connection with the issuance of bonds.

Added by Stats. 1982, Ch. 1368, Sec. 1.

Section 1263.020 - Date right to compensation deemed to have accrued

Except as otherwise provided by law, the right to compensation shall be deemed to have accrued at the date of filing the complaint.

Added by Stats. 1975, Ch. 1275.

Section 1263.025 - Independent appraisal of property public entity offers to purchase under threat of eminent domain

(a) A public entity shall offer to pay the reasonable costs, not to exceed five thousand dollars ($5,000), of an independent appraisal ordered by the owner of a property that the public entity offers to purchase under a threat of eminent domain, at the time the public entity makes the offer to purchase the property. The independent appraisal shall be conducted by an appraiser licensed by the Office of Real Estate Appraisers.

(b) For purposes of this section, an offer to purchase a property "under a threat of eminent domain" is an offer to purchase a property pursuant to any of the following:

(1) Eminent domain.

(2) Following adoption of a resolution of necessity for the property pursuant to Section 1240.040.

(3) Following a statement that the public entity may take the property by eminent domain.

Added by Stats 2006 ch 594 (SB 1210), s 8, eff. 1/1/2007.

Article 2 - DATE OF VALUATION

Section 1263.110 - Date on which deposit made; deposit not deemed to have been made

(a) Unless an earlier date of valuation is applicable under this article, if the plaintiff deposits the probable compensation in accordance with Article 1 (commencing with Section 1255.010) of Chapter 6 or the amount of the award in accordance with Article 2 (commencing with Section 1268.110) of Chapter 11, the date of valuation is the date on which the deposit is made.

(b) Whether or not the plaintiff has taken possession of the property or obtained an order for possession, if the court determines pursuant to Section 1255.030 that the probable amount of compensation exceeds the amount previously deposited pursuant to Article 1 (commencing with Section 1255.010) of Chapter 6 and the amount on deposit is not increased accordingly within the time allowed under Section 1255.030, no deposit shall be deemed to have been made for the purpose of this section.

Added by Stats. 1975, Ch. 1275.

Section 1263.120 - Issued brought to trial within one year after commencement of proceeding
If the issue of compensation is brought to trial within one year after commencement of the proceeding, the date of valuation is the date of commencement of the proceeding.
Added by Stats. 1975, Ch. 1275.

Section 1263.130 - Issue not brought to trial within one year after commencement of proceeding
Subject to Section 1263.110, if the issue of compensation is not brought to trial within one year after commencement of the proceeding, the date of valuation is the date of the commencement of the trial unless the delay is caused by the defendant, in which case the date of valuation is the date of commencement of the proceeding.
Added by Stats. 1975, Ch. 1275.

Section 1263.140 - New trial ordered but not commenced within one year after commencement of proceeding
Subject to Section 1263.110, if a new trial is ordered by the trial or appellate court and the new trial is not commenced within one year after the commencement of the proceeding, the date of valuation is the date of the commencement of such new trial unless, in the interest of justice, the court ordering the new trial orders a different date of valuation.
Added by Stats. 1975, Ch. 1275.

Section 1263.150 - Mistrial declared and retrial not commenced within one year after commencement of proceeding
Subject to Section 1263.110, if a mistrial is declared and the retrial is not commenced within one year after the commencement of the proceeding, the date of valuation is the date of the commencement of the retrial of the case unless, in the interest of justice, the court declaring the mistrial orders a different date of valuation.
Added by Stats. 1975, Ch. 1275.

Article 3 - COMPENSATION FOR IMPROVEMENTS

Section 1263.205 - Improvements pertaining to the realty defined; determining whether property can be removed without substantial economic loss
(a) As used in this article, "improvements pertaining to the realty" include any machinery or equipment installed for use on property taken by eminent domain, or on the remainder if such property is part of a larger parcel, that cannot be removed without a substantial economic loss or without substantial damage to the property on which it is installed, regardless of the method of installation.
(b) In determining whether particular property can be removed "without a substantial economic loss" within the meaning of this section, the value of the property in place considered as a part of the realty should be compared with its value if it were removed and sold.
Added by Stats. 1975, Ch. 1275.

Section 1263.210 - All improvements taken into account in determining compensation
(a) Except as otherwise provided by statute, all improvements pertaining to the realty shall be taken into account in determining compensation.
(b) Subdivision (a) applies notwithstanding the right or obligation of a tenant, as against the owner of any other interest in real property, to remove such improvement at the expiration of his term.
Added by Stats. 1975, Ch. 1275.

Section 1263.230 - Removed or destroyed improvements not taken into account
(a) Improvements pertaining to the realty shall not be taken into account in determining compensation to the extent that they are removed or destroyed before the earliest of the following times:
   (1) The time the plaintiff takes title to the property.
   (2) The time the plaintiff takes possession of the property.
   (3) If the defendant moves from the property in compliance with an order for possession, the date specified in the order; except that, if the defendant so moves prior to such date and gives the plaintiff written notice thereof, the date 24 hours after such notice is received by the plaintiff.
(b) Where improvements pertaining to the realty are removed or destroyed by the defendant at any time, such improvements shall not be taken into account in determining compensation. Where such removal or destruction damages the remaining property, such damage shall be taken into account in determining compensation to the extent it reduces the value of the remaining property.
Added by Stats. 1975, Ch. 1275.

Section 1263.240 - Improvement made subsequent to date of service of summons
Improvements pertaining to the realty made subsequent to the date of service of summons shall not be taken into account in determining compensation unless one of the following is established:
(a) The improvement is one required to be made by a public utility to its utility system.
(b) The improvement is one made with the written consent of the plaintiff.
(c) The improvement is one authorized to be made by a court order issued after a noticed hearing and upon a finding by the court that the hardship to the defendant of not permitting the improvement outweighs the hardship to the plaintiff of permitting the improvement. The court may, at the time it makes an order under this subdivision authorizing the improvement to be made, limit the extent to which the improvement shall be taken into account in determining compensation.
Added by Stats. 1975, Ch. 1275.

Section 1263.250 - Defendant harvesting and marketing crops
(a) The acquisition of property by eminent domain shall not prevent the defendant from harvesting and marketing crops planted before or after the service of summons. If the plaintiff takes possession of the property at a time that prevents the defendant from harvesting and marketing the crops, the fair market value of the crops in place at the date the plaintiff is authorized to take possession of the property shall be included in the compensation awarded for the property taken.
(b) Notwithstanding subdivision (a), the plaintiff may obtain a court order precluding the defendant from planting crops after service of summons, in which case the compensation awarded for the property taken shall include an amount sufficient to compensate for loss caused by the limitation on the defendant's right to use the property.
Added by Stats. 1975, Ch. 1275.

Section 1263.260 - Notice of election to remove improvements
Notwithstanding Section 1263.210, the owner of improvements pertaining to the realty may elect to remove any or all such improvements by serving on the plaintiff within 60 days after service of summons written notice of such election. If the plaintiff fails within 30 days thereafter to serve on the owner written notice of refusal to allow removal of such improvements, the owner may remove such improvements and shall be compensated for their reasonable removal and relocation cost not to exceed the market value of the improvements. Where such removal will cause damage to the structure in which the improvements are located, the defendant shall cause no more damage to the structure than is reasonably necessary in removing the improvements, and the structure shall be valued as if the removal had caused no damage to the structure.
Added by Stats. 1975, Ch. 1275.

Section 1263.270 - Improvement located in part upon property taken and in part upon property not taken
Where an improvement pertaining to the realty is located in part upon property taken and in part upon property not taken, the court may, on motion of any party and a determination that justice so requires, direct the plaintiff to acquire the entire improvement, including the part located

on property not taken, together with an easement or other interest reasonably necessary for the demolition, removal, or relocation of the improvement.
Added by Stats. 1975, Ch. 1275.

Article 4 - MEASURE OF COMPENSATION FOR PROPERTY TAKEN

Section 1263.310 - Measure of compensation fair market value
Compensation shall be awarded for the property taken. The measure of this compensation is the fair market value of the property taken.
Added by Stats. 1975, Ch. 1275.

Section 1263.320 - Fair market value defined; no relevant, comparable market
(a) The fair market value of the property taken is the highest price on the date of valuation that would be agreed to by a seller, being willing to sell but under no particular or urgent necessity for so doing, nor obliged to sell, and a buyer, being ready, willing, and able to buy but under no particular necessity for so doing, each dealing with the other with full knowledge of all the uses and purposes for which the property is reasonably adaptable and available.
(b) The fair market value of property taken for which there is no relevant, comparable market is its value on the date of valuation as determined by any method of valuation that is just and equitable.
Amended by Stats. 1992, Ch. 7, Sec. 2. Effective January 1, 1993.

Section 1263.321 - Determining value of nonprofit special use property
A just and equitable method of determining the value of nonprofit, special use property for which there is no relevant, comparable market is as set forth in Section 824 of the Evidence Code, but subject to the exceptions set forth in subdivision (c) of Section 824 of the Evidence Code.
Added by Stats. 1992, Ch. 7, Sec. 3. Effective January 1, 1993.

Section 1263.330 - Increase or decrease in value not included
The fair market value of the property taken shall not include any increase or decrease in the value of the property that is attributable to any of the following:
(a) The project for which the property is taken.
(b) The eminent domain proceeding in which the property is taken.
(c) Any preliminary actions of the plaintiff relating to the taking of the property.
Added by Stats. 1975, Ch. 1275.

Article 5 - COMPENSATION FOR INJURY TO REMAINDER

Section 1263.410 - Generally
(a) Where the property acquired is part of a larger parcel, in addition to the compensation awarded pursuant to Article 4 (commencing with Section 1263.310) for the part taken, compensation shall be awarded for the injury, if any, to the remainder.
(b) Compensation for injury to the remainder is the amount of the damage to the remainder reduced by the amount of the benefit to the remainder. If the amount of the benefit to the remainder equals or exceeds the amount of the damage to the remainder, no compensation shall be awarded under this article. If the amount of the benefit to the remainder exceeds the amount of damage to the remainder, such excess shall be deducted from the compensation provided in Section 1263.510, if any, but shall not be deducted from the compensation required to be awarded for the property taken or from the other compensation required by this chapter.
Added by Stats. 1975, Ch. 1275.

Section 1263.420 - Damage to remainder
Damage to the remainder is the damage, if any, caused to the remainder by either or both of the following:
(a) The severance of the remainder from the part taken.
(b) The construction and use of the project for which the property is taken in the manner proposed by the plaintiff whether or not the damage is caused by a portion of the project located on the part taken.
Added by Stats. 1975, Ch. 1275.

Section 1263.430 - Benefit to remainder
Benefit to the remainder is the benefit, if any, caused by the construction and use of the project for which the property is taken in the manner proposed by the plaintiff whether or not the benefit is caused by a portion of the project located on the part taken.
Added by Stats. 1975, Ch. 1275.

Section 1263.440 - Delay in time when damage or benefit actually realized; date of valuation base for determining amount of damage or benefit
(a) The amount of any damage to the remainder and any benefit to the remainder shall reflect any delay in the time when the damage or benefit caused by the construction and use of the project in the manner proposed by the plaintiff will actually be realized.
(b) The value of the remainder on the date of valuation, excluding prior changes in value as prescribed in Section 1263.330, shall serve as the base from which the amount of any damage and the amount of any benefit to the remainder shall be determined.
Added by Stats. 1975, Ch. 1275.

Section 1263.450 - Features mitigating damage or providing benefit
Compensation for injury to the remainder shall be based on the project as proposed. Any features of the project which mitigate the damage or provide benefit to the remainder, including but not limited to easements, crossings, underpasses, access roads, fencing, drainage facilities, and cattle guards, shall be taken into account in determining the compensation for injury to the remainder.
Added by Stats. 1975, Ch. 1275.

Article 6 - COMPENSATION FOR LOSS OF GOODWILL

Section 1263.510 - Proof required for compensation for loss; goodwill defined; leaseback agreement
(a) The owner of a business conducted on the property taken, or on the remainder if the property is part of a larger parcel, shall be compensated for loss of goodwill if the owner proves all of the following:
    (1) The loss is caused by the taking of the property or the injury to the remainder.
    (2) The loss cannot reasonably be prevented by a relocation of the business or by taking steps and adopting procedures that a reasonably prudent person would take and adopt in preserving the goodwill.
    (3) Compensation for the loss will not be included in payments under Section 7262 of the Government Code.
    (4) Compensation for the loss will not be duplicated in the compensation otherwise awarded to the owner.
(b) Within the meaning of this article, "goodwill" consists of the benefits that accrue to a business as a result of its location, reputation for dependability, skill or quality, and any other circumstances resulting in probable retention of old or acquisition of new patronage.
(c) If the public entity and the owner enter into a leaseback agreement pursuant to Section 1263.615, the following shall apply:
    (1) No additional goodwill shall accrue during the lease.
    (2) The entering of a leaseback agreement shall not be a factor in determining goodwill. Any liability for goodwill shall be established and paid at the time of acquisition of the property by eminent domain or subsequent to notice that the property may be taken by eminent domain.
Amended by Stats 2006 ch 602 (SB 1650),s 2, eff. 1/1/2007.

Section 1263.520 - State tax returns made available to plaintiff
The owner of a business who claims compensation under this article shall make available to the court, and the court shall, upon such terms and conditions as will preserve their confidentiality, make available to the plaintiff, the state tax returns of the business for audit for confidential use solely for the purpose of determining the amount of compensation under this article. Nothing in this section affects any right a party may otherwise have to discovery or to require the production of documents, papers, books, and accounts.
Added by Stats. 1975, Ch. 1275.

Section 1263.530 - Temporary interference with or interruption of business
Nothing in this article is intended to deal with compensation for inverse condemnation claims for temporary interference with or interruption of business.
Added by Stats. 1975, Ch. 1275.

Article 7 - MISCELLANEOUS PROVISIONS

Section 1263.610 - Agreement to relocate structure or carry work on property not taken
A public entity and the owner of property to be acquired for public use may make an agreement that the public entity will:
(a) Relocate for the owner any structure if such relocation is likely to reduce the amount of compensation otherwise payable to the owner by an amount equal to or greater than the cost of such relocation.
(b) Carry out for the owner any work on property not taken, including work on any structure, if the performance of the work is likely to reduce the amount of compensation otherwise payable to the owner by an amount equal to or greater than the cost of the work.
Added by Stats. 1975, Ch. 1275.

Section 1263.615 - One-year leaseback agreement offered to owner
(a) A public entity shall offer a one-year leaseback agreement to the owner of a property to be acquired by any method set forth in subdivision (b) for that property owner's continued use of the property upon acquisition, subject to the property owner's payment of fair market rents and compliance with other conditions set forth in subdivision (c), unless the public entity states in writing that the development, redevelopment, or use of the property for its stated public use is scheduled to begin within two years of its acquisition. This section shall not apply if the public entity states in writing that a leaseback of the property would create or allow the continuation of a public nuisance to the surrounding community.
(b) The following property acquisitions are subject to the requirements of this section:
(1) Any acquisition by a public entity pursuant to eminent domain.
(2) Any acquisition by a public entity following adoption of a resolution of necessity pursuant to Article 2 (commencing with Section 1245.210) of Chapter 4 for the property.
(3) Any acquisition by a public entity prior to the adoption of a resolution of necessity pursuant to Article 2 (commencing with Section 1245.210) of Chapter 4 for the property, but subsequent to a written notice that the public entity may take the property by eminent domain.
(c) The following conditions shall apply to any leaseback offered pursuant to this section:
(1) The lessee shall be responsible for any additional waste or nuisance on the property, and for any other liability arising from the continued use of the property.
(2) The lessor may demand a security deposit to cover any potential liability arising from the leaseback. The security deposit shall be reasonable in light of the use of the leased property.
(3) The lessor shall be indemnified from any legal liability and attorney's fees resulting from any lawsuit against the lessee or lessor, arising from the operation of the lessee's business or use of the property.
(4) The lessor shall require the lessee to carry adequate insurance to cover potential liabilities arising from the lease and use of the property, and shall require that insurance to name the lessor as an additional insured.
(5) Additional goodwill shall not accrue during any lease.
(6) The lessee shall be subject to unlawful detainer proceedings as provided by law.
(d) A public entity shall offer to renew a leaseback agreement for one-year terms, subject to any rent adjustment to reflect inflation and upon compliance with other conditions set forth in subdivision (c), unless the public entity states in writing that the development, redevelopment, or use of the property for its stated public use is scheduled to begin within two years of the termination date of the lease. At least 60 days prior to the lease termination date, the public entity lessor shall either offer a one-year renewal of the lease or send a statement declaring that the lease will not be renewed because the development, redevelopment, or use of the property is scheduled to begin within two years of the lease termination date. The lessee shall either accept or reject a lease renewal offer at least 30 days prior to the lease termination date. The lessee's failure to accept a renewal offer in a timely manner shall constitute a rejection of the renewal offer. A lessor's failure to offer a renewal or give the notice as required shall extend the lease term for 60-day increments until an offer or notice is made, and if a notice of termination is given after the lease termination date, the lessee shall have no less than 60 days to vacate the property. A lessee's failure to accept within 30 days a renewal offer made subsequent to the lease termination date shall constitute a rejection of the offer.
(e) A party who holds over after expiration of the lease shall be subject to unlawful detainer proceedings and shall also be subject to the lessor for holdover damages.
(f) A leaseback entered into pursuant to this section shall not affect the amount of compensation otherwise payable to the property owner for the property to be acquired.
Added by Stats 2006 ch 602 (SB 1650),s 3, eff. 1/1/2007.

Section 1263.620 - Cessation of construction of improvement or installation of machinery or equipment in response to service of summons
(a) Where summons is served during construction of an improvement or installation of machinery or equipment on the property taken or on the remainder if such property is part of a larger parcel, and the owner of the property ceases the construction or installation due to such service, the owner shall be compensated for his expenses reasonably incurred for work necessary for either of the following purposes:
(1) To protect against the risk of injury to persons or to other property created by the uncompleted improvement.
(2) To protect the partially installed machinery or equipment from damage, deterioration, or vandalism.
(b) The compensation provided in this section is recoverable only if the work was preceded by notice to the plaintiff except in the case of an emergency. The plaintiff may agree with the owner (1) that the plaintiff will perform work necessary for the purposes of this section or (2) as to the amount of compensation payable under this section.
Added by Stats. 1975, Ch. 1275.

Article 8 - REMEDIATION OF HAZARDOUS MATERIALS ON PROPERTY TO BE ACQUIRED BY SCHOOL DISTRICTS

Section 1263.710 - [Operative Until 1/1/2024] Remedial action and removal defined; required action defined
(a) As used in this article, "remedial action" and "removal" shall have the meanings accorded to those terms in Sections 25322 and 25323, respectively, of the Health and Safety Code.
(b) As used in this article, "required action" means any removal or other remedial action with regard to hazardous materials that is necessary to comply with any requirement of federal, state, or local law.

Repealed and added by Stats. 1995, Ch. 247, Sec. 2. Effective January 1, 1996.

This section is set out more than once due to postponed, multiple, or conflicting amendments.

Section 1263.710 - [Operative 1/1/2024] Remedial action and removal defined; required action defined

(a) As used in this article, "remedial action" and "removal" shall have the meanings accorded to those terms in Sections 78125 and 78135, respectively, of the Health and Safety Code.

(b) As used in this article, "required action" means any removal or other remedial action with regard to hazardous materials that is necessary to comply with any requirement of federal, state, or local law.

Amended by Stats 2022 ch 258 (AB 2327),s 10, eff. 1/1/2023, op. 1/1/2024.

Repealed and added by Stats. 1995, Ch. 247, Sec. 2. Effective January 1, 1996.

This section is set out more than once due to postponed, multiple, or conflicting amendments.

Section 1263.711 - Hazardous material defined

As used in this article, "hazardous material" shall have the same meaning as that term is defined in Section 25260 of the Health and Safety Code, except that under no circumstances shall petroleum which is naturally occurring on a site be considered a hazardous material.

Added by Stats. 1995, Ch. 247, Sec. 2. Effective January 1, 1996.

Section 1263.720 - Duty of court upon determination that hazardous material present within property

(a) Upon petition of any party to the proceeding, the court in which the proceeding is brought shall specially set for hearing the issue of whether any hazardous material is present within the property to be taken.

(b) If the court determines that any hazardous material is present within the property to be taken, the court shall do all of the following:

(1) Identify those measures constituting the required action with regard to the hazardous material, the probable cost of the required action, and the party that shall be designated by the court to cause the required action to be performed.

(2) Designate a trustee to monitor the completion of the required action and to hold funds, deducted from amounts that are otherwise to be paid to the defendant pursuant to this title, to defray the probable cost of the required action.

(3) Transfer to the trustee funds necessary to defray the probable cost of the required action from amounts deposited with the court pursuant to Article 1 (commencing with Section 1255.010) of Chapter 6 or pursuant to Section 1268.110. In the case of any payment to be made directly to the defendant pursuant to Section 1268.010, the plaintiff shall first pay to the trustee the amount necessary to defray the probable cost of the required action, as identified by the court, and shall pay the remainder of the judgment to the defendant. The total amount transferred or paid to the trustee pursuant to this paragraph shall not exceed an amount equal to 75 percent of the following, as applicable:

(A) Prior to entry of judgment, the amount deposited as the probable amount of compensation pursuant to Article 1 (commencing with Section 1255.010) of Chapter 6.

(B) Subsequent to entry of judgment, the fair market value of the property taken, as determined pursuant to Article 4 (commencing with Section 1263.310). If the amount determined as fair market value pursuant to that article exceeds the amount deposited pursuant to Article 1 (commencing with Section 1255.010) of Chapter 6, that excess shall be available, subject to the 75 percent limit set forth in this paragraph, for transfer to the trustee for the purposes of this paragraph or for reimbursement of the plaintiff for payments made to the trustee pursuant to this paragraph. If the amount determined as fair market value pursuant to Article 4 (commencing with Section 1263.310) is less than the amount deposited pursuant to Article 1 (commencing with Section 1255.010) of Chapter 6, the plaintiff shall be entitled to a return of amounts thereby deposited, a judgment against the defendant, or both, as necessary to ensure that the total amount transferred or paid to the trustee pursuant to this paragraph not exceed an amount equal to 75 percent of the fair market value of the property taken, as determined pursuant to Article 4 (commencing with Section 1263.310).

(4) Establish a procedure by which the trustee shall make one or more payments from the funds it receives pursuant to paragraph (3) to the party causing the required action to be performed, upon completion of all or specified portions of the required action. Any amount of those funds that remains following the completion of all of the required action shall be applied in accordance with the provisions of this title that govern the disposition of the deposit amounts referred to in paragraph (3).

(c) The actual and reasonable costs of the trustee incurred pursuant to this section shall be paid by the plaintiff.

Repealed and added by Stats. 1995, Ch. 247, Sec. 2. Effective January 1, 1996.

Section 1263.730 - Amount available to complete required action insufficient

Where the required action is caused to be performed by the plaintiff, and the amount available to the trustee under this article is insufficient to meet the actual cost incurred by the plaintiff to complete the required action, the plaintiff may either apply to the court for a new hearing regarding identification of the probable cost, or complete the required action at its own expense and bring an action against the defendant to recover the additional costs.

Repealed and added by Stats. 1995, Ch. 247, Sec. 2. Effective January 1, 1996.

Section 1263.740 - Presence of hazardous material not considered in appraising property

The presence of any hazardous material within a property shall not be considered in appraising the property, for purposes of Section 1263.720, pursuant to Article 1 (commencing with Section 1255.010) of Chapter 6, or pursuant to Article 4 (commencing with Section 1263.310).

Repealed and added by Stats. 1995, Ch. 247, Sec. 2. Effective January 1, 1996.

Section 1263.750 - Remedies available to plaintiff; plaintiff entitled to compensation for benefit if plaintiff abandons proceedings

(a) Notwithstanding any action taken pursuant to this article, the plaintiff shall have available all remedies in law that are available to a purchaser of real property with respect to any cost, loss, or liability for which the plaintiff is not reimbursed under this article.

(b) If the plaintiff abandons the proceeding at any time, the plaintiff shall be entitled to compensation for the benefit, if any, conferred on the property by reason of the remedial action performed pursuant to this article. That benefit shall be applied as an offset to the amount of any entitlement to damages on the part of the defendant pursuant to Section 1268.620 or, if it exceeds the amount of those damages, shall constitute a lien upon the property, to the extent of that excess, when recorded with the county recorder in the county in which the real property is located. The lien shall contain the legal description of the real property, the assessor's parcel number, and the name of the owner of record as shown on the latest equalized assessment roll. The lien shall be enforceable upon the transfer or sale of the property, and the priority of the lien shall be as of the date of recording. In determining the amount of the benefit, if any, neither party shall have the burden of proof. For the purposes of this subdivision, "benefit" means the extent to which the remedial action has enhanced the fair market value of the property.

Repealed and added by Stats. 1995, Ch. 247, Sec. 2. Effective January 1, 1996.

Section 1263.760 - Satisfaction of requirements of section 7267.2, Government Code

An offer by the plaintiff to purchase the property subject to this article shall be deemed to satisfy the requirements of Section 7267.2 of the Government Code.

Repealed and added by Stats. 1995, Ch. 247, Sec. 2. Effective January 1, 1996.

Section 1263.770 - Applicability of article to school districts

This article shall only apply to the acquisition of property by school districts.

Repealed and added by Stats. 1995, Ch. 247, Sec. 2. Effective January 1, 1996.

Chapter 10 - DIVIDED INTERESTS
Article 1 - GENERAL PROVISIONS

Section 1265.010 - Compensation for other property interests not limited by chapter

Although this chapter provides rules governing compensation for particular interests in property, it does not otherwise limit or affect the right to compensation for any other interest in property.

Added by Stats. 1975, Ch. 1275.

Article 2 - LEASES

Section 1265.110 - Termination of lease

Where all the property subject to a lease is acquired for public use, the lease terminates.

Added by Stats. 1975, Ch. 1275.

Section 1265.120 - Termination of lease as to part of property taken

Except as provided in Section 1265.130, where part of the property subject to a lease is acquired for public use, the lease terminates as to the part taken and remains in force as to the remainder, and the rent reserved in the lease that is allocable to the part taken is extinguished.

Added by Stats. 1975, Ch. 1275.

Section 1265.130 - Petition to terminate lease where part of property subject to lease taken

Where part of the property subject to a lease is acquired for public use, the court may, upon petition of any party to the lease, terminate the lease if the court determines that an essential part of the property subject to the lease is taken or that the remainder of the property subject to the lease is no longer suitable for the purposes of the lease.

Added by Stats. 1975, Ch. 1275.

Section 1265.140 - Time of termination

The termination or partial termination of a lease pursuant to this article shall be at the earlier of the following times:

(a) The time title to the property is taken by the person who will put it to the public use.

(b) The time the plaintiff is authorized to take possession of the property as stated in an order for possession.

Added by Stats. 1975, Ch. 1275.

Section 1265.150 - Right of lessee to compensation not affected

Nothing in this article affects or impairs any right a lessee may have to compensation for the taking of his lease in whole or in part or for the taking of any other property in which he has an interest.

Added by Stats. 1975, Ch. 1275.

Section 1265.160 - Rights and obligations of parties to lease not affected

Nothing in this article affects or impairs the rights and obligations of the parties to a lease to the extent that the lease provides for such rights and obligations in the event of the acquisition of all or a portion of the property for public use.

Added by Stats. 1975, Ch. 1275.

Article 3 - ENCUMBRANCES

Section 1265.210 - Lien defined

As used in this article, "lien" means a mortgage, deed of trust, or other security interest in property whether arising from contract, statute, common law, or equity.

Added by Stats. 1975, Ch. 1275.

Section 1265.220 - Lien and indebtedness secured by lien not due at time of entry of judgment

Where property acquired by eminent domain is encumbered by a lien and the indebtedness secured thereby is not due at the time of the entry of judgment, the amount of such indebtedness may be, at the option of the plaintiff, deducted from the judgment and the lien shall be continued until such indebtedness is paid; but the amount for which, as between the plaintiff and the defendant, the plaintiff is liable under Article 5 (commencing with Section 1268.410) of Chapter 11 may not be deducted from the judgment.

Added by Stats. 1975, Ch. 1275.

Section 1265.225 - Partial taking of property secured by lien

(a) Where there is a partial taking of property encumbered by a lien, the lienholder may share in the award only to the extent determined by the court to be necessary to prevent an impairment of the security, and the lien shall continue upon the part of the property not taken as security for the unpaid portion of the indebtedness.

(b) Notwithstanding subdivision (a), the lienholder and the property owner may at any time after commencement of the proceeding agree that some or all of the award shall be apportioned to the lienholder on the indebtedness.

Added by Stats. 1975, Ch. 1275.

Section 1265.230 - Partial taking of property encumbered by lien and portion of property taken encumbered by junior lien

(a) This section applies only where there is a partial taking of property encumbered by a lien and the part taken or some portion of it is also encumbered by a junior lien that extends to only a portion of the property encumbered by the senior lien. This section provides only for allocation of the portion of the award, if any, that will be available for payment to the junior and senior lienholders and does not provide for determination of the amount of such portion.

(b) As used in this section, "impairment of security" means the security of the lienholder remaining after the taking, if any, is of less value in proportion to the remaining indebtedness than the value of the security before the taking was in proportion to the indebtedness secured thereby.

(c) The portion of the award that will be available for payment to the senior and junior lienholders shall be allocated first to the senior lien up to the full amount of the indebtedness secured thereby and the remainder, if any, to the junior lien.

(d) If the allocation under subdivision (c) would result in an impairment of the junior lienholder's security, the allocation to the junior lien shall be adjusted so as to preserve the junior lienholder's security to the extent that the remaining amount allocated to the senior lien, if paid to the senior lienholder, would not result in an impairment of the senior lienholder's security.

(e) The amounts allocated to the senior and junior liens by this section are the amounts of indebtedness owing to such senior and junior lienholders that are secured by their respective liens on the property taken, and any other indebtedness owing to the senior or junior lienholders shall not be considered as secured by the property taken. If the plaintiff makes the election provided in Section 1265.220, the indebtedness that is deducted from the judgment is the indebtedness so determined, and the lien shall continue until that amount of indebtedness is paid.

Added by Stats. 1975, Ch. 1275.

Section 1265.240 - Prepayment penalty not included in amount payable to lienholder

Where the property acquired for public use is encumbered by a lien, the amount payable to the lienholder shall not include any penalty for prepayment.

Added by Stats. 1975, Ch. 1275.

Section 1265.250 - Property acquired encumbered by lien of fixed lien special assessment

(a) As used in this section:

(1) "Fixed lien special assessment" means a nonrecurring assessment levied on property in a fixed amount by a local public entity for the capital expenditure for a specific improvement, whether collectible in a lump sum or in installments.

(2) "Special annual assessment" means a recurring assessment levied on property annually in an indeterminate amount by a local public entity, whether for the capital expenditure for a specific improvement or for other purposes.

(b) If property acquired by eminent domain is encumbered by the lien of a fixed lien special assessment or of a bond representing the fixed lien special assessment:

(1) The amount of the lien shall be paid to the lienholder from the award or withheld from the award for payment pursuant to Section 1265.220.

(2) Where there is a partial taking of the property, the amount of the lien prescribed in Section 1265.225 shall be paid to the lienholder from the award, or at the option of the lienholder the applicable statutory procedure, if any, for segregation and apportionment of the lien may be invoked and the amount apportioned to the part taken shall be paid to the lienholder from the award.

(c) If property acquired by eminent domain is encumbered by the lien of a special annual assessment:

(1) The amount of the lien prorated to, but not including, the date of apportionment determined pursuant to Section 5082 of the Revenue and Taxation Code, shall be paid to the lienholder from the award. As between the plaintiff and defendant, the plaintiff is liable for the amount of the lien prorated from and including the date of apportionment determined pursuant to Section 5082 of the Revenue and Taxation Code.

(2) Where there is a partial taking of the property, the amount of the lien, reduced by the amount for which the plaintiff is liable pursuant to this paragraph, shall be paid to the lienholder from the award. As between the plaintiff and defendant, the plaintiff is liable for the amount of the lien allocable to the part taken for the current assessment year, determined to the extent practicable in the same manner and by the same method as the amount of the assessment on the property for the current assessment year was determined, prorated from and including the date of apportionment determined pursuant to Section 5082 of the Revenue and Taxation Code.

Added by Stats. 1980, Ch. 122, Sec. 2.

Article 4 - FUTURE INTERESTS

Section 1265.410 - Acquisition violates use restriction coupled with contingent future interest granting possession upon violation

(a) Where the acquisition of property for public use violates a use restriction coupled with a contingent future interest granting a right to possession of the property upon violation of the use restriction:

(1) If violation of the use restriction was otherwise reasonably imminent, the owner of the contingent future interest is entitled to compensation for its value, if any.

(2) If violation of the use restriction was not otherwise reasonably imminent but the benefit of the use restriction was appurtenant to other property, the owner of the contingent future interest is entitled to compensation to the extent that the failure to comply with the use restriction damages the dominant premises to which the restriction was appurtenant and of which he was the owner.

(b) Where the acquisition of property for public use violates a use restriction coupled with a contingent future interest granting a right to possession of the property upon violation of the use restriction but the contingent future interest is not compensable under subdivision (a), if the use restriction is that the property be devoted to a particular charitable or public use, the compensation for the property shall be devoted to the same or similar use coupled with the same contingent future interest.

Added by Stats. 1975, Ch. 1275.

Section 1265.420 - Acquired property subject to life tenancy

Where property acquired for public use is subject to a life tenancy, upon petition of the life tenant or any other person having an interest in the property, the court may order any of the following:

(a) An apportionment and distribution of the award based on the value of the interest of life tenant and remainderman.

(b) The compensation to be used to purchase comparable property to be held subject to the life tenancy.

(c) The compensation to be held in trust and invested and the income (and, to the extent the instrument that created the life tenancy permits, principal) to be distributed to the life tenant for the remainder of the tenancy.

(d) Such other arrangement as will be equitable under the circumstances.

Added by Stats. 1975, Ch. 1275.

Chapter 11 - POSTJUDGMENT PROCEDURE

Article 1 - PAYMENT OF JUDGMENT; FINAL ORDER OF CONDEMNATION

Section 1268.010 - Payment of full amount required by judgment

(a) Not later than 30 days after final judgment, or 30 days after the conclusion of any other court proceedings, including any federal court proceedings, commenced by the defendant challenging the judgment or any of the condemnation proceedings, whichever date is later, the plaintiff shall pay the full amount required by the judgment.

(b) Payment shall be made by either or both of the following methods:

(1) Payment of money directly to the defendant. Any amount which the defendant has previously withdrawn pursuant to Article 2 (commencing with Section 1255.210) of Chapter 6 shall be credited as a payment to him on the judgment.

(2) Deposit of money with the court pursuant to Section 1268.110. Upon entry of judgment, a deposit made pursuant to Article 1 (commencing with Section 1255.010) of Chapter 6 is deemed to be a deposit made pursuant to Section 1268.110 if the full amount required by the judgment is deposited or paid.

Amended by Stats. 1981, Ch. 831, Sec. 1.

Section 1268.020 - Failure to timely pay full amount required by judgment

(a) If the plaintiff fails to pay the full amount required by the judgment within the time specified in Section 1268.010, the defendant may:

(1) If the plaintiff is a public entity, enforce the judgment as provided in Division 3.6 (commencing with Section 810) of Title 1 of the Government Code.

(2) If the plaintiff is not a public entity, enforce the judgment as in a civil case.

(b) Upon noticed motion of the defendant, the court shall enter judgment dismissing the eminent domain proceeding if all of the following are established:

(1) The plaintiff failed to pay the full amount required by the judgment within the time specified in Section 1268.010.

(2) The defendant has filed in court and served upon the plaintiff, by registered or certified mail, a written notice of the plaintiff's failure to pay the full amount required by the judgment within the time specified in Section 1268.010.

(3) The plaintiff has failed for 20 days after service of the notice under paragraph (2) to pay the full amount required by the judgment in the manner provided in subdivision (b) of Section 1268.010.

(c) The defendant may elect to exercise the remedy provided by subdivision (b) without attempting to use the remedy provided by subdivision (a).

(d) As used in this section, "public entity" does not include the Regents of the University of California.

Amended by Stats. 1980, Ch. 215, Sec. 1.

Section 1268.030 - Final order if full amount paid

(a) Upon application of any party, the court shall make a final order of condemnation if the full amount of the judgment has been paid as required by Section 1268.010 or satisfied pursuant to Section 1268.020.
(b) The final order of condemnation shall describe the property taken and identify the judgment authorizing the taking.
(c) The party upon whose application the order was made shall serve notice of the making of the order on all other parties affected thereby. Any party affected by the order may thereafter record a certified copy of the order in the office of the recorder of the county in which the property is located and shall serve notice of recordation upon all other parties affected thereby. Title to the property vests in the plaintiff upon the date of recordation.
Added by Stats. 1975, Ch. 1275.

Article 2 - DEPOSIT AND WITHDRAWAL OF AWARD

Section 1268.110 - Deposit of full amount of award with interest after entry of judgment
(a) Except as provided in subdivision (b), the plaintiff may, at any time after entry of judgment, deposit with the court for the persons entitled thereto the full amount of the award, together with interest then due thereon, less any amounts previously paid directly to the defendants or deposited pursuant to Article 1 (commencing with Section 1255.010) of Chapter 6.
(b) A deposit may be made under this section notwithstanding an appeal, a motion for a new trial, or a motion to vacate or set aside the judgment but may not be made after the judgment has been reversed, vacated, or set aside.
(c) Any amount deposited pursuant to this article on a judgment that is later reversed, vacated, or set aside shall be deemed to be an amount deposited pursuant to Article 1 (commencing with Section 1255.010) of Chapter 6.
Added by Stats. 1975, Ch. 1275.

Section 1268.120 - Notice of deposit
If the deposit is made under Section 1268.110 prior to apportionment of the award, the plaintiff shall serve a notice that the deposit has been made on all of the parties who have appeared in the proceeding. If the deposit is made after apportionment of the award, the plaintiff shall serve a notice that the deposit has been made on all of the parties to the proceeding determined by the order apportioning the award to have an interest in the money deposited. The notice of deposit shall state that a deposit has been made and the date and the amount of the deposit. Service of the notice shall be made in the manner provided in Section 1268.220 for the service of an order for possession. Service of an order for possession under Section 1268.220 is sufficient compliance with this section.
Added by Stats. 1975, Ch. 1275.

Section 1268.130 - Deposit of additional amount to secure further compensation, costs and interest
At any time after the plaintiff has made a deposit upon the award pursuant to Section 1268.110, the court may, upon motion of any defendant, order the plaintiff to deposit such additional amount as the court determines to be necessary to secure payment of any further compensation, costs, or interest that may be recovered in the proceeding. After the making of such an order, the court may, on motion of any party, order an increase or a decrease in such additional amount. A defendant may withdraw the amount deposited under this section or a portion thereof only if it is determined that he is entitled to recover such amount in the proceeding.
Added by Stats. 1975, Ch. 1275.

Section 1268.140 - Application by defendant for payment from deposit
(a) After entry of judgment, any defendant who has an interest in the property for which a deposit has been made may apply for and obtain a court order that he be paid from the deposit the amount to which he is entitled upon his filing either of the following:
  (1) A satisfaction of the judgment.
  (2) A receipt for the money which shall constitute a waiver by operation of law of all claims and defenses except a claim for greater compensation.
(b) If the award has not been apportioned at the time the application is made, the applicant shall give notice of the application to all the other defendants who have appeared in the proceeding and who have an interest in the property. If the award has been apportioned at the time the application is made, the applicant shall give such notice to the other defendants as the court may require.
(c) Upon objection to the withdrawal made by any party to the proceeding, the court, in its discretion, may require the applicant to file an undertaking in the same manner and upon the conditions prescribed in Section 1255.240 for withdrawal of a deposit prior to entry of judgment.
(d) If the judgment is reversed, vacated, or set aside, a defendant may withdraw a deposit only pursuant to Article 2 (commencing with Section 1255.210) of Chapter 6.
Added by Stats. 1975, Ch. 1275.

Section 1268.150 - Money ordered deposited in state treasury or upon request in county treasury
(a) Except as provided in subdivision (b), when money is deposited as provided in this article, the court shall order the money to be deposited in the State Treasury or, upon written request of the plaintiff filed with the deposit, in the county treasury. If the money is deposited in the State Treasury pursuant to this subdivision, it shall be held, invested, deposited, and disbursed in the manner specified in Article 10 (commencing with Section 16429) of Chapter 2 of Part 2 of Division 4 of Title 2 of the Government Code, and interest earned or other increment derived from its investment shall be apportioned and disbursed in the manner specified in that article. As between the parties to the proceeding, money deposited pursuant to this subdivision shall remain at the risk of the plaintiff until paid or made payable to the defendant by order of the court.
(b) If after entry of judgment but prior to apportionment of the award the defendants are unable to agree as to the withdrawal of all or a portion of any amount deposited, the court shall upon motion of any defendant order that the amount deposited be invested in United States government obligations or interest-bearing accounts in an institution whose accounts are insured by an agency of the federal government for the benefit of the defendants who shall be entitled to the interest earned on the investments in proportion to the amount of the award they receive when the award is apportioned.
Added by Stats. 1975, Ch. 1275.

Section 1268.160 - Withdrawal in amount in excess of amount party entitled
(a) Any amount withdrawn by a party pursuant to this article in excess of the amount to which he is entitled as finally determined in the eminent domain proceeding shall be paid to the parties entitled thereto. The court shall enter judgment accordingly.
(b) The judgment so entered shall not include interest except that any amount that is to be paid to a defendant shall include legal interest from the date of its withdrawal by another defendant.
(c) If the judgment so entered is not paid within 30 days after its entry, the court may, on motion, enter judgment against the sureties, if any, for the amount of such judgment.
(d) The court may, in its discretion and with such security as it deems appropriate, grant a party obligated to pay under this section a stay of execution for any amount to be paid to a plaintiff. Such stay of execution shall not exceed one year following entry of judgment under this section.
Added by Stats. 1975, Ch. 1275.

Section 1268.170 - Rights not waived by making deposit
By making a deposit pursuant to this article, the plaintiff does not waive the right to appeal from the judgment, the right to move to abandon, or the right to request a new trial.
Added by Stats. 1975, Ch. 1275.

Article 3 - POSSESSION AFTER JUDGMENT

Section 1268.210 - Application for order of possession and authorization to take possession

(a) If the plaintiff is not in possession of the property to be taken, the plaintiff may, at any time after entry of judgment, apply ex parte to the court for an order for possession, and the court shall authorize the plaintiff to take possession of the property pending conclusion of the litigation if:

    (1) The judgment determines that the plaintiff is entitled to take the property; and

    (2) The plaintiff has paid to or deposited for the defendants, pursuant to Article 1 (commencing with Section 1255.010) of Chapter 6 or Article 2 (commencing with Section 1268.110), an amount not less than the amount of the award, together with the interest then due thereon.

(b) The court's order shall state the date after which the plaintiff is authorized to take possession of the property. Where deposit is made, the order shall state such fact and the date and the amount of the deposit.

(c) Where the judgment is reversed, vacated, or set aside, the plaintiff may obtain possession of the property only pursuant to Article 3 (commencing with Section 1255.410) of Chapter 6.

Added by Stats. 1975, Ch. 1275.

Section 1268.220 - Service of copy of order of possession

(a) The plaintiff shall serve a copy of the order for possession upon each defendant and his attorney, either personally or by mail:

    (1) At least 30 days prior to the date possession is to be taken of property lawfully occupied by a person dwelling thereon or by a farm or business operation.

    (2) At least 10 days prior to the date possession is to be taken in any case not covered by paragraph (1).

(b) A single service upon or mailing to one of several persons having a common business or residence address is sufficient.

Added by Stats. 1975, Ch. 1275.

Section 1268.230 - Rights not waived by taking possession

By taking possession pursuant to this article, the plaintiff does not waive the right to appeal from the judgment, the right to move to abandon, or the right to request a new trial.

Added by Stats. 1975, Ch. 1275.

Section 1268.240 - Public entity's right to exercise police power not limited

Nothing in this article limits the right of a public entity to exercise its police power in emergency situations.

Added by Stats. 1975, Ch. 1275.

Article 4 - INTEREST

Section 1268.310 - Dates from which interest computed

The compensation awarded in the proceeding shall draw interest, computed as prescribed by Section 1268.350, from the earliest of the following dates:

(a) The date of entry of judgment.

(b) The date the plaintiff takes possession of the property.

(c) The date after which the plaintiff is authorized to take possession of the property as stated in an order for possession.

Amended by Stats. 1986, Ch. 1372, Sec. 1.

Section 1268.311 - Computation in inverse condemnation proceeding

In any inverse condemnation proceeding in which interest is awarded, the interest shall be computed as prescribed by Section 1268.350.

Added by Stats. 1986, Ch. 1372, Sec. 2.

Section 1268.320 - Dates computation of interest ceases

The compensation awarded in the proceeding shall cease to draw interest at the earliest of the following dates:

(a) As to any amount deposited pursuant to Article 1 (commencing with Section 1255.010) of Chapter 6 (deposit of probable compensation prior to judgment), the date such amount is withdrawn by the person entitled thereto.

(b) As to the amount deposited in accordance with Article 2 (commencing with Section 1268.110) (deposit of amount of award), the date of such deposit.

(c) As to any amount paid to the person entitled thereto, the date of such payment.

Added by Stats. 1975, Ch. 1275.

Section 1268.330 - Value of continued possession offset against interest; rents and other income received offset against interest

If, after the date that interest begins to accrue, the defendant:

(a) Continues in actual possession of the property, the value of that possession shall be offset against the interest. For the purpose of this section, the value of possession of the property shall be presumed to be the rate of interest calculated as prescribed by Section 1268.350 on the compensation awarded. This presumption is one affecting the burden of proof.

(b) Receives rents or other income from the property attributable to the period after interest begins to accrue, the net amount of these rents and other income shall be offset against the interest.

Amended by Stats. 1986, Ch. 1372, Sec. 3.

Section 1268.340 - Interest assessed by court

Interest, including interest accrued due to possession of property by the plaintiff prior to judgment, and any offset against interest as provided in Section 1268.330, shall be assessed by the court rather than by jury.

Added by Stats. 1975, Ch. 1275.

Section 1268.350 - Rate of interest payable for calendar quarter

(a) As used in this section, "apportionment rate" means the apportionment rate calculated by the Controller as the rate of earnings by the Surplus Money Investment Fund for each calendar quarter.

(b) The rate of interest payable under this article for each calendar quarter, or fraction thereof, for which interest is due, shall be the apportionment rate for the immediately preceding calendar quarter.

(c) Each district office of the Department of Transportation shall quote the apportionment rate to any person upon request.

Amended by Stats 2006 ch 311 (SB 1586),s 1, eff. 1/1/2007.

Section 1268.360 - Computation of interest payable for calendar quarter

The interest payable for each calendar quarter shall draw interest, computed as prescribed by Section 1268.350, in each succeeding calendar quarter for which interest is due.

Amended by Stats 2006 ch 311 (SB 1586),s 2, eff. 1/1/2007.

Article 5 - PRORATION OF PROPERTY TAXES

Section 1268.410 - Liability of plaintiff

As between the plaintiff and defendant, the plaintiff is liable for any ad valorem taxes, penalties, and costs upon property acquired by eminent domain prorated from and including the date of apportionment determined pursuant to Section 5082 of the Revenue and Taxation Code.

Amended by Stats. 1979, Ch. 31.

Section 1268.420 - Acquisition makes property exempt from taxes

(a) Except as provided in subdivision (b):
  (1) If the acquisition of property by eminent domain will make the property exempt property as defined in Section 5081 of the Revenue and Taxation Code, any ad valorem taxes, penalties, or costs on the property for which the plaintiff is liable pursuant to Section 1268.410 are not collectible.
  (2) If the acquisition of property by eminent domain will not make the property exempt property as defined in Section 5081 of the Revenue and Taxation Code, the plaintiff shall be deemed to be the assessee for the purposes of collection of any ad valorem taxes, penalties, and costs on the property for which the plaintiff is liable pursuant to Section 1268.410.
(b) To the extent there is a dismissal or partial dismissal of the eminent domain proceeding, the amount of any unpaid ad valorem taxes, penalties, and costs on the property for which the plaintiff would be liable pursuant to Section 1268. 410 until the entry of judgment of dismissal shall be awarded to the defendant. The amount awarded shall be paid to the tax collector from the award or, if unpaid for any reason, are collectible from the defendant.
Repealed and added by Stats. 1979, Ch. 31.

Section 1268.430 - Liability of plaintiff if defendant has paid
(a) If the defendant has paid any amount for which, as between the plaintiff and defendant, the plaintiff is liable under this article, the plaintiff shall pay to the defendant a sum equal to such amount.
(b) The amount the defendant is entitled to be paid under this section shall be claimed in the manner provided for claiming costs and at the following times:
  (1) If the plaintiff took possession of the property prior to judgment, at the time provided for claiming costs.
  (2) If the plaintiff did not take possession of the property prior to judgment, not later than 30 days after the plaintiff took title to the property.
Added by Stats. 1975, Ch. 1275.

Section 1268.440 - Refund of taxes paid on exempt property
(a) If taxes have been paid on property that is exempt property as defined in Section 5081 of the Revenue and Taxation Code, the amount of the taxes that, if unpaid, would have been subject to cancellation under Article 5 (commencing with Section 5081) of Chapter 4 of Part 9 of Division 1 of the Revenue and Taxation Code shall be deemed to be erroneously collected and shall be refunded in the manner provided in Article 1 (commencing with Section 5096) of Chapter 5 of Part 9 of Division 1 of the Revenue and Taxation Code to the person who paid the taxes.
(b) The public entity shall be deemed to be the person who paid the taxes if the public entity reimbursed the defendant for the taxes under a cost bill filed in the eminent domain proceeding pursuant to Section 1268.430. A claim for refund of taxes filed by a public entity pursuant to this section shall contain a copy of the cost bill under which taxes were reimbursed or a declaration under penalty of perjury by the public entity that the taxes were reimbursed under a cost bill.
(c) Taxes paid on either the secured or unsecured roll may be refunded pursuant to this section.
Added by Stats. 1979, Ch. 31.

Section 1268.450 - Separate valuation of property on assessment roll
If property acquired by eminent domain does not have a separate valuation on the assessment roll, any party to the eminent domain proceeding may, at any time after the taxes on the property are subject to cancellation under Article 5 (commencing with Section 5081) of Chapter 4 of Part 9 of Division 1 of the Revenue and Taxation Code, apply to the tax collector for a separate valuation of the property in accordance with Article 3 (commencing with Section 2821) of Chapter 3 of Part 5 of Division 1 of the Revenue and Taxation Code notwithstanding any provision in that article to the contrary.
Added by Stats. 1979, Ch. 31.

Article 6 - ABANDONMENT

Section 1268.510 - Notice of abandonment; setting abandonment aside; dismissal of proceeding
(a) At any time after the filing of the complaint and before the expiration of 30 days after final judgment, the plaintiff may wholly or partially abandon the proceeding by serving on the defendant and filing in court a written notice of such abandonment.
(b) The court may, upon motion made within 30 days after the filing of such notice, set the abandonment aside if it determines that the position of the moving party has been substantially changed to his detriment in justifiable reliance upon the proceeding and such party cannot be restored to substantially the same position as if the proceeding had not been commenced.
(c) Upon denial of a motion to set aside such abandonment or, if no such motion is filed, upon the expiration of the time for filing such a motion, the court shall, on motion of any party, enter judgment wholly or partially dismissing the proceeding.
Added by Stats. 1975, Ch. 1275.

Article 7 - LITIGATION EXPENSES AND DAMAGES UPON DISMISSAL OR DEFEAT OF RIGHT TO TAKE

Section 1268.610 - Award to defendant of litigation expenses
(a) Subject to subdivisions (b) and (c), the court shall award the defendant his or her litigation expenses whenever:
  (1) The proceeding is wholly or partly dismissed for any reason.
  (2) Final judgment in the proceeding is that the plaintiff cannot acquire property it sought to acquire in the proceeding.
(b) Where there is a partial dismissal or a final judgment that the plaintiff cannot acquire a portion of the property originally sought to be acquired, or a dismissal of one or more plaintiffs pursuant to Section 1260.020, the court shall award the defendant only those litigation expenses, or portion thereof, that would not have been incurred had the property sought to be acquired following the dismissal or judgment been the property originally sought to be acquired.
(c) If the plaintiff files a notice of abandonment as to a particular defendant, or a request for dismissal of a particular defendant, and the court determines that the defendant did not own or have any interest in the property that the plaintiff sought to acquire in the proceeding, the court shall award that defendant only those litigation expenses incurred up to the time of filing the notice of abandonment or request for dismissal.
(d) Litigation expenses under this section shall be claimed in and by a cost bill to be prepared, served, filed, and taxed as in a civil action. If the proceeding is dismissed upon motion of the plaintiff, the cost bill shall be filed within 30 days after notice of entry of judgment.
Amended by Stats 2001 ch 192 (AB 1463), s 1, eff. 1/1/2002.

Section 1268.620 - Proceeding dismissed or judgment that plaintiff cannot acquire property
If, after the defendant moves from property in compliance with an order or agreement for possession or in reasonable contemplation of its taking by the plaintiff, the proceeding is dismissed with regard to that property for any reason or there is a final judgment that the plaintiff cannot acquire that property, the court shall:
(a) Order the plaintiff to deliver possession of the property to the persons entitled to it; and
(b) Make such provision as shall be just for the payment of all damages proximately caused by the proceeding and its dismissal as to that property.
Added by Stats. 1975, Ch. 1275.

Article 8 - COSTS

Section 1268.710 - Defendants allowed costs
The defendants shall be allowed their costs, including the costs of determining the apportionment of the award made pursuant to subdivision (b) of Section 1260.220, except that the costs of determining any issue as to title between two or more defendants shall be borne by the defendants in such proportion as the court may direct.
Added by Stats. 1975, Ch. 1275.

Section 1268.720 - Defendant allowed costs on appeal
Unless the court otherwise orders, whether or not he is the prevailing party, the defendant in the proceeding shall be allowed his costs on appeal. This section does not apply to an appeal involving issues between defendants.
Added by Stats. 1975, Ch. 1275.

Chapter 12 - ARBITRATION OF COMPENSATION IN ACQUISITIONS OF PROPERTY FOR PUBLIC USE

Section 1273.010 - Agreement to arbitrate
(a) Any person authorized to acquire property for public use may enter into an agreement to arbitrate any controversy as to the compensation to be made in connection with the acquisition of the property.
(b) Where property is already appropriated to a public use, the person authorized to compromise or settle the claim arising from a taking or damaging of such property for another public use may enter into an agreement to arbitrate any controversy as to the compensation to be made in connection with such taking or damaging.
(c) For the purposes of this section, in the case of a public entity, "person" refers to the particular department, officer, commission, board, or governing body authorized to acquire property on behalf of the public entity or to compromise or settle a claim arising from the taking or damaging of the entity's property.
Added by Stats. 1975, Ch. 1275.

Section 1273.020 - Payment of arbitrator's expenses and fees, witness fees and mileage and attorney's fees
(a) Notwithstanding Sections 1283.2 and 1284.2, the party acquiring the property shall pay all of the expenses and fees of the neutral arbitrator and the statutory fees and mileage of all witnesses subpoenaed in the arbitration, together with other expenses of the arbitration incurred or approved by the neutral arbitrator, not including attorney's fees or expert witness fees or other expenses incurred by other parties for their own benefit.
(b) An agreement authorized by this chapter may require that the party acquiring the property pay reasonable attorney's fees or expert witness fees, or both, to any other party to the arbitration. If the agreement requires the payment of such fees, the amount of the fees is a matter to be determined in the arbitration proceeding unless the agreement prescribes otherwise.
(c) The party acquiring the property may pay the expenses and fees referred to in subdivisions (a) and (b) from funds available for the acquisition of the property or other funds available for the purpose.
Added by Stats. 1975, Ch. 1275.

Section 1273.030 - Rules applicable to agreements
(a) Except as specifically provided in this chapter, agreements authorized by this chapter are subject to Title 9 (commencing with Section 1280) of this part.
(b) An agreement authorized by this chapter may be made whether or not an eminent domain proceeding has been commenced to acquire the property. If a proceeding has been commenced or is commenced, any petition or response relating to the arbitration shall be filed and determined in the proceeding.
(c) Notwithstanding Section 1281.4, an agreement authorized by this chapter does not waive or restrict the power of any person to commence and prosecute an eminent domain proceeding, including the taking of possession prior to judgment, except that, upon motion of a party to the proceeding, the court shall stay the determination of compensation until any petition for an order to arbitrate is determined and, if arbitration is ordered, until arbitration is had in accordance with the order.
(d) The effect and enforceability of an agreement authorized by this chapter is not defeated or impaired by contention or proof by any party to the agreement that the party acquiring the property pursuant to the agreement lacks the power or capacity to take the property by eminent domain.
(e) Notwithstanding the rules as to venue provided by Sections 1292 and 1292.2, any petition relating to arbitration authorized by this chapter shall be filed in the superior court in the county in which the property, or any portion of the property, is located.
Added by Stats. 1975, Ch. 1275.

Section 1273.040 - Terms and conditions specified in agreement; abandonment
(a) Except as provided in subdivision (b), an agreement authorized by this chapter may specify the terms and conditions under which the party acquiring the property may abandon the acquisition, the arbitration proceeding, and any eminent domain proceeding that may have been, or may be, filed. Unless the agreement provides that the acquisition may not be abandoned, the party acquiring the property may abandon the acquisition, the arbitration proceeding, and any eminent domain proceeding at any time not later than the time for filing and serving a petition or response to vacate an arbitration award under Sections 1288, 1288.2, and 1290.6.
(b) If the proceeding to acquire the property is abandoned after the arbitration agreement is executed, the party from whom the property was to be acquired is entitled to recover (1) all expenses reasonably and necessarily incurred (i) in preparing for the arbitration proceeding and for any judicial proceedings in connection with the acquisition of the property, (ii) during the arbitration proceeding and during any judicial proceedings in connection with the acquisition, and (iii) in any subsequent judicial proceedings in connection with the acquisition and (2) reasonable attorney's fees, appraisal fees, and fees for the services of other experts where such fees were reasonably and necessarily incurred to protect his interests in connection with the acquisition of the property. Unless the agreement otherwise provides, the amount of such expenses and fees shall be determined by arbitration in accordance with the agreement.
Added by Stats. 1975, Ch. 1275.

Section 1273.050 - Acknowledgment and recording of agreement
(a) An agreement authorized by this chapter may be acknowledged and recorded, and rerecorded, in the same manner and with the same effect as a conveyance of real property except that two years after the date the agreement is recorded, or rerecorded, the record ceases to be notice to any person for any purpose.
(b) In lieu of recording the agreement, there may be recorded a memorandum thereof, executed by the parties to the agreement, containing at least the following information: the names of the parties to the agreement, a description of the property, and a statement that an arbitration agreement affecting such property has been entered into pursuant to this chapter. Such memorandum when acknowledged and recorded, or rerecorded, in the same manner as a conveyance of real property has the same effect as if the agreement itself were recorded or rerecorded.
Added by Stats. 1975, Ch. 1275.

Title 8 - CHANGE OF NAMES

Section 1275 - Superior court jurisdiction

Applications for change of names must be determined by the Superior Courts.
Amended by Stats. 1983, Ch. 486, Sec. 1.

Section 1276 - Applications generally

(a)

(1) All applications for change of names shall be made to the superior court of the county where the person whose name is proposed to be changed resides, except as specified in subdivision (e) or (g), either (A) by petition signed by the person or, if the person is under 18 years of age, by one of the person's parents, by any guardian of the person, or as specified in subdivision (e), or, if both parents are deceased and there is no guardian of the person, then by some near relative or friend of the person, or (B) as provided in Section 7638 of the Family Code.

(2) The petition or pleading shall specify the place of birth and residence of the person, the person's present name, the name proposed, and the reason for the change of name.

(b) In a proceeding for a change of name commenced by the filing of a petition, if the person whose name is to be changed is under 18 years of age, the petition shall, if neither parent of the person has signed the petition, name, as far as known to the person proposing the name change, the parents of the person and their place of residence, if living, or, if neither parent is living, near relatives of the person, and their place of residence.

(c) In a proceeding for a change of name commenced by the filing of a petition, if the person whose name is proposed to be changed is under 18 years of age and the petition is signed by only one parent, the petition shall specify the address, if known, of the other parent if living. If the petition is signed by a guardian, the petition shall specify the name and address, if known, of the parent or parents, if living, or the grandparents, if the addresses of both parents are unknown or if both parents are deceased, of the person whose name is proposed to be changed.

(d) In a proceeding for a change of name commenced by the filing of a petition, if the person whose name is proposed to be changed is 12 years of age or older, has been relinquished to an adoption agency by the person's parent or parents, and has not been legally adopted, the petition shall be signed by the person and the adoption agency to which the person was relinquished. The near relatives of the person and their place of residence shall not be included in the petition unless they are known to the person whose name is proposed to be changed.

(e) All petitions for the change of the name of a minor submitted by a guardian appointed by the juvenile court or the probate court, by a court-appointed dependency attorney appointed as guardian ad litem pursuant to rules adopted under Section 326.5 of the Welfare and Institutions Code, or by an attorney for a minor who is alleged or adjudged to be a person described in Section 601 or 602 of the Welfare and Institutions Code shall be made in the court having jurisdiction over the minor. All petitions for the change of name of a nonminor dependent may be made in the juvenile court.

(f) If the petition is signed by a guardian, the petition shall specify relevant information regarding the guardianship, the likelihood that the child will remain under the guardian's care until the child reaches the age of majority, and information suggesting that the child will not likely be returned to the custody of the child's parents.

(g)

(1) On or after January 1, 2023, an application for a change of name may be made to a superior court for a person whose name is proposed to be changed, even if the person does not reside within the State of California, if the person is seeking to change their name on at least one of the following documents:

(A) A birth certificate that was issued within this state to the person whose name is proposed to be changed.

(B) A birth certificate that was issued within this state to the legal child of the person whose name is proposed to be changed.

(C) A marriage license and certificate or a confidential marriage license and certificate that was issued within this state to the person whose name is proposed to be changed.

(2) For the purposes of this subdivision, the superior court in the county where the birth under subparagraph (A) or (B) of paragraph (1) occurred or marriage under subparagraph (C) of paragraph (1) was entered shall be a proper venue for the proceeding. The name change shall be adjudicated in accordance with California law.

Amended by Stats 2021 ch 577 (AB 218),s 1.5, eff. 1/1/2022.
Amended by Stats 2021 ch 401 (AB 1578),s 7, eff. 1/1/2022.
Amended by Stats 2018 ch 776 (AB 3250),s 9, eff. 1/1/2019.
Amended by Stats 2006 ch 567 (AB 2303),s 10, eff. 1/1/2007.
Amended by Stats 2000 ch 111 (AB 2155), s 1, eff. 1/1/2001.

Section 1277 - Order to show cause; publication; participant in address confidentiality program; participant in state Witness Relocation and Assistance Program; application part of Uniform Parentage Act action; guardian files petition

(a)

(1) If a proceeding for a change of name is commenced by the filing of a petition, except as provided in subdivisions (b), (c), (d), and (f), or Section 1277.5, the court shall thereupon make an order reciting the filing of the petition, the name of the person by whom it is filed, and the name proposed. The order shall direct all persons interested in the matter to appear before the court at a time and place specified, which shall be not less than 6 weeks nor more than 12 weeks from the time of making the order, unless the court orders a different time, to show cause why the application for change of name should not be granted. The order shall direct all persons interested in the matter to make known any objection that they may have to the granting of the petition for change of name by filing a written objection, which includes the reasons for the objection, with the court at least two court days before the matter is scheduled to be heard and by appearing in court at the hearing to show cause why the petition for change of name should not be granted. The order shall state that, if no written objection is timely filed, the court may grant the petition without a hearing.

(2)

(A) A copy of the order to show cause shall be published pursuant to Section 6064 of the Government Code in a newspaper of general circulation to be designated in the order published in the county. If a newspaper of general circulation is not published in the county, a copy of the order to show cause shall be posted by the clerk of the court in three of the most public places in the county in which the court is located, for a like period. Proof shall be made to the satisfaction of the court of this publication or posting at the time of the hearing of the application.

(B)

(i) On or after January 1, 2023, if the person whose name is proposed to be changed does not live in the county where the petition is filed, pursuant to subdivision (g) of Section 1276, the copy of the order to show cause shall be published pursuant to Section 6064 of the Government Code in a newspaper of general circulation published in the county of the person's residence. If a newspaper of general circulation is not published in the county of the person's residence, a copy of the order to show cause shall be posted by the clerk of the court in the county of the person's residence or a similarly situated local official in three of the most public places in the county of the person's residence, for a like period. If the place where the person seeking the name change lives does not have counties, publication shall be made according to the requirements of this paragraph in the local subdivision or territory of the person's residence. Proof shall be made to the satisfaction of the court of this publication or posting at the time of the hearing of the application.

(ii) If the person is unable to publish or post a copy of the order to show cause pursuant to clause (i), the court may allow an alternate method of publication or posting or may waive this requirement after sufficient evidence of diligent efforts to publish or post a copy of the order has been submitted to the satisfaction of the court.

(3) Four weekly publications shall be sufficient publication of the order to show cause. If the order is published in a daily newspaper, publication once a week for four successive weeks shall be sufficient.

(4) If a petition has been filed for a minor by a parent and the other parent, if living, does not join in consenting thereto, the petitioner shall cause, not less than 30 days before the hearing, to be served notice of the time and place of the hearing or a copy of the order to show cause on the other parent pursuant to Section 413.10, 414.10, 415.10, or 415.40. If notice of the hearing cannot reasonably be accomplished pursuant to Section 415.10 or 415.40, the court may order that notice be given in a manner that the court determines is reasonably calculated to give actual notice to the nonconsenting parent. In that case, if the court determines that notice by publication is reasonably calculated to give actual notice to the nonconsenting parent, the court may determine that publication of the order to show cause pursuant to this subdivision is sufficient notice to the nonconsenting parent.

(b)

(1) If the petition for a change of name alleges a reason or circumstance described in paragraph (2), and the petitioner has established that the petitioner is an active participant in the address confidentiality program created pursuant to Chapter 3.1 (commencing with Section 6205) of Division 7 of Title 1 of the Government Code, and that the name the petitioner is seeking to acquire is on file with the Secretary of State, the action for a change of name is exempt from the requirement for publication of the order to show cause under subdivision (a), and the petition and the order of the court shall, in lieu of reciting the proposed name, indicate that the proposed name is confidential and is on file with the Secretary of State pursuant to the provisions of the address confidentiality program.

(2) The procedure described in paragraph (1) applies to petitions alleging any of the following reasons or circumstances:

(A) To avoid domestic violence, as defined in Section 6211 of the Family Code.

(B) To avoid stalking, as defined in Section 646.9 of the Penal Code.

(C) To avoid sexual assault, as defined in Section 1036.2 of the Evidence Code.

(D) To avoid human trafficking, as defined in Section 236.1 of the Penal Code.

(3) For any petition under this subdivision, the current legal name of the petitioner shall be kept confidential by the court and shall not be published or posted in the court's calendars, indexes, or register of actions, as required by Article 7 (commencing with Section 69840) of Chapter 5 of Title 8 of Title 8 of the Government Code, or by any means or in any public forum, including a hardcopy or an electronic copy, or any other type of public media or display.

(4) Notwithstanding paragraph (3), the court may, at the request of the petitioner, issue an order reciting the name of the petitioner at the time of the filing of the petition and the new legal name of the petitioner as a result of the court's granting of the petition.

(5) A petitioner may request that the court file the petition and any other papers associated with the proceeding under seal. The court may consider the request at the same time as the petition for name change, and may grant the request in any case in which the court finds that all of the following factors apply:

(A) There exists an overriding interest that overcomes the right of public access to the record.

(B) The overriding interest supports sealing the record.

(C) A substantial probability exists that the overriding interest will be prejudiced if the record is not sealed.

(D) The proposed order to seal the records is narrowly tailored.

(E) No less restrictive means exist to achieve the overriding interest.

(c) If the petition is filed for a minor or nonminor dependent who is under the jurisdiction of the juvenile court, the action for a change of name is exempt from the requirement for publication of the order to show cause under subdivision (a).

(d) A proceeding for a change of name for a witness participating in the state Witness Relocation and Assistance Program established by Title 7.5 (commencing with Section 14020) of Part 4 of the Penal Code who has been approved for the change of name by the program is exempt from the requirement for publication of the order to show cause under subdivision (a).

(e) If an application for change of name is brought as part of an action under the Uniform Parentage Act (Part 3 (commencing with Section 7600) of Division 12 of the Family Code), whether as part of a petition or cross-complaint or as a separate order to show cause in a pending action thereunder, service of the application shall be made upon all other parties to the action in a like manner as prescribed for the service of a summons, as set forth in Article 3 (commencing with Section 415.10) of Chapter 4 of Title 5 of Part 2. Upon the setting of a hearing on the issue, notice of the hearing shall be given to all parties in the action in a like manner and within the time limits prescribed generally for the type of hearing (whether trial or order to show cause) at which the issue of the change of name is to be decided.

(f) If a guardian files a petition to change the name of the guardian's minor ward pursuant to Section 1276:

(1) The guardian shall provide notice of the hearing to any living parent of the minor by personal service at least 30 days before the hearing.

(2) If either or both parents are deceased or cannot be located, the guardian shall cause, not less than 30 days before the hearing, to be served a notice of the time and place of the hearing or a copy of the order to show cause on the child's grandparents, if living, pursuant to Section 413.10, 414.10, 415.10, or 415.40.

Amended by Stats 2021 ch 577 (AB 218),s 2.5, eff. 1/1/2022.
Amended by Stats 2021 ch 401 (AB 1578),s 8, eff. 1/1/2022.
Amended by Stats 2018 ch 818 (AB 2201),s 1, eff. 1/1/2019.
Amended by Stats 2018 ch 776 (AB 3250),s 10, eff. 1/1/2019.
Added by Stats 2017 ch 853 (SB 179),s 4, eff. 1/1/2018.

Section 1277.5 - Name change to conform to gender identity

(a)

(1) If a proceeding for a change of name to conform the petitioner's name to the petitioner's gender identity is commenced by the filing of a petition, the court shall thereupon make an order reciting the filing of the petition, the name of the person by whom it is filed, and the name proposed. The order shall direct all persons interested in the matter to make known any objection to the change of name by filing a written objection, which includes any reasons for the objection, within six weeks of the making of the order, and shall state that if no objection showing good cause to oppose the name change is timely filed, the court shall, without hearing, enter the order that the change of name is granted.

(2) If a petition is filed to change the name of a minor to conform to gender identity that does not include the signatures of both living parents, the petition and the order to show cause made in accordance with paragraph (1) shall be served on the parent who did not sign the petition, pursuant to Section 413.10, 414.10, 415.10, or 415.40, within 30 days from the date on which the order is made by the court. If service cannot reasonably be accomplished pursuant to Section 415.10 or 415.40, the court may order that service be accomplished in a manner that the court determines is reasonably calculated to give actual notice to the parent who did not sign the petition.

(b) The proceeding for a change of name to conform the petitioner's name to the petitioner's gender identity is exempt from any requirement for publication.

(c) A hearing date shall not be set in the proceeding unless an objection is timely filed and shows good cause for opposing the name change. Objections based solely on concerns that the proposed change is not the petitioner's actual gender identity or gender assigned at birth shall not constitute good cause. At the hearing, the court may examine under oath any of the petitioners, remonstrants, or other persons touching the petition or application, and may make an order changing the name or dismissing the petition or application as the court may deem right and proper.

Amended by Stats 2018 ch 776 (AB 3250),s 11, eff. 1/1/2019.
Added by Stats 2017 ch 853 (SB 179),s 5, eff. 1/1/2018.

Section 1278 - Hearing

(a)

(1) Except as provided in subdivisions (c) and (d), the petition or application shall be heard at the time designated by the court, only if objections are filed by a person who can, in those objections, show to the court good cause against the change of name. At the hearing, the court may examine on oath any of the petitioners, remonstrants, or other persons touching the petition or application, and may make an order changing the name, or dismissing the petition or application, as the court may deem right and proper.

(2) If no objection is filed at least two court days before the date set for hearing, the court may, without hearing, enter the order that the change of name is granted.

(b) If the provisions of subdivision (b) of Section 1277 apply, the court shall not disclose the proposed name unless the court finds by clear and convincing evidence that the allegations of domestic violence, stalking, or sexual assault in the petition are false.

(c) If the application for a change of name is brought as part of an action under the Uniform Parentage Act (Part 3 (commencing with Section 7600) of Division 12 of the Family Code), the hearing on the issue of the change of name shall be conducted pursuant to statutes and rules of court governing those proceedings, whether the hearing is conducted upon an order to show cause or upon trial.

(d) If the petition for a change of name is filed by a guardian on behalf of a minor ward, the court shall first find that the ward is likely to remain in the guardian's care until the age of majority and that the ward is not likely to be returned to the custody of the parents. Upon making those findings, the court shall consider the petition and may grant the petition only if it finds that the proposed name change is in the best interest of the child.

(e) This section shall become operative on September 1, 2018.

Added by Stats 2017 ch 853 (SB 179),s 7, eff. 1/1/2018.

Section 1278.5 - Parents do not join in consent in proceeding to change minor's name

In any proceeding pursuant to this title in which a petition has been filed to change the name of a minor, and both parents, if living, do not join in consent, the court may deny the petition in whole or in part if it finds that any portion of the proposed name change is not in the best interest of the child.

Amended by Stats 2006 ch 567 (AB 2303),s 13, eff. 1/1/2007.

Section 1279 - [Repealed]

Repealed by Stats 2000 ch 506 (SB 1350), s 4, eff. 1/1/2001.

Section 1279.5 - Common law right not abrogated; petition by prisoners; petition by persons required to register as sex offenders

(a) Except as provided in subdivision (e) or (f), this title does not abrogate the common law right of a person to change his or her name.

(b) A person under the jurisdiction of the Department of Corrections and Rehabilitation or sentenced to county jail has the right to petition the court to obtain a name or gender change pursuant to this title or Article 7 (commencing with Section 103425) of Chapter 11 of Part 1 of Division 102 of the Health and Safety Code.

(c) A person under the jurisdiction of the Department of Corrections and Rehabilitation shall provide a copy of the petition for a name change to the department, in a manner prescribed by the department, at the time the petition is filed. A person sentenced to county jail shall provide a copy of the petition for name change to the sheriff's department, in a manner prescribed by the department, at the time the petition is filed.

(d) In all documentation of a person under the jurisdiction of the Department of Corrections and Rehabilitation or imprisoned within a county jail, the new name of a person who obtains a name change shall be used, and prior names shall be listed as an alias.

(e) Notwithstanding any other law, a court shall deny a petition for a name change pursuant to this title made by a person who is required to register as a sex offender under Section 290 of the Penal Code, unless the court determines that it is in the best interest of justice to grant the petition and that doing so will not adversely affect the public safety. If a petition for a name change is granted for an individual required to register as a sex offender, the individual shall, within five working days, notify the chief of police of the city in which he or she is domiciled, or the sheriff of the county if he or she is domiciled in an unincorporated area, and additionally with the chief of police of a campus of a University of California or California State University if he or she is domiciled upon the campus or in any of its facilities.

(f) For the purpose of this section, the court shall use the California Law Enforcement Telecommunications System (CLETS) and Criminal Justice Information System (CJIS) to determine whether or not an applicant for a name change is required to register as a sex offender pursuant to Section 290 of the Penal Code. Each person applying for a name change shall declare under penalty of perjury that he or she is not required to register as a sex offender pursuant to Section 290 of the Penal Code. If a court is not equipped with CLETS or CJIS, the clerk of the court shall contact an appropriate local law enforcement agency, which shall determine whether or not the petitioner is required to register as a sex offender pursuant to Section 290 of the Penal Code.

(g) This section shall become operative on September 1, 2018.

Added by Stats 2017 ch 856 (SB 310),s 3, eff. 1/1/2018.

Section 1279.6 - Prohibited acts by trade or business

No person engaged in a trade or business of any kind or in the provision of a service of any kind shall do any of the following:

(a) Refuse to do business with a person, or refuse to provide the service to a person, regardless of the person's marital status, because he or she has chosen to use or regularly uses his or her birth name, former name, or name adopted upon solemnization of marriage or registration of domestic partnership.

(b) Impose, as a condition of doing business with a person, or as a condition of providing the service to a person, a requirement that the person, regardless of his or her marital status, use a name other than his or her birth name, former name, or name adopted upon solemnization of marriage or registration of domestic partnership, if the person has chosen to use or regularly uses that name.

Amended by Stats 2007 ch 567 (AB 102),s 3, eff. 1/1/2008.

Title 9 - ARBITRATION

Chapter 1 - GENERAL PROVISIONS

Section 1280 - Definitions

As used in this title:

(a) "Agreement" includes, but is not limited to, agreements providing for valuations, appraisals, and similar proceedings and agreements between employers and employees or between their respective representatives.

(b) "Award" includes, but is not limited to, an award made pursuant to an agreement not in writing.

(c) "Consumer" means an individual who seeks, uses, or acquires, by purchase or lease, any goods or services for personal, family, or household purposes.

(d) "Controversy" means any question arising between parties to an agreement whether the question is one of law or of fact or both.

(e) "Drafting party" means the company or business that included a predispute arbitration provision in a contract with a consumer or employee. The term includes any third party relying upon, or otherwise subject to the arbitration provision, other than the employee or consumer.

(f) "Employee" means any current employee, former employee, or applicant for employment. The term includes any person who is, was, or who claims to have been misclassified as an independent contractor or otherwise improperly placed into a category other than employee or applicant for employment.

(g) "Neutral arbitrator" means an arbitrator who is (1) selected jointly by the parties or by the arbitrators selected by the parties, or (2) appointed by the court when the parties or the arbitrators selected by the parties fail to select an arbitrator who was to be selected jointly by the parties.

(h) "Party to the arbitration" means a party to the arbitration agreement, including any of the following:

(1) A party who seeks to arbitrate a controversy pursuant to the agreement.

(2) A party against whom such arbitration is sought pursuant to the agreement.

(3) A party who is made a party to the arbitration by order of the neutral arbitrator upon that party's application, upon the application of any other party to the arbitration, or upon the neutral arbitrator's own determination.

(i) "Written agreement" includes a written agreement that has been extended or renewed by an oral or implied agreement.

Amended by Stats 2019 ch 870 (SB 707),s 2, eff. 1/1/2020.

Section 1280.2 - Reference to title applies to amendments and additions

Whenever reference is made in this title to any portion of the title or of any other law of this State, the reference applies to all amendments and additions thereto now or hereafter made.

Repealed and added by Stats. 1961, Ch. 461.

Chapter 2 - ENFORCEMENT OF ARBITRATION AGREEMENTS

Section 1281 - Generally

A written agreement to submit to arbitration an existing controversy or a controversy thereafter arising is valid, enforceable and irrevocable, save upon such grounds as exist for the revocation of any contract.

Repealed and added by Stats. 1961, Ch. 461.

Section 1281.1 - Request to arbitrate deemed made pursuant to written agreement

For the purposes of this article, any request to arbitrate made pursuant to subdivision (a) of Section 1299.4 shall be considered as made pursuant to a written agreement to submit a controversy to arbitration.

Added by Stats 2000 ch 906 (SB 402), s 1, eff. 1/1/2001.

Section 1281.12 - Time limitations contained in agreement tolled by commencement of civil action by party to agreement

If an arbitration agreement requires that arbitration of a controversy be demanded or initiated by a party to the arbitration agreement within a period of time, the commencement of a civil action by that party based upon that controversy, within that period of time, shall toll the applicable time limitations contained in the arbitration agreement with respect to that controversy, from the date the civil action is commenced until 30 days after a final determination by the court that the party is required to arbitrate the controversy, or 30 days after the final termination of the civil action that was commenced and initiated the tolling, whichever date occurs first.

Added by Stats 2006 ch 266 (AB 1553),s 1, eff. 1/1/2007.

Section 1281.2 - Grounds for not ordering parties to arbitrate controversy

On petition of a party to an arbitration agreement alleging the existence of a written agreement to arbitrate a controversy and that a party to the agreement refuses to arbitrate that controversy, the court shall order the petitioner and the respondent to arbitrate the controversy if it determines that an agreement to arbitrate the controversy exists, unless it determines that:

(a) The right to compel arbitration has been waived by the petitioner; or

(b) Grounds exist for rescission of the agreement.

(c) A party to the arbitration agreement is also a party to a pending court action or special proceeding with a third party, arising out of the same transaction or series of related transactions and there is a possibility of conflicting rulings on a common issue of law or fact. For purposes of this section, a pending court action or special proceeding includes an action or proceeding initiated by the party refusing to arbitrate after the petition to compel arbitration has been filed, but on or before the date of the hearing on the petition. This subdivision shall not be applicable to an agreement to arbitrate disputes as to the professional negligence of a health care provider made pursuant to Section 1295.

(d) The petitioner is a state or federally chartered depository institution that, on or after January 1, 2018, is seeking to apply a written agreement to arbitrate, contained in a contract consented to by a respondent consumer, to a purported contractual relationship with that respondent consumer that was created by the petitioner fraudulently without the respondent consumer's consent and by unlawfully using the respondent consumer's personal identifying information, as defined in Section 1798.92 of the Civil Code. If the court determines that a written agreement to arbitrate a controversy exists, an order to arbitrate that controversy may not be refused on the ground that the petitioner's contentions lack substantive merit. If the court determines that there are other issues between the petitioner and the respondent which are not subject to arbitration and which are the subject of a pending action or special proceeding between the petitioner and the respondent and that a determination of such issues may make the arbitration unnecessary, the court may delay its order to arbitrate until the determination of such other issues or until such earlier time as the court specifies.

If the court determines that a party to the arbitration is also a party to litigation in a pending court action or special proceeding with a third party as set forth under subdivision (c), the court (1) may refuse to enforce the arbitration agreement and may order intervention or joinder of all parties in a single action or special proceeding; (2) may order intervention or joinder as to all or only certain issues; (3) may order arbitration among the parties who have agreed to arbitration and stay the pending court action or special proceeding pending the outcome of the arbitration proceeding; or (4) may stay arbitration pending the outcome of the court action or special proceeding.

Amended by Stats 2018 ch 106 (AB 3247),s 1, eff. 1/1/2019.

Amended by Stats 2017 ch 480 (SB 33),s 1, eff. 1/1/2018.

Section 1281.3 - Consolidation of separate arbitration proceedings

A party to an arbitration agreement may petition the court to consolidate separate arbitration proceedings, and the court may order consolidation of separate arbitration proceedings when:

(1) Separate arbitration agreements or proceedings exist between the same parties; or one party is a party to a separate arbitration agreement or proceeding with a third party; and

(2) The disputes arise from the same transactions or series of related transactions; and

(3) There is common issue or issues of law or fact creating the possibility of conflicting rulings by more than one arbitrator or panel of arbitrators. If all of the applicable arbitration agreements name the same arbitrator, arbitration panel, or arbitration tribunal, the court, if it orders consolidation, shall order all matters to be heard before the arbitrator, panel, or tribunal agreed to by the parties. If the applicable arbitration agreements name separate arbitrators, panels, or tribunals, the court, if it orders consolidation, shall, in the absence of an agreed method of selection by all parties to the consolidated arbitration, appoint an arbitrator in accord with the procedures set forth in Section 1281.6.

In the event that the arbitration agreements in consolidated proceedings contain inconsistent provisions, the court shall resolve such conflicts and determine the rights and duties of the various parties to achieve substantial justice under all the circumstances.

The court may exercise its discretion under this section to deny consolidation of separate arbitration proceedings or to consolidate separate arbitration proceedings only as to certain issues, leaving other issues to be resolved in separate proceedings.

This section shall not be applicable to an agreement to arbitrate disputes as to the professional negligence of a health care provider made pursuant to Section 1295.

Added by Stats. 1978, Ch. 260.

Section 1281.4 - Stay of action or proceeding until arbitration had in accordance with order or issue to arbitrate determined

If a court of competent jurisdiction, whether in this State or not, has ordered arbitration of a controversy which is an issue involved in an action or proceeding pending before a court of this State, the court in which such action or proceeding is pending shall, upon motion of a party to such action or proceeding, stay the action or proceeding until an arbitration is had in accordance with the order to arbitrate or until such earlier time as the court specifies.

If an application has been made to a court of competent jurisdiction, whether in this State or not, for an order to arbitrate a controversy which is an issue involved in an action or proceeding pending before a court of this State and such application is undetermined, the court in which such action or proceeding is pending shall, upon motion of a party to such action or proceeding, stay the action or proceeding until the application for an order to arbitrate is determined and, if arbitration of such controversy is ordered, until an arbitration is had in accordance with the order to arbitrate or until such earlier time as the court specifies.

If the issue which is the controversy subject to arbitration is severable, the stay may be with respect to that issue only.

Added by Stats. 1961, Ch. 461.

Section 1281.5 - Arbitration by claimant to enforce lien

(a) Any person who proceeds to record and enforce a claim of lien by commencement of an action pursuant to Chapter 4 (commencing with Section 8400) of Title 2 of Part 6 of Division 4 of the Civil Code, does not thereby waive any right of arbitration the person may have pursuant to a written agreement to arbitrate, if, in filing an action to enforce the claim of lien, the claimant does either of the following:

(1) Includes an allegation in the complaint that the claimant does not intend to waive any right of arbitration, and intends to move the court, within 30 days after service of the summons and complaint, for an order to stay further proceedings in the action.

(2) At the same time that the complaint is filed, the claimant files an application that the action be stayed pending the arbitration of any issue, question, or dispute that is claimed to be arbitrable under the agreement and that is relevant to the action to enforce the claim of lien.

(b) Within 30 days after service of the summons and complaint, the claimant shall file and serve a motion and notice of motion pursuant to Section 1281.4 to stay the action pending the arbitration of any issue, question, or dispute that is claimed to be arbitrable under the agreement and that is relevant to the action to enforce the claim of lien. The failure of a claimant to comply with this subdivision is a waiver of the claimant's right to compel arbitration.

(c) The failure of a defendant to file a petition pursuant to Section 1281.2 at or before the time the defendant answers the complaint filed pursuant to subdivision (a) is a waiver of the defendant's right to compel arbitration.

Amended by Stats 2010 ch 697 (SB 189),s 25, eff. 1/1/2011, op. 7/1/2012.

Amended by Stats 2003 ch 22 (SB 113), eff. 7/1/2003.

Amended by Stats 2002 ch 784 (SB 1316),s 82, eff. 1/1/2003.

Section 1281.6 - Method of appointing arbitrator; petition made to court to appoint neutral arbitrator

If the arbitration agreement provides a method of appointing an arbitrator, that method shall be followed. If the arbitration agreement does not provide a method for appointing an arbitrator, the parties to the agreement who seek arbitration and against whom arbitration is sought may agree on a method of appointing an arbitrator and that method shall be followed. In the absence of an agreed method, or if the agreed method fails or for any reason cannot be followed, or when an arbitrator appointed fails to act and his or her successor has not been appointed, the court, on petition of a party to the arbitration agreement, shall appoint the arbitrator.

When a petition is made to the court to appoint a neutral arbitrator, the court shall nominate five persons from lists of persons supplied jointly by the parties to the arbitration or obtained from a governmental agency concerned with arbitration or private disinterested association concerned with arbitration. The parties to the agreement who seek arbitration and against whom arbitration is sought may within five days of receipt of notice of the nominees from the court jointly select the arbitrator whether or not the arbitrator is among the nominees. If the parties fail to select an arbitrator within the five-day period, the court shall appoint the arbitrator from the nominees.

Amended by Stats 2001 ch 362 (SB 475), s 3, eff. 1/1/2002.

Section 1281.7 - Petition filed in lieu of answer to complaint

A petition pursuant to Section 1281.2 may be filed in lieu of filing an answer to a complaint. The petitioning defendant shall have 15 days after any denial of the petition to plead to the complaint.

Added by Stats. 1987, Ch. 1080, Sec. 9.

Section 1281.8 - Application for provisional remedy in connection with arbitrable controversy

(a) As used in this section, "provisional remedy" includes the following:

(1) Attachments and temporary protective orders issued pursuant to Title 6.5 (commencing with Section 481.010) of Part 2.

(2) Writs of possession issued pursuant to Article 2 (commencing with Section 512.010) of Chapter 2 of Title 7 of Part 2.

(3) Preliminary injunctions and temporary restraining orders issued pursuant to Section 527.

(4) Receivers appointed pursuant to Section 564.

(b) A party to an arbitration agreement may file in the court in the county in which an arbitration proceeding is pending, or if an arbitration proceeding has not commenced, in any proper court, an application for a provisional remedy in connection with an arbitrable controversy, but only upon the ground that the award to which the applicant may be entitled may be rendered ineffectual without provisional relief. The application shall be accompanied by a complaint or by copies of the demand for arbitration and any response thereto. If accompanied by a complaint, the application shall also be accompanied by a statement stating whether the party is or is not reserving the party's right to arbitration.

(c) A claim by the party opposing issuance of a provisional remedy, that the controversy is not subject to arbitration, shall not be grounds for denial of any provisional remedy.

(d) An application for a provisional remedy under subdivision (b) shall not operate to waive any right of arbitration which the applicant may have pursuant to a written agreement to arbitrate, if, at the same time as the application for a provisional remedy is presented, the applicant also presents to the court an application that all other proceedings in the action be stayed pending the arbitration of any issue, question, or dispute which is claimed to be arbitrable under the agreement and which is relevant to the action pursuant to which the provisional remedy is sought.

Added by Stats. 1989, Ch. 470, Sec. 2.

Section 1281.85 - Ethical standards for neutral arbitrators

(a) Beginning July 1, 2002, a person serving as a neutral arbitrator pursuant to an arbitration agreement shall comply with the ethics standards for arbitrators adopted by the Judicial Council pursuant to this section. The Judicial Council shall adopt ethical standards for all neutral arbitrators effective July 1, 2002. These standards shall be consistent with the standards established for arbitrators in the judicial arbitration program and may expand but may not limit the disclosure and disqualification requirements established by this chapter. The standards shall address the disclosure of interests, relationships, or affiliations that may constitute conflicts of interest, including prior service as an arbitrator or other dispute resolution neutral entity, disqualifications, acceptance of gifts, and establishment of future professional relationships.

(b) Subdivision (a) does not apply to an arbitration conducted pursuant to the terms of a public or private sector collective bargaining agreement.

(c) The ethics requirements and standards of this chapter are nonnegotiable and shall not be waived.

Amended by Stats 2009 ch 133 (AB 1090),s 1, eff. 1/1/2010.
Amended by Stats 2002 ch 176 (SB 1707),s 1, eff. 1/1/2003.
Added by Stats 2001 ch 362 (SB 475), s 4, eff. 1/1/2002.

Section 1281.9 - Disclosures by neutral arbitrators

(a) In any arbitration pursuant to an arbitration agreement, when a person is to serve as a neutral arbitrator, the proposed neutral arbitrator shall disclose all matters that could cause a person aware of the facts to reasonably entertain a doubt that the proposed neutral arbitrator would be able to be impartial, including all of the following:

(1) The existence of any ground specified in Section 170.1 for disqualification of a judge. For purposes of paragraph (8) of subdivision (a) of Section 170.1, the proposed neutral arbitrator shall disclose whether or not he or she has a current arrangement concerning prospective employment or other compensated service as a dispute resolution neutral or is participating in, or, within the last two years, has participated in, discussions regarding such prospective employment or service with a party to the proceeding.

(2) Any matters required to be disclosed by the ethics standards for neutral arbitrators adopted by the Judicial Council pursuant to this chapter.

(3) The names of the parties to all prior or pending noncollective bargaining cases in which the proposed neutral arbitrator served or is serving as a party arbitrator for any party to the arbitration proceeding or for a lawyer for a party and the results of each case arbitrated to conclusion, including the date of the arbitration award, identification of the prevailing party, the names of the parties' attorneys and the amount of monetary damages awarded, if any. In order to preserve confidentiality, it shall be sufficient to give the name of any party who is not a party to the pending arbitration as "claimant" or "respondent" if the party is an individual and not a business or corporate entity.

(4) The names of the parties to all prior or pending noncollective bargaining cases involving any party to the arbitration or lawyer for a party for which the proposed neutral arbitrator served or is serving as neutral arbitrator, and the results of each case arbitrated to conclusion, including the date of the arbitration award, identification of the prevailing party, the names of the parties' attorneys and the amount of monetary damages awarded, if any. In order to preserve confidentiality, it shall be sufficient to give the name of any party not a party to the pending arbitration as "claimant" or "respondent" if the party is an individual and not a business or corporate entity.

(5) Any attorney-client relationship the proposed neutral arbitrator has or had with any party or lawyer for a party to the arbitration proceeding.

(6) Any professional or significant personal relationship the proposed neutral arbitrator or his or her spouse or minor child living in the household has or has had with any party to the arbitration proceeding or lawyer for a party.

(b) Subject only to the disclosure requirements of law, the proposed neutral arbitrator shall disclose all matters required to be disclosed pursuant to this section to all parties in writing within 10 calendar days of service of notice of the proposed nomination or appointment.

(c) For purposes of this section, "lawyer for a party" includes any lawyer or law firm currently associated in the practice of law with the lawyer hired to represent a party.

(d) For purposes of this section, "prior cases" means noncollective bargaining cases in which an arbitration award was rendered within five years prior to the date of the proposed nomination or appointment.

(e) For purposes of this section, "any arbitration" does not include an arbitration conducted pursuant to the terms of a public or private sector collective bargaining agreement.

Amended by Stats 2002 ch 1094 (AB 2504),s 2, eff. 1/1/2003.
Amended by Stats 2001 ch 362 (SB 475), s 5, eff. 1/1/2002.

Section 1281.91 - Disqualification of neutral arbitrators

(a) A proposed neutral arbitrator shall be disqualified if he or she fails to comply with Section 1281.9 and any party entitled to receive the disclosure serves a notice of disqualification within 15 calendar days after the proposed nominee or appointee fails to comply with Section 1281.9.

(b)

(1) If the proposed neutral arbitrator complies with Section 1281.9, the proposed neutral arbitrator shall be disqualified on the basis of the disclosure statement after any party entitled to receive the disclosure serves a notice of disqualification within 15 calendar days after service of the disclosure statement.

(2) A party shall have the right to disqualify one court-appointed arbitrator without cause in any single arbitration, and may petition the court to disqualify a subsequent appointee only upon a showing of cause.

(c) The right of a party to disqualify a proposed neutral arbitrator pursuant to this section shall be waived if the party fails to serve the notice pursuant to the times set forth in this section, unless the proposed nominee or appointee makes a material omission or material misrepresentation in his or her disclosure. Except as provided in subdivision (d), in no event may a notice of disqualification be given after a hearing of any contested issue of fact relating to the merits of the claim or after any ruling by the arbitrator regarding any contested matter. Nothing in this subdivision shall limit the right of a party to vacate an award pursuant to Section 1286.2, or to disqualify an arbitrator pursuant to any other law or statute.

(d) If any ground specified in Section 170.1 exists, a neutral arbitrator shall disqualify himself or herself upon the demand of any party made before the conclusion of the arbitration proceeding. However, this subdivision does not apply to arbitration proceedings conducted under a collective bargaining agreement between employers and employees or their respective representatives.

Added by Stats 2001 ch 362 (SB 475), s 6, eff. 1/1/2002.

Section 1281.92 - Private arbitration company administering consumer arbitration

(a) No private arbitration company may administer a consumer arbitration, or provide any other services related to a consumer arbitration, if the company has, or within the preceding year has had, a financial interest, as defined in Section 170.5, in any party or attorney for a party.

(b) No private arbitration company may administer a consumer arbitration, or provide any other services related to a consumer arbitration, if any party or attorney for a party has, or within the preceding year has had, any type of financial interest in the private arbitration company.

(c) This section shall operate only prospectively so as not to prohibit the administration of consumer arbitrations on the basis of financial interests held prior to January 1, 2003.

(d) This section applies to all consumer arbitration agreements subject to this article, and to all consumer arbitration proceedings conducted in California.

(e) This section shall become operative on January 1, 2003.

Added by Stats 2002 ch 952 (AB 2574),s 1, eff. 1/1/2003.

Section 1281.95 - Declaration by arbitrator in arbitration pursuant to construction contract; disqualification

(a) In a binding arbitration of any claim for more than three thousand dollars ($3,000) pursuant to a contract for the construction or improvement of residential property consisting of one to four units, the arbitrator shall, within 10 days following his or her appointment, provide to each party a written declaration under penalty of perjury. This declaration shall disclose (1) whether the arbitrator or his or her employer or arbitration service had or has a personal or professional affiliation with either party, and (2) whether the arbitrator or his or her employer or arbitration service has been selected or designated as an arbitrator by either party in another transaction.

(b) If the arbitrator discloses an affiliation with either party, discloses that the arbitrator has been selected or designated as an arbitrator by either party in another arbitration, or fails to comply with this section, he or she may be disqualified from the arbitration by either party.
(c) A notice of disqualification shall be served within 15 days after the arbitrator makes the required disclosures or fails to comply. The right of a party to disqualify an arbitrator shall be waived if the party fails to serve the notice of disqualification pursuant to this subdivision unless the arbitration makes a material omission or material misrepresentation in his or her disclosure. Nothing in this section shall limit the right of a party to vacate an award pursuant to Section 1286.2, or to disqualify an arbitrator pursuant to any other law or statute.
Amended by Stats 2002 ch 1008 (AB 3028),s 5, eff. 1/1/2003.

Section 1281.96 - Information required by private arbitration company administering consumer arbitration
(a) Except as provided in paragraph (2) of subdivision (c), a private arbitration company that administers or is otherwise involved in a consumer arbitration, shall collect, publish at least quarterly, and make available to the public on the internet website of the private arbitration company, if any, and on paper upon request, a single cumulative report that contains all of the following information regarding each consumer arbitration within the preceding five years:
  (1) Whether arbitration was demanded pursuant to a pre-dispute arbitration clause and, if so, whether the pre-dispute arbitration clause designated the administering private arbitration company.
  (2) The name of the nonconsumer party, if the nonconsumer party is a corporation or other business entity, and whether the nonconsumer party was the initiating party or the responding party, if known.
  (3) The nature of the dispute involved as one of the following: goods; credit; other banking or finance; insurance; health care; construction; real estate; telecommunications, including software and Internet usage; debt collection; personal injury; employment; or other. If the dispute involved employment, the amount of the employee's annual wage divided into the following ranges: less than one hundred thousand dollars ($100,000), one hundred thousand dollars ($100,000) to two hundred fifty thousand dollars ($250,000), inclusive, and over two hundred fifty thousand dollars ($250,000). If the employee chooses not to provide wage information, it may be noted.
  (4) Whether the consumer or nonconsumer party was the prevailing party. As used in this section, "prevailing party" includes the party with a net monetary recovery or an award of injunctive relief.
  (5) The total number of occasions, if any, the nonconsumer party has previously been a party in an arbitration administered by the private arbitration company.
  (6) The total number of occasions, if any, the nonconsumer party has previously been a party in a mediation administered by the private arbitration company.
  (7) Whether the consumer party was represented by an attorney and, if so, the name of the attorney and the full name of the law firm that employs the attorney, if any.
  (8) The date the private arbitration company received the demand for arbitration, the date the arbitrator was appointed, and the date of disposition by the arbitrator or private arbitration company.
  (9) The type of disposition of the dispute, if known, identified as one of the following: withdrawal, abandonment, settlement, award after hearing, award without hearing, default, or dismissal without hearing. If a case was administered in a hearing, indicate whether the hearing was conducted in person, by telephone or video conference, or by documents only.
  (10) The amount of the claim, whether equitable relief was requested or awarded, the amount of any monetary award, the amount of any attorney's fees awarded, and any other relief granted, if any.
  (11) The name of the arbitrator, the arbitrator's total fee for the case, the percentage of the arbitrator's fee allocated to each party, whether a waiver of any fees was granted, and, if so, the amount of the waiver.
  (12) Demographic data, reported in the aggregate, relative to ethnicity, race, disability, veteran status, gender, gender identity, and sexual orientation of all arbitrators as self-reported by the arbitrators. Demographic data disclosed or released pursuant to this paragraph shall also indicate the percentage of respondents who declined to respond.
(b) The information required by this section shall be made available in a format that allows the public to search and sort the information using readily available software, and shall be directly accessible from a conspicuously displayed link on the internet website of the private arbitration company with the identifying description: "consumer case information."
(c)
  (1) If the information required by subdivision (a) is provided by the private arbitration company in compliance with subdivision (b) and may be downloaded without a fee, the company may charge the actual cost of copying to any person who requests the information on paper. If the information required by subdivision (a) is not accessible by the internet in compliance with subdivision (b), the company shall provide that information without charge to any person who requests the information on paper.
  (2) Notwithstanding paragraph (1), a private arbitration company that receives funding pursuant to Chapter 8 (commencing with Section 465) of Division 1 of the Business and Professions Code and that administers or conducts fewer than 50 consumer arbitrations per year may collect and publish the information required by subdivision (a) semiannually, provide the information only on paper, and charge the actual cost of copying.
(d) This section shall apply to any consumer arbitration commenced on or after January 1, 2003.
(e) A private arbitration company shall not have any liability for collecting, publishing, or distributing the information required by this section.
(f) It is the intent of the Legislature that private arbitration companies comply with all legal obligations of this section.
(g) The amendments to subdivision (a) made by the act adding this subdivision shall not apply to any consumer arbitration administered by a private arbitration company before January 1, 2015.
Amended by Stats 2019 ch 870 (SB 707),s 3, eff. 1/1/2020.
Amended by Stats 2014 ch 870 (AB 802),s 1, eff. 1/1/2015.
Added by Stats 2002 ch 1158 (AB 2656),s 1, eff. 1/1/2003.

Section 1281.97 - Material breach for failure to pay fees before arbitration can proceed
(a)
  (1) In an employment or consumer arbitration that requires, either expressly or through application of state or federal law or the rules of the arbitration provider, the drafting party to pay certain fees and costs before the arbitration can proceed, if the fees or costs to initiate an arbitration proceeding are not paid within 30 days after the due date the drafting party is in material breach of the arbitration agreement, is in default of the arbitration, and waives its right to compel arbitration under Section 1281.2.
  (2) After an employee or consumer meets the filing requirements necessary to initiate an arbitration, the arbitration provider shall immediately provide an invoice for any fees and costs required before the arbitration can proceed to all of the parties to the arbitration. The invoice shall be provided in its entirety, shall state the full amount owed and the date that payment is due, and shall be sent to all parties by the same means on the same day. To avoid delay, absent an express provision in the arbitration agreement stating the number of days in which the parties to the arbitration must pay any required fees or costs, the arbitration provider shall issue all invoices to the parties as due upon receipt.
(b) If the drafting party materially breaches the arbitration agreement and is in default under subdivision (a), the employee or consumer may do either of the following:
  (1) Withdraw the claim from arbitration and proceed in a court of appropriate jurisdiction.

(2) Compel arbitration in which the drafting party shall pay reasonable attorney's fees and costs related to the arbitration.
(c) If the employee or consumer withdraws the claim from arbitration and proceeds with an action in a court of appropriate jurisdiction under paragraph (1) of subdivision (b), the statute of limitations with regard to all claims brought or that relate back to any claim brought in arbitration shall be tolled as of the date of the first filing of a claim in a court, arbitration forum, or other dispute resolution forum.
(d) If the employee or consumer proceeds with an action in a court of appropriate jurisdiction, the court shall impose sanctions on the drafting party in accordance with Section 1281.99.
Amended by Stats 2021 ch 222 (SB 762),s 2, eff. 1/1/2022.
Added by Stats 2019 ch 870 (SB 707),s 4, eff. 1/1/2020.

Section 1281.98 - Failure to pay fees and costs during pendency of proceeding
(a)
    (1) In an employment or consumer arbitration that requires, either expressly or through application of state or federal law or the rules of the arbitration provider, that the drafting party pay certain fees and costs during the pendency of an arbitration proceeding, if the fees or costs required to continue the arbitration proceeding are not paid within 30 days after the due date, the drafting party is in material breach of the arbitration agreement, is in default of the arbitration, and waives its right to compel the employee or consumer to proceed with that arbitration as a result of the material breach.
    (2) The arbitration provider shall provide an invoice for any fees and costs required for the arbitration proceeding to continue to all of the parties to the arbitration. The invoice shall be provided in its entirety, shall state the full amount owed and the date that payment is due, and shall be sent to all parties by the same means on the same day. To avoid delay, absent an express provision in the arbitration agreement stating the number of days in which the parties to the arbitration must pay any required fees or costs, the arbitration provider shall issue all invoices to the parties as due upon receipt. Any extension of time for the due date shall be agreed upon by all parties.
(b) If the drafting party materially breaches the arbitration agreement and is in default under subdivision (a), the employee or consumer may unilaterally elect to do any of the following:
    (1) Withdraw the claim from arbitration and proceed in a court of appropriate jurisdiction. If the employee or consumer withdraws the claim from arbitration and proceeds with an action in a court of appropriate jurisdiction, the statute of limitations with regard to all claims brought or that relate back to any claim brought in arbitration shall be tolled as of the date of the first filing of a claim in any court, arbitration forum, or other dispute resolution forum.
    (2) Continue the arbitration proceeding, if the arbitration provider agrees to continue administering the proceeding, notwithstanding the drafting party's failure to pay fees or costs. The neutral arbitrator or arbitration provider may institute a collection action at the conclusion of the arbitration proceeding against the drafting party that is in default of the arbitration for payment of all fees associated with the employment or consumer arbitration proceeding, including the cost of administering any proceedings after the default.
    (3) Petition the court for an order compelling the drafting party to pay all arbitration fees that the drafting party is obligated to pay under the arbitration agreement or the rules of the arbitration provider.
    (4) Pay the drafting party's fees and proceed with the arbitration proceeding. As part of the award, the employee or consumer shall recover all arbitration fees paid on behalf of the drafting party without regard to any findings on the merits in the underlying arbitration.
(c) If the employee or consumer withdraws the claim from arbitration and proceeds in a court of appropriate jurisdiction pursuant to paragraph (1) of subdivision (b), both of the following apply:
    (1) The employee or consumer may bring a motion, or a separate action, to recover all attorney's fees and all costs associated with the abandoned arbitration proceeding. The recovery of arbitration fees, interest, and related attorney's fees shall be without regard to any findings on the merits in the underlying action or arbitration.
    (2) The court shall impose sanctions on the drafting party in accordance with Section 1281.99.
(d) If the employee or consumer continues in arbitration pursuant to paragraphs (2) through (4) of subdivision (b), inclusive, the arbitrator shall impose appropriate sanctions on the drafting party, including monetary sanctions, issue sanctions, evidence sanctions, or terminating sanctions.
Amended by Stats 2021 ch 222 (SB 762),s 3, eff. 1/1/2022.
Added by Stats 2019 ch 870 (SB 707),s 5, eff. 1/1/2020.

Section 1281.99 - Sanctions
(a) The court shall impose a monetary sanction against a drafting party that materially breaches an arbitration agreement pursuant to subdivision (a) of Section 1281.97 or subdivision (a) of Section 1281.98, by ordering the drafting party to pay the reasonable expenses, including attorney's fees and costs, incurred by the employee or consumer as a result of the material breach.
(b) In addition to the monetary sanction described in subdivision (a), the court may order any of the following sanctions against a drafting party that materially breaches an arbitration agreement pursuant to subdivision (a) of Section 1281.97 or subdivision (a) of Section 1281.98, unless the court finds that the one subject to the sanction acted with substantial justification or that other circumstances make the imposition of the sanction unjust.
    (1) An evidence sanction by an order prohibiting the drafting party from conducting discovery in the civil action.
    (2) A terminating sanction by one of the following orders:
        (A) An order striking out the pleadings or parts of the pleadings of the drafting party.
        (B) An order rendering a judgment by default against the drafting party.
    (3) A contempt sanction by an order treating the drafting party as in contempt of court.
Added by Stats 2019 ch 870 (SB 707),s 6, eff. 1/1/2020.

Chapter 3 - CONDUCT OF ARBITRATION PROCEEDINGS

Section 1282 - Powers and duties of arbitrators
Unless the arbitration agreement otherwise provides, or unless the parties to the arbitration otherwise provide by an agreement which is not contrary to the arbitration agreement as made or as modified by all of the parties thereto:
(a) The arbitration shall be by a single neutral arbitrator.
(b) If there is more than one arbitrator, the powers and duties of the arbitrators, other than the powers and duties of a neutral arbitrator, may be exercised by a majority of them if reasonable notice of all proceedings has been given to all arbitrators.
(c) If there is more than one neutral arbitrator:
    (1) The powers and duties of a neutral arbitrator may be exercised by a majority of the neutral arbitrators.
    (2) By unanimous agreement of the neutral arbitrators, the powers and duties may be delegated to one of their number but the power to make or correct the award may not be so delegated.
(d) If there is no neutral arbitrator, the powers and duties of a neutral arbitrator may be exercised by a majority of the arbitrators.
Amended by Stats. 1997, Ch. 445, Sec. 3. Effective January 1, 1998.

Section 1282.2 - Hearing
Unless the arbitration agreement otherwise provides, or unless the parties to the arbitration otherwise provide by an agreement which is not contrary to the arbitration agreement as made or as modified by all the parties thereto:
(a)

(1) The neutral arbitrator shall appoint a time and place for the hearing and cause notice thereof to be served personally or by registered or certified mail on the parties to the arbitration and on the other arbitrators not less than seven days before the hearing. Appearance at the hearing waives the right to notice.

(2) With the exception of matters arising out of collective-bargaining agreements, those described in Section 1283.05, actions involving personal injury or death, or as provided in the parties' agreement to arbitrate, in the event the aggregate amount in controversy exceeds fifty thousand dollars ($50,000) and the arbitrator is informed thereof by any party in writing by personal service, registered or certified mail, prior to designating a time and place of hearing pursuant to paragraph (1), the neutral arbitrator by the means prescribed in paragraph (1) shall appoint a time and place for hearing not less than 60 days before the hearing, and the following provisions shall apply:

(A) Either party shall within 15 days of receipt of the notice of hearing have the right to demand in writing, served personally or by registered or certified mail, that the other party provide a list of witnesses it intends to call designating which witnesses will be called as expert witnesses and a list of documents it intends to introduce at the hearing provided that the demanding party provides such lists at the time of its demand. A copy of such demand and the demanding party's lists shall be served on the arbitrator.

(B) Such lists shall be served personally or by registered or certified mail on the requesting party 15 days thereafter. Copies thereof shall be served on the arbitrator.

(C) Listed documents shall be made available for inspection and copying at reasonable times prior to the hearing.

(D) Time limits provided herein may be waived by mutual agreement of the parties if approved by the arbitrator.

(E) The failure to list a witness or a document shall not bar the testimony of an unlisted witness or the introduction of an undesignated document at the hearing, provided that good cause for omission from the requirements of subparagraph (A) is shown, as determined by the arbitrator.

(F) The authority of the arbitrator to administer and enforce this paragraph shall be as provided in subdivisions (b) to (e), inclusive, of Section 1283.05.

(b) The neutral arbitrator may adjourn the hearing from time to time as necessary. On request of a party to the arbitration for good cause, or upon his own determination, the neutral arbitrator may postpone the hearing to a time not later than the date fixed by the agreement for making the award, or to a later date if the parties to the arbitration consent thereto.

(c) The neutral arbitrator shall preside at the hearing, shall rule on the admission and exclusion of evidence and on questions of hearing procedure and shall exercise all powers relating to the conduct of the hearing.

(d) The parties to the arbitration are entitled to be heard, to present evidence and to cross-examine witnesses appearing at the hearing, but rules of evidence and rules of judicial procedure need not be observed. On request of any party to the arbitration, the testimony of witnesses shall be given under oath.

(e) If a court has ordered a person to arbitrate a controversy, the arbitrators may hear and determine the controversy upon the evidence produced notwithstanding the failure of a party ordered to arbitrate, who has been duly notified, to appear.

(f) If an arbitrator, who has been duly notified, for any reason fails to participate in the arbitration, the arbitration shall continue but only the remaining neutral arbitrator or neutral arbitrators may make the award.

(g) If a neutral arbitrator intends to base an award upon information not obtained at the hearing, he shall disclose the information to all parties to the arbitration and give the parties an opportunity to meet it.

Amended by Stats. 1981, Ch. 714, Sec. 72.

Section 1282.4 - Representation by attorney

(a) A party to the arbitration has the right to be represented by an attorney at any proceeding or hearing in arbitration under this title. A waiver of this right may be revoked; but if a party revokes that waiver, the other party is entitled to a reasonable continuance for the purpose of procuring an attorney.

(b) Notwithstanding any other law, including Section 6125 of the Business and Professions Code, an attorney admitted to the bar of any other state may represent the parties in the course of, or in connection with, an arbitration proceeding in this state, provided that the attorney, if not admitted to the State Bar of California, satisfies all of the following:

(1) He or she timely serves the certificate described in subdivision (c).

(2) The attorney's appearance is approved in writing on that certificate by the arbitrator, the arbitrators, or the arbitral forum.

(3) The certificate bearing approval of the attorney's appearance is filed with the State Bar of California and served on the parties as described in this section.

(c) Within a reasonable period of time after the attorney described in subdivision (b) indicates an intention to appear in the arbitration, the attorney shall serve a certificate in a form prescribed by the State Bar of California on the arbitrator, arbitrators, or arbitral forum, the State Bar of California, and all other parties and counsel in the arbitration whose addresses are known to the attorney. The certificate shall state all of the following:

(1) The case name and number, and the name of the arbitrator, arbitrators, or arbitral forum assigned to the proceeding in which the attorney seeks to appear.

(2) The attorney's residence and office address.

(3) The courts before which the attorney has been admitted to practice and the dates of admission.

(4) That the attorney is currently a member in good standing of, and eligible to practice law before, the bar of those courts.

(5) That the attorney is not currently on suspension or disbarred from the practice of law before the bar of any court.

(6) That the attorney is not a resident of the State of California.

(7) That the attorney is not regularly employed in the State of California.

(8) That the attorney is not regularly engaged in substantial business, professional, or other activities in the State of California.

(9) That the attorney agrees to be subject to the jurisdiction of the courts of this state with respect to the law of this state governing the conduct of attorneys to the same extent as a member of the State Bar of California.

(10) The title of the court and the cause in which the attorney has filed an application to appear as counsel pro hac vice in this state or filed a certificate pursuant to this section in the preceding two years, the date of each application or certificate, and whether or not it was granted. If the attorney has made repeated appearances, the certificate shall reflect the special circumstances that warrant the approval of the attorney's appearance in the arbitration.

(11) The name, address, and telephone number of the active member of the State Bar of California who is the attorney of record.

(d) The arbitrator, arbitrators, or arbitral forum may approve the attorney's appearance if the attorney has complied with subdivision (c). Failure to timely file and serve the certificate described in subdivision (c) shall be grounds for disapproval of the appearance and disqualification from serving as an attorney in the arbitration in which the certificate was filed. In the absence of special circumstances, repeated appearances shall be grounds for disapproval of the appearance and disqualification from serving as an attorney in the arbitration in which the certificate was filed.

(e) Within a reasonable period of time after the arbitrator, arbitrators, or arbitral forum approves the certificate, the attorney shall file the certificate with the State Bar of California and serve the certificate as described in Section 1013a on all parties and counsel in the arbitration whose addresses are known to the attorney.

(f) An attorney who fails to file or serve the certificate required by this section or files or serves a certificate containing false information or who otherwise fails to comply with the standards of professional conduct required of members of the State Bar of California shall be subject to the disciplinary jurisdiction of the State Bar with respect to that certificate or any of his or her acts occurring in the course of the arbitration.
(g) Notwithstanding any other law, including Section 6125 of the Business and Professions Code, an attorney who is a member in good standing of the bar of any state may represent the parties in connection with rendering legal services in this state in the course of and in connection with an arbitration pending in another state.
(h) Notwithstanding any other law, including Section 6125 of the Business and Professions Code, any party to an arbitration arising under collective bargaining agreements in industries and provisions subject to either state or federal law may be represented in the course of, and in connection with, those proceedings by any person, regardless of whether that person is licensed to practice law in this state.
(i) Nothing in this section shall apply to Division 4 (commencing with Section 3200) of the Labor Code.
(j)

(1) In enacting the amendments to this section made by Assembly Bill 2086 of the 1997-98 Regular Session, it is the intent of the Legislature to respond to the holding in Birbrower v. Superior Court (1998) 17 Cal.4th 119, to provide a procedure for nonresident attorneys who are not licensed in this state to appear in California arbitration proceedings.

(2) In enacting subdivision (h), it is the intent of the Legislature to make clear that any party to an arbitration arising under a collective bargaining agreement governed by the laws of this state may be represented in the course of and in connection with those proceedings by any person regardless of whether that person is licensed to practice law in this state.

(3) Except as otherwise specifically provided in this section, in enacting the amendments to this section made by Assembly Bill 2086 of the 1997-98 Regular Session, it is the Legislature's intent that nothing in this section is intended to expand or restrict the ability of a party prior to the decision in Birbrower to elect to be represented by any person in a nonjudicial arbitration proceeding, to the extent those rights or abilities existed prior to that decision. To the extent that Birbrower is interpreted to expand or restrict that right or ability pursuant to the laws of this state, it is hereby abrogated except as specifically provided in this section.

(4) In enacting subdivision (i), it is the intent of the Legislature to make clear that nothing in this section shall affect those provisions of law governing the right of injured workers to elect to be represented by any person, regardless of whether that person is licensed to practice law in this state, as set forth in Division 4 (commencing with Section 3200) of the Labor Code.

Amended by Stats 2014 ch 71 (SB 1304),s 20, eff. 1/1/2015.
Amended by Stats 2013 ch 76 (AB 383),s 24, eff. 1/1/2014.
Amended by Stats 2012 ch 53 (AB 1631),s 1, eff. 1/1/2013.
Amended by Stats 2010 ch 277 (SB 877),s 1, eff. 1/1/2011.
Amended by Stats 2006 ch 357 (AB 2482),s 1, eff. 1/1/2007.
Amended by Stats 2005 ch 607 (AB 415),s 1, eff. 10/6/2005.
Amended by Stats 2000 ch 1011 (SB 2153), s 2, eff. 1/1/2001.

Section 1282.5 - Transcription of arbitration proceedings
(a)

(1) A party to an arbitration has the right to have a certified shorthand reporter transcribe any deposition, proceeding, or hearing. The transcript shall be the official record of the deposition, proceeding, or hearing.

(2) A party requesting a certified shorthand reporter shall make his or her request in or at either of the following:

(A) A demand for arbitration, or a response, answer, or counterclaim to a demand for arbitration.

(B) A pre-hearing scheduling conference at which a deposition, proceeding, or hearing is being calendared.

(b) If an arbitration agreement does not provide for a certified shorthand reporter, the party requesting the transcript shall incur the expense of the certified shorthand reporter. However, in a consumer arbitration, a certified shorthand reporter shall be provided upon request of an indigent consumer, as defined in Section 1284.3, at the expense of the nonconsumer party.
(c) If an arbitrator refuses to allow a party to have a certified shorthand reporter transcribe any deposition, proceeding, or hearing pursuant to this section, the party may petition the court for an order to compel the arbitrator to grant the party's request. The petition may include a request for an order to stay any deposition, proceeding, or hearing related to the arbitration pending the court's determination of the petition.
(d) This section does not add grounds for vacating an arbitration award pursuant to subdivision (a) of Section 1286.2 or for correcting an arbitration award pursuant to Section 1286.6.

Added by Stats 2016 ch 626 (SB 1007),s 1, eff. 1/1/2017.

Section 1282.6 - Subpoenas
(a) A subpoena requiring the attendance of witnesses, and a subpoena duces tecum for the production of books, records, documents and other evidence, at an arbitration proceeding or a deposition under Section 1283, and if Section 1283.05 is applicable, for the purposes of discovery, shall be issued as provided in this section. In addition, the neutral arbitrator upon their own determination may issue subpoenas for the attendance of witnesses and subpoenas duces tecum for the production of books, records, documents, and other evidence.
(b) Subpoenas shall be issued, as of course, signed but otherwise in blank, to the party requesting them, by a neutral association, organization, governmental agency, or office if the arbitration agreement provides for administration of the arbitration proceedings by, or under the rules of, a neutral association, organization, governmental agency or office, or by the neutral arbitrator.
(c) The party serving the subpoena shall fill it in before service. Subpoenas shall be served and enforced in accordance with Chapter 2 (commencing with Section 1985) of Title 3 of Part 4 of this code.

Amended by Stats 2022 ch 420 (AB 2960),s 11, eff. 1/1/2023.
Amended by Stats. 1982, Ch. 108, Sec. 1.

Section 1282.8 - Oaths
The neutral arbitrator may administer oaths.

Added by Stats. 1961, Ch. 461.

Section 1283 - Depositions
On application of a party to the arbitration, the neutral arbitrator may order the deposition of a witness to be taken for use as evidence and not for discovery if the witness cannot be compelled to attend the hearing or if exceptional circumstances exist as to make it desirable, in the interest of justice and with due regard to the importance of presenting the testimony of witnesses orally at the hearing, to allow the deposition to be taken. The deposition shall be taken in the manner prescribed by law for the taking of depositions in civil actions. If the neutral arbitrator orders the taking of the deposition of a witness who resides outside the state, the party who applied for the taking of the deposition shall obtain a commission, letters rogatory, or a letter of request therefor from the superior court in accordance with Chapter 10 (commencing with Section 2026.010) of Title 4 of Part 4.

Amended by Stats 2005 ch 294 (AB 333),s 4, eff. 1/1/2006

Section 1283.05 - Procedure for taking depositions and discovery
To the extent provided in Section 1283.1 depositions may be taken and discovery obtained in arbitration proceedings as follows:

(a) After the appointment of the arbitrator or arbitrators, the parties to the arbitration shall have the right to take depositions and to obtain discovery regarding the subject matter of the arbitration, and, to that end, to use and exercise all of the same rights, remedies, and procedures, and be subject to all of the same duties, liabilities, and obligations in the arbitration with respect to the subject matter thereof, as provided in Chapter 2 (commencing with Section 1985) of Title 3 of Part 4, and in Title 4 (commencing with Section 2016.010) of Part 4, as if the subject matter of the arbitration were pending before a superior court of this state in a civil action other than a limited civil case, subject to the limitations as to depositions set forth in subdivision (e) of this section.

(b) The arbitrator or arbitrators themselves shall have power, in addition to the power of determining the merits of the arbitration, to enforce the rights, remedies, procedures, duties, liabilities, and obligations of discovery by the imposition of the same terms, conditions, consequences, liabilities, sanctions, and penalties as can be or may be imposed in like circumstances in a civil action by a superior court of this state under the provisions of this code, except the power to order the arrest or imprisonment of a person.

(c) The arbitrator or arbitrators may consider, determine, and make such orders imposing such terms, conditions, consequences, liabilities, sanctions, and penalties, whenever necessary or appropriate at any time or stage in the course of the arbitration, and such orders shall be as conclusive, final, and enforceable as an arbitration award on the merits, if the making of any such order that is equivalent to an award or correction of an award is subject to the same conditions, if any, as are applicable to the making of an award or correction of an award.

(d) For the purpose of enforcing the duty to make discovery, to produce evidence or information, including books and records, and to produce persons to testify at a deposition or at a hearing, and to impose terms, conditions, consequences, liabilities, sanctions, and penalties upon a party for violation of any such duty, such party shall be deemed to include every affiliate of such party as defined in this section. For such purpose:

(1) The personnel of every such affiliate shall be deemed to be the officers, directors, managing agents, agents, and employees of such party to the same degree as each of them, respectively, bears such status to such affiliate; and

(2) The files, books, and records of every such affiliate shall be deemed to be in the possession and control of, and capable of production by, such party. As used in this section, "affiliate" of the party to the arbitration means and includes any party or person for whose immediate benefit the action or proceeding is prosecuted or defended, or an officer, director, superintendent, member, agent, employee, or managing agent of such party or person.

(e) Depositions for discovery shall not be taken unless leave to do so is first granted by the arbitrator or arbitrators.

Amended by Stats 2004 ch 182 (AB 3081),s 16, eff. 7/1/2005

Section 1283.1 - Provisions of section 1283.05 deemed incorporated into agreement

(a) All of the provisions of Section 1283.05 shall be conclusively deemed to be incorporated into, made a part of, and shall be applicable to, every agreement to arbitrate any dispute, controversy, or issue arising out of or resulting from any injury to, or death of, a person caused by the wrongful act or neglect of another.

(b) Only if the parties by their agreement so provide, may the provisions of Section 1283.05 be incorporated into, made a part of, or made applicable to, any other arbitration agreement.

Amended by Stats. 1970, Ch. 1045.

Section 1283.2 - Witness fees and mileage

Except for the parties to the arbitration and their agents, officers and employees, all witnesses appearing pursuant to subpoena are entitled to receive fees and mileage in the same amount and under the same circumstances as prescribed by law for witnesses in civil actions in the superior court. The fee and mileage of a witness subpoenaed upon the application of a party to the arbitration shall be paid by such party. The fee and mileage of a witness subpoenaed soley upon the determination of the neutral arbitrator shall be paid in the manner provided for the payment of the neutral arbitrator's expenses.

Added by Stats. 1961, Ch. 461.

Section 1283.4 - Award requirements

The award shall be in writing and signed by the arbitrators concurring therein. It shall include a determination of all the questions submitted to the arbitrators the decision of which is necessary in order to determine the controversy.

Added by Stats. 1961, Ch. 461.

Section 1283.6 - Service of copy of award

The neutral arbitrator shall serve a signed copy of the award on each party to the arbitration personally or by registered or certified mail or as provided in the agreement.

Added by Stats. 1961, Ch. 461.

Section 1283.8 - Time for making award

The award shall be made within the time fixed therefor by the agreement or, if not so fixed, within such time as the court orders on petition of a party to the arbitration. The parties to the arbitration may extend the time either before or after the expiration thereof. A party to the arbitration waives the objection that an award was not made within the time required unless he gives the arbitrators written notice of his objection prior to the service of a signed copy of the award on him.

Added by Stats. 1961, Ch. 461.

Section 1284 - Application to correct award

The arbitrators, upon written application of a party to the arbitration, may correct the award upon any of the grounds set forth in subdivisions (a) and (c) of Section 1286.6 not later than 30 days after service of a signed copy of the award on the applicant.

Application for such correction shall be made not later than 10 days after service of a signed copy of the award on the applicant. Upon or before making such application, the applicant shall deliver or mail a copy of the application to all of the other parties to the arbitration.

Any party to the arbitration may make written objection to such application. The objection shall be made not later than 10 days after the application is delivered or mailed to the objector. Upon or before making such objection, the objector shall deliver or mail a copy of the objection to the applicant and all the other parties to the arbitration.

The arbitrators shall either deny the application or correct the award. The denial of the application or the correction of the award shall be in writing and signed by the arbitrators concurring therein, and the neutral arbitrator shall serve a signed copy of such denial or correction on each party to the arbitration personally or by registered or certified mail or as provided in the agreement. If no denial of the application or correction of the award is served within the 30-day period provided in this section, the application for correction shall be deemed denied on the last day thereof.

Repealed and added by Stats. 1961, Ch. 461.

Section 1284.2 - Payment of expenses and fees

Unless the arbitration agreement otherwise provides or the parties to the arbitration otherwise agree, each party to the arbitration shall pay his pro rata share of the expenses and fees of the neutral arbitrator, together with other expenses of the arbitration incurred or approved by the neutral arbitrator, not including counsel fees or witness fees or other expenses incurred by a party for his own benefit.

Added by Stats. 1961, Ch. 461.

Section 1284.3 - Fees and costs assessed in consumer arbitration

(a) No neutral arbitrator or private arbitration company shall administer a consumer arbitration under any agreement or rule requiring that a consumer who is a party to the arbitration pay the fees and costs incurred by an opposing party if the consumer does not prevail in the arbitration, including, but not limited to, the fees and costs of the arbitrator, provider organization, attorney, or witnesses.

(b)

(1) All fees and costs charged to or assessed upon a consumer party by a private arbitration company in a consumer arbitration, exclusive of arbitrator fees, shall be waived for an indigent consumer. For the purposes of this section, "indigent consumer" means a person having a gross monthly income that is less than 300 percent of the federal poverty guidelines. Nothing in this section shall affect the ability of a private arbitration company to shift fees that would otherwise be charged or assessed upon a consumer party to a nonconsumer party.

(2) Prior to requesting or obtaining any fee, a private arbitration company shall provide written notice of the right to obtain a waiver of fees to a consumer or prospective consumer in a manner calculated to bring the matter to the attention of a reasonable consumer, including, but not limited to, prominently placing a notice in its first written communication to the consumer and in any invoice, bill, submission form, fee schedule, rules, or code of procedure.

(3) Any consumer requesting a waiver of fees or costs may establish his or her eligibility by making a declaration under oath on a form provided to the consumer by the private arbitration company for signature stating his or her monthly income and the number of persons living in his or her household. No private arbitration company may require a consumer to provide any further statement or evidence of indigence.

(4) Any information obtained by a private arbitration company about a consumer's identity, financial condition, income, wealth, or fee waiver request shall be kept confidential and may not be disclosed to any adverse party or any nonparty to the arbitration, except a private arbitration company may not keep confidential the number of waiver requests received or granted, or the total amount of fees waived.

(c) This section applies to all consumer arbitration agreements subject to this article, and to all consumer arbitration proceedings conducted in California.

Added by Stats 2002 ch 1101 (AB 2915),s 1, eff. 1/1/2003.

Chapter 4 - ENFORCEMENT OF THE AWARD
Article 1 - CONFIRMATION, CORRECTION OR VACATION OF THE AWARD

Section 1285 - Petition to confirm, correct or vacate award

Any party to an arbitration in which an award has been made may petition the court to confirm, correct or vacate the award. The petition shall name as respondents all parties to the arbitration and may name as respondents any other persons bound by the arbitration award.

Repealed and added by Stats. 1961, Ch. 461.

Section 1285.2 - Response to petition

A response to a petition under this chapter may request the court to dismiss the petition or to confirm, correct or vacate the award.

Added by Stats. 1961, Ch. 461.

Section 1285.4 - Petition requirements

A petition under this chapter shall:

(a) Set forth the substance of or have attached a copy of the agreement to arbitrate unless the petitioner denies the existence of such an agreement.

(b) Set forth names of the arbitrators.

(c) Set forth or have attached a copy of the award and the written opinion of the arbitrators, if any.

Added by Stats. 1961, Ch. 461.

Section 1285.6 - Response requirements

Unless a copy thereof is set forth in or attached to the petition, a response to a petition under this chapter shall:

(a) Set forth the substance of or have attached a copy of the agreement to arbitrate unless the respondent denies the existence of such an agreement.

(b) Set forth the names of the arbitrators.

(c) Set forth or have attached a copy of the award and the written opinion of the arbitrators, if any.

Added by Stats. 1961, Ch. 461.

Section 1285.8 - Petition or response to set forth grounds for correcting of vacating award

A petition to correct or vacate an award, or a response requesting such relief, shall set forth the grounds on which the request for such relief is based.

Added by Stats. 1961, Ch. 461.

Section 1286 - Duty of court if petition and response duly served and filed

If a petition or response under this chapter is duly served and filed, the court shall confirm the award as made, whether rendered in this state or another state, unless in accordance with this chapter it corrects the award and confirms it as corrected, vacates the award or dismisses the proceedings.

Amended by Stats. 1978, Ch. 260.

Section 1286.2 - Grounds for vacating award

(a) Subject to Section 1286.4, the court shall vacate the award if the court determines any of the following:

(1) The award was procured by corruption, fraud or other undue means.

(2) There was corruption in any of the arbitrators.

(3) The rights of the party were substantially prejudiced by misconduct of a neutral arbitrator.

(4) The arbitrators exceeded their powers and the award cannot be corrected without affecting the merits of the decision upon the controversy submitted.

(5) The rights of the party were substantially prejudiced by the refusal of the arbitrators to postpone the hearing upon sufficient cause being shown therefor or by the refusal of the arbitrators to hear evidence material to the controversy or by other conduct of the arbitrators contrary to the provisions of this title.

(6) An arbitrator making the award either:

(A) failed to disclose within the time required for disclosure a ground for disqualification of which the arbitrator was then aware; or

(B) was subject to disqualification upon grounds specified in Section 1281.91 but failed upon receipt of timely demand to disqualify himself or herself as required by that provision. However, this subdivision does not apply to arbitration proceedings conducted under a collective bargaining agreement between employers and employees or between their respective representatives.

(b) Petitions to vacate an arbitration award pursuant to Section 1285 are subject to the provisions of Section 128.7.

Amended by Stats 2001 ch 362 (SB 475), s 7, eff. 1/1/2002.

Section 1286.4 - Petition or response required to be duly served and filed to vacate award

The court may not vacate an award unless:

(a) A petition or response requesting that the award be vacated has been duly served and filed; or

(b) A petition or response requesting that the award be corrected has been duly served and filed and;

(1) All petitioners and respondents are before the court; or

(2) All petitioners and respondents have been given reasonable notice that the court will be requested at the hearing to vacate the award or that the court on its own motion has determined to vacate the award and all petitioners and respondents have been given an opportunity to show why the award should not be vacated.
Added by Stats. 1961, Ch. 461.

Section 1286.6 - Grounds for correcting award
Subject to Section 1286.8, the court, unless it vacates the award pursuant to Section 1286.2, shall correct the award and confirm it as corrected if the court determines that:
(a) There was an evident miscalculation of figures or an evident mistake in the description of any person, thing or property referred to in the award;
(b) The arbitrators exceeded their powers but the award may be corrected without affecting the merits of the decision upon the controversy submitted; or
(c) The award is imperfect in a matter of form, not affecting the merits of the controversy.
Added by Stats. 1961, Ch. 461.

Section 1286.8 - Petition and response required to be duly served and filed to correct award
The court may not correct an award unless:
(a) A petition or response requesting that the award be corrected has been duly served and filed; or
(b) A petition or response requesting that the award be vacated has been duly served and filed and:
(1) All petitioners and respondents are before the court; or
(2) All petitioners and respondents have been given reasonable notice that the court will be requested at the hearing to correct the award or that the court on its own motion has determined to correct the award and all petitioners and respondents have been given an opportunity to show why the award should not be corrected.
Added by Stats. 1961, Ch. 461.

Section 1287 - Rehearing if award vacated
If the award is vacated, the court may order a rehearing before new arbitrators. If the award is vacated on the grounds set forth in paragraph (4) or (5) of subdivision (a) of Section 1286.2, the court with the consent of the parties to the court proceeding may order a rehearing before the original arbitrators.
If the arbitration agreement requires that the award be made within a specified period of time, the rehearing may nevertheless be held and the award made within an equal period of time beginning with the date of the order for rehearing but only if the court determines that the purpose of the time limit agreed upon by the parties to the arbitration agreement will not be frustrated by the application of this provision.
Amended by Stats 2012 ch 162 (SB 1171),s 15, eff. 1/1/2013.

Section 1287.2 - Dismissal of proceeding as to respondent
The court shall dismiss the proceeding under this chapter as to any person named as a respondent if the court determines that such person was not bound by the arbitration award and was not a party to the arbitration.
Added by Stats. 1961, Ch. 461.

Section 1287.4 - Judgment confirming award
If an award is confirmed, judgment shall be entered in conformity therewith. The judgment so entered has the same force and effect as, and is subject to all the provisions of law relating to, a judgment in a civil action of the same jurisdictional classification; and it may be enforced like any other judgment of the court in which it is entered, in an action of the same jurisdictional classification.
Amended by Stats. 1998, Ch. 931, Sec. 124. Effective September 28, 1998.

Section 1287.6 - Force and effect of judgment
An award that has not been confirmed or vacated has the same force and effect as a contract in writing between the parties to the arbitration.
Added by Stats. 1961, Ch. 461.

Article 2 - LIMITATIONS OF TIME

Section 1288 - Time for serving and filing petitions
A petition to confirm an award shall be served and filed not later than four years after the date of service of a signed copy of the award on the petitioner. A petition to vacate an award or to correct an award shall be served and filed not later than 100 days after the date of the service of a signed copy of the award on the petitioner.
Repealed and added by Stats. 1961, Ch. 461.

Section 1288.2 - Time for serving and filing response
A response requesting that an award be vacated or that an award be corrected shall be served and filed not later than 100 days after the date of service of a signed copy of the award upon:
(a) The respondent if he was a party to the arbitration; or
(b) The respondent's representative if the respondent was not a party to the arbitration.
Added by Stats. 1961, Ch. 461.

Section 1288.4 - Time for serving and filing petition after service of award on petitioner
No petition may be served and filed under this chapter until at least 10 days after service of the signed copy of the award upon the petitioner.
Added by Stats. 1961, Ch. 461.

Section 1288.6 - Service and filing petition after determination of application to arbitrators for correction
If an application is made to the arbitrators for correction of the award, a petition may not be served and filed under this chapter until the determination of that application.
Added by Stats. 1961, Ch. 461.

Section 1288.8 - Date for service of award if application made to arbitrators for correction
If an application is made to the arbitrators for correction of the award, the date of the service of the award for the purposes of this article shall be deemed to be whichever of the following dates is the earlier:
(a) The date of service upon the petitioner of a signed copy of the correction of the award or of the denial of the application.
(b) The date that such application is deemed to be denied under Section 1284.
Added by Stats. 1961, Ch. 461.

Chapter 5 - GENERAL PROVISIONS RELATING TO JUDICIAL PROCEEDINGS
Article 1 - PETITIONS AND RESPONSES

Section 1290 - Generally
A proceeding under this title in the courts of this State is commenced by filing a petition. Any person named as a respondent in a petition may file a response thereto. The allegations of a petition are deemed to be admitted by a respondent duly served therewith unless a response is duly served and filed. The allegations of a response are deemed controverted or avoided.
Repealed and added by Stats. 1961, Ch. 461.

Section 1290.2 - Petition heard in manner for making and hearing motions
A petition under this title shall be heard in a summary way in the manner and upon the notice provided by law for the making and hearing of motions, except that not less than 10 days' notice of the date set for the hearing on the petition shall be given.
Added by Stats. 1961, Ch. 461.

Section 1290.4 - Service of petition, notice of hearing and other papers
(a) A copy of the petition and a written notice of the time and place of the hearing thereof and any other papers upon which the petition is based shall be served in the manner provided in the arbitration agreement for the service of such petition and notice.
(b) If the arbitration agreement does not provide the manner in which such service shall be made and the person upon whom service is to be made has not previously appeared in the proceeding and has not previously been served in accordance with this subdivision:
(1) Service within this State shall be made in the manner provided by law for the service of summons in an action.
(2) Service outside this State shall be made by mailing the copy of the petition and notice and other papers by registered or certified mail. Personal service is the equivalent of such service by mail. Proof of service by mail shall be made by affidavit showing such mailing together with the return receipt of the United States Post Office bearing the signature of the person on whom service was made. Notwithstanding any other provision of this title, if service is made in the manner provided in this paragraph, the petition may not be heard until at least 30 days after the date of such service.
(c) If the arbitration agreement does not provide the manner in which such service shall be made and the person on whom service is to be made has previously appeared in the proceeding or has previously been served in accordance with subdivision (b) of this section, service shall be made in the manner provided in Chapter 5 (commencing with Section 1010) of Title 14 of Part 2 of this code.
Added by Stats. 1961, Ch. 461.

Section 1290.6 - Time for serving and filing response
A response shall be served and filed within 10 days after service of the petition except that if the petition is served in the manner provided in paragraph (2) of subdivision (b) of Section 1290.4, the response shall be served and filed within 30 days after service of the petition. The time provided in this section for serving and filing a response may be extended by an agreement in writing between the parties to the court proceeding or, for good cause, by order of the court.
Added by Stats. 1961, Ch. 461.

Section 1290.8 - Manner of serving response
A response shall be served as provided in Chapter 5 (commencing with Section 1010) of Title 14 of Part 2 of this code.
Added by Stats. 1961, Ch. 461.

Section 1291 - Statement of decision
A statement of decision shall be made by the court, if requested pursuant to Section 632, whenever an order or judgment, except a special order after final judgment, is made that is appealable under this title.
Amended by Stats. 1983, Ch. 302, Sec. 2.

Section 1291.2 - Preference of proceedings
In all proceedings brought under the provisions of this title, all courts wherein such proceedings are pending shall give such proceedings preference over all other civil actions or proceedings, except older matters of the same character and matters to which special precedence may be given by law, in the matter of setting the same for hearing and in hearing the same to the end that all such proceedings shall be quickly heard and determined.
Added by Stats. 1961, Ch. 461.

Article 2 - VENUE, JURISDICTION AND COSTS

Section 1292 - Place for filing petition made prior to commencement of arbitration
Except as otherwise provided in this article, any petition made prior to the commencement of arbitration shall be filed in a court having jurisdiction in:
(a) The county where the agreement is to be performed or was made.
(b) If the agreement does not specify a county where the agreement is to be performed and the agreement was not made in any county in this state, the county where any party to the court proceeding resides or has a place of business.
(c) In any case not covered by subdivision (a) or (b) of this section, in any county in this state.
Amended by Stats. 1993, Ch. 1261, Sec. 2. Effective January 1, 1994.

Section 1292.2 - Place for filing petition made after commencement of arbitration
Except as otherwise provided in this article, any petition made after the commencement or completion of arbitration shall be filed in a court having jurisdiction in the county where the arbitration is being or has been held, or, if not held exclusively in any one county of this state, or if held outside of this state, then the petition shall be filed as provided in Section 1292.
Amended by Stats. 1993, Ch. 1261, Sec. 3. Effective January 1, 1994.

Section 1292.4 - Petition for order to arbitrate filed in pending action or proceeding
If a controversy referable to arbitration under an alleged agreement is involved in an action or proceeding pending in a superior court, a petition for an order to arbitrate shall be filed in such action or proceeding.
Added by Stats. 1961, Ch. 461.

Section 1292.6 - Retention of jurisdiction to determine subsequent petition involving same agreement and same controversy
After a petition has been filed under this title, the court in which such petition was filed retains jurisdiction to determine any subsequent petition involving the same agreement to arbitrate and the same controversy, and any such subsequent petition shall be filed in the same proceeding.
Added by Stats. 1961, Ch. 461.

Section 1292.8 - Place for making motion for stay on ground issue subject to arbitration
A motion for a stay of an action on the ground that an issue therein is subject to arbitration shall be made in the court where the action is pending.
Added by Stats. 1961, Ch. 461.

Section 1293 - Consent to jurisdiction of state courts to enforce agreement
The making of an agreement in this State providing for arbitration to be had within this State shall be deemed a consent of the parties thereto to the jurisdiction of the courts of this State to enforce such agreement by the making of any orders provided for in this title and by entering of judgment on an award under the agreement.
Repealed and added by Stats. 1961, Ch. 461.

Section 1293.2 - Awarding costs upon judicial proceeding
The court shall award costs upon any judicial proceeding under this title as provided in Chapter 6 (commencing with Section 1021) of Title 14 of Part 2 of this code.
Added by Stats. 1961, Ch. 461.

Article 3 - APPEALS

Section 1294 - Orders or judgments from which party may appeal

An aggrieved party may appeal from:
(a) An order dismissing or denying a petition to compel arbitration.
(b) An order dismissing a petition to confirm, correct or vacate an award.
(c) An order vacating an award unless a rehearing in arbitration is ordered.
(d) A judgment entered pursuant to this title.
(e) A special order after final judgment.
Repealed and added by Stats. 1961, Ch. 461.

Section 1294.2 - Review by court upon appeal

The appeal shall be taken in the same manner as an appeal from an order or judgment in a civil action. Upon an appeal from any order or judgment under this title, the court may review the decision and any intermediate ruling, proceeding, order or decision which involves the merits or necessarily affects the order or judgment appealed from, or which substantially affects the rights of a party. The court may also on such appeal review any order on motion for a new trial. The respondent on the appeal, or party in whose favor the judgment or order was given may, without appealing from such judgment, request the court to and it may review any of the foregoing matters for the purpose of determining whether or not the appellant was prejudiced by the error or errors upon which he relies for reversal or modification of the judgment or order from which the appeal is taken. The provisions of this section do not authorize the court to review any decision or order from which an appeal might have been taken.

Added by Stats. 1961, Ch. 461.

Section 1294.4 - Expedited appeal process for a person filing a claim arising under the Elder and Dependent Adult Civil Protection Act

(a) Except as provided in subdivision (b), in an appeal filed pursuant to subdivision (a) of Section 1294 involving a claim under the Elder and Dependent Adult Civil Protection Act (Chapter 11 (commencing with Section 15600) of Part 3 of Division 9 of the Welfare and Institutions Code) in which a party has been granted a preference pursuant to Section 36 of this code, the court of appeal shall issue its decision no later than 100 days after the notice of appeal is filed.
(b) The court of appeal may grant an extension of time in the appeal only if good cause is shown and the extension will promote the interests of justice.
(c) The Judicial Council shall, on or before July 1, 2017, adopt rules of court to do both of the following:
   (1) Implement subdivisions (a) and (b).
   (2) Establish a shortened notice of appeal period for the cases described in subdivision (a).
Added by Stats 2016 ch 628 (SB 1065),s 2, eff. 1/1/2017.

Title 9.1 - ARBITRATION OF MEDICAL MALPRACTICE

Section 1295 - Form of provisions in medical services contract containing provisions for arbitration

(a) Any contract for medical services which contains a provision for arbitration of any dispute as to professional negligence of a health care provider shall have such provision as the first article of the contract and shall be expressed in the following language: "It is understood that any dispute as to medical malpractice, that is as to whether any medical services rendered under this contract were unnecessary or unauthorized or were improperly, negligently or incompetently rendered, will be determined by submission to arbitration as provided by California law, and not by a lawsuit or resort to court process except as California law provides for judicial review of arbitration proceedings. Both parties to this contract, by entering into it, are giving up their constitutional right to have any such dispute decided in a court of law before a jury, and instead are accepting the use of arbitration."
(b) Immediately before the signature line provided for the individual contracting for the medical services must appear the following in at least 10-point bold red type:"NOTICE: BY SIGNING THIS CONTRACT YOU ARE AGREEING TO HAVE ANY ISSUE OF MEDICAL MALPRACTICE DECIDED BY NEUTRAL ARBITRATION AND YOU ARE GIVING UP YOUR RIGHT TO A JURY OR COURT TRIAL. SEE ARTICLE 1 OF THIS CONTRACT."
(c) Once signed, such a contract governs all subsequent open-book account transactions for medical services for which the contract was signed until or unless rescinded by written notice within 30 days of signature. Written notice of such rescission may be given by a guardian or conservator of the patient if the patient is incapacitated or a minor.
(d) Where the contract is one for medical services to a minor, it shall not be subject to disaffirmance if signed by the minor's parent or legal guardian.
(e) Such a contract is not a contract of adhesion, nor unconscionable nor otherwise improper, where it complies with subdivisions (a), (b), and (c) of this section.
(f) Subdivisions (a), (b), and (c) shall not apply to any health care service plan contract offered by an organization registered pursuant to Article 2.5 (commencing with Section 12530) of Division 3 of Title 2 of the Government Code, or licensed pursuant to Chapter 2.2 (commencing with Section 1340) of Division 2 of the Health and Safety Code, which contains an arbitration agreement if the plan complies with paragraph (10) of subdivision (b) of Section 1363 of the Health and Safety Code, or otherwise has a procedure for notifying prospective subscribers of the fact that the plan has an arbitration provision, and the plan contracts conform to subdivision (h) of Section 1373 of the Health and Safety Code.
(g) For the purposes of this section:
   (1) "Health care provider" means any person licensed or certified pursuant to Division 2 (commencing with Section 500) of the Business and Professions Code, or licensed pursuant to the Osteopathic Initiative Act, or the Chiropractic Initiative Act, or licensed pursuant to Chapter 2.5 (commencing with Section 1440) of Division 2 of the Health and Safety Code; and any clinic, health dispensary, or health facility, licensed pursuant to Division 2 (commencing with Section 1200) of the Health and Safety Code. "Health care provider" includes the legal representatives of a health care provider;
   (2) "Professional negligence" means a negligent act or omission to act by a health care provider in the rendering of professional services, which act or omission is the proximate cause of a personal injury or wrongful death, provided that such services are within the scope of services for which the provider is licensed and which are not within any restriction imposed by the licensing agency or licensed hospital.
Amended by Stats 2023 ch 42 (AB 118),s 1, eff. 7/10/2023.
Amended by Stats. 1976, Ch. 1185.

Title 9.2 - PUBLIC CONSTRUCTION CONTRACT ARBITRATION

Section 1296 - Agreement that arbitrator's decision supported by law and substantial evidence

The parties to a construction contract with a public agency may expressly agree in writing that in any arbitration to resolve a dispute relating to the contract, the arbitrator's award shall be supported by law and substantial evidence. If the agreement so provides, a court shall, subject to Section 1286.4, vacate the award if after review of the award it determines either that the award is not supported by substantial evidence or that it is based on an error of law.

Added by Stats. 1979, Ch. 46.

Title 9.3 - ARBITRATION AND CONCILIATION OF INTERNATIONAL COMMERCIAL DISPUTES

Chapter 1 - APPLICATION AND INTERPRETATION

Article 1 - SCOPE OF APPLICATION

Section 1297.11 - Applicability of title generally

This title applies to international commercial arbitration and conciliation, subject to any agreement which is in force between the United States and any other state or states.

Added by Stats. 1988, Ch. 23, Sec. 1. Effective March 7, 1988.

Section 1297.12 - Applicability only if place of arbitration or conciliation in state

This title, except Article 2 (commencing with Section 1297.81) of Chapter 2 and Article 3 (commencing with Section 1297.91) of Chapter 2, applies only if the place of arbitration or conciliation is in the State of California.

Added by Stats. 1988, Ch. 23, Sec. 1. Effective March 7, 1988.

Section 1297.13 - Conditions making agreement international

An arbitration or conciliation agreement is international if any of the following applies:

(a) The parties to an arbitration or conciliation agreement have, at the time of the conclusion of that agreement, their places of business in different states.

(b) One of the following places is situated outside the state in which the parties have their places of business:

  (i) The place of arbitration or conciliation if determined in, or pursuant to, the arbitration or conciliation agreement.

  (ii) Any place where a substantial part of the obligations of the commercial relationship is to be performed.

  (iii) The place with which the subject matter of the dispute is most closely connected.

(c) The parties have expressly agreed that the subject matter of the arbitration or conciliation agreement relates to commercial interests in more than one state.

(d) The subject matter of the arbitration or conciliation agreement is otherwise related to commercial interests in more than one state.

Added by Stats. 1988, Ch. 23, Sec. 1. Effective March 7, 1988.

Section 1297.14 - Place of business if party has more than one place of business

For the purposes of Section 1297.13, if a party has more than one place of business, the place of business is that which has the closest relationship to the arbitration agreement, and if a party does not have a place of business, reference is to be made to his habitual residence.

Added by Stats. 1988, Ch. 23, Sec. 1. Effective March 7, 1988.

Section 1297.15 - States of United States considered one state

For the purposes of Section 1297.13, the states of the United States, including the District of Columbia, shall be considered one state.

Added by Stats. 1988, Ch. 23, Sec. 1. Effective March 7, 1988.

Section 1297.16 - Relationships making agreement commercial

An arbitration or conciliation agreement is commercial if it arises out of a relationship of a commercial nature including, but not limited to, any of the following:

(a) A transaction for the supply or exchange of goods or services.

(b) A distribution agreement.

(c) A commercial representation or agency.

(d) An exploitation agreement or concession.

(e) A joint venture or other, related form of industrial or business cooperation.

(f) The carriage of goods or passengers by air, sea, rail, or road.

(g) Construction.

(h) Insurance.

(i) Licensing.

(j) Factoring.

(k) Leasing.

(l) Consulting.

(m) Engineering.

(n) Financing.

(o) Banking.

(p) The transfer of data or technology.

(q) Intellectual or industrial property, including trademarks, patents, copyrights and software programs.

(r) Professional services.

Added by Stats. 1988, Ch. 23, Sec. 1. Effective March 7, 1988.

Section 1297.17 - Other state laws not affected

This title shall not affect any other law in force in California by virtue of which certain disputes may not be submitted to arbitration or may be submitted to arbitration only in accordance with provisions other than those of this title. Notwithstanding the foregoing, this title supersedes Sections 1280 to 1284.2, inclusive, with respect to international commercial arbitration and conciliation.

Added by Stats. 1988, Ch. 23, Sec. 1. Effective March 7, 1988.

Article 2 - INTERPRETATION

Section 1297.21 - Definitions

For the purposes of this title:

(a) "Arbitral award" means any decision of the arbitral tribunal on the substance of the dispute submitted to it and includes an interim, interlocutory, or partial arbitral award.

(b) "Arbitral tribunal" means a sole arbitrator or a panel of arbitrators.

(c) "Arbitration" means any arbitration whether or not administered by a permanent arbitral institution.

(d) "Conciliation" means any conciliation whether or not administered by a permanent conciliation institution.

(e) "Chief Justice" means the Chief Justice of California or his or her designee.

(f) "Court" means a body or an organ of the judicial system of a state.

(g) "Party" means a party to an arbitration or conciliation agreement.

(h) "Superior court" means the superior court in the county in this state selected pursuant to Section 1297.61.

(i) "Supreme Court" means the Supreme Court of California.

Added by Stats. 1988, Ch. 23, Sec. 1. Effective March 7, 1988.

Section 1297.22 - Right of parties to authorize third party to make determination

Where a provision of this title, except Article 1 (commencing with Section 1297.281) of Chapter 6, leaves the parties free to determine a certain issue, such freedom includes the right of the parties to authorize a third party, including an institution, to make that determination.
Added by Stats. 1988, Ch. 23, Sec. 1. Effective March 7, 1988.

Section 1297.23 - Reference to agreement to include rules referred to in agreement
Where a provision of this title refers to the fact that the parties have agreed or that they may agree, or in any other way refers to an agreement of the parties, such agreement shall be deemed to include any arbitration or conciliation rules referred to in that agreement.
Added by Stats. 1988, Ch. 23, Sec. 1. Effective March 7, 1988.

Section 1297.24 - Reference to claim applies to counterclaim
Where this title, other than Article 8 (commencing with Section 1297. 251) of Chapter 5, Article 5 (commencing with Section 1297.321) of Chapter 6, or subdivision (a) of Section 1297.322, refers to a claim, it also applies to a counterclaim, and where it refers to a defense, it also applies to a defense to that counterclaim.
Added by Stats. 1988, Ch. 23, Sec. 1. Effective March 7, 1988.

Article 3 - RECEIPT OF WRITTEN COMMUNICATIONS

Section 1297.31 - When communication deemed received
Unless otherwise agreed by the parties, any written communication is deemed to have been received if it is delivered to the addressee personally or if it is delivered at his place of business, habitual residence, or mailing address, and the communication is deemed to have been received on the day it is so delivered.
Added by Stats. 1988, Ch. 23, Sec. 1. Effective March 7, 1988.

Section 1297.32 - Communication sent to addresse's last known place of business, residence or mailing address
If none of the places referred to in Section 1297.31 can be found after making a reasonable inquiry, a written communication is deemed to have been received if it is sent to the addressee's last known place of business, habitual residence, or mailing address by registered mail or by any other means which provides a record of the attempt to deliver it.
Added by Stats. 1988, Ch. 23, Sec. 1. Effective March 7, 1988.

Section 1297.33 - Inapplicable to communications in respect to court proceedings
This article does not apply to written communications in respect of court proceedings.
Added by Stats. 1988, Ch. 23, Sec. 1. Effective March 7, 1988.

Article 4 - WAIVER OF RIGHT TO OBJECT

Section 1297.41 - Proceeding to arbitration without timely stating objection
A party who knows that any provision of this title, or any requirement under the arbitration agreement, has not been complied with and yet proceeds with the arbitration without stating his or her objection to noncompliance without undue delay or, if a time limit is provided for stating that objection, within that period of time, shall be deemed to have waived his right to object.
Added by Stats. 1988, Ch. 23, Sec. 1. Effective March 7, 1988.

Section 1297.42 - Any provision of this title defined
For purposes of Section 1297.41, "any provision of this title" means any provision of this title in respect of which the parties may otherwise agree.
Added by Stats. 1988, Ch. 23, Sec. 1. Effective March 7, 1988.

Article 5 - EXTENT OF JUDICIAL INTERVENTION

Section 1297.51 - Intervention by court
In matters governed by this title, no court shall intervene except where so provided in this title, or applicable federal law.
Added by Stats. 1988, Ch. 23, Sec. 1. Effective March 7, 1988.

Article 6 - FUNCTIONS

Section 1297.61 - Functions performed by superior courts
The functions referred to in Sections 1297.114, 1297.115, 1297.116, 1297.134, 1297.135, 1297.136, 1297.165, 1297.166, and 1297.167 shall be performed by the superior court of the county in which the place of arbitration is located. The functions referred to in Section 1297.81 shall be performed by the superior court selected pursuant to Article 2 (commencing with Section 1292) of Chapter 5 of Title 9.
Added by Stats. 1988, Ch. 23, Sec. 1. Effective March 7, 1988.

Chapter 2 - ARBITRATION AGREEMENTS AND JUDICIAL MEASURES IN AID OF ARBITRATION

Article 1 - DEFINITION AND FORM OF ARBITRATION AGREEMENTS

Section 1297.71 - Arbitration agreement defined
An "arbitration agreement" is an agreement by the parties to submit to arbitration all or certain disputes which have arisen or which may arise between them in respect of a defined legal relationship, whether contractual or not. An arbitration agreement may be in the form of an arbitration clause in a contract or in the form of a separate agreement.
Added by Stats. 1988, Ch. 23, Sec. 1. Effective March 7, 1988.

Section 1297.72 - Agreement to be in writing
An arbitration agreement shall be in writing. An agreement is in writing if it is contained in a document signed by the parties or in an exchange of letters, telex, telegrams, or other means of telecommunication which provide a record of this agreement, or in an exchange of statements of claim and defense in which the existence of an agreement is alleged by one party and not denied by another. The reference in a contract to a document containing an arbitration clause constitutes an arbitration agreement provided that the contract is in writing and the reference is such as to make that clause part of the contract.
Added by Stats. 1988, Ch. 23, Sec. 1. Effective March 7, 1988.

Article 2 - STAY OF PROCEEDINGS

Section 1297.81 - Application for order to stay proceedings and compel arbitration
When a party to an international commercial arbitration agreement as defined in this title commences judicial proceedings seeking relief with respect to a matter covered by the agreement to arbitrate, any other party to the agreement may apply to the superior court for an order to stay the proceedings and to compel arbitration.
Added by Stats. 1988, Ch. 23, Sec. 1. Effective March 7, 1988.

Section 1297.82 - Timely request granted
A timely request for a stay of judicial proceedings made under Section 1297.81 shall be granted.
Added by Stats. 1988, Ch. 23, Sec. 1. Effective March 7, 1988.

Article 3 - INTERIM MEASURES

Section 1297.91 - Request for interim measures not incompatible with agreement

It is not incompatible with an arbitration agreement for a party to request from a superior court, before or during arbitral proceedings, an interim measure of protection, or for the court to grant such a measure.
Added by Stats. 1988, Ch. 23, Sec. 1. Effective March 7, 1988.

Section 1297.92 - Request for enforcement of award of arbitral tribunal
Any party to an arbitration governed by this title may request from the superior court enforcement of an award of an arbitral tribunal to take any interim measure of protection of an arbitral tribunal pursuant to Article 2 (commencing with Section 1297.171) of Chapter 4. Enforcement shall be granted pursuant to the law applicable to the granting of the type of interim relief requested.
Added by Stats. 1988, Ch. 23, Sec. 1. Effective March 7, 1988.

Section 1297.93 - Measures court may grant in connection with pending arbitration
Measures which the court may grant in connection with a pending arbitration include, but are not limited to:
(a) An order of attachment issued to assure that the award to which applicant may be entitled is not rendered ineffectual by the dissipation of party assets.
(b) A preliminary injunction granted in order to protect trade secrets or to conserve goods which are the subject matter of the arbitral dispute.
Added by Stats. 1988, Ch. 23, Sec. 1. Effective March 7, 1988.

Section 1297.94 - Preclusive effect given to findings of fact of arbitral tribunal
In considering a request for interim relief, the court shall give preclusive effect to any and all findings of fact of the arbitral tribunal including the probable validity of the claim which is the subject of the award for interim relief and which the arbitral tribunal has previously granted in the proceeding in question, provided that such interim award is consistent with public policy.
Added by Stats. 1988, Ch. 23, Sec. 1. Effective March 7, 1988.

Section 1297.95 - Preclusive effect to tribunal's findings given until court finding on jurisdiction
Where the arbitral tribunal has not ruled on an objection to its jurisdiction, the court shall not grant preclusive effect to the tribunal's findings until the court has made an independent finding as to the jurisdiction of the arbitral tribunal. If the court rules that the arbitral tribunal did not have jurisdiction, the application for interim measures of relief shall be denied. Such a ruling by the court that the arbitral tribunal lacks jurisdiction is not binding on the arbitral tribunal or subsequent judicial proceeding.
Added by Stats. 1988, Ch. 23, Sec. 1. Effective March 7, 1988.

Chapter 3 - COMPOSITION OF ARBITRAL TRIBUNALS
Article 1 - NUMBER OF ARBITRATORS
Section 1297.101 - Generally
The parties may agree on the number of arbitrators. Otherwise, there shall be one arbitrator.
Added by Stats. 1988, Ch. 23, Sec. 1. Effective March 7, 1988.

Article 2 - APPOINTMENT OF ARBITRATORS
Section 1297.111 - Person of any nationality
A person of any nationality may be an arbitrator.
Added by Stats. 1988, Ch. 23, Sec. 1. Effective March 7, 1988.

Section 1297.112 - Parties may agree on procedure for appointing
Subject to Sections 1297.115 and 1297.116, the parties may agree on a procedure for appointing the arbitral tribunal.
Added by Stats. 1988, Ch. 23, Sec. 1. Effective March 7, 1988.

Section 1297.113 - Appointment in arbitration with three arbitrators and two parties
Failing such agreement referred to in Section 1297.112, in an arbitration with three arbitrators and two parties, each party shall appoint one arbitrator, and the two appointed arbitrators shall appoint the third arbitrator.
Added by Stats. 1988, Ch. 23, Sec. 1. Effective March 7, 1988.

Section 1297.114 - Failure to timely agree on appointment
If the appointment procedure in Section 1297.113 applies and either a party fails to appoint an arbitrator within 30 days after receipt of a request to do so from the other party, or the two appointed arbitrators fail to agree on the third arbitrator within 30 days after their appointment, the appointment shall be made, upon request of a party, by the superior court.
Added by Stats. 1988, Ch. 23, Sec. 1. Effective March 7, 1988.

Section 1297.115 - Appointment on failure to agree on sole arbitrator
Failing any agreement referred to in Section 1297.112, in an arbitration with a sole arbitrator, if the parties fail to agree on the arbitrator, the appointment shall be made, upon request of a party, by the superior court.
Added by Stats. 1988, Ch. 23, Sec. 1. Effective March 7, 1988.

Section 1297.116 - Necessary measures taken by superior court
The superior court, upon the request of a party, may take the necessary measures, unless the agreement on the appointment procedure provides other means for securing the appointment, where, under an appointment procedure agreed upon by the parties, any of the following occurs:
(a) A party fails to act as required under that procedure.
(b) The parties, or two appointed arbitrators, fail to reach an agreement expected of them under that procedure.
(c) A third party, including an institution, fails to perform any function entrusted to it under that procedure.
Added by Stats. 1988, Ch. 23, Sec. 1. Effective March 7, 1988.

Section 1297.117 - Decision of superior court final
A decision on a matter entrusted to the superior court pursuant to Sections 1297.114, 127.115, and 1297.116 is final and is not subject to appeal.
Added by Stats. 1988, Ch. 23, Sec. 1. Effective March 7, 1988.

Section 1297.118 - Considerations by superior court in appointing arbitrator
The superior court, in appointing an arbitrator, shall have due regard to all of the following:
(a) Any qualifications required of the arbitrator by the agreement of the parties.
(b) Other considerations as are likely to secure the appointment of an independent and impartial arbitrator.
(c) In the case of a sole or third arbitrator, the advisability of appointing an arbitrator of a nationality other than those of the parties.
Added by Stats. 1988, Ch. 23, Sec. 1. Effective March 7, 1988.

Section 1297.119 - Immunity of arbitrator
An arbitrator has the immunity of a judicial officer from civil liability when acting in the capacity of arbitrator under any statute or contract. The immunity afforded by this section shall supplement, and not supplant, any otherwise applicable common law or statutory immunity.
Added by Stats. 1994, Ch. 228, Sec. 1. Effective January 1, 1995.

Article 3 - GROUNDS FOR CHALLENGE
Section 1297.121 - Disclosure of information causing impartiality to be question

Except as otherwise provided in this title, all persons whose names have been submitted for consideration for appointment or designation as arbitrators or conciliators, or who have been appointed or designated as such, shall, within 15 days, make a disclosure to the parties of any information which might cause their impartiality to be questioned including, but not limited to, any of the following instances:

(a) The person has a personal bias or prejudice concerning a party, or personal knowledge of disputed evidentiary facts concerning the proceeding.

(b) The person served as a lawyer in the matter in controversy, or the person is or has been associated with another who has participated in the matter during such association, or he or she has been a material witness concerning it.

(c) The person served as an arbitrator or conciliator in another proceeding involving one or more of the parties to the proceeding.

(d) The person, individually or a fiduciary, or such person's spouse or minor child residing in such person's household, has a financial interest in the subject matter in controversy or in a party to the proceeding, or any other interest that could be substantially affected by the outcome of the proceeding.

(e) The person, his or her spouse, or a person within the third degree of relationship to either of them, or the spouse of such a person meets any of the following conditions:

   (i) The person is or has been a party to the proceeding, or an officer, director, or trustee of a party.

   (ii) The person is acting or has acted as a lawyer in the proceeding.

   (iii) The person is known to have an interest that could be substantially affected by the outcome of the proceeding.

   (iv) The person is likely to be a material witness in the proceeding.

(f) The person has a close personal or professional relationship with a person who meets any of the following conditions:

   (i) The person is or has been a party to the proceeding, or an officer, director, or trustee of a party.

   (ii) The person is acting or has acted as a lawyer or representative in the proceeding.

   (iii) The person is or expects to be nominated as an arbitrator or conciliator in the proceedings.

   (iv) The person is known to have an interest that could be substantially affected by the outcome of the proceeding.

   (v) The person is likely to be a material witness in the proceeding.

Added by Stats. 1988, Ch. 23, Sec. 1. Effective March 7, 1988.

Section 1297.122 - Waiver of disclosure

The obligation to disclose information set forth in Section 1297.121 is mandatory and cannot be waived as to the parties with respect to persons serving either as the sole arbitrator or sole conciliator or as the chief or prevailing arbitrator or conciliator. The parties may otherwise agree to waive such disclosure.

Added by Stats. 1988, Ch. 23, Sec. 1. Effective March 7, 1988.

Section 1297.123 - Continuation of duty to disclose

From the time of appointment and throughout the arbitral proceedings, an arbitrator, shall, without delay, disclose to the parties any circumstances referred to in Section 1297.121 which were not previously disclosed.

Added by Stats. 1988, Ch. 23, Sec. 1. Effective March 7, 1988.

Section 1297.124 - Justifiable doubts as to independence or impartiality or qualifications

Unless otherwise agreed by the parties or the rules governing the arbitration, an arbitrator may be challenged only if circumstances exist that give rise to justifiable doubts as to his or her independence or impartiality, or as to his or her possession of the qualifications upon which the parties have agreed.

Added by Stats. 1988, Ch. 23, Sec. 1. Effective March 7, 1988.

Section 1297.125 - Challenge for reasons becoming apparent after appointment

A party may challenge an arbitrator appointed by it, or in whose appointment it has participated, only for reasons of which it becomes aware after the appointment has been made.

Added by Stats. 1988, Ch. 23, Sec. 1. Effective March 7, 1988.

Article 4 - CHALLENGE PROCEDURE

Section 1297.131 - Parties may agree on procedure

The parties may agree on a procedure for challenging an arbitrator and the decision reached pursuant to that procedure shall be final.

Added by Stats. 1988, Ch. 23, Sec. 1. Effective March 7, 1988.

Section 1297.132 - Time for sending written statement of reasons for challenge

Failing any agreement referred to in Section 1297.131, a party which intends to challenge an arbitrator shall, within 15 days after becoming aware of the constitution of the arbitral tribunal or after becoming aware of any circumstances referred to in Sections 1297.124 and 1297.125, whichever shall be later, send a written statement of the reasons for the challenge to the arbitral tribunal.

Added by Stats. 1988, Ch. 23, Sec. 1. Effective March 7, 1988.

Section 1297.133 - Arbitral tribunal to decide challenge

Unless the arbitrator challenged under Section 1297.132 withdraws from his or her office or the other party agrees to the challenge, the arbitral tribunal shall decide on the challenge.

Added by Stats. 1988, Ch. 23, Sec. 1. Effective March 7, 1988.

Section 1297.134 - Requesting superior court to decide on challenge

If a challenge following the procedure under Section 1297.133 is not successful, the challenging party may request the superior court, within 30 days after having received notice of the decision rejecting the challenge, to decide on the challenge. If a challenge is based upon the grounds set forth in Section 1297.121, and the superior court determines that the facts support a finding that such ground or grounds fairly exist, then the challenge should be sustained.

Added by Stats. 1988, Ch. 23, Sec. 1. Effective March 7, 1988.

Section 1297.135 - Decision of superior court final

The decision of the superior court under Section 1297.134 is final and is not subject to appeal.

Added by Stats. 1988, Ch. 23, Sec. 1. Effective March 7, 1988.

Section 1297.136 - Continuation with arbitral proceedings while request pending

While a request under Section 1297.134 is pending, the arbitral tribunal, including the challenged arbitrator, may continue with the arbitral proceedings and make an arbitral award.

Added by Stats. 1988, Ch. 23, Sec. 1. Effective March 7, 1988.

Article 5 - FAILURE OR IMPOSSIBILITY TO ACT

Section 1297.141 - Termination of mandate of arbitrator

The mandate of an arbitrator terminates if he becomes de jure or de facto unable to perform his or her functions or for other reasons fails to act without undue delay, and he withdraws from his or her office or the parties agree to the termination of his or her mandate.

Added by Stats. 1988, Ch. 23, Sec. 1. Effective March 7, 1988.

Section 1297.142 - Requesting superior court to decide remaining controversy

If a controversy remains concerning any of the grounds referred to in Section 1297.141, a party may request the superior court to decide on the termination of the mandate.
Added by Stats. 1988, Ch. 23, Sec. 1. Effective March 7, 1988.

Section 1297.143 - Decision of superior court final
A decision of the superior court under Section 1297.142 is not subject to appeal.
Added by Stats. 1988, Ch. 23, Sec. 1. Effective March 7, 1988.

Section 1297.144 - Acceptance of validity of ground referred to in section 1297.132 not implied
If, under this section or Section 1297.132, an arbitrator withdraws from office or a party agrees to the termination of the mandate of an arbitrator, this does not imply acceptance of the validity of any ground referred to in Section 1297.132.
Added by Stats. 1988, Ch. 23, Sec. 1. Effective March 7, 1988.

Article 6 - TERMINATION OF MANDATE AND SUBSTITUTION OF ARBITRATORS

Section 1297.151 - Termination upon withdrawal of arbitrator
In addition to the circumstances referred to under Article 4 (commencing with Section 1297.131) and Article 5 (commencing with Section 1297.141) of this chapter, the mandate of an arbitrator terminates upon his or her withdrawal from office for any reason, or by or pursuant to agreement of the parties.
Added by Stats. 1988, Ch. 23, Sec. 1. Effective March 7, 1988.

Section 1297.152 - Appointment of substitute arbitrator
Where the mandate of an arbitrator terminates, a substitute arbitrator shall be appointed according to the rules that were applicable to the appointment of the arbitrator being replaced.
Added by Stats. 1988, Ch. 23, Sec. 1. Effective March 7, 1988.

Section 1297.153 - Hearings previously held repeated
Unless otherwise agreed by the parties:
(a) Where the sole or presiding arbitrator is replaced, any hearings previously held shall be repeated.
(b) Where an arbitrator other than the sole or presiding arbitrator is replaced, any hearings previously held may be repeated at the discretion of the arbitral tribunal.
Added by Stats. 1988, Ch. 23, Sec. 1. Effective March 7, 1988.

Section 1297.154 - Order or ruling prior to replacement not invalid
Unless otherwise agreed by the parties, an order or ruling of the arbitral tribunal made prior to the replacement of an arbitrator under this section is not invalid because there has been a change in the composition of the tribunal.
Added by Stats. 1988, Ch. 23, Sec. 1. Effective March 7, 1988.

Chapter 4 - JURISDICTION OF ARBITRAL TRIBUNALS

Article 1 - COMPETENCE OF AN ARBITRAL TRIBUNAL TO RULE ON ITS JURISDICTION

Section 1297.161 - Arbitration clause forming part of contract treated as agreement independent of other terms of contract
The arbitral tribunal may rule on its own jurisdiction, including ruling on any objections with respect to the existence or validity of the arbitration agreement, and for that purpose, an arbitration clause which forms part of a contract shall be treated as an agreement independent of the other terms of the contract, and a decision by the arbitral tribunal that the contract is null and void shall not entail ipso jure the invalidity of the arbitration clause.
Added by Stats. 1988, Ch. 23, Sec. 1. Effective March 7, 1988.

Section 1297.162 - Raising plea tribunal without jurisdiction
A plea that the arbitral tribunal does not have jurisdiction shall be raised not later than the submission of the statement of defense. However, a party is not precluded from raising such a plea by the fact that he or she has appointed, or participated in the appointment of, an arbitrator.
Added by Stats. 1988, Ch. 23, Sec. 1. Effective March 7, 1988.

Section 1297.163 - Raising plea that tribunal exceeding jurisdiction
A plea that the arbitral tribunal is exceeding the scope of its authority shall be raised as soon as the matter alleged to be beyond the scope of its authority is raised during the arbitral proceedings.
Added by Stats. 1988, Ch. 23, Sec. 1. Effective March 7, 1988.

Section 1297.164 - Admission of later plea if delay justified
The arbitral tribunal may, in either of the cases referred to in Sections 1297.162 and 1297.163, admit a later plea if it considers the delay justified.
Added by Stats. 1988, Ch. 23, Sec. 1. Effective March 7, 1988.

Section 1297.165 - Plea rules on as preliminary question or award on merits
The arbitral tribunal may rule on a plea referred to in Sections 1297.162 and 1297.163 either as a preliminary question or in an award on the merits.
Added by Stats. 1988, Ch. 23, Sec. 1. Effective March 7, 1988.

Section 1297.166 - Time for requesting superior court to decide matter
If the arbitral tribunal rules as a preliminary question that it has jurisdiction, any party shall request the superior court, within 30 days after having received notice of that ruling, to decide the matter or shall be deemed to have waived objection to such finding.
Added by Stats. 1988, Ch. 23, Sec. 1. Effective March 7, 1988.

Section 1297.167 - Continuation of proceedings while request pending
While a request under Section 1297.166 is pending, the arbitral tribunal may continue with the arbitral proceedings and make an arbitral award.
Added by Stats. 1988, Ch. 23, Sec. 1. Effective March 7, 1988.

Article 2 - INTERIM MEASURES ORDERED BY ARBITRAL TRIBUNALS

Section 1297.171 - Authority to take measures of protection
Unless otherwise agreed by the parties, the arbitral tribunal may, at the request of a party, order a party to take any interim measure of protection as the arbitral tribunal may consider necessary in respect of the subject matter of the dispute.
Added by Stats. 1988, Ch. 23, Sec. 1. Effective March 7, 1988.

Section 1297.172 - Appropriate security provided
The arbitral tribunal may require a party to provide appropriate security in connection with a measure ordered under Section 1297.171.
Added by Stats. 1988, Ch. 23, Sec. 1. Effective March 7, 1988.

Chapter 5 - MANNER AND CONDUCT OF ARBITRATION

Article 1 - EQUAL TREATMENT OF PARTIES

Section 1297.181 - Generally
The parties shall be treated with equality and each party shall be given a full opportunity to present his or her case.
Added by Stats. 1988, Ch. 23, Sec. 1. Effective March 7, 1988.

Article 1.5 - REPRESENTATION BY FOREIGN AND OUT-OF-STATE ATTORNEYS

Section 1297.185 - "Qualified attorney" defined

For purposes of this article, a "qualified attorney" means an individual who is not admitted to practice law in this state but is all of the following:

(a) Admitted to practice law in a state or territory of the United States or the District of Columbia or a member of a recognized legal profession in a foreign jurisdiction, the members of which are admitted or otherwise authorized to practice as attorneys or counselors at law or the equivalent.

(b) Subject to effective regulation and discipline by a duly constituted professional body or public authority of that jurisdiction.

(c) In good standing in every jurisdiction in which he or she is admitted or otherwise authorized to practice.

Added by Stats 2018 ch 134 (SB 766),s 1, eff. 1/1/2019.

Section 1297.186 - Provision of services in international commercial arbitration or related conciliation, mediation, or alternative dispute resolution proceeding

(a) Notwithstanding any other law, including Section 6125 of the Business and Professions Code, a qualified attorney may provide legal services in an international commercial arbitration or related conciliation, mediation, or alternative dispute resolution proceeding, if any of the following conditions is satisfied:

(1) The services are undertaken in association with an attorney who is admitted to practice in this state and who actively participates in the matter.

(2) The services arise out of or are reasonably related to the attorney's practice in a jurisdiction in which the attorney is admitted to practice.

(3) The services are performed for a client who resides in or has an office in the jurisdiction in which the attorney is admitted or otherwise authorized to practice.

(4) The services arise out of or are reasonably related to a matter that has a substantial connection to a jurisdiction in which the attorney is admitted or otherwise authorized to practice.

(5) The services arise out of a dispute governed primarily by international law or the law of a foreign or out-of-state jurisdiction.

(b) This section does not apply to a dispute or controversy concerning any of the following:

(1) An individual's acquisition or lease of goods or services primarily for personal, family, or household use.

(2) An individual's coverage under a health insurance plan or an interaction between an individual and a healthcare provider.

(3) An application for employment in California.

(4) The terms and conditions of, or right to, employment in California, unless the dispute or controversy primarily concerns intellectual property rights, including those involving trademarks, patents, copyright, and software programs.

(c) This section does not affect the right of an attorney admitted to practice law in this state to provide legal services in an international commercial arbitration or related conciliation, mediation, or alternative dispute resolution proceeding, or the right of representation established in Section 1297.351.

Added by Stats 2018 ch 134 (SB 766),s 1, eff. 1/1/2019.

Section 1297.187 - Permission to appear pro hac vice

A qualified attorney rendering legal services pursuant to this article shall not appear in a court of this state unless he or she has applied for and received permission to appear as counsel pro hac vice pursuant to the California Rules of Court, as applicable.

Added by Stats 2018 ch 134 (SB 766),s 1, eff. 1/1/2019.

Section 1297.188 - Disciplinary authority

(a) A qualified attorney rendering legal services pursuant to this article is subject to the jurisdiction of the courts and disciplinary authority of this state with respect to the California Rules of Professional Conduct and the laws governing the conduct of attorneys to the same extent as a member of the State Bar of California.

(b) The State Bar of California may report complaints and evidence of disciplinary violations against an attorney practicing pursuant to this article to the appropriate disciplinary authority of any jurisdiction in which the attorney is admitted or otherwise authorized to practice law. This section does not limit or affect the authority of the State Bar to report information about an attorney to authorities in any jurisdiction in which the attorney is admitted or otherwise authorized to practice law.

(c) On or before May 1 of each year, the State Bar shall submit a report to the Supreme Court that specifies the number and nature of any complaints that it has received during the prior calendar year against attorneys who provide legal services pursuant to this article and any actions it has taken in response to those complaints.

Added by Stats 2018 ch 134 (SB 766),s 1, eff. 1/1/2019.

Section 1297.189 - Court rules

The Supreme Court may issue rules implementing this article.

Added by Stats 2018 ch 134 (SB 766),s 1, eff. 1/1/2019.

Article 2 - DETERMINATION OF RULES OF PROCEDURE

Section 1297.191 - Parties may agree on procedure

Subject to this title, the parties may agree on the procedure to be followed by the arbitral tribunal in conducting the proceedings.

Added by Stats. 1988, Ch. 23, Sec. 1. Effective March 7, 1988.

Section 1297.192 - Arbitration conducted in manner tribunal considers appropriate

Failing any agreement referred to in Section 1297.191, the arbitral tribunal may, subject to this title, conduct the arbitration in the manner it considers appropriate.

Added by Stats. 1988, Ch. 23, Sec. 1. Effective March 7, 1988.

Section 1297.193 - Power of tribunal under section 1297.192

The power of the arbitral tribunal under Section 1297.192 includes the power to determine the admissibility, relevance, materiality, and weight of any evidence.

Added by Stats. 1988, Ch. 23, Sec. 1. Effective March 7, 1988.

Article 3 - PLACE OF ARBITRATION

Section 1297.201 - Parties may agree

The parties may agree on the place of arbitration.

Added by Stats. 1988, Ch. 23, Sec. 1. Effective March 7, 1988.

Section 1297.202 - Place determined by tribunal failing agreement

Failing any agreement referred to in Section 1297.201, the place of arbitration shall be determined by the arbitral tribunal having regard to the circumstances of the case, including the convenience of the parties.

Added by Stats. 1988, Ch. 23, Sec. 1. Effective March 7, 1988.

Section 1297.203 - Meeting at any place tribunal considers appropriate

Notwithstanding Section 1297.201, the arbitral tribunal may, unless otherwise agreed by the parties, meet at any place it considers appropriate for consultation among its members, for hearing witnesses, experts, or the parties, or for inspection of documents, goods, or other property.

Added by Stats. 1988, Ch. 23, Sec. 1. Effective March 7, 1988.

Article 4 - COMMENCEMENT OF ARBITRAL PROCEEDINGS

Section 1297.211 - Generally

Unless otherwise agreed by the parties, the arbitral proceedings in respect of a particular dispute commence on the date on which a request for that dispute to be referred to arbitration is received by the respondent.

Added by Stats. 1988, Ch. 23, Sec. 1. Effective March 7, 1988.

Article 5 - LANGUAGE

Section 1297.221 - Parties may agree upon language used

The parties may agree upon the language or languages to be used in the arbitral proceedings.

Added by Stats. 1988, Ch. 23, Sec. 1. Effective March 7, 1988.

Section 1297.222 - Tribunal to determine language failing agreement

Failing any agreement referred to in Section 1297.221, the arbitral tribunal shall determine the language or languages to be used in the arbitral proceedings.

Added by Stats. 1988, Ch. 23, Sec. 1. Effective March 7, 1988.

Section 1297.223 - Applicability of agreement or determination

The agreement or determination, unless otherwise specified, shall apply to any written statement by a party, any hearing, and any arbitral award, decision, or other communication by the arbitral tribunal.

Added by Stats. 1988, Ch. 23, Sec. 1. Effective March 7, 1988.

Section 1297.224 - Documentary evidence accompanied by translation

The arbitral tribunal may order that any documentary evidence shall be accompanied by a translation into the language or languages agreed upon by the parties or determined by the arbitral tribunal.

Added by Stats. 1988, Ch. 23, Sec. 1. Effective March 7, 1988.

Article 6 - STATEMENTS OF CLAIM AND DEFENSE

Section 1297.231 - Generally

Within the period of time agreed upon by the parties or determined by the arbitral tribunal, the claimant shall state the facts supporting his or her claim, the points at issue, and the relief or remedy sought, and the respondent shall state his or her defense in respect of these particulars, unless the parties have otherwise agreed as to the required elements of those statements.

Added by Stats. 1988, Ch. 23, Sec. 1. Effective March 7, 1988.

Section 1297.232 - Submission of relevant documents with statements

The parties may submit with their statements all documents they consider to be relevant or may add a reference to the documents or other evidence they will submit.

Added by Stats. 1988, Ch. 23, Sec. 1. Effective March 7, 1988.

Section 1297.233 - Amendment or supplementation of claim or defense

Unless otherwise agreed by the parties, either party may amend or supplement his or her claim or defense during the course of the arbitral proceedings, unless the arbitral tribunal considers it inappropriate to allow the amendment or supplement having regard to the delay in making it.

Added by Stats. 1988, Ch. 23, Sec. 1. Effective March 7, 1988.

Article 7 - HEARINGS AND WRITTEN PROCEEDINGS

Section 1297.241 - Tribunal to decide

Unless otherwise agreed by the parties, the arbitral tribunal shall decide whether to hold oral hearings for the presentation of evidence or for oral argument, or whether the proceedings shall be conducted on the basis of documents and other materials.

Added by Stats. 1988, Ch. 23, Sec. 1. Effective March 7, 1988.

Section 1297.242 - Holding oral hearings if requested

Unless the parties have agreed that no oral hearings shall be held, the arbitral tribunal shall hold oral hearings at an appropriate state of the proceedings, if so requested by a party.

Added by Stats. 1988, Ch. 23, Sec. 1. Effective March 7, 1988.

Section 1297.243 - Notice of hearing or meeting

The parties shall be given sufficient advance notice of any hearing and of any meeting of the arbitral tribunal for the purpose of inspection of documents, goods, or other property.

Added by Stats. 1988, Ch. 23, Sec. 1. Effective March 7, 1988.

Section 1297.244 - Information communicated to parties

All statements, documents, or other information supplied to, or applications made to, the arbitral tribunal by one party shall be communicated to the other party, and any expert report or evidentiary document on which the arbitral tribunal may rely in making its decision shall be communicated to the parties.

Added by Stats. 1988, Ch. 23, Sec. 1. Effective March 7, 1988.

Section 1297.245 - Held in camera

Unless otherwise agreed by the parties, all oral hearings and meetings in arbitral proceedings shall be held in camera.

Added by Stats. 1988, Ch. 23, Sec. 1. Effective March 7, 1988.

Article 8 - DEFAULT OF A PARTY

Section 1297.251 - Failure of claimant to communicate statement of claim

Unless otherwise agreed by the parties, where, without showing sufficient cause, the claimant fails to communicate his or her statement of claim in accordance with Sections 1297.231 and 1297.232, the arbitral tribunal shall terminate the proceedings.

Added by Stats. 1988, Ch. 23, Sec. 1. Effective March 7, 1988.

Section 1297.252 - Failure of respondent to communicate statement of defense

Unless otherwise agreed by the parties, where, without showing sufficient cause, the respondent fails to communicate his or her statement of defense in accordance with Sections 1297.231 and 1297.232, the arbitral tribunal shall continue the proceedings without treating that failure in itself as an admission of the claimant's allegations.

Added by Stats. 1988, Ch. 23, Sec. 1. Effective March 7, 1988.

Section 1297.253 - Failure to appear at oral hearing or produce documentary evidence

Unless otherwise agreed by the parties, where, without showing sufficient cause, a party fails to appear at an oral hearing or to produce documentary evidence, the arbitral tribunal may continue with the proceedings and make the arbitral award on the evidence before it.

Added by Stats. 1988, Ch. 23, Sec. 1. Effective March 7, 1988.

Article 9 - EXPERT APPOINTED BY ARBITRAL TRIBUNAL

Section 1297.261 - Generally

Unless otherwise agreed by the parties, the arbitral tribunal may appoint one or more experts to report to it on specific issues to be determined by the arbitral tribunal, and require a party to give the expert any relevant information or to produce, or to provide access to, any relevant documents, goods, or other property for his or her inspection.

Added by Stats. 1988, Ch. 23, Sec. 1. Effective March 7, 1988.

Section 1297.262 - Participation of expert in oral hearing

Unless otherwise agreed by the parties, if a party so requests or if the arbitral tribunal considers it necessary, the expert shall, after delivery of his or her written or oral report, participate in an oral hearing where the parties have the opportunity to question the expert and to present expert witnesses on the points at issue.

Added by Stats. 1988, Ch. 23, Sec. 1. Effective March 7, 1988.

Article 10 - COURT ASSISTANCE IN TAKING EVIDENCE AND CONSOLIDATING ARBITRATIONS

Section 1297.271 - Request for superior court assistance

The arbitral tribunal, or a party with the approval of the arbitral tribunal, may request from the superior court assistance in taking evidence and the court may execute the request within its competence and according to its rules on taking evidence. In addition, a subpoena may issue as provided in Section 1282.6, in which case the witness compensation provisions of Section 1283.2 shall apply.

Added by Stats. 1988, Ch. 23, Sec. 1. Effective March 7, 1988.

Section 1297.272 - Power of court where consolidation of arbitrations agreed to by parties

Where the parties to two or more arbitration agreements have agreed, in their respective arbitration agreements or otherwise, to consolidate the arbitrations arising out of those arbitration agreements, the superior court may, on application by one party with the consent of all the other parties to those arbitration agreements, do one or more of the following:

(a) Order the arbitrations to be consolidated on terms the court considers just and necessary.

(b) Where all the parties cannot agree on an arbitral tribunal for the consolidated arbitration, appoint an arbitral tribunal in accordance with Section 1297.118.

(c) Where all the parties cannot agree on any other matter necessary to conduct the consolidated arbitration, make any other order it considers necessary.

Added by Stats. 1988, Ch. 23, Sec. 1. Effective March 7, 1988.

Section 1297.273 - Authority of parties to agree to consolidation of arbitrations

Nothing in this article shall be construed to prevent the parties to two or more arbitrations from agreeing to consolidate those arbitrations and taking any steps that are necessary to effect that consolidation.

Added by Stats. 1988, Ch. 23, Sec. 1. Effective March 7, 1988.

Chapter 6 - MAKING OF ARBITRAL AWARD AND TERMINATION OF PROCEEDINGS

Article 1 - RULES APPLICABLE TO SUBSTANCE OF DISPUTE

Section 1297.281 - Dispute decided by tribunal in accordance with rules of law designated by parties

The arbitral tribunal shall decide the dispute in accordance with the rules of law designated by the parties as applicable to the substance of the dispute.

Added by Stats. 1988, Ch. 23, Sec. 1. Effective March 7, 1988.

Section 1297.282 - Construction of designation of law or legal system

Any designation by the parties of the law or legal system of a given state shall be construed, unless otherwise expressed, as directly referring to the substantive law of that state and not to its conflict of laws rules.

Added by Stats. 1988, Ch. 23, Sec. 1. Effective March 7, 1988.

Section 1297.283 - Failure of designation

Failing any designation of the law under Section 1297.282 by the parties, the arbitral tribunal shall apply the rules of law it considers to be appropriate given all the circumstances surrounding the dispute.

Added by Stats. 1988, Ch. 23, Sec. 1. Effective March 7, 1988.

Section 1297.284 - Decision ex aequo et bono or amiable compositeur

The arbitral tribunal shall decide ex aequo et bono or as amiable compositeur, if the parties have expressly authorized it to do so.

Added by Stats. 1988, Ch. 23, Sec. 1. Effective March 7, 1988.

Section 1297.285 - Decision in accordance with contract terms taking into account usage of trade

In all cases, the arbitral tribunal shall decide in accordance with the terms of the contract and shall take into account the usages of the trade applicable to the transaction.

Added by Stats. 1988, Ch. 23, Sec. 1. Effective March 7, 1988.

Article 2 - DECISIONMAKING BY PANEL OF ARBITRATORS

Section 1297.291 - Generally

Unless otherwise agreed by the parties, in arbitral proceedings with more than one arbitrator, any decision of the arbitral tribunal shall be made by a majority of all of its members.

Notwithstanding this section, if authorized by the parties or all the members of the arbitral tribunal, questions of procedure may be decided by a presiding arbitrator.

Added by Stats. 1988, Ch. 23, Sec. 1. Effective March 7, 1988.

Article 3 - SETTLEMENT

Section 1297.301 - Generally

It is not incompatible with an arbitration agreement for an arbitral tribunal to encourage settlement of the dispute and, with the agreement of the parties, the arbitral tribunal may use mediation, conciliation, or other procedures at any time during the arbitral proceedings to encourage settlement.

Added by Stats. 1988, Ch. 23, Sec. 1. Effective March 7, 1988.

Section 1297.302 - Termination of proceedings upon settlement during arbitral proceedings

If, during arbitral proceedings, the parties settle the dispute, the arbitral tribunal shall terminate the proceedings and, if requested by the parties and not objected to by the arbitral tribunal, record the settlement in the form of an arbitral award on agreed terms.

Added by Stats. 1988, Ch. 23, Sec. 1. Effective March 7, 1988.

Section 1297.303 - Law governing award on agreed terms

An arbitral award on agreed terms shall be made in accordance with Article 4 (commencing with Section 1297.311) of this chapter and shall state that it is an arbitral award.

Added by Stats. 1988, Ch. 23, Sec. 1. Effective March 7, 1988.

Section 1297.304 - Status and effect of award on agreed terms

An arbitral award on agreed terms has the same status and effect as any other arbitral award on the substance of the dispute.
Added by Stats. 1988, Ch. 23, Sec. 1. Effective March 7, 1988.

Article 4 - FORM AND CONTENT OF ARBITRAL AWARD

Section 1297.311 - Award in writing and signed by tribunal members
An arbitral award shall be made in writing and shall be signed by the members of the arbitral tribunal.
Added by Stats. 1988, Ch. 23, Sec. 1. Effective March 7, 1988.

Section 1297.312 - Signature of majority of tribunal members sufficient
For the purposes of Section 1297.311, in arbitral proceedings with more than one arbitrator, the signatures of the majority of all the members of the arbitral tribunal shall be sufficient so long as the reason for any omitted signature is stated.
Added by Stats. 1988, Ch. 23, Sec. 1. Effective March 7, 1988.

Section 1297.313 - Award to state reasons upon which award based, exception
The arbitral award shall state the reasons upon which it is based, unless the parties have agreed that no reasons are to be given, or the award is an arbitral award on agreed terms under Article 3 (commencing with Section 1297.301) of this chapter.
Added by Stats. 1988, Ch. 23, Sec. 1. Effective March 7, 1988.

Section 1297.314 - Award to state date and place of arbitration
The arbitral award shall state its date and the place of arbitration as determined in accordance with Article 3 (commencing with Section 1297.201) of Chapter 5 and the award shall be deemed to have been made at that place.
Added by Stats. 1988, Ch. 23, Sec. 1. Effective March 7, 1988.

Section 1297.315 - Signed copy delivered to parties
After the arbitral award is made, a signed copy shall be delivered to each party.
Added by Stats. 1988, Ch. 23, Sec. 1. Effective March 7, 1988.

Section 1297.316 - Interim award
The arbitral tribunal may, at any time during the arbitral proceedings, make an interim arbitral award on any matter with respect to which it may make a final arbitral award. The interim award may be enforced in the same manner as a final arbitral award.
Added by Stats. 1988, Ch. 23, Sec. 1. Effective March 7, 1988.

Section 1297.317 - Interest
Unless otherwise agreed by the parties, the arbitral tribunal may award interest.
Added by Stats. 1988, Ch. 23, Sec. 1. Effective March 7, 1988.

Section 1297.318 - Costs
(a) Unless otherwise agreed by the parties, the costs of an arbitration shall be at the discretion of the arbitral tribunal.
(b) In making an order for costs, the arbitral tribunal may include as costs any of the following:
 (1) The fees and expenses of the arbitrators and expert witnesses.
 (2) Legal fees and expenses.
 (3) Any administration fees of the institution supervising the arbitration, if any.
 (4) Any other expenses incurred in connection with the arbitral proceedings.
(c) In making an order for costs, the arbitral tribunal may specify any of the following:
 (1) The party entitled to costs.
 (2) The party who shall pay the costs.
 (3) The amount of costs or method of determining that amount.
 (4) The manner in which the costs shall be paid.
Added by Stats. 1988, Ch. 23, Sec. 1. Effective March 7, 1988.

Article 5 - TERMINATION OF PROCEEDINGS

Section 1297.321 - Generally; award final upon expiration of applicable periods
The arbitral proceedings are terminated by the final arbitral award or by an order of the arbitral tribunal under Section 1297.322. The award shall be final upon the expiration of the applicable periods in Article 6 (commencing with Section 1297.331) of this chapter.
Added by Stats. 1988, Ch. 23, Sec. 1. Effective March 7, 1988.

Section 1297.322 - When order for termination issued
The arbitral tribunal shall issue an order for the termination of the arbitral proceedings where any of the following occurs:
(a) The claimant withdraws his or her claim, unless the respondent objects to the order and the arbitral tribunal recognizes a legitimate interest on the respondent's part in obtaining a final settlement of the dispute.
(b) The parties agree on the termination of the proceedings.
(c) The arbitral tribunal finds that the continuation of the proceedings has for any other reason become unnecessary or impossible.
Added by Stats. 1988, Ch. 23, Sec. 1. Effective March 7, 1988.

Section 1297.323 - Termination of tribunal mandate
Subject to Article 6 (commencing with Section 1297.331) of this chapter, the mandate of the arbitral tribunal terminates with the termination of the arbitral proceedings.
Added by Stats. 1988, Ch. 23, Sec. 1. Effective March 7, 1988.

Article 6 - CORRECTION AND INTERPRETATION OF AWARDS AND ADDITIONAL AWARDS

Section 1297.331 - Time for requesting correction or interpretation
Within 30 days after receipt of the arbitral award, unless another period of time has been agreed upon by the parties:
(a) A party may request the arbitral tribunal to correct in the arbitral award any computation errors, any clerical or typographical errors, or any other errors of a similar nature.
(b) A party may, if agreed by the parties, request the arbitral tribunal to give an interpretation of a specific point or part of the arbitral award.
Added by Stats. 1988, Ch. 23, Sec. 1. Effective March 7, 1988.

Section 1297.332 - Time for making correction or interpretation
If the arbitral tribunal considers any request made under Section 1297.331 to be justified, it shall make the correction or give the interpretation within 30 days after receipt of the request and the interpretation shall form part of the arbitral award.
Added by Stats. 1988, Ch. 23, Sec. 1. Effective March 7, 1988.

Section 1297.333 - Correction of error on tribunal's initiative, time period
The arbitral tribunal may correct any error of the type referred to in subdivision (a) of Section 1297.331, on its own initiative, within 30 days after the date of the arbitral award.
Added by Stats. 1988, Ch. 23, Sec. 1. Effective March 7, 1988.

Section 1297.334 - Time for requesting additional award
Unless otherwise agreed by the parties, a party may request, within 30 days after receipt of the arbitral award, the arbitral tribunal to make an additional arbitral award as to the claims presented in the arbitral proceedings but omitted from the arbitral award.
Added by Stats. 1988, Ch. 23, Sec. 1. Effective March 7, 1988.

Section 1297.335 - Time for making additional award
If the arbitral tribunal considers any request made under Section 1297.334 to be justified, it shall make the additional arbitral award within 60 days after receipt of the request.
Added by Stats. 1988, Ch. 23, Sec. 1. Effective March 7, 1988.

Section 1297.336 - Extension of periods of time
The arbitral tribunal may extend, if necessary, the period of time within which it shall make a correction, give an interpretation, or make an additional arbitral award under Section 1297.331 or 1297.334.
Added by Stats. 1988, Ch. 23, Sec. 1. Effective March 7, 1988.

Section 1297.337 - Applicability of Article 4
Article 4 (commencing with Section 1297.311) of this chapter applies to a correction or interpretation of the arbitral award or to an additional arbitral award made under this section.
Added by Stats. 1988, Ch. 23, Sec. 1. Effective March 7, 1988.

Chapter 7 - CONCILIATION
Article 1 - APPOINTMENT OF CONCILIATORS

Section 1297.341 - Policy of state; selection of conciliators
It is the policy of the State of California to encourage parties to an international commercial agreement or transaction which qualifies for arbitration or conciliation pursuant to Section 1297.13, to resolve disputes arising from such agreements or transactions through conciliation. The parties may select or permit an arbitral tribunal or other third party to select one or more persons to serve as the conciliator or conciliators who shall assist the parties in an independent and impartial manner in their attempt to reach an amicable settlement of their dispute.
Added by Stats. 1988, Ch. 23, Sec. 1. Effective March 7, 1988.

Section 1297.342 - Guided by principles of objectivity, fairness and justice
The conciliator or conciliators shall be guided by principles of objectivity, fairness, and justice, giving consideration to, among other things, the rights and obligations of the parties, the usages of the trade concerned and the circumstances surrounding the dispute, including any previous practices between the parties.
Added by Stats. 1988, Ch. 23, Sec. 1. Effective March 7, 1988.

Section 1297.343 - Manner of conducting proceedings
The conciliator or conciliators may conduct the conciliation proceedings in such a manner as they consider appropriate, taking into account the circumstances of the case, the wishes of the parties, and the desirability of a speedy settlement of the dispute. Except as otherwise provided in this title, other provisions of this code, the Evidence Code, or the California Rules of Court, shall not apply to conciliation proceedings brought under this title.
Added by Stats. 1988, Ch. 23, Sec. 1. Effective March 7, 1988.

Article 2 - REPRESENTATION AND ASSISTANCE

Section 1297.351 - Generally
The parties may appear in person or be represented or assisted by any person of their choice. A person assisting or representing a party need not be a member of the legal profession or licensed to practice law in California.
Added by Stats. 1988, Ch. 23, Sec. 1. Effective March 7, 1988.

Article 3 - REPORT OF CONCILIATORS

Section 1297.361 - Draft settlement
At any time during the proceedings, the conciliator or conciliators may prepare a draft conciliation settlement which may include the assessment and apportionment of costs between the parties, and send copies to the parties, specifying the time within which they must signify their approval.
Added by Stats. 1988, Ch. 23, Sec. 1. Effective March 7, 1988.

Section 1297.362 - Authority to require party to accept settlement proposed
No party may be required to accept any settlement proposed by the conciliator or conciliators.
Added by Stats. 1988, Ch. 23, Sec. 1. Effective March 7, 1988.

Article 4 - CONFIDENTIALITY

Section 1297.371 - Generally
When persons agree to participate in conciliation under this title:
(a) Evidence of anything said or of any admission made in the course of the conciliation is not admissible in evidence, and disclosure of any such evidence shall not be compelled, in any civil action in which, pursuant to law, testimony may be compelled to be given. However, this subdivision does not limit the admissibility of evidence if all parties participating in conciliation consent to its disclosure.
(b) In the event that any such evidence is offered in contravention of this section, the arbitration tribunal or the court shall make any order which it considers to be appropriate to deal with the matter, including, without limitation, orders restricting the introduction of evidence, or dismissing the case without prejudice.
(c) Unless the document otherwise provides, no document prepared for the purpose of, or in the course of, or pursuant to, the conciliation, or any copy thereof, is admissible in evidence, and disclosure of any such document shall not be compelled, in any arbitration or civil action in which, pursuant to law, testimony may be compelled to be given.
Added by Stats. 1988, Ch. 23, Sec. 1. Effective March 7, 1988.

Article 5 - STAY OF ARBITRATION AND RESORT TO OTHER PROCEEDINGS

Section 1297.381 - Agreement stay judicial or arbitration proceedings
The agreement of the parties to submit a dispute to conciliation shall be deemed an agreement between or among those parties to stay all judicial or arbitral proceedings from the commencement of conciliation until the termination of conciliation proceedings.
Added by Stats. 1988, Ch. 23, Sec. 1. Effective March 7, 1988.

Section 1297.382 - Limitations periods tolled and periods of prescription extended
All applicable limitation periods including periods of prescription shall be tolled or extended upon the commencement of conciliation proceedings to conciliate a dispute under this title and all limitation periods shall remain tolled and periods of prescription extended as to all parties to the conciliation proceedings until the 10th day following the termination of conciliation proceedings. For purposes of this article, conciliation proceedings are deemed to have commenced as soon as (a) a party has requested conciliation of a particular dispute or disputes, and (b) the other party or parties agree to participate in the conciliation proceeding.
Added by Stats. 1988, Ch. 23, Sec. 1. Effective March 7, 1988.

Article 6 - TERMINATION

Section 1297.391 - Termination as to all parties by declaration of conciliator or parties or signing settlement

The conciliation proceedings may be terminated as to all parties by any of the following:

(a) A written declaration of the conciliator or conciliators, after consultation with the parties, to the effect that further efforts at conciliation are no longer justified, on the date of the declaration.

(b) A written declaration of the parties addressed to the conciliator or conciliators to the effect that the conciliation proceedings are terminated, on the date of the declaration.

(c) The signing of a settlement agreement by all of the parties, on the date of the agreement.

Added by Stats. 1988, Ch. 23, Sec. 1. Effective March 7, 1988.

Section 1297.392 - Termination as to particular parties by declaration or signing settlement

The conciliation proceedings may be terminated as to particular parties by either of the following:

(a) A written declaration of a party to the other party and the conciliator or conciliators, if appointed, to the effect that the conciliation proceedings shall be terminated as to that particular party, on the date of the declaration.

(b) The signing of a settlement agreement by some of the parties, on the date of the agreement.

Added by Stats. 1988, Ch. 23, Sec. 1. Effective March 7, 1988.

Section 1297.393 - Participation of conciliator in arbitral or judicial proceedings of same dispute

No person who has served as conciliator may be appointed as an arbitrator for, or take part in any arbitral or judicial proceedings in, the same dispute unless all parties manifest their consent to such participation or the rules adopted for conciliation or arbitration otherwise provide.

Added by Stats. 1988, Ch. 23, Sec. 1. Effective March 7, 1988.

Section 1297.394 - Rights or remedies not waived by submitting to conciliation

By submitting to conciliation, no party shall be deemed to have waived any rights or remedies which that party would have had if conciliation had not been initiated, other than those set forth in any settlement agreement which results from the conciliation.

Added by Stats. 1988, Ch. 23, Sec. 1. Effective March 7, 1988.

Article 7 - ENFORCEABILITY OF DECREE

Section 1297.401 - Generally

If the conciliation succeeds in settling the dispute, and the result of the conciliation is reduced to writing and signed by the conciliator or conciliators and the parties or their representatives, the written agreement shall be treated as an arbitral award rendered by an arbitral tribunal duly constituted in and pursuant to the laws of this state, and shall have the same force and effect as a final award in arbitration.

Added by Stats. 1988, Ch. 23, Sec. 1. Effective March 7, 1988.

Article 8 - COSTS

Section 1297.411 - Conciliator to fix costs and give notice; included in costs

Upon termination of the conciliation proceedings, the conciliator shall fix the costs of the conciliation and give written notice thereof to the parties. As used in this article, "costs" includes only the following:

(a) A reasonable fee to be paid to the conciliator or conciliators.

(b) The travel and other reasonable expenses of the conciliator or conciliators.

(c) The travel and other reasonable expenses of witnesses requested by the conciliator or conciliators with the consent of the parties.

(d) The cost of any expert advice requested by the conciliator or conciliators with the consent of the parties.

(e) The cost of any court.

Added by Stats. 1988, Ch. 23, Sec. 1. Effective March 7, 1988.

Section 1297.412 - Apportionment

These costs shall be borne equally by the parties unless the settlement agreement provides for a different apportionment. All other expenses incurred by a party shall be borne by that party.

Added by Stats. 1988, Ch. 23, Sec. 1. Effective March 7, 1988.

Article 9 - EFFECT ON JURISDICTION

Section 1297.421 - Consent to participate not deemed consent to jurisdiction of court of state if conciliation fails

Neither the request for conciliation, the consent to participate in the conciliation proceedings, the participation in such proceedings, nor the entering into a conciliation agreement or settlement shall be deemed as consent to the jurisdiction of any court in this state in the event conciliation fails.

Added by Stats. 1988, Ch. 23, Sec. 1. Effective March 7, 1988.

Article 10 - IMMUNITY OF CONCILIATORS AND PARTIES

Section 1297.431 - Immunity while present in state for conciliation purposes

Neither the conciliator or conciliators, the parties, nor their representatives shall be subject to service of process on any civil matter while they are present in this state for the purpose of arranging for or participating in conciliation pursuant to this title.

Added by Stats. 1988, Ch. 23, Sec. 1. Effective March 7, 1988.

Section 1297.432 - Immunity of conciliator

No person who serves as a conciliator shall be held liable in an action for damages resulting from any act or omission in the performance of his or her role as a conciliator in any proceeding subject to this title.

Added by Stats. 1988, Ch. 23, Sec. 1. Effective March 7, 1988.

Title 9.4 - REAL ESTATE CONTRACT ARBITRATION

Section 1298 - Provision in contracts; format

(a) Whenever any contract to convey real property, or contemplated to convey real property in the future, including marketing contracts, deposit receipts, real property sales contracts as defined in Section 2985 of the Civil Code, leases together with options to purchase, or ground leases coupled with improvements, but not including powers of sale contained in deeds of trust or mortgages, contains a provision for binding arbitration of any dispute between the principals in the transaction, the contract shall have that provision clearly titled "ARBITRATION OF DISPUTES." If a provision for binding arbitration is included in a printed contract, it shall be set out in at least 8-point bold type or in contrasting red in at least 8-point type, and if the provision is included in a typed contract, it shall be set out in capital letters.

(b) Whenever any contract or agreement between principals and agents in real property sales transactions, including listing agreements, as defined in Section 1086 of the Civil Code, contains a provision requiring binding arbitration of any dispute between the principals and agents in the transaction, the contract or agreement shall have that provision clearly titled "ARBITRATION OF DISPUTES." If a provision for binding arbitration is included in a printed contract, it shall be set out in at least 8-point bold type or in contrasting red in at least 8-point type, and if the provision is included in a typed contract, it shall be set out in capital letters.

(c) Immediately before the line or space provided for the parties to indicate their assent or nonassent to the arbitration provision described in subdivision (a) or (b), and immediately following that arbitration provision, the following shall appear: "NOTICE: BY INITIALLING IN THE

SPACE BELOW YOU ARE AGREEING TO HAVE ANY DISPUTE ARISING OUT OF THE MATTERS INCLUDED IN THE 'ARBITRATION OF DISPUTES' PROVISION DECIDED BY NEUTRAL ARBITRATION AS PROVIDED BY CALIFORNIA LAW AND YOU ARE GIVING UP ANY RIGHTS YOU MIGHT POSSESS TO HAVE THE DISPUTE LITIGATED IN A COURT OR JURY TRIAL. BY INITIALLING IN THE SPACE BELOW YOU ARE GIVING UP YOUR JUDICIAL RIGHTS TO DISCOVERY AND APPEAL, UNLESS THOSE RIGHTS ARE SPECIFICALLY INCLUDED IN THE 'ARBITRATION OF DISPUTES' PROVISION. IF YOU REFUSE TO SUBMIT TO ARBITRATION AFTER AGREEING TO THIS PROVISION, YOU MAY BE COMPELLED TO ARBITRATE UNDER THE AUTHORITY OF THE CALIFORNIA CODE OF CIVIL PROCEDURE. YOUR AGREEMENT TO THIS ARBITRATION PROVISION IS VOLUNTARY."

"WE HAVE READ AND UNDERSTAND THE FOREGOING AND AGREE TO SUBMIT DISPUTES ARISING OUT OF THE MATTERS INCLUDED IN THE 'ARBITRATION OF DISPUTES' PROVISION TO NEUTRAL ARBITRATION."

If the above provision is included in a printed contract, it shall be set out either in at least 10-point bold type or in contrasting red print in at least 8-point bold type, and if the provision is included in a typed contract, it shall be set out in capital letters.

(d) Nothing in this section shall be construed to diminish the authority of any court of competent jurisdiction with respect to real property transactions in areas involving court supervision or jurisdiction, including, but not limited to, probate, marital dissolution, foreclosure of liens, unlawful detainer, or eminent domain.

(e) In the event an arbitration provision is contained in an escrow instruction, it shall not preclude the right of an escrowholder to institute an interpleader action.

Title head amended by Stats 2007 ch 130 (AB 299),s 38, eff. 1/1/2008.

Amended by Stats. 1989, Ch. 22, Sec. 1. Effective May 25, 1989. Operative July 1, 1989, by Sec. 2 of Ch. 22.

Section 1298.5 - Recording notice of pending action not waiver of right to arbitration

Any party to an action who proceeds to record a notice of pending action pursuant to Section 409 shall not thereby waive any right of arbitration which that person may have pursuant to a written agreement to arbitrate, nor any right to petition the court to compel arbitration pursuant to Section 1281.2, if, in filing an action to record that notice, the party at the same time presents to the court an application that the action be stayed pending the arbitration of any dispute which is claimed to be arbitrable and which is relevant to the action.

Added by Stats. 1988, Ch. 881, Sec. 1. Operative July 1, 1989, by Section 1298.8.

Section 1298.7 - Rights of action not precluded by contract provision or agreement to arbitrate

In the event an arbitration provision is included in a contract or agreement covered by this title, it shall not preclude or limit any right of action for bodily injury or wrongful death, or any right of action to which Section 337.1 or 337.15 is applicable.

Added by Stats. 1988, Ch. 881, Sec. 1. Operative July 1, 1989, by Section 1298.8.

Section 1298.8 - Effective date of title

This title shall become operative on July 1, 1989, and shall only apply to contracts or agreements entered into on or after that date.

Added by Stats. 1988, Ch. 881, Sec. 1. Note: This section delayed the initial operation of Title 9.3 (now numbered 9.4), commencing with Section 1298.

Title 9.5 - ARBITRATION OF FIREFIGHTER AND LAW ENFORCEMENT OFFICER LABOR DISPUTES

Section 1299 - Legislative findings and declaration; legislative intent

The Legislature hereby finds and declares that strikes taken by firefighters and law enforcement officers against public employers are a matter of statewide concern, are a predictable consequence of labor strife and poor morale that is often the outgrowth of substandard wages and benefits, and are not in the public interest. The Legislature further finds and declares that the dispute resolution procedures contained in this title provide the appropriate method for resolving public sector labor disputes that could otherwise lead to strikes by firefighters or law enforcement officers. It is the intent of the Legislature to protect the health and welfare of the public by providing impasse remedies necessary to afford public employers the opportunity to safely alleviate the effects of labor strife that would otherwise lead to strikes by firefighters and law enforcement officers. It is further the intent of the Legislature that, in order to effectuate its predominant purpose, this title be construed to apply broadly to all public employers, including, but not limited to, charter cities, counties, and cities and counties in this state.

It is not the intent of the Legislature to alter the scope of issues subject to collective bargaining between public employers and employee organizations representing firefighters or law enforcement officers.

The provisions of this title are intended by the Legislature to govern the resolution of impasses reached in collective bargaining between public employers and employee organizations representing firefighters and law enforcement officers over economic issues that remain in dispute over their respective interests. However, the provisions of this title are not intended by the Legislature to be used as a procedure to determine the rights of any firefighter or law enforcement officer in any grievance initiated as a result of a disciplinary action taken by any public employer. The Legislature further intends that this title shall not apply to any law enforcement policy that pertains to how law enforcement officers interact with members of the public or pertains to police-community relations, such as policies on the use of police powers, enforcement priorities and practices, or supervision, oversight, and accountability covering officer behavior toward members of the public, to any community-oriented policing policy or to any process employed by an employer to investigate firefighter or law enforcement officer behavior that could lead to discipline against any firefighter or law enforcement officer, nor to contravene any provision of a charter that governs an employer that is a city, county, or city and county, which provision prescribes a procedure for the imposition of any disciplinary action taken against a firefighter or law enforcement officer.

Added by Stats 2000 ch 906 (SB 402), s 2, eff. 1/1/2001.

Section 1299.2 - Applicability of title

This title shall apply to all employers of firefighters and law enforcement officers.

Added by Stats 2000 ch 906 (SB 402), s 2, eff. 1/1/2001.

Section 1299.3 - Definitions

As used in this title:

(a) "Employee" means any firefighter or law enforcement officer represented by an employee organization, as defined in subdivision (b).

(b) "Employee organization" means any organization recognized by the employer for the purpose of representing firefighters or law enforcement officers in matters relating to wages, hours, and other terms and conditions of employment within the scope of arbitration.

(c) "Employer" means any local agency employing employees, as defined in subdivision (a), or any entity, except the State of California, acting as an agent of any local agency, either directly or indirectly.

(d) "Firefighter" means any person who is employed to perform firefighting, fire prevention, fire training, hazardous materials response, emergency medical services, fire or arson investigation, or any related duties, without respect to the rank, job title, or job assignment of that person.

(e) "Law enforcement officer" means any person who is a peace officer, as defined in Section 830.1 of, subdivisions (b) and (d) of Section 830.31 of, subdivisions (a), (b), and (c) of Section 830.32 of, subdivisions (a), (b), and (d) of Section 830.33 of, subdivisions (a) and (b) of Section

830.35 of, subdivision (a) of Section 830.5 of, and subdivision (a) of Section 830.55 of, the Penal Code, without respect to the rank, job title, or job assignment of that person.

(f) "Local agency" means any governmental subdivision, district, public and quasi-public corporation, joint powers agency, public agency or public service corporation, town, city, county, city and county, or municipal corporation, whether incorporated or not or whether chartered or not.

(g) "Scope of arbitration" means economic issues, including salaries, wages and overtime pay, health and pension benefits, vacation and other leave, reimbursements, incentives, differentials, and all other forms of remuneration. The scope of arbitration shall not include any issue that is protected by what is commonly referred to as the "management rights" clause contained in Section 3504 of the Government Code. Notwithstanding the foregoing, any employer that is not exempt under Section 1299.9 may supersede this subdivision by adoption of an ordinance that establishes a broader definition of "scope of arbitration."

Amended by Stats 2002 ch 664 (AB 3034),s 52, eff. 1/1/2003.
Added by Stats 2000 ch 906 (SB 402), s 2, eff. 1/1/2001.

Section 1299.4 - Submission of differences to arbitration panel

(a) If an impasse has been declared after the parties have exhausted their mutual efforts to reach agreement over matters within the scope of arbitration, and the parties are unable to agree to the appointment of a mediator, or if a mediator agreed to by the parties is unable to effect settlement of a dispute between the parties after his or her appointment, the employee organization may, by written notification to the employer, request that their differences be submitted to an arbitration panel.

(b) Within three days after receipt of the written notification, each party shall designate a person to serve as its member of an arbitration panel. Within five days thereafter, or within additional periods to which they mutually agree, the two members of the arbitration panel appointed by the parties shall designate an impartial person with experience in labor and management dispute resolution to act as chairperson of the arbitration panel.

(c) In the event that the parties are unable or unwilling to agree upon a third person to serve as chairperson, the two members of the arbitration panel shall jointly request from the American Arbitration Association a list of seven impartial and experienced persons who are familiar with matters of employer-employee relations. The two panel members may as an alternative, jointly request a list of seven names from the California State Mediation and Conciliation Service, or a list from either entity containing more or less than seven names, so long as the number requested is an odd number. If after five days of receipt of the list, the two panel members cannot agree on which of the listed persons shall serve as chairperson, they shall, within two days, alternately strike names from the list, with the first panel member to strike names being determined by lot. The last person whose name remains on the list shall be chairperson.

(d) Employees as defined by this chapter shall not be permitted to engage in strikes that endanger public safety.

(e) No employer shall interfere with, intimidate, restrain, coerce, or discriminate against an employee organization or employee because of an exercise of rights under this title.

(f) No employer shall refuse to meet and confer or condition agreement upon a memorandum of understanding based upon an employee organization's exercise of rights under this title.

Added by Stats 2000 ch 906 (SB 402), s 2, eff. 1/1/2001.

Section 1299.5 - inquiries and investigation, hearings and other action by panel

(a) The arbitration panel shall, within 10 days after its establishment or any additional periods to which the parties agree, meet with the parties or their representatives, either jointly or separately, make inquiries and investigations, hold hearings, and take any other action including further mediation, that the arbitration panel deems appropriate.

(b) For the purpose of its hearings, investigations, or inquiries, the arbitration panel may subpoena witnesses, administer oaths, take the testimony of any person, and issue subpoenas duces tecum to require the production and examination of any employer's or employee organization's records, books, or papers relating to any subject matter before the panel.

Added by Stats 2000 ch 906 (SB 402), s 2, eff. 1/1/2001.

Section 1299.6 - Submission of last best offer of settlement by parties; decision of panel

(a) The arbitration panel shall direct that five days prior to the commencement of its hearings, each of the parties shall submit the last best offer of settlement as to each of the issues within the scope of arbitration, as defined in this title, made in bargaining as a proposal or counterproposal and not previously agreed to by the parties prior to any arbitration request made pursuant to subdivision (a) of Section 1299.4. The arbitration panel, within 30 days after the conclusion of the hearing, or any additional period to which the parties agree, shall separately decide on each of the disputed issues submitted by selecting, without modification, the last best offer that most nearly complies with the applicable factors described in subdivision (c). This subdivision shall be applicable except as otherwise provided in subdivision (b).

(b) Notwithstanding the terms of subdivision (a), the parties by mutual agreement may elect to submit as a package the last best offer of settlement made in bargaining as a proposal or counterproposal on those issues within the scope of arbitration, as defined in this title, not previously agreed to by the parties prior to any arbitration request made pursuant to subdivision (a) of Section 1299.4. The arbitration panel, within 30 days after the conclusion of the hearing, or any additional period to which the parties agree, shall decide on the disputed issues submitted by selecting, without modification, the last best offer package that most nearly complies with the applicable factors described in subdivision (c).

(c) The arbitration panel, unless otherwise agreed to by the parties, shall limit its findings to issues within the scope of arbitration and shall base its findings, opinions, and decisions upon those factors traditionally taken into consideration in the determination of those matters within the scope of arbitration, including but not limited to the following factors, as applicable:

(1) The stipulations of the parties.

(2) The interest and welfare of the public.

(3) The financial condition of the employer and its ability to meet the costs of the award.

(4) The availability and sources of funds to defray the cost of any changes in matters within the scope of arbitration.

(5) Comparison of matters within the scope of arbitration of other employees performing similar services in corresponding fire or law enforcement employment.

(6) The average consumer prices for goods and services, commonly known as the Consumer Price Index.

(7) The peculiarity of requirements of employment, including, but not limited to, mental, physical, and educational qualifications; job training and skills; and hazards of employment.

(8) Changes in any of the foregoing that are traditionally taken into consideration in the determination of matters within the scope of arbitration.

Added by Stats 2000 ch 906 (SB 402), s 2, eff. 1/1/2001.

Section 1299.7 - Copy of decision delivered or mailed to parties; decision not binding for period of five days after service; disclosure and binding effect after five day period; rejection by employer

(a) The arbitration panel shall mail or otherwise deliver a copy of the decision to the parties. However, the decision of the arbitration panel shall not be publicly disclosed, and shall not be binding, for a period of five days after service to the parties. During that five-day period, the parties may meet privately, attempt to resolve their differences and, by mutual agreement, amend or modify the decision of the arbitration panel.

(b) At the conclusion of the five-day period, which may be extended by the parties, the arbitration panel's decision, as may be amended or modified by the parties pursuant to subdivision (a), shall be publicly disclosed and, unless the governing body acts in accordance with subdivision (c), shall be binding on all parties, and, if specified by the arbitration panel, be incorporated into and made a part of any existing memorandum of understanding as defined in Section 3505.1 of the Government Code.

(c) The employer may by unanimous vote of all the members of the governing body reject the decision of the arbitration panel, except as specifically provided to the contrary in a city, county, or city and county charter with respect to the rejection of an arbitration award.

Amended by Stats 2003 ch 877 (SB 440),s 1, eff. 1/1/2004.
Added by Stats 2000 ch 906 (SB 402), s 2, eff. 1/1/2001.

Section 1299.8 - Applicability of Title 9

Unless otherwise provided in this title, Title 9 (commencing with Section 1280) shall be applicable to any arbitration proceeding undertaken pursuant to this title.

Added by Stats 2000 ch 906 (SB 402), s 2, eff. 1/1/2001.

Section 1299.9 - Inapplicability to city, county or city and county with charter provisions for procedure for resolving disputes

(a) The provisions of this title shall not apply to any employer that is a city, county, or city and county, governed by a charter that was amended prior to January 1, 2004, to incorporate a procedure requiring the submission of all unresolved disputes relating to wages, hours, and other terms and conditions of employment within the scope of arbitration to an impartial and experienced neutral person or panel for final and binding determination, provided however that the charter amendment is not subsequently repealed or amended in a form that would no longer require the submission of all unresolved disputes relating to wages, hours, and other terms and conditions of employment within the scope of arbitration to an impartial and experienced neutral person or panel, for final and binding determination.

(b) Unless otherwise agreed to by the parties, the costs of the arbitration proceeding and the expenses of the arbitration panel, except those of the employer representative, shall be borne by the employee organization.

Amended by Stats 2003 ch 877 (SB 440),s 2, eff. 1/1/2004.
Added by Stats 2000 ch 906 (SB 402), s 2, eff. 1/1/2001.

Title 10 - UNCLAIMED PROPERTY
Chapter 1 - GENERAL PROVISIONS
Article 1 - DEFINITIONS

Section 1300 - Definitions

For the purposes of this title, the following definitions shall apply:

(a) "Property," unless specifically qualified, includes all classes of property, real, personal and mixed.

(b) "Unclaimed property," unless specifically qualified, means all property (1) which is unclaimed, abandoned, escheated, permanently escheated, or distributed to the state, or (2) which, under any provision of law, will become unclaimed, abandoned, escheated, permanently escheated, or distributed to the state, or (3) to the possession of which the state is or will become entitled, if not claimed by the person or persons entitled thereto within the time allowed by law, whether or not there has been a judicial determination that such property is unclaimed, abandoned, escheated, permanently escheated, or distributed to the state.

(c) "Escheat," unless specifically qualified, means the vesting in the state of title to property the whereabouts of whose owner is unknown or whose owner is unknown or which a known owner has refused to accept, whether by judicial determination or by operation of law, subject to the right of claimants to appear and claim the escheated property or any portion thereof. When used in reference to the law of another state, "escheat" includes the transfer to the state of the right to the custody of such property.

(d) "Permanent escheat" means the absolute vesting in the state of title to property the whereabouts of whose owner is unknown or whose owner is unknown or which a known owner has refused to accept, pursuant to judicial determination, pursuant to a proceeding of escheat as provided by Chapter 5 (commencing with Section 1410) of this title, or pursuant to operation of law, and the barring of all claims to the property by the former owner thereof or his successors.

(e) "Controller" means the State Controller.

(f) "Treasurer" means the State Treasurer.

(g) "Domicile," in the case of a corporation, refers to the place where the corporation is incorporated.

Amended by Stats. 1968, Ch. 356.

Section 1301 - Construction of references to section, article or chapter

For the purposes of this title, unless otherwise specified, (1) a reference to a section refers to a section of this code; (2) a reference to an article refers to an article of the chapter of this title in which such reference is made; and (3) a reference to a chapter refers to a chapter of this title.

Added by Stats. 1951, Ch. 1708.

Article 2 - PURPOSE AND SCOPE

Section 1305 - Purpose

It is the purpose of this title to provide for the receipt, custody, investment, management, disposal, escheat and permanent escheat of various classes of unclaimed property, to the possession of which the State is, or may become, entitled under the provisions of this title or under other provision of law.

Added by Stats. 1951, Ch. 1708.

Section 1306 - Inapplicability to money or property held by state

The provisions of this title do not apply to money or other property held by the State or any officer thereof as trustee or bailee under the terms of an express contract to which the State or any officer thereof is a party.

Added by Stats. 1951, Ch. 1708.

Chapter 2 - RECEIPT AND EXPENDITURE OF FUNDS
Article 1 - DEPOSIT OF UNCLAIMED PROPERTY

Section 1310 - Cash transmitted to Treasurer and person property transmitted to Controller for deposit

Whenever, under the provisions of this title or under any other provision of law, unclaimed money or other unclaimed property is payable into the State Treasury, the person responsible for making such payment shall, if it is cash, transmit it to the Treasurer, and if it is personal property other than cash, transmit it to the Controller for deposit in the State Treasury.

Added by Stats. 1951, Ch. 1708.

Section 1311 - Notice to Controller of transmission of money or property to Treasurer or Controller

Any person transmitting money or other property to the Treasurer or Controller under the provisions of this title shall, at the time of such transmittal, furnish written notice thereof to the Controller, setting forth the amount of cash transmitted, the nature and description of the personal property other than cash transmitted, the name and last known address of the person entitled to such property or for whose benefit such property is transmitted, a reference to the specific statutory provision under which such property is transmitted, and if such property represents the proceeds of an estate of a decedent, or an unclaimed amount payable pursuant to an allowed and approved claim against such an estate, the name of the decedent, the county and court in which probate or escheat proceedings, if any, were held, the number of the action, if any; and, in the case of all classes of property so transmitted, such other identifying information available from the records of the person making such transmittal, as the Controller may require.

Added by Stats. 1951, Ch. 1708.

Section 1312 - Order or decree of distribution in decedent's estate or vesting title in state

Whenever money or other property is paid to the State or any officer or employee thereof under the provisions of this title, and such money or other property has been covered by a decree of distribution in a decedent's estate, or by an order or decree of a court ordering such payment or adjudging that title to such property has vested in the State, the person transmitting such money or other property to the Treasurer or Controller shall, at the time of such transmittal, furnish to the Controller a certified copy of each court order or decree, and of each court order correcting or amending the same, covering such money or other property.

Added by Stats. 1951, Ch. 1708.

Section 1313 - Unclaimed Property Fund

A fund is hereby created in the State Treasury, to be known as the Unclaimed Property Fund.

All money, except permanently escheated money, paid to the state or any officer or employee thereof for deposit in the State Treasury under the provisions of this title shall, on order of the Controller, be deposited in the Unclaimed Property Fund.

All property other than money, including the proceeds from the sale or other disposition thereof, except permanently escheated property received by, or coming into the possession of, the state or any officer or employee thereof under the provisions of this title shall, on order of the Controller, be deposited in the State Treasury to be held in the Unclaimed Property Fund.

Amended by Stats. 1978, Ch. 1183.

Section 1314 - Account in Fund covering accountability for money deposited in Fund

The Controller shall maintain a separate account in the Unclaimed Property Fund covering the accountability for money deposited in the Unclaimed Property Fund under each article of Chapter 6. All real and personal property distributed to the State or delivered into the possession of the State or any officer or employee thereof under the provisions of this title, shall be accounted for by the Controller in the name of the account in the Unclaimed Property Fund to which the proceeds thereof, if converted into cash, would be credited under the provisions of this title. All personal property deposited in the State Treasury under the provisions of this title shall be held by the Treasurer in the name of the same account in the Unclaimed Property Fund for which such property is accounted by the Controller, as herein provided.

Added by Stats. 1951, Ch. 1708.

Section 1315 - Recording unclaimed money or property of deceased person received by state

If unclaimed money or other property in an estate of a deceased person, or if any unclaimed amount payable pursuant to an allowed and approved claim against such an estate, is received by the State or any officer or employee thereof and deposited in the State Treasury under the provisions of this title, it shall be recorded on the books of the Controller to the credit, or in the name, of such estate, for the benefit of the person entitled thereto or his successors in interest.

Added by Stats. 1951, Ch. 1708.

Section 1316 - Recording unclaimed money or property received by state for benefit of heirs, devisees, legatees, creditors, etc.

If unclaimed money or other property is received by the State or any officer or employee thereof and deposited in the State Treasury under the provisions of this title for the benefit of known heirs, devisees, legatees or creditors of an estate of a deceased person, or for the benefit of known claimants, payees, or other persons entitled thereto, it shall be recorded on the books of the Controller to the credit, or in the name, of such heirs, devisees, legatees, creditors, claimants, payees, or other persons entitled thereto.

Added by Stats. 1951, Ch. 1708.

Section 1317 - Amount of canceled warrant credited to Fund transferred to General Fund

The amount of each canceled warrant credited to the Unclaimed Property Fund under the provisions of Section 17072 of the Government Code shall, on order of the Controller, be transferred to the General Fund.

Amended by Stats. 1978, Ch. 1183.

Section 1318 - Deposit of interest and other income derived from investment of money in Fund

All interest received and other income derived from the investment of moneys in the Unclaimed Property Fund, as provided in Section 13470 of the Government Code, shall, on order of the Controller, be deposited in the General Fund.

Amended by Stats. 1978, Ch. 1183.

Section 1319 - Deposit and credit of rents, interest, dividends or other income received and held by state

Except as otherwise provided in Section 1318, all rents, interest, dividends or other income or increment derived from real or personal property received and held by the State in the name of the Unclaimed Property Fund under the provisions of this title shall, on order of the Controller, be deposited in the Unclaimed Property Fund, and shall be credited by the Controller to the account maintained by him, in the name of which such property is accounted, as provided in Chapter 2. Any moneys deposited in the Unclaimed Property Fund under the provisions of this section shall be held for the benefit of the person or persons entitled to the property from which such moneys were derived, or their successors in interest; and shall be subject to claim in the same manner as such property may be claimed; but the period in which such moneys shall be available for claim by and payment to the person or persons entitled thereto shall not extend beyond the period in which the property from which such moneys were derived is available for claim and payment under the provisions of this title.

Added by Stats. 1951, Ch. 1708.

Section 1320 - Deposit of rents, interest, dividends or other income or increment derived from property escheated to state

Except as otherwise provided in Section 1318, all rents, interest, dividends or other income or increment derived from real or personal property that has permanently escheated to the state, shall, on order of the Controller, be deposited in the General Fund.

All moneys deposited in the General Fund under the provisions of this section shall be deemed to have permanently escheated to the state as of the date of permanent escheat of the property from which such moneys were derived.

Amended by Stats. 1978, Ch. 1183.

Section 1321 - Immunity of person delivering money or property to state or holder of money or property

Any person delivering money or other property to the Treasurer or Controller under the provisions of this title shall, upon such delivery, be relieved and held harmless by the State from all or any claim or claims which exist at that time with reference to such money or other property, or which may thereafter be made, or which may come into existence, on account of, or in respect to, such money or other property.

No action shall be maintained against any person who is the holder of such money or other property, nor against any officer as agent thereof, for:

(a) The recovery of such money or other property delivered to the Treasurer or Controller pursuant to this title, or for interest thereon subsequent to the date of the report thereof, if any, to the Controller; or

(b) Damages alleged to have resulted from such delivery to the Treasurer or Controller. No owner of money or other property shall be entitled to receive interest thereon or with respect thereto from and after the date on which a report of such money or other property is made to the Controller pursuant to any provision of this title, whether or not he was entitled to such interest prior to such report.

As used in this section, "person" and "holder" have the respective meanings set forth in Section 1461 of this code.

Added by Stats. 1953, Ch. 279.

Article 2 - APPROPRIATION

Section 1325 - Purposes for which money in Fund continuously appropriated to Controller for expenditure

Notwithstanding Section 13340 of the Government Code, all money in the Unclaimed Property Fund is hereby continuously appropriated to the Controller, without regard to fiscal years, for expenditure for any of the following purposes:

(a) For refund, to the person making such deposit, of amounts, including overpayments, deposited in error in such fund.

(b) For payment of the cost of title searches and appraisals incurred by the Controller covering real or personal property held in the name of an account in such fund.

(c) For payment of the cost incurred by the Controller covering indemnity bonds required in order to have duplicate certificates of ownership issued in order to replace lost certificates, covering personal property held in the name of an account in such fund.

(d) For payment of amounts required to be paid by the state as trustee, bailee, or successor in interest to the preceding owner, pursuant to the provisions of trust deeds, mortgages, or other liens on real property held in the name of an account in such fund.

(e) For payment of costs incurred by the Controller for the repair, maintenance and upkeep of real and personal property held in the name of an account in such fund.

(f) For payment of costs of official advertising in connection with the sale of real or personal property held in the name of an account in such fund.

(g) For payment to taxing agencies of the amounts deducted by the Controller from allowed and approved claims, in accordance with the provisions of subdivision (c) of Section 4986.5 of the Revenue and Taxation Code.

(h) For transfer to the Inheritance Tax Fund, on order of the Controller, of the amount of any inheritance taxes determined to be due and payable to the state by any claimant, with respect to any real or personal property, including cash, claimed by that person under the provisions of this title.

(i) For payment and delivery to claimants of money or other property held to the credit, or in the name, of an account in such fund, under the provisions of this title.

(j) For transfer to the General Fund, on order of the Controller, of any money or other property in the Unclaimed Property Fund which becomes permanently escheated to the state under the provisions of this title. Any expenditure made by the Controller pursuant to the provisions of this section shall be charged against any balance credited to the particular account in the Unclaimed Property Fund, in the name of which is held the real or personal property for which the expenditure is made; and if sufficient balance is not available in such account, the expenditure may be made from any appropriation from the General Fund for the support of the Controller, or, in the case of official advertising, from any appropriation available therefor, to be reimbursed from the proceeds of any subsequent sale of the property for which such expenditure is made.

Amended by Stats. 1993, Ch. 692, Sec. 1. Effective January 1, 1994.

Chapter 3 - PAYMENT OF CLAIMS

Article 1 - GENERAL

Section 1335 - Immunity of state upon payment or delivering money or property to claimant

When payment or delivery of money or other property has been made to any claimant under the provisions of this chapter, no suit shall thereafter be maintained by any other claimant against the State or any officer thereof for or on account of such property.

Added by Stats. 1951, Ch. 1708.

Article 2 - REFUND OF ERRONEOUS RECEIPTS

Section 1345 - Generally

If any person has erroneously delivered any unclaimed moneys or other unclaimed property to the state or any officer or employee thereof, and the moneys or other property is deposited in the Unclaimed Property Fund or is held by the Controller or Treasurer in the name of any account in that fund pursuant to this title, the moneys or other property delivered in error may be refunded or returned to that person on order of the Controller.

Amended by Stats 2016 ch 31 (SB 836),s 11, eff. 6/27/2016.
Amended by Stats 2006 ch 538 (SB 1852),s 68, eff. 1/1/2007.

Section 1346 - Transfer of erroneously delivered cash to Unclaimed Property Fund or adjustment of records to show proper account if other than cash

If any person has erroneously delivered any unclaimed moneys or other unclaimed property to the state or any officer or employee thereof, and the moneys or other property is deposited in, or transferred to, the General Fund, or is held by the Controller or Treasurer in the name of that fund, pursuant to this title, the moneys or other property delivered in error, if cash, shall on order of the Controller, be transferred from the General Fund to the Unclaimed Property Fund, and, if other than cash, the records of the Controller and Treasurer shall be adjusted to show that it is held in the name of the proper account in the Unclaimed Property Fund; and the moneys or other property may be refunded or returned to that person on order of the Controller.

Amended by Stats 2016 ch 31 (SB 836),s 12, eff. 6/27/2016.
Amended by Stats 2006 ch 538 (SB 1852),s 69, eff. 1/1/2007.

Section 1347 - Property held as permanently escheated subsequently determined not to be escheated

Whenever money deposited in the Unclaimed Property Fund is transferred to the General Fund under the provisions of this title, and whenever the records of the Controller and Treasurer covering property other than money held in the name of any account in the Unclaimed Property Fund are adjusted to record such property as held in the name of the General Fund, as permanently escheated property under the provisions of this title, if it is subsequently determined that such money or other property is not, in fact, permanently escheated, such money or other property, if cash, shall, on order of the Controller, be retransferred from the General Fund to the Unclaimed Property Fund; and, if the property is other than money, the records of the Controller and Treasurer shall be adjusted to show that it is held in the name and for the benefit of the proper account in the Unclaimed Property Fund.

Amended by Stats. 1978, Ch. 1183.

Article 3 - CLAIMS

Section 1350 - Persons who may claim money or property

Unless otherwise provided in this title, all money or other property deposited in the State Treasury under the provisions of this title may be claimed by the person entitled thereto at any time prior to the date on which such money or other property has become permanently escheated, as provided by this title.

Added by Stats. 1951, Ch. 1708.

Section 1351 - Money or property deposited becoming property of state by escheat

Unless otherwise provided in this title, all money or other property deposited in the State Treasury under the provisions of this title, if not claimed by the person entitled thereto within five years from the date of such deposit, shall become the property of the State by escheat; and upon request by the Controller, the Attorney General shall commence a proceeding under the provisions of Section 1410, or, in lieu of such proceeding, the Controller may take action as provided by Article 2 of Chapter 5, to have it adjudged, determined or established that the title to such money or other property has vested in the State.

Added by Stats. 1951, Ch. 1708.

Section 1352 - Property held for third persons or title subject to rights of third persons

(a) Whenever unclaimed money or other property is deposited in the State Treasury under this title, and, except as otherwise provided by law, whenever there is in the possession of the state or its officers any money or other property which is held for third persons or the title to which has vested in the state subject to the rights of third persons, and the period during which it may be claimed by a person entitled thereto has not terminated, the period and person being prescribed by law, if the value of the money or other property to which the claimant is entitled is less than sixty thousand dollars ($60,000), any such person may present his or her claim for it to the Controller. The claim shall be made in the form prescribed by the Controller, which shall set forth the information required by Section 1355 or any other information that the Controller may deem necessary to establish right or title to the money or other property in the claimant.

(b) Property assigned or distributed to a name distributee may be claimed by the distributee himself or herself or his or her legal guardian or conservator, as provided in subdivision (a) regardless of the amount. This subdivision does not apply to the heirs or estate of a distributee, or to property distributed to the state for lack of known heirs.

(c) Any person aggrieved by a decision of the Controller may commence an action, naming the Controller as a defendant, to establish his or her claim in the superior court in any county or city and county in which the Attorney General has an office pursuant to Section 1541.

Amended by Stats. 1990, Ch. 450, Sec. 1. Effective July 31, 1990.

Section 1353 - Superior court jurisdiction to determine title to money or property

Except as otherwise provided in Sections 401 or 1352, whenever money or other property is deposited in the State Treasury under the provisions of this title, and, except as otherwise provided by law, when there is in the possession of the State or its officers any money or other property which is to be held for third persons or the title to which has vested in the State subject to the rights of third persons, the Superior Court of the County of Sacramento shall have full and exclusive jurisdiction to determine the title to such money or other property and all claims thereto.

If the period in which such money or other property may be claimed by a person entitled thereto has not terminated, such period and person being prescribed by law, any such person may file a petition in the Superior Court of the County of Sacramento, or as provided in Section 401, showing his claim or right to the money or other property or the proceeds thereof, or any portion thereof.

The petition shall be verified, and, among other things, must, insofar as they are applicable or material to the matters at issue, state the facts required to be stated in a petition filed under Section 1355. If the money or other property at issue did not come into the possession of the State or its officers in connection with estates of deceased persons, the petition shall, in addition to the foregoing facts, state any material facts necessary to establish a prima facie right or title in the petitioner. Upon the filing of the petition, the same proceedings shall be had as are required in Section 1355.

If, upon trial of the issues, the court is satisfied of the claimant's right or title to the money or other property claimed, it shall grant him a certificate to that effect under its seal. Upon presentation of such certificate, the Controller shall draw his warrant on the Treasurer for the amount of money covered thereby; and if the certificate covers any property other than money, a certified copy of the certificate filed with the officer of the State having possession of the property shall serve as sufficient authority to the officer for the delivery of such property to the claimant.

Added by Stats. 1951, Ch. 1708.

Section 1354 - Recovery on claim made or petition filed by representative of estate

Whenever any claim is made or petition filed by the representative of an estate or other person, under the provisions of this chapter, or under any other provision of law, to recover money or other property deposited in the State Treasury or held by the State or any officer thereof to the credit, or in the name, of any account in the Unclaimed Property Fund, no recovery will be allowed unless it affirmatively appears that there are heirs or legatees who will receive such money or other property or creditors of the deceased owner of the claim whose claims are valid and are not barred, and whose claims were in existence prior to the death of such deceased owner of the claim. Where only creditors exist, and there are no heirs or legatees, said claims shall be allowed only to the extent necessary to pay such claims and the reasonable costs of administration of the estate, including court costs, administrator's fees and attorney's fees. This section shall apply to all claims which are pending at the time that this section goes into effect as well as to claims arising hereafter.

Added by Stats. 1951, Ch. 1708.

Section 1355 - Petition filed in Superior Court of Sacramento County showing claim or right to money or property

Within five years after date of entry of judgment in any proceeding had under the provisions of Chapter 5, or within five years after completion of notice by publication in an escheat action taken under the provisions of Section 1415, a person not a party or privy to such proceeding or action, if not otherwise barred, may file a petition in the Superior Court of the County of Sacramento, or as provided in Section 401, showing his claim or right to the money or other property, or the proceeds thereof.

Said petition shall be verified; and, in a proceeding for the recovery by the petitioner as heir, devisee, or legatee, or the successor in interest of an heir, devisee or legatee, of money or other property received by the State from the estate of a decedent under the provisions of Article 1 of Chapter 6, such petition, among other things must state:

The full name, and the place and date of birth of the decedent whose estate, or any part thereof, is claimed.

The full name of such decedent's father and the maiden name of his mother, the places and dates of their respective births, the place and date of their marriage, the full names of all children the issue of such marriage, with the date of birth of each, and the place and date of death of all children of such marriage who have died unmarried and without issue.

Whether or not such decedent was ever married, and if so, where, when and to whom.

How, when and where such marriage, if any, was dissolved.

Whether or not said decedent was ever remarried, and, if so, where, when and to whom.

The full names, and the dates and places of birth of all lineal descendants, if any, of said decedent; the dates and places of death of any thereof who died prior to the filing of such petition; and the places of residence of all who are then surviving, with the degree of relationship of each of such survivors to said decedent.

Whether any of the brothers or sisters of such decedent every married, and, if so, where, when and whom.

The full names, and the places and dates of birth of all children who are the issue of the marriage of any such brother or sister of the decedent, and the date and place of death of all deceased nephews and nieces of said decedent.

Whether or not said decedent, if of foreign birth, ever became a naturalized citizen of the United States, and, if so, when, where, and by what court citizenship was conferred.

The post-office names of the cities, towns or other places, each in its appropriate connection, wherein are preserved the records of the births, marriages and deaths hereinbefore enumerated, and, if known, the title of the public official or other person having custody of such records.

The nationality of each of the heirs of the decedent.

The street address of each of the heirs of the decedent.

If, for any reason, the petitioner is unable to set forth any of the matters or things hereinbefore required, he shall clearly state such reason in his petition.

At least 20 days before the hearing of the petition, a copy of the petition and notice of hearing must be served on the Attorney General and on the Controller, and the Attorney General may answer the same at his discretion.

If such claim includes a claim to real property or any interest therein, the petitioner shall record in the office of the county recorder of the county in which the real property is situated, a notice of the pendency of the petition containing the object of the action and a description of the property in the county affected thereby. From the time of filing such notice for record only, shall a purchaser or encumbrancer of the property be deemed to have constructive notice of the pendency of the action, and only of its pendency against parties designated by their real names.

The court must thereupon try the issue as issues are tried in civil actions; and if it is determined that such person is entitled to the money or other property or the proceeds thereof, it must order the property, if it has not been sold, to be delivered to him, or if it has been sold and the proceeds thereof paid into the State Treasury, it must order the Controller to draw his warrant on the Treasurer for the payment of the same, but without interest or cost to the State. A copy of such order, under the seal of the court, shall be a sufficient voucher for drawing such warrant.

All persons who fail to appear and file their petitions within the time limited are forever barred; saving, however, to infants and persons of unsound mind, the right to appear and file their petitions at any time within the time limited, or within one year after their respective disabilities cease.

Amended by Stats. 1951, Ch. 1738.

Chapter 4 - MANAGEMENT OF UNCLAIMED PROPERTY
Article 1 - GENERAL PROVISIONS

Section 1360 - Definitions
For the purposes of this chapter, the following definitions shall apply:
(a) "Personal property" means personal property falling within the definition of "unclaimed property" under the provisions of this title;
(b) "Real property" means real property falling within the definition of "unclaimed property" under the provisions of this title;
(c) "Securities" includes stocks, bonds, notes, debentures, certificates of deposit, shares, and all other evidences of ownership or indebtedness, and all forms of chose in action and the interests in property represented thereby, falling within the definition of unclaimed property under the provisions of this title.
Added by Stats. 1951, Ch. 1708.

Section 1361 - Care and custody of property assumed by state for benefit of those entitled
The care and custody of all property delivered to the Treasurer or Controller pursuant to this title is assumed by the State for the benefit of those entitled thereto, and the State is responsible for the payment of all claims established thereto pursuant to law, less any lawful deductions.
Added by Stats. 1951, Ch. 1708.

Article 2 - POWERS OF THE CONTROLLER

Section 1365 - Generally
In connection with all unclaimed property, the Controller has all of the powers necessary in order to safeguard and conserve the interests of all parties, including the State, having any vested or expectant interest in such unclaimed property. His powers include, but are not limited to, the authority to incur obligations the payment of which is authorized by the provisions of Section 1325.
Added by Stats. 1951, Ch. 1708.

Article 3 - SALE OR DISPOSAL OF PROPERTY

Section 1370 - Power of Controller to sell or lease personal property
The Controller may sell or lease personal property at any time, and in any manner, and may execute those leases on behalf and in the name of the State of California.
Amended by Stats 2016 ch 31 (SB 836),s 13, eff. 6/27/2016.
Amended by Stats 2006 ch 538 (SB 1852),s 70, eff. 1/1/2007.

Section 1371 - Power of Controller as to securities, accounts, debts, contractual rights or other choses in action
The Controller may sell, cash, redeem, exchange, or otherwise dispose of any securities and all other classes of personal property, and may sell, cash, redeem, exchange, compromise, adjust, settle, or otherwise dispose of any accounts, debts, contractual rights, or other choses in action if, in his or her opinion, that action on his or her part is necessary or will tend to safeguard and conserve the interests of all parties, including the state, having any vested or expectant interest in the property.
Amended by Stats 2016 ch 31 (SB 836),s 14, eff. 6/27/2016.
Amended by Stats 2006 ch 538 (SB 1852),s 71, eff. 1/1/2007.

Section 1372 - Power of controller to sign, endorse or authenticate securities, bills of sale, documents or other instruments
The Controller may sign, endorse, or otherwise authenticate, in the name and on behalf of the State, subscribing his name, as Controller, under such writing, any securities, bills of sale, documents, or other instruments required, under customary business practice, for the consummation of the transactions authorized by this chapter. For all purposes, such endorsement is conclusive and binding against the State and the heirs, devisees, legatees, or other claimants of the property covered by such endorsement.
Added by Stats. 1951, Ch. 1708.

Section 1373 - Sale or lease at public auction; notice
The Controller may lease or sell any real property for cash at public auction to the highest bidder.
Before such sale or lease, notice thereof shall be published pursuant to Government Code Section 6063 in a newspaper published in the county in which the real property is situated, or in an adjoining county, if there is no newspaper published in such county. The notice is sufficient for all the purposes of such lease or sale if the real property is described sufficiently to identify it. The cost of publication shall be a charge against the proceeds of the lease or sale, or, if the lease or sale is not consummated, such cost shall be a legal charge against the appropriation for official advertising.
If the value of the property to be sold does not appear to exceed one thousand dollars ($1,000) in the determination of the Controller, notice of sale thereof may be published pursuant to Government Code Section 6061.
Amended by Stats. 1963, Ch. 752.

Section 1374 - Authority of Controller to reject bids
The Controller may reject any and all bids made at sales or public auctions held under the provisions of this chapter.
Added by Stats. 1951, Ch. 1708.

Section 1375 - Power of Controller to sell or lease real property at private sale
Any real property may be sold or leased by the Controller at private sale without published notice.
Amended by Stats 2016 ch 31 (SB 836),s 15, eff. 6/27/2016.
Amended by Stats 2006 ch 538 (SB 1852),s 72, eff. 1/1/2007.

Section 1376 - Execution of deed covering real property and bill of sale covering personal property
Upon receipt of the proceeds of any sale made pursuant to this chapter, the Controller shall execute, in the name and on behalf of the State of California, a deed covering the real property, and a bill of sale covering the personal property, sold. He may execute leases for real or personal property in the name and on behalf of the State of California.
Added by Stats. 1951, Ch. 1708.

Section 1377 - Creating obligation not already obligation of owners, heirs, devisees, etc.
The Controller shall not enter into any transaction which shall create or impose upon the owners, heirs, devisees, legatees, or other claimants of the property involved, any obligation under an executory contract, the performance of which is not already an obligation of such owners, heirs, devisees, legatees, or other claimants prior to the consummation of the transactions authorized by this chapter.
Added by Stats. 1951, Ch. 1708.

Section 1378 - Immunity of state on account of transaction entered into by Controller
No suit shall be maintained by any person against the State or any officer thereof, for or on account of any transaction entered into by the Controller pursuant to this chapter.
Added by Stats. 1951, Ch. 1708.

Section 1379 - Power of Controller to destroy personal property other than cash deposited in Treasury
The Controller may destroy or otherwise dispose of any personal property other than cash deposited in the State Treasury under this title, if that property is determined by him or her to be valueless or of such little value that the costs of conducting a sale would probably exceed the amount that would be realized from the sale, and neither the Treasurer nor Controller shall be held to respond in damages at the suit of any person claiming loss by reason of that destruction or disposition.
Amended by Stats 2016 ch 31 (SB 836),s 16, eff. 6/27/2016.
Amended by Stats 2006 ch 538 (SB 1852),s 73, eff. 1/1/2007.

Section 1380 - Transaction exempt from section 11009, Government Code
All sales, exchanges, or other transactions entered into by the Controller pursuant to this chapter are exempt from the provisions of Section 11009 of the Government Code.
Added by Stats. 1951, Ch. 1708.

Section 1381 - Transactions conclusive against everyone except purchaser or encumbrancer for valuable consideration
All sales, leases or other transactions entered into by the Controller pursuant to this chapter shall be conclusive against everyone, except a purchaser or encumbrancer who in good faith and for a valuable consideration acquires a title or interest by an instrument in writing that is first duly recorded.
Added by Stats. 1951, Ch. 1738.

Section 1382 - Real property to which article applies
Any provision of this article which authorizes the Controller to sell real property applies to any real property distributed or escheated to, or the title to which has vested in, the State of California by court order or decree of distribution, if such real property is held in the name of the Unclaimed Property Fund under the provision of this title, whether or not such real property has permanently escheated to the State.
This section does not apply to the disposition of tax-deeded lands under Chapter 7, 8 or 9 of Part 6 of Division 1 of the Revenue and Taxation Code.
Added by Stats. 1953, Ch. 281.

Article 4 - DISPOSAL OF PROCEEDS OF SALE OR LEASE

Section 1390 - Proceeds deposited in Unclaimed Property Fund
The Controller shall deliver to the Treasurer the proceeds of any sale or lease of property, other than permanently escheated property, made pursuant to this chapter; and, on order of the Controller, the amount thereof shall be deposited in the Unclaimed Property Fund. Such amount shall be credited by the Controller to the account in said fund, in the name of which the property sold or leased was held. All moneys deposited in the Unclaimed Property Fund under the provisions of this section shall be held for the benefit of those entitled to claim the property sold or leased; but the period in which such moneys shall be available for claim by and payment to the persons entitled thereto shall not extend beyond the period in which such property is available for claim and payment under the provisions of this title.
Added by Stats. 1951, Ch. 1708.

Section 1391 - Proceeds deposited in General Fund
The Controller shall deliver to the Treasurer the proceeds of any sale or lease of permanently escheated property made pursuant to this chapter; and, on order of the Controller, the amount thereof shall be deposited in the General Fund. All moneys deposited in the General Fund under the provisions of this section shall be deemed to have permanently escheated to the state as of the date of permanent escheat of the property from which such moneys were derived.
Amended by Stats. 1978, Ch. 1183.

Section 1392 - Credit of proceeds to estate from which property affected by transaction received
The proceeds of any transaction by the Controller under the provisions of this chapter in connection with property received and held by the state under the provisions of Article 1 (commencing with Section 1440) of Chapter 6 of this title shall be credited by the Controller to the estate from which the property affected by the transaction was received; or, if such property has permanently escheated to the state, to the account in the General Fund to which the permanently escheated cash derived from estates of deceased persons is credited.
Amended by Stats. 1978, Ch. 1183.

Section 1393 - Credit of proceeds to unlocated heirs, devisees or legatees
The proceeds of any transaction by the Controller under the provisions of this chapter, in connection with property received and held by the state under the provisions of Article 1 (commencing with Section 1440) of Chapter 6 of this title, for the benefit of unlocated heirs, devisees or legatees of estates of deceased persons, shall be credited by the Controller to such heirs, devisees or legatees of the property affected by such transaction; or, if such property has permanently escheated to the state, to the account in the General Fund to which the permanently escheated cash derived from estates of deceased persons is credited.
Amended by Stats. 1978, Ch. 1183.

Section 1394 - Credit of proceeds to persons entitled or to account in General Fund
The proceeds of any transaction by the Controller under the provisions of this chapter in connection with property received and held by the state under the provisions of this title, for the benefit of the persons entitled thereto, shall be credited by the Controller to such persons; or, if the property affected by such transaction has permanently escheated to the state, to the account in the General Fund in the name of which such permanently escheated property was recorded.
Amended by Stats. 1978, Ch. 1183.

Chapter 5 - ESCHEAT PROCEEDINGS

Article 1 - ESCHEAT PROCEEDINGS ON UNCLAIMED PROPERTY

Section 1410 - Generally
The Attorney General shall, from time to time, commence actions on behalf of the state for the purpose of having it adjudged that title to unclaimed property to which the state has become entitled by escheat has vested in the state, and for the purpose of having it adjudged that property has been actually abandoned or that the owner thereof has died and there is no person entitled thereto and the same has escheated and vested in the state. Such actions shall be brought in the Superior Court for the County of Sacramento; except that if any real property covered by the petition is not situated in the County of Sacramento, an action respecting the real property shall be commenced in the superior court for the

county in which such real property or any part thereof is situated. The Attorney General shall cause to be recorded in the office of the county recorder of the county in which the real property is situated, a notice of the pendency of the petition containing the names of the parties, and the object of the action and a description of the property in the county affected thereby. From the time of filing such notice for record only, shall a purchaser or encumbrancer of the property affected thereby be deemed to have constructive notice of the pendency of the action, and only of the pendency against parties designated by their real names.

Such action shall be commenced by filing a petition. The provisions of Section 1420, relating to the facts to be set forth in the petition, joinder of parties and causes of action, and the provisions of Section 1423, relating to appearances and pleadings, shall be applicable to any proceeding had under this section.

Upon the filing of the petition, the court shall make an order requiring all persons interested in the property or estate to appear on a day not more than 90 days nor less than 60 days from the date of the order and show cause, if any they have, why title to the property should not vest in the State of California.

Service of process in such actions shall be made by delivery of a copy of the order, together with a copy of the petition, to each person who claims title to any property covered by the petition and who is known to the Attorney General or the Controller or who has theretofore filed in the office of the Controller a written request for such service of process, stating his name and address, including street number, or post-office box number, if any, and by publishing the order at least once a week for two consecutive weeks in a newspaper published in the county in which the action is filed, the last publication to be at least 10 days prior to the date set for the hearing.

Upon completion of the service of process, as provided in this section, the court shall have full and complete jurisdiction over the estate, the property, and the person of everyone having or claiming any interest in the property, and shall have full and complete jursidiction to hear and determine the issues therein, and to render an appropriate judgment.

In addition to the foregoing publication of the order, a notice shall be given by publication, at least once a week for two successive weeks in a newspaper published in the county from which the property was forwarded to the State Treasury or is situated, of each estate and item of property from such county or situated in such county in excess of one thousand dollars ($1,000). Such notice shall state that a petition has been filed and an order made as hereinbefore provided and shall list each estate and item in excess of one thousand dollars ($1,000) and show the amount of the property, if money, or a description thereof, if other than money, and the name of the owner or claimant and his last known address. Any omission or defect in the giving of such additional notice shall not affect the jurisdiction of the court.

If it appears from the facts found or admitted that the state is entitled to the property or any part thereof mentioned in the petition, judgment shall be rendered that title to such property or part thereof, as the case may be, has vested in the state by escheat.

No costs of suit shall be allowed against any party in any action or proceeding had under this section.

Amended by Stats. 1984, Ch. 268, Sec. 1. Effective June 30, 1984.

Article 2 - ESCHEAT BY NOTICE AND PUBLICATION

Section 1415 - Generally

Whenever any money or other personal property of a value of one thousand dollars ($1,000) or less has heretofore been, or is hereafter, deposited in the State Treasury and the same is subject to being declared escheated to the state or being declared vested in the state as abandoned property, or otherwise, under any laws of this state, in lieu of the procedure provided for elsewhere in this chapter, the Controller may, from time to time, prepare a return listing such property and give notice thereof in the manner hereinafter provided. Such return shall list each item and show (1) the amount of the property, if money, or a description thereof if other than money; (2) the name of the owner or claimant and his last known address, if known; (3) the name and address of the person delivering the property to the State Treasury, if known but where the property is received from an estate, only the name of the decedent together with the name of the county and the number of the proceeding need be given; (4) the facts and circumstances by virtue of which it is claimed the property has escheated or vested in the state; and (5) such other information as the Controller may desire to include to assist in identifying each item.

When such return has been completed, the Controller shall prepare, date, and attach thereto a notice that the property listed in the return has escheated or vested in the state. Copies of such return and notice shall then be displayed and be open to public inspection during business hours in at least three offices of the Controller, one in the City of Sacramento, one in the City and County of San Francisco, and one in the City of Los Angeles.

The Controller shall then cause notice to be given by publication in one newspaper of general circulation published in the City of Sacramento, and also by publication in one newspaper of general circulation published in the City and County of San Francisco, and also by publication in one newspaper of general circulation published in the City of Los Angeles, at least once each calendar week for two consecutive weeks, that said return and notice that the property listed in the return has escheated or vested in the state has been prepared and is on display and open to public inspection during business hours, giving the addresses and room numbers of the locations where the same may be inspected.

Such publication shall be made within 90 days after attaching the notice to the return. Notice by such publication shall be deemed completed 120 days after attaching the notice to the return.

Within five years after such notice by publication is completed, any person entitled to such property may claim it in the manner provided in Chapter 3 of this title. All persons who fail to make such claim within the time limited are forever barred; saving, however, to infants and persons of unsound mind, the right to appear and claim such property at any time within the time limited, or within one year after their respective disabilities cease.

Amended by Stats. 1984, Ch. 268, Sec. 2. Effective June 30, 1984.

Article 3 - ESCHEAT PROCEEDINGS IN DECEDENTS' ESTATES

Section 1420 - Generally

(a) At any time after two years after the death of any decedent who leaves property to which the state is entitled by reason of it having escheated to the state, the Attorney General shall commence a proceeding on behalf of the state in the Superior Court for the County of Sacramento to have it adjudged that the state is so entitled. The action shall be commenced by filing a petition, which shall be treated as the information elsewhere referred to in this title.

(b) The petition shall set forth a description of the property, the name of the person last in possession thereof, the name of the person, if any, claiming the property, or portion thereof, and the facts and circumstances by virtue of which it is claimed the property has escheated.

(c) Upon the filing of the petition, the court shall make an order requiring all persons interested in the estate to appear and show cause, if any, within 60 days from the date of the order, why the estate should not vest in the state. The order must be published at least once a week for four consecutive weeks in a newspaper published in the County of Sacramento, the last publication to be at least 10 days prior to the date set for the hearing. Upon the completion of the publication of the order, the court shall have full and complete jurisdiction over the estate, the property, and the person of everyone having or claiming any interest in the property, and shall have full and complete jurisdiction to hear and determine the issues therein, and render the appropriate judgment thereon.

(d) If proceedings for the administration of the estate have been instituted, a copy of the order must be filed with the papers in the estate. If proceedings for the administration of any estate of the decedent have been instituted and none of the persons entitled to succeed thereto have appeared and made claim to the property, or any portion thereof, before the decree of final distribution therein is made, or before the commencement of a proceeding by the Attorney General, or if the court shall find that the persons as have appeared are not entitled to the property of the estate, or any portion thereof, the court shall, upon final settlement of the proceedings for the administration of the estate, after the payment of all debts and expenses of administration, distribute all moneys and other property remaining to the State of California. In any proceeding brought by the Attorney General under this chapter, any two or more parties and any two or more causes of action may be joined in the same proceedings and in the same petition without being separately stated, and it shall be sufficient to allege in the petition that the decedent left no heirs to take the estate and the failure of heirs to appear and set up their claims in any proceeding, or in any proceedings for the administration of the estate, shall be sufficient proof upon which to base the judgment in any proceeding or decree of distribution.

(e) If proceedings for the administration of any estate have not been commenced within six months from the death of any decedent the Attorney General may direct the public administrator to commence the same forthwith.

Amended by Stats 2003 ch 62 (SB 600),s 26, eff. 1/1/2004.

Amended by Stats 2002 ch 784 (SB 1316),s 83, eff. 1/1/2003.

Section 1421 - Action by Attorney General to determine state's rights to property or intervention in proceeding affecting estate and contesting claimants' rights

Whenever the Attorney General is informed that any estate has escheated or is about to escheat to the state, or that the property involved in any action or special proceeding has escheated or is about to escheat to the state, the Attorney General may commence an action on behalf of the state to determine its rights to the property or may intervene on its behalf in any action or special proceeding affecting the estate and contest the rights of any claimant or claimants thereto. The Attorney General may also apply to the superior court or any judge thereof for an order directing the county treasurer to deposit in the State Treasury all money, and to deliver to the Controller for deposit in the State Treasury, all other personal property, in the possession of the county treasurer, which may become payable to the State Treasury pursuant to Section 7643 of the Probate Code.

Amended by Stats. 1988, Ch. 1199, Sec. 9. Operative July 1, 1989, by Sec. 119 of Ch. 1199.

Section 1422 - Appointment of receiver to take charge of estate

The court, upon the information being filed, and upon application of the Attorney General, either before or after answer, upon notice to the party claiming the estate, if known, may, upon sufficient cause therefor being shown, appoint a receiver to take charge of such estate, or any part thereof, or to receive the rents, income and profits of the same until the title of such estate is finally settled.

Added by Stats. 1951, Ch. 1708.

Section 1423 - Appearance and answer by persons named in information

All persons named in the information may appear and answer, and may traverse or deny the facts stated therein at any time before the time for answering expires, and any other person claiming an interest in such estate may appear and be made a defendant, by motion for that purpose in open court within the time allowed for answering, and if no such person appears and answers within the time, then judgment must be rendered that the State is the owner of the property in such information claimed.

If any person appears and denies the title set up by the State, or traverses any material fact set forth in the information, the issue of fact must be tried as issues of fact are tried in civil actions.

If, after the issues are tried, it appears from the facts found or admitted that the State has good title to the property in the information mentioned, or any part thereof, judgment must be rendered that the State is the owner and entitled to the possession thereof, and that it recover costs of suit against the defendants who have appeared and answered.

In any judgment rendered, or that has heretofore been rendered by any court escheating property to the State, on motion of the Attorney General, the court must make an order that such property, unless it consists of money, be sold by the sheriff of the county where it is situate, at public sale, for cash, after giving notice of the time and place of sale, as may be prescribed by the court in such order; that the sheriff, within five days after such sale, make a report thereof to the court, and upon the hearing of such report, the court may examine the report and witnesses in relation thereto, and if the proceedings were unfair, or if the sum bid disproportionate to the value, or if it appears that a sum exceeding said bid, exclusive of the expense of a new sale, may be obtained, the court may vacate the sale, and direct another to be had, of which notice must be given, and the sale in all respects conducted as if no previous sale had taken place. If an offer greater in amount than that named in the report is made to the court in writing by a responsible person, the court may, in its discretion, accept such offer and confirm the sale to such person, or order a new sale.

If it appears to the court that the sale was legally made and fairly conducted and that the sum bid is not disproportionate to the value of the property sold, and that a sum exceeding such bid, exclusive of the expense of a new sale, cannot be obtained, or if the increased bid above mentioned is made and accepted by the court, the court must make an order confirming the sale and directing the sheriff, in the name of the State, to execute to the purchaser or purchasers a conveyance of said property sold; and said conveyance vests in the purchaser or purchasers all the right and title of the State therein.

The sheriff shall, out of the proceeds of such sale, pay the cost of said proceedings incurred on behalf of the State, including the expenses of making such sale, and also an attorney's fee, if additional counsel was employed in said proceedings, to be fixed by the court, not exceeding 10 percent on the amount of such sale; and the residue thereof shall be paid by said sheriff into the State Treasury.

Added by Stats. 1951, Ch. 1708.

Section 1424 - Distributing or vesting clause of judgment or decree creating trust in favor of unknown or unidentified persons

If, in any proceeding had under this title, the judgment or decree distributes or vests unclaimed property or any portion thereof to or in the State of California and the distributing or vesting clause contains words otherwise creating a trust in favor of certain unknown or unidentified persons as a class, such judgment or decree shall vest in the State of California both legal and equitable title to such property; saving, however, the right of claimants to appear and claim the property, as provided in this title.

Added by Stats. 1951, Ch. 1708.

Article 4 - PERMANENT ESCHEAT

Section 1430 - Generally

(a) Upon the expiration of five years after the date of entry of judgment in any proceeding pursuant to this chapter, or upon the expiration of five years after completion of notice by publication in an escheat action taken pursuant to Section 1415, the property covered by that proceeding or action shall permanently escheat to the state, except as provided in subdivision (b).

(b) Infants and persons of unsound mind shall have the right to appear and claim such property as provided in this title if born before the expiration of the five-year period; but it shall be presumed that there are no infants nor persons of unsound mind who are or will be entitled to claim this property unless and until they appear and claim the property as provided in this title. This presumption shall be conclusive in favor of any purchaser in good faith and for a valuable consideration from the state and everyone subsequently claiming under him or her, saving however, to infants and persons of unsound mind the right of recourse to the proceeds of any sale or other disposition of any such property by the state and as herein provided.

(c) Except as otherwise provided in this subdivision, a named beneficiary of property that escheats pursuant to this title or, if the beneficiary is deceased or a court renders a judgment that the beneficiary is dead, a blood relative of the named beneficiary may claim property described in subdivision (a) at any time within five years after the date of entry of judgment in any proceeding under this chapter. The named beneficiary or, if a court has rendered a judgment that the named beneficiary is dead, the blood relative of the named beneficiary shall be entitled to immediate payment upon this claim. If a court has not rendered a judgment that the named beneficiary is dead, payment of the claim of a blood relative of the named beneficiary shall be made on the day before the expiration of the five-year period described in this section. This subdivision shall not apply to authorize a claim by any person, including any issue or blood relative of that person, whose interest or inheritance was specifically restricted or barred by a provision in the donating or transferring instrument.

Amended by Stats. 1997, Ch. 671, Sec. 1. Effective January 1, 1998.

Section 1431 - Transfer of permanently escheated money to General Fund; adjustment of records of permanently escheated property

When money in the Unclaimed Property Fund has become permanently escheated to the state, the amount thereof shall, on order of the Controller, be transferred to the General Fund. When property other than money held by the Controller or Treasurer in the name of any account in the Unclaimed Property Fund has become permanently escheated to the state, the records of the Controller and Treasurer shall be adjusted to show that such property is held in the name of the General Fund.

Amended by Stats. 1980, Ch. 676, Sec. 69.

Chapter 6 - DISPOSITION OF UNCLAIMED PROPERTY

Article 1 - ESTATES OF DECEASED PERSONS

Section 1440 - Money or property deemed paid under provisions of article

Whenever, under the provisions of this title or under any other provision of law, any unclaimed money or other property in an estate of a deceased person, or any unclaimed amount payable pursuant to an allowed and approved claim against such an estate, is paid to the State or any officer or employee thereof for deposit in the State Treasury, it shall be deemed to have been so paid under the provisions of this article.

Added by Stats. 1951, Ch. 1708.

Section 1441 - Money or property permanently escheated without further proceeding

Money or other property distributed to the state under Chapter 6 (commencing with Section 11900) of Part 10 of Division 7 of the Probate Code, if not claimed within five years from the date of the order for distribution, as provided in Chapter 3, is permanently escheated to the state without further proceeding; saving, however, to infants and persons of unsound mind, the right to appear and file their claims within the time limited pursuant to Section 1430, or within one year after their respective disabilities cease; provided, however, that any such property shall be conclusively presumed to be permanently escheated to the state as to all persons in favor of a purchaser in good faith and for a valuable consideration from the state and anyone subsequently claiming under that purchaser, saving however, to infants and persons of unsound mind the right of recourse to the proceeds of any sale or other disposition of that property by the state and as herein provided.

Amended by Stats. 1995, Ch. 105, Sec. 1. Effective January 1, 1996.

Section 1442 - Claim to money or other property by person entitled

Except as otherwise provided in Section 1441, any money or other property paid into the State Treasury under the provisions of this article may be claimed by the person entitled thereto, as provided in Chapter 3.

Added by Stats. 1951, Ch. 1708.

Section 1443 - Money or property deemed paid or delivered for deposit in State Treasury

Notwithstanding any other provision of law, all money or other property paid or delivered to the state or any officer or employee thereof under the provisions of Section 7643 or 11428, Chapter 6 (commencing with Section 11900) of Part 10 of Division 7, or Section 6800, of the Probate Code, or under any other section of the Probate Code, or any amendment thereof adopted after the effective date of this section, shall be deemed to be paid or delivered for deposit in the State Treasury under the provisions of this article, and shall be transmitted, received, accounted for, and disposed of, as provided in this title.

Amended by Stats. 1988, Ch. 1199, Sec. 11. Operative July 1, 1989, by Sec. 119 of Ch. 1199.

Section 1444 - Money or property deposited in county treasury paid to Treasurer or Controller

At the time of the next county settlement following the expiration of one year from the date of its deposit in the county treasury, all money or other property distributed in the administration of an estate of a deceased person and heretofore or hereafter deposited in the county treasury to the credit of known heirs, legatees, or devisees, and any money or other property remaining on deposit to the credit of an estate after final distribution to such known heirs, legatees or devisees, shall be paid to the Treasurer or Controller as provided in Chapter 2.

Added by Stats. 1951, Ch. 1708.

Section 1444.5 - Money or property on deposit with county treasurer received from public administrator deemed permanently escheated to state

Notwithstanding any other provision of law, any money on deposit with the county treasurer of a county received from a public administrator of the county in trust and to the account of the estate of a deceased person or the creditor of a deceased person, in an amount of fifty dollars ($50) or less as to any one estate or creditor, and not covered by a decree of distribution, which was received or remained on hand after the final accounting in such deceased person's estate and the discharge of such public administrator as representative of the estate, and where the money has so remained on deposit in trust for a period of 15 years or more unclaimed by any heir, devisee or legatee of such deceased person, or by any creditor having an allowed and approved claim against the deceased person's estate remaining unpaid, shall be deemed permanently escheated to the State of California. The total of any such moneys so held in trust unclaimed for such period may be paid in a lump sum by the county treasurer, from such funds as he may have on hand for the purpose, to the State Treasurer, at the time of the next county settlement after the effective date of this section, or at any county settlement thereafter. Such lump sum payment may be made by designating it to have been made under this section, without the necessity of any further report or statement of the estates or claimants concerned, without the necessity of any order of court, and without being subject to the provisions of Section 1311 or 1312. Upon receipt by the State Treasurer, any permanently escheated money received by him under this section shall forthwith be deposited in the School Land Fund, subject only to the rights of minors and persons of unsound mind saved to them by Section 1430.

This section shall also apply in all respects to any money on deposit with a county treasurer received from the coroner of the county in trust and to the account of a deceased person, and any such money shall be held, deemed permanently escheated, reported and paid over in like manner as hereinabove set forth.

Added by Stats. 1957, Ch. 1375.

Section 1445 - Petition by county treasurer for order directing payment of money or property into State Treasury

If money or other property is deposited in a county treasury, and if the deposits belong (1) to known decedents' estates on which letters testamentary or letters of administration have never been issued or (2) to known decedents' estates on which letters testamentary or letters of administration have been issued but no decree of distribution has been rendered, due to the absence of any parties interested in the estate or the failure of such parties diligently to protect their interests by taking reasonable steps for the purpose of securing a distribution of the estate, the county treasurer shall, within one year following the expiration of five years from the date of such deposit, file a petition in the superior court of the county in which the deposit is held, setting forth the fact that the money or other personal property has remained in the county treasury under such circumstances for such five-year period, and petitioning the court for an order directing him to pay such money or other property into the State Treasury.

At the time of the next county settlement following the date of the making of the order by the court, unless earlier payment is required by the Controller, the county treasurer shall pay such money or other property to the Treasurer or Controller as provided in Chapter 2.

Added by Stats. 1951, Ch. 1708.

Section 1446 - Unclaimed money or other property belonging to person who dies while confined in state institution subject to jurisdiction of Director of Corrections

Notwithstanding any other provision of law, all unclaimed money or other property belonging to any person who dies while confined in any state institution subject to the jurisdiction of the Director of Corrections, which is paid or delivered to the State or any officer or employee thereof under the provisions of Section 5061 of the Penal Code, or under any amendment thereof adopted after the effective date of this section, shall be deemed to be paid or delivered for deposit in the State Treasury under the provisions of this article, and shall be transmitted, received, accounted for, and disposed of, as provided in this part.

Added by Stats. 1951, Ch. 1708.

Section 1447 - Money or other property belonging to person who dies while confined in state institution subject to jurisdiction of State Department of State Hospitals

Notwithstanding any other law, all unclaimed money or other property belonging to a person who dies while confined in a state institution subject to the jurisdiction of the State Department of State Hospitals, which is paid or delivered to the state or an officer or employee thereof under the provisions of Section 166 of the Welfare and Institutions Code, or under any amendment thereof adopted after the effective date of Chapter 1708 of the Statutes of 1951 shall be deemed to be paid or delivered for deposit in the State Treasury under the provisions of this article, and shall be transmitted, received, accounted for, and disposed of, as provided in this part.

Amended by Stats 2014 ch 144 (AB 1847),s 7, eff. 1/1/2015.

Section 1448 - Unclaimed money or property belonging to person who dies while confined in state institution subject to jurisdiction of Youth Authority

Notwithstanding any other provision of law, all unclaimed money or other property belonging to any person who dies while confined in any state institution subject to the jurisdiction of the Youth Authority, which is paid or delivered to the State or any officer thereof under the provisions of Section 1015 of the Welfare and Institutions Code or under any amendment thereof adopted after the effective date of this section, shall be deemed to be paid or delivered for deposit in the State Treasury under the provisions of this article, and shall be transmitted, received, accounted for, and disposed of, as provided in this part.

Added by Stats. 1951, Ch. 1708.

Section 1449 - Presumptively abandoned money or property paid or delivered to Treasurer or Controller under section 7644, Probate Code

Notwithstanding any other provision of law, all presumptively abandoned money or other property paid or delivered to the Treasurer or Controller under the provisions of Section 7644 of the Probate Code shall be deemed to be paid or delivered for deposit in the State Treasury under the provisions of this article, and shall be transmitted, received, accounted for, and disposed of as provided in this title.

Amended by Stats. 1988, Ch. 1199, Sec. 12. Operative July 1, 1989, by Sec. 119 of Ch. 1199.

Article 2 - ABANDONED PROPERTY

Section 1476 - Generally

The expiration of any period of time specified by law, during which an action or proceeding may be commenced or enforced to secure payment of a claim for money or recovery of property, shall not prevent any such money or other property from being deemed abandoned property, nor affect any duty to file a report required by this title or to deliver to the Treasurer or Controller any such abandoned property; and shall not serve as a defense in any action or proceeding brought under the provisions of this article to compel the filing of any report or the delivery of any abandoned property required by this article or to enforce or collect any penalty provided by this article.

Added by Stats. 1951, Ch. 1708.

Chapter 7 - UNCLAIMED PROPERTY LAW
Article 1 - SHORT TITLE; DEFINITIONS; APPLICATION

Section 1500 - Title of law

This chapter may be cited as the Unclaimed Property Law.

Amended by Stats. 1968, Ch. 356.

Section 1501 - Definitions

As used in this chapter, unless the context otherwise requires:

(a) "Apparent owner" means the person who appears from the records of the holder to be entitled to property held by the holder.

(b) "Banking organization" means any national or state bank, trust company, banking company, land bank, savings bank, safe-deposit company, private banker, or any similar organization.

(c) "Business association" means any private corporation, joint stock company, business trust, partnership, or any association for business purposes of two or more individuals, whether or not for profit, including, but not by way of limitation, a banking organization, financial organization, life insurance corporation, and utility.

(d) "Financial organization" means any federal or state savings and loan association, building and loan association, credit union, investment company, or any similar organization.

(e) "Holder" means any person in possession of property subject to this chapter belonging to another, or who is trustee in case of a trust, or is indebted to another on an obligation subject to this chapter.

(f) "Life insurance corporation" means any association or corporation transacting the business of insurance on the lives of persons or insurance appertaining thereto, including, but not by way of limitation, endowments, and annuities.

(g) "Owner" means a depositor in case of a deposit, a beneficiary in case of a trust, or creditor, claimant, or payee in case of other choses in action, or any person having a legal or equitable interest in property subject to this chapter, or his or her legal representative.

(h) "Person" means any individual, business association, government or governmental subdivision or agency, two or more persons having a joint or common interest, or any other legal or commercial entity, whether that person is acting in his or her own right or in a representative or fiduciary capacity.

(i) "Employee benefit plan distribution" means any money, life insurance, endowment or annuity policy or proceeds thereof, securities or other intangible property, or any tangible property, distributable to a participant, former participant, or the beneficiary or estate or heirs of a participant or former participant or beneficiary, from a trust or custodial fund established under a plan to provide health and welfare, pension, vacation, severance, retirement benefit, death benefit, stock purchase, profit sharing, employee savings, supplemental unemployment insurance benefits or similar benefits, or which is established under a plan by a business association functioning as or in conjunction with a labor union which receives for distribution residuals on behalf of employees working under collective-bargaining agreements.

(j) "Residuals" means payments pursuant to a collective bargaining agreement of additional compensation for domestic and foreign uses of recorded materials.

Amended by Stats. 1990, Ch. 450, Sec. 2. Effective July 31, 1990.

Section 1501.5 - Property received by state not to permanently escheat to state

(a) Notwithstanding any provision of law to the contrary, property received by the state under this chapter shall not permanently escheat to the state.

(b) The Legislature finds and declares that this section is declaratory of the existing law and sets forth the intent of the Legislature regarding the Uniform Disposition of Unclaimed Property Act (Chapter 1809, Statutes of 1959) and all amendments thereto and revisions thereof. Any opinions, rulings, orders, judgments, or other statements to the contrary by any court are erroneous and inconsistent with the intent of the Legislature.

(c) It is the intent of the Legislature that property owners be reunited with their property. In making changes to the unclaimed property program, the Legislature intends to adopt a more expansive notification program that will provide all of the following:

(1) Notification by the state to all owners of unclaimed property prior to escheatment.

(2) A more expansive postescheatment policy that takes action to identify those owners of unclaimed property.

(3) A waiting period of not less than seven years from delivery of property to the state prior to disposal of any unclaimed property deemed to have no commercial value.

Amended by Stats 2014 ch 913 (AB 2747),s 10, eff. 1/1/2015.

Amended by Stats 2007 ch 179 (SB 86),s 1, eff. 8/24/2007.

Section 1502 - Inapplicability of chapter

(a) This chapter does not apply to any of the following:

(1) Any property in the official custody of a municipal utility district.

(2) Any property in the official custody of a local agency if such property may be transferred to the general fund of such agency under the provisions of Sections 50050-50053 of the Government Code.

(3) Any property in the official custody of a court if the property may be transferred to the Trial Court Operations Fund under Section 68084.1 of the Government Code.

(b) None of the provisions of this chapter applies to any type of property received by the state under the provisions of Chapter 1 (commencing with Section 1300) to Chapter 6 (commencing with Section 1440), inclusive, of this title.

Amended by Stats 2007 ch 738 (AB 1248),s 6, eff. 1/1/2008.

Amended by Stats 2004 ch 227 (SB 1102),s 13, eff. 8/16/2004.

Section 1503 - When holder not required to report under old act

(a) As used in this section:

(1) "Old act" means this chapter as it existed prior to January 1, 1969.

(2) "New act" means this chapter as it exists on and after January 1, 1969.

(3) "Property not subject to the old act" means property that was not presumed abandoned under the old act and would never have been presumed abandoned under the old act had the old act continued in existence on and after January 1, 1969, without change.

(b) The holder is not required to file a report concerning, or to pay or deliver to the Controller, any property not subject to the old act if an action by the owner against the holder to recover that property was barred by an applicable statute of limitations prior to January 1, 1969.

(c) The holder is not required to file a report concerning, or to pay or deliver to the Controller, any property not subject to the old act, or any property that was not required to be reported under the old act, unless on January 1, 1969, the property has been held by the holder for less than the escheat period. "Escheat period" means the period referred to in Sections 1513 to 1521, inclusive, of the new act, whichever is applicable to the particular property.

Amended by Stats. 1990, Ch. 450, Sec. 3. Effective July 31, 1990.

Section 1504 - Property escheated under laws of another state

(a) As used in this section:

(1) "Old act" means this chapter as it existed prior to January 1, 1969.

(2) "New act" means this chapter as it exists on and after January 1, 1969.

(3) "Property not subject to the old act" means property that was not presumed abandoned under the old act and would never have been presumed abandoned under the old act had the old act continued in existence on and after January 1, 1969, without change.

(b) This chapter does not apply to any property that was escheated under the laws of another state prior to September 18, 1959.

(c) This chapter does not require the holder to pay or deliver any property not subject to the old act to this state if the property was escheated under the laws of another state prior to January 1, 1969, and was delivered to the custody of that state prior to January 1, 1970, in compliance with the laws of that state. Nothing in this subdivision affects or limits the right of the State Controller to recover such property from the other state.

Added by Stats. 1968, Ch. 356.

Section 1505 - Duty to report or pay or deliver property arising prior to January 1, 1969

This chapter does not affect any duty to file a report with the State Controller or to pay or deliver any property to him that arose prior to January 1, 1969, under the provisions of this chapter as it existed prior to January 1, 1969. Such duties may be enforced by the State Controller, and the penalties for failure to perform such duties may be imposed, under the provisions of this chapter as it existed prior to January 1, 1969. The provisions of this chapter as it existed prior to January 1, 1969, are continued in existence for the purposes of this section.

Repealed and added by Stats. 1968, Ch. 356.

Section 1506 - Construction of provisions as restatements and continuations

The provisions of this chapter as it exists on and after January 1, 1969, insofar as they are substantially the same as the provisions of this chapter as it existed prior to January 1, 1969, relating to the same subject matter, shall be construed as restatements and continuations thereof and not as new enactments.

Added by Stats. 1968, Ch. 356.

Article 2 - ESCHEAT OF UNCLAIMED PERSONAL PROPERTY

Section 1510 - When intangible personal property escheats to state

Unless otherwise provided by statute of this state, intangible personal property escheats to this state under this chapter if the conditions for escheat stated in Sections 1513 through 1521 exist, and if:

(a) The last known address, as shown on the records of the holder, of the apparent owner is in this state.

(b) No address of the apparent owner appears on the records of the holder and:

(1) The last known address of the apparent owner is in this state; or

(2) The holder is domiciled in this state and has not previously paid the property to the state of the last known address of the apparent owner; or

(3) The holder is a government or governmental subdivision or agency of this state and has not previously paid the property to the state of the last known address of the apparent owner.

(c) The last known address, as shown on the records of the holder, of the apparent owner is in a state that does not provide by law for the escheat of such property and the holder is (1) domiciled in this state or (2) a government or governmental subdivision or agency of this state.

(d) The last known address, as shown on the records of the holder, of the apparent owner is in a foreign nation and the holder is (1) domiciled in this state or (2) a government or governmental subdivision or agency of this state.

Amended by Stats. 1978, Ch. 1183.

Section 1511 - Money order, travelers check or similar written instrument

(a) Any sum payable on a money order, travelers check, or other similar written instrument (other than a third-party bank check) on which a business association is directly liable escheats to this state under this chapter if the conditions for escheat stated in Section 1513 exist and if:

(1) The books and records of such business association show that such money order, travelers check, or similar written instrument was purchased in this state;

(2) The business association has its principal place of business in this state and the books and records of the business association do not show the state in which such money order, travelers check, or similar written instrument was purchased; or

(3) The business association has its principal place of business in this state, the books and records of the business association show the state in which such money order, travelers check, or similar written instrument was purchased, and the laws of the state of purchase do not provide for the escheat of the sum payable on such instrument.

(b) Notwithstanding any other provision of this chapter, this section applies to sums payable on money orders, travelers checks, and similar written instruments deemed abandoned on or after February 1, 1965, except to the extent that such sums have been paid over to a state prior to January 1, 1974. For the purposes of this subdivision, the words "deemed abandoned" have the same meaning as those words have as used in Section 604 of Public Law Number 93-495 (October 28, 1974), 88th Statutes at Large 1500.

Repealed and added by Stats. 1975, Ch. 25.

Section 1513 - Property held or owing by business association

(a) Subject to Sections 1510 and 1511, the following property held or owing by a business association escheats to this state:

(1)

(A) Except as provided in paragraph (6), any demand, savings, or matured time deposit, or account subject to a negotiable order of withdrawal, made with a banking organization, together with any interest or dividends thereon, excluding, from demand deposits and accounts subject to a negotiable order of withdrawal only, any reasonable service charges that may lawfully be withheld and that do not, where made in this state, exceed those set forth in schedules filed by the banking organization from time to time with the Controller, if the owner, for more than three years, has not done any of the following:

(i) Increased or decreased the amount of the deposit, cashed an interest check, or presented the passbook or other similar evidence of the deposit for the crediting of interest.

(ii) Corresponded electronically or in writing with the banking organization concerning the deposit.

(iii) Otherwise indicated an interest in the deposit as evidenced by a memorandum or other record on file with the banking organization.

(B) A deposit or account shall not, however, escheat to the state if, during the previous three years, the owner has owned another deposit or account with the banking organization or the owner has owned an individual retirement account or funds held by the banking organization under a retirement plan for self-employed individuals or a similar account or plan established pursuant to the internal revenue laws of the United States or the laws of this state, as described in paragraph (6), and, with respect to that deposit, account, or plan, the owner has done any of the acts described in clause (i), (ii), or (iii) of subparagraph (A), and the banking organization has communicated electronically or in writing with the owner, at the address to which communications regarding that deposit, account, or plan are regularly sent, with regard to the deposit or account that would otherwise escheat under subparagraph (A). For purposes of this subparagraph, "communications" includes account statements or statements required under the internal revenue laws of the United States.

(C) No banking organization may discontinue any interest or dividends on any savings deposit because of the inactivity contemplated by this section.

(2)

(A) Except as provided in paragraph (6), any demand, savings, or matured time deposit, or matured investment certificate, or account subject to a negotiable order of withdrawal, or other interest in a financial organization or any deposit made therewith, and any interest or dividends thereon, excluding, from demand deposits and accounts subject to a negotiable order of withdrawal only, any reasonable service charges that may lawfully be withheld and that do not, where made in this state, exceed those set forth in schedules filed by the financial organization from time to time with the Controller, if the owner, for more than three years, has not done any of the following:

(i) Increased or decreased the amount of the funds or deposit, cashed an interest check, or presented an appropriate record for the crediting of interest or dividends.

(ii) Corresponded electronically or in writing with the financial organization concerning the funds or deposit.

(iii) Otherwise indicated an interest in the funds or deposit as evidenced by a memorandum or other record on file with the financial organization.

(B) A deposit or account shall not, however, escheat to the state if, during the previous three years, the owner has owned another deposit or account with the financial organization or the owner has owned an individual retirement account or funds held by the financial organization under a retirement plan for self-employed individuals or a similar account or plan established pursuant to the internal revenue laws of the United States or the laws of this state, as described in paragraph (6), and, with respect to that deposit, account, or plan, the owner has done any of the acts described in clause (i), (ii), or (iii) of subparagraph (A), and the financial organization has communicated electronically or in writing with the owner, at the address to which communications regarding that deposit, account, or plan are regularly sent, with regard to the deposit or account that would otherwise escheat under subparagraph (A). For purposes of this subparagraph, "communications" includes account statements or statements required under the internal revenue laws of the United States.

(C) No financial organization may discontinue any interest or dividends on any funds paid toward purchase of shares or other interest, or on any deposit, because of the inactivity contemplated by this section.

(3) Any sum payable on a traveler's check issued by a business association that has been outstanding for more than 15 years from the date of its issuance, if the owner, for more than 15 years, has not corresponded in writing with the business association concerning it, or otherwise indicated an interest as evidenced by a memorandum or other record on file with the association.

(4) Any sum payable on any other written instrument on which a banking or financial organization is directly liable, including, by way of illustration but not of limitation, any draft, cashier's check, teller's check, or certified check, that has been outstanding for more than three years from the date it was payable, or from the date of its issuance if payable on demand, if the owner, for more than three years, has not corresponded electronically or in writing with the banking or financial organization concerning it, or otherwise indicated an interest as evidenced by a memorandum or other record on file with the banking or financial organization.

(5) Any sum payable on a money order issued by a business association, including a banking or financial organization, that has been outstanding for more than seven years from the date it was payable, or from the date of its issuance if payable on demand, excluding any reasonable service charges that may lawfully be withheld and that do not, when made in this state, exceed those set forth in schedules filed by the business association from time to time with the Controller, if the owner, for more than seven years, has not corresponded electronically or in writing with the business association, banking, or financial organization concerning it, or otherwise indicated an interest as evidenced by a memorandum or other record on file with the business association. For the purposes of this subdivision, "reasonable service charge" means a service charge that meets all of the following requirements:

(A) It is uniformly applied to all of the issuer's money orders.

(B) It is clearly disclosed to the purchaser at the time of purchase and to the recipient of the money order.
(C) It does not begin to accrue until three years after the purchase date, and it stops accruing after the value of the money order escheats.
(D) It is permitted by contract between the issuer and the purchaser.
(E) It does not exceed 25 cents ($0.25) per month or the aggregate amount of twenty-one dollars ($21).

(6)
(A) Any funds held by a business association in an individual retirement account or under a retirement plan for self-employed individuals or similar account or plan established pursuant to the internal revenue laws of the United States or of this state, if the owner, for more than three years after the funds become payable or distributable, has not done any of the following:
(i) Increased or decreased the principal.
(ii) Accepted payment of principal or income.
(iii) Corresponded electronically or in writing concerning the property or otherwise indicated an interest.

(B) Funds held by a business association in an individual retirement account or under a retirement plan for self-employed individuals or a similar account or plan created pursuant to the internal revenue laws of the United States or the laws of this state shall not escheat to the state if, during the previous three years, the owner has owned another such account, plan, or any other deposit or account with the business association and, with respect to that deposit, account, or plan, the owner has done any of the acts described in clause (i), (ii), or (iii) of subparagraph (A), and the business association has communicated electronically or in writing with the owner, at the address to which communications regarding that deposit, account, or plan are regularly sent, with regard to the account or plan that would otherwise escheat under subparagraph (A). For purposes of this subparagraph, "communications" includes account statements or statements required under the internal revenue laws of the United States.

(C) These funds are not payable or distributable within the meaning of this subdivision unless either of the following is true:
(i) Under the terms of the account or plan, distribution of all or a part of the funds would then be mandatory.
(ii) For an account or plan not subject to mandatory distribution requirement under the internal revenue laws of the United States or the laws of this state, the owner has attained $70^{1}/_{2}$ years of age.

(7) Any wages or salaries that have remained unclaimed by the owner for more than one year after the wages or salaries become payable.
(b) For purposes of this section, "service charges" means service charges imposed because of the inactivity contemplated by this section.
(c) A holder shall, commencing on or before January 1, 2018, regard the following transactions that are initiated electronically and are reflected in the books and records of the banking or financial organization as evidence that an owner has increased or decreased the amount of the funds or deposit in an account, for purposes of paragraphs (1) and (2) of subdivision (a):
(1) A single or recurring debit transaction authorized by the owner.
(2) A single or recurring credit transaction authorized by the owner
(3) Recurring transactions authorized by the owner that represent payroll deposits or deductions.
(4) Recurring credits authorized by the owner or a responsible party that represent the deposit of any federal benefits, including social security benefits, veterans' benefits, and pension payments.

Amended by Stats 2016 ch 463 (AB 2258),s 1, eff. 1/1/2017.
Amended by Stats 2011 ch 305 (SB 495),s 1, eff. 1/1/2012.
Amended by Stats 2009 ch 522 (AB 1291),s 1, eff. 1/1/2010.
Amended by Stats 2003 ch 304 (AB 378),s 1, eff. 1/1/2004.
Amended October 10, 1999 (Bill Number: AB 777) (Chapter 835).

Section 1513.5 - Notice by banking or financial organization that deposit, account, shares, etc. may escheat to state
(a) Except as provided in subdivision (c), if the holder has in its records an address for the apparent owner, which the holder's records do not disclose to be inaccurate, every banking or financial organization shall make reasonable efforts to notify any owner by mail or, if the owner has consented to electronic notice, electronically, that the owner's deposit, account, shares, or other interest in the banking or financial organization will escheat to the state pursuant to clause (i), (ii), or (iii) of subparagraph (A) of paragraph (1), (2), or (6) of subdivision (a) of Section 1513. The holder shall give notice either:
(1) Not less than two years nor more than two and one-half years after the date of last activity by, or communication with, the owner with respect to the account, deposit, shares, or other interest, as shown on the record of the banking or financial organization.
(2) Not less than 6 nor more than 12 months before the time the account, deposit, shares, or other interest becomes reportable to the Controller in accordance with this chapter.
(b) The notice required by this section shall specify the time that the deposit, account, shares, or other interest will escheat and the effects of escheat, including the necessity for filing a claim for the return of the deposit, account, shares, or other interest. The face of the notice shall contain a heading at the top that reads as follows: "THE STATE OF CALIFORNIA REQUIRES US TO NOTIFY YOU THAT YOUR UNCLAIMED PROPERTY MAY BE TRANSFERRED TO THE STATE IF YOU DO NOT CONTACT US," or substantially similar language. The notice required by this section shall, in boldface type or in a font a minimum of two points larger than the rest of the notice, exclusive of the heading, (1) specify that since the date of last activity, or for the last two years, there has been no owner activity on the deposit, account, shares, or other interest; (2) identify the deposit, account, shares, or other interest by number or identifier, which need not exceed four digits; (3) indicate that the deposit, account, shares, or other interest is in danger of escheating to the state; and (4) specify that the Unclaimed Property Law requires banking and financial organizations to transfer funds of a deposit, account, shares, or other interest if it has been inactive for three years. It shall also include a form, as prescribed by the Controller, by which the owner may declare an intention to maintain the deposit, account, shares, or other interest. If that form is filled out, signed by the owner, and returned to the banking or financial organization, it shall satisfy the requirement of clause (iii) of subparagraph (A) of paragraph (1), clause (iii) of subparagraph (A) of paragraph (2), or clause (iii) of subparagraph (A) of paragraph (6) of subdivision (a) of Section 1513. In lieu of returning the form, the banking or financial organization may provide a telephone number or other electronic means to enable the owner to contact that organization. The contact, as evidenced by a memorandum or other record on file with the banking or financial organization, shall satisfy the requirement of clause (iii) of subparagraph (A) of paragraph (1), clause (iii) of subparagraph (A) of paragraph (2), or clause (iii) of subparagraph (A) of paragraph (6) of subdivision (a) of Section 1513. If the deposit, account, shares, or other interest has a value greater than two dollars ($2), the banking or financial organization may impose a service charge on the deposit, account, shares, or other interest for this notice in an amount not to exceed the administrative cost of mailing or electronically sending the notice and form and in no case to exceed two dollars ($2).
(c) Notice as provided by subdivisions (a) and (b) shall not be required for deposits, accounts, shares, or other interests of less than fifty dollars ($50), and, except as provided in subdivision (b), no service charge may be made for notice on these items.
(d) In addition to the notices required pursuant to subdivision (a), the holder may give additional notice as described in subdivision (b) at any time between the date of last activity by, or communication with, the owner and the date the holder transfers the deposit, account, shares, or other interest to the Controller.
(e) At the time a new account is opened with a banking or financial organization, the organization shall provide a written notice to the person opening the account informing the person that his or her property may be transferred to the appropriate state if no activity occurs in the account within the time period specified by state law. If the person opening the account has consented to electronic notice, that notice may be provided electronically.

Amended by Stats 2013 ch 362 (AB 212),s 1, eff. 1/1/2014.
Amended by Stats 2011 ch 305 (SB 495),s 2, eff. 1/1/2012.
Amended by Stats 2009 ch 522 (AB 1291),s 2, eff. 1/1/2010.
Amended by Stats 2002 ch 813 (AB 1772),s 1, eff. 1/1/2004

Section 1514 - Proceeds of contents of safe deposit box or other safekeeping repository

(a) The contents of, or the proceeds of sale of the contents of, any safe deposit box or any other safekeeping repository, held in this state by a business association, escheat to this state if unclaimed by the owner for more than three years from the date on which the lease or rental period on the box or other repository expired, or from the date of termination of any agreement because of which the box or other repository was furnished to the owner without cost, whichever last occurs.

(b) If a business association has in its records an address for an apparent owner of the contents of, or the proceeds of sale of the contents of, a safe deposit box or other safekeeping repository described in subdivision (a), and the records of the business association do not disclose the address to be inaccurate, the business association shall make reasonable efforts to notify the owner by mail, or, if the owner has consented to electronic notice, electronically, that the owner's contents, or the proceeds of the sale of the contents, will escheat to the state pursuant to this section. The business association shall give notice not less than 6 months and not more than 12 months before the time the contents, or the proceeds of the sale of the contents, become reportable to the Controller in accordance with this chapter.

(c) The face of the notice shall contain a heading at the top that reads as follows: "THE STATE OF CALIFORNIA REQUIRES US TO NOTIFY YOU THAT YOUR UNCLAIMED PROPERTY MAY BE TRANSFERRED TO THE STATE IF YOU DO NOT CONTACT US," or substantially similar language. The notice required by this subdivision shall specify the date that the property will escheat and the effects of escheat, including the necessity for filing a claim for the return of the property. The notice required by this section shall, in boldface type or in a font a minimum of two points larger than the rest of the notice, exclusive of the heading, do all of the following:

(1) Identify the safe deposit box or other safekeeping repository by number or identifier.

(2) State that the lease or rental period on the box or repository has expired or the agreement has terminated.

(3) Indicate that the contents of, or the proceeds of sale of the contents of, the safe deposit box or other safekeeping repository will escheat to the state unless the owner requests the contents or their proceeds.

(4) Specify that the Unclaimed Property Law requires business associations to transfer the contents of, or the proceeds of sale of the contents of, a safe deposit box or other safekeeping repository to the Controller if they remain unclaimed for more than three years.

(5) Advise the owner to make arrangements with the business association to either obtain possession of the contents of, or the proceeds of sale of the contents of, the safe deposit box or other safekeeping repository, or enter into a new agreement with the business association to establish a leasing or rental arrangement. If an owner fails to establish such an arrangement prior to the end of the period described in subdivision (a), the contents or proceeds shall escheat to this state.

(d) In addition to the notice required pursuant to subdivision (b), the business association may give additional notice in accordance with subdivision (c) at any time between the date on which the lease or rental period for the safe deposit box or repository expired, or from the date of the termination of any agreement, through which the box or other repository was furnished to the owner without cost, whichever is earlier, and the date the business association transfers the contents of, or the proceeds of sale of the contents of, the safe deposit box or other safekeeping repository to the Controller.

(e) The contents of, or the proceeds of sale of the contents of, a safe deposit box or other safekeeping repository shall not escheat to the state if, as of June 30 or the fiscal yearend next preceding the date on which a report is required to be filed under Section 1530, the owner has owned, with a banking organization providing the safe deposit box or other safekeeping repository, any demand, savings, or matured time deposit, or account subject to a negotiable order of withdrawal, which has not escheated under Section 1513 and is not reportable under subdivision (d) of Section 1530.

(f) The contents of, or the proceeds of sale of the contents of, a safe deposit box or other safekeeping repository shall not escheat to the state if, as of June 30 or the fiscal yearend next preceding the date on which a report is required to be filed under Section 1530, the owner has owned, with a financial organization providing the safe deposit box or other safekeeping repository, any demand, savings, or matured time deposit, or matured investment certificate, or account subject to a negotiable order of withdrawal, or other interest in a financial organization or any deposit made therewith, and any interest or dividends thereon, which has not escheated under Section 1513 and is not reportable under subdivision (d) of Section 1530.

(g) The contents of, or the proceeds of sale of the contents of, a safe deposit box or other safekeeping repository shall not escheat to the state if, as of June 30 or the fiscal yearend next preceding the date on which a report is required to be filed under Section 1530, the owner has owned, with a banking or financial organization providing the safe deposit box or other safekeeping repository, any funds in an individual retirement account or under a retirement plan for self-employed individuals or similar account or plan pursuant to the internal revenue laws of the United States or the income tax laws of this state, which has not escheated under Section 1513 and is not reportable under subdivision (d) of Section 1530.

(h) In the event the owner is in default under the safe deposit box or other safekeeping repository agreement and the owner has owned any demand, savings, or matured time deposit, account, or plan described in subdivision (e), (f), or (g), the banking or financial organization may pay or deliver the contents of, or the proceeds of sale of the contents of, the safe deposit box or other safekeeping repository to the owner after deducting any amount due and payable from those proceeds under that agreement. Upon making that payment or delivery under this subdivision, the banking or financial organization shall be relieved of all liability to the extent of the value of those contents or proceeds.

(i) For new accounts opened for a safe deposit box or other safekeeping repository with a business association on and after January 1, 2011, the business association shall provide a written notice to the person leasing the safe deposit box or safekeeping repository informing the person that his or her property, or the proceeds of sale of the property, may be transferred to the appropriate state upon running of the time period specified by state law from the date the lease or rental period on the safe deposit box or repository expired, or from the date of termination of any agreement because of which the box or other repository was furnished to the owner without cost, whichever is earlier.

(j) A business association may directly escheat the contents of a safe deposit box or other safekeeping repository without exercising its rights under Article 2 (commencing with Section 1630) of Chapter 17 of Division 1 of the Financial Code.

Amended by Stats 2012 ch 162 (SB 1171),s 16, eff. 1/1/2013.
Amended by Stats 2011 ch 305 (SB 495),s 3, eff. 1/1/2012.
Amended by Stats 2009 ch 522 (AB 1291),s 3, eff. 1/1/2010.

Section 1515 - Funds held or owing by life insurance corporation under life or endowment insurance policy or annuity contract

(a) Subject to Section 1510, funds held or owing by a life insurance corporation under any life or endowment insurance policy or annuity contract which has matured or terminated escheat to this state if unclaimed and unpaid for more than three years after the funds became due and payable as established from the records of the corporation.

(b) If a person other than the insured or annuitant is entitled to the funds and no address of that person is known to the corporation or if it is not definite and certain from the records of the corporation what person is entitled to the funds, it is presumed that the last known address of the person entitled to the funds is the same as the last known address of the insured or annuitant according to the records of the corporation. This presumption is a presumption affecting the burden of proof.

(c) A life insurance policy not matured by actual proof of the death of the insured according to the records of the corporation is deemed to be matured and the proceeds due and payable if:

(1) The insured has attained, or would have attained if he or she were living, the limiting age under the mortality table on which the reserve is based.

(2) The policy was in force at the time the insured attained, or would have attained, the limiting age specified in paragraph (1).

(3) Neither the insured nor any other person appearing to have an interest in the policy has, within the preceding three years, according to the records of the corporation (i) assigned, readjusted, or paid premiums on the policy, (ii) subjected the policy to loan, or (iii) corresponded in writing with the life insurance corporation concerning the policy.

(d) Any funds otherwise payable according to the records of the corporation are deemed due and payable although the policy or contract has not been surrendered as required.

Amended by Stats. 1993, Ch. 692, Sec. 3. Effective January 1, 1994.

Section 1515.5 - Property distributable in course of demutualization or reorganization of insurance company deemed abandoned

Property distributable in the course of a demutualization or related reorganization of an insurance company is deemed abandoned as follows:

(a) On the date of the demutualization or reorganization, if the instruments or statements reflecting the distribution are not mailed to the owner because the address on the books and records for the holder is known to be incorrect.

(b) Two years after the date of the demutualization or reorganization, if instruments or statements reflecting the distribution are mailed to the owner and returned by the post office as undeliverable and the owner has done neither of the following:

(1) Communicated in writing with the holder or its agent regarding the property.

(2) Otherwise communicated with the holder or its agent regarding the property as evidenced by a memorandum or other record on file with the holder or its agent.

(c) Three years after the date of the demutualization or reorganization, if instruments or statements reflecting the distribution are mailed to the owner and not returned by the post office as undeliverable and the owner has done neither of the following:

(1) Communicated in writing with the holder or its agent regarding the property.

(2) Otherwise communicated with the holder or its agent regarding the property as evidenced by a memorandum or other record on file with the holder or its agent.

Added by Stats 2003 ch 304 (AB 378),s 2, eff. 1/1/2004.

Section 1516 - Dividend, profit, distribution, etc. held or owing by business organization for shareholder, certificate holder, member, etc.

(a) Subject to Section 1510, any dividend, profit, distribution, interest, payment on principal, or other sum held or owing by a business association for or to its shareholder, certificate holder, member, bondholder, or other security holder, or a participating patron of a cooperative, who has not claimed it, or corresponded in writing with the business association concerning it, within three years after the date prescribed for payment or delivery, escheats to this state.

(b) Subject to Section 1510, any intangible interest in a business association, as evidenced by the stock records or membership records of the association, escheats to this state if (1) the interest in the association is owned by a person who for more than three years has neither claimed a dividend or other sum referred to in subdivision (a) nor corresponded in writing with the association or otherwise indicated an interest as evidenced by a memorandum or other record on file with the association, and (2) the association does not know the location of the owner at the end of the three-year period. With respect to the interest, the business association shall be deemed the holder.

(c) Subject to Section 1510, any dividends or other distributions held for or owing to a person at the time the stock or other security to which they attach escheats to this state also escheat to this state as of the same time.

(d) If the business association has in its records an address for the apparent owner, which the business association's records do not disclose to be inaccurate, with respect to any interest that may escheat pursuant to subdivision (b), the business association shall make reasonable efforts to notify the owner by mail or, if the owner has consented to electronic notice, electronically, that the owner's interest in the business association will escheat to the state. The notice shall be given not less than 6 nor more than 12 months before the time the interest in the business association becomes reportable to the Controller in accordance with this chapter. The face of the notice shall contain a heading at the top that reads as follows: "THE STATE OF CALIFORNIA REQUIRES US TO NOTIFY YOU THAT YOUR UNCLAIMED PROPERTY MAY BE TRANSFERRED TO THE STATE IF YOU DO NOT CONTACT US," or substantially similar language. The notice required by this subdivision shall specify the time that the interest will escheat and the effects of escheat, including the necessity for filing a claim for the return of the interest. The notice required by this section shall, in boldface type or in a font a minimum of two points larger than the rest of the notice, exclusive of the heading, (1) specify that since the date of last activity, or for the last two years, there has been no owner activity on the deposit, account, shares, or other interest; (2) identify the deposit, account, shares, or other interest by number or identifier, which need not exceed four digits; (3) indicate that the deposit, account, shares, or other interest is in danger of escheating to the state; and (4) specify that the Unclaimed Property Law requires business associations to transfer funds of a deposit, account, shares, or other interest if it has been inactive for three years. It shall also include a form, as prescribed by the Controller, by which the owner may confirm the owner's current address. If that form is filled out, signed by the owner, and returned to the holder, it shall be deemed that the business association knows the location of the owner. In lieu of returning the form, the business association may provide a telephone number or other electronic means to enable the owner to contact the association. With that contact, as evidenced by a memorandum or other record on file with the business association, the business association shall be deemed to know the location of the owner. The business association may impose a service charge on the deposit, account, shares, or other interest for this notice and form in an amount not to exceed the administrative cost of mailing or electronically sending the notice and form, and in no case to exceed two dollars ($2).

(e) In addition to the notice required pursuant to subdivision (d), the holder may give additional notice as described in subdivision (d) at any time between the date of last activity by, or communication with, the owner and the date the holder transfers the deposit, shares, or other interest to the Controller.

(f) The interest that escheats pursuant to subdivision (b) shall not be reportable pursuant to Section 1530 unless and until the per share value, as set forth in Section 1172.80 of Title 2 of the California Code of Regulations, is equal to or greater than one cent ($0.01) or the aggregate value of the security held exceeds one thousand dollars ($1,000).

Amended by Stats 2022 ch 420 (AB 2960),s 12, eff. 1/1/2023.
Amended by Stats 2011 ch 305 (SB 495),s 4, eff. 1/1/2012.
Amended by Stats 2009 ch 522 (AB 1291),s 4, eff. 1/1/2010.
Amended by Stats 2002 ch 813 (AB 1772),s 2, eff. 1/1/2004

Section 1517 - Property distributable in course of dissolution of business organization or insurer

(a) All property distributable in the course of a voluntary or involuntary dissolution or liquidation of a business association that is unclaimed by the owner within six months after the date of final distribution or liquidation escheats to this state.

(b) All property distributable in the course of voluntary or involuntary dissolution or liquidation of an insurer or other person brought under Article 14 (commencing with Section 1010) of Chapter 1 of Part 2 of Division 1 of the Insurance Code, that is unclaimed by the owner after six months of the date of final distribution, shall be transferred to the Department of Insurance, with any proceeds of sale of property and other funds to be deposited in the Insurance Fund for expenditure as provided in Section 12937 of the Insurance Code.

(c) This section applies to all tangible personal property located in this state and, subject to Section 1510, to all intangible personal property.
Amended by Stats. 1996, Ch. 187, Sec. 1. Effective July 19, 1996.

Section 1518 - Personal property held in fiduciary capacity

(a)

(1) All tangible personal property located in this state and, subject to Section 1510, all intangible personal property, including intangible personal property maintained in a deposit or account, and the income or increment on such tangible or intangible property, held in a fiduciary capacity for the benefit of another person escheats to this state if for more than three years after it becomes payable or distributable, the owner has not done any of the following:

(A) Increased or decreased the principal.

(B) Accepted payment of principal or income.

(C) Corresponded in writing concerning the property.

(D) Otherwise indicated an interest in the property as evidenced by a memorandum or other record on file with the fiduciary.

(2) Notwithstanding paragraph (1), tangible or intangible property, and the income or increment on the tangible or intangible property, held in a fiduciary capacity for another person shall not escheat to the state if the requirements of subparagraphs (A) and (B) are satisfied.

(A) During the previous three years, the fiduciary took one of the following actions:

(i) Held another deposit or account for the benefit of the owner.

(ii) Maintained a deposit or account on behalf of the owner in an individual retirement account.

(iii) Held funds or other property under a retirement plan for a self-employed individual, or similar account or plan, established pursuant to the internal revenue laws of the United States or the laws of this state.

(B) During the previous three years, the owner has done any of the acts described in subparagraph (A), (B), (C), or (D) of paragraph (1) with respect to the deposit, account, or plan described in subparagraph (A), and the fiduciary has communicated electronically or in writing with the owner at the address to which communications regarding that deposit, account, or plan are regularly sent, with regard to the deposit, account, or plan that would otherwise escheat under this subdivision. "Communications," for purposes of this subparagraph, includes account statements or statements required under the internal revenue laws of the United States.

(b) Funds in an individual retirement account or a retirement plan for self-employed individuals or similar account or plan established pursuant to the internal revenue laws of the United States or of this state are not payable or distributable within the meaning of subdivision (a) unless either of the following is true:

(1) Under the terms of the account or plan, distribution of all or part of the funds would then be mandatory.

(2) For an account or plan not subject to mandatory distribution requirement under the internal revenue laws of the United States or the laws of this state, the owner has attained $70^{1}/_{2}$ years of age.

(c) For the purpose of this section, when a person holds property as an agent for a business association, he or she is deemed to hold the property in a fiduciary capacity for the business association alone, unless the agreement between him or her and the business association clearly provides the contrary. For the purposes of this chapter, if a person holds property in a fiduciary capacity for a business association alone, he or she is the holder of the property only insofar as the interest of the business association in the property is concerned and the association is deemed to be the holder of the property insofar as the interest of any other person in the property is concerned.

Amended by Stats 2011 ch 305 (SB 495),s 5, eff. 1/1/2012.

Section 1518.5 - Funds maintained in a preneed funeral trust or similar account; escheat

(a) Subject to Section 1510, funds maintained in a preneed funeral trust or similar account or plan escheat to the state if, for more than three years after the funds became payable and distributable pursuant to subdivision (b), as established from the records of the funeral establishment or trustee, the beneficiary or trustor has not corresponded electronically or in writing concerning the property or otherwise indicated an interest, as evidenced by a memorandum or other record on file with the funeral establishment or trustee.

(b) For the purposes of this section, the corpus of a preneed funeral trust or similar account or plan, together with any income accrued, less a revocation fee not to exceed the amount reserved pursuant to Section 7735 of the Business and Professions Code, becomes payable and distributable under any of the following circumstances:

(1) The beneficiary of the trust attained, or would have attained if living, 105 years of age.

(2) Forty-five years have passed since execution of the preneed funeral agreement.

(3) The holder received notification of the death or presumed death of the beneficiary and has not provided the contracted funeral merchandise or services.

(4) The preneed funeral trust is a preneed installment trust and the amount due to the funeral establishment from the trustor has not been paid during the three preceding years and neither the trustor nor the beneficiary has communicated with either the funeral establishment or the trustee about the preneed funeral installment trust during that three-year period.

(c) For purposes of this section, except subdivision (d), the funeral establishment obligated to provide preneed funeral services under the trust or similar account or plan is the holder. For purposes of subdivision (d), the trustee is the holder.

(d)

(1) All funds, including accrued income and revocation fees reserved pursuant to Section 7735 of the Business and Professions Code, maintained in a preneed funeral trust or similar account or plan held by a trustee for a funeral establishment that has been dissolved, closed, or had its license revoked shall escheat to the state if unclaimed by the funeral establishment, beneficiary, trustor, or legal representative of either the beneficiary or trustor within six months after the date of final distribution or liquidation.

(2) Notwithstanding paragraph (1), the revocation fee pursuant to Section 7735 of the Business and Professions Code shall not be retained by the funeral establishment.

(e) Escheatment of preneed funeral trust funds to the Controller shall release the funeral establishment from the obligation of furnishing the personal property, funeral merchandise, or services originally arranged in the preneed funeral agreement associated with the trust. However, if the funeral establishment provided personal property, or funeral merchandise or services to the beneficiary after funds have escheated, the funeral establishment shall be entitled to recover the escheated funds upon submission to the Controller of a death certificate and a statement detailing the personal property or funeral merchandise or services provided pursuant to Section 1560.

(f) Nothing in this section, or any other law or regulation, shall require escheatment of any funds received by a funeral establishment, cemetery, or other person from property or funeral merchandise or services provided under Chapter 4 (commencing with Section 8600) of Part 3 of Division 8 of the Health and Safety Code.

(g) A trustee or a funeral establishment shall not charge the trust, a trustor, or a beneficiary any fees or costs associated with a search or verification conducted pursuant to this section. However, a trustee or funeral establishment may incorporate fees or costs associated with a search or verification as part of the administration of the trust pursuant to Section 7735 of the Business and Professions Code.

(h) Delivery of the corpus of the trust, and the income accrued to the trust, to the funeral establishment, the trustor, the beneficiary, or the Controller pursuant to this article shall relieve the trustee of any further liability with regard to those funds.

(i) This section shall become operative on January 1, 2023.

Added by Stats 2021 ch 514 (AB 293),s 5, eff. 1/1/2022.

Section 1519 - Personal property held for owner by government
All tangible personal property located in this state, and, subject to Section 1510, all intangible personal property, held for the owner by any government or governmental subdivision or agency, that has remained unclaimed by the owner for more than three years escheats to this state.
Amended by Stats. 1990, Ch. 450, Sec. 10. Effective July 31, 1990.

Section 1519.5 - Sums held by business organization ordered refunded by court or administrative agency
Subject to Section 1510, any sums held by a business association that have been ordered to be refunded by a court or an administrative agency including, but not limited to, the Public Utilities Commission, which have remained unclaimed by the owner for more than one year after becoming payable in accordance with the final determination or order providing for the refund, whether or not the final determination or order requires any person entitled to a refund to make a claim for it, escheats to this state.

It is the intent of the Legislature that the provisions of this section shall apply retroactively to all funds held by business associations on or after January 1, 1977, and which remain undistributed by the business association as of the effective date of this act.

Further, it is the intent of the Legislature that nothing in this section shall be construed to change the authority of a court or administrative agency to order equitable remedies.
Added by Stats. 1984, Ch. 1096, Sec. 1.

Section 1520 - Personal property held and owing in ordinary course of holder's business
(a) All tangible personal property located in this state and, subject to Section 1510, all intangible personal property, except property of the classes mentioned in Sections 1511, 1513, 1514, 1515, 1515.5, 1516, 1517, 1518, 1518.5, 1519, and 1521, including any income or increment thereon and deducting any lawful charges, that is held or owing in the ordinary course of the holder's business and has remained unclaimed by the owner for more than three years after it became payable or distributable escheats to this state.

(b) Except as provided in subdivision (a) of Section 1513.5, subdivision (b) of Section 1514, and subdivision (d) of Section 1516, if the holder has in its records an address for the apparent owner of property valued at fifty dollars ($50) or more, which the holder's records do not disclose to be inaccurate, the holder shall make reasonable efforts to notify the owner by mail or, if the owner has consented to electronic notice, electronically, that the owner's property will escheat to the state pursuant to this chapter. The notice shall be mailed not less than 6 nor more than 12 months before the time when the owner's property held by the business becomes reportable to the Controller in accordance with this chapter. The face of the notice shall contain a heading at the top that reads as follows: "THE STATE OF CALIFORNIA REQUIRES US TO NOTIFY YOU THAT YOUR UNCLAIMED PROPERTY MAY BE TRANSFERRED TO THE STATE IF YOU DO NOT CONTACT US," or substantially similar language. The notice required by this subdivision shall specify the time when the property will escheat and the effects of escheat, including the need to file a claim in order for the owner's property to be returned to the owner. The notice required by this section shall, in boldface type or in a font a minimum of two points larger than the rest of the notice, exclusive of the heading, (1) specify that since the date of last activity, or for the last two years, there has been no owner activity on the deposit, account, shares, or other interest; (2) identify the deposit, account, shares, or other interest by number or identifier, which need not exceed four digits; (3) indicate that the deposit, account, shares, or other interest is in danger of escheating to the state; and (4) specify that the Unclaimed Property Law requires holders to transfer funds of a deposit, account, shares, or other interest if it has been inactive for three years. It shall also include a form, as prescribed by the Controller, by which the owner may confirm the owner's current address. If that form is filled out, signed by the owner, and returned to the holder, it shall be deemed that the account, or other device in which the owner's property is being held, remains currently active and recommences the escheat period. In lieu of returning the form, the holder may provide a telephone number or other electronic means to enable the owner to contact the holder. With that contact, as evidenced by a memorandum or other record on file with the holder, the account or other device in which the owner's property is being held shall be deemed to remain currently active and shall recommence the escheat period. The holder may impose a service charge on the deposit, account, shares, or other interest for this notice in an amount not to exceed the administrative cost of mailing or electronically sending the notice and form, and in no case to exceed two dollars ($2).

(c) In addition to the notice required pursuant to subdivision (b), the holder may give additional notice as described in subdivision (b) at any time between the date of last activity by, or communication with, the owner and the date the holder transfers the property to the Controller.

(d) For purposes of this section, "lawful charges" means charges that are specifically authorized by statute, other than the Unclaimed Property Law, or by a valid, enforceable contract.

(e) This section shall become operative on January 1, 2023.
Added by Stats 2021 ch 514 (AB 293),s 7, eff. 1/1/2022.

Section 1520.5 - Gift certificates
Section 1520 does not apply to gift certificates subject to Title 1.4A (commencing with Section 1749.45) of Part 4 of Division 3 of the Civil Code. However, Section 1520 applies to any gift certificate that has an expiration date and that is given in exchange for money or any other thing of value.
Amended by Stats 2003 ch 116 (AB 1092),s 3, eff. 1/1/2004.

Section 1521 - Employee benefit plan distributions
(a) Except as provided in subdivision (b), and subject to Section 1510, all employee benefit plan distributions and any income or other increment thereon escheats to the state if the owner has not, within three years after it becomes payable or distributable, accepted the distribution, corresponded in writing concerning the distribution, or otherwise indicated an interest as evidenced by a memorandum or other record on file with the fiduciary of the trust or custodial fund or administrator of the plan under which the trust or fund is established. As used in this section, "fiduciary" means any person exercising any power, authority, or responsibility of management or disposition with respect to any money or other property of a retirement system or plan, and "administrator" means the person specifically so designated by the plan, trust agreement, contract, or other instrument under which the retirement system or plan is operated, or if none is designated, the employer.

(b) Except as provided in subdivision (c), an employee benefit plan distribution and any income or other increment thereon shall not escheat to this state if, at the time the distribution shall become payable to a participant in an employee benefit plan, the plan contains a provision for forfeiture or expressly authorizes the administrator to declare a forfeiture of a distribution to a beneficiary thereof who cannot be found after a period of time specified in the plan, and the trust or fund established under the plan has not terminated prior to the date on which the distribution would become forfeitable in accordance with the provision.

(c) A participant entitled to an employee benefit plan distribution in the form of residuals shall be relieved from a forfeiture declared under subdivision (b) upon the making of a claim therefor.
Amended by Stats. 1990, Ch. 450, Sec. 12. Effective July 31, 1990.

Section 1522 - Charge or fee imposed because of inactive or unclaimed status
No service, handling, maintenance or other charge or fee of any kind which is imposed because of the inactive or unclaimed status contemplated by this chapter, may be deducted or withheld from any property subject to escheat under this chapter, unless specifically permitted by this chapter.

Even when specifically permitted by this chapter, such charges or fees may not be excluded, withheld or deducted from property subject to this chapter if, under its policy or procedure, the holder would not have excluded, withheld or deducted such charges or fees in the event the property had been claimed by the owner prior to being reported or remitted to the Controller.
Amended by Stats. 1981, Ch. 831, Sec. 3.

Section 1523 - Policyholder entitled to Proposition 103 rebate not located
If an insurer, after a good faith effort to locate and deliver to a policyholder a Proposition 103 rebate ordered or negotiated pursuant to Section 1861.01 of the Insurance Code, determines that a policyholder cannot be located, all funds attributable to that rebate escheat to the state and shall be delivered to the Controller. The funds subject to escheat on or after July 1, 1997, shall be transferred by the Controller to the Department of Insurance for deposit in the Insurance Fund in the following amounts and for the following purposes:
(a) Up to the amount that will repay principal and interest on the General Fund loan authorized by Item 0845-001-0001 of the Budget Act of 1996 for expenditure as provided in Section 12936 of the Insurance Code.
(b) The sum of four million dollars ($4,000,000) for expenditure during the 1998-1999 fiscal year as provided in Section 12967 of the Insurance Code.
Amended by Stats. 1998, Ch. 963, Sec. 1. Effective September 29, 1998.

Section 1528 - Unclaimed funds held by domestic fraternal benefit society
This chapter does not apply to unclaimed funds held by a life insurance corporation which is organized or admitted as a domestic fraternal benefit society under Chapter 10 (commencing with Section 10970) of Part 2 of Division 2 of the Insurance Code, so long as such funds are used for scholarship funds, exclusive of costs of administration thereof.
Added by Stats. 1974, Ch. 1050.

Article 3 - IDENTIFICATION OF ESCHEATED PROPERTY

Section 1530 - Report required by persons holding funds or other property escheated to state
(a) Every person holding funds or other property escheated to this state under this chapter shall report to the Controller as provided in this section.
(b) The report shall be on a form prescribed or approved by the Controller and shall include:
   (1) Except with respect to traveler's checks and money orders, the name, if known, and last known address, if any, of each person appearing from the records of the holder to be the owner of any property of value of at least fifty dollars ($50) escheated under this chapter. This paragraph shall become inoperative on July 1, 2014.
   (2) Except with respect to traveler's checks and money orders, the name, if known, and last known address, if any, of each person appearing from the records of the holder to be the owner of any property of value of at least twenty-five dollars ($25) escheated under this chapter. This paragraph shall become operative on July 1, 2014.
   (3) In the case of escheated funds of life insurance corporations, the full name of the insured or annuitant, and his or her last known address, according to the life insurance corporation's records.
   (4) In the case of the contents of a safe deposit box or other safekeeping repository or in the case of other tangible property, a description of the property and the place where it is held and may be inspected by the Controller. The report shall set forth any amounts owing to the holder for unpaid rent or storage charges and for the cost of opening the safe deposit box or other safekeeping repository, if any, in which the property was contained.
   (5) The nature and identifying number, if any, or description of any intangible property and the amount appearing from the records to be due, except that items of value under twenty-five dollars ($25) each may be reported in aggregate.
   (6) Except for any property reported in the aggregate, the date when the property became payable, demandable, or returnable, and the date of the last transaction with the owner with respect to the property.
   (7) Other information which the Controller prescribes by rule as necessary for the administration of this chapter.
(c) If the holder is a successor to other persons who previously held the property for the owner, or if the holder has changed his or her name while holding the property, he or she shall file with his or her report all prior known names and addresses of each holder of the property.
(d) The report shall be filed before November 1 of each year as of June 30 or fiscal yearend next preceding, but the report of life insurance corporations, and the report of all insurance corporation demutualization proceeds subject to Section 1515.5, shall be filed before May 1 of each year as of December 31 next preceding. The initial report for property subject to Section 1515.5 shall be filed on or before May 1, 2004, with respect to conditions in effect on December 31, 2003, and all property shall be determined to be reportable under Section 1515.5 as if that section were in effect on the date of the insurance company demutualization or related reorganization. The Controller may postpone the reporting date upon his or her own motion or upon written request by any person required to file a report.
(e) The report, if made by an individual, shall be verified by the individual; if made by a partnership, by a partner; if made by an unincorporated association or private corporation, by an officer; and if made by a public corporation, by its chief fiscal officer or other employee authorized by the holder.
Amended by Stats 2014 ch 71 (SB 1304),s 21, eff. 1/1/2015.
Amended by Stats 2013 ch 362 (AB 212),s 2, eff. 1/1/2014.
Amended by Stats 2003 ch 304 (AB 378),s 4, eff. 1/1/2004.

Section 1531 - Notice within one year after payment or delivery of escheated property
(a) Within one year after payment or delivery of escheated property as required by Section 1532, the Controller shall cause a notice to be published in a manner that the Controller determines to be reasonable, which may include, but not be limited to, newspapers, Internet Web sites, radio, television, or other media. In carrying out this duty, the Controller shall not use any of the following:
   (1) Money appropriated for the Controller's audit programs.
   (2) More money than the Legislature appropriates for this subdivision's purpose.
   (3) A photograph in a notice.
   (4) An elected official's name in a notice.
(b) Within 165 days after the final date for filing the report required by Section 1530, the Controller shall mail a notice to each person having an address listed in the report who appears to be entitled to property of the value of fifty dollars ($50) or more escheated under this chapter. If the report filed pursuant to Section 1530 includes a social security number, the Controller shall request the Franchise Tax Board to provide a current address for the apparent owner on the basis of that number. The Controller shall mail the notice to the apparent owner for whom a current address is obtained if the address is different from the address previously reported to the Controller. If the Franchise Tax Board does not provide an address or a different address, then the Controller shall mail the notice to the address listed in the report required by Section 1530.
(c) The mailed notice shall contain all of the following:
   (1) A statement that, according to a report filed with the Controller, property is being held to which the addressee appears entitled.
   (2) The name and address of the person holding the property and any necessary information regarding changes of name and address of the holder.
   (3) A statement that, if satisfactory proof of claim is not presented by the owner to the holder by the date specified in the notice, the property will be placed in the custody of the Controller and may be sold or destroyed pursuant to this chapter, and all further claims concerning the property or, if sold, the net proceeds of its sale, must be directed to the Controller.
(d) This section is intended to inform owners about the possible existence of unclaimed property identified pursuant to this chapter.
Amended by Stats 2017 ch 200 (AB 772),s 1, eff. 1/1/2018.
Amended by Stats 2007 ch 179 (SB 86),s 2, eff. 8/24/2007.

Section 1531.5 - Notification program designed to inform owners about possible existence of unclaimed property

(a) The Controller shall establish and conduct a notification program designed to inform owners about the possible existence of unclaimed property received pursuant to this chapter.
(b) Any notice sent pursuant to this section shall not contain a photograph or likeness of an elected official.
(c)
  (1) Notwithstanding any other law, upon the request of the Controller, a state or local governmental agency may furnish to the Controller from its records the address or other identification or location information that could reasonably be used to locate an owner of unclaimed property.
  (2) If the address or other identification or location information requested by the Controller is deemed confidential under any laws or regulations of this state, it shall nevertheless be furnished to the Controller. However, neither the Controller nor any officer, agent, or employee of the Controller shall use or disclose that information except as may be necessary in attempting to locate the owner of unclaimed property.
  (3) This subdivision shall not be construed to require disclosure of information in violation of federal law.
  (4) If a fee or charge is customarily made for the information requested by the Controller, the Controller shall pay that customary fee or charge.
(d) Costs for administering this section shall be subject to the level of appropriation in the annual Budget Act.
Added by Stats 2007 ch 179 (SB 86),s 3, eff. 8/24/2007.

Section 1531.6 - Notice to owners of savings bonds, war bond or military award
(a) In addition to the notices required pursuant to this chapter, the Controller may mail a separate notice to an apparent owner of a United States savings bond, war bond, or military award whose name is shown on or can be associated with the contents of a safe deposit box or other safekeeping repository and is different from the reported owner of the safe deposit box or other safekeeping repository.
(b) A notice sent pursuant to this section shall not contain a photograph or likeness of an elected official.
(c)
  (1) Notwithstanding any other law, upon request of the Controller, a state or local governmental agency may furnish to the Controller from its records the address or other identification or location information that could reasonably be used to locate an owner of unclaimed property.
  (2) If the address or other identification or location information requested by the Controller is deemed confidential under any law or regulation of the state, it shall nevertheless be furnished to the Controller. However, neither the Controller nor any officer, agent, or employee of the Controller shall use or disclose that information, except as may be necessary in attempting to locate the owner of unclaimed property.
  (3) This subdivision shall not be construed to require disclosure of information in violation of federal law.
  (4) If a fee or charge is customarily made for the information requested by the Controller, the Controller shall pay the customary fee or charge.
(d) Costs for administering this section shall be subject to the level of appropriation in the annual Budget Act.
Added by Stats 2015 ch 297 (AB 355),s 1, eff. 1/1/2016.

Section 1532 - Payment or delivery of escheated property by persons filing report
(a) Every person filing a report as provided by Section 1530 shall, no sooner than seven months and no later than seven months and 15 days after the final date for filing the report, pay or deliver to the Controller all escheated property specified in the report. Any payment of unclaimed cash in an amount of at least two thousand dollars ($2,000) shall be made by electronic funds transfer pursuant to regulations adopted by the Controller. The Controller may postpone the date for payment or delivery of the property, and the date for any report required by subdivision (b), upon the Controller's own motion or upon written request by any person required to pay or deliver the property or file a report as required by this section.
(b) If a person establishes their right to receive any property specified in the report to the satisfaction of the holder before that property has been delivered to the Controller, or it appears that, for any other reason, the property may not be subject to escheat under this chapter, the holder shall not pay or deliver the property to the Controller but shall instead file a report with the Controller, on a form and in a format prescribed or approved by the Controller, containing information pertaining to the property subject to escheat.
(c) Any property not paid or delivered pursuant to subdivision (b) that is later determined by the holder to be subject to escheat under this chapter shall not be subject to the interest provision of Section 1577.
(d) The holder of any interest under subdivision (b) of Section 1516 shall deliver a duplicate certificate to the Controller or shall register the securities in uncertificated form in the name of the Controller. Upon delivering a duplicate certificate or providing evidence of registration of the securities in uncertificated form to the Controller, the holder, any transfer agent, registrar, or other person acting for or on behalf of the holder in executing or delivering the duplicate certificate or registering the uncertificated securities, shall be relieved from all liability of every kind to any person including, but not limited to, any person acquiring the original certificate or the duplicate of the certificate issued to the Controller for any losses or damages resulting to that person by the issuance and delivery to the Controller of the duplicate certificate or the registration of the uncertificated securities to the Controller.
(e) Payment of any intangible property to the Controller shall be made at the office of the Controller in Sacramento or at another location as the Controller by regulation may designate. Except as otherwise agreed by the Controller and the holder, tangible personal property shall be delivered to the Controller at the place where it is held.
(f) Payment is deemed complete on the date the electronic funds transfer is initiated if the settlement to the state's demand account occurs on or before the banking day following the date the transfer is initiated. If the settlement to the state's demand account does not occur on or before the banking day following the date the transfer is initiated, payment is deemed to occur on the date settlement occurs.
(g) Any person required to pay cash by electronic funds transfer who makes the payment by means other than an authorized electronic funds transfer shall be liable for a civil penalty of 2 percent of the amount of the payment that is due pursuant to this section, in addition to any other penalty provided by law. Penalties are due at the time of payment. If the Controller finds that a holder's failure to make payment by an appropriate electronic funds transfer in accordance with the Controller's procedures is due to reasonable cause and circumstances beyond the holder's control, and occurred notwithstanding the exercise of ordinary care and in the absence of willful neglect, that holder shall be relieved of the penalties.
(h) An electronic funds transfer shall be accomplished by an automated clearinghouse debit, an automated clearinghouse credit, a Federal Reserve Wire Transfer (Fedwire), or by an international funds transfer. Banking costs incurred for the automated clearinghouse debit transaction by the holder shall be paid by the state. Banking costs incurred by the state for the automated clearinghouse credit transaction may be paid by the holder originating the credit. Banking costs incurred for the Fedwire transaction charged to the holder and the state shall be paid by the person originating the transaction. Banking costs charged to the holder and to the state for an international funds transfer may be charged to the holder.
(i) For purposes of this section:
  (1) "Electronic funds transfer" means any transfer of funds, other than a transaction originated by check, draft, or similar paper instrument, that is initiated through an electronic terminal, telephonic instrument, modem, computer, or magnetic tape, so as to order, instruct, or authorize a financial institution to credit or debit an account.
  (2) "Automated clearinghouse" means any federal reserve bank, or an organization established by agreement with the National Automated Clearing House Association or any similar organization, that operates as a clearinghouse for transmitting or receiving entries between banks or bank accounts and that authorizes an electronic transfer of funds between those banks or bank accounts.

(3) "Automated clearinghouse debit" means a transaction in which the state, through its designated depository bank, originates an automated clearinghouse transaction debiting the holder's bank account and crediting the state's bank account for the amount of payment.

(4) "Automated clearinghouse credit" means an automated clearinghouse transaction in which the holder, through its own bank, originates an entry crediting the state's bank account and debiting the holder's bank account.

(5) "Fedwire" means any transaction originated by the holder and utilizing the national electronic payment system to transfer funds through federal reserve banks, pursuant to which the holder debits its own bank account and credits the state's bank account.

(6) "International funds transfer" means any transaction originated by the holder and utilizing the international electronic payment system to transfer funds, pursuant to which the holder debits its own bank account, and credits the funds to a United States bank that credits the Unclaimed Property Fund.

Amended by Stats 2021 ch 103 (SB 308),s 1, eff. 1/1/2022.
Amended by Stats 2011 ch 305 (SB 495),s 7, eff. 1/1/2012.
Amended by Stats 2009 ch 522 (AB 1291),s 6, eff. 1/1/2010.
Amended by Stats 2007 ch 179 (SB 86),s 4, eff. 8/24/2007.
Amended by Stats 2004 ch 520 (AB 2530),s 2, eff. 1/1/2005

Section 1532.1 - Payment or delivery of property escheating to state pursuant to section 1514

Notwithstanding Sections 1531 and 1532, property that escheats to the state pursuant to Section 1514 shall not be paid or delivered to the state until the earlier of (a) the time when the holder is requested to do so by the Controller or (b) within one year after the final date for filing the report required by Section 1530 as specified in subdivision (d) of Section 1530. Within one year after receipt of property as provided by this section, the Controller shall cause a notice to be published as provided in Section 1531.

Amended by Stats. 1996, Ch. 762, Sec. 8. Effective January 1, 1997.

Section 1533 - Not in interest of state to take custody of tangible personal property

Tangible personal property may be excluded from the notices required by Section 1531, shall not be delivered to the State Controller, and shall not escheat to the state, if the State Controller, in his discretion, determines that it is not in the interest of the state to take custody of the property and notifies the holder in writing, within 120 days from receipt of the report required by Section 1530, of his determination not to take custody of the property.

Added by Stats. 1968, Ch. 356.

Article 4 - PAYMENT OF CLAIMS

Section 1540 - Generally

(a) Any person, excluding another state, who claims to have been the owner, as defined in subdivision (d), of property paid or delivered to the Controller under this chapter may file a claim to the property or to the net proceeds from its sale. The claim shall be on a form prescribed by the Controller and shall be verified by the claimant.

(b) The Controller shall consider each claim within 180 days after it is filed to determine if the claimant is the owner, as defined in subdivision (d), and may hold a hearing and receive evidence. The Controller shall give written notice to the claimant if the Controller denies the claim in whole or in part. The notice may be given by mailing it to the address, if any, stated in the claim as the address to which notices are to be sent. If no address is stated in the claim, the notice may be mailed to the address, if any, of the claimant as stated in the claim. A notice of denial need not be given if the claim fails to state either an address to which notices are to be sent or an address of the claimant.

(c) Interest shall not be payable on any claim paid under this chapter.

(d) Notwithstanding subdivision (g) of Section 1501, for purposes of filing a claim pursuant to this section, "owner" means the person who had legal right to the property before its escheat, the person's heirs or estate representative, the person's guardian or conservator, or a public administrator acting pursuant to the authority granted in Sections 7660 and 7661 of the Probate Code. An "owner" also means a nonprofit civic, charitable, or educational organization that granted a charter, sponsorship, or approval for the existence of the organization that had the legal right to the property before its escheat but that has dissolved or is no longer in existence, if the charter, sponsorship, approval, organization bylaws, or other governing documents provide that unclaimed or surplus property shall be conveyed to the granting organization upon dissolution or cessation to exist as a distinct legal entity. Only an owner, as defined in this subdivision, may file a claim with the Controller pursuant to this article.

(e) Following a public hearing, the Controller shall adopt guidelines and forms that shall provide specific instructions to assist owners in filing claims pursuant to this article.

(f) Notwithstanding any other provision, property reported to, and received by, the Controller pursuant to this chapter in the name of a state agency, including the University of California and the California State University, or a local agency, including a school district and community college district, may be transferred by the Controller directly to the state or local agency without the filing of a claim. Property transferred pursuant to this subdivision is immune from suit pursuant to Section 1566 in the same manner as if the state or local agency had filed a claim to the property. For purposes of this subdivision, "local agency" means a city, county, city and county, or district.

Amended by Stats 2020 ch 36 (AB 3364),s 26, eff. 1/1/2021.
Amended by Stats 2019 ch 320 (AB 1637),s 1, eff. 1/1/2020.
Amended by Stats 2014 ch 330 (AB 1712),s 1, eff. 1/1/2015.
Amended by Stats 2013 ch 128 (AB 1275),s 1, eff. 1/1/2014.
Amended by Stats 2005 ch 706 (AB 1742),s 15, eff. 1/1/2006
Amended by Stats 2002 ch 1124 (AB 3000),s 3, eff. 9/30/2002.

Section 1541 - Action to establish claim

Any person aggrieved by a decision of the Controller or as to whose claim the Controller has failed to make a decision within 180 days after the filing of the claim, may commence an action, naming the Controller as a defendant, to establish his or her claim in the superior court in any county or city and county in which the Attorney General has an office. The action shall be brought within 90 days after the decision of the Controller or within 270 days from the filing of the claim if the Controller fails to make a decision. The summons and a copy of the complaint shall be served upon the Controller and the Attorney General and the Controller shall have 60 days within which to respond by answer. The action shall be tried without a jury.

Amended by Stats. 2003, Ch. 228, Sec. 9. Effective August 11, 2003.

Section 1542 - Claim of another state

(a) At any time after property has been paid or delivered to the Controller under this chapter, another state is entitled to recover the property if:

(1) The property escheated to this state under subdivision (b) of Section 1510 because no address of the apparent owner of the property appeared on the records of the holder when the property was escheated under this chapter, the last known address of the apparent owner was in fact in that other state, and, under the laws of that state, the property escheated to that state.

(2) The last known address of the apparent owner of the property appearing on the records of the holder is in that other state and, under the laws of that state, the property has escheated to that state.

(3) The property is the sum payable on a travelers check, money order, or other similar instrument that escheated to this state under Section 1511, the travelers check, money order, or other similar instrument was in fact purchased in that other state, and, under the laws of that state, the property escheated to that state.

(4) The property is funds held or owing by a life insurance corporation that escheated to this state by application of the presumption provided by subdivision (b) of Section 1515, the last known address of the person entitled to the funds was in fact in that other state, and, under the laws of that state, the property escheated to that state.

(b) The claim of another state to recover escheated property under this section shall be presented in writing to the Controller, who shall consider the claim within 180 days after it is presented. The Controller may hold a hearing and receive evidence. The Controller shall allow the claim upon determination that the other state is entitled to the escheated property.

(c) Paragraphs (1) and (2) of subdivision (a) do not apply to property described in paragraph (3) or (4) of that subdivision.

Amended by Stats. 2003, Ch. 228, Sec. 10. Effective August 11, 2003.

Section 1543 - Unclaimed property; secure payment of claims

Notwithstanding Section 1540, the Controller may do any of the following to streamline the secure payment of claims:

(a) Minimize the number of documents a claimant is required to submit for property valued at less than five thousand dollars ($5,000).

(b) Allow electronic submission of documentation to the Controller's internet website for any claim deemed appropriate by the Controller.

(c) Authorize direct deposit by electronic fund transfer for the payment of an approved claim.

Added by Stats 2022 ch 270 (AB 1208),s 1, eff. 1/1/2023.

Article 5 - ADMINISTRATION OF UNCLAIMED PROPERTY

Section 1560 - Generally

(a) Upon the payment or delivery of escheated property to the Controller, the state shall assume custody and shall be responsible for the safekeeping of the property. Any person who pays or delivers escheated property to the Controller under this chapter and who, prior to escheat, if the person's records contain an address for the apparent owner that the holder's records do not disclose to be inaccurate, has made reasonable efforts to notify the owner by mail or, if the owner has consented to electronic notice, electronically, in substantial compliance with Sections 1513.5, 1514, 1516, and 1520, that the owner's property, deposit, account, shares, or other interest will escheat to the state, is relieved of all liability to the extent of the value of the property so paid or delivered for any claim that then exists or that thereafter may arise or be made in respect to the property. Property removed from a safe-deposit box or other safekeeping repository shall be received by the Controller subject to any valid lien of the holder for rent and other charges, the rent and other charges to be paid out of the proceeds remaining after the Controller has deducted therefrom their selling cost.

(b) Any holder who has paid moneys to the Controller pursuant to this chapter may make payment to any person appearing to that holder to be entitled thereto, and upon filing proof of the payment and proof that the payee was entitled thereto, the Controller shall forthwith reimburse the holder for the payment without deduction of any fee or other charges. Where reimbursement is sought for a payment made on a negotiable instrument, including a traveler's check or money order, the holder shall be reimbursed under this subdivision upon filing proof that the instrument was duly presented to them and that payment was made thereon to a person who appeared to the holder to be entitled to payment.

(c) The holder shall be reimbursed under this section even if they made the payment to a person whose claim against them was barred because of the expiration of any period of time as those described in Section 1570.

(d) Any holder who has delivered personal property, including a certificate of any interest in a business association, to the Controller pursuant to this chapter may reclaim the personal property if still in the possession of the Controller without payment of any fee or other charges upon filing proof that the owner thereof has claimed such personal property from the holder. The Controller may, in their discretion, accept an affidavit of the holder stating the facts that entitle the holder to reimbursement under this subdivision as sufficient proof for the purposes of this subdivision.

(e) Any holder who has delivered funds maintained under a preneed funeral trust or similar account or plan to the Controller pursuant to this chapter and has fulfilled the services of the preneed funeral trust escheated to the Controller shall be reimbursed under this section upon submission of a death certificate for the beneficiary and a statement detailing the personal property or funeral merchandise or services provided.

(f) This section shall become operative on January 1, 2023.

Added by Stats 2021 ch 514 (AB 293),s 9, eff. 1/1/2022.

Section 1561 - Claim of property paid or delivered to Controller by holder; payment or delivery of property because of mistake of law or fact

(a) If the holder pays or delivers escheated property to the State Controller in accordance with this chapter and thereafter any person claims the property from the holder or another state claims the property from the holder under that state's laws relating to escheat, the State Controller shall, upon written notice of such claim, defend the holder against the claim and indemnify him against any liability on the claim.

(b) If any holder, because of mistake of law or fact, pays or delivers any property to the State Controller that has not escheated under this chapter and thereafter claims the property from the State Controller, the State Controller shall, if he has not disposed of the property in accordance with this chapter, refund or redeliver the property to the holder without deduction for any fee or other charge.

(c) As used in this section, "escheated property" means property which this chapter provides escheats to this state, whether or not it is determined that another state had a superior right to escheat such property at the time it was paid or delivered to the State Controller or at some time thereafter.

Added by Stats. 1968, Ch. 356.

Section 1562 - Dividends, interest or other increments realized or accruing prior to liquidation or conversion into money

When property other than money is delivered to the State Controller under this chapter, any dividends, interest or other increments realized or accruing on such property at or prior to liquidation or conversion thereof into money, shall upon receipt be credited to the owner's account by the State Controller. Except for amounts so credited the owner is not entitled to receive income or other increments on money or other property paid or delivered to the State Controller under this chapter. All interest received and other income derived from the investment of moneys deposited in the Unclaimed Property Fund under the provisions of this chapter shall, on order of the State Controller, be transferred to the General Fund.

Added by renumbering Section 1514 by Stats. 1968, Ch. 356.

Section 1563 - Sale of escheated property

(a) Except as provided in subdivisions (b) and (c), all escheated property delivered to the Controller under this chapter shall be sold by the Controller to the highest bidder at public sale in whatever city in the state affords in the Controller's judgment the most favorable market for the property involved, or the Controller may conduct the sale by electronic media, including, but not limited to, the internet, if in the Controller's judgment it is cost effective to conduct the sale of the property involved in that manner. However, no sale shall be made pursuant to this subdivision until 18 months after the final date for filing the report required by Section 1530. The Controller may decline the highest bid and reoffer the property for sale if the Controller considers the price bid insufficient. The Controller need not offer any property for sale if, in the Controller's opinion, the probable cost of sale exceeds the value of the property. Any sale of escheated property held under this section shall be preceded by a single publication of notice thereof, at least one week in advance of sale, in an English language newspaper of general circulation in the county where the property is to be sold.

(b) Securities listed on an established stock exchange shall be sold at the prevailing prices on that exchange. Other securities may be sold over the counter at prevailing prices or by any other method that the Controller may determine to be advisable. These securities shall be sold by the

Controller no sooner than 18 months, but no later than 20 months, after the actual date of filing of the report required by Section 1530. If securities delivered to the Controller by a holder of the securities remain in the custody of the Controller, a person making a valid claim for those securities under this chapter shall be entitled to receive the securities from the Controller. If the securities have been sold, the person shall be entitled to receive the net proceeds received by the Controller from the sale of the securities. United States government savings bonds and United States war bonds shall be presented to the United States for payment. Subdivision (a) does not apply to the property described in this subdivision.

(c)

(1)All escheated property consisting of military awards, decorations, equipment, artifacts, memorabilia, documents, photographs, films, literature, and any other item relating to the military history of California and Californians that is delivered to the Controller is exempt from subdivision (a) and may, at the discretion of the Controller, be held in trust for the Controller at the California State Military Museum and Resource Center, or successor entity. All escheated property held in trust pursuant to this subdivision is subject to the applicable regulations of the United States Army governing Army museum activities as described in Section 179 of the Military and Veterans Code. A person claiming an interest in the escheated property may file a claim to the property pursuant to Article 4 (commencing with Section 1540).

(2)The California State Military Museum and Resource Center, or successor entity, shall be responsible for the costs of storage and maintenance of escheated property delivered by the Controller under this subdivision.

(d) The purchaser at any sale conducted by the Controller pursuant to this chapter shall receive title to the property purchased, free from all claims of the owner or prior holder thereof and of all persons claiming through or under them. The Controller shall execute all documents necessary to complete the transfer of title.

Amended by Stats 2022 ch 420 (AB 2960),s 13, eff. 1/1/2023.
Amended by Stats 2016 ch 31 (SB 836),s 17, eff. 6/27/2016.
Amended by Stats 2015 ch 297 (AB 355),s 2, eff. 1/1/2016.
Amended by Stats 2007 ch 179 (SB 86),s 5, eff. 8/24/2007.
Amended by Stats 2003 ch 265 (AB 542),s 2, eff. 1/1/2004.
Amended by Stats 2000 ch 16 (AB 938), s 2, eff. 5/5/2000.
Amended by Stats 2000 ch 924 (AB 2935), s 2, eff. 1/1/2001.

Section 1564 - Money received deposited in Abandoned Property Account in Unclaimed Property Fund

(a) All money received under this chapter, including the proceeds from the sale of property under Section 1563, shall be deposited in the Unclaimed Property Fund in an account titled "Abandoned Property."

(b) Notwithstanding Section 13340 of the Government Code, all money in the Abandoned Property Account in the Unclaimed Property Fund is hereby continuously appropriated to the Controller, without regard to fiscal years, for expenditure in accordance with law in carrying out and enforcing the provisions of this chapter, including, but not limited to, the following purposes:

(1) For payment of claims allowed by the Controller under the provisions of this chapter.

(2) For refund, to the person making such deposit, of amounts, including overpayments, deposited in error in such fund.

(3) For payment of the cost of appraisals incurred by the Controller covering property held in the name of an account in such fund.

(4) For payment of the cost incurred by the Controller for the purchase of lost instrument indemnity bonds, or for payment to the person entitled thereto, for any unpaid lawful charges or costs which arose from holding any specific property or any specific funds which were delivered or paid to the Controller, or which arose from complying with this chapter with respect to such property or funds.

(5) For payment of amounts required to be paid by the state as trustee, bailee, or successor in interest to the preceding owner.

(6) For payment of costs incurred by the Controller for the repair, maintenance, and upkeep of property held in the name of an account in such fund.

(7) For payment of costs of official advertising in connection with the sale of property held in the name of an account in such fund.

(8) For transfer to the General Fund as provided in subdivision (c).

(9) For transfer to the Inheritance Tax Fund of the amount of any inheritance taxes determined to be due and payable to the state by any claimant with respect to any property claimed by him or her under the provisions of this chapter.

(c) At the end of each month, or more often if he or she deems it advisable, the Controller shall transfer all money in the Abandoned Property Account in excess of fifty thousand dollars ($50,000) to the General Fund. Before making this transfer, the Controller shall record the name and last known address of each person appearing from the holders' report to be entitled to the escheated property and the name and last known address of each insured person or annuitant, and with respect to each policy or contract listed in the report of a life insurance corporation, its number, and the name of the corporation. The record shall be available for public inspection at all reasonable business hours.

Amended by Stats. 1993, Ch. 692, Sec. 7. Effective January 1, 1994.

Section 1564.5 - Abandoned IOLTA Property Account

(a) Notwithstanding any law, including, but not limited to, Section 1564, all money received under this chapter from funds held in an Interest on Lawyers' Trust Account (IOLTA) that escheat to the state shall be administered as set forth in this section. The money shall be deposited into the Abandoned IOLTA Property Account, which is hereby established within the Unclaimed Property Fund.

(b) Twenty-five percent of the money in the Abandoned IOLTA Property Account shall be deposited into the IOLTA Claims Reserve Subaccount, which is hereby established within the Abandoned IOLTA Property Account. Notwithstanding Section 13340 of the Government Code, funds in the subaccount are continuously appropriated to the Controller for the payment of all refunds and claims pursuant to this chapter related to escheated IOLTA funds.

(c) The balance of the funds in the Abandoned IOLTA Property Account, excluding funds in the subaccount, shall be transferred on an annual basis to the Public Interest Attorney Loan Repayment Account established pursuant to Section 6032.5 of the Business and Professions Code. Before making this transfer, the Controller shall record the name and last known address of each person appearing from the holders' report to be entitled to the escheated property. The record shall be available for public inspection at all reasonable business hours.

Amended by Stats 2018 ch 390 (AB 2350),s 1, eff. 1/1/2019.
Added by Stats 2015 ch 488 (SB 134),s 2, eff. 1/1/2016.

Section 1565 - Property of no apparent commercial value delivered to Controller

Any property delivered to the Controller pursuant to this chapter that has no apparent commercial value shall be retained by the Controller for a period of not less than seven years from the date the property is delivered to the Controller. If the Controller determines that any property delivered to him or her pursuant to this chapter has no apparent commercial value, he or she may at any time thereafter destroy or otherwise dispose of the property, and in that event no action or proceeding shall be brought or maintained against the state or any officer thereof, or against the holder for, or on account of any action taken by, the Controller pursuant to this chapter with respect to the property.

Amended by Stats 2011 ch 305 (SB 495),s 8, eff. 1/1/2012.
Amended by Stats 2007 ch 179 (SB 86),s 6, eff. 8/24/2007.

Section 1566 - Immunity upon payment of delivery to claimant; transactions entered into by Controller

(a) When payment or delivery of money or other property has been made to any claimant under the provisions of this chapter, no suit shall thereafter be maintained by any other claimant against the state or any officer or employee thereof for or on account of such property.

(b) Except as provided in Section 1541, no suit shall be maintained by any person against the state or any officer or employee thereof for or on account of any transaction entered into by the State Controller pursuant to this chapter.
Added by Stats. 1968, Ch. 356.

Section 1567 - Examination of property by Director of Parks and Recreation
The Director of Parks and Recreation may examine any tangible personal property delivered to the Controller under this chapter for purposes of determining whether such property would be useful under the provisions of Section 512 of the Public Resources Code. If the director makes such a determination with respect to the property, the Controller may deliver the property to the director for use in carrying out the purposes of Section 512 of the Public Resources Code. Upon the termination of any such use, the director shall return the property to the Controller.
Amended by Stats. 1981, Ch. 714, Sec. 73.

Article 6 - COMPLIANCE AND ENFORCEMENT

Section 1570 - Expiration of period of time during which proceeding commenced or enforced to obtain payment
The expiration of any period of time specified by statute or court order, during which an action or proceeding may be commenced or enforced to obtain payment or recovery of property from the holder, does not prevent the money or property from being escheated, nor affect any duty to file a report required by this chapter or to pay or deliver escheated property to the State Controller.
Added by renumbering Section 1515 by Stats. 1968, Ch. 356.

Section 1571 - Examination person believed to be holder who has failed to report property
(a) The Controller may at reasonable times and upon reasonable notice examine the records of any person if the Controller has reason to believe that the person is a holder who has failed to report property that should have been reported pursuant to this chapter.
(b) When requested by the Controller, the examination shall be conducted by any licensing or regulating agency otherwise empowered by the laws of this state to examine the records of the holder. For the purpose of determining compliance with this chapter, the Commissioner of Financial Protection and Innovation is vested with full authority to examine the records of any banking organization and any savings association doing business within this state but not organized under the laws of or created in this state.
(c) Following a public hearing, the Controller shall adopt guidelines as to the policies and procedures governing the activity of third-party auditors who are hired by the Controller.
(d) Following a public hearing, the Controller shall adopt guidelines, on or before July 1, 1999, establishing forms, policies, and procedures to enable a person to dispute or appeal the results of any record examination conducted pursuant to this section.
Amended by Stats 2022 ch 452 (SB 1498),s 42, eff. 1/1/2023.
Amended by Stats 2014 ch 913 (AB 2747),s 11, eff. 1/1/2015.

Section 1572 - Actions by Controller
(a) The State Controller may bring an action in a court of appropriate jurisdiction, as specified in this section, for any of the following purposes:
  (1) To enforce the duty of any person under this chapter to permit the examination of the records of such person.
  (2) For a judicial determination that particular property is subject to escheat by this state pursuant to this chapter.
  (3) To enforce the delivery of any property to the State Controller as required under this chapter.
(b) The State Controller may bring an action under this chapter in any court of this state of appropriate jurisdiction in any of the following cases:
  (1) Where the holder is any person domiciled in this state, or is a government or governmental subdivision or agency of this state.
  (2) Where the holder is any person engaged in or transacting business in this state, although not domiciled in this state.
  (3) Where the property is tangible personal property and is held in this state.
(c) In any case where no court of this state can obtain jurisdiction over the holder, the State Controller may bring an action in any federal or state court with jurisdiction over the holder.
Added by Stats. 1968, Ch. 356.

Section 1573 - Agreement to provide information to another state
The State Controller may enter into an agreement to provide information needed to enable another state to determine unclaimed property it may be entitled to escheat if such other state or an official thereof agrees to provide this state with information needed to enable this state to determine unclaimed property it may be entitled to escheat. The State Controller may, by regulation, require the reporting of information needed to enable him to comply with agreements made pursuant to this section and may, by regulation, prescribe the form, including verification, of the information to be reported and the times for filing the reports.
Added by Stats. 1968, Ch. 356.

Section 1574 - Action by Attorney General in name of another state to enforce unclaimed property laws
At the request of another state, the Attorney General of this state may bring an action in the name of the other state, in any court of appropriate jurisdiction of this state or federal court within this state, to enforce the unclaimed property laws of the other state against a holder in this state of property subject to escheat by the other state, if:
(a) The courts of the other state cannot obtain jurisdiction over the holder;
(b) The other state has agreed to bring actions in the name of this state at the request of the Attorney General of this state to enforce the provisions of this chapter against any person in the other state believed by the State Controller to hold property subject to escheat under this chapter, where the courts of this state cannot obtain jurisdiction over such person; and
(c) The other state has agreed to pay reasonable costs incurred by the Attorney General in bringing the action.
Added by Stats. 1968, Ch. 356.

Section 1575 - Request by Attorney General that another state bring action to enforce provisions of chapter
(a) If the State Controller believes that a person in another state holds property subject to escheat under this chapter and the courts of this state cannot obtain jurisdiction over that person, the Attorney General of this state may request an officer of the other state to bring an action in the name of this state to enforce the provisions of this chapter against such person.
(b) This state shall pay all reasonable costs incurred by the other state in any action brought under the authority of this section. The State Controller may agree to pay to any state bringing such an action a reward not to exceed fifteen percent of the value, after deducting reasonable costs, of any property recovered for this state as a direct or indirect result of such action. Any costs or rewards paid pursuant to this section shall be paid from the Abandoned Property Account in the Unclaimed Property Fund and shall not be deducted from the amount that is subject to be claimed by the owner in accordance with this chapter.
Added by Stats. 1968, Ch. 356.

Section 1576 - Willfully failing to render report; willfully refusing to pay or deliver escheated property
(a) Any person who willfully fails to render any report or perform other duties, including use of the report format described in Section 1530, required under this chapter shall be punished by a fine of one hundred dollars ($100) for each day such report is withheld or such duty is not performed, but not more than ten thousand dollars ($10,000).
(b) Any person who willfully refuses to pay or deliver escheated property to the Controller as required under this chapter shall be punished by a fine of not less than five thousand dollars ($5,000) nor more than fifty thousand dollars ($50,000).
(c) No person shall be considered to have willfully failed to report, pay, or deliver escheated property, or perform other duties unless he or she has failed to respond within a reasonable time after notification by certified mail by the Controller's office of his or her failure to act.

Amended by Stats. 1996, Ch. 762, Sec. 10. Effective January 1, 1997.

Section 1577 - Interest payable for failure to report, pay or deliver unclaimed property; waiver

(a) In addition to any damages, penalties, or fines for which a person may be liable under other provisions of law, any person who fails to report, pay, or deliver unclaimed property within the time prescribed by this chapter, unless that failure is due to reasonable cause, shall pay to the Controller interest at the rate of 12 percent per annum on that property or value thereof from the date the property should have been reported, paid, or delivered.

(b) If a holder reports and pays or delivers unclaimed property within the time prescribed by this chapter, but files a report that is not in substantial compliance with the requirements of Section 1530 or 1532, the interest payable on the unclaimed property that is paid or delivered in the time prescribed by this chapter shall not exceed ten thousand dollars ($10,000).

(c) The Controller may waive the interest payable under this section if the holder's failure to file a report that is in substantial compliance with the requirements of Section 1530 or 1532 is due to reasonable cause.

(d) The Controller shall waive the interest payable under this section if the holder participates in and completes all of the requirements of the California Voluntary Compliance Program under Section 1577.5, subject to the right to reinstate, as specified.

Amended by Stats 2022 ch 282 (AB 2280),s 2, eff. 1/1/2023.
Amended by Stats 2009 ch 522 (AB 1291),s 8, eff. 1/1/2010.
Amended by Stats 2003 ch 304 (AB 378),s 5, eff. 1/1/2004.

Section 1577.5 - California Voluntary Compliance Program

(a) This section shall be known, and may be cited, as the "California Voluntary Compliance Program."

(b) The Controller may establish a program for the voluntary compliance of holders for the purpose of resolving unclaimed property that is due and owing to the state under this chapter.

(c) A holder that has not reported unclaimed property in accordance with Section 1530 may request to enroll in the program using a form prescribed by the Controller.

(d) The Controller, in their discretion, may enroll eligible holders in the program. A holder is ineligible to participate in the program if any of the following apply:

(1) At the time the holder's request to enroll is received by the Controller, the holder is the subject of an examination of records or has received notification from the Controller of an impending examination under Section 1571.

(2) At the time the holder's request to enroll is received by the Controller, the holder is the subject of a civil or criminal prosecution involving compliance with this chapter.

(3) The Controller has notified the holder of an interest assessment under Section 1577 within the previous five years, and the interest assessment remains unpaid at the time of the holder's request to enroll. A holder subject to an outstanding interest assessment may file or refile a request to enroll in the program after resolving the outstanding interest assessment.

(4) The Controller has waived interest assessed against the holder under this section within the previous five years. Notwithstanding the foregoing, if a holder acquired or merged with another entity within the five-year period, the holder may request to enroll in the program for the purpose of resolving unclaimed property that may be due and owing to the state as a result of the acquisition or merger.

(e) The Controller shall waive interest assessed under Section 1577 for a holder enrolled in the program if the holder does all the following within the prescribed timeframes and satisfies the other requirements of this section:

(1) Enrolls in and participates in an unclaimed property educational training program provided by the Controller within three months after the date on which the Controller notified the holder of their enrollment in the program, unless the Controller sets a different date.

(2) Reviews their books and records for unclaimed property for at least the previous 10 years, starting from June 30 or the fiscal yearend preceding the date on which the report required by paragraph (4) is due.

(3) Makes reasonable efforts to notify owners of reportable property by mail or electronically, as applicable, pursuant to Sections 1513.5, 1514, 1516, or 1520, no less than 30 days prior to submitting the report required by paragraph (4).

(4) Reports to the Controller as required by subdivisions (b), (c), and (e) of Section 1530 within six months after the date on which the Controller notified the holder of their enrollment in the program. Upon written request by the enrolled holder, the Controller may postpone the reporting date for a period not to exceed 18 months after the date on which the Controller notified the holder of their enrollment in the program.

(5) Submits to the Controller an updated report and pays or delivers to the Controller all escheated property specified in the report as required by Section 1532, no sooner than seven months and no later than seven months and 15 days after the Controller received the report submitted pursuant to paragraph (4).

(f) The Controller may reinstate interest waived under subdivision (d) of Section 1577 if the holder does not pay or deliver all escheated property specified in the report submitted pursuant to and within the timeframe prescribed by paragraph (5) of subdivision (e).

(g) The Controller may adopt guidelines and forms that provide specific procedures for the administration of the program.

(h) This section shall become operative only upon an appropriation by the Legislature in the annual Budget Act for this purpose.

Added by Stats 2022 ch 282 (AB 2280),s 4, eff. 1/1/2023.

Article 7 - MISCELLANEOUS

Section 1580 - Power of Controller to make rules and regulations

The State Controller is hereby authorized to make necessary rules and regulations to carry out the provisions of this chapter.
Amended by Stats. 1978, Ch. 1183.

Section 1581 - Records required by business selling travelers checks, money orders or similar instruments in state

(a) Any business association that sells in this state its travelers checks, money orders, or other similar written instruments (other than third-party bank checks) on which such business association is directly liable, or that provides such travelers checks, money orders, or similar written instruments to others for sale in this state, shall maintain a record indicating those travelers checks, money orders, or similar written instruments that are purchased from it in this state.

(b) The record required by this section may be destroyed after it has been retained for such reasonable time as the State Controller shall designate by regulation.

(c) Any business association that willfully fails to comply with this section is liable to the state for a civil penalty of five hundred dollars ($500) for each day of such failure to comply, which penalty may be recovered in an action brought by the State Controller.
Amended by Stats. 1975, Ch. 25.

Section 1582 - Validity of agreement to locate, deliver or recover property reported

(a)

(1) An agreement to locate, deliver, recover, or assist in the recovery of property reported under Section 1530 is invalid if either of the following apply:

(A) The agreement is entered into between the date a report is filed under subdivision (d) of Section 1530 and the date the property is paid or delivered under Section 1532.

(B) The agreement requires the owner to pay a fee or compensation prior to approval of the claim and payment of the recovered property to the owner by the Controller.

(2)An agreement to locate, deliver, recover, or assist in the recovery of property reported under Section 1530 made after payment or delivery under Section 1532 is valid if it meets all of the following requirements:

(A)The agreement is in writing and includes a disclosure of the nature and value of the property, that the Controller is in possession of the property, and the address where the owner can directly claim the property from the Controller.

(B)The agreement is signed by the owner after receipt of the disclosure described in subparagraph (A).

(C)The fee or compensation agreed upon is not in excess of 10 percent of the recovered property.

(3)This subdivision shall not be construed to prevent an owner from asserting, at any time, that an agreement to locate property is based upon an excessive or unjust consideration.

(b)Notwithstanding any other provision of law, records of the Controller's office pertaining to unclaimed property are not available for public inspection or copying until after publication of notice of the property or, if publication of notice of the property is not required, until one year after delivery of the property to the Controller.

Amended by Stats 2022 ch 282 (AB 2280),s 5, eff. 1/1/2023.

Amended by Stats. 1990, Ch. 450, Sec. 16. Effective July 31, 1990.

Chapter 8 - PROPERTY IN CUSTODY OF FEDERAL OFFICERS, AGENCIES, AND DEPARTMENTS

Section 1600 - Policy of state to discover property in custody of United States

It is the policy of this State:

(a) To discover property in the custody of officers, departments, and agencies of the United States, which property is unclaimed by owners whose addresses are known or presumed to be in this State;

(b) To provide a procedure for judicial determination of the right of the State to receive custody of such unclaimed property; and

(c) To authorize expenditure of state funds to pay the proportionate cost of the State in discovering such unclaimed property and to hold the United States harmless against claims concerning such property when delivered to the custody of the State in accordance with this chapter.

Added by Stats. 1959, Ch. 1801.

Section 1601 - Definitions

As used in this chapter:

(a) "Unclaimed property" means any tangible personal property or intangible personal property, including choses in action in amounts certain, and all debts owed or entrusted funds or other property held by any federal agency or any officer or employee thereof, whether occasioned by contract or operation of law or otherwise, except bonuses and gratuities, which has remained unclaimed by the owner for:

(1) Twenty years from the date of maturity or call for payment, if arising from transactions under the public debt; or

(2) Twenty years after the last transaction concerning principal or interest, if deposits in the postal savings system; or

(3) Five years after the property first became payable, demandable, or returnable, if arising from any other transaction.

(b) "Owner" means any person, including his or her legal representative, who has or had a legal or equitable interest in unclaimed property. The owner shall be conclusively presumed to be the person to whom unclaimed property was or is payable or returnable according to the records of the United States Government. If two or more persons are interested in the property, and the extent of their respective interests is unknown, it shall be presumed that their interests in such property are equal.

(c) "Person" includes any individual, partnership, corporation, limited liability company, unincorporated association, or other legal entity.

Amended by Stats. 1994, Ch. 1010, Sec. 64. Effective January 1, 1995.

Section 1602 - Agreement for payments of state's share of costs incurred by United States in examining records

The Controller is authorized to enter into agreements establishing the time and manner for payments of this State's proportionate share of the actual and necessary cost incurred by the United States in examining records and reporting information to this State as such share of such cost shall be determined pursuant to federal law. Said agreements may provide for single payments at stated times over a period of years. The State Controller shall make all payments at the time and in the manner provided in said agreements.

Added by Stats. 1959, Ch. 1801.

Section 1603 - United States held harmless against claim concerning property delivered to state

The State hereby undertakes to hold the United States harmless against any claim concerning property delivered to the custody of the State in accordance with the provisions of this chapter. In the event an action or proceeding on such claim is brought against the United States the Attorney General shall intervene therein. The State consents to suit by such claimant in such contingency and any defense in favor of the United States shall be available to and urged by the State.

Added by Stats. 1959, Ch. 1801.

Section 1604 - Property subject to delivery to state if last known address of owner in state

(a) All unclaimed intangible property, together with all interest and other increments accruing thereto, is subject to delivery to this state if the last known address of the owner is in this state. If the last known address of an owner is in this state, any other owner's address which is unknown shall be presumed to be in this state. If the last known addresses of owners are in this state and in one or more other states, the addresses of other owners whose addresses are unknown shall be presumed to be within this state if the federal agency having custody of the unclaimed property initially acquired possession in this state. If the records of the United States do not disclose the address of any owner of unclaimed property, such address shall be presumed to be within this state if the federal agency having custody of such property initially acquired possession in this state. All addresses presumed to be within this state are presumed to be within the County of Sacramento. For the purposes of this chapter, it shall be presumed that the situs of unclaimed intangible property is in this state if the last known or presumed address of the owner is in this state.

(b) All unclaimed tangible property is subject to delivery to this state if the federal agency having custody of the unclaimed property initially acquired possession in this state.

Amended by Stats. 1968, Ch. 356.

Section 1605 - Certification by Governor that United States will be compensated for cost of examining records

The Governor shall certify to the Comptroller General or other proper officer of the United States that the law of this State provides effective means whereby the United States shall be compensated at reasonable times for this State's proportionate share of the actual and necessary cost of examining records and for reporting information and whereby the United States shall be held harmless in the event of claim for property delivered to this State in accordance with the provisions of this chapter.

Such certification shall be made on the thirtieth day of June next following the effective date of any federal statute requiring such certification.

Added by Stats. 1959, Ch. 1801.

Section 1606 - Request that Comptroller General report previously unreported information

On the thirtieth day of June next following the date of certification by the Governor, and annually thereafter, the Controller shall request the Comptroller General or other proper officer of the United States to report all previously unreported information relating to unclaimed property as determined by that officer pursuant to federal law.

Added by Stats. 1959, Ch. 1801.

Section 1607 - Copy of report posted at superior court courthouses; claim against United States by person asserting interest in property

When a report is received from the Comptroller General or other proper officer of the United States, the Controller shall prepare and forward a copy thereof to the clerk of the superior court of each county within this state and the clerk shall post a copy at the courthouse for a period of 60 days. Any person asserting an interest in property mentioned in the report may elect to claim against the United States under the laws of the United States, in which event and within 90 days following the date of initial posting by the clerk the person shall notify the Controller of the asserted interest and intention to so claim. The Controller shall omit the property from any claim by the state until such time as the asserted interest may be finally determined against the claimant. The interest may not thereafter be asserted against the state.
Amended by Stats 2003 ch 62 (SB 600),s 27, eff. 1/1/2004.
Amended by Stats 2002 ch 784 (SB 1316),s 84, eff. 1/1/2003.

Section 1608 - Expiration of period of time for commencing proceeding not to affect state's right to acquire possession of property
The expiration of any period of time specified by statute or court order, during which an action or proceeding may be commenced or enforced to obtain payment of a claim for funds or delivery of property shall not affect the right of this State to acquire possession of unclaimed property in accordance with the provisions of this chapter.
Added by Stats. 1959, Ch. 1801.

Section 1609 - Proceeding commenced by Attorney General to determine state's right to custody of property
Within 120 days following the date of initial posting by the clerk of the superior court, the Attorney General shall commence a proceeding by filing a petition to determine the state's right to custody of all property mentioned in such report and unclaimed within the time and in the manner provided by Section 1607. The proceeding shall be commenced and heard in the superior court in the County of Sacramento and venue shall not be affected by the provisions of Section 401, Code of Civil Procedure.
The petition shall name as respondents all persons known to have been interested and "all persons unknown claiming any title or interest in or to the property described or referred to in the petition." If the records of the United States fail to disclose with reasonable certainty the identity or number of owners or claimants of specific funds or other personal property, or the extent of their interests therein, such persons may be designated and described as a class, to wit, as "all unknown owners or claimants to the funds or property mentioned in or affected by ____," and, as the case may be, the petition shall identify and set forth the court actions or proceedings to the credit of which such funds or other property are held, or the accounts or other identifying references under which they are carried upon the records of the United States. The petition shall describe or refer to the property, and may include one or more items, as the Attorney General may be advised, without prejudice to his right to commence subsequent proceedings relating to other items not included. The petition shall also state the name of the owner and his last address as known or as presumed under this chapter, and shall set forth the facts and circumstances by virtue of which it is claimed that such funds or property are subject to custody by the state. Any number of respondents may be joined whether they reside in the same or different counties, and any number of causes of action may be joined and need not be separately stated.
Amended by Stats 2002 ch 784 (SB 1316),s 85, eff. 1/1/2003.

Section 1610 - Notice of proceeding
No summons or other process shall issue to direct the appearance and answer of a respondent. Commencing within five days after filing petition, notice of the proceeding shall be published once each week for three consecutive weeks in a newspaper of general circulation published within the County of Sacramento. At the time the notice is first published, a copy of the petition and notice shall be posted at the courthouse in the county where each defendant was last known or presumed to have had an address. Such petition and such notice shall remain posted for 45 days. The notice of proceeding shall advise that the State seeks custody of unclaimed property held by the United States. The names but not the addresses of the respondents shall be contained in the notice with a statement that such persons are believed to live or to have lived within the State and are believed to be or to have been owners of the unclaimed property. The notice shall not contain a description of the unclaimed property but shall advise that such description together with the last known or presumed addresses of owners may be determined by examining the petition filed in the proceeding. The petition and its place of filing shall be sufficiently identified and described. The notice shall advise that persons claiming an interest must answer the petition within the time prescribed by law, which time shall be stated, if they elect to pursue their claims against the United States, otherwise their rights to property shall be preserved subject to delayed delivery as provided by law. The notice shall advise that Section 1611, Code of Civil Procedure, should be consulted for the time, form, and costs of an answer.
The notice shall be deemed completed 45 days after the date of first publication, whereupon the court shall have full and complete jurisdiction over the property described in the petition and not claimed within the time or in the manner provided in Section 1611, and shall have full and complete jurisdiction to determine the right of the State to custody and to render an appropriate judgment therefor.
Added by Stats. 1959, Ch. 1801.

Section 1611 - Response to petition
Any person, whether or not named in the petition, may within 15 days after completion of notice respond to the petition by answer describing the property, asserting an interest as owner or successor, and declaring an intention to claim the same from the United States under the laws of the United States. Such answer shall not be filed unless accompanied by the sum of ten dollars ($10) for deposit in court, and no other answer or response shall be filed by or on behalf of a claimant. The court shall strike from the petition and dismiss from the proceeding all property described in the answer. The funds on deposit shall be transmitted by the court to the Controller and shall be received for deposit in the abandoned property account in the Unclaimed Property Fund as total reimbursement for costs and services expended on behalf of the claimant. Such dismissal shall be without prejudice to a subsequent petition should it appear that the claimant is not entitled to the property, and the interest asserted in said answer shall not thereafter be asserted against the State.
Added by Stats. 1959, Ch. 1801.

Section 1612 - Application for judgment, findings and declaration by court
Within 20 days following expiration of time for filing answer under Section 1611, the Attorney General shall apply to the court for a judgment relating to all property set forth in the petition and not claimed by answer. The court shall find that such property appears to be or to have been owned by persons residing within this State and remains unclaimed by such persons. The court shall declare that the property, which shall be described, is subject to custody of the State and shall be delivered to and received by the State of California to be retained until such time as it may be claimed pursuant to law.
Added by Stats. 1959, Ch. 1801.

Section 1613 - Request for delivery or payment of property described in judgment
The Controller shall request delivery or payment of all unclaimed property described in the judgment declaring the right of the State to receive custody of such property. The request shall be accompanied by a certified copy of said judgment and shall be directed to such officer, agency, or department of the United States as may be designated for such purposes by federal law. The Controller shall furnish receipts for all property delivered or paid.
Added by Stats. 1959, Ch. 1801.

Section 1614 - Deposit or sale of property received
Property received under this chapter shall be deposited or sold by the State Controller as though received under Chapter 7 (commencing with Section 1500) of this title. Property received under this chapter shall not be subject to claim within two years following the date upon which it is paid to or received by the state. Thereafter, claims shall be made in the manner provided in Chapter 7 (commencing with Section 1500) of this title.

Amended by Stats. 1968, Ch. 356.

Section 1615 - Money in abandoned property account appropriated for expenditure by Controller

All money in the abandoned property account in the Unclaimed Property Fund is hereby continuously appropriated to the State Controller without regard to fiscal years, for expenditure in accordance with this chapter for the following purposes:

(a) For payment of the proportionate costs of this State pursuant to the terms of any contract entered with the United States;

(b) For payment of sums necessary to indemnify the United States for losses occasioned by claims to property delivered to the custody of this State.

Added by Stats. 1959, Ch. 1801.

Title 11 - MONEY JUDGMENTS OF OTHER JURISDICTIONS
Chapter 1 - SISTER STATE MONEY JUDGMENTS

Section 1710.10 - Definitions

As used in this chapter:

(a) "Judgment creditor" means the person or persons who can bring an action to enforce a sister state judgment.

(b) "Judgment debtor" means the person or persons against whom an action to enforce a sister state judgment can be brought.

(c) "Sister state judgment" means that part of any judgment, decree, or order of a court of a state of the United States, other than California, which requires the payment of money, but does not include a support order as defined in Section 155 of the Family Code.

Title heading amended by Stats 2017 ch 168 (AB 905),s 1, eff. 1/1/2018.

Chapter heading amended by Stats 2017 ch 168 (AB 905),s 2, eff. 1/1/2018.

Amended by Stats. 1992, Ch. 163, Sec. 64. Effective January 1, 1993. Operative January 1, 1994, by Sec. 161 of Ch. 163.

Section 1710.15 - Application by judgment creditor for entry of judgment based on sister state judgment

(a) A judgment creditor may apply for the entry of a judgment based on a sister state judgment by filing an application pursuant to Section 1710.20.

(b) The application shall be executed under oath and shall include all of the following:

(1) A statement that an action in this state on the sister state judgment is not barred by the applicable statute of limitations.

(2) A statement, based on the applicant's information and belief, that no stay of enforcement of the sister state judgment is currently in effect in the sister state.

(3) A statement of the amount remaining unpaid under the sister state judgment and, if accrued interest on the sister state judgment is to be included in the California judgment, a statement of the amount of interest accrued on the sister state judgment (computed at the rate of interest applicable to the judgment under the law of the sister state), a statement of the rate of interest applicable to the judgment under the law of the sister state, and a citation to the law of the sister state establishing the rate of interest.

(4) A statement that no action based on the sister state judgment is currently pending in any court in this state and that no judgment based on the sister state judgment has previously been entered in any proceeding in this state.

(5) Where the judgment debtor is an individual, a statement setting forth the name and last known residence address of the judgment debtor. Where the judgment debtor is a corporation, a statement of the corporation's name, place of incorporation, and whether the corporation, if foreign, has qualified to do business in this state under the provisions of Chapter 21 (commencing with Section 2100) of Division 1 of Title 1 of the Corporations Code. Where the judgment debtor is a partnership, a statement of the name of the partnership, whether it is a foreign partnership, and, if it is a foreign partnership, whether it has filed a statement pursuant to Section 15800 of the Corporations Code designating an agent for service of process. Except for facts which are matters of public record in this state, the statements required by this paragraph may be made on the basis of the judgment creditor's information and belief.

(6) A statement setting forth the name and address of the judgment creditor.

(c) A properly authenticated copy of the sister state judgment shall be attached to the application.

Amended by Stats. 1985, Ch. 106, Sec. 11.

Section 1710.20 - Filing application; proper county

(a) An application for entry of a judgment based on a sister state judgment shall be filed in a superior court.

(b) Subject to the power of the court to transfer proceedings under this chapter pursuant to Title 4 (commencing with Section 392) of Part 2, the proper county for the filing of an application is any of the following:

(1) The county in which any judgment debtor resides.

(2) If no judgment debtor is a resident, any county in this state.

(c) A case in which the sister state judgment amounts to twenty-five thousand dollars ($25,000) or less is a limited civil case.

Amended by Stats 2002 ch 784 (SB 1316),s 86, eff. 1/1/2003.

Section 1710.25 - Amounts of judgment entered

(a) Upon the filing of the application, the clerk shall enter a judgment based upon the application for the total of the following amounts as shown therein:

(1) The amount remaining unpaid under the sister state judgment.

(2) The amount of interest accrued on the sister state judgment (computed at the rate of interest applicable to the judgment under the law of the sister state).

(3) The amount of the fee for filing the application for entry of the sister state judgment.

(b) Entry shall be made in the same manner as entry of an original judgment of the court. From the time of entry, interest shall accrue on the judgment so entered at the rate of interest applicable to a judgment entered in this state.

Amended by Stats. 1984, Ch. 311, Sec. 4.

Section 1710.30 - Service of notice of entry of judgment

(a) Notice of entry of judgment shall be served promptly by the judgment creditor upon the judgment debtor in the manner provided for service of summons by Article 3 (commencing with Section 415.10) of Chapter 4 of Title 5 of Part 2. Notice shall be in a form prescribed by the Judicial Council and shall inform the judgment debtor that the judgment debtor has 30 days within which to make a motion to vacate the judgment.

(b) The fee for service of the notice of entry of judgment under this section is an item of costs recoverable in the same manner as statutory fees for service of a writ as provided in Chapter 5 (commencing with Section 685.010) of Division 1 of Title 9 of Part 2, but such fee may not exceed the amount allowed to a public officer or employee in this state for such service.

Amended by Stats. 1982, Ch. 497, Sec. 79. Operative July 1, 1983, by Sec. 185 of Ch. 497.

Section 1710.35 - Effect of judgment

Except as otherwise provided in this chapter, a judgment entered pursuant to this chapter shall have the same effect as an original money judgment of the court and may be enforced or satisfied in like manner.

Amended by Stats. 1984, Ch. 311, Sec. 5.

Section 1710.40 - Vacation of judgment

(a) A judgment entered pursuant to this chapter may be vacated on any ground which would be a defense to an action in this state on the sister state judgment, including the ground that the amount of interest accrued on the sister state judgment and included in the judgment entered pursuant to this chapter is incorrect.
(b) Not later than 30 days after service of notice of entry of judgment pursuant to Section 1710.30, proof of which has been made in the manner provided by Article 5 (commencing with Section 417.10) of Chapter 4 of Title 5 of Part 2, the judgment debtor, on written notice to the judgment creditor, may make a motion to vacate the judgment under this section.
(c) Upon the hearing of the motion to vacate the judgment under this section, the judgment may be vacated upon any ground provided in subdivision (a) and another and different judgment entered, including, but not limited to, another and different judgment for the judgment creditor if the decision of the court is that the judgment creditor is entitled to such different judgment. The decision of the court on the motion to vacate the judgment shall be given and filed with the clerk of court in the manner provided in Sections 632, 634, and 635, except that the court is not required to make any written findings and conclusions if the amount of the judgment as entered under Section 1710.25 does not exceed one thousand dollars ($1,000).
Amended by Stats. 1977, Ch. 232.

Section 1710.45 - Writ of execution or enforcement on judgment
(a) Except as otherwise provided in this section, a writ of execution on a judgment entered pursuant to this chapter shall not issue, nor may the judgment be enforced by other means, until at least 30 days after the judgment creditor serves notice of entry of the judgment upon the judgment debtor, proof of which has been made in the manner provided by Article 5 (commencing with Section 417.10) of Chapter 4 of Title 5 of Part 2.
(b) A writ of execution may be issued, or other enforcement sought, before service of the notice of entry of judgment if the judgment debtor is any of the following:
(1) An individual who does not reside in this state.
(2) A foreign corporation not qualified to do business in this state under the provisions of Chapter 21 (commencing with Section 2100) of Division 1 of Title 1 of the Corporations Code.
(3) A foreign partnership which has not filed a statement pursuant to Section 15700 of the Corporations Code designating an agent for service of process.
(c) The court may order that a writ of execution be issued, or may permit enforcement by other means, before service of the notice of entry of judgment if the court finds upon an ex parte showing that great or irreparable injury would result to the judgment creditor if issuance of the writ or enforcement were delayed as provided in subdivision (a).
(d) Property levied upon pursuant to a writ issued under subdivision (b) or (c) or otherwise sought to be applied to the satisfaction of the judgment shall not be sold or distributed before 30 days after the judgment creditor serves notice of entry of the judgment upon the judgment debtor, proof of which has been made in the manner provided by Article 5 (commencing with Section 417.10) of Chapter 4 of Title 5 of Part 2. However, if property levied upon is perishable, it may be sold in order to prevent its destruction or loss of value, but the proceeds of the sale shall not be distributed to the judgment creditor before the date sale of nonperishable property is permissible.
Amended by Stats. 1982, Ch. 497, Sec. 80. Operative July 1, 1983, by Sec. 185 of Ch. 497.

Section 1710.50 - Stay of enforcement
(a) The court shall grant a stay of enforcement where:
(1) An appeal from the sister state judgment is pending or may be taken in the state which originally rendered the judgment. Under this paragraph, enforcement shall be stayed until the proceedings on appeal have been concluded or the time for appeal has expired.
(2) A stay of enforcement of the sister state judgment has been granted in the sister state. Under this paragraph, enforcement shall be stayed until the sister state stay of enforcement expires or is vacated.
(3) The judgment debtor has made a motion to vacate pursuant to Section 1710.40. Under this paragraph, enforcement shall be stayed until the judgment debtor's motion to vacate is determined.
(4) Any other circumstance exists where the interests of justice require a stay of enforcement.
(b) The court may grant a stay of enforcement under this section on its own motion, on ex parte motion, or on noticed motion.
(c) The court shall grant a stay of enforcement under this section on such terms and conditions as are just including but not limited to the following:
(1) The court may require an undertaking in an amount it determines to be just, but the amount of the undertaking shall not exceed double the amount of the judgment creditor's claim.
(2) If a writ of execution has been issued, the court may order that it remain in effect.
(3) If property of the judgment debtor has been levied upon under a writ of execution, the court may order the levying officer to retain possession of the property capable of physical possession and to maintain the levy on other property.
Added by Stats. 1974, Ch. 211.

Section 1710.55 - Entry of judgment based on sister state judgment prohibited
No judgment based on a sister state judgment may be entered pursuant to this chapter in any of the following cases:
(a) A stay of enforcement of the sister state judgment is currently in effect in the sister state.
(b) An action based on the sister state judgment is currently pending in any court in this state.
(c) A judgment based on the sister state judgment has previously been entered in any proceeding in this state.
Added by Stats. 1974, Ch. 211.

Section 1710.60 - Action to enforce sister state judgment
(a) Except as provided in subdivision (b), nothing in this chapter affects any right a judgment creditor may have to bring an action to enforce a sister state judgment.
(b) No action to enforce a sister state judgment may be brought where a judgment based on such sister state judgment has previously been entered pursuant to this chapter.
Added by Stats. 1974, Ch. 211.

Section 1710.65 - Action by judgment creditor based on part of judgment not requiring payment of money
The entry of a judgment based on a sister state judgment pursuant to this chapter does not limit the right of the judgment creditor to bring an action based on the part of a judgment of a sister state which does not require the payment of money, nor does the bringing of such an action limit the right of the judgment creditor to obtain entry of judgment based on the sister state judgment pursuant to this chapter.
Added by Stats. 1974, Ch. 211.

Chapter 2 - FOREIGN-COUNTRY MONEY JUDGMENTS
Section 1713 - Title of act
This chapter may be cited as the Uniform Foreign-Country Money Judgments Recognition Act.
Added by Stats 2007 ch 212 (SB 639),s 2, eff. 1/1/2008.

Section 1714 - Definitions
As used in this chapter:
(a) "Foreign country" means a government other than any of the following:

(1) The United States.
(2) A state, district, commonwealth, territory, or insular possession of the United States.
(3) A federally recognized Indian nation, tribe, pueblo, band, or Alaska Native village.
(4) Any other government with regard to which the decision in this state as to whether to recognize a judgment of that government's courts is initially subject to determination under the Full Faith and Credit Clause of the United States Constitution.
(b) "Foreign-country judgment" means a judgment of a court of a foreign country.
Amended by Stats 2017 ch 168 (AB 905),s 3, eff. 1/1/2018.
Amended by Stats 2014 ch 243 (SB 406),s 2, eff. 1/1/2015.
Added by Stats 2007 ch 212 (SB 639),s 2, eff. 1/1/2008.

Section 1715 - Applicability of chapter

(a) Except as otherwise provided in subdivision (b), this chapter applies to a foreign-country judgment to the extent that the judgment both:
(1) Grants or denies recovery of a sum of money.
(2) Under the law of the foreign country where rendered, is final, conclusive, and enforceable.
(b) This chapter does not apply to a foreign-country judgment, even if the judgment grants or denies recovery of a sum of money, to the extent that the judgment is any of the following:
(1) A judgment for taxes.
(2) A fine or other penalty.
(3)
(A) A judgment for divorce, support, or maintenance, or other judgment rendered in connection with domestic relations.
(B) A judgment for divorce, support, or maintenance, or other judgment rendered in connection with domestic relations may be recognized by a court of this state pursuant to Section 1723.
(c) A party seeking recognition of a foreign-country judgment has the burden of establishing that the foreign-country judgment is entitled to recognition under this chapter.
Added by Stats 2007 ch 212 (SB 639),s 2, eff. 1/1/2008.

Section 1716 - State required to recognize judgments to which chapter applies; judgments state shall not to recognize; judgments state not required to recognize

(a) Except as otherwise provided in subdivisions (b), (c), (d), and (f), a court of this state shall recognize a foreign-country judgment to which this chapter applies.
(b) A court of this state shall not recognize a foreign-country judgment if any of the following apply:
(1) The judgment was rendered under a judicial system that does not provide impartial tribunals or procedures compatible with the requirements of due process of law.
(2) The foreign court did not have personal jurisdiction over the defendant.
(3) The foreign court did not have jurisdiction over the subject matter.
(c)
(1) A court of this state shall not recognize a foreign-country judgment if any of the following apply:
(A) The defendant in the proceeding in the foreign court did not receive notice of the proceeding in sufficient time to enable the defendant to defend.
(B) The judgment was obtained by fraud that deprived the losing party of an adequate opportunity to present its case.
(C) The judgment or the cause of action or claim for relief on which the judgment is based is repugnant to the public policy of this state or of the United States.
(D) The proceeding in the foreign court was contrary to an agreement between the parties under which the dispute in question was to be determined otherwise than by proceedings in that foreign court.
(E) In the case of jurisdiction based only on personal service, the foreign court was a seriously inconvenient forum for the trial of the action.
(F) The judgment was rendered in circumstances that raise substantial doubt about the integrity of the rendering court with respect to the judgment.
(G) The specific proceeding in the foreign court leading to the judgment was not compatible with the requirements of due process of law.
(2) Notwithstanding an applicable ground for nonrecognition under paragraph (1), the court may nonetheless recognize a foreign-country judgment if the party seeking recognition of the judgment demonstrates good reason to recognize the judgment that outweighs the ground for nonrecognition.
(d) A court of this state is not required to recognize a foreign-country judgment if the judgment conflicts with another final and conclusive judgment.
(e) If the party seeking recognition of a foreign-country judgment has met its burden of establishing recognition of the foreign-country judgment pursuant to subdivision (c) of Section 1715, a party resisting recognition of a foreign-country judgment has the burden of establishing that a ground for nonrecognition stated in subdivision (b), (c), or (d) exists.
(f) A court of this state shall not recognize a foreign-country judgment for defamation if that judgment is not recognizable under Section 4102 of Title 28 of the United States Code.
Amended by Stats 2017 ch 168 (AB 905),s 5, eff. 1/1/2018.
Amended by Stats 2009 ch 579 (SB 320),s 1, eff. 1/1/2010.
Added by Stats 2007 ch 212 (SB 639),s 2, eff. 1/1/2008.

Section 1717 - Bases for personal jurisdiction

(a) For the purpose of paragraph (2) of subdivision (b) of Section 1716, a foreign court lacks personal jurisdiction over a defendant if either of the following conditions is met:
(1) The foreign court lacks a basis for exercising personal jurisdiction that would be sufficient according to the standards governing personal jurisdiction in this state.
(2) The foreign court lacks personal jurisdiction under its own law.
(b) A foreign-country judgment shall not be refused recognition for lack of personal jurisdiction under paragraph (1) of subdivision (a) if any of the following apply:
(1) The defendant was served with process personally in the foreign country.
(2) The defendant voluntarily appeared in the proceeding, other than for the purpose of protecting property seized or threatened with seizure in the proceeding or of contesting the jurisdiction of the court over the defendant.
(3) The defendant, before the commencement of the proceeding, had agreed to submit to the jurisdiction of the foreign court with respect to the subject matter involved.
(4) The defendant was domiciled in the foreign country when the proceeding was instituted or was a corporation or other form of business organization that had its principal place of business in, or was organized under the laws of, the foreign country.

(5) The defendant had a business office in the foreign country and the proceeding in the foreign court involved a cause of action or claim for relief arising out of business done by the defendant through that office in the foreign country.

(6) The defendant operated a motor vehicle or airplane in the foreign country and the proceeding involved a cause of action or claim for relief arising out of that operation.

(c) The list of bases for personal jurisdiction in subdivision (b) is not exclusive. The courts of this state may recognize bases of personal jurisdiction other than those listed in subdivision (b) as sufficient for the purposes of paragraph (1) of subdivision (a).

Amended by Stats 2017 ch 168 (AB 905),s 6, eff. 1/1/2018.
Amended by Stats 2009 ch 579 (SB 320),s 2, eff. 1/1/2010.
Added by Stats 2007 ch 212 (SB 639),s 2, eff. 1/1/2008.

Section 1718 - Recognition issue raise by filing action; raised by filing counterclaim, cross-claim or affirmative defense

(a) If recognition of a foreign-country judgment is sought as an original matter, the issue of recognition shall be raised by filing an action seeking recognition of the foreign-country judgment.

(b) If recognition of a foreign-country judgment is sought in a pending action, the issue of recognition may be raised by counterclaim, cross-claim, or affirmative defense.

Added by Stats 2007 ch 212 (SB 639),s 2, eff. 1/1/2008.

Section 1719 - Conclusive effect of judgment; enforcement

If the court in a proceeding under Section 1718 finds that the foreign-country judgment is entitled to recognition under this chapter then, to the extent that the foreign-country judgment grants or denies recovery of a sum of money, the foreign-country judgment is both of the following:

(a) Conclusive between the parties to the same extent as the judgment of a sister state entitled to full faith and credit in this state would be conclusive.

(b) Enforceable in the same manner and to the same extent as a judgment rendered in this state.

Added by Stats 2007 ch 212 (SB 639),s 2, eff. 1/1/2008.

Section 1720 - Stay if appeal pending or will be taken

If a party establishes that an appeal from a foreign-country judgment is pending or will be taken in the foreign country, the court may stay any proceedings with regard to the foreign-country judgment until the appeal is concluded, the time for appeal expires, or the appellant has had sufficient time to prosecute the appeal and has failed to do so.

Added by Stats 2007 ch 212 (SB 639),s 2, eff. 1/1/2008.

Section 1721 - Time for commencing action to recognize judgment

An action to recognize a foreign-country judgment shall be commenced within the earlier of the time during which the foreign-country judgment is effective in the foreign country or 10 years from the date that the foreign-country judgment became effective in the foreign country.

Added by Stats 2007 ch 212 (SB 639),s 2, eff. 1/1/2008.

Section 1722 - Need to promote uniformity of law

In applying and construing this uniform act, consideration shall be given to the need to promote uniformity of the law with respect to its subject matter among states that enact it.

Added by Stats 2007 ch 212 (SB 639),s 2, eff. 1/1/2008.

Section 1723 - Recognition under principles of comity or otherwise

This chapter does not prevent the recognition under principles of comity or otherwise of a foreign-country judgment not within the scope of this chapter.

Added by Stats 2007 ch 212 (SB 639),s 2, eff. 1/1/2008.

Section 1724 - Effective date

(a) This chapter applies to all actions commenced on or after the effective date of this chapter in which the issue of recognition of a foreign-country judgment is raised.

(b) The former Uniform Foreign Money-Judgments Recognition Act (Chapter 2 (commencing with Section 1713) of Title 11 of Part 3) applies to all actions commenced before the effective date of this chapter in which the issue of recognition of a foreign-country judgment is raised.

Added by Stats 2007 ch 212 (SB 639),s 2, eff. 1/1/2008.

Section 1725 - Declaratory relief

(a) If all of the following conditions are satisfied, a person against whom a foreign-country defamation judgment was rendered may seek declaratory relief with respect to liability for the judgment or a determination that the judgment is not recognizable under section 1716:

(1) The person is a resident or other person or entity amenable to jurisdiction in this state.

(2) The person either has assets in this state that may be subject to an enforcement proceeding to satisfy the foreign-country defamation judgment or may have to take actions in this state to comply with the foreign-country defamation judgment.

(3) The publication at issue was published in this state.

(b) A court of this state has jurisdiction to determine a declaratory relief action or issue a determination pursuant to this section and has personal jurisdiction over the person or entity who obtained the foreign-country defamation judgment.

(c) This section shall apply to a foreign-country defamation judgment regardless of when it was rendered.

Added by Stats 2017 ch 168 (AB 905),s 7, eff. 1/1/2018.

Chapter 3 - TRIBAL COURT CIVIL MONEY JUDGMENT ACT

Section 1730 - Short title

This chapter shall be known and may be cited as the Tribal Court Civil Money Judgment Act.

Amended by Stats 2017 ch 168 (AB 905),s 10, eff. 1/1/2018.
Chapter heading added by Stats 2017 ch 168 (AB 905),s 9, eff. 1/1/2018.
Title heading repealed by Stats 2017 ch 168 (AB 905),s 8, eff. 1/1/2018.
Added by Stats 2014 ch 243 (SB 406),s 4, eff. 1/1/2015.

Section 1731 - [Effective Until 1/1/2024] Scope

(a) This chapter governs the procedures by which the superior courts of the State of California recognize and enter tribal court money judgments of any federally recognized Indian tribe. Determinations regarding recognition and entry of a tribal court money judgment pursuant to state law shall have no effect upon the independent authority of that judgment. To the extent not inconsistent with this chapter, the Code of Civil Procedure shall apply.

(b) This chapter does not apply to any of the following tribal court money judgments:

(1) For taxes, fines, or other penalties.

(2) For which federal law requires that states grant full faith and credit recognition, including child support orders under the Full Faith and Credit for Child Support Orders Act (28 U.S.C. Sec. 1738B) , except for the purposes of recognizing a tribal court order establishing the right of a child or other dependent of a participant in a retirement plan or other plan of deferred compensation to an assignment of all or a portion of the benefits payable.

(3) For which state law provides for recognition, including child support orders recognized under the Uniform Child Custody Jurisdiction and Enforcement Act (Part 3 (commencing with Section 3400) of Division 8 of the Family Code), other forms of family support orders under the Uniform Interstate Family Support Act (Part 6 (commencing with Section 5700.101) of Division 9 of the Family Code), except for the purposes of recognizing a tribal court order establishing the right of a spouse, former spouse, child, or other dependent of a participant in a retirement plan or other plan of deferred compensation to an assignment of all or a portion of the benefits payable.

(4) For decedents' estates, guardianships, conservatorships, internal affairs of trusts, powers of attorney, or other tribal court money judgments that arise in proceedings that are or would be governed by the Probate Code.

(c) Nothing in this chapter shall be deemed or construed to expand or limit the jurisdiction of either the state or any Indian tribe.

Amended by Stats 2021 ch 58 (AB 627),s 1, eff. 1/1/2022.
Amended by Stats 2017 ch 168 (AB 905),s 11, eff. 1/1/2018.
Amended by Stats 2015 ch 493 (SB 646),s 1, eff. 1/1/2016.
Added by Stats 2014 ch 243 (SB 406),s 4, eff. 1/1/2015.

This section is set out more than once due to postponed, multiple, or conflicting amendments.

Section 1731 - [Effective 1/1/2024] Scope

(a) This chapter governs the procedures by which the superior courts of the State of California recognize and enter tribal court money judgments of any federally recognized Indian tribe. Determinations regarding recognition and entry of a tribal court money judgment pursuant to state law shall have no effect upon the independent authority of that judgment. To the extent not inconsistent with this chapter, the Code of Civil Procedure shall apply.

(b) This chapter does not apply to any of the following tribal court money judgments:

(1) For taxes, fines, or other penalties, except for tribal taxes as described in clause 3 of subparagraph (B) of paragraph (3) of subdivision (d) of Section 1616 of Article 10 of Chapter 4 of Division 2 of Title 18 of the California Code of Regulations, and related interest or penalties.

(2) For which federal law requires that states grant full faith and credit recognition, including child support orders under the Full Faith and Credit for Child Support Orders Act (28 U.S.C. Sec. 1738B), except for the purposes of recognizing a tribal court order establishing the right of a child or other dependent of a participant in a retirement plan or other plan of deferred compensation to an assignment of all or a portion of the benefits payable.

(3) For which state law provides for recognition, including child support orders recognized under the Uniform Child Custody Jurisdiction and Enforcement Act (Part 3 (commencing with Section 3400) of Division 8 of the Family Code), other forms of family support orders under the Uniform Interstate Family Support Act (Part 6 (commencing with Section 5700.101) of Division 9 of the Family Code), except for the purposes of recognizing a tribal court order establishing the right of a spouse, former spouse, child, or other dependent of a participant in a retirement plan or other plan of deferred compensation to an assignment of all or a portion of the benefits payable.

(4) For decedents' estates, guardianships, conservatorships, internal affairs of trusts, powers of attorney, or other tribal court money judgments that arise in proceedings that are or would be governed by the Probate Code.

(c) Nothing in this chapter shall be deemed or construed to expand or limit the jurisdiction of either the state or any Indian tribe.

Amended by Stats 2023 ch 138 (AB 1139),s 1, eff. 1/1/2024.
Amended by Stats 2021 ch 58 (AB 627),s 1, eff. 1/1/2022.
Amended by Stats 2017 ch 168 (AB 905),s 11, eff. 1/1/2018.
Amended by Stats 2015 ch 493 (SB 646),s 1, eff. 1/1/2016.
Added by Stats 2014 ch 243 (SB 406),s 4, eff. 1/1/2015.

This section is set out more than once due to postponed, multiple, or conflicting amendments.

Section 1732 - Definitions

For purposes of this chapter:

(a) "Applicant" means the person or persons who can bring an action to enforce a tribal court money judgment.

(b) "Civil action or proceeding" means any action or proceeding that is not criminal, except for those actions or proceedings expressly excluded by subdivision (b) of Section 1731.

(c) "Due process" includes, but is not limited to, the right to be represented by legal counsel, to receive reasonable notice and an opportunity for a hearing, to call and cross-examine witnesses, and to present evidence and argument to an impartial decisionmaker.

(d) "Good cause" means a substantial reason, taking into account the prejudice or irreparable harm a party will suffer if a hearing is not held on an objection or not held within the time periods established by this chapter.

(e) "Respondent" means the person or persons against whom an action to enforce a tribal court money judgment can be brought.

(f) "Tribal court" means any court or other tribunal of any federally recognized Indian nation, tribe, pueblo, band, or Alaska Native village, duly established under tribal or federal law, including Courts of Indian Offenses organized pursuant to Part 11 of Title 25 of the Code of Federal Regulations.

(g) "Tribal court money judgment" means any written judgment, decree, or order of a tribal court for a specified amount of money that was issued in a civil action or proceeding that is final, conclusive, and enforceable by the tribal court in which it was issued and is duly authenticated in accordance with the laws and procedures of the tribe or tribal court.

Amended by Stats 2017 ch 168 (AB 905),s 12, eff. 1/1/2018.
Added by Stats 2014 ch 243 (SB 406),s 4, eff. 1/1/2015.

Section 1733 - Application for entry of judgment

(a) An application for entry of a judgment under this chapter shall be filed in a superior court.

(b) Subject to the power of the court to transfer proceedings under this chapter pursuant to Title 4 (commencing with Section 392) of Part 2, and except as provided in Section 1733.1, the proper county for the filing of an application is either of the following:

(1) The county in which any respondent resides or owns property.

(2) If no respondent is a resident, any county in this state.

(c) A case in which the tribal court money judgment amounts to twenty-five thousand dollars ($25,000) or less is a limited civil case.

Amended by Stats 2021 ch 58 (AB 627),s 2, eff. 1/1/2022.
Amended by Stats 2017 ch 168 (AB 905),s 13, eff. 1/1/2018.
Added by Stats 2014 ch 243 (SB 406),s 4, eff. 1/1/2015.

Section 1733.1 - Joint application for the recognition of a tribal court order

(a)

(1) If the parties to the underlying tribal court proceeding agree, the parties may file a joint application for the recognition of a tribal court order that establishes a right to child support, spousal support payments, or marital property rights to such spouse, former spouse, child, or other dependent of a participant in a retirement plan or other plan of deferred compensation, which order assigns all or a portion of the benefits payable with respect to the participant to an alternate payee.

(2) If one of the parties to a tribal court order described in paragraph (1) does not agree to join in the application, the other party may proceed by having the tribal court execute a certificate in lieu of the signature of the other party. The Judicial Council shall adopt a format for the certificate.

(3) The application shall be on a form adopted by the Judicial Council, executed under penalty of perjury by parties to the proceeding submitting the application.

(4) The application shall include the name, current address, telephone number, and email address of each party, the name and mailing address of the issuing tribal court, and a certified copy of the order to be recognized.

(b) The filing fee for an application filed under this section is one hundred dollars ($100).

(c) An application filed pursuant to this section may be filed in the county in which either one of the parties resides.

(d) Entry of the tribal court order under this section does not confer any jurisdiction on a court of this state to modify or enforce the tribal court order.

Amended by Stats 2022 ch 420 (AB 2960),s 14, eff. 1/1/2023.
Amended by Stats 2022 ch 28 (SB 1380),s 29, eff. 1/1/2023. Not implemented per s 168.
Added by Stats 2021 ch 58 (AB 627),s 3, eff. 1/1/2022.

Section 1734 - Form of application

(a) An applicant may apply for recognition and entry of a judgment based on a tribal court money judgment by filing an application in superior court pursuant to Section 1733.

(b) The application shall be executed under penalty of perjury and include all of the following information:

(1) The name and address of the tribal court that issued the judgment to be enforced and the date of the tribal court money judgment or any renewal thereof.

(2) The name and address of the party seeking recognition.

(3)

(A) Any of the following statements, as applicable:

(i) If the respondent is an individual, the name and last known residence address of the respondent.

(ii) If the respondent is a corporation, the corporation's name, place of incorporation, and whether the corporation, if foreign, has qualified to do business in this state under the provisions of Chapter 21 (commencing with Section 2100) of Division 1 of Title 1 of the Corporations Code.

(iii) If the respondent is a partnership, the name of the partnership, whether it is a foreign partnership, and if it is a foreign partnership, whether it has filed a statement pursuant to Section 15800 of the Corporations Code designating an agent for service of process.

(iv) If the respondent is a limited liability company, the company's name, whether it is a foreign company, and if so, whether it has filed a statement pursuant to Section 17060 of the Corporations Code.

(B) Except for facts that are matters of public record in this state, the statements required by this paragraph may be made on the basis of the applicant's information and belief.

(4) A statement that an action in this state to enforce the tribal court money judgment is not barred by the applicable statute of limitations.

(5) A statement, based on the applicant's information and belief, that the tribal court money judgment is final and that no stay of enforcement of the tribal court money judgment is currently in effect.

(6) A statement that includes all of the following:

(A) The amount of the award granted in the tribal court money judgment that remains unpaid.

(B) If accrued interest on the tribal court money judgment is to be included in the California judgment, the amount of interest accrued on the tribal court money judgment, computed at the rate of interest applicable to the judgment under the law of the tribal jurisdiction in which the tribal court money judgment was issued.

(C) The rate of interest applicable to the money judgment under the law of the jurisdiction in which the tribal court money judgment was issued.

(D) A citation to the supporting authority.

(7) A statement that no action based on the tribal court money judgment is currently pending in any state court and that no judgment based on the tribal court money judgment has previously been entered in any proceeding in this state.

(c) All of the following items shall be attached to the application:

(1) An authenticated copy of the tribal court money judgment, certified by the judge or clerk of the tribal court.

(2) A copy of the tribal court rules of procedure pursuant to which the tribal court money judgment was entered.

(3) A declaration under penalty of perjury by the tribal court clerk, applicant, or applicant's attorney stating, based on personal knowledge, that the case that resulted in the entry of the judgment was conducted in compliance with the tribal court's rules of procedure.

Added by Stats 2014 ch 243 (SB 406),s 4, eff. 1/1/2015.

Section 1735 - Service; notice

(a) Promptly upon the filing of an application pursuant to Section 1734, the applicant shall serve upon the respondent a notice of filing of the application to recognize and enter the tribal court money judgment, together with a copy of the application and any documents filed with the application. The notice of filing shall be in a form that shall be prescribed by the Judicial Council, and shall inform the respondent that the respondent has 30 days from service of the notice of filing to file objections to the enforcement of the tribal court money judgment. The notice shall include the name and address of the applicant and the applicant's attorney, if any, and the text of Sections 1736 and 1737.

(b) Except as provided in subdivision (c), service shall be made in the manner provided for service of summons by Article 3 (commencing with Section 415.10) of Chapter 4 of Title 5 of Part 2.

(c) If a respondent is the State of California or any of its officers, employees, departments, agencies, boards, or commissions, service of the notice of filing on that respondent may be by mail to the office of the Attorney General.

(d) The fee for service of the notice of filing under this section is an item of costs recoverable in the same manner as statutory fees for service of a writ as provided in Chapter 5 (commencing with Section 685.010) of Division 1 of Title 9 of Part 2, but the recoverable amount for that fee shall not exceed the amount allowed to a public officer or employee of this state for that service.

(e) The applicant shall file a proof of service of the notice promptly following service.

Amended by Stats 2021 ch 58 (AB 627),s 4, eff. 1/1/2022.
Added by Stats 2014 ch 243 (SB 406),s 4, eff. 1/1/2015.

Section 1736 - Entry of judgment

(a) If no objections are timely filed in accordance with Section 1737, the clerk shall certify that no objections were timely filed, and a judgment shall be entered.

(b) The judgment entered by the superior court shall be based on and contain the provisions and terms of the tribal court money judgment. The judgment shall be entered in the same manner, have the same effect, and be enforceable in the same manner as any civil judgment, order, or decree of a court of this state, except as provided in Section 1733.1.

Amended by Stats 2021 ch 58 (AB 627),s 5, eff. 1/1/2022.

Added by Stats 2014 ch 243 (SB 406),s 4, eff. 1/1/2015.

Section 1737 - Objections

(a) Any objection to the recognition and entry of the tribal court money judgment sought under Section 1734 shall be served and filed within 30 days of service of the notice of filing. If any objection is filed within this time period, the superior court shall set a time period for replies and set the matter for a hearing. The hearing shall be held by the superior court within 45 days from the date the objection is filed unless good cause exists for a later hearing. The only grounds for objecting to the recognition or enforcement of a tribal court money judgment are the grounds set forth in subdivisions (b), (c), and (d).

(b) A tribal court money judgment shall not be recognized and entered if the respondent demonstrates to the superior court that at least one of the following occurred:

(1) The tribal court did not have personal jurisdiction over the respondent.

(2) The tribal court did not have jurisdiction over the subject matter.

(3) The judgment was rendered under a judicial system that does not provide impartial tribunals or procedures compatible with the requirements of due process of law.

(c)

(1) The superior court shall decline to recognize and enter a tribal court money judgment if any one of the following grounds applies:

(A) The defendant in the proceeding in the tribal court did not receive notice of the proceeding in sufficient time to enable the defendant to defend.

(B) The judgment was obtained by fraud that deprived the losing party of an adequate opportunity to present its case.

(C) The judgment or the cause of action or claim for relief on which the judgment is based is repugnant to the public policy of the state or of the United States.

(D) The proceeding in the tribal court was contrary to an agreement between the parties under which the dispute in question was to be determined otherwise than by proceedings in that tribal court.

(E) In the case of jurisdiction based on personal service only, the tribal court was a seriously inconvenient forum for the trial of the action.

(F) The judgment was rendered under circumstances that raise substantial doubt about the integrity of the rendering court with respect to the judgment.

(G) The specific proceeding in the tribal court leading to the judgment was not compatible with the requirements of due process of law.

(H) The judgment includes recovery for a claim of defamation, unless the court determines that the defamation law applied by the tribal court provided at least as much protection for freedom of speech and the press as provided by both the United States and California Constitutions.

(2) Notwithstanding an applicable ground for nonrecognition under paragraph (1), the court may nonetheless recognize a tribal court money judgment if the applicant demonstrates good reason to recognize the judgment that outweighs the ground for nonrecognition.

(d) The superior court may, in its discretion, decline to recognize and enter a tribal court money judgment if the judgment conflicts with another final and conclusive judgment.

(e) If objections have been timely filed, the applicant has the burden of establishing that the tribal court money judgment is entitled to recognition. If the applicant has met its burden, a party resisting recognition of the tribal court money judgment has the burden of establishing that a ground for nonrecognition exists pursuant to subdivision (b), (c), or (d).

Amended by Stats 2021 ch 58 (AB 627),s 6, eff. 1/1/2022.
Amended by Stats 2017 ch 168 (AB 905),s 14, eff. 1/1/2018.
Added by Stats 2014 ch 243 (SB 406),s 4, eff. 1/1/2015.

Section 1738 - Stay

The superior court shall grant a stay of enforcement if the respondent establishes one of the following to the superior court:

(a) An appeal from the tribal court money judgment is pending or may be taken in the tribal court, in which case the superior court shall stay state execution of the tribal court money judgment until the proceeding on appeal has been concluded or the time for appeal has expired.

(b) A stay of enforcement of the tribal court money judgment has been granted by the tribal court, in which case the superior court shall stay enforcement of the tribal court money judgment until the stay of execution expires or is vacated.

(c) Any other circumstance exists where the interests of justice require a stay of enforcement.

Added by Stats 2014 ch 243 (SB 406),s 4, eff. 1/1/2015.

Section 1739 - Action to recognize judgment

An action to recognize a tribal court money judgment or any renewal thereof shall be commenced within the earlier of the following periods:

(a)The time during which the tribal court money judgment is effective within the territorial jurisdiction of the tribal court.

(b) Ten years from the date that the tribal court money judgment became effective in the tribal jurisdiction.

Added by Stats 2014 ch 243 (SB 406),s 4, eff. 1/1/2015.

Section 1740 - Resolution of issues with tribal court judge

(a) The superior court may, after notice to all parties, attempt to resolve any issues raised regarding a tribal court money judgment by contacting the tribal court judge who issued the judgment.

(b) The superior court shall allow the parties to participate in, and shall prepare a record of, any communication made with the tribal court judge pursuant to this section.

Added by Stats 2014 ch 243 (SB 406),s 4, eff. 1/1/2015.

Section 1741 - Construction with other law

(a) The Uniform Foreign-Country Money Judgments Recognition Act (Chapter 2 (commencing with Section 1713)) applies to all actions commenced in superior court before January 1, 2015, in which the issue of recognition of a tribal court money judgment is raised.

(b) This chapter applies to all actions to enforce tribal court money judgments as defined herein commenced in superior court on or after January 1, 2015. A judgment entered under this chapter shall not limit the right of a party to seek enforcement of any part of a judgment, order, or decree entered by a tribal court that is not encompassed by the judgment entered under this chapter.

Amended by Stats 2017 ch 168 (AB 905),s 15, eff. 1/1/2018.
Added by Stats 2014 ch 243 (SB 406),s 4, eff. 1/1/2015.

Section 1742 - [Repealed]

Repealed by Stats 2017 ch 168 (AB 905),s 16, eff. 1/1/2018.
Added by Stats 2014 ch 243 (SB 406),s 4, eff. 1/1/2015.

Title 11.6 - CIVIL ACTION MEDIATION

Section 1775 - Legislative findings and declaration

The Legislature finds and declares that:

(a) The peaceful resolution of disputes in a fair, timely, appropriate, and cost-effective manner is an essential function of the judicial branch of state government under Article VI of the California Constitution.

(b) In the case of many disputes, litigation culminating in a trial is costly, time consuming, and stressful for the parties involved. Many disputes can be resolved in a fair and equitable manner through less formal processes.

(c) Alternative processes for reducing the cost, time, and stress of dispute resolution, such as mediation, have been effectively used in California and elsewhere. In appropriate cases mediation provides parties with a simplified and economical procedure for obtaining prompt and equitable resolution of their disputes and a greater opportunity to participate directly in resolving these disputes. Mediation may also assist to reduce the backlog of cases burdening the judicial system. It is in the public interest for mediation to be encouraged and used where appropriate by the courts.

(d) Mediation and similar alternative processes can have the greatest benefit for the parties in a civil action when used early, before substantial discovery and other litigation costs have been incurred. Where appropriate, participants in disputes should be encouraged to utilize mediation and other alternatives to trial for resolving their differences in the early stages of a civil action.

(e) As a pilot project in Los Angeles County and in other counties which elect to apply this title, courts should be able to refer cases to appropriate dispute resolution processes such as judicial arbitration and mediation as an alternative to trial, consistent with the parties' right to obtain a trial if a dispute is not resolved through an alternative process.

(f) The purpose of this title is to encourage the use of court-annexed alternative dispute resolution methods in general, and mediation in particular. It is estimated that the average cost to the court for processing a civil case of the kind described in Section 1775.3 through judgment is three thousand nine hundred forty-three dollars ($3,943) for each judge day, and that a substantial portion of this cost can be saved if these cases are resolved before trial. The Judicial Council, through the Administrative Office of the Courts, shall conduct a survey to determine the number of cases resolved by alternative dispute resolution authorized by this title, and shall estimate the resulting savings realized by the courts and the parties. The results of the survey shall be included in the report submitted pursuant to Section 1775.14. The programs authorized by this title shall be deemed successful if they result in estimated savings of at least two hundred fifty thousand dollars ($250,000) to the courts and corresponding savings to the parties.

Added by Stats. 1993, Ch. 1261, Sec. 4. Effective January 1, 1994.

Section 1775.1 - Mediation defined; act performed by party may also be performed by counsel

(a) As used in this title, "mediation" means a process in which a neutral person or persons facilitate communication between the disputants to assist them in reaching a mutually acceptable agreement.

(b) Unless otherwise specified in this title or ordered by the court, any act to be performed by a party may also be performed by his or her counsel of record.

Amended by Stats 2002 ch 784 (SB 1316),s 87, eff. 1/1/2003.

Section 1775.2 - Title applicable to Los Angeles County courts; election by other county courts to apply title; effective date

(a) This title shall apply to the courts of the County of Los Angeles.

(b) A court of any county, at the option of the presiding judge, may elect whether or not to apply this title to eligible actions filed in that court, and this title shall not apply in any court which has not so elected. An election under this subdivision may be revoked by the court at any time.

(c) Courts are authorized to apply this title to all civil actions pending or commenced on or after January 1, 1994.

Added by Stats. 1993, Ch. 1261, Sec. 4. Effective January 1, 1994.

Section 1775.3 - Civil actions which may be submitted to mediation by presiding judge or designate

(a) In the courts of the County of Los Angeles and in other courts that elect to apply this title, all at-issue civil actions in which arbitration is otherwise required pursuant to Section 1141.11, whether or not the action includes a prayer for equitable relief, may be submitted to mediation by the presiding judge or the judge designated under this title as an alternative to judicial arbitration pursuant to Chapter 2.5 (commencing with Section 1141.10) of Title 3.

(b) Any civil action otherwise within the scope of this title in which a party to the action is a public agency or public entity may be submitted to mediation pursuant to subdivision (a).

Added by Stats. 1993, Ch. 1261, Sec. 4. Effective January 1, 1994.

Section 1775.4 - Action ordered into arbitration not order into mediation; action ordered into mediation not ordered into arbitration

An action that has been ordered into arbitration pursuant to Section 1141.11 or 1141.12 may not be ordered into mediation under this title, and an action that has been ordered into mediation pursuant to Section 1775.3 may not be ordered into arbitration pursuant to Section 1141.11.

Added by Stats. 1993, Ch. 1261, Sec. 4. Effective January 1, 1994.

Section 1775.5 - Amount in controversy

The court shall not order a case into mediation where the amount in controversy exceeds fifty thousand dollars ($50,000). The determination of the amount in controversy shall be made in the same manner as provided in Section 1141.16 and, in making this determination, the court shall not consider the merits of questions of liability, defenses, or comparative negligence.

Added by Stats. 1993, Ch. 1261, Sec. 4. Effective January 1, 1994.

Section 1775.6 - Time for selection of mediator; method of selection and qualification

In actions submitted to mediation pursuant to Section 1775.3, a mediator shall be selected for the action within 30 days of its submission to mediation. The method of selection and qualification of the mediator shall be as the parties determine. If the parties are unable to agree on a mediator within 15 days of the date of submission of the action to mediation, the court may select a mediator pursuant to standards adopted by the Judicial Council.

Added by Stats. 1993, Ch. 1261, Sec. 4. Effective January 1, 1994.

Section 1775.7 - Time periods specified in Chapter 1.5 not suspended; computing five-year period specified in section 583.310

(a) Submission of an action to mediation pursuant to this title shall not suspend the running of the time periods specified in Chapter 1.5 (commencing with Section 583.110) of Title 8 of Part 2, except as provided in this section.

(b) If an action is or remains submitted to mediation pursuant to this title more than four years and six months after the plaintiff has filed the action, then the time beginning on the date four years and six months after the plaintiff has filed the action and ending on the date on which a statement of nonagreement is filed pursuant to Section 1775.9 shall not be included in computing the five-year period specified in Section 583.310.

Added by Stats. 1993, Ch. 1261, Sec. 4. Effective January 1, 1994.

Section 1775.8 - Compensation of court-appointed mediators; payment of administrative costs

(a) The compensation of court-appointed mediators shall be the same as the compensation of arbitrators pursuant to Section 1141.18, except that no compensation shall be paid prior to the filing of a statement of nonagreement by the mediator pursuant to Section 1775.9 or prior to settlement of the action by the parties.

(b) All administrative costs of mediation, including compensation of mediators, shall be paid in the same manner as for arbitration pursuant to Section 1141.28. Funds allocated for the payment of arbitrators under the judicial arbitration program shall be equally available for the payment of mediators under this title.

Added by Stats. 1993, Ch. 1261, Sec. 4. Effective January 1, 1994.

Section 1775.9 - Statement of nonagreement filed by mediator

(a) In the event that the parties to mediation are unable to reach a mutually acceptable agreement and any party to the mediation wishes to terminate the mediation, then the mediator shall file a statement of nonagreement. This statement shall be in a form to be developed by the Judicial Council.
(b) Upon the filing of a statement of nonagreement, the matter shall be calendared for trial, by court or jury, both as to law and fact, insofar as possible, so that the trial shall be given the same place on the active list as it had prior to mediation, or shall receive civil priority on the next setting calendar.
Added by Stats. 1993, Ch. 1261, Sec. 4. Effective January 1, 1994.

Section 1775.10 - Confidentiality of statements made by parties
All statements made by the parties during the mediation shall be subject to Sections 703.5 and 1152, and Chapter 2 (commencing with Section 1115) of Division 9, of the Evidence Code.
Amended by Stats. 1997, Ch. 772, Sec. 2. Effective January 1, 1998.

Section 1775.11 - Discovery
Any party who participates in mediation pursuant to Section 1775.3 shall retain the right to obtain discovery to the extent available under the Civil Discovery Act, Title 4 (commencing with Section 2016.010) of Part 4.
Amended by Stats 2004 ch 182 (AB 3081),s 17, eff. 7/1/2005

Section 1775.12 - Reference to mediation or statement of nonagreement in subsequent trial irregularity
Any reference to the mediation or the statement of nonagreement filed pursuant to Section 1775.9 during any subsequent trial shall constitute an irregularity in the proceedings of the trial for the purposes of Section 657.
Added by Stats. 1993, Ch. 1261, Sec. 4. Effective January 1, 1994.

Section 1775.13 - Other alternative dispute resolution programs not preempted
It is the intent of the Legislature that nothing in this title be construed to preempt other current or future alternative dispute resolution programs operating in the trial courts.
Added by Stats. 1993, Ch. 1261, Sec. 4. Effective January 1, 1994.

Section 1775.14 - Report by Judicial Council to Legislature
(a) On or before January 1, 1998, the Judicial Council shall submit a report to the Legislature concerning court alternative dispute resolution programs. This report shall include, but not be limited to, a review of programs operated in Los Angeles County and other courts that have elected to apply this title, and shall examine, among other things, the effect of this title on the judicial arbitration programs of courts that have participated in that program.
(b) The Judicial Council shall, by rule, require that each court applying this title file with the Judicial Council data that will enable the Judicial Council to submit the report required by subdivision (a).
Amended by Stats 2006 ch 538 (SB 1852),s 74, eff. 1/1/2007.

Section 1775.15 - Rules
Notwithstanding any other provision of law except the provisions of this title, the Judicial Council shall provide by rule for all of the following:
(a) The procedures to be followed in submitting actions to mediation under this act.
(b) Coordination of the procedures and processes under this act with those under the trial Court Delay Reduction Act, Article 5 (commencing with Section 68600) of Chapter 2 of Title 8 of the Government Code.
(c) Exceptions for cause from provisions of this title. In providing for exceptions, the Judicial Council shall take into consideration whether the civil action might not be amenable to mediation.
Added by Stats. 1993, Ch. 1261, Sec. 4. Effective January 1, 1994.

Title 11.7 - RECOVERY OF PREFERENCES AND EXEMPT PROPERTY IN AN ASSIGNMENT FOR THE BENEFIT OF CREDITORS

Section 1800 - Definitions
(a) As used in this section, the following terms have the following meanings:
  (1) "Insolvent" means:
    (A) With reference to a person other than a partnership, a financial condition such that the sum of the person's debts is greater than all of the person's property, at a fair valuation, exclusive of both of the following:
      (i) Property transferred, concealed, or removed with intent to hinder, delay, or defraud the person's creditors.
      (ii) Property that is exempt from property of the estate pursuant to the election of the person made pursuant to Section 1801.
    (B) With reference to a partnership, financial condition such that the sum of the partnership's debts are greater than the aggregate of, at a fair valuation, both of the following:
      (i) All of the partnership's property, exclusive of property of the kind specified in clause (i) of subparagraph (A).
      (ii) The sum of the excess of the value of each general partner's separate property, exclusive of property of the kind specified in clause (ii) of subparagraph (A), over the partner's separate debts.
  (2) "Inventory" means personal property leased or furnished, held for sale or lease, or to be furnished under a contract for service, raw materials, work in process, or materials used or consumed in a business, including farm products such as crops or livestock, held for sale or lease.
  (3) "Insider" means:
    (A) If the assignor is an individual, any of the following:
      (i) A relative of the assignor or of a general partner of the assignor.
      (ii) A partnership in which the assignor is a general partner.
      (iii) A general partner of the assignor.
      (iv) A corporation of which the assignor is a director, officer, or person in control.
    (B) If the assignor is a corporation, any of the following:
      (i) A director of the assignor.
      (ii) An officer of the assignor.
      (iii) A person in control of the assignor.
      (iv) A partnership in which the assignor is a general partner.
      (v) A general partner of the assignor.
      (vi) A relative of a general partner, director, officer, or person in control of the assignor.
    (C) If the assignor is a partnership, any of the following:
      (i) A general partner in the assignor.
      (ii) A relative of a general partner in, general partner of, or person in control of the assignor.
      (iii) A partnership in which the assignor is a general partner.
      (iv) A general partner of the assignor.
      (v) A person in control of the assignor.

(D) An affiliate of the assignor or an insider of an affiliate as if the affiliate were the assignor.

(E) A managing agent of the assignor. As used in this paragraph, the following terms have the following meanings:

"Relative" means an individual related by affinity or consanguinity within the third degree as determined by the common law, or an individual in a step or adoptive relationship within the third degree.

An "affiliate" means a person that directly or indirectly owns, controls, or holds, with power to vote, 20 percent or more of the outstanding voting securities of the assignor, or 20 percent or more of whose outstanding voting securities are directly or indirectly owned, controlled, or held with power to vote by the assignor, excluding securities held in a fiduciary or agency capacity without sole discretionary power to vote, or held solely to secure a debt if the holder has not in fact exercised the power to vote, or a person who operates the business of the assignor under a lease or operating agreement or whose business is operated by the assignor under a lease or operating agreement.

(4) "Judicial lien" means a lien obtained by judgment, levy, sequestration, or other legal or equitable process or proceeding.

(5) "New value" means money or money's worth in goods, services, or new credit, or release by a transferee of property previously transferred to the transferee in a transaction that is neither void nor voidable by the assignor or the assignee under any applicable law, but does not include an obligation substituted for an existing obligation.

(6) "Receivable" means a right to payment, whether or not the right has been earned by performance.

(7) "Security agreement" means an agreement that creates or provides for a security interest.

(8) "Security interest" means a lien created by an agreement.

(9) "Statutory lien" means a lien arising solely by force of a statute on specified circumstances or conditions, or lien of distress for rent, whether or not statutory, but does not include a security interest or judicial lien, whether or not the interest or lien is provided by or is dependent on a statute and whether or not the interest or lien is made fully effective by statute.

(10) "Transfer" means every mode, direct or indirect, absolute or conditional, voluntary or involuntary, or disposing of or parting with property or with an interest in property, including retention of title as a security interest.

(b) Except as provided in subdivision (c), the assignee of any general assignment for the benefit of creditors, as defined in Section 493.010, may recover any transfer of property of the assignor that is all of the following:

(1) To or for the benefit of a creditor.

(2) For or on account of an antecedent debt owed by the assignor before the transfer was made.

(3) Made while the assignor was insolvent.

(4) Made on or within 90 days before the date of the making of the assignment or made between 90 days and one year before the date of making the assignment if the creditor, at the time of the transfer, was an insider and had reasonable cause to believe the debtor was insolvent at the time of the transfer.

(5) Enables the creditor to receive more than another creditor of the same class.

(c) The assignee may not recover under this section a transfer as follows:

(1) To the extent that the transfer was both of the following:

(A) Intended by the assignor and the creditor to or for whose benefit the transfer was made to be a contemporaneous exchange for new value given to the assignor.

(B) In fact a substantially contemporaneous exchange.

(2) To the extent that the transfer was all of the following:

(A) In payment of a debt incurred in the ordinary course of business or financial affairs of the assignor and the transferee.

(B) Made in the ordinary course of business or financial affairs of the assignor and the transferee.

(C) Made according to ordinary business terms.

(3) Of a security interest in property acquired by the assignor that meets both of the following:

(A) To the extent the security interest secures new value that was all of the following:

(i) Given at or after the signing of a security agreement that contains a description of the property as collateral.

(ii) Given by or on behalf of the secured party under the agreement.

(iii) Given to enable the assignor to acquire the property.

(iv) In fact used by the assignor to acquire the property.

(B) That is perfected within 20 days after the security interest attaches.

(4) To or for the benefit of a creditor, to the extent that, after the transfer, the creditor gave new value to or for the benefit of the assignor that meets both of the following:

(A) Not secured by an otherwise unavoidable security interest.

(B) On account of which new value the assignor did not make an otherwise unavoidable transfer to or for the benefit of the creditor.

(5) Of a perfected security interest in inventory or a receivable or the proceeds of either, except to the extent that the aggregate of all the transfers to the transferee caused a reduction, as of the date of the making of the assignment and to the prejudice of other creditors holding unsecured claims, of any amount by which the debt secured by the security interest exceeded the value of all security interest for the debt on the later of the following:

(A) Ninety days before the date of the making of the assignment.

(B) The date on which new value was first given under the security agreement creating the security interest.

(6) That is the fixing of a statutory lien.

(7) That is payment to a claimant, as defined in Section 8004 of the Civil Code, in exchange for the claimant's waiver or release of any potential or asserted claim of lien, stop payment notice, or right to recover on a payment bond, or any combination thereof.

(8) To the extent that the transfer was a bona fide payment of a debt to a spouse, former spouse, or child of the debtor, for alimony to, maintenance for, or support of, the spouse or child, in connection with a separation agreement, divorce decree, or other order of a court of record, or a determination made in accordance with state or territorial law by a governmental unit, or property settlement agreement; but not to the extent that either of the following occurs:

(A) The debt is assigned to another entity voluntarily, by operation of law or otherwise, in which case the assignee may not recover that portion of the transfer that is assigned to the state or any political subdivision of the state pursuant to Part D of Title IV of the Social Security Act (42 U.S.C. Sec. 601 et seq.) and passed on to the spouse, former spouse, or child of the debtor.

(B) The debt includes a liability designated as alimony, maintenance, or support, unless the liability is actually in the nature of alimony, maintenance, or support.

(d) An assignee of any general assignment for the benefit of creditors, as defined in Section 493.010, may avoid a transfer of property of the assignor transferred to secure reimbursement of a surety that furnished a bond or other obligation to dissolve a judicial lien that would have been avoidable by the assignee under subdivision (b). The liability of the surety under the bond or obligation shall be discharged to the extent of the value of the property recovered by the assignee or the amount paid to the assignee.

(e)

(1) For the purposes of this section:

(A) A transfer of real property other than fixtures, but including the interest of a seller or purchaser under a contract for the sale of real property, is perfected when a bona fide purchaser of the property from the debtor, against whom applicable law permits the transfer to be perfected, cannot acquire an interest that is superior to the interest of the transferee.

(B) A transfer of a fixture or property other than real property is perfected when a creditor on a simple contract cannot acquire a judicial lien that is superior to the interest of the transferee.

(2) For the purposes of this section, except as provided in paragraph (3), a transfer is made at any of the following times:

(A) At the time the transfer takes effect between the transferor and the transferee, if the transfer is perfected at, or within 10 days after, the time, except as provided in subparagraph (B) of paragraph (3) of subdivision (c).

(B) At the time the transfer is perfected, if the transfer is perfected after the 10 days.

(C) Immediately before the date of making the assignment if the transfer is not perfected at the later of:

(i) The making of the assignment.

(ii) Ten days after the transfer takes effect between the transferor and the transferee.

(3) For the purposes of this section, a transfer is not made until the assignor has acquired rights in the property transferred.

(f) For the purposes of this section, the assignor is presumed to have been insolvent on and during the 90 days immediately preceding the date of making the assignment.

(g) An action by an assignee under this section must be commenced within one year after making the assignment.

Amended by Stats 2010 ch 697 (SB 189),s 26, eff. 1/1/2011, op. 7/1/2012.

Amended by Stats 2006 ch 538 (SB 1852),s 75, eff. 1/1/2007.

EFFECTIVE 1/1/2000. Amended July 28, 1999 (Bill Number: SB 219) (Chapter 202).

Section 1801 - Exempt property

In any general assignment for the benefit of creditors (as defined in Section 493.010), the assignor, if an individual, may choose to retain as exempt property either the property which is otherwise exempt under Chapter 4 (commencing with Section 703.010) of Division 2 of Title 9 of Part 2 or, in the alternative, the following property:

(a) The assignor's aggregate interest, not to exceed seven thousand five hundred dollars ($7,500) in value, in real property or personal property that the assignor or a dependent of the assignor uses as a residence, in a cooperative that owns property that the assignor or a dependent of the assignor uses as a residence, or in a burial plot for the assignor or a dependent of the assignor.

(b) The assignor's interest, not to exceed one thousand two hundred dollars ($1,200) in value, in one motor vehicle.

(c) The assignor's interest, not to exceed two hundred dollars ($200) in value in any particular item, in household furnishings, household goods, wearing apparel, appliances, books, animals, crops, or musical instruments, that are held primarily for the personal, family, or household use of the assignor or a dependent of the assignor.

(d) The assignor's aggregate interest, not to exceed five hundred dollars ($500) in value, in jewelry held primarily for the personal, family, or household use of the assignor or a dependent of the assignor.

(e) The assignor's aggregate interest, not to exceed in value four hundred dollars ($400) plus any unused amount of the exemption provided under subdivision (a), in any property.

(f) The assignor's aggregate interest, not to exceed seven hundred fifty dollars ($750) in value, in any implements, professional books, or tools, of the trade of the assignor or the trade of a dependent of the assignor.

(g) Any unmatured life insurance contract owned by the assignor, other than a credit life insurance contract.

(h) The assignor's aggregate interest, not to exceed in value four thousand dollars ($4,000) in any accrued dividend or interest under, or loan value of, any unmatured life insurance contract owned by the assignor under which the insured is the assignor or an individual of whom the assignor is a dependent.

(i) Professionally prescribed health aids for the assignor or a dependent of the assignor.

(j) The assignor's right to receive any of the following:

(1) A social security benefit, unemployment compensation, or a local public assistance benefit except that this paragraph does not preclude the application of Section 1255.7 of the Unemployment Insurance Code.

(2) A veterans' benefit.

(3) A disability, illness, or unemployment benefit except that this paragraph does not preclude the application of Section 1255.7 of the Unemployment Insurance Code.

(4) Alimony, support, or separate maintenance, to the extent reasonably necessary for the support of the assignor and any dependent of the assignor.

(5) A payment under a stock bonus, pension, profit sharing, annuity, or similar plan or contract on account of illness, disability, death, age, or length of service, to the extent reasonably necessary for the support of the assignor and any dependent of the assignor, unless:

(i) The plan or contract was established by or under the auspices of an employer of which the assignor was a partner, officer, director or controlling person at the time the assignor's rights under the plan or contract arose;

(ii) The payment is on account of age or length of service; and

(iii) Such plan or contract does not qualify under Section 401(a)(a), 403(a)(a), 403(b)(b), 408, or 409 of the Internal Revenue Code of 1954 (26 U.S.C. 401(a), 403(a), 403(b), 408, or 409).

(k) The assignor's right to receive, or property that is traceable to any of the following:

(1) An award under a crime victim's reparation law.

(2) A payment on account of the wrongful death of an individual of whom the assignor was a dependent, to the extent reasonably necessary for the support of the assignor and any dependent of the assignor.

(3) A payment under a life insurance contract that insured the life of an individual of whom the assignor was a dependent on the date of such individual's death, to the extent reasonably necessary for the support of the assignor and any dependent of the assignor.

(4) A payment, not to exceed seven thousand five hundred dollars ($7,500), on account of personal bodily injury, as compensation for pain and suffering or actual pecuniary loss (other than loss of future earnings), of the assignor or an individual of whom the assignor is a dependent.

(5) A payment in compensation of loss of future earnings of the assignor or an individual of whom the assignor is or was a dependent, to the extent reasonably necessary for the support of the assignor and any dependent of the assignor. In this section, "dependent" includes spouse, whether or not actually dependent, "assignor" means each spouse, if the assignment is made by a married couple, and "value" means fair market value as of the date of the making of the assignment.

Amended by Stats. 1983, Ch. 155, Sec. 23. Effective June 30, 1983. Operative July 1, 1983, by Sec. 32 of Ch. 155.

Section 1802 - Notice of assignment given by assignee

(a) In any general assignment for the benefit of creditors, as defined in Section 493.010, the assignee shall, within 30 days after the assignment has been accepted in writing, give written notice of the assignment to the assignor's creditors, equityholders, and other parties in interest as set forth on the list provided by the assignor pursuant to subdivision (c).

(b) In the notice given pursuant to subdivision (a), the assignee shall establish a date by which creditors must file their claims to be able to share in the distribution of proceeds of the liquidation of the assignor's assets. That date shall be not less than 150 days and not greater than 180 days after the date of the first giving of the written notice to creditors and parties in interest.
(c) The assignor shall provide to the assignee at the time of the making of the assignment a list of creditors, equityholders, and other parties in interest, signed under penalty of perjury, which shall include the names, addresses, cities, states, and ZIP Codes for each person together with the amount of that person's anticipated claim in the assignment proceedings.
Added by Stats. 1992, Ch. 1348, Sec. 8. Effective January 1, 1993.

Title 12 - TRIBAL INJUNCTIONS

Section 1811 - Injunction against gaming or authorization of gaming
(a) Following the issuance of the bonds as specified in Section 63048.65 of the Government Code and during the term of the bonds, if it reasonably appears that the exclusive right of an Indian tribe with a designated tribal compact, as defined in subdivision (b) of Section 63048.6 of the Government Code, pursuant to Section 3.2(a)(a) of that compact has been violated, the tribe may seek a preliminary and permanent injunction against that gaming or the authorization of that gaming as a substantial impairment of the rights specified in Section 3.2(a)(a), in order to afford the tribe stability in its gaming operation and to maintain the bargained-for source of payment and security of the bonds. However, no remedy other than an injunction shall be available against the state or any of its political subdivisions for a violation of Section 3.2(a)(a). The Legislature hereby finds and declares that any such violation of the exclusive right to gaming under Section 3.2(a)(a) is a substantial impairment of the rights specified in that section and will cause irreparable harm that cannot be adequately remedied by damages. No undertaking shall be required on the part of the tribes in connection with any action to seek the preliminary or permanent injunction.
(b) Notwithstanding any other provision of law, the parties to an action brought pursuant to subdivision (a) may petition the Supreme Court for a writ of mandate from any order granting or denying a preliminary injunction. Any such petition shall be filed within 15 days following the notice of entry of the superior court order, and no extension of that period shall be allowed. In any case in which a petition has been filed within the time allowed therefor, the Supreme Court shall make any orders, as it may deem proper in the circumstances.
Added by Stats 2004 ch 91 (AB 687), s 2, eff. 6/30/2004.

Title 13 - INSPECTION WARRANTS

Section 1822.50 - Defined
An inspection warrant is an order, in writing, in the name of the people, signed by a judge of a court of record, directed to a state or local official, commanding him to conduct any inspection required or authorized by state or local law or regulation relating to building, fire, safety, plumbing, electrical, health, labor, or zoning.
Amended by Stats. 1980, Ch. 230, Sec. 1.

Section 1822.51 - Issued upon cause; supported by affidavit
An inspection warrant shall be issued upon cause, unless some other provision of state or federal law makes another standard applicable. An inspection warrant shall be supported by an affidavit, particularly describing the place, dwelling, structure, premises, or vehicle to be inspected and the purpose for which the inspection is made. In addition, the affidavit shall contain either a statement that consent to inspect has been sought and refused or facts or circumstances reasonably justifying the failure to seek such consent.
Amended by Stats. 1984, Ch. 476, Sec. 2.

Section 1822.52 - Cause deemed to exist
Cause shall be deemed to exist if either reasonable legislative or administrative standards for conducting a routine or area inspection are satisfied with respect to the particular place, dwelling, structure, premises, or vehicle, or there is reason to believe that a condition of nonconformity exists with respect to the particular place, dwelling, structure, premises, or vehicle.
Added by Stats. 1968, Ch. 1097.

Section 1822.53 - Examination of applicant and other witnesses by judge
Before issuing an inspection warrant, the judge may examine on oath the applicant and any other witness, and shall satisfy himself of the existence of grounds for granting such application.
Added by Stats. 1968, Ch. 1097.

Section 1822.54 - Issuance of warrant
If the judge is satisfied that the proper standard for issuance of the warrant has been met, he or she shall issue the warrant particularly describing each place, dwelling, structure, premises, or vehicle to be inspected and designating on the warrant the purpose and limitations of the inspection, including the limitations required by this title.
Amended by Stats. 1984, Ch. 476, Sec. 3.

Section 1822.55 - Time period warrant effective; execution and return; void after expiration of time
An inspection warrant shall be effective for the time specified therein, but not for a period of more than 14 days, unless extended or renewed by the judge who signed and issued the original warrant, upon satisfying himself that such extension or renewal is in the public interest. Such inspection warrant must be executed and returned to the judge by whom it was issued within the time specified in the warrant or within the extended or renewed time. After the expiration of such time, the warrant, unless executed, is void.
Added by Stats. 1968, Ch. 1097.

Section 1822.56 - Inspection pursuant to warrant
An inspection pursuant to this warrant may not be made between 6:00 p.m. of any day and 8:00 a.m. of the succeeding day, nor in the absence of an owner or occupant of the particular place, dwelling, structure, premises, or vehicle unless specifically authorized by the judge upon a showing that such authority is reasonably necessary to effectuate the purpose of the regulation being enforced. An inspection pursuant to a warrant shall not be made by means of forcible entry, except that the judge may expressly authorize a forcible entry where facts are shown sufficient to create a reasonable suspicion of a violation of a state or local law or regulation relating to building, fire, safety, plumbing, electrical, health, labor, or zoning, which, if such violation existed, would be an immediate threat to health or safety, or where facts are shown establishing that reasonable attempts to serve a previous warrant have been unsuccessful. Where prior consent has been sought and refused, notice that a warrant has been issued must be given at least 24 hours before the warrant is executed, unless the judge finds that immediate execution is reasonably necessary in the circumstances shown.
Amended by Stats. 1980, Ch. 230, Sec. 2.

Section 1822.57 - Willfully refusing to permit inspection
Any person who willfully refuses to permit an inspection lawfully authorized by warrant issued pursuant to this title is guilty of a misdemeanor.
Added by Stats. 1968, Ch. 1097.

Section 1822.58 - Inspections by Department of Fish and Game of places fish or aquatic plants held or stored
A warrant may be issued under the requirements of this title to authorize personnel of the Department of Fish and Game to conduct inspections of locations where fish, amphibia, or aquatic plants are held or stored under Division 12 (commencing with Section 15000) of the Fish and Game Code.
Added by Stats. 1982, Ch. 1486, Sec. 1.

Section 1822.59 - Inspection by Department of Food and Agriculture for purposes of animal or plant disease eradication

(a) Notwithstanding the provisions of Section 1822.54, for purposes of an animal or plant pest or disease eradication effort pursuant to Division 4 (commencing with Section 5001) or Division 5 (commencing with Section 9101) of the Food and Agricultural Code, the judge may issue a warrant under the requirements of this title describing a specified geographic area to be inspected by authorized personnel of the Department of Food and Agriculture.

(b) A warrant issued pursuant to this section may only authorize the inspection of the exterior of places, dwellings, structures, premises or vehicles, and only in areas urban in character. The warrant shall state the geographical area which it covers and the purpose of and limitations on the inspection.

(c) A warrant may be issued pursuant to this section whether or not the property owners in the area have refused to consent to the inspection. A peace officer may use reasonable force to enter a property to be inspected if so authorized by the warrant.

Added by Stats. 1984, Ch. 476, Sec. 4.

Section 1822.60 - Department of Justice inspections conducted under section 19827(a), Business and Professions Code

A warrant may be issued under the requirements of this title to authorize personnel of the Department of Justice to conduct inspections as provided in subdivision (a) of Section 19827 of the Business and Professions Code.

Amended by Stats 2007 ch 176 (SB 82),s 51, eff. 8/24/2007.

Part 4 - MISCELLANEOUS PROVISIONS
Title 1 - OF THE GENERAL PRINCIPLES OF EVIDENCE

Section 1855 - Copy of map injured, destroyed, lost or stolen offered for record in place of original map

When any map which has been recorded in the office of the recorder of any county is injured, destroyed, lost, or stolen, any person interested may file in the superior court of the county in which the map was originally filed or recorded a verified petition in writing alleging that the map has been injured, destroyed, lost, or stolen without fault of the person making the application, and that the petitioner has a true and correct copy of the original map which he or she offers for record in the place of the original map. The petition shall be accompanied by a copy of the true copy offered for recording.

Upon the filing of the petition the clerk shall set it for hearing by the court, and give notice of the hearing by causing notice of the time and place of the hearing to be posted at the courthouse in the county where the court is held at least 10 days prior to the hearing. A copy of the petition and a copy of the true copy offered for record shall be served upon the recorder of the county in which the proceedings are brought at least 10 days prior to the hearing. The court may order any further notice to be given as it deems proper. At the time set for the hearing the court shall take evidence for and against the petition, and if it appears to the court from the evidence presented that the copy of the map submitted is a true copy of the original map, it shall decree that the copy is a true copy of the original map, and order the copy placed of record in the office of the recorder in the place of the original map.

A certified copy of the decree shall accompany the true copy of the map for record. When presented to the county recorder for record, he or she shall place of record the copy of the map in the place of the original map.

When placed of record the copy shall have the same effect as the original map, and conveyances of property referring to the original map shall have the same effect as though the original map had not been injured, destroyed, lost, or stolen, and conveyances thereafter made referring to the copy of the original map shall be deemed to refer also to the original map.

Added by renumbering Section 1855b by Stats. 1987, Ch. 56, Sec. 23.

Section 1856 - Contradiction of terms of agreement by evidence of prior agreement or contemporaneous oral agreement; evidence explaining or supplementing terms

(a) Terms set forth in a writing intended by the parties as a final expression of their agreement with respect to the terms included therein may not be contradicted by evidence of a prior agreement or of a contemporaneous oral agreement.

(b) The terms set forth in a writing described in subdivision (a) may be explained or supplemented by evidence of consistent additional terms unless the writing is intended also as a complete and exclusive statement of the terms of the agreement.

(c) The terms set forth in a writing described in subdivision (a) may be explained or supplemented by course of dealing or usage of trade or by course of performance.

(d) The court shall determine whether the writing is intended by the parties as a final expression of their agreement with respect to the terms included therein and whether the writing is intended also as a complete and exclusive statement of the terms of the agreement.

(e) Where a mistake or imperfection of the writing is put in issue by the pleadings, this section does not exclude evidence relevant to that issue.

(f) Where the validity of the agreement is the fact in dispute, this section does not exclude evidence relevant to that issue.

(g) This section does not exclude other evidence of the circumstances under which the agreement was made or to which it relates, as defined in Section 1860, or to explain an extrinsic ambiguity or otherwise interpret the terms of the agreement, or to establish illegality or fraud.

(h) As used in this section, "agreement" includes trust instruments, deeds, wills, and contracts between parties.

Amended by Stats 2013 ch 81 (AB 824),s 1, eff. 1/1/2014.

Section 1857 - Interpretation of language of writing

The language of a writing is to be interpreted according to the meaning it bears in the place of its execution, unless the parties have reference to a different place.

Enacted 1872.

Section 1858 - Office of judge in construction of statute or instrument

In the construction of a statute or instrument, the office of the Judge is simply to ascertain and declare what is in terms or in substance contained therein, not to insert what has been omitted, or to omit what has been inserted; and where there are several provisions or particulars, such a construction is, if possible, to be adopted as will give effect to all.

Enacted 1872.

Section 1859 - Intention of Legislature or intention of parties in construction of statute or instrument

In the construction of a statute the intention of the Legislature, and in the construction of the instrument the intention of the parties, is to be pursued, if possible; and when a general and particular provision are inconsistent, the latter is paramount to the former. So a particular intent will control a general one that is inconsistent with it.

Enacted 1872.

Section 1860 - Circumstances under which instrument made

For the proper construction of an instrument, the circumstances under which it was made, including the situation of the subject of the instrument, and of the parties to it, may also be shown, so that the Judge be placed in the position of those whose language he is to interpret.

Enacted 1872.

Section 1861 - Presumption terms of writing used in primary and general acceptation; evidence of local, technical or peculiar signification

The terms of a writing are presumed to have been used in their primary and general acceptation, but evidence is nevertheless admissible that they have a local, technical, or otherwise peculiar signification, and were so used and understood in the particular instance, in which case the agreement must be construed accordingly.
Enacted 1872.

Section 1862 - Words of instrument partly in writing and partly in printed form inconsistent
When an instrument consists partly of written words and partly of a printed form, and the two are inconsistent, the former controls the latter.
Enacted 1872.

Section 1864 - Terms of agreement intended in different sense by different parties
When the terms of an agreement have been intended in a different sense by the different parties to it, that sense is to prevail against either party in which he supposed the other understood it, and when different constructions of a provision are otherwise equally proper, that is to be taken which is most favorable to the party in whose favor the provision was made.
Enacted 1872.

Section 1865 - Construction of written notice
A written notice, as well as every other writing, is to be construed according to the ordinary acceptation of its terms. Thus a notice to the drawers or indorsers of a bill of exchange or promissory note, that it has been protested for want of acceptance or payment, must be held to import that the same has been duly presented for acceptance or payment and the same refused, and that the holder looks for payment to the person to whom the notice is given.
Enacted 1872.

Section 1866 - Statute or instrument susceptible to two interpretations
When a statute or instrument is equally susceptible of two interpretations, one in favor of natural right, and the other against it, the former is to be adopted.
Enacted 1872.

Title 2 - OF THE KINDS AND DEGREES OF EVIDENCE
Chapter 2 - WITNESSES
Section 1878 - Witness defined
A witness is a person whose declaration under oath is received as evidence for any purpose, whether such declaration be made on oral examination, or by deposition or affidavit.
Enacted 1872.

Chapter 3 - WRITINGS
Article 2 - PUBLIC WRITINGS
Section 1895 - Law either written or unwritten
Laws, whether organic or ordinary, are either written or unwritten.
Enacted 1872.

Section 1896 - Written law defined
A written law is that which is promulgated in writing, and of which a record is in existence.
Enacted 1872.

Section 1897 - Organic laws; statutes; written laws contained in constitution and statutes
The organic law is the Constitution of Government, and is altogether written. Other written laws are denominated statutes. The written law of this State is therefore contained in its Constitution and statutes, and in the Constitution and statutes of the United States.
Enacted 1872.

Section 1898 - Public or private statutes
Statutes are public or private. A private statute is one which concerns only certain designated individuals, and affects only their private rights. All other statutes are public, in which are included statutes creating or affecting corporations.
Enacted 1872.

Section 1899 - Unwritten law defined
Unwritten law is the law not promulgated and recorded, as mentioned in Section 1896, but which is, nevertheless, observed and administered in the Courts of the country. It has no certain repository, but is collected from the reports of the decisions of the Courts, and the treatises of learned men.
Enacted 1872.

Section 1904 - Judicial record defined
A judicial record is the record or official entry of the proceedings in a Court of justice, or of the official act of a judicial officer, in an action or special proceeding.
Enacted 1872.

Section 1908 - Effect of judgment or final order
(a) The effect of a judgment or final order in an action or special proceeding before a court or judge of this state, or of the United States, having jurisdiction to pronounce the judgment or order, is as follows:
    (1) In case of a judgment or order against a specific thing, or in respect to the probate of a will, or the administration of the estate of a decedent, or in respect to the personal, political, or legal condition or relation of a particular person, the judgment or order is conclusive upon the title to the thing, the will, or administration, or the condition or relation of the person.
    (2) In other cases, the judgment or order is, in respect to the matter directly adjudged, conclusive between the parties and their successors in interest by title subsequent to the commencement of the action or special proceeding, litigating for the same thing under the same title and in the same capacity, provided they have notice, actual or constructive, of the pendency of the action or proceeding.
(b) A person who is not a party but who controls an action, individually or in cooperation with others, is bound by the adjudications of litigated matters as if he were a party if he has a proprietary or financial interest in the judgment or in the determination of a question of fact or of a question of law with reference to the same subject matter or transaction; if the other party has notice of his participation, the other party is equally bound. At any time prior to a final judgment, as defined in Section 577, a determination of whether the judgment, verdict upon which it was entered, or a finding upon which it was entered is to be binding upon a nonparty pursuant to this subdivision or whether such nonparty is entitled to the benefit of this subdivision may, on the noticed motion of any party or any nonparty that may be affected by this subdivision, be made in the court in which the action was tried or in which the action is pending on appeal. If no such motion is made before the judgment becomes final, the determination may be made in a separate action. If appropriate, a judgment may be entered or ordered to be entered pursuant to such determination.
Amended by Stats. 1975, Ch. 225.

Section 1908.5 - Alleging conclusive judgment or order in pleadings

When a judgment or order of a court is conclusive, the judgment or order must be alleged in the pleadings if there be an opportunity to do so; if there be no such opportunity, the judgment or order may be used as evidence.
Added by Stats. 1965, Ch. 299.

Section 1909 - Disputable presumption created by judicial orders
Other judicial orders of a Court or Judge of this State, or of the United States, create a disputable presumption, according to the matter directly determined, between the same parties and their representatives and successors in interest by title subsequent to the commencement of the action or special proceeding, litigating for the same thing under the same title and in the same capacity.
Enacted 1872.

Section 1910 - Parties deemed same
The parties are deemed to be the same when those between whom the evidence is offered were on opposite sides in the former case, and a judgment or other determination could in that case have been made between them alone, though other parties were joined with both or either.
Enacted 1872.

Section 1911 - That deemed adjudged in former judgment
That only is deemed to have been adjudged in a former judgment which appears upon its face to have been so adjudged, or which was actually and necessarily included therein or necessary thereto.
Enacted 1872.

Section 1912 - Party bound by record and party stands in relation to surety
Whenever, pursuant to the last four sections, a party is bound by a record, and such party stands in the relation of a surety for another, the latter is also bound from the time that he has notice of the action or proceeding, and an opportunity at the surety's request to join in the defense.
Enacted 1872.

Section 1913 - Effect of judicial record on sister state
(a) Subject to subdivision (b), the effect of a judicial record of a sister state is the same in this state as in the state where it was made, except that it can only be enforced in this state by an action or special proceeding.
(b) The authority of a guardian, conservator, or committee, or of a personal representative, does not extend beyond the jurisdiction of the government under which that person was invested with authority, except to the extent expressly authorized by Article 4 (commencing with Section 2011) of Chapter 8 of Part 3 of Division 4 of the Probate Code or another statute.
Amended by Stats 2014 ch 553 (SB 940),s 1, eff. 1/1/2015, op. 1/1/2016.

Section 1914 - Effect of judicial record of court of admiralty of foreign country
The effect of the judicial record of a Court of admiralty of a foreign country is the same as if it were the record of a Court of admiralty of the United States.
Enacted 1872.

Section 1916 - Grounds for impeaching judicial record
Any judicial record may be impeached by evidence of a want of jurisdiction in the Court or judicial officer, of collusion between the parties, or of fraud in the party offering the record, in respect to the proceedings.
Enacted 1872.

Section 1917 - Jurisdiction to sustain record
The jurisdiction sufficient to sustain a record is jurisdiction over the cause, over the parties, and over the thing, when a specific thing is the subject of the judgment.
Enacted 1872.

Article 3 - PRIVATE WRITINGS

Section 1929 - Either sealed or unsealed
Private writings are either:
1. Sealed; or,
2. Unsealed.
Enacted 1872.

Section 1930 - Seal defined
A seal is a particular sign, made to attest, in the most formal manner, the execution of an instrument.
Enacted 1872.

Section 1931 - Public seal of state; private seal; seal of sister state or foreign country regarded in state
Section Nineteen Hundred and Thirty-one. A public seal in this State is a stamp or impression made by a public officer with an instrument provided by law, to attest the execution of an official or public document, upon the paper, or upon any substance attached to the paper, which is capable of receiving a visible impression. A private seal may be made in the same manner by any instrument, or it may be made by the scroll of a pen, or by writing the word "seal" against the signature of the writer. A scroll or other sign, made in a sister State or foreign country, and there recognized as a seal, must be so regarded in this State.
Amended by Code Amendments 1873-74, Ch. 383.

Section 1932 - No difference between sealed and unsealed writings
Section Nineteen Hundred and Thirty-two. There shall be no difference hereafter, in this State, between sealed and unsealed writings. A writing under seal may therefore be changed, or altogether discharged by a writing not under seal.
Amended by Code Amendments 1873-74, Ch. 383.

Section 1933 - Execution of instrument
The execution of an instrument is the subscribing and delivering it, with or without affixing a seal.
Enacted 1872.

Section 1934 - Agreement in writing without seal for compromise or settlement of debt
An agreement, in writing, without a seal, for the compromise or settlement of a debt, is as obligatory as if a seal were affixed.
Enacted 1872.

Section 1935 - Subscribing witness
A subscribing witness is one who sees a writing executed or hears it acknowledged, and at the request of the party thereupon signs his name as a witness.
Enacted 1872.

Section 1950 - Removal of record from office where kept
Section Nineteen Hundred and Fifty. The record of a conveyance of real property, or any other record, a transcript of which is admissible in evidence, must not be removed from the office where it is kept, except upon the order of a Court, in cases where the inspection of the record is shown to be essential to the just determination of the cause or proceeding pending, or where the Court is held in the same building with such office.
Amended by Code Amendments 1873-74, Ch. 383.

Section 1952 - Exhibits, depositions or administrative record introduced at trial of civil action or proceeding
(a) The clerk shall retain in his or her custody any exhibit, deposition, or administrative record introduced in the trial of a civil action or proceeding or filed in the action or proceeding until the final determination thereof or the dismissal of the action or proceeding, except that the court may order the exhibit, deposition, or administrative record returned to the respective party or parties at any time upon oral stipulation in open court or by written stipulation by the parties or for good cause shown.
(b) No exhibit or deposition shall be ordered destroyed or otherwise disposed of pursuant to this section where a party to the action or proceeding files a written notice with the court requesting the preservation of any exhibit, deposition, or administrative record for a stated time, but not to exceed one year.
(c) Upon the conclusion of the trial of a civil action or proceeding at which any exhibit or deposition has been introduced, the court shall order that the exhibit or deposition be destroyed or otherwise disposed of by the clerk. The operative destruction or disposition date shall be 60 days following final determination of the action or proceeding. Final determination includes final determination on appeal. Written notice of the order shall be sent by first-class mail to the parties by the clerk.
(d) Upon the conclusion of any posttrial hearing at which any exhibit, deposition, or administrative record has been introduced, the court shall order that the exhibit or deposition be destroyed or otherwise disposed of by the clerk. The operative date of destruction or disposition shall be 60 days following the conclusion of the hearing, or if an appeal is taken, upon final determination of the appeal. Written notice of the order shall be sent by first-class mail to the parties by the clerk.
Amended by Stats. 1991, Ch. 1090, Sec. 7.

Section 1952.2 - Return of exhibits, depositions and administrative records
Notwithstanding any other provisions of law, upon a judgment becoming final, at the expiration of the appeal period, unless an appeal is pending, the court, in its discretion, and on its own motion by a written order signed by the judge, filed in the action, and an entry thereof made in the register of actions, may order the clerk to return all of the exhibits, depositions, and administrative records introduced or filed in the trial of a civil action or proceeding to the attorneys for the parties introducing or filing the same.
Amended by Stats. 1991, Ch. 1090, Sec. 8.

Section 1952.3 - Destruction of exhibit, deposition or administrative record
Notwithstanding any other provision of the law, the court, on its own motion, may order the destruction or other disposition of any exhibit, deposition, or administrative record introduced in the trial or posttrial hearing of a civil action or proceeding or filed in the action or proceeding that, if appeal has not been taken from the decision of the court in the action or proceeding, remains in the custody of the court or clerk five years after time for appeal has expired, or, if appeal has been taken, remains in the custody of the court or clerk five years after final determination thereof, or that remains in the custody of the court or clerk for a period of five years after any of the following:
(a) A motion for a new trial has been granted and a memorandum to set the case for trial has not been filed, or a motion to set for trial has not been made within five years.
(b) The dismissal of the action or proceeding. In addition, the court on its own motion, may order the destruction or other disposition of any exhibit, deposition, or administrative record that remains in the custody of the court or clerk for a period of 10 years after the introduction or filing of the action or proceeding if, in the discretion of the court, the exhibit, deposition, or administrative record should be disposed of or destroyed.
The order shall be entered in the register of actions of each case in which the order is made.
No exhibit, deposition, or administrative record shall be ordered destroyed or otherwise disposed of pursuant to this section if a party to the action or proceeding files a written notice with the court requesting the preservation of any exhibit, deposition, or administrative record for a stated time, but not to exceed one year.
Any sealed file shall be retained for at least two years after the date on which destruction would otherwise be authorized pursuant to this section.
Amended by Stats. 1991, Ch. 1090, Sec. 9.

Article 4 - RECORDS DESTROYED IN FIRE OR CALAMITY

Section 1953 - Record includes
As used in this article "record" includes all or any part of any judgment, decree, order, document, paper, process, or file.
Added by Stats. 1953, Ch. 52.

Section 1953.01 - Application for order authorizing record be supplied by copy of original
Whenever in any action or special proceeding, civil or criminal, in any court of this State any record is lost, injured, or destroyed by reason of conflagration or other public calamity, any person interested therein may apply by a duly verified petition in writing to the court for an order authorizing such defect to be supplied by a duly certified copy of the original, where such copy can be obtained.
Added by Stats. 1953, Ch. 52.

Section 1953.02 - Court order that copy of record have same effect as original
Upon notice given pursuant to Sections 1010 to 1020, inclusive, of this code, and its being shown to the satisfaction of the court that the record has been so lost, injured, or destroyed, the court shall make an order that the certified copy shall thereafter have the same effect in all respects as the original would have had.
Added by Stats. 1953, Ch. 52.

Section 1953.03 - Application that copy of record cannot be obtained and unless supplied or remedied damage to applicant may result
Whenever in any action or special proceeding, civil or criminal, in any court of this State any record is lost, injured, or destroyed by reason of conflagration or other public calamity, and a certified copy of the original cannot be supplied, any person interested therein may make written application to the court, verified by affidavit, showing such loss, injury, or destruction, and that a certified copy of the record cannot be obtained by the person making the application, and that such loss, injury, or destruction occurred by conflagration, or other calamity, without the fault or neglect of the person making the application, and that such loss, injury, or destruction, unless supplied or remedied may result in damage to the person making the application. Thereupon the court shall cause notice of the application to be given pursuant to Sections 1010 to 1020, inclusive, of this code.
Added by Stats. 1953, Ch. 52.

Section 1953.04 - Order reciting substance of lost, injured or destroyed record
Upon the hearing if the court is satisfied that the statements contained in the written application are true, it shall make an order reciting the substance and effect of the lost, injured, or destroyed record. The order shall have the same effect that the original would have had if it had not been lost, injured, or destroyed, so far as concerns the person making the application, and the persons who have been notified, pursuant to Section 1953.03.
Added by Stats. 1953, Ch. 52.

Section 1953.05 - Restored record in proceeding in rem
The record in all cases where the proceeding is in rem, including probate, guardianship, conservatorship, and insolvency proceedings, may be supplied in like manner upon like notice to all persons who have appeared therein, and upon notice by publication or postings for not less than 10 days, as the court may order, to all persons who have not appeared. When restored the record shall have the same effect as the original upon all

persons who have been personally served with notice of the application, and as to all other persons it shall be prima facie evidence of the contents of the original.

Amended by Stats. 1979, Ch. 730.

Section 1953.06 - Certified copy of transcript of record filed in reviewing court

If an appeal to a reviewing court has been taken in any action or special proceeding in any trial court in which the record has been subsequently lost or destroyed by conflagration or other public calamity and a transcript of such record has been filed in the reviewing court, any person interested in the action or special proceeding may obtain a certified copy of all or any portion of the transcript from the clerk of the reviewing court and may file such certified copy in the office of the clerk of the court from which the appeal was taken. Thereupon the certified copy may be made the basis of any further proceedings or processes in the trial court in such action or special proceeding to all intents and purposes as if the original record were on file.

Amended by Stats. 1967, Ch. 17.

Article 4.5 - PRIVATE RECORDS DESTROYED IN DISASTER OR CALAMITY

Section 1953.10 - Application for order establishing record

Any person, corporation, copartnership, organization, institution, business, member of profession or calling interested in establishing the existence, substance, genuineness, or authenticity of any memorandum, book, map, chart, manuscript, writing, account, entry, record, print, document, representation, or combination thereof that has been damaged, rendered wholly or partially illegible, destroyed in whole or in part or lost by explosion, conflagration, earthquake, disaster or other public calamity, may apply by duly verified petition to the court for an order establishing, reciting, or declaring the existence, substance, genuineness or authenticity of the same.

Added by Stats. 1961, Ch. 1311.

Section 1953.11 - Notice of petition and hearing

Notice of the filing of the petition and of the time and place of the hearing thereof shall be given to such persons, if any, as the court shall designate by its order. Such order shall specify how such notice shall be given and may be by publication, posting, personal service or otherwise as the court shall direct. Upon the hearing of the petition proof shall be submitted to the court that notice has been given as prescribed in such order.

Added by Stats. 1961, Ch. 1311.

Section 1953.12 - Order reciting existence of record

Upon the hearing the court shall receive such evidence as may be required and if the court is satisfied that the statements contained in the petition are true, it shall make an order reciting the existence, substance, genuineness or authenticity of the destroyed or lost memorandum, book, map, chart, manuscript, writing, account, entry, print, document, representation or combination thereof.

Added by Stats. 1961, Ch. 1311.

Section 1953.13 - Order deemed in lieu of original and of same effect as original

The order of court made upon such hearing shall refer to the memorandum, book, map, chart, manuscript, writing, account, entry, record, print, document, representation or combination thereof which is the subject of said petition and such court order shall be deemed in lieu of the original and have the same effect as if the original had not been damaged, destroyed or otherwise rendered wholly or partially illegible.

Added by Stats. 1961, Ch. 1311.

Chapter 6 - INDISPENSABLE EVIDENCE

Section 1971 - Creating, granting, assigning, surrendering or declaring estate or interest in real property

No estate or interest in real property, other than for leases for a term not exceeding one year, nor any power over or concerning it, or in any manner relating thereto, can be created, granted, assigned, surrendered, or declared, otherwise than by operation of law, or a conveyance or other instrument in writing, subscribed by the party creating, granting, assigning, surrendering, or declaring the same, or by the party's lawful agent thereunto authorized by writing.

Amended by Stats. 1986, Ch. 820, Sec. 19. Operative July 1, 1987, by Sec. 43 of Ch. 820.

Section 1972 - Power to compel specific performance; trust not prevented from arising or being extinguished

(a) Section 1971 shall not be construed to abridge the power of any court to compel the specific performance of an agreement, in case of part performance thereof.

(b) Section 1971 does not affect the creation of a trust under Division 9 (commencing with Section 15000) of the Probate Code nor prevent any trust from arising or being extinguished by implication or operation of law.

Amended by Stats. 1986, Ch. 820, Sec. 20. Operative July 1, 1987, by Sec. 43 of Ch. 820.

Section 1974 - Charging person upon representation as to credit of third person

No evidence is admissible to charge a person upon a representation as to the credit of a third person, unless such representation, or some memorandum thereof, be in writing, and either subscribed by or in the handwriting of the party to be charged. This section is a Statute of Frauds provision and is to be applied in a manner that is consistent with the manner in which subdivision 2 of Section 1624 of the Civil Code is applied.

Amended by Stats. 1970, Ch. 720.

Title 3 - OF THE PRODUCTION OF EVIDENCE

Chapter 2 - MEANS OF PRODUCTION

Section 1985 - Subpoenas or subpoenas duces tecum

(a) The process by which the attendance of a witness is required is the subpoena. It is a writ or order directed to a person and requiring the person's attendance at a particular time and place to testify as a witness. It may also require a witness to bring any books, documents, electronically stored information, or other things under the witness's control which the witness is bound by law to produce in evidence. When a county recorder is using the microfilm system for recording, and a witness is subpoenaed to present a record, the witness shall be deemed to have complied with the subpoena if the witness produces a certified copy thereof.

(b) A copy of an affidavit shall be served with a subpoena duces tecum issued before trial, showing good cause for the production of the matters and things described in the subpoena, specifying the exact matters or things desired to be produced, setting forth in full detail the materiality thereof to the issues involved in the case, and stating that the witness has the desired matters or things in his or her possession or under his or her control.

(c) The clerk, or a judge, shall issue a subpoena or subpoena duces tecum signed and sealed but otherwise in blank to a party requesting it, who shall fill it in before service. An attorney at law who is the attorney of record in an action or proceeding, may sign and issue a subpoena to require attendance before the court in which the action or proceeding is pending or at the trial of an issue therein, or upon the taking of a deposition in an action or proceeding pending therein; the subpoena in such a case need not be sealed. An attorney at law who is the attorney of record in an action or proceeding, may sign and issue a subpoena duces tecum to require production of the matters or things described in the subpoena.

Amended by Stats 2012 ch 72 (SB 1574),s 1, eff. 1/1/2013.

Section 1985.1 - Agreement to appear at time other than time specified in subpoena; failure to appear pursuant to agreement

Any person who is subpoenaed to appear at a session of court, or at the trial of an issue therein, may, in lieu of appearance at the time specified in the subpoena, agree with the party at whose request the subpoena was issued to appear at another time or upon such notice as may be agreed upon. Any failure to appear pursuant to such agreement may be punished as a contempt by the court issuing the subpoena. The facts establishing or disproving such agreement and the failure to appear may be proved by an affidavit of any person having personal knowledge of the facts.
Added by Stats. 1969, Ch. 140.

Section 1985.2 - Notice contained in subpoena requiring attendance of witness
Any subpoena which requires the attendance of a witness at any civil trial shall contain the following notice in a type face designed to call attention to the notice:
Contact the attorney requesting this subpoena, listed above, before the date on which you are required to be in court, if you have any question about the time or date for you to appear, or if you want to be certain that your presence in court is required.
Added by Stats. 1978, Ch. 431.

Section 1985.3 - Service on consumer whose records are being sought
(a) For purposes of this section, the following definitions apply:
  (1) "Personal records" means the original, any copy of books, documents, other writings, or electronically stored information pertaining to a consumer and which are maintained by any "witness" which is a physician, dentist, ophthalmologist, optometrist, chiropractor, physical therapist, acupuncturist, podiatrist, veterinarian, veterinary hospital, veterinary clinic, pharmacist, pharmacy, hospital, medical center, clinic, radiology or MRI center, clinical or diagnostic laboratory, state or national bank, state or federal association (as defined in Section 5102 of the Financial Code), state or federal credit union, trust company, anyone authorized by this state to make or arrange loans that are secured by real property, security brokerage firm, insurance company, title insurance company, underwritten title company, escrow agent licensed pursuant to Division 6 (commencing with Section 17000) of the Financial Code or exempt from licensure pursuant to Section 17006 of the Financial Code, attorney, accountant, institution of the Farm Credit System, as specified in Section 2002 of Title 12 of the United States Code, or telephone corporation which is a public utility, as defined in Section 216 of the Public Utilities Code, or psychotherapist, as defined in Section 1010 of the Evidence Code, or a private or public preschool, elementary school, secondary school, or postsecondary school as described in Section 76244 of the Education Code.
  (2) "Consumer" means any individual, partnership of five or fewer persons, association, or trust which has transacted business with, or has used the services of, the witness or for whom the witness has acted as agent or fiduciary.
  (3) "Subpoenaing party" means the person or persons causing a subpoena duces tecum to be issued or served in connection with any civil action or proceeding pursuant to this code, but shall not include the state or local agencies described in Section 7465 of the Government Code, or any entity provided for under Article VI of the California Constitution in any proceeding maintained before an adjudicative body of that entity pursuant to Chapter 4 (commencing with Section 6000) of Division 3 of the Business and Professions Code.
  (4) "Deposition officer" means a person who meets the qualifications specified in Section 2020.420.
(b) Prior to the date called for in the subpoena duces tecum for the production of personal records, the subpoenaing party shall serve or cause to be served on the consumer whose records are being sought a copy of the subpoena duces tecum, of the affidavit supporting the issuance of the subpoena, if any, and of the notice described in subdivision (e), and proof of service as indicated in paragraph (1) of subdivision (c). This service shall be made as follows:
  (1) To the consumer personally, or at his or her last known address, or in accordance with Chapter 5 (commencing with Section 1010) of Title 14 of Part 3, or, if he or she is a party, to his or her attorney of record. If the consumer is a minor, service shall be made on the minor's parent, guardian, conservator, or similar fiduciary, or if one of them cannot be located with reasonable diligence, then service shall be made on any person having the care or control of the minor or with whom the minor resides or by whom the minor is employed, and on the minor if the minor is at least 12 years of age.
  (2) Not less than 10 days prior to the date for production specified in the subpoena duces tecum, plus the additional time provided by Section 1013 if service is by mail.
  (3) At least five days prior to service upon the custodian of the records, plus the additional time provided by Section 1013 if service is by mail.
(c) Prior to the production of the records, the subpoenaing party shall do either of the following:
  (1) Serve or cause to be served upon the witness a proof of personal service or of service by mail attesting to compliance with subdivision (b).
  (2) Furnish the witness a written authorization to release the records signed by the consumer or by his or her attorney of record. The witness may presume that any attorney purporting to sign the authorization on behalf of the consumer acted with the consent of the consumer, and that any objection to release of records is waived.
(d) A subpoena duces tecum for the production of personal records shall be served in sufficient time to allow the witness a reasonable time, as provided in Section 2020.410, to locate and produce the records or copies thereof.
(e) Every copy of the subpoena duces tecum and affidavit, if any, served on a consumer or his or her attorney in accordance with subdivision (b) shall be accompanied by a notice, in a typeface designed to call attention to the notice, indicating that (1) records about the consumer are being sought from the witness named on the subpoena; (2) if the consumer objects to the witness furnishing the records to the party seeking the records, the consumer must file papers with the court or serve a written objection as provided in subdivision (g) prior to the date specified for production on the subpoena; and (3) if the party who is seeking the records will not agree in writing to cancel or limit the subpoena, an attorney should be consulted about the consumer's interest in protecting his or her rights of privacy. If a notice of taking of deposition is also served, that other notice may be set forth in a single document with the notice required by this subdivision.
(f) A subpoena duces tecum for personal records maintained by a telephone corporation which is a public utility, as defined in Section 216 of the Public Utilities Code, shall not be valid or effective unless it includes a consent to release, signed by the consumer whose records are requested, as required by Section 2891 of the Public Utilities Code.
(g) Any consumer whose personal records are sought by a subpoena duces tecum and who is a party to the civil action in which this subpoena duces tecum is served may, prior to the date for production, bring a motion under Section 1987.1 to quash or modify the subpoena duces tecum. Notice of the bringing of that motion shall be given to the witness and deposition officer at least five days prior to production. The failure to provide notice to the deposition officer shall not invalidate the motion to quash or modify the subpoena duces tecum but may be raised by the deposition officer as an affirmative defense in any action for liability for improper release of records. Any other consumer or nonparty whose personal records are sought by a subpoena duces tecum may, prior to the date of production, serve on the subpoenaing party, the witness, and the deposition officer, a written objection that cites the specific grounds on which production of the personal records should be prohibited.
No witness or deposition officer shall be required to produce personal records after receipt of notice that the motion has been brought by a consumer, or after receipt of a written objection from a nonparty consumer, except upon order of the court in which the action is pending or by agreement of the parties, witnesses, and consumers affected.
The party requesting a consumer's personal records may bring a motion under Section 1987.1 to enforce the subpoena within 20 days of service of the written objection. The motion shall be accompanied by a declaration showing a reasonable and good faith attempt at informal resolution of the dispute between the party requesting the personal records and the consumer or the consumer's attorney.

(h) Upon good cause shown and provided that the rights of witnesses and consumers are preserved, a subpoenaing party shall be entitled to obtain an order shortening the time for service of a subpoena duces tecum or waiving the requirements of subdivision (b) where due diligence by the subpoenaing party has been shown.

(i) Nothing contained in this section shall be construed to apply to any subpoena duces tecum which does not request the records of any particular consumer or consumers and which requires a custodian of records to delete all information which would in any way identify any consumer whose records are to be produced.

(j) This section shall not apply to proceedings conducted under Division 1 (commencing with Section 50), Division 4 (commencing with Section 3200), Division 4.5 (commencing with Section 6100), or Division 4.7 (commencing with Section 6200), of the Labor Code.

(k) Failure to comply with this section shall be sufficient basis for the witness to refuse to produce the personal records sought by a subpoena duces tecum.

(l) If the subpoenaing party is the consumer, and the consumer is the only subject of the subpoenaed records, notice to the consumer, and delivery of the other documents specified in subdivision (b) to the consumer, is not required under this section.

Amended by Stats 2012 ch 72 (SB 1574),s 2, eff. 1/1/2013.
Amended by Stats 2005 ch 300 (AB 496),s 6, eff. 1/1/2006
Amended by Stats 2004 ch 182 (AB 3081),s 18, eff. 1/1/2005
Amended September 21, 1999 (Bill Number: AB 794) (Chapter 444).

Section 1985.4 - Procedure applicable to records containing personal information

The procedures set forth in Section 1985.3 are applicable to a subpoena duces tecum for records containing "personal information," as defined in Section 1798.3 of the Civil Code that are otherwise exempt from public disclosure under a provision listed in Section 7920.505 of the Government Code that are maintained by a state or local agency as defined in Section 7920.510 or 7920.540 of the Government Code. For the purposes of this section, "witness" means a state or local agency as defined in Section 7920.510 or 7920.540 of the Government Code and "consumer" means any employee of any state or local agency as defined in Section 7920.510 or 7920.540 of the Government Code, or any other natural person. Nothing in this section shall pertain to personnel records as defined in Section 832.8 of the Penal Code.

Amended by Stats 2021 ch 615 (AB 474),s 57, eff. 1/1/2022, op. 1/1/2023.
Amended by Stats. 1988, Ch. 441, Sec. 1.

Section 1985.5 - Subpoena requiring attendance before officer or commissioner out of court

If a subpena requires the attendance of a witness before an officer or commissioner out of court, it shall, for a refusal to be sworn, or to answer as a witness, or to subscribe an affidavit or deposition when required, also require the witness to attend a session of the court issuing the subpena at a time and place thereof to be fixed by said officer or commissioner.

Added by Stats. 1941, Ch. 405.

Section 1985.6 - Service on employee whose records are being sought

(a) For purposes of this section, the following terms have the following meanings:

(1) "Deposition officer" means a person who meets the qualifications specified in Section 2020.420.

(2) "Employee" means any individual who is or has been employed by a witness subject to a subpoena duces tecum. "Employee" also means any individual who is or has been represented by a labor organization that is a witness subject to a subpoena duces tecum.

(3) "Employment records" means the original or any copy of books, documents, other writings, or electronically stored information pertaining to the employment of any employee maintained by the current or former employer of the employee, or by any labor organization that has represented or currently represents the employee.

(4) "Labor organization" has the meaning set forth in Section 1117 of the Labor Code.

(5) "Subpoenaing party" means the person or persons causing a subpoena duces tecum to be issued or served in connection with any civil action or proceeding, but does not include the state or local agencies described in Section 7465 of the Government Code, or any entity provided for under Article VI of the California Constitution in any proceeding maintained before an adjudicative body of that entity pursuant to Chapter 4 (commencing with Section 6000) of Division 3 of the Business and Professions Code.

(b) Prior to the date called for in the subpoena duces tecum of the production of employment records, the subpoenaing party shall serve or cause to be served on the employee whose records are being sought a copy of: the subpoena duces tecum; the affidavit supporting the issuance of the subpoena, if any; the notice described in subdivision (e); and proof of service as provided in paragraph (1) of subdivision (c). This service shall be made as follows:

(1) To the employee personally, or at his or her last known address, or in accordance with Chapter 5 (commencing with Section 1010) of Title 14 of Part 2, or, if he or she is a party, to his or her attorney of record. If the employee is a minor, service shall be made on the minor's parent, guardian, conservator, or similar fiduciary, or if one of them cannot be located with reasonable diligence, then service shall be made on any person having the care or control of the minor, or with whom the minor resides, and on the minor if the minor is at least 12 years of age.

(2) Not less than 10 days prior to the date for production specified in the subpoena duces tecum, plus the additional time provided by Section 1013 if service is by mail.

(3) At least five days prior to service upon the custodian of the employment records, plus the additional time provided by Section 1013 if service is by mail.

(c) Prior to the production of the records, the subpoenaing party shall either:

(1) Serve or cause to be served upon the witness a proof of personal service or of service by mail attesting to compliance with subdivision (b).

(2) Furnish the witness a written authorization to release the records signed by the employee or by his or her attorney of record. The witness may presume that the attorney purporting to sign the authorization on behalf of the employee acted with the consent of the employee, and that any objection to the release of records is waived.

(d) A subpoena duces tecum for the production of employment records shall be served in sufficient time to allow the witness a reasonable time, as provided in Section 2020.410, to locate and produce the records or copies thereof.

(e) Every copy of the subpoena duces tecum and affidavit served on an employee or his or her attorney in accordance with subdivision (b) shall be accompanied by a notice, in a typeface designed to call attention to the notice, indicating that (1) employment records about the employee are being sought from the witness named on the subpoena; (2) the employment records may be protected by a right of privacy; (3) if the employee objects to the witness furnishing the records to the party seeking the records, the employee shall file papers with the court prior to the date specified for production on the subpoena; and (4) if the subpoenaing party does not agree in writing to cancel or limit the subpoena, an attorney should be consulted about the employee's interest in protecting his or her rights of privacy. If a notice of taking of deposition is also served, that other notice may be set forth in a single document with the notice required by this subdivision.

(f)

(1) Any employee whose employment records are sought by a subpoena duces tecum may, prior to the date for production, bring a motion under Section 1987.1 to quash or modify the subpoena duces tecum. Notice of the bringing of that motion shall be given to the witness and the deposition officer at least five days prior to production. The failure to provide notice to the deposition officer does not invalidate the motion to quash or modify the subpoena duces tecum but may be raised by the deposition officer as an affirmative defense in any action for liability for improper release of records.

(2) Any nonparty employee whose employment records are sought by a subpoena duces tecum may, prior to the date of production, serve on the subpoenaing party, the deposition officer, and the witness a written objection that cites the specific grounds on which production of the employment records should be prohibited.

(3) No witness or deposition officer shall be required to produce employment records after receipt of notice that the motion has been brought by an employee, or after receipt of a written objection from a nonparty employee, except upon order of the court in which the action is pending or by agreement of the parties, witnesses, and employees affected.

(4) The party requesting an employee's employment records may bring a motion under subdivision (c) of Section 1987 to enforce the subpoena within 20 days of service of the written objection. The motion shall be accompanied by a declaration showing a reasonable and good faith attempt at informal resolution of the dispute between the party requesting the employment records and the employee or the employee's attorney.

(g) Upon good cause shown and provided that the rights of witnesses and employees are preserved, a subpoenaing party shall be entitled to obtain an order shortening the time for service of a subpoena duces tecum or waiving the requirements of subdivision (b) if due diligence by the subpoenaing party has been shown.

(h) This section may not be construed to apply to any subpoena duces tecum that does not request the records of any particular employee or employees and that requires a custodian of records to delete all information that would in any way identify any employee whose records are to be produced.

(i) This section does not apply to proceedings conducted under Division 1 (commencing with Section 50), Division 4 (commencing with Section 3200), Division 4.5 (commencing with Section 6100), or Division 4.7 (commencing with Section 6200), of the Labor Code.

(j) Failure to comply with this section shall be sufficient basis for the witness to refuse to produce the employment records sought by subpoena duces tecum.

(k) If the subpoenaing party is the employee, and the employee is the only subject of the subpoenaed records, notice to the employee, and delivery of the other documents specified in subdivision (b) to the employee, are not required under this section.

Amended by Stats 2012 ch 72 (SB 1574),s 3, eff. 1/1/2013.
Amended by Stats 2006 ch 538 (SB 1852),s 76, eff. 1/1/2007.
Amended by Stats 2005 ch 300 (AB 496),s 7.5, eff. 1/1/2006
Amended by Stats 2005 ch 294 (AB 333),s 5, eff. 1/1/2006
Amended by Stats 2004 ch 101 (SB 1465), s 1, eff. 7/1/2005.
Amended September 21, 1999 (Bill Number: AB 794) (Chapter 444).

Section 1985.7 - Order to show cause why medical provider's records should not be produced

When a medical provider fails to comply with Section 1158 of the Evidence Code, in addition to any other available remedy, the demanding party may apply to the court for an order to show cause why the records should not be produced.

Any order to show cause issued pursuant to this section shall be served upon respondent in the same manner as a summons. It shall be returnable no sooner than 20 days after issuance unless ordered otherwise upon a showing of substantial hardship. The court shall impose monetary sanctions pursuant to Section 1158 of the Evidence Code unless it finds that the person subject to the sanction acted with substantial justification or that other circumstances make the imposition of the sanction unjust.

Added by Stats. 1996, Ch. 1159, Sec. 12. Effective January 1, 1997.

Section 1985.8 - Production of electronically stored information

(a)

(1) A subpoena in a civil proceeding may require that electronically stored information, as defined in Section 2016.020, be produced and that the party serving the subpoena, or someone acting on the party's request, be permitted to inspect, copy, test, or sample the information.

(2) Any subpoena seeking electronically stored information shall comply with the requirements of this chapter.

(b) A party serving a subpoena requiring production of electronically stored information may specify the form or forms in which each type of information is to be produced.

(c) If a person responding to a subpoena for production of electronically stored information objects to the specified form or forms for producing the information, the subpoenaed person may provide an objection stating the form or forms in which it intends to produce each type of information.

(d) Unless the subpoenaing party and the subpoenaed person otherwise agree or the court otherwise orders, the following shall apply:

(1) If a subpoena requiring production of electronically stored information does not specify a form or forms for producing a type of electronically stored information, the person subpoenaed shall produce the information in the form or forms in which it is ordinarily maintained or in a form that is reasonably usable.

(2) A subpoenaed person need not produce the same electronically stored information in more than one form.

(e) The subpoenaed person opposing the production, inspection, copying, testing, or sampling of electronically stored information on the basis that information is from a source that is not reasonably accessible because of undue burden or expense shall bear the burden of demonstrating that the information is from a source that is not reasonably accessible because of undue burden or expense.

(f) If the person from whom discovery of electronically stored information is subpoenaed establishes that the information is from a source that is not reasonably accessible because of undue burden or expense, the court may nonetheless order discovery if the subpoenaing party shows good cause, subject to any limitations imposed under subdivision (i).

(g) If the court finds good cause for the production of electronically stored information from a source that is not reasonably accessible, the court may set conditions for the discovery of the electronically stored information, including allocation of the expense of discovery.

(h) If necessary, the subpoenaed person, at the reasonable expense of the subpoenaing party, shall, through detection devices, translate any data compilations included in the subpoena into a reasonably usable form.

(i) The court shall limit the frequency or extent of discovery of electronically stored information, even from a source that is reasonably accessible, if the court determines that any of the following conditions exists:

(1) It is possible to obtain the information from some other source that is more convenient, less burdensome, or less expensive.

(2) The discovery sought is unreasonably cumulative or duplicative.

(3) The party seeking discovery has had ample opportunity by discovery in the action to obtain the information sought.

(4) The likely burden or expense of the proposed discovery outweighs the likely benefit, taking into account the amount in controversy, the resources of the parties, the importance of the issues in the litigation, and the importance of the requested discovery in resolving the issues.

(j) If a subpoenaed person notifies the subpoenaing party that electronically stored information produced pursuant to a subpoena is subject to a claim of privilege or of protection as attorney work product, as described in Section 2031.285, the provisions of Section 2031.285 shall apply.

(k) A party serving a subpoena requiring the production of electronically stored information shall take reasonable steps to avoid imposing undue burden or expense on a person subject to the subpoena.

(l) An order of the court requiring compliance with a subpoena issued under this section shall protect a person who is neither a party nor a party's officer from undue burden or expense resulting from compliance.

(m)

(1) Absent exceptional circumstances, the court shall not impose sanctions on a subpoenaed person or any attorney of a subpoenaed person for failure to provide electronically stored information that has been lost, damaged, altered, or overwritten as the result of the routine, good faith operation of an electronic information system.

(2) This subdivision shall not be construed to alter any obligation to preserve discoverable information.

Amended by Stats 2012 ch 72 (SB 1574),s 4, eff. 1/1/2013.

Added by Stats 2009 ch 5 (AB 5),s 2, eff. 6/29/2009.

Section 1986 - When subpoena obtainable

A subpoena is obtainable as follows:

(a) To require attendance before a court, or at the trial of an issue therein, or upon the taking of a deposition in an action or proceeding pending therein, it is obtainable from the clerk of the court in which the action or proceeding is pending.

(b) To require attendance before a commissioner appointed to take testimony by a court of a foreign country, or of the United States, or of any other state in the United States, or before any officer or officers empowered by the laws of the United States to take testimony, it may be obtained from the clerk of the superior court of the county in which the witness is to be examined.

(c) To require attendance out of court, in cases not provided for in subdivision (a), before a judge, justice, or other officer authorized to administer oaths or take testimony in any matter under the laws of this state, it is obtainable from the judge, justice, or other officer before whom the attendance is required. If the subpoena is to require attendance before a court, or at the trial of an issue therein, it is obtainable from the clerk, as of course, upon the application of the party desiring it. If it is obtained to require attendance before a commissioner or other officer upon the taking of a deposition, it must be obtained, as of course, from the clerk of the superior court of the county wherein the attendance is required upon the application of the party requiring it.

Amended by Stats 2007 ch 263 (AB 310),s 14, eff. 1/1/2008.

Section 1986.1 - Testimony or other evidence given by journalist

(a) No testimony or other evidence given by a journalist under subpoena in a civil or criminal proceeding may be construed as a waiver of the immunity rights provided by subdivision (b) of Section 2 of Article I of the California Constitution.

(b)

(1) Because important constitutional rights of a third-party witness are adjudicated when rights under subdivision (b) of Section 2 of Article I of the California Constitution are asserted, except in circumstances that pose a clear and substantial threat to the integrity of the criminal investigation or present an imminent risk of death or serious bodily harm, a journalist who is subpoenaed in any civil or criminal proceeding shall be given at least five days' notice by the party issuing the subpoena that his or her appearance will be required.

(2) To protect against the inadvertent disclosure by a third party of information protected by Section 2 of Article I of the California Constitution, a party issuing a subpoena in any civil or criminal proceeding to a third party that seeks the records of a journalist shall, except in circumstances that pose a clear and substantial threat to the integrity of the criminal investigation or present an imminent risk of death or serious bodily harm, provide notice of the subpoena to the journalist and the publisher of the newspaper, magazine, or other publication or station operations manager of the broadcast station that employs or contracts with the journalist, as applicable, at least five days prior to issuing the subpoena. The party issuing the subpoena shall include in the notice, at a minimum, an explanation of why the requested records will be of material assistance to the party seeking them and why alternate sources of information are not sufficient to avoid the need for the subpoena.

(c) If a trial court holds a journalist in contempt of court in a criminal proceeding notwithstanding subdivision (b) of Section 2 of Article I of the California Constitution, the court shall set forth findings, either in writing or on the record, stating at a minimum, why the information will be of material assistance to the party seeking the evidence, and why alternate sources of the information are not sufficient to satisfy the defendant's right to a fair trial under the Sixth Amendment to the United States Constitution and Section 15 of Article I of the California Constitution.

(d) As used in this section, "journalist" means the persons specified in subdivision (b) of Section 2 of Article I of the California Constitution.

Amended by Stats 2013 ch 519 (SB 558),s 1, eff. 1/1/2014.

Added by Stats 2000 ch 377 (AB 1860), s 1, eff. 1/1/2001.

Section 1986.5 - Fees and mileage of person subpoenaed and required to give deposition

Any person who is subpoenaed and required to give a deposition shall be entitled to receive the same witness fees and mileage as if the subpoena required him or her to attend and testify before a court in which the action or proceeding is pending. Notwithstanding this requirement, the only fees owed to a witness who is required to produce business records under Section 1560 of the Evidence Code pursuant to a subpoena duces tecum, but who is not required to personally attend a deposition away from his or her place of business, shall be those prescribed in Section 1563 of the Evidence Code.

Amended by Stats. 1986, Ch. 603, Sec. 4.

Section 1987 - Service of subpoena

(a) Except as provided in Sections 68097.1 to 68097.8, inclusive, of the Government Code, the service of a subpoena is made by delivering a copy, or a ticket containing its substance, to the witness personally, giving or offering to the witness at the same time, if demanded by him or her, the fees to which he or she is entitled for travel to and from the place designated, and one day's attendance there. The service shall be made so as to allow the witness a reasonable time for preparation and travel to the place of attendance. The service may be made by any person. If service is to be made on a minor, service shall be made on the minor's parent, guardian, conservator, or similar fiduciary, or if one of those persons cannot be located with reasonable diligence, service shall be made on any person having the care or control of the minor or with whom the minor resides or by whom the minor is employed, and on the minor if the minor is 12 years of age or older. If the minor is alleged to come within the description of Section 300, 601, or 602 of the Welfare and Institutions Code and the minor is not in the custody of a parent or guardian, regardless of the age of the minor, service also shall be made upon the designated agent for service of process at the county child welfare department or the probation department under whose jurisdiction the minor has been placed.

(b) In the case of the production of a party to the record of any civil action or proceeding or of a person for whose immediate benefit an action or proceeding is prosecuted or defended or of anyone who is an officer, director, or managing agent of any such party or person, the service of a subpoena upon any such witness is not required if written notice requesting the witness to attend before a court, or at a trial of an issue therein, with the time and place thereof, is served upon the attorney of that party or person. The notice shall be served at least 10 days before the time required for attendance unless the court prescribes a shorter time. If entitled thereto, the witness, upon demand, shall be paid witness fees and mileage before being required to testify. The giving of the notice shall have the same effect as service of a subpoena on the witness, and the parties shall have those rights and the court may make those orders, including the imposition of sanctions, as in the case of a subpoena for attendance before the court.

(c) If the notice specified in subdivision (b) is served at least 20 days before the time required for attendance, or within any shorter period of time as the court may order, it may include a request that the party or person bring with him or her books, documents, electronically stored information, or other things. The notice shall state the exact materials or things desired and that the party or person has them in his or her possession or under his or her control. Within five days thereafter, or any other time period as the court may allow, the party or person of whom the request is made may serve written objections to the request or any part thereof, with a statement of grounds. Thereafter, upon noticed motion of the requesting party, accompanied by a showing of good cause and of materiality of the items to the issues, the court may order production of items to which objection was made, unless the objecting party or person establishes good cause for nonproduction or production under limitations or conditions. The procedure of this subdivision is alternative to the procedure provided by Sections 1985 and 1987.5 in the cases herein provided for, and no subpoena duces tecum shall be required. Subject to this subdivision, the notice provided in this subdivision shall have the same effect as is provided in subdivision (b) as to a notice for attendance of that party or person.

Amended by Stats 2012 ch 72 (SB 1574),s 5, eff. 1/1/2013.

Amended by Stats 2002 ch 1008 (AB 3028),s 6, eff. 1/1/2003.

Section 1987.1 - Motion for order quashing, modifying or directing compliance with subpoena including protective orders

(a) If a subpoena requires the attendance of a witness or the production of books, documents, electronically stored information, or other things before a court, or at the trial of an issue therein, or at the taking of a deposition, the court, upon motion reasonably made by any person described in subdivision (b), or upon the court's own motion after giving counsel notice and an opportunity to be heard, may make an order quashing the subpoena entirely, modifying it, or directing compliance with it upon those terms or conditions as the court shall declare, including protective orders. In addition, the court may make any other order as may be appropriate to protect the person from unreasonable or oppressive demands, including unreasonable violations of the right of privacy of the person.

(b) The following persons may make a motion pursuant to subdivision (a):

(1) A party.

(2) A witness.

(3) A consumer described in Section 1985.3.

(4) An employee described in Section 1985.6.

(5) A person whose personally identifying information, as defined in subdivision (b) of Section 1798.79.8 of the Civil Code, is sought in connection with an underlying action involving that person's exercise of free speech rights.

(c) Nothing in this section shall require any person to move to quash, modify, or condition any subpoena duces tecum of personal records of any consumer served under paragraph (1) of subdivision (b) of Section 1985.3 or employment records of any employee served under paragraph (1) of subdivision (b) of Section 1985.6.

Amended by Stats 2012 ch 72 (SB 1574),s 6, eff. 1/1/2013.

Amended by Stats 2008 ch 742 (AB 2433),s 1, eff. 1/1/2009.

Amended by Stats 2007 ch 113 (AB 1126),s 3, eff. 1/1/2008.

Section 1987.2 - Reasonable expenses in making or opposing motions

(a) Except as specified in subdivision (c), in making an order pursuant to motion made under subdivision (c) of Section 1987 or under Section 1987.1, the court may in its discretion award the amount of the reasonable expenses incurred in making or opposing the motion, including reasonable attorney's fees, if the court finds the motion was made or opposed in bad faith or without substantial justification or that one or more of the requirements of the subpoena was oppressive.

(b)

(1) Notwithstanding subdivision (a), absent exceptional circumstances, the court shall not impose sanctions on a subpoenaed person or the attorney of a subpoenaed person for failure to provide electronically stored information that has been lost, damaged, altered, or overwritten as the result of the routine, good faith operation of an electronic information system.

(2) This subdivision shall not be construed to alter any obligation to preserve discoverable information.

(c) If a motion is filed under Section 1987.1 for an order to quash or modify a subpoena from a court of this state for personally identifying information, as defined in subdivision (b) of Section 1798.79.8 of the Civil Code, for use in an action pending in another state, territory, or district of the United States, or in a foreign nation, and that subpoena has been served on any Internet service provider, or on the provider of any other interactive computer service, as defined in Section 230(f)(2)(f)(2) of Title 47 of the United States Code, if the moving party prevails, and if the underlying action arises from the moving party's exercise of free speech rights on the Internet and the respondent has failed to make a prima facie showing of a cause of action, the court shall award the amount of the reasonable expenses incurred in making the motion, including reasonable attorney's fees.

Amended by Stats 2012 ch 72 (SB 1574),s 7, eff. 1/1/2013.

Amended by Stats 2008 ch 742 (AB 2433),s 2, eff. 1/1/2009.

Section 1987.3 - Subpoena served on custodian of records and personal appearance not required

When a subpoena duces tecum is served upon a custodian of records or other qualified witness as provided in Article 4 (commencing with Section 1560) of Chapter 2 of Division 11 of the Evidence Code, and his personal attendance is not required by the terms of the subpoena, Section 1989 shall not apply.

Added by Stats. 1970, Ch. 590.

Section 1987.5 - Service of copy of affidavit upon which subpoena based

The service of a subpoena duces tecum is invalid unless at the time of such service a copy of the affidavit upon which the subpoena is based is served on the person served with the subpoena. In the case of a subpoena duces tecum which requires appearance and the production of matters and things at the taking of a deposition, the subpoena shall not be valid unless a copy of the affidavit upon which the subpoena is based and the designation of the materials to be produced, as set forth in the subpoena, is attached to the notice of taking the deposition served upon each party or its attorney as provided in Chapter 3 (commencing with Section 2002) and in Title 4 (commencing with Section 2016.010). If matters and things are produced pursuant to a subpoena duces tecum in violation of this section, any other party to the action may file a motion for, and the court may grant, an order providing appropriate relief, including, but not limited to, exclusion of the evidence affected by the violation, a retaking of the deposition notwithstanding any other limitation on discovery proceedings, or a continuance. The party causing the subpoena to be served shall retain the original affidavit until final judgment in the action, and shall file the affidavit with the court only upon reasonable request by any party or witness affected thereby. This section does not apply to deposition subpoenas commanding only the production of business records for copying under Article 4 (commencing with Section 2020.410) of Chapter 6 of Title 4.

Amended by Stats 2004 ch 182 (AB 3081),s 20, eff. 7/1/2005

Section 1988 - Witness concealed so as to prevent service

If a witness is concealed in a building or vessel, so as to prevent the service of subpoena upon him, any Court or Judge, or any officer issuing the subpoena, may, upon proof by affidavit of the concealment, and of the materiality of the witness, make an order that the Sheriff of the county serve the subpoena; and the Sheriff must serve it accordingly, and for that purpose may break into the building or vessel where the witness is concealed.

Enacted 1872.

Section 1989 - Witness not obliged to attend unless resident within state at time of service

A witness, including a witness specified in subdivision (b) of Section 1987, is not obliged to attend as a witness before any court, judge, justice or any other officer, unless the witness is a resident within the state at the time of service.

Amended by Stats. 1981, Ch. 184, Sec. 3.

Section 1990 - Requiring person present in court or before judicial officer to testify

A person present in Court, or before a judicial officer, may be required to testify in the same manner as if he were in attendance upon a subpoena issued by such Court or officer.

Enacted 1872.

Section 1991 - Disobedience to subpoena, refusal to be sworn or to answer as witness or to subscribe affidavit or deposition

Disobedience to a subpoena, or a refusal to be sworn, or to answer as a witness, or to subscribe an affidavit or deposition when required, may be punished as a contempt by the court issuing the subpoena.

When the subpoena, in any such case, requires the attendance of the witness before an officer or commissioner out of court, it is the duty of the officer or commissioner to report any disobedience or refusal to be sworn or to answer a question or to subscribe an affidavit or deposition when required, to the court issuing the subpoena. The witness shall not be punished for any refusal to be sworn or to answer a question or to subscribe an affidavit or deposition, unless, after a hearing upon notice, the court orders the witness to be sworn, or to so answer or subscribe and then only for disobedience to the order.

Any judge, justice, or other officer mentioned in subdivision (c) of Section 1986, may report any disobedience or refusal to be sworn or to answer a question or to subscribe an affidavit or deposition when required to the superior court of the county in which attendance was required; and the court thereupon has power, upon notice, to order the witness to perform the omitted act, and any refusal or neglect to comply with the order may be punished as a contempt of court.

In lieu of the reporting of the refusal as hereinabove provided, the party seeking to obtain the deposition or to have the deposition or affidavit signed, at the time of the refusal may request the officer or commissioner to notify the witness that at a time stated, not less than five days nor more than 20 days from the date of the refusal, he or she will report the refusal of the witness to the court and that the party will, at that time, or as soon thereafter as he or she may be heard, apply to the court for an order directing the witness to be sworn, or to answer as a witness, or subscribe the deposition or affidavit, as the case may be, and that the witness is required to attend that session of the court.

The officer or commissioner shall enter in the record of the proceedings an exact transcription of the request made of him or her that he or she notify the witness that the party will apply for an order directing the witness to be sworn or to answer as a witness or subscribe the deposition or affidavit, and of his or her notice to the witness, and the transcription shall be attached to his or her report to the court of the refusal of the witness. The report shall be filed by the officer with the clerk of the court issuing the subpoena, and the witness shall attend that session of the court, and for failure or refusal to do so may be punished for contempt.

At the time so specified by the officer, or at a subsequent time to which the court may have continued the matter, if the officer has theretofore filed a report showing the refusal of the witness, the court shall hear the matter, and without further notice to the witness, may order the witness to be sworn or to answer as a witness or subscribe the deposition or affidavit, as the case may be, and may in the order specify the time and place at which compliance shall be made or to which the taking of the deposition is continued. Thereafter if the witness refuses to comply with the order he or she may be punished for contempt.

Amended by Stats. 1987, Ch. 56, Sec. 24.

Section 1991.1 - Disobedience to subpoena requiring attendance before officer out of court

Disobedience to a subpoena requiring attendance of a witness before an officer out of court in a deposition taken pursuant to Title 4 (commencing with Section 2016.010), or refusal to be sworn as a witness at that deposition, may be punished as contempt, as provided in subdivision (e) of Section 2023.030, without the necessity of a prior order of court directing compliance by the witness.

Amended by Stats 2004 ch 182 (AB 3081),s 21, eff. 7/1/2005

Section 1991.2 - Inapplicability of section 1991 to act or omission occurring in deposition pursuant to Title 4

The provisions of Section 1991 do not apply to any act or omission occurring in a deposition taken pursuant to Title 4 (commencing with Section 2016.010). The provisions of Chapter 7 (commencing with Section 2023.010) of Title 4 are exclusively applicable.

Amended by Stats 2005 ch 294 (AB 333),s 6, eff. 1/1/2006

Section 1992 - Amount forfeited to aggrieved party and damages for failure to appear

A person failing to appear pursuant to a subpoena or a court order also forfeits to the party aggrieved the sum of five hundred dollars ($500), and all damages that he or she may sustain by the failure of the person to appear pursuant to the subpoena or court order, which forfeiture and damages may be recovered in a civil action.

Amended by Stats 2005 ch 474 (AB 1150),s 1, eff. 1/1/2006

Section 1993 - Warrant for arrest of person as alternative to warrant for contempt

(a)

(1) As an alternative to issuing a warrant for contempt pursuant to paragraph (5) or (9) of subdivision (a) of Section 1209, the court may issue a warrant for the arrest of a witness who failed to appear pursuant to a subpoena or a person who failed to appear pursuant to a court order. The court, upon proof of the service of the subpoena or order, may issue a warrant to the sheriff of the county in which the witness or person may be located and the sheriff shall, upon payment of fees as provided in Section 26744.5 of the Government Code, arrest the witness or person and bring him or her before the court.

(2) Before issuing a warrant for a failure to appear pursuant to a subpoena pursuant to this section, the court shall issue a "failure to appear" notice informing the person subject to the subpoena that a failure to appear in response to the notice may result in the issuance of a warrant. This notice requirement may be omitted only upon a showing that the appearance of the person subject to the subpoena is material to the case and that urgency dictates the person's immediate appearance.

(b) The warrant shall contain all of the following:

(1) The title and case number of the action.

(2) The name and physical description of the person to be arrested.

(3) The last known address of the person to be arrested.

(4) The date of issuance and county in which it is issued.

(5) The signature or name of the judicial officer issuing the warrant, the title of his or her office, and the name of the court.

(6) A command to arrest the person for failing to appear pursuant to the subpoena or court order, and specifying the date of service of the subpoena or court order.

(7) A command to bring the person to be arrested before the issuing court, or the nearest court if in session, for the setting of bail in the amount of the warrant or to release on the person's own recognizance. Any person so arrested shall be released from custody if he or she cannot be brought before the court within 12 hours of arrest, and the person shall not be arrested if the court will not be in session during the 12-hour period following the arrest.

(8) A statement indicating the expiration date of the warrant as determined by the court.

(9) The amount of bail.

(10) An endorsement for nighttime service if good cause is shown, as provided in Section 840 of the Penal Code.

(11) A statement indicating whether the person may be released upon a promise to appear, as provided by Section 1993.1. The court shall permit release upon a promise to appear, unless it makes a written finding that the urgency and materiality of the person's appearance in court precludes use of the promise to appear process.

(12) The date and time to appear in court if arrested and released pursuant to paragraph (11).

Amended by Stats 2010 ch 680 (AB 2394),s 15, eff. 1/1/2011.

Amended by Stats 2006 ch 277 (AB 2369),s 3, eff. 1/1/2007.

Added by Stats 2005 ch 474 (AB 1150),s 3, eff. 1/1/2006.
Repealed by Stats 2005 ch 474 (AB 1150),s 2, eff. 1/1/2006.

Section 1993.1 - Release of person arrested upon promise to appear; notice to appear

(a) If authorized by the court as provided by paragraph (11) of subdivision (b) of Section 1993, the sheriff may release the person arrested upon his or her promise to appear as provided in this section.

(b) The sheriff shall prepare in duplicate a written notice to appear in court, containing the title of the case, case number, name and address of the person, the offense charged, and the time when, and place where, the person shall appear in court. In addition, the notice shall advise the person arrested of the provisions of Section 1992.

(c) The date and time specified in the notice to appear in court shall be that determined by the issuing court pursuant to paragraph (12) of subdivision (b) of Section 1993.

(d) The sheriff shall deliver one copy of the notice to appear to the arrested person, and the arrested person, in order to secure release, shall give his or her written promise to appear in court as specified in the notice by signing the duplicate notice, which shall be retained by the sheriff, and the sheriff may require the arrested person, if he or she has no satisfactory identification, to place a right thumbprint, or a left thumbprint or fingerprint if the person has a missing or disfigured right thumb, on the notice to appear. Except for law enforcement purposes relating to the identity of the arrestee, no person or entity may sell, give away, allow the distribution of, include in a database, or create a database with, this print. Upon the signing of the duplicate notice, the arresting officer shall immediately release the person arrested from custody.

(e) The sheriff shall, as soon as practicable, file the original notice with the issuing court. The notice may be electronically transmitted to the court.

(f) The person arrested shall be released unless one of the following is a reason for nonrelease, in which case the arresting officer either may release the person or shall indicate, on a form to be established by his or her employing law enforcement agency, which of the following was a reason for the nonrelease:

(1) The person arrested was so intoxicated that he or she could have been a danger to himself or herself or to others.

(2) The person arrested required medical examination or medical care or was otherwise unable to care for his or her own safety.

(3) There were one or more additional outstanding arrest warrants for the person.

(4) The person arrested demanded to be taken before a magistrate or refused to sign the notice to appear.

Added by Stats 2005 ch 474 (AB 1150),s 4, eff. 1/1/2006.

Section 1993.2 - Failure to appear after being released on promise to appear

If a person arrested on a civil bench warrant issued pursuant to Section 1993 fails to appear after being released on a promise to appear, the court may issue another warrant to bring the person before the court or assess a civil assessment in the amount of not more than one thousand dollars ($1,000), which shall be collected as follows:

(a) The assessment shall not become effective until at least 10 calendar days after the court mails a warning notice to the person by first-class mail to the address shown on the promise to appear or to the person's last known address. If the person appears within the time specified in the notice and shows good cause for the failure to appear or for the failure to pay a fine, the court shall vacate the assessment.

(b) The assessment imposed under subdivision (a) may be enforced in the same manner as a money judgment in a limited civil case, and shall be subject to the due process requirements governing defense of actions and collection of civil money judgments generally.

Added by Stats 2005 ch 474 (AB 1150),s 5, eff. 1/1/2006.

Section 1994 - Cause of commitment and question refused specified in warrant of commitment

Every warrant of commitment, issued by a court or officer pursuant to this chapter, shall specify therein, particularly, the cause of the commitment, and if it be for refusing to answer a question, that question shall be stated in the warrant.

Amended by Stats 2005 ch 474 (AB 1150),s 6, eff. 1/1/2006

Section 1995 - Order for examination if witness confined in jail

If the witness be a prisoner, confined in a jail within this state, an order for his examination in the jail upon deposition, or for his temporary removal and production before a court or officer may be made as follows:

1. By the court itself in which the action or special proceeding is pending, unless it be a small claims court.

2. By a justice of the Supreme Court, or a judge of the superior court of the county where the action or proceeding is pending, if pending before a small claims court, or before a judge or other person out of court.

Amended by Stats. 1977, Ch. 1257.

Section 1996 - Order made upon motion

Such order can only be made on the motion of a party, upon affidavit showing the nature of the action or proceeding, the testimony expected from the witness, and its materiality.

Enacted 1872.

Section 1997 - Production required if witness confined in jail in county where action pending; otherwise examination upon deposition

If the witness be imprisoned in a jail in the county where the action or proceeding is pending, his production may be required. In all other cases his examination, when allowed, must be taken upon deposition.

Amended by Stats. 1941, Ch. 802.

Chapter 3 - MANNER OF PRODUCTION

Article 1 - MODE OF TAKING THE TESTIMONY OF WITNESSES

Section 2002 - Three modes

The testimony of witnesses is taken in three modes:

1. By affidavit;
2. By deposition;
3. By oral examination.

Enacted 1872.

Section 2003 - Affidavit

An affidavit is a written declaration under oath, made without notice to the adverse party.

Enacted 1872.

Section 2004 - Deposition

A deposition is a written declaration, under oath, made upon notice to the adverse party, for the purpose of enabling him to attend and cross-examine. In all actions and proceedings where the default of the defendant has been duly entered, and in all proceedings to obtain letters of administration, or for the probate of wills and the issuance of letters testamentary thereon, where, after due and legal notice, those entitled to contest the application have failed to appear, the entry of said defaults, and the failure of said persons to appear after notice, shall be deemed to be a waiver of the right to any further notice of any application or proceeding to take testimony by deposition in such action or proceeding.

Amended by Stats. 1907, Ch. 527.

Section 2005 - Oral examination

An oral examination is an examination in presence of the jury or tribunal which is to decide the fact or act upon it, the testimony being heard by the jury or tribunal from the lips of the witness.
Enacted 1872.

Article 2 - AFFIDAVITS

Section 2009 - Use of affidavit
An affidavit may be used to verify a pleading or a paper in a special proceeding, to prove the service of a summons, notice, or other paper in an action or special proceeding, to obtain a provisional remedy, the examination of a witness, or a stay of proceedings, and in uncontested proceedings to establish a record of birth, or upon a motion, and in any other case expressly permitted by statute.
Amended by Stats. 1965, Ch. 299.

Section 2010 - Evidence of publication given by affidavit
Evidence of the publication of a document or notice required by law, or by an order of a Court or Judge, to be published in a newspaper, may be given by the affidavit of the printer of the newspaper, or his foreman or principal clerk, annexed to a copy of the document or notice, specifying the times when, and the paper in which, the publication was made.
Enacted 1872.

Section 2011 - Place of filing; prima facie evidence of facts stated
Section Two Thousand and Eleven. If such affidavit be made in an action or special proceeding pending in a Court, it may be filed with the Court or a Clerk thereof. If not so made, it may be filed with the Clerk of the county where the newspaper is printed. In either case the original affidavit, or a copy thereof, certified by the Judge of the Court or Clerk having it in custody, is prima facie evidence of the facts stated therein.
Amended by Code Amendments 1873-74, Ch. 383.

Section 2012 - Taken before officer authorized to administer oaths
An affidavit to be used before any court, judge, or officer of this state may be taken before any officer authorized to administer oaths.
Amended by Stats. 1907, Ch. 393.

Section 2013 - Affidavit taken in another state to be used in state
Section Two Thousand and Thirteen. An affidavit taken in another State of the United States, to be used in this State, may be taken before a Commissioner appointed by the Governor of this State to take affidavits and depositions in such other State, or before any Notary Public in another State, or before any Judge or Clerk of a Court of record having a seal.
Amended by Code Amendments 1873-74, Ch. 383.

Section 2014 - Affidavit taken in foreign county to be used in state
Section Two Thousand and Fourteen. An affidavit taken in a foreign country to be used in this State, may be taken before an Embassador, Minister, Consul, Vice Consul, or Consular Agent of the United States, or before any Judge of a Court of record having a seal in such foreign country.
Amended by Code Amendments 1873-74, Ch. 383.

Section 2015 - Certification required when affidavit before judge or court in another state or foreign country
When an affidavit is taken before a Judge or a Court in another State, or in a foreign country, the genuineness of the signature of the Judge, the existence of the Court, and the fact that such Judge is a member thereof, must be certified by the Clerk of the Court, under the seal thereof.
Enacted 1872.

Section 2015.3 - Force and effect of certificate of sheriff, marshal or clerk of superior court
The certificate of a sheriff, marshal, or the clerk of the superior court, has the same force and effect as his or her affidavit.
Amended by Stats 2002 ch 784 (SB 1316),s 88, eff. 1/1/2003.

Section 2015.5 - Certificate or declaration under penalty of perjury of truth and correctness of matter
Whenever, under any law of this state or under any rule, regulation, order or requirement made pursuant to the law of this state, any matter is required or permitted to be supported, evidenced, established, or proved by the sworn statement, declaration, verification, certificate, oath, or affidavit, in writing of the person making the same (other than a deposition, or an oath of office, or an oath required to be taken before a specified official other than a notary public), such matter may with like force and effect be supported, evidenced, established or proved by the unsworn statement, declaration, verification, or certificate, in writing of such person which recites that it is certified or declared by him or her to be true under penalty of perjury, is subscribed by him or her, and (1), if executed within this state, states the date and place of execution, or (2), if executed at any place, within or without this state, states the date of execution and that it is so certified or declared under the laws of the State of California. The certification or declaration may be in substantially the following form:
(a) If executed within this state: "I certify (or declare) under penalty of perjury that the foregoing is true and correct":_____
_____(Date and Place)(Signature)
(b) If executed at any place, within or without this state: "I certify (or declare) under penalty of perjury under the laws of the State of California that the foregoing is true and correct":

_____
(Date)(Signature)
Amended by Stats. 1980, Ch. 889, Sec. 1. Operative July 1, 1981, by Sec. 6 of Ch. 889.

Section 2015.6 - Affirmation in lieu of oath
Whenever, under any law of this State or under any rule, regulation, order or requirement made pursuant to law, an oath is required to be taken by a person appointed to discharge specific duties in a particular action, proceeding or matter, whether or not pending in court, including but not limited to a person appointed as executor, administrator, guardian, conservator, appraiser, receiver, or elisor, an unsworn written affirmation may be made and executed, in lieu of such oath. Such affirmation shall commence "I solemnly affirm," shall state the substance of the other matter required by the oath, the date and place of execution and shall be subscribed by him.
Added by Stats. 1961, Ch. 1364.

Title 4 - CIVIL DISCOVERY ACT
Chapter 1 - GENERAL PROVISIONS

Section 2016.010 - Title of act
This title may be cited as the "Civil Discovery Act."
Added by Stats 2004 ch 182 (AB 3081),s 23, eff. 7/1/2005.

Section 2016.020 - Definitions
As used in this title:
(a) "Action" includes a civil action and a special proceeding of a civil nature.
(b) "Court" means the trial court in which the action is pending, unless otherwise specified.
(c) "Document" and "writing" mean a writing, as defined in Section 250 of the Evidence Code.
(d) "Electronic" means relating to technology having electrical, digital, magnetic, wireless, optical, electromagnetic, or similar capabilities.
(e) "Electronically stored information" means information that is stored in an electronic medium.

Amended by Stats 2009 ch 5 (AB 5),s 3, eff. 6/29/2009.
Added by Stats 2004 ch 182 (AB 3081),s 23, eff. 7/1/2005.

Section 2016.030 - Modification of procedures by stipulation

Unless the court orders otherwise, the parties may by written stipulation modify the procedures provided by this title for any method of discovery permitted under Section 2019.010.
Added by Stats 2004 ch 182 (AB 3081),s 23, eff. 7/1/2005.

Section 2016.040 - Meet and confer declaration in support of motion

A meet and confer declaration in support of a motion shall state facts showing a reasonable and good faith attempt at an informal resolution of each issue presented by the motion.
Added by Stats 2004 ch 182 (AB 3081),s 23, eff. 7/1/2005.

Section 2016.050 - Applicability of sections 1011 and 1013

Sections 1011 and 1013 apply to any method of discovery or service of a motion provided for in this title.
Amended by Stats 2017 ch 64 (SB 543),s 2, eff. 1/1/2018.
Added by Stats 2004 ch 182 (AB 3081),s 23, eff. 7/1/2005.

Section 2016.060 - Last day to perform act falls on Saturday, Sunday or holiday

When the last day to perform or complete any act provided for in this title falls on a Saturday, Sunday, or holiday as specified in Section 10, the time limit is extended until the next court day closer to the trial date.
Added by Stats 2004 ch 171 (AB 3078),s 4, eff. 7/1/2005.
Added by Stats 2004 ch 182 (AB 3081),, 23.5 eff. 7/1/2005.
See Stats 2004 ch 171 (AB 3078), s 7.
See Stats 2004 ch 182 (AB 3081), s 62.

Section 2016.070 - Applicability to discovery in aid of enforcement of money judgment

This title applies to discovery in aid of enforcement of a money judgment only to the extent provided in Article 1 (commencing with Section 708.010) of Chapter 6 of Title 9 of Part 2.
Added by Stats 2004 ch 182 (AB 3081),s 23, eff. 7/1/2005.

Section 2016.080 - Court conducted informal discovery conference; request by party; timing

(a) If an informal resolution is not reached by the parties, as described in Section 2016.040, the court may conduct an informal discovery conference upon request by a party or on the court's own motion for the purpose of discussing discovery matters in dispute between the parties.
(b) If a party requests an informal discovery conference, the party shall file a declaration described in Section 2016.040 with the court. Any party may file a response to a declaration filed pursuant to this subdivision. If a court is in session and does not grant, deny, or schedule the party's request within 10 calendar days after the initial request, the request shall be deemed denied.
(c)
(1) If a court grants or orders an informal discovery conference, the court may schedule and hold the conference no later than 30 calendar days after the court granted the request or issued its order, and before the discovery cutoff date.
(2) If an informal discovery conference is granted or ordered, the court may toll the deadline for filing a discovery motion or make any other appropriate discovery order.
(d) If an informal discovery conference is not held within 30 calendar days from the date the court granted the request, the request for an informal discovery conference shall be deemed denied, and any tolling period previously ordered by the court shall continue to apply to that action.
(e) The outcome of an informal discovery conference does not bar a party from filing a discovery motion or prejudice the disposition of a discovery motion.
(f) This section does not prevent the parties from stipulating to the timing of discovery proceedings as described in Section 2024.060.
(g) This section shall remain in effect only until January 1, 2023, and as of that date is repealed, unless a later enacted statute that is enacted before January 1, 2023, deletes or extends that date.
Amended by Stats 2018 ch 92 (SB 1289),s 44, eff. 1/1/2019.
Added by Stats 2017 ch 189 (AB 383),s 1, eff. 1/1/2018.

Section 2016.090 - Initial disclosures

(a) The following shall apply only to a civil action upon an order of the court following stipulation by all parties to the action:
(1) Within 45 days of the order of the court, a party shall, without awaiting a discovery request, provide to the other parties an initial disclosure that includes all of the following information:
(A) The names, addresses, telephone numbers, and email addresses of all persons likely to have discoverable information, along with the subjects of that information, that the disclosing party may use to support its claims or defenses, unless the use would be solely for impeachment.
(B) A copy, or a description by category and location, of all documents, electronically stored information, and tangible things that the disclosing party has in its possession, custody, or control and may use to support its claims or defenses, unless the use would be solely for impeachment.
(C) Any agreement under which an insurance company may be liable to satisfy, in whole or in part, a judgment entered in the action or to indemnify or reimburse for payments made to satisfy the judgment.
(D) Any agreement under which a person, as defined in Section 175 of the Evidence Code, may be liable to satisfy, in whole or in part, a judgment entered in the action or to indemnify or reimburse for payments made to satisfy the judgment. Only those provisions of an agreement that are material to the terms of the insurance, indemnification, or reimbursement are required to be included in the initial disclosure. Material provisions include, but are not limited to, the identities of parties to the agreement and the nature and limits of the coverage.
(2) A party shall make its initial disclosures based on the information then reasonably available to it. A party is not excused from making its initial disclosures because it has not fully investigated the case, because it challenges the sufficiency of another party's disclosures, or because another party has not made its disclosures.
(3) A party that has made its initial disclosures, as described in paragraph (1), or that has responded to another party's discovery request, shall supplement or correct a disclosure or response in the following situations:
(A) In a timely manner if the party learns that in some material respect the disclosure or response is incomplete or incorrect and the additional or corrective information has not otherwise been made known to the other parties during the disclosure or discovery process.
(B) As ordered by the court.
(4) A party's obligations under this section may be enforced by a court on its own motion or the motion of a party to compel disclosure.
(5) A party's disclosures under this section shall be verified under penalty of perjury as being true and correct to the best of the party's knowledge.
(b) Notwithstanding subdivision (a), this section does not apply to the following actions:
(1) An unlawful detainer action, as defined in Section 1161.
(2) An action in the small claims division of a court, as defined in Section 116.210.
Added by Stats 2019 ch 836 (SB 17),s 1, eff. 1/1/2020.

Chapter 2 - SCOPE OF DISCOVERY
Article 1 - GENERAL PROVISIONS

Section 2017.010 - Generally
Unless otherwise limited by order of the court in accordance with this title, any party may obtain discovery regarding any matter, not privileged, that is relevant to the subject matter involved in the pending action or to the determination of any motion made in that action, if the matter either is itself admissible in evidence or appears reasonably calculated to lead to the discovery of admissible evidence. Discovery may relate to the claim or defense of the party seeking discovery or of any other party to the action. Discovery may be obtained of the identity and location of persons having knowledge of any discoverable matter, as well as of the existence, description, nature, custody, condition, and location of any document, electronically stored information, tangible thing, or land or other property.
Amended by Stats 2012 ch 72 (SB 1574),s 8, eff. 1/1/2013.
Added by Stats 2004 ch 182 (AB 3081),s 23, eff. 7/1/2005.

Section 2017.020 - Limiting scope of discovery by motion for protective order
(a) The court shall limit the scope of discovery if it determines that the burden, expense, or intrusiveness of that discovery clearly outweighs the likelihood that the information sought will lead to the discovery of admissible evidence. The court may make this determination pursuant to a motion for protective order by a party or other affected person. This motion shall be accompanied by a meet and confer declaration under Section 2016.040.

(b) The court shall impose a monetary sanction under Chapter 7 (commencing with Section 2023.010) against any party, person, or attorney who unsuccessfully makes or opposes a motion for a protective order, unless it finds that the one subject to the sanction acted with substantial justification or that other circumstances make the imposition of the sanction unjust.

(c)
  (1) Notwithstanding subdivision (b), or any other section of this title, absent exceptional circumstances, the court shall not impose sanctions on a party or any attorney of a party for failure to provide electronically stored information that has been lost, damaged, altered, or overwritten as the result of the routine, good faith operation of an electronic information system.
  (2) This subdivision shall not be construed to alter any obligation to preserve discoverable information.
Amended by Stats 2012 ch 72 (SB 1574),s 9, eff. 1/1/2013.
Added by Stats 2004 ch 182 (AB 3081),s 23, eff. 7/1/2005.

Article 2 - SCOPE OF DISCOVERY IN SPECIFIC CONTEXTS

Section 2017.210 - Existence and contents of agreement under which insurance carrier may be liable
A party may obtain discovery of the existence and contents of any agreement under which any insurance carrier may be liable to satisfy in whole or in part a judgment that may be entered in the action or to indemnify or reimburse for payments made to satisfy the judgment. This discovery may include the identity of the carrier and the nature and limits of the coverage. A party may also obtain discovery as to whether that insurance carrier is disputing the agreement's coverage of the claim involved in the action, but not as to the nature and substance of that dispute. Information concerning the insurance agreement is not by reason of disclosure admissible in evidence at trial.
Added by Stats 2004 ch 182 (AB 3081),s 23, eff. 7/1/2005.

Section 2017.220 - Civil action alleging sexual harassment, sexual assault or sexual battery
(a) In any civil action alleging conduct that constitutes sexual harassment, sexual assault, or sexual battery, any party seeking discovery concerning the plaintiff's sexual conduct with individuals other than the alleged perpetrator shall establish specific facts showing that there is good cause for that discovery, and that the matter sought to be discovered is relevant to the subject matter of the action and reasonably calculated to lead to the discovery of admissible evidence. This showing shall be made by a noticed motion, accompanied by a meet and confer declaration under Section 2016.040, and shall not be made or considered by the court at an ex parte hearing.

(b) The court shall impose a monetary sanction under Chapter 7 (commencing with Section 2023.010) against any party, person, or attorney who unsuccessfully makes or opposes a motion for discovery under subdivision (a), unless it finds that the one subject to the sanction acted with substantial justification or that other circumstances make the imposition of the sanction unjust.
Added by Stats 2004 ch 182 (AB 3081),s 23, eff. 7/1/2005.

Article 3 - VIOLATION OF THE ELDER ABUSE AND DEPENDENT ADULT CIVIL PROTECTION ACT

Section 2017.310 - Confidential settlement agreement
(a) Notwithstanding any other provision of law, it is the policy of the State of California that confidential settlement agreements are disfavored in any civil action the factual foundation for which establishes a cause of action for a violation of the Elder Abuse and Dependent Adult Civil Protection Act (Chapter 11(commencing with Section 15600) of Part 3 of Division 9 of the Welfare and Institutions Code).

(b) Provisions of a confidential settlement agreement described in subdivision (a) may not be recognized or enforced by the court absent a showing of any of the following:
  (1) The information is privileged under existing law.
  (2) The information is not evidence of abuse of an elder or dependent adult, as described in Sections 15610.30, 15610.57, and 15610.63 of the Welfare and Institutions Code.
  (3) The party seeking to uphold the confidentiality of the information has demonstrated that there is a substantial probability that prejudice will result from the disclosure and that the party's interest in the information cannot be adequately protected through redaction.

(c) Nothing in paragraph (1), (2), or (3) of subdivision (b) permits the sealing or redacting of a defendant's name in any information made available to the public.

(d) Except as expressly provided in this section, nothing in this section is intended to alter, modify, or amend existing law.

(e) Nothing in this section may be deemed to prohibit the entry or enforcement of that part of a confidentiality agreement, settlement agreement, or stipulated agreement between the parties that requires the nondisclosure of the amount of any money paid in a settlement of a claim.

(f) Nothing in this section applies to or affects an action for professional negligence against a health care provider.
Added by Stats 2004 ch 182 (AB 3081),s 23, eff. 7/1/2005.

Section 2017.320 - Information protected from disclosure by stipulated protective order
(a) In any civil action the factual foundation for which establishes a cause of action for a violation of the Elder Abuse and Dependent Adult Civil Protection Act (Chapter 11 (commencing with Section 15600) of Part 3 of Division 9 of the Welfare and Institutions Code), any information that is acquired through discovery and is protected from disclosure by a stipulated protective order shall remain subject to the protective order, except for information that is evidence of abuse of an elder or dependent adult as described in Sections 15610.30, 15610.57, and 15610.63 of the Welfare and Institutions Code.

(b) In that instance, after redacting information in the document that is not evidence of abuse of an elder or dependent adult as described in Sections 15610.30, 15610.57, and 15610.63 of the Welfare and Institutions Code, a party may file that particularized information with the court.

The party proposing to file the information shall offer to meet and confer with the party from whom the information was obtained at least one week prior to filing that information with the court.

(c) The filing party shall give concurrent notice of the filing with the court and its basis to the party from whom the information was obtained.

(d) Any filed information submitted to the court shall remain confidential under any protective order for 30 days after the filing and shall be part of the public court record thereafter, unless an affected party petitions the court and shows good cause for a court protective order.

(e) The burden of showing good cause shall be on the party seeking the court protective order.

(f) A stipulated protective order may not be recognized or enforced by the court to prevent disclosure of information filed with the court pursuant to subdivision (b), absent a showing of any of the following:

(1) The information is privileged under existing law.

(2) The information is not evidence of abuse of an elder or dependent adult as described in Sections 15610.30, 15610.57, and 15610.63 of the Welfare and Institutions Code.

(3) The party seeking to uphold the confidentiality of the information has demonstrated that there is a substantial probability that prejudice will result from the disclosure and that the party's interest in the information cannot be adequately protected through redaction.

(g) If the court denies the petition for a court protective order, it shall redact any part of the filed information it finds is not evidence of abuse of an elder or dependent adult, as described in Sections 15610.30, 15610.57, and 15610.63 of the Welfare and Institutions Code. Nothing in this subdivision or in paragraph (1), (2), or (3) of subdivision (f) permits the sealing or redacting of a defendant's name in any information made available to the public.

(h) Nothing in this section applies to or affects an action for professional negligence against a health care provider.

Added by Stats 2004 ch 182 (AB 3081),s 23, eff. 7/1/2005.

Chapter 3 - USE OF TECHNOLOGY IN CONDUCTING DISCOVERY IN A COMPLEX CASE

Section 2017.710 - [Repealed]
Repealed by Stats 2012 ch 72 (SB 1574),s 10, eff. 1/1/2013.
Added by Stats 2004 ch 182 (AB 3081),s 23, eff. 7/1/2005.

Section 2017.720 - [Repealed]
Repealed by Stats 2012 ch 72 (SB 1574),s 11, eff. 1/1/2013.
Added by Stats 2004 ch 182 (AB 3081),s 23, eff. 7/1/2005.

Section 2017.730 - [Repealed]
Repealed by Stats 2012 ch 72 (SB 1574),s 12, eff. 1/1/2013.
Added by Stats 2004 ch 182 (AB 3081),s 23, eff. 7/1/2005.

Section 2017.740 - [Repealed]
Repealed by Stats 2012 ch 72 (SB 1574),s 13, eff. 1/1/2013.
Added by Stats 2004 ch 182 (AB 3081),s 23, eff. 7/1/2005.

Chapter 4 - ATTORNEY WORK PRODUCT

Section 2018.010 - Client defined
For purposes of this chapter, "client" means a "client" as defined in Section 951 of the Evidence Code.
Added by Stats 2004 ch 182 (AB 3081),s 23, eff. 7/1/2005.

Section 2018.020 - Policy of state
It is the policy of the state to do both of the following:

(a) Preserve the rights of attorneys to prepare cases for trial with that degree of privacy necessary to encourage them to prepare their cases thoroughly and to investigate not only the favorable but the unfavorable aspects of those cases.

(b) Prevent attorneys from taking undue advantage of their adversary's industry and efforts.

Added by Stats 2004 ch 182 (AB 3081),s 23, eff. 7/1/2005.

Section 2018.030 - Generally
(a) A writing that reflects an attorney's impressions, conclusions, opinions, or legal research or theories is not discoverable under any circumstances.

(b) The work product of an attorney, other than a writing described in subdivision (a), is not discoverable unless the court determines that denial of discovery will unfairly prejudice the party seeking discovery in preparing that party's claim or defense or will result in an injustice.

Added by Stats 2004 ch 182 (AB 3081),s 23, eff. 7/1/2005.

Section 2018.040 - Restatement of existing law
This chapter is intended to be a restatement of existing law relating to protection of work product. It is not intended to expand or reduce the extent to which work product is discoverable under existing law in any action.
Added by Stats 2004 ch 182 (AB 3081),s 23, eff. 7/1/2005.

Section 2018.050 - Lawyer suspected of participating in crime of fraud
Notwithstanding Section 2018.040, when a lawyer is suspected of knowingly participating in a crime or fraud, there is no protection of work product under this chapter in any official investigation by a law enforcement agency or proceeding or action brought by a public prosecutor in the name of the people of the State of California if the services of the lawyer were sought or obtained to enable or aid anyone to commit or plan to commit a crime or fraud.
Added by Stats 2004 ch 182 (AB 3081),s 23, eff. 7/1/2005.

Section 2018.060 - In camera hearing
Nothing in this chapter is intended to limit an attorney's ability to request an in camera hearing as provided for in People v. Superior Court (Laff) (2001) 25 Cal.4th 703.
Added by Stats 2004 ch 182 (AB 3081),s 23, eff. 7/1/2005.

Section 2018.070 - Discovery by State Bar
(a) The State Bar may discover the work product of an attorney against whom disciplinary charges are pending when it is relevant to issues of breach of duty by the lawyer and requisite client approval has been granted.

(b) Where requested and for good cause, discovery under this section shall be subject to a protective order to ensure the confidentiality of the work product except for its use by the State Bar in disciplinary investigations and its consideration under seal in State Bar Court proceedings.

(c) For purposes of this chapter, whenever a client has initiated a complaint against an attorney, the requisite client approval shall be deemed to have been granted.

Added by Stats 2004 ch 182 (AB 3081),s 23, eff. 7/1/2005.

Section 2018.080 - Action between attorney and client or former client
In an action between an attorney and a client or a former client of the attorney, no work product privilege under this chapter exists if the work product is relevant to an issue of breach by the attorney of a duty to the client arising out of the attorney-client relationship.
Added by Stats 2004 ch 182 (AB 3081),s 23, eff. 7/1/2005.

Chapter 5 - METHODS AND SEQUENCE OF DISCOVERY
Article 1 - GENERAL PROVISIONS

Section 2019.010 - Methods of discovery
Any party may obtain discovery by one or more of the following methods:
(a) Oral and written depositions.
(b) Interrogatories to a party.
(c) Inspections of documents, things, and places.
(d) Physical and mental examinations.
(e) Requests for admissions.
(f) Simultaneous exchanges of expert trial witness information.
Added by Stats 2004 ch 182 (AB 3081),s 23, eff. 7/1/2005.

Section 2019.020 - Methods used in sequence
(a) Except as otherwise provided by a rule of the Judicial Council, a local court rule, or a local uniform written policy, the methods of discovery may be used in any sequence, and the fact that a party is conducting discovery, whether by deposition or another method, shall not operate to delay the discovery of any other party.
(b) Notwithstanding subdivision (a), on motion and for good cause shown, the court may establish the sequence and timing of discovery for the convenience of parties and witnesses and in the interests of justice.
Added by Stats 2004 ch 182 (AB 3081),s 23, eff. 7/1/2005.

Section 2019.030 - Restricting frequency or extent of use of discovery
(a) The court shall restrict the frequency or extent of use of a discovery method provided in Section 2019.010 if it determines either of the following:
　(1) The discovery sought is unreasonably cumulative or duplicative, or is obtainable from some other source that is more convenient, less burdensome, or less expensive.
　(2) The selected method of discovery is unduly burdensome or expensive, taking into account the needs of the case, the amount in controversy, and the importance of the issues at stake in the litigation.
(b) The court may make these determinations pursuant to a motion for a protective order by a party or other affected person. This motion shall be accompanied by a meet and confer declaration under Section 2016.040.
(c) The court shall impose a monetary sanction under Chapter 7 (commencing with Section 2023.010) against any party, person, or attorney who unsuccessfully makes or opposes a motion for a protective order, unless it finds that the one subject to the sanction acted with substantial justification or that other circumstances make the imposition of the sanction unjust.
Added by Stats 2004 ch 182 (AB 3081), 23 eff. 7/1/2005.

Section 2019.040 - Electronically stored information
(a) When any method of discovery permits the production, inspection, copying, testing, or sampling of documents or tangible things, that method shall also permit the production, inspection, copying, testing, or sampling of electronically stored information.
(b) All procedures available under this title to compel, prevent, or limit the production, inspection, copying, testing, or sampling of documents or tangible things shall be available to compel, prevent, or limit the production, inspection, copying, testing, or sampling of electronically stored information.
Added by Stats 2012 ch 72 (SB 1574),s 14, eff. 1/1/2013.

Article 2 - METHODS AND SEQUENCE OF DISCOVERY IN SPECIFIC CONTEXTS

Section 2019.210 - Action alleging misappropriation of trade secret
In any action alleging the misappropriation of a trade secret under the Uniform Trade Secrets Act (Title 5 (commencing with Section 3426) of Part 1 of Division 4 of the Civil Code), before commencing discovery relating to the trade secret, the party alleging the misappropriation shall identify the trade secret with reasonable particularity subject to any orders that may be appropriate under Section 3426.5 of the Civil Code.
Added by Stats. 2004, Ch. 182, Sec. 23. Effective January 1, 2005. Operative July 1, 2005, by Sec. 64 of Ch. 182.

Chapter 6 - NONPARTY DISCOVERY
Article 1 - GENERAL PROVISIONS

Section 2020.010 - Methods to obtain discovery
(a) Any of the following methods may be used to obtain discovery within the state from a person who is not a party to the action in which the discovery is sought:
　(1) An oral deposition under Chapter 9 (commencing with Section 2025.010).
　(2) A written deposition under Chapter 11 (commencing with Section 2028.010).
　(3) A deposition for production of business records and things under Article 4 (commencing with Section 2020.410) or Article 5 (commencing with Section 2020.510).
(b) Except as provided in subdivision (a) of Section 2025.280, the process by which a nonparty is required to provide discovery is a deposition subpoena.
Added by Stats 2004 ch 182 (AB 3081),s 23, eff. 7/1/2005.

Section 2020.020 - Demand of deposition subpoena
A deposition subpoena may command any of the following:
(a) Only the attendance and the testimony of the deponent, under Article 3 (commencing with Section 2020.310).
(b) Only the production of business records for copying, under Article 4 (commencing with Section 2020.410).
(c) The attendance and the testimony of the deponent, as well as the production of business records, other documents, electronically stored information, and tangible things, under Article 5 (commencing with Section 2020.510).
Amended by Stats 2012 ch 72 (SB 1574),s 15, eff. 1/1/2013.
Added by Stats 2004 ch 182 (AB 3081),s 23, eff. 7/1/2005.

Section 2020.030 - Provisions applicable to deposition subpoena
Except as modified in this chapter, the provisions of Chapter 2 (commencing with Section 1985) of Title 3 of Part 4 of this code, and of Article 4 (commencing with Section 1560) of Chapter 2 of Division 11 of the Evidence Code, apply to a deposition subpoena.
Added by Stats 2004 ch 182 (AB 3081),s 23, eff. 7/1/2005.

Article 2 - PROCEDURES APPLICABLE TO ALL TYPES OF DEPOSITION SUBPOENAS

Section 2020.210 - Court-issued subpoena; attorney issued subpoena
(a) The clerk of the court in which the action is pending shall issue a deposition subpoena signed and sealed, but otherwise in blank, to a party requesting it, who shall fill it in before service.

(b) Instead of a court-issued deposition subpoena, an attorney of record for any party may sign and issue a deposition subpoena. A deposition subpoena issued under this subdivision need not be sealed. A copy may be served on the nonparty, and the attorney may retain the original.
Added by Stats 2004 ch 182 (AB 3081),ss 23, 23 eff. 7/1/2005.

Section 2020.220 - Service of subpoena
(a) Subject to subdivision (c) of Section 2020.410, service of a deposition subpoena shall be effected a sufficient time in advance of the deposition to provide the deponent a reasonable opportunity to locate and produce any designated business records, documents, electronically stored information, and tangible things, as described in Article 4 (commencing with Section 2020.410), and, where personal attendance is commanded, a reasonable time to travel to the place of deposition.

(b) Any person may serve the subpoena by personal delivery of a copy of it as follows:

(1) If the deponent is a natural person, to that person.

(2) If the deponent is an organization, to any officer, director, custodian of records, or to any agent or employee authorized by the organization to accept service of a subpoena.

(c) Personal service of any deposition subpoena is effective to require all of the following of any deponent who is a resident of California at the time of service:

(1) Personal attendance and testimony, if the subpoena so specifies.

(2) Any specified production, inspection, testing, and sampling.

(3) The deponent's attendance at a court session to consider any issue arising out of the deponent's refusal to be sworn, or to answer any question, or to produce specified items, or to permit inspection or photocopying, if the subpoena so specifies, or specified testing and sampling of the items produced.

(d) Unless the subpoenaing party and the subpoenaed person otherwise agree or the court otherwise orders, the following shall apply:

(1) If a subpoena requiring production of electronically stored information does not specify a form or forms for producing a type of electronically stored information, the person subpoenaed shall produce the information in the form or forms in which it is ordinarily maintained or in a form that is reasonably usable.

(2) A subpoenaed person need not produce the same electronically stored information in more than one form.

(e) The subpoenaed person opposing the production, inspection, copying, testing, or sampling of electronically stored information on the basis that the information is from a source that is not reasonably accessible because of undue burden or expense shall bear the burden of demonstrating that the information is from a source that is not reasonably accessible because of undue burden or expense.

(f) If the person from whom discovery of electronically stored information is subpoenaed establishes that the information is from a source that is not reasonably accessible because of undue burden or expense, the court may nonetheless order discovery if the subpoenaing party shows good cause, subject to any limitations imposed under subdivision (i).

(g) If the court finds good cause for the production of electronically stored information from a source that is not reasonably accessible, the court may set conditions for the discovery of the electronically stored information, including allocation of the expense of discovery.

(h) If necessary, the subpoenaed person, at the reasonable expense of the subpoenaing party, shall, through detection devices, translate any data compilations included in the subpoena into a reasonably usable form.

(i) The court shall limit the frequency or extent of discovery of electronically stored information, even from a source that is reasonably accessible, if the court determines that any of the following conditions exists:

(1) It is possible to obtain the information from some other source that is more convenient, less burdensome, or less expensive.

(2) The discovery sought is unreasonably cumulative or duplicative.

(3) The party seeking discovery has had ample opportunity by discovery in the action to obtain the information sought.

(4) The likely burden or expense of the proposed discovery outweighs the likely benefit, taking into account the amount in controversy, the resources of the parties, the importance of the issues in the litigation, and the importance of the requested discovery in resolving the issues.

(j) If a subpoenaed person notifies the subpoenaing party that electronically stored information produced pursuant to a subpoena is subject to a claim of privilege or of protection as attorney work product, as described in Section 2031.285, the provisions of Section 2031.285 shall apply.

(k) A party serving a subpoena requiring the production of electronically stored information shall take reasonable steps to avoid imposing undue burden or expense on a person subject to the subpoena.

(l) An order of the court requiring compliance with a subpoena issued under this section shall protect a person who is neither a party nor a party's officer from undue burden or expense resulting from compliance.

(m)

(1) Absent exceptional circumstances, the court shall not impose sanctions on a subpoenaed person or any attorney of a subpoenaed person for failure to provide electronically stored information that has been lost, damaged, altered, or overwritten as the result of the routine, good faith operation of an electronic information system.

(2) The subdivision shall not be construed to alter any obligation to preserve discoverable information.

Amended by Stats 2012 ch 72 (SB 1574),s 16, eff. 1/1/2013.

Added by Stats 2004 ch 182 (AB 3081),s 23, eff. 7/1/2005.

Section 2020.230 - Witness fee and mileage if personal appearance of deponent required
(a) If a deposition subpoena requires the personal attendance of the deponent, under Article 3 (commencing with Section 2020.310) or Article 5 (commencing with Section 2020.510), the party noticing the deposition shall pay to the deponent in cash or by check the same witness fee and mileage required by Chapter 1 (commencing with Section 68070) of Title 8 of the Government Code for attendance and testimony before the court in which the action is pending. This payment, whether or not demanded by the deponent, shall be made, at the option of the party noticing the deposition, either at the time of service of the deposition subpoena, or at the time the deponent attends for the taking of testimony.

(b) Service of a deposition subpoena that does not require the personal attendance of a custodian of records or other qualified person, under Article 4 (commencing with Section 2020.410), shall be accompanied, whether or not demanded by the deponent, by a payment in cash or by check of the witness fee required by paragraph (6) of subdivision (b) of Section 1563 of the Evidence Code.

Added by Stats 2004 ch 182 (AB 3081),s 23, eff. 7/1/2005.

Section 2020.240 - Disobedience of subpoena by deponent
A deponent who disobeys a deposition subpoena in any manner described in subdivision (c) of Section 2020.220 may be punished for contempt under Chapter 7 (commencing with Section 2023.010) without the necessity of a prior order of court directing compliance by the witness. The deponent is also subject to the forfeiture and the payment of damages set forth in Section 1992.

Added by Stats 2004 ch 182 (AB 3081),s 23, eff. 7/1/2005.

Article 3 - SUBPOENA COMMANDING ONLY ATTENDANCE AND TESTIMONY OF THE DEPONENT

Section 2020.310 - Rules applicable
The following rules apply to a deposition subpoena that commands only the attendance and the testimony of the deponent:

(a) The subpoena shall specify the time when and the place where the deponent is commanded to attend the deposition.

(b) The subpoena shall set forth a summary of all of the following:
- **(1)** The nature of a deposition.
- **(2)** The rights and duties of the deponent.
- **(3)** The penalties for disobedience of a deposition subpoena, as described in Section 2020.240.

(c) If the deposition will be recorded using audio or video technology by, or at the direction of, the noticing party under Section 2025.340, the subpoena shall state that it will be recorded in that manner.

(d) If the deposition testimony will be conducted using instant visual display, the subpoena shall state that it will be conducted in that manner.

(e) If the deponent is an organization, the subpoena shall describe with reasonable particularity the matters on which examination is requested. The subpoena shall also advise the organization of its duty to make the designation of employees or agents who will attend the deposition, as described in Section 2025.230.

Added by Stats 2004 ch 182 (AB 3081),s 23, eff. 7/1/2005.

Article 4 - SUBPOENA COMMANDING ONLY PRODUCTION OF BUSINESS RECORDS FOR COPYING 2020.410

Section 2020.410 - Generally

(a) A deposition subpoena that commands only the production of business records for copying shall designate the business records to be produced either by specifically describing each individual item or by reasonably particularizing each category of item, and shall specify the form in which any electronically stored information is to be produced, if a particular form is desired.

(b) Notwithstanding subdivision (a), specific information identifiable only to the deponent's records system, like a policy number or the date when a consumer interacted with the witness, is not required.

(c) A deposition subpoena that commands only the production of business records for copying need not be accompanied by an affidavit or declaration showing good cause for the production of the business records designated in it. It shall be directed to the custodian of those records or another person qualified to certify the records. It shall command compliance in accordance with Section 2020.430 on a date that is no earlier than 20 days after the issuance, or 15 days after the service, of the deposition subpoena, whichever date is later.

(d) If, under Section 1985.3 or 1985.6, the one to whom the deposition subpoena is directed is a witness, and the business records described in the deposition subpoena are personal records pertaining to a consumer, the service of the deposition subpoena shall be accompanied either by a copy of the proof of service of the notice to the consumer described in subdivision (e) of Section 1985.3, or subdivision (b) of Section 1985.6, as applicable, or by the consumer's written authorization to release personal records described in paragraph (2) of subdivision (c) of Section 1985.3, or paragraph (2) of subdivision (c) of Section 1985.6, as applicable.

Amended by Stats 2012 ch 72 (SB 1574),s 17, eff. 1/1/2013.
Added by Stats 2004 ch 182 (AB 3081),s 23, eff. 7/1/2005.

Section 2020.420 - Deposition officer

The officer for a deposition seeking discovery only of business records for copying under this article shall be a professional photocopier registered under Chapter 20 (commencing with Section 22450) of Division 8 of the Business and Professions Code, or a person exempted from the registration requirements of that chapter under Section 22451 of the Business and Professions Code. This deposition officer shall not be financially interested in the action, or a relative or employee of any attorney of the parties. Any objection to the qualifications of the deposition officer is waived unless made before the date of production or as soon thereafter as the ground for that objection becomes known or could be discovered by reasonable diligence.

Added by Stats 2004 ch 182 (AB 3081),s 23, eff. 7/1/2005.

Section 2020.430 - Delivery required by custodian of records to deposition officer

(a) Except as provided in subdivision (e), if a deposition subpoena commands only the production of business records for copying, the custodian of the records or other qualified person shall, in person, by messenger, or by mail, deliver both of the following only to the deposition officer specified in the subpoena:
- **(1)** A true, legible, and durable copy of the records.
- **(2)** An affidavit in compliance with Section 1561 of the Evidence Code.

(b) If the delivery required by subdivision (a) is made to the office of the deposition officer, the records shall be enclosed, sealed, and directed as described in subdivision (c) of Section 1560 of the Evidence Code.

(c) If the delivery required by subdivision (a) is made at the office of the business whose records are the subject of the deposition subpoena, the custodian of those records or other qualified person shall do one of the following:
- **(1)** Permit the deposition officer specified in the deposition subpoena to make a copy of the originals of the designated business records during normal business hours, as defined in subdivision (e) of Section 1560 of the Evidence Code.
- **(2)** Deliver to the deposition officer a true, legible, and durable copy of the records on receipt of payment in cash or by check, by or on behalf of the party serving the deposition subpoena, of the reasonable costs of preparing that copy, together with an itemized statement of the cost of preparation, as determined under subdivision (b) of Section 1563 of the Evidence Code. This copy need not be delivered in a sealed envelope.

(d) Unless the parties, and if the records are those of a consumer as defined in Section 1985.3 or 1985.6, the consumer, stipulate to an earlier date, the custodian of the records shall not deliver to the deposition officer the records that are the subject of the deposition subpoena prior to the date and time specified in the deposition subpoena. The following legend shall appear in boldface type on the deposition subpoena immediately following the date and time specified for production: "Do not release the requested records to the deposition officer prior to the date and time stated above."

(e) This section does not apply if the subpoena directs the deponent to make the records available for inspection or copying by the subpoenaing party's attorney or a representative of that attorney at the witness' business address under subdivision (e) of Section 1560 of the Evidence Code.

(f) The provisions of Section 1562 of the Evidence Code concerning the admissibility of the affidavit of the custodian or other qualified person apply to a deposition subpoena served under this article.

Added by Stats 2004 ch 182 (AB 3081),s 23, eff. 7/1/2005.

Section 2020.440 - Copy of records provided by deposition officer

Promptly on or after the deposition date and after the receipt or the making of a copy of business records under this article, the deposition officer shall provide that copy to the party at whose instance the deposition subpoena was served, and a copy of those records to any other party to the action who then or subsequently, within a period of six months following the settlement of the case, notifies the deposition officer that the party desires to purchase a copy of those records.

Added by Stats 2004 ch 182 (AB 3081),s 23, eff. 7/1/2005.

Article 5 - SUBPOENA COMMANDING BOTH PRODUCTION OF BUSINESS RECORDS AND ATTENDANCE AND TESTIMONY OF THE DEPONENT 2020.510

Section 2020.510 - Generally

(a) A deposition subpoena that commands the attendance and the testimony of the deponent, as well as the production of business records, documents, electronically stored information, and tangible things, shall:
  (1) Comply with the requirements of Section 2020.310.
  (2) Designate the business records, documents, electronically stored information, and tangible things to be produced either by specifically describing each individual item or by reasonably particularizing each category of item.
  (3) Specify any testing or sampling that is being sought.
  (4) Specify the form in which any electronically stored information is to be produced, if a particular form is desired.
(b) A deposition subpoena under subdivision (a) need not be accompanied by an affidavit or declaration showing good cause for the production of the documents and things designated.
(c) If, as described in Section 1985.3, the person to whom the deposition subpoena is directed is a witness, and the business records described in the deposition subpoena are personal records pertaining to a consumer, the service of the deposition subpoena shall be accompanied either by a copy of the proof of service of the notice to the consumer described in subdivision (e) of Section 1985.3, or by the consumer's written authorization to release personal records described in paragraph (2) of subdivision (c) of Section 1985.3.
(d) If, as described in Section 1985.6, the person to whom the deposition subpoena is directed is a witness and the business records described in the deposition subpoena are employment records pertaining to an employee, the service of the deposition subpoena shall be accompanied either by a copy of the proof of service of the notice to the employee described in subdivision (e) of Section 1985.6, or by the employee's written authorization to release personal records described in paragraph (2) of subdivision (c) of Section 1985.6.
Amended by Stats 2012 ch 72 (SB 1574),s 18, eff. 1/1/2013.
Amended by Stats 2007 ch 113 (AB 1126),s 4, eff. 1/1/2008.
Added by Stats 2004 ch 182 (AB 3081),s 23, eff. 7/1/2005.

Chapter 7 - SANCTIONS

Section 2023.010 - Misuses of discovery process
Misuses of the discovery process include, but are not limited to, the following:
(a) Persisting, over objection and without substantial justification, in an attempt to obtain information or materials that are outside the scope of permissible discovery.
(b) Using a discovery method in a manner that does not comply with its specified procedures.
(c) Employing a discovery method in a manner or to an extent that causes unwarranted annoyance, embarrassment, or oppression, or undue burden and expense.
(d) Failing to respond or to submit to an authorized method of discovery.
(e) Making, without substantial justification, an unmeritorious objection to discovery.
(f) Making an evasive response to discovery.
(g) Disobeying a court order to provide discovery.
(h) Making or opposing, unsuccessfully and without substantial justification, a motion to compel or to limit discovery.
(i) Failing to confer in person, by telephone, or by letter with an opposing party or attorney in a reasonable and good faith attempt to resolve informally any dispute concerning discovery, if the section governing a particular discovery motion requires the filing of a declaration stating facts showing that an attempt at informal resolution has been made.
Added by Stats 2004 ch 182 (AB 3081),s 23, eff. 7/1/2005.

Section 2023.020 - Monetary sanction
Notwithstanding the outcome of the particular discovery motion, the court shall impose a monetary sanction ordering that any party or attorney who fails to confer as required pay the reasonable expenses, including attorney's fees, incurred by anyone as a result of that conduct.
Added by Stats 2004 ch 182 (AB 3081),s 23, eff. 7/1/2005.

Section 2023.030 - Sanctions for misuse of discovery process
To the extent authorized by the chapter governing any particular discovery method or any other provision of this title, the court, after notice to any affected party, person, or attorney, and after opportunity for hearing, may impose the following sanctions against anyone engaging in conduct that is a misuse of the discovery process:
(a) The court may impose a monetary sanction ordering that one engaging in the misuse of the discovery process, or any attorney advising that conduct, or both pay the reasonable expenses, including attorney's fees, incurred by anyone as a result of that conduct. The court may also impose this sanction on one unsuccessfully asserting that another has engaged in the misuse of the discovery process, or on any attorney who advised that assertion, or on both. If a monetary sanction is authorized by any provision of this title, the court shall impose that sanction unless it finds that the one subject to the sanction acted with substantial justification or that other circumstances make the imposition of the sanction unjust.
(b) The court may impose an issue sanction ordering that designated facts shall be taken as established in the action in accordance with the claim of the party adversely affected by the misuse of the discovery process. The court may also impose an issue sanction by an order prohibiting any party engaging in the misuse of the discovery process from supporting or opposing designated claims or defenses.
(c) The court may impose an evidence sanction by an order prohibiting any party engaging in the misuse of the discovery process from introducing designated matters in evidence.
(d) The court may impose a terminating sanction by one of the following orders:
  (1) An order striking out the pleadings or parts of the pleadings of any party engaging in the misuse of the discovery process.
  (2) An order staying further proceedings by that party until an order for discovery is obeyed.
  (3) An order dismissing the action, or any part of the action, of that party.
  (4) An order rendering a judgment by default against that party.
(e) The court may impose a contempt sanction by an order treating the misuse of the discovery process as a contempt of court.
(f)
  (1) Notwithstanding subdivision (a), or any other section of this title, absent exceptional circumstances, the court shall not impose sanctions on a party or any attorney of a party for failure to provide electronically stored information that has been lost, damaged, altered, or overwritten as the result of the routine, good faith operation of an electronic information system.
  (2) This subdivision shall not be construed to alter any obligation to preserve discoverable information.
Amended by Stats 2012 ch 72 (SB 1574),s 19, eff. 1/1/2013.
Added by Stats 2004 ch 182 (AB 3081),s 23, eff. 7/1/2005.

Section 2023.040 - Request for sanction
A request for a sanction shall, in the notice of motion, identify every person, party, and attorney against whom the sanction is sought, and specify the type of sanction sought. The notice of motion shall be supported by a memorandum of points and authorities, and accompanied by a declaration setting forth facts supporting the amount of any monetary sanction sought.
Added by Stats 2004 ch 182 (AB 3081),s 23, eff. 7/1/2005.

Section 2023.050 - Court-imposed sanctions

(a) Notwithstanding any other law, and in addition to any other sanctions imposed pursuant to this chapter, a court shall impose a two hundred and fifty dollar ($250) sanction, payable to the requesting party, upon a party, person, or attorney if, upon reviewing a request for a sanction made pursuant to Section 2023.040, the court finds any of the following:

(1) The party, person, or attorney did not respond in good faith to a request for the production of documents made pursuant to Section 2020.010, 2020.410, 2020.510, or 2025.210, or to an inspection demand made pursuant to Section 2031.010.

(2) The party, person, or attorney produced requested documents within seven days before the court was scheduled to hear a motion to compel production of the records pursuant to Section 2025.450, 2025.480, or 2031.320 that is filed by the requesting party as a result of the other party, person, or attorney's failure to respond in good faith.

(3) The party, person, or attorney failed to confer in person, by telephone, letter, or other means of communication in writing, as defined in Section 250 of the Evidence Code, with the party or attorney requesting the documents in a reasonable and good faith attempt to resolve informally any dispute concerning the request.

(b) Notwithstanding paragraph (3) of subdivision (o) of Section 6068 of the Business and Professions Code, the court may, in its discretion, require an attorney who is sanctioned pursuant to subdivision (a) to report the sanction, in writing, to the State Bar within 30 days of the imposition of the sanction.

(c) The court may excuse the imposition of the sanction required by subdivision (a) if the court makes written findings that the one subject to the sanction acted with substantial justification or that other circumstances make the imposition of the sanction unjust.

(d) Sanctions pursuant to this section shall be imposed only after notice to the party, person, or attorney against whom the sanction is proposed to be imposed and opportunity for that party, person, or attorney to be heard.

(e) For purposes of this section, there is a rebuttable presumption that a natural person acted in good faith if that person was not represented by an attorney in the action at the time the conduct that is sanctionable under subdivision (a) occurred. This presumption may only be overcome by clear and convincing evidence.

Added by Stats 2019 ch 836 (SB 17),s 2, eff. 1/1/2020.

Chapter 8 - TIME FOR COMPLETION OF DISCOVERY

Section 2024.010 - Motion for leave to complete discovery proceedings or motion concerning discovery heard closer to initial trial date or to reopen discovery after new trial date set

As used in this chapter, discovery is considered completed on the day a response is due or on the day a deposition begins.

Added by Stats 2004 ch 182 (AB 3081),s 23, eff. 1/1/2005, op. 7/1/2005.

Section 2024.020 - Time to complete proceedings or have motions heard

(a) Except as otherwise provided in this chapter, any party shall be entitled as a matter of right to complete discovery proceedings on or before the 30th day, and to have motions concerning discovery heard on or before the 15th day, before the date initially set for the trial of the action.

(b) Except as provided in Section 2024.050, a continuance or postponement of the trial date does not operate to reopen discovery proceedings.

Added by Stats 2004 ch 182 (AB 3081),s 23, eff. 7/1/2005.

Section 2024.030 - Time for completion of proceedings concerning witnesses and have motion heard

Any party shall be entitled as a matter of right to complete discovery proceedings pertaining to a witness identified under Chapter 18 (commencing with Section 2034.010) on or before the 15th day, and to have motions concerning that discovery heard on or before the 10th day, before the date initially set for the trial of the action.

Added by Stats 2004 ch 182 (AB 3081),s 23, eff. 7/1/2005.

Section 2024.040 - Time limit on completing discovery in action to arbitrate; inapplicability to summary proceedings to obtain possession of real property and eminent domain

(a) The time limit on completing discovery in an action to be arbitrated under Chapter 2.5 (commencing with Section 1141.10) of Title 3 of Part 3 is subject to Judicial Council Rule. After an award in a case ordered to judicial arbitration, completion of discovery is limited by Section 1141.24.

(b) This chapter does not apply to either of the following:

(1) Summary proceedings for obtaining possession of real property governed by Chapter 4 (commencing with Section 1159) of Title 3 of Part 3. Except as provided in Sections 2024.050 and 2024.060, discovery in these proceedings shall be completed on or before the fifth day before the date set for trial.

(2) Eminent domain proceedings governed by Title 7 (commencing with Section 1230.010) of Part 3.

Amended by Stats 2012 ch 162 (SB 1171),s 17, eff. 1/1/2013.
Added by Stats 2004 ch 182 (AB 3081),s 23, eff. 7/1/2005.

Section 2024.050 - Motion to grant leave to complete proceedings and have motion heard closer to initial trial date or after new trial date set

(a) On motion of any party, the court may grant leave to complete discovery proceedings, or to have a motion concerning discovery heard, closer to the initial trial date, or to reopen discovery after a new trial date has been set. This motion shall be accompanied by a meet and confer declaration under Section 2016.040.

(b) In exercising its discretion to grant or deny this motion, the court shall take into consideration any matter relevant to the leave requested, including, but not limited to, the following:

(1) The necessity and the reasons for the discovery.

(2) The diligence or lack of diligence of the party seeking the discovery or the hearing of a discovery motion, and the reasons that the discovery was not completed or that the discovery motion was not heard earlier.

(3) Any likelihood that permitting the discovery or hearing the discovery motion will prevent the case from going to trial on the date set, or otherwise interfere with the trial calendar, or result in prejudice to any other party.

(4) The length of time that has elapsed between any date previously set, and the date presently set, for the trial of the action.

(c) The court shall impose a monetary sanction under Chapter 7 (commencing with Section 2023.010) against any party, person, or attorney who unsuccessfully makes or opposes a motion to extend or to reopen discovery, unless it finds that the one subject to the sanction acted with substantial justification or that other circumstances make the imposition of the sanction unjust.

Added by Stats 2004 ch 182 (AB 3081),s 23, eff. 7/1/2005.

Section 2024.060 - Agreement to extend time for completion of proceedings and hearing motions

Parties to an action may, with the consent of any party affected by it, enter into an agreement to extend the time for the completion of discovery proceedings or for the hearing of motions concerning discovery, or to reopen discovery after a new date for trial of the action has been set. This agreement may be informal, but it shall be confirmed in a writing that specifies the extended date. In no event shall this agreement require a court to grant a continuance or postponement of the trial of the action.

Added by Stats 2004 ch 182 (AB 3081),s 23, eff. 7/1/2005.

Chapter 9 - ORAL DEPOSITION INSIDE CALIFORNIA

Article 1 - GENERAL PROVISIONS

Section 2025.010 - Generally

Any party may obtain discovery within the scope delimited by Chapter 2 (commencing with Section 2017.010), and subject to the restrictions set forth in Chapter 5 (commencing with Section 2019.010), by taking in California the oral deposition of any person, including any party to the action. The person deposed may be a natural person, an organization such as a public or private corporation, a partnership, an association, or a governmental agency.
Amended by Stats 2016 ch 86 (SB 1171),s 41, eff. 1/1/2017.
Added by Stats 2004 ch 182 (AB 3081),s 23, eff. 7/1/2005.

Article 2 - DEPOSITION NOTICE

Section 2025.210 - Service of notice
Subject to Sections 2025.270 and 2025.610, an oral deposition may be taken as follows:
(a) The defendant may serve a deposition notice without leave of court at any time after that defendant has been served or has appeared in the action, whichever occurs first.
(b) The plaintiff may serve a deposition notice without leave of court on any date that is 20 days after the service of the summons on, or appearance by, any defendant. On motion with or without notice, the court, for good cause shown, may grant to a plaintiff leave to serve a deposition notice on an earlier date.
Added by Stats 2004 ch 182 (AB 3081),s 23, eff. 7/1/2005.

Section 2025.220 - Notice requirements
(a) A party desiring to take the oral deposition of any person shall give notice in writing. The deposition notice shall state all of the following, in at least 12-point type:
  (1) The address where the deposition will be taken.
  (2) The date of the deposition, selected under Section 2025.270, and the time it will commence.
  (3) The name of each deponent, and the address and telephone number, if known, of any deponent who is not a party to the action. If the name of the deponent is not known, the deposition notice shall set forth instead a general description sufficient to identify the person or particular class to which the person belongs.
  (4) The specification with reasonable particularity of any materials or category of materials, including any electronically stored information, to be produced by the deponent.
  (5) Any intention by the party noticing the deposition to record the testimony by audio or video technology, in addition to recording the testimony by the stenographic method as required by Section 2025.330 and any intention to record the testimony by stenographic method through the instant visual display of the testimony. If the deposition will be conducted using instant visual display, a copy of the deposition notice shall also be given to the deposition officer. Any offer to provide the instant visual display of the testimony or to provide rough draft transcripts to any party which is accepted prior to, or offered at, the deposition shall also be made by the deposition officer at the deposition to all parties in attendance. Any party or attorney requesting the provision of the instant visual display of the testimony, or rough draft transcripts, shall pay the reasonable cost of those services, which may be no greater than the costs charged to any other party or attorney.
  (6) Any intention to reserve the right to use at trial a video recording of the deposition testimony of a treating or consulting physician or of an expert witness under subdivision (d) of Section 2025.620. In this event, the operator of the video camera shall be a person who is authorized to administer an oath, and shall not be financially interested in the action or be a relative or employee of any attorney of any of the parties.
  (7) The form in which any electronically stored information is to be produced, if a particular form is desired.
  (8)
    (A) A statement disclosing the existence of a contract, if any is known to the noticing party, between the noticing party or a third party who is financing all or part of the action and either of the following for any service beyond the noticed deposition:
      (i) The deposition officer.
      (ii) The entity providing the services of the deposition officer.
    (B) A statement disclosing that the party noticing the deposition, or a third party financing all or part of the action, directed his or her attorney to use a particular officer or entity to provide services for the deposition, if applicable.
(b) Notwithstanding subdivision (a), where under Article 4 (commencing with Section 2020.410) only the production by a nonparty of business records for copying is desired, a copy of the deposition subpoena shall serve as the notice of deposition.
Amended by Stats 2018 ch 268 (AB 3019),s 1, eff. 1/1/2019.
Amended by Stats 2015 ch 346 (AB 1197),s 2, eff. 1/1/2016.
Amended by Stats 2012 ch 72 (SB 1574),s 20, eff. 1/1/2013.
Added by Stats 2004 ch 182 (AB 3081),s 23, eff. 7/1/2005.

Section 2025.230 - Designation of persons to testify if deponent named not natural person
If the deponent named is not a natural person, the deposition notice shall describe with reasonable particularity the matters on which examination is requested. In that event, the deponent shall designate and produce at the deposition those of its officers, directors, managing agents, employees, or agents who are most qualified to testify on its behalf as to those matters to the extent of any information known or reasonably available to the deponent.
Added by Stats 2004 ch 182 (AB 3081),s 23, eff. 7/1/2005.

Section 2025.240 - Notice given to every party appearing in action; service on consumer or employee
(a) The party who prepares a notice of deposition shall give the notice to every other party who has appeared in the action. The deposition notice, or the accompanying proof of service, shall list all the parties or attorneys for parties on whom it is served.
(b) If, as defined in subdivision (a) of Section 1985.3 or subdivision (a) of Section 1985.6, the party giving notice of the deposition is a subpoenaing party, and the deponent is a witness commanded by a deposition subpoena to produce personal records of a consumer or employment records of an employee, the subpoenaing party shall serve on that consumer or employee all of the following:
  (1) A notice of the deposition.
  (2) The notice of privacy rights specified in subdivision (e) of Section 1985.3 or in subdivision (e) of Section 1985.6.
  (3) A copy of the deposition subpoena.
(c) If the attendance of the deponent is to be compelled by service of a deposition subpoena under Chapter 6 (commencing with Section 2020.010), an identical copy of that subpoena shall be served with the deposition notice.
Amended by Stats 2007 ch 113 (AB 1126),s 5, eff. 1/1/2008.
Added by Stats 2004 ch 182 (AB 3081),s 23, eff. 7/1/2005.

Section 2025.250 - Place for taking deposition
(a) Unless the court orders otherwise under Section 2025.260, the deposition of a natural person, whether or not a party to the action, shall be taken at a place that is, at the option of the party giving notice of the deposition, either within 75 miles of the deponent's residence, or within the county where the action is pending and within 150 miles of the deponent's residence.
(b) The deposition of an organization that is a party to the action shall be taken at a place that is, at the option of the party giving notice of the deposition, either within 75 miles of the organization's principal executive or business office in California, or within the county where the action is pending and within 150 miles of that office.

(c) Unless the organization consents to a more distant place, the deposition of any other organization shall be taken within 75 miles of the organization's principal executive or business office in California.

(d) If an organization has not designated a principal executive or business office in California, the deposition shall be taken at a place that is, at the option of the party giving notice of the deposition, either within the county where the action is pending, or within 75 miles of any executive or business office in California of the organization.

Amended by Stats 2005 ch 294 (AB 333),s 7, eff. 1/1/2006
Added by Stats 2004 ch 182 (AB 3081),s 23, eff. 7/1/2005.

Section 2025.260 - Motion that deponent attend deposition at place more distant than permitted

(a) A party desiring to take the deposition of a natural person who is a party to the action or an officer, director, managing agent, or employee of a party may make a motion for an order that the deponent attend for deposition at a place that is more distant than that permitted under Section 2025.250. This motion shall be accompanied by a meet and confer declaration under Section 2016.040.

(b) In exercising its discretion to grant or deny this motion, the court shall take into consideration any factor tending to show whether the interests of justice will be served by requiring the deponent's attendance at that more distant place, including, but not limited to, the following:

(1) Whether the moving party selected the forum.

(2) Whether the deponent will be present to testify at the trial of the action.

(3) The convenience of the deponent.

(4) The feasibility of conducting the deposition by written questions under Chapter 11 (commencing with Section 2028.010), or of using a discovery method other than a deposition.

(5) The number of depositions sought to be taken at a place more distant than that permitted under Section 2025.250.

(6) The expense to the parties of requiring the deposition to be taken within the distance permitted under Section 2025.250.

(7) The whereabouts of the deponent at the time for which the deposition is scheduled.

(c) The order may be conditioned on the advancement by the moving party of the reasonable expenses and costs to the deponent for travel to the place of deposition.

(d) The court shall impose a monetary sanction under Chapter 7 (commencing with Section 2023.010) against any party, person, or attorney who unsuccessfully makes or opposes a motion to increase the travel limits for a party deponent, unless it finds that the one subject to the sanction acted with substantial justification or that other circumstances make the imposition of the sanction unjust.

Added by Stats 2004 ch 182 (AB 3081),s 23, eff. 7/1/2005.

Section 2025.270 - Scheduling

(a) An oral deposition shall be scheduled for a date at least 10 days after service of the deposition notice.

(b) Notwithstanding subdivision (a), in an unlawful detainer action or other proceeding under Chapter 4 (commencing with Section 1159) of Title 3 of Part 3, an oral deposition shall be scheduled for a date at least five days after service of the deposition notice, but not later than five days before trial.

(c) Notwithstanding subdivisions (a) and (b), if, as defined in Section 1985.3 or 1985.6, the party giving notice of the deposition is a subpoenaing party, and the deponent is a witness commanded by a deposition subpoena to produce personal records of a consumer or employment records of an employee, the deposition shall be scheduled for a date at least 20 days after issuance of that subpoena.

(d) On motion or ex parte application of any party or deponent, for good cause shown, the court may shorten or extend the time for scheduling a deposition, or may stay its taking until the determination of a motion for a protective order under Section 2025.420.

Amended by Stats 2007 ch 113 (AB 1126),s 6, eff. 1/1/2008.
Added by Stats 2004 ch 182 (AB 3081),s 23, eff. 7/1/2005.

Section 2025.280 - Force and effect of notice

(a) The service of a deposition notice under Section 2025.240 is effective to require any deponent who is a party to the action or an officer, director, managing agent, or employee of a party to attend and to testify, as well as to produce any document, electronically stored information, or tangible thing for inspection and copying.

(b) The attendance and testimony of any other deponent, as well as the production by the deponent of any document, electronically stored information, or tangible thing for inspection and copying, requires the service on the deponent of a deposition subpoena under Chapter 6 (commencing with Section 2020.010).

(c) A deponent required by notice or subpoena to produce electronically stored information shall provide a means of gaining direct access to, or a translation into a reasonably usable form of, any electronically stored information that is password protected or otherwise inaccessible.

Amended by Stats 2016 ch 467 (AB 2427),s 2, eff. 1/1/2017.
Amended by Stats 2012 ch 72 (SB 1574),s 21, eff. 1/1/2013.
Added by Stats 2004 ch 182 (AB 3081),s 23, eff. 7/1/2005.

Section 2025.290 - Time limits on examination by other than witness' counsel of record

(a) Except as provided in subdivision (b), or by any court order, including a case management order, a deposition examination of the witness by all counsel, other than the witness' counsel of record, shall be limited to seven hours of total testimony. The court shall allow additional time, beyond any limits imposed by this section, if needed to fairly examine the deponent or if the deponent, another person, or any other circumstance impedes or delays the examination.

(b) This section shall not apply under any of the following circumstances:

(1) If the parties have stipulated that this section will not apply to a specific deposition or to the entire proceeding.

(2) To any deposition of a witness designated as an expert pursuant to Sections 2034.210 to 2034.310, inclusive.

(3) To any case designated as complex by the court pursuant to Rule 3.400 of the California Rules of Court, unless a licensed physician attests in a declaration served on the parties that the deponent suffers from an illness or condition that raises substantial medical doubt of survival of the deponent beyond six months, in which case the deposition examination of the witness by all counsel, other than the witness' counsel of record, shall be limited to two days of no more than seven hours of total testimony each day, or 14 hours of total testimony.

(4) To any case brought by an employee or applicant for employment against an employer for acts or omissions arising out of or relating to the employment relationship.

(5) To any deposition of a person who is designated as the most qualified person to be deposed under Section 2025.230.

(6) To any party who appeared in the action after the deposition has concluded, in which case the new party may notice another deposition subject to the requirements of this section.

(c) It is the intent of the Legislature that any exclusions made by this section shall not be construed to create any presumption or any substantive change to existing law relating to the appropriate time limit for depositions falling within the exclusion. Nothing in this section shall be construed to affect the existing right of any party to move for a protective order or the court's discretion to make any order that justice requires to limit a deposition in order to protect any party, deponent, or other natural person or organization from unwarranted annoyance, embarrassment, oppression, undue burden, or expense.

Added by Stats 2012 ch 346 (AB 1875),s 1, eff. 1/1/2013.

Section 2025.295 - Duration of deposition examination of plaintiff suffering from mesothelioma or silicosis

(a) Notwithstanding Section 2025.290, in any civil action for injury or illness that results in mesothelioma or silicosis, a deposition examination of the plaintiff by all counsel, other than the plaintiff's counsel of record, shall be limited to seven hours of total testimony if a licensed physician attests in a declaration served on the parties that the deponent suffers from mesothelioma or silicosis, raising substantial medical doubt of the survival of the deponent beyond six months.
(b) Notwithstanding the presumptive time limit in subdivision (a), upon request by a defendant, a court may, in its discretion, grant one of the following up to:
  (1) An additional three hours of deposition testimony for no more than 10 hours of total deposition conducted by the defendants if there are more than 10 defendants appearing at the deposition.
  (2) An additional seven hours of deposition testimony for no more than 14 hours of total deposition conducted by the defendants if there are more than 20 defendants appearing at the deposition.
(c) The court may grant the additional time provided for in paragraphs (1) and (2) of subdivision (b) only if it finds that an extension, in the instant case, is in the interest of fairness, which includes consideration of the number of defendants appearing at the deposition, and determines that the health of the deponent does not appear to be endangered by the grant of additional time.
Added by Stats 2019 ch 212 (SB 645),s 1, eff. 1/1/2020.

Article 3 - CONDUCT OF DEPOSITION

Section 2025.310 - Physical presence
(a) At the election of the deponent or the deposing party, the deposition officer may attend the deposition at a different location than the deponent via remote means. A deponent is not required to be physically present with the deposition officer when being sworn in at the time of the deposition.
(b) Subject to Section 2025.420, any party or attorney of record may, but is not required to, be physically present at the deposition at the location of the deponent. If a party or attorney of record elects to be physically present at the location of the deponent, all physically present participants in the deposition shall comply with local health and safety ordinances, rules, and orders.
(c) The procedures to implement this section shall be established by court order in the specific action or proceeding or by the California Rules of Court.
(d) An exercise of the authority granted by subdivision (a) or (b) does not waive any other provision of this title, including, but not limited to, provisions regarding the time, place, or manner in which a deposition shall be conducted.
(e) This section does not alter or amend who may lawfully serve as a deposition officer pursuant to this title or who otherwise may administer oaths pursuant to Sections 2093 and 2094 of this code or Section 8201 of the Government Code.
Amended by Stats 2022 ch 92 (SB 1037),s 1, eff. 1/1/2023.
Amended by Stats 2020 ch 112 (SB 1146),s 3, eff. 9/18/2020.
Added by Stats 2004 ch 182 (AB 3081),s 23, eff. 7/1/2005.

Section 2025.320 - Conducted under supervision of deposition officer
Except as provided in Section 2020.420, the deposition shall be conducted under the supervision of an officer who is authorized to administer an oath and is subject to all of the following requirements:
(a) The officer shall not be financially interested in the action and shall not be a relative or employee of any attorney of the parties, or of any of the parties.
(b) Services and products offered or provided by the deposition officer or the entity providing the services of the deposition officer to any party or to any party's attorney or third party who is financing all or part of the action shall be offered to all parties or their attorneys attending the deposition. No service or product may be offered or provided by the deposition officer or by the entity providing the services of the deposition officer to any party or any party's attorney or third party who is financing all or part of the action unless the service or product is offered or provided to all parties or their attorneys attending the deposition. All services and products offered or provided shall be made available at the same time to all parties or their attorneys.
(c) The deposition officer or the entity providing the services of the deposition officer shall not provide to any party or any party's attorney or third party who is financing all or part of the action any service or product consisting of the deposition officer's notations or comments regarding the demeanor of any witness, attorney, or party present at the deposition. The deposition officer or entity providing the services of the deposition officer shall not collect any personal identifying information about the witness as a service or product to be provided to any party or third party who is financing all or part of the action.
(d) Upon the request of any party or any party's attorney attending a deposition, any party or any party's attorney attending the deposition shall enter in the record of the deposition all services and products made available to that party or party's attorney or third party who is financing all or part of the action by the deposition officer or by the entity providing the services of the deposition officer. A party in the action who is not represented by an attorney shall be informed by the noticing party or the party's attorney that the unrepresented party may request this statement.
(e) Any objection to the qualifications of the deposition officer is waived unless made before the deposition begins or as soon thereafter as the ground for that objection becomes known or could be discovered by reasonable diligence.
(f) Violation of this section by any person may result in a civil penalty of up to five thousand dollars ($5,000) imposed by a court of competent jurisdiction.
Added by Stats 2004 ch 182 (AB 3081),s 23, eff. 7/1/2005.

Section 2025.330 - Taking testimony
(a) The deposition officer shall put the deponent under oath or affirmation.
(b) Unless the parties agree or the court orders otherwise, the testimony, as well as any stated objections, shall be taken stenographically. If taken stenographically, it shall be by a person certified pursuant to Article 3 (commencing with Section 8020) of Chapter 13 of Division 3 of the Business and Professions Code.
(c) The party noticing the deposition may also record the testimony by audio or video technology if the notice of deposition stated an intention also to record the testimony by either of those methods, or if all the parties agree that the testimony may also be recorded by either of those methods. Any other party, at that party's expense, may make an audio or video record of the deposition, provided that the other party promptly, and in no event less than three calendar days before the date for which the deposition is scheduled, serves a written notice of this intention to make an audio or video record of the deposition testimony on the party or attorney who noticed the deposition, on all other parties or attorneys on whom the deposition notice was served under Section 2025.240, and on any deponent whose attendance is being compelled by a deposition subpoena under Chapter 6 (commencing with Section 2020.010). If this notice is given three calendar days before the deposition date, it shall be made by personal service under Section 1011.
(d) Examination and cross-examination of the deponent shall proceed as permitted at trial under the provisions of the Evidence Code.
(e) In lieu of participating in the oral examination, parties may transmit written questions in a sealed envelope to the party taking the deposition for delivery to the deposition officer, who shall unseal the envelope and propound them to the deponent after the oral examination has been completed.
Amended by Stats 2005 ch 294 (AB 333),s 8, eff. 1/1/2006
Added by Stats 2004 ch 182 (AB 3081),s 23, eff. 7/1/2005.

Section 2025.340 - Deposition recorded by means of audio or video technology
If a deposition is being recorded by means of audio or video technology by, or at the direction of, any party, the following procedure shall be observed:
(a) The area used for recording the deponent's oral testimony shall be suitably large, adequately lighted, and reasonably quiet.
(b) The operator of the recording equipment shall be competent to set up, operate, and monitor the equipment in the manner prescribed in this section. Except as provided in subdivision (c), the operator may be an employee of the attorney taking the deposition unless the operator is also the deposition officer.
(c) If a video recording of deposition testimony is to be used under subdivision (d) of Section 2025.620, the operator of the recording equipment shall be a person who is authorized to administer an oath, and shall not be financially interested in the action or be a relative or employee of any attorney of any of the parties, unless all parties attending the deposition agree on the record to waive these qualifications and restrictions.
(d) Services and products offered or provided by the deposition officer or the entity providing the services of the deposition officer to any party or to any party's attorney or third party who is financing all or part of the action shall be offered or provided to all parties or their attorneys attending the deposition. No service or product may be offered or provided by the deposition officer or by the entity providing the services of the deposition officer to any party or any party's attorney or third party who is financing all or part of the action unless the service or product is offered or provided to all parties or their attorneys attending the deposition. All services and products offered or provided shall be made available at the same time to all parties or their attorneys.
(e) The deposition officer or the entity providing the services of the deposition officer shall not provide to any party or any other person or entity any service or product consisting of the deposition officer's notations or comments regarding the demeanor of any witness, attorney, or party present at the deposition. The deposition officer or the entity providing the services of the deposition officer shall not collect any personal identifying information about the witness as a service or product to be provided to any party or third party who is financing all or part of the action.
(f) Upon the request of any party or any party's attorney attending a deposition, any party or any party's attorney attending the deposition shall enter in the record of the deposition all services and products made available to that party or party's attorney or third party who is financing all or part of the action by the deposition officer or by the entity providing the services of the deposition officer. A party in the action who is not represented by an attorney shall be informed by the noticing party that the unrepresented party may request this statement.
(g) The operator shall not distort the appearance or the demeanor of participants in the deposition by the use of camera or sound recording techniques.
(h) The deposition shall begin with an oral or written statement on camera or on the audio recording that includes the operator's name and business address, the name and business address of the operator's employer, the date, time, and place of the deposition, the caption of the case, the name of the deponent, a specification of the party on whose behalf the deposition is being taken, and any stipulations by the parties.
(i) Counsel for the parties shall identify themselves on camera or on the audio recording.
(j) The oath shall be administered to the deponent on camera or on the audio recording.
(k) If the length of a deposition requires the use of more than one unit of tape or electronic storage, the end of each unit and the beginning of each succeeding unit shall be announced on camera or on the audio recording.
(l) At the conclusion of a deposition, a statement shall be made on camera or on the audio recording that the deposition is ended and shall set forth any stipulations made by counsel concerning the custody of the audio or video recording and the exhibits, or concerning other pertinent matters.
(m) A party intending to offer an audio or video recording of a deposition in evidence under Section 2025.620 shall notify the court and all parties in writing of that intent and of the parts of the deposition to be offered. That notice shall be given within sufficient time for objections to be made and ruled on by the judge to whom the case is assigned for trial or hearing, and for any editing of the recording. Objections to all or part of the deposition shall be made in writing. The court may permit further designations of testimony and objections as justice may require. With respect to those portions of an audio or video record of deposition testimony that are not designated by any party or that are ruled to be objectionable, the court may order that the party offering the recording of the deposition at the trial or hearing suppress those portions, or that an edited version of the deposition recording be prepared for use at the trial or hearing. The original audio or video record of the deposition shall be preserved unaltered. If no stenographic record of the deposition testimony has previously been made, the party offering an audio or video recording of that testimony under Section 2025.620 shall accompany that offer with a stenographic transcript prepared from that recording.
Added by Stats 2004 ch 182 (AB 3081),s 23, eff. 7/1/2005.

Article 4 - OBJECTIONS, SANCTIONS, PROTECTIVE ORDERS, MOTIONS TO COMPEL, AND SUSPENSION OF DEPOSITIONS

Section 2025.410 - Generally
(a) Any party served with a deposition notice that does not comply with Article 2 (commencing with Section 2025.210) waives any error or irregularity unless that party promptly serves a written objection specifying that error or irregularity at least three calendar days prior to the date for which the deposition is scheduled, on the party seeking to take the deposition and any other attorney or party on whom the deposition notice was served.
(b) If an objection is made three calendar days before the deposition date, the objecting party shall make personal service of that objection pursuant to Section 1011 on the party who gave notice of the deposition. Any deposition taken after the service of a written objection shall not be used against the objecting party under Section 2025.620 if the party did not attend the deposition and if the court determines that the objection was a valid one.
(c) In addition to serving this written objection, a party may also move for an order staying the taking of the deposition and quashing the deposition notice. This motion shall be accompanied by a meet and confer declaration under Section 2016.040. The taking of the deposition is stayed pending the determination of this motion.
(d) The court shall impose a monetary sanction under Chapter 7 (commencing with Section 2023.010) against any party, person, or attorney who unsuccessfully makes or opposes a motion to quash a deposition notice, unless it finds that the one subject to the sanction acted with substantial justification or that other circumstances make the imposition of the sanction unjust.
(e)
(1) Notwithstanding subdivision (d), absent exceptional circumstances, the court shall not impose sanctions on any party, person, or attorney for failure to provide electronically stored information that has been lost, damaged, altered, or overwritten as the result of the routine, good faith operation of an electronic information system.
(2) This subdivision shall not be construed to alter any obligation to preserve discoverable information.
Amended by Stats 2012 ch 72 (SB 1574),s 22, eff. 1/1/2013.
Added by Stats 2004 ch 182 (AB 3081),s 23, eff. 7/1/2005.

Section 2025.420 - Motion for protective order
(a) Before, during, or after a deposition, any party, any deponent, or any other affected natural person or organization may promptly move for a protective order. The motion shall be accompanied by a meet and confer declaration under Section 2016.040.

(b) The court, for good cause shown, may make any order that justice requires to protect any party, deponent, or other natural person or organization from unwarranted annoyance, embarrassment, or oppression, or undue burden and expense. This protective order may include, but is not limited to, one or more of the following directions:

(1) That the deposition not be taken at all.

(2) That the deposition be taken at a different time.

(3) That a video recording of the deposition testimony of a treating or consulting physician or of any expert witness, intended for possible use at trial under subdivision (d) of Section 2025.620, be postponed until the moving party has had an adequate opportunity to prepare, by discovery deposition of the deponent, or other means, for cross-examination.

(4) That the deposition be taken at a place other than that specified in the deposition notice, if it is within a distance permitted by Sections 2025.250 and 2025.260.

(5) That the deposition be taken only on certain specified terms and conditions.

(6) That the deponent's testimony be taken by written, instead of oral, examination.

(7) That the method of discovery be interrogatories to a party instead of an oral deposition.

(8) That the testimony be recorded in a manner different from that specified in the deposition notice.

(9) That certain matters not be inquired into.

(10) That the scope of the examination be limited to certain matters.

(11) That all or certain of the writings or tangible things designated in the deposition notice not be produced, inspected, copied, tested, or sampled, or that conditions be set for the production of electronically stored information designated in the deposition notice.

(12) That designated persons, other than the parties to the action and their officers and counsel, be excluded from attending the deposition.

(13) That a trade secret or other confidential research, development, or commercial information not be disclosed or be disclosed only to specified persons or only in a specified way.

(14) That the parties simultaneously file specified documents enclosed in sealed envelopes to be opened as directed by the court.

(15) That the deposition be sealed and thereafter opened only on order of the court.

(16) That examination of the deponent be terminated. If an order terminates the examination, the deposition shall not thereafter be resumed, except on order of the court.

(c) The party, deponent, or any other affected natural person or organization that seeks a protective order regarding the production, inspection, copying, testing, or sampling of electronically stored information on the basis that the information is from a source that is not reasonably accessible because of undue burden or expense shall bear the burden of demonstrating that the information is from a source that is not reasonably accessible because of undue burden or expense.

(d) If the party or affected person from whom discovery of electronically stored information is sought establishes that the information is from a source that is not reasonably accessible because of undue burden or expense, the court may nonetheless order discovery if the demanding party shows good cause, subject to any limitations imposed under subdivision (f).

(e) If the court finds good cause for the production of electronically stored information from a source that is not reasonably accessible, the court may set conditions for the discovery of the electronically stored information, including allocation of the expense of discovery.

(f) The court shall limit the frequency or extent of discovery of electronically stored information, even from a source that is reasonably accessible, if the court determines that any of the following conditions exist:

(1) It is possible to obtain the information from some other source that is more convenient, less burdensome, or less expensive.

(2) The discovery sought is unreasonably cumulative or duplicative.

(3) The party seeking discovery has had ample opportunity by discovery in the action to obtain the information sought.

(4) The likely burden or expense of the proposed discovery outweighs the likely benefit, taking into account the amount in controversy, the resources of the parties, the importance of the issues in the litigation, and the importance of the requested discovery in resolving the issues.

(g) If the motion for a protective order is denied in whole or in part, the court may order that the deponent provide or permit the discovery against which protection was sought on those terms and conditions that are just.

(h) The court shall impose a monetary sanction under Chapter 7 (commencing with Section 2023.010) against any party, person, or attorney who unsuccessfully makes or opposes a motion for a protective order, unless it finds that the one subject to the sanction acted with substantial justification or that other circumstances make the imposition of the sanction unjust.

(i)

(1) Notwithstanding subdivision (h), absent exceptional circumstances, the court shall not impose sanctions on any party, deponent, or other affected natural person or organization or any of their attorneys for failure to provide electronically stored information that has been lost, damaged, altered, or overwritten as the result of the routine, good faith operation of an electronic information system.

(2) This subdivision shall not be construed to alter any obligation to preserve discoverable information.

Amended by Stats 2012 ch 72 (SB 1574),s 23, eff. 1/1/2013.

Added by Stats 2004 ch 182 (AB 3081),s 23, eff. 7/1/2005.

Section 2025.430 - Failure of party giving notice of deposition to attend or proceed

If the party giving notice of a deposition fails to attend or proceed with it, the court shall impose a monetary sanction under Chapter 7 (commencing with Section 2023.010) against that party, or the attorney for that party, or both, and in favor of any party attending in person or by attorney, unless it finds that the one subject to the sanction acted with substantial justification or that other circumstances make the imposition of the sanction unjust.

Added by Stats 2004 ch 182 (AB 3081),s 23, eff. 7/1/2005.

Section 2025.440 - Failure of deponent to attend because party giving notice failed to serve deposition subpoena

(a) If a deponent does not appear for a deposition because the party giving notice of the deposition failed to serve a required deposition subpoena, the court shall impose a monetary sanction under Chapter 7 (commencing with Section 2023.010) against that party, or the attorney for that party, or both, in favor of any other party who, in person or by attorney, attended at the time and place specified in the deposition notice in the expectation that the deponent's testimony would be taken, unless the court finds that the one subject to the sanction acted with substantial justification or that other circumstances make the imposition of the sanction unjust.

(b) If a deponent on whom a deposition subpoena has been served fails to attend a deposition or refuses to be sworn as a witness, the court may impose on the deponent the sanctions described in Section 2020.240.

Added by Stats 2004 ch 182 (AB 3081),s 23, eff. 7/1/2005.

Section 2025.450 - Motion to compel deponent testimony and production

(a) If, after service of a deposition notice, a party to the action or an officer, director, managing agent, or employee of a party, or a person designated by an organization that is a party under Section 2025.230, without having served a valid objection under Section 2025.410, fails to appear for examination, or to proceed with it, or to produce for inspection any document, electronically stored information, or tangible thing described in the deposition notice, the party giving the notice may move for an order compelling the deponent's attendance and testimony, and the production for inspection of any document, electronically stored information, or tangible thing described in the deposition notice.

(b) A motion under subdivision (a) shall comply with both of the following:

(1) The motion shall set forth specific facts showing good cause justifying the production for inspection of any document, electronically stored information, or tangible thing described in the deposition notice.

(2) The motion shall be accompanied by a meet and confer declaration under Section 2016.040, or, when the deponent fails to attend the deposition and produce the documents, electronically stored information, or things described in the deposition notice, by a declaration stating that the petitioner has contacted the deponent to inquire about the nonappearance.

(c) In a motion under subdivision (a) relating to the production of electronically stored information, the party or party-affiliated deponent objecting to or opposing the production, inspection, copying, testing, or sampling of electronically stored information on the basis that the information is from a source that is not reasonably accessible because of the undue burden or expense shall bear the burden of demonstrating that the information is from a source that is not reasonably accessible because of undue burden or expense.

(d) If the party or party-affiliated deponent from whom discovery of electronically stored information is sought establishes that the information is from a source that is not reasonably accessible because of the undue burden or expense, the court may nonetheless order discovery if the demanding party shows good cause, subject to any limitations imposed under subdivision (f).

(e) If the court finds good cause for the production of electronically stored information from a source that is not reasonably accessible, the court may set conditions for the discovery of the electronically stored information, including allocation of the expense of discovery.

(f) The court shall limit the frequency or extent of discovery of electronically stored information, even from a source that is reasonably accessible, if the court determines that any of the following conditions exists:

(1) It is possible to obtain the information from some other source that is more convenient, less burdensome, or less expensive.

(2) The discovery sought is unreasonably cumulative or duplicative.

(3) The party seeking discovery has had ample opportunity by discovery in the action to obtain the information sought.

(4) The likely burden or expense of the proposed discovery outweighs the likely benefit, taking into account the amount in controversy, the resources of the parties, the importance of the issues in the litigation, and the importance of the requested discovery in resolving the issues.

(g)

(1) If a motion under subdivision (a) is granted, the court shall impose a monetary sanction under Chapter 7 (commencing with Section 2023.010) in favor of the party who noticed the deposition and against the deponent or the party with whom the deponent is affiliated, unless the court finds that the one subject to the sanction acted with substantial justification or that other circumstances make the imposition of the sanction unjust.

(2) On motion of any other party who, in person or by attorney, attended at the time and place specified in the deposition notice in the expectation that the deponent's testimony would be taken, the court shall impose a monetary sanction under Chapter 7 (commencing with Section 2023.010) in favor of that party and against the deponent or the party with whom the deponent is affiliated, unless the court finds that the one subject to the sanction acted with substantial justification or that other circumstances make the imposition of the sanction unjust.

(h) If that party or party-affiliated deponent then fails to obey an order compelling attendance, testimony, and production, the court may make those orders that are just, including the imposition of an issue sanction, an evidence sanction, or a terminating sanction under Chapter 7 (commencing with Section 2023.010) against that party deponent or against the party with whom the deponent is affiliated. In lieu of, or in addition to, this sanction, the court may impose a monetary sanction under Chapter 7 (commencing with Section 2023.010) against that deponent or against the party with whom that party deponent is affiliated, and in favor of any party who, in person or by attorney, attended in the expectation that the deponent's testimony would be taken pursuant to that order.

(i)

(1) Notwithstanding subdivisions (g) and (h), absent exceptional circumstances, the court shall not impose sanctions on a party or any attorney of a party for failure to provide electronically stored information that has been lost, damaged, altered, or overwritten as the result of the routine, good faith operation of an electronic information system.

(2) This subdivision shall not be construed to alter any obligation to preserve discoverable information.

Amended by Stats 2012 ch 72 (SB 1574),s 24, eff. 1/1/2013.
Added by Stats 2004 ch 182 (AB 3081),s 23, eff. 7/1/2005.

Section 2025.460 - Waiver unless objection made

(a) The protection of information from discovery on the ground that it is privileged or that it is a protected work product under Chapter 4 (commencing with Section 2018.010) is waived unless a specific objection to its disclosure is timely made during the deposition.

(b) Errors and irregularities of any kind occurring at the oral examination that might be cured if promptly presented are waived unless a specific objection to them is timely made during the deposition. These errors and irregularities include, but are not limited to, those relating to the manner of taking the deposition, to the oath or affirmation administered, to the conduct of a party, attorney, deponent, or deposition officer, or to the form of any question or answer. Unless the objecting party demands that the taking of the deposition be suspended to permit a motion for a protective order under Sections 2025.420 and 2025.470, the deposition shall proceed subject to the objection.

(c) Objections to the competency of the deponent, or to the relevancy, materiality, or admissibility at trial of the testimony or of the materials produced are unnecessary and are not waived by failure to make them before or during the deposition.

(d) If a deponent objects to the production of electronically stored information on the grounds that it is from a source that is not reasonably accessible because of undue burden or expense and that the deponent will not search the source in the absence of an agreement with the deposing party or court order, the deponent shall identify in its objection the types or categories of sources of electronically stored information that it asserts are not reasonably accessible. By objecting and identifying information of a type or category of source or sources that are not reasonably accessible, the deponent preserves any objections it may have relating to that electronically stored information.

(e) If a deponent fails to answer any question or to produce any document, electronically stored information, or tangible thing under the deponent's control that is specified in the deposition notice or a deposition subpoena, the party seeking that answer or production may adjourn the deposition or complete the examination on other matters without waiving the right at a later time to move for an order compelling that answer or production under Section 2025.480.

(f) Notwithstanding subdivision (a), if a deponent notifies the party that took a deposition that electronically stored information produced pursuant to the deposition notice or subpoena is subject to a claim of privilege or of protection as attorney work product, as described in Section 2031.285, the provisions of Section 2031.285 shall apply.

Amended by Stats 2012 ch 72 (SB 1574),s 25, eff. 1/1/2013.
Added by Stats 2004 ch 182 (AB 3081),s 23, eff. 7/1/2005.

Section 2025.470 - Suspension of taking of testimony

The deposition officer may not suspend the taking of testimony without the stipulation of all parties present unless any party attending the deposition, including the deponent, demands that the deposition officer suspend taking the testimony to enable that party or deponent to move for a protective order under Section 2025.420 on the ground that the examination is being conducted in bad faith or in a manner that unreasonably annoys, embarrasses, or oppresses that deponent or party.

Added by Stats 2004 ch 182 (AB 3081),s 23, eff. 7/1/2005.

Section 2025.480 - Motion to compel answer or production

(a) If a deponent fails to answer any question or to produce any document, electronically stored information, or tangible thing under the deponent's control that is specified in the deposition notice or a deposition subpoena, the party seeking discovery may move the court for an order compelling that answer or production.
(b) This motion shall be made no later than 60 days after the completion of the record of the deposition, and shall be accompanied by a meet and confer declaration under Section 2016.040.
(c) Notice of this motion shall be given to all parties and to the deponent either orally at the examination, or by subsequent service in writing. If the notice of the motion is given orally, the deposition officer shall direct the deponent to attend a session of the court at the time specified in the notice.
(d) In a motion under subdivision (a) relating to the production of electronically stored information, the deponent objecting to or opposing the production, inspection, copying, testing, or sampling of electronically stored information on the basis that the information is from a source that is not reasonably accessible because of the undue burden or expense shall bear the burden of demonstrating that the information is from a source that is not reasonably accessible because of undue burden or expense.
(e) If the deponent from whom discovery of electronically stored information is sought establishes that the information is from a source that is not reasonably accessible because of the undue burden or expense, the court may nonetheless order discovery if the deposing party shows good cause, subject to any limitations imposed under subdivision (g).
(f) If the court finds good cause for the production of electronically stored information from a source that is not reasonably accessible, the court may set conditions for the discovery of the electronically stored information, including allocation of the expense of discovery.
(g) The court shall limit the frequency or extent of discovery of electronically stored information, even from a source that is reasonably accessible, if the court determines that any of the following conditions exists:
    (1) It is possible to obtain the information from some other source that is more convenient, less burdensome, or less expensive.
    (2) The discovery sought is unreasonably cumulative or duplicative.
    (3) The party seeking discovery has had ample opportunity by discovery in the action to obtain the information sought.
    (4) The likely burden or expense of the proposed discovery outweighs the likely benefit, taking into account the amount in controversy, the resources of the parties, the importance of the issues in the litigation, and the importance of the requested discovery in resolving the issues.
(h) Not less than five days prior to the hearing on this motion, the moving party shall lodge with the court a certified copy of any parts of the stenographic transcript of the deposition that are relevant to the motion. If a deposition is recorded by audio or video technology, the moving party is required to lodge a certified copy of a transcript of any parts of the deposition that are relevant to the motion.
(i) If the court determines that the answer or production sought is subject to discovery, it shall order that the answer be given or the production be made on the resumption of the deposition.
(j) The court shall impose a monetary sanction under Chapter 7 (commencing with Section 2023.010) against any party, person, or attorney who unsuccessfully makes or opposes a motion to compel an answer or production, unless it finds that the one subject to the sanction acted with substantial justification or that other circumstances make the imposition of the sanction unjust.
(k) If a deponent fails to obey an order entered under this section, the failure may be considered a contempt of court. In addition, if the disobedient deponent is a party to the action or an officer, director, managing agent, or employee of a party, the court may make those orders that are just against the disobedient party, or against the party with whom the disobedient deponent is affiliated, including the imposition of an issue sanction, an evidence sanction, or a terminating sanction under Chapter 7 (commencing with Section 2023.010). In lieu of or in addition to this sanction, the court may impose a monetary sanction under Chapter 7 (commencing with Section 2023.010) against that party deponent or against any party with whom the deponent is affiliated.
(l)
    (1) Notwithstanding subdivisions (j) and (k), absent exceptional circumstances, the court shall not impose sanctions on a deponent or any attorney of a deponent for failure to provide electronically stored information that has been lost, damaged, altered, or overwritten as the result of the routine, good faith operation of an electronic information system.
    (2) This subdivision shall not be construed to alter any obligation to preserve discoverable information.
Amended by Stats 2012 ch 72 (SB 1574),s 26, eff. 1/1/2013.
Amended by Stats 2005 ch 22 (SB 1108),s 21, eff. 1/1/2006
Added by Stats 2004 ch 182 (AB 3081),s 23, eff. 7/1/2005.

Article 5 - TRANSCRIPT OR RECORDING

Section 2025.510 - Generally

(a) Unless the parties agree otherwise, the testimony at a deposition recorded by stenographic means shall be transcribed.
(b) The party noticing the deposition shall bear the cost of the transcription, unless the court, on motion and for good cause shown, orders that the cost be borne or shared by another party.
(c) Notwithstanding subdivision (b) of Section 2025.320, any other party or the deponent, at the expense of that party or deponent, may obtain a copy of the transcript.
(d) If the deposition officer receives a request from a party for an original or a copy of the deposition transcript, or any portion thereof, and the full or partial transcript will be available to that party prior to the time the original or copy would be available to any other party, the deposition officer shall immediately notify all other parties attending the deposition of the request, and shall, upon request by any party other than the party making the original request, make that copy of the full or partial deposition transcript available to all parties at the same time.
(e) Stenographic notes of depositions shall be retained by the reporter for a period of not less than eight years from the date of the deposition, where no transcript is produced, and not less than one year from the date on which the transcript is produced. The notes may be either on paper or electronic media, as long as it allows for satisfactory production of a transcript at any time during the periods specified.
(f) At the request of any other party to the action, including a party who did not attend the taking of the deposition testimony, any party who records or causes the recording of that testimony by means of audio or video technology shall promptly do both of the following:
    (1) Permit that other party to hear the audio recording or to view the video recording.
    (2) Furnish a copy of the audio or video recording to that other party on receipt of payment of the reasonable cost of making that copy of the recording.
(g) If the testimony at the deposition is recorded both stenographically and by audio or video technology, the stenographic transcript shall be the official record of that testimony for the purpose of the trial and any subsequent hearing or appeal.
(h)
    (1) The requesting attorney or party appearing in propria persona shall timely pay the deposition officer or the entity providing the services of the deposition officer for the transcription or copy of the transcription described in subdivision (b) or (c), and any other deposition product or service that is requested either orally or in writing.
    (2) This subdivision shall apply unless responsibility for the payment is otherwise provided by law or unless the deposition officer or entity is notified in writing at the time the services or products are requested that the party or another identified person will be responsible for payment.
    (3) This subdivision does not prohibit or supersede an agreement between an attorney and a party allocating responsibility for the payment of deposition costs to the party.

(4) Nothing in the case of Serrano v. Stefan Merli Plastering Co., Inc. (2008) 162 Cal.App.4th 1014 shall be construed to alter the standards by which a court acquires personal jurisdiction over a nonparty to an action.

(5) The requesting attorney or party appearing in propria persona, upon the written request of a deposition officer who has obtained a final judgment for payment of services provided pursuant to this subdivision, shall provide to the deposition officer an address that can be used to effectuate service for the purpose of Section 708.110 in the manner specified in Section 415.10.

(i) For purposes of this section, "deposition product or service" means any product or service provided in connection with a deposition that qualifies as shorthand reporting, as described in Section 8017 of the Business and Professions Code, and any product or service derived from that shorthand reporting.

Amended by Stats 2014 ch 913 (AB 2747),s 12, eff. 1/1/2015.
Amended by Stats 2012 ch 125 (AB 2372),s 1, eff. 1/1/2013.
Amended by Stats 2007 ch 115 (AB 1211),s 1, eff. 1/1/2008.
Added by Stats 2004 ch 182 (AB 3081),s 23, eff. 7/1/2005.

Section 2025.520 - Notice that transcript of testimony available; changing form or substance of answer or approving or disapproving transcript

(a) If the deposition testimony is stenographically recorded, the deposition officer shall send written notice to the deponent and to all parties attending the deposition when the original transcript of the testimony for each session of the deposition is available for reading, correcting, and signing, unless the deponent and the attending parties agree on the record that the reading, correcting, and signing of the transcript of the testimony will be waived or that the reading, correcting, and signing of a transcript of the testimony will take place after the entire deposition has been concluded or at some other specific time.

(b) For 30 days following each notice under subdivision (a), unless the attending parties and the deponent agree on the record or otherwise in writing to a longer or shorter time period, the deponent may change the form or the substance of the answer to a question, and may either approve the transcript of the deposition by signing it, or refuse to approve the transcript by not signing it.

(c) Alternatively, within this same period, the deponent may change the form or the substance of the answer to any question and may approve or refuse to approve the transcript by means of a letter to the deposition officer signed by the deponent which is mailed by certified or registered mail with return receipt requested. A copy of that letter shall be sent by first-class mail to all parties attending the deposition.

(d) For good cause shown, the court may shorten the 30-day period for making changes, approving, or refusing to approve the transcript.

(e) The deposition officer shall indicate on the original of the transcript, if the deponent has not already done so at the office of the deposition officer, any action taken by the deponent and indicate on the original of the transcript, the deponent's approval of, or failure or refusal to approve, the transcript. The deposition officer shall also notify in writing the parties attending the deposition of any changes which the deponent timely made in person.

(f) If the deponent fails or refuses to approve the transcript within the allotted period, the deposition shall be given the same effect as though it had been approved, subject to any changes timely made by the deponent.

(g) Notwithstanding subdivision (f), on a seasonable motion to suppress the deposition, accompanied by a meet and confer declaration under Section 2016.040, the court may determine that the reasons given for the failure or refusal to approve the transcript require rejection of the deposition in whole or in part.

(h) The court shall impose a monetary sanction under Chapter 7 (commencing with Section 2023.010) against any party, person, or attorney who unsuccessfully makes or opposes a motion to suppress a deposition under this section, unless the court finds that the one subject to the sanction acted with substantial justification or that other circumstances make the imposition of the sanction unjust.

Added by Stats 2004 ch 182 (AB 3081),s 23, eff. 7/1/2005.

Section 2025.530 - Notice that audio or video recording available; changing substance of answer; signing deposition or statement refusing to sign

(a) If there is no stenographic transcription of the deposition, the deposition officer shall send written notice to the deponent and to all parties attending the deposition that the audio or video recording made by, or at the direction of, any party, is available for review, unless the deponent and all these parties agree on the record to waive the hearing or viewing of the audio or video recording of the testimony.

(b) For 30 days following a notice under subdivision (a), the deponent, either in person or by signed letter to the deposition officer, may change the substance of the answer to any question.

(c) The deposition officer shall set forth in a writing to accompany the recording any changes made by the deponent, as well as either the deponent's signature identifying the deposition as the deponent's own, or a statement of the deponent's failure to supply the signature, or to contact the officer within the period prescribed by subdivision (b).

(d) When a deponent fails to contact the officer within the period prescribed by subdivision (b), or expressly refuses by a signature to identify the deposition as the deponent's own, the deposition shall be given the same effect as though signed.

(e) Notwithstanding subdivision (d), on a reasonable motion to suppress the deposition, accompanied by a meet and confer declaration under Section 2016.040, the court may determine that the reasons given for the refusal to sign require rejection of the deposition in whole or in part.

(f) The court shall impose a monetary sanction under Chapter 7 (commencing with Section 2023.010) against any party, person, or attorney who unsuccessfully makes or opposes a motion to suppress a deposition under this section, unless it finds that the one subject to the sanction acted with substantial justification or that other circumstances make the imposition of the sanction unjust.

Added by Stats 2004 ch 182 (AB 3081),s 23, eff. 7/1/2005.

Section 2025.540 - Certification by deposition officer

(a) The deposition officer shall certify on the transcript of the deposition, or in a writing accompanying an audio or video record of deposition testimony, as described in Section 2025.530, that the deponent was duly sworn and that the transcript or recording is a true record of the testimony given.

(b) When prepared as a rough draft transcript, the transcript of the deposition may not be certified and may not be used, cited, or transcribed as the certified transcript of the deposition proceedings. The rough draft transcript may not be cited or used in any way or at any time to rebut or contradict the certified transcript of deposition proceedings as provided by the deposition officer.

Added by Stats 2004 ch 182 (AB 3081),s 23, eff. 7/1/2005.

Section 2025.550 - Transcript of deposition transmitted to attorney for party who noticed deposition

(a) The certified transcript of a deposition shall not be filed with the court. Instead, the deposition officer shall securely seal that transcript in an envelope or package endorsed with the title of the action and marked: "Deposition of (here insert name of deponent)," and shall promptly transmit it to the attorney for the party who noticed the deposition. This attorney shall store it under conditions that will protect it against loss, destruction, or tampering.

(b) The attorney to whom the transcript of a deposition is transmitted shall retain custody of it until six months after final disposition of the action. At that time, the transcript may be destroyed, unless the court, on motion of any party and for good cause shown, orders that the transcript be preserved for a longer period.

Added by Stats 2004 ch 182 (AB 3081),s 23, eff. 7/1/2005.

Section 2025.560 - Retention of audio or video recording of deposition by operator

(a) An audio or video recording of deposition testimony made by, or at the direction of, any party, including a certified recording made by an operator qualified under subdivisions (b) to (f), inclusive, of Section 2025.340, shall not be filed with the court. Instead, the operator shall retain custody of that recording and shall store it under conditions that will protect it against loss, destruction, or tampering, and preserve as far as practicable the quality of the recording and the integrity of the testimony and images it contains.
(b) At the request of any party to the action, including a party who did not attend the taking of the deposition testimony, or at the request of the deponent, that operator shall promptly do both of the following:

(1) Permit the one making the request to hear or to view the recording on receipt of payment of a reasonable charge for providing the facilities for hearing or viewing the recording.

(2) Furnish a copy of the audio or video recording to the one making the request on receipt of payment of the reasonable cost of making that copy of the recording.

(c) The attorney or operator who has custody of an audio or video recording of deposition testimony made by, or at the direction of, any party, shall retain custody of it until six months after final disposition of the action. At that time, the audio or video recording may be destroyed or erased, unless the court, on motion of any party and for good cause shown, orders that the recording be preserved for a longer period.
Amended by Stats 2009 ch 88 (AB 176),s 18, eff. 1/1/2010.
Added by Stats 2004 ch 182 (AB 3081),s 23, eff. 7/1/2005.

Section 2025.570 - Copy of transcript or recording made available by deposition officer

(a) Notwithstanding subdivision (b) of Section 2025.320, unless the court issues an order to the contrary, a copy of the transcript of the deposition testimony made by, or at the direction of, any party, or an audio or video recording of the deposition testimony, if still in the possession of the deposition officer, shall be made available by the deposition officer to any person requesting a copy, on payment of a reasonable charge set by the deposition officer.
(b) If a copy is requested from the deposition officer, the deposition officer shall mail a notice to all parties attending the deposition and to the deponent at the deponent's last known address advising them of all of the following:

(1) The copy is being sought.

(2) The name of the person requesting the copy.

(3) The right to seek a protective order under Section 2025.420.

(c) If a protective order is not served on the deposition officer within 30 days of the mailing of the notice, the deposition officer shall make the copy available to the person requesting the copy.
(d) This section shall apply only to recorded testimony taken at depositions occurring on or after January 1, 1998.
Added by Stats 2004 ch 182 (AB 3081),s 23, eff. 7/1/2005.

Article 6 - POST-DEPOSITION PROCEDURES 2025.610

Section 2025.610 - Leave to take subsequent deposition

(a) Once any party has taken the deposition of any natural person, including that of a party to the action, neither the party who gave, nor any other party who has been served with a deposition notice pursuant to Section 2025.240 may take a subsequent deposition of that deponent.
(b) Notwithstanding subdivision (a), for good cause shown, the court may grant leave to take a subsequent deposition, and the parties, with the consent of any deponent who is not a party, may stipulate that a subsequent deposition be taken.
(c) This section does not preclude taking one subsequent deposition of a natural person who has previously been examined under either or both of the following circumstances:

(1) The person was examined as a result of that person's designation to testify on behalf of an organization under Section 2025.230.

(2) The person was examined pursuant to a court order under Section 485.230, for the limited purpose of discovering pursuant to Section 485.230 the identity, location, and value of property in which the deponent has an interest.

(d) This section does not authorize the taking of more than one subsequent deposition for the limited purpose of Section 485.230.
Added by Stats 2004 ch 182 (AB 3081),s 23, eff. 7/1/2005.

Section 2025.620 - Use of deposition at trial or other hearing

At the trial or any other hearing in the action, any part or all of a deposition may be used against any party who was present or represented at the taking of the deposition, or who had due notice of the deposition and did not serve a valid objection under Section 2025.410, so far as admissible under the rules of evidence applied as though the deponent were then present and testifying as a witness, in accordance with the following provisions:
(a) Any party may use a deposition for the purpose of contradicting or impeaching the testimony of the deponent as a witness, or for any other purpose permitted by the Evidence Code.
(b) An adverse party may use for any purpose, a deposition of a party to the action, or of anyone who at the time of taking the deposition was an officer, director, managing agent, employee, agent, or designee under Section 2025.230 of a party. It is not ground for objection to the use of a deposition of a party under this subdivision by an adverse party that the deponent is available to testify, has testified, or will testify at the trial or other hearing.
(c) Any party may use for any purpose the deposition of any person or organization, including that of any party to the action, if the court finds any of the following:

(1) The deponent resides more than 150 miles from the place of the trial or other hearing.

(2) The deponent, without the procurement or wrongdoing of the proponent of the deposition for the purpose of preventing testimony in open court, is any of the following:

(A) Exempted or precluded on the ground of privilege from testifying concerning the matter to which the deponent's testimony is relevant.

(B) Disqualified from testifying.

(C) Dead or unable to attend or testify because of existing physical or mental illness or infirmity.

(D) Absent from the trial or other hearing and the court is unable to compel the deponent's attendance by its process.

(E) Absent from the trial or other hearing and the proponent of the deposition has exercised reasonable diligence but has been unable to procure the deponent's attendance by the court's process.

(3) Exceptional circumstances exist that make it desirable to allow the use of any deposition in the interests of justice and with due regard to the importance of presenting the testimony of witnesses orally in open court.

(d) Any party may use a video recording of the deposition testimony of a treating or consulting physician or of any expert witness even though the deponent is available to testify if the deposition notice under Section 2025.220 reserved the right to use the deposition at trial, and if that party has complied with subdivision (m) of Section 2025.340.
(e) Subject to the requirements of this chapter, a party may offer in evidence all or any part of a deposition, and if the party introduces only part of the deposition, any other party may introduce any other parts that are relevant to the parts introduced.
(f) Substitution of parties does not affect the right to use depositions previously taken.
(g) When an action has been brought in any court of the United States or of any state, and another action involving the same subject matter is subsequently brought between the same parties or their representatives or successors in interest, all depositions lawfully taken and duly filed in

the initial action may be used in the subsequent action as if originally taken in that subsequent action. A deposition previously taken may also be used as permitted by the Evidence Code.
Added by Stats 2004 ch 182 (AB 3081),s 23, eff. 7/1/2005.

Chapter 10 - ORAL DEPOSITION OUTSIDE CALIFORNIA

Section 2026.010 - Generally

(a) Any party may obtain discovery by taking an oral deposition, as described in Section 2025.010, in another state of the United States, or in a territory or an insular possession subject to its jurisdiction. Except as modified in this section, the procedures for taking oral depositions in California set forth in Chapter 9 (commencing with Section 2025.010) apply to an oral deposition taken in another state of the United States, or in a territory or an insular possession subject to its jurisdiction.

(b) If a deponent is a party to the action or an officer, director, managing agent, or employee of a party, the service of the deposition notice is effective to compel that deponent to attend and to testify, as well as to produce any document, electronically stored information, or tangible thing for inspection, copying, testing, or sampling. The deposition notice shall specify a place in the state, territory, or insular possession of the United States that is within 75 miles of the residence or a business office of a deponent.

(c) If the deponent is not a party to the action or an officer, director, managing agent, or employee of a party, a party serving a deposition notice under this section shall use any process and procedures required and available under the laws of the state, territory, or insular possession where the deposition is to be taken to compel the deponent to attend and to testify, as well as to produce any document, electronically stored information, or tangible thing for inspection, copying, testing, sampling, and any related activity.

(d) A deposition taken under this section shall be conducted in either of the following ways:

(1) Under the supervision of a person who is authorized to administer oaths by the laws of the United States or those of the place where the examination is to be held, and who is not otherwise disqualified under Section 2025.320 and subdivisions (b) to (f), inclusive, of Section 2025.340.

(2) Before a person appointed by the court.

(e) An appointment under subdivision (d) is effective to authorize that person to administer oaths and to take testimony.

(f) On request, the clerk of the court shall issue a commission authorizing the deposition in another state or place. The commission shall request that process issue in the place where the examination is to be held, requiring attendance and enforcing the obligations of the deponents to produce documents and electronically stored information and answer questions. The commission shall be issued by the clerk to any party in any action pending in its venue without a noticed motion or court order. The commission may contain terms that are required by the foreign jurisdiction to initiate the process. If a court order is required by the foreign jurisdiction, an order for a commission may be obtained by ex parte application.
Amended by Stats 2012 ch 72 (SB 1574),s 27, eff. 1/1/2013.
Added by Stats 2004 ch 182 (AB 3081),s 23, eff. 7/1/2005.

Section 2027.010 - Taking deposition in foreign country

(a) Any party may obtain discovery by taking an oral deposition, as described in Section 2025.010, in a foreign nation. Except as modified in this section, the procedures for taking oral depositions in California set forth in Chapter 9 (commencing with Section 2025.010) apply to an oral deposition taken in a foreign nation.

(b) If a deponent is a party to the action or an officer, director, managing agent, or employee of a party, the service of the deposition notice is effective to compel the deponent to attend and to testify, as well as to produce any document, electronically stored information, or tangible thing for inspection, copying, testing, or sampling.

(c) If a deponent is not a party to the action or an officer, director, managing agent or employee of a party, a party serving a deposition notice under this section shall use any process and procedures required and available under the laws of the foreign nation where the deposition is to be taken to compel the deponent to attend and to testify, as well as to produce any document, electronically stored information, or tangible thing for inspection, copying, testing, sampling, and any related activity.

(d) A deposition taken under this section shall be conducted under the supervision of any of the following:

(1) A person who is authorized to administer oaths or their equivalent by the laws of the United States or of the foreign nation, and who is not otherwise disqualified under Section 2025.320 and subdivisions (b) to (f), inclusive, of Section 2025.340.

(2) A person or officer appointed by commission or under letters rogatory.

(3) Any person agreed to by all the parties.

(e) On motion of the party seeking to take an oral deposition in a foreign nation, the court in which the action is pending shall issue a commission, letters rogatory, or a letter of request, if it determines that one is necessary or convenient. The commission, letters rogatory, or letter of request may include any terms and directions that are just and appropriate. The deposition officer may be designated by name or by descriptive title in the deposition notice and in the commission. Letters rogatory or a letter of request may be addressed: "To the Appropriate Judicial Authority in [name of foreign nation]."
Amended by Stats 2012 ch 72 (SB 1574),s 28, eff. 1/1/2013.
Added by Stats 2004 ch 182 (AB 3081),s 23, eff. 7/1/2005.

Chapter 11 - DEPOSITION BY WRITTEN QUESTIONS

Section 2028.010 - Generally

Any party may obtain discovery by taking a deposition by written questions instead of by oral examination. Except as modified in this chapter, the procedures for taking oral depositions set forth in Chapters 9 (commencing with Section 2025.010) and 10 (commencing with Section 2026.010) apply to written depositions.
Added by Stats 2004 ch 182 (AB 3081),s 23, eff. 7/1/2005.

Section 2028.020 - Notice

The notice of a written deposition shall comply with Sections 2025.220 and 2025.230, and with subdivision (c) of Section 2020.240, except as follows:

(a) The name or descriptive title, as well as the address, of the deposition officer shall be stated.

(b) The date, time, and place for commencement of the deposition may be left to future determination by the deposition officer.
Added by Stats 2004 ch 182 (AB 3081),s 23, eff. 7/1/2005.

Section 2028.030 - Service of questions with notice; time for serving cross questions; redirect questions; recross questions; extension of time

(a) The questions to be propounded to the deponent by direct examination shall accompany the notice of a written deposition.

(b) Within 30 days after the deposition notice and questions are served, a party shall serve any cross questions on all other parties entitled to notice of the deposition.

(c) Within 15 days after being served with cross questions, a party shall serve any redirect questions on all other parties entitled to notice of the deposition.

(d) Within 15 days after being served with redirect questions, a party shall serve any recross questions on all other parties entitled to notice of the deposition.

(e) The court may, for good cause shown, extend or shorten the time periods for the interchange of cross, redirect, and recross questions.
Added by Stats 2004 ch 182 (AB 3081),s 23, eff. 7/1/2005.

Section 2028.040 - Objection to form of question

(a) A party who objects to the form of any question shall serve a specific objection to that question on all parties entitled to notice of the deposition within 15 days after service of the question. A party who fails to timely serve an objection to the form of a question waives it.

(b) The objecting party shall promptly move the court to sustain the objection. This motion shall be accompanied by a meet and confer declaration under Section 2016.040. Unless the court has sustained that objection, the deposition officer shall propound to the deponent that question subject to that objection as to its form.

(c) The court shall impose a monetary sanction under Chapter 7 (commencing with Section 2023.010) against any party, person, or attorney who unsuccessfully makes or opposes a motion to sustain an objection, unless it finds that the one subject to the sanction acted with substantial justification or that other circumstances make the imposition of the sanction unjust.
Added by Stats 2004 ch 182 (AB 3081),s 23, eff. 7/1/2005.

Section 2028.050 - Objection to question on ground that it calls for privileged information or protected work product

(a) A party who objects to any question on the ground that it calls for information that is privileged or is protected work product under Chapter 4 (commencing with Section 2018.010) shall serve a specific objection to that question on all parties entitled to notice of the deposition within 15 days after service of the question. A party who fails to timely serve that objection waives it.

(b) The party propounding any question to which an objection is made on those grounds may then move the court for an order overruling that objection. This motion shall be accompanied by a meet and confer declaration under Section 2016.040 The deposition officer shall not propound to the deponent any question to which a written objection on those grounds has been served unless the court has overruled that objection.

(c) The court shall impose a monetary sanction under Chapter 7 (commencing with Section 2023.010) against any party, person, or attorney who unsuccessfully makes or opposes a motion to overrule an objection, unless it finds that the one subject to the sanction acted with substantial justification or that other circumstances make the imposition of the sanction unjust.
Added by Stats 2004 ch 182 (AB 3081),s 23, eff. 7/1/2005.

Section 2028.060 - Forwarding copy of questions on direct examination to deponent for study prior to deposition

(a) The party taking a written deposition may forward to the deponent a copy of the questions on direct examination for study prior to the deposition.

(b) No party or attorney shall permit the deponent to preview the form or the substance of any cross, redirect, or recross questions.
Added by Stats 2004 ch 182 (AB 3081),s 23, eff. 7/1/2005.

Section 2028.070 - Court orders

In addition to any appropriate order listed in Section 2025.420, the court may order any of the following:

(a) That the deponent's testimony be taken by oral, instead of written, examination.

(b) That one or more of the parties receiving notice of the written deposition be permitted to attend in person or by attorney and to propound questions to the deponent by oral examination.

(c) That objections under Sections 2028.040 and 2028.050 be sustained or overruled.

(d) That the deposition be taken before an officer other than the one named or described in the deposition notice.
Added by Stats 2004 ch 182 (AB 3081),s 23, eff. 7/1/2005.

Section 2028.080 - Delivery of copy of notice and questions served to deposition officer

The party taking a written deposition shall deliver to the officer designated in the deposition notice a copy of that notice and of all questions served under Section 2028.030. The deposition officer shall proceed promptly to propound the questions and to take and record the testimony of the deponent in response to the questions.
Added by Stats 2004 ch 182 (AB 3081),s 23, eff. 7/1/2005.

Chapter 12 - DISCOVERY IN ACTION PENDING OUTSIDE CALIFORNIA

Section 2029.010 - [Repealed]
Repealed by Stats 2008 ch 231 (AB 2193),s 2, eff. 1/1/2009.
Chapter heading amended by Stats 2008 ch 231 (AB 2193),s 1, eff. 1/1/2009.
Amended by Stats 2005 ch 294 (AB 333),s 9, eff. 1/1/2006.
Added by Stats 2004 ch 182 (AB 3081),s 23, eff. 7/1/2005.

Article 1 - INTERSTATE AND INTERNATIONAL DEPOSITIONS AND DISCOVERY ACT

Section 2029.100 - Title of act

This article may be cited as the Interstate and International Depositions and Discovery Act.
Added by Stats 2008 ch 231 (AB 2193),s 3, eff. 1/1/2009.

Section 2029.200 - Definitions

In this article:

(a)"Foreign jurisdiction" means either of the following:

(1)A state other than this state.

(2)A foreign nation.

(b)"Foreign penal civil action" means a civil action authorized by the law of a state other than this state in which the sole purpose is to punish an offense against the public justice of that state.

(c)"Foreign subpoena" means a subpoena issued under authority of a court of record of a foreign jurisdiction.

(d)"Person" means an individual, corporation, business trust, estate, trust, partnership, limited liability company, association, joint venture, public corporation, government, or governmental subdivision, agency, or instrumentality, or any other legal or commercial entity.

(e)"State" means a state of the United States, the District of Columbia, Puerto Rico, the Virgin Islands, a federally recognized Indian tribe, or any territory or insular possession subject to the jurisdiction of the United States.

(f)"Subpoena" means a document, however denominated, issued under authority of a court of record requiring a person to do any of the following:

(1)Attend and give testimony at a deposition.

(2)Produce and permit inspection, copying, testing, or sampling of designated books, documents, records, electronically stored information, or tangible things in the possession, custody, or control of the person.

(3)Permit inspection of premises under the control of the person.
Amended by Stats 2022 ch 628 (AB 2091),s 3, eff. 9/27/2022.
Amended by Stats 2012 ch 72 (SB 1574),s 29, eff. 1/1/2013.
Added by Stats 2008 ch 231 (AB 2193),s 3, eff. 1/1/2009.

Section 2029.300 - Request for issuance of subpoena

(a) To request issuance of a subpoena under this section, a party shall submit the original or a true and correct copy of a foreign subpoena to the clerk of the superior court in the county in which discovery is sought to be conducted in this state. A request for the issuance of a subpoena under this section does not constitute making an appearance in the courts of this state.

(b) In addition to submitting a foreign subpoena under subdivision (a), a party seeking discovery shall do both of the following:

(1) Submit an application requesting that the superior court issue a subpoena with the same terms as the foreign subpoena. The application shall be on a form prescribed by the Judicial Council pursuant to Section 2029.390. No civil case cover sheet is required.

(2) Pay the fee specified in Section 70626 of the Government Code.

(c) When a party submits a foreign subpoena to the clerk of the superior court in accordance with subdivision (a), and satisfies the requirements of subdivision (b), the clerk shall promptly issue a subpoena for service upon the person to which the foreign subpoena is directed.

(d) A subpoena issued under this section shall satisfy all of the following conditions:

(1) It shall incorporate the terms used in the foreign subpoena.

(2) It shall contain or be accompanied by the names, addresses, and telephone numbers of all counsel of record in the proceeding to which the subpoena relates and of any party not represented by counsel.

(3) It shall bear the caption and case number of the out-of-state case to which it relates.

(4) It shall state the name of the court that issues it.

(5) It shall be on a form prescribed by the Judicial Council pursuant to Section 2029.390.

(e) Notwithstanding subdivision (a), a subpoena shall not be issued pursuant to this section in any of the following circumstances:

(1) If the foreign subpoena is based on a violation of another state's laws that interfere with a person's right to allow a child to receive gender-affirming health care or gender-affirming mental health care. For the purpose of this paragraph, "gender-affirming health care" and "gender-affirming mental health care" shall have the same meaning as provided in Section 16010.2 of the Welfare and Institutions Code.

(2) If the submitted foreign subpoena relates to a foreign penal civil action and would require disclosure of information related to sensitive services. For purposes of this paragraph, "sensitive services" has the same meaning as defined in Section 791.02 of the Insurance Code.

Amended by Stats 2022 ch 810 (SB 107),s 2.5, eff. 1/1/2023.
Amended by Stats 2022 ch 628 (AB 2091),s 4, eff. 9/27/2022.
Added by Stats 2008 ch 231 (AB 2193),s 3, eff. 1/1/2009.

Section 2029.350 - Subpoena issued by attorney

(a) Notwithstanding Sections 1986 and 2029.300, if a party to a proceeding pending in a foreign jurisdiction retains an attorney licensed to practice in this state, who is an active member of the State Bar, and that attorney receives the original or a true and correct copy of a foreign subpoena, the attorney may issue a subpoena under this article.

(b)

(1) Notwithstanding subdivision (a), an authorized attorney shall not issue a subpoena pursuant to subdivision (a) if the foreign subpoena is based on a violation of another state's laws that interfere with a person's right to allow a child to receive gender-affirming health care or gender-affirming mental health care.

(2) For the purpose of this subdivision, "gender-affirming health care" and "gender-affirming mental health care" shall have the same meaning as provided in Section 16010.2 of the Welfare and Institutions Code.

(c) Notwithstanding subdivision (a), an attorney shall not issue a subpoena under this article based on a foreign subpoena that relates to a foreign penal civil action and that would require disclosure of information related to sensitive services. For purposes of this subdivision, "sensitive services" has the same meaning as defined in Section 791.02 of the Insurance Code.

(d) A subpoena issued under this section shall satisfy all of the following conditions:

(1) It shall incorporate the terms used in the foreign subpoena.

(2) It shall contain or be accompanied by the names, addresses, and telephone numbers of all counsel of record in the proceeding to which the subpoena relates and of any party not represented by counsel.

(3) It shall bear the caption and case number of the out-of-state case to which it relates.

(4) It shall state the name of the superior court of the county in which the discovery is to be conducted.

(5) It shall be on a form prescribed by the Judicial Council pursuant to Section 2029.390.

Amended by Stats 2022 ch 810 (SB 107),s 3.5, eff. 1/1/2023.
Amended by Stats 2022 ch 628 (AB 2091),s 5, eff. 9/27/2022.
Added by Stats 2008 ch 231 (AB 2193),s 3, eff. 1/1/2009.

Section 2029.390 - Preparation of application form and new subpoena forms

On or before January 1, 2010, the Judicial Council shall do all of the following:

(a) Prepare an application form to be used for purposes of Section 2029.300.

(b) Prepare one or more new subpoena forms that include clear instructions for use in issuance of a subpoena under Section 2029.300 or 2029.350. Alternatively, the Judicial Council may modify one or more existing subpoena forms to include clear instructions for use in issuance of a subpoena under Section 2029.300 or 2029.350.

Added by Stats 2008 ch 231 (AB 2193),s 3, eff. 1/1/2009.

Section 2029.400 - Personal service of subpoena

A subpoena issued under this article shall be personally served in compliance with the law of this state, including, without limitation, Section 1985.

Added by Stats 2008 ch 231 (AB 2193),s 3, eff. 1/1/2009.

Section 2029.500 - Applicability of laws or rules governing depositions, production or inspection

Titles 3 (commencing with Section 1985) and 4 (commencing with Section 2016.010) of Part 4, and any other law or court rule of this state governing a deposition, a production of documents or other tangible items, or an inspection of premises, including any law or court rule governing payment of court costs or sanctions, apply to discovery under this article.

Added by Stats 2008 ch 231 (AB 2193),s 3, eff. 1/1/2009.

Section 2029.600 - Request for relief

(a) If a dispute arises relating to discovery under this article, any request for a protective order or to enforce, quash, or modify a subpoena, or for other relief may be filed in the superior court in the county in which discovery is to be conducted and, if so filed, shall comply with the applicable rules or statutes of this state.

(b) A request for relief pursuant to this section shall be referred to as a petition notwithstanding any statute under which a request for the same relief would be referred to as a motion or by another term if it was brought in a proceeding pending in this state.

(c) A petition for relief pursuant to this section shall be accompanied by a civil case cover sheet.

Added by Stats 2008 ch 231 (AB 2193),s 3, eff. 1/1/2009.

Section 2029.610 - First appearance fee; requirements of petition, response, other document filed

(a) On filing a petition under Section 2029.600, a petitioner who is a party to the out-of-state proceeding shall pay a first appearance fee as specified in Section 70611 of the Government Code. A petitioner who is not a party to the out-of-state proceeding shall pay the fee specified in subdivision (c) of Section 70626 of the Government Code.
(b) The court in which the petition is filed shall assign it a case number.
(c) On responding to a petition under Section 2029.600, a party to the out-of-state proceeding shall pay a first appearance fee as specified in Section 70612 of the Government Code. A person who is not a party to the out-of-state proceeding may file a response without paying a fee.
(d) Any petition, response, or other document filed under this section shall satisfy all of the following conditions:
  (1) It shall bear the caption and case number of the out-of-state case to which it relates.
  (2) The first page shall state the name of the court in which the document is filed.
  (3) The first page shall state the case number assigned by the court under subdivision (b).
  (4) The first page shall state whether or not the person filing the document is a party to the out-of-state case.
Amended by Stats 2011 ch 308 (SB 647),s 4, eff. 1/1/2012.
Added by Stats 2008 ch 231 (AB 2193),s 3, eff. 1/1/2009.

Section 2029.620 - Petition for relief if another dispute later arises relating to discovery in same case
(a) If a petition has been filed under Section 2029.600 and another dispute later arises relating to discovery being conducted in the same county for purposes of the same out-of-state proceeding, the deponent or other disputant may file a petition for appropriate relief in the same superior court as the previous petition.
(b) The first page of the petition shall clearly indicate that it is not the first petition filed in that court that relates to the out-of-state case.
(c)
  (1) If the petitioner in the new dispute is a party to the out-of-state case who previously paid a first appearance fee under this article, the petitioner shall pay a motion fee as specified in subdivision (a) of Section 70617 of the Government Code. If the petitioner in the new dispute is a party to the out-of-state case but has not previously paid a first appearance fee under this article, the petitioner shall pay a first appearance fee as specified in Section 70611 of the Government Code.
  (2) If the petitioner in the new dispute is not a party to the out-of-state case, the petitioner shall pay the fee specified in subdivision (c) of Section 70626 of the Government Code, unless the petitioner previously paid that fee. If the petitioner previously paid the fee specified in subdivision (c) of Section 70626 of the Government Code, the petitioner shall pay a motion fee as specified in subdivision (a) of Section 70617 of the Government Code.
(d) If a person responding to the new petition is not a party to the out-of-state case, or is a party who previously paid a first appearance fee under this article, that person does not have to pay a fee for responding. If a person responding to the new petition is a party to the out-of-state case but has not previously paid a first appearance fee under this article, that person shall pay a first appearance fee as specified in Section 70612 of the Government Code.
(e) Any petition, response, or other document filed under this section shall satisfy all of the following conditions:
  (1) It shall bear the caption and case number of the out-of-state case to which it relates.
  (2) The first page shall state the name of the court in which the document is filed.
  (3) The first page shall state the same case number that the court assigned to the first petition relating to the out-of-state case.
  (4) The first page shall state whether or not the person filing the document is a party to the out-of-state case.
(f) A petition for relief pursuant to this section shall be accompanied by a civil case cover sheet.
Amended by Stats 2011 ch 308 (SB 647),s 5, eff. 1/1/2012.
Added by Stats 2008 ch 231 (AB 2193),s 3, eff. 1/1/2009.

Section 2029.630 - Petition requirements
A petition under Section 2029.600 or Section 2029.620 is subject to the requirements of Section 1005 relating to notice and to filing and service of papers.
Added by Stats 2008 ch 231 (AB 2193),s 3, eff. 1/1/2009.

Section 2029.640 - Relief without obtaining subpoena or being subpoenaed
If a party to a proceeding pending in a foreign jurisdiction seeks discovery from a witness in this state by properly issued notice or by agreement, it is not necessary for that party to obtain a subpoena under this article to be able to seek relief under Section 2029.600 or 2029.620. The deponent or any other party may also seek relief under Section 2029.600 or 2029.620 in those circumstances, regardless of whether the deponent was subpoenaed under this article.
Added by Stats 2008 ch 231 (AB 2193),s 3, eff. 1/1/2009.

Section 2029.650 - Petition for extraordinary writ
(a) If a superior court issues an order granting, denying, or otherwise resolving a petition under Section 2029.600 or 2029.620, a person aggrieved by the order may petition the appropriate court of appeal for an extraordinary writ. No order or other action of a court under this article is appealable in this state.
(b) Pending its decision on the writ petition, the court of appeal may stay the order of the superior court, the discovery that is the subject of that order, or both.
Added by Stats 2008 ch 231 (AB 2193),s 3, eff. 1/1/2009.

Section 2029.700 - Sections referred to as California version of Uniform Interstate Depositions and Discovery Act
(a) Sections 2029.100, 2029.200, 2029.300, 2029.400, 2029.500, 2029.600, 2029.800, 2029.900, and this section, collectively, constitute and may be referred to as the "California version of the Uniform Interstate Depositions and Discovery Act."
(b) In applying and construing this uniform act, consideration shall be given to the need to promote uniformity of the law with respect to its subject matter among the states that enact it.
Added by Stats 2008 ch 231 (AB 2193),s 3, eff. 1/1/2009.

Section 2029.800 - Applicability to cases pending on operative date
This article applies to requests for discovery in cases pending on or after the operative date of this section.
Added by Stats 2008 ch 231 (AB 2193),s 3, eff. 1/1/2009.

Section 2029.900 - Operative date
Section 2029.390 is operative on January 1, 2009. The remainder of this article is operative on January 1, 2010.
Added by Stats 2008 ch 231 (AB 2193),s 3, eff. 1/1/2009.

Chapter 13 - WRITTEN INTERROGATORIES
Article 1 - PROPOUNDING INTERROGATORIES
Section 2030.010 - Generally
(a) Any party may obtain discovery within the scope delimited by Chapter 2 (commencing with Section 2017.010), and subject to the restrictions set forth in Chapter 5 (commencing with Section 2019.010), by propounding to any other party to the action written interrogatories to be answered under oath.

(b) An interrogatory may relate to whether another party is making a certain contention, or to the facts, witnesses, and writings on which a contention is based. An interrogatory is not objectionable because an answer to it involves an opinion or contention that relates to fact or the application of law to fact, or would be based on information obtained or legal theories developed in anticipation of litigation or in preparation for trial.

Amended by Stats 2015 ch 303 (AB 731),s 42, eff. 1/1/2016.
Added by Stats 2004 ch 182 (AB 3081),s 23, op. 7/1/2005.

Section 2030.020 - Propounding interrogatories without leave of court

(a) A defendant may propound interrogatories to a party to the action without leave of court at any time.

(b) A plaintiff may propound interrogatories to a party without leave of court at any time that is 10 days after the service of the summons on, or appearance by, that party, whichever occurs first.

(c) Notwithstanding subdivision (b), in an unlawful detainer action or other proceeding under Chapter 4 (commencing with Section 1159) of Title 3 of Part 3, a plaintiff may propound interrogatories to a party without leave of court at any time that is five days after service of the summons on, or appearance by, that party, whichever occurs first.

(d) Notwithstanding subdivisions (b) and (c), on motion with or without notice, the court, for good cause shown, may grant leave to a plaintiff to propound interrogatories at an earlier time.

Amended by Stats 2007 ch 113 (AB 1126),s 7, eff. 1/1/2008.
Added by Stats 2004 ch 182 (AB 3081),s 23, eff. 7/1/2005.

Section 2030.030 - Number of interrogatories

(a) A party may propound to another party either or both of the following:

(1) Thirty-five specially prepared interrogatories that are relevant to the subject matter of the pending action.

(2) Any additional number of official form interrogatories, as described in Chapter 17 (commencing with Section 2033.710), that are relevant to the subject matter of the pending action.

(b) Except as provided in Section 2030.070, no party shall, as a matter of right, propound to any other party more than 35 specially prepared interrogatories. If the initial set of interrogatories does not exhaust this limit, the balance may be propounded in subsequent sets.

(c) Unless a declaration as described in Section 2030.050 has been made, a party need only respond to the first 35 specially prepared interrogatories served, if that party states an objection to the balance, under Section 2030.240, on the ground that the limit has been exceeded.

Added by Stats 2004 ch 182 (AB 3081),s 23, eff. 7/1/2005.

Section 2030.040 - Propounding greater number of interrogatories

(a) Subject to the right of the responding party to seek a protective order under Section 2030.090, any party who attaches a supporting declaration as described in Section 2030.050 may propound a greater number of specially prepared interrogatories to another party if this greater number is warranted because of any of the following:

(1) The complexity or the quantity of the existing and potential issues in the particular case.

(2) The financial burden on a party entailed in conducting the discovery by oral deposition.

(3) The expedience of using this method of discovery to provide to the responding party the opportunity to conduct an inquiry, investigation, or search of files or records to supply the information sought.

(b) If the responding party seeks a protective order on the ground that the number of specially prepared interrogatories is unwarranted, the propounding party shall have the burden of justifying the number of these interrogatories.

Added by Stats 2004 ch 182 (AB 3081),s 23, eff. 7/1/2005.

Section 2030.050 - Declaration for additional discovery

Any party who is propounding or has propounded more than 35 specially prepared interrogatories to any other party shall attach to each set of those interrogatories a declaration containing substantially the following:

DECLARATION FOR ADDITIONAL DISCOVERY

I, _____, declare:

1. I am (a party to this action or proceeding appearing in propria persona) (presently the attorney for _____, a party to this action or proceeding).

2. I am propounding to _____ the attached set of interrogatories.

3. This set of interrogatories will cause the total number of specially prepared interrogatories propounded to the party to whom they are directed to exceed the number of specially prepared interrogatories permitted by Section 2030.030 of the Code of Civil Procedure.

4. I have previously propounded a total of _____ interrogatories to this party, of which _____ interrogatories were not official form interrogatories.

5. This set of interrogatories contains a total of _____ specially prepared interrogatories.

6. I am familiar with the issues and the previous discovery conducted by all of the parties in the case.

7. I have personally examined each of the questions in this set of interrogatories.

8. This number of questions is warranted under Section 2030.040 of the Code of Civil Procedure because _____. (Here state each factor described in Section 2030.040 that is relied on, as well as the reasons why any factor relied on is applicable to the instant lawsuit.)

9. None of the questions in this set of interrogatories is being propounded for any improper purpose, such as to harass the party, or the attorney for the party, to whom it is directed, or to cause unnecessary delay or needless increase in the cost of litigation. I declare under penalty of perjury under the laws of California that the foregoing is true and correct, and that this declaration was executed on _____.

_____ (Signature) _____

Attorney for

Amended by Stats 2005 ch 22 (SB 1108),s 22, eff. 1/1/2006
Added by Stats 2004 ch 182 (AB 3081),s 23, eff. 7/1/2005.

Section 2030.060 - Requirements of interrogatories

(a) A party propounding interrogatories shall number each set of interrogatories consecutively.

(b) In the first paragraph immediately below the title of the case, there shall appear the identity of the propounding party, the set number, and the identity of the responding party.

(c) Each interrogatory in a set shall be separately set forth and identified by number or letter.

(d) Each interrogatory shall be full and complete in and of itself. No preface or instruction shall be included with a set of interrogatories unless it has been approved under Chapter 17 (commencing with Section 2033.710).

(e) Any term specially defined in a set of interrogatories shall be typed with all letters capitalized wherever that term appears.

(f) No specially prepared interrogatory shall contain subparts, or a compound, conjunctive, or disjunctive question.

(g) An interrogatory may not be made a continuing one so as to impose on the party responding to it a duty to supplement an answer to it that was initially correct and complete with later acquired information.

Added by Stats 2004 ch 182 (AB 3081),s 23, eff. 7/1/2005.
Section 2030.070 - Supplemental interrogatory
(a) In addition to the number of interrogatories permitted by Sections 2030.030 and 2030.040, a party may propound a supplemental interrogatory to elicit any later acquired information bearing on all answers previously made by any party in response to interrogatories.
(b) A party may propound a supplemental interrogatory twice before the initial setting of a trial date, and, subject to the time limits on discovery proceedings and motions provided in Chapter 8 (commencing with Section 2024.010), once after the initial setting of a trial date.
(c) Notwithstanding subdivisions (a) and (b), on motion, for good cause shown, the court may grant leave to a party to propound an additional number of supplemental interrogatories.
Added by Stats 2004 ch 182 (AB 3081),s 23, eff. 7/1/2005.
Section 2030.080 - Service of copies of interrogatories
(a) The party propounding interrogatories shall serve a copy of them on the party to whom the interrogatories are directed.
(b) The propounding party shall also serve a copy of the interrogatories on all other parties who have appeared in the action. On motion, with or without notice, the court may relieve the party from this requirement on its determination that service on all other parties would be unduly expensive or burdensome.
Added by Stats 2004 ch 182 (AB 3081),s 23, eff. 7/1/2005.
Section 2030.090 - Motion for protective order
(a) When interrogatories have been propounded, the responding party, and any other party or affected natural person or organization may promptly move for a protective order. This motion shall be accompanied by a meet and confer declaration under Section 2016.040.
(b) The court, for good cause shown, may make any order that justice requires to protect any party or other natural person or organization from unwarranted annoyance, embarrassment, or oppression, or undue burden and expense. This protective order may include, but is not limited to, one or more of the following directions:
    (1) That the set of interrogatories, or particular interrogatories in the set, need not be answered.
    (2) That, contrary to the representations made in a declaration submitted under Section 2030.050, the number of specially prepared interrogatories is unwarranted.
    (3) That the time specified in Section 2030.260 to respond to the set of interrogatories, or to particular interrogatories in the set, be extended.
    (4) That the response be made only on specified terms and conditions.
    (5) That the method of discovery be an oral deposition instead of interrogatories to a party.
    (6) That a trade secret or other confidential research, development, or commercial information not be disclosed or be disclosed only in a certain way.
    (7) That some or all of the answers to interrogatories be sealed and thereafter opened only on order of the court.
(c) If the motion for a protective order is denied in whole or in part, the court may order that the party provide or permit the discovery against which protection was sought on terms and conditions that are just.
(d) The court shall impose a monetary sanction under Chapter 7 (commencing with Section 2023.010) against any party, person, or attorney who unsuccessfully makes or opposes a motion for a protective order under this section, unless it finds that the one subject to the sanction acted with substantial justification or that other circumstances make the imposition of the sanction unjust.
Added by Stats 2004 ch 182 (AB 3081),s 23, eff. 7/1/2005.
Article 2 - RESPONSE TO INTERROGATORIES
Section 2030.210 - Methods of responding; requirements
(a) The party to whom interrogatories have been propounded shall respond in writing under oath separately to each interrogatory by any of the following:
    (1) An answer containing the information sought to be discovered.
    (2) An exercise of the party's option to produce writings.
    (3) An objection to the particular interrogatory.
(b) In the first paragraph of the response immediately below the title of the case, there shall appear the identity of the responding party, the set number, and the identity of the propounding party.
(c) Each answer, exercise of option, or objection in the response shall bear the same identifying number or letter and be in the same sequence as the corresponding interrogatory. The text of that interrogatory need not be repeated, except as provided in paragraph (6) of subdivision (d).
(d) In order to facilitate the discovery process:
    (1) Except as provided in paragraph (5), upon request by the responding party, the propounding party shall provide the interrogatories in an electronic format to the responding party within three court days of the request.
    (2) Except as provided in paragraph (5), upon request by the propounding party after receipt of the responses to the interrogatories, the responding party shall provide the responses in an electronic format to the propounding party within three court days of the request.
    (3) A party may provide the interrogatories or responses to the interrogatories requested pursuant to paragraphs (1) and (2) in any format agreed upon by the parties. If the parties are unable to agree on a format, the interrogatories or responses to interrogatories shall be provided in plain text format.
    (4) A party may transmit the interrogatories or responses to the interrogatories requested pursuant to paragraphs (1) and (2) by any method agreed upon by the parties. If the parties are unable to agree on a method of transmission, the interrogatories or responses to interrogatories shall be transmitted by electronic mail to an email address provided by the requesting party.
    (5) If the interrogatories or responses to interrogatories were not created in an electronic format, a party is not required to create the interrogatories or response to interrogatories in an electronic format for the purpose of transmission to the requesting party.
    (6) A responding party who has requested and received the interrogatories in an electronic format pursuant to paragraph (1) shall include the text of the interrogatory immediately preceding the response.
Amended by Stats 2019 ch 190 (AB 1349),s 1, eff. 1/1/2020.
Added by Stats 2004 ch 182 (AB 3081),s 23, eff. 7/1/2005.
Section 2030.220 - Answers
(a) Each answer in a response to interrogatories shall be as complete and straightforward as the information reasonably available to the responding party permits.
(b) If an interrogatory cannot be answered completely, it shall be answered to the extent possible.
(c) If the responding party does not have personal knowledge sufficient to respond fully to an interrogatory, that party shall so state, but shall make a reasonable and good faith effort to obtain the information by inquiry to other natural persons or organizations, except where the information is equally available to the propounding party.
Added by Stats 2004 ch 182 (AB 3081),s 23, eff. 7/1/2005.
Section 2030.230 - Specification of writings from which answer may be derived or ascertained
If the answer to an interrogatory would necessitate the preparation or the making of a compilation, abstract, audit, or summary of or from the documents of the party to whom the interrogatory is directed, and if the burden or expense of preparing or making it would be substantially the

same for the party propounding the interrogatory as for the responding party, it is a sufficient answer to that interrogatory to refer to this section and to specify the writings from which the answer may be derived or ascertained. This specification shall be in sufficient detail to permit the propounding party to locate and to identify, as readily as the responding party can, the documents from which the answer may be ascertained. The responding party shall then afford to the propounding party a reasonable opportunity to examine, audit, or inspect these documents and to make copies, compilations, abstracts, or summaries of them.

Added by Stats 2004 ch 182 (AB 3081),s 23, eff. 7/1/2005.

Section 2030.240 - Objection

(a) If only a part of an interrogatory is objectionable, the remainder of the interrogatory shall be answered.

(b) If an objection is made to an interrogatory or to a part of an interrogatory, the specific ground for the objection shall be set forth clearly in the response. If an objection is based on a claim of privilege, the particular privilege invoked shall be clearly stated. If an objection is based on a claim that the information sought is protected work product under Chapter 4 (commencing with Section 2018.010), that claim shall be expressly asserted.

Added by Stats 2004 ch 182 (AB 3081),s 23, eff. 7/1/2005.

Section 2030.250 - Signing responses under oath

(a) The party to whom the interrogatories are directed shall sign the response under oath unless the response contains only objections.

(b) If that party is a public or private corporation, or a partnership, association, or governmental agency, one of its officers or agents shall sign the response under oath on behalf of that party. If the officer or agent signing the response on behalf of that party is an attorney acting in that capacity for the party, that party waives any lawyer-client privilege and any protection for work product under Chapter 4 (commencing with Section 2018.010) during any subsequent discovery from that attorney concerning the identity of the sources of the information contained in the response.

(c) The attorney for the responding party shall sign any responses that contain an objection.

Added by Stats 2004 ch 182 (AB 3081),s 23, eff. 7/1/2005.

Section 2030.260 - Time for service of original response on propounding party; time from date of service to respond; service of copy of responses on other parties

(a) Within 30 days after service of interrogatories, the party to whom the interrogatories are propounded shall serve the original of the response to them on the propounding party, unless on motion of the propounding party the court has shortened the time for response, or unless on motion of the responding party the court has extended the time for response.

(b) Notwithstanding subdivision (a), in an unlawful detainer action or other proceeding under Chapter 4 (commencing with Section 1159) of Title 3 of Part 3, the party to whom the interrogatories are propounded shall have five days from the date of service to respond, unless on motion of the propounding party the court has shortened the time for response, or unless on motion of the responding party the court has extended the time for response.

(c) The party to whom the interrogatories are propounded shall also serve a copy of the response on all other parties who have appeared in the action. On motion, with or without notice, the court may relieve the party from this requirement on its determination that service on all other parties would be unduly expensive or burdensome.

Amended by Stats 2007 ch 113 (AB 1126),s 8, eff. 1/1/2008.
Added by Stats 2004 ch 182 (AB 3081),s 23, eff. 7/1/2005.

Section 2030.270 - Agreement to extend time for service of response

(a) The party propounding interrogatories and the responding party may agree to extend the time for service of a response to a set of interrogatories, or to particular interrogatories in a set, to a date beyond that provided in Section 2030.260.

(b) This agreement may be informal, but it shall be confirmed in a writing that specifies the extended date for service of a response.

(c) Unless this agreement expressly states otherwise, it is effective to preserve to the responding party the right to respond to any interrogatory to which the agreement applies in any manner specified in Sections 2030.210, 2030.220, 2030.230, and 2030.240.

Added by Stats 2004 ch 182 (AB 3081),s 23, eff. 7/1/2005.

Section 2030.280 - Filing with court; retention of originals by propounding party

(a) The interrogatories and the response thereto shall not be filed with the court.

(b) The propounding party shall retain both the original of the interrogatories, with the original proof of service affixed to them, and the original of the sworn response until six months after final disposition of the action. At that time, both originals may be destroyed, unless the court on motion of any party and for good cause shown orders that the originals be preserved for a longer period.

Added by Stats 2004 ch 182 (AB 3081),s 23, eff. 7/1/2005.

Section 2030.290 - Failure to serve timely response; motion for order compelling response

If a party to whom interrogatories are directed fails to serve a timely response, the following rules apply:

(a) The party to whom the interrogatories are directed waives any right to exercise the option to produce writings under Section 2030.230, as well as any objection to the interrogatories, including one based on privilege or on the protection for work product under Chapter 4 (commencing with Section 2018.010). The court, on motion, may relieve that party from this waiver on its determination that both of the following conditions are satisfied:

    (1) The party has subsequently served a response that is in substantial compliance with Sections 2030.210, 2030.220, 2030.230, and 2030.240.

    (2) The party's failure to serve a timely response was the result of mistake, inadvertence, or excusable neglect.

(b) The party propounding the interrogatories may move for an order compelling response to the interrogatories.

(c) The court shall impose a monetary sanction under Chapter 7 (commencing with Section 2023.010) against any party, person, or attorney who unsuccessfully makes or opposes a motion to compel a response to interrogatories, unless it finds that the one subject to the sanction acted with substantial justification or that other circumstances make the imposition of the sanction unjust. If a party then fails to obey an order compelling answers, the court may make those orders that are just, including the imposition of an issue sanction, an evidence sanction, or a terminating sanction under Chapter 7 (commencing with Section 2023.010). In lieu of or in addition to that sanction, the court may impose a monetary sanction under Chapter 7 (commencing with Section 2023.010).

Added by Stats 2004 ch 182 (AB 3081),s 23, eff. 7/1/2005.

Section 2030.300 - Motion for order compelling further response

(a) On receipt of a response to interrogatories, the propounding party may move for an order compelling a further response if the propounding party deems that any of the following apply:

    (1) An answer to a particular interrogatory is evasive or incomplete.

    (2) An exercise of the option to produce documents under Section 2030.230 is unwarranted or the required specification of those documents is inadequate.

    (3) An objection to an interrogatory is without merit or too general.

(b)

    (1) A motion under subdivision (a) shall be accompanied by a meet and confer declaration under Section 2016.040.

(2) In lieu of a separate statement required under the California Rules of Court, the court may allow the moving party to submit a concise outline of the discovery request and each response in dispute.

(c) Unless notice of this motion is given within 45 days of the service of the verified response, or any supplemental verified response, or on or before any specific later date to which the propounding party and the responding party have agreed in writing, the propounding party waives any right to compel a further response to the interrogatories.

(d) The court shall impose a monetary sanction under Chapter 7 (commencing with Section 2023.010) against any party, person, or attorney who unsuccessfully makes or opposes a motion to compel a further response to interrogatories, unless it finds that the one subject to the sanction acted with substantial justification or that other circumstances make the imposition of the sanction unjust.

(e) If a party then fails to obey an order compelling further response to interrogatories, the court may make those orders that are just, including the imposition of an issue sanction, an evidence sanction, or a terminating sanction under Chapter 7 (commencing with Section 2023.010). In lieu of, or in addition to, that sanction, the court may impose a monetary sanction under Chapter 7 (commencing with Section 2023.010).

Amended by Stats 2018 ch 317 (AB 2230),s 3, eff. 1/1/2019, op. 1/1/2020.
Amended by Stats 2013 ch 18 (AB 1183),s 1, eff. 1/1/2014.
Added by Stats 2004 ch 182 (AB 3081),s 23, eff. 7/1/2005.

Section 2030.310 - Amended answer to response; motion that initial answer binding on responding party

(a) Without leave of court, a party may serve an amended answer to any interrogatory that contains information subsequently discovered, inadvertently omitted, or mistakenly stated in the initial interrogatory. At the trial of the action, the propounding party or any other party may use the initial answer under Section 2030.410, and the responding party may then use the amended answer.

(b) The party who propounded an interrogatory to which an amended answer has been served may move for an order that the initial answer to that interrogatory be deemed binding on the responding party for the purpose of the pending action. This motion shall be accompanied by a meet and confer declaration under Section 2016.040.

(c) The court shall grant a motion under subdivision (b) if it determines that all of the following conditions are satisfied:

(1) The initial failure of the responding party to answer the interrogatory correctly has substantially prejudiced the party who propounded the interrogatory.

(2) The responding party has failed to show substantial justification for the initial answer to that interrogatory.

(3) The prejudice to the propounding party cannot be cured either by a continuance to permit further discovery or by the use of the initial answer under Section 2030.410.

(d) The court shall impose a monetary sanction under Chapter 7 (commencing with Section 2023.010) against any party, person, or attorney who unsuccessfully makes or opposes a motion to deem binding an initial answer to an interrogatory, unless it finds that the one subject to the sanction acted with substantial justification or that other circumstances make the imposition of the sanction unjust.

Added by Stats 2004 ch 182 (AB 3081),s 23, eff. 7/1/2005.

Article 3 - USE OF INTERROGATORY ANSWER

Section 2030.410 - Generally

At the trial or any other hearing in the action, so far as admissible under the rules of evidence, the propounding party or any party other than the responding party may use any answer or part of an answer to an interrogatory only against the responding party. It is not ground for objection to the use of an answer to an interrogatory that the responding party is available to testify, has testified, or will testify at the trial or other hearing.

Added by Stats 2004 ch 182 (AB 3081),s 23, eff. 7/1/2005.

Chapter 14 - INSPECTION, COPYING, TESTING, SAMPLING, AND PRODUCTION OF DOCUMENTS, ELECTRONICALLY STORED INFORMATION, TANGIBLE THINGS, LAND, AND OTHER PROPERTY

Article 1 - INSPECTION DEMAND

Section 2031.010 - Generally

(a) Any party may obtain discovery within the scope delimited by Chapter 2 (commencing with Section 2017.010), and subject to the restrictions set forth in Chapter 5 (commencing with Section 2019.010), by inspecting, copying, testing, or sampling documents, tangible things, land or other property, and electronically stored information in the possession, custody, or control of any other party to the action.

(b) A party may demand that any other party produce and permit the party making the demand, or someone acting on the demanding party's behalf, to inspect and to copy a document that is in the possession, custody, or control of the party on whom the demand is made.

(c) A party may demand that any other party produce and permit the party making the demand, or someone acting on the demanding party's behalf, to inspect and to photograph, test, or sample any tangible things that are in the possession, custody, or control of the party on whom the demand is made.

(d) A party may demand that any other party allow the party making the demand, or someone acting on the demanding party's behalf, to enter on any land or other property that is in the possession, custody, or control of the party on whom the demand is made, and to inspect and to measure, survey, photograph, test, or sample the land or other property, or any designated object or operation on it.

(e) A party may demand that any other party produce and permit the party making the demand, or someone acting on the demanding party's behalf, to inspect, copy, test, or sample electronically stored information in the possession, custody, or control of the party on whom demand is made.

Amended by Stats 2016 ch 86 (SB 1171),s 42, eff. 1/1/2017.
Chapter heading amended by Stats 2012 ch 72 (SB 1574),s 30, eff. 1/1/2013.
Amended by Stats 2009 ch 5 (AB 5),s 4, eff. 6/29/2009.
Added by Stats 2004 ch 182 (AB 3081),s 23, eff. 7/1/2005.

Section 2031.020 - Demand for inspection without leave of court

(a) A defendant may make a demand for inspection, copying, testing, or sampling without leave of court at any time.

(b) A plaintiff may make a demand for inspection, copying, testing, or sampling without leave of court at any time that is 10 days after the service of the summons on, or appearance by, the party to whom the demand is directed, whichever occurs first.

(c) Notwithstanding subdivision (b), in an unlawful detainer action or other proceeding under Chapter 4 (commencing with Section 1159) of Title 3 of Part 3, a plaintiff may make a demand for inspection, copying, testing, or sampling without leave of court at any time that is five days after service of the summons on, or appearance by, the party to whom the demand is directed, whichever occurs first.

(d) Notwithstanding subdivisions (b) and (c), on motion with or without notice, the court, for good cause shown, may grant leave to a plaintiff to make a demand for inspection, copying, testing, or sampling at an earlier time.

Amended by Stats 2009 ch 5 (AB 5),s 5, eff. 6/29/2009.
Amended by Stats 2007 ch 113 (AB 1126),s 9, eff. 1/1/2008.
Added by Stats 2004 ch 182 (AB 3081),s 23, eff. 7/1/2005.

Section 2031.030 - Requirements of demand

(a)
    (1) A party demanding inspection, copying, testing, or sampling shall number each set of demands consecutively.
    (2) A party demanding inspection, copying, testing, or sampling of electronically stored information may specify the form or forms in which each type of electronically stored information is to be produced.
(b) In the first paragraph immediately below the title of the case, there shall appear the identity of the demanding party, the set number, and the identity of the responding party.
(c) Each demand in a set shall be separately set forth, identified by number or letter, and shall do all of the following:
    (1) Designate the documents, tangible things, land or other property, or electronically stored information to be inspected, copied, tested, or sampled either by specifically describing each individual item or by reasonably particularizing each category of item.
    (2) Specify a reasonable time for the inspection, copying, testing, or sampling that is at least 30 days after service of the demand, unless the court for good cause shown has granted leave to specify an earlier date. In an unlawful detainer action or other proceeding under Chapter 4 (commencing with Section 1159) of Title 3 of Part 3, the demand shall specify a reasonable time for the inspection, copying, testing, or sampling that is at least five days after service of the demand, unless the court, for good cause shown, has granted leave to specify an earlier date.
    (3) Specify a reasonable place for making the inspection, copying, testing, or sampling, and performing any related activity.
    (4) Specify any inspection, copying, testing, sampling, or related activity that is being demanded, as well as the manner in which that activity will be performed, and whether that activity will permanently alter or destroy the item involved.
Amended by Stats 2009 ch 5 (AB 5),s 6, eff. 6/29/2009.
Amended by Stats 2007 ch 113 (AB 1126),s 10, eff. 1/1/2008.
Added by Stats 2004 ch 182 (AB 3081),s 23, eff. 7/1/2005.

Section 2031.040 - Service of copy of demand
The party making a demand for inspection, copying, testing, or sampling shall serve a copy of the demand on the party to whom it is directed and on all other parties who have appeared in the action.
Amended by Stats 2009 ch 5 (AB 5),s 7, eff. 6/29/2009.
Added by Stats 2004 ch 182 (AB 3081),s 23, eff. 7/1/2005.

Section 2031.050 - Supplemental demand
(a) In addition to the demands for inspection, copying, testing, or sampling permitted by this chapter, a party may propound a supplemental demand to inspect, copy, test, or sample any later acquired or discovered documents, tangible things, land or other property, or electronically stored information in the possession, custody, or control of the party on whom the demand is made.
(b) A party may propound a supplemental demand for inspection, copying, testing, or sampling twice before the initial setting of a trial date, and, subject to the time limits on discovery proceedings and motions provided in Chapter 8 (commencing with Section 2024.010), once after the initial setting of a trial date.
(c) Notwithstanding subdivisions (a) and (b), on motion, for good cause shown, the court may grant leave to a party to propound an additional number of supplemental demands for inspection, copying, testing, or sampling.
Amended by Stats 2009 ch 5 (AB 5),s 8, eff. 6/29/2009.
Added by Stats 2004 ch 182 (AB 3081),s 23, eff. 7/1/2005.

Section 2031.060 - Motion for protective order
(a) When an inspection, copying, testing, or sampling of documents, tangible things, places, or electronically stored information has been demanded, the party to whom the demand has been directed, and any other party or affected person, may promptly move for a protective order. This motion shall be accompanied by a meet and confer declaration under Section 2016.040.
(b) The court, for good cause shown, may make any order that justice requires to protect any party or other person from unwarranted annoyance, embarrassment, or oppression, or undue burden and expense. This protective order may include, but is not limited to, one or more of the following directions:
    (1) That all or some of the items or categories of items in the demand need not be produced or made available at all.
    (2) That the time specified in Section 2031.260 to respond to the set of demands, or to a particular item or category in the set, be extended.
    (3) That the place of production be other than that specified in the demand.
    (4) That the inspection, copying, testing, or sampling be made only on specified terms and conditions.
    (5) That a trade secret or other confidential research, development, or commercial information not be disclosed, or be disclosed only to specified persons or only in a specified way.
    (6) That the items produced be sealed and thereafter opened only on order of the court.
(c) The party or affected person who seeks a protective order regarding the production, inspection, copying, testing, or sampling of electronically stored information on the basis that the information is from a source that is not reasonably accessible because of undue burden or expense shall bear the burden of demonstrating that the information is from a source that is not reasonably accessible because of undue burden or expense.
(d) If the party or affected person from whom discovery of electronically stored information is sought establishes that the information is from a source that is not reasonably accessible because of undue burden or expense, the court may nonetheless order discovery if the demanding party shows good cause, subject to any limitations imposed under subdivision (f).
(e) If the court finds good cause for the production of electronically stored information from a source that is not reasonably accessible, the court may set conditions for the discovery of the electronically stored information, including allocation of the expense of discovery.
(f) The court shall limit the frequency or extent of discovery of electronically stored information, even from a source that is reasonably accessible, if the court determines that any of the following conditions exist:
    (1) It is possible to obtain the information from some other source that is more convenient, less burdensome, or less expensive.
    (2) The discovery sought is unreasonably cumulative or duplicative.
    (3) The party seeking discovery has had ample opportunity by discovery in the action to obtain the information sought.
    (4) The likely burden or expense of the proposed discovery outweighs the likely benefit, taking into account the amount in controversy, the resources of the parties, the importance of the issues in the litigation, and the importance of the requested discovery in resolving the issues.
(g) If the motion for a protective order is denied in whole or in part, the court may order that the party to whom the demand was directed provide or permit the discovery against which protection was sought on terms and conditions that are just.
(h) Except as provided in subdivision (i), the court shall impose a monetary sanction under Chapter 7 (commencing with Section 2023.010) against any party, person, or attorney who unsuccessfully makes or opposes a motion for a protective order, unless it finds that the one subject to the sanction acted with substantial justification or that other circumstances make the imposition of the sanction unjust.
(i)
    (1) Notwithstanding subdivision (h), absent exceptional circumstances, the court shall not impose sanctions on a party or any attorney of a party for failure to provide electronically stored information that has been lost, damaged, altered, or overwritten as the result of the routine, good faith operation of an electronic information system.
    (2) This subdivision shall not be construed to alter any obligation to preserve discoverable information.
Amended by Stats 2021 ch 124 (AB 938),s 15, eff. 1/1/2022.

Amended by Stats 2009 ch 5 (AB 5),s 9, eff. 6/29/2009.
Added by Stats 2004 ch 182 (AB 3081),s 23, eff. 7/1/2005.

Article 2 - RESPONSE TO INSPECTION DEMAND

Section 2031.210 - Requirements of response

(a) The party to whom a demand for inspection, copying, testing, or sampling has been directed shall respond separately to each item or category of item by any of the following:

(1) A statement that the party will comply with the particular demand for inspection, copying, testing, or sampling by the date set for the inspection, copying, testing, or sampling pursuant to paragraph (2) of subdivision (c) of Section 2031.030 and any related activities.

(2) A representation that the party lacks the ability to comply with the demand for inspection, copying, testing, or sampling of a particular item or category of item.

(3) An objection to the particular demand for inspection, copying, testing, or sampling.

(b) In the first paragraph of the response immediately below the title of the case, there shall appear the identity of the responding party, the set number, and the identity of the demanding party.

(c) Each statement of compliance, each representation, and each objection in the response shall bear the same number and be in the same sequence as the corresponding item or category in the demand, but the text of that item or category need not be repeated.

(d) If a party objects to the discovery of electronically stored information on the grounds that it is from a source that is not reasonably accessible because of undue burden or expense and that the responding party will not search the source in the absence of an agreement with the demanding party or court order, the responding party shall identify in its response the types or categories of sources of electronically stored information that it asserts are not reasonably accessible. By objecting and identifying information of a type or category of source or sources that are not reasonably accessible, the responding party preserves any objections it may have relating to that electronically stored information.

Amended by Stats 2009 ch 5 (AB 5),s 10, eff. 6/29/2009.
Amended by Stats 2007 ch 738 (AB 1248),s 7, eff. 1/1/2008.
Added by Stats 2004 ch 182 (AB 3081),s 23, eff. 7/1/2005.

Section 2031.220 - Statement that party to whom demand directed will comply demand

A statement that the party to whom a demand for inspection, copying, testing, or sampling has been directed will comply with the particular demand shall state that the production, inspection, copying, testing, or sampling, and related activity demanded, will be allowed either in whole or in part, and that all documents or things in the demanded category that are in the possession, custody, or control of that party and to which no objection is being made will be included in the production.

Amended by Stats 2009 ch 5 (AB 5),s 11, eff. 6/29/2009.
Added by Stats 2004 ch 182 (AB 3081),s 23, eff. 7/1/2005.

Section 2031.230 - Statement of inability to comply with demand

A representation of inability to comply with the particular demand for inspection, copying, testing, or sampling shall affirm that a diligent search and a reasonable inquiry has been made in an effort to comply with that demand. This statement shall also specify whether the inability to comply is because the particular item or category has never existed, has been destroyed, has been lost, misplaced, or stolen, or has never been, or is no longer, in the possession, custody, or control of the responding party. The statement shall set forth the name and address of any natural person or organization known or believed by that party to have possession, custody, or control of that item or category of item.

Amended by Stats 2009 ch 5 (AB 5),s 12, eff. 6/29/2009.
Added by Stats 2004 ch 182 (AB 3081),s 23, eff. 7/1/2005.

Section 2031.240 - Objections

(a) If only part of an item or category of item in a demand for inspection, copying, testing, or sampling is objectionable, the response shall contain a statement of compliance, or a representation of inability to comply with respect to the remainder of that item or category.

(b) If the responding party objects to the demand for inspection, copying, testing, or sampling of an item or category of item, the response shall do both of the following:

(1) Identify with particularity any document, tangible thing, land, or electronically stored information falling within any category of item in the demand to which an objection is being made.

(2) Set forth clearly the extent of, and the specific ground for, the objection. If an objection is based on a claim of privilege, the particular privilege invoked shall be stated. If an objection is based on a claim that the information sought is protected work product under Chapter 4 (commencing with Section 2018.010), that claim shall be expressly asserted.

(c)

(1) If an objection is based on a claim of privilege or a claim that the information sought is protected work product, the response shall provide sufficient factual information for other parties to evaluate the merits of that claim, including, if necessary, a privilege log.

(2) It is the intent of the Legislature to codify the concept of a privilege log as that term is used in California case law. Nothing in this subdivision shall be construed to constitute a substantive change in case law.

Amended by Stats 2012 ch 232 (AB 1354),s 1, eff. 1/1/2013.
Amended by Stats 2009 ch 5 (AB 5),s 13, eff. 6/29/2009.
Added by Stats 2004 ch 182 (AB 3081),s 23, eff. 7/1/2005.

Section 2031.250 - Signing response under oath

(a) The party to whom the demand for inspection, copying, testing, or sampling is directed shall sign the response under oath unless the response contains only objections.

(b) If that party is a public or private corporation or a partnership or association or governmental agency, one of its officers or agents shall sign the response under oath on behalf of that party. If the officer or agent signing the response on behalf of that party is an attorney acting in that capacity for a party, that party waives any lawyer-client privilege and any protection for work product under Chapter 4 (commencing with Section 2018.010) during any subsequent discovery from that attorney concerning the identity of the sources of the information contained in the response.

(c) The attorney for the responding party shall sign any responses that contain an objection.

Amended by Stats 2009 ch 5 (AB 5),s 14, eff. 6/29/2009.
Added by Stats 2004 ch 182 (AB 3081),s 23, eff. 7/1/2005.

Section 2031.260 - Time for service of original of response; time from date of service to respond

(a) Within 30 days after service of a demand for inspection, copying, testing, or sampling, the party to whom the demand is directed shall serve the original of the response to it on the party making the demand, and a copy of the response on all other parties who have appeared in the action, unless on motion of the party making the demand, the court has shortened the time for response, or unless on motion of the party to whom the demand has been directed, the court has extended the time for response.

(b) Notwithstanding subdivision (a), in an unlawful detainer action or other proceeding under Chapter 4 (commencing with Section 1159) of Title 3 of Part 3, the party to whom a demand for inspection, copying, testing, or sampling is directed shall have at least five days from the date of

service of the demand to respond, unless on motion of the party making the demand, the court has shortened the time for the response, or unless on motion of the party to whom the demand has been directed, the court has extended the time for response.
Amended by Stats 2009 ch 5 (AB 5),s 15, eff. 6/29/2009.
Amended by Stats 2007 ch 113 (AB 1126),s 11, eff. 1/1/2008.
Added by Stats 2004 ch 182 (AB 3081),s 23, eff. 7/1/2005.

Section 2031.270 - Agreement to extend date of inspection or time of service of response

(a) The party demanding inspection, copying, testing, or sampling and the responding party may agree to extend the date for the inspection, copying, testing, or sampling or the time for service of a response to a set of demands, or to particular items or categories of items in a set, to a date or dates beyond those provided in Sections 2031.030, 2031.210, 2031.260, and 2031.280.

(b) This agreement may be informal, but it shall be confirmed in a writing that specifies the extended date for inspection, copying, testing, or sampling, or for the service of a response.

(c) Unless this agreement expressly states otherwise, it is effective to preserve to the responding party the right to respond to any item or category of item in the demand to which the agreement applies in any manner specified in Sections 2031.210, 2031.220, 2031.230, 2031.240, and 2031.280.

Amended by Stats 2009 ch 5 (AB 5),s 16, eff. 6/29/2009.
Amended by Stats 2007 ch 738 (AB 1248),s 8, eff. 1/1/2008.
Added by Stats 2004 ch 182 (AB 3081),s 23, eff. 7/1/2005.

Section 2031.280 - Production of documents in response to demand

(a) Any documents or category of documents produced in response to a demand for inspection, copying, testing, or sampling shall be identified with the specific request number to which the documents respond.

(b) The documents shall be produced on the date specified in the demand pursuant to paragraph (2) of subdivision (c) of Section 2031.030, unless an objection has been made to that date. If the date for inspection has been extended pursuant to Section 2031.270, the documents shall be produced on the date agreed to pursuant to that section.

(c) If a party responding to a demand for production of electronically stored information objects to a specified form for producing the information, or if no form is specified in the demand, the responding party shall state in its response the form in which it intends to produce each type of information.

(d) Unless the parties otherwise agree or the court otherwise orders, the following shall apply:

(1) If a demand for production does not specify a form or forms for producing a type of electronically stored information, the responding party shall produce the information in the form or forms in which it is ordinarily maintained or in a form that is reasonably usable.

(2) A party need not produce the same electronically stored information in more than one form.

(e) If necessary, the responding party at the reasonable expense of the demanding party shall, through detection devices, translate any data compilations included in the demand into reasonably usable form.

Amended by Stats 2019 ch 208 (SB 370),s 1, eff. 1/1/2020.
Amended by Stats 2009 ch 5 (AB 5),s 17, eff. 6/29/2009.
Amended by Stats 2007 ch 738 (AB 1248),s 9, eff. 1/1/2008.
Added by Stats 2004 ch 182 (AB 3081),s 23, eff. 7/1/2005.

Section 2031.285 - Electronically stored information produced subject to claim of privilege or protection as attorney work product

(a) If electronically stored information produced in discovery is subject to a claim of privilege or of protection as attorney work product, the party making the claim may notify any party that received the information of the claim and the basis for the claim.

(b) After being notified of a claim of privilege or of protection under subdivision (a), a party that received the information shall immediately sequester the information and either return the specified information and any copies that may exist or present the information to the court conditionally under seal for a determination of the claim.

(c)

(1) Prior to the resolution of the motion brought under subdivision (d), a party shall be precluded from using or disclosing the specified information until the claim of privilege is resolved.

(2) A party who received and disclosed the information before being notified of a claim of privilege or of protection under subdivision (a) shall, after that notification, immediately take reasonable steps to retrieve the information.

(d)

(1) If the receiving party contests the legitimacy of a claim of privilege or protection, he or she may seek a determination of the claim from the court by making a motion within 30 days of receiving the claim and presenting the information to the court conditionally under seal.

(2) Until the legitimacy of the claim of privilege or protection is resolved, the receiving party shall preserve the information and keep it confidential and shall be precluded from using the information in any manner.

Added by Stats 2009 ch 5 (AB 5),s 18, eff. 6/29/2009.

Section 2031.290 - Demand and response filed with court; retention by demanding party until final disposition

(a) The demand for inspection, copying, testing, or sampling, and the response to it, shall not be filed with the court.

(b) The party demanding an inspection, copying, testing, or sampling shall retain both the original of the demand, with the original proof of service affixed to it, and the original of the sworn response until six months after final disposition of the action. At that time, both originals may be destroyed, unless the court, on motion of any party and for good cause shown, orders that the originals be preserved for a longer period.

Amended by Stats 2009 ch 5 (AB 5),s 19, eff. 6/29/2009.
Added by Stats 2004 ch 182 (AB 3081),s 23, eff. 7/1/2005.

Section 2031.300 - Failure to serve timely response; motion to compel response

If a party to whom a demand for inspection, copying, testing, or sampling is directed fails to serve a timely response to it, the following rules shall apply:

(a) The party to whom the demand for inspection, copying, testing, or sampling is directed waives any objection to the demand, including one based on privilege or on the protection for work product under Chapter 4 (commencing with Section 2018.010). The court, on motion, may relieve that party from this waiver on its determination that both of the following conditions are satisfied:

(1) The party has subsequently served a response that is in substantial compliance with Sections 2031.210, 2031.220, 2031.230, 2031.240, and 2031.280.

(2) The party's failure to serve a timely response was the result of mistake, inadvertence, or excusable neglect.

(b) The party making the demand may move for an order compelling response to the demand.

(c) Except as provided in subdivision (d), the court shall impose a monetary sanction under Chapter 7 (commencing with Section 2023.010) against any party, person, or attorney who unsuccessfully makes or opposes a motion to compel a response to a demand for inspection, copying, testing, or sampling, unless it finds that the one subject to the sanction acted with substantial justification or that other circumstances make the imposition of the sanction unjust. If a party then fails to obey the order compelling a response, the court may make those orders that are just, including the imposition of an issue sanction, an evidence sanction, or a terminating sanction under Chapter 7 (commencing with Section

2023.010). In lieu of or in addition to this sanction, the court may impose a monetary sanction under Chapter 7 (commencing with Section 2023.010).

(d)

(1) Notwithstanding subdivision (c), absent exceptional circumstances, the court shall not impose sanctions on a party or any attorney of a party for failure to provide electronically stored information that has been lost, damaged, altered, or overwritten as a result of the routine, good faith operation of an electronic information system.

(2) This subdivision shall not be construed to alter any obligation to preserve discoverable information.

Amended by Stats 2009 ch 5 (AB 5),s 20, eff. 6/29/2009.
Amended by Stats 2005 ch 22 (SB 1108),s 23, eff. 1/1/2006
Added by Stats 2004 ch 182 (AB 3081),s 23, eff. 7/1/2005.

Section 2031.310 - Motion for order compelling further response

(a) On receipt of a response to a demand for inspection, copying, testing, or sampling, the demanding party may move for an order compelling further response to the demand if the demanding party deems that any of the following apply:

(1) A statement of compliance with the demand is incomplete.

(2) A representation of inability to comply is inadequate, incomplete, or evasive.

(3) An objection in the response is without merit or too general.

(b) A motion under subdivision (a) shall comply with each of the following:

(1) The motion shall set forth specific facts showing good cause justifying the discovery sought by the demand.

(2) The motion shall be accompanied by a meet and confer declaration under Section 2016.040.

(3) In lieu of a separate statement required under the California Rules of Court, the court may allow the moving party to submit a concise outline of the discovery request and each response in dispute.

(c) Unless notice of this motion is given within 45 days of the service of the verified response, or any supplemental verified response, or on or before any specific later date to which the demanding party and the responding party have agreed in writing, the demanding party waives any right to compel a further response to the demand.

(d) In a motion under subdivision (a) relating to the production of electronically stored information, the party or affected person objecting to or opposing the production, inspection, copying, testing, or sampling of electronically stored information on the basis that the information is from a source that is not reasonably accessible because of the undue burden or expense shall bear the burden of demonstrating that the information is from a source that is not reasonably accessible because of undue burden or expense.

(e) If the party or affected person from whom discovery of electronically stored information is sought establishes that the information is from a source that is not reasonably accessible because of the undue burden or expense, the court may nonetheless order discovery if the demanding party shows good cause, subject to any limitations imposed under subdivision (g).

(f) If the court finds good cause for the production of electronically stored information from a source that is not reasonably accessible, the court may set conditions for the discovery of the electronically stored information, including allocation of the expense of discovery.

(g) The court shall limit the frequency or extent of discovery of electronically stored information, even from a source that is reasonably accessible, if the court determines that any of the following conditions exists:

(1) It is possible to obtain the information from some other source that is more convenient, less burdensome, or less expensive.

(2) The discovery sought is unreasonably cumulative or duplicative.

(3) The party seeking discovery has had ample opportunity by discovery in the action to obtain the information sought.

(4) The likely burden or expense of the proposed discovery outweighs the likely benefit, taking into account the amount in controversy, the resources of the parties, the importance of the issues in the litigation, and the importance of the requested discovery in resolving the issues.

(h) Except as provided in subdivision (j), the court shall impose a monetary sanction under Chapter 7 (commencing with Section 2023.010) against any party, person, or attorney who unsuccessfully makes or opposes a motion to compel further response to a demand, unless it finds that the one subject to the sanction acted with substantial justification or that other circumstances make the imposition of the sanction unjust.

(i) Except as provided in subdivision (j), if a party fails to obey an order compelling further response, the court may make those orders that are just, including the imposition of an issue sanction, an evidence sanction, or a terminating sanction under Chapter 7 (commencing with Section 2023.010). In lieu of, or in addition to, that sanction, the court may impose a monetary sanction under Chapter 7 (commencing with Section 2023.010).

(j)

(1) Notwithstanding subdivisions (h) and (i), absent exceptional circumstances, the court shall not impose sanctions on a party or any attorney of a party for failure to provide electronically stored information that has been lost, damaged, altered, or overwritten as the result of the routine, good faith operation of an electronic information system.

(2) This subdivision shall not be construed to alter any obligation to preserve discoverable information.

Amended by Stats 2018 ch 317 (AB 2230),s 4, eff. 1/1/2019, op. 1/1/2020.
Amended by Stats 2013 ch 18 (AB 1183),s 2, eff. 1/1/2014.
Amended by Stats 2009 ch 5 (AB 5),s 21, eff. 6/29/2009.
Added by Stats 2004 ch 182 (AB 3081),s 23, eff. 7/1/2005.

Section 2031.320 - Motion to compel compliance with demand; failure to obey order compelling inspection

(a) If a party filing a response to a demand for inspection, copying, testing, or sampling under Sections 2031.210, 2031.220, 2031.230, 2031.240, and 2031.280 thereafter fails to permit the inspection, copying, testing, or sampling in accordance with that party's statement of compliance, the demanding party may move for an order compelling compliance.

(b) Except as provided in subdivision (d), the court shall impose a monetary sanction under Chapter 7 (commencing with Section 2023.010) against any party, person, or attorney who unsuccessfully makes or opposes a motion to compel compliance with a demand, unless it finds that the one subject to the sanction acted with substantial justification or that other circumstances make the imposition of the sanction unjust.

(c) Except as provided in subdivision (d), if a party then fails to obey an order compelling inspection, copying, testing, or sampling, the court may make those orders that are just, including the imposition of an issue sanction, an evidence sanction, or a terminating sanction under Chapter 7 (commencing with Section 2023.010). In lieu of or in addition to that sanction, the court may impose a monetary sanction under Chapter 7 (commencing with Section 2023.010).

(d)

(1) Notwithstanding subdivisions (b) and (c), absent exceptional circumstances, the court shall not impose sanctions on a party or any attorney of a party for failure to provide electronically stored information that has been lost, damaged, altered, or overwritten as the result of the routine, good faith operation of an electronic information system.

(2) This subdivision shall not be construed to alter any obligation to preserve discoverable information.

Amended by Stats 2009 ch 5 (AB 5),s 22, eff. 6/29/2009.
Added by Stats 2004 ch 182 (AB 3081),s 23, eff. 7/1/2005.

Article 3 - INSPECTION AND PRODUCTION OF DOCUMENTS AND OTHER PROPERTY IN SPECIFIC CONTEXTS

Section 2031.510 - Boundary of land patented in dispute or validity of state patent or grant
(a) In any action, regardless of who is the moving party, where the boundary of land patented or otherwise granted by the state is in dispute, or the validity of any state patent or grant dated before 1950 is in dispute, all parties shall have the duty to disclose to all opposing parties all nonprivileged relevant written evidence then known and available, including evidence against interest, relating to the above issues.
(b) This evidence shall be disclosed within 120 days after the filing with the court of proof of service upon all named defendants. Thereafter, the parties shall have the continuing duty to make all subsequently discovered relevant and nonprivileged written evidence available to the opposing parties.
Added by Stats 2004 ch 182 (AB 3081),s 23, eff. 7/1/2005.

Chapter 15 - PHYSICAL OR MENTAL EXAMINATION
Article 1 - GENERAL PROVISIONS

Section 2032.010 - Construction
(a) This chapter does not affect genetic testing under Chapter 2 (commencing with Section 7550) of Part 2 of Division 12 of the Family Code.
(b) This chapter does not require the disclosure of the identity of an expert consulted by an attorney in order to make the certification required in an action for professional negligence under Section 411.35.
Amended by Stats 2018 ch 876 (AB 2684),s 2, eff. 1/1/2019.
Added by Stats 2004 ch 182 (AB 3081),s 23, eff. 7/1/2005.

Section 2032.020 - Generally
(a) Any party may obtain discovery, subject to the restrictions set forth in Chapter 5 (commencing with Section 2019.010), by means of a physical or mental examination of (1) a party to the action, (2) an agent of any party, or (3) a natural person in the custody or under the legal control of a party, in any action in which the mental or physical condition (including the blood group) of that party or other person is in controversy in the action.
(b) A physical examination conducted under this chapter shall be performed only by a licensed physician or other appropriate licensed health care practitioner.
(c)
(1) A mental examination conducted under this chapter shall be performed only by a licensed physician, or by a licensed clinical psychologist who holds a doctoral degree in psychology and has had at least five years of postgraduate experience in the diagnosis of emotional and mental disorders.
(2) If an action involves allegations of sexual abuse of a minor, including any act listed in paragraphs (1) to (3), inclusive, of subdivision (a) of Section 1002, and the examinee is less than 15 years of age, the licensed physician or clinical psychologist shall have expertise in child abuse and trauma.
Amended by Stats 2017 ch 133 (SB 755),s 1, eff. 1/1/2018.
Added by Stats 2004 ch 182 (AB 3081),s 23, eff. 7/1/2005.

Article 2 - PHYSICAL EXAMINATION OF PERSONAL INJURY PLAINTIFF

Section 2032.210 - Plaintiff includes
As used in this article, "plaintiff" includes a cross-complainant, and "defendant" includes a cross-defendant.
Added by Stats 2004 ch 182 (AB 3081),s 23, eff. 7/1/2005.

Section 2032.220 - Demand by defendant in case in which plaintiff seeking recovery for person injuries
(a) In any case in which a plaintiff is seeking recovery for personal injuries, any defendant may demand one physical examination of the plaintiff, if both of the following conditions are satisfied:
(1) The examination does not include any diagnostic test or procedure that is painful, protracted, or intrusive.
(2) The examination is conducted at a location within 75 miles of the residence of the examinee.
(b) A defendant may make a demand under this article without leave of court after that defendant has been served or has appeared in the action, whichever occurs first.
(c) A demand under subdivision (a) shall specify the time, place, manner, conditions, scope, and nature of the examination, as well as the identity and the specialty, if any, of the physician who will perform the examination.
(d) A physical examination demanded under subdivision (a) shall be scheduled for a date that is at least 30 days after service of the demand. On motion of the party demanding the examination, the court may shorten this time.
(e) The defendant shall serve a copy of the demand under subdivision (a) on the plaintiff and on all other parties who have appeared in the action.
Added by Stats 2004 ch 182 (AB 3081),s 23, eff. 7/1/2005.

Section 2032.230 - Response by plaintiff by written statement; time for service of response by plaintiff; extension of time
(a) The plaintiff to whom a demand for a physical examination under this article is directed shall respond to the demand by a written statement that the examinee will comply with the demand as stated, will comply with the demand as specifically modified by the plaintiff, or will refuse, for reasons specified in the response, to submit to the demanded physical examination.
(b) Within 20 days after service of the demand the plaintiff to whom the demand is directed shall serve the original of the response to it on the defendant making the demand, and a copy of the response on all other parties who have appeared in the action. On motion of the defendant making the demand, the court may shorten the time for response. On motion of the plaintiff to whom the demand is directed, the court may extend the time for response.
Added by Stats 2004 ch 182 (AB 3081),s 23, eff. 7/1/2005.

Section 2032.240 - Waiver of objection to demand if response not timely served; motion for order compelling response and compliance
(a) If a plaintiff to whom a demand for a physical examination under this article is directed fails to serve a timely response to it, that plaintiff waives any objection to the demand. The court, on motion, may relieve that plaintiff from this waiver on its determination that both of the following conditions are satisfied:
(1) The plaintiff has subsequently served a response that is in substantial compliance with Section 2032.230.
(2) The plaintiff's failure to serve a timely response was the result of mistake, inadvertence, or excusable neglect.
(b) The defendant may move for an order compelling response and compliance with a demand for a physical examination.
(c) The court shall impose a monetary sanction under Chapter 7 (commencing with Section 2023.010) against any party, person, or attorney who unsuccessfully makes or opposes a motion to compel response and compliance with a demand for a physical examination, unless it finds that the one subject to the sanction acted with substantial justification or that other circumstances make the imposition of the sanction unjust.
(d) If a plaintiff then fails to obey the order compelling response and compliance, the court may make those orders that are just, including the imposition of an issue sanction, an evidence sanction, or a terminating sanction under Chapter 7 (commencing with Section 2023.010). In lieu of or in addition to that sanction the court may impose a monetary sanction under Chapter 7 (commencing with Section 2023.010).

Added by Stats 2004 ch 182 (AB 3081),s 23, eff. 7/1/2005.

Section 2032.250 - Motion for order compelling compliance with demand

(a) If a defendant who has demanded a physical examination under this article, on receipt of the plaintiff's response to that demand, deems that any modification of the demand, or any refusal to submit to the physical examination is unwarranted, that defendant may move for an order compelling compliance with the demand. This motion shall be accompanied by a meet and confer declaration under Section 2016.040.

(b) The court shall impose a monetary sanction under Chapter 7 (commencing with Section 2023.010) against any party, person, or attorney who unsuccessfully makes or opposes a motion to compel compliance with a demand for a physical examination, unless it finds that the one subject to the sanction acted with substantial justification or that other circumstances make the imposition of the sanction unjust.

Added by Stats 2004 ch 182 (AB 3081),s 23, eff. 7/1/2005.

Section 2032.260 - Demand and response filed with court; retention by defendant of originals until final disposition

(a) The demand for a physical examination under this article and the response to it shall not be filed with the court.

(b) The defendant shall retain both the original of the demand, with the original proof of service affixed to it, and the original response until six months after final disposition of the action. At that time, the original may be destroyed, unless the court, on motion of any party and for good cause shown, orders that the originals be preserved for a longer period.

Added by Stats 2004 ch 182 (AB 3081),s 23, eff. 7/1/2005.

Article 3 - MOTION FOR PHYSICAL OR MENTAL EXAMINATION

Section 2032.310 - Leave of court required; motion for examination; service of notice of motion

(a) If any party desires to obtain discovery by a physical examination other than that described in Article 2 (commencing with Section 2032.210), or by a mental examination, the party shall obtain leave of court.

(b) A motion for an examination under subdivision (a) shall specify the time, place, manner, conditions, scope, and nature of the examination, as well as the identity and the specialty, if any, of the person or persons who will perform the examination. The motion shall be accompanied by a meet and confer declaration under Section 2016.040.

(c) Notice of the motion shall be served on the person to be examined and on all parties who have appeared in the action.

Added by Stats 2004 ch 182 (AB 3081),s 23, eff. 7/1/2005.

Section 2032.320 - Granting motion

(a) The court shall grant a motion for a physical or mental examination under Section 2032.310 only for good cause shown.

(b) If a party stipulates as provided in subdivision (c), the court shall not order a mental examination of a person for whose personal injuries a recovery is being sought except on a showing of exceptional circumstances.

(c) A stipulation by a party under this subdivision shall include both of the following:

(1) A stipulation that no claim is being made for mental and emotional distress over and above that usually associated with the physical injuries claimed.

(2) A stipulation that no expert testimony regarding this usual mental and emotional distress will be presented at trial in support of the claim for damages.

(d) An order granting a physical or mental examination shall specify the person or persons who may perform the examination, as well as the time, place, manner, diagnostic tests and procedures, conditions, scope, and nature of the examination.

(e) If the place of the examination is more than 75 miles from the residence of the person to be examined, an order to submit to it shall be entered only if both of the following conditions are satisfied:

(1) The court determines that there is good cause for the travel involved.

(2) The order is conditioned on the advancement by the moving party of the reasonable expenses and costs to the examinee for travel to the place of examination.

Added by Stats 2004 ch 182 (AB 3081),s 23, eff. 7/1/2005.

Section 2032.340 - Mental examination of child less than 15 years of age; duration

(a) If any action involving allegations of sexual abuse of a minor, including any act listed in paragraphs (1) to (3), inclusive, of subdivision (a) of Section 1002, the mental examination of a child less than 15 years of age shall not exceed three hours, inclusive of breaks.

(b) Notwithstanding subdivision (a), the court may grant an extension of the three-hour limit for good cause.

Added by Stats 2017 ch 133 (SB 755),s 2, eff. 1/1/2018.

Article 4 - FAILURE TO SUBMIT TO OR PRODUCE ANOTHER FOR PHYSICAL OR MENTAL EXAMINATION

Section 2032.410 - Party required to submit to examination

If a party is required to submit to a physical or mental examination under Articles 2 (commencing with Section 2032.210) or 3 (commencing with Section 2032.310), or under Section 2016.030, but fails to do so, the court, on motion of the party entitled to the examination, may make those orders that are just, including the imposition of an issue sanction, an evidence sanction, or a terminating sanction under Chapter 7 (commencing with Section 2023.010). In lieu of or in addition to that sanction, the court may, on motion of the party, impose a monetary sanction under Chapter 7 (commencing with Section 2023.010).

Added by Stats 2004 ch 182 (AB 3081),s 23, eff. 7/1/2005.

Section 2032.420 - Party required to produce another for examination

If a party is required to produce another for a physical or mental examination under Articles 2 (commencing with Section 2032.210) or 3 (commencing with Section 2032.310), or under Section 2032.030, but fails to do so, the court, on motion of the party entitled to the examination, may make those orders that are just, including the imposition of an issue sanction, an evidence sanction, or a terminating sanction under Chapter 7 (commencing with Section 2023.010), unless the party failing to comply demonstrates an inability to produce that person for examination. In lieu of or in addition to that sanction, the court may impose a monetary sanction under Chapter 7 (commencing with Section 2023.010).

Added by Stats 2004 ch 182 (AB 3081),s 23, eff. 7/1/2005.

Article 5 - CONDUCT OF EXAMINATION

Section 2032.510 - Attorney or party permitted to attend as observer

(a) The attorney for the examinee or for a party producing the examinee, or that attorney's representative, shall be permitted to attend and observe any physical examination conducted for discovery purposes, and to record stenographically or by audio technology any words spoken to or by the examinee during any phase of the examination.

(b) The observer under subdivision (a) may monitor the examination, but shall not participate in or disrupt it.

(c) If an attorney's representative is to serve as the observer, the representative shall be authorized to so act by a writing subscribed by the attorney which identifies the representative.

(d) If in the judgment of the observer the examiner becomes abusive to the examinee or undertakes to engage in unauthorized diagnostic tests and procedures, the observer may suspend it to enable the party being examined or producing the examinee to make a motion for a protective order.

(e) If the observer begins to participate in or disrupt the examination, the person conducting the physical examination may suspend the examination to enable the party at whose instance it is being conducted to move for a protective order.
(f) The court shall impose a monetary sanction under Chapter 7 (commencing with Section 2023.010) against any party, person, or attorney who unsuccessfully makes or opposes a motion for a protective order under this section, unless it finds that the one subject to the sanction acted with substantial justification or that other circumstances make the imposition of the sanction unjust.
Amended by Stats 2005 ch 294 (AB 333),s 10, eff. 1/1/2006
Added by Stats 2004 ch 182 (AB 3081),s 23, eff. 7/1/2005.

Section 2032.520 - Additional X-rays of area taken
If an examinee submits or authorizes access to X-rays of any area of his or her body for inspection by the examining physician, no additional X-rays of that area may be taken by the examining physician except with consent of the examinee or on order of the court for good cause shown.
Added by Stats 2004 ch 182 (AB 3081),s 23, eff. 7/1/2005.

Section 2032.530 - Right to record mental examination by audio technology
(a) The examiner and examinee shall have the right to record a mental examination by audio technology.
(b) Nothing in this title shall be construed to alter, amend, or affect existing case law with respect to the presence of the attorney for the examinee or other persons during the examination by agreement or court order.
Amended by Stats 2005 ch 294 (AB 333),s 11, eff. 1/1/2006
Added by Stats 2004 ch 182 (AB 3081),s 23, eff. 7/1/2005.

Article 6 - REPORTS OF EXAMINATION

Section 2032.610 - Delivering of copies of reports required by demanding party
(a) If a party submits to, or produces another for, a physical or mental examination in compliance with a demand under Article 2 (commencing with Section 2032.210), an order of court under Article 3 (commencing with Section 2032.310), or an agreement under Section 2016.030, that party has the option of making a written demand that the party at whose instance the examination was made deliver both of the following to the demanding party:
  (1) A copy of a detailed written report setting out the history, examinations, findings, including the results of all tests made, diagnoses, prognoses, and conclusions of the examiner.
  (2) A copy of reports of all earlier examinations of the same condition of the examinee made by that or any other examiner.
(b) If the option under subdivision (a) is exercised, a copy of the requested reports shall be delivered within 30 days after service of the demand, or within 15 days of trial, whichever is earlier.
(c) In the circumstances described in subdivision (a), the protection for work product under Chapter 4 (commencing with Section 2018.010) is waived, both for the examiner's writings and reports and to the taking of the examiner's testimony.
Added by Stats 2004 ch 182 (AB 3081),s 23, eff. 7/1/2005.

Section 2032.620 - Motion for order compelling delivery of reports
(a) If the party at whose instance an examination was made fails to make a timely delivery of the reports demanded under Section 2032.610, the demanding party may move for an order compelling their delivery. This motion shall be accompanied by a meet and confer declaration under Section 2016.040.
(b) The court shall impose a monetary sanction under Chapter 7 (commencing with Section 2023.010) against any party, person, or attorney who unsuccessfully makes or opposes a motion to compel delivery of medical reports under this section, unless it finds that the one subject to the sanction acted with substantial justification or that other circumstances make the imposition of the sanction unjust.
(c) If a party then fails to obey an order compelling delivery of demanded medical reports, the court may make those orders that are just, including the imposition of an issue sanction, an evidence sanction, or a terminating sanction under Chapter 7 (commencing with Section 2023.010). In lieu of or in addition to those sanctions, the court may impose a monetary sanction under Chapter 7 (commencing with Section 2023.010). The court shall exclude at trial the testimony of any examiner whose report has not been provided by a party.
Added by Stats 2004 ch 182 (AB 3081),s 23, eff. 7/1/2005.

Section 2032.630 - Waivers by demanding and obtaining report or taking deposition of examiner
By demanding and obtaining a report of a physical or mental examination under Section 2032.610 or 2032.620, or by taking the deposition of the examiner, other than under Article 3 (commencing with Section 2034.410) of Chapter 18, the party who submitted to, or produced another for, a physical or mental examination waives in the pending action, and in any other action involving the same controversy, any privilege, as well as any protection for work product under Chapter 4 (commencing with Section 2018.010), that the party or other examinee may have regarding reports and writings as well as the testimony of every other physician, psychologist, or licensed health care practitioner who has examined or may thereafter examine the party or other examinee in respect of the same physical or mental condition.
Added by Stats 2004 ch 182 (AB 3081),s 23, eff. 7/1/2005.

Section 2032.640 - Receipt of existing report of any examination
A party receiving a demand for a report under Section 2032.610 is entitled at the time of compliance to receive in exchange a copy of any existing written report of any examination of the same condition by any other physician, psychologist, or licensed health care practitioner. In addition, that party is entitled to receive promptly any later report of any previous or subsequent examination of the same condition, by any physician, psychologist, or licensed health care practitioner.
Added by Stats 2004 ch 182 (AB 3081),s 23, eff. 7/1/2005.

Section 2032.650 - Motion for order compelling delivery of medical reports
(a) If a party who has demanded and received delivery of medical reports under Section 2032.610 fails to deliver existing or later reports of previous or subsequent examinations under Section 2032.640, a party who has complied with Section 2032.610 may move for an order compelling delivery of medical reports. This motion shall be accompanied by a meet and confer declaration under Section 2016.040.
(b) The court shall impose a monetary sanction under Chapter 7 (commencing with Section 2023.010) against any party, person, or attorney who unsuccessfully makes or opposes a motion to compel delivery of medical reports under this section, unless it finds that the one subject to the sanction acted with substantial justification or that other circumstances make the imposition of the sanction unjust.
(c) If a party then fails to obey an order compelling delivery of medical reports, the court may make those orders that are just, including the imposition of an issue sanction, an evidence sanction, or a terminating sanction under Chapter 7 (commencing with Section 2023.010). In lieu of or in addition to the sanction, the court may impose a monetary sanction under Chapter 7 (commencing with Section 2023.010). The court shall exclude at trial the testimony of any health care practitioner whose report has not been provided by a party ordered to do so by the court.
Added by Stats 2004 ch 182 (AB 3081),s 23, eff. 7/1/2005.

Chapter 16 - REQUESTS FOR ADMISSION
Article 1 - REQUESTS FOR ADMISSION

Section 2033.010 - Generally
Any party may obtain discovery within the scope delimited by Chapter 2 (commencing with Section 2017.010), and subject to the restrictions set forth in Chapter 5 (commencing with Section 2019.010), by a written request that any other party to the action admit the genuineness of specified

documents, or the truth of specified matters of fact, opinion relating to fact, or application of law to fact. A request for admission may relate to a matter that is in controversy between the parties.

Amended by Stats 2016 ch 86 (SB 1171),s 43, eff. 1/1/2017.

Added by Stats 2004 ch 182 (AB 3081),s 23, eff. 7/1/2005.

Section 2033.020 - Request for admission without leave of court

(a) A defendant may make requests for admission by a party without leave of court at any time.

(b) A plaintiff may make requests for admission by a party without leave of court at any time that is 10 days after the service of the summons on, or appearance by, that party, whichever occurs first.

(c) Notwithstanding subdivision (b), in an unlawful detainer action or other proceeding under Chapter 4 (commencing with Section 1159) of Title 3 of Part 3, a plaintiff may make requests for admission by a party without leave of court at any time that is five days after service of the summons on, or appearance by, that party, whichever occurs first.

(d) Notwithstanding subdivisions (b) and (c), on motion with or without notice, the court, for good cause shown, may grant leave to a plaintiff to make requests for admission at an earlier time.

Amended by Stats 2007 ch 113 (AB 1126),s 12, eff. 1/1/2008.

Added by Stats 2004 ch 182 (AB 3081),s 23, eff. 7/1/2005.

Section 2033.030 - Number of admissions requested

(a) No party shall request, as a matter of right, that any other party admit more than 35 matters that do not relate to the genuineness of documents. If the initial set of admission requests does not exhaust this limit, the balance may be requested in subsequent sets.

(b) Unless a declaration as described in Section 2033.050 has been made, a party need only respond to the first 35 admission requests served that do not relate to the genuineness of documents, if that party states an objection to the balance under Section 2033.230 on the ground that the limit has been exceeded.

(c) The number of requests for admission of the genuineness of documents is not limited except as justice requires to protect the responding party from unwarranted annoyance, embarrassment, oppression, or undue burden and expense.

Added by Stats 2004 ch 182 (AB 3081),s 23, eff. 7/1/2005.

Section 2033.040 - Requesting greater number of admissions

(a) Subject to the right of the responding party to seek a protective order under Section 2033.080, any party who attaches a supporting declaration as described in Section 2033.050 may request a greater number of admissions by another party if the greater number is warranted by the complexity or the quantity of the existing and potential issues in the particular case.

(b) If the responding party seeks a protective order on the ground that the number of requests for admission is unwarranted, the propounding party shall have the burden of justifying the number of requests for admission.

Added by Stats 2004 ch 182 (AB 3081),s 23, eff. 7/1/2005.

Section 2033.050 - Declaration for additional discovery

Any party who is requesting or who has already requested more than 35 admissions not relating to the genuineness of documents by any other party shall attach to each set of requests for admissions a declaration containing substantially the following words:

DECLARATION FOR ADDITIONAL DISCOVERY

I, _____, declare:

1. I am (a party to this action or proceeding appearing in propria persona) (presently the attorney for _____, a party to this action or proceeding).

2. I am propounding to _____ the attached set of requests for admission.

3. This set of requests for admission will cause the total number of requests propounded to the party to whom they are directed to exceed the number of requests permitted by Section 2033.030 of the Code of Civil Procedure.

4. I have previously propounded a total of _____ requests for admission to this party.

5. This set of requests for admission contains a total of _____ requests.

6. I am familiar with the issues and the previous discovery conducted by all of the parties in this case.

7. I have personally examined each of the requests in this set of requests for admission.

8. This number of requests for admission is warranted under Section 2033.040 of the Code of Civil Procedure because _____. (Here state the reasons why the complexity or the quantity of issues in the instant lawsuit warrant this number of requests for admission.)

9. None of the requests in this set of requests is being propounded for any improper purpose, such as to harass the party, or the attorney for the party, to whom it is directed, or to cause unnecessary delay or needless increase in the cost of litigation. I declare under penalty of perjury under the laws of California that the foregoing is true and correct, and that this declaration was executed on _____.

_____ (Signature) _____

Attorney for

Added by Stats 2004 ch 182 (AB 3081),s 23, eff. 7/1/2005.

Section 2033.060 - Request for admissions

(a) A party requesting admissions shall number each set of requests consecutively.

(b) In the first paragraph immediately below the title of the case, there shall appear the identity of the party requesting the admissions, the set number, and the identity of the responding party.

(c) Each request for admission in a set shall be separately set forth and identified by letter or number.

(d) Each request for admission shall be full and complete in and of itself. No preface or instruction shall be included with a set of admission requests unless it has been approved under Chapter 17 (commencing with Section 2033.710).

(e) Any term specially defined in a request for admission shall be typed with all letters capitalized whenever the term appears.

(f) No request for admission shall contain subparts, or a compound, conjunctive, or disjunctive request unless it has been approved under Chapter 17 (commencing with Section 2033.710).

(g) A party requesting an admission of the genuineness of any documents shall attach copies of those documents to the requests, and shall make the original of those documents available for inspection on demand by the party to whom the requests for admission are directed.

(h) No party shall combine in a single document requests for admission with any other method of discovery.

Added by Stats 2004 ch 182 (AB 3081),s 23, eff. 7/1/2005.

Section 2033.070 - Service of copy of request

The party requesting admissions shall serve a copy of them on the party to whom they are directed and on all other parties who have appeared in the action.

Added by Stats 2004 ch 182 (AB 3081),s 23, eff. 7/1/2005.

Section 2033.080 - Protective order

(a) When requests for admission have been made, the responding party may promptly move for a protective order. This motion shall be accompanied by a meet and confer declaration under Section 2016.040.

(b) The court, for good cause shown, may make any order that justice requires to protect any party from unwarranted annoyance, embarrassment, oppression, or undue burden and expense. This protective order may include, but is not limited to, one or more of the following directions:

(1) That the set of admission requests, or particular requests in the set, need not be answered at all.

(2) That, contrary to the representations made in a declaration submitted under Section 2033.050, the number of admission requests is unwarranted.

(3) That the time specified in Section 2033.250 to respond to the set of admission requests, or to particular requests in the set, be extended.

(4) That a trade secret or other confidential research, development, or commercial information not be admitted or be admitted only in a certain way.

(5) That some or all of the answers to requests for admission be sealed and thereafter opened only on order of the court.

(c) If the motion for a protective order is denied in whole or in part, the court may order that the responding party provide or permit the discovery against which protection was sought on terms and conditions that are just.

(d) The court shall impose a monetary sanction under Chapter 7 (commencing with Section 2023.010) against any party, person, or attorney who unsuccessfully makes or opposes a motion for a protective order under this section, unless it finds that the one subject to the sanction acted with substantial justification or that other circumstances make the imposition of the sanction unjust.

Added by Stats 2004 ch 182 (AB 3081),s 23, eff. 7/1/2005.

Article 2 - RESPONSE TO REQUESTS FOR ADMISSION

Section 2033.210 - Requirements

(a) The party to whom requests for admission have been directed shall respond in writing under oath separately to each request.

(b) Each response shall answer the substance of the requested admission, or set forth an objection to the particular request.

(c) In the first paragraph of the response immediately below the title of the case, there shall appear the identity of the responding party, the set number, and the identity of the requesting party.

(d) Each answer or objection in the response shall bear the same identifying number or letter and be in the same sequence as the corresponding request. The text of that request need not be repeated, except as provided in paragraph (6) of subdivision (e).

(e) In order to facilitate the discovery process:

(1) Except as provided in paragraph (5), upon request by the responding party, the propounding party shall provide the requests for admission in an electronic format to the responding party within three court days of the request.

(2) Except as provided in paragraph (5), upon request by the propounding party after receipt of the responses to the requests for admission, the responding party shall provide the responses in an electronic format to the propounding party within three court days of the request.

(3) A party may provide the requests for admission or responses to the requests for admission requested pursuant to paragraphs (1) and (2) in any format agreed upon by the parties. If the parties are unable to agree on a format, the requests for admission or responses to the requests for admission shall be provided in plain text format.

(4) A party may transmit the requests for admission or responses to the requests for admission requested pursuant to paragraphs (1) and (2) by any method agreed upon by the parties. If the parties are unable to agree on a method of transmission, the requests for admission or responses to the requests for admission shall be transmitted by electronic mail to an email address provided by the requesting party.

(5) If the requests for admission or responses to the requests for admission were not created in an electronic format, a party is not required to create the requests for admission or responses in an electronic format for the purpose of transmission to the requesting party.

(6) A responding party who has requested and received requests for admission in an electronic format pursuant to paragraph (1) shall include the text of the request immediately preceding the response.

Amended by Stats 2019 ch 190 (AB 1349),s 2, eff. 1/1/2020.
Added by Stats 2004 ch 182 (AB 3081),s 23, eff. 7/1/2005.

Section 2033.220 - Answers

(a) Each answer in a response to requests for admission shall be as complete and straightforward as the information reasonably available to the responding party permits.

(b) Each answer shall:

(1) Admit so much of the matter involved in the request as is true, either as expressed in the request itself or as reasonably and clearly qualified by the responding party.

(2) Deny so much of the matter involved in the request as is untrue.

(3) Specify so much of the matter involved in the request as to the truth of which the responding party lacks sufficient information or knowledge.

(c) If a responding party gives lack of information or knowledge as a reason for a failure to admit all or part of a request for admission, that party shall state in the answer that a reasonable inquiry concerning the matter in the particular request has been made, and that the information known or readily obtainable is insufficient to enable that party to admit the matter.

Amended by Stats 2005 ch 22 (SB 1108),s 24, eff. 1/1/2006
Added by Stats 2004 ch 182 (AB 3081),s 23, eff. 7/1/2005.

Section 2033.230 - Objections

(a) If only a part of a request for admission is objectionable, the remainder of the request shall be answered.

(b) If an objection is made to a request or to a part of a request, the specific ground for the objection shall be set forth clearly in the response. If an objection is based on a claim of privilege, the particular privilege invoked shall be clearly stated. If an objection is based on a claim that the matter as to which an admission is requested is protected work product under Chapter 4 (commencing with Section 2018.010), that claim shall be expressly asserted.

Added by Stats 2004 ch 182 (AB 3081),s 23, eff. 7/1/2005.

Section 2033.240 - Signing response under oath

(a) The party to whom the requests for admission are directed shall sign the response under oath, unless the response contains only objections.

(b) If that party is a public or private corporation, or a partnership or association or governmental agency, one of its officers or agents shall sign the response under oath on behalf of that party. If the officer or agent signing the response on behalf of that party is an attorney acting in that capacity for the party, that party waives any lawyer-client privilege and any protection for work product under Chapter 4 (commencing with Section 2018.010) during any subsequent discovery from that attorney concerning the identity of the sources of the information contained in the response.

(c) The attorney for the responding party shall sign any response that contains an objection.

Added by Stats 2004 ch 182 (AB 3081),s 23, eff. 7/1/2005.

Section 2033.250 - Time for service of response; time for response from date of service

(a) Within 30 days after service of requests for admission, the party to whom the requests are directed shall serve the original of the response to them on the requesting party, and a copy of the response on all other parties who have appeared, unless on motion of the requesting party the court has shortened the time for response, or unless on motion of the responding party the court has extended the time for response.
(b) Notwithstanding subdivision (a), in an unlawful detainer action or other proceeding under Chapter 4 (commencing with Section 1159) of Title 3 of Part 3, the party to whom the request is directed shall have at least five days from the date of service to respond, unless on motion of the requesting party the court has shortened the time for response, or unless on motion of the responding party the court has extended the time for response.
Amended by Stats 2007 ch 113 (AB 1126),s 13, eff. 1/1/2008.
Added by Stats 2004 ch 182 (AB 3081),s 23, eff. 7/1/2005.

Section 2033.260 - Agreement to extension of time
(a) The party requesting admissions and the responding party may agree to extend the time for service of a response to a set of admission requests, or to particular requests in a set, to a date beyond that provided in Section 2033.250.
(b) This agreement may be informal, but it shall be confirmed in a writing that specifies the extended date for service of a response.
(c) Unless this agreement expressly states otherwise, it is effective to preserve to the responding party the right to respond to any request for admission to which the agreement applies in any manner specified in Sections 2033.210, 2033.220, and 2033.230.
(d) Notice of this agreement shall be given by the responding party to all other parties who were served with a copy of the request.
Added by Stats 2004 ch 182 (AB 3081),s 23, eff. 7/1/2005.

Section 2033.270 - Request and response filed with court; retention of originals by requesting party
(a) The requests for admission and the response to them shall not be filed with the court.
(b) The party requesting admissions shall retain both the original of the requests for admission, with the original proof of service affixed to them, and the original of the sworn response until six months after final disposition of the action. At that time, both originals may be destroyed, unless the court, on motion of any party and for good cause shown, orders that the originals be preserved for a longer period.
Added by Stats 2004 ch 182 (AB 3081),s 23, eff. 7/1/2005.

Section 2033.280 - Failure to timely serve response
If a party to whom requests for admission are directed fails to serve a timely response, the following rules apply:
(a) The party to whom the requests for admission are directed waives any objection to the requests, including one based on privilege or on the protection for work product under Chapter 4 (commencing with Section 2018.010). The court, on motion, may relieve that party from this waiver on its determination that both of the following conditions are satisfied:
  (1) The party has subsequently served a response that is in substantial compliance with Sections 2033.210, 2033.220, and 2033.230.
  (2) The party's failure to serve a timely response was the result of mistake, inadvertence, or excusable neglect.
(b) The requesting party may move for an order that the genuineness of any documents and the truth of any matters specified in the requests be deemed admitted, as well as for a monetary sanction under Chapter 7 (commencing with Section 2023.010).
(c) The court shall make this order, unless it finds that the party to whom the requests for admission have been directed has served, before the hearing on the motion, a proposed response to the requests for admission that is in substantial compliance with Section 2033.220. It is mandatory that the court impose a monetary sanction under Chapter 7 (commencing with Section 2023.010) on the party or attorney, or both, whose failure to serve a timely response to requests for admission necessitated this motion.
Amended by Stats 2005 ch 294 (AB 333),s 12, eff. 1/1/2006
Added by Stats 2004 ch 182 (AB 3081),s 23, eff. 7/1/2005.

Section 2033.290 - Motion compelling further response
(a) On receipt of a response to requests for admissions, the party requesting admissions may move for an order compelling a further response if that party deems that either or both of the following apply:
  (1) An answer to a particular request is evasive or incomplete.
  (2) An objection to a particular request is without merit or too general.
(b)
  (1) A motion under subdivision (a) shall be accompanied by a meet and confer declaration under Section 2016.040.
  (2) In lieu of a separate statement required under the California Rules of Court, the court may allow the moving party to submit a concise outline of the discovery request and each response in dispute.
(c) Unless notice of this motion is given within 45 days of the service of the verified response, or any supplemental verified response, or any specific later date to which the requesting party and the responding party have agreed in writing, the requesting party waives any right to compel further response to the requests for admission.
(d) The court shall impose a monetary sanction under Chapter 7 (commencing with Section 2023.010) against any party, person, or attorney who unsuccessfully makes or opposes a motion to compel further response, unless it finds that the one subject to the sanction acted with substantial justification or that other circumstances make the imposition of the sanction unjust.
(e) If a party then fails to obey an order compelling further response to requests for admission, the court may order that the matters involved in the requests be deemed admitted. In lieu of, or in addition to, this order, the court may impose a monetary sanction under Chapter 7 (commencing with Section 2023.010).
Amended by Stats 2018 ch 317 (AB 2230),s 5, eff. 1/1/2019, op. 1/1/2020.
Amended by Stats 2013 ch 18 (AB 1183),s 3, eff. 1/1/2014.
Added by Stats 2004 ch 182 (AB 3081),s 23, eff. 7/1/2005.

Section 2033.300 - Withdrawal or amendment of admission
(a) A party may withdraw or amend an admission made in response to a request for admission only on leave of court granted after notice to all parties.
(b) The court may permit withdrawal or amendment of an admission only if it determines that the admission was the result of mistake, inadvertence, or excusable neglect, and that the party who obtained the admission will not be substantially prejudiced in maintaining that party's action or defense on the merits.
(c) The court may impose conditions on the granting of the motion that are just, including, but not limited to, the following:
  (1) An order that the party who obtained the admission be permitted to pursue additional discovery related to the matter involved in the withdrawn or amended admission.
  (2) An order that the costs of any additional discovery be borne in whole or in part by the party withdrawing or amending the admission.
Added by Stats 2004 ch 182 (AB 3081),s 23, eff. 7/1/2005.

Article 3 - EFFECT OF ADMISSION

Section 2033.410 - Matter conclusively established; binding only on party
(a) Any matter admitted in response to a request for admission is conclusively established against the party making the admission in the pending action, unless the court has permitted withdrawal or amendment of that admission under Section 2033.300.

(b) Notwithstanding subdivision (a), any admission made by a party under this section is binding only on that party and is made for the purpose of the pending action only. It is not an admission by that party for any other purpose, and it shall not be used in any manner against that party in any other proceeding.

Added by Stats 2004 ch 182 (AB 3081),s 23, eff. 7/1/2005.

Section 2033.420 - Motion to pay reasonable expenses

(a) If a party fails to admit the genuineness of any document or the truth of any matter when requested to do so under this chapter, and if the party requesting that admission thereafter proves the genuineness of that document or the truth of that matter, the party requesting the admission may move the court for an order requiring the party to whom the request was directed to pay the reasonable expenses incurred in making that proof, including reasonable attorney's fees.

(b) The court shall make this order unless it finds any of the following:

(1) An objection to the request was sustained or a response to it was waived under Section 2033.290.

(2) The admission sought was of no substantial importance.

(3) The party failing to make the admission had reasonable ground to believe that that party would prevail on the matter.

(4) There was other good reason for the failure to admit.

Added by Stats 2004 ch 182 (AB 3081),s 23, eff. 7/1/2005.

Chapter 17 - FORM INTERROGATORIES AND REQUESTS FOR ADMISSION

Section 2033.710 - Generally

The Judicial Council shall develop and approve official form interrogatories and requests for admission of the genuineness of any relevant documents or of the truth of any relevant matters of fact for use in any civil action in a state court based on personal injury, property damage, wrongful death, unlawful detainer, breach of contract, family law, or fraud and for any other civil actions the Judicial Council deems appropriate.

Added by Stats 2004 ch 182 (AB 3081),s 23, eff. 7/1/2005.

Section 2033.720 - Official form interrogatories for victims receiving complete restitution payment

(a) The Judicial Council shall develop and approve official form interrogatories for use by a victim who has not received complete payment of a restitution order made pursuant to Section 1202.4 of the Penal Code.

(b) Notwithstanding whether a victim initiates or maintains an action to satisfy the unpaid restitution order, a victim may propound the form interrogatories approved pursuant to this section once each calendar year. The defendant subject to the restitution order shall, in responding to the interrogatories propounded, provide current information regarding the nature, extent, and location of any assets, income, and liabilities in which the defendant claims a present or future interest.

Added by Stats 2004 ch 182 (AB 3081),s 23, eff. 7/1/2005.

Section 2033.730 - Advisory committee

(a) In developing the form interrogatories and requests for admission required by Sections 2033.710 and 2033.720, the Judicial Council shall consult with a representative advisory committee which shall include, but not be limited to, representatives of all of the following:

(1) The plaintiff's bar.

(2) The defense bar.

(3) The public interest bar.

(4) Court administrators.

(5) The public.

(b) The form interrogatories and requests for admission shall be drafted in nontechnical language.

Added by Stats 2004 ch 182 (AB 3081),s 23, eff. 7/1/2005.

Section 2033.740 - Use optional; available through clerk of court; rules to govern use

(a) Use of the form interrogatories and requests for admission approved by the Judicial Council shall be optional.

(b) The form interrogatories and requests for admission shall be made available through the office of the clerk of the appropriate trial court.

(c) The Judicial Council shall promulgate any necessary rules to govern the use of the form interrogatories and requests for admission.

Added by Stats 2004 ch 182 (AB 3081),s 23, eff. 7/1/2005.

Chapter 18 - SIMULTANEOUS EXCHANGE OF EXPERT WITNESS INFORMATION

Article 1 - GENERAL PROVISIONS

Section 2034.010 - Inapplicability to eminent domain proceedings

This chapter does not apply to exchanges of lists of experts and valuation data in eminent domain proceedings under Chapter 7 (commencing with Section 1258.010) of Title 7 of Part 3.

Added by Stats 2004 ch 182 (AB 3081),s 23, eff. 7/1/2005.

Article 2 - DEMAND FOR EXCHANGE OF EXPERT WITNESS INFORMATION

Section 2034.210 - Generally

After the setting of the initial trial date for the action, any party may obtain discovery by demanding that all parties simultaneously exchange information concerning each other's expert trial witnesses to the following extent:

(a) Any party may demand a mutual and simultaneous exchange by all parties of a list containing the name and address of any natural person, including one who is a party, whose oral or deposition testimony in the form of an expert opinion any party expects to offer in evidence at the trial.

(b) If any expert designated by a party under subdivision (a) is a party or an employee of a party, or has been retained by a party for the purpose of forming and expressing an opinion in anticipation of the litigation or in preparation for the trial of the action, the designation of that witness shall include or be accompanied by an expert witness declaration under Section 2034.260.

(c) Any party may also include a demand for the mutual and simultaneous production for inspection and copying of all discoverable reports and writings, if any, made by any expert described in subdivision (b) in the course of preparing that expert's opinion.

Added by Stats 2004 ch 182 (AB 3081),s 23, eff. 7/1/2005.

Section 2034.220 - Demand without leave of court

Any party may make a demand for an exchange of information concerning expert trial witnesses without leave of court. A party shall make this demand no later than the 10th day after the initial trial date has been set, or 70 days before that trial date, whichever is closer to the trial date.

Added by Stats 2004 ch 182 (AB 3081),s 23, eff. 7/1/2005.

Section 2034.230 - Requirements of demand

(a) A demand for an exchange of information concerning expert trial witnesses shall be in writing and shall identify, below the title of the case, the party making the demand. The demand shall state that it is being made under this chapter.

(b) The demand shall specify the date for the exchange of lists of expert trial witnesses, expert witness declarations, and any demanded production of writings. The specified date of exchange shall be 50 days before the initial trial date, or 20 days after service of the demand, whichever is closer to the trial date, unless the court, on motion and a showing of good cause, orders an earlier or later date of exchange.

Added by Stats 2004 ch 182 (AB 3081),s 23, eff. 7/1/2005.

Section 2034.240 - Service of demand

The party demanding an exchange of information concerning expert trial witnesses shall serve the demand on all parties who have appeared in the action.

Added by Stats 2004 ch 182 (AB 3081),s 23, eff. 7/1/2005.

Section 2034.250 - Motion for protective order

(a) A party who has been served with a demand to exchange information concerning expert trial witnesses may promptly move for a protective order. This motion shall be accompanied by a meet and confer declaration under Section 2016.040.

(b) The court, for good cause shown, may make any order that justice requires to protect any party from unwarranted annoyance, embarrassment, oppression, or undue burden and expense. The protective order may include, but is not limited to, one or more of the following directions:

(1) That the demand be quashed because it was not timely served.

(2) That the date of exchange be earlier or later than that specified in the demand.

(3) That the exchange be made only on specified terms and conditions.

(4) That the production and exchange of any reports and writings of experts be made at a different place or at a different time than specified in the demand.

(5) That some or all of the parties be divided into sides on the basis of their identity of interest in the issues in the action, and that the designation of any experts as described in subdivision (b) of Section 2034.210 be made by any side so created.

(6) That a party or a side reduce the list of employed or retained experts designated by that party or side under subdivision (b) of Section 2034.210.

(c) If the motion for a protective order is denied in whole or in part, the court may order that the parties against whom the motion is brought, provide or permit the discovery against which the protection was sought on those terms and conditions that are just.

(d) The court shall impose a monetary sanction under Chapter 7 (commencing with Section 2023.010) against any party, person, or attorney who unsuccessfully makes or opposes a motion for a protective order under this section, unless it finds that the one subject to the sanction acted with substantial justification or that other circumstances make the imposition of the sanction unjust.

Added by Stats 2004 ch 182 (AB 3081),s 23, eff. 7/1/2005.

Section 2034.260 - Procedure and requirements of exchange

(a) All parties who have appeared in the action shall exchange information concerning expert witnesses in writing on or before the date of exchange specified in the demand. The exchange of information may occur at a meeting of the attorneys for the parties involved or by serving the information on the other party by any method specified in Section 1011 or 1013, on or before the date of exchange.

(b) The exchange of expert witness information shall include either of the following:

(1) A list setting forth the name and address of a person whose expert opinion that party expects to offer in evidence at the trial.

(2) A statement that the party does not presently intend to offer the testimony of an expert witness.

(c) If a witness on the list is an expert as described in subdivision (b) of Section 2034.210, the exchange shall also include or be accompanied by an expert witness declaration signed only by the attorney for the party designating the expert, or by that party if that party has no attorney. This declaration shall be under penalty of perjury and shall contain all of the following:

(1) A brief narrative statement of the qualifications of each expert.

(2) A brief narrative statement of the general substance of the testimony that the expert is expected to give.

(3) A representation that the expert has agreed to testify at the trial.

(4) A representation that the expert will be sufficiently familiar with the pending action to submit to a meaningful oral deposition concerning the specific testimony, including an opinion and its basis, that the expert is expected to give at trial.

(5) A statement of the expert's hourly and daily fee for providing deposition testimony and for consulting with the retaining attorney.

Amended by Stats 2018 ch 92 (SB 1289),s 45, eff. 1/1/2019.
Amended by Stats 2017 ch 64 (SB 543),s 3, eff. 1/1/2018.
Added by Stats 2004 ch 182 (AB 3081),s 23, eff. 7/1/2005.

Section 2034.270 - Demand includes demand for production of reports and writings

If a demand for an exchange of information concerning expert trial witnesses includes a demand for production of reports and writings as described in subdivision (c) of Section 2034.210, all parties shall produce and exchange, at the place and on the date specified in the demand, all discoverable reports and writings, if any, made by any designated expert described in subdivision (b) of Section 2034.210.

Added by Stats 2004 ch 182 (AB 3081),s 23, eff. 7/1/2005.

Section 2034.280 - Supplemental expert witness list

(a) Within 20 days after the exchange described in Section 2034.260, any party who engaged in the exchange may submit a supplemental expert witness list containing the name and address of any experts who will express an opinion on a subject to be covered by an expert designated by an adverse party to the exchange, if the party supplementing an expert witness list has not previously retained an expert to testify on that subject.

(b) This supplemental list shall be accompanied by an expert witness declaration under subdivision (c) of Section 2034.260 concerning those additional experts, and by all discoverable reports and writings, if any, made by those additional experts.

(c) The party shall also make those experts available immediately for a deposition under Article 3 (commencing with Section 2034.410), which deposition may be taken even though the time limit for discovery under Chapter 8 (commencing with Section 2024.010) has expired.

Added by Stats 2004 ch 182 (AB 3081),s 23, eff. 7/1/2005.

Section 2034.290 - Demand and lists filed with court; retention of originals by demanding party

(a) A demand for an exchange of information concerning expert trial witnesses, and any expert witness lists and declarations exchanged shall not be filed with the court.

(b) The party demanding the exchange shall retain both the original of the demand, with the original proof of service affixed, and the original of all expert witness lists and declarations exchanged in response to the demand until six months after final disposition of the action. At that time, all originals may be destroyed unless the court, on motion of any party and for good cause shown, orders that the originals be preserved for a longer period.

(c) Notwithstanding subdivisions (a) and (b), a demand for exchange of information concerning expert trial witnesses, and all expert witness lists and declarations exchanged in response to it, shall be lodged with the court when their contents become relevant to an issue in any pending matter in the action.

Added by Stats 2004 ch 182 (AB 3081),s 23, eff. 7/1/2005.

Section 2034.300 - Exclusion of evidence of expert opinion of party not in compliance

Except as provided in Section 2034.310 and in Articles 4 (commencing with Section 2034.610) and 5 (commencing with Section 2034.710), on objection of any party who has made a complete and timely compliance with Section 2034.260, the trial court shall exclude from evidence the expert opinion of any witness that is offered by any party who has unreasonably failed to do any of the following:

(a) List that witness as an expert under Section 2034.260.

(b) Submit an expert witness declaration.

(c) Produce reports and writings of expert witnesses under Section 2034.270.
(d) Make that expert available for a deposition under Article 3 (commencing with Section 2034.410).
Added by Stats 2004 ch 182 (AB 3081),s 23, eff. 7/1/2005.

Section 2034.310 - Calling expert not previously designated as witness
A party may call as a witness at trial an expert not previously designated by that party if either of the following conditions is satisfied:
(a) That expert has been designated by another party and has thereafter been deposed under Article 3 (commencing with Section 2034.410).
(b) That expert is called as a witness to impeach the testimony of an expert witness offered by any other party at the trial. This impeachment may include testimony to the falsity or nonexistence of any fact used as the foundation for any opinion by any other party's expert witness, but may not include testimony that contradicts the opinion.
Added by Stats 2004 ch 182 (AB 3081),s 23, eff. 7/1/2005.

Article 3 - DEPOSITION OF EXPERT WITNESS

Section 2034.410 - Generally
On receipt of an expert witness list from a party, any other party may take the deposition of any person on the list. The procedures for taking oral and written depositions set forth in Chapters 9 (commencing with Section 2025.010), 10 (commencing with Section 2026.010), and 11 (commencing with Section 2028.010) apply to a deposition of a listed trial expert witness except as provided in this article.
Added by Stats 2004 ch 182 (AB 3081),s 23, eff. 7/1/2005.

Section 2034.415 - Production of materials
An expert described in subdivision (b) of Section 2034.210 whose deposition is noticed pursuant to Section 2025.220 shall, no later than three business days before his or her deposition, produce any materials or category of materials, including any electronically stored information, called for by the deposition notice.
Added by Stats 2016 ch 467 (AB 2427),s 3, eff. 1/1/2017.

Section 2034.420 - Location of expert's deposition
The deposition of any expert described in subdivision (b) of Section 2034.210 shall be taken at a place that is within 75 miles of the courthouse where the action is pending. On motion for a protective order by the party designating an expert witness, and on a showing of exceptional hardship, the court may order that the deposition be taken at a more distant place from the courthouse.
Amended by Stats 2008 ch 303 (AB 2619),s 1, eff. 1/1/2009.
Added by Stats 2004 ch 182 (AB 3081),s 23, eff. 7/1/2005.

Section 2034.430 - Payment of expert's hourly or daily fee
(a) Except as provided in subdivision (f), this section applies to an expert witness, other than a party or an employee of a party, who is any of the following:
   (1) An expert described in subdivision (b) of Section 2034.210.
   (2) A treating physician and surgeon or other treating health care practitioner who is to be asked during the deposition to express opinion testimony, including opinion or factual testimony regarding the past or present diagnosis or prognosis made by the practitioner or the reasons for a particular treatment decision made by the practitioner, but not including testimony requiring only the reading of words and symbols contained in the relevant medical record or, if those words and symbols are not legible to the deponent, the approximation by the deponent of what those words or symbols are.
   (3) An architect, professional engineer, or licensed land surveyor who was involved with the original project design or survey for which that person is asked to express an opinion within the person's expertise and relevant to the action or proceeding.
(b) A party desiring to depose an expert witness described in subdivision (a) shall pay the expert's reasonable and customary hourly or daily fee for any time spent at the deposition from the time noticed in the deposition subpoena, or from the time of the arrival of the expert witness should that time be later than the time noticed in the deposition subpoena, until the time the expert witness is dismissed from the deposition, regardless of whether the expert is actually deposed by any party attending the deposition.
(c) If any counsel representing the expert or a nonnoticing party is late to the deposition, the expert's reasonable and customary hourly or daily fee for the time period determined from the time noticed in the deposition subpoena until the counsel's late arrival, shall be paid by that tardy counsel.
(d) Notwithstanding subdivision (c), the hourly or daily fee charged to the tardy counsel shall not exceed the fee charged to the party who retained the expert, except where the expert donated services to a charitable or other nonprofit organization.
(e) A daily fee shall only be charged for a full day of attendance at a deposition or where the expert was required by the deposing party to be available for a full day and the expert necessarily had to forgo all business that the expert would otherwise have conducted that day but for the request that the expert be available all day for the scheduled deposition.
(f) In a worker's compensation case arising under Division 4 (commencing with Section 3201) or Division 4.5 (commencing with Section 6100) of the Labor Code, a party desiring to depose any expert on another party's expert witness list shall pay the fee under this section.
Amended by Stats 2008 ch 303 (AB 2619),s 2, eff. 1/1/2009.
Added by Stats 2004 ch 182 (AB 3081),s 23, eff. 7/1/2005.

Section 2034.440 - Responsibility for fee charged by expert for preparing for deposition
The party designating an expert is responsible for any fee charged by the expert for preparing for a deposition and for traveling to the place of the deposition, as well as for any travel expenses of the expert.
Added by Stats 2004 ch 182 (AB 3081),s 23, eff. 7/1/2005.

Section 2034.450 - Delivery of expert's fee
(a) The party taking the deposition of an expert witness shall either accompany the service of the deposition notice with a tender of the expert's fee based on the anticipated length of the deposition, or tender that fee at the commencement of the deposition.
(b) The expert's fee shall be delivered to the attorney for the party designating the expert.
(c) If the deposition of the expert takes longer than anticipated, the party giving notice of the deposition shall pay the balance of the expert's fee within five days of receipt of an itemized statement from the expert.
Added by Stats 2004 ch 182 (AB 3081),s 23, eff. 7/1/2005.

Section 2034.460 - Service of notice accompanied by fee effective to require party to produce expert
(a) The service of a proper deposition notice accompanied by the tender of the expert witness fee described in Section 2034.430 is effective to require the party employing or retaining the expert to produce the expert for the deposition.
(b) If the party noticing the deposition fails to tender the expert's fee under Section 2034.430, the expert shall not be deposed at that time unless the parties stipulate otherwise.
Added by Stats 2004 ch 182 (AB 3081),s 23, eff. 7/1/2005.

Section 2034.470 - Motion for order setting compensation of expert
(a) If a party desiring to take the deposition of an expert witness under this article deems that the hourly or daily fee of that expert for providing deposition testimony is unreasonable, that party may move for an order setting the compensation of that expert. Notice of this motion shall also be given to the expert.

(b) A motion under subdivision (a) shall be accompanied by a meet and confer declaration under Section 2016.040. In any attempt at an informal resolution under Section 2016.040, either the party or the expert shall provide the other with all of the following:

(1) Proof of the ordinary and customary fee actually charged and received by that expert for similar services provided outside the subject litigation.

(2) The total number of times the presently demanded fee has ever been charged and received by that expert.

(3) The frequency and regularity with which the presently demanded fee has been charged and received by that expert within the two-year period preceding the hearing on the motion.

(c) In addition to any other facts or evidence, the expert or the party designating the expert shall provide, and the court's determination as to the reasonableness of the fee shall be based on, proof of the ordinary and customary fee actually charged and received by that expert for similar services provided outside the subject litigation.

(d) In an action filed after January 1, 1994, the expert or the party designating the expert shall also provide, and the court's determination as to the reasonableness of the fee shall also be based on, both of the following:

(1) The total number of times the presently demanded fee has ever been charged and received by that expert.

(2) The frequency and regularity with which the presently demanded fee has been charged and received by that expert within the two-year period preceding the hearing on the motion.

(e) The court may also consider the ordinary and customary fees charged by similar experts for similar services within the relevant community and any other factors the court deems necessary or appropriate to make its determination.

(f) Upon a determination that the fee demanded by that expert is unreasonable, and based upon the evidence and factors considered, the court shall set the fee of the expert providing testimony.

(g) The court shall impose a monetary sanction under Chapter 7 (commencing with Section 2023.010) against any party, person, or attorney who unsuccessfully makes or opposes a motion to set the expert witness fee, unless it finds that the one subject to the sanction acted with substantial justification or that other circumstances make the imposition of the sanction unjust.

Added by Stats 2004 ch 182 (AB 3081),s 23, eff. 7/1/2005.

Article 4 - MOTION TO AUGMENT OR AMEND EXPERT WITNESS LIST OR DECLARATION

Section 2034.610 - Generally

(a) On motion of any party who has engaged in a timely exchange of expert witness information, the court may grant leave to do either or both of the following:

(1) Augment that party's expert witness list and declaration by adding the name and address of any expert witness whom that party has subsequently retained.

(2) Amend that party's expert witness declaration with respect to the general substance of the testimony that an expert previously designated is expected to give.

(b) A motion under subdivision (a) shall be made at a sufficient time in advance of the time limit for the completion of discovery under Chapter 8 (commencing with Section 2024.010) to permit the deposition of any expert to whom the motion relates to be taken within that time limit. Under exceptional circumstances, the court may permit the motion to be made at a later time.

(c) The motion shall be accompanied by a meet and confer declaration under Section 2016.040.

Added by Stats 2004 ch 182 (AB 3081),s 23, eff. 7/1/2005.

Section 2034.620 - Conditions required to be satisfied to grant leave to amend or augment or amend

The court shall grant leave to augment or amend an expert witness list or declaration only if all of the following conditions are satisfied:

(a) The court has taken into account the extent to which the opposing party has relied on the list of expert witnesses.

(b) The court has determined that any party opposing the motion will not be prejudiced in maintaining that party's action or defense on the merits.

(c) The court has determined either of the following:

(1) The moving party would not in the exercise of reasonable diligence have determined to call that expert witness or have decided to offer the different or additional testimony of that expert witness.

(2) The moving party failed to determine to call that expert witness, or to offer the different or additional testimony of that expert witness as a result of mistake, inadvertence, surprise, or excusable neglect, and the moving party has done both of the following:

(A) Sought leave to augment or amend promptly after deciding to call the expert witness or to offer the different or additional testimony.

(B) Promptly thereafter served a copy of the proposed expert witness information concerning the expert or the testimony described in Section 2034.260 on all other parties who have appeared in the action.

(d) Leave to augment or amend is conditioned on the moving party making the expert available immediately for a deposition under Article 3 (commencing with Section 2034.410), and on any other terms as may be just, including, but not limited to, leave to any party opposing the motion to designate additional expert witnesses or to elicit additional opinions from those previously designated, a continuance of the trial for a reasonable period of time, and the awarding of costs and litigation expenses to any party opposing the motion.

Added by Stats 2004 ch 182 (AB 3081),s 23, eff. 7/1/2005.

Section 2034.630 - Monetary sanction for unsuccessfully opposing motion

The court shall impose a monetary sanction under Chapter 7 (commencing with Section 2023.010) against any party, person, or attorney who unsuccessfully makes or opposes a motion to augment or amend expert witness information, unless it finds that the one subject to the sanction acted with substantial justification or that other circumstances make the imposition of the sanction unjust.

Added by Stats 2004 ch 182 (AB 3081),s 23, eff. 7/1/2005.

Article 5 - MOTION TO SUBMIT TARDY EXPERT WITNESS INFORMATION

Section 2034.710 - Generally

(a) On motion of any party who has failed to submit expert witness information on the date specified in a demand for that exchange, the court may grant leave to submit that information on a later date.

(b) A motion under subdivision (a) shall be made a sufficient time in advance of the time limit for the completion of discovery under Chapter 8 (commencing with Section 2024.010) to permit the deposition of any expert to whom the motion relates to be taken within that time limit. Under exceptional circumstances, the court may permit the motion to be made at a later time.

(c) The motion shall be accompanied by a meet and confer declaration under Section 2016.040.

Added by Stats 2004 ch 182 (AB 3081),s 23, eff. 7/1/2005.

Section 2034.720 - Conditions required to be satisfied to grant leave

The court shall grant leave to submit tardy expert witness information only if all of the following conditions are satisfied:

(a) The court has taken into account the extent to which the opposing party has relied on the absence of a list of expert witnesses.

(b) The court has determined that any party opposing the motion will not be prejudiced in maintaining that party's action or defense on the merits.

(c) The court has determined that the moving party did all of the following:

(1) Failed to submit the information as the result of mistake, inadvertence, surprise, or excusable neglect.

(2) Sought leave to submit the information promptly after learning of the mistake, inadvertence, surprise, or excusable neglect.

(3) Promptly thereafter served a copy of the proposed expert witness information described in Section 2034.260 on all other parties who have appeared in the action.

(d) The order is conditioned on the moving party making the expert available immediately for a deposition under Article 3 (commencing with Section 2034.410), and on any other terms as may be just, including, but not limited to, leave to any party opposing the motion to designate additional expert witnesses or to elicit additional opinions from those previously designated, a continuance of the trial for a reasonable period of time, and the awarding of costs and litigation expenses to any party opposing the motion.

Added by Stats 2004 ch 182 (AB 3081),s 23, eff. 7/1/2005.

Section 2034.730 - Monetary sanction for unsuccessfully opposing motion

The court shall impose a monetary sanction under Chapter 7 (commencing with Section 2023.010) against any party, person, or attorney who unsuccessfully makes or opposes a motion to submit tardy expert witness information, unless it finds that the one subject to the sanction acted with substantial justification or that other circumstances make the imposition of the sanction unjust.

Added by Stats 2004 ch 182 (AB 3081),s 23, eff. 7/1/2005.

Chapter 19 - PERPETUATION OF TESTIMONY OR PRESERVATION OF EVIDENCE BEFORE FILING ACTION

Section 2035.010 - Generally

(a) One who expects to be a party or expects a successor in interest to be a party to an action that may be cognizable in a court of the state, whether as a plaintiff, or as a defendant, or in any other capacity, may obtain discovery within the scope delimited by Chapter 2 (commencing with Section 2017.010), and subject to the restrictions set forth in Chapter 5 (commencing with Section 2019.010), for the purpose of perpetuating that person's own testimony or that of another natural person or organization, or of preserving evidence for use in the event an action is subsequently filed.

(b) One shall not employ the procedures of this chapter for purposes of either ascertaining the possible existence of a cause of action or a defense to it, or of identifying those who might be made parties to an action not yet filed.

Amended by Stats 2016 ch 86 (SB 1171),s 44, eff. 1/1/2017.

Amended by Stats 2005 ch 294 (AB 333),s 13, eff. 1/1/2006

Added by Stats 2004 ch 182 (AB 3081),s 23, eff. 7/1/2005.

Section 2035.020 - Methods for discovery

The methods available for discovery conducted for the purposes set forth in Section 2035.010 are all of the following:

(a) Oral and written depositions.

(b) Inspections of documents, things, and places.

(c) Physical and mental examinations.

Added by Stats 2004 ch 182 (AB 3081),s 23, eff. 7/1/2005.

Section 2035.030 - Petition

(a) One who desires to perpetuate testimony or preserve evidence for the purposes set forth in Section 2035.010 shall file a verified petition in the superior court of the county of the residence of at least one expected adverse party, or, if no expected adverse party is a resident of the State of California, in the superior court of a county where the action or proceeding may be filed.

(b) The petition shall be titled in the name of the one who desires the perpetuation of testimony or the preservation of evidence. The petition shall set forth all of the following:

(1) The expectation that the petitioner or the petitioner's successor in interest will be a party to an action cognizable in a court of the State of California.

(2) The present inability of the petitioner and, if applicable, the petitioner's successor in interest either to bring that action or to cause it to be brought.

(3) The subject matter of the expected action and the petitioner's involvement. A copy of any written instrument the validity or construction of which may be called into question, or which is connected with the subject matter of the proposed discovery, shall be attached to the petition.

(4) The particular discovery methods described in Section 2035.020 that the petitioner desires to employ.

(5) The facts that the petitioner desires to establish by the proposed discovery.

(6) The reasons for desiring to perpetuate or preserve these facts before an action has been filed.

(7) The name or a description of those whom the petitioner expects to be adverse parties so far as known.

(8) The name and address of those from whom the discovery is to be sought.

(9) The substance of the information expected to be elicited from each of those from whom discovery is being sought.

(c) The petition shall request the court to enter an order authorizing the petitioner to engage in discovery by the described methods for the purpose of perpetuating the described testimony or preserving the described evidence.

Amended by Stats 2005 ch 294 (AB 333),s 14, eff. 1/1/2006

Added by Stats 2004 ch 182 (AB 3081),s 23, eff. 7/1/2005.

Section 2035.040 - Service of notice of petition

(a) The petitioner shall cause service of a notice of the petition under Section 2035.030 to be made on each natural person or organization named in the petition as an expected adverse party. This service shall be made in the same manner provided for the service of a summons.

(b) The service of the notice shall be accompanied by a copy of the petition. The notice shall state that the petitioner will apply to the court at a time and place specified in the notice for the order requested in the petition.

(c) This service shall be effected at least 20 days prior to the date specified in the notice for the hearing on the petition.

(d) If after the exercise of due diligence, the petitioner is unable to cause service to be made on any expected adverse party named in the petition, the court in which the petition is filed shall make an order for service by publication.

(e) If any expected adverse party served by publication does not appear at the hearing, the court shall appoint an attorney to represent that party for all purposes, including the cross-examination of any person whose testimony is taken by deposition. The court shall order that the petitioner pay the reasonable fees and expenses of any attorney so appointed.

Added by Stats 2004 ch 182 (AB 3081),s 23, eff. 7/1/2005.

Section 2035.050 - Determining whether to make order

(a) If the court determines that all or part of the discovery requested under this chapter may prevent a failure or delay of justice, it shall make an order authorizing that discovery. In determining whether to authorize discovery by a petitioner who expects a successor in interest to be a party to an action, the court shall consider, in addition to other appropriate factors, whether the requested discovery could be conducted by the petitioner's successor in interest, instead of by the petitioner.

(b) The order shall identify any witness whose deposition may be taken, and any documents, things, or places that may be inspected, and any person whose physical or mental condition may be examined.

(c) Any authorized depositions, inspections, and physical or mental examinations shall then be conducted in accordance with the provisions of this title relating to those methods of discovery in actions that have been filed.

Amended by Stats 2005 ch 294 (AB 333),s 15, eff. 1/1/2006

Added by Stats 2004 ch 182 (AB 3081),s 23, eff. 7/1/2005.

Section 2035.060 - Use of deposition

If a deposition to perpetuate testimony has been taken either under the provisions of this chapter, or under comparable provisions of the laws of the state in which it was taken, or the federal courts, or a foreign nation in which it was taken, that deposition may be used, in any action involving the same subject matter that is brought in a court of the State of California, in accordance with Section 2025.620 against any party, or the successor in interest of any party, named in the petition as an expected adverse party.

Amended by Stats 2005 ch 294 (AB 333),s 16, eff. 1/1/2006

Added by Stats 2004 ch 182 (AB 3081),s 23, eff. 7/1/2005.

Chapter 20 - PERPETUATION OF TESTIMONY OR PRESERVATION OF INFORMATION PENDING APPEAL

Section 2036.010 - Generally

If an appeal has been taken from a judgment entered by a court of the state, or if the time for taking an appeal has not expired, a party may obtain discovery within the scope delimited by Chapter 2 (commencing with Section 2017.010), and subject to the restrictions set forth in Chapter 5 (commencing with Section 2019.010), for purposes of perpetuating testimony or preserving information for use in the event of further proceedings in that court.

Amended by Stats 2016 ch 86 (SB 1171),s 45, eff. 1/1/2017.

Added by Stats 2004 ch 182 (AB 3081),s 23, eff. 7/1/2005.

Section 2036.020 - Methods of discovery

The methods available for discovery for the purpose set forth in Section 2036.010 are all of the following:

(a) Oral and written depositions.

(b) Inspections of documents, things, and places.

(c) Physical and mental examinations.

Added by Stats 2004 ch 182 (AB 3081),s 23, eff. 7/1/2005.

Section 2036.030 - Requirements of motion

(a) A party who desires to obtain discovery pending appeal shall obtain leave of the court that entered the judgment. This motion shall be made on the same notice and service of parties as is required for discovery sought in an action pending in that court.

(b) The motion for leave to conduct discovery pending appeal shall set forth all of the following:

(1) The names and addresses of the natural persons or organizations from whom the discovery is being sought.

(2) The particular discovery methods described in Section 2036.020 for which authorization is being sought.

(3) The reasons for perpetuating testimony or preserving evidence.

Added by Stats 2004 ch 182 (AB 3081),s 23, eff. 7/1/2005.

Section 2036.040 - Order authorizing discovery

(a) If the court determines that all or part of the discovery requested under this chapter may prevent a failure or delay of justice in the event of further proceedings in the action in that court, it shall make an order authorizing that discovery.

(b) The order shall identify any witness whose deposition may be taken, and any documents, things, or places that may be inspected, and any person whose physical or mental condition may be examined.

(c) Any authorized depositions, inspections, and physical and mental examinations shall then be conducted in accordance with the provisions of this title relating to these methods of discovery in a pending action.

Added by Stats 2004 ch 182 (AB 3081),s 23, eff. 7/1/2005.

Section 2036.050 - Use of deposition

If a deposition to perpetuate testimony has been taken under the provisions of this chapter, it may be used in any later proceeding in accordance with Section 2025.620.

Added by Stats 2004 ch 182 (AB 3081),s 23, eff. 7/1/2005.

Title 5 - OF THE RIGHTS AND DUTIES OF WITNESSES

Section 2064 - Duty to attend and answer

A witness, served with a subpoena, must attend at the time appointed, with any papers under his control lawfully required by the subpoena, and answer all pertinent and legal questions; and, unless sooner discharged, must remain until the testimony is closed.

Amended by Stats. 1907, Ch. 395.

Section 2065 - Notice that witness may be entitled to fees and mileage

Any witness who is subpoenaed in any civil or administrative action or proceeding shall be given written notice on the subpoena that the witness may be entitled to receive fees and mileage. Such notice shall indicate generally the manner in which the request for fees and mileage should be made.

Added by Stats. 1979, Ch. 67.

Title 6 - OF EVIDENCE IN PARTICULAR CASES, AND MISCELLANEOUS AND GENERAL PROVISIONS

Chapter 1 - EVIDENCE IN PARTICULAR CASES

Section 2074 - Offer equivalent to actual production and tender

An offer in writing to pay a particular sum of money, or to deliver a written instrument or specific personal property, is, if not accepted, equivalent to the actual production and tender of the money, instrument, or property.

Enacted 1872.

Section 2075 - Receipt for payment of money or delivery of instrument or property

Whoever pays money, or delivers an instrument or property, is entitled to a receipt therefor from the person to whom the payment or delivery is made, and may demand a proper signature to such receipt as a condition of the payment or delivery.

Enacted 1872.

Section 2076 - Objection required

The person to whom a tender is made must, at the time, specify any objection he may have to the money, instrument, or property, or he must be deemed to have waived it; and if the objection be to the amount of money, the terms of the instrument, or the amount or kind of property, he must specify the amount, terms, or kind which he requires, or be precluded from objecting afterwards.

Enacted 1872.

Section 2077 - Rules for construing descriptive part of conveyance of real property
Section Two Thousand and Seventy-seven. The following are the rules for construing the descriptive part of a conveyance of real property, when the construction is doubtful and there are no other sufficient circumstances to determine it:
One-Where there are certain definite and ascertained particulars in the description, the addition of others which are indefinite, unknown, or false, does not frustrate the conveyance, but it is to be construed by the first mentioned particulars.
Two-When permanent and visible or ascertained boundaries or monuments are inconsistent with the measurement, either of lines, angles, or surfaces, the boundaries or monuments are paramount.
Three-Between different measurements which are inconsistent with each other, that of angles is paramount to that of surfaces, and that of lines paramount to both.
Four-When a road, or stream of water not navigable, is the boundary, the rights of the grantor to the middle of the road or the thread of the stream are included in the conveyance, except where the road or thread of the stream is held under another title.
Five-When tide water is the boundary, the rights of the grantor to ordinary high-water mark are included in the conveyance. When a navigable lake, where there is no tide, is the boundary, the rights of the grantor to low-water mark are included in the conveyance.
Six-When the description refers to a map, and that reference is inconsistent with other particulars, it controls them if it appears that the parties acted with reference to the map; otherwise the map is subordinate to other definite and ascertained particulars.
Amended by Code Amendments 1873-74, Ch. 383.

Chapter 3 - ADMINISTRATION OF OATHS AND AFFIRMATIONS

Section 2093 - Persons having power to administer oaths and affirmations
(a) A court, judge or clerk of a court, justice, notary public, and officer or person authorized to take testimony in an action or proceeding, or to decide upon evidence, has the power to administer oaths and affirmations.
(b)
(1) A shorthand reporter certified pursuant to Article 3 (commencing with Section 8020) of Chapter 13 of Division 3 of the Business and Professions Code has the power to administer oaths and affirmations and may perform the duties of the deposition officer pursuant to Chapter 9 (commencing with Section 2025.010) of Title 4. The certified shorthand reporter is entitled to receive fees for services rendered during a deposition, including fees for deposition services, as specified in subdivision (c) of Section 8211 of the Government Code.
(2) This subdivision also applies to depositions taken by telephone or other remote electronic means as specified in Chapter 2 (commencing with Section 2017.010) and Chapter 9 (commencing with Section 2025.010) of Title 4.
(c)
(1) A former judge or justice of a court of record in the state who retired or resigned from office may administer oaths and affirmations, if the former judge or justice requests and receives a certification from the Commission on Judicial Performance pursuant to paragraph (2).
(2) The Commission on Judicial Performance shall issue a certification enabling a former judge or justice to administer oaths and affirmations if the following conditions are satisfied:
(A) The former judge or justice was not removed from office; was not censured and barred from receiving an assignment, appointment, or reference of work from any California state court; did not retire or resign from office with an agreement with the commission that the former judge or justice would not receive an assignment, appointment or reference of work from any California state court; and, at the time of the former judge or justice's retirement, resignation, or request for certification, a formal disciplinary proceeding was not pending or was resolved on the merits in the judge or justice's favor after his or her retirement or resignation and before the request for certification.
(B) A medical certification provided to the commission by the former judge or justice pursuant to paragraph (3) establishes one of the following:
(i) The former judge or justice does not have a medical condition that would impair his or her ability to administer oaths or affirmations.
(ii) The former judge or justice has a medical condition that may impair his or her ability to administer oaths and affirmations, but the condition does not impair his or her ability at the present time.
(3) The Commission on Judicial Performance may require an applicant to obtain a medical certification in order to receive or renew a certification to administer oaths and affirmations if, at the time of resignation or retirement, there is evidence in a disability application file or in a disciplinary investigation file of possible cognitive impairment affecting the judge or justice, or if the former judge or justice previously received a two-year certification to administer oaths and affirmations from the commission. The commission shall supply the required forms to an applicant upon request.
(4) If an applicant's medical certification indicates that the applicant has a medical condition that may impair his or her ability to administer oaths and affirmations, but the condition does not impair his or her ability at the time the medical certification is submitted with the application, the Commission on Judicial Performance shall issue a certification to administer oaths and affirmations pursuant to paragraph (2), but the certification is only valid for a period of two years from the date of issuance.
(5) Notwithstanding paragraph (1), a former judge or justice of a court of record who received a certification to administer oaths and affirmations from the Commission on Judicial Performance prior to January 1, 2018, may continue to administer oaths and affirmations until the expiration of the certification, at which time he or she may reapply for certification pursuant to paragraph (2).
(6) The Commission on Judicial Performance may charge a regulatory fee not to exceed fifteen dollars ($15) for each certification application submitted pursuant to this subdivision to cover its costs, including costs to review a medical certification.
(d) A rule or regulation regarding the confidentiality of proceedings of the Commission on Judicial Performance does not prohibit the commission from issuing a certificate as provided for in this section.
(e) The administration of an oath or affirmation pursuant to this section without pay does not violate Section 75060.6 of the Government Code.
Amended by Stats 2018 ch 92 (SB 1289),s 46, eff. 1/1/2019.
Amended by Stats 2017 ch 82 (AB 740),s 1, eff. 1/1/2018.
Amended by Stats 2016 ch 86 (SB 1171),s 46, eff. 1/1/2017.
Amended by Stats 2015 ch 308 (AB 1028),s 1, eff. 1/1/2016.
Amended by Stats 2004 ch 182 (AB 3081),s 24, eff. 7/1/2005
Amended by Stats 2001 ch 812 (AB 223), s 12, eff. 1/1/2002.

Section 2094 - Administered by obtaining affirmative response to questions
(a) An oath, affirmation, or declaration in an action or a proceeding, may be administered by obtaining an affirmative response to one of the following questions:
(1) "Do you solemnly state that the evidence you shall give in this issue (or matter) shall be the truth, the whole truth, and nothing but the truth, so help you God?"
(2) "Do you solemnly state, under penalty of perjury, that the evidence that you shall give in this issue (or matter) shall be the truth, the whole truth, and nothing but the truth?"

(b) In the alternative to the forms prescribed in subdivision (a), the court may administer an oath, affirmation, or declaration in an action or a proceeding in a manner that is calculated to awaken the person's conscience and impress the person's mind with the duty to tell the truth. The court shall satisfy itself that the person testifying understands that his or her testimony is being given under penalty of perjury.

Amended by Stats 2002 ch 806 (AB 3027),s 17, eff. 1/1/2003.
Amended by Stats 2000 ch 688 (AB 1669), s 13, eff. 1/1/2001.

Section 2095 through 2097 - [Repealed]
Repealed by Stats 2000 ch 688 (AB 1669), ss 14-16, eff. 1/1/2001.

Title 7 - UNIFORM FEDERAL LIEN REGISTRATION ACT

Section 2100 - Applicability of title
This title applies only to federal tax liens and to other federal liens notices of which under any Act of Congress or any regulation adopted pursuant thereto are required or permitted to be filed in the same manner as notices of federal tax liens.

Added by Stats. 1979, Ch. 330.

Section 2101 - Filing notices
(a) Notices of liens, certificates, and other notices affecting federal tax liens or other federal liens must be filed in accordance with this title.
(b) Notices of liens upon real property for obligations payable to the United States and certificates and notices affecting the liens shall be filed for record in the office of the recorder of the county in which the real property subject to the liens is situated.
(c) Notices of federal liens upon personal property, whether tangible or intangible, for obligations payable to the United States and certificates and notices affecting the liens shall be filed as follows:

(1) If the person against whose interest the lien applies is a corporation, a limited liability company, or a partnership whose principal executive office is in this state, as these entities are defined in the internal revenue laws of the United States, in the office of the Secretary of State.

(2) If the person against whose interest the lien applies is a trust that is not covered by paragraph (1), in the office of the Secretary of State.

(3) If the person against whose interest the lien applies is the estate of a decedent, in the office of the Secretary of State.

(4) In all other cases, in the office of the recorder of the county where the person against whose interest the lien applies resides at the time of filing of the notice of lien.

Amended by Stats. 1997, Ch. 892, Sec. 2. Effective January 1, 1998.

Section 2102 - Certification entitles notices to be filed
Certification of notices of liens, certificates, or other notices affecting federal liens by the Secretary of the Treasury of the United States or his or her delegate, or by any official or entity of the United States responsible for filing or certifying of notice of any other lien, entitles them to be filed and no other attestation, certification, or acknowledgment is necessary.

Added by Stats. 1979, Ch. 330.

Section 2103 - Presentation of notices to filing officer
(a) If a notice of federal lien, a refiling of a notice of federal lien, or a notice of revocation of any certificate described in subdivision (b) is presented to a filing officer who is:

(1) The Secretary of State, he or she shall cause the notice to be filed, indexed, and marked in accordance with the provisions of Sections 9515, 9516, and 9522 of the Commercial Code as if the notice were a financing statement within the meaning of that code; or

(2) A county recorder, he or she shall accept for filing, file for record in the manner set forth in Section 27320 of the Government Code, and index the document by the name of the person against whose interest the lien applies in the general index.

(b) If a certificate of release, nonattachment, discharge, or subordination of any lien is presented to the Secretary of State for filing he or she shall:

(1) Cause a certificate of release or nonattachment to be filed, indexed, and marked as if the certificate were a termination statement within the meaning of the Commercial Code.

(2) Cause a certificate of discharge or subordination to be filed, indexed, and marked as if the certificate were a release of collateral within the meaning of the Commercial Code.

(c) If a refiled notice of federal lien referred to in subdivision (a) or any of the certificates or notices referred to in subdivision (b) is presented for filing to a county recorder, he or she shall accept for filing, file for record in the manner set forth in Section 27320 of the Government Code, and index the document by the name of the person against whose interest the lien applies in the general index.

(d) Upon request of any person, the filing officer shall issue his or her certificate showing whether there is on file, on the date and hour stated therein, any notice of lien or certificate or notice affecting any lien filed after January 1, 1968, under this title or former Chapter 14 (commencing with Section 7200) of Division 7 of Title 1 of the Government Code, naming a particular person, and if a notice or certificate is on file, giving the date and hour of filing of each notice or certificate. Upon request, the filing officer shall furnish a copy of any notice of federal lien, or notice or certificate affecting a federal lien. If the filing officer is a county recorder, the fee for a certificate for each name searched shall be set by the filing officer in an amount that covers actual costs, and the fee for copies shall be in accordance with Section 27366 of the Government Code. If the filing officer is the Secretary of State, the certificate shall be issued as part of a combined certificate pursuant to Section 9528 of the Commercial Code, and the fee for the certificate and copies shall be in accordance with that section.

Amended by Stats 2012 ch 494 (SB 1532),s 2, eff. 1/1/2013.
Amended by Stats 2009 ch 606 (SB 676),s 1, eff. 1/1/2010.
EFFECTIVE 7/01/2001. Amended October 10, 1999 (Bill Number: SB 45) (Chapter 991).

Section 2104 - Fees
The fee charged for recording and indexing each notice of lien or certificate or notice affecting the lien filed with the county recorder shall be the same as those established by Article 5 (commencing with Section 27360) of Chapter 6 of Part 3 of Division 2 of Title 3 of the Government Code for the recording and indexing of documents.

The fee for filing and indexing each notice of lien or certificate or notice affecting the lien with the office of the Secretary of State is set forth in subdivision (a) of Section 12194 of the Government Code.

The officer shall bill the district directors of internal revenue or other appropriate federal officials on a monthly basis for fees for documents recorded or filed by the county recorder or the Secretary of State.

Amended by Stats. 1999, Ch. 1000, Sec. 13. Effective January 1, 2000.

Section 2105 - Federal tax lien notices filed prior to January 2, 1968
Filing officers with whom notices of federal tax liens, certificates and notices affecting such liens have been filed on or before January 1, 1968, shall, after that date, continue to maintain a file labeled "federal tax lien notices filed prior to January 2, 1968" containing notices and certificates filed in numerical order of receipt. If a notice of lien was filed on or before January 1, 1968, any certificate or notice affecting the lien shall be filed in the same office.

Added by Stats. 1979, Ch. 330.

Section 2106 - Application and construction of title

This title shall be applied and construed to effectuate its general purpose to make uniform the law with respect to the subject of this title among states enacting it.

Added by Stats. 1979, Ch. 330.

Section 2106.5 - Filing by electronic or magnetic means

This title shall be applied and construed to permit the transmission, filing, recording, and indexing of notices of federal tax liens and all certificates that relate to or affect those liens, including, but not limited to, certificates of release, discharge, subordination, and nonattachment, by electronic or magnetic means, using computerized data processing, telecommunications, and other similar information technologies available to the filing offices.

Added by Stats. 1998, Ch. 463, Sec. 1. Effective January 1, 1999.

Section 2107 - Title of act

This title may be cited as the Uniform Federal Lien Registration Act.

Added by Stats. 1979, Ch. 330.

Made in the USA
Las Vegas, NV
18 May 2024